이 책의 구성과 특징

파트 기초 학습

파트별로 최신 출제 경향, 단계별 문제 풀이 전략, 빈출 유형 분석을 수록하여, 유형 세부 학습 전에 토익 리스닝의 기초를 다질 수 있게 하였다.

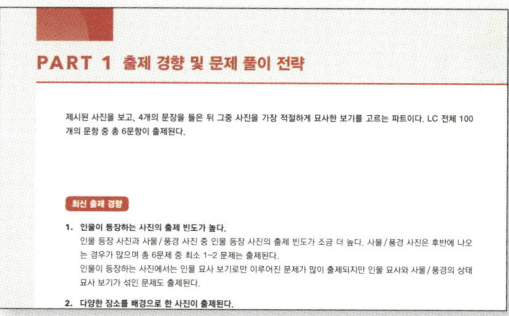

유형별 전략

❶ 핵심 포인트

토익 리스닝에 가장 자주 출제되는 유형들을 선별하고 각 유형에 맞는 핵심 전략을 제시하였다. 학습한 내용을 실전 맛보기와 CHECK UP 문제에 바로바로 적용해보며 확실하게 익힐 수 있다.

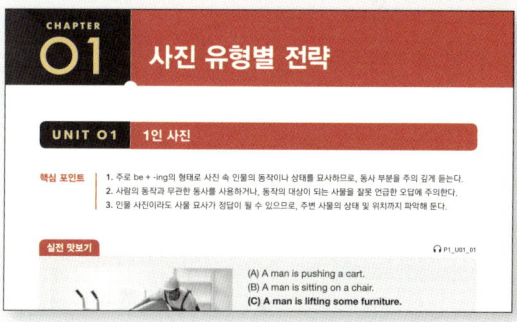

❷ PART 1 빈출 표현 / PART 2 빈출 질문 및 응답

PART 1에서 가장 자주 출제되는 필수 표현들과, PART 2에서 반드시 알아야 할 빈출 질문 및 응답 유형을 엄선하여 수록하였다.

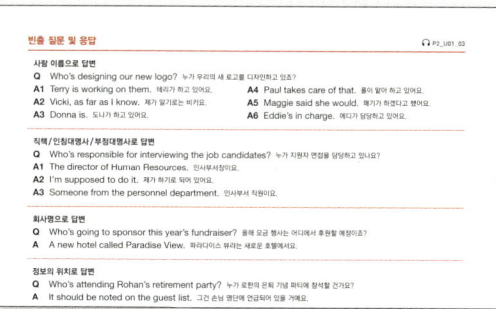

❸ PART 3, 4 빈출 질문 / 빈출 단서

PART 3, 4의 빈출 질문 패턴과 각 문제 유형에서 자주 쓰이는 단서 유형들을 수록하여, 지문 속에서 빠르게 답을 찾아내는 능력을 키울 수 있도록 하였다.

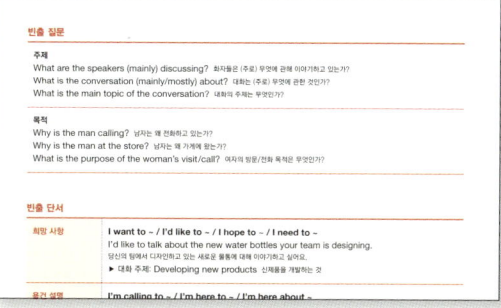

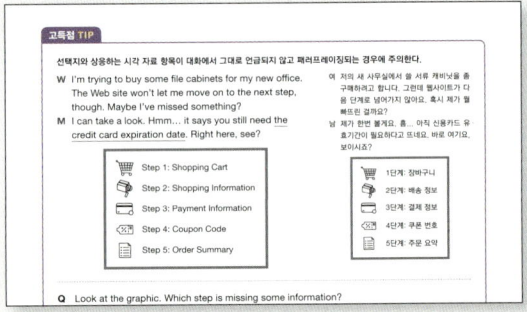
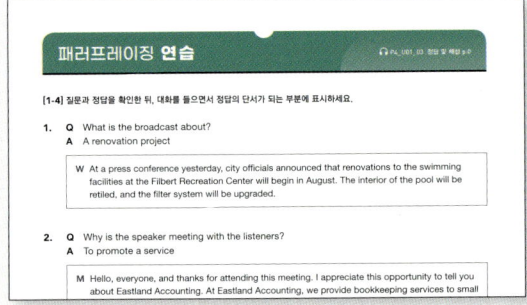

학습 일정표

PART 1, 2, 3, 4를 순차적으로 학습하는

4주 완성 A코스

	DAY 1	DAY 2	DAY 3	DAY 4	DAY 5	DAY 6
1주	PART 1 UNIT 01~02	PART 1 UNIT 03~04	PART 1 UNIT 05~06	PART 1 UNIT 07, PART TEST	PART 2 UNIT 01~02	PART 2 UNIT 03~04
	월 일	월 일	월 일	월 일	월 일	월 일

	DAY 7	DAY 8	DAY 9	DAY 10	DAY 11	DAY 12
2주	PART 2 UNIT 05~06	PART 2 UNIT 07~08	PART 2 UNIT 09~10	PART 2 UNIT 11~12	PART 2 UNIT 13~14, PART TEST 1, 2	PART 3 UNIT 01~02
	월 일	월 일	월 일	월 일	월 일	월 일

	DAY 13	DAY 14	DAY 15	DAY 16	DAY 17	DAY 18
3주	PART 3 UNIT 03~04	PART 3 UNIT 05~06	PART 3 UNIT 07~08	PART 3 UNIT 09~10	PART 3 UNIT 11~12, PART TEST	PART 4 UNIT 01~02
	월 일	월 일	월 일	월 일	월 일	월 일

	DAY 19	DAY 20	DAY 21	DAY 22	DAY 23	DAY 24
4주	PART 4 UNIT 03~04	PART 4 UNIT 05~06	PART 4 UNIT 07~08	PART 4 UNIT 09~10	PART 4 UNIT 11~12	PART 4 UNIT 13~15, PART TEST
	월 일	월 일	월 일	월 일	월 일	월 일

PART 1, 2, 3, 4를 동시에 학습하는

4주 완성 B코스

	DAY 1	DAY 2	DAY 3	DAY 4	DAY 5	DAY 6
1주	PART 1 UNIT 01~02 월 일	PART 2 UNIT 01~02 월 일	PART 2 UNIT 03~04 월 일	PART 3 UNIT 01~02 월 일	PART 3 UNIT 03~04 월 일	PART 4 UNIT 01~02 월 일

	DAY 7	DAY 8	DAY 9	DAY 10	DAY 11	DAY 12
2주	PART 4 UNIT 03~04 월 일	PART 1 UNIT 03~04 월 일	PART 2 UNIT 05~06 월 일	PART 2 UNIT 07~08 월 일	PART 3 UNIT 05~06 월 일	PART 3 UNIT 07~08 월 일

	DAY 13	DAY 14	DAY 15	DAY 16	DAY 17	DAY 18
3주	PART 4 UNIT 05~06 월 일	PART 4 UNIT 07~08 월 일	PART 1 UNIT 05~06 월 일	PART 2 UNIT 09~10 월 일	PART 2 UNIT 11~12 월 일	PART 3 UNIT 09~10 월 일

	DAY 19	DAY 20	DAY 21	DAY 22	DAY 23	DAY 24
4주	PART 4 UNIT 09~10 월 일	PART 4 UNIT 11~12 월 일	PART 1 UNIT 07, PART TEST 월 일	PART 2 UNIT 13~14, PART TEST 1, 2 월 일	PART 3 UNIT 11~12, PART TEST 월 일	PART 4 UNIT 13~15, PART TEST 월 일

TOEIC 소개

TOEIC은 Test of English for International Communication(국제적인 의사소통을 위한 영어 시험)의 약자로, 영어가 모국어가 아닌 사람들이 비즈니스 현장 및 일상생활에서 필요한 실용 영어 능력을 갖추었는가를 평가하는 시험이다.

시험 구성

구성	파트		문항 수	시간	배점
Listening Comprehension	Part 1	사진 묘사	6	45분	495점
	Part 2	질의 응답	25		
	Part 3	짧은 대화	39		
	Part 4	짧은 담화	30		
Reading Comprehension	Part 5	단문 빈칸 채우기	30	75분	495점
	Part 6	장문 빈칸 채우기	16		
	Part 7 독해	단일 지문	29		
		이중 지문	10		
		삼중 지문	15		
합계	7 Parts		200문항	120분	990점

(Listening Comprehension 문항 수 100, Reading Comprehension 문항 수 100)

출제 범위 및 주제

업무 및 일상생활에서 쓰이는 실용적인 주제들이 출제된다. 특정 문화나 특정 직업 분야에만 해당되는 주제는 출제하지 않으며, 듣기 평가의 경우 미국, 영국, 호주 등 다양한 국가의 발음이 섞여 출제된다.

일반 업무	계약, 협상, 영업, 홍보, 마케팅, 사업 계획
금융/재무	예산, 투자, 세금, 청구, 회계
개발	연구, 제품 개발
제조	공장 경영, 생산 조립 라인, 품질 관리
인사	채용, 승진, 퇴직, 직원 교육, 입사 지원
사무실	회의, 메모/전화/팩스/이메일, 사무 장비 및 가구
행사	학회, 연회, 회식, 시상식, 박람회, 제품 시연회
부동산	건축, 부동산 매매/임대, 기업 부지, 전기/수도/가스 설비
여행/여가	교통수단, 공항/역, 여행 일정, 호텔 및 자동차 예약/연기/취소, 영화, 전시, 공연

접수 방법

- 한국 TOEIC 위원회 사이트(www.toeic.co.kr)에서 인터넷 접수 기간을 확인하고 접수한다.
- 시험 접수 시 최근 6개월 이내에 촬영한 jpg 형식의 사진 파일이 필요하므로 미리 준비한다.
- 시험 10~12일 전부터는 특별 추가 접수 기간에 해당하여 추가 비용이 발생하므로, 접수 일정을 미리 확인하여 정기 접수 기간 내에 접수하도록 한다.

시험 당일 준비물

- 신분증: 주민등록증, 운전면허증, 기간 만료 전 여권, 공무원증 등 규정 신분증만 인정
     (중·고등학생의 경우 학생증, 청소년증도 인정)
- 필기구: 연필, 지우개 (볼펜, 사인펜은 사용 불가)

시험 진행

오전 시험	오후 시험	진행 내용
09:30 – 09:45	02:30 – 02:45	답안지 작성 오리엔테이션
09:45 – 09:50	02:45 – 02:50	쉬는 시간
09:50 – 10:05	02:50 – 03:05	신분증 확인
10:05 – 10:10	03:05 – 03:10	문제지 배부 및 파본 확인
10:10 – 10:55	03:10 – 03:55	듣기 평가 (LC)
10:55 – 12:10	03:55 – 05:10	독해 평가 (RC)

성적 확인

- 미리 안내된 성적 발표일(시험일로부터 약 12일 후)에 한국 TOEIC 위원회 사이트(www.toeic.co.kr) 및 공식 애플리케이션을 통해 성적을 확인할 수 있다.
- 성적표 수령은 온라인 출력 또는 우편 수령 중에서 선택할 수 있다.
- 온라인 출력과 우편 수령 모두 1회 발급만 무료이며, 그 이후에는 유료로 발급된다.

LC 파트별 문제 유형

PART 1 사진 묘사

파트 소개	제시된 사진을 보고, 4개의 문장을 들은 뒤 그중 사진을 가장 잘 묘사한 문장을 고르는 파트
문항 수	6문항
사진 유형	1인 사진 2인 이상 사진 사물·풍경 사진

문제지 형태

1.

2.

🔊

Number 1.

Look at the picture marked number 1 in your test book.

(A) She's putting on an apron.
(B) She's opening a kitchen cupboard.
(C) She's filling up a cup.
(D) She's drinking a glass of water.

PART 2 질의 응답

파트 소개	질문과 3개의 응답을 듣고, 질문에 가장 적절한 응답을 고르는 파트
문항 수	25문항
질문 유형	의문사 의문문, 조동사·Be동사 의문문, 부정 의문문, 제안·요청 의문문, 부가 의문문, 선택 의문문, 간접 의문문, 평서문

문제지 형태

PART 2

Directions: You will hear a question or statement and three responses spoken in English. They will not be printed in your test book and will be spoken only one time. Select the best response to the question or statement and mark the letter (A), (B), or (C) on your answer sheet.

7. Mark your answer on your answer sheet.

8. Mark your answer on your answer sheet.

9. Mark your answer on your answer sheet.

10. Mark your answer on your answer sheet.

11. Mark your answer on your answer sheet.

12. Mark your answer on your answer sheet.

13. Mark your answer on your answer sheet.

14. Mark your answer on your answer sheet.

15. Mark your answer on your answer sheet.

16. Mark your answer on your answer sheet.

17. Mark your answer on your answer sheet.

18. Mark your answer on your answer sheet.

19. Mark your answer on your answer sheet.

20. Mark your answer on your answer sheet.

21. Mark your answer on your answer sheet.

22. Mark your answer on your answer sheet.

23. Mark your answer on your answer sheet.

24. Mark your answer on your answer sheet.

25. Mark your answer on your answer sheet.

26. Mark your answer on your answer sheet.

27. Mark your answer on your answer sheet.

28. Mark your answer on your answer sheet.

29. Mark your answer on your answer sheet.

30. Mark your answer on your answer sheet.

31. Mark yo

Number 7.

Who has the key to the storage closet?

(A) Yes, it's quite spacious.
(B) Becky can open it for you.
(C) This store has reasonable prices.

PART 3 짧은 대화

파트 소개	두 명 또는 세 명의 대화를 듣고, 이와 관련된 3개의 문제에 대해 가장 적절한 답을 고르는 파트
문항 수	39문항 (13개 대화문×3문항)
대화 유형	2인 대화 2인 대화+시각 자료 3인 대화
문제 유형	주제·목적, 화자·장소, 문제점·이유, 세부사항, 제안·요청, 다음에 할·일어날 일, 의도 파악, 시각 자료 연계

문제지 형태

PART 3

Directions: You will hear some conversations between two or more people. You will be asked to answer three questions about what the speakers say in each conversation. Select the best response to each question and mark the letter (A), (B), (C), or (D) on your answer sheet. The conversations will not be printed in your test book and will be

32. What did the man do last month?
(A) He started a new job.
(B) He gave a presentation.
(C) He applied for a position.
(D) He attended a conference.

33. What is the woman asked to do?
(A) Lead a training session
(B) Renew a contract
(C) Assess job candidates
(D) Submit a proposal

34. What does the man plan to send to the woman?
(A) A neighborhood map
(B) A list of dates
(C) A feedback survey
(D) A confirmation code

35. Where are the speakers?
(A) At a supermarket
(B) At a restaurant
(C) At a cooking school
(D) At a department store

36. Why does the man look at a schedule?
(A) To check a location
(B) To confirm a presenter's name
(C) To read a guest list
(D) To review a price

37. What will the woman probably do next?
(A) Call a friend
(B) Pay for a ticket
(C) Return an item

38. Who a
(A) Ba
(B) Pa
(C) Da
(D) Fa

39. What
(A) A
(B) A
(C) A
(D) Ar

40. What
(A) Pa
(B) Fir
(C) Tra
(D) Lo

41. What
(A) An
(B) A
(C) A
(D) A

42. Where
(A) At
(B) At
(C) At
(D) At

43. What
do?
(A) Re
(B) Se
(C) Approve a budget

🔊

Questions 32-34 refer to the following conversation.

M Hello, I'd like to speak to Charlotte Willis.

W This is she.

M Hi, Ms. Willis. This is Jack Anderson. I met you briefly after the talk you gave at last month's conference in Dallas. I work for Dunbar Inc.

W Oh, yes. I remember you.

M Great! Well, I was wondering whether you do private sessions. I think your sales techniques would be perfect for our team, so we'd like to hire you for our next training event. Would that be possible?

W I'm interested, but it would depend on when you need it done.

M How about I e-mail you the dates that work best for us? Then you could let me know whether you're available.

PART 4 짧은 담화

파트 소개	한 사람이 말하는 담화를 듣고, 이와 관련된 3개의 문제에 대해 가장 적절한 답을 고르는 파트
문항 수	30문항 (10개 담화문×3문항)
담화 유형	전화 메시지, 사내 공지, 공공장소 안내, 연설·강연·소개, 광고, 방송, 관광·견학 등
문제 유형	주제·목적, 화자·청자·장소, 문제점·이유, 세부사항, 제안·요청, 다음에 할·일어날 일, 의도 파악, 시각 자료 연계

문제지 형태

PART 4

Directions: You will hear some talks given by a single speaker. You will be asked to answer three questions about what the speaker says in each talk. Select the best response to each question and mark the letter (A), (B), (C), or (D) on your answer sheet. The talks will not be printed in your test book and will be spoken only one time.

71. What department is the speaker most likely calling from?
    (A) Marketing
    (B) Finance
    (C) Sales
    (D) Customer service

72. Why did the company change a policy?
    (A) It will form a partnership.
    (B) It is hiring new staff.
    (C) It will expand overseas.
    (D) It is trying to save money.

73. What will the speaker send to the listener?
    (A) An updated schedule
    (B) A company memo
    (C) A security code
    (D) A complaint form

74. What is the workshop about?
    (A) Interior design
    (B) Cooking
    (C) Creative writing
    (D) Hiking

75. What does the speaker suggest the listeners do?
    (A) Make adjustments
    (B) Bring supplies
    (C) Work together
    (D) Take notes

76. What does the speaker say the group will do on May 8?

77. Who i
    (A) Re
    (B) Co
    (C) Ba
    (D) Cu

78. What
    (A) Us
    (B) Re
    (C) Ha
    (D) In

79. What
    (A) Int
    (B) Ch
    (C) Sh
    (D) As

80. What
    (A) A
    (B) A
    (C) An interior paint
    (D) A beverage mix

81. What is special about the product?
    (A) Its effects last for a long time.
    (B) It is not harmful to animals.
    (C) It has eco-friendly packaging.
    (D) It is produced locally.

82. What does the speaker encourage the listeners to do?
    (A) Try a free sample
    (B) Sign a new contract
    (C) View a photo gallery

Questions 71-73 refer to the following telephone message.

Hi, Aisha. It's William calling you back. To answer your question, our team has not processed your bonus payment yet. The company recently changed the payment policy because of the bank's fees. We will now send payments only once a month to cut down on costs. I hope you understand. I'll e-mail you a copy of the memo that explained this. I think you must have missed it. Thanks.

미국식 발음과 영국식 발음의 차이

토익 리스닝에서는 미국, 캐나다, 영국, 호주 총 네 나라의 발음이 나온다. 이중 캐나다는 미국과, 호주는 영국과 발음이 거의 비슷하기 때문에 크게 미국식 발음과 영국식 발음의 차이를 익혀 두면 토익 리스닝에 대비할 수 있다.

1 자음 [r]

미국에서는 혀를 굴리면서 부드럽게 'ㄹ'로 발음하는 반면, 영국에서는 음절의 끝소리 [r]을 발음하지 않는다.

	car	**door**	**enter**	**there**
미국식	[카ㄹ]	[도어ㄹ]	[엔터ㄹ]	[데어ㄹ]
영국식	[카]	[도어]	[엔터]	[데어]

- She's closing a **door**. 그녀는 문을 닫고 있다.
- I just started working **there**. 저는 이제 막 그곳에서 일하기 시작했어요.

2 자음 [t]

모음 사이에 낀 [t]를 미국에서는 'ㄷ'나 'ㄹ'로 부드럽게 발음하지만, 영국에서는 'ㅌ' 소리 그대로 강하게 발음한다.

	computer	**letter**	**meeting**	**waiting**
미국식	[컴퓨러]	[레러]	[미링]	[웨이링]
영국식	[컴퓨터]	[레터]	[미팅]	[웨이팅]

- A worker is typing on a **computer**. 직원이 컴퓨터로 타자를 치고 있다.
- I have a **meeting** this afternoon. 저는 오늘 오후에 회의가 있어요.

3 모음 [a]

미국에서는 '애'에 가깝게, 영국에서는 '아'에 가깝게 발음한다.

	ask	pass	last	plant
미국식	[애스크]	[패스]	[래스트]	[플랜트]
영국식	[아스크]	[파스]	[라스트]	[플란트]

- You should **ask** Emily. 에밀리에게 물어보셔야 해요.
- The man is watering a **plant**. 남자가 식물에 물을 주고 있다.

4 모음 [o]

미국에서는 '아', 영국에서는 '오'에 가까운 소리로 발음한다.

	topic	box	copy	job
미국식	[타픽]	[박스]	[카피]	[잡]
영국식	[토픽]	[복스]	[코피]	[좁]

- I'll send you a **copy**. 제가 한 부 보내드릴게요.
- Here are the **topics** we're going to cover. 우리가 다룰 주제들이 여기 있습니다.

그 외 반드시 외워 두어야 할 발음

	schedule	advertisement	produce	fragile
미국식	[스케쥴]	[애드버타이즈먼트]	[프로듀스]	[프레절]
영국식	[쉐쥴]	[어드버티스먼트]	[프로쥬스]	[프레자일]

실전에서 바로 써먹는
쉬운 토익 공식 인강

toeic.eduwill.net

PART

1

출제 경향 및 문제 풀이 전략

제시된 사진을 보고, 4개의 문장을 들은 뒤 그중 사진을 가장 적절하게 묘사한 보기를 고르는 파트이다. LC 전체 100개의 문항 중 총 6문항이 출제된다.

최신 출제 경향

1. **인물이 등장하는 사진의 출제 빈도가 높다.**
   인물 등장 사진과 사물/풍경 사진 중 인물 등장 사진의 출제 빈도가 조금 더 높다. 사물/풍경 사진은 후반에 나오는 경우가 많으며 총 6문제 중 최소 1~2 문제는 출제된다.
   인물이 등장하는 사진에서는 인물 묘사 보기로만 이루어진 문제가 많이 출제되지만 인물 묘사와 사물/풍경의 상태 묘사 보기가 섞인 문제도 출제된다.

2. **다양한 장소를 배경으로 한 사진이 출제된다.**
   실내 업무 장소와 야외를 배경으로 한 사진의 출제 빈도가 높지만 집, 편의 시설, 길거리 등 다양한 장소의 사진이 출제되고 있다.

문제 풀이 전략

STEP 1 사진 파악하기
동작: 시계를 걸고 있음
상태: 앞치마를 매고 있음

STEP 2 오답 소거하며 정답 선택하기
(A) 그는 시계를 걸고 있다. (○, 시계를 걸고 있음)
(B) 그는 나무를 쌓고 있다. (×, 나무를 쌓고 있지 않음)
(C) 그는 벽을 칠하고 있다. (×, 벽을 칠하고 있지 않음)
(D) 그는 앞치마를 매는 중이다. (×, 이미 앞치마를 착용한 상태임)

(A) He's hanging a clock.
(B) He's stacking some wood.
(C) He's painting a wall.
(D) He's putting on an apron.

빈출 오답 유형 분석

1. 사진 속 인물의 동작/상태를 잘못 묘사한 오답

사진 속 인물의 동작이나 상태를 잘못된 동사 어휘로 묘사한 오답이 나온다.

(✗) He's **moving** a sofa. 그는 소파를 옮기고 있다.
(○) He's **sitting on** a sofa. 그는 소파에 앉아 있다.

→ moving(옮기고 있다)은 인물의 동작을 잘못 묘사한 오답이다.

2. 사진에 없는 인물이나 사물을 묘사한 오답

사진에 등장하지 않는 인물이나 사물을 묘사한 오답이 나온다.

(✗) One of the people is positioned in front of a **podium**.
사람들 중 한 명이 연단 앞에 위치해 있다.
(○) One of the people is positioned in front of a **whiteboard**.
사람들 중 한 명이 화이트보드 앞에 위치해 있다.

→ 사진에 없는 podium(연단)을 이용한 오답이다.

3. 사진 속 인물이나 사물의 위치를 잘못 묘사한 오답

사진 속 인물이나 사물의 위치를 틀리게 묘사한 오답이 나온다.

(✗) There's a potted plant **on the windowsill**.
창턱에 화분에 심어진 식물이 있다.
(○) There's a potted plant **on the countertop**.
조리대 위에 화분에 심어진 식물이 있다.

→ on the windowsill(창턱 위에)은 사물의 위치를 잘못 묘사한 오답이다.

4. 혼동을 유도하는 어휘를 이용한 오답

사진에는 없지만 연상되는 어휘를 이용하거나 발음이나 형태가 비슷해 헷갈릴 수 있는 어휘를 이용한 오답이 나온다.

(✗) A market is full of **shoppers**. 상점이 쇼핑객들로 가득 차 있다.
(○) Some fruit has been put on display. 과일들이 진열되어 있다.

→ 상점에서 연상되는 쇼핑객을 이용한 오답이다.

사진은 사람의 등장 유무에 따라, 그리고 사진이 찍힌 장소가 어디냐에 따라 구분할 수 있다.

사진 유형별

1. 1인 사진

사람이 한 명만 등장하는 사진으로, 사진 속 인물의 동작이나 상태를 주로 묘사한다. 사물의 상태／위치, 배경을 묘사하는 표현들이 정답으로 출제될 수도 있다.

She's holding a cup.
그녀는 컵을 들고 있다.

2. 2인 이상 사진

2인 이상의 여러 명의 사람들이 등장하는 사진으로, 인물들의 공통된 모습 또는 두드러지는 어떤 한 사람이나 일부의 모습을 묘사한다. 사물의 상태／위치, 배경을 묘사하는 표현들이 정답으로 출제되기도 한다.

Some people are listening to a presentation.
몇몇 사람들이 발표를 듣고 있다.

3. 사물·풍경 사진

사람이 없고 사물이나 배경만 등장하는 사진으로, 사진 속 사물의 위치나 상태 또는 전반적인 풍경을 묘사하는 경우가 많다.

A dining area has been set up outdoors.
식사 공간이 야외에 준비되어 있다.

사진 장소별

1. 실내 업무 장소 사진

실내 업무 장소를 배경으로 한 사진으로, 사무실 / 회의실 / 실험실 / 작업실 등이 있다.

The woman is typing on a keyboard.
여자가 키보드에 타자를 치고 있다.

2. 야외·교통수단 사진

야외 장소를 배경으로 하거나 교통수단이 등장하는 사진으로, 실외 작업 모습이나 교통수단 관련 차량, 공항, 항구 등이 있다.

The people are gathered under a tree.
사람들이 나무 아래에 모여 있다.

3. 여가·편의 시설 사진

여가 활동 관련 사진이나 편의 시설을 배경으로 한 사진으로, 공연장 / 전시회 / 쇼핑 장소 / 도서관 / 식당 / 카페 등이 있다.

They're browsing for library books.
그들은 도서관 책을 둘러보고 있다.

4. 집·기타 장소 사진

집을 배경으로 한 사진으로, 요리 / 청소 등 가사 활동과 집 내부 사진이 등장한다.

He's preparing some food.
그는 음식을 준비하고 있다.

| UNIT 01 | 1인 사진 |

핵심 포인트
1. 주로 be + -ing의 형태로 사진 속 인물의 동작이나 상태를 묘사하므로, 동사 부분을 주의 깊게 듣는다.
2. 사람의 동작과 무관한 동사를 사용하거나, 동작의 대상이 되는 사물을 잘못 언급한 오답에 주의한다.
3. 인물 사진이라도 사물 묘사가 정답이 될 수 있으므로, 주변 사물의 상태 및 위치까지 파악해 둔다.

실전 맛보기

 P1_U01_01

(A) A man is pushing a cart.
(B) A man is sitting on a chair.
(C) A man is lifting some furniture.
(D) A man is putting on a hard hat.

(A) 남자가 카트를 밀고 있다. (×) 사진에 카트가 보이지만 남자가 밀고(pushing) 있지는 않으므로 오답
(B) 남자가 의자에 앉아 있다. (×) 남자가 의자에 앉아(sitting) 있지 않으므로 오답
(C) 남자가 가구를 들어 올리고 있다. (○) 남자가 소파(가구)를 들어 올리는 모습을 적절하게 묘사한 정답
(D) 남자가 안전모를 착용하고 있다. (×) 남자가 안전모를 착용하는(putting on) 중이 아니라 이미 착용한 상태이므로 오답

CHECK UP

P1_U01_02 정답 및 해설 p.2

1.

(A)　　　(B)　　　(C)　　　(D)

2.

(A)　　　(B)　　　(C)　　　(D)

동작	holding a cup 컵을 들고 있다	planting some vegetables 채소를 심고 있다
	taking some notes 메모를 하고 있다	watering some plants 식물에 물을 주고 있다
	painting a wall 벽을 칠하고 있다	assembling some shelves 선반을 조립하고 있다
	pushing a wheelbarrow 손수레를 밀고 있다	shoveling snow 눈을 삽으로 치우고 있다
	playing an instrument 악기를 연주하고 있다	stacking some boxes 상자들을 쌓고 있다
	reading a street sign 거리 표지판을 읽고 있다	washing dishes in the sink
	folding some laundry 빨래를 개고 있다	싱크대에서 설거지를 하고 있다
	riding a bicycle 자전거를 타고 있다	weighing some food on a scale
	hanging a poster 포스터를 걸고 있다	저울로 음식의 무게를 달고 있다
	pointing at a screen 화면을 가리키고 있다	turning on/off a lamp 램프를 켜고/끄고 있다
	drinking from a coffee cup	plugging/unplugging in an appliance
	커피잔으로 무언가를 마시고 있다	가전제품의 플러그를 꽂고/뽑고 있다
	paying for some merchandise	packing/unpacking a suitcase
	물건값을 지불하고 있다	여행 가방을 싸고/풀고 있다
	pressing a button on a telephone	loading/unloading a vehicle
	전화기의 버튼을 누르고 있다	차에 짐을 싣고/내리고 있다
착용 동작/ 상태	wearing glasses 안경을 쓰고 있다	putting on a sweater 스웨터를 입는 중이다
	wearing an apron 앞치마를 입고 있다	tying his shoe 신발 끈을 매고 있다
	wearing gloves 장갑을 끼고 있다	buttoning his coat 코트의 단추를 채우고 있다
	wearing headphones 헤드폰을 끼고 있다	zipping up his jacket 재킷의 지퍼를 잠그고 있다
	wearing a lab coat 실험실 가운을 입고 있다	taking off[removing] a hat 모자를 벗고 있다
시선/ 자세	looking in a bag 가방 안을 보고 있다	holding onto a railing 난간을 잡고 있다
	looking through a drawer 서랍을 살펴보고 있다	kneeling down 무릎을 꿇고 있다
	looking out a window 창밖을 보고 있다	leaning over a container 용기 위로 몸을 구부리고 있다
	looking at a clock on the wall	leaning against the wall 벽에 기대고 있다
	벽에 걸린 시계를 보고 있다	reaching for a bottle 병에 손을 뻗고 있다
	reviewing a document 서류를 검토하고 있다	bending over/down 몸을 구부리고/숙이고 있다
	resting on a bench 벤치에 앉아 쉬고 있다	standing next to a window 창문 옆에 서 있다

고득점 TIP

동작 – 상태 혼동 동사를 이용한 오답에 주의한다.

putting on a jacket (○) 재킷을 입는 중이다 → 입고 있는 동작
wearing a jacket (×) 재킷을 입고 있다 → 입은 채로 있는 상태

getting on a bicycle (×) 자전거에 타는 중이다 → 타려는 동작
riding a bicycle (○) 자전거에 타고 있다 → 타고 있는 상태

대화를 듣고 알맞은 답을 고른 뒤, 다시 들으면서 빈칸을 채우세요.

1.

(A) He's _____.

(B) He's _____.

(C) He's _____.

(D) He's _____.

(A)　　　　(B)　　　　(C)　　　　(D)

2.

(A) She's _____.

(B) She's _____.

(C) She's _____.

(D) She's _____.

(A)　　　　(B)　　　　(C)　　　　(D)

3.

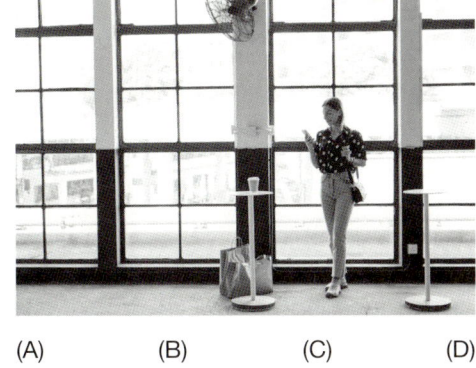

(A) The woman is _____.

(B) Some windows are _____.

(C) The woman is _____.

(D) Some bags have _____.

(A)　　　　(B)　　　　(C)　　　　(D)

🎧 P1_U01_05 정답 및 해설 p.3

사진을 적절하게 묘사한 보기를 고르세요.

1.

(A)   (B)   (C)   (D)

2.

(A)   (B)   (C)   (D)

3.

(A)   (B)   (C)   (D)

4.

(A)   (B)   (C)   (D)

5.

(A)   (B)   (C)   (D)

6.

(A)   (B)   (C)   (D)

핵심 포인트
1. 사진 속 특정 인물의 개별 동작 또는 여러 인물들의 공통 동작을 be + -ing의 형태로 묘사하는 경우가 많다.
2. 다수의 사람을 workers나 travelers와 같은 주어를 사용해 묘사하기도 하므로 이에 유의한다.
3. 복수 주어가 나오면 인물들의 공통 동작에, 1인 주어가 나오면 특정 인물의 개별 동작 또는 상태에 주의해서 듣도록 한다.

실전 맛보기
🎧 P1_U02_01

(A) They're looking at a document.
(B) They're adjusting a computer monitor.
(C) One of the people is taking off a pair of glasses.
(D) One of the people is drinking from a glass.

(A) 그들은 문서를 보고 있다. (○) 두 사람이 문서를 보고 있는 모습을 적절하게 묘사한 정답
(B) 그들은 컴퓨터 모니터를 조절하고 있다. (×) 사진에 컴퓨터 모니터(computer monitor)가 보이지만 두 사람이 이것을 조절하고(adjusting) 있는 것은 아니므로 오답
(C) 사람들 중 한 명이 안경을 벗고 있다. (×) 여자가 안경(a pair of glasses)을 벗는(taking off) 중이 아니라 착용한 상태이므로 오답
(D) 사람들 중 한 명이 유리잔에 든 것을 마시고 있다. (×) 사진에 유리잔(glass)은 보이지만 이것으로 무언가를 마시고 있는 사람은 보이지 않으므로 오답

CHECK UP
 P1_U02_02 정답 및 해설 p.5

1.

(A)   (B)   (C)   (D)

2.

(A)   (B)   (C)   (D)

동작	walking across a bridge 다리를 건너고 있다	approaching a doorway 출입구에 다가가고 있다
	crossing a street 길을 건너고 있다	assembling some furniture 가구를 조립하고 있다
	entering a building 건물에 들어가고 있다	setting the table 테이블을 차리고 있다
	leaving an office 사무실에서 나가고 있다	greeting each other 인사를 나누고 있다
	leading a tour group 단체 관광을 인솔하고 있다	attending an art exhibit 미술 전시회에 참석하고 있다
	visiting a library 도서관에 방문하고 있다	arranging some chairs 의자를 배열하고 있다
	fixing some equipment 장비를 수리하고 있다	rolling up his sleeves 소매를 말아 올리고 있다
	waiting for a bus 버스를 기다리고 있다	stepping off a shuttle 셔틀버스에서 내리고 있다
	playing a board game 보드게임을 하고 있다	handing out flyers 전단을 나눠주고 있다
	exercising on the grass 잔디 위에서 운동을 하고 있다	setting up a tent 텐트를 설치하고 있다
	dining at a restaurant 식당에서 식사를 하고 있다	adjusting some blinds 블라인드를 조정하고 있다
	shaking hands 악수를 하고 있다	handing a book to the woman 여자에게 책을 건네주고 있다
	exchanging business cards 명함을 주고받고 있다	passing a box to another 다른 사람에게 상자를 건네고 있다
	stacking boxes 상자들을 쌓고 있다	
	holding some containers 용기 몇 개를 들고 있다	
시선/ 자세	facing each other 서로를 마주 보고 있다	be seated at a table 테이블에 앉아 있다
	facing a screen 화면을 보고 있다	be seated in a circle 둥글게 둘러앉아 있다
	watching a performance 공연을 보고 있다	be seated in a waiting area 대기실에 앉아 있다
	looking at a display case 진열장을 보고 있다	be gathered in an auditorium 강당에 모여 있다
	examining a document 서류를 검토하고 있다	be gathered around a desk 책상 주위에 모여 있다
	riding a bicycle 자전거를 타고 있다	standing behind a podium 연단 뒤에 서 있다
	resting on a bench 벤치에서 쉬고 있다	standing in line 줄을 지어 서 있다
	inspecting an engine 엔진을 살펴보고 있다	leaning against a windowsill 창턱에 기대고 있다

PART 1 UNIT 02

고득점 TIP

사물 주어로 인물의 동작을 묘사할 수 있다. 이 경우에는 항상 현재진행 수동태(be + being + p.p.)로 쓰인다.

Some handouts are being distributed.
유인물이 배포되고 있다.
= One of the people is distributing some handouts.
　사람들 중 한 명이 유인물을 배포하고 있다.

A cart is being used to move boxes.
카트가 상자들을 옮기는 데 사용되고 있다.
= One of the workers is using a cart to move boxes.
　작업자들 중 한 명이 상자들을 나르기 위해 카트를 사용하고 있다.

대화를 듣고 알맞은 답을 고른 뒤, 다시 들으면서 빈칸을 채우세요.

1.

(A) They're _____.

(B) The woman is _____.

(C) They're _____.

(D) The man is _____.

(A)   (B)   (C)   (D)

2.

(A) One of the men is _____.

(B) One of the men is _____.

(C) The men are _____.

(D) The men are _____.

(A)   (B)   (C)   (D)

3.

(A) Some books are _____.

(B) Some books are _____.

(C) The people are _____.

(D) The people are _____.

(A)   (B)   (C)   (D)

사진을 적절하게 묘사한 보기를 고르세요.

1.

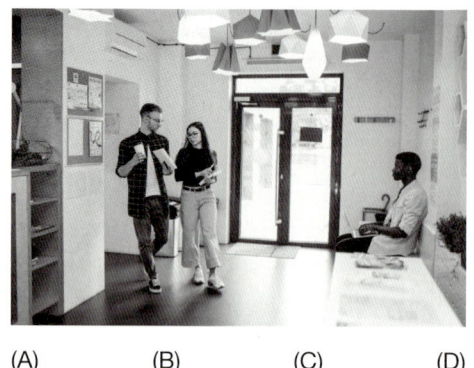

(A)   (B)   (C)   (D)

2.

(A)   (B)   (C)   (D)

3.

(A)   (B)   (C)   (D)

4.

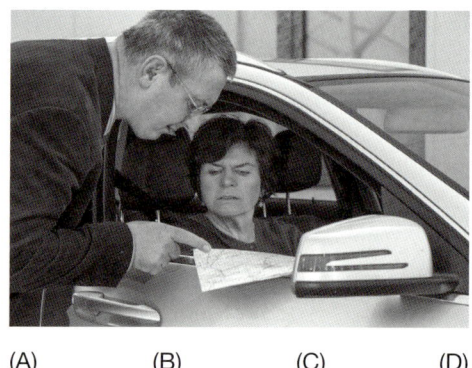

(A)   (B)   (C)   (D)

5.

(A)   (B)   (C)   (D)

6.

(A)   (B)   (C)   (D)

핵심 포인트

1. 눈에 띄는 주요 사물의 위치 및 상태뿐만 아니라 그 외 주변 사물이나 전반적인 풍경까지 빠르게 사진을 파악한다.
2. 사진에 등장하지 않는 사람이나 사물을 이용한 오답에 주의한다.
3. 사물의 위치를 나타내는 전치사(구)와 부사구를 주의 깊게 듣는다.

실전 맛보기 　　🎧 P1_U03_01

(A) Some dishes have been put in a sink.
(B) Some cups have been lined up on a shelf.
(C) Some towels are hanging from a faucet.
(D) A potted plant is being watered.

(A) 몇 개의 접시들이 싱크대에 놓여 있다. (×) 사진에 싱크대(sink)는 보이지만 접시들이 보이지 않으므로 오답

(B) 몇 개의 컵들이 선반 위에 일렬로 놓여 있다. (○) 선반에 일렬로 놓여 있는 컵들을 적절하게 묘사한 정답

(C) 몇 개의 수건들이 수도꼭지에 걸려 있다. (×) 사진에 수건(towels)과 수도꼭지(faucet)는 보이지만 수건이 수도꼭지에 걸려 있지 않으므로 오답

(D) 화분에 물이 뿌려지고 있다. (×) 사진에 있는 화분(potted plant)에 물이 뿌려지고(being watered) 있는 상태가 아니므로 오답

CHECK UP 　　🎧 P1_U03_02 정답 및 해설 p.8

1.

(A) 　　(B) 　　(C) 　　(D)

2.

(A) 　　(B) 　　(C) 　　(D)

상태	Some floor tiles are in a pattern. 바닥 타일이 일정한 패턴으로 되어 있다.
	Some light fixtures are mounted on the walls. 조명 기구들이 벽면에 설치되어 있다.
	Some tires have been removed from a car. 자동차에서 타이어 몇 개가 빠져있다.
	Notices have been posted on a bulletin board. 게시판에 공고문들이 게시되어 있다.
	Fruit and vegetables have been put on display. 과일과 채소가 진열되어 있다.
	Products are displayed on shelves. 상품들이 선반에 진열되어 있다.
	Tools are propped against a wall. 공구가 벽에 기대어져 있다.
	Some bookshelves are separated by an aisle. 책꽂이가 통로로 구분되어 있다.
	Sets of utensils have been arranged on napkins. 식기 세트들이 냅킨 위에 정리되어 있다.
위치	Some furniture has been stacked near a fence. 가구들이 울타리 근처에 쌓여 있다.
	Some potted plants have been placed in a courtyard. 화분에 심은 화초 몇 개가 뜰에 놓여 있다.
	A plant has been placed in front of a window. 식물이 창문 앞에 놓여 있다.
	A cushion has been set on an armchair. 쿠션이 안락의자에 놓여 있다.
	Some boxes are stacked on a filing cabinet. 박스 몇 개가 서류 캐비닛 위에 쌓여 있다.
	Some bricks are piled next to a building. 벽돌들이 건물 옆에 쌓여 있다.

풍경 묘사 빈출 표현

도로/ 건물	A pathway is paved with stones. 길이 돌로 포장되어 있다.
	The walkway is covered in fallen leaves. 인도가 낙엽으로 덮여 있다.
	A bus is being driven down a road. 버스가 도로를 따라 운행되고 있다.
	A fence surrounds a fountain. 울타리가 분수를 에워싸고 있다.
	There are some vehicles lining the side of a street. 길가에 줄지어 있는 차량들이 있다.
	Some trees are lining a walkway. 나무들이 보도를 따라 늘어서 있다.
	Some motorbikes have been parked in a row. 오토바이 몇 대가 일렬로 주차되어 있다.
자연	A bridge crosses over a waterway. 다리가 수로 위를 가로지르고 있다.
	Some trees border a pond. 나무들이 연못을 둘러싸고 있다.
	There's a deck overlooking a lake. 호수가 내려다보이는 갑판이 있다.

고득점 TIP

사물을 구체적으로 명시하지 않고 포괄적인 의미의 단어를 사용하여 묘사하기도 한다.

Some **furniture** has been stacked.
가구들이 쌓여 있다.
→ 테이블과 의자를 가구(furniture)로 묘사

Sound **equipment** has been set up on a stage.
음향 장비가 무대에 설치되어 있다.
→ 스피커와 마이크 등을 음향 장비(sound equipment)로 묘사

대화를 듣고 알맞은 답을 고른 뒤, 다시 들으면서 빈칸을 채우세요.

1.

(A) All chairs are _____.

(B) Napkins are _____.

(C) Chairs have _____.

(D) Light fixtures are _____.

(A)   (B)   (C)   (D)

2.

(A) Some light fixtures are _____.

(B) Some curtains are _____.

(C) Some sofas have _____.

(D) Some cushions have _____.

(A)   (B)   (C)   (D)

3.

(A) A passenger is _____.

(B) A bus is _____.

(C) Some roads are _____.

(D) Some trees are _____.

(A)   (B)   (C)   (D)

사진을 적절하게 묘사한 보기를 고르세요.

1.

(A)   (B)   (C)   (D)

2.

(A)   (B)   (C)   (D)

3.

(A)   (B)   (C)   (D)

4.

(A)   (B)   (C)   (D)

5.

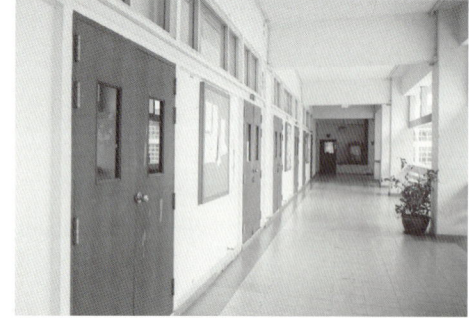

(A)   (B)   (C)   (D)

6.

(A)   (B)   (C)   (D)

UNIT 04 실내 업무 장소 사진

빈출 상황 및 사진

🎧 P1_U04_01

사무실/회의실 서류 검토, 사무기기 사용, 발표, 동료 간 대화 등

They're reviewing some documents at a desk.
그들은 책상에서 서류를 검토하고 있다.

The presenter is standing behind a podium.
발표자가 연단 뒤에 서 있다.

The woman is shaking hands with one of the men.
여자가 남자들 중 한 명과 악수를 하고 있다.

Some folders have been placed on top of a file cabinet.
몇몇 서류철들이 서류 보관함 위에 놓여 있다.

The woman is writing on a document.
여자가 서류에 무언가를 적고 있다.

The woman is refilling a printer with paper.
여자가 인쇄기에 종이를 다시 채우고 있다.

She's using some office equipment.
여자가 사무기기를 사용하고 있다.

A drawer has been left open.
서랍이 열려 있다.

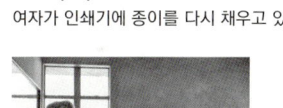

The man is talking on a mobile phone.
남자가 휴대폰으로 통화를 하고 있다.

The woman is typing on a keyboard.
여자가 키보드에 타자를 치고 있다.

They're exchanging business cards.
그들은 명함을 교환하고 있다.

She's stapling some papers together.
그녀는 종이를 스테이플러로 찍고 있다.

Some binders have been lined up on a shelf.
바인더들이 선반에 정렬되어 있다.

The audience is facing a screen.
청중이 스크린을 마주 보고 있다.

Several papers are pinned to a cork board.
몇몇 종이들이 코르크 판에 꽂혀 있다.

실험실/작업실 실험 복장, 기계 조작, 공구 및 장비 등

The woman is using a microscope.
여자가 현미경을 사용하고 있다.

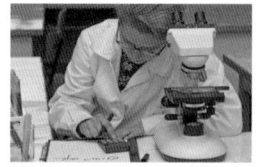

She's pressing a button on a device.
그녀는 장치의 버튼을 누르고 있다.

She's wearing a lab coat.
그녀는 실험실 가운을 입고 있다.

The man is fixing a bicycle.
남자가 자전거를 수리하고 있다.

He's operating some machinery.
그는 기계를 작동하고 있다.

The man is using a hammer.
남자가 망치를 사용하고 있다.

Some tools are spread out on a table.
장비가 테이블 위에 널려 있다.

The man is putting on protective work gear.
남자가 보호용 작업 장비를 착용하고 있다.

The worker is cleaning up some debris.
작업자가 잔해를 치우고 있다.

CHECK UP　　　　　🎧 P1_U04_02 정답 및 해설 p.11

1.

(A)　　　(B)　　　(C)　　　(D)

2.

(A)　　　(B)　　　(C)　　　(D)

대화를 듣고 알맞은 답을 고른 뒤, 다시 들으면서 빈칸을 채우세요.

1.

(A) The audience is _____.

(B) The audience is _____.

(C) The speaker is _____.

(D) The speaker is _____.

(A)   (B)   (C)   (D)

2.

(A) Some shelves are _____.

(B) A laptop is _____.

(C) The woman is _____.

(D) The woman is _____.

(A)   (B)   (C)   (D)

3.

(A) The man is _____.

(B) The man is _____.

(C) The man is _____.

(D) The man is _____.

(A)   (B)   (C)   (D)

사진을 적절하게 묘사한 보기를 고르세요.

1.

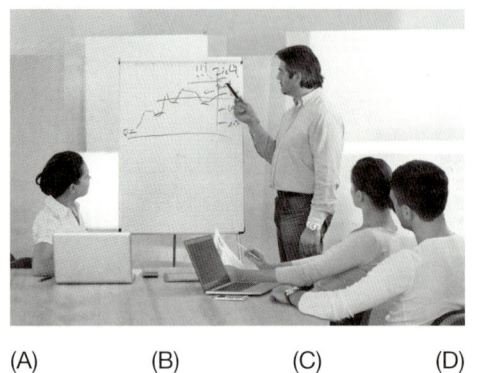

(A)   (B)   (C)   (D)

2.

(A)   (B)   (C)   (D)

3.

(A)   (B)   (C)   (D)

4.

(A)   (B)   (C)   (D)

5.

(A)   (B)   (C)   (D)

6.

(A)   (B)   (C)   (D)

빈출 상황 및 사진

🎧 P1_U05_01

실외 작업　건물 주변 관리, 정원, 건물 공사, 도로 / 보도 공사 등

Some people are planting a tree.
사람들이 나무를 심고 있다.

A man is trimming some bushes.
남자가 관목을 다듬고 있다.

A woman is watering some flowers.
여자가 꽃에 물을 주고 있다.

He's sawing off a branch.
그는 나뭇가지를 톱질해서 자르고 있다.

Leaves are being raked into piles.
나뭇잎을 긁어 모아 무더기로 쌓고 있다.

He's mowing the lawn.
그는 잔디를 깎고 있다.

A man is pushing a wheelbarrow.
남자가 손수레를 밀고 있다.

Snow is being shoveled from a walkway.
보도에서 눈을 삽으로 치우고 있다.

A construction vehicle has been parked near a building.
공사 차량이 건물 근처에 주차되어 있다.

A portion of the roof is unfinished.
지붕의 일부가 마무리되지 않았다.

They're lifting a wooden plank.
그들은 나무 판자를 들어 올리고 있다.

The workers are doing construction work on a house.
작업자들이 주택 공사를 하고 있다.

A man is climbing up a ladder.
남자가 사다리를 올라가고 있다.

A man is using a shovel to move some dirt.
남자가 삽을 이용해 흙을 옮기고 있다.

Some bricks are piled near a building.
몇몇 벽돌들이 건물 근처에 쌓여 있다.

교통수단 관련 차량, 역, 정류장, 비행기, 공항, 항구 등

Some boxes have been stored inside a vehicle.
상자들이 차량 안에 보관되어 있다.

Some travelers are waiting in line.
여행자들이 줄을 서서 기다리고 있다.

Some traffic cones have been placed near a truck.
원뿔형 도로 표지물들이 트럭 근처에 놓여 있다.

The men are unloading a chair from a vehicle.
남자들이 차량에서 의자를 내리고 있다.

A bus is being driven down a road.
버스가 도로를 따라 운행되고 있다.

A bridge crosses over a waterway.
다리가 수로 위를 가로지르고 있다.

Some bicycles are parked outside.
자전거들이 외부에 주차되어 있다.

There are some vehicles lining the side of a street.
길가에 줄지어 있는 차량들이 있다.

Some passengers are waiting for a train.
승객들이 기차를 기다리고 있다.

CHECK UP

 P1_U05_02 정답 및 해설 p.14

1.

(A)   (B)   (C)   (D)

2.

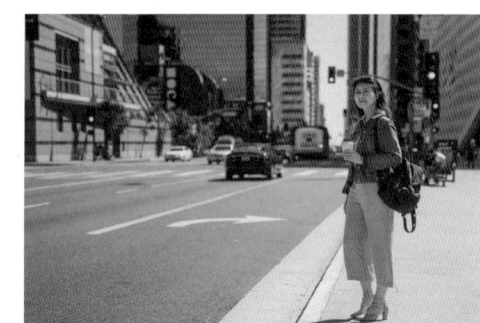

(A)   (B)   (C)   (D)

대화를 듣고 알맞은 답을 고른 뒤, 다시 들으면서 빈칸을 채우세요.

1.

(A) Passengers are _____.
(B) A passenger is _____.
(C) A counter is _____.
(D) Passengers are _____.

(A)　　　　(B)　　　　(C)　　　　(D)

2.

(A) Some crates are _____.
(B) Some bicycles are _____.
(C) A tree is _____.
(D) A railing is _____.

(A)　　　　(B)　　　　(C)　　　　(D)

3.

(A) There are _____.
(B) There's _____.
(C) He's _____.
(D) He's _____.

(A)　　　　(B)　　　　(C)　　　　(D)

실전 문제

사진을 적절하게 묘사한 보기를 고르세요.

1.

(A)   (B)   (C)   (D)

2.

(A)   (B)   (C)   (D)

3.

(A)   (B)   (C)   (D)

4.

(A)   (B)   (C)   (D)

5.

(A)   (B)   (C)   (D)

6.

(A)   (B)   (C)   (D)

빈출 상황 및 사진

🎧 P1_U06_01

여가 활동　공원, 운동, 공연장, 전시회, 기타 취미 생활

A man is jogging down a street.
남자가 거리를 따라 조깅을 하고 있다.

Some park benches are empty.
몇몇 공원 벤치가 비어 있다.

They're strolling along a tree-lined path.
그들은 나무가 늘어선 길을 따라 거닐고 있다.

He's fishing from a pier.
그는 부두에서 낚시를 하고 있다.

Some people are playing instruments.
몇몇 사람들이 악기를 연주하고 있다.

Some people are watching a performance.
몇몇 사람들이 공연을 보고 있다.

편의 시설　쇼핑 장소, 도서관, 약국, 진열대, 계산대 등

A cashier is standing at a cash register.
계산대 점원이 계산대에 서 있다.

A woman is browsing for library books.
여자가 도서관 책을 둘러보고 있다.

Products are displayed on shelves.
제품들이 선반 위에 진열되어 있다.

A customer is paying for some merchandise.
손님이 물건값을 지불하고 있다.

They're waiting in line at a checkout counter.
그들은 계산대에서 줄을 서서 기다리고 있다.

He's weighing some fruit on a scale.
그는 저울에 과일의 무게를 달고 있다.

She's holding some clothes.
그녀는 옷을 들고 있다.

They're across the desk from each other.
그들은 책상을 가운데 두고 마주보고 있다.

She's looking at some packages.
그녀는 포장지를 살펴보고 있다.

식당 / 카페 메뉴 주문, 식사, 요리, 서빙 등

They're ordering food in a restaurant.
그들은 식당에서 음식을 주문하고 있다.

One of the women is writing down an order.
여자들 중 한 명이 주문을 적고 있다.

She's serving a meal in the restaurant.
그녀는 식당에서 식사를 갖다주고 있다.

He's filling a cup with coffee.
그는 커피로 컵을 채우고 있다.

She's preparing some food.
그녀는 음식을 준비하고 있다.

All seats are unoccupied.
모든 좌석들이 비어 있다.

Some large cooking pots are on a counter.
큰 조리용 냄비 몇 개가 조리대 위에 있다.

Some food has been arranged on a tray.
음식이 쟁반 위에 정렬되어 있다.

A pizza is being taken out of an oven.
피자가 오븐에서 꺼내지고 있다.

CHECK UP

P1_U06_02 정답 및 해설 p.17

1.

(A)   (B)   (C)   (D)

2.

(A)   (B)   (C)   (D)

대화를 듣고 알맞은 답을 고른 뒤, 다시 들으면서 빈칸을 채우세요.

1.

(A) The diners are _____.

(B) One of the women is _____.

(C) A server is _____.

(D) A server is _____.

(A)　　　　(B)　　　　(C)　　　　(D)

2.

(A) The people are _____.

(B) The woman is _____.

(C) The man is _____.

(D) The people are _____.

(A)　　　　(B)　　　　(C)　　　　(D)

3.

(A) The people are _____.

(B) One of the men is _____.

(C) The people are _____.

(D) The people are _____.

(A)　　　　(B)　　　　(C)　　　　(D)

사진을 적절하게 묘사한 보기를 고르세요.

1.

(A)　　　(B)　　　(C)　　　(D)

2.

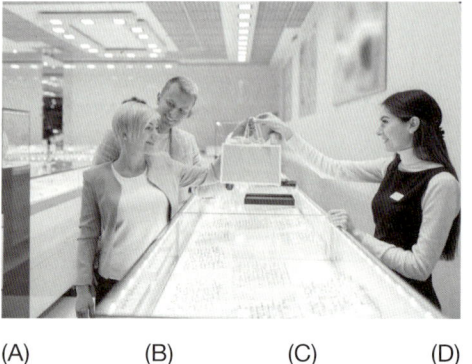

(A)　　　(B)　　　(C)　　　(D)

3.

(A)　　　(B)　　　(C)　　　(D)

4.

(A)　　　(B)　　　(C)　　　(D)

5.

(A)　　　(B)　　　(C)　　　(D)

6.

(A)　　　(B)　　　(C)　　　(D)

빈출 상황 및 사진

🎧 P1_U07_01

가정집 가구, 가정용품, 집 내부 장식 등

Some pictures are hanging on a wall.
그림 몇 개가 벽에 걸려 있다.

A flower vase has been placed on a counter.
꽃병이 조리대 위에 놓여 있다.

A pillow has been set on an armchair.
베개가 안락의자 위에 놓여 있다.

A potted plant is positioned in a corner.
화분에 심은 화초가 구석에 위치해 있다.

Some cushions are arranged on a bed.
쿠션 몇 개가 침대 위에 정리되어 있다.

Plates have been stacked by a windowsill.
접시들이 창틀 옆에 포개져 있다.

A vase has been filled with flowers.
화병이 꽃으로 가득 차 있다.

There is a curtain covering a window.
창문을 가리는 커튼이 있다.

A light fixture is hanging above a dining area.
조명 기구가 식탁 공간 위에 걸려 있다.

A wall is decorated with a pattern design.
벽이 무늬 있는 디자인으로 도배되어 있다.

The view out of the window is completely blocked by curtains.
창문 밖 경관이 커튼으로 완전히 차단되어 있다.

A drawer has been left open.
서랍이 열려 있다.

Some appliances are on a counter.
가전제품들이 조리대 위에 있다.

A seating area has been arranged on a rug.
좌석이 있는 구역이 러그 위에 마련되어 있다.

The refrigerator doors are closed.
냉장고 문이 닫혀 있다.

가사 활동 요리, 청소 등의 집안일

The woman is turning on a stove.
여자가 가스레인지를 켜고 있다.

The woman is scrubbing the countertop.
여자가 조리대를 문질러 닦고 있다.

She's reading a book on a sofa.
그녀는 소파에서 책을 읽고 있다.

A man is preparing some food.
남자가 음식을 준비하고 있다.

She's pushing a button on an appliance.
그녀는 가전제품의 버튼을 누르고 있다.

The woman is looking inside a refrigerator.
여자가 냉장고 안을 들여다보고 있다.

A man is washing dishes in the sink.
남자가 싱크대에서 설거지를 하고 있다.

They're lifting some furniture.
그들은 가구를 들고 있다.

A man is folding some laundry.
남자가 세탁물을 접고 있다.

CHECK UP

🎧 P1_U07_02 정답 및 해설 p.19

1.

(A)　　　　(B)　　　　(C)　　　　(D)

2.

(A)　　　　(B)　　　　(C)　　　　(D)

🎧 P1_U07_03 정답 및 해설 p.20

대화를 듣고 알맞은 답을 고른 뒤, 다시 들으면서 빈칸을 채우세요.

1.

(A)   (B)   (C)   (D)

(A) He's _____.

(B) He's _____.

(C) He's _____.

(D) He's _____.

2.

(A)   (B)   (C)   (D)

(A) Some pictures are _____.

(B) Some furniture is _____.

(C) A mirror has _____.

(D) A sofa has _____.

3.

(A)   (B)   (C)   (D)

(A) She's _____.

(B) She's _____.

(C) She's _____.

(D) She's _____.

사진을 적절하게 묘사한 보기를 고르세요.

1.

(A) (B) (C) (D)

2.

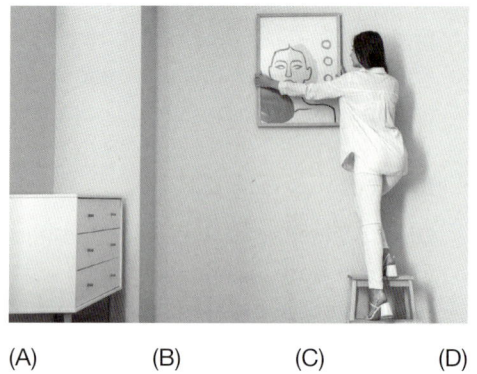

(A) (B) (C) (D)

3.

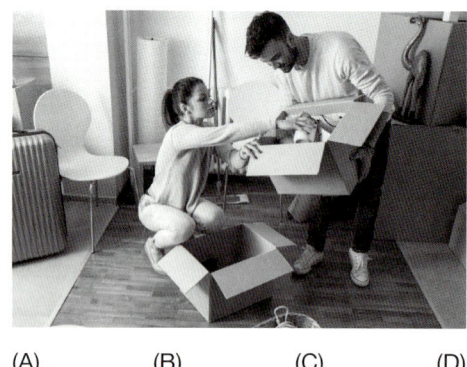

(A) (B) (C) (D)

4.

(A) (B) (C) (D)

5.

(A) (B) (C) (D)

6.

(A) (B) (C) (D)

LISTENING TEST

In the Listening test, you will be asked to demonstrate how well you understand spoken English. The entire Listening test will last approximately 45 minutes. There are four parts, and directions are given for each part. You must mark your answers on the separate answer sheet. Do not write your answers in your test book.

PART 1

Directions: For each question in this part, you will hear four statements about a picture in your test book. When you hear the statements, you must select the one statement that best describes what you see in the picture. Then find the number of the question on your answer sheet and mark your answer. The statements will not be printed in your test book and will be spoken only one time.

Statement (C), "He's making a phone call," is the best description of the picture, so you should select answer (C) and mark it on your answer sheet.

1.

2.

3.

4.

5.

6.

고난도 문제
해설 강의

toeic.eduwill.net

PART

2

출제 경향 및 문제 풀이 전략

PART 2 출제 경향 및 문제 풀이 전략

질문과 3개의 응답을 듣고, 질문에 가장 적절한 응답을 고르는 파트이다. LC 전체 100개의 문항 중 총 25문항이 출제된다.

최신 출제 경향

1. 의문사 의문문과 비의문사 의문문의 출제 빈도는 비슷하다.
의문사 의문문과 평서문을 포함한 비의문사 의문문은 각각 평균 13문제씩 비슷한 비율로 출제된다.

2. 답변 패턴이 다양하다.
질문에 대한 직접적인 답변도 많이 출제되지만 간접적인 답변의 출제 비율이 높아지면서 예측하기 어려운 답변이 나오는 경우가 많아지고 있다. 따라서 학습자들은 이에 대비해 다양한 간접적인 답변을 접하고 익혀야 한다.

3. 평서문의 출제 빈도가 높다.
의문문이 아닌 서술 문장 형태의 평서문의 출제 빈도가 높아졌다. 평서문은 정해진 답변 패턴이 없기 때문에 PART 2의 난이도가 높아졌다고 할 수 있다.

문제 풀이 전략

M Who set up the display? ·

W

(A) A new line of shampoos.
(B) Mr. Erickson did. ·
(C) I rarely shop there.

STEP 1 질문 파악하기
질문의 앞부분과 키워드를 주의 깊게 듣고 질문을 파악한다.
남 누가 진열품을 설치했나요?

STEP 2 오답 소거하며 정답 선택하기
여
(A) 새로운 종류의 샴푸 제품입니다. (×, 질문의 display에서 신제품을 진열하는 상황을 연상하도록 유도해 혼동을 줌)
(B) 에릭슨 씨가 했습니다. (○, 진열한 사람을 묻는 Who 의문에 사람 이름(Mr. Erickson)으로 적절하게 답변함)
(C) 저는 거의 그곳에서 쇼핑하지 않아요. (×, 질문의 display (진열)에서 연상되는 shop(쇼핑하다)을 이용해 혼동을 줌)

1. 의문사 의문문에 Yes/No로 답변한 오답

Yes/No로 답할 수 없는 의문사 의문문에 Yes/No를 이용한 오답이 나온다.

Q Why isn't the museum open today? 박물관이 오늘 왜 문을 안 열었나요?

A (✕) Yes, I'm sure. 네, 확실해요.

A (○) Because it's a national holiday. 국경일이기 때문이에요.

→ 이유를 묻는 Why 의문문에 Yes로 답한 오답이다.

2. 질문 속 의문사가 아닌 다른 의문사에 맞게 답변한 오답

질문 속 의문사가 아닌 다른 의문사 의문문에 적절한 답변을 이용한 오답이 나온다.

Q When will the printer be repaired? 프린터는 언제 고쳐질 건가요?

A (✕) On my desk. 제 책상 위에요.

A (○) Probably this afternoon. 아마도 오늘 오후에요.

→ When 의문문에 의문사 Where에 맞게 답변한 오답이다.

3. 질문 속 어휘를 반복한 오답

질문 속 특정 어휘를 다시 반복해 혼동을 유도하는 오답이 나온다.

Q Do you think our **customer**s will like our new logo?
고객들이 우리의 새로운 로고를 좋아할 거라고 생각하나요?

A (✕) I stayed late to help a **customer**. 저는 고객을 돕기 위해 늦게까지 있었어요.

A (○) Yes, it's very attractive. 네, 그건 굉장히 멋져요.

→ 질문 속 customer를 반복한 오답이다.

4. 유사한 발음을 이용한 오답

질문에 나온 단어와 유사한 발음을 지닌 어휘를 이용해 혼동을 유도하기도 한다.

Q Who gave the presentation on the **launch** event? 출시 행사에서 누가 발표를 했나요?

A (✕) I already ate **lunch**. 저는 이미 점심을 먹었어요.

A (○) The project manager, I believe. 프로젝트 책임자였을 거예요.

→ launch와 유사한 발음을 가진 lunch를 이용한 오답이다.

5. 유사 의미 또는 연상 관계의 단어들을 이용한 오답

질문에 사용된 단어들과 유사한 의미를 지닌 단어, 또는 연상 관계에 있는 단어들을 이용하여 오답 함정을 만들기도 한다.

Q You **transferred** to this branch recently, didn't you? 최근에 이 지점으로 옮기셨죠, 그렇지 않나요?

A (✕) No, we used a **moving** company. 아니요, 우리는 이사 업체를 이용했어요.

A (○) Yes, just last week. 네, 지난주에 왔어요.

→ transfer(옮기다)와 유사한 의미의 단어 move(옮기다)를 이용한 오답이다.

Part 2에서는 질문을 듣고 질문의 앞부분과 키워드를 파악하는 것이 가장 중요하다. 따라서 본 교재에서는 Part 2를 질문 유형에 따라 크게 의문사 의문문과 기타 의문문으로 구분하였다.

의문사 의문문

1. Who 의문문

의문사 Who(누구)로 시작하는 질문으로, 사람과 관련된 내용으로 답변할 수 있다.

Q Who's in charge of the conference this year? 누가 올해 회의 담당인가요?
A I think it is Mr. Nixon. 닉슨 씨인 것 같아요.

2. What · Which 의문문

의문사 What(무엇)이나 Which(어느 것)로 시작하는 질문으로, 의문사 뒤 세부 정보와 관련된 내용으로 답변할 수 있다.

Q What kind of ice cream did you buy? 어떤 종류의 아이스크림을 샀나요?
A I got the strawberry flavor. 딸기 맛을 샀어요.

Q Which bags are on sale? 어느 가방이 할인 판매 중인가요?
A The ones on the right. 오른쪽에 있는 것들이요.

3. When 의문문

의문사 When(언제)으로 시작하는 질문으로, 시간과 관련된 내용으로 응답한다.

Q When does the shop close? 그 상점은 언제 닫나요?
A At 8 o'clock tonight. 오늘 밤 8시에요.

4. Where 의문문

의문사 Where(어디)로 시작하는 질문으로, 주로 장소나 출처와 관련된 내용으로 응답한다.

Q Where is the career workshop being held? 커리어 워크숍은 어디에서 열리고 있나요?
A In conference room. 회의실에서요.

5. How 의문문

의문사 How(어떻게/얼마나)로 시작하는 질문으로, 방법이나 수단 외에도 의견, 수량 등을 묻기도 한다.

Q How was your vacation? 휴가는 어땠어요?
A It was great. 아주 좋았어요.

6. Why 의문문

의문사 Why(왜)로 시작하는 질문으로, 이유나 목적과 관련된 내용으로 응답한다.

Q Why did William move to Boston? 윌리엄은 왜 보스턴으로 이사했나요?
A To start a different job. 다른 일을 시작하기 위해서요.

기타 의문문

1. 조동사/Be동사 의문문

조동사/Be동사로 시작하는 질문으로, 긍정 또는 부정을 나타내거나 부연 설명하는 내용으로 응답한다.

Q Did you finish preparing your presentation? 발표 준비를 끝냈나요?
A No, it's due tomorrow. 아니요, 그건 내일까지예요.

Q Are you ready to go to dinner? 저녁 먹으러 갈 준비가 되었나요?
A I need to finish this report. 전 이 보고서를 끝내야 해요.

2. 부정 의문문

조동사나 Be동사에 not이 붙은 질문으로, Yes/No 답변이 흔하지만 그렇지 않은 답변도 적지 않게 출제된다.

Q Hasn't the new catalogue come in yet? 새 카탈로그가 아직 입고되지 않았나요?
A It should be here by afternoon. 오후까지는 올 거예요.

3. 제안·요청 의문문

의문문 형태이지만 무언가를 권유하거나 요청하는 문장으로, 해당 사항을 수락하거나 거절하는 내용으로 응답한다.

Q Can you please fix my computer? 제 컴퓨터 좀 고쳐주실 수 있나요?
A Sorry, I'm right in the middle of something. 죄송해요, 제가 지금 뭘 좀 하는 중이라서요.

4. 부가 의문문

평서문 뒤에 aren't you?, didn't you?와 같은 꼬리말이 붙은 질문으로, 일반 의문문과 같이 긍정 또는 부정을 나타내거나 부연 설명하는 내용으로 응답한다.

Q I haven't seen Martha since last night, have you? 어젯밤부터 마사가 안 보여요. 당신은 봤나요?
A No, I haven't. / She is on a business trip. 아니요, 저도 못 봤어요. / 그녀는 출장 중이에요.

5. 선택 의문문

접속사 or(또는)를 이용해 두 가지 사항 중에 어느 것을 선택할지 묻는 질문이다.

Q Do you prefer to take the bus or the train? 버스 타길 선호하세요, 아니면 기차를 선호하세요?
A I'd rather take the bus. 저는 차라리 버스를 타겠어요.

6. 간접 의문문

일반 의문문 안에 의문사 의문문이 포함되어 있는 형태의 질문으로, 질문 속 의문사와 관련된 내용으로 응답한다.

Q Do you know how I can turn on this machine? 이 기계를 어떻게 켜는지 아세요?
A Yes, let me show you. 네, 제가 보여드릴게요.

7. 평서문

의문문이 아닌 서술 문장 형태로, 정해진 답변 패턴이 없기 때문에 난이도가 가장 높다.

Q I haven't received the updated employee list yet. 업데이트된 직원 명단을 아직 받지 못했어요.
A I can forward it to you right now. 제가 지금 보내드릴게요.

의문사 의문문

UNIT 01 | Who 의문문

핵심 포인트

1. 어떤 일의 담당자가 누구인지, 누가 맡을 예정인지, 누가 일을 처리했는지를 묻는 질문의 비중이 가장 높으며, 사람 이름이나 직책명으로 답하는 경우가 많다.
2. 인칭대명사로 시작하지만 엉뚱한 내용이 이어지는 답변도 있으므로 끝까지 놓치지 않고 듣는다.
3. 잘 모르겠다거나 다른 이에게 물어보라는 등의 간접 응답의 출제 비율이 높아지고 있으므로 유의한다.

실전 맛보기

🎧 P2_U01_01

Who will book the hotel for the business trip?

(A) I prefer a room with a view.

(B) Mr. Lang, the administrative assistant.

(C) Probably in the afternoon of the 15th.

출장 시 묵을 호텔은 누가 예약할 건가요?

(A) 저는 전망이 좋은 방을 선호해요. (×) '호텔'에서 연상되는 '전망이 좋은 방'을 이용한 오답

(B) 사무 보조인 랑 씨요. (O) 사람 이름과 직책으로 적절하게 답변한 정답

(C) 아마 15일 오후에요. (×) 시점으로 대답한 오답

CHECK UP

🎧 P2_U01_02 정답 및 해설 p.25

1. (A) (B) (C) **2.** (A) (B) (C)

3. (A) (B) (C) **4.** (A) (B) (C)

사람 이름으로 답변

Q Who's designing our new logo? 누가 우리의 새 로고를 디자인하고 있죠?

A1 Terry is working on them. 테리가 하고 있어요.

A2 Vicki, as far as I know. 제가 알기로는 비키요.

A3 Donna is. 도나가 하고 있어요.

A4 Paul takes care of that. 폴이 맡아 하고 있어요.

A5 Maggie said she would. 매기가 하겠다고 했어요.

A6 Eddie's in charge. 에디가 담당하고 있어요.

직책 / 인칭대명사 / 부정대명사로 답변

Q Who's responsible for interviewing the job candidates? 누가 지원자 면접을 담당하고 있나요?

A1 The director of Human Resources. 인사부서장이요.

A2 I'm supposed to do it. 제가 하기로 되어 있어요.

A3 Someone from the personnel department. 인사부서 직원이요.

회사명으로 답변

Q Who's going to sponsor this year's fundraiser? 올해 모금 행사는 어디에서 후원할 예정이죠?

A A new hotel called Paradise View. 파라다이스 뷰라는 새로운 호텔에서요.

정보의 위치로 답변

Q Who's attending Rohan's retirement party? 누가 로한의 은퇴 기념 파티에 참석할 건가요?

A It should be noted on the guest list. 그건 손님 명단에 언급되어 있을 거예요.

모른다거나 남에게 물어보라는 답변

Q Who's in charge of organizing the research symposium? 누가 연구 심포지엄 준비를 담당하나요?

A1 I'm not sure. 잘 모르겠어요.

A2 You'll have to ask Linda. 린다에게 물어보셔야 할 거예요.

A3 You'd better ask Linda. 린다에게 물어보는 게 좋을 거예요.

우회 답변 / 제3의 답변

Q Who's leading the focus group meeting next week? 누가 다음 주에 포커스 그룹 회의를 이끌죠?

A1 It's been delayed until July. 그건 7월로 연기되었어요.

A2 It hasn't been decided yet. 아직 결정되지 않았어요.

A3 We're still deciding. 아직 결정하는 중이에요.

A4 I'll have to check my notes. 메모한 걸 확인해 봐야겠어요.

A5 That will be announced later today. 그건 오늘 늦게 공지될 거예요.

A6 Didn't you get the e-mail this morning? 오늘 아침에 이메일 못 받으셨어요?

고득점 TIP

1. 단순히 질문의 표면적인 의미가 아닌 질문의 의도나 대화가 벌어지고 있는 상황을 짐작하여 정답을 찾아야 하는 경우도 있다.

   Q Who was in the break room last? 누가 마지막으로 휴게실에 있었나요?

   A I noticed that it was messy, too. 저도 지저분하다고 느꼈어요.

2. Who로 물어보는 질문이지만 시간이나 일정에 관련된 내용이 정답이 될 수도 있으므로 Who 의문사만 듣고 무조건 When에 관련된 답변을 소거해서는 안 된다.

   Q Who's going to submit the budget report today? 오늘 누가 예산안을 제출할 거죠?

   A I thought it's due tomorrow. 기한이 내일까지라고 생각했어요.

대화를 듣고 알맞은 답을 고른 뒤, 다시 들으면서 빈칸을 채우세요.

1. (A) (B) (C)

Q Who is _____ on the city project?

(A) I'm _____.

(B) It starts _____.

(C) The _____.

2. (A) (B) (C)

Q Who's leading the _____?

(A) _____ does it.

(B) Certainly, _____.

(C) _____ do you need?

3. (A) (B) (C)

Q Who is _____ for the position?

(A) There were so many _____.

(B) _____.

(C) Probably _____.

4. (A) (B) (C)

Q Who _____ this order form?

(A) Some _____.

(B) _____.

(C) _____.

5. (A) (B) (C)

Q Who _____?

(A) Press _____.

(B) Jeff, _____.

(C) Yes, _____.

대화를 듣고 알맞은 답을 고르세요.

1. Mark your answer on your answer sheet.　　　(A)　　(B)　　(C)

2. Mark your answer on your answer sheet.　　　(A)　　(B)　　(C)

3. Mark your answer on your answer sheet.　　　(A)　　(B)　　(C)

4. Mark your answer on your answer sheet.　　　(A)　　(B)　　(C)

5. Mark your answer on your answer sheet.　　　(A)　　(B)　　(C)

6. Mark your answer on your answer sheet.　　　(A)　　(B)　　(C)

7. Mark your answer on your answer sheet.　　　(A)　　(B)　　(C)

8. Mark your answer on your answer sheet.　　　(A)　　(B)　　(C)

9. Mark your answer on your answer sheet.　　　(A)　　(B)　　(C)

10. Mark your answer on your answer sheet.　　　(A)　　(B)　　(C)

11. Mark your answer on your answer sheet.　　　(A)　　(B)　　(C)

12. Mark your answer on your answer sheet.　　　(A)　　(B)　　(C)

13. Mark your answer on your answer sheet.　　　(A)　　(B)　　(C)

14. Mark your answer on your answer sheet.　　　(A)　　(B)　　(C)

15. Mark your answer on your answer sheet.　　　(A)　　(B)　　(C)

UNIT 02 What·Which 의문문

핵심 포인트
1. 의문사 What과 Which 뒤에 나오는 명사를 주의해서 듣고, What 뒤에 명사가 나오지 않을 때는 동사를 주의해서 듣는다.
2. Which 의문문에서는 대명사 one을 포함한 답변이 정답으로 출제되는 경우가 많다. 하지만, 복수를 선택하거나 우회적인 내용의 정답이 출제될 수 있으므로 유의한다.

실전 맛보기
🎧 P2_U02_01

What's the size of this apartment unit?
(A) Of course. I love the view.
(B) Yes, he works in my department.
(C) Around eight hundred square feet.

이 아파트 한 가구의 면적이 어떻게 되나요?
(A) 물론이죠. 저는 전망이 아주 마음에 들어요. (×) '아파트'에서 연상되는 '전망'을 이용한 오답
(B) 네, 그는 제 부서에서 일하고 있어요. (×) apartment와 department의 유사 발음을 이용한 오답
(C) 약 800평방피트 정도 됩니다. (○) 아파트의 면적을 나타내는 숫자로 적절하게 답변한 정답

Which office are the interns using?
(A) The one next to the sales team's office.
(B) We'll do it in turn.
(C) It's on my desk.

인턴들은 어느 사무실을 사용하나요?
(A) 영업팀 사무실 옆방이요. (○) one은 office를 가리키는 대명사이므로 정답
(B) 차례대로 할 거예요. (×) intern과의 발음의 유사성을 이용한 오답
(C) 그것은 제 책상 위에 있어요. (×) office와 연상되는 desk를 이용한 오답

CHECK UP
🎧 P2_U02_02 정답 및 해설 p.29

1. (A) (B) (C)   **2.** (A) (B) (C)

3. (A) (B) (C)   **4.** (A) (B) (C)

What 빈출 질문 및 응답

| 시간 | **Q** What time is the new employee orientation tomorrow? 내일 신입사원 오리엔테이션은 몇 시인가요? |
| | **A** At 10 in the morning, I think. 아침 10시인 것 같아요. |

| 종류 | **Q** What kind of food does your restaurant serve? 당신의 식당은 어떤 종류의 음식을 제공하나요? |
| | **A** Italian, mostly. 주로 이탈리안 음식이요. |

방법	**Q** What's the best way to get to the convention center? 컨벤션 센터로 가는 가장 좋은 방법이 무엇인가요?
	A1 A taxi is probably the best. 아마 택시가 가장 나을 거예요.
	A2 I'd take the bus. 저라면 버스를 타겠어요.
	A3 Let's take a look at the train schedule. 열차 시간표를 한번 봅시다.

| 가격 | **Q** What's the price of this sweater? 이 스웨터의 가격은 얼마인가요? |
| | **A** It's on sale for 45 dollars. 할인해서 45달러예요. |

의견	**Q** What do you think about our new logo? 우리 새로운 로고에 대해 어떻게 생각하시나요?
	A1 We should make the font smaller. 글씨를 좀 더 작게 해야겠어요.
	A2 Actually, I like the old one. 사실 저는 이전 것이 좋아요.

| 의무 | **Q** What should we bring to the training session? 우리는 교육 때 무엇을 가져가야 하나요? |
| | **A** Just a pen will be fine. 펜 하나면 될 거예요. |

Which, Which of 빈출 질문 및 응답

대명사 one을 사용한 대답

Q Which photograph should we use for the article? 그 기사에 어떤 사진을 써야 하죠?
A1 The one with the CEO. CEO가 함께 있는 거요.
A2 The third one on the right. 오른쪽 세 번째 거요.
A3 I prefer the one that was taken in the office. 사무실에서 찍은 게 더 좋아요.

모두 다 좋다고 할 때

Q Which of these dates is more convenient for you? 이 날짜들 중 어느 날이 당신에게 더 편한가요?
A1 They are all good for me. 다 좋아요.
A2 They all work for me. 다 괜찮아요.

고득점 TIP

Which로 물어볼 경우 무조건 one이 쓰인 것을 정답으로 골라서는 안 된다.

Q Which company was hired to renovate the building? 건물 개조를 위해 어떤 회사가 고용됐나요?
(A) That project has been postponed. 그 프로젝트는 연기되었어요. (○)
(B) One of our most popular designs. 우리의 가장 인기 있는 디자인 중 하나요. (×)
(C) A 7-story building. 7층 건물이에요. (×)

대화를 듣고 알맞은 답을 고른 뒤, 다시 들으면서 빈칸을 채우세요.

1. (A)   (B)   (C)

Q _____ the banquet hall?

(A) The _____ there.

(B) There was an _____.

(C) Yes, _____.

2. (A)   (B)   (C)

Q _____ produces these umbrellas?

(A) Probably _____.

(B) Yes, it's going _____.

(C) _____ Louisville.

3. (A)   (B)   (C)

Q Which parking lot is _____ the Macy Theater?

(A) I suggest _____.

(B) The new theater _____.

(C) No, it's not _____.

4. (A)   (B)   (C)

Q _____ of the president's speech?

(A) _____ next month.

(B) She really _____.

(C) _____.

5. (A)   (B)   (C)

Q What _____ do you need?

(A) _____.

(B) _____.

(C) _____ documents.

대화를 듣고 알맞은 답을 고르세요.

1. Mark your answer on your answer sheet. (A) (B) (C)

2. Mark your answer on your answer sheet. (A) (B) (C)

3. Mark your answer on your answer sheet. (A) (B) (C)

4. Mark your answer on your answer sheet. (A) (B) (C)

5. Mark your answer on your answer sheet. (A) (B) (C)

6. Mark your answer on your answer sheet. (A) (B) (C)

7. Mark your answer on your answer sheet. (A) (B) (C)

8. Mark your answer on your answer sheet. (A) (B) (C)

9. Mark your answer on your answer sheet. (A) (B) (C)

10. Mark your answer on your answer sheet. (A) (B) (C)

11. Mark your answer on your answer sheet. (A) (B) (C)

12. Mark your answer on your answer sheet. (A) (B) (C)

13. Mark your answer on your answer sheet. (A) (B) (C)

14. Mark your answer on your answer sheet. (A) (B) (C)

15. Mark your answer on your answer sheet. (A) (B) (C)

PART 2 UNIT 02

핵심 포인트

1. 의문사 When 뒤에 나오는 Be동사/조동사의 시제(과거, 현재, 미래)를 주의해서 듣는다.
2. 전치사와 함께 구체적인 시간을 언급하거나 다양한 시간 관련 표현들이 자주 등장하므로 반드시 익혀 두도록 한다.
3. 시간 관련 표현이 오답으로 나오는 경우도 있으므로 이러한 함정에 빠지지 않도록 유의한다.
4. 미래에 일어날 일의 시점을 묻는 질문에 이미 그 일을 했다고 답하는 패턴의 문제가 종종 출제되고 있으므로 유의한다.

실전 맛보기　　　　　　　　　　　　　　　　　　　　　　　🎧 P2_U03_01

When can you review the stack of résumés with me?

(A) How about after lunch?
(B) Yes, we're reviewing her application now.
(C) Behind the office building.

··

언제 저와 이 쌓인 이력서들을 검토하실 수 있나요?

(A) 점심 식사 후에 어때요? (O) 점심 식사 후라는 시점을 제안한 정답
(B) 네, 우리는 그녀의 지원서를 지금 검토하고 있어요. (×) 의문사 의문문에 Yes로 답변한 오답
(C) 사무실 건물 뒤에요. (×) 위치로 답변한 오답

CHECK UP　　　　　　　　　　　　　　　　🎧 P2_U03_02 정답 및 해설 p.34

1. (A)　　　　(B)　　　　(C)　　　　　**2.** (A)　　　　(B)　　　　(C)

3. (A)　　　　(B)　　　　(C)　　　　　**4.** (A)　　　　(B)　　　　(C)

시제별 질문과 답변

Q When did we last conduct a safety inspection? 우리가 마지막으로 안전 검사를 한 게 언제예요?
A About two months ago. 두 달 전쯤에요.

Q When does the museum open? 박물관은 언제 문을 열죠?
A Not until 10:00 in the morning. 아침 10시 넘어야 해요.

Q When are they going to replace the copy machine? 언제 그들은 복사기를 교체할 건가요?
A Before the end of the month. 이달 말 이전에요.

우회적 답변 / 제3의 답변

Q When will our pasta be ready? 저희 파스타는 언제 나오나요?
A1 I'll check with our chef. 주방장에게 물어볼게요.
A2 The kitchen is very busy tonight. 오늘 밤 주방이 너무 바쁘네요.

Q When are you moving to your new office? 언제 새 사무실로 옮기세요?
A1 The schedule is not fixed yet. 일정이 아직 정해지지 않았어요.
A2 I already moved a few days ago. 벌써 며칠 전에 옮겼어요.

Q When are the new employees starting? 신입사원들은 언제부터 출근하죠?
A1 There are two people left to interview. 두 명 더 면접을 봐야 해요.
A2 We're a bit behind schedule. 일정이 좀 늦어졌어요.

빈출 표현   🎧 P2_U03_04

과거	Sometime last week. 지난주쯤에요.
	A couple of days ago. 며칠 전에요.
	In February, as far as I know. 제가 알기로는 2월이요.
	Last quarter, if I remember correctly. 제 기억이 맞다면 지난 분기요.

현재	At 10 A.M. every day. 매일 오전 10시에요.
	Every night at nine. 매일 밤 9시에요.
	On weekdays at 6. 평일 6시에요.
	Usually around lunchtime 보통 점심시간 쯤에요.
	On the first Tuesday of every month. 매달 첫 화요일마다요.

미래	Earlier would be better. 빠를수록 좋아요.
	The same time as last night. 어젯밤과 같은 시간에요.
	Monday might work well. 월요일이 좋을 것 같아요.
	It's scheduled for 3 o'clock. 3시로 예정되어 있어요.
	Wednesday the 9th is convenient. 9일 수요일이 편해요.

고득점 TIP

시점을 묻는 질문에 회의, 워크숍과 같은 행사를 의미하는 단어가 포함된 답변이 정답이 될 수도 있다.

Q When will the new partnership be announced? 새로운 파트너십은 언제 발표될까요?
A At the board meeting next week. 다음 주 이사회에서요.

대화를 듣고 알맞은 답을 고른 뒤, 다시 들으면서 빈칸을 채우세요.

1. (A) (B) (C)

Q When did Samantha _____ the supply room?

(A) _____.

(B) _____ boxes.

(C) She cleaned _____.

2. (A) (B) (C)

Q _____ inventory of our stock?

(A) Our toasters _____.

(B) _____.

(C) Yes, _____ the shelves.

3. (A) (B) (C)

Q When _____ to work on our project?

(A) Come to _____.

(B) It _____, right?

(C) _____ my calendar.

4. (A) (B) (C)

Q When will you _____?

(A) _____ he has a good _____.

(B) _____ by phone.

(C) _____.

5. (A) (B) (C)

Q _____ the morning mail delivery?

(A) _____ nine _____.

(B) _____ over there.

(C) Thanks, but _____.

대화를 듣고 알맞은 답을 고르세요.

1. Mark your answer on your answer sheet.　　　　　(A)　　(B)　　(C)

2. Mark your answer on your answer sheet.　　　　　(A)　　(B)　　(C)

3. Mark your answer on your answer sheet.　　　　　(A)　　(B)　　(C)

4. Mark your answer on your answer sheet.　　　　　(A)　　(B)　　(C)

5. Mark your answer on your answer sheet.　　　　　(A)　　(B)　　(C)

6. Mark your answer on your answer sheet.　　　　　(A)　　(B)　　(C)

7. Mark your answer on your answer sheet.　　　　　(A)　　(B)　　(C)

8. Mark your answer on your answer sheet.　　　　　(A)　　(B)　　(C)

9. Mark your answer on your answer sheet.　　　　　(A)　　(B)　　(C)

10. Mark your answer on your answer sheet.　　　　　(A)　　(B)　　(C)

11. Mark your answer on your answer sheet.　　　　　(A)　　(B)　　(C)

12. Mark your answer on your answer sheet.　　　　　(A)　　(B)　　(C)

13. Mark your answer on your answer sheet.　　　　　(A)　　(B)　　(C)

14. Mark your answer on your answer sheet.　　　　　(A)　　(B)　　(C)

15. Mark your answer on your answer sheet.　　　　　(A)　　(B)　　(C)

PART 2 UNIT 03

핵심 포인트
1. 전치사를 포함한 장소/위치로 답하는 경우가 많지만 전치사를 이용한 오답에 유의한다.
2. 해당 정보를 확인할 수 있는 방법을 말해주거나 반문으로 답하는 간접적인 응답의 출제 비율이 높아지고 있다.
3. 빠르게 발음하면 Where과 When의 발음이 비슷하게 들릴 수 있으므로 이를 함정으로 이용한 When 관련 답변이 종종 오답으로 출제된다.

실전 맛보기 🎧 P2_U04_01

Where will the journalism convention be held in May?

(A) She actually owns the newspaper.
(B) Probably on the 15th.
(C) In Boston, I think.

저널리즘 회의는 5월에 어디에서 열릴까요?

(A) 그녀는 사실 신문사를 운영하고 있어요. (×) '저널리즘'에서 연상되는 '신문사'를 이용한 오답
(B) 아마 15일에요. (×) When 질문에 해당하는 오답
(C) 보스턴인 것 같아요. (O) 장소(Boston)로 적절하게 답변한 정답

CHECK UP 🎧 P2_U04_02 정답 및 해설 p.39

1. (A)   (B)   (C)   **2.** (A)   (B)   (C)

3. (A)   (B)   (C)   **4.** (A)   (B)   (C)

장소 / 위치로 답변

Q Where is the investment seminar being held this year? 투자 세미나가 이번 해에는 어디에서 열리나요?

A The same hotel as last year. 작년과 같은 호텔에서요.

Q Where can I find an extra stapler? 여분의 스테이플러를 어디에서 찾을 수 있나요?

A In the bottom desk drawer. 책상 서랍 맨 아래 칸에서요.

사람으로 답변

Q Where are the keys to the storeroom? 창고 열쇠는 어디에 있나요?

A Helen had them last. 마지막으로 헬렌이 그것들을 가지고 있었어요.

반문으로 답변

Q Where is the presentation remote clicker? 프레젠테이션용 리모컨이 어디에 있죠?

A Didn't Helen use it at the meeting yesterday? 헬렌이 어제 회의할 때 쓰지 않았나요?

우회적 답변 / 제3의 답변

Q Where should we put the new printer? 새 프린터를 어디에 놓아야 하나요?

A You'd better ask Terry. 테리에게 물어보는 게 좋겠어요.

Q Where did you buy this coffee machine? 이 커피 머신 어디에서 샀어요?

A It was a gift. 선물로 받았어요.

빈출 표현 🎧 P2_U04_04

in **on** **at**	in the top drawer 맨 위 서랍에 in aisle two 2번 통로에 in the lobby 로비에 in the supply room 비품실에 in Berlin, Germany 독일 베를린에 on the 5th floor 5층에 on the top shelf 선반 맨 위 칸에 on a Web site 웹사이트에	on the next block 다음 블록에 on George Street 조지 가에 on the other side of town 도시 반대쪽에 at the back of the building 건물 뒤에 at the end of aisle three 3번 통로 끝에 at a hotel in London 런던에 있는 호텔에 at the supermarket on the corner 모퉁이에 있는 슈퍼마켓에
그 외	near the entrance 입구 근처에 behind the office building 사무실 건물 뒤에 down the street 길 끝에 by the loading dock 하역장 옆에 across from the pharmacy 약국 건너편에	just around the corner 모퉁이를 돌아서 바로 A town 35 minutes away. 35분 거리의 마을에서요. You can register online. 온라인에서 등록할 수 있어요. Next to the door would be good. 문 옆이 좋을 거예요.

고득점 TIP

건물의 위치를 묻는 질문에 사물의 위치로 답한 표현이 오답으로 출제될 수 있다. 단순히 장소/위치 관련 전치사(in, on, at, by 등)만 듣고 정답을 선택하지 않도록 한다.

Q Where's the nearest pharmacy? 가장 가까운 약국은 어디에 있나요?

(A) In the first drawer. (×) 첫 번째 서랍에요.

(B) The closest one is on Hewes Street. (○) 가장 가까운 곳은 휴즈 거리에 있어요.

대화를 듣고 알맞은 답을 고른 뒤, 다시 들으면서 빈칸을 채우세요.

1. (A)　(B)　(C)

Q ＿＿＿＿＿＿ the new branch office ＿＿＿＿＿＿?

(A) Approximately ＿＿＿＿＿＿＿＿＿.

(B) Should I ＿＿＿＿＿＿＿＿＿ them?

(C) It's just ＿＿＿＿＿＿＿＿＿.

2. (A)　(B)　(C)

Q Where are the old ＿＿＿＿＿＿＿＿＿?

(A) Thank you for ＿＿＿＿＿＿＿＿.

(B) ＿＿＿＿＿＿＿＿＿ storage closet.

(C) He wasn't ＿＿＿＿＿＿＿＿.

3. (A)　(B)　(C)

Q Where can we ＿＿＿＿＿＿＿＿＿?

(A) Three ＿＿＿＿＿＿＿＿.

(B) There is ＿＿＿＿＿＿＿＿.

(C) The ＿＿＿＿＿＿＿＿ as last year.

4. (A)　(B)　(C)

Q ＿＿＿＿＿＿ I get my ID ＿＿＿＿＿＿?

(A) ＿＿＿＿＿＿＿＿.

(B) ＿＿＿＿＿＿＿＿ security office.

(C) She's ＿＿＿＿＿＿＿＿.

5. (A)　(B)　(C)

Q ＿＿＿＿＿＿＿＿＿ clients for a meal?

(A) ＿＿＿＿＿＿＿＿ still interested.

(B) I don't ＿＿＿＿＿＿＿＿ clients.

(C) ＿＿＿＿＿＿＿＿ reservation.

대화를 듣고 알맞은 답을 고르세요.

1. Mark your answer on your answer sheet.　　　(A)　　(B)　　(C)

2. Mark your answer on your answer sheet.　　　(A)　　(B)　　(C)

3. Mark your answer on your answer sheet.　　　(A)　　(B)　　(C)

4. Mark your answer on your answer sheet.　　　(A)　　(B)　　(C)

5. Mark your answer on your answer sheet.　　　(A)　　(B)　　(C)

6. Mark your answer on your answer sheet.　　　(A)　　(B)　　(C)

7. Mark your answer on your answer sheet.　　　(A)　　(B)　　(C)

8. Mark your answer on your answer sheet.　　　(A)　　(B)　　(C)

9. Mark your answer on your answer sheet.　　　(A)　　(B)　　(C)

10. Mark your answer on your answer sheet.　　　(A)　　(B)　　(C)

11. Mark your answer on your answer sheet.　　　(A)　　(B)　　(C)

12. Mark your answer on your answer sheet.　　　(A)　　(B)　　(C)

13. Mark your answer on your answer sheet.　　　(A)　　(B)　　(C)

14. Mark your answer on your answer sheet.　　　(A)　　(B)　　(C)

15. Mark your answer on your answer sheet.　　　(A)　　(B)　　(C)

핵심 포인트

1. How 다음에 조동사나 be동사가 나오면 '어떻게'의 의미이거나 방법, 수단, 또는 의견을 묻는 질문이다.
2. How 다음에 나오는 형용사나 부사에 따라 기간/수량/빈도/가격 등 묻는 내용이 결정되므로 질문의 앞부분을 특히 유의해서 들어야 한다.
3. How soon ~?(시기)/How deep ~?(깊이)/How quickly ~?(속도) 등 다양한 형용사와 부사를 이용한 질문이 출제되기도 한다.

실전 맛보기 🎧 P2_U05_01

How did the product demonstration go yesterday?

(A) Everything went really well.
(B) Let me show you a few more.
(C) It's about 2:30.

어제 제품 시연은 어떻게 되었나요?

(A) 모든 게 다 잘 됐어요. (○) How did... go?는 "~이 어떻게 되었나?"는 질문이므로 정답.
(B) 몇 개 더 보여드릴게요. (×) demonstration에서 연상되는 내용을 이용한 오답
(C) 2시 30분쯤이요. (×) When에 관한 답변이므로 오답

CHECK UP 🎧 P2_U05_02 정답 및 해설 p.43

1. (A)   (B)   (C)   **2.** (A)   (B)   (C)

3. (A)   (B)   (C)   **4.** (A)   (B)   (C)

방법 수단	**How do I...?**
	Q How do I sign up for the seminar? 그 세미나에 어떻게 등록하죠?
	A You need to fill out a form online. 온라인에서 양식을 작성하셔야 돼요.
	Q How do I get to the city hall from here? 여기에서 시청으로 어떻게 가죠?
	A Turn left at the next corner. 다음 모퉁이에서 왼쪽으로 돌아가세요.
의견	**How was...? / How did you like...? / How did... go?**
	Q How was the trade show yesterday? 어제 열렸던 무역박람회는 어땠나요?
	A It was very successful! 굉장히 성공적이었어요!
	Q How did you like the café? 그 카페는 마음에 들었나요?
	A It was great. Well worth the drive. 훌륭했어요. 운전해서 찾아간 보람이 있었어요.
	Q How did yesterday's meeting with the clients go? 어제 고객들과의 미팅은 어땠나요?
	A Deborah met with them. 데보라가 고객들을 만났어요.
수량	**How many...?**
	Q How many chairs need to be set up for the seminar? 세미나를 위해 얼마나 많은 의자를 설치해야 하나요?
	A1 At least twenty. 적어도 스무 개요.
	A2 Tracy has the list of attendees. 트레이시에게 참가자 리스트가 있어요.
	A3 You should call Jonathan, the planner. 기획자인 조나단에게 전화해 보셔야 해요.
가격	**How much...?**
	Q How much does this toaster oven cost? 이 오븐 토스터는 얼마인가요?
	A It's on sale for 450 dollars. 세일해서 450달러에요.
기간	**How long...?**
	Q How long have you worked with John? 존과 함께 일을 한 지 얼마나 됐나요?
	A1 About four years. 약 4년 동안이요.
	A2 I just started working here. 저는 이제 막 여기서 일하기 시작했어요.
빈도	**How often...?**
	Q How often does the tennis club meet? 테니스 클럽은 얼마나 자주 만나나요?
	A1 Twice a month. 한 달에 두 번이요.
	A2 Once every two weeks. 2주에 한 번이요.
기타	**How soon...?**
	Q How soon can you start reviewing the applications? 신청서 검토를 언제 시작할 수 있나요?
	A I'll start now. 지금 시작할게요.

고득점 TIP

특정 정보를 묻는 의문사 의문문에는 Yes/No 답변이 불가하지만, How about ~?(~하는 게 어때요?)으로 시작하는 의문문에는 Yes/No로 답변이 가능하다.

Q   How about shortening our business hours?   영업시간을 단축하는 게 어때요?

A   Yes, that's a good idea.   그래요, 좋은 생각이에요.

PART 2   UNIT 05

대화를 듣고 알맞은 답을 고른 뒤, 다시 들으면서 빈칸을 채우세요.

1. (A) (B) (C) **Q** _____ holiday party yesterday?

(A) Yes, _____.

(B) _____.

(C) _____.

2. (A) (B) (C) **Q** How _____ at headquarters?

(A) _____.

(B) _____.

(C) _____ working hours.

3. (A) (B) (C) **Q** _____ for catering?

(A) Yes, _____.

(B) Just fill _____.

(C) About _____.

4. (A) (B) (C) **Q** _____ go back to London to visit?

(A) _____.

(B) Well, I _____

(C) Yeah, it's one _____.

5. (A) (B) (C) **Q** How much _____?

(A) _____.

(B) _____ summer catalog.

(C) _____ with the computer.

대화를 듣고 알맞은 답을 고르세요.

1. Mark your answer on your answer sheet.   (A)   (B)   (C)

2. Mark your answer on your answer sheet.   (A)   (B)   (C)

3. Mark your answer on your answer sheet.   (A)   (B)   (C)

4. Mark your answer on your answer sheet.   (A)   (B)   (C)

5. Mark your answer on your answer sheet.   (A)   (B)   (C)

6. Mark your answer on your answer sheet.   (A)   (B)   (C)

7. Mark your answer on your answer sheet.   (A)   (B)   (C)

8. Mark your answer on your answer sheet.   (A)   (B)   (C)

9. Mark your answer on your answer sheet.   (A)   (B)   (C)

10. Mark your answer on your answer sheet.   (A)   (B)   (C)

11. Mark your answer on your answer sheet.   (A)   (B)   (C)

12. Mark your answer on your answer sheet.   (A)   (B)   (C)

13. Mark your answer on your answer sheet.   (A)   (B)   (C)

14. Mark your answer on your answer sheet.   (A)   (B)   (C)

15. Mark your answer on your answer sheet.   (A)   (B)   (C)

PART 2

UNIT 05

핵심 포인트

1. 'Why + 조동사' 다음에 나오는 주어와 동사를 집중해서 듣도록 한다.
2. because/for 또는 to부정사를 이용해 답하는 경우가 많지만 이 표현들이 생략된 형태의 정답도 자주 출제된다.
3. because/for 또는 to부정사로 시작하는 함정도 있으므로 끝까지 놓치지 않고 듣는다.

실전 맛보기 🎧 P2_U06_01

Why was Granson Road closed this morning?

(A) We rode together in my car.
(B) The morning meeting was canceled.
(C) The city recently approved some repairs.

오늘 아침 그랜슨 도로가 왜 폐쇄되었나요?

(A) 우리는 제 차를 함께 탔어요. (×) road와 발음이 같은 rode를 이용한 오답
(B) 아침 회의가 취소됐어요. (×) morning을 반복한 오답
(C) 시에서 최근 보수를 승인했어요. (○) 도로 폐쇄의 원인이 보수 때문이라고 우회적으로 답변한 정답

CHECK UP 🎧 P2_U06_02 정답 및 해설 p.48

| 1. | (A) | (B) | (C) | 2. | (A) | (B) | (C) |
| 3. | (A) | (B) | (C) | 4. | (A) | (B) | (C) |

이유 / 원인으로 답변

Q Why will the museum be closed tomorrow? 왜 박물관이 내일 문을 닫죠?
A1 Because it's a national holiday. 공휴일이라서요.
A2 It's closed on Mondays. 월요일마다 문을 닫아요.
A3 I heard it will be renovated. 보수 공사를 한다고 들었어요.

Q Why do you work so late these days? 요즘 왜 이렇게 늦게까지 일하세요?
A I have a deadline coming up. 마감일이 다가오고 있어서요.

목적으로 답변

Q Why did Mitchell leave early today? 미첼은 왜 오늘 일찍 떠났죠?
A1 To pick Mr. Torres up from the train station. 기차역으로 토레스 씨를 마중 나가기 위해서요.
A2 For a client meeting. 고객과의 미팅을 위해서요.

반문으로 답변

Q Why do we have another meeting about the budget? 왜 또 예산안에 대해 회의하는 거죠?
A Have you seen last quarter's sales figures? 지난 분기 매출액 보셨어요?

Q Why haven't the tables been set up in the garden? 테이블이 왜 정원에 설치되지 않았죠?
A Have you seen the weather forecast? 일기예보 보셨어요?

Q Why aren't the trainees in the conference room now? 왜 교육생들이 지금 회의실에 없는 거죠?
A Didn't you get an e-mail with the updated schedule? 수정된 일정을 이메일로 못 받으셨어요?

모른다거나 다른 사람에게 물어보라는 답변

Q Why am I not authorized to access this Web site? 저는 왜 이 웹사이트에 접속 권한이 없죠?
A1 I'm not really sure. 잘 모르겠어요.
A2 You'd better check with your manager. 매니저에게 확인해 보는 게 좋겠어요.

빈출 표현

P2_U06_04

원인 이유	Because a machine is broken. 기계가 고장 났기 때문이에요.
	Because the network is down. 네트워크가 먹통이기 때문이에요.
	Because not enough people enrolled. 등록한 사람들이 충분하지 않기 때문이에요.
	Because it's supposed to rain all weekend. 주말 내내 비가 내릴 거기 때문이에요.
	Because there's a problem with the Web site. 웹사이트에 문제가 있기 때문이에요.
	There was a scheduling conflict. 일정이 겹쳤어요.
	We missed the submission deadline. 제출 마감일을 놓쳤어요.

고득점 TIP

질문의 의도에 불평이 담겨 있다는 것을 파악하고 이에 되묻거나 해결책을 제시하는 답변이 정답이 될 수도 있다.

Q Why are they cleaning the carpets now? 왜 그들은 지금 카펫을 청소하고 있는 거죠?
A Is the noise bothering you? 소음이 신경 쓰이나요?

PART 2 UNIT 06

연습 문제

대화를 듣고 알맞은 답을 고른 뒤, 다시 들으면서 빈칸을 채우세요.

1. (A) (B) (C)   **Q** _____ Macon Airlines?

(A) Yes, _____ a ticket.

(B) An _____.

(C) _____ it's the cheapest.

2. (A) (B) (C)   **Q** _____ they received the _____?

(A) I forgot _____.

(B) The _____.

(C) _____.

3. (A) (B) (C)   **Q** Why was the _____?

(A) _____.

(B) Every summer _____.

(C) _____ weather.

4. (A) (B) (C)   **Q** Why is Mr. Gonzalo _____?

(A) _____.

(B) _____.

(C) It's a _____.

5. (A) (B) (C)   **Q** _____ my credit card been _____?

(A) A _____ car.

(B) You'll have to _____.

(C) The _____ for returns.

대화를 듣고 알맞은 답을 고르세요.

1. Mark your answer on your answer sheet. (A) (B) (C)

2. Mark your answer on your answer sheet. (A) (B) (C)

3. Mark your answer on your answer sheet. (A) (B) (C)

4. Mark your answer on your answer sheet. (A) (B) (C)

5. Mark your answer on your answer sheet. (A) (B) (C)

6. Mark your answer on your answer sheet. (A) (B) (C)

7. Mark your answer on your answer sheet. (A) (B) (C)

8. Mark your answer on your answer sheet. (A) (B) (C)

9. Mark your answer on your answer sheet. (A) (B) (C)

10. Mark your answer on your answer sheet. (A) (B) (C)

11. Mark your answer on your answer sheet. (A) (B) (C)

12. Mark your answer on your answer sheet. (A) (B) (C)

13. Mark your answer on your answer sheet. (A) (B) (C)

14. Mark your answer on your answer sheet. (A) (B) (C)

15. Mark your answer on your answer sheet. (A) (B) (C)

PART 2 UNIT 06

핵심 포인트

1. Do 의문문은 사실이나 의견을, Have 의문문은 경험이나 상태를 확인하는 내용으로 출제되는데 Yes/No 가 나온 뒤 부연 설명이 이어지거나 Yes/No를 생략한 답변이 주로 정답으로 나온다.

2. Can 의문문은 가능 상황을, Will 의문문은 미래 계획을, Should 의문문은 의무적 상황을 확인하는 등 조동사 종류와 그 쓰임이 다양하므로 이에 맞는 다양한 정답 패턴을 익혀 둬야 한다.

3. 질문의 주어와 답변의 주어가 일치하지 않는 경우도 있으므로 주어를 정확하게 파악한다.

실전 맛보기   🎧 P2_U07_01

Did the football jerseys sell out as we expected?

(A) There are a few boxes left in the stockroom.
(B) It could be a competitive tournament.
(C) I like to go swimming instead.

....

축구 셔츠가 우리가 예상한 대로 다 팔렸나요?

(A) 창고에 몇 상자 남아 있어요. (○) No를 생략한 채 부정의 의미로 답변한 정답
(B) 경쟁이 치열한 토너먼트가 될 거예요. (×) 축구에서 연상되는 토너먼트를 이용한 오답
(C) 대신 수영을 하러 가고 싶어요. (×) 축구처럼 운동 종목의 하나인 수영을 이용한 오답

CHECK UP   🎧 P2_U07_02 정답 및 해설 p.53

1. (A)   (B)   (C)   **2.** (A)   (B)   (C)

3. (A)   (B)   (C)   **4.** (A)   (B)   (C)

Do/ Does/ Did	**Q**	**Do** you sell gift cards in your store? 가게에서 기프트 카드를 파나요?
	A	Yes, they're in the last aisle. 네, 제일 끝 통로에 있어요.
	Q	**Does** your restaurant offer delivery service? 당신의 식당은 배달 서비스를 제공하나요?
	A	Yes, except on Sundays. 네, 일요일만 제외하고요.
	Q	**Did** you take the bus to get here? 버스 타고 오셨어요?
	A	No, I drove. 아니요, 운전해서 왔어요.
Have	**Q**	Have you met Mr. Lee, the new HR director? 새 인사부장으로 온 이 씨를 만나봤어요?
	A	I've been in meetings all day. 전 하루 종일 회의에 참석했어요.
	Q	Have you finished reviewing the contract? 계약서 검토를 다 했나요?
	A1	It's longer than I thought. 그건 생각보다 길어요.
	A2	I need to finish this report first. 이 보고서를 먼저 끝내야 해요.
Can	**Q**	Can you send me a link to that Web site? 그 웹사이트 링크를 제게 보내주실 수 있으세요?
	A1	Sorry, I can't connect to the Internet. 미안해요, 인터넷 연결이 안 돼요.
	A2	OK, I'll do that now. 네, 지금 보낼게요.
	Q	Can we afford to replace all these computers? 이 컴퓨터들을 전부 교체할 형편이 될까요?
	A	There's a sale on electronics tomorrow. 내일 전자제품 세일을 한대요.
	Q	Can I speak to you for a minute? 잠깐 얘기할 시간 있으세요?
	A	Sorry, my client is waiting outside. 죄송한데, 제 고객이 밖에서 기다리고 있어서요.
Will	**Q**	Will we discuss the new project at Thursday's meeting? 목요일 회의에서 새 프로젝트에 대해 논의할 건가요?
	A	Haven't you seen the agenda? 의제를 못 봤나요?
	Q	Will you be at the meeting in the afternoon? 오후에 회의에 참석하시나요?
	A1	Yes, I'll be there. 네, 갈 거예요.
	A2	I have a dentist appointment. 치과 예약이 있어요.
Should	**Q**	Should we reserve a conference room for the interview? 면접을 위해 회의실을 예약해야 할까요?
	A	No, we hired someone last week. 아니요, 우린 지난 주에 다른 사람을 고용했어요.

고득점 TIP

Yes/No로 답변 후 엉뚱한 주어를 이용하거나 연상 어휘를 이용한 오답에 주의한다.

Q Do you have Carol's work e-mail address? 캐롤의 사내 메일 주소를 아나요?

A No, they didn't find anymore. (×) 아니요, 그들은 더 이상 찾지 못했어요. → Carol은 she에 해당

A Yes, he moved to London. (×) 네, 그는 런던으로 이사했어요. → address(주소)와 move(옮기다)를 이용한 오답

대화를 듣고 알맞은 답을 고른 뒤, 다시 들으면서 빈칸을 채우세요.

1. (A) (B) (C)

Q _____ be inspected for a leak?

(A) It _____ last weekend.

(B) That's _____.

(C) _____ the reception desk.

2. (A) (B) (C)

Q _____ been delayed?

(A) Has he _____ on it?

(B) I can _____ on my phone.

(C) I was late again _____.

3. (A) (B) (C)

Q _____ Thomas _____ Friday's staff meeting?

(A) Sure, _____.

(B) Yes, _____.

(C) We _____.

4. (A) (B) (C)

Q Did you _____ for the computer?

(A) _____ 50 dollars.

(B) They're _____.

(C) _____ in Sales.

5. (A) (B) (C)

Q Have you ever _____ team?

(A) Yes, back _____ for Fordman's.

(B) The bank _____ it.

(C) The _____ them.

대화를 듣고 알맞은 답을 고르세요.

1. Mark your answer on your answer sheet. (A) (B) (C)

2. Mark your answer on your answer sheet. (A) (B) (C)

3. Mark your answer on your answer sheet. (A) (B) (C)

4. Mark your answer on your answer sheet. (A) (B) (C)

5. Mark your answer on your answer sheet. (A) (B) (C)

6. Mark your answer on your answer sheet. (A) (B) (C)

7. Mark your answer on your answer sheet. (A) (B) (C)

8. Mark your answer on your answer sheet. (A) (B) (C)

9. Mark your answer on your answer sheet. (A) (B) (C)

10. Mark your answer on your answer sheet. (A) (B) (C)

11. Mark your answer on your answer sheet. (A) (B) (C)

12. Mark your answer on your answer sheet. (A) (B) (C)

13. Mark your answer on your answer sheet. (A) (B) (C)

14. Mark your answer on your answer sheet. (A) (B) (C)

15. Mark your answer on your answer sheet. (A) (B) (C)

핵심 포인트

1. Be동사의 시제와 질문의 주어를 주의해서 듣는다.
2. Yes/No가 포함된 직접적인 정답 유형이 자주 출제되지만 Yes/No가 생략된 채 우회적으로 표현하는 응답의 출제 비율이 높아지고 있으므로 유의한다.
3. be + -ing는 현재진행형 시제뿐만 아니라 미래 계획을 나타내는 시제로도 쓰이므로 유의한다.

실전 맛보기　🎧 P2_U08_01

Are you going on the Boston sightseeing tour?
(A) Where did you see her?
(B) I gave him a quick tour.
(C) No, I lived there for ten years.

보스턴 관광 여행을 갈 건가요?
(A) 어디서 그녀를 보았나요? (×) sightseeing과 일부 음절이 같은 see를 이용한 오답
(B) 그에게 간단히 구경시켜 줬어요. (×) 질문의 tour를 이용한 오답
(C) 아니요, 저는 거기에서 10년 동안 살았어요. (○) 그곳에 오래 살아서 관광을 갈 필요가 없다는 뜻의 정답

CHECK UP　🎧 P2_U08_02 정답 및 해설 p.57

1. (A)　(B)　(C)　　**2.** (A)　(B)　(C)

3. (A)　(B)　(C)　　**4.** (A)　(B)　(C)

현재

Are...?

Q　Are these brochures about your company?　이 책자들은 당신의 회사에 관한 건가요?
A　Yes. Feel free to take one.　네. 얼마든지 가져가세요.

Q　Are you still serving lunch?　아직 점심 식사 되나요?
A　Yes, until 3 o'clock.　네, 3시까지 돼요.

Is...?

Q　Is there a café on this level of the hotel?　호텔 이 층에 카페가 있나요?
A　No, you have to go to the first floor.　아니요, 1층으로 가셔야 해요.

Q　Is Rick out of the office today?　오늘 릭이 자리를 비웠나요?
A　No, he's just gone for lunch.　아니요, 그는 점심을 먹으러 갔어요.

Q　Is it too late to order dinner?　저녁을 주문하기에 너무 늦었나요?
A　We just closed the kitchen.　우린 방금 주방을 마감했어요.

과거

Were...?

Q　Were you able to reserve the hotel you wanted?　당신이 원하는 호텔을 예약할 수 있었나요?
A　No, it was all booked up.　아니요, 전부 예약이 꽉 찼었어요.

Was...?

Q　Was this library renovated recently?　이 도서관은 최근에 보수되었나요?
A　Yes, that's what I heard.　네, 제가 들은 바로는 그래요.

미래

Are you/we/they going to...?

Q　Are you going to apply for the manager position?　그 관리직에 지원할 건가요?
A　I missed the deadline.　마감일을 놓쳤어요.

Is 주어 doing...?

Q　Is Ms. Jimmie attending today's seminar?　지미 씨가 오늘 세미나에 참석하나요?
A　Robert has the guest list.　로버트에게 손님 명단이 있어요.

Q　Is the flight going to be delayed?　비행기가 연착될까요?
A　Yes, that's what the information board says.　네, 안내판에 그렇게 나와 있어요.

고득점 TIP

긍정/부정의 답변 후 질문 속 어휘에서 연상 가능한 단어를 이용한 오답에 주의한다.

Q　Is there a fee to use my credit card abroad?　제 신용카드를 해외에서 사용할 때 수수료를 내나요?
A　Right—it expires soon. (×)　맞아요. 그건 곧 만료돼요.

대화를 듣고 알맞은 답을 고른 뒤, 다시 들으면서 빈칸을 채우세요.

1. (A) (B) (C)

Q Are you _____ today?

(A) Yes, _____.

(B) No, _____.

(C) I'm _____.

2. (A) (B) (C)

Q _____ to the new advertising campaign?

(A) Thanks _____.

(B) No, I'm busy with _____.

(C) _____.

3. (A) (B) (C)

Q _____ ink cartridge _____ with the printer?

(A) The model number _____.

(B) _____.

(C) Some _____.

4. (A) (B) (C)

Q _____ for everyone?

(A) _____ some fresh air.

(B) _____ the message.

(C) Please _____.

5. (A) (B) (C)

Q Is Ms. Crawford _____ today?

(A) There are _____.

(B) A new _____.

(C) I just saw _____.

대화를 듣고 알맞은 답을 고르세요.

1. Mark your answer on your answer sheet.	(A) (B) (C)
2. Mark your answer on your answer sheet.	(A) (B) (C)
3. Mark your answer on your answer sheet.	(A) (B) (C)
4. Mark your answer on your answer sheet.	(A) (B) (C)
5. Mark your answer on your answer sheet.	(A) (B) (C)
6. Mark your answer on your answer sheet.	(A) (B) (C)
7. Mark your answer on your answer sheet.	(A) (B) (C)
8. Mark your answer on your answer sheet.	(A) (B) (C)
9. Mark your answer on your answer sheet.	(A) (B) (C)
10. Mark your answer on your answer sheet.	(A) (B) (C)
11. Mark your answer on your answer sheet.	(A) (B) (C)
12. Mark your answer on your answer sheet.	(A) (B) (C)
13. Mark your answer on your answer sheet.	(A) (B) (C)
14. Mark your answer on your answer sheet.	(A) (B) (C)
15. Mark your answer on your answer sheet.	(A) (B) (C)

부정 의문문

핵심 포인트
1. 부정 의문문의 답변은 not을 생략한 긍정 의문문의 답변과 동일하며, 긍정이면 Yes, 부정이면 No로 응답하는 직접적인 정답 유형이 자주 출제된다.
2. Yes/No로 응답한 후 이어지는 부연 설명이 Yes/No와 일치하지 않는 오답 유형도 종종 출제되니 끝까지 놓치지 않고 듣는다.
3. Yes/No를 생략하거나 확인해 보겠다는 등 우회적인 답변의 비율이 높아지고 있으므로 유의한다.

실전 맛보기
🎧 P2_U09_01

Isn't your suitcase over the weight limit?

(A) A direct flight to Atlanta.
(B) I'll wait for you here.
(C) Yes, I paid an additional fee.

··

당신의 여행 가방은 중량 제한 초과 아닌가요?

(A) 애틀랜타행 직항 항공편이요. (×) '여행 가방'에서 연상되는 '애틀랜타행 직항 항공편'을 이용한 오답
(B) 여기서 당신을 기다릴게요. (×) weight와 유사한 발음을 가진 wait를 이용한 오답
(C) 네, 저는 추가 비용을 지불했어요. (○) 중량이 초과되어 추가 비용을 냈다고 부연 설명한 정답

CHECK UP
🎧 P2_U09_02 정답 및 해설 p.62

1. (A) (B) (C)   **2.** (A) (B) (C)

3. (A) (B) (C)   **4.** (A) (B) (C)

Aren't/Isn't...?

Q Aren't you organizing this year's fundraiser? 당신이 올해 모금 행사를 준비하지 않나요?

A No, Mr. Chung is handling it. 아니요, 그건 정 씨가 맡고 있어요.

Q Aren't we planning to hold a company retreat this year? 올해는 회사 야유회를 주최할 계획이 없나요?

A Our budget's been cut. 예산이 삭감되었어요.

Q Isn't there a pharmacy on 12th Street? 12번가에 약국이 있지 않나요?

A Yes, it's near the bakery. 네, 빵집 근처에 있어요.

Q Isn't the workshop scheduled for tomorrow? 워크숍이 내일로 예정되어 있지 않나요?

A No, it was postponed. 아니요, 그건 연기되었어요.

Don't/Doesn't/Didn't...?

Q Don't you have a copy of the budget report? 예산 보고서 사본을 가지고 있지 않나요?

A Simone is still working on them. 시몬이 아직 작업을 하고 있어요.

Q Doesn't Glen work in the design department? 글렌이 디자인 부서에서 일하고 있지 않나요?

A Actually, he's in IT. 사실 그는 IT부서예요.

Q Didn't you register for the festival next week? 다음 주 축제에 등록하지 않았나요?

A No, I'll be busy at that time. 아니요, 제가 그때 바빠요.

Haven't...?

Q Haven't the new interns arrived yet? 새 인턴들은 아직 도착하지 않았나요?

A Helen's talking to them now. 헬렌이 지금 그들에게 이야기를 하고 있어요.

Can't...?

Q Can't we use a different color for the magazine title? 잡지 제목에 다른 색상을 쓰면 안 될까요?

A Let's discuss it tomorrow. 내일 논의합시다.

Won't...?

Q Won't we need a permit to hold this event? 이 행사를 주최하려면 허가가 필요하지 않을까요?

A They recently changed the policy. 그들은 최근 정책을 바꿨어요.

Shouldn't...?

Q Shouldn't the keynote speaker have arrived by now? 기조 연설자가 지금쯤은 도착했어야 하지 않을까요?

A No, he'll be here at 2 o'clock. 아니요, 그는 2시에 올 거예요.

고득점 TIP

Don't you...?로 물어본다고 해서 섣불리 'I'로 시작하는 답변을 정답으로 단정해서는 안 된다.

Q Don't you work upstairs? 위층 사무실에서 일하지 않으세요?

(A) No, I prefer to take the stairs. (×) 아뇨, 저는 계단을 이용하는 게 좋아요.

(B) Yes, you're working on the second floor, right? (○) 네, 2층에서 일하시죠?

(A)는 주어가 'I'로 시작하지만 work를 walk로 잘못 알아들을 수 있다는 점을 이용한 오답이다. work upstairs는 '위층에서 일하다'는 뜻이며, walk upstairs는 '걸어서 올라가다'는 뜻이다.

대화를 듣고 알맞은 답을 고른 뒤, 다시 들으면서 빈칸을 채우세요.

1. (A) (B) (C)   **Q** _____ go to the festival yesterday?

(A) I _____.

(B) All big name _____.

(C) _____ start?

2. (A) (B) (C)   **Q** _____ coming today?

(A) I'd like to _____.

(B) Class _____.

(C) _____ by 4:00 P.M.

3. (A) (B) (C)   **Q** _____ finished the drawings?

(A) I _____.

(B) _____ them today.

(C) You may _____.

4. (A) (B) (C)   **Q** Isn't the _____?

(A) I think _____.

(B) It's _____ here.

(C) The _____ at 9.

5. (A) (B) (C)   **Q** _____ for help from management?

(A) He was just _____.

(B) _____ have any.

(C) That might _____.

대화를 듣고 알맞은 답을 고르세요.

1. Mark your answer on your answer sheet.   (A)   (B)   (C)

2. Mark your answer on your answer sheet.   (A)   (B)   (C)

3. Mark your answer on your answer sheet.   (A)   (B)   (C)

4. Mark your answer on your answer sheet.   (A)   (B)   (C)

5. Mark your answer on your answer sheet.   (A)   (B)   (C)

6. Mark your answer on your answer sheet.   (A)   (B)   (C)

7. Mark your answer on your answer sheet.   (A)   (B)   (C)

8. Mark your answer on your answer sheet.   (A)   (B)   (C)

9. Mark your answer on your answer sheet.   (A)   (B)   (C)

10. Mark your answer on your answer sheet.   (A)   (B)   (C)

11. Mark your answer on your answer sheet.   (A)   (B)   (C)

12. Mark your answer on your answer sheet.   (A)   (B)   (C)

13. Mark your answer on your answer sheet.   (A)   (B)   (C)

14. Mark your answer on your answer sheet.   (A)   (B)   (C)

15. Mark your answer on your answer sheet.   (A)   (B)   (C)

PART 2

UNIT 09

핵심 포인트
1. 수락과 반대를 뜻하는 전형적인 표현이 정답으로 자주 출제되므로 빈출 응답 표현을 익히도록 한다.
2. Could you...? 또는 Would you...?로 물어볼 경우 Sure, OK, Yes, Sorry로 응답한 다음 주어가 'I' 로 시작하는 경우가 많다. 하지만, 'I' 다음 엉뚱한 내용의 함정이 있을 수 있으므로 주의해야 한다.
3. 수락할 수 없는 이유나 요청한 일을 이미 완료했음을 나타내는 답변 등의 간접적인 응답의 출제 비율이 높아지고 있으므로 유의한다.

실전 맛보기 🎧 P2_U10_01

Could you explain the projector settings to Fiona?

(A) Yes, they set up a booth.
(B) I enjoyed her presentation.
(C) Sure, I have time now.

....

피오나에게 프로젝터 설정을 설명해 줄 수 있나요?

(A) 네, 그들이 부스를 설치했어요. (×) Yes로 답변이 가능하지만 settings와 set up을 이용한 오답
(B) 저는 그녀의 발표를 즐겼어요. (×) 주어가 I 로 시작하는 오답
(C) 물론이죠, 지금 시간이 돼요. (○) 시간이 있다며 요청을 수락한 정답

CHECK UP 🎧 P2_U10_02 정답 및 해설 p.67

1. (A)　　(B)　　(C)　　　　**2.** (A)　　(B)　　(C)

3. (A)　　(B)　　(C)　　　　**4.** (A)　　(B)　　(C)

제안	**Q Why don't we** hold a photo contest? 사진 콘테스트를 여는 게 어때요?

A1 That's a great suggestion. 좋은 제안이네요.   **A2** OK, that sounds good. 좋은 생각이에요.

A3 I think that's a great idea. 좋은 생각인 것 같아요.   **A4** That works for me. 저는 찬성이에요.

Q How about hiring a security guard? 경비원을 고용하는 게 어때요?

A There's not much money in the budget. 예산이 넉넉하지 않아요.

Q Would you like to go to the movie with us on Friday? 금요일에 우리랑 같이 영화 보러 갈래요?

A Absolutely, I haven't seen one in a while. 물론이죠, 한동안 영화를 못 봤네요.

Q Can I help you move your desk? 책상 옮기는 거 도와드릴까요?

A I think I can manage on my own. 저 혼자 할 수 있을 것 같아요.

요청

Q Can you recommend a dentist? 치과의사 추천 좀 해 줄 수 있을까요?

A Sure, I'll give you his number. 물론이죠, 그의 번호를 줄게요.

Q Could you give me a ride to work tomorrow? 내일 출근할 때 좀 태워줄 수 있어요?

A I'd be happy to. 물론이죠.

Q Would you take charge of organizing the conference this year?
올해 콘퍼런스 준비를 맡아 주시겠어요?

A What's the budget? 예산이 얼마나 책정되어 있나요?

Q Would you mind helping me repair the door? 제가 이 문을 고치는 걸 도와주시겠어요?

A Sure, where is the toolbox? 물론이죠, 공구 상자가 어디에 있나요?

수락

Yes, I'll be sure to do that. 네, 꼭 그렇게 할게요.
OK, I'll take care of that. 알았어요, 제가 처리할게요.
Sure. I don't mind doing that. 그럼요. 전 그렇게 해도 괜찮아요.
Absolutely, I'll do that right away. 물론이죠, 제가 지금 바로 할게요.
Sure, I'll be available around 2 o'clock. 물론이죠, 2시쯤에 시간이 될 거예요.

거절

Sorry, I don't have time right now. 죄송해요, 제가 지금 시간이 없어요.
I have plans that day. 제가 그날에는 계획이 있어요.
I'll be on vacation then. 제가 그때 휴가 중일 거예요.
Sorry, I'm right in the middle of something. 죄송해요, 제가 지금 뭘 좀 하는 중이라서요.
Could you ask David instead? 데이비드에게 대신 부탁하시겠어요?
Sorry, I'm on my way to a meeting. 죄송해요, 전 지금 회의에 가는 중이에요.
You'll need to call technical support. 기술 지원팀에 전화해야 할 거예요.

고득점 TIP

Would you mind...?는 직역하면 '~가 언짢으신가요?'라는 뜻이기 때문에 Yes로 답하면 거절, No로 답하면 수락을 뜻한다.

Q Would you mind reviewing the budget? 그 예산안 검토 좀 해 주시겠어요?

A No, I'll take care of that. (= Sure, I'll take care of that.) 알았어요, 제가 처리할게요.

대화를 듣고 알맞은 답을 고른 뒤, 다시 들으면서 빈칸을 채우세요.

1. (A) (B) (C)

Q _____ in the front row?

(A) _____ over there.

(B) The national _____.

(C) Of course, _____.

2. (A) (B) (C)

Q _____ a 20-minute break?

(A) I think _____.

(B) Don't we already _____?

(C) How about _____?

3. (A) (B) (C)

Q Could you pick up _____?

(A) _____ home.

(B) _____.

(C) _____.

4. (A) (B) (C)

Q _____ reviewing these design portfolios?

(A) Sure, give _____.

(B) _____.

(C) Some _____.

5. (A) (B) (C)

Q Can you get _____ at the pharmacy?

(A) _____ after a meal.

(B) Yes, _____.

(C) I think _____.

대화를 듣고 알맞은 답을 고르세요.

1. Mark your answer on your answer sheet.   (A)   (B)   (C)

2. Mark your answer on your answer sheet.   (A)   (B)   (C)

3. Mark your answer on your answer sheet.   (A)   (B)   (C)

4. Mark your answer on your answer sheet.   (A)   (B)   (C)

5. Mark your answer on your answer sheet.   (A)   (B)   (C)

6. Mark your answer on your answer sheet.   (A)   (B)   (C)

7. Mark your answer on your answer sheet.   (A)   (B)   (C)

8. Mark your answer on your answer sheet.   (A)   (B)   (C)

9. Mark your answer on your answer sheet.   (A)   (B)   (C)

10. Mark your answer on your answer sheet.   (A)   (B)   (C)

11. Mark your answer on your answer sheet.   (A)   (B)   (C)

12. Mark your answer on your answer sheet.   (A)   (B)   (C)

13. Mark your answer on your answer sheet.   (A)   (B)   (C)

14. Mark your answer on your answer sheet.   (A)   (B)   (C)

15. Mark your answer on your answer sheet.   (A)   (B)   (C)

핵심 포인트

1. 부가 의문문은 [평서문, + 꼬리 의문문?]의 형태로 구성되며, 꼬리 의문문은 평서문의 내용을 확인하는 차원에서 물어보는 것이므로 평서문 내용에 집중해서 듣도록 한다.
2. 평서문 뒤에 붙은 꼬리 의문문의 형태와 상관없이 묻는 내용에 대해 긍정이면 Yes, 부정이면 No로 답변한다.
3. Yes/No로 응답한 후 부연 설명이 이어지는 응답 유형에서 부연 설명의 내용이 Yes/No와 일치하는지 주의해서 듣는다.

실전 맛보기

🎧 P2_U11_01

I can keep these library books for three weeks, can't I?

(A) Usually nonfiction books.
(B) Yes, that's our policy.
(C) No, I don't have a card.

이 도서관 책들을 3주 동안 가지고 있을 수 있죠, 그렇지 않나요?

(A) 보통 논픽션 책들이요. (×) books를 반복한 오답
(B) 네, 그게 저희 정책이에요. (O) Yes로 응답한 후 그게 정책이라고 부연 설명한 정답
(C) 아니요, 저한테 카드가 없어요. (×) No로 응답했지만 부연 설명이 일치하지 않는 오답

CHECK UP

🎧 P2_U11_02 정답 및 해설 p.71

1.	(A)	(B)	(C)	**2.**	(A)	(B)	(C)
3.	(A)	(B)	(C)	**4.**	(A)	(B)	(C)

be

Q Today's meeting wasn't well attended, **was it**? 오늘 회의에 참석자가 많지 않았죠, 그렇죠?
A Many employees are out on vacation. 많은 직원들이 휴가로 없어요.

Q The small suitcase is still in stock, **isn't it**? 작은 여행 가방은 아직 재고가 있죠, 그렇지 않나요?
A No, we sold the last one. 아니요, 마지막 남은 하나를 팔았어요.

Q Lisa is going to Scott's retirement party, **isn't she**? 리사는 스콧의 은퇴 기념 파티에 갈 거죠, 그렇지 않나요?
A I don't think they worked together. 그들은 같이 일하지 않았을 거예요.

Q There's a pharmacy on Oak Street, **isn't there**? 오크 가에 약국이 있죠, 그렇지 않나요?
A No, that's a bank now. 아니요, 이제 거긴 은행이에요.

do

Q Your phone needs to be fixed, **doesn't it**? 당신의 휴대전화를 수리해야 하죠, 그렇지 않나요?
A No, it's working fine. 아니요, 작동이 잘 돼요.

Q Ms. Joe transferred to a different department, **didn't she**? 조 씨는 다른 부서로 옮겼죠, 그렇지 않나요?
A Yes, she's in sales now. 네, 그녀는 이제 영업부예요.

have

Q You've already ordered computers, **haven't you**? 이미 컴퓨터들을 주문했죠, 그렇지 않나요?
A Yes, they should arrive soon. 네, 곧 도착할 거예요.

Q The printer has been fixed, **hasn't it**? 인쇄기는 수리됐죠, 그렇지 않나요?
A Yes, it works fine now. 네, 지금 잘 작동해요.

Q The shuttle hasn't left yet, **has it**? 셔틀버스는 아직 떠나지 않았죠, 그렇죠?
A No, you've got 10 minutes. 네, 10분 남았어요.

can

Q I can take a shuttle to the train station, **can't I**? 저는 기차역까지 셔틀을 탈 수 있죠, 그렇지 않나요?
A Yes, it leaves at 4:45 P.M. 네, 그건 오후 4시 45분에 떠나요.

should

Q We should ask Henry to join the seminar, **shouldn't we**?
헨리에게 세미나에 참가하라고 해야 하죠, 그렇지 않나요?
A I already did. 제가 이미 했어요.

right

Q The prototype will be ready by next Monday, **right**? 시제품은 다음 주 월요일까지 준비되는 거죠?
A Actually, we need a few more days. 실은 며칠 더 필요해요.

don't you think?

Q We should take the 12:30 train, **don't you think**?
우리는 12시 30분 기차를 타야 하죠, 그렇게 생각하지 않나요?
A The one after that seems to leave too late. 그 다음 기차는 너무 늦게 출발하는 것 같네요.

고득점 TIP

부가 의문문에 의문문이나 반문으로 답하는 경우도 정답이 될 수 있다.

Q You can't reschedule the interview, can you? 면접 일정을 다시 잡을 수는 없지요, 그렇죠?
A Can I get back to you later? 나중에 다시 알려드려도 될까요?

Q You're going to attend the training session tomorrow, right? 내일 교육에 참석할 거죠, 그렇죠?
A Do you think that's necessary? 그 교육이 필요할까요?

대화를 듣고 알맞은 답을 고른 뒤, 다시 들으면서 빈칸을 채우세요.

1. (A) (B) (C) **Q** _____ is half an hour late, _____?

                    (A) Yes, _____.

                    (B) They _____.

                    (C) To _____.

2. (A) (B) (C) **Q** _____ the new business cards, _____?

                    (A) Please _____ on the back.

                    (B) A small _____.

                    (C) _____ for mine.

3. (A) (B) (C) **Q** The new Italian restaurant _____, _____?

                    (A) _____.

                    (B) _____ version.

                    (C) _____.

4. (A) (B) (C) **Q** _____ to be free this afternoon, _____?

                    (A) _____ 20 dollars.

                    (B) Yes, _____.

                    (C) Yes, to _____.

5. (A) (B) (C) **Q** You _____ women's clothing, _____?

                    (A) OK. We'll check _____.

                    (B) No, I have a _____.

                    (C) _____ at the bottom.

대화를 듣고 알맞은 답을 고르세요.

1. Mark your answer on your answer sheet.　　　　(A)　　(B)　　(C)

2. Mark your answer on your answer sheet.　　　　(A)　　(B)　　(C)

3. Mark your answer on your answer sheet.　　　　(A)　　(B)　　(C)

4. Mark your answer on your answer sheet.　　　　(A)　　(B)　　(C)

5. Mark your answer on your answer sheet.　　　　(A)　　(B)　　(C)

6. Mark your answer on your answer sheet.　　　　(A)　　(B)　　(C)

7. Mark your answer on your answer sheet.　　　　(A)　　(B)　　(C)

8. Mark your answer on your answer sheet.　　　　(A)　　(B)　　(C)

9. Mark your answer on your answer sheet.　　　　(A)　　(B)　　(C)

10. Mark your answer on your answer sheet.　　　　(A)　　(B)　　(C)

11. Mark your answer on your answer sheet.　　　　(A)　　(B)　　(C)

12. Mark your answer on your answer sheet.　　　　(A)　　(B)　　(C)

13. Mark your answer on your answer sheet.　　　　(A)　　(B)　　(C)

14. Mark your answer on your answer sheet.　　　　(A)　　(B)　　(C)

15. Mark your answer on your answer sheet.　　　　(A)　　(B)　　(C)

PART 2

UNIT 11

핵심 포인트

1. 질문에 나오는 두 가지의 선택 사항에 집중해서 듣도록 한다.
2. 두 가지 선택 사항 중 한 가지를 고르는 정답이 주로 출제된다. 정답에는 질문에 언급된 단어가 그대로 사용되는 경우가 많지만 질문에 나온 단어들을 그대로 사용하지 않는 경우도 있으므로 주의해서 들어야 한다.
3. 선택 사항에 대해 아직 결정을 내리지 못했다거나 구체적인 질문을 하는 경우 등 여러 가지 제3의 답변이 정답으로 출제되기도 한다.

실전 맛보기 🎧 P2_U12_01

Would you like me to order two vegetable platters or three for the reception?

(A) Sure, I'd like that.
(B) Two should be plenty.
(C) Okay, I'll remind the receptionist.

환영회 때 채소 두 접시를 주문할까요, 아니면 세 접시를 주문할까요?

(A) 좋습니다. 그걸로 할게요. (×) 질문의 Would you like...에 사용된 would like를 이용한 오답
(B) 2개면 충분할 거예요. (○) 둘 중 하나로 적절하게 답변한 정답
(C) 알겠어요, 안내원에게 알려 줄게요. (×) reception과 파생 관계인 receptionist를 이용한 오답

CHECK UP 🎧 P2_U12_02 정답 및 해설 p.76

1. (A) (B) (C) **2.** (A) (B) (C)

3. (A) (B) (C) **4.** (A) (B) (C)

Would you... or ...?

Q Would you like a refund or an exchange? 환불을 원하세요, 아니면 교환을 원하세요?

A A refund, please. 환불이요.

Q Would you like to see the doctor on Monday or Thursday? 월요일에 진찰을 받으시겠어요, 목요일에 받으시겠어요?

A Thursday works better. 목요일이 더 나아요.

Q Would you prefer to fly in the morning or the afternoon? 아침 비행기가 좋으세요, 저녁 비행기가 좋으세요?

A Whichever one is cheaper. 아무거나 싼 거요.

Do you want... or ...?

Q Do you want to take a bus or a taxi to the airport? 공항으로 버스를 타고 갈까요, 택시를 타고 갈까요?

A Let's take the bus. 버스를 타죠.

Q Do you want your commercial to run at eight or nine P.M.? 저녁 8시에 광고가 나가길 원하세요, 9시에 나가길 원하세요?

A I'd prefer nine. 9시요.

Are you... or ...? / Is it... or ...?

Q Are you going to buy the backpack or suitcase? 배낭을 사시겠어요, 여행 가방을 사시겠어요?

A I decided to get the suitcase. 여행 가방을 사기로 했어요.

Q Was it James or Patricia who reviewed the finance report?
그 재무 보고서를 검토한 사람이 제임스인가요 패트리샤인가요?

A Well, I'm not really sure. 글쎄요, 잘 모르겠어요.

복합 질문 (문장 or 문장)

Q Should we release the film this spring or would summer be better?
영화를 올 봄에 개봉해야 할까요, 여름이 좋을까요?

A Summer is better. 여름이 나을 거예요.

Q Have you finished reviewing the data or do you need more time?
자료 검토는 다 했나요, 아니면 시간이 더 필요한가요?

A I'm finishing it now. 지금 마무리하고 있어요.

고득점 TIP

1. 두 가지 선택 사항 중 하나에 해당하지만 질문에 언급된 단어를 그대로 사용하지 않고도 정답이 되는 경우가 빈번하다.

Q Have you moved or are you at the same address? 당신은 이사를 갔나요, 아니면 주소가 그대로인가요?

A I still live at Maple Street. 저는 아직 메이플 가에 살고 있어요. (= I'm at the same address.)

2. 선택 사항에 대해 되묻는 답변이 정답이 될 수도 있다.

Q Are you driving or taking a bus to the beach? 해변까지 자가용으로 갈 건가요, 버스를 탈 건가요?

A Do the buses run often? 버스가 자주 있나요?

대화를 듣고 알맞은 답을 고른 뒤, 다시 들으면서 빈칸을 채우세요.

1. (A)　(B)　(C)

Q Will you ＿＿＿＿＿＿＿＿＿＿ Sunday or Monday?

(A) ＿＿＿＿＿＿＿＿＿＿, here you are.

(B) ＿＿＿＿＿＿＿＿.

(C) ＿＿＿＿＿＿＿＿.

2. (A)　(B)　(C)

Q Should I send you ＿＿＿＿＿ or give you ＿＿＿＿＿?

(A) It ＿＿＿＿＿＿＿＿.

(B) I'll ＿＿＿＿＿＿＿＿.

(C) ＿＿＿＿＿＿＿＿, please.

3. (A)　(B)　(C)

Q Do you prefer to work ＿＿＿＿＿, or work ＿＿＿＿＿?

(A) It's ＿＿＿＿＿＿＿＿.

(B) I'm ＿＿＿＿＿＿＿＿.

(C) I ＿＿＿＿＿＿＿＿.

4. (A)　(B)　(C)

Q Can I pay ＿＿＿＿＿, or do I have to ＿＿＿＿＿?

(A) We ＿＿＿＿＿＿＿＿.

(B) Yes, that's ＿＿＿＿＿＿＿＿.

(C) No, it's ＿＿＿＿＿＿＿＿.

5. (A)　(B)　(C)

Q Are you ready ＿＿＿＿＿ or are you ＿＿＿＿＿?

(A) The ＿＿＿＿＿＿＿＿ tomorrow.

(B) I need ＿＿＿＿＿＿＿＿ .

(C) Is Samuel ＿＿＿＿＿＿＿＿?

대화를 듣고 알맞은 답을 고르세요.

1. Mark your answer on your answer sheet. (A) (B) (C)

2. Mark your answer on your answer sheet. (A) (B) (C)

3. Mark your answer on your answer sheet. (A) (B) (C)

4. Mark your answer on your answer sheet. (A) (B) (C)

5. Mark your answer on your answer sheet. (A) (B) (C)

6. Mark your answer on your answer sheet. (A) (B) (C)

7. Mark your answer on your answer sheet. (A) (B) (C)

8. Mark your answer on your answer sheet. (A) (B) (C)

9. Mark your answer on your answer sheet. (A) (B) (C)

10. Mark your answer on your answer sheet. (A) (B) (C)

11. Mark your answer on your answer sheet. (A) (B) (C)

12. Mark your answer on your answer sheet. (A) (B) (C)

13. Mark your answer on your answer sheet. (A) (B) (C)

14. Mark your answer on your answer sheet. (A) (B) (C)

15. Mark your answer on your answer sheet. (A) (B) (C)

UNIT 13 간접 의문문

핵심 포인트

1. 질문 속 의문문의 의문사, 주어, 동사를 주의해서 듣는다.
2. 질문 속 의문사에 맞게 직접적인 정보를 알려주는 정답이 자주 출제되지만, 해당 정보를 알려줄 수 없다거나 해당 정보를 얻는 방법을 알려주는 등 간접적인 응답도 종종 정답으로 출제된다.

실전 맛보기

P2_U13_01

Could you demonstrate how to change the air filter?

(A) Your change is thirty-five cents.
(B) It stays fresh for a long time.
(C) The instructions are online.

이 공기 필터를 어떻게 교체하는지 보여주실 수 있나요?

(A) 거스름돈은 35센트입니다. (×) 질문의 동사 change를 다른 의미로 사용한 오답
(B) 그건 오랫동안 신선함을 유지해요. (×) '공기 필터'에서 연상되는 '신선함'을 이용한 오답
(C) 설명서가 온라인에 있어요. (○) 온라인에서 설명서를 볼 수 있다는 방법으로 답변한 정답

CHECK UP

P2_U13_02 정답 및 해설 p.81

1. (A)   (B)   (C)   **2.** (A)   (B)   (C)

3. (A)   (B)   (C)   **4.** (A)   (B)   (C)

who 간접 의문문

Q Do you know who reviewed the finance report? 누가 재정 보고서를 검토했는지 아시나요?

A Well, I'm not really sure. 글쎄요, 저는 잘 모르겠어요.

Q Do you know who the owner of this bag is? 이 가방의 주인이 누구인지 아세요?

A It belongs to Brian. 브라이언 거예요.

what 간접 의문문

Q Could you tell me what happened at last Friday's seminar?
지난 금요일 세미나에서 무슨 일이 있었는지 알려주실 수 있나요?

A I was on vacation. 저는 휴가 중이었어요.

Q Did you see what was posted on the bulletin board? 게시판에 뭐가 공고됐는지 봤나요?

A An updated training schedule. 업데이트된 교육 일정이요.

when 간접 의문문

Q Do you know when the library opens? 도서관이 언제 여는지 아시나요?

A At 9 A.M. every day. 매일 오전 9시에요.

Q Did you find out when the clients will visit? 고객들이 언제 방문하는지 알아봤나요?

A Yes, they're coming next Monday. 네, 그들은 다음 주 월요일에 와요.

where 간접 의문문

Q Can you tell me where the company cafeteria is? 회사 구내식당이 어디에 있는지 말해 주실 수 있나요?

A It's on the third floor. 3층에 있어요.

Q Do you know where the community center is? 커뮤니티 센터가 어디에 있는지 아세요?

A1 Yes, I've been there several times. 네, 거기에 몇 번 가 봤어요.

A2 Actually, it closed at six o'clock. 사실, 거긴 6시에 문을 닫았어요.

how 간접 의문문

Q Can you show me how to operate this new cash register? 이 새로운 금전 등록기를 어떻게 사용하는지 보여줄 수 있나요?

A I can help you in 10 minutes. 10분 뒤에 도와드릴게요.

Q Can you tell me how to get to the museum? 박물관에 어떻게 가는지 말해줄 수 있나요?

A Yes, just give me a minute. 네, 잠시 기다려 주세요.

why 간접 의문문

Q Do you know why she left early yesterday? 그녀가 어제 왜 일찍 떠났는지 아시나요?

A She had a dentist appointment. 그녀는 치과 진료가 예약돼 있었어요.

고득점 TIP

의문문 속 의문사가 where일 때 발음이 비슷한 when에 맞게 응답한 답변이 오답으로 출제될 수도 있다.

Q Do you know where Marita went? 마리타가 어디 갔는지 아시나요?

A Isn't it at 12:30? (×) 12시 30분에 아닌가요?

A Probably to the break room. (○) 아마 휴게실로요.

대화를 듣고 알맞은 답을 고른 뒤, 다시 들으면서 빈칸을 채우세요.

1. (A) (B) (C)

Q Can I ask _____ the nearest _____ is?

(A) It's _____.

(B) _____ so.

(C) It's just _____.

2. (A) (B) (C)

Q Do you know _____ to room 3?

(A) It's _____.

(B) Here is _____.

(C) _____ the next meeting.

3. (A) (B) (C)

Q Can you explain _____ this ticket machine?

(A) _____ a first-class seat.

(B) Ten _____.

(C) Yes, _____ please.

4. (A) (B) (C)

Q Do you know _____ this carpet is?

(A) The _____.

(B) You'll need to _____.

(C) Yes, she's _____.

5. (A) (B) (C)

Q Do you know _____ is?

(A) _____ the artist?

(B) Yes, I _____.

(C) A _____.

대화를 듣고 알맞은 답을 고르세요.

1. Mark your answer on your answer sheet.　　　　(A)　　(B)　　(C)

2. Mark your answer on your answer sheet.　　　　(A)　　(B)　　(C)

3. Mark your answer on your answer sheet.　　　　(A)　　(B)　　(C)

4. Mark your answer on your answer sheet.　　　　(A)　　(B)　　(C)

5. Mark your answer on your answer sheet.　　　　(A)　　(B)　　(C)

6. Mark your answer on your answer sheet.　　　　(A)　　(B)　　(C)

7. Mark your answer on your answer sheet.　　　　(A)　　(B)　　(C)

8. Mark your answer on your answer sheet.　　　　(A)　　(B)　　(C)

9. Mark your answer on your answer sheet.　　　　(A)　　(B)　　(C)

10. Mark your answer on your answer sheet.　　　　(A)　　(B)　　(C)

11. Mark your answer on your answer sheet.　　　　(A)　　(B)　　(C)

12. Mark your answer on your answer sheet.　　　　(A)　　(B)　　(C)

13. Mark your answer on your answer sheet.　　　　(A)　　(B)　　(C)

14. Mark your answer on your answer sheet.　　　　(A)　　(B)　　(C)

15. Mark your answer on your answer sheet.　　　　(A)　　(B)　　(C)

PART 2

UNIT 13

핵심 포인트

1. 문장 전체의 내용을 집중해서 듣고 무엇에 대해 말하고 있는지 파악한 후 답변을 듣도록 한다.
2. 평서문임에도 Yes/No로 시작하는 응답이 종종 출제되므로 뒤에 따라오는 부연 설명이 Yes/No와 일치하는지 주의해서 듣는다.

실전 맛보기

🎧 P2_U14_01

There were a lot of empty seats at the leadership lecture.

(A) Another popular event was happening next door.
(B) My major at university was economics.
(C) An aisle seat is better.

리더십 강의에 빈자리가 많았어요.

(A) 또 다른 인기 있는 행사가 옆방에서 열리고 있었어요. (O) 상황의 원인을 간접적으로 제시한 정답
(B) 저는 대학에서 경제학을 전공했어요. (×) '강의'에서 연상되는 '대학 전공'을 이용한 오답
(C) 통로 쪽 자리가 더 좋아요. (×) seat을 반복한 오답

CHECK UP

🎧 P2_U14_02 정답 및 해설 p.86

1.	(A)	(B)	(C)	**2.**	(A)	(B)	(C)
3.	(A)	(B)	(C)	**4.**	(A)	(B)	(C)

문제점 언급

Q My flight has been canceled because of the weather.　날씨 때문에 제 항공편이 취소되었어요.

A I'll reschedule our meeting then.　그러면 우리 회의 일정을 다시 잡아볼게요.

정보 전달 / 상황 설명

Q The textile delivery has arrived.　원단 배달이 도착했어요.

A Okay, just put the invoice on my desk.　네, 청구서는 제 책상 위에 놔주세요.

의견 제시

Q I'd like to live closer to the office.　회사에서 가까운 곳에 살고 싶어요.

A Didn't you just move?　얼마 전에 이사하지 않았나요?

제안 / 요청

Q I think we should hire an illustrator.　우리 삽화가를 고용해야 할 것 같아요.

A That's not such a bad idea.　그렇게 나쁜 생각은 아니네요.

Q I'd like you to present your proposal at today's meeting.　오늘 회의에서 당신의 제안서를 발표해 줬으면 해요.

A1 Sorry, but I'm just too busy.　미안하지만 제가 너무 바빠요.

A2 Sure, I'd be happy to.　물론이죠.

감정 표현

Q Our new interns have been doing a great job.　우리 새 인턴들이 정말 잘하고 있어요.

A I agree.　저도 그렇게 생각해요.

빈출 표현: 반문으로 답변하는 경우　　　　　　　　　　　　　　🎧 P2_U14_04

Q Your office looks really different.
당신의 사무실은 정말 달라 보이네요.

A When was the last time you were here?
여기에 마지막으로 온 게 언제죠?

Q I finished the building inspection.
건물 점검을 마쳤어요.

A Did you find any problems?
무슨 문제점이라도 있던가요?

Q I'm planning to repaint the walls of the office.
사무실 벽을 다시 페인트칠할 계획이에요.

A What color were you thinking?
무슨 색으로 생각하고 있나요?

Q We need a project assistant by the end of this month.　이달 말까지는 프로젝트 보조가 필요해요.

A Have you considered Ella Morita?
엘라 모리타를 고려해 보셨나요?

Q Please pick up Ms. Ann at the airport tomorrow morning.　내일 아침 공항으로 앤 씨를 마중 나와 주세요.

A What time should I leave?
저는 몇 시에 떠나야 하나요?

Q The new café on 15th Street has delicious food.　15번가에 새로 생긴 카페는 음식이 맛있어요.

A Oh, you've been there?
오, 거기에 갔었군요?

고득점 TIP

의견을 제시하는 평서문에 동의/부정 또는 수락/거절을 하기 위해 Yes/No로 응답하는 답변이 정답이 될 수도 있다.

Q Maybe we should reschedule the meeting.　아마 우린 회의 일정을 다시 잡아야 할 것 같아요.

A No, I need to talk to the team today.　안 돼요, 오늘 팀에 이야기해야 해요. (일정을 바꿀 수 없다는 뜻)

대화를 듣고 알맞은 답을 고른 뒤, 다시 들으면서 빈칸을 채우세요.

1. (A) (B) (C)

Q The new backpacks _____ well.

(A) Yeah, there are _____.

(B) Please _____.

(C) _____ in the afternoon.

2. (A) (B) (C)

Q _____, your table _____ yet.

(A) Around _____.

(B) I'm _____.

(C) That's a _____.

3. (A) (B) (C)

Q That was an amazing _____.

(A) The violin soloist _____.

(B) Sorry, I'm _____.

(C) How did _____?

4. (A) (B) (C)

Q _____ to a quieter _____.

(A) _____ Singapore last year.

(B) A new _____.

(C) Room 503 _____.

5. (A) (B) (C)

Q _____ in the meeting room _____.

(A) It's _____.

(B) _____ at 3.

(C) Please _____ team.

대화를 듣고 알맞은 답을 고르세요.

1. Mark your answer on your answer sheet.   (A)   (B)   (C)

2. Mark your answer on your answer sheet.   (A)   (B)   (C)

3. Mark your answer on your answer sheet.   (A)   (B)   (C)

4. Mark your answer on your answer sheet.   (A)   (B)   (C)

5. Mark your answer on your answer sheet.   (A)   (B)   (C)

6. Mark your answer on your answer sheet.   (A)   (B)   (C)

7. Mark your answer on your answer sheet.   (A)   (B)   (C)

8. Mark your answer on your answer sheet.   (A)   (B)   (C)

9. Mark your answer on your answer sheet.   (A)   (B)   (C)

10. Mark your answer on your answer sheet.   (A)   (B)   (C)

11. Mark your answer on your answer sheet.   (A)   (B)   (C)

12. Mark your answer on your answer sheet.   (A)   (B)   (C)

13. Mark your answer on your answer sheet.   (A)   (B)   (C)

14. Mark your answer on your answer sheet.   (A)   (B)   (C)

15. Mark your answer on your answer sheet.   (A)   (B)   (C)

PART 2

UNIT 14

PART 2

Directions: You will hear a question or statement and three responses spoken in English. They will not be printed in your test book and will be spoken only one time. Select the best response to the question or statement and mark the letter (A), (B), or (C) on your answer sheet.

7. Mark your answer on your answer sheet.

8. Mark your answer on your answer sheet.

9. Mark your answer on your answer sheet.

10. Mark your answer on your answer sheet.

11. Mark your answer on your answer sheet.

12. Mark your answer on your answer sheet.

13. Mark your answer on your answer sheet.

14. Mark your answer on your answer sheet.

15. Mark your answer on your answer sheet.

16. Mark your answer on your answer sheet.

17. Mark your answer on your answer sheet.

18. Mark your answer on your answer sheet.

19. Mark your answer on your answer sheet.

20. Mark your answer on your answer sheet.

21. Mark your answer on your answer sheet.

22. Mark your answer on your answer sheet.

23. Mark your answer on your answer sheet.

24. Mark your answer on your answer sheet.

25. Mark your answer on your answer sheet.

26. Mark your answer on your answer sheet.

27. Mark your answer on your answer sheet.

28. Mark your answer on your answer sheet.

29. Mark your answer on your answer sheet.

30. Mark your answer on your answer sheet.

31. Mark your answer on your answer sheet.

전체 영국·호주 음성 + 고난도 문제(우회 답변)

PART 2

Directions: You will hear a question or statement and three responses spoken in English. They will not be printed in your test book and will be spoken only one time. Select the best response to the question or statement and mark the letter (A), (B), or (C) on your answer sheet.

7. Mark your answer on your answer sheet.

8. Mark your answer on your answer sheet.

9. Mark your answer on your answer sheet.

10. Mark your answer on your answer sheet.

11. Mark your answer on your answer sheet.

12. Mark your answer on your answer sheet.

13. Mark your answer on your answer sheet.

14. Mark your answer on your answer sheet.

15. Mark your answer on your answer sheet.

16. Mark your answer on your answer sheet.

17. Mark your answer on your answer sheet.

18. Mark your answer on your answer sheet.

19. Mark your answer on your answer sheet.

20. Mark your answer on your answer sheet.

21. Mark your answer on your answer sheet.

22. Mark your answer on your answer sheet.

23. Mark your answer on your answer sheet.

24. Mark your answer on your answer sheet.

25. Mark your answer on your answer sheet.

26. Mark your answer on your answer sheet.

27. Mark your answer on your answer sheet.

28. Mark your answer on your answer sheet.

29. Mark your answer on your answer sheet.

30. Mark your answer on your answer sheet.

31. Mark your answer on your answer sheet.

고난도 문제
해설 강의

toeic.eduwill.net

PART

3

출제 경향 및 문제 풀이 전략

PART 3 출제 경향 및 문제 풀이 전략

두 명 또는 세 명의 대화를 듣고, 이와 관련된 3개의 문제에 알맞은 답을 고르는 파트이다. LC 전체 100문항 중에서 총 39문항(13개 대화문×3문항)이 출제되며, 매회 3인 대화문 2개가 포함된다.

최신 출제 경향

1. 문제 유형 세부사항을 묻는 문제의 출제 빈도가 높다.
대화에서 언급된 구체적인 정보를 묻는 세부사항 문제가 10~20문항 정도로 가장 많이 출제된다. 화자의 신분을 묻는 문제, 화자가 제안하거나 요청하는 것을 묻는 문제 또한 꾸준히 출제되고 있다. 화자가 한 말의 의도를 파악하는 문제는 2문항, 시각 자료와 연계하여 푸는 문제는 3문항으로 매회 고정되어 출제된다.

2. 대화 주제 회사 관련 대화의 출제 빈도가 높다.
Part 3 대화는 크게 회사 관련 대화와 일상생활 관련 대화로 나눌 수 있는데, 그중 회사 관련 대화가 매회 총 13개의 대화 중 평균 9개 정도로 출제 빈도가 높은 편이다. 사내 업무, 인사, 행사, 사무기기 및 시설 등 회사에서 일어날 수 있는 다양한 주제의 대화가 출제된다.

문제 풀이 전략

STEP 1 질문 파악하기
대화가 나오기 전, 질문을 읽고 키워드를 통해 묻는 내용을 파악하고, 정답의 단서가 어느 부분에서 나올지 예상한다.

STEP 2 대화 속 단서 찾기
파악한 키워드를 바탕으로 대화를 들으면서 단서가 되는 내용을 찾는다.

STEP 3 정답 선택하기
대화에서 들은 단서 내용을 동일하게 또는 다른 어휘로 바꾸어 적절하게 표현한 보기를 정답으로 선택한다.

32. What industry do the speakers most likely work in?

(A) Healthcare
(B) Construction
(C) Advertising
(D) Agriculture

33. According to the man, what is the problem?

(A) There was a shortage of materials.
(B) There has been bad weather recently.
(C) There was a lack of skilled workers.
~~(D) There was... some~~

M Marjorie, **³²I'm afraid we have an issue with the building site on Spring Avenue.** The site manager says they're nearly two weeks behind schedule.

W Oh, no! We need to finish on time. The business has already advertised a grand opening date.

M I know. But... uh... **³³we've had a lot of storms in the past couple of weeks.** So, it was impossible to do some of the tasks.

W I guess our only choice is to schedule the crew for additional hours. We'll have to provide overtime pay, but I think it will be worth it.

문제 유형별

전체 내용 관련 문제	**1. 주제·목적** 대화의 주제 또는 화자의 전화/방문 목적을 묻는 문제
	2. 화자·장소 직업/근무지 등 화자의 신분을 묻거나, 대화가 일어나는 장소를 묻는 문제
세부 내용 관련 문제	**3. 문제점·이유** 화자의 걱정/문제점에 대해 묻는 문제, 화자가 ~하는 이유를 묻는 문제
	4. 세부사항 무엇/누구/언제/어디 등 대화에서 언급된 구체적인 정보를 묻는 문제
	5. 제안·요청사항 화자가 상대방에게 제안하거나 부탁/요청하는 것을 묻는 문제
	6. 다음에 할·일어날 일 화자가 다음에 할 일 또는 미래에 일어날 일을 묻는 문제
	7. 화자의 의도 파악 화자가 한 말의 의미나 그 말을 통해 암시하는 것, 또는 그것을 말한 이유를 묻는 문제
	8. 시각 자료 연계 목록/지도/그래프 등 다양한 유형의 시각 자료가 함께 제시되는 문제

대화 주제별

회사 관련 대화	**9. 회사 업무·인사** 회사에서 이루어지는 기본적인 업무나 채용/승진 등의 인사와 관련된 대화
	10. 사내 행사·시설 회사 내/외부에서 개최되는 각종 행사 및 회사 내 사무기기나 시설과 관련된 대화
일상생활 관련 대화	**11. 쇼핑·여가·일상** 상점/병원/도서관 등 일상생활에서 접할 수 있는 다양한 편의 시설에서 일어나는 대화
	12. 교통·여행·주거 교통수단, 여행 및 출장, 부동산 임대 등과 관련된 대화

UNIT 01 주제·목적 문제

핵심 포인트
1. 주로 대화 초반에 단서가 언급되므로, 대화 초반부를 놓치지 않고 듣는다.
2. 대화 주제가 후반부에 등장하는 경우도 종종 있으므로, 대화 초반부를 듣고서 주제가 파악되지 않는다면 나머지 2문제를 먼저 해결한 뒤 마지막에 푼다.

실전 맛보기
🎧 P3_U01_01

What is the purpose of the man's call?	남자의 전화 목적은 무엇인가?
(A) To arrange an interview	(A) 면접 일정을 잡기 위해
(B) To promote an insurance plan	(B) 보험 상품을 홍보하기 위해
(C) To confirm an appointment	**(C) 예약을 확인하기 위해**
(D) To introduce an employee	(D) 직원을 소개하기 위해

M Hi, Ms. Gilbert. This is Anthony from the Kirkland Dental Clinic. I'm calling to confirm that you'll be attending your annual checkup tomorrow at 4 o'clock.	**남** 안녕하세요, 길버트 씨. 저는 커클랜드 치과의 앤서니입니다. 내일 4시에 연례 건강검진에 오시기로 되어 있음을 확인하기 위해 전화 드립니다.
W Oh, I'm afraid I can't make it. I have an important meeting scheduled then. Could I change it to next week?	**여** 아, 죄송하지만 못 갈 것 같습니다. 그때 중요한 회의가 잡혔어요. 다음 주로 바꿀 수 있을까요?
M Let's see… Dr. Hwang is available on Tuesday morning at 9 or on Thursday afternoon at 2:30. Would one of those times work for you?	**남** 한번 볼게요… 황 박사님이 화요일 오전 9시나 목요일 오후 2시 30분에 시간이 되십니다. 그 시간들 중 하나면 괜찮으시겠어요?
W I can come on Tuesday morning.	**여** 화요일 오전에 갈 수 있습니다.
M Great! I'll rebook that for you, Ms. Gilbert. And don't forget to bring your insurance card if you have one.	**남** 좋습니다! 그렇게 다시 예약해 드리겠습니다, 길버트 씨. 그리고 보험증이 있으시면 가져오시는 것을 잊지 마세요.

CHECK UP
🎧 P3_U01_02 정답 및 해설 p.100

1. Why is the man calling?

    (A) To update his contact information
    (B) To ask about a payment
    (C) To request a copy of a contract
    (D) To correct a mistake on an invoice

2. What are the speakers discussing?

    (A) Some survey results
    (B) A job opening
    (C) Some new product ideas
    (D) A marketing plan

주제

What are the speakers (mainly) discussing? 화자들은 (주로) 무엇에 관해 이야기하고 있는가?
What is the conversation (mainly/mostly) about? 대화는 (주로) 무엇에 관한 것인가?
What is the main topic of the conversation? 대화의 주제는 무엇인가?

목적

Why is the man calling? 남자는 왜 전화하고 있는가?
Why is the man at the store? 남자는 왜 가게에 왔는가?
What is the purpose of the woman's visit/call? 여자의 방문/전화 목적은 무엇인가?

빈출 단서

희망 사항	**I want to ~ / I'd like to ~ / I hope to ~ / I need to ~** I'd like to talk about the new water bottles your team is designing. 당신의 팀에서 디자인하고 있는 새로운 물통에 대해 이야기하고 싶어요. ▶ 대화 주제: Developing new products 신제품을 개발하는 것
용건 설명	**I'm calling to ~ / I'm here to ~ / I'm here about ~** I'm calling to confirm your medical checkup with us tomorrow at 9 A.M. 내일 오전 9시에 있을 귀하의 건강검진을 확정하기 위해 전화 드립니다. ▶ 전화 목적: To confirm an appointment 예약을 확정하기 위해
논의 요청/ 진행 상황 확인	**Let's discuss ~ / Can we talk about ~? / Did you finish ~? / How is ~ coming along?** Did you finish compiling the results from the focus group? 소비자 그룹에서 나온 결과 자료 취합을 다 끝냈나요? ▶ 대화 주제: The results of a focus group 소비자 그룹 결과
관심 유발	**Have you seen ~? / Did you hear ~? / I'm curious ~** W Did you hear our museum just acquired a large impressionist art collection? 우리 박물관에서 대량의 인상파 미술 소장품들을 구했다는 거 들었어요? M Really? Who was the donor? 정말요? 기증자는 누구였나요? ▶ 대화 주제: Receiving a donation 기증품을 받는 것

고득점 TIP

전화나 방문 목적을 묻는 문제의 선택지에는 목적(To ~)뿐만 아니라 이유를 나타내는 완전한 문장도 나올 수 있다.

W Thanks for visiting Avon Appliances.
M Hi, I broke a component of the drill I bought here last week. I'm wondering if you have a service for fixing that.

여 에이번 가전제품점에 방문해 주셔서 감사합니다.
남 안녕하세요, 제가 지난주에 이곳에서 산 드릴의 부품을 망가뜨렸어요. 그것을 수리하는 서비스가 있는지 궁금합니다.

Q Why is the man at the store? 남자는 왜 가게에 왔는가?
A1 To inquire about a repair 수리에 대해 문의하기 위해
A2 Some equipment is broken. 기기가 고장 났다.

[1-4] 질문과 정답을 확인한 뒤, 대화를 들으면서 정답의 단서가 되는 부분에 표시하세요.

1. **Q** What is the main topic of the conversation?

   A Arranging a group tour

> **W** I need a team-building activity for the members of my department, so I'm planning a group activity.
>
> **M** No problem. We offer a variety of tours to suit any budget.

2. **Q** Why is the man calling?

   A To request temporary staff

> **M** Hello. This is Alan from Ingram Accounting. We need to hire a temporary worker for our busy season, which starts in January.
>
> **W** I can help you with that. What kind of duties do you need covered?

3. **Q** What is the conversation mainly about?

   A Renovating a building

> **W** I've got great news, Naveen! We were approved for a grant from the federal government. Now we have enough to repair the historic Westbury Chapel. This will be an exciting project for our town.
>
> **M** I'm so glad to hear that we'll finally be able to make the necessary repairs. It'll look so much better once the work is all finished.

4. **Q** What is the purpose of the woman's call?

   A To arrange a job interview

> **W** Good morning. I'm calling from Cruz Recruitment. You applied for a position at BC Sales, and I'd like you to come in next week for an interview.
>
> **M** That's great. I'm free on Thursday and Friday.
>
> **W** Alright. How about Thursday at 9:30 A.M.?

[5-6] 대화를 듣고 정답의 단서가 알맞게 패러프레이징된 답을 고르세요.

5. What are the speakers discussing?

   (A) Training staff members
   (B) Purchasing some machines

6. Why is the woman calling the man?

   (A) To make an appointment
   (B) To pay a bill

대화를 듣고 알맞은 답을 고른 뒤, 다시 들으면서 빈칸을 채우세요.

1. Why is the woman calling the man?

(A) To discuss a schedule change
(B) To cancel a meeting
(C) To find a hotel in Houston
(D) To confirm the price of a flight

W Brandon, I just got off the phone with Margaret in Houston. _____ _____ from Houston because of a meeting that the marketing team has scheduled.
M Okay, would you like me to _____ returning on Tuesday afternoon?
W Yes, and make sure it is a direct flight. I want to spend as little time as possible traveling.
M No problem.

2. What is the conversation mainly about?

(A) A colleague's promotion
(B) A new employee
(C) A marketing campaign
(D) A business conference

3. What does the woman say she will do?

(A) Train a new marketing team leader
(B) Contact senior executives
(C) Work overtime on a project
(D) Prepare an event for her coworker

W Did you hear that Tyson has been _____ _____? All the senior executives agreed to promote him out of the three candidates.
M That was fast! Wasn't he just transferred to the marketing team? I guess the senior executives all valued his leadership and commitment. He deserves it.
W I agree with that. Anyway, I'm going to _____ _____ to celebrate this achievement. Would you like to help me out with it?

4. Why is the woman calling?

(A) To buy a new house
(B) To find a space for her business
(C) To take an art class
(D) To complain about some tenants

5. What problem does the man mention?

(A) The building is not in a favorable location.
(B) The site is smaller than expected.
(C) The rent is higher than the woman's budget.
(D) All studios are currently unavailable.

W Hello, my name is Diane Madsen. I'm _____ _____ for my art class. Are you renting out units at Rossline Studios on 5th Street?
M Yes, we are. Could you tell me when you are planning to move in?
W Well, August would be perfect, as I want to get everything ready before I open my class in September.
M I'm afraid _____ until August or later. However, that may change. Why don't I talk to the tenants first and I'll let you know later?

대화를 듣고 알맞은 답을 고르세요.

1. What is the purpose of the woman's visit?

(A) To update an address
(B) To apply for a job
(C) To book a consultation
(D) To make a complaint

2. What does the woman say about her neighbor?

(A) He recommended a business.
(B) He works as a technician.
(C) He was disappointed with a service.
(D) He has recently moved.

3. What does the man suggest the woman do?

(A) Call another branch
(B) Pay in installments
(C) Read a pamphlet
(D) Purchase some insurance

4. What is the main topic of the conversation?

(A) Hiring policies
(B) Quarterly profits
(C) Rental fees
(D) Delivery schedules

5. What does the man suggest doing?

(A) Conducting a survey
(B) Changing a business model
(C) Redesigning a Web site
(D) Running more advertisements

6. Who most likely is Ruth Castro?

(A) A building owner
(B) A computer technician
(C) A business consultant
(D) A factory worker

7. Why is the woman calling the Dove Botanical Gardens?

(A) To request a tour
(B) To cancel a reservation
(C) To inquire about fees
(D) To purchase a ticket

8. What did the woman see on a Web site?

(A) Some reviews
(B) Some images
(C) Driving directions
(D) Opening times

9. What does the man say is no longer available?

(A) A group discount
(B) A transportation service
(C) A meal option
(D) A full refund

10. What event are the speakers discussing?

(A) A career fair
(B) A food festival
(C) A fund-raiser
(D) A film screening

11. Why does the woman say, "I'm moving to a new apartment this weekend"?

(A) To correct some misinformation
(B) To reject an invitation
(C) To update an address
(D) To ask for assistance

12. What does the man say he will do?

(A) Search for a different event
(B) Take some pictures
(C) Pick up some brochures
(D) Cover the woman's shift

13. What is the topic of the conversation?

(A) The company's overtime policy
(B) The inconvenience of traveling for business
(C) The location of a parking area
(D) The reimbursement of travel expenses

14. What does Susan say about the company's policy?

(A) It has recently changed.
(B) It doesn't cover much.
(C) It doesn't include parking.
(D) It needs to be updated.

15. What will the man probably do next?

(A) Make a complaint about a policy
(B) Update some software on his computer
(C) Send information to the women
(D) Print a list of employees

Midlands Natural History Museum

Hall 1	Ocean Life
Hall 2	Ancient Societies
Hall 3	Space
Hall 4	Fossil Room

16. What is the purpose of the woman's visit?

(A) To promote a Web site
(B) To lead a tour
(C) To apply for a job
(D) To take some photographs

17. Look at the graphic. Which exhibition hall is currently not available?

(A) Hall 1
(B) Hall 2
(C) Hall 3
(D) Hall 4

18. What does the man recommend doing?

(A) Visiting a different branch
(B) Providing some contact information
(C) Taking an informational brochure
(D) Speaking to a manager

핵심 포인트

1. 주제·목적 문제와 마찬가지로 주로 초반에 단서가 언급되므로, 대화 초반부에 나오는 직업, 장소 표현을 놓치지 않고 듣는다.
2. 화자의 직업이나 대화 장소가 직접적으로 언급되지 않는다면, 대화 곳곳에 등장하는 키워드를 통해 정답을 유추한다.
3. 화자 문제는 신분이나 직업뿐만 아니라 업종, 근무지, 부서 등을 묻는 다양한 형태로 출제될 수 있다.

실전 맛보기

🎧 P3_U02_01

Who most likely is the man?	남자는 누구인 것 같은가?
(A) An event planner	(A) 행사 기획자
(B) An art instructor	**(B) 미술 강사**
(C) A city official	(C) 시 공무원
(D) A business consultant	(D) 사업 컨설턴트

W I had a great time in your class today, Charlie. I feel like I learned a lot.	여 오늘 당신의 수업은 정말 즐거웠어요, 찰리. 많은 것을 배운 것 같아요.
M Great! I'm really impressed with the progress you've made so far. Your paintings are looking better and better every week.	남 좋네요! 지금까지 당신이 보인 진전에 정말 깊은 인상을 받았어요. 당신의 그림들은 매주 점점 더 좋아 보여요.
W Thank you. I know the summer schedule hasn't been announced yet, but do you plan to open another class for that term?	여 고마워요. 아직 여름 시간표는 발표되지 않았지만, 여름 학기에 또 다른 수업을 열 계획인가요?
M I'm not sure yet. It depends on the demand. However, I'll make an announcement as soon as anything is finalized.	남 아직 잘 모르겠어요. 그것은 수요에 달려 있어요. 하지만, 무엇이든 확정되자마자 공지할게요.
W That would be perfect. I'd love the chance to continue developing my skills.	여 그래 주시면 좋겠어요. 계속해서 제 능력을 발전시킬 기회를 가지고 싶어요.

CHECK UP

🎧 P3_U02_02 정답 및 해설 p.108

1. Where are the speakers?

(A) At a bookstore
(B) At a concert hall
(C) At a musical instrument shop
(D) At an art school

2. What industry do the speakers most likely work in?

(A) Journalism
(B) Healthcare
(C) Real estate
(D) Technology

빈출 질문

화자

Who (most likely) is the man? 남자는 누구인가?

Where do the speakers (most likely) work? 화자들은 어디에서 일하는가?

What kind of business does the woman (most likely) work for? 여자는 어떤 종류의 업체에서 일하는가?

What field/industry/department do the speakers (most likely) work in? 화자들은 어떤 분야/업계/부서에서 일하는가?

장소

Where (most likely) is the man? 남자는 어디에 있는가?

Where does the conversation (most likely) take place? 대화는 어디에서 일어나는가?

빈출 단서

환영 인사	**Welcome to ~ / You've reached ~ / Thanks for coming to ~** You've reached Greenway Apartments. How can I help you? 그린웨이 아파트에 전화하셨습니다. 어떻게 도와드릴까요? ▶ 화자 직업: A property manager 건물 관리자
자기소개	**This is ~ / I'm calling from ~ / I own ~** Hello, I'm Ruth Torres calling from Easy Travel World magazine. 안녕하세요, 저는 쉬운 세계여행 잡지사에서 전화 드리는 루스 토레스입니다. ▶ 화자 근무지: At a magazine publisher 잡지사에서
상대방 정보	**You must be ~ / your first day at ~ / I'm interested in having you ~** Hi, you must be Walter from Waco Contractors. Welcome to Woodland Banner House. 안녕하세요, 당신이 와코 시공사에서 오신 월터 씨군요. 우드랜드 배너 하우스에 오신 것을 환영합니다. ▶ 화자 직업: A building contractor 건설업자
간접 키워드	**W** Please come in. I'm rearranging this display of antique lamps. If you need help finding anything, just let me know. 들어오세요. 저는 이 골동품 램프들의 진열을 바꾸고 있어요. 뭐든 찾는 데 도움이 필요하시면, 제게 알려주세요. **M** Can you show me wireframe eyeglasses? Something from the late 19th century would be great. 철사 프레임의 안경을 보여 주실 수 있나요? 19세기 후반의 물건이면 좋을 것 같아요. ▶ 대화 장소: At an antique store 골동품 가게에서

고득점 TIP

화자들의 공통 직업이나 근무지를 묻는 문제는 we나 our, us와 같이 '우리'를 나타내는 표현을 잘 듣는다.

W Rico, I finally had some time to visit the building that our law office will move into. I took a few photos. Take a look.

M I love the modern style!

W Me, too. And it's on a busy road, which will increase our exposure in town.

여 리코, 제가 드디어 우리 법률 사무소가 이전할 건물에 방문할 시간이 좀 있었어요. 사진을 몇 장 찍어 왔어요. 한번 보세요.

남 현대적인 스타일이 아주 마음에 드네요!

여 저도요. 그리고 번화가에 있어서, 시내에서 우리가 노출되는 빈도가 늘어날 거예요.

Q Where do the speakers work? 화자들은 어디에서 일하는가?

A At a law office 법률 사무소에서

[1-4] 질문과 정답을 확인한 뒤, 대화를 들으면서 정답의 단서가 되는 부분에 표시하세요.

1. **Q** Who is the man?

   A A city official

> **W** I'm pleased to welcome to the studio our special guest today, Mr. Joseph Warren. He's the director of the city's department of transportation.
> **M** Thanks for inviting me, Cecilia.

2. **Q** Where does the conversation most likely take place?

   A On a train

> **M** Ms. Santos, I've checked the platform of the station, and there are no other passengers trying to board the passenger cars.
> **W** Great. The luggage has been secured in the cargo car. So, we're ready to announce to the passengers that we'll be departing the station shortly.

3. **Q** Where does the conversation take place?

   A At a restaurant

> **M** Alice, could you help me change the tablecloths on the tables in our dining area? The wait staff will be arriving soon to serve our diners.
> **W** Sure, I can help with that.
> **M** Thanks! And I've ordered a new oven, so that should arrive later this week.

4. **Q** Where does the man work?

   A At an appliance manufacturer

> **M** Thanks for agreeing to take on this consulting job, Ms. Lucas. We recently released new refrigerator and air conditioner models. However, we've been getting bad reviews, which is affecting our company's reputation.
> **W** Don't worry. I'll devise some strategies to help improve your image.

[5-6] 대화를 듣고 정답의 단서가 알맞게 패러프레이징된 답을 고르세요.

5. What type of company do the speakers most likely work for?

   (A) Advertising
   (B) Finance

6. Where most likely are the speakers?

   (A) At a hardware store
   (B) At a construction site

대화를 듣고 알맞은 답을 고른 뒤, 다시 들으면서 빈칸을 채우세요.

1. Where do the speakers work?

(A) At a restaurant
(B) At a department store
(C) At a real estate agency
(D) At a bank

> W How are the trainees in your department doing?
> M You mean the new _____? They're doing really well. In fact, I plan to promote all of them to full-time cashiers.
> W That's great news. I wonder if some of them could _____. We're short-staffed again.
> M Well, after the training is completed, I'll send you the names of those who may be interested in changing departments.

2. What field do the speakers most likely work in?

(A) Telecommunications
(B) Entertainment
(C) Tourism
(D) Advertising

> W Alex, I heard you did a great job leading the meeting with Allstar Autos. They really liked the new _____. You're setting up more meetings with new clients this month, right?
> M Yes, but I've been thinking of doing video conferences rather than meeting face to face.
> W Aren't there always problems with the video conference system?
> M Well... I've just read an article about a new system that we might want to purchase. _____ when I get back to my desk.

3. What does the man say he will do?

(A) Return some equipment
(B) Provide information to the woman
(C) Attend a meeting with a client
(D) Exchange a purchased product

4. Where most likely are the speakers?

(A) At a catering company
(B) At an office supply store
(C) At a print shop
(D) At a hotel

> M Good morning. What can I do for you?
> W Hi, I'm here to make a change to my wedding invitation. The order is under my fiancé's name. His last name is Monfort.
> M OK... let's see... Oh, here's the order. It looks like _____, so it'll be no problem to adjust it. What change would you like to make?
> W We've decided to _____ _____, not The Rose Inn.

5. According to the woman, what has changed about the event?

(A) The time
(B) The venue
(C) The sponsor
(D) The date

대화를 듣고 알맞은 답을 고르세요.

1. Where is the conversation taking place?

(A) At a travel agency
(B) At an airport
(C) At a luggage store
(D) At a bus station

2. What problem does the man mention?

(A) A part is broken.
(B) A fee has increased.
(C) A bag is too heavy.
(D) A catalog had an error.

3. What does the woman offer to do?

(A) Issue a refund
(B) Extend a warranty
(C) Place an order
(D) Contact a manager

4. Where does the conversation take place?

(A) At a department store
(B) At a hotel
(C) At an airport
(D) At a bus stop

5. What problem does the woman mention?

(A) A service has been discontinued.
(B) A passport has expired.
(C) A fee has not been paid.
(D) A reservation was lost.

6. What will the man most likely do next?

(A) Complete a form
(B) Provide a confirmation code
(C) Print an itinerary
(D) Make a phone call

7. Where does the conversation take place?

(A) At a shopping center
(B) At a sports stadium
(C) At a concert hall
(D) At a bus terminal

8. Why is the woman unable to use the ticket?

(A) It has expired.
(B) It has been damaged.
(C) It is for the wrong date.
(D) It is missing some information.

9. What will Gilbert give the woman?

(A) A receipt
(B) A map
(C) A parking pass
(D) Some change

10. Which industry do the speakers most likely work in?

(A) Insurance
(B) Publishing
(C) Entertainment
(D) Banking

11. What does the woman say about a parking area?

(A) It is conveniently located.
(B) It has specific spots for employees.
(C) It is temporarily closed for repairs.
(D) It can be used for a small fee.

12. What does the woman imply when she says, "there are few employees living there"?

(A) A bus journey takes a long time.
(B) An office relocation has been canceled.
(C) A subway station has closed.
(D) A service is no longer available.

13. Who most likely is the man?

(A) A computer programmer
(B) An illustrator
(C) A musician
(D) A film director

14. How did the woman learn about the man's work?

(A) By visiting a Web site
(B) By reading his résumé
(C) By purchasing one of his projects
(D) By attending a conference

15. What does the man request?

(A) A sample text
(B) A job application
(C) A business card
(D) A contract

Printing Rates (per 1,000)

Size	Standard Paper	Glossy Paper
Small	$90	$100
Medium	$110	$130
Large	$145	$150

16. What kind of business do the speakers work for?

(A) A library
(B) An auto repair shop
(C) A bakery
(D) A print shop

17. What does the man say about glossy paper?

(A) It is easier to fold than standard paper.
(B) It is too expensive for a budget.
(C) It makes colors look brighter.
(D) It is more durable than standard paper.

18. Look at the graphic. How much will the speakers most likely be charged?

(A) $100
(B) $110
(C) $130
(D) $150

핵심 포인트

1. 부정적인 의미를 지닌 표현과 함께 걱정거리가 언급되는 부분을 주의 깊게 듣는다.
2. because(~하기 때문에)나 so(그래서)와 같이 원인과 결과를 나타내는 표현이 포함된 문장에 주목한다.
3. 주로 문장 형태의 긴 선택지로 출제되므로, 선택지를 미리 읽고 내용을 파악해 두는 것이 좋다.

실전 맛보기
🎧 P3_U03_01

What problem does the man mention?	남자는 어떤 문제를 언급하는가?
(A) Tickets are not selling well.	(A) 티켓이 잘 팔리지 않고 있다.
(B) Some equipment is not working.	(B) 일부 장비가 작동하지 않고 있다.
(C) A shipment did not arrive.	**(C) 택배가 도착하지 않았다.**
(D) An employee is absent.	(D) 직원이 결근했다.

M I'm excited that the Manchester Orchestra has agreed to give a performance at our theater.	남 맨체스터 오케스트라가 우리 극장에서 공연하기로 해서 신나요.
W Yes, hosting such a prestigious group will be great for our reputation. We need to start promoting ticket sales as soon as possible. Have you received the promotional brochures I ordered?	여 네, 그렇게 명성 있는 그룹을 모시는 것은 우리의 평판에 굉장히 좋을 거예요. 우리는 가능한 한 빨리 티켓 판매를 홍보하기 시작해야 해요. 제가 주문한 홍보 책자를 받으셨어요?
M The shipment was supposed to be delivered yesterday, but there's no sign of it.	남 택배가 어제 배송될 예정이었지만, 올 기미가 전혀 안 보여요.
W Hmm… we'd better call the print shop to find out what's going on. I'd like to start passing those brochures out to audience members.	여 흠… 무슨 일이 있는지 알아보기 위해 인쇄소에 전화해 보는 것이 좋겠어요. 그 책자들을 관객들에게 나눠 주기 시작했으면 해요.
M I'm not very busy, so I can take care of that now.	남 제가 그다지 바쁘지 않으니, 지금 그것을 처리할 수 있어요.

CHECK UP
🎧 P3_U03_02 정답 및 해설 p.116

1. What problem does the man mention?

(A) A client has canceled a contract.
(B) A speaker cannot make it to an event.
(C) A board meeting has been postponed.
(D) A workshop has been overbooked.

2. Why did the woman choose the man for a project?

(A) He has recently finished some other work duties.
(B) He assisted with the same event last year.
(C) He has a large network of business contacts.
(D) He has an impressive educational background.

문제점

What is the (man's) problem? (남자의) 문제는 무엇인가?

What problem does the woman mention/have? 여자는 어떤 문제를 언급하는가/가지고 있는가?

What is the man concerned about? 남자는 무엇에 대해 걱정하는가?

이유

Why does the man apologize? 남자는 왜 사과하는가?

Why does the woman want to ~? 여자는 왜 ~하고 싶어 하는가?

Why is the woman surprised/pleased/excited? 여자는 왜 놀랐는가/기뻐하는가/신이 났는가?

빈출 단서

반전	**but / however / unfortunately / actually** I want to order a new charging cable for my mobile phone, but it says you don't have any available online. 제 핸드폰에 쓸 충전 케이블을 새로 주문하고 싶은데, 온라인에 재고가 없다고 나와 있어요. ▶ 걱정하는 이유: A product has been difficult to obtain. 제품을 구하기 어렵다.
부정적 의미	**not possible / not able to ~ / too ~ / bad news** The space is a bit too small. I'd like to expand my business, but the class would be too crowded. 공간이 너무 작아요. 저는 사업을 확장하고 싶은데, 반이 너무 붐빌 거예요. ▶ 문제점: A space is not large enough. 공간이 충분히 크지 않다.
문제/걱정	**problem / trouble / issue / concern / worried / help / advice** Some of the users had trouble adjusting the settings and we really need to improve that. 사용자들 중 몇 명이 설정을 조정하는 데 어려움을 겪었고 우리는 그것을 반드시 개선해야 합니다. ▶ 문제점: Some settings are difficult to change. 몇 가지 설정이 바꾸기가 어렵다.
원인/결과	**because (of) ~ / due to ~ / so ~** I'll be out of the office tomorrow for a dentist appointment. So I won't be able to make the meeting. 저는 내일 치과 예약 때문에 사무실을 나갈 예정이에요. 그래서 회의에 참석할 수 없을 겁니다. ▶ 회의 불참 이유: She has to go to a dental appointment. 그녀는 치과 예약에 가야 한다.

고득점 TIP

화자의 감정을 묻는 문제는 감탄사가 단서로 주어질 수 있다.

W How long will it take to install the new floor tiles?

M About four weeks.

W Wow, that's much longer than I expected. I didn't realize it was such a big project.

여 새 바닥 타일을 까는 데 얼마나 걸릴까요?
남 4주 정도요.
여 우와, 제가 예상했던 것보다 훨씬 더 오래 걸리네요. 그렇게 큰 프로젝트인 줄 몰랐어요.

Q Why is the woman surprised? 여자는 왜 놀랐는가?

A A project will take a long time to complete. 프로젝트를 완료하는 데 시간이 오래 걸릴 것이다.

[1-4] 질문과 정답을 확인한 뒤, 대화를 들으면서 정답의 단서가 되는 부분에 표시하세요.

1. **Q** What problem does the woman mention?

A An appliance has leaked.

> **M** Welcome to the Clearview Towers property management office. How may I help you?
>
> **W** My name is Justine Romo, and I live in unit 433. I was running my dishwasher this morning, but it seems there's a leak. After it had been running for a while, I saw water all over the floor.

2. **Q** What problem does the man mention?

A Some expenses are not covered.

> **W** Good morning, Mr. Ennis. You said you had a concern about the contract?
>
> **M** Yes. There's no provision for our travel expenses. This is important, as our band is coming from out of town.

3. **Q** Why is the man excited about his new apartment?

A It is close to a park.

> **W** I heard you are moving to the Victoria neighborhood.
>
> **M** Yes, to an apartment on Dayton Street. It's located near Spruce Park, so I'm excited to move there.

4. **Q** Why is the man unable to help the woman?

A He has to answer a phone call.

> **W** Now that I'm checked in, would you mind showing me how to get to your on-site gym?
>
> **M** I can in a moment, but my phone's ringing and I need to take this call.

[5-6] 대화를 듣고 정답의 단서가 알맞게 패러프레이징된 답을 고르세요.

5. Why is the man concerned?

(A) A client is upset.

(B) A location is remote.

6. What is the problem?

(A) Some equipment is not working properly.

(B) A passenger did not arrive on time.

대화를 듣고 알맞은 답을 고른 뒤, 다시 들으면서 빈칸을 채우세요.

1. What is the problem?

(A) A light is not working.

(B) Some documents are missing.

(C) An appliance is too noisy.

(D) The staff lounge is too hot.

W Excuse me, could you check the refrigerator in the staff lounge when you're finished here?

M Another employee already told me about that, so I checked it a little while ago. The fan in the back is starting to _____ _____, it seems.

W How soon can you fix it? _____ _____.

M I'll need to get a replacement part, so I'll fix it tomorrow.

---

2. Where does the woman most likely work?

(A) At a bank

(B) At a bookstore

(C) At a driver's license center

(D) At a public library

3. Why will the man return tomorrow?

(A) To get an application form

(B) To attend a free event

(C) To provide an extra document

(D) To request a new credit card

M Excuse me, I just moved here, and I'd like to _____ to check out some books. How can I do that?

W First, you'll need to fill out the application form. Then you'll need to show your driver's license and proof of address, such as your credit card statement or utility bill.

M Well, I have my driver's license with me, but I'll have to come back tomorrow _____ ___.

W That's fine. Once you do that, we can _____ _____.

---

4. What problem does the woman mention?

(A) An item was never received.

(B) An account password isn't working.

(C) A card has expired.

(D) Some information was deleted.

5. What will the woman most likely do tomorrow?

(A) Repair some equipment

(B) Deliver a document

(C) Apply for another card

(D) Shop for supplies

W Hi, my name is Kendra Wood. I just opened a business account here. However, _____ _____ from you yet.

M Sorry. Let me look up your information. Hmm… It says it was delivered on Monday and signed for by Mr. Kahleem.

W Oh, really? I didn't ask him. I'm glad it arrived. I need to _____ tomorrow with it. I guess I should have checked around the office before coming here.

대화를 듣고 알맞은 답을 고르세요.

1. What is the woman preparing for?

(A) A meeting agenda
(B) A keynote speech
(C) A nomination form
(D) A conference registration

2. What is the woman concerned about?

(A) Losing a document
(B) Working long hours
(C) Missing a deadline
(D) Exceeding a budget

3. Why does the woman thank the man?

(A) He agreed to work late.
(B) He gave her some information.
(C) He offered to proofread a document.
(D) He will introduce her to a client.

4. Why is the woman pleased?

(A) A bank will extend its hours.
(B) A loan application was approved.
(C) She was offered a promotion.
(D) She will transfer to a new branch.

5. What does the man mean when he says, "we're in the middle of our peak season"?

(A) He does not have time to help the woman.
(B) There is extra money to spend on a project.
(C) A suggested timeline would be a problem.
(D) The business is doing well.

6. What does the man say about his friend?

(A) He is currently looking for a job.
(B) He can advise them on a decision.
(C) He will visit the business soon.
(D) He attended an industry conference.

7. What does the woman want to do?

(A) Exchange an item
(B) Place a rush order
(C) Purchase a gift card
(D) Get a refund

8. What problem does the man mention?

(A) A shop is about to close.
(B) An item is out of stock.
(C) Prices have recently increased.
(D) A coupon is no longer valid.

9. What does the man say he will do?

(A) He will give her store credit.
(B) He will call the warehouse.
(C) He will contact the woman.
(D) He will check the store's Web site.

10. What is the woman planning to do?

(A) Attend a business dinner
(B) Visit a friend
(C) Pick up a car
(D) Buy a new home appliance

11. What information does the man provide?

(A) Where to catch a bus
(B) Where to buy a ticket
(C) How to find a taxi
(D) How to pay for parking

12. What is the woman's problem?

(A) She does not have enough money.
(B) Her car is being repaired.
(C) She is late for a meeting.
(D) There are no parking spaces.

13. Where is the conversation most likely taking place?

(A) At a business institute
(B) At a supermarket
(C) At a medical clinic
(D) At a manufacturing facility

14. What problem are the women discussing?

(A) A light will not turn on.
(B) A shipment will arrive late.
(C) A door cannot be opened.
(D) A heater has malfunctioned.

15. What will happen in an hour?

(A) A business will close for the day.
(B) A training session will begin.
(C) A room will be cleaned.
(D) A patient will have an appointment.

	Lunch Shift	Dinner Shift
Monday	Victoria	Nicole
Tuesday	Teresa	Gabriel
Wednesday	Kinoka	Victoria
Thursday	Closed for holiday	

16. Why does the woman want to take time off?

(A) To visit family members
(B) To leave for a trip
(C) To go to a doctor
(D) To attend a seminar

17. Look at the graphic. Who will the woman most likely speak to?

(A) Nicole
(B) Teresa
(C) Gabriel
(D) Kinoka

18. What does the woman say she will do later today?

(A) Give the man a call
(B) Print a new schedule
(C) Stop by the restaurant
(D) Work an extra shift

PART 3

UNIT 03

핵심 포인트

1. What, Who, How 등의 의문사로 세부 내용을 묻는 다양한 문제가 출제된다.
2. 질문의 핵심 키워드가 대화에서 언급되는 부분에 주목한다. 대화 속 정답 단서는 대부분 패러프레이징되어 선택지에 제시된다.
3. 3인 대화에서는 같은 성별의 화자들에 대한 내용을 묻는 문제가 나올 수 있으므로, 화자들이 공통적으로 언급하는 내용을 주의 깊게 듣는다.

실전 맛보기

🎧 P3_U04_01

What is the woman preparing for?	여자는 무엇을 준비하고 있는가?
(A) A training session	(A) 교육
(B) A business trip	(B) 출장
(C) A grand opening	**(C) 개점**
(D) A live performance	(D) 라이브 공연

M Thank you for visiting Kea Furniture. How may I help you?	남 케아 가구점을 방문해 주셔서 감사합니다. 어떻게 도와드릴까요?
W Good morning. I've heard that you can design custom-made wooden furniture.	여 안녕하세요. 주문 제작 목재 가구를 디자인하신다고 들었어요.
M That's correct. We can adjust any of our products to the exact size you need. Is there a specific project you had in mind?	남 맞습니다. 저희 제품 중 어느 것이든 당신이 필요로 하는 정확한 크기로 맞출 수 있습니다. 생각해 두신 구체적인 프로젝트가 있나요?
W Yes, I'd like some benches for the café area of my new bakery. They need to fit perfectly in the corner, and I'd like them to be ready by opening day, June 18.	여 네, 제가 새로 열 제과점의 카페 구역에 놓을 벤치들을 원해요. 그것들은 구석에 딱 맞아야 하고, 개점일인 6월 18일까지 준비되었으면 좋겠어요.
M Alright. If you have time now, I can get one of our staff members to discuss the project with you.	남 알겠습니다. 지금 시간이 있으시면, 저희 직원들 중 한 명이 그 프로젝트에 관해 당신과 이야기를 나누도록 할 수 있습니다.
W That would be great. Thanks!	여 그러면 좋겠어요. 감사해요!

CHECK UP

🎧 P3_U04_02 정답 및 해설 p.124

1. What is the woman responsible for?

(A) Catering a dinner
(B) Publishing a book
(C) Calling all the guests
(D) Coordinating an event

2. What does the man say about a parking meter?

(A) It is out of order.
(B) It is convenient.
(C) It will expire soon.
(D) Its fee is expensive.

What 의문사

What did the man ~? 남자는 무엇을 ~했는가?
What does the woman say about ~? 여자는 ~에 대해 무엇이라고 말하는가?
According to the woman, what is ~? 여자에 따르면, ~는 무엇인가?

기타 의문사

Who will the speakers ~? 화자들은 누구를 ~할 것인가?
When/Where will the man ~? 남자는 언제/어디로 ~할 것인가?
How did the woman learn about ~? 여자는 ~에 대해 어떻게 알게 되었는가?

빈출 단서 패러프레이징

품사 전환	**단어의 앞뒤 순서를 바꾸면서 품사를 바꾸어 제시** We are celebrating our company's 20th anniversary this week. 저희는 이번 주에 회사의 20주년 기념일을 축하할 거예요. ▶ 참석할 행사: An anniversary celebration 기념일 축하 행사
동의어/반의어 이용	**동일한 의미를 가진 다른 단어 또는 유사한 표현으로 바꾸거나, 반대되는 의미를 가진 단어에 부정을 나타내는 not을 붙여서 제시** It's made out of a treated material that makes the fibers extremely resistant to stains. 그것은 약품 처리된 물질로 만들어져 있어서 섬유가 얼룩에 몹시 강해지도록 합니다. ▶ 제품에 대해 말하는 것: It does not stain easily. 그것은 쉽게 얼룩지지 않는다.
상위어 이용	**해당 단어의 의미를 포괄하는 상위 개념의 단어로 바꾸어 제시** I e-mailed you a copy of the report this morning. 오늘 오전에 당신에게 이메일로 보고서 사본을 보냈어요. ▶ 최근에 한 일: Send a document 문서 보내기
함축	**수식어구를 생략하고 핵심 동사와 명사만 남기거나, 긴 문장을 단어나 구 또는 짧은 문장으로 함축하여 제시** I think we should look for a firm that has worked with clients like us for years. 저는 우리 같은 고객들과 몇 년간 일해온 회사를 찾아야 한다고 생각해요. ▶ 회사의 조건: It has relevant experience. 그곳은 관련 경험을 가지고 있다.

고득점 TIP

과거에 일어난 일을 묻는 문제는 날짜, 요일 등 지난 특정 시점을 나타내는 표현을 잘 들어야 한다.

W Hey, Adam. Can you believe how big that snowstorm was on Saturday?

M Yeah, it's the worst one I've seen in years. I'm guessing we'll be really busy at the warehouse this week unloading delayed deliveries.

여 저기요, 애덤. 토요일에 친 눈보라가 얼마나 대단했는지 믿어지나요?

남 그러니까요, 제가 몇 년 동안 본 것 중에 최악이었어요. 이번 주에 우리는 밀린 배송품을 내리느라 창고에서 아주 바쁠 것 같네요.

Q According to the speakers, what happened on Saturday?
화자들에 따르면, 토요일에 무슨 일이 일어났는가?

A There was a snowstorm. 눈보라가 쳤다.

[1-4] 질문과 정답을 확인한 뒤, 대화를 들으면서 정답의 단서가 되는 부분에 표시하세요.

1. **Q** What does the woman say about a consultation program?

A It was very popular.

> **M** Erica, you're planning the office's Health Week this year, right?
> **W** Yes, I had a personal trainer offer consultations with employees about workouts. A lot of people signed up. It was very well received.

2. **Q** Where will the woman most likely go next?

A To a bank

> **W** We've just received the new electric mixers from Davis Manufacturing, so we need to set up a display.
> **M** I can start working on that now.
> **W** Thank you. I'll help you when I get back, but first I need to go and deposit yesterday's cash.

3. **Q** How does the woman suggest changing a poster?

A By using fewer fonts

> **M** I sent you the first draft of the poster to advertise our new theater show. Did you get a chance to look at it yet? I'd like your opinion.
> **W** Well, I like the combination of colors, but having so many different fonts is distracting. I think you'd better just use one or two.

4. **Q** What product feature does the woman say she is concerned about?

A Durability

> **M** I'm excited about the new hiking boots we'll be releasing this spring. I think a lot of our customers will be interested in them.
> **W** Yes, I agree. However, we have to make sure we don't rush the testing process. It's important for the boots to be durable enough for long hikes on rough trails.

[5-6] 대화를 듣고 정답의 단서가 알맞게 패러프레이징된 답을 고르세요.

5. What does the woman say she has to do?

(A) Speak to a bandmate
(B) Get driving directions

6. What does the man warn the woman about?

(A) His car is having problems.
(B) Other people will be with him.

🎧 P3_U04_04 정답 및 해설 p.127

대화를 듣고 알맞은 답을 고른 뒤, 다시 들으면서 빈칸을 채우세요.

1. According to the woman, who will be arriving soon?

(A) A friend
(B) A coworker
(C) A boss
(D) A client

> **W** I have only half an hour, so I'd like to order something that can be made quickly. Will the salad take long?
> **M** Not at all. Plus, today we have a special on the ricotta cheese salad.
> **W** Sounds good. _____ asked me to order for her, since _____. So, can I get two special salads and two coffees, please?
> **M** Okay, I'll be back shortly.

2. What does the woman want to do?

(A) Apply for a job abroad
(B) Request a loan
(C) Get an official document
(D) Exchange a purchased item

3. Where will the woman probably go next?

(A) To a different counter
(B) To the woman's office
(C) To another branch
(D) To a downstairs café

> **W** Excuse me. I'd like to _____. I'll be doing some international travel. I was told it normally takes about a week to receive a passport, but is there any way I can get it sooner?
> **M** Yes, there's an option for the express service, but you will need to pay an additional fee of 30 dollars. It takes about two business days.
> **W** That's fine. I'll apply for the express service. Can I do that here?
> **M** Sorry, you should _____ _____.

4. When will the business change its service hours?

(A) Today
(B) Tomorrow
(C) Next week
(D) Next month

5. What would the man like to do with the voicemail?

(A) Hire a professional service for it
(B) Shorten the message
(C) Get some feedback from customers
(D) Add a security feature

> **M** Maria, have you heard that the company has decided to _____ starting from next week?
> **W** Yes, it'll be great for business. But now we need to _____ right away to include our new schedule.
> **M** Right, I forgot about that. You know, the sound quality isn't very good. I'm wondering how much _____ would cost.
> **W** One of my friends recently hired someone to do that for her company. I'll call her and find out how much she paid.

대화를 듣고 알맞은 답을 고르세요.

1. What does the woman's company most likely produce?

(A) Computer accessories
(B) Gardening supplies
(C) Kitchen appliances
(D) Workout equipment

2. Why does the woman apologize?

(A) A device will not turn on.
(B) An item is the wrong size.
(C) Some components were missing.
(D) The man was overcharged.

3. What does the man ask about?

(A) A delivery charge
(B) A return policy
(C) A product catalog
(D) A mailing list

4. How did the man learn about the business?

(A) By reading a sign outside
(B) By receiving an e-mail
(C) By performing an online search
(D) By speaking to a coworker

5. What has the man recently done?

(A) Completed a degree
(B) Opened a business
(C) Moved into the area
(D) Won a competition

6. What will the woman ask a colleague to do?

(A) Issue a parking pass
(B) Give the man a tour
(C) Bring some paperwork
(D) Adjust a membership fee

7. Why is the woman calling?

(A) To make a payment
(B) To sign up for a service
(C) To report an error
(D) To request a repair

8. What does the man say about a software program?

(A) It will be replaced soon.
(B) It requires a password.
(C) It has recently been upgraded.
(D) It restarts automatically.

9. What does the man say might be necessary?

(A) Submitting a document
(B) Visiting the office
(C) Closing an account
(D) Contacting a manager

10. What kind of job are the women training for?

(A) Electrician
(B) Safety inspector
(C) Architect
(D) Real estate agent

11. What does the man warn the women about?

(A) A labor shortage
(B) A software issue
(C) An additional fee
(D) A waiting list

12. What does Marcy ask about?

(A) A meal break
(B) A textbook
(C) A tour
(D) A password

13. What does the man have to do by Friday?

(A) Meet with a team leader
(B) Submit a report
(C) Sign a contract
(D) Negotiate with clients

14. What does the man imply when he says, "I won't be back until Thursday"?

(A) He thinks a contract has been completed.
(B) He wants to postpone a meeting with the woman.
(C) He had his flight change unexpectedly.
(D) He does not have time to finish a task.

15. What does the woman suggest the man do?

(A) Hire an assistant
(B) Ask for an extension
(C) Cancel his business trip
(D) Call a representative

Feature	Rating (out of 10)
Style	9.9
Packaging	9.8
Durability	9.1
Ease of use	8.7

16. What kind of product are the speakers discussing?

(A) Some headphones
(B) A tablet computer
(C) A printer
(D) A smartphone

17. Look at the graphic. What rating is the woman particularly pleased about?

(A) 9.9
(B) 9.8
(C) 9.1
(D) 8.7

18. What does the woman hope to do?

(A) Improve a product's energy efficiency
(B) Hire a celebrity for an advertisement
(C) Promote the product at a music festival
(D) Make improvements to a Web site

UNIT O5 제안·요청사항 문제

핵심 포인트

1. 주로 마지막 문제로 출제되며, 대화 후반부에서 단서가 언급된다.
2. 질문을 미리 읽고 화자의 성별을 확인한 뒤, 해당 화자의 말 속에서 무언가를 제안하거나 요청하는 표현을 놓치지 않고 듣는다.
3. 상대방에게 무언가를 하라고 제안하는 것뿐만 아니라 자신이 해 주겠다는 제안 내용도 출제될 수 있으므로 질문을 정확하게 파악해야 한다.

실전 맛보기

P3_U05_01

What does the man ask the woman to do?	남자는 여자에게 무엇을 해 달라고 요청하는가?
(A) Provide company information	**(A) 회사 정보 제공하기**
(B) Proofread a document	(B) 문서 교정하기
(C) Attend an interview	(C) 면접 참석하기
(D) Send an invitation	(D) 초대장 보내기

W Amir, the employee orientation is coming up, and I'm wondering if you would be willing to give the welcome speech at the session.	**여** 아미르, 직원 오리엔테이션이 다가오고 있는데, 당신이 그 시간에 환영사를 할 의향이 있는지 궁금해요.
M I've never done anything like that before, but I'll give it a try. What do I need to include in the speech?	**남** 전에 그런 것을 해 본 적이 전혀 없지만, 한번 해 볼게요. 제가 연설에 무엇을 포함해야 하죠?
W You just need to welcome the attendees and tell them a little bit about our company.	**여** 참석자들을 환영하고 우리 회사에 대해 조금 이야기하기만 하면 돼요.
M Hmm… I know a lot about our current operations, but not much about the company's history. Could you please send me some details about that?	**남** 흠… 저는 현재 사업에 대해서는 많이 알고 있지만, 회사의 역사에 관해서는 많이 알지 못해요. 그것에 관한 세부 정보를 좀 보내 주시겠어요?
W Sure. I have some documents that I think would be helpful.	**여** 물론이죠. 도움이 될 것 같은 문서들이 제게 좀 있어요.

CHECK UP

P3_U05_02 정답 및 해설 p.132

1. What does the woman recommend the man do?

(A) Attend an anniversary party
(B) Give a presentation at an event
(C) Ask employees for help at a meeting
(D) Update employees' contact numbers

2. What does the man ask the woman to do?

(A) Oversee a project
(B) Provide some feedback
(C) Confirm a schedule
(D) Call a client

제안

What does the man suggest (doing)? 남자는 무엇을 (할 것을) 제안하는가?

What does the woman recommend the man do? 여자는 남자에게 무엇을 하라고 추천하는가?

What does the man offer to do? 남자는 무엇을 해 주겠다고 제안하는가?

요청

What does the man ask/tell the woman to do? 남자는 여자에게 무엇을 해 달라고 요청하는가?

What does the woman ask for? 여자는 무엇을 요청하는가?

What is the man asked to do? 남자는 무엇을 하도록 요청받는가?

빈출 단서

권고/추천	**Why don't you ~? / (Maybe) We should ~ / I suggest ~** Maybe we should post some frequently asked questions and answers on the bulletin board in the cafeteria area. 아마도 우리는 구내식당 구역에 있는 게시판에 자주 묻는 질문과 답변 몇 개를 게시해야 할 거예요. ▶ 제안사항: Posting information 정보를 게시하는 것
제공	**I can ~ / I'll ~ if you'd like / I'm happy to ~** I can give the manager a call to see what time will be convenient. 제가 관리자에게 전화해서 몇 시가 편할지 알아볼 수 있어요. ▶ 제안사항: Call a manager 관리자에게 전화하기
지시/부탁	**Can/Could/Will/Would you ~? / Please ~** Would you get some price quotes from local party rental companies? 지역의 파티 렌탈 업체에서 견적서를 좀 받아 주시겠어요? ▶ 요청사항: Get some cost estimates 견적서 받기

고득점 TIP

질문에 쓰인 동사가 수동형(asked)이면 질문 속 화자가 아닌 상대방 화자의 말에서 단서를 찾아야 한다.

W I make a lot of deliveries for my business, so I need a reliable van.

M I understand. All of our vans are in great condition, and they have a lot of space in the back. So, I think they'll be perfect. Did you bring your driver's license? If so, you can take one for a test drive.

여 저는 업무상 배달을 많이 해서, 믿을 만한 승합차가 필요해요.

남 알겠습니다. 저희 승합차들은 모두 상태가 아주 좋고, 뒤쪽에 공간이 많아요. 그래서 그것들이 딱 좋을 것 같아요. 운전면허증을 가져오셨나요? 그렇다면, 시험 운전을 위해 한 대 타 보셔도 됩니다.

Q What is the woman asked to provide? 여자는 무엇을 제공하도록 요청받는가?

A A driver's license 운전면허증

[1-4] 질문과 정답을 확인한 뒤, 대화를 들으면서 정답의 단서가 되는 부분에 표시하세요.

1. **Q** What does the man offer to do?

A Send a list of suggestions

> **W** I'm excited about my business trip to Berlin. It'll be my first time visiting Germany. You used to work in Berlin, right?
>
> **M** Yes, for two years. I can e-mail you some recommendations for places to go in your free time.

2. **Q** What does the man suggest doing?

A Buying multiple items

> **M** Here is our section of camping lanterns. All of them are lightweight as well as water-resistant. Will you be camping by yourself or in a group?
>
> **W** There will be about 10 of us.
>
> **M** In that case, I suggest getting more than one. Our store has a variety of options to choose from.

3. **Q** What does the man ask the woman to do?

A Find a fabric supplier

> **W** I love the designs you've created for our new trousers, Liam. However, the linen supplier we currently use doesn't have a wide range of colors.
>
> **M** We'll need to find a new one then. Could you please do some research about this?

4. **Q** What task does the woman ask the man to do?

A Make an announcement

> **W** Brian, please announce to everyone that we'll begin boarding in about five minutes. I'd like passengers to start getting their IDs ready.
>
> **M** Alright, I'll do that right now.

[5-6] 대화를 듣고 정답의 단서가 알맞게 패러프레이징된 답을 고르세요.

5. What does the woman ask the man to do?

(A) Bring supplies to the restaurant

(B) Substitute for a coworker

6. What does the man suggest the woman do?

(A) Check an invoice

(B) Perform another task first

대화를 듣고 알맞은 답을 고른 뒤, 다시 들으면서 빈칸을 채우세요.

1. What does the woman ask the man to do?

(A) Make a list of comments
(B) Schedule another meeting
(C) Demonstrate a product
(D) Check some figures in a report

M Thanks for coming out to today's sales meeting, everyone. What are your thoughts on the quarterly profit report?
W I was quite surprised. I didn't realize how popular our tablets are.
M Yes, we've sold a lot. But I think we should focus on the products that aren't selling well.
W Hmm... maybe the marketing department should start a new campaign. Will you _____ _____ to share with them?

2. What are the speakers discussing?

(A) A business relocation
(B) A rival company
(C) A clearance sale
(D) A job opening

3. What does the woman suggest they do?

(A) Open some overseas locations
(B) Change their target reader
(C) Translate foreign books
(D) Hire skilled book designers

M Have you heard about Lighthouse Publishing Company? One of their books is _____ _____.
W Really? I heard they have just brought in Erik Benson. His designs are great, which will contribute further to their success.
M But they're not doing well overseas.
W Well, once their commercials begin, I know they will succeed there, too. We don't want to lose market share to them, so we'd better _____.

4. What problem does the man mention?

(A) A budget must be reduced.
(B) An employee will relocate.
(C) An office has become unavailable.
(D) An item is out of stock.

5. What is the woman asked to do?

(A) Design an office
(B) Order some equipment
(C) Adjust a document
(D) Take some measurements

W You said you needed to talk to me.
M That's right. I talked to accounting, and they said _____ for Mr. Jeong's office by 250 dollars.
W I see. Well, we could use that extra table in my office instead of buying a new one. And he can probably use just one filing cabinet instead of two.
M Good idea. _____ so accounting can sign off on it.

대화를 듣고 알맞은 답을 고르세요.

1. What does the woman mean when she says, "I'm completely booked next week"?

(A) She cannot attend an event.
(B) She needs the man's help.
(C) She wants to cancel an appointment.
(D) She has to stay in Portland.

2. What does Mr. Turner want to discuss?

(A) Carpet
(B) Furniture
(C) Light fixtures
(D) Wall colors

3. What does the woman ask the man to do?

(A) Test a new product
(B) Introduce her to a client
(C) Pick up some brochures
(D) Provide some samples

4. What problem are the speakers mainly discussing?

(A) A supplier has raised its prices.
(B) The company received poor reviews.
(C) A city festival has been canceled.
(D) Competition in an industry has increased.

5. What does the woman suggest?

(A) Changing an event date
(B) Hiring a consultant
(C) Providing some training
(D) Running a promotion

6. What does the man offer to do?

(A) Contact some businesses
(B) Revise a contract
(C) Work additional hours
(D) Prepare a meeting agenda

7. Who most likely is the man?

(A) A Web designer
(B) A magazine journalist
(C) A marketing consultant
(D) A talk show host

8. What did Hartway Tech recently confirm?

(A) A competition for customers
(B) The replacement of an executive
(C) The launch of an educational program
(D) A partnership with another company

9. What does the woman encourage the man to do?

(A) Apply for a position
(B) Watch a video
(C) Join a mailing list
(D) Review some charts

10. What does the woman say she wants to do?

(A) Attend a lecture
(B) Take some photographs
(C) Go on a tour
(D) Buy some souvenirs

11. What does the man give the woman some information about?

(A) Artists' backgrounds
(B) Payment options
(C) A membership program
(D) Upcoming events

12. What does the man suggest doing?

(A) Trying a new food
(B) Visiting a Web site
(C) Keeping a ticket
(D) Making a group reservation

13. Who most likely is the man?

    (A) A tour guide
    (B) A marketing manager
    (C) A journalist
    (D) A secretary

14. Why is Mr. Johnson absent?

    (A) He has another meeting.
    (B) He is having transportation issues.
    (C) He is going to a show.
    (D) He forgot about the appointment.

15. What is the man asked to bring?

    (A) An exhibition brochure
    (B) A security badge
    (C) A driver's license
    (D) A work portfolio

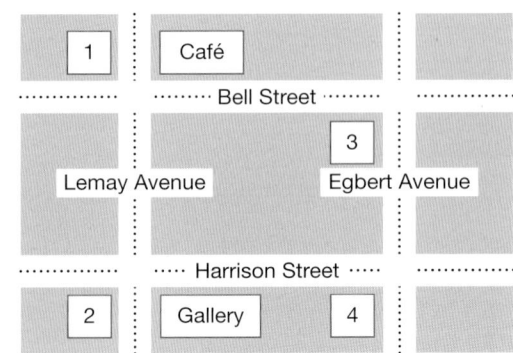

16. Why is the man unable to attend his original appointment?

    (A) He needs a repair done at his home.
    (B) He has an urgent work project.
    (C) He is taking a business trip.
    (D) He is picking up a friend at the airport.

17. Look at the graphic. Where does the woman work?

    (A) In location 1
    (B) In location 2
    (C) In location 3
    (D) In location 4

18. What does the woman ask for?

    (A) Some haircare products
    (B) Some photographs
    (C) An ID card
    (D) A confirmation number

핵심 포인트

1. 화자가 다음에 할 일 또는 앞으로 일어날 일을 묻는 문제로, 주로 대화 후반부에서 will, now, next 등 미래를 나타내는 표현과 함께 단서 문장이 언급된다.
2. 앞으로 일어날 일을 묻는 문제의 경우 대부분 선택지가 완전한 문장으로 제시되므로, 주어까지 미리 읽고 키워드를 파악해 두는 것이 좋다.

실전 맛보기

P3_U06_01

What will the woman do next?	여자는 다음에 무엇을 할 것인가?
(A) Rearrange some tables	(A) 테이블 다시 배열하기
(B) Give a building tour	(B) 건물 구경시켜 주기
(C) Set up some equipment	**(C) 장비 설치하기**
(D) Contact the receptionist	(D) 접수 담당자에게 연락하기

M Hi, Nadia. The representatives from Dayton Enterprises will be arriving in about an hour. Is everything ready?

W Well, the caterer has just dropped off the refreshments, so I've set those up on a table at the back of the conference room. The chairs have been arranged, and the receptionist knows that she should send our visitors to the second floor.

M Great! I hope our guests get a good impression of our company. They'll be listening to three presentations today, right?

W That's right. I still need to set up the projector and laptop for those. I'll take care of it now.

남 안녕하세요, 나디아. 데이턴 산업의 대표들이 약 한 시간 후에 도착할 거예요. 모든 것이 준비됐나요?

여 음, 음식 공급 업체가 방금 다과를 가져다주어서, 회의실 뒤쪽 테이블에 그것들을 준비해 놓았어요. 의자들을 배열해 두었고, 그리고 접수 담당자가 우리 방문객들을 2층으로 보내야 한다고 알고 있어요.

남 좋아요! 손님들이 우리 회사에 대해 좋은 인상을 받길 바라요. 그들은 오늘 세 개의 발표를 들을 예정이죠, 맞죠?

여 맞아요. 아직 제가 그 발표들을 위한 프로젝터와 노트북 컴퓨터를 설치해야 해요. 지금 처리할게요.

CHECK UP

P3_U06_02 정답 및 해설 p.141

1. What will the man most likely do next?

(A) Recommend a book
(B) Provide address information
(C) Transfer the woman's call
(D) Process a payment

2. What will happen tomorrow?

(A) The client will send a payment.
(B) The client will renew a contract.
(C) The speakers will give a presentation.
(D) The speakers will launch a product.

다음에 할 일

What will the man (most likely) do next? 남자는 다음에 무엇을 할 것인가?

What does the woman say she will do? 여자는 무엇을 할 것이라고 말하는가?

다음에 일어날 일

What will happen ~? ~에 무슨 일이 일어날 것인가?

What event will take place ~? ~에 무슨 행사가 개최될 것인가?

빈출 단서

계획	**I'll ~ / I'm going to ~ / I just need to ~ / There's going to be ~** I'm going to set up the sign here about our special promotion on birthday cakes. 생일 케이크 특별 판매에 관해 제가 이곳에 표지판을 설치할게요. ▶ 다음에 할 일: Put up a sign 표지판 세우기
제안	**Let's ~ / Let me ~ / I can/could ~** Let's take our lunch break now and revise the drawing after we eat. 우리 지금 점심시간을 가지고, 먹고 나서 도안을 수정합시다. ▶ 다음에 할 일: Take a lunch break 점심시간 가지기
요청	**Can/Could/Will/Would you ~? / Please ~** Kevin, can you talk to someone in technical support to see if they can speed up the process? 케빈, 기술지원부의 누군가에게 이야기해서 그들이 절차를 빠르게 할 수 있는지 알아봐 줄 수 있나요? ▶ 다음에 할 일: Contact Technical Support 기술지원부에 연락하기

PART 3 UNIT 06

고득점 TIP

한 화자의 말에서 자신이 할 일과 상대방이 할 일이 둘 다 나오는 경우, 주어를 혼동하지 않도록 주의한다.

W We were supposed to install the security cameras in the hallways today, but the devices we need have been delayed.

M This seems to keep happening. I'll arrange a meeting with our supplier to deal with the issue. In the meantime, could you talk to the maintenance team about doing a different task first?

여 우리가 오늘 복도에 보안 카메라를 설치하기로 되어 있었지만, 우리에게 필요한 장치들의 배송이 지연되고 있어요.

남 이런 일이 계속 일어나는 것 같아요. 제가 이 문제를 처리하기 위해 우리 공급 업체와 회의를 잡을게요. 그러는 동안, 당신은 관리팀에게 다른 업무를 먼저 하라고 말해 주시겠어요?

Q1 What will the man most likely do next? 남자는 다음에 무엇을 할 것 같은가?

A Arrange a meeting 회의 잡기

Q2 What will the woman probably do next? 여자는 아마도 다음에 무엇을 할 것인가?

A Contact some employees 몇몇 직원들에게 연락하기

[1-4] 질문과 정답을 확인한 뒤, 대화를 들으면서 정답의 단서가 되는 부분에 표시하세요.

1. **Q** What does the woman say she will do next?

   A Calculate a price

> **M** Hmm… I like the layout of the kitchen you've designed, but I'm not sure about the material for the countertops. Would it be possible to get marble countertops instead of granite?
> **W** Of course, let me figure out the final cost.

2. **Q** What does the man say is happening this week?

   A A free item is available with purchase.

> **W** Hi. I need a coffee machine, but I'm not sure which brand is best.
> **M** Well, Ellison is a popular choice. And this week the store is offering a free coffee mug with every purchase of an Ellison product.

3. **Q** What will the woman most likely do next?

   A Print a document

> **W** The number of tourists visiting the area has been declining steadily. You can see on this graph how this year compares to previous years. This is part of the reason our hotel chain has been struggling.
> **M** I'd like to share this with the board of directors. Please get me a printout of this information right away.

4. **Q** What will happen on Friday?

   A Some office repairs

> **M** Thanks for getting back to me. I wanted you to know that there's going to be repair work in our office on Friday. So, we need to find a different place to meet.
> **W** That's fine with me. Why don't we reserve a table at the Indigo Restaurant, as it's conveniently located for both of us?

[5-6] 대화를 듣고 정답의 단서가 알맞게 패러프레이징된 답을 고르세요.

5. What will the woman do next?

   (A) Make an announcement
   (B) Check a weather forecast

6. According to the man, what will happen next Wednesday?

   (A) A training program will start.
   (B) A group will visit a building.

대화를 듣고 알맞은 답을 고른 뒤, 다시 들으면서 빈칸을 채우세요.

1. What will the speakers do next?

(A) Request new seats
(B) Buy some souvenirs
(C) Have something to eat
(D) Contact their clients

M I just finished checking in for our flight. We're departing from Gate 52.
W Okay. I hope this meeting goes well. I'm a bit nervous. The client is very demanding.
M It'll be fine. The last time we were in Vancouver, they were very happy with your designs. Now… um… we still have about 40 minutes left before the flight. Let's relax and _____.
W Sounds great.

2. What are the speakers mainly discussing?

(A) A new book
(B) A business trip
(C) An employee
(D) An article

3. What does the man say he will do?

(A) Attend a meeting
(B) Send another article
(C) Call his employee
(D) Stop by his coworker's office

W Mr. Howard, I haven't received _____ _____ yet.
M Well, I e-mailed it to Eric Rivers for editing, and I'm waiting for his comments.
W Okay, I'll ask him to forward it to me as soon as possible. The article also needs to be done by tomorrow because I have to send it to the printer then.
M Actually, _____ _____ in a few minutes. Would you like me to ask him to stop by your desk as soon as the meeting ends?

4. What does the man say will happen tomorrow morning?

(A) New brochures will be delivered.
(B) Some catered food will be prepared.
(C) A new customer will visit the company.
(D) The woman will call the print shop.

5. What will the woman most likely do next?

(A) Attend a meeting
(B) Update a Web site
(C) Call a potential customer
(D) Proofread the brochures

W Hi, Daniel. I wanted to let you know that Mr. Baldwin from All-Tech is _____ _____. However, he said there wasn't enough information on our Web site. I'd send him a brochure, but we've run out.
M Don't worry. I called the print shop yesterday and asked them to reprint more as soon as possible. _____ _____ tomorrow morning.
W Great. Thanks. I'll call Mr. Baldwin to get his mailing address.

실전 문제

대화를 듣고 알맞은 답을 고르세요.

1. What did the woman do this morning?

(A) She bought a newspaper.
(B) She saw an advertisement.
(C) She worked out at a gym.
(D) She picked up some supplies.

2. What does the woman think the business should prepare for?

(A) Facing competition from other businesses
(B) Undergoing a facility inspection
(C) Having more members sign up
(D) Budgeting for price increases

3. What does the man say he will do?

(A) Adjust a schedule
(B) Check a Web site
(C) Print a contract
(D) Send a message

4. Where most likely do the speakers work?

(A) At an amusement park
(B) At a sports stadium
(C) At a movie theater
(D) At an aquarium

5. What is scheduled to happen next week?

(A) Group discounts will become available.
(B) The hours of operation will change.
(C) A new Web site will be launched.
(D) Another branch of the business will open.

6. What will the woman most likely do next?

(A) Place an order
(B) Design a poster
(C) Adjust a work schedule
(D) Print a price list

7. Who most likely is the woman?

(A) A maintenance worker
(B) A business owner
(C) A security officer
(D) A computer technician

8. Why does the man say, "some clients are meeting me in half an hour"?

(A) To cancel a request
(B) To express excitement
(C) To give permission
(D) To request an exception

9. What does the woman say she will do?

(A) Visit the man's office
(B) Call the man back
(C) Print a document
(D) Check a policy

10. What are the men preparing for?

(A) A writing competition
(B) A book-signing event
(C) An art class
(D) A musical performance

11. Who most likely is Ms. Ferguson?

(A) A music instructor
(B) A newspaper reporter
(C) A financial expert
(D) A building owner

12. What will Ted most likely do next?

(A) Make some beverages
(B) Print some signs
(C) Call a supervisor
(D) Take a break

13. Where most likely are the speakers?

(A) At a department store
(B) At an airport
(C) At a hotel
(D) At a bus station

14. What does the woman want to do?

(A) Find a place to eat
(B) Receive compensation for damage
(C) Check the weight of some luggage
(D) Exchange her ticket

15. What will the woman most likely do next?

(A) Show a passport
(B) Speak to a manager
(C) Fill out a form
(D) Look at a map

#711   #718

#720   #725

16. Look at the graphic. Which order is the man picking up?

(A) #711
(B) #718
(C) #720
(D) #725

17. According to the man, what event will take place today?

(A) A training workshop
(B) An anniversary party
(C) A welcome reception
(D) An awards dinner

18. What does the man inquire about?

(A) Storing an item
(B) Placing another order
(C) Making a payment
(D) Adding a card

PART 3   UNIT 06

핵심 포인트
1. 질문에 제시된 인용구를 미리 확인한 뒤, 대화 속 해당 문장의 앞뒤 대사에 주목한다.
2. 문장의 사전적 의미가 아니라 문맥상 알맞은 의미나 화자의 의도를 파악해야 하므로, 대화의 전체적인 흐름과 맥락을 이해해야 답을 고를 수 있다.

실전 맛보기

🎧 P3_U07_01

Why does the man say, "the IT team is very good"?	남자는 왜 "IT 팀이 아주 잘해요"라고 말하는가?
(A) To volunteer for a task	(A) 자진하여 일을 맡기 위해
(B) To recommend a solution	**(B) 해결 방법을 추천하기 위해**
(C) To update a schedule	(C) 일정을 업데이트하기 위해
(D) To reject an offer	(D) 제안을 거절하기 위해

W Benjamin, have you used this projector before? I think I have everything hooked up to my laptop correctly, but I just keep getting a blue screen.	여 벤저민, 전에 이 프로젝터 사용한 적 있어요? 모든 것을 제 노트북 컴퓨터에 제대로 연결한 것 같은데, 계속 파란색 화면만 나와요.
M Hmm… I don't have any experience with that. I haven't had to give any presentations yet. But you know, the IT team is very good.	남 흠… 저는 그런 경험이 한 번도 없어요. 아직 발표해야 했던 적이 전혀 없거든요. 하지만 있잖아요, IT 팀이 아주 잘해요.
W Well, I've tried calling them a few times, but I keep getting a busy signal. It must be because they're so busy these days. Maybe I can stop by there in person to report the issue.	여 음, 그들에게 몇 번 전화를 해 봤지만, 계속 통화 중 신호만 나와요. 요즘 그들이 아주 바쁘기 때문이 틀림없어요. 아마도 직접 들러서 이 문제를 알리면 될 것 같아요.
M Good luck. I hope you figure it out.	남 행운을 빌어요. 그것을 해결하길 바라요.

CHECK UP

🎧 P3_U07_02 정답 및 해설 p.149

1. What does the man imply when he says, "I work until 6 o'clock"?

(A) He will meet the woman later.
(B) He cannot go to the store.
(C) He is on a tight deadline.
(D) He will check the microscopes soon.

2. Why does the man say, "we just announced it two days ago"?

(A) To remind the woman of a deadline
(B) To decline an offer
(C) To reassure the woman
(D) To make a request

의미 / 암시하는 것

What does the woman mean/imply when she says, "~"? 여자는 "~"라고 말할 때 무엇을 의미/암시하는가?

목적

Why does the man say, "~"? 남자는 왜 "~"라고 말하는가?

빈출 의도

동의	W Our VIP clients will arrive on Thursday afternoon. I'd like to take them to the Violet Bistro for dinner. What are your thoughts? 우리의 VIP 고객들이 목요일 오후에 도착할 거예요. 저는 저녁 식사 때 그들을 바이올렛 비스트로에 데려가려고 해요. 당신의 생각은 어떤가요? M That place has great reviews. 그곳은 후기가 좋아요. ▶ 목적: To agree with a suggestion 제안에 동의하기 위해
반대	W I still need one more person to help with the advisory committee for the upcoming restructuring. Who would be a good fit? 저는 곧 있을 개편을 위한 자문 위원회를 도울 사람이 아직 한 명 더 필요해요. 누가 적임자일까요? M Maybe Greg would be interested. 아마도 그레그가 관심이 있을 거예요. W Greg? He's only worked here for a month. 그레그요? 그는 이곳에서 일한 지 한 달밖에 되지 않았는데요. ▶ 목적: To disagree with a suggestion 제안에 반대하기 위해
거절	M We've finally reached an agreement with the Duvall Corporation. I'll be flying to Toronto to sign the paperwork. Oh, and you're having your retirement party soon, right? 우리는 마침내 듀발 기업과 합의에 이르렀어요. 저는 서류에 서명을 하러 토론토에 갈 거예요. 아, 그리고 당신은 곧 은퇴 기념 파티를 할 거죠, 맞죠? W Yes, on Friday, April 10th. Will you be there? 네, 4월 10일 금요일이에요. 당신도 올 건가요? M My return flight is on the 12th. 제가 돌아오는 비행편은 12일이에요. ▶ 의미: He will not be able to attend an event. 그는 행사에 참석할 수 없을 것이다.
제안	W We need a specialty cake for the anniversary party. Cake Creations is just across the street. Should we order from there? 우리는 기념일 파티를 위해 특별한 케이크가 필요해요. 케이크 크리에이션이 바로 길 건너에 있어요. 그곳에서 주문을 해야 할까요? M I've used Paradise Bakery on a few occasions. Everyone seemed to enjoy their cakes. 저는 파라다이스 제과점을 몇 번 이용했어요. 모두가 그곳 케이크를 좋아하는 것 같았고요. ▶ 목적: To suggest an alternative 대안을 제시하기 위해
요청	W Make sure to submit an expense report for your business trip. 당신의 출장에 대한 지출 품의서를 반드시 제출해 주세요. M Um... I've never filed a travel expense report. 음... 저는 출장비 지출 품의서를 제출해 본 적이 없어요. W I'll ask Mr. Petrov in the accounting department to show you how. 제가 회계 부서의 페트로프 씨에게 요청해서 어떻게 하는지 당신에게 보여달라고 할게요. ▶ 목적: To ask for assistance 도움을 요청하기 위해

강조	**M** I've tried to set up a meeting with the head designers several times. We still have to finalize some decisions about the material for the straps on our backpacks. 저는 수석 디자이너들과 회의를 잡으려고 여러 번 시도했어요. 우리는 여전히 배낭끈의 재질에 관한 몇 가지 결정을 내려야 해요. **W** What should we do about this? The school year is starting in three months. 이걸 어떻게 해야 하나요? 세 달 뒤면 학기가 시작해요. ▶ 목적: To emphasize the need for urgency 서두르는 것의 필요성을 강조하기 위해
감정	**M** I thought the electrician I sent had fixed your light. 제가 보낸 전기 기술자가 당신의 조명을 고쳤을 거라 생각했어요. **W** He was here for a few hours yesterday, but the light is flickering again. This should be a simple repair. 그분이 어제 몇 시간 동안 여기 계셨는데, 조명이 또다시 깜박거려요. 이건 간단한 수리 작업이에요. **M** I'm very sorry that your issue isn't resolved yet. 당신의 문제가 아직 해결되지 않은 것에 대해 정말 죄송해요. ▶ 의미: She is unhappy with a service. 그녀는 서비스에 불만이다.
기타	**M** Thank you for inviting me to this interview, Ms. Iverson. You said you're looking for someone to take care of the finances for your restaurant? 저를 면접에 불러 주셔서 감사합니다, 아이버슨 씨. 당신의 식당에서 재무를 맡을 사람을 찾고 있다고 하셨죠? **W** Yes, she's moving to a new city. We have four different retail branches, so the job would be quite complex and challenging. 네, 그녀가 새로운 도시로 이사를 가거든요. 저희는 네 개의 직영 대리점을 가지고 있기 때문에, 일이 꽤 복잡하고 어려울 거예요. **M** I've run my own accounting firm for 20 years. 저는 20년 동안 제 회계 법인을 운영해 왔어요. ▶ 의미: He is qualified for a job. 그는 일을 맡을 자격이 있다.

고득점 TIP

상대방의 제안이나 요청 바로 뒤에 대답하는 문장이 인용 어구로 쓰이면 반대나 거절의 의미일 가능성이 높다.

W When do you need these quarterly reports done?
M Could you do it today?
W Well, the paperwork for Mr. Riley is due at 3 o'clock.

여 이 분기 보고서는 언제까지 끝내야 하나요?
남 오늘 해 주시겠어요?
여 음, 라일리 씨를 위한 서류 작업을 3시까지 마쳐야 해요.

- -

Q Why does the woman say, "the paperwork for Mr. Riley is due at 3 o'clock"?
여자는 왜 "라일리 씨를 위한 서류 작업을 3시까지 마쳐야 해요"라고 말하는가?

A To explain that she cannot help right now 지금 당장 도와줄 수 없음을 설명하기 위해

대화를 듣고 알맞은 답을 고른 뒤, 다시 들으면서 빈칸을 채우세요.

1. What does the woman mean when she says, "I sent it to the printer this morning"?

(A) She knows how to get to a site.

(B) She missed the assigned deadline.

(C) She has been too busy to read a message.

(D) She cannot make a change.

> M Francesca, I'm wondering if you are still working on the invitation.
> W You mean the one for the awards ceremony?
> M That's right. Could you _____ _____? I think a lot of people have never been to that venue before.
> W I sent it to the printer this morning. I guess people will need to just look up the directions online if they need them.

2. Why does the woman say, "We're shooting the commercial on Friday"?

(A) To show concern

(B) To ask for assistance

(C) To make a job offer

(D) To reject a suggestion

3. What does the man plan to do tomorrow?

(A) Unload a furniture truck

(B) Issue a partial refund

(C) Send an updated catalog

(D) Confirm a delivery schedule

> M Hello, Ms. Hodge? This is Tony from Fremont Furniture. I'm calling about your order of three leather sofas for your hotel's lobby. They were supposed to be delivered today, but I'm afraid _____.
> W We're shooting the commercial on Friday. Our site needs to look its best.
> M I'm very sorry for the inconvenience. Our supplier is having some distribution issues, but I think we can still get the sofas to you within a few days. I'll call you tomorrow _____.

4. How did the speakers most likely meet each other?

(A) They live in the same neighborhood.

(B) They attended the same university.

(C) They got hired by the same restaurant.

(D) They volunteer for the same charity.

5. Why does the man say, "I live within walking distance"?

(A) To express relief

(B) To suggest a place to eat

(C) To reject an offer

(D) To adjust a schedule

> W Victor, did you hear that _____ _____ next weekend? It's a way to show appreciation for the work we've been doing.
> M I must have missed the e-mail about that. Do you know when and where it will take place?
> W Yes, it's at the Lakeside Restaurant on Saturday at 7 P.M. If you'd like, _____ _____.
> M I live within walking distance. But thanks for letting me know.

실전 문제

대화를 듣고 알맞은 답을 고르세요.

1. What type of business do the speakers most likely work for?

(A) A photography studio
(B) A magazine publisher
(C) A catering company
(D) A travel agency

2. Why does the woman say, "Nicholas is in Los Angeles"?

(A) To praise an employee
(B) To express surprise
(C) To reject some assistance
(D) To clarify a decision

3. Why will the man go to Nicholas's office?

(A) To look for some flight information
(B) To get some chairs for a meeting
(C) To download a file from a computer
(D) To set up some equipment

4. Where are the speakers?

(A) At a business institute
(B) At a fitness center
(C) At a photography studio
(D) At an art gallery

5. Why does the woman say, "we've got the lowest prices in the region"?

(A) To justify a wait time
(B) To correct a Web site error
(C) To apologize for a mistake
(D) To reject a request

6. What will the woman give the man?

(A) A coupon
(B) A business card
(C) A map
(D) A brochure

7. What are the speakers mainly discussing?

(A) An e-mail
(B) An interior design
(C) A client
(D) A commercial

8. What does the man mean when he says, "I just got in"?

(A) He just came back from the client's office.
(B) He just received an e-mail.
(C) He went to pick up a package.
(D) He didn't have a chance to look over something.

9. What will the man most likely do next?

(A) Look for some notes
(B) Call someone about the design
(C) Print a floor plan
(D) Meet with a customer

10. What does the woman need help doing?

(A) Meeting with some investors
(B) Conducting some interviews
(C) Giving a presentation
(D) Testing a product

11. Why does the man say, "it's nearly 10 now"?

(A) To praise an employee's hard work
(B) To complain about a delay
(C) To suggest taking a break
(D) To explain that he won't be prepared

12. What does the woman say she will do tomorrow?

(A) Welcome some visitors
(B) Give a speech
(C) Contact a colleague
(D) Finalize a contract

13. What does the man mean when he says, "the cupcakes were gone in the first 20 minutes"?

(A) The woman should look for some lost items.

(B) He was disappointed about arriving late.

(C) The woman should order a lot of cupcakes.

(D) He thinks a break time was too short.

14. Who has recently joined the company?

(A) A senior accountant

(B) A sales manager

(C) A graphic designer

(D) A marketing consultant

15. What does the man warn the woman about?

(A) A business closure

(B) A food allergy

(C) A processing time

(D) An approaching deadline

16. Which department does the woman work in?

(A) Product Development

(B) Technical Support

(C) Accounting

(D) Human Resources

17. What is the woman preparing for?

(A) A press conference

(B) A board meeting

(C) A staff award

(D) A job fair

18. What does the man imply when he says, "I uploaded the files to the database"?

(A) The woman should change an access code.

(B) The woman will not need assistance.

(C) He has lost some files.

(D) He knows why a system is running slowly.

핵심 포인트

1. 목록/표, 지도/평면도, 그래프, 쿠폰, 기타 그림 등의 다양한 시각 자료가 나올 수 있다. 모든 시각 자료는 대화가 나오기 전에 미리 읽고 키워드를 파악해 두어야 한다.
2. 선택지와 상응하는 네 가지 항목이 대화에서 언급되는 부분에 주목한다. 만약 대화에서 여러 개의 항목이 언급된다면, 시각 자료와 대화의 내용이 일치하는지 비교하면서 듣는다.

실전 맛보기

🎧 P3_U08_01

Airline	Departure / Arrival
Comfort Ways	7:50 / 9:10
Best Fly	12:10 / 13:30
Rolling Clouds	13:25 / 14:50
North Alliance	17:05 / 18:15

Look at the graphic. Which airline will the man use for his trip?

(A) Comfort Ways
(B) Best Fly
(C) Rolling Clouds
(D) North Alliance

항공사	출발 / 도착
컴포트 웨이즈	7:50 / 9:10
베스트 플라이	12:10 / 13:30
롤링 클라우즈	13:25 / 14:50
노스 얼라이언스	17:05 / 18:15

시각 자료를 보시오. 남자는 그의 여행을 위해 어떤 항공사를 이용할 것인가?

(A) 컴포트 웨이즈
(B) 베스트 플라이
(C) 롤링 클라우즈
(D) 노스 얼라이언스

W Shawn, how are you planning to get to the SAP Convention in Seattle? I need to report the travel expenses for the business trip.

M Jerry and I will go there the night before in Jerry's car and get a place to stay for the night.

W Hmm… but since Highway 57 is closed, I think taking a plane would be a better option.

M Oh, that sounds reasonable. The cost would be about the same since we wouldn't have to pay for lodging. We can take the early-morning plane on the day of the convention.

W That sounds great. You can check the flight schedule and let me know.

여 숀, 시애틀에서 있는 SAP 컨벤션에 어떻게 갈 계획이에요? 제가 출장 여행 경비를 보고해야 해요.

남 제리와 저는 전날 밤에 제리의 차로 가서 그날 밤에 묵을 곳을 구할 거예요.

여 흠… 하지만 57번 고속도로가 폐쇄되었기 때문에, 비행기를 타는 것이 더 나은 선택 같은데요.

남 아, 일리가 있는 말이네요. 우리가 숙박비를 지불하지 않아도 될 테니 비용은 거의 같을 거예요. 회의 당일에 이른 아침 비행기를 타면 돼요.

여 좋은 생각이에요. 항공 시간표를 확인하고 제게 알려 주시면 됩니다.

시각 자료 연계 세부사항

Look at the graphic. What/Which/Who/Where/When/How ~?

시각 자료를 보시오. 무엇이/어떤 것이/누가/어디에서/언제/어떻게 ~?

빈출 시각 자료

목록 / 표

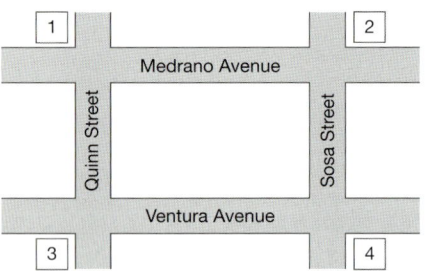

Keith Edwin, July 19 Agenda

9:00 A.M.	Reception for new staff members
10:00 A.M.	Departmental meeting
2:00 P.M.	Employee evaluations
4:00 P.M.	Investor conference call
5:00 P.M.	Contract review

Now that you won't have the call with investors, could Mr. Desmond from Willow Incorporated meet with you at that time?

투자자들과의 전화 회의가 없을테니, 그 시간에 윌로우 사의 데스몬드 씨를 만나시겠어요?

▶ 데스몬드 씨를 만날 시간: 4:00 P.M.

지도 / 평면도

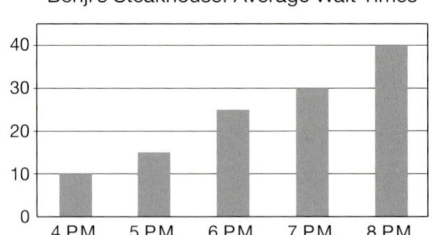

You can usually find parking on the street near the intersection of Medrano and Sosa. That's where you should check first.

당신은 보통 메드라노 가와 소사 가의 교차로 근처 거리에서 주차장을 찾을 수 있어요. 그곳을 가장 먼저 확인해 보셔야 해요.

▶ 추천하는 장소: Location 2

그래프

Benji's Steakhouse: Average Wait Times

I'm meeting with the representatives from Jackson Metals at Benji's Steakhouse to discuss the contract. I'm going to take them at 7 o'clock.

저는 계약을 논의하기 위해 잭슨 금속 업체의 대표자들과 벤지 스테이크하우스에서 만날 거예요. 그들을 7시에 데려가려고 해요.

▶ 기다려야 할 시간: 30 minutes

PART 3 UNIT 08

그림	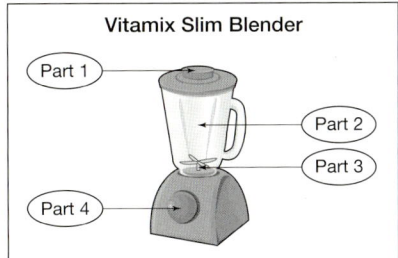 Its blade is made of extra durable stainless steel, so it's guaranteed to last. 날개가 아주 내구성 있는 스테인리스 스틸로 만들어져 있어서, 확실히 오래갈 거예요. ▶ 강조하는 요소: Part 3

기타 양식	**EMPLOYEE SURVEY FORM**
	1. Department: _____
	2. Time at Company:
	   ☐ Less than 5 years ☐ 5 years+
	3. Opinion about proposal:
	   ☐ Agree ☐ Disagree ☐ Not sure
	4. Comments: _____
	
	On the survey form, you can include an explanation of why you think this is a bad idea.
	조사 양식에서, 당신은 이것이 별로라고 생각하는 이유에 대한 설명을 넣을 수 있어요.
	▶ 언급하는 설문 항목: Item 4

고득점 TIP

선택지와 상응하는 시각 자료 항목이 대화에서 그대로 언급되지 않고 패러프레이징되는 경우에 주의한다.

W I'm trying to buy some file cabinets for my new office. The Web site won't let me move on to the next step, though. Maybe I've missed something?

M I can take a look. Hmm… it says you still need <u>the credit card expiration date</u>. Right here, see?

여 저의 새 사무실에서 쓸 서류 캐비닛을 좀 구매하려고 합니다. 그런데 웹사이트가 다음 단계로 넘어가지 않아요. 혹시 제가 뭘 빠뜨린 걸까요?

남 제가 한번 볼게요. 흠… 아직 신용카드 유효기간이 필요하다고 뜨네요. 바로 여기요, 보이시죠?

 Step 1: Shopping Cart
 Step 2: Shopping Information
 Step 3: Payment Information
 Step 4: Coupon Code
 Step 5: Order Summary

 1단계: 장바구니
 2단계: 배송 정보
 3단계: 결제 정보
 4단계: 쿠폰 번호
 5단계: 주문 요약

Q Look at the graphic. Which step is missing some information?
시각 자료를 보시오. 어떤 단계에서 정보가 누락되었는가?

A Step 3 3단계

대화를 듣고 알맞은 답을 고른 뒤, 다시 들으면서 빈칸을 채우세요.

Extension	Title
567	Accounting Manager
569	HR Manager
573	IT Manager
575	General Manager

1. Look at the graphic. Which extension number will the man most likely call?

(A) 567
(B) 569
(C) 573
(D) 575

W Jason, have you had a chance to try out the new software yet? It has a lot of nice new features, but it doesn't run very fast.
M Are the other team members experiencing the same problem?
W Yeah. Many of my team members have said the same thing. I think we should report it to someone in charge.
M _____ and ask them to look into this issue.

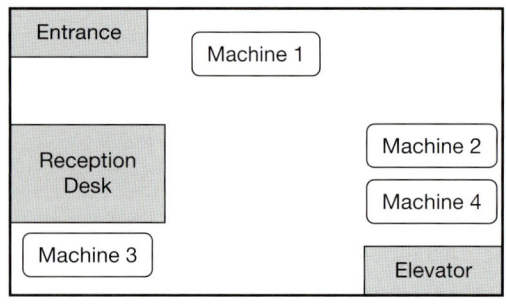

2. Why did the man visit the site?

(A) To perform some research
(B) To deliver some documents
(C) To give a demonstration
(D) To attend a job interview

3. Look at the graphic. Which machine is not working?

(A) Machine 1
(B) Machine 2
(C) Machine 3
(D) Machine 4

M Hello, could you please let me know where I can find Tiffany Henson's office? My name is Ross Preston, and I'm here to show Ms. Henson _____ _____.
W Her office is number 304, but she doesn't usually get to the office until nine.
M That's fine. I'm quite early because traffic was light. I'll just get a snack while I wait.
W Oh… um… in that case, don't use _____. It's been _____.

실전 문제

대화를 듣고 알맞은 답을 고르세요.

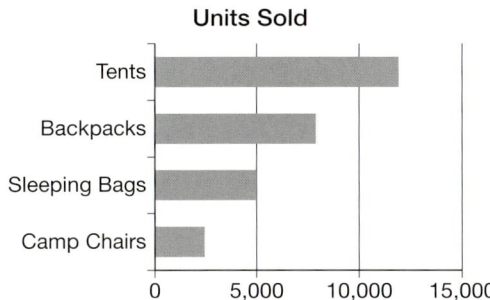

Units Sold

Tents	
Backpacks	
Sleeping Bags	
Camp Chairs	

0   5,000   10,000   15,000

Order Form

Item	Quantity	Total Price
Vests	24	$180
Hats	4	$40
Trousers	12	$150
Shirts	36	$360

1. What are the speakers preparing for?

(A) A career fair
(B) A product launch
(C) A board meeting
(D) A political debate

2. Look at the graphic. Which product does the man refer to?

(A) Tents
(B) Backpacks
(C) Sleeping Bags
(D) Camp Chairs

3. What did the man recently do?

(A) He visited the headquarters.
(B) He renewed some contracts.
(C) He attended a workshop.
(D) He rented an office space.

4. Where do the speakers most likely work?

(A) At an advertising agency
(B) At a supermarket
(C) At an accounting office
(D) At a beverage manufacturer

5. Look at the graphic. Which quantity does the man say should be changed?

(A) 24
(B) 4
(C) 12
(D) 36

6. What does the man plan to do next?

(A) Update a schedule
(B) Check some prices
(C) Speak to some customers
(D) Unload a truck

Cups for Sale

Wine Glass $12		Glass $8	
Coffee Mug $5		Pitcher $20	

7. What kind of business do the speakers work for?

(A) A coffee shop
(B) An environmental agency
(C) A law firm
(D) A catering company

8. Look at the graphic. How much will the speakers pay per item?

(A) $12
(B) $8
(C) $5
(D) $20

9. What does the woman offer to do?

(A) Keep track of a receipt
(B) Use her own credit card
(C) Unlock an entrance
(D) Move a vehicle

Bank Transfer Request:
Sender Information

1. Name *Geroge Norton*

2. Address *181 Walker Street, Detroit,*
   MI 48219

3. Bank Name *Osseo Bank*

4. Branch Number *054*

5. Account Number *420532947*

10. According to the woman, what is Mr. Norton excited about doing?

(A) Starting a new job
(B) Taking golf lessons
(C) Joining a tournament
(D) Meeting new people

11. Look at the graphic. Which line contained an error?

(A) Line 2
(B) Line 3
(C) Line 4
(D) Line 5

12. Why does the woman plan to call the reception desk?

(A) To request a pass for Mr. Norton
(B) To get Mr. Norton's contact details
(C) To report a computer error
(D) To schedule a tour

UNIT 09	회사 업무·인사 관련 대화

핵심 포인트

1. 회사 내 일반 업무나 채용, 승진 등의 인사에 대한 논의, 일정 확인, 업무 요청과 같은 업무 관련 대화가 파트 3에서 가장 많이 출제되며, 상황 언급 → 도움 요청/제안 → 수락 또는 거절의 대화 흐름이 자주 나온다.
2. 제안/요청사항이나 다음에 할 일을 묻는 문제가 자주 출제된다.

실전 맛보기
🎧 P3_U09_01

M Rebecca, are you busy right now? **¹Since you have worked on national campaigns before**, I'm wondering if you could give me some advice.	남 레베카, 지금 바빠요? **¹당신이 전에 전국적인 캠페인 작업을 했으니** 제게 조언을 좀 해 줄 수 있는지 궁금해요.
W **¹Is this about the ads you're creating for Cityview Enterprises?**	여 **¹시티뷰 산업을 위해 당신이 만들고 있는 광고에 관한 것인가요?**
M Yes. We need to be ready to present the concept to the client by Friday. **²It isn't much time, so I'm not sure we'll complete it by then.**	남 네. 우리는 금요일까지 고객에게 콘셉트를 제출할 준비를 해야 해요. **²시간이 많지 않아서, 그때까지 그것을 끝낼지 잘 모르겠어요.**
W I wouldn't mind looking over what you have so far. Maybe I can help move things along.	여 당신이 지금까지 한 것을 검토하는 것은 마다하지 않을게요. 아마도 제가 일이 빨리 진행되도록 도울 수 있을 거예요.
M Thanks a lot! **³I'll e-mail you the files with everything I've done.**	남 정말 고마워요! **³제가 한 모든 것이 담긴 파일을 당신에게 이메일로 보낼게요.**

1. Where do the speakers most likely work? 화자
   At an advertising agency

2. What does the man say he is concerned about? 문제점
   A tight deadline

3. What will the man most likely do next? 다음에 할 일
   Send the woman some work

1. 화자들은 어디에서 일하는 것 같은가?
   광고 대행사에서

2. 남자는 무엇에 관해 우려하고 있다고 말하는가?
   빠듯한 마감 기한

3. 남자는 다음에 무엇을 할 것 같은가?
   여자에게 작업물 보내기

CHECK UP
🎧 P3_U09_02 정답 및 해설 p.160

1. What will the man do on Monday?
   (A) Start a new job
   (B) Have an interview
   (C) Lead a tour
   (D) Participate in a training

2. What does the woman ask the man to do?
   (A) Submit a form
   (B) Prepare a report
   (C) Bring identification
   (D) Update a résumé

3. What has the woman received from the man?
   (A) Some work samples
   (B) A signed contract
   (C) A letter of reference
   (D) A membership card

빈출 상황

진행 상황 점검	Steve, how's the development of the payroll software coming? 스티브, 급여 소프트웨어 개발은 어떻게 되어 가나요?
일정 확인	I'll be ready to present the results at the sales meeting tomorrow. 저는 내일 영업 회의에서 결과를 발표할 준비가 될 거예요.
업무 요청	Do you have time to help me prepare for our end of the season warehouse sale? 제가 우리의 시즌 마감 창고 세일을 준비하는 것을 도와주실 시간이 있나요?
채용 / 면접	You recently applied for a position here and I'm hoping you can come in for an interview. 귀하께서 최근에 이곳 일자리에 지원하셨는데 면접을 보러 오실 수 있기를 희망하고 있습니다.
승진 / 전근 / 은퇴	I just heard at the staff meeting that our store manager, Mr. Harris, is going to retire next month. 저는 방금 직원 회의에서 우리 지점 관리자인 해리스 씨가 다음 달에 은퇴할 예정이라고 들었어요.

빈출 표현

🎧 P3_U09_03

회사 업무

set up[hold] a meeting 회의를 열다	revise a document 문서를 수정하다
arrange a video conference 화상 회의를 잡다	worth the investment 투자할 가치가 있다
meet a deadline 마감일을 맞추다	provide funds for ~에 자금을 제공하다
request a deadline extension 마감일 연장을 요청하다	finalize a budget 예산을 최종 승인하다
behind/ahead of schedule 일정보다 뒤처진/앞선	advertising strategy 광고 전략
have a scheduling conflict 일정이 겹치다	breakdown of the costs and benefits 비용 편익 분석
be in charge of ~을 담당하다	reduce the cost of ~의 비용을 절감하다
do research 조사하다	bring a lot of attention 많은 관심을 끌다
come up with an idea 아이디어를 내놓다	expand a product line 제품 라인을 확장하다
make some prototypes 견본을 만들다	apply for a grant 보조금을 신청하다
compile the results 결과를 정리하다	update an agenda 안건 목록을 업데이트하다
get started on ~에 착수하다	be responsible for ~에 대한 책임이 있다
put together a presentation 발표를 준비하다	sign a contract 계약서에 서명하다

인사

make a job offer 일자리를 제안하다	take over (직무 등을) 인계받다
job opening 일자리 공석	orientation for new hires 신규 입사자 교육
advertise a position 구직 광고를 내다	identification badges 사원증
post a job description 직무 내용 설명서를 게시하다	hire more employees 더 많은 직원들을 고용하다
meet the requirements 자격 요건을 충족하다	level of experience 경력 수준
submit a résumé 이력서를 제출하다	join the team 팀에 합류하다
apply for a position 일자리에 지원하다	hire a temporary worker 임시 직원을 고용하다
review an application 지원서를 검토하다	have a background in ~에 이력이 있다
interview a job candidate 입사 지원자 면접을 보다	have in mind 염두에 두다
choose the final candidate 최종 후보를 선택하다	oversee the training 교육을 감독하다
train a new staff member 신입 직원을 교육하다	come in for an interview 면접을 보러 오다
get a promotion 승진하다	start one's career 경력을 쌓기 시작하다
transfer 전근 가다, 전근 시키다	employee evaluation 직원 평가

[1-4] 질문과 정답을 확인한 뒤, 대화를 들으면서 정답의 단서가 되는 부분에 표시하세요.

1. **Q** What position are the speakers trying to fill?

A Software developer

> **M** We have a lot of great candidates for the open position, don't you think?
> **W** Definitely. I'm confident that we'll find the right person to work on developing our new software.
> **M** Shall we meet tomorrow to discuss the decision further?

2. **Q** What problem does the woman mention?

A Some settings are difficult to change.

> **M** How have the reviews for our new copy machine been so far?
> **W** Most people are satisfied with it. However, several reviewers reported that they had trouble adjusting the settings.
> **M** Hmm… we'd better make the R&D team aware of this issue.

3. **Q** What does the man ask the woman to do?

A Submit an article

> **M** Your blog is very impressive, Ms. Stewart. Would you be willing to write a special article on summer fashion trends? You can e-mail me the draft as soon as it's ready.
> **W** Sure, I'm highly interested in contributing to your magazine.

4. **Q** What does the man say he likes about a company?

A It offers opportunities for growth.

> **W** Thank you for attending this interview, Mr. Jones. It seems that you have a lot of experience in the field. Why did you decide to apply for this role?
> **M** Well, I know that this firm provides good opportunities for training and education. I can picture myself being here for the long term.

[5-6] 대화를 듣고 정답의 단서가 알맞게 패러프레이징된 답을 고르세요.

5. What does the woman offer the man?

(A) A job promotion
(B) An event invitation

6. What does the woman say about a new product?

(A) It is energy efficient.
(B) It is inexpensive.

대화를 듣고 알맞은 답을 고른 뒤, 다시 들으면서 빈칸을 채우세요.

1. What does the woman think the man should do?

(A) Train some new employees
(B) Sign up for a class
(C) Apply for a new position
(D) Check an event's budget

W Harvey, you've just completed your certification for performing financial audits, right?
M Yes. I was taking courses on the weekend. Why do you ask?
W Well, _____ at our Worthington branch. It has a competitive salary and excellent benefits. I think you'd do a great job. Would you _____ _____?
M That's a great opportunity. I'll do that.

2. What does the man say about Mr. Rentz?

(A) He wants to extend his contract.
(B) He does not like new projects.
(C) He sent a new proposal.
(D) He is concerned about a budget.

3. What will the speakers most likely do next?

(A) Make a detailed schedule
(B) Visit Mr. Rentz's office
(C) Give a second presentation
(D) Ask staff to join a team

M I had a meeting with Mr. Rentz at Amvac Chemicals yesterday. I'm not sure if he'll use our service or not. He likes our approach to international companies. However, _____ _____.
W That must be why he wasn't interested in our proposal last time.
M Well, this time, he asked me to send him more details. We should start _____ _____ right away.
W That's fine with me.

4. What did the woman misunderstand?

(A) A manager's name
(B) A meeting time
(C) A meeting venue
(D) A lunch menu

5. What does the man suggest the woman do?

(A) Provide more details
(B) Return after lunch
(C) Wait in the lobby
(D) Meet another person

W Good morning. I'm Audrey Coolidge from CPA Accounting Firm. I have an appointment at 1 o'clock with the manager, Mr. Johnson, to confirm the contract details.
M Actually, Mr. Johnson is scheduled for a meeting with you at 2 P.M., not 1 P.M.
W Oh, _____. Well, is he available now by any chance?
M Unfortunately, he's at a business luncheon. _____ _____? He's familiar with all the details of the contract.

대화를 듣고 알맞은 답을 고르세요.

1. Which department does the man work in?

   (A) Sales
   (B) Finance
   (C) Graphic design
   (D) Product development

2. What does the woman say will happen next month?

   (A) A staff celebration will be held.
   (B) A new regulation will go into effect.
   (C) Some people will visit the company.
   (D) Some new employees will be hired.

3. Why does the woman reject the man's offer?

   (A) A supervisor's approval is required.
   (B) The deadline is approaching soon.
   (C) There is not enough room in a budget.
   (D) A task has already been completed.

4. Who is the woman?

   (A) A job applicant
   (B) An interviewer
   (C) An administrative assistant
   (D) An advertisement executive

5. Why is the woman pleased?

   (A) She likes the job position.
   (B) She has enough references.
   (C) She was offered a job.
   (D) She has not missed a deadline.

6. What does the man ask the woman to do?

   (A) Negotiate her pay
   (B) Send her résumé today
   (C) Provide some references
   (D) Schedule an interview

7. What is the conversation mainly about?

   (A) Finding new investors
   (B) Responding to employee complaints
   (C) Developing a training program
   (D) Filling a job opening

8. What impressed the woman about Ms. Solomon?

   (A) Her business network
   (B) Her educational background
   (C) Her communication skills
   (D) Her long career history

9. What does the man plan to do this afternoon?

   (A) Create a handbook
   (B) Make an announcement
   (C) Review some documents
   (D) Attend an interview

10. Who most likely are the speakers?

    (A) Investors
    (B) Librarians
    (C) Real estate agents
    (D) Maintenance workers

11. What does the woman say she has done?

    (A) Sent a package
    (B) Practiced a presentation
    (C) Set up a display
    (D) Read a book

12. What does the woman suggest when she says, "Professor Kirkland won't use a projector"?

    (A) She is surprised by a decision.
    (B) She will remove a screen.
    (C) A task will not take long.
    (D) An order should be canceled.

13. Where most likely are the speakers?

(A) At a coffee shop
(B) At a technology firm
(C) At a gym
(D) At a newspaper stand

14. Why does the man thank the women?

(A) They offered to get him new equipment.
(B) They selected him for a promotion.
(C) They approved his vacation request.
(D) They asked him to give a talk.

15. What does Beth say she will do this week?

(A) Meet a client
(B) Prepare a contract
(C) Make an announcement
(D) Test a product

	Echo	Wexford
Same-day pickup		✔
Delivery	✔	✔
Clothing alterations	✔	
Repairs	✔	✔

16. According to the woman, what has caused a problem?

(A) A supplier is unreliable.
(B) Competition has increased.
(C) It is difficult to find skilled employees.
(D) Some machinery must be replaced.

17. Look at the graphic. What service does the woman want to focus on?

(A) Same-day pickup
(B) Delivery
(C) Clothing alterations
(D) Repairs

18. What will the man probably do next?

(A) Contact a business
(B) Design an advertisement
(C) Read a newspaper article
(D) Adjust a price list

핵심 포인트 | 1. 기념 행사, 직원 교육, 학회, 워크숍 등의 각종 행사를 준비하거나 행사에 참석하여 이야기하는 내용, 또는 회사 내 기기나 시설 등의 고장으로 인해 수리 보수를 요청하는 내용이 자주 출제된다.
2. 대화에서 언급된 문제점이나 이유를 묻는 문제가 자주 출제된다.

실전 맛보기

P3_U10_01

W Mr. Torres, ¹we're going to have to stop production on the leather two-seater sofas. We've had some quality-control issues with the back panels. The edges aren't smooth. Do you know why this could be happening?

M Well, ²I think it's an issue with the blade on the machine. It's probably worn out and needs to be replaced.

W ³We have some replacement parts in the storage room. I can go and see if we have the right part there.

M Thank you. That would be helpful. Just let me know if I need to order anything.

여 토레스 씨, ¹우리가 2인용 가죽 소파의 생산을 중단해야 할 거예요. 뒤판에 일부 품질 관리 문제가 있어 왔어요. 가장자리가 매끄럽지 않아요. 왜 이런 일이 일어나는지 알아요?

남 음, ²기계의 날에 문제가 있는 것 같아요. 아마도 닳아서 교체해야 할 거예요.

여 ³창고에 교체 부품들이 좀 있어요. 제가 가서 적절한 부품이 있는지 확인할게요.

남 고마워요. 그러면 도움이 되겠네요. 제가 주문해야 하는 것이 있으면 알려 주세요.

---

1. Where do the speakers most likely work? 화자
    At a furniture factory

2. What does the man think has caused a problem? 문제점
    A machine component is too old.

3. What does the woman offer to do? 제안사항
    Check a storage area

1. 화자들은 어디에서 일하는 것 같은가?
   가구 공장에서

2. 남자는 무엇이 문제를 일으켰다고 생각하는가?
   기계의 부품이 너무 낡았다.

3. 여자는 무엇을 해 주겠다고 제안하는가?
   보관 창고 확인하기

CHECK UP

P3_U10_02 정답 및 해설 p.168

1. What is the conversation mainly about?

    (A) A training session
    (B) A policy change
    (C) An industry conference
    (D) A business trip

2. What does the man want to do?

    (A) Reduce some expenses
    (B) Make an activity more interesting
    (C) Take some time off
    (D) Improve enrollment figures

3. What does the woman suggest doing?

    (A) Reserving a space off-site
    (B) Hiring a consultant
    (C) Assigning participants to groups
    (D) Preparing a questionnaire

행사 준비	We don't have enough outdoor seating for a big event. We'd have to rent some folding chairs and tables. 우리에게는 대규모 행사를 위한 야외 좌석이 충분하지 않아요. 우린 접이식 의자와 테이블을 빌려 와야 할 거에요.
행사 참석	Excuse me, we're attending the workshop. Is this the room where the networking session will start? 실례합니다, 저희는 워크숍에 참석 중인데요. 상호 교류 시간이 이곳에서 시작하는 게 맞나요?
사무기기 고장	I'm trying to copy the handout for today's meeting, but it's only printing blank pages. 오늘 회의에 쓸 인쇄물을 복사하려고 하는데, 빈 페이지만 인쇄되고 있어요.
시스템 오류	The new software seems to be causing some problems with logging into the system. 새로운 소프트웨어가 시스템에 로그인하는 데 어떤 문제를 일으키고 있는 것 같습니다.

빈출 표현

P3_U10_03

사내 행사	upcoming performance 다가오는 공연	plan a conference 학회를 기획하다
	make plans for ~의 계획을 세우다	cover expenses 비용을 부담하다
	do a product demonstration 제품 시연을 하다	choose a venue 장소를 고르다
	sponsor an event 행사를 후원하다	book a band 밴드를 섭외하다
	arrange for transportation 교통편을 마련하다	retirement celebration 은퇴 기념 행사
	provide refreshments 다과를 제공하다	charity auction 자선 경매
	place a catering order 출장 요리를 주문하다	employee appreciation party 직원 감사 파티
	celebrate an award 수상을 축하하다	shareholder's meeting 주주총회
	get some price quotes 견적서를 받다	company retreat 회사 야유회
	set up a display booth 전시 부스를 설치하다	fund-raiser 기금 모금 행사
	print out handouts 유인물을 인쇄하다	job[recruitment] fair 취업 박람회
	be ready for a trade show 무역 박람회를 준비하다	product launch 제품 출시
	organize an annual event 연례행사를 준비하다	keynote speaker 기조 연설자
시설	break down 고장 나다	fix a leak 누수를 고치다
	out of order 고장 난	repair a ventilation system 환기 장치를 수리하다
	have some issues 문제가 있다	set up equipment 장비를 설치하다
	receive a maintenance request 수리 요청을 받다	closed for renovations 보수를 위해 닫은
	report a problem 문제를 보고하다	install light fixtures 조명을 설치하다
	shut down a machine 기계를 멈추다	unexpected repairs 예상치 못한 수리
	review some instructions 설명서를 검토하다	post an announcement 공지를 게시하다
	take a look 한번 보다	cause a problem 문제를 야기하다
	inspect a facility 시설을 점검하다	head over to ~로 가다
	routine maintenance 정기적인 유지 보수	call a technician 기술자에게 전화하다
	order some equipment 장비를 주문하다	send someone over 사람을 보내다
	run out of ~가 떨어지다	diagnose a problem 문제를 진단하다
	work properly 제대로 작동하다	speed up the process 절차를 빠르게 하다

[1-4] 질문과 정답을 확인한 뒤, 대화를 들으면서 정답의 단서가 되는 부분에 표시하세요.

1. **Q** Why is the man concerned?

A A space may be too small.

> **M** Which venue are you considering for the upcoming social media marketing workshop?
> **W** Last time we rented the Concord Center. I was thinking about doing that again.
> **M** Hmm… we're expecting a lot of attendees, so maybe it won't fit everyone.

2. **Q** Where do the speakers work?

A At a hotel

> **W** Did you hear that we're removing all of the carpets in the guest rooms? We're going with wooden flooring instead.
> **M** That'll look great, and it will be easier to clean each hotel room. But I'm worried some people will think the atmosphere is not very cozy.

3. **Q** What does the man remind the woman about?

A A retirement party

> **M** Do you want to walk to the conference room together, Katelyn? Ravi's retirement celebration is starting soon.
> **W** Oh, I had forgotten that was today!
> **M** Then I guess it's a good thing I stopped by. You might have missed it.

4. **Q** Who will the man give a presentation to?

A Potential investors

> **W** Hi, David. I got your message about needing someone from IT to set up a projector and screen.
> **M** Yes, thanks. My team has got a meeting in the conference room at 2 P.M. for some people we hope will become investors.

[5-6] 대화를 듣고 정답의 단서가 알맞게 패러프레이징된 답을 고르세요.

5. What problem is being discussed?

(A) A colleague has missed an important deadline.

(B) An e-mail system is not functioning properly.

6. Why is the woman excited about an event?

(A) The guest speaker has an excellent reputation.

(B) The attendees can receive professional certification.

대화를 듣고 알맞은 답을 고른 뒤, 다시 들으면서 빈칸을 채우세요.

1. What kind of event is the man planning?

(A) A fund-raising event

(B) A launch party

(C) A prize drawing

(D) A sports competition

M Hello, Ms. Clayton? I'm calling from Sedalia Swimwear. We're planning to _____ _____ on May 25. Since you're a well-known local athlete, we were wondering if you would like to help promote the product and attend _____.

W Well, I'd have to try the swimsuit myself first.

M Of course. I can send you a sample so you can see how great the quality is.

2. What problem does the woman mention?

(A) An item wasn't ordered.

(B) An event has been postponed.

(C) A contract has recently expired.

(D) A warranty has been canceled.

3. What does the woman say about Digicom products?

(A) They are easy to operate.

(B) They cost more than competitors' products.

(C) Their warranty coverage is restrictive.

(D) Their reviews are very good.

W Do you have a minute, Mr. McGuire? I've just realized that _____ _____ for the new conference room, we forgot to _____.

M That was a huge oversight. Have you looked into our options?

W Well, I don't think we should purchase another Digicom product. _____.

M Okay. Order whatever you think is best. Just don't spend over 200 dollars. That should be plenty to get something suitable.

4. What does the woman want to do?

(A) Attend a workshop

(B) Apply for a job

(C) Give a presentation

(D) Hire a photographer

5. What does the man say he will send the woman?

(A) An address

(B) A portfolio

(C) A contract

(D) A picture

W Hello. I'm Clair Appaw from Merits. _____ _____ for our corporate banquet on May 27th. One of my colleagues recommended you, so I'm wondering if you're available.

M Let's see… Yes, my calendar is clear on that day. How long do you think the event will last?

W We're planning to take group pictures right after lunch. It shouldn't take more than two hours.

M That's fine. _____ to go over. Can I have your e-mail address, please?

대화를 듣고 알맞은 답을 고르세요.

1. Why is the man concerned about holding an event at Collins Park?

(A) It does not have a picnic area.
(B) It has limited parking space.
(C) It is usually very crowded.
(D) It is not suitable in rainy weather.

2. What does the woman say they need to consider?

(A) The start time
(B) The menu items
(C) The travel distance
(D) The overall expenses

3. Why will the man contact Foley Incorporated?

(A) To check a policy
(B) To arrange transportation
(C) To recruit employees
(D) To order some food

4. Where is the conversation most likely taking place?

(A) At a fitness center
(B) At a business institute
(C) At an appliance store
(D) At a library

5. What problem does the man describe?

(A) A door is locked.
(B) A room is too hot.
(C) An employee is absent.
(D) A space is double-booked.

6. What does the man ask the woman to do?

(A) Post a notice
(B) Look for a business card
(C) Issue some refunds
(D) Pay a repairperson

7. According to the woman, what is the problem?

(A) Her parking pass has expired.
(B) Her computer will not turn on.
(C) She cannot access a database.
(D) She will be absent from a meeting.

8. What has the business recently done?

(A) Launched a new Web site
(B) Increased its security measures
(C) Relocated to a new building
(D) Expanded its management team

9. According to the man, what can be found on a Web site?

(A) Some photographs
(B) An updated schedule
(C) Some e-mail addresses
(D) Some instructions

10. What type of business do the speakers most likely work for?

(A) An advertising agency
(B) A book publisher
(C) A television studio
(D) A law firm

11. What problem with the trade fair does the man mention?

(A) Its booths have been fully booked.
(B) Its fees exceed the planned budget.
(C) Its attendance has been declining.
(D) Its location is too far away.

12. What will the speakers' company do next month?

(A) Upgrade a Web site
(B) Renew a contract
(C) Hire more employees
(D) Move to a new office

13. What kind of event will take place in December?

(A) An awards ceremony
(B) A gallery opening
(C) A retirement party
(D) A trade show

14. Why does the man say, "I usually hire Pomona Catering"?

(A) To express surprise
(B) To correct a misunderstanding
(C) To reject a proposal
(D) To make a suggestion

15. What will the woman do this afternoon?

(A) Try some samples
(B) Send some invitations
(C) Contact a business
(D) Visit a venue

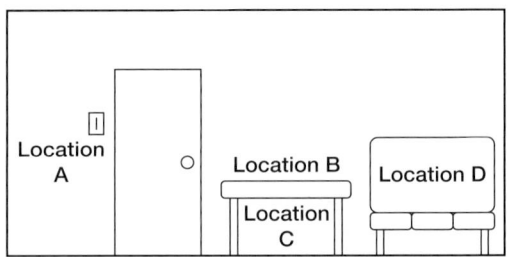

16. What made the woman buy the appliance?

(A) It is available in many colors.
(B) It does not use much energy.
(C) It has a variety of settings.
(D) It is a compact size.

17. What is the man concerned about?

(A) The appliance could be confusing to use.
(B) The appliance may be too noisy.
(C) The appliance will be hard to clean.
(D) The appliance has a short power cord.

18. Look at the graphic. Where does the woman suggest placing the appliance?

(A) At Location A
(B) At Location B
(C) At Location C
(D) At Location D

PART 3　UNIT 10

핵심 포인트

1. 상점이나 식당을 비롯하여 병원, 은행, 헬스장 등 우리가 일상생활에서 접할 수 있는 다양한 편의 시설에서 일어나는 대화로, 상품 구매 및 환불, 각종 시설이나 서비스 이용에 관한 내용이 주로 나온다.
2. 장소나 화자를 묻는 문제, 상품 및 서비스 관련 세부 정보를 묻는 문제가 자주 출제된다.

실전 맛보기

🎧 P3_U11_01

M ¹Thanks for shopping at Evergreen Camping Supplies. Is there anything I can help you find?	**남** ¹에버그린 캠핑용품점에서 쇼핑해 주셔서 감사합니다. 제가 찾아 드릴 것이 있나요?
W Yes. ²I'm interested in the Trail-X backpack made by Roe Outdoors. It was supposed to be released this week. Do you sell it in this store?	**여** 네. 로 아웃도어 사에서 만든 ²트레일 엑스 배낭에 관심이 있어요. 이번 주에 출시될 예정이었어요. 이 가게에서 그걸 판매하나요?
M Yes, we do, but ²I'm afraid we've already sold out. It was much more popular than we expected.	**남** 네, 그렇습니다만, ²유감스럽게도 이미 다 팔렸습니다. 저희가 예상했던 것보다 훨씬 더 인기가 많았어요.
W That doesn't surprise me. This is the third store I've been to. I'd rather not get a different brand. Do you know when you'll have more?	**여** 놀랍지도 않아요. 여기가 제가 들른 세 번째 가게예요. 전 다른 브랜드는 사고 싶지 않아요. 언제 더 들어오는지 아시나요?
M Let me just check the system… uh, we'll get a new shipment on Saturday morning, so ³you should come back on the weekend.	**남** 제가 시스템을 확인해 볼게요… 어, 토요일 아침에 새로 배송을 받을 거예요, 그러니 ³주말에 다시 오셔야 합니다.

---

1. Who most likely is the man? 화자
A sales clerk

2. What does the man say about the backpack? It is not currently available. 세부사항

3. What does the man suggest doing? 제안사항
Returning on the weekend

1. 남자는 누구인 것 같은가?
판매원

2. 남자는 배낭에 관해 무엇이라고 말하는가?
그것은 지금 구할 수 없다.

3. 남자는 무엇을 할 것을 제안하는가?
주말에 다시 오는 것

CHECK UP

🎧 P3_U11_02 정답 및 해설 p.176

1. Why is the man calling?
(A) To buy a new product
(B) To get a discount coupon
(C) To check his order's status
(D) To complain about a shipping price

2. What does the man say he will do?
(A) Cancel an order
(B) Visit a business
(C) Pay a late fee
(D) Send an e-mail

3. What did the man receive last week?
(A) A receipt
(B) A coupon
(C) A product catalog
(D) A feedback survey

상품 구매	Hi, I'm interested in buying 50 top hats for a school performance. Do you have them in stock? 안녕하세요, 저는 학교 공연을 위해 중산모자 50개를 구매하는 데 관심이 있어요. 그것들의 재고가 있나요?
교환/환불	I purchased this laptop computer yesterday and I'm having a problem. The keyboard isn't working, and I'd like to exchange it. 제가 어제 이 노트북 컴퓨터를 구매했는데 문제가 있어요. 키보드가 작동을 하지 않아서, 교환을 하고 싶습니다.
서비스 이용	I'm here to pick up a package. I found this notice on my door indicating I missed a delivery. 저는 소포를 찾으러 이곳에 왔습니다. 제가 배송을 놓쳤다는 것을 알려주는 이 안내문을 문에서 발견했어요.
시설 이용	I'm wondering what your fitness center offers. Do you have sessions with personal trainers? 이곳 헬스장에서 무엇을 제공하는지 궁금합니다. 개인 트레이너들의 수업이 있나요?
예약 확인	Hello, this is Kim from the Harry's. I'm calling to confirm your appointment for tomorrow at 9. 안녕하세요, 해리스의 킴입니다. 귀하의 내일 9시 예약을 확정하고자 전화 드려요.

빈출 표현 🎧 P3_U11_03

쇼핑		
	on display 진열된	get a discount 할인을 받다
	sold out 매진된	get an extended warranty 연장된 보증을 받다
	in stock/out of stock 재고가 있는/없는	for an extra charge 추가 비용을 내면
	look around 둘러보다	price list 가격표
	have a promotion 판촉 행사를 하다	in other sizes 다른 치수로
	place an order 주문하다	resistant to stains 얼룩에 강한
	make a payment 대금을 지불하다	figure out the cost 비용을 계산하다
	issue a refund 환불해 주다	offer free delivery 무료 배송을 해 주다
	clearance sale 재고 정리 세일	check our stock 재고를 확인하다
	compensate 보상하다	be included in the price 가격에 포함되다
	show a receipt 영수증을 보여 주다	come in handy 쓸모가 있다
	not have any available 이용 가능한 것이 없다	lifetime repair service 평생 수리 서비스
	process one's order 주문을 처리하다	take an order over the phone 전화로 주문을 받다

여가/일상		
	book[reserve] a table 테이블을 예약하다	reserve a ticket 표를 예약하다
	pay a bill 계산서를 지불하다	sign up for a subscription 구독 신청을 하다
	dietary restriction 식이 제한	attend a class 강의에 참석하다
	have an appointment 예약이 있다	pay by the hour 시간제로 지불하다
	schedule a check-up 검진 일정을 잡다	reschedule for another day 다른 날로 다시 예약하다
	see a doctor 진찰을 받다	confirm an appointment 예약을 확정하다
	transfer money 송금하다	register for a class 수업에 등록하다
	apply for a loan 대출을 신청하다	fill out an application form 신청서를 작성하다
	deposit 예금하다; 예금	make a reservation 예약하다
	make a withdrawal 인출하다	free of charge 무료로
	set up[open] an account 계좌를 개설하다	at no extra cost 추가 비용 없이
	work out 운동하다	purchase a membership 회원권을 구매하다
	renew a membership 멤버십을 갱신하다	have a variety of options 다양한 선택사항이 있다

[1-4] 질문과 정답을 확인한 뒤, 대화를 들으면서 정답의 단서가 되는 부분에 표시하세요.

1. **Q** Why does the man ask for assistance?

A He does not have a qualification.

> **W** Hi. I have a business account here, but I'm thinking of moving some of the funds into a different investment type, like stocks.
>
> **M** I'm not qualified to give financial advice, but I can get one of our advisors to help you.

2. **Q** What can customers do at the store?

A Design their own products

> **W** Thank you for visiting Rivera Jewelry. Can I help you find anything?
>
> **M** Actually, I heard that you allow customers to design their own jewelry. I'd like to make a unique ring as a gift.
>
> **W** Of course. What did you have in mind?

3. **Q** What does the man suggest?

A Buying a reusable item

> **W** Hi. I'd like to order a drink to-go. A large latte with caramel syrup, please.
>
> **M** Alright. And we've just started selling reusable cups. If you buy the cup, you can get 25 cents off every time you use it.

4. **Q** What new policy does the woman tell the man about?

A He does not need an appointment.

> **M** Hi, my name is Terry Williams, and I'm calling to make an appointment with Dr. Lee. I need to get a flu shot. Do you have any openings this week?
>
> **W** Actually, our policy has changed. Patients no longer need to see the doctor to get a flu shot. You can just come in anytime during the clinic's opening hours.

[5-6] 대화를 듣고 정답의 단서가 알맞게 패러프레이징된 답을 고르세요.

5. What service does the woman mention?

(A) Unlimited repairs
(B) Free installation

6. What does the woman suggest that the man do?

(A) Visit another branch
(B) Use an online resource

대화를 듣고 알맞은 답을 고른 뒤, 다시 들으면서 빈칸을 채우세요.

1. Who most likely is the woman?

(A) A hotel manager
(B) A restaurant server
(C) A professional chef
(D) A supermarket employee

W Would you like me to _____, sir? We're running a special today. If you order a slice of our raspberry cheesecake, you can get a free cup of coffee.
M Thanks, but the lunch portion was more than enough. _____. That was an excellent meal, though.
W The chef will be glad to hear that. I'll be back in just a moment.

2. What event are the speakers talking about?

(A) A jazz concert
(B) An art exhibition
(C) A new movie
(D) An opera

3. What does the man want to do?

(A) Call the theater
(B) Find out about other events
(C) Buy a ticket from someone
(D) Check a Web site

W I can't wait for this Saturday. Lena invited me _____. It's been a long time since I went to one.
M Really? I hope you have a good time. I've never been to the opera, but I'd like to see one sometime.
W I think some of her friends said they probably won't be able to make it. They might want to sell their tickets.
M That sounds great. Please let her know _____ if one is available.

4. Where most likely are the speakers?

(A) At a clothing factory
(B) At a fabric store
(C) At an interior design firm
(D) At a restaurant

5. What does the man suggest the woman do?

(A) Go to another shop
(B) Search a Web site
(C) Come back next week
(D) Check a stock room

W Excuse me. _____ in this color? I need it for a garment I'm working on.
M Hmm... I'm afraid we're out of that particular color at the moment. _____ _____ down the street? They might sell it.
W Thanks for the tip, but I have a gift certificate for your store. I'd prefer to make use of that. I'm not in any rush anyway. I can come back another time.

대화를 듣고 알맞은 답을 고르세요.

1. What is mentioned about the scarf?

(A) It comes in different colors.
(B) It is part of a new line.
(C) There is just one left.
(D) It arrived in the morning.

2. What does the man offer to do?

(A) Gift wrap a present
(B) Discount an item
(C) Call another store
(D) Order a product

3. What event is being held tomorrow?

(A) An employee picnic
(B) A charity fund-raiser
(C) A grand opening
(D) A retirement party

4. What did the woman do last month?

(A) She moved to a new city.
(B) She graduated from university.
(C) She lost a library book.
(D) She attended a community event.

5. What is the conversation mainly about?

(A) A job opening
(B) A registration procedure
(C) Professional development workshops
(D) Apartment lease terms

6. According to the man, what can be found on a Web site?

(A) A photo gallery
(B) Upcoming events
(C) An account's status
(D) Operating hours

7. Where does the man need to send the package?

(A) To a hotel
(B) To an apartment
(C) To an art gallery
(D) To an office building

8. What does the woman ask the man to do?

(A) Give her an address
(B) Complete a form
(C) Pay the courier
(D) Lift a box

9. What does the man say about the box?

(A) It is small and expensive.
(B) It has non-refundable items.
(C) It is missing.
(D) It needs special care.

10. What kind of class is the man interested in?

(A) Photography
(B) Cooking
(C) Painting
(D) Music

11. Why does the woman suggest registering early?

(A) To receive a voucher
(B) To save time
(C) To ensure availability
(D) To get a discount

12. Why does the woman say, "our schedule will change in the summer"?

(A) To propose a possible solution
(B) To express disappointment
(C) To apologize for a delay
(D) To justify a cost

13. Where do the women work?

(A) At a cafeteria
(B) At a jewelry shop
(C) At a shoe store
(D) At a community center

14. Why does the man want to make a purchase?

(A) He will give a gift.
(B) He will start a new job.
(C) He will attend a wedding.
(D) He will take a trip.

15. What does the man want Hannah to do?

(A) Recommend a brand
(B) Take some measurements
(C) Explain a policy
(D) Check a stock room

Thursday Schedule	
9 A.M. – 11 A.M.	Doug
11 A.M. – 1 P.M.	Violet
1 P.M. – 3 P.M.	James
3 P.M. – 5 P.M.	Carol

16. Where does the man work?

(A) At a hair salon
(B) At a dental clinic
(C) At a movie theater
(D) At a financial institution

17. What problem does the man mention?

(A) A delivery was not made on time.
(B) The business will close soon.
(C) A schedule contained an error.
(D) An employee has moved out of town.

18. Look at the graphic. Who will most likely help the woman?

(A) Doug
(B) Violet
(C) James
(D) Carol

PART 3

UNIT 11

핵심 포인트

1. 교통수단, 도로 상황, 길 안내 등에 관한 교통 관련 대화가 출제된다.
2. 여행이나 출장을 준비하는 내용이나 공항, 호텔 등 여행 관련 장소에서 일어나는 대화가 출제된다.
3. 부동산 임대, 이사, 관리사무소 직원과의 대화 등 주거와 관련된 대화가 출제된다.
4. 장소나 화자를 묻는 문제, 세부 정보를 묻는 문제가 자주 출제된다.

실전 맛보기

🎧 P3_U12_01

M Alina Towers Property Management Office. How can I help you?

W Hello, I'm flying to Boston next week for a job interview. ¹I'd like to look at some apartments while I'm there. I'm particularly interested in your two-bedroom apartments. ¹Could someone show me around on the afternoon of the 10th?

M Sure. There are a few units available. How about 1 o'clock?

W Okay. Also, ²would it be possible to leave my luggage there while I'm looking at the units?

M Hmm… ³I'm not sure if that's allowed for security reasons. Let me ask my coworker.

남 앨리나 타워 부동산 관리사무소입니다. 어떻게 도와드릴까요?

여 안녕하세요, 제가 다음 주에 채용 면접을 위해 비행편으로 보스턴에 가려고 합니다. ¹그곳에 있는 동안 아파트를 좀 보고 싶어요. 특히 침실이 두 개인 아파트에 관심이 있습니다. ¹10일 오후에 제가 둘러보도록 안내해 주실 분이 계실까요?

남 물론입니다. 이용할 수 있는 몇 세대가 있어요. 1시는 어떠세요?

여 좋습니다. 또한, ²제가 세대들을 둘러보는 동안 제 짐을 그곳에 두는 것이 가능할까요?

남 흠… ³보안상의 이유로 그것이 허용되는지 잘 모르겠어요. 제 동료에게 물어볼게요.

---

1. Why is the woman calling? 목적
   To schedule a tour

2. What special request does the woman make? 세부사항
   Leaving items at the man's office

3. What will the man probably do next? 다음에 할 일
   Ask about a rule

1. 여자는 왜 전화하고 있는가?
   둘러보는 일정을 잡기 위해

2. 여자는 어떤 특별한 요청을 하는가?
   남자의 사무실에 물품을 두는 것

3. 남자는 아마도 다음에 무엇을 할 것인가?
   규정에 대해 물어보기

CHECK UP

🎧 P3_U12_02 정답 및 해설 p.183

1. How did the woman find out about the agency?
   (A) She read a review online.
   (B) A coworker told her about it.
   (C) She saw a flyer in a store window.
   (D) Her company uses it for business travel.

2. According to the man, what is available this month?
   (A) Free upgrades
   (B) New accommodations
   (C) Lower prices
   (D) Guided tours

3. What does the man tell the woman to do?
   (A) Watch a promotional video
   (B) Purchase a map
   (C) Fill out a passport application
   (D) Check a Web site

대중교통 이용	Hi, I'm trying to catch the next train to the city. 안녕하세요, 저는 시내로 가는 다음 기차를 타려고 해요.
항공편 문의	I'm checking in for Flight 3887 to San Francisco, and I'm wondering if I can change my seat. 샌프란시스코로 가는 3887 항공편에 탑승 수속을 하려는데, 제 좌석을 바꿀 수 있는지 궁금합니다.
호텔 이용	I was looking forward to an ocean view room. I've requested that when I made the reservation. 저는 바다 전망 객실을 기대하고 있었어요. 예약을 할 때 요청사항을 남겼었거든요.
부동산 임대	Will there be any three-bedroom apartments available next month? 다음 달에 이용 가능한 침실 3개짜리 아파트가 있을까요?
관리사무소	Hi, I live in 3B. I tried to use the stove but it won't turn on. 안녕하세요, 저는 3B호에 살고 있는데요, 가스레인지를 쓰려고 했는데 켜지지 않습니다.

빈출 표현

🎧 P3_U12_03

교통 / 여행	
get a traffic update 교통 정보 업데이트를 받다	tourist attraction 관광 명소
traffic report 교통 정보	accommodations 숙박 시설
get on board 탑승하다	buy a souvenir 기념품을 사다
close down the road 도로를 폐쇄하다	carry-on luggage 기내용 짐
arrive on time 제시간에 도착하다	weight limit 무게 제한
traffic congestion 교통 혼잡	confirm the details 세부사항을 확정하다
arrange a ride 차편을 마련하다	view of the city lights 도시 불빛 전망
use public transportation 대중교통을 이용하다	offer a voucher 상품권을 제공하다
road construction 도로 공사	start boarding the plane 항공기 탑승을 시작하다
baggage claim ticket 수하물 보관 티켓	be ready for takeoff 이륙 준비가 되다
travel itinerary 여행 일정표	connecting flight 연결 항공편
flight delay 항공편 지연	cover the cost 비용을 감당하다
travel expenses 여행 경비	tour package 여행 상품

주거	
meet a real estate agent 부동산 중개업자를 만나다	potential office space 쓸 수 있는 사무실 공간
find a space 공간을 찾다	property listings 부동산 목록
relocate to ~로 이사하다	be renovated 개조되다
property 토지, 부동산	affordable 가격이 적당한
rent out 임대하다	lease a land 땅을 임대하다
renew a lease 임대 계약을 갱신하다	retile the floor 바닥 타일을 다시 깔다
give a tour 구경시켜 주다	give an estimate 견적을 내다
neighborhood 동네, 인근	take measurements 치수를 재다
have a lot of space 공간이 넓다	meet one's criteria ~의 기준을 충족하다
in a great location 위치가 좋은	redecorate the interior 실내 장식을 새로 하다
show someone around 구경시켜 주다	residential area 주거 지역
have new appliances 새 전자제품이 갖추어져 있다	studio 원룸
rental application 임대 신청서	tenant 세입자

[1-4] 질문과 정답을 확인한 뒤, 대화를 들으면서 정답의 단서가 되는 부분에 표시하세요.

1. **Q** Why will the woman be going to Seattle?

A To give a presentation

> W Hi, Omar. It's Lori. I'm wondering if you've booked my plane tickets for Seattle yet.
> M You mean for your business trip to present at the conference? I was going to choose the flights today.

2. **Q** What does the man plan to do in two months?

A Open a business

> W Hi, Mr. Baek. This is Vivian from Jackson Realty. There's a commercial space that I think would be perfect for your accounting firm. Do you have time to look at it this week?
> M Sure! I hope to get my business up and running in two months, so I need to find somewhere soon so I can open on time.

3. **Q** Why is a street blocked off?

A Some charging stations are being installed.

> M Excuse me. I saw the sign saying this road is temporarily closed. I'm wondering what's going on. Are you part of the construction team?
> W Yes. The road has to stay closed while we put in some charging stations for electric cars. You'll have to use another route.

4. **Q** What does the woman notice about a suitcase?

A It is over a weight limit.

> W You're all checked in for your flight, Mr. Hubbard, but... um... it seems that your suitcase is five kilograms over the airline's baggage allowance. You'll have to pay an additional fee.
> M Oh, I didn't realize that. Do you take credit cards?

[5-6] 대화를 듣고 정답의 단서가 알맞게 패러프레이징된 답을 고르세요.

5. What does the man say about a train pass?

(A) It has recently had a price increase.
(B) It is cheaper to purchase before a trip.

6. Who most likely is the woman?

(A) A construction worker
(B) A property manager

대화를 듣고 알맞은 답을 고른 뒤, 다시 들으면서 빈칸을 채우세요.

1. Why did Jamie miss the meeting?

(A) She didn't have the schedule.

(B) She toured a new school.

(C) She was stuck on a road.

(D) She took an alternate route.

> **M** Jaime, I noticed you weren't at the meeting this morning. Is everything okay?
> **W** Yes, _____ on Hershey Street.
> **M** There always seems to be heavy congestion there. Why don't you take South Street instead?
> **W** Actually, I have to take Hershey Street to drop my son off at school. I'll just have to leave home a little earlier from now on.

2. When will the move take place?

(A) On March 14

(B) On March 15

(C) On April 14

(D) On April 15

> **W** Hi, there. I saw your leaflet for moving services. I'm planning on moving my store to a larger space in another city. Could you help?
> **M** Of course! Which city are you moving to, and on what date would you prefer? We're booked up quite a bit for March, and we are closed on Wednesdays.
> **W** We're moving to Atlanta. _____ _____?
> **M** Perfect! But we need to know _____ _____. We want to prepare the packaging in advance.

3. What does the man ask about?

(A) Fragile items

(B) A special discount

(C) Company policies

(D) A delivery fee

4. What problem does the woman mention?

(A) She does not know where to go.

(B) She damaged her suitcase.

(C) She needs a later flight.

(D) She has lost her ticket.

> **W** Excuse me. I'm booked on the 12:15 flight to Chicago, but I'm not sure _____ _____.
> **M** Let's see… according to my computer, that flight is boarding at Gate 23. It's in Terminal 3.
> **W** Isn't that quite a long walk from here?
> **M** Yes, so _____ to save time. There's no charge for it, and it departs from right over there. The next one should be here in just a few minutes.

5. What does the man suggest doing?

(A) Replacing an item

(B) Making an announcement

(C) Using a shuttle

(D) Paying for an upgrade

PART 3 UNIT 12

대화를 듣고 알맞은 답을 고르세요.

1. Where most likely are the speakers?

(A) At a music festival
(B) At a subway station
(C) At a ticket counter
(D) At a bus stop

2. What does the woman think caused the delay?

(A) A shortage of bus drivers
(B) An event downtown
(C) Construction on Martin Street
(D) Some severe weather

3. What does the woman suggest doing?

(A) Waiting for the next bus
(B) Attending an event
(C) Taking alternate transportation
(D) Checking a schedule online

4. According to the woman, what event is taking place in Bristol tomorrow?

(A) A marathon
(B) A bike race
(C) A job fair
(D) A conference

5. What does the woman recommend the man do?

(A) Book a plane ticket
(B) Travel through Bristol
(C) Take another train
(D) Request a refund

6. What does the man imply when he says, "what else can I do"?

(A) He wants to hear another idea.
(B) He must take the train at midnight.
(C) He cannot go to Cornwall.
(D) He will check another train's schedule.

7. What does the man ask about?

(A) Giving a talk at a conference
(B) Meeting a client in Toronto
(C) Getting reimbursed for business expenses
(D) Changing some travel arrangements

8. What does the man plan to do on Friday?

(A) Visit some friends
(B) See a city's famous sites
(C) Attend a workshop
(D) Confirm a decision

9. What will be sent to the man?

(A) An itinerary
(B) An address
(C) An access code
(D) A request form

10. Where is the conversation taking place?

(A) At an airport
(B) At a travel agency
(C) At a ticket counter
(D) At a hotel

11. What does the woman say about Towson Travel?

(A) It is located near the ocean.
(B) It has a large selection of activities.
(C) It provides free tours around the city.
(D) It has the area's most affordable prices.

12. What does the woman offer to do?

(A) Give a special price
(B) Send the man a ticket
(C) Lend the man some equipment
(D) Provide a complimentary meal

13. Where is the conversation taking place?

(A) At an apartment building
(B) At a warehouse
(C) At a department store
(D) At a financial institution

14. What does the woman tell Mr. Ortiz about?

(A) A return policy
(B) An outstanding bill
(C) A scheduling problem
(D) A move-in procedure

15. What will Kevin do for Mr. Ortiz?

(A) Lead him on a building tour
(B) Give him a parking pass
(C) Print a floor layout
(D) Check that a key works

Re-pavement Schedule	
Jul. 1–2 (Fri–Sat)	Grant Ave.
Jul. 7–8 (Thu–Fri)	Sears St.
Jul. 13–14 (Wed–Thu)	Parker St.
Jul. 18–19 (Mon–Tue)	Boarder Ave.

16. Who most likely is the woman?

(A) A building tenant
(B) A government employee
(C) A field manager
(D) A construction worker

17. Look at the graphic. Where most likely is the man's building located?

(A) On Grant Avenue
(B) On Sears Street
(C) On Parker Street
(D) On Boarder Avenue

18. What will the man do after this call?

(A) Call City Hall
(B) Post a sign
(C) Move his car
(D) Change his work schedule

PART 3

Directions: You will hear some conversations between two or more people. You will be asked to answer three questions about what the speakers say in each conversation. Select the best response to each question and mark the letter (A), (B), (C), or (D) on your answer sheet. The conversations will not be printed in your test book and will be spoken only one time.

32. What does the woman request?
    (A) Taking some time off
    (B) Getting a pay raise
    (C) Moving to a larger office
    (D) Changing a meeting time

33. Why was a team busier than usual?
    (A) Some equipment stopped working.
    (B) Some important files were lost.
    (C) A client changed a deadline.
    (D) A colleague got transferred.

34. What will the woman most likely do next?
    (A) Post a notice in the lounge
    (B) Check some figures
    (C) Visit a Web site
    (D) Talk to an HR representative

35. What will take place on Saturday?
    (A) An open house
    (B) A photography class
    (C) A city tour
    (D) A product launch

36. What does the woman think participants will be interested in?
    (A) An expert's advice
    (B) A reasonable price
    (C) A beautiful view
    (D) A security feature

37. What does the man plan to do tomorrow?
    (A) Update a calendar
    (B) Submit a financial report
    (C) Print some brochures
    (D) Speak to a consultant

38. What type of products does the speakers' company make?
    (A) Healthy snacks
    (B) Hand lotions
    (C) Vitamin supplements
    (D) Energy drinks

39. What is the woman worried about?
    (A) A safety issue
    (B) A poor review
    (C) An increased cost
    (D) An environmental problem

40. What does the man say he will do?
    (A) Change a supplier
    (B) Conduct some research
    (C) Test some packaging
    (D) Place an order

41. What does the man ask for?
    (A) A parking pass
    (B) An identification card
    (C) A work schedule
    (D) A building map

42. Why does the woman say, "we've changed our software recently"?
    (A) To explain a problem
    (B) To recommend a product
    (C) To propose an alternative
    (D) To express agreement

43. What will the woman most likely do next?
    (A) Check a form
    (B) Call a repair person
    (C) Speak to a supervisor
    (D) Print a document

44. What type of business do the speakers work for?

(A) A radio station
(B) A movie theater
(C) An electronics store
(D) A furniture manufacturer

45. What do the men express concern about?

(A) A competitor's low prices
(B) A regulation change
(C) Some poor reviews
(D) Some absent employees

46. What does the woman say about Sinclair Interiors?

(A) It can work on short notice.
(B) It provides high-quality services.
(C) It has helped the business before.
(D) It has the least expensive services.

47. Where most likely are the speakers?

(A) At an auto repair shop
(B) At a health clinic
(C) At a moving company
(D) At a manufacturing facility

48. What does the man ask about?

(A) Where some crew members can be found
(B) How some machinery should be assembled
(C) When an order will be shipped
(D) Whether some upgrades have been completed

49. What will the man do on Wednesday?

(A) Complete a questionnaire
(B) Submit a report
(C) Give a demonstration
(D) Unpack some boxes

50. What does the woman ask the man about?

(A) A payment method
(B) An entrance fee
(C) A closing time
(D) A bus route

51. What does the man mean when he says, "it'll be rainy all afternoon"?

(A) A wait time may be longer than usual.
(B) The woman may want to change her plans.
(C) An event is likely to be delayed.
(D) He is disappointed he forgot his umbrella.

52. Where does the man recommend going?

(A) To an antique shop
(B) To a shopping center
(C) To an art gallery
(D) To a movie theater

53. What is the woman planning to do?

(A) Have a room renovated
(B) Buy some home appliances
(C) Enroll in design classes
(D) Move to a new house

54. According to the man, what can the woman receive?

(A) An online tool
(B) An on-site consultation
(C) A free sample
(D) An extended warranty

55. What is available until the end of the month?

(A) A loyalty card
(B) An installment plan
(C) A discounted price
(D) A particular brand

56. Where most likely are the speakers?

    (A) At a restaurant
    (B) At a laboratory
    (C) At an orchard
    (D) At a travel agency

57. What will the men teach the woman how to do first?

    (A) Clean some machinery
    (B) Use a software program
    (C) Make a repair
    (D) Process a payment

58. What does Scott give to the woman?

    (A) Some business cards
    (B) Some protective gear
    (C) A name tag
    (D) A user manual

59. Who most likely is the woman?

    (A) A hotel owner
    (B) A famous chef
    (C) A restaurant employee
    (D) An event planner

60. What should the man do to use a separate room?

    (A) Sign up for a membership
    (B) Reserve it at least a week early
    (C) Visit the business as a group
    (D) Pay an extra fee

61. Why is the man inquiring about the menu?

    (A) He cannot find the menu online.
    (B) He is worried about the amount of food.
    (C) The budget he has is limited.
    (D) Someone in his party has dietary restrictions.

Bronze Plan	50 Minutes	$50
Silver Plan	100 Minutes	$75
Gold Plan	150 Minutes	$85
Platinum Plan	Unlimited Minutes	$100

62. Look at the graphic. Which plan will the woman most likely sign up for?

    (A) The Bronze Plan
    (B) The Silver Plan
    (C) The Gold Plan
    (D) The Platinum Plan

63. What does the woman say about her current cell phone?

    (A) It is very expensive.
    (B) It is hard to use.
    (C) It was bigger than she expected.
    (D) It is not functioning properly.

64. According to the man, what happened at the store earlier today?

    (A) A new model was delivered.
    (B) A display case was broken.
    (C) A policy was changed.
    (D) A device was returned.

Client Visit and Tour	
Activity	Time
Greetings and Introductions	2:00 P.M.
Factory Tour	2:15 P.M.
Presentation: Company History	2:45 P.M.
Coffee and Desserts	3:15 P.M.

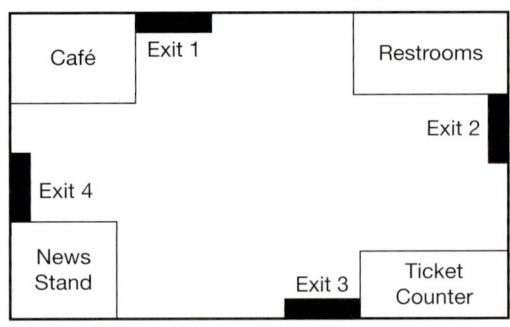

65. Where most likely is this conversation taking place?

(A) At a university
(B) At a recruiting agency
(C) At a manufacturing plant
(D) At a real estate office

66. What problem does the woman mention?

(A) A client visit has been postponed.
(B) An electric door is malfunctioning.
(C) A sales receipt has gone missing.
(D) A piece of equipment has broken down.

67. Look at the graphic. What time will the presentation take place?

(A) At 2:00 P.M.
(B) At 2:15 P.M.
(C) At 2:45 P.M.
(D) At 3:15 P.M.

68. What do the speakers plan to do at 11 o'clock?

(A) Participate in a business course
(B) Lead a seminar
(C) Tour a commercial property
(D) Meet an investor

69. Look at the graphic. Where will the speakers meet?

(A) At Exit 1
(B) At Exit 2
(C) At Exit 3
(D) At Exit 4

70. What does the woman say she wants to do?

(A) Reschedule an appointment
(B) Purchase a beverage
(C) Confirm an address
(D) Find a gift

고난도 문제
해설 강의

실전에서 바로 써먹는
쉬운 토익 공식 인강

toeic.eduwill.net

PART 4

출제 경향 및 문제 풀이 전략

PART 4 출제 경향 및 문제 풀이 전략

한 사람이 말하는 짧은 담화를 듣고, 이와 관련된 3개의 문제에 알맞은 답을 고르는 파트이다. LC 전체 100문항 중에서 총 30문항(10개 담화문×3문항)이 출제된다.

최신 출제 경향

1. 문제 유형 세부사항을 묻는 문제의 출제 빈도가 높다.
담화에서 언급된 구체적인 정보를 묻는 세부사항 문제가 10~15문항 정도로 가장 많이 출제된다. 화자/청자의 신분을 묻는 문제, 화자가 제안하거나 요청하는 것을 묻는 문제 또한 꾸준히 출제되고 있다. 화자가 한 말의 의도를 파악하는 문제는 3문항, 시각 자료와 연계하여 푸는 문제는 2문항으로 매회 고정되어 출제된다.

2. 담화 유형 사내 공지와 전화 메시지의 출제 빈도가 높다.
Part 4에서는 전화 메시지, 공지, 연설, 방송 등 다양한 유형의 담화가 출제되는데, 그중 회사에서 일어나는 공지가 가장 많이 출제되고, 음성 메시지나 부재중 자동 응답 메시지와 같은 전화 메시지의 출제 빈도도 높은 편이다. 매회 총 10개의 담화 중 절반 이상이 위의 두 가지 유형으로 출제되는 경우가 많다.

문제 풀이 전략

STEP 1 질문 파악하기
담화가 나오기 전, 질문을 읽고 키워드를 통해 묻는 내용을 파악하고, 정답의 단서가 어느 부분에서 나올지 예상한다.

STEP 2 담화 속 단서 찾기
파악한 키워드를 바탕으로 담화를 들으면서 단서가 되는 내용을 찾는다.

STEP 3 정답 선택하기
담화에서 들은 단서 내용을 동일하게 또는 다른 어휘로 바꾸어 적절하게 표현한 보기를 정답으로 선택한다.

71. Who most likely is the speaker?
(A) A personnel manager
(B) A marketing director
(C) A financial consultant
(D) A company president

72. Why does the speaker say, "I was away on a business trip all week"?
(A) To ask for some help
(B) To change his schedule
(C) To give an excuse
(D) To cancel a meeting

73. What does the speaker ask the listener to do?
(A) Send additional information
(B) Consult with a client

M Hello, Rika. ⁷¹This is Philip Kim from personnel. ⁷²I'm sorry for the late response to your e-mail. I was away on a business trip all week. I did see your e-mail requesting our team to approve publishing a job posting for your department. However, the detailed job description is missing from your request. ⁷³Can you send me a new request with the job description added? Once our team reviews and approves it, the posting should be published on our Web site. Please let me know if you have any other questions. Thank you.

유형 분석

문제 유형별

전체 내용 관련 문제	**1. 주제·목적** 메시지 주제, 회의 목적 등 담화의 주제나 목적을 묻는 문제 **2. 화자·청자·장소** 직업/근무지 등 화자나 청자의 신분을 묻거나, 담화가 일어나는 장소를 묻는 문제
세부 내용 관련 문제	**3. 문제점·이유** 화자의 걱정/문제점에 대해 묻는 문제, 화자나 청자가 ~하는 이유를 묻는 문제 **4. 세부사항** 무엇/누구/언제/어디 등 담화에서 언급된 구체적인 정보를 묻는 문제 **5. 제안·요청사항** 화자가 청자에게 제안하거나 부탁/요청하는 것을 묻는 문제 **6. 다음에 할·일어날 일** 화자나 청자가 다음에 할 일 또는 미래에 일어날 일을 묻는 문제 **7. 화자의 의도 파악** 화자가 한 말의 의미나 그 말을 통해 암시하는 것, 또는 그것을 말한 이유를 묻는 문제 **8. 시각 자료 연계** 목록/지도/그래프 등 다양한 유형의 시각 자료가 함께 제시되는 문제

담화 유형별

회사 / 일상생활 관련 담화	**9. 전화 메시지** 전화 건 사람이 자동 응답기에 남긴 음성 메시지, 회사나 관공서에서 미리 녹음해 둔 부재중 자동 응답 메시지 **10. 사내 공지** 새로운 정책이나 제도 등을 알리는 사내 공지, 업무 관련 다양한 안건에 대해 논의하는 회의 발췌록 **11. 공공장소 안내** 운영 시간이나 특별 행사 등과 관련하여 공공장소나 교통수단에서 이루어지는 안내 방송 **12. 연설·강연·소개** 컨퍼런스나 개관식 같은 각종 행사에서의 기조연설이나 짧은 강연 및 인물 소개 **13. 광고** 제품이나 서비스, 업체, 행사 및 이벤트 등을 홍보하기 위한 광고 **14. 방송** 지역 뉴스, 일기 예보, 교통 안내 등의 라디오 방송 및 일반 교양 프로그램 **15. 관광·견학** 유적지 같은 여행 장소나 공장 등 다양한 시설물에서 관광이나 견학을 이끄는 가이드의 안내

UNIT 01 · 주제·목적 문제

핵심 포인트

1. 주로 첫 번째나 두 번째 문제로 출제된다.
2. 담화 도입부의 인사말 바로 다음에 단서가 언급되는 경우가 많다. 담화 초반부를 듣고서 주제나 목적이 파악되지 않는다면, 담화를 끝까지 들은 뒤 전체 맥락을 통해 정답을 찾는다.

실전 맛보기

🎧 P4_U01_01

Why is the speaker calling?

(A) To request a repair
(B) To promote a service
(C) To confirm a delivery schedule
(D) To explain a refund process

화자는 왜 전화하고 있는가?

(A) 수리를 요청하기 위해
(B) 서비스를 홍보하기 위해
(C) 배송 일정을 확인하기 위해
(D) 환불 절차를 설명하기 위해

W Good morning. This is Tina from Bellevue Appliances. I'm calling about the delivery of the washing machine that you ordered a few days ago. You said you would be home this afternoon between two and four so that we could deliver it. I just want to make sure that this is still the case. If so, you don't need to take any further action. However, if you need to change the time or day, please call the store as soon as possible to let us know. Thank you.

여 안녕하세요. 저는 벨뷰 가전제품점의 티나입니다. 며칠 전에 주문하신 세탁기의 배송과 관련하여 전화드립니다. 저희가 세탁기를 배달할 수 있도록 오늘 오후 2시에서 4시 사이에 댁에 계시겠다고 하셨지요. 여전히 그러하신지 확인하려고 합니다. 그러시다면, 더 이상의 조치를 취하실 필요가 없습니다. 하지만, 시간이나 날짜를 바꾸셔야 한다면 가능한 한 빨리 매장으로 전화하셔서 저희에게 알려주세요. 감사합니다.

CHECK UP

🎧 P4_U01_02 정답 및 해설 p.201

1. What is the speaker discussing?

(A) An educational session
(B) A software error
(C) An industry conference
(D) A guidebook

2. What is the purpose of the talk?

(A) To recruit employees
(B) To announce a job promotion
(C) To introduce a product
(D) To assess customer reviews

빈출 질문

주제

What is the speaker (mainly) discussing? 화자는 (주로) 무엇에 관해 이야기하고 있는가?

What is the message/announcement/broadcast (mainly) about? 메시지/공지/방송은 (주로) 무엇에 관한 것인가?

What is the topic of the workshop/meeting? 워크숍/회의의 주제는 무엇인가?

What (type of product/company) is being advertised? 무엇이(어떤 종류의 제품/회사가) 광고되고 있는가?

목적

Why is the speaker calling? 화자는 왜 전화하고 있는가?

What is the purpose of the talk/meeting/call? 담화/회의/전화의 목적은 무엇인가?

빈출 단서

전화 메시지	**I'm calling to tell you ~ / I'm calling about ~ / I wanted to let you know ~** I'm calling about the property our development company just purchased. 저희 개발 회사에서 매입한 부동산 관련하여 전화 드립니다. ▶ 메시지 주제: A property 부동산
사내 공지	**I'm happy to announce ~ / I want to remind ~ / The final item on our agenda is ~** The final item on our agenda is the new security software we're implementing. 마지막 안건은 우리가 새롭게 시행할 보안 소프트웨어입니다. ▶ 공지 주제: Some new software 새로운 소프트웨어
연설/강연	**Today I'll be presenting ~ / In today's workshop, you'll learn ~** In today's workshop, you'll learn how to measure employee performance. 오늘 워크숍에서, 여러분은 직원 성과를 측정하는 법을 배우게 될 겁니다. ▶ 워크숍 주제: Evaluating employee results 직원 성과를 평가하는 것
광고	**Are you looking for ~? / Do you need ~? / If you're having trouble -ing, find ~** Are you looking for a place to go for a delicious meal? 맛있는 식사를 위한 장소를 찾고 계신가요? ▶ 광고 대상: A restaurant 식당
방송	**In local news, ~ / Now to business news, ~ / On today's show, we'll be discussing ~** Now to business news. A local company Silver Motors Incorporated released a new application. 경제 소식입니다. 지역 업체인 실버 모터스 사에서 새로운 앱을 출시했습니다. ▶ 방송 주제: A mobile application 모바일 앱

고득점 TIP

광고에서는 광고 대상을 묻는 문제가 출제될 가능성이 매우 높고, 단서는 대부분 첫 문장에서 주어진다.

M Are you looking for fresh locally made cheese? Then don't forget to visit Augusta Dairy Farm.

남 지역에서 갓 만든 치즈를 찾고 계시나요? 그렇다면 오거스타 낙농장을 방문하는 것을 잊지 마세요.

Q What type of product is being advertised? 어떤 종류의 제품이 광고되고 있는가?

A Cheese 치즈

[1-4] 질문과 정답을 확인한 뒤, 대화를 들으면서 정답의 단서가 되는 부분에 표시하세요.

1. **Q** What is the broadcast about?

A A renovation project

> **W** At a press conference yesterday, city officials announced that renovations to the swimming facilities at the Filbert Recreation Center will begin in August. The interior of the pool will be retiled, and the filter system will be upgraded.

2. **Q** Why is the speaker meeting with the listeners?

A To promote a service

> **M** Hello, everyone, and thanks for attending this meeting. I appreciate this opportunity to tell you about Eastland Accounting. At Eastland Accounting, we provide bookkeeping services to small businesses in a variety of fields.

3. **Q** What most likely is being advertised?

A A commercial real estate service

> **W** Are you hoping to find the perfect office space for a new business or looking to expand and need an additional location? Whatever you require, officesearch.com is the solution.

4. **Q** What is the speaker discussing?

A A Web site update

> **M** Last on today's agenda, I wanted to let you know about some updates to the company's internal Web site. You can now track your working hours, request time off, and give feedback all in the same place.

[5-6] 대화를 듣고 정답의 단서가 알맞게 패러프레이징된 답을 고르세요.

5. Why is the speaker calling?

(A) To invite the listener to travel with him

(B) To ask the listener to conduct a workshop

6. What is the topic of the broadcast?

(A) A merger between two businesses

(B) A leadership change at a company

대화를 듣고 알맞은 답을 고른 뒤, 다시 들으면서 빈칸을 채우세요.

1. What is the news report mainly about?

(A) An acquisition of a company

(B) A new factory

(C) A product review

(D) A company's name change

> **M** Good morning. You're listening to KWRP's morning business report. Brook Services announced today that _____ Brook Equity Research. The company has been the industry's leading provider of investment research for the last 32 years. The reason for the change is that _____ _____. President Donald Vance states that the company will grow by nearly 10 percent in the coming year. Investors are looking forward to this growth.

2. What is being advertised?

(A) A hiking tour

(B) A cruise

(C) A resort package

(D) A flight

3. What change has recently occurred at the business?

(A) The grounds were expanded.

(B) Some dining options were improved.

(C) A pool was renovated.

(D) Outdoor activities were added.

> **W** Are you planning to get away for a relaxing weekend? Well, now is your chance to go at a great price. Luxurious Skytop Grounds is offering 40 percent off _____ through the end of March. We've never offered such great prices. Choose from our many _____ _____, or simply lounge by one of our pools. And, speaking of pools, we've just _____ _____. Every night is filled with entertainment to please all ages at Skytop Grounds. Visit our Web site today at www.skytopgrounds.com.

4. What kind of business is the speaker calling?

(A) A home improvement company

(B) A car dealership

(C) A telecommunication company

(D) A plumbing service

5. Why is the speaker calling?

(A) To inquire about an open position

(B) To file a complaint

(C) To change a delivery address

(D) To find out a product price

> **M** Hello, this is Travis Kurowski. In March, I hired your company _____ _____. It looked great when you finished, but now it's cracking and there are some holes forming. It's only been two months, so... _____. According to your policy on your Web site, you guarantee a response to any complaints within 24 hours. Please call me as soon as you get this. My number's 555-2289. Thank you.

PART 4

UNIT 01

대화를 듣고 알맞은 답을 고르세요.

1. What is the advertisement about?

(A) An air conditioner
(B) A refrigerator
(C) A dishwasher
(D) A vacuum cleaner

2. Why should the listeners visit the company's Web site?

(A) To watch a video
(B) To become a product tester
(C) To leave a comment
(D) To see a list of stores

3. What is mentioned about the voucher?

(A) What it looks like
(B) How much it is worth
(C) When it will expire
(D) How it will be sent

4. What is the topic of the meeting?

(A) A privacy policy
(B) A job opening
(C) A corporate merger
(D) A funding reduction

5. Why does the speaker say, "He doesn't know much about our operations"?

(A) To explain an error
(B) To ask for more time
(C) To provide reassurance
(D) To criticize a decision

6. Why is the speaker unable to respond to questions now?

(A) She has to leave the meeting early.
(B) She thinks some information is confidential.
(C) She needs to complete a training program.
(D) She is waiting for a reply from a client.

7. What is the purpose of the talk?

(A) To present an award
(B) To announce a promotion
(C) To introduce a marketing campaign
(D) To thank some team members

8. What does the speaker say about Mr. Allen?

(A) He was a founding member of the company.
(B) He will transfer from another branch.
(C) He has recently published a book.
(D) He has a lot of experience.

9. Why should the listeners e-mail the speaker?

(A) To sign up for a training session
(B) To suggest a venue
(C) To participate in a meal
(D) To share their questions

10. What is the broadcast mainly about?

(A) A singing contest
(B) A community fund-raiser
(C) A grand opening
(D) A beach cleanup project

11. What was given to participants?

(A) A game ticket
(B) A bag
(C) A water bottle
(D) A store coupon

12. According to the speaker, what will Ms. Fenbury prepare?

(A) An online workshop
(B) A musical performance
(C) A museum exhibit
(D) A photo gallery

13. What is the purpose of the meeting?

(A) To plan an advertising strategy
(B) To adjust a commission structure
(C) To analyze customer feedback
(D) To train new employees

14. Who most likely is Gene Richmond?

(A) A business owner
(B) A hiring manager
(C) A freelance writer
(D) A salesperson

15. What will the listeners most likely do next?

(A) Review a contract
(B) Take a vote
(C) Listen to a talk
(D) Discuss market trends

Mr. Lowry's Garden

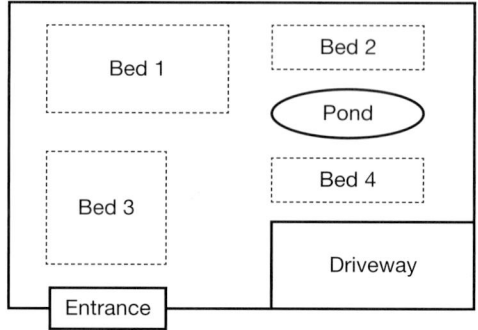

16. Why is the speaker calling?

(A) To thank the listener for a review
(B) To introduce a new service
(C) To apologize for a delay to a task
(D) To give the results of an assessment

17. Look at the graphic. Which bed is the speaker concerned about?

(A) Bed 1
(B) Bed 2
(C) Bed 3
(D) Bed 4

18. What will the speaker do this afternoon?

(A) Send a product list
(B) Take some photographs
(C) Order some flowers
(D) Visit the listener

PART 4 UNIT 01

핵심 포인트
1. 담화 초반부, 특히 첫 문장의 인사말에서 신분이나 직업, 장소를 나타내는 표현을 주의 깊게 듣는다.
2. 말하고 있는 화자뿐만 아니라 이를 듣고 있을 청자의 신분을 묻는 문제도 출제되므로, 질문 속 주어를 미리 파악해 두어야 한다.

실전 맛보기

🎧 P4_U02_01

Where does the listener work?

(A) At a construction company
(B) At a hotel
(C) At an art gallery
(D) At a hospital

청자는 어디에서 일하는가?

(A) 건설회사에서
(B) 호텔에서
(C) 미술관에서
(D) 병원에서

M Good morning. This message is for the general manager of the Kettering Hotel. I wanted to give you some feedback about my recent stay. Although the room was spacious and clean, your site was not relaxing at all. There was noisy construction going on outside my window every morning. This made it very difficult to relax. I understand that you cannot control what is happening at nearby properties. However, you should inform guests about an issue such as this in advance. That way, they can make an informed decision.

남 안녕하세요. 이 메시지는 케터링 호텔의 총괄 지배인에게 전하는 것입니다. 제가 최근 머물렀을 때에 대한 피드백을 드리고자 합니다. 방은 널찍하고 깨끗했지만, 장소가 전혀 편안하지 않았습니다. 매일 아침 제 창밖에서 시끄러운 공사가 계속되고 있었습니다. 이로 인해 느긋하게 쉬기가 매우 어려웠습니다. 당신이 주변 사유지에서 일어나는 일을 통제할 수 없다는 것을 이해합니다. 하지만, 숙박객들에게 이 같은 문제에 대해 사전에 알려 주셔야 합니다. 그래야 그들이 잘 알고 결정할 수 있습니다.

CHECK UP

🎧 P4_U02_02 정답 및 해설 p.209

1. Where most likely are the listeners?

   (A) At a research laboratory
   (B) At a hair salon
   (C) At a fitness center
   (D) At a dental clinic

2. Who is the speaker?

   (A) A television director
   (B) A government official
   (C) A radio host
   (D) A property manager

빈출 질문

화자·청자

Who (most likely) is/are the speaker/listeners? 화자는/청자들은 누구인가?
Where does/do the speaker/listeners (most likely) work? 화자는/청자들은 어디에서 일하는가?
Who is the intended audience for the announcement? 공지의 대상인 청중은 누구인가?

장소

Where is/are the speaker/listeners? 화자는/청자들은 어디에 있는가?
Where is the announcement being made? 공지는 어디에서 이루어지고 있는가?

빈출 단서

전화 메시지	**This is ~ calling from ~ / This message is for ~ / Thank you for calling ~ / You've reached ~** Hello, this is Barbara Morris calling from Saint Louis Savings and Loan. 안녕하세요, 저는 세인트루이스 저축 금융에서 전화 드리는 바바라 모리스입니다. ▶ 화자 근무지: At a bank 은행에서
공공장소 안내	**Attention ~ / This is an announcement for ~ / For those of you who ~** Attention all passengers waiting to board Flight 511 to Mexico. 멕시코로 가는 511 항공편 탑승을 기다리고 계시는 모든 승객 여러분 주목해 주세요. ▶ 담화 장소: At an airport 공항에서
연설/강연	**Thank you for attending ~ / Welcome to this seminar on ~ / We have ~ here at today's workshop** Thank you for attending this annual gathering for industry leaders in microchip manufacturing. 마이크로칩 제조 업계의 선두 주자들을 위한 연례 모임에 참석해 주셔서 감사합니다. ▶ 청자 업계: Manufacturing 제조업
관광/견학	**Welcome to ~ / I'll be leading you on ~ / I want to welcome you all to this tour of ~** Welcome to this tour of Cartersville Automotive company. 이곳 카터스빌 자동차 회사 견학에 오신 것을 환영합니다. ▶ 담화 장소: At an automobile factory 자동차 공장에서

고득점 TIP

담화 초반부를 듣고서 장소가 파악되지 않는다면, 담화 곳곳의 간접 키워드나 전체 맥락을 통해 정답을 찾는다.

W Okay, everyone. I hope that you enjoyed the snacks. Now it's time to return to the orientation activities. I'd like to go over the safety features of the equipment you'll be using here at the factory. Also, I'm pleased to tell you that management has recently approved a plan to expand the plant.

여 자, 여러분. 간식을 맛있게 드셨기를 바랍니다. 이제 오리엔테이션 활동으로 돌아갈 시간입니다. 여러분이 이곳 공장에서 사용하게 될 장비의 안전장치들을 살펴보겠습니다. 또한, 최근에 경영진이 공장을 확장하는 계획을 승인했다는 사실을 알려 드리게 되어 기쁩니다.

Q Where do the listeners most likely work? 청자들은 어디에서 일하는 것 같은가?
A At a manufacturing company 제조 회사에서

[1-4] 질문과 정답을 확인한 뒤, 대화를 들으면서 정답의 단서가 되는 부분에 표시하세요.

1. **Q** Where are the listeners?

    A At a cooking class

> **W** Welcome, everyone, to Home Italian. I'm Gina, and I'm looking forward to teaching you how to make delicious dishes in this cooking series. For our first class, you'll learn how to make a simple tomato-based sauce that tastes great on pasta.

2. **Q** Who most likely are the listeners?

    A Salespeople

> **M** You're all doing a great job with appliance sales, and this is our best month so far. Now, you should know that we're offering a great deal on Omaha brand dishwashers. When customers ask you for suggestions, please be sure to mention this promotion.

3. **Q** Who is the speaker?

    A A company president

> **W** Good afternoon. As president of Macon Technology, I'm delighted to be presenting at this shareholder's meeting. We have a lot of exciting news about projects for the upcoming year that I'm going to share with you today.

4. **Q** Where is the tour taking place?

    A At a ceramics factory

> **M** It is my pleasure to welcome you all to Layton Manufacturing. Our town is known for the beautiful ceramics produced by its factories. The tradition has been carried on for over a hundred years.

[5-6] 대화를 듣고 정답의 단서가 알맞게 패러프레이징된 답을 고르세요.

5. What type of company does the speaker work for?

    (A) An advertising agency

    (B) A law firm

6. Where is the announcement being made?

    (A) At a grocery store

    (B) At a restaurant

대화를 듣고 알맞은 답을 고른 뒤, 다시 들으면서 빈칸을 채우세요.

1. Where most likely is the speaker?

(A) At a trade show
(B) At a business conference
(C) At a group interview
(D) At an employee orientation

M Hello and thank you for attending the North Star _____. Before we begin today's events, I have two announcements. First, the men's room on the first floor is currently under construction, so we ask that you use the one on the second floor. And the second announcement is about Emmanuel Durand. Due to a scheduling conflict, he will be our first presenter of the day, as he must head out immediately after.

2. What kind of business does the speaker most likely work for?

(A) An accounting firm
(B) A delivery company
(C) A manufacturing facility
(D) A law firm

3. What are the listeners advised to do?

(A) Welcome a new employee
(B) Report to a manager
(C) Attend a reception
(D) Evaluate their work

W Hello, everyone. I'd like to take this time to introduce our newest employee. Regina Glover is _____ at Hart & Collins. While she won't be spending any time in court, she will be a vital member of our team. She is filling the position of Human Resources Manager. I was thrilled when I heard the news that she accepted our offer last week. We are very lucky to have her. Please take the time to introduce yourself and _____.

4. Who most likely is the speaker?

(A) An architect
(B) A banker
(C) A lawyer
(D) A journalist

5. What will the listeners do next?

(A) Watch a video
(B) Try some samples
(C) Introduce themselves
(D) Read some handouts

M It's wonderful to see so many people here for today's lecture. Thanks for coming. A lot has changed in the industry _____ _____. One of the popular trends these days is to incorporate recycled goods into the design. I'll tell you all about the advantages and disadvantages of various building materials during this talk. However, first I'd like to discuss _____ _____ to you when you arrived. Please take a moment to _____ _____.

PART 4

UNIT 02

대화를 듣고 알맞은 답을 고르세요.

1. What type of business does the speaker work for?

   (A) A construction company
   (B) A real estate agency
   (C) An advertising agency
   (D) A coffee shop

2. According to the speaker, how can the listeners learn about some coffee shops?

   (A) By reading a handout
   (B) By attending a meeting
   (C) By talking to the speaker
   (D) By receiving an e-mail

3. What does the speaker ask the listeners to do?

   (A) Attend a staff training session
   (B) Think of ways to promote the business
   (C) Research a competitor's menu
   (D) Tell people about a job opening

4. Where do the listeners most likely work?

   (A) At a clothing store
   (B) At an electronics manufacturer
   (C) At a pharmaceutical company
   (D) At a car dealership

5. What has Charles Kent recently done?

   (A) He set a new sales record.
   (B) He transferred from another branch.
   (C) He got a job promotion.
   (D) He was featured on the news.

6. What will the speaker do next?

   (A) Respond to some concerns
   (B) Assign the listeners to groups
   (C) Show some sales figures
   (D) Award a prize

7. Where does the speaker most likely work?

   (A) At a hotel
   (B) At a restaurant
   (C) At a bakery
   (D) At a store

8. What is the purpose of the message?

   (A) To advertise a sale
   (B) To correct a mistake
   (C) To explain a return policy
   (D) To ask for a payment

9. What does the speaker ask the listener to do?

   (A) E-mail some information
   (B) Visit the business
   (C) Review a service
   (D) Book a delivery time

10. Where is the talk most likely taking place?

    (A) On a boat tour
    (B) On a group hike
    (C) At a sports tournament
    (D) At a holiday festival

11. What does the speaker imply when he says, "the storm was last night"?

    (A) The site is not as busy as usual.
    (B) The speaker's colleague will be late.
    (C) A change could not be predicted.
    (D) A weather report was inaccurate.

12. What will the speaker give to the listeners?

    (A) Some food
    (B) Some clothing
    (C) An admission ticket
    (D) A map

13. Who most likely are the listeners?

(A) Health inspectors
(B) Food critics
(C) Delivery drivers
(D) Kitchen staff

14. According to the speaker, what can customers do from next week?

(A) Order through a mobile app
(B) Get discounts on bulk orders
(C) Join a loyalty program
(D) Enjoy vegetarian options

15. What benefit does the speaker mention?

(A) Reducing costs
(B) Saving time
(C) Improving safety
(D) Creating jobs

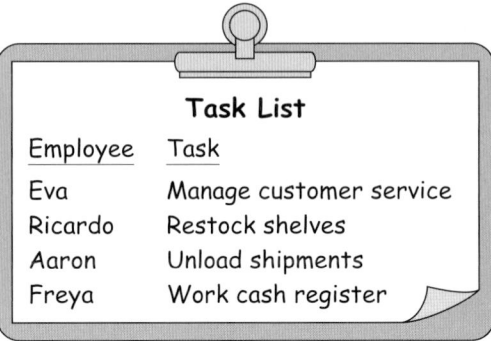

Task List

Employee	Task
Eva	Manage customer service
Ricardo	Restock shelves
Aaron	Unload shipments
Freya	Work cash register

16. Where most likely is the talk taking place?

(A) At a hardware store
(B) At a shoe store
(C) At a bookstore
(D) At a furniture store

17. What does the speaker say will happen today?

(A) A clearance sale will be held.
(B) Some new merchandise will be designed.
(C) Some demonstrations will be given.
(D) The business will be closed for training.

18. Look at the graphic. What task will Jessica do today?

(A) Manage customer service
(B) Restock shelves
(C) Unload shipments
(D) Work cash register

핵심 포인트

1. 문제점을 묻는 문제는 파트 3에 비해 출제 비율이 매우 낮다.
2. 단서 문장을 찾는 것은 어렵지 않은 편이지만, 담화 내용이 패러프레이징되어 출제되는 경우가 많으므로 선택지를 미리 읽고 내용을 파악해 두어야 한다.

실전 맛보기

P4_U03_01

Why does the speaker congratulate the listeners?	화자는 왜 청자들을 축하하는가?
(A) An award nomination was received.	(A) 수상 후보로 지명되었다.
(B) A product has sold out.	(B) 상품이 매진되었다.
(C) A negotiation was finalized.	(C) 협상이 마무리되었다.
(D) A client is satisfied.	**(D) 고객이 만족해한다.**

W May I have your attention please, everyone? I just talked to Andrew Larson, the head of Yuma Footwear. He said that he was very pleased with the television commercial you designed for their new line of hiking boots. Congratulations! You got the project done on time and to a high standard. Mr. Larson said that he plans to get in touch with us again next quarter to request an even bigger project. This is great for our business. Keep up the good work!

여 주목해 주시겠습니까, 여러분? 제가 방금 유마 풋웨어의 책임자인 앤드루 라슨과 얘기를 나눴습니다. 그가 자사의 등산화 신제품 라인을 위해 여러분이 고안한 TV 광고가 매우 마음에 든다고 했습니다. 축하합니다! 여러분은 시간에 맞춰 높은 수준으로 그 프로젝트를 마쳤습니다. 라슨 씨는 다음 분기에 다시 우리에게 연락해 훨씬 더 큰 프로젝트를 요청할 계획이라고 했습니다. 이것은 우리 사업에 굉장히 잘된 일입니다. 앞으로도 계속해서 잘해 주세요!

CHECK UP

P4_U03_02 정답 및 해설 p.216

1. What problem does the speaker mention?

(A) Some payments have not been made.
(B) An address is incorrect.
(C) He cannot log on to a Web site.
(D) He has not received his tickets.

2. Why are the listeners asked to visit a Web site?

(A) To review a set of rules
(B) To find a list of winners
(C) To register for an event
(D) To pick out a prize

문제점

What problem does the speaker mention/report? 화자는 어떤 문제를 언급/보고하는가?

What problem is mainly discussed? 어떤 문제가 주로 이야기되는가?

What is the speaker concerned about? 화자는 무엇에 대해 걱정하는가?

이유

Why does the speaker apologize? 화자는 왜 사과하는가?

Why does the speaker congratulate ~? 화자는 왜 ~를 축하하는가?

Why should the listeners visit a Web site? 청자들은 왜 웹사이트를 방문해야 하는가?

빈출 단서

결함/고장	**have some issues / not working / broke down / defective** Our Web site is having some issues. The link to view men's clothes isn't working. 저희 웹사이트에 문제가 있습니다. 남자 옷을 볼 수 있는 링크가 작동하지 않습니다. ▶ 문제점: A link is not working. 링크가 작동하지 않는다.
지연/변경	**have been delayed / still haven't received / won't be able to attend / unavailable** Unfortunately, our first order of the new smartphone model has been delayed. 유감스럽게도, 새로운 스마트폰 모델의 첫 주문이 지연되고 있습니다. ▶ 문제점: An order has been delayed. 주문이 지연되었다.
부족	**facing a shortage / not enough / higher than the budget** As you know, trucking businesses like ours are facing a severe driver shortage. 아시다시피, 저희와 같은 트럭 운송 업체들은 심각한 운전 인력난을 겪고 있습니다. ▶ 문제점: A staff shortage 직원 부족
사과/감사/축하	**We apologize for ~ / I'm sorry about ~ / Thanks to ~ / I want to thank you for ~ /** **Congratulations (on) ~ / I'd like to congratulate ~** We're having technical difficulties with the audio. I'm very sorry about this. 저희는 오디오에 기술적 문제를 겪고 있습니다. 이것에 대해 진심으로 사과드립니다. ▶ 사과하는 이유: A sound system is broken. 음향 장치가 고장 났다.

고득점 TIP

문제점 문제는 전화 메시지나 회의 발췌록에서 출제되는 경우가 많다.

M Hi, Charlotte. It's Robert from JD Realty. I'm calling to tell you that the apartment you viewed yesterday is available for move-in two weeks earlier than expected, so that fits your schedule perfectly. The only issue is that the monthly rent is a little higher than your budget.

남 안녕하세요, 샬롯. JD 부동산의 로버트예요. 당신이 어제 봤던 아파트에 예상보다 2주 더 일찍 입주할 수 있어서, 당신의 일정에 딱 맞는다는 걸 알려 드리려고 전화드렸어요. 유일한 문제는 월 임대료가 당신의 예산보다 조금 더 비싸다는 것이에요.

Q What problem does the speaker mention? 화자는 어떤 문제를 언급하는가?

A A rental fee is higher than expected. 임대료가 예상보다 비싸다.

[1-4] 질문과 정답을 확인한 뒤, 대화를 들으면서 정답의 단서가 되는 부분에 표시하세요.

1. **Q** What problem with the product does the speaker mention?

A It makes too much noise.

> **M** Good afternoon, everyone. To begin today's meeting, I'd like to address an issue with our recently released washing machine. A lot of customers have complained that it is noisier than expected. As we want to ensure the best experience for people using our products, we need to find a way to resolve this problem.

2. **Q** Why does the speaker ask the listeners to arrive early?

A To receive some clothing

> **W** I'd just like to remind everyone that we'll start offering our new menu from Monday. This is also the day that we will change our uniforms to complement the rebranding of our restaurant. Please come for your shift a bit earlier than usual to pick up the new shirt and apron set. Thank you.

3. **Q** Why does the speaker apologize?

A Not enough chairs are available.

> **M** Thank you for being here for this morning's staff meeting. I'm sorry that there are not enough chairs set up. We usually don't meet with all of the departments together, so I hope some of you don't mind standing.

4. **Q** What problem is an industry experiencing?

A A loss of revenue

> **W** In national news, an analysis of hundreds of trucking companies has revealed an alarming trend in the industry. Price increases have caused companies to lose thousands of dollars each year. The lost revenue comes mostly from the rising cost of gasoline.

[5-6] 대화를 듣고 정답의 단서가 알맞게 패러프레이징된 답을 고르세요.

5. Why does the speaker request to be contacted by phone?

(A) He is away from the office.
(B) His computer is not working.

6. What problem does the speaker mention?

(A) Some orchestra members were absent.
(B) Attendance has been poor.

대화를 듣고 알맞은 답을 고른 뒤, 다시 들으면서 빈칸을 채우세요.

1. According to the speaker, what is the problem?

(A) Some staff members were late for work.

(B) A venue has been changed.

(C) Too many people came to the event.

(D) Some supplies are not ready yet.

> **W** Thanks, everyone, for volunteering to work for the company picnic. As you know, this is the largest event organized by our company, so your help means a lot. Unfortunately, we have to make a slight change to our schedule. The food has already arrived, but we can't start setting up yet since _____ _____. So, while waiting for the truck, I'd like some of you to help me with decorating the tables.

2. What kind of business does the speaker most likely work for?

(A) A catering company

(B) A news agency

(C) A bank

(D) A print shop

3. What problem does the speaker mention?

(A) Some employees are inexperienced.

(B) An e-mail system is not working.

(C) The price of some items has risen.

(D) The business is overbooked on the day.

> **M** Hello, this message is for Mr. Donald Jeffrey. This is Andrew Harris. I received your e-mail regarding _____ _____ on June 10th. Unfortunately, some of the food options aren't available at the prices you mentioned. I think you must have been looking at an older version of our brochure. _____ _____ since that was printed. So, the new total is higher than the budget you proposed. But, we have several other options I'd love to discuss with you. Please call me back.

4. What does Fly4you plan to do in January?

(A) Upgrade their seating

(B) Add more frequent service

(C) Offer a free timetable

(D) Lower ticket prices

5. Why are the listeners encouraged to visit a Web site?

(A) To request a map

(B) To purchase a ticket

(C) To view a revised schedule

(D) To register for travel insurance

> **W** When it comes to traveling abroad, Fly4you takes you to more cities around the world than any other airline. And, starting in January, we'll be _____ _____ in Europe to make your travel even easier and faster. Our fares are usually two-thirds of the price of other airlines. In addition, all of our flights are equipped with spacious and comfortable seating. _____ _____, visit our Web site at www.Fly4youair.com. We hope you travel with us soon.

PART 4

UNIT 03

대화를 듣고 알맞은 답을 고르세요.

1. Who are the listeners?

(A) Gym employees
(B) Painting instructors
(C) Restaurant servers
(D) Factory workers

2. According to the speaker, what has caused a problem?

(A) A shipment arrived late.
(B) A window has been broken.
(C) Some construction work is noisy.
(D) Some products have been discontinued.

3. What does the speaker say she will do?

(A) Waive a fee
(B) Call a repairperson
(C) Put up a notice
(D) Speak to a supervisor

4. Why does the speaker apologize?

(A) Some seats are uncomfortable.
(B) An area was not cleaned.
(C) The tickets are sold out.
(D) A service is behind schedule.

5. According to the speaker, when will the bus most likely depart for Manhattan?

(A) In 10 minutes
(B) In 20 minutes
(C) In 30 minutes
(D) In an hour

6. What kind of facility is next to Gate 10?

(A) A cafeteria
(B) A phone booth
(C) A ticket counter
(D) A vending machine

7. Why did the speaker change a classroom?

(A) It offers a quieter environment.
(B) It is in a more convenient location.
(C) It has newly purchased equipment.
(D) It can accommodate more students.

8. What will the listeners learn to do in today's workshop?

(A) Resize images
(B) Create a search bar
(C) Add a banner
(D) Change a text color

9. According to the speaker, what can listeners do with a code?

(A) Give some feedback
(B) Get a discount
(C) Access a software program
(D) Enroll in another class

10. Who will perform at the June 10 event?

(A) Dancers
(B) Comedians
(C) Singers
(D) Actors

11. Why is the fund-raiser being held?

(A) To purchase new equipment
(B) To complete building repairs
(C) To make a stage larger
(D) To hire more employees

12. What will volunteers do on Friday?

(A) Manage a parking lot
(B) Arrange some seats
(C) Pass out flyers
(D) Sell performance tickets

13. What type of business is being discussed?

(A) A furniture store
(B) A laundry facility
(C) A restaurant
(D) A factory

14. According to the advertisement, why is the business recruiting workers?

(A) It has secured a new partner.
(B) It has launched a new service.
(C) It has opened a second location.
(D) It has extended its business hours.

15. What does the speaker mean when she says, "a lot of customers have shown interest"?

(A) An advertising campaign has worked.
(B) A product will sell out soon.
(C) Employees are likely to work a lot.
(D) The management team is effective.

Performance Review	
Selina's Story	★★
A Song in My Heart	★
The Forest Journey	★★★
Wonderful World	★★★★

16. What kind of business does the speaker most likely work for?

(A) An accounting firm
(B) An employment agency
(C) A law firm
(D) A financial institution

17. Look at the graphic. Which show did the speaker buy tickets for?

(A) Selina's Story
(B) A Song in My Heart
(C) The Forest Journey
(D) Wonderful World

18. Why does the speaker want to meet with the listener tomorrow?

(A) To introduce a client
(B) To make presentation slides
(C) To select a restaurant
(D) To review some reports

핵심 포인트

1. What뿐만 아니라 Who, When, How 등의 의문사로 다양한 세부 내용을 묻는 문제가 출제된다.
2. 질문의 핵심 어구를 미리 파악하여 담화에서 어떤 내용이 나올지 예측하면서 듣는다.

실전 맛보기 🎧 P4_U04_01

What does the speaker say about the trade show?	화자는 무역 박람회에 대해 무엇이라고 말하는가?
(A) It will offer booths in two sizes.	(A) 그것은 두 가지 크기의 부스를 제공할 것이다.
(B) The location is too far away this year.	(B) 올해는 장소가 너무 멀다.
(C) Booths may not be available for long.	**(C) 부스가 오랫동안 남아 있지 않을 수도 있다.**
(D) The participation fee has increased.	(D) 참가비가 인상되었다.

W Hi, Michael. This is Jill. I wanted to tell you about an idea I had for our hand lotion. I was thinking that we could start offering it in two different sizes. A lot of our customers would probably like a more portable version of the product. Also, I'd like to talk about booking a booth at this year's trade show. Registration just started today, but the booths are expected to sell out quickly. If we want to participate in the event, we'd better reserve one right away.	여 안녕하세요, 마이클. 질이에요. 우리 핸드 로션에 대해 제가 생각한 아이디어를 당신에게 말해 주고 싶었어요. 그것을 두 가지 다른 크기로 제공하기 시작할 수 있겠다고 생각하고 있었어요. 우리 고객들 중 다수가 아마도 휴대하기 더 좋은 형태의 제품을 좋아할 거예요. 또한, 올해의 무역박람회에 부스를 예약하는 것에 관해서도 얘기하고 싶어요. 오늘 막 등록이 시작되었지만, 부스가 빨리 매진될 것으로 예상돼요. 우리가 이 행사에 참가하고자 한다면, 당장 하나를 예약하는 것이 좋겠어요.

CHECK UP 🎧 P4_U04_02 정답 및 해설 p.224

1. Who is Gabriela Rowan?

(A) A professional musician
(B) A financial donor
(C) A city official
(D) An event planner

2. What will the listeners receive for volunteering?

(A) A gift certificate
(B) A cash bonus
(C) A T-shirt
(D) A day off

What 의문사

What did/does/will the speaker ~? 화자는 무엇을 ~했는가/하는가/할 것인가?

What does the speaker say about ~? 화자는 ~에 대해 무엇이라고 말하는가?

기타 의문사

Who is ~? ~는 누구인가?

When/Where will ~? 언제/어디에서 ~할 것인가?

How can the listeners ~? 청자들은 어떻게 ~할 수 있는가?

빈출 단서

계획	**will ~ / be going to ~** I'm going to give you an employee identification card which you'll have to scan each time you enter the building. 제가 직원 신분증을 드릴 건데요, 당신은 건물에 출입할 때마다 그것을 스캔해야 합니다. ▶ 받을 것: An identification card 신분증
시간	**at ~ / in ~ / on ~** I work the night shift, so it's best to call me in the morning. 저는 야간 근무를 하기 때문에, 아침에 저에게 전화 주시는 것이 가장 좋습니다. ▶ 연락 받기를 원하는 때: In the morning 오전에
장소	**at ~ / in ~ / on ~** This event will take place at the Stanford Library. 이 행사는 스탠포드 도서관에서 열릴 것입니다. ▶ 행사가 열릴 장소: At a library 도서관에서
방법	**If you ~ / Please ~ / by ~** If you leave a review on our Web site, you'll get a discount on any purchases made during the month of May. 저희 웹사이트에 후기를 남겨 주시면, 5월에 하시는 모든 구매에 할인을 받으실 겁니다. ▶ 할인 받는 방법: By leaving an online review 온라인 후기를 남김으로써

고득점 TIP

화자가 청자들에게 상기시키는(remind about) 것을 묻는 문제는 Remember ~(~을 기억해 주세요)와 같은 표현을 잘 들어야 한다.

M Next, we'll be touring the sculpture garden located at the rear of the Logan Mansion. Temperatures dropped last night, and it's still very cold outside. So, remember that the walkways may be quite icy. We'll walk a little more slowly than usual so no one slips.

남 다음으로, 우리는 로건 맨션의 뒤편에 위치한 조각 공원을 둘러보겠습니다. 어젯밤에 기온이 떨어져서, 아직 밖이 매우 춥습니다. 따라서, 보도가 꽤 얼어 있을지도 모른다는 것을 기억하세요. 미끄러지지 않게 우리는 평소보다 조금 더 천천히 걷겠습니다.

Q What does the speaker remind the listeners about? 화자는 청자들에게 무엇에 관해 상기시키는가?

A Icy walkways 빙판길

[1-4] 질문과 정답을 확인한 뒤, 대화를 들으면서 정답의 단서가 되는 부분에 표시하세요.

1. **Q** What can the flight attendants help with?

A Completing a form

> **M** Good morning, passengers. We are on schedule for our arrival in New York and will be landing in approximately half an hour. If you are having any difficulty filling out your customs or immigration forms, please notify one of our flight attendants to receive assistance.

2. **Q** What did the company do last year?

A It changed an advertising strategy.

> **W** I'd like to give you an update on our exercise bikes. Last year, we switched our advertising to include targeted ads on popular blogs. This has been a great move. The new strategy has led to a 30 percent increase in sales.

3. **Q** When was the speaker first inspired to write a book?

A While traveling abroad

> **M** It is an honor to speak here today at the Southfield Public Library. I'd like to thank everyone who has come to listen to this talk about my recently published book. I actually first got the idea for the plot when I was on vacation overseas in Singapore.

4. **Q** What is the Crestview neighborhood known for?

A Its long history

> **W** The next stop on our tour will be the Crestview neighborhood. I think you'll all enjoy exploring this area. It is known for having the oldest homes in the city. Many of them were built over 300 years ago.

[5-6] 대화를 듣고 정답의 단서가 알맞게 패러프레이징된 답을 고르세요.

5. How can the listeners receive a discount?

(A) By making a purchase online
(B) By buying tickets for a group

6. What does the speaker say about a building?

(A) It requires an entry code.
(B) It does not have a parking area.

대화를 듣고 알맞은 답을 고른 뒤, 다시 들으면서 빈칸을 채우세요.

1. What does the speaker say about the repair?

(A) It can be done by an expert.

(B) It will be more expensive than expected.

(C) It has been delayed.

(D) It will not involve many steps.

> **W** This is a message for Dan White. I'm Michelle from Hampton Computer Services. I'm calling about the monitor you dropped off to be repaired last Thursday. I told you we'd be able to have it back to you by tomorrow. Unfortunately, we are still waiting for a part to arrive. _____ _____, so I'll call you back then when I know more. I'm sorry for the inconvenience caused.

2. What are the listeners invited to do on the company Web site?

(A) Fill out a questionnaire

(B) Provide pictures of a house

(C) Compare houses for sale

(D) Read customer comments

3. What is available if customers are not happy with the service?

(A) A cleaning service

(B) A discount coupon

(C) A full refund

(D) A store voucher

> **M** Are you looking for an easy way to move your furniture and belongings? Well, Top Movers is here for you. One of our qualified and professional employees can visit your house to offer you a price quotation. Plus, you can save up to 20 percent on our price quote just by _____ _____ at our Web site, www.topmovers.com. Remember, if you are not satisfied with our service for any reason, we will _____ _____, no questions asked.

4. What is a special feature of the product?

(A) A light weight

(B) A competitive price

(C) A long battery life

(D) A compact size

5. What are the listeners advised to do?

(A) Write down their ideas

(B) Visit the display booth

(C) Vote on a design

(D) Move to the front

> **W** I'm delighted to share with you our most recent invention. The T17 Electric Drone is everything that has been missing in drone technology. Moreover, _____ _____ than any drone out there. Members of our design team are here to walk you through the process we took to create it. Just a reminder, _____ _____ in the space provided on the back of the brochure. That way, you'll have them fresh in your mind during the feedback session.

PART 4 UNIT 04

대화를 듣고 알맞은 답을 고르세요.

1. What does the speaker most likely specialize in?

(A) Software development
(B) Food production
(C) Fashion design
(D) Real estate

2. What does the speaker want to do?

(A) Use a different supplier
(B) Hire an assistant
(C) Change a color
(D) Perform further tests

3. Why does the speaker say, "it's similar to the Pacifica brand"?

(A) To give a compliment
(B) To reject a suggestion
(C) To confirm a strategy
(D) To recommend a business

4. Who is Deanna Caruso?

(A) A radio host
(B) A journalist
(C) A professional athlete
(D) A restaurant owner

5. Why is the cookbook popular?

(A) It has a lot of healthy meal ideas.
(B) It makes it easy to substitute ingredients.
(C) It contains a lot of pictures.
(D) Its recipes do not require a lot of steps.

6. According to the speaker, when will a Web site be launched?

(A) Tomorrow
(B) This Friday
(C) Next week
(D) Next month

7. Where is the announcement taking place?

(A) At an office building
(B) At a park
(C) At a hotel
(D) At a museum

8. What does the speaker say about the garden?

(A) It will receive new plants soon.
(B) It can be visited for free.
(C) It will feature outdoor art exhibits.
(D) It can accommodate private parties.

9. What has changed about the original plan?

(A) The construction budget
(B) The layout of chairs
(C) The closing time
(D) The number of visitors

10. Why does the speaker congratulate the listeners?

(A) The company has been nominated for an award.
(B) Customers gave some positive reviews.
(C) A new product is selling well.
(D) A project was completed early.

11. According to the speaker, what will one of the listeners be able to do?

(A) Give a presentation
(B) Get a promotion
(C) Select team assignments
(D) Take a business trip

12. What does the speaker suggest doing on a Web site?

(A) Reading a job description
(B) Creating an account
(C) Downloading a form
(D) Registering for an event

13. What does the service offer?

(A) Free deliveries
(B) Alerts on discounts
(C) Mobile banking
(D) Local news

14. What should people provide on the Web site?

(A) A brand preference
(B) A phone number
(C) An e-mail address
(D) A credit card number

15. How can the listeners get a free gift?

(A) By spending a certain amount
(B) By recommending a friend
(C) By signing up in August
(D) By completing a survey

Debra Rooney: Schedule for March 9	
9:00 A.M.	Design team briefing
9:30 A.M.	Newspaper phone interview
10:00 A.M.	Management meeting
11:00 A.M.	Online training

16. What kind of business does the speaker work for?

(A) An accounting agency
(B) A post office
(C) A pharmaceutical company
(D) A financial institution

17. What does the speaker want to discuss in a meeting?

(A) Canceling a project
(B) Running more tests
(C) Reducing expenses
(D) Finding investors

18. Look at the graphic. Which activity on the speaker's schedule got canceled?

(A) Design team briefing
(B) Newspaper phone interview
(C) Management meeting
(D) Online training

핵심 포인트 | 1. 화자가 청자에게 권고, 추천, 요청, 지시하는 내용을 묻는 문제로, 주로 담화 중반 이후에 단서가 언급된다.
2. 특히 명령문이나 please, suggest, recommend와 같은 제안/요청 표현이 나오면 해당 문장을 주의 깊게 듣는다.

실전 맛보기

🎧 P4_U05_01

What does the speaker suggest doing?

(A) Hiring temporary workers
(B) Holding a contest
(C) Lowering ticket prices
(D) Purchasing some software

화자는 무엇을 할 것을 제안하는가?

(A) 임시 직원을 고용하는 것
(B) 대회를 개최하는 것
(C) 티켓 가격을 인하하는 것
(D) 소프트웨어를 구입하는 것

M Hi, Maggie. It's Jacob. I wanted to discuss some ideas for promoting the sports activities in town. Last year, we posted photos from local sports events on social media. However, a lot of our residents have commented that they didn't look very professional. Although we don't have room in the budget to hire someone to edit the photos, I think we should consider buying some photo-editing software. That way, we can make some improvements to the photos we use without spending much. Please let me know what you think.

남 안녕하세요, 매기. 제이콥이에요. 시내에서 스포츠 활동을 홍보하기 위한 몇 가지 아이디어를 좀 논의하고 싶어서요. 작년에 우리는 지역 스포츠 행사에서 찍은 사진들을 소셜 미디어에 올렸는데요. 하지만 많은 주민들이 그것들이 전문가의 솜씨로 보이지 않는다고 평가했어요. 사진을 편집할 사람을 고용할 예산의 여유는 없지만, 사진 편집용 소프트웨어 구입을 고려해야 한다고 생각해요. 그렇게 하면, 많은 비용을 들이지 않고 우리가 이용하는 사진들을 개선할 수 있을 거예요. 어떻게 생각하시는지 알려 주세요.

CHECK UP

🎧 P4_U05_02 정답 및 해설 p.232

1. What are the listeners asked to do by this weekend?

(A) Stock new products
(B) Clean a warehouse
(C) Take inventory
(D) Wear a new uniform

2. What are the listeners advised to do?

(A) Check a Web site
(B) Contact a manager
(C) Receive text alerts
(D) Take a different route

제안

What does the speaker suggest/recommend? 화자는 무엇을 제안/추천하는가?

What does the speaker encourage the listener to do? 화자는 청자에게 무엇을 하라고 독려하는가?

What are the listeners advised to do? 청자들은 무엇을 하도록 권고받는가?

What does the speaker offer to do? 화자는 무엇을 해 주겠다고 제안하는가?

요청

What does the speaker ask/remind the listeners to do? 화자는 청자들에게 무엇을 하라고 요청하는가/상기시키는가?

What are the listeners asked/invited to do? 청자들은 무엇을 하도록 요청받는가?

빈출 단서

권고 / 추천	**I encourage/suggest/recommend ~ / I think we should ~ / We should consider -ing** I encourage you to take notes at that time since many of the tips I give aren't printed in your manual. 제가 알려드리는 비법들 중 대다수는 설명서에 적혀 있지 않기 때문에 메모를 하시는 것을 권장합니다. ▶ 제안사항: Take notes 메모하기
제공 / 제의	**I'll ~ / I'd like to ~ / I'd be happy to ~** I'd be happy to arrange a visit to your office so your staff can try them out. 직원들이 그것들을 써볼 수 있도록 당신의 사무실 방문 일정을 기꺼이 잡겠습니다. ▶ 제안사항: Arrange a visit 방문 일정 잡기
지시 / 부탁	**Please ~ / Make sure ~ / We invite you to ~ / Don't forget to ~** Don't forget to sign your contract and payment forms tomorrow morning when you come in. 내일 아침에 들어오시면 당신의 계약서와 납부서에 서명하는 것을 잊지 마세요. ▶ 요청사항: Sign some paperwork 몇몇 서류에 서명하기

고득점 TIP

offer to do(자신이 해 주겠다고 제안하는 행동) 문제와 offer ~(~에게 제공하는 것) 문제를 혼동하지 않는다.

W You said you were thinking about placing a bulk order for staff uniforms. I'd like to send a box of fabric samples for you to check out.

여 당신은 직원 유니폼을 대량 주문할 생각이라고 하셨죠. 확인해 보실 수 있도록 직물 샘플 상자를 보내 드리려고 합니다.

Q What does the speaker offer to do? 화자는 무엇을 해 주겠다고 제안하는가?

A Send some samples 몇몇 샘플 보내기

M I know you'll love this hand lotion as soon as you try it. That's why I'm offering a 100 percent money-back guarantee.

남 틀림없이 여러분은 이 핸드로션을 써 보자마자 아주 마음에 들어 하실 겁니다. 그것이 제가 100% 환불 보장을 해 드리는 이유입니다.

Q What is the speaker offering customers? 화자는 고객들에게 무엇을 제공하는가?

A A full refund 전액 환불

[1-4] 질문과 정답을 확인한 뒤, 대화를 들으면서 정답의 단서가 되는 부분에 표시하세요.

1. **Q** What does the speaker ask the listener to do?

  A Fill out a form

> **M** Our customers' opinions matter to us, and we use their feedback to make improvements. So, I hope you fill out the customer satisfaction survey that was sent to you by e-mail.

2. **Q** What are the listeners asked to do?

  A Register for a training session

> **W** You cannot use the new machinery until you have been certified. Therefore, training sessions will be held throughout the week. Please sign up for one that suits your schedule. The sign-up sheet is in the break room.

3. **Q** What does the speaker suggest the listeners do?

  A Take a shuttle bus

> **M** This weekend, the city's annual Independence Day parade will be held in downtown area. The city center will be crowded, and parking will be very limited. So, I recommend taking one of the hotel's complimentary shuttle buses if you plan to attend this event.

4. **Q** What are the listeners encouraged to do in May?

  A Take a test ride

> **W** Our new bicycle folds into a compact size for easy storage. Nevertheless, it has the excellent performance you would expect from a standard bicycle. Stop by any Coney's retail location during the month of May to take a free spin on one and try it out.

[5-6] 대화를 듣고 정답의 단서가 알맞게 패러프레이징된 답을 고르세요.

5. What does the speaker suggest?

  (A) Hiring a new analyst
  (B) Surveying some customers

6. What does the speaker invite the listeners to do?

  (A) Have some refreshments
  (B) Share their suggestions

대화를 듣고 알맞은 답을 고른 뒤, 다시 들으면서 빈칸을 채우세요.

1. What does the speaker suggest the listeners do before 9 o'clock?

(A) Check some equipment
(B) Download a map
(C) Drink some water
(D) Take some pictures

M Good morning, everyone. My name is Kyle, and I'll be leading you on today's hike. We'll be taking the Eagleview Trail. It is one of the most difficult trails in the park, so that's why we only offer it to experienced hikers. We'll start our hike at 9 o'clock, which is in about 10 minutes. Before then, feel free to _____ _____ to make sure it is in good condition.

2. What does the speaker say about the survey?

(A) It was taken too quickly.
(B) It was confusing to participants.
(C) It reflects everyone's opinion.
(D) It will be created by Gary.

3. What is the listener asked to do?

(A) Call the speaker
(B) Find detailed information
(C) Make a reservation
(D) Conduct another survey

M Hello, Gary. This is Stanley. _____ _____ on where to go for the company retreat this year. We really wanted everyone's opinion this year, and, thankfully, _____. Unfortunately, the beach you suggested was the least popular. But don't worry, the other places we are looking at apparently have a lot to do. I'll e-mail you the results in a minute. Please _____ _____ of the top two places. We can choose one after we know a bit more.

4. What will be the final activity?

(A) Taking a test
(B) Watching a video
(C) Reviewing a policy
(D) Having a discussion

5. What does the speaker ask the listeners to do?

(A) Sign a document
(B) Perform an inspection
(C) Write down questions
(D) Get into small groups

W Thank you all for coming in on a Saturday morning. Our insurance company has asked for some additions to our driving safety policy, so that is the reason for this class. At the end of the class, everyone is required to _____ _____ provided by the insurance company. It covers a few tips on how to avoid road accidents. Also, you should _____ _____ on the back of the handout before turning it in, to verify you've seen and understood the film.

대화를 듣고 알맞은 답을 고르세요.

1. What event are the listeners attending?

(A) A music class
(B) An awards ceremony
(C) A company picnic
(D) A community fund-raiser

2. What does the speaker remind the listeners to do?

(A) Show identification
(B) Join a mailing list
(C) Keep a ticket
(D) Pick up a gift

3. According to the speaker, why should the listeners visit a Web site?

(A) To register for an event
(B) To view some images
(C) To select a design
(D) To find out a winner

4. Where is the announcement taking place?

(A) On a cruise ship
(B) On a hotel shuttle
(C) At a bus terminal
(D) At an airport

5. According to the speaker, how will a project help travelers?

(A) By reducing ticket costs
(B) By adding more food options
(C) By making journeys shorter
(D) By expanding a parking area

6. What does the speaker encourage the listeners to do?

(A) Inspect their luggage
(B) Check for closures
(C) Purchase tickets early
(D) Go to a different entrance

7. What did the listener design?

(A) A video game
(B) A digital thermometer
(C) A security system
(D) A smartphone application

8. What does the speaker offer to do?

(A) Introduce a colleague
(B) Proofread a manual
(C) Print some paperwork
(D) Call a technician

9. Why does the speaker say, "a detailed manual will work"?

(A) To provide a guarantee
(B) To suggest canceling a session
(C) To promote a new design
(D) To justify a high fee

10. Which department does the speaker work in?

(A) Sales
(B) Accounting
(C) Personnel
(D) Purchasing

11. According to the speaker, what has caused a problem?

(A) Some items were not delivered on time.
(B) The supplier increased a price.
(C) Some workers are inexperienced.
(D) Some equipment is broken.

12. What does the speaker ask the listener to do?

(A) Change a packaging design
(B) Find workers for the weekend
(C) Attend a staff meeting
(D) Review a production goal

13. What is the purpose of the talk?

(A) To introduce a new employee
(B) To demonstrate a revised procedure
(C) To announce an upcoming inspection
(D) To report a production increase

14. What are the listeners invited to do?

(A) Clear any blocked exits
(B) Check the fire extinguishers
(C) Test the fire alarms
(D) Review emergency procedures

15. Who is Mr. Firth?

(A) An inspector
(B) A manager
(C) A firefighter
(D) A client

Item	Reference #
Table lamp	48-J
Wooden desk	60-P
Desk chair	72-W
File cabinet	91-C

16. Why did the speaker go to Tokyo?

(A) To lead a workshop
(B) To give a speech
(C) To inspect a facility
(D) To accept an award

17. Look at the graphic. Which reference number will arrive today?

(A) 48-J
(B) 60-P
(C) 72-W
(D) 91-C

18. What does the speaker invite the listener to do on Thursday?

(A) Attend a conference
(B) Try some product samples
(C) Look at some properties
(D) Meet a job candidate

PART 4

UNIT 05

핵심 포인트 | 1. 주로 마지막 문제로 출제되며, 담화 이후에 화자/청자가 할 일이나 앞으로 일어날 일을 묻는다.
2. 담화 후반부에서 화자가 미래 시제로 다음에 할 일을 말하거나, 시간이나 요일, 날짜 등의 특정 시점과 함께 향후 계획이 언급되는 부분을 주의 깊게 듣는다.

실전 맛보기

P4_U06_01

What will the listeners do next?	청자들은 다음에 무엇을 할 것인가?
(A) Work in small groups	**(A) 소그룹으로 활동하기**
(B) Sign some paperwork	(B) 서류에 서명하기
(C) Move to another room	(C) 다른 방으로 옮기기
(D) Enjoy some refreshments	(D) 다과 즐기기

W Good morning. My name is Anna Russel, and I'd like to welcome you all to Talbert Consulting. We had a lot of applicants for this year's recruitment drive, so congratulations on being selected. You all had a chance to chat during the staff breakfast, and I'd like to dive right into the orientation materials. Let's start by completing the first activity in the handbook in groups of three or four people. You can get together with the people sitting around you. If you have any questions, I'll be walking around the room.

여 안녕하세요. 제 이름은 안나 러셀이고, 여러분 모두 탤버트 컨설팅 사와 함께하게 되신 것을 환영합니다. 올해의 채용 행사에 많은 분들이 지원하셨기에, 선발되신 것을 축하드립니다. 여러분 모두 직원 조찬 동안 담소를 나눌 기회를 가지셨으니, 오리엔테이션 자료로 바로 들어가겠습니다. 서너 명으로 조를 이뤄서 안내서의 첫 번째 활동을 완수하는 것으로 시작하겠습니다. 주변에 앉은 사람들과 모이면 됩니다. 질문이 있으시면, 제가 방을 돌아다니고 있을 때 하시면 됩니다.

CHECK UP

P4_U06_02 정답 및 해설 p.240

1. What will the speaker most likely do next?

(A) Present an award
(B) Take a group photo
(C) Introduce some donors
(D) Conduct a tour

2. What will happen on August 11?

(A) A group interview will be held.
(B) A contract will be renewed.
(C) A special offer will end.
(D) A new branch will open.

빈출 질문

다음에 할 일

What will the speaker/listeners do next? 화자는/청자들은 다음에 무엇을 할 것인가?

What does the speaker plan to do? 화자는 무엇을 하려고 계획하는가?

다음에 일어날 일

What will happen in/at/on ~? ~에(서) 무슨 일이 일어날 것인가?

What will take place after ~? ~한 다음에 무슨 일이 일어날 것인가?

빈출 단서

계획	**I'll ~ / I'm going to ~ / You'll get to ~ / 주어 will be -ing**
	I'm going to show you a short video about how quickly these solar panels can be put onto your buildings.
	이 태양 전지판이 여러분의 건물에 얼마나 빠르게 설치될 수 있는지에 관한 짧은 영상을 보여드리겠습니다.
	▶ 다음에 할 일: Watch a video 영상 시청하기
의무	**We need to ~ / 주어 should ~ / It's time to ~**
	We need to choose a new board member, so Madeleine is passing around ballots now.
	우리는 새로운 임원을 결정해야 하므로, 지금 매들린이 투표용지를 나누어 주고 있습니다.
	▶ 다음에 할 일: Vote for a board member 임원을 위해 투표하기
제안	**Let's (start by) ~ / Let me ~ / I'd like us to ~**
	Let's start by looking at the types of tables we offer on our online catalog.
	우리가 온라인 카탈로그에서 제공하는 테이블 종류를 살펴보는 것으로 시작해 봅시다.
	▶ 다음에 할 일: Look at a catalog 카탈로그 보기
요청	**Please ~ / 명령문**
	Please take a moment and sign the new employee documents.
	잠시 시간을 내서 신규 직원 서류에 서명해 주세요.
	▶ 다음에 할 일: Sign some documents 서류에 서명하기
특정 시점	**시간 / 요일 / 날짜 / Before/After ~**
	This offer is only good until May 20. 이 가격 할인은 5월 20일까지만 유효합니다.
	▶ 5월 20일에 일어날 일: A special offer will end. 특별 할인이 끝날 것이다.

고득점 TIP

다음에 할 일이나 일어날 일을 묻는 문제가 나오면, 담화 속에서 분위기를 환기하는 표현을 잘 듣는다.

Now ~ / Next ~ / Before moving to the next part ~ / Before we continue ~

M You can explore the exhibition at your own pace later. But now, let's turn left here and take a look at the video screen, which is showing a brief film.

남 여러분은 나중에 자신에게 맞는 속도로 전시회를 둘러보실 수 있습니다. 하지만 지금은 왼쪽으로 돌아서 비디오 화면을 보죠. 짧은 영화가 상영되고 있습니다.

Q What will the listeners do next? 청자들은 다음에 무엇을 할 것인가?

A View a film 영화 보기

[1-4] 질문과 정답을 확인한 뒤, 대화를 들으면서 정답의 단서가 되는 부분에 표시하세요.

1. **Q** What will the listeners most likely do next?
A Watch another video

> **W** So, whenever you receive a customer complaint, please transfer the call to a supervisor right away. The next video in this training session will show you how to do so on our phone system. It will load automatically in just a moment.

2. **Q** What will the speaker do next?
A Give a demonstration

> **M** Before the items are packaged, they must be weighed carefully on our scale, which is by the entrance. Let me take you there now to show you the features of the scale and how to reset it before each weighing session. There are just a few steps, so I don't think you'll have any issues with it.

3. **Q** What will happen on Monday?
A New labels will be used.

> **W** We have recently partnered with Brenson Couriers to improve the speed of our deliveries. We will be adopting their tracking system, so we must use their labels on the packages we are processing. Therefore, on Monday morning, every workstation will need to be restocked with their labels.

4. **Q** What will the listeners most likely do next?
A Go on a tour

> **M** Our firm has been growing rapidly, so it's great to welcome you all to the team. Now, a lot of new employees find the layout of this building to be very confusing. So, let's start by showing you around the different rooms that you'll need to be familiar with.

[5-6] 대화를 듣고 정답의 단서가 알맞게 패러프레이징된 답을 고르세요.

5. What will happen next?

(A) Some prizes will be given out.
(B) Some paperwork will be completed.

6. What will the speaker do next?

(A) Create survey questions
(B) Distribute information

대화를 듣고 알맞은 답을 고른 뒤, 다시 들으면서 빈칸을 채우세요.

1. What are the listeners asked to do next?

(A) Come up with some ideas
(B) Read a sales report
(C) Sample some products
(D) View a chart

M My name is Joshua Ellis, and I'm a market analyst from Conway Analytics. I've been researching the possible reasons for the slow sales of your new line of low-fat yogurts. Although people enjoy the taste, it seems that there are not very many flavor options. That's why consumers are choosing other brands. So, I'd like us to _____ _____ that you think would be popular. Then we'll see how those compare to what's currently available.

2. Who most likely are the listeners?

(A) Event managers
(B) Science experts
(C) Software developers
(D) Journalists

3. What does the speaker say will happen next month?

(A) A building will undergo renovations.
(B) A new product will be released.
(C) Members will gather for a meal.
(D) A Web site will be launched.

W I think this is one of the best meetings I've ever had with distinguished _____. Before we end this meeting, I want to mention a few things. First, our next meeting will be held at the Grand Convention Center on Parker Street on Friday, September 21, which is two days later than what we had originally planned. So, don't forget to update your calendars. Also, remember that we need some volunteers _____ _____. Please visit our Web site for more details.

4. What does the speaker say about last Saturday?

(A) An event had to be canceled.
(B) The site was closed in the morning.
(C) They received some referrals.
(D) There weren't enough volunteers.

M Hi, this message is for Stella Weiss. This is Gerald from the animal rescue shelter. I want to thank you so much for volunteering at our adoption event last Saturday. _____ _____, your presence really meant a lot. You expressed interest in coming in a few mornings a week, right? I think we can find a regular task for you. I'll _____ of what needs to be done. Call me back and let me know which one you'd like to sign up for. Thanks!

5. What will the speaker most likely do next?

(A) Check a policy
(B) Call a staff member
(C) Send a document
(D) Complete a registration form

대화를 듣고 알맞은 답을 고르세요.

1. What will happen at 11 o'clock?

(A) Some job interviews will take place.
(B) Some winners will be announced.
(C) A press conference will be held.
(D) A flight from Chicago will depart.

2. What was the speaker supposed to do?

(A) Donate some money
(B) Join a competition
(C) Present at a conference
(D) Conduct an interview

3. Why does the speaker say, "Diana worked on the project"?

(A) To reject a colleague's criticism
(B) To correct a misunderstanding
(C) To show appreciation for some help
(D) To suggest a replacement

4. What is the broadcast about?

(A) Social media
(B) Résumé writing
(C) Career classes
(D) Internet security

5. What did Pamela Abbot do in February?

(A) She traveled overseas.
(B) She published a book.
(C) She launched a Web site.
(D) She attended a workshop.

6. According to the speaker, what will happen tonight?

(A) An agreement will be signed.
(B) A registration period will begin.
(C) An award winner will be announced.
(D) A video will be uploaded.

7. Where most likely are the listeners?

(A) At an art institute
(B) At a museum
(C) At a research laboratory
(D) At a gardening shop

8. According to the speaker, what information on a lable is incorrect?

(A) The material
(B) The weight
(C) The date of creation
(D) The country of origin

9. What will the listeners do next?

(A) Have some refreshments
(B) Write down some questions
(C) Take some pictures
(D) Visit a gift shop

10. According to the speaker, what will take place next week?

(A) A music festival
(B) A career fair
(C) A sports competition
(D) An anniversary party

11. What industry does the speaker most likely work in?

(A) Transportation
(B) Finance
(C) Technology
(D) Medicine

12. Why should the listeners talk to the speaker?

(A) To ask questions about a policy
(B) To suggest some improvements
(C) To volunteer for an extra shift
(D) To schedule a training session

13. Why did the speaker call a meeting?

(A) To ask for volunteers
(B) To prepare for a conference
(C) To discuss a vacation policy
(D) To introduce a new product

14. What benefit does the speaker mention?

(A) Some paper forms are easier to read.
(B) Employees can save a lot of time.
(C) The company will be more profitable.
(D) Customers will be more satisfied.

15. What will Bernard do next?

(A) Distribute a handout
(B) Explain a sign-in process
(C) Present a financial report
(D) Introduce a speaker

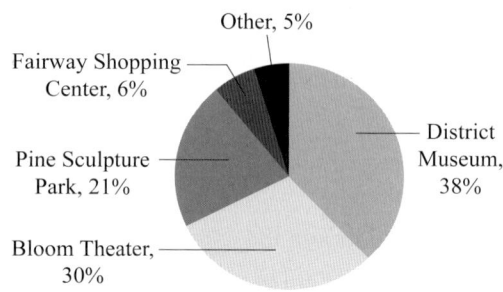

16. Who is the speaker?

(A) A food vendor
(B) A business consultant
(C) A city official
(D) An event coordinator

17. Look at the graphic. Which location does not have an ice cream shop?

(A) Fairway Shopping Center
(B) Pine Sculpture Park
(C) Bloom Theater
(D) District Museum

18. What does the speaker plan to do?

(A) Conduct another survey
(B) Assess rental options
(C) Introduce new flavors
(D) Adjust a price

PART 4 UNIT 06

핵심 포인트

1. 제시된 인용구의 앞뒤 대사에 특히 주목하고, 어조에서 드러나는 화자의 감정 또한 중요한 단서가 될 수 있으므로 주의 깊게 듣는다.
2. 문장의 문맥상 의미가 아닌 일부 사전적 의미를 이용한 그럴듯한 오답에 주의한다.

실전 맛보기 ∩ P4_U07_01

Why does the speaker say, "this event is great for our community"?

(A) To encourage the listeners to volunteer
(B) To show agreement with the listeners' comments
(C) To remind the listeners about a schedule change
(D) To thank the listeners for their suggestions

화자는 왜 "이 행사는 우리 지역사회에 매우 좋은 것입니다"라고 말하는가?

(A) 청자들에게 자원봉사를 하라고 권하기 위해
(B) 청자들의 의견에 동의를 표하기 위해
(C) 청자들에게 일정 변경을 상기시키기 위해
(D) 제안에 대해 청자들에게 감사하기 위해

M Alright, before you begin exploring the national park on your own, I'd like to tell you about our upcoming mountain bike race. It is amazing how much planning has to go into such an event… for example, setting up the trails, providing refreshments, directing the athletes, and cleaning up afterward. If you would like to donate your time, there are sign-up forms at the visitor center. Don't forget… this event is great for our community. Anyway, I hope you enjoy the rest of your time at the park and that you visit again soon.

남 좋습니다, 여러분이 독자적으로 국립공원 탐방을 시작하기 전에, 다가오는 저희 산악자전거 경주에 대해 말씀드리겠습니다. 이런 행사에는 놀라울 정도로 많은 계획이 필요합니다 … 예를 들면, 코스 준비, 다과 제공, 선수 안내, 끝난 후 청소 같은 것들입니다. 여러분의 시간을 기부하고 싶으시면, 방문객 센터에 신청서가 있습니다. 잊지 마세요… 이 행사는 우리 지역사회에 매우 좋은 것입니다. 어쨌든, 남은 시간 공원에서 즐겁게 보내시고 여러분이 곧 다시 찾아 주시기를 바랍니다.

CHECK UP ∩ P4_U07_02 정답 및 해설 p.248

1. What does the speaker mean when she says, "this artist is very popular"?

   (A) An event is expected to be crowded.
   (B) Some artwork will increase in value.
   (C) The proposed price is fair.
   (D) Some items will probably sell quickly.

2. Why does the speaker say, "what people like about our business is the friendly service"?

   (A) To justify a price
   (B) To give reassurance
   (C) To reject a suggestion
   (D) To praise the listener

의미 / 암시하는 것

What does the speaker mean when she says, "~"? 화자는 "~"라고 말할 때 무엇을 의미하는가?

What does the speaker imply when he says, "~"? 화자는 "~"라고 말할 때 무엇을 암시하는가?

목적

Why does the speaker say, "~"? 화자는 왜 "~"라고 말하는가?

빈출 의도

설명	Unfortunately, the hallway lights will not be installed today. We noticed a major crack in the ceiling, which we need to investigate further. It could be related to the lighting situation.
	안타깝게도, 복도 조명은 오늘 설치되지 않을 것입니다. 우리는 천장에 큰 균열이 있는 것을 발견했는데, 그 균열을 더 조사해 보아야 합니다. 그것은 조명과 관련되어 있을 수 있습니다.
	▶ 목적: To explain why some work will be delayed 일부 작업이 지연되는 이유를 설명하기 위해
강조	In February, Jane Hammel opened a small consulting firm from her home. Now just six months later, her company has over 50 major clients. We'll be talking to Ms. Hammel today to find out more about her journey.
	2월에, 제인 하멜은 그녀의 집에서 작은 컨설팅 회사를 열었습니다. 겨우 6개월이 지난 지금, 그녀의 회사에는 50명 이상의 주요 고객이 있습니다. 우리는 오늘 하멜 씨의 여정에 대해 더 알아보기 위해 그녀와 이야기를 나눌 것입니다.
	▶ 의미: A business is successful. 사업이 성공적이다.
권장	The original owner of the site was a big fan of horse-riding, and you'll see as we move outside how the grounds are perfectly suited for this hobby. Remember, admission to Danbury Manor includes unguided access to the horse stables.
	이 지역의 원래 주인은 승마의 열성 팬이었고, 우리가 밖으로 이동할 때 여러분은 그 장소가 어떻게 이 취미에 완벽하게 들어맞는 곳인지 알게 될 것입니다. 기억하세요, 댄버리 저택의 입장권에는 마구간으로의 자유로운 접근이 포함되어 있습니다.
	▶ 목적: To encourage the listeners to explore the horse stables 청자들이 마구간을 살펴보도록 장려하기 위해
안심	Our office building will look much better after the renovations. Now, I've heard employees say that the construction will make it difficult to focus on their tasks. Well, work will only take place on weekends.
	우리 사옥은 개조 후에 훨씬 더 좋아 보일 것입니다. 자, 저는 직원들이 공사가 업무에 집중하기 어렵게 만들 거라고 말하는 것을 들었는데요. 음, 작업은 주말에만 있을 것입니다.
	▶ 목적: To provide reassurance 안심시키기 위해
정정	Thanks for leaving an online review and giving a five-star rating for the washing machine's quality. But we were surprised by one thing. You wrote that you wish the washing machine had a delay timer. The Pro-Wash model has that feature.
	온라인 후기를 남겨 주시고 세탁기 품질에 별 5개 등급을 주셔서 감사합니다. 그런데 저희는 한 가지 사실에 놀랐습니다. 당신은 세탁기에 시간 지연 타이머가 있었으면 좋겠다고 썼습니다. 프로워시 모델에는 그 기능이 있습니다.
	▶ 목적: To correct a misunderstanding 오해를 바로잡기 위해

방법	We've already called in a technician to make the necessary repairs, and he will be here shortly. Despite this issue, we need to stay on schedule with your appointments. There are two associates at the front desk. 우리는 필요한 수리를 하기 위해 이미 기술자를 불렀고, 그가 곧 도착할 것입니다. 이러한 문제에도 불구하고, 우리는 여러분의 예약 일정에 맞추어야 합니다. 프런트에 직원 두 명이 있습니다. ▶ 목적: To give the listeners instructions 청자들에게 안내사항을 전달하기 위해
가능	Adding solar panels to buildings in this district was previously prohibited, as officials were worried it might ruin the historic atmosphere. However, some new members were elected to the city council recently. It's worth looking into. 이 지역의 건물들에 태양 전지판을 설치하는 것은 이전에는 금지되었는데, 공무원들이 그것이 역사적인 분위기를 망칠 수 있다고 우려했기 때문입니다. 하지만, 최근에 몇몇 새로운 의원들이 시의회에 선출되었습니다. 그것은 주의 깊게 살펴볼 가치가 있습니다. ▶ 의미: A policy could change. 정책이 변경될 수 있다.
불가능	I would love for you to visit our site and learn more about our operations. I'd like to arrange that, so please let me know when is convenient for you. Just keep in mind our company will be going through an annual inspection on July 7. 저는 당신이 현장에 방문하셔서 저희 사업을 좀 더 봐 주시면 좋겠습니다. 그것의 일정을 잡고 싶으니, 언제가 편하신지 제게 알려 주세요. 저희 회사는 7월 7일에 연례 점검을 받을 예정이라는 것만 기억해 주세요. ▶ 목적: To indicate unavailability 불가능을 나타내기 위해
기타	We'll take the shuttle from the airport to the train station, and our train is scheduled to depart at 1:25 P.M. I wish we had time to explore the unique shops that are found all around the station. But let's just say, we won't be doing any shopping. 우리는 공항에서 기차역까지 셔틀을 탈 것이고, 우리 열차는 오후 1시 25분에 출발할 예정입니다. 저는 우리에게 역 주변에 있는 독특한 가게들을 둘러볼 시간이 있었으면 좋겠습니다. 하지만 말씀드리죠, 우리는 쇼핑은 하지 않을 것입니다. ▶ 의미: Time will be limited. 시간이 제한될 것이다.

고득점 TIP

다른 사람을 칭찬하는 말은 그 사람이 앞으로 어떠한 일을 해낼 것임을 나타내려는 의도로 많이 쓰인다.

M We plan to promote the new loyalty program for our airline on several social media platforms. This will be the best way to advertise its features. Now, some of you may be wondering about having to take on additional work. Fortunately, Ling is a social media expert.

남 우리는 몇몇 소셜 미디어 플랫폼에서 우리 항공사의 새로운 고객 보상 프로그램을 홍보할 계획입니다. 이는 그것의 특징을 광고하는 가장 좋은 방법일 것입니다. 자, 여러분 중 일부는 추가적으로 업무를 맡아야 하는지에 대해 궁금해할지도 모릅니다. 다행스럽게도, 링이 소셜 미디어 전문가입니다.

Q What does the speaker mean when he says, "Ling is a social media expert"?
화자는 "링이 소셜 미디어 전문가입니다"라고 말할 때 무엇을 의미하는가?

A Ling will complete a project. 링이 프로젝트를 완수할 것이다.

대화를 듣고 알맞은 답을 고른 뒤, 다시 들으면서 빈칸을 채우세요.

1. Why does the speaker say, "they don't know who made it"?

(A) To ask for a correction
(B) To correct a misunderstanding
(C) To suggest a different process
(D) To request some information

M Welcome, everyone, to the semi-final round of our televised baking contest. We have just five bakers left in our competition, and after today, it will be four. These bakers have really shown their talent throughout the competition. Now, a lot of people think that _____ _____. But don't forget, when they taste the food, they don't know who made it. That way, _____ at all times.

2. Why does the speaker say, "I know what you're thinking"?

(A) To make a complaint
(B) To address some confusion
(C) To explain a delay
(D) To refuse an offer

3. What can the listeners do at the museum?

(A) See a reproduction of the old city
(B) Attend a history lecture
(C) Watch a video on Bristol
(D) Purchase photos from long ago

W Welcome to today's Walking Tour of Historical Bristol. We're here on Luther Avenue. Now, I know what you're thinking, the buildings on your left are _____ than the buildings on your right. Actually, there used to be a wall here, and these buildings were built at different times. Due to population growth, the wall was knocked down to make room for new housing. At the end of this tour, we'll visit the history museum, where we can see a model that _____.

4. What does the speaker give to the listeners?

(A) An itinerary
(B) A visitor's pass
(C) Building maps
(D) Advertising pamphlets

5. What does the speaker imply when she says, "I'll double-check that"?

(A) She thinks some financial figures are incorrect.
(B) She does not know the clients' interests.
(C) She will verify that the weather will be nice.
(D) She is concerned about some contract terms.

W Here you go. These are all the _____ _____ in the Chicago area. We need to build a strong relationship with our clients through a special activity. So far, we've spent all of our time in meetings, so we haven't been able to get any closer to them. Thankfully, I think _____ _____, so we can do an outdoor activity if we want. Just in case, I'll double-check that. Please let me know what you might prefer.

PART 4

UNIT 07

대화를 듣고 알맞은 답을 고르세요.

1. What event will take place in August?

(A) An annual parade
(B) A park cleanup project
(C) An art festival
(D) A fund-raising dinner

2. What does the speaker mean when he says, "there is another major event that day"?

(A) A site is not available.
(B) A goal may not be reached.
(C) An event date will be changed.
(D) Traffic congestion is expected.

3. What will the listeners do next?

(A) View a map
(B) Select a venue
(C) Discuss some posters
(D) Have some refreshments

4. Which department does the speaker most likely work for?

(A) Finance
(B) Graphic design
(C) Maintenance
(D) Public relations

5. What does the speaker imply when he says, "We can work around that"?

(A) A business trip has been approved.
(B) A receipt is not always required.
(C) A work schedule is flexible.
(D) A budget is large enough.

6. What did the speaker send in an e-mail?

(A) An upcoming event
(B) A new assignment
(C) A credit card application
(D) A company policy

7. Where does the speaker most likely work?

(A) At an architecture firm
(B) At a publishing company
(C) At a laboratory
(D) At a department store

8. Why does the speaker say, "The office was full every weekend"?

(A) To complain about a parking issue
(B) To suggest moving to a new building
(C) To emphasize the listeners' hard work
(D) To confirm an attendance list

9. What does the speaker remind the listeners about?

(A) How to treat sensitive information
(B) Where to find a company's Web site
(C) Who will be eligible for a project
(D) When to turn in some forms

10. What did the speaker do for the listener?

(A) Send a document
(B) Recommend a shop
(C) Clean a garment
(D) Issue a refund

11. What does the speaker mean when she says, "it's already 4:30"?

(A) A task took longer than she anticipated.
(B) There is not much time left before an event.
(C) She would like to postpone a meeting.
(D) She is late for an appointment.

12. What does the speaker offer to do?

(A) Deliver an item
(B) Supply an estimate
(C) Contact a client
(D) Cancel a reservation

13. Where does the speaker work?

(A) At a software company
(B) At a sporting goods store
(C) At a medical clinic
(D) At a manufacturing facility

14. Why does the speaker say, "this is not our usual display"?

(A) To thank the listeners
(B) To criticize a mistake
(C) To justify a timeline
(D) To reject a request

15. What does the speaker say will happen on Friday?

(A) A celebrity will sign autographs.
(B) A journalist will visit the business.
(C) A discount will go into effect.
(D) A television commercial will be filmed.

16. What is being advertised?

(A) A uniform manufacturer
(B) A laundry service
(C) A cleaning company
(D) A landscaping firm

17. What does the speaker imply when she says, "This never happens in the industry"?

(A) The service was out of date.
(B) Some information may be incorrect.
(C) There are a lot of customers.
(D) The special offer is impressive.

18. According to the speaker, what can be found on a Web site?

(A) A map of locations
(B) Feedback from customers
(C) An employee directory
(D) Promotional items

핵심 포인트

1. 목록/표, 지도/평면도, 그래프, 쿠폰, 기타 그림 등의 다양한 시각 자료가 나올 수 있다. 모든 시각 자료는 담화가 나오기 전에 미리 읽고 키워드를 파악해 두어야 한다.
2. 선택지와 상응하는 네 가지 항목이 담화에서 언급되는 부분에 주목한다. 최고/최저를 나타내는 표현이나 순서, 위치, 방향 등을 나타내는 표현 또한 주의 깊게 들어야 한다.

실전 맛보기

🎧 P4_U08_01

Westfall Bank Services	
Counter 1	Withdrawals and deposits
Counter 2	Opening an account
Counter 3	Foreign currency exchange
Counter 4	Loan applications

Look at the graphic. Which counter is experiencing additional delays?

(A) Counter 1
(B) Counter 2
(C) Counter 3
(D) Counter 4

웨스트폴 은행 서비스	
1번 창구	입출금
2번 창구	계좌 개설
3번 창구	환전
4번 창구	대출 신청

시각 자료를 보시오. 어떤 창구가 추가 지연을 겪고 있는가?

(A) 1번 창구
(B) 2번 창구
(C) 3번 창구
(D) 4번 창구

M Thank you for visiting Westfall Bank. We'd like to remind you to line up for the correct counter according to the sign. Also, please note that we are having some software issues. So, if you are here to open a new account, you may have to wait longer than expected. We apologize for the inconvenience and hope to resolve the problem soon. Also, if you are applying for a loan, be sure that you have all of the correct paperwork with you before you speak to a staff member. Thank you.

남 웨스트폴 은행을 방문해 주셔서 감사합니다. 안내판에 따라 정확한 창구에 줄을 서 주실 것을 다시 한번 알려 드립니다. 또한, 일부 소프트웨어 문제가 있다는 것을 알아 두시기 바랍니다. 따라서, 신규 계좌를 개설하러 오셨다면, 예상보다 오래 기다리셔야 할 수도 있습니다. 불편을 드려 죄송하며 곧 문제를 해결하기를 희망합니다. 또한, 대출을 신청하시려면, 직원과 상담하기 전에 반드시 정확한 서류를 모두 지참해 주시기 바랍니다. 감사합니다.

시각 자료 연계 세부사항

Look at the graphic. What/Which/Who/Where/When/How ~?

시각 자료를 보시오. 무엇이/어떤 것이/누가/어디에서/언제/어떻게 ~?

빈출 단서

항목명	

① 직접 언급

All of the bus fares are more expensive now except for the fare for the North Route, which has not increased. 인상되지 않은 북부 노선을 제외하면 이제 모든 버스 요금은 더 비쌉니다.

▶ 인상되지 않은 요금: $4.50

Downtown Route	$3.75
North Route	$4.50
East Route	$4.00
West Route	$3.25

② 간접 언급

I saw you listed on the employee directory page for the Rivendell Herald. It seemed that you'd be the right person for this matter. I'd like to get news coverage for a local business I'm opening. It's a bakery that makes cakes for any occasion. I'm wondering if you would be willing to write an article about us.

저는 리벤델 헤럴드의 직원 명부 페이지에 당신이 기재되어 있는 걸 봤어요. 당신이 이 문제에 적임자인 것 같았습니다. 제가 개업하는 지역 사업체의 뉴스 보도를 받고 싶어요. 모든 행사를 위한 케이크를 만드는 제과점이에요. 당신이 우리에 대한 기사를 쓸 의향이 있는지 궁금합니다.

▶ 메시지 대상: Robert Norton

Rivendell Herald Employee Directory	
Harvey Snyder	Sports Editor
Marta Zavala	Art Critic
Robert Norton	Business Reporter
Eve Lanigan	Science News

순서	

the first / the second / the last / before / after

For those of you who didn't hear the announcement earlier, the session right after lunch today has been canceled.

아까 공지를 못 들으신 분들을 위해 말씀드리자면, 오늘 점심 식사 직후의 세션은 취소되었습니다.

▶ 취소된 세션: Using Color

Product Design Workshops	
10 A.M.	Copyright Issues
11 A.M.	Design Tools
Noon	Lunch
1 P.M.	Using Color
2 P.M.	Brand Identity

위치 / 방향	**next to / between / in front of / across from / leading to / on the corner of** Let's go there now so you can drop off your belongings. It's next to the elevator, right across from the reference library. 지금 그곳으로 가서 여러분의 짐을 내려놓을 수 있도록 하죠. 그곳은 엘리베이터 옆이고, 자료실 바로 맞은편에 있습니다.

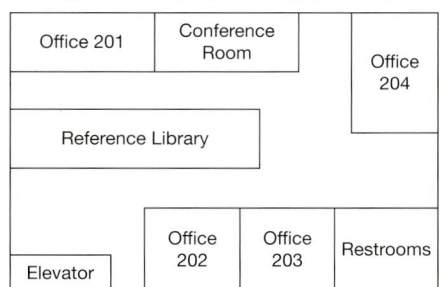

▶ 지금 갈 사무실: Office 202

최상급 / 비교급	**the most expensive / the least popular / the highest / the largest / more than** It's no surprise that the largest group was concerned about the cost. However, we plan to focus on the least popular factor. At 17 percent, there is still an opportunity to reach a lot of customers. 가장 큰 집단이 비용을 염려한 것은 놀랄 일이 아닙니다. 하지만, 우리는 가장 대중적이지 않은 요소에 초점을 맞출 계획입니다. 그것은 17%로, 여전히 많은 고객들에게 다가갈 수 있는 기회가 있습니다.

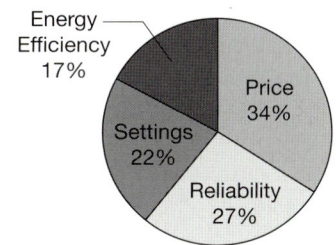

▶ 목표로 삼을 요소: Energy Efficiency

고득점 TIP

지도나 배치도에서는 위치, 방향뿐만 아니라 공간 크기에 차이가 없는지도 미리 봐 두는 것이 좋다.

W Medina Incorporated has reserved three of our private rooms. However, we can still accept regular customers, as the smallest room has not been booked. Service in that room will continue as usual.

여 메디나 사에서 우리의 프라이빗룸 세 개를 예약했습니다. 하지만, 가장 작은 방은 예약되지 않았기 때문에, 우리는 여전히 일반 손님들도 받을 수 있습니다. 그 방에서 서비스는 평소와 같이 계속될 것입니다.

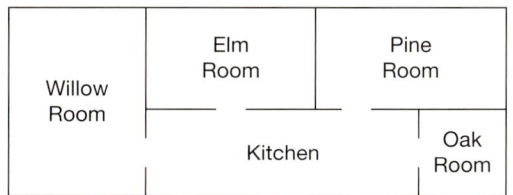

Q Look at the graphic. Which room can regular customers use?
시각 자료를 보시오. 일반 손님들은 어느 방을 이용할 수 있는가?

A Oak Room 오크룸

대화를 듣고 알맞은 답을 고른 뒤, 다시 들으면서 빈칸을 채우세요.

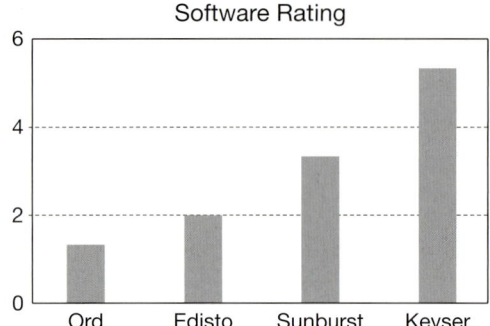

Software Rating

| Ord | Edisto | Sunburst | Keyser |

M I have some good news, everyone. We had some surplus funds in the budget, so I was able to buy some new accounting software for our company. I looked into several programs. In the end, I decided to _____ _____. It had a lot of additional features that I think we will find useful. I'll start inputting our financial records into the new software from tomorrow.

1. Look at the graphic. Which accounting software did the speaker purchase?

(A) Ord
(B) Edisto
(C) Sunburst
(D) Keyser

Interior Paints	
Brand of Paint	**Price**
Blake Interior Latex	$29.99
Stroop Interior Latex	$31.99
Smith-Wright Interior Latex	$32.99
Lance Paints Acrylic Latex	$34.99

M Hello, Mr. Walker. This is Victor from Blake Hardware. I just spoke to our supplier, and the paint you ordered this morning is going to come in later than expected. We would deliver it on Wednesday instead of Monday. As an apology, I'll _____. I understand if you want to cancel your order instead. However, Smith-Wright does have the best quality in paint, so I think _____ _____. If you have any questions, please call me back at 555-3574. Thank you.

2. What does the speaker offer to do?

(A) Contact a supplier
(B) Cancel a fee
(C) Send an invoice
(D) Recommend a product

3. Look at the graphic. How much will Mr. Walker pay for his order?

(A) $29.99
(B) $31.99
(C) $32.99
(D) $34.99

PART 4

UNIT 08

실전 문제

대화를 듣고 알맞은 답을 고르세요.

Renway Business Complex

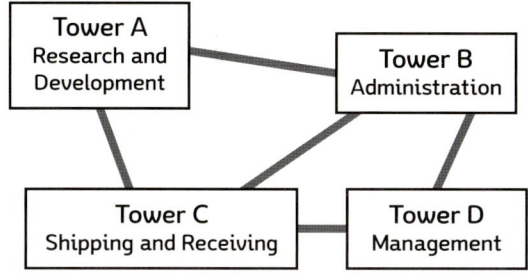

TRAINING SCHEDULE	
Time	**Presenter and Topic**
8:00-8:15	Ms. Lions: Introduction
8:15-8:45	Mr. Scott: Getting Started
8:45-9:30	Mr. Ben: Advanced Features
9:30-10:00	Ms. Lockhart: Personalization

1. Why did the speaker take a long time to reply?

(A) She had a lot of business meetings.
(B) She was unsure about her schedule.
(C) She lost the listener's contact details.
(D) She did not get a message.

2. What products does the listener's company sell?

(A) Furniture
(B) Jewelry
(C) Kitchenware
(D) Cosmetics

3. Look at the graphic. Where will the speaker meet the listener on Wednesday?

(A) At Tower A
(B) At Tower B
(C) At Tower C
(D) At Tower D

4. What will the listeners learn about?

(A) A messaging system
(B) A research database
(C) A graphic design program
(D) A security alarm

5. What are the listeners asked to do?

(A) Practice using a system
(B) Review a manual
(C) Complete a survey
(D) Attend a reception

6. Look at the graphic. What topic will Mr. Thomas cover?

(A) Introduction
(B) Getting Started
(C) Advanced Features
(D) Personalization

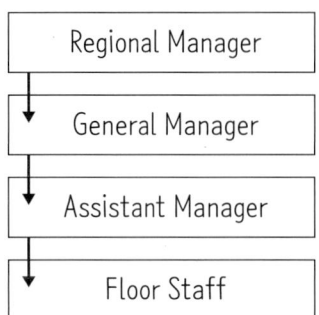

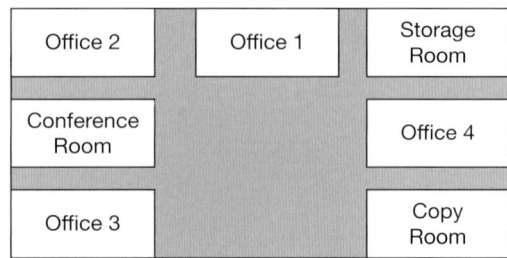

7. According to the speaker, what has caused a problem?

(A) Lack of applicants
(B) Heavier workload
(C) Untrained employees
(D) Outdated technology

8. Look at the graphic. Which position was recently added?

(A) Regional Manager
(B) General Manager
(C) Assistant Manager
(D) Floor Staff

9. What will the speaker do after the meeting?

(A) Post a document
(B) Send an e-mail
(C) Apply to a program
(D) Update a Web site

10. Look at the graphic. Which office will the manager most likely take?

(A) Office 1
(B) Office 2
(C) Office 3
(D) Office 4

11. Why did the speaker call the furniture company?

(A) To address a complaint
(B) To order extra lamps
(C) To ask for a refund
(D) To change an address

12. What does the speaker say about the lighting?

(A) The wrong size was chosen.
(B) The style was perfect for the room.
(C) Too many items were ordered.
(D) The price was not affordable.

PART 4 UNIT 08

UNIT 09 전화 메시지

핵심 포인트 │ 1. 전화 건 사람이 수신자에게 남긴 음성 메시지가 주로 나오며, 회사나 공공기관의 자동 응답 메시지도 가끔 출제된다. 인사말 및 화자 소개 → 전화 목적 및 세부사항 → 요청사항의 흐름으로 전개되는 경우가 많다.
2. 메시지의 목적이나 화자/청자의 정보를 묻는 문제가 자주 출제된다.

실전 맛보기
🎧 P4_U09_01

W Hi, Ms. Brantley. ¹This is Amika Sano from Hartland Bank. I'm currently processing your application for a loan for your bakery. I have most of the information that I need. However, ²you forgot to submit your business plan. So, please send one to me as soon as possible. ³It should be in a specific format. We've created some samples for our customers' reference. They are available on our Web site. If you need extra help, please feel free to get in touch. My number is 555-7935.

여 안녕하세요, 브랜틀리 씨. ¹하트랜드 은행의 아미카 사노입니다. 지금 당신의 제과점을 위한 대출 신청을 처리 중입니다. 필요한 정보가 대부분 제게 있어요. 하지만, ²당신은 사업 계획서 제출을 잊으셨어요. 그러니 최대한 빨리 제게 그것을 보내 주세요. ³그것은 특별한 형식을 갖추어야 합니다. 저희가 고객들이 참고할 수 있도록 몇몇 샘플들을 만들었습니다. 그것들은 저희 웹사이트에서 이용할 수 있습니다. 추가로 도움이 필요하시면, 언제든 연락 주세요. 제 번호는 555-7935입니다.

1. Which field does the speaker work in? 화자
   Finance

2. What should the listener send to the speaker?
   A business plan 세부사항

3. Why does the speaker say, "They are available on our Web site"? 화자의 의도 파악
   To suggest using some documents as a guide

1. 화자는 어떤 분야에서 일하는가?
   금융

2. 청자는 화자에게 무엇을 보내야 하는가?
   사업 계획서

3. 화자는 왜 "그것들은 저희 웹사이트에서 이용할 수 있습니다"라고 말하는가?
   문서를 길잡이로 이용할 것을 제안하기 위해

CHECK UP
🎧 P4_U09_02 정답 및 해설 p.259

1. What service does the speaker's company provide?
   (A) Appliance repair
   (B) Furniture rental
   (C) Musical entertainment
   (D) Business accounting

2. Why is the speaker unable to fulfill a request?
   (A) A vehicle is not working.
   (B) An employee is absent.
   (C) Some supplies are sold out.
   (D) Some instructions were unclear.

3. What does the speaker offer to do?
   (A) Issue a refund
   (B) Give a demonstration
   (C) Come to work early
   (D) Provide a discount

빈출 상황

예약/주문 확인	I'm calling from Morgan's Dental Clinic with some important information about your upcoming appointment this Friday at 2 P.M. 이번 주 금요일 오후 2시에 있을 예약에 대한 중요한 정보가 있어서 모건 치과에서 전화 드립니다.
채용 제안	Thank you again for applying to our company. Good news, we'd like to offer you the position. 저희 회사에 지원해 주셔서 다시 한번 감사합니다. 좋은 소식은, 귀하께 일자리를 제안 드리고 싶습니다.
업무 논의	I'd like to get together to discuss some ideas about making the business district more attractive for the winter season. 겨울 시즌을 맞아 상업 지역을 더 매력적으로 만드는 것에 대한 논의를 하기 위해 모였으면 좋겠어요.
휴점 안내	This summer, our building is closed for major renovations. 이번 여름에, 저희 건물은 대대적인 보수공사로 인해 문을 닫습니다.

빈출 표현

🎧 P4_U09_03

returning your call 답신 전화를 하는	be closed until ~까지 문을 닫다
look for ~을 찾다	apologize for the inconvenience 불편에 대해 사과하다
arrange for 준비하다	out of town 도시를 떠나 있는
set up a time 시간을 잡다	give someone a call ~에게 전화를 하다
confirm one's appointment 예약을 확정하다	reach someone ~에게 연락하다
schedule a meeting 회의를 잡다	receive an e-mail 이메일을 받다
make arrangements 준비하다	ahead of time 예정보다 빨리
put in an order 주문하다	upcoming event 곧 있을 행사
delivery time 배송 시간	be looking forward to -ing ~을 기대 중이다
be impressed by ~에 감명을 받다	plan the next step 다음 단계를 계획하다
give an update 최신 소식을 알려 주다	be wondering if ~인지 궁금해 하다
call to see if ~인지 알아보려고 전화하다	need extra help 추가적인 도움을 필요로 하다
discuss an idea 아이디어에 대해 논의하다	unfortunately 유감스럽게도
let someone know ~에게 알려 주다	available 시간이 있는
check on the progress 진척 상황을 알아보다	possible option 선택 가능한 옵션
make a change 변경하다	stay on the line 전화를 끊지 않고 기다리다
be surprised by ~에 놀라다	convenient for ~에게 편한
keep in mind 명심하다	immediate assistance 즉각적인 도움
be scheduled to ~하기로 예정되어 있다	in person 직접
make up for the inconvenience 불편에 대해 보상하다	hear from someone ~에게서 듣다
send by e-mail 이메일로 보내다	if you're interested 관심이 있으시다면
propose a date 날짜를 제안하다	when you get the chance 가능하실 때
show A to B A에게 B를 보여 주다	This is a message for ~에게 남기는 메시지입니다
have time tomorrow 내일 시간이 있다	I'm calling to tell you ~을 말씀드리고자 전화드립니다
have bad news 나쁜 소식이 있다	I'm worried about ~이 걱정됩니다
has been delayed 지연되었다	You'll be happy to know ~라는 걸 알면 기쁘실 거예요
won't be able to ~할 수 없을 것이다	Please call me back at ~로 다시 전화해 주세요
be supposed to ~하기로 되어 있다	talk to you soon 조만간 다시 연락드릴게요

[1-4] 질문과 정답을 확인한 뒤, 대화를 들으면서 정답의 단서가 되는 부분에 표시하세요.

1. **Q** What does the speaker ask the listener to do?

  A Change a task assignment

> **W** I've just received a report about a water leak in the employee kitchen. Could you schedule the maintenance team to work on that for a few hours today instead of painting the hallway on the second floor?

2. **Q** What does the speaker say she likes about the center?

  A The technical support

> **W** Thank you for giving me a tour of your convention center yesterday. I would like to go forward with the booking, as your site seems perfect for us. I was especially interested in the option to use your technical staff. This will make it much easier to set up for our video presentations.

3. **Q** What is the speaker excited to report?

  A A fund-raising goal was met.

> **M** Hi, Christine. This is Douglas Conway from the Nashville Art Museum. I've got some exciting news for you. We reached our goal of raising ten thousand dollars to make upgrades to the community garden on our property. I'm wondering if you could write a press release about this.

4. **Q** What is the message mainly about?

  A A roadwork project

> **M** Hi, this is Juan Rodriguez, the head of the state's transportation department. I'm calling about our proposed highway expansion project. I would like to discuss the preliminary designs at your earliest convenience.

[5-6] 대화를 듣고 정답의 단서가 알맞게 패러프레이징된 답을 고르세요.

5. What is the purpose of the call?

  (A) To explain a delay
  (B) To place an order

6. What is the Starburst Café offering all week?

  (A) Discounted meals
  (B) Free beverages

대화를 듣고 알맞은 답을 고른 뒤, 다시 들으면서 빈칸을 채우세요.

1. Where does the speaker work?

(A) At a car rental agency

(B) At a recycling center

(C) At a computer repair shop

(D) At an accounting firm

> **W** Hello, Mr. Daniels. This is Liz Marrota, the manager of Benson Tech. I'm calling to tell you about _____ _____ yesterday. I'm afraid I have bad news. While we were able to retrieve the data from your hard drive, the mainboard is too broken to save. Please call me back at 555-4638 to plan the next step. Thank you.

2. What does the speaker say about the order?

(A) It will cost more than expected.

(B) It was shipped to the wrong address.

(C) It was damaged in transit.

(D) It is currently unavailable.

3. How can the listener cancel the order?

(A) By visiting the business in person

(B) By sending a copy of the receipt

(C) By calling the store directly

(D) By completing a request form

> **M** This is a message for Mr. Baker. This is Dan from Lansing Books. The book you ordered… um… *Structures of Europe*, _____ _____. We won't be able to deliver it on Friday as originally planned. Unfortunately, we are unsure how long it will be before we get more. If you would like to cancel this order, _____ _____ at your earliest convenience. You would receive a full refund, of course. The number is on your order form. We apologize for the inconvenience this may cause.

4. Where does the speaker work?

(A) At a construction firm

(B) At an electronics manufacturer

(C) At a real estate agency

(D) At an interior design company

5. What does the speaker say about Lilian Meyer?

(A) She will attend an industry event.

(B) She is available to answer questions.

(C) She plans to schedule a meeting.

(D) She is the company's newest employee.

> **M** Hello. You've reached the voicemail of Brian Baldwin of Hillside Incorporated. We are proud to be the area's top-rated _____ _____. I'm sorry I am unable to take your call at this time. I will be out of town for the rest of the week due to an industry event. I will return on Monday, June 7. In the meantime, if you need immediate assistance, _____ _____ to Lilian Meyer at extension number 21. Thank you.

대화를 듣고 알맞은 답을 고르세요.

1. What is the message about?

(A) Building a new house
(B) Renting an apartment
(C) Moving downtown
(D) Living abroad

2. According to the speaker, why is the listener preferred?

(A) He wants a long-term lease.
(B) He is a reliable person.
(C) He was approved for a loan.
(D) He had a professional recommendation.

3. When is the deadline for the listener to decide?

(A) This afternoon
(B) Tomorrow morning
(C) This weekend
(D) The day after tomorrow

4. What is the message mainly about?

(A) A change in ownership
(B) An error in monthly bills
(C) A new communications package
(D) A loss of Internet service

5. According to the speaker, what caused a problem?

(A) A shortage of employees
(B) A severe storm
(C) A technology upgrade
(D) A change in regulations

6. What are the listeners encouraged to do?

(A) Complete a questionnaire
(B) Report problems to the company
(C) Log into an account
(D) Authorize a payment

7. What is the purpose of the call?

(A) To confirm a deadline
(B) To explain a delay
(C) To discuss a reservation
(D) To request a payment

8. According to the speaker, what can the listener do for free?

(A) Get an upgrade
(B) Have a meal
(C) Attend a show
(D) Ride a shuttle bus

9. What does the speaker suggest when he says, "we expect a lot of interest in it"?

(A) He will make time for an event.
(B) A price is likely to increase soon.
(C) The listener made a good suggestion.
(D) The listener should act quickly.

10. Where does the speaker most likely work?

(A) At a hardware store
(B) At a clothing manufacturer
(C) At a shipping company
(D) At a carpet store

11. What does the speaker say about this Friday?

(A) An annual sale will begin.
(B) The business will close early.
(C) Some new products will arrive.
(D) A business may be busier than usual.

12. What can customers receive this week?

(A) Free cleaning supplies
(B) Overnight delivery
(C) An extended warranty
(D) A store voucher

13. Where does the speaker work?

    (A) At an advertising firm
    (B) At a grocery store
    (C) At a print shop
    (D) At a hair salon

14. What does the speaker say about the flyers?

    (A) She would like to add more graphics.
    (B) She was expecting different colors.
    (C) She thinks there will not be enough.
    (D) She is considering changing the size.

15. What will happen tomorrow?

    (A) A ticket for a trip will be purchased.
    (B) Some new forms will be reviewed.
    (C) A meeting with a client will be held.
    (D) A document will be posted online.

Mountain Coffee Shop	☕
Sunday	8 A.M.–4 P.M.
Monday–Wednesday	Closed
Thursday	9 A.M.–6 P.M.
Friday	8 A.M.–9 P.M.
Saturday	7 A.M.–8 P.M.

16. Why will the speaker meet with the listener?

    (A) To conduct an interview
    (B) To sign a contract
    (C) To renew a subscription
    (D) To share some samples

17. Look at the graphic. Which day does the speaker plan to meet the listener?

    (A) Sunday
    (B) Thursday
    (C) Friday
    (D) Saturday

18. What does the speaker say about the Bluebell Diner?

    (A) It offers free parking.
    (B) It is located outside the city.
    (C) It has a lot of space.
    (D) It has recently changed its menu.

UNIT 10 사내 공지

핵심 포인트

1. 주로 회의록에서 발췌된 것으로, 회사 내 새로운 소식을 알리거나 업무 관련 다양한 안건에 대해 논의하는 내용이 나오며, 회의/공지 주제 → 세부사항 → 제안/요청사항의 흐름으로 전개된다.
2. 주제나 세부사항을 묻는 문제가 자주 출제된다.

실전 맛보기

🎧 P4_U10_01

M Before we end our staff meeting, ¹I'd like to remind you about the renovations that are starting at our office tomorrow. New windows will be installed, and the walls will be painted. Now, ²some staff members have told me they're worried that they'll have trouble focusing on their work assignments due to interruptions from the noise. Fortunately, to minimize this issue, the crew will complete most of the work on the weekend. Oh, that reminds me... ³please cover your computer and work phone in a sheet of plastic before you leave work. You can get the necessary supplies from Amanda. Thanks.

남 직원 회의를 마치기 전에, ¹여러분에게 내일 우리 사무실에서 시작되는 보수 작업에 대해 다시 한번 알려 드리겠습니다. 창문이 새로 설치될 것이며, 벽에 페인트칠을 할 것입니다. 자, ²몇몇 직원들이 소음 방해로 인해 업무에 집중하는 데 어려움이 있을까 봐 걱정스럽다고 제게 말했습니다. 다행스럽게도, 이러한 문제를 최소화하기 위해서, 작업반이 주말에 대부분의 작업을 완료할 것입니다. 아, 그러고 보니 생각나는데요... ³퇴근하기 전에 비닐 한 장으로 여러분의 컴퓨터와 업무용 전화기를 덮으시기 바랍니다. 필요한 용품은 아만다에게 받으시면 됩니다. 감사합니다.

1. What is the announcement mainly about? 주제
   A renovation project

2. According to the speaker, why have some employees expressed concern? 이유
   Some work may be disrupted.

3. What are the listeners asked to do before they leave? 요청사항
   Put a protective cover over their equipment

1. 공지는 주로 무엇에 관한 것인가?
   보수 프로젝트

2. 화자에 따르면, 일부 직원들은 왜 우려를 표했는가?
   일부 작업이 지장을 받을지도 모른다.

3. 청자들은 퇴근하기 전에 무엇을 하도록 요청받는가?
   자신들의 장비에 보호용 커버 씌우기

CHECK UP

🎧 P4_U10_02 정답 및 해설 p.266

1. What has the company recently done?
   (A) Launched a product line
   (B) Received an award nomination
   (C) Opened a new branch
   (D) Hired a consultant

2. According to the speaker, why will the company hold a special event?
   (A) To introduce an employee
   (B) To promote a service
   (C) To recruit staff members
   (D) To celebrate an anniversary

3. What will be given to one of the listeners?
   (A) A gift voucher
   (B) Extra time off
   (C) A free meal
   (D) Some office supplies

빈출 상황

업무 방안 논의	So, the purpose of today's meeting is to generate story ideas for the upcoming issues of our magazine. 자, 오늘 회의의 목적은 우리 잡지의 다음 호에 관한 스토리 아이디어를 내는 것입니다.
매출/실적 평가	Today I'll be presenting on the results of the promotional event we held last quarter. 오늘은 우리가 지난 분기에 진행한 판촉 홍보 행사의 결과에 대해 발표하겠습니다.
제도 변경 공지	Finally, a reminder that we're planning to institute a new incentive program. 마지막으로, 우리가 새로운 인센티브 프로그램을 시행할 계획이라는 것을 다시 한번 알려 드립니다.
사내 행사 안내	Before we end our staff meeting, I want to remind everyone that our bank branch is hosting a document shredding event. 직원 회의를 마치기 전에, 우리 은행 지점이 문서 파쇄 행사를 열 것이라는 사실을 모두에게 상기시켜 주고 싶습니다.
건물 이용 안내	Please be aware that next week, the main parking area in front of our office building will be closed for repaving. 다음 주에, 우리 사옥 앞 메인 주차장 구역이 재포장 공사를 위해 닫을 것이라는 것에 유의해 주세요.

빈출 표현

🎧 P4_U10_03

call a meeting 회의를 소집하다
have an announcement 공지사항이 있다
have some good news 좋은 소식이 있다
staff meeting agenda 직원 회의 안건
from now on 지금부터
face a severe shortage 심각한 부족을 겪다
introduce a new product 신제품을 소개하다
install new software 새로운 소프트웨어를 설치하다
branch out (새로운 분야로) 진출하다
last[previous] quarter 지난 분기
keep up with demand 수요를 따라잡다
increase sales 매출액을 증가시키다
host an event 행사를 개최하다
purchase new equipment 새로운 장비를 구매하다
have trouble -ing ~하는 데 어려움을 겪다
attract new recruits 신규 직원들을 끌어모으다
production process 생산 절차
assembly line 생산 라인
drop in sales 매출 감소
be required to ~하도록 요구받다
be on schedule 일정대로 되다
now more than ever 어느 때보다도 더
generate ideas 아이디어를 생각해 내다
employee satisfaction survey 직원 만족도 조사
have a contract signed 계약을 체결시키다
submit a vacation request 휴가 신청서를 제출하다

member of the board of directors 이사회 회원
head of the department 부서장
discuss the results 결과에 대해 논의하다
set up a window display 진열장을 설치하다
work overtime 초과근무를 하다
institute a new program 새로운 프로그램을 시행하다
customer feedback 고객 의견
closed for repaving 재포장 공사를 위해 닫은
minimize issues 문제를 최소화하다
take over one's responsibility ~의 책임을 맡다
investigate further 더 조사하다
go over a plan 계획을 점검하다
needless to say 말할 필요도 없이
have an update on ~에 대한 최신 소식이 있다
remind everyone that ~라는 점을 모두에게 상기시키다
Before you begin your shifts 여러분의 근무를 시작하기 전에
To address this concern 이 문제를 해결하기 위해
I'd like to touch on ~에 관해 언급하고 싶습니다
Please be aware that ~라는 것에 유의해 주세요
I'm happy to announce that ~를 알리게 되어 기쁩니다
We have a lot of ground to cover 이야기할 것들이 많습니다
You can let employees know that
직원들에게 ~라고 알려 주세요
I need someone to volunteer 자원해 줄 사람이 필요합니다
I appreciate your hard work and dedication
여러분의 노고와 헌신에 감사드립니다

[1-4] 질문과 정답을 확인한 뒤, 대화를 들으면서 정답의 단서가 되는 부분에 표시하세요.

1. **Q** What will Ms. Nelson do tomorrow?

A Give a presentation

> **M** I've invited Sandra Nelson, our senior technician, to today's meeting. She'll go over her research with our team before sharing it formally at a conference tomorrow. This will help you become familiar with the main findings.

2. **Q** What are the listeners supposed to do next?

A Log into a Web site

> **W** Welcome, everyone, and thank you for coming to this orientation. Let's begin by activating your accounts on our employee Web site. There you will see links to things like your work assignments, time-off requests, and payment summaries.

3. **Q** What were the listeners asked to draft by today?

A Job descriptions

> **M** At the end of our last meeting, I asked everyone to submit a detailed description of your work responsibilities by today. These will help me to make sure that all responsibilities are covered and that there are no overlapping duties.

4. **Q** What does the speaker remind the listeners about?

A A budget limit

> **W** I think a gift for each employee would help to show our appreciation for everything they've done this year. I know that concert tickets are a popular option. But don't forget that our budget is only 50 dollars per employee.

[5-6] 대화를 듣고 정답의 단서가 알맞게 패러프레이징된 답을 고르세요.

5. What type of product is being discussed?

(A) A beverage

(B) A clothing item

6. What does the speaker say she will do?

(A) Adjust the price of a product

(B) Assign more staff members to a project

대화를 듣고 알맞은 답을 고른 뒤, 다시 들으면서 빈칸을 채우세요.

1. What are the listeners asked to do?

(A) Place their belongings in a vehicle
(B) Meet at a hotel for lunch
(C) Be cautious during the activities
(D) Participate in all sessions

M I hope everyone got a good night's sleep. Today should be a lot of fun. It will also hopefully bring us closer together and allow us to work better as a team. Okay then... ah, I have an announcement as you finish your breakfast. Please _____ _____ as soon as you check out of the hotel. We'll be taking the vans to the horse-riding sessions, so we want to make sure we have everything.

---

2. Who most likely are the listeners?

(A) Managers
(B) Customers
(C) Job applicants
(D) Stockholders

3. What does the speaker ask the listeners to do?

(A) Send in product reviews
(B) Meet with a manager
(C) Create an idea for an advertisement
(D) Visit some potential clients

M Thanks for _____ today. We have a lot to cover, so let's get started right away. I'd like to touch on page 6 of the packet I gave you. As you can see from the profit chart, it could've been a lot worse. We anticipated negative feedback following the product reviews, but in-store profits have been surprisingly positive. Therefore, we would like to launch a new advertising campaign. I'd like you all to _____ _____ by tomorrow.

---

4. What kind of products does the speaker's business sell?

(A) Automotive parts
(B) Wooden furniture
(C) Home appliances
(D) Gardening supplies

5. According to the speaker, why is the business popular?

(A) It offers long warranties.
(B) It has knowledgeable employees.
(C) It has low prices.
(D) It is open for extended hours.

W I have some good news, everyone. We found a site for another store in the southern region. More people are getting interested in ____ _____, as well as our seeds, soil, and plants. This new store will help us keep up with demand. The main reason that our business is so popular is because of you. _____ _____ and can answer questions. So, I just want you to know that I appreciate your hard work and dedication.

실전 문제

대화를 듣고 알맞은 답을 고르세요.

1. Who most likely are the listeners?

   (A) Small business owners
   (B) Prospective investors
   (C) Sales clerks
   (D) Product developers

2. What is the speaker mainly talking about?

   (A) A storage container
   (B) A foam mattress
   (C) A power tool
   (D) A protective case

3. Why does the speaker think a product will sell well?

   (A) It will come in a variety of colors.
   (B) It will have an eco-friendly design.
   (C) It will be made locally.
   (D) It will look modern.

4. What will take place on Thursday?

   (A) A training session
   (B) A site inspection
   (C) A press conference
   (D) A corporate merger

5. What does the speaker ask the listeners to do?

   (A) Confirm their availability
   (B) Submit some questions by e-mail
   (C) Read a manual carefully
   (D) Leave some rooms unlocked

6. What does the speaker say about a company picnic?

   (A) It will not be affected by the weather.
   (B) The attendees should bring food.
   (C) It will begin earlier than originally planned.
   (D) Family guests are allowed to participate.

7. What industry do the listeners most likely work in?

   (A) Healthcare
   (B) Transportation
   (C) Education
   (D) Finance

8. What does the speaker mean when he says, "the form is brief"?

   (A) A task can be finished quickly.
   (B) Some questions should be added.
   (C) A file was not printed completely.
   (D) The proposed deadline is reasonable.

9. What will the speaker send the listeners each month?

   (A) A team assignment
   (B) A client list
   (C) A work schedule
   (D) A budget summary

10. What happened recently?

    (A) A new regulation was passed.
    (B) A supplier has signed a contract.
    (C) A service received positive reviews.
    (D) An open position was filled.

11. What does the company plan to do?

    (A) Form a business partnership
    (B) Conduct an employee survey
    (C) Relocate its headquarters
    (D) Change a commission structure

12. Why does the speaker thank Vanna DeRose?

    (A) She hired some employees.
    (B) She will go on a business trip.
    (C) She is doing some research.
    (D) She is negotiating a contract.

13. What is mentioned about the new insurance package?

(A) It will be updated every year.
(B) It is less expensive than those of competitors.
(C) It will be offered at 15 percent off.
(D) It is intended only for senior citizens.

14. What happened last month?

(A) Employees were rewarded for their hard work.
(B) Some complaints were made about poor service.
(C) A job training workshop was held.
(D) The company was ranked second in the market.

15. Why should the listeners visit a Web site?

(A) To get more information
(B) To post a notice
(C) To download a coupon
(D) To check a schedule

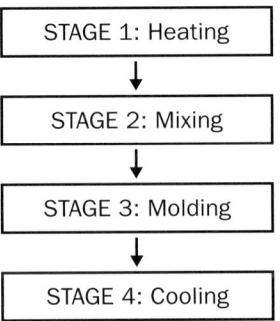

STAGE 1: Heating

STAGE 2: Mixing

STAGE 3: Molding

STAGE 4: Cooling

16. What has the speaker decided?

(A) The safety protocols should be updated.
(B) Two managers should be assigned to each shift.
(C) Nighttime hours should be added to the schedule.
(D) Some temporary workers should be hired.

17. Look at the graphic. In which stage does the speaker think a problem occurred?

(A) Stage 1
(B) Stage 2
(C) Stage 3
(D) Stage 4

18. What will the speaker do after the meeting?

(A) Order some parts
(B) Call a repairperson
(C) Conduct some tests
(D) Unload a shipment

PART 4

UNIT 10

핵심 포인트 | 1. 상점이나 공연장 같은 공공장소 및 공항, 기차역 등의 교통수단에서 이루어지는 안내 방송으로, 인사말 및 공지 주제 → 세부사항 → 요청사항의 흐름으로 전개되는 경우가 많다.
2. 담화 장소, 요청사항 또는 다음에 할 일을 묻는 문제가 자주 출제된다.

실전 맛보기

🎧 P4_U11_01

M ¹Attention, all passengers for flight 2833 with service to Amsterdam. ²For those of you who have a confirmed ticket but have not been assigned a seat yet, please report to the service counter here at Gate 40. You will be issued a new boarding pass. We will begin boarding shortly, starting with our first-class passengers and families with small children or anyone who needs additional time. ³I'd like to reassure you that we are on schedule for our original departure time of 7:55. Thank you.

남 ¹암스테르담으로 운항하는 2833 항공편의 모든 승객들에게 알립니다. ²확정된 티켓을 가지고 계시지만 아직 좌석을 배정받지 못한 분들은 이곳 40번 탑승구의 서비스 카운터로 오시기 바랍니다. 탑승권을 새로 발급받으실 것입니다. 저희는 곧 탑승을 시작할 것이며, 1등석 승객들과 어린아이들이 있는 가족, 혹은 시간이 더 필요하신 분부터 먼저 타시겠습니다. ³원래 출발 시간인 7시 55분에 맞춰 예정대로 진행되고 있으니 안심하시기 바랍니다. 감사합니다.

1. Where is the announcement most likely taking place? 장소
   At an airport

2. According to the speaker, what do some listeners still need to do? 세부사항
   Receive a boarding pass

3. What does the speaker say to reassure the listeners? 세부사항
   A departure time has not changed.

1. 공지는 어디서 이루어지고 있는 것 같은가?
   공항에서

2. 화자에 따르면, 몇몇 청자들은 여전히 무엇을 해야 하는가?
   탑승권 받기

3. 화자는 청자들을 안심시키기 위해 무엇이라고 말하는가?
   출발 시간이 변경되지 않았다.

CHECK UP

🎧 P4_U11_02 정답 및 해설 p.275

1. Where is the announcement being made?

   (A) At a sports facility
   (B) At a concert hall
   (C) At an art gallery
   (D) At a public park

2. Why does the speaker say, "the café is open until 10"?

   (A) To make a change to a reservation
   (B) To reject a meal invitation
   (C) To correct a misunderstanding
   (D) To recommend getting refreshments

3. According to the speaker, why should the listeners keep a ticket?

   (A) To get a discount
   (B) To be issued a refund
   (C) To enter a prize drawing
   (D) To enroll in a loyalty program

특별 행사 안내	Don't forget next Friday at 1 o'clock we will be holding our annual fashion show. 다음 주 금요일 1시에 우리가 연례 패션쇼를 개최한다는 것을 잊지 마세요.
영업시간 안내	This is a reminder that the West Town Mall has extended hours today because of the upcoming holiday. 웨스트 타운 몰이 다가오는 휴일로 인해 오늘 영업시간을 연장했다는 것을 다시 한번 알려 드립니다.
탑승 / 출발 / 도착	We'll be landing in Toronto in about 15 minutes, so please keep your seat belt fastened for the remainder of the flight. 약 15분 후에 토론토에 착륙할 예정이오니, 남은 비행 시간 동안 안전벨트를 매 주시기 바랍니다.
지연 / 변경 알림	We're having some technical issues with the sound system, and the show will be delayed for at least an hour. 음향 시스템에 기술적인 문제가 있어서, 공연이 적어도 한 시간은 지연될 것입니다.

빈출 표현

🎧 P4_U11_03

공공장소		
patron 고객		customer service desk 고객 서비스 창구
performance 공연		temporarily closed 일시적으로 폐쇄된
inform 알리다		technical issues 기술적 문제
make an announcement 공지하다		sold out 매진된
be scheduled to ~하기로 되어 있다		not functioning properly 제대로 작동하지 않는
note that ~에 유의하다		report to ~로 가다
sound system 음향 시스템		special deal 특별 할인 행사
wait time 대기 시간		address the situation 상황을 해결하다
free admission 무료 입장권		resolve the issue 문제를 해결하다
renovation 보수 공사		fix the problem 문제를 고치다
prohibited 금지된		Don't miss this opportunity to ~할 기회를 놓치지 마세요
call a technician 기술자를 부르다		We apologize for the inconvenience 불편을 끼쳐 드려 죄송합니다
fill out a form 양식을 작성하다		
take a moment 시간을 내다		

교통수단		
take off 이륙하다		departure time 출발 시각
land in ~에 착륙하다		boarding pass 탑승권
keep your seat belt fastened 안전벨트를 매다		personal belongings 개인 소지품
need assistance 도움을 필요로 하다		feel free to 자유롭게 ~하다
flight attendant 승무원		board the train 열차에 탑승하다
passenger 승객		overhead rack (짐 넣는) 선반
ticket counter 매표소		under your seat 좌석 아래에
foggy weather 안개가 짙은 날씨		round-trip domestic flight 국내 왕복 항공권
due to heavy rain 폭우 때문에		in-flight services 기내 서비스
be still on 여전히 진행 중이다		enroll in our loyalty program 고객 보상 프로그램에 등록하다
begin boarding 탑승을 시작하다		expect to arrive on time 정시에 도착할 것으로 예상하다
stay on schedule 일정에 맞추다		Thank you for your compliance 협조해 주셔서 감사합니다
arrive shortly 곧 도착하다		
weather conditions 기상 상태		

[1-4] 질문과 정답을 확인한 뒤, 대화를 들으면서 정답의 단서가 되는 부분에 표시하세요.

1. **Q** What does the speaker tell some of the listeners to do on a Web site?

A Complete some forms

> **M** You can pick up your conference packet at the table right outside the main auditorium. And if you have not completed the registration forms yet, please visit our Web site and fill them out before you go to the table. You can use your smartphone or borrow a tablet from one of our staff members.

2. **Q** What does the speaker say about the Tuesday evening film?

A Ticket prices are reduced.

> **W** Attention, Summit Cinema patrons. Tickets for the 7 P.M. screening of The Mountaineers are nearly sold out. You can reserve tickets online for future movies on our Web site. And don't forget that tickets are half price for the movie screening on Tuesday evening. Visit our Web site for more information.

3. **Q** Why does the speaker apologize to the listeners?

A There was a delay.

> **M** Good afternoon, everyone, and welcome aboard this flight to Atlanta. We apologize for the delay at takeoff. We had an issue with the meals for our in-flight service, but the problem has been resolved.

4. **Q** What does the speaker say about a ballroom?

A An invitation is needed for entry.

> **W** Attention, visitors to Alvarez Convention Center. The ballroom is now open for entry for the Carlyle Incorporated Awards Dinner. For those attending the event, please make sure that you have your invitation with you.

[5-6] 대화를 듣고 정답의 단서가 알맞게 패러프레이징된 답을 고르세요.

5. What does the speaker say is now available?

(A) Free Internet service
(B) Reclining seats

6. What does the speaker say has happened recently?

(A) Employees have been trained.
(B) Lines have grown.

대화를 듣고 알맞은 답을 고른 뒤, 다시 들으면서 빈칸을 채우세요.

1. Why has a train been delayed?

    (A) It requires additional fuel.

    (B) It needs a different driver.

    (C) It has a mechanical problem.

    (D) It is overbooked.

M May I have your attention for the following announcement? We regret to inform you that the 4:15 train to Boston has been delayed _____. We have called a technician and hope to fix the problem quickly. However, we do not know how long this process will take. Passengers are invited to take the 4:40 train instead. A new ticket will not be required. Simply show your ticket to a staff member. Thank you for your patience.

2. What is the purpose of the announcement?

    (A) To remind listeners about a closure

    (B) To report a found item

    (C) To apologize for a shipment delay

    (D) To introduce a new service

W Attention, Mapleton Supermarket shoppers. A customer _____ and turned it in to our staff. Please take a moment to see if you are missing it. If so, please come to _____, which is located near Aisle 18. We will hold the bag securely until it has been claimed. It will need to be properly identified to be released. Thank you for shopping with us today. It is our pleasure to serve you.

3. Where should some listeners go?

    (A) To a check-out counter

    (B) To the front entrance

    (C) To a manager's office

    (D) To a parking area

4. Where most likely are the listeners?

    (A) At a ferry terminal

    (B) At an airport

    (C) At a bus station

    (D) At a train station

M Attention, all passengers. The northern wing of the facility is temporarily closed due to repairs. Visitors are prohibited from entering the area. Thank you for your compliance. For the next few weeks, _____ to Jacksonville, Wrightham, and Tawney City will leave from Gate Area C instead. To find your exact gate number, we recommend _____ _____ about 20 to 30 minutes _____. We wish you a safe and comfortable journey, and thank you for traveling with us today.

5. What does the speaker recommend doing?

    (A) Checking some information in advance

    (B) Signing up for an account

    (C) Printing a copy of an itinerary

    (D) Using a text alert system

대화를 듣고 알맞은 답을 고르세요.

1. What is the speaker mainly discussing?

(A) A clearance sale
(B) A poetry reading
(C) A community fund-raiser
(D) A writing workshop

2. What does the speaker suggest doing?

(A) Sitting near the front
(B) Checking a start time
(C) Making a purchase in advance
(D) Submitting questions in writing

3. According to the speaker, why should the listeners visit a Web site?

(A) To share their opinions
(B) To learn about new products
(C) To buy tickets for an event
(D) To join a mailing list

4. Where is the announcement most likely being made?

(A) At a car repair shop
(B) At a travel agency
(C) At a train station
(D) At a bus stop

5. According to the speaker, what was the cause of a delay?

(A) A ticketing error
(B) Poor weather conditions
(C) A late shipment
(D) Some faulty equipment

6. What are the listeners asked to do?

(A) Report problems to the speaker
(B) Keep their personal belongings with them
(C) Move to a different area
(D) Have their ticket ready to present

7. What had caused a delay?

(A) Some tickets were incorrect.
(B) Weather conditions were bad.
(C) There were some technical issues.
(D) A staff member arrived late.

8. What does the speaker remind the listeners about?

(A) Putting away their bags
(B) Showing their boarding pass
(C) Fastening their seat belts
(D) Repositioning their tray tables

9. What can the listeners receive if they join a loyalty program?

(A) Access to a private lounge
(B) A complimentary beverage
(C) Additional loyalty points
(D) A voucher for an upgrade

10. Where does the announcement take place?

(A) At a shopping center
(B) At a library
(C) At a hotel
(D) At a concert hall

11. According to the speaker, what will be available at the ticket counter?

(A) Beverages
(B) Posters
(C) Coupons
(D) Catalogs

12. What has recently been done at the site?

(A) Some parking areas were repaved.
(B) A ticketing system was upgraded.
(C) Some seats were replaced.
(D) A building was expanded.

13. Where is the announcement taking place?

(A) At a farm
(B) At a clothing store
(C) At a grocery store
(D) At an electronics store

14. According to the speaker, what can be found at the cash registers?

(A) Menus
(B) Gift certificates
(C) Shopping bags
(D) Questionnaires

15. What does the speaker imply when she says, "Don't be shy"?

(A) She thinks everyone should try a new product.
(B) She wants people to share their opinions freely.
(C) She hopes the listeners will come back frequently.
(D) She encourages the use of gift certificates.

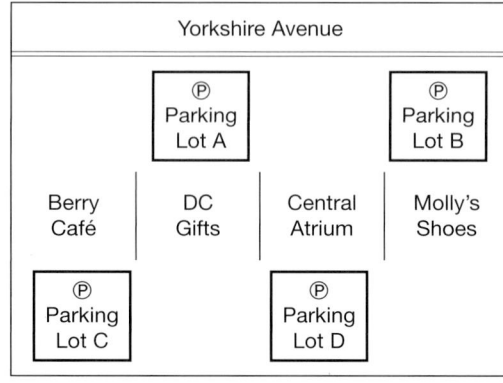

16. What change does the speaker announce?

(A) Different music performances
(B) A cancellation of parking fees
(C) Longer business hours
(D) Added food vendors

17. Look at the graphic. Where can the listeners take a shuttle?

(A) At Parking Lot A
(B) At Parking Lot B
(C) At Parking Lot C
(D) At Parking Lot D

18. What event will happen tomorrow?

(A) A community festival
(B) A grand opening
(C) A cooking demonstration
(D) A fashion show

PART 4 UNIT 11

핵심 포인트 | 1. 각종 모임 및 행사의 연설이나 강연은 인사말 및 본인 소개 → 행사/강연 주제 → 세부사항 → 다음에 할 일 순으로 전개되는 경우가 많으며, 화자/청자, 담화 세부사항, 다음에 할 일을 묻는 문제가 자주 출제된다.
2. 발표자, 수상자 등 특정 인물을 소개하는 담화 또한 종종 출제되는데, 해당 인물의 이력이나 업적을 소개 하는 내용이 주를 이루고 이것이 세부사항 문제로 출제되는 경우가 많다.

실전 맛보기
P4_U12_01

M It's an honor to be here as the guest speaker at today's event. ¹The topic of my lecture will be the benefits of producing goods from recycled materials. ²Many companies avoid exploring this process because it is difficult to find suppliers that can reliably provide the necessary raw materials. However, you can overcome this obstacle with the right planning. In fact, ³if you'd like to find out more about supply chains, I'd recommend James Draper's workshop next month.

남 오늘 행사에 초청 연사로 참석하게 되어 영광 입니다. ¹제 강연의 주제는 재활용 재료를 이 용한 제품 생산의 이점이 될 것입니다. ²필요 한 원자재를 확실하게 공급할 수 있는 공급업 체를 찾기가 어렵기 때문에, 많은 회사들이 이 과정을 검토하는 것을 피합니다. 하지만, 올바른 계획으로 이러한 장애물을 극복할 수 있습니다. 실제로, ³공급망에 관해 더 알아보 시려면, 다음 달에 있는 제임스 드레이퍼의 워크숍을 추천드립니다.

---

1. What is the talk mainly about? 주제
   Manufacturing with recycled materials

2. What difficulty does the speaker mention about a process? 세부사항
   Finding reliable suppliers

3. According to the speaker, how can the listeners get more information? 세부사항
   By attending a workshop

1. 담화는 주로 무엇에 관한 것인가?
   재활용 재료로 제조하는 것

2. 화자는 과정에 대해 어떤 어려움을 언급하는가?
   믿을만한 공급업체를 찾는 것

3. 화자에 따르면, 청자들은 어떻게 더 많은 정보 를 얻을 수 있는가?
   워크숍에 참석함으로써

CHECK UP
P4_U12_02 정답 및 해설 p.282

1. What event is taking place?
   (A) A trade show
   (B) A sports competition
   (C) A career fair
   (D) An awards ceremony

2. What can the listeners do during the presentation?
   (A) Browse a catalog
   (B) Complete a form
   (C) Try a new application
   (D) Watch a video

3. What does the speaker ask the listeners to do?
   (A) Get into groups
   (B) Put on headphones
   (C) Read a manual
   (D) Enter their name

기조연설	Thank you all for coming to the opening ceremony of the new headquarters building. As the company's president, I'm honored to welcome you to this beautiful and modern facility. 신사옥 개관식에 참석해 주신 모든 분들께 감사드립니다. 회사 대표로서, 저는 여러분이 아름답고 현대적인 이 시설에 오신 것을 환영하게 되어 영광입니다.
설명/교육	I'm going to give you a step-by-step guide to repainting a room. The first thing you need to do is calculate the amount of paint you will need. 방을 새로 칠하는 단계별 가이드를 드리겠습니다. 가장 먼저 해야 할 일은 여러분에게 필요할 페인트의 양을 계산하는 것입니다.
제품 발표	Thanks for visiting our exhibit at the National Technology Trade Fair. Today I'd like to present our speech-recognition software, Talk-Pro. 국내 기술 무역 박람회에서 저희 전시에 방문해 주셔서 감사합니다. 오늘 저희의 음성 인식 소프트웨어 토크프로를 발표하고자 합니다.
인물 소개	Today's keynote speaker is Arlene Spencer, who is a highly respected journalist specializing in political coverage. 오늘의 기조연설자는 알린 스펜서인데, 그녀는 정치 보도를 전문으로 하는 매우 존경받는 언론인입니다.

PART 4

UNIT 12

빈출 표현

🎧 P4_U12_03

trade fair 무역 박람회
annual gathering 연례 모임
trade show 무역 박람회
awards ceremony 시상식
press conference 기자 회견
career symposium 직업 토론회
opening ceremony 개업식
shareholders meeting 주주총회
training session 교육 시간
professional development 전문성 개발
panel discussion on ~에 대한 공개 토론
field of medicine 의약 분야
technological innovation 기술 혁신
product demonstration 제품 시연
present the latest product 최신 제품을 발표하다
celebrate the 10th anniversary 10주년 기념일을 축하하다
announce the winner 수상자를 발표하다
give[present] an award 시상하다
hard work and commitment 노고와 헌신
raffle 경품 추첨
choose a prize 상품을 고르다
split into small groups 소규모 그룹으로 나누다
develop business leadership skills
비즈니스 리더십 능력을 키우다

expert advice 전문가의 조언
keynote speaker 기조연설자
guest speaker 초청 연사
chair of the committee 위원회 의장
industry specialists 업계 전문가
property consultant 부동산 컨설턴트
employee of the month 이달의 직원
a leading expert in ~ 분야 최고의 전문가
run the operation 사업체를 운영하다
establish 설립하다
start a company 회사를 차리다
begin one's career 경력을 쌓기 시작하다
in the field of ~ 분야에서
serve the public 대중을 위해 봉사하다
with over 10 years of experience 10년 이상의 경력을 가진
to celebrate our success 우리의 성공을 축하하기 위해
It's an honor to ~하게 되어 영광입니다
We're pleased to be with ~와 함께하게 되어 기쁩니다
In today's workshop, you'll learn how to
오늘 워크숍에서, 여러분은 ~하는 법을 배우게 될 겁니다
I'm happy to announce that ~을 알려 드리게 되어 기쁩니다
I'll be showing you how to
~하는 법을 여러분에게 보여 드릴 것입니다

[1-4] 질문과 정답을 확인한 뒤, 대화를 들으면서 정답의 단서가 되는 부분에 표시하세요.

1.   **Q**   What type of event are the listeners attending?

    A   An industry conference

> **W**   I'd like to welcome you all to the annual conference on wastewater management. Our first speaker today is Carl Armstrong, the head of Goodwin Industries. He'll be discussing the best ways to reuse wastewater and the systems needed to do so.

2.   **Q**   What does the speaker thank Shobe Services for?

    A   Installing a fence

> **M**   It is a pleasure to welcome you all to the opening of Fairview Park. We hope everyone in the community will enjoy this outdoor space. I would especially like to thank Shobe Services, who put up the wooden fence at the south end of the park.

3.   **Q**   What does the speaker encourage the listeners to do?

    A   Sign up for a special event

> **W**   I hope everyone is enjoying the conference so far. Please note that the closing dinner led by Joe Thorson is not included with the event registration. We still have spots available for that. If you don't have a ticket and would like to attend, please sign up. There's a registration table near the rear entrance.

4.   **Q**   According to the speaker, who created Work-Well?

    A   A medical doctor

> **M**   Thank you all for attending this press conference. We are excited to introduce Work-Well, a well-being program designed to help office workers minimize their stress through a series of targeted stretches. Dr. Aubrey Ramirez, a physician who is a leading expert in health and wellness, developed the program last year.

[5-6] 대화를 듣고 정답의 단서가 알맞게 패러프레이징된 답을 고르세요.

5.   What will be discussed during the session?

    (A) An election of city council members

    (B) A proposal for a new law

6.   What aspect of the speaker's job does she like?

    (A) The opportunity for job promotion

    (B) The ability to choose her own projects

대화를 듣고 알맞은 답을 고른 뒤, 다시 들으면서 빈칸을 채우세요.

1. What industry do the listeners work in?

(A) Insurance
(B) Aviation
(C) Medicine
(D) Automotive

M Good morning, and welcome to this annual gathering. It's wonderful to _____ _____ to learn more about the field. Our keynote speaker will be Megan Frazier, an industry specialist who will be talking about communications technology. Ms. Frazier has been in the field for decades, and she started her own company a few years ago to develop new strategies for dealing with increasingly crowded airspace. After the talk, you will have the opportunity to ask questions.

2. What are the instructions for?

(A) Editing a video
(B) Opening a bank account
(C) Using a security camera
(D) Installing some software

3. What are the listeners asked to do at the end of the process?

(A) Double-click the start icon
(B) Use the pause button
(C) Restart the computer
(D) Download the application

W This is an instructional video to help you _____ _____ onto your computer. As the instructions play, you can click the pause button at any time. The installation process will take approximately seven minutes, so please make sure you are available for the entire time. At the end of the process, you will be asked to _____ _____ to complete the installation. Now, let's begin by double-clicking the blue start icon on top of your screen.

4. Who most likely are the listeners?

(A) Professional chefs
(B) Festival volunteers
(C) Elected officials
(D) Job applicants

5. What does the speaker remind the listeners about?

(A) Some survey results will be announced.
(B) A prize drawing will be held.
(C) A special guest will give a talk.
(D) Meals should be ordered in advance.

M I'd like to welcome you all to this appreciation dinner. The city holds the International Food Festival every year, and it would not be possible _____. We want to thank you for your hard work and commitment. Please enjoy your meal and the live music. And don't forget to _____ _____. There are a number of exciting prizes to be given away, and we will announce the winners at the end of the event. Have a wonderful evening!

PART 4

UNIT 12

대화를 듣고 알맞은 답을 고르세요.

1. Where most likely do the listeners work?

(A) At a museum
(B) At a post office
(C) At a bakery
(D) At a bookstore

2. What will the listeners learn about today?

(A) Safety guidelines
(B) Brochure designs
(C) Customer complaints
(D) Cleaning techniques

3. What does the speaker suggest when she says, "you should speak with Adam"?

(A) Adam has the necessary supplies.
(B) Adam will confirm group assignments.
(C) She is correcting an error on the schedule.
(D) She plans to watch Adam's demonstration.

4. What is the purpose of the talk?

(A) To cancel a workshop
(B) To honor an employee
(C) To gather feedback
(D) To launch a new product

5. What will the listeners receive later today?

(A) An event souvenir
(B) A work report
(C) A contract
(D) A survey form

6. What does the speaker reassure the listeners about?

(A) They can attend the next event.
(B) Their information will not be revealed.
(C) Their schedule will not be changed.
(D) They can record the presentations.

7. Who is the speaker?

(A) A fitness instructor
(B) A safety inspector
(C) A government official
(D) A building designer

8. What is the talk mainly about?

(A) The venue for an outdoor festival
(B) The construction of a stadium
(C) The sale of some public property
(D) The expansion of a bicycle path

9. According to the speaker, what is the purpose of the project?

(A) To generate tax revenue
(B) To reduce the amount of traffic
(C) To encourage people to exercise
(D) To attract tourists to the area

10. Where does the speaker most likely work?

(A) At a university
(B) At a publishing company
(C) At an Internet provider
(D) At an interior design firm

11. What does the speaker say about Mr. Wilder?

(A) He will give a presentation.
(B) He will replace Mr. Cooper.
(C) He has lived abroad.
(D) He has won an award.

12. What will take place next Friday?

(A) Some maintenance work
(B) A training session
(C) A staff meeting
(D) A welcoming party

13. Where is the speaker?

(A) At a grand opening
(B) At a group interview
(C) At a trade fair
(D) At an awards ceremony

14. What does the speaker say about young professionals?

(A) They are skilled with technical devices.
(B) They want to start their own businesses.
(C) They are concerned about the environment.
(D) They do not have enough experience.

15. According to the speaker, what will employees now be able to do?

(A) Back up their e-mail
(B) Submit nominations
(C) Work from home
(D) Open new accounts

16. Why was the film special for the speaker?

(A) Its budget was very big.
(B) Its script was written by a friend.
(C) It was filmed in an interesting location.
(D) It starred a famous actor.

17. Look at the graphic. Which item does the speaker point out?

(A) Item 1
(B) Item 2
(C) Item 3
(D) Item 4

18. What will the speaker most likely do next?

(A) Distribute some handouts
(B) Answer some questions
(C) Introduce a colleague
(D) Show some images

핵심 포인트

1. 제품 및 서비스, 업체 등을 홍보하는 내용으로, 주의 환기 및 광고 대상 → 특징 및 장점 → 할인 혜택 등의 추가 정보 순으로 전개된다.
2. 광고 주제 및 대상, 특징이나 혜택 등의 세부사항을 묻는 문제가 자주 출제된다.

실전 맛보기

🎧 P4_U13_01

W ¹Are you looking for delicious gourmet chocolate? If so, Shanta Foods has what you need. Our high-quality chocolate is locally made and is sold all over the world. We use only premium ingredients at our factory. ²You can visit the site and take a group tour to see how we make our products. Anyone can take the tour at no cost. And ³to view videos showing you how to use our products in a variety of delicious recipes, visit www.shantafoods.com. We hope to see you soon at Shanta Foods.

여 ¹맛있는 고급 초콜릿을 찾고 계신가요? 그렇다면, 샨타 푸드에 당신에게 필요한 것이 있습니다. 저희의 고급 초콜릿은 지역에서 만들어지고 전 세계에서 팔립니다. 저희 공장에서는 프리미엄 재료만 사용합니다. ²현장을 방문하셔서 저희가 어떻게 제품을 만드는지 보기 위해 단체 견학을 하실 수 있습니다. 누구든 무료로 견학할 수 있습니다. 그리고 ³여러 가지 맛있는 조리법으로 저희 제품을 이용하는 방법을 보여 드리는 영상을 시청하시려면 www.shantafoods.com을 방문하세요. 곧 샨타 푸드에서 뵙기를 기대합니다.

1. What type of food product is being advertised?
   Chocolate 주제

2. What does the speaker say is available at no cost? 세부사항
   A group tour

3. According to the speaker, what can the listeners do on a Web site? 세부사항
   Access some videos

1. 어떤 종류의 식품이 광고되고 있는가?
   초콜릿

2. 화자는 무엇이 무료로 이용 가능하다고 말하는가?
   단체 견학

3. 화자에 따르면, 청자들은 웹사이트에서 무엇을 할 수 있는가?
   영상 이용하기

CHECK UP

🎧 P4_U13_02 정답 및 해설 p.290

1. What type of class is being advertised?
   (A) Presentations
   (B) Business writing
   (C) Accounting
   (D) Computer programming

2. According to the speaker, why are the classes unique?
   (A) The fee is lower than similar courses.
   (B) A certificate will be issued at the end.
   (C) They are available in person and online.
   (D) They include feedback from experts.

3. How can the listeners get additional information?
   (A) By attending an event
   (B) By sending an e-mail
   (C) By visiting a Web site
   (D) By calling the institute

빈출 상황

제품/서비스 광고	If you're having trouble sleeping, find Gravity Mattress today. We guarantee you'll have a good night's sleep. 잠을 자는 데 어려움이 있다면, 오늘 그래비티 매트리스를 찾아보세요. 저희는 당신의 숙면을 보장합니다.
업체 광고	Are you looking for a place to go for a delicious meal? Then come to Danny's Seafood. 맛있는 식사를 위해 갈 만한 장소를 찾고 있나요? 그렇다면 대니스 해산물 전문점으로 오세요.
견학/교육 프로그램 광고	The Linked Institute is offering a new course about project management. 링크드 협회에서는 프로젝트 관리에 관한 새로운 강의를 제공하고 있습니다.
부동산 광고	If you're looking for a new office space for your company, consider moving to Infinity Building. 당신의 회사를 위한 새로운 사무실 공간을 찾고 있다면, 인피니티 빌딩으로 이사하는 것을 고려해 보세요.
구인 광고	Are you looking for a rewarding career? Consider becoming a sales associate at Northland Shop. 보람 있는 직업을 찾고 있나요? 노스랜드 상점의 영업 사원이 되는 것을 고려해 보세요.

빈출 표현

🎧 P4_U13_03

home repair 집수리
office space 사무실 공간
release 출시; 출시하다
hold an event 행사를 열다
folding bicycle 접이식 자전거
financial needs 재정적 필요
rewarding career 보람 있는 직업, 보수가 좋은 직업
guided tour 안내원을 동반하는 견학
unique experience 이색적인 경험
private room 사적인 공간
family gathering 가족 모임
accommodate 수용하다
technical skills 전문 능력
install 설치하다
renovation 보수 공사
high quality 고품질
convenience 편의, 편리한 것
a wide variety of 매우 다양한
locally made 현지에서 생산된
highly anticipated 몹시 기대되는
first-class 최고의
experienced 경력이 풍부한
specially designed 특별하게 디자인된
highly skilled 고도로 숙련된
well-trained 잘 훈련된
popular features 인기 있는 사양
exceptional customer service 뛰어난 고객 서비스
comfortable to ~하기에 편한

compact shape 아담한 형태
up-to-date information 최신 정보
reasonable price 합리적인 가격
fit your budget 예산에 맞다
special offer 특가 판매
free of charge 무료의
complimentary 무료의
affordable price 저렴한 가격
A as well as B B뿐만 아니라 A도
offer 10 percent off 10퍼센트 할인을 제공하다
leave a review 후기를 남기다
place an order 주문하다
be good until ~까지 유효하다
for a limited time 한시적으로
qualify for ~의 자격을 얻다
receive an automatic discount 자동 할인을 받다
enter the promotional code 할인 코드를 입력하다
schedule a consultation 상담 일정을 잡다
stop by ~에 들르다
Do you need ~? ~이 필요한가요?
Are you looking for ~? ~을 찾고 계신가요?
Do you want to improve ~? ~을 향상시키고 싶나요?
If you're having trouble -ing ~하는 데 어려움이 있다면
If you're interested in ~하는 데 관심이 있다면
If you're tired of ~에 싫증이 났다면
We guarantee that 저희는 ~을 보장합니다
We hope to see you soon at ~에서 곧 뵙기를 희망합니다
Visit our Web site to 저희 웹사이트를 방문하셔서 ~하세요

[1-4] 질문과 정답을 확인한 뒤, 대화를 들으면서 정답의 단서가 되는 부분에 표시하세요.

1. **Q** What is the advertisement about?

A A sports drink

> **W** Do you work out regularly? Then you need a way to keep your body hydrated and fueled. Fire-Flex is a new line of performance beverages that will surely quench your thirst when you're working out. They also deliver a targeted combination of vitamins to nourish your muscles and reduce fatigue.

2. **Q** What is being offered to new customers?

A A free consultation

> **M** It's time to start planning for your future with help from Vernon Investments. If you've never used our services before, sign up today to get a complimentary consultation with one of our investment advisors.

3. **Q** How can the listeners receive a free gift?

A By signing up for an account

> **W** We're pleased to introduce our new loyalty program where you can earn points on every purchase at Tino's Department Store. Anyone who registers for a customer account with our store will receive a free tote bag with the Tino's logo. More information is available at our customer service desk.

4. **Q** What can customers receive if they make a purchase before April 30th?

A Some training

> **M** Our photo editing software will help to make all of your projects look as if they were created by a professional. And, if you purchase the software before April 30th, we'll give you a free instructional session. This will help you to become familiar with all of the features.

[5-6] 대화를 듣고 정답의 단서가 알맞게 패러프레이징된 답을 고르세요.

5. According to the speaker, what has the business recently done?

(A) It completed a renovation project.
(B) It hired a new chef.

6. What does the speaker encourage the listeners to do?

(A) Order in advance
(B) Leave a review

대화를 듣고 알맞은 답을 고른 뒤, 다시 들으면서 빈칸을 채우세요.

1. How can the listeners get more information?

(A) By visiting a Web site
(B) By e-mailing a manager
(C) By calling the company
(D) By viewing a video

W If you're having trouble getting motivated about going to work every day, it might be time for a change. At Utica Automotive Company, you can have an exciting as well as lucrative career in car sales. You'll get to meet lots of people while working in a supportive environment. We're currently hiring people with great communication skills, even those who are not experienced in sales. To find out more, _____ from 8 A.M. to 6 P.M. at 555-1212.

2. What is being advertised?

(A) A remodeling company
(B) A marketing firm
(C) A delivery company
(D) An instant messaging service

3. According to the speaker, why should the listeners contact the business?

(A) To request a discount
(B) To check a price
(C) To set up an account
(D) To apply for a job

M In today's fast-paced world, no one can afford to lag behind. That's why Rapid Express _____ _____ on the market today. We will deliver packages 15 percent faster than any other company working today. We guarantee that all international packages will be delivered within 48 hours and all domestic packages within 24 hours. Contact us now to see _____ for your specific package. Call us at 555-0147. We'll save you time and help you deliver results.

4. What type of event is being advertised?

(A) An annual festival
(B) A large plant sale
(C) An amusement park opening
(D) A gardening supply exposition

5. According to the speaker, what is available on a Web site?

(A) The hours of operation
(B) A list of events
(C) A discount voucher
(D) The location of the events

W Brooklyn Botanical Garden is proud to _____ of our Spring and Sunshine Festival. This weekend, we will offer over 60 events celebrating the gorgeous trees and the return of spring. The two-day festival will begin next Saturday, the 30th of April. Bring your whole family. In fact, you can _____ from our Web site. It will give your whole family, up to two adults and two children, admission to the gardens for the price of two adult tickets. Come celebrate spring with Brooklyn Botanical Gardens.

PART 4

UNIT 13

대화를 듣고 알맞은 답을 고르세요.

1. What is being advertised?

(A) An office security system
(B) A videoconference software program
(C) An Internet service provider
(D) A new version of a smartphone

2. What benefit of the product does the speaker mention?

(A) It is affordable.
(B) It has many features.
(C) It is easy to use.
(D) It comes with a guarantee.

3. According to the speaker, what can the listeners do in January?

(A) Have a representative visit
(B) Try a product for free
(C) Enter a prize drawing
(D) Watch a demonstration

4. How does the factory tour end?

(A) Some catalogs are distributed.
(B) The participants paint an item.
(C) A group photograph is taken.
(D) An employee responds to questions.

5. According to the speaker, what is sold in the gift shop?

(A) Dishes
(B) Snacks
(C) Maps
(D) Clothing

6. What does the speaker remind the listeners about?

(A) Whom to contact
(B) When a site closes
(C) What footwear to use
(D) Where to leave belongings

7. What type of product is being advertised?

(A) A blender
(B) A microwave oven
(C) A coffee machine
(D) A refrigerator

8. What feature of the R-60 does the speaker highlight?

(A) It is energy efficient.
(B) It has an affordable price.
(C) It has a compact shape.
(D) It is durable.

9. What does the speaker imply when she says, "You can't miss it"?

(A) The listeners should be careful.
(B) Attendance is mandatory.
(C) A special offer will end soon.
(D) A display is easy to find.

10. What is being advertised?

(A) A film screening
(B) An art festival
(C) A sports competition
(D) A book sale

11. According to the speaker, what can the listeners do online?

(A) Request a refund
(B) Get driving directions
(C) Reserve a seat
(D) Make a donation

12. What will happen at the end of the event?

(A) An award will be presented.
(B) A prize drawing will be held.
(C) A reporter will film an interview.
(D) A person will sign autographs.

13. What is being advertised?

(A) An apartment building
(B) A sports stadium
(C) A music hall
(D) An office complex

14. What benefit of the site does the speaker highlight?

(A) New appliances
(B) Access to public transportation
(C) A spacious parking lot
(D) Outdoor recreation areas

15. According to the speaker, how can the listeners get more information?

(A) By sending an e-mail
(B) By browsing a Web site
(C) By taking a tour
(D) By calling the business

Little Italy Buffet	
Buffet Meals	**Price**
All-you-can-eat lunch: Adult	$11.99
All-you-can-eat lunch: Child	$9.99
All-you-can-eat dinner: Adult	$12.99
All-you-can-eat dinner: Child	$10.99

16. What has the business recently done?

(A) It expanded its menu.
(B) It added outdoor seating.
(C) It extended its hours of operation.
(D) It opened a new location.

17. Look at the graphic. How much is the adult lunch buffet in April?

(A) $11.99
(B) $9.99
(C) $12.99
(D) $10.99

18. Why are the listeners asked to call the business?

(A) To make a reservation
(B) To get food delivered to their house
(C) To leave a review
(D) To report dietary restrictions

핵심 포인트

1. 지역 뉴스 및 교통 상황, 또는 일반 교양 프로그램에서 방송 주제나 초대 손님을 소개하는 내용이 주로 나온다. 일기 예보는 최근 출제 빈도가 낮은 편이다.
2. 프로그램 및 주제 → 주요 소식 → 다음 방송 안내 순으로 전개되는 경우가 많으며, 방송 주제나 세부사항을 묻는 문제가 자주 출제된다.

실전 맛보기

🎧 P4_U14_01

M And now it's time for the local news. ¹The city council has approved funding to renovate the north swimming pool area at the Stratford Community Center. The floor tiles will be replaced, and upgrades will be made to the pool's filtration system. ²Those who are interested in seeing what the completed pool will look like can view copies of the designs on the city's Web site. The work will begin in April. ³If you enjoy swimming, don't worry. The opening hours for the south swimming pool will remain the same.

남 지금은 지역 뉴스 시간입니다. ¹시 의회는 스트래트퍼드 지역 문화 센터의 북쪽 수영장을 보수하기 위한 자금을 승인했습니다. 바닥 타일이 교체될 것이며, 수영장 여과 시스템이 업그레이드될 것입니다. ²보수가 끝난 수영장이 어떤 모습일지 확인하는 데 관심 있으신 분들은 시 웹사이트에서 설계도 사본을 볼 수 있습니다. 이 작업은 4월에 시작될 것입니다. ³여러분이 수영하는 것을 즐기신다면, 걱정하지 마세요. 남쪽 수영장의 운영 시간은 그대로 유지될 것입니다.

1. What is the focus of the broadcast? 주제
   A renovation project

2. According to the speaker, what can the listeners find on a Web site? 세부사항
   Some designs

3. What does the speaker say to reassure the listeners? 세부사항
   Some services will not be interrupted.

1. 방송의 주제는 무엇인가?
   보수 공사

2. 화자에 따르면, 청자들은 웹사이트에서 무엇을 찾을 수 있는가?
   설계도

3. 화자는 청자들을 안심시키기 위해 무엇이라고 말하는가?
   일부 서비스는 중단되지 않을 것이다.

CHECK UP

🎧 P4_U14_02 정답 및 해설 p.298

1. What is the broadcast about?
   (A) An industry conference
   (B) A career development workshop
   (C) A software program
   (D) A job opening

2. According to the speaker, why should the listeners visit a Web site?
   (A) To read some reviews
   (B) To download a coupon
   (C) To request a free trial
   (D) To view a schedule

3. What will the listeners hear next?
   (A) An advertisement
   (B) A traffic report
   (C) A political debate
   (D) A weather forecast

빈출 상황

경제 뉴스	Uptown Manufacturing announced that it has chosen Jeffrey Schultz to take over as CEO. 업타운 제조사에서 제프리 슐츠가 대표이사직을 인수하도록 결정했다고 발표했습니다.
지역 소식	For those of you in the neighborhood, the annual film festival starts in Montreal today and continues throughout the weekend. 지역에 계신 분들께 알립니다. 연례 영화제가 오늘 몬트리올에서 시작해 주말 동안 계속됩니다.
교통 상황	Motorists traveling south on Highway 70 are reminded that there's road construction near the exit to Atlantic City. 70번 고속도로를 타고 남쪽으로 가는 운전자들에게 애틀랜틱시티로 나가는 출구 근처에 도로 공사가 있다는 것을 다시 한번 알립니다.
일기 예보	And now for the local weather report. It looks like the snow will clear up this afternoon. 그리고 이제 지역 일기 예보입니다. 오늘 오후에는 눈이 그칠 것으로 보입니다.
기타 방송 프로그램	Today I'm delighted to have on the show Jordan Russell, the chief designer of Forest Park. 오늘 저는 포레스트 파크의 수석 디자이너인 조던 러셀을 방송에 모시게 되어 기쁩니다.

빈출 표현

🎧 P4_U14_03

뉴스/ 프로그램			
local news 지역 뉴스		increase in prices 가격 인상	
industrial news 산업 뉴스		lower supply 줄어든 공급	
regional business news 지역 경제 뉴스		approve funding 자금 제공을 승인하다	
architectural news 건축계 소식		lead to ~로 이어지다	
automobile industry 자동차 산업		lost revenue 수익 손실	
host 진행자		generate profits 이익을 창출하다	
radio station 라디오 방송국		on air 방송 중인	
an important reminder 중요한 알림		commercial break 광고 시간	
spokesperson 대변인		interview with ~와의 인터뷰	
election 선출		special guest 특별 초대 손님	
launch 출시하다		world-renowned 세계적으로 유명한	
be founded by ~에 의해 설립되다		expert in ~의 전문가	
be awarded a license 허가를 받다		Thanks for tuning in to ~를 들어 주셔서 감사합니다	
release a new application 새로운 앱을 출시하다		On today's episode 오늘 방송에서는	
expand into international markets 국제 시장에 진출하다		~ will be joining us ~가 이 자리에 함께할 것입니다	
		Stay tuned 채널을 고정해 주세요	

교통/날씨			
traffic conditions 교통 상황		be closed for ~로 인해 폐쇄되다	
commuter 통근자		take a detour 우회하다	
motorist 운전자		take an alternative route 다른 길로 가다	
travel 이동하다		cause a lot of noise and traffic jams 많은 소음과 교통체증을 유발하다	
highway 고속도로		weather report 일기 예보	
road construction 도로 공사		inclement weather 악천후	
resurface 재포장하다		snowstorm 눈보라	
lane 차선		clear up (날이) 개다	
exit to ~로 나가는 출구		with no chance of ~할 확률이 없는	
traffic congestion 교통 혼잡		precipitation 강수량	
significant delay 심각한 지연		be in the forecast 예보가 있다	
heavy traffic 극심한 교통량			

[1-4] 질문과 정답을 확인한 뒤, 대화를 들으면서 정답의 단서가 되는 부분에 표시하세요.

1. **Q** What will Walston Enterprises do next month?

    A Start an internship program

> **M** At a press conference this morning, a representative from Walston Enterprises announced that the company will launch an internship program next month. Walston is the leading provider of marketing services in the technology sector. It is seeking to help the next generation of marketers as well as identifying potential employees.

2. **Q** According to the speaker, why is a business successful?

    A It offers a wide selection.

> **W** Thanks for tuning in to *City Life*, the show about what to do in and around Lexington. Today we're looking at Carson Resort. This is one of the most visited attractions in Lexington. Its popularity is due largely to the variety of activities it provides.

3. **Q** What will take place in Lodgeville in September?

    A A sporting event

> **M** Event planners in Lodgeville are still looking for volunteers to assist with the annual marathon in September. The race is expected to attract visitors from across the state as people come to watch the athletes compete.

4. **Q** How will the recent donation be used?

    A To pay for translators

> **W** You're listening to *Nature News* on Radio 103.4 FM. Our guest today is Patrick Miller, head of the National Parks Service. He'll be discussing a Web site upgrade aimed at attracting international visitors to the parks. For example, thanks to a recent private donation, the department will be able to hire translators for the Web site's contents.

[5-6] 대화를 듣고 정답의 단서가 알맞게 패러프레이징된 답을 고르세요.

5. According to the speaker, what are experts anticipating?

    (A) Higher prices

    (B) Greater variety

6. What problem does the speaker mention?

    (A) An increase in the cost of materials

    (B) A shortage of skilled employees

대화를 듣고 알맞은 답을 고른 뒤, 다시 들으면서 빈칸을 채우세요.

1. What does the speaker say she is excited about?

(A) A sports tournament
(B) An art exhibition
(C) A dance performance
(D) A singing contest

> **W** Now let's take a look at what's in the forecast for this weekend. Both Saturday and Sunday will be cool and sunny with no chance of rain. That's perfect weather for the Summer Festival at Camden Park. The New York Dance Group will be _____, so I'm really looking forward to that. I'm glad we'll have nice weather for it. Remember, you don't need tickets for the festival. However, you may want to bring your own chairs.

2. Who will be interviewed?

(A) A doctor
(B) An author
(C) A politician
(D) A journalist

3. What will the listeners hear next?

(A) Some news reports
(B) A sports update
(C) Traffic reports
(D) Some commercials

> **M** This is *Fresh Horizons*, and I'm Steven Shapiro. On today's episode, Olivia Mann will be joining us. She is a professor of Psychology at Pearfield University. She will be telling us about her book, *How We Think*, _____ _____. But, before we get to Ms. Mann, let's look at the weather report. Tonight and tomorrow, we have a slight chance of precipitation. Then, on Sunday it's going to clear up. Now, we will be right back with Olivia Mann after _____ _____.

4. What is the speaker discussing?

(A) Road damage
(B) Bus services
(C) Heavy traffic
(D) Parking issues

5. What does the speaker recommend doing?

(A) Allowing some extra time
(B) Attending a meeting
(C) Reporting road accidents
(D) Using a residential street

> **W** Let's take a look at the rush hour traffic. As usual, _____ headed into the city center. This has been an ongoing problem and a source of stress for commuters. Most experts say that it is unlikely to change without adding a carpool lane. If you think this is a good idea and would like to voice your opinion, you should _____ _____ to join in the debate.

대화를 듣고 알맞은 답을 고르세요.

1. According to the speaker, what will Mr. Kirwin do this summer?

(A) Invest in a business
(B) Take a world tour
(C) Teach a class
(D) Release a product line

2. What will Mr. Kirwin talk about on today's program?

(A) His career history
(B) His new book
(C) His educational goals
(D) His art exhibit

3. What are the listeners encouraged to do?

(A) Call with questions
(B) Enter a contest
(C) Buy tickets in advance
(D) Join a mailing list

---

4. What kind of food is the radio program about?

(A) A dairy product
(B) A beverage
(C) A fruit
(D) A vegetable

5. What will Gina Diaz discuss about a food item?

(A) Its production
(B) Its growing popularity
(C) Its health benefits
(D) Its cost

6. Why should the listeners visit a Web site?

(A) To get some recipes
(B) To post a comment
(C) To check a schedule
(D) To search for a store

7. What is the cause of a delay?

(A) Road construction is in progress.
(B) A vehicle has broken down.
(C) Lines are being painted on a highway.
(D) There is inclement weather.

8. What will some drivers have to do?

(A) Take a detour
(B) Use public transportation
(C) Park at another site
(D) Pay a toll

9. According to the speaker, how can the listeners get more information?

(A) By calling the radio station
(B) By downloading a mobile application
(C) By reading a brochure
(D) By listening to another broadcast

---

10. What will be built in the community?

(A) A community center
(B) A park
(C) A hospital
(D) A library

11. What benefit of the project is mentioned?

(A) It will conserve wildlife.
(B) It will improve the employment rate.
(C) It will increase tourism.
(D) It will boost population growth.

12. Who will be interviewed after the break?

(A) A governor
(B) An instructor
(C) Community residents
(D) Wildlife experts

---

13. What is the news report mainly about?

(A) A community award
(B) A corporate merger
(C) A local business
(D) A product recall

14. What does the speaker imply when she says, "10 more vans were recently added"?

(A) A service has become popular.
(B) There was an error with an order.
(C) A business needs more information.
(D) Some new investors are needed.

15. Who will Mr. Evans meet with next week?

(A) Marketing experts
(B) Store owners
(C) Local doctors
(D) City officials

Date	Temperature	Chance of Rain
April 7	11°C	25%
April 8	15°C	20%
April 9	12°C	5%
April 10	14°C	10%
April 11	9°C	15%

16. Look at the graphic. When will a grand opening event be held?

(A) April 8
(B) April 9
(C) April 10
(D) April 11

17. What has been relocated to the Valley Amusement Park?

(A) A beach house
(B) A famous statue
(C) A roller coaster
(D) An outdoor stage

18. What are park visitors advised to do?

(A) Bring their own lunch
(B) Wear comfortable footwear
(C) Pack an umbrella
(D) Purchase a group ticket

핵심 포인트 | 1. 가이드나 안내원이 다양한 장소 및 시설물의 관광, 견학을 이끄는 담화로, 인사말 및 자기소개 → 관광/견학 세부사항 → 당부 및 다음 일정 안내와 같은 흐름으로 전개된다.
2. 장소, 세부사항, 제안/요청사항이나 다음에 할 일을 묻는 문제가 자주 출제된다.

실전 맛보기

🎧 P4_U15_01

M ¹Thank you for signing up for this tour of our hybrid car manufacturing plant. Here at Abida Automotive, we value innovation and quality. We'll be starting on the production floor, so ²please wear the hard hats and safety goggles I gave you when you arrived. You will be able to take a close look at the assembly process for two different models. ³At the end of the tour, you will have the opportunity to test drive one of the models if you'd like. Then you'll be able to see the amazing features for yourself.

남 ¹이번 저희 하이브리드 승용차 제조공장 견학에 신청해 주셔서 감사합니다. 이곳 아비다 자동차는 혁신과 품질을 소중하게 생각합니다. 생산 현장에서 시작할 예정이니 ²여러분이 도착하셨을 때 제가 드린 안전모와 보호 안경을 착용해 주시기 바랍니다. 두 개의 서로 다른 모델들의 조립 과정을 자세히 살펴보실 수 있을 것입니다. ³견학이 끝날 때, 여러분은 원하시면 모델들 중 하나를 시승해 볼 기회를 가지게 될 것입니다. 그러면 여러분이 직접 놀라운 기능들을 확인하실 수 있을 것입니다.

1. Where most likely are the listeners? 장소
At an automobile factory

2. What does the speaker ask the listeners to do?
Wear protective gear 요청사항

3. How will the listeners end the tour? 세부사항
By trying some products

1. 청자들은 어디에 있는 것 같은가?
자동차 공장에

2. 화자는 청자들에게 무엇을 하라고 요청하는가?
보호 장비 착용하기

3. 청자들은 어떻게 견학을 끝낼 것인가?
일부 제품을 이용해 봄으로써

CHECK UP

🎧 P4_U15_02 정답 및 해설 p.306

1. What kind of tour is the speaker leading?

(A) A boat tour
(B) A train tour
(C) A bicycle tour
(D) A walking tour

2. What is the village of Pendleton famous for?

(A) Diverse wildlife
(B) Unique architecture
(C) Handmade jewelry
(D) Traditional music

3. What does the speaker imply when he says, "The forecast said it will be windy"?

(A) The listeners should prepare warm clothing.
(B) A trip may take longer than usual.
(C) Some safety rules must be followed.
(D) A previous report was incorrect.

빈출 상황

여행지 이동	Attention everyone. The next stop is on quite a busy road, so please watch your step as you exit the tour bus. 모두 주목해 주세요. 다음에 내릴 곳은 꽤 혼잡한 도로이니, 관광버스에서 내리실 때 발밑을 조심하시길 바랍니다.
유적지 답사	I want to welcome you all to this tour of the historic Herz Mansion designed by renowned architect Lukas Herz. 유명한 건축가 루카스 헤르츠가 설계한 역사적인 헤르츠 저택의 관광에 오신 여러분 모두 환영합니다.
공장 견학	Today I'll be showing you our process of taking raw materials and turning them into components for the computer industry. 오늘 저는 원료를 가져와서 컴퓨터 산업을 위한 부품으로 바꾸는 과정을 여러분에게 보여드릴 것입니다.
기타 문화시설 관람	As you walk around the Victoria Museum today, you'll learn about the entire history of railway. 오늘 빅토리아 박물관을 둘러보면서, 여러분은 철도의 모든 역사에 대해 배울 것입니다.

빈출 표현

🎧 P4_U15_03

tour guide 여행 가이드
historic building 역사적인 건물
manufacturing plant 제조 공장
assembly process 조립 공정
art gallery 미술관
village 마을, 부락
mansion 저택
facility 시설
landmark 주요 지형지물
filming location 영화 촬영지
wildlife tour 야생 동물 관람
permanent exhibit 상설 전시
planetarium 천문관
preserved 보존된
exterior 외관
artifact 유물
artisan 장인
handcraft 수공예; 손으로 만들다
packaging 포장
renowned architect 유명한 건축가
talented artists 재능 있는 예술가들
be founded by ~에 의해 설립되다
be known for ~로 알려져 있다
be crowded with ~로 붐비다
family owned and operated 가족이 소유하고 운영하는
date back to 시기가 ~까지 거슬러 올라가다
the Middle Ages 중세 시대
the 18th century 18세기

remarkable[notable] 주목할 만한
impressive 인상적인
unique features 독특한 특징
on display 전시 중인
hands-on experience 실제 체험
safety rules 안전 수칙
wear a hard hat 안전모를 쓰다
at all times 항상
flash photography 플래시 촬영
along with ~와 함께
complimentary breakfast 무료 아침 식사
walking distance 도보로 갈 수 있는 거리
explore 탐험하다
gift shop 기념품점
souvenir 기념품
hand out 나누어 주다
point out 가리키다
make sure 반드시 ~하다
move on to ~로 이동하다
get back to ~로 돌아가다
be allowed to ~하도록 허용되다
leave in about 10 minutes 약 10분 뒤에 출발하다
remain with the group 일행과 함께 있다
stay in the area 지역에 머무르다
last approximately one hour 한 시간 정도 계속되다
take a close look at ~을 자세히 보다
take plenty of photos 사진을 많이 찍다
end the tour 견학을 마치다

[1-4] 질문과 정답을 확인한 뒤, 대화를 들으면서 정답의 단서가 되는 부분에 표시하세요.

1. **Q** What will the listeners have the opportunity to do on a tour?

A Learn about a house

> **M** I hope you will all enjoy this tour of the historic Terrick Mansion, which was built in the 1700s. Our tour today will cover just the mansion itself. I would be happy to answer any questions you may have along the way.

2. **Q** Why does the speaker plan to stop regularly?

A To keep the group together

> **W** As we go higher on the hiking trail, you'll begin to get an amazing view of the valley below. You are welcome to hike at your own pace. However, please don't lose sight of the group as we go. I'll stop regularly to let people catch up and make sure we're all still together.

3. **Q** According to the speaker, what is the Hewitt Estate famous for?

A Being used as a film location

> **M** The pillars at the front of the historic Hewitt Estate are made from marble that was imported from Italy. The home is well-known for being the filming location of the movie *The Queen's Secret*, so it will probably look familiar to you.

4. **Q** Where are the listeners?

A At a ceramics factory

> **W** We hope you will all enjoy this tour of our ceramics manufacturing plant. At Wayfair Ceramics, we are dedicated to creating stylish designs that will look great in your home. And we make our products to last for a long time.

[5-6] 대화를 듣고 정답의 단서가 알맞게 패러프레이징된 답을 고르세요.

5. What does the speaker say about the company?

(A) It has opened a second location.

(B) It is a family-run operation.

6. According to the speaker, why do people like the exhibit?

(A) It is updated frequently.

(B) It is very educational.

대화를 듣고 알맞은 답을 고른 뒤, 다시 들으면서 빈칸을 채우세요.

1. What does the speaker invite the listeners to do?

(A) Visit the on-site café
(B) Attend a workshop
(C) Join a loyalty program
(D) Participate in a fund-raiser

W As we tour the Crescent Museum today, you'll see a wide range of artifacts from the Middle Ages. Our permanent exhibit is one of the nation's largest collections of sculptures, mosaics, and tapestries from this period. The tour will last approximately one hour. After that, we are _____ in which you can make a craft using a book-binding technique from the 10th century. _____. The event is available at no additional cost.

2. What does the speaker say about Christian Maggio?

(A) He designed the bank.
(B) He was the first bank teller.
(C) He will show them around the place.
(D) He made coins and bills.

3. What will the listeners do next?

(A) Watch a video
(B) Purchase some souvenirs
(C) Visit a tourist attraction
(D) Have refreshments

M Now, we are approaching the last stop on this tour. On your right, you'll notice an old red brick building. This is the first bank in our country, _____ Christian Maggio and built in the early 18th century. Construction of this bank took much longer than expected due to the unusually cold weather that winter. Before we finish our tour, let's _____ and have a look at the mint, where you can see the entire process of making coins and bills.

4. What will the listeners see on the tour?

(A) Modern machinery
(B) Famous paintings
(C) Exotic animals
(D) Historic architecture

5. How can the listeners get a coupon?

(A) By making a purchase in the gift shop
(B) By signing up with a group
(C) By posting a picture online
(D) By filling out a survey

W I'd like to welcome you all to the Guildford Zoo. On our tour today, you'll have the opportunity to _____ _____ such as lions, flamingos, and giraffes. Please feel free to take as many pictures as you like, but remember that flash photography is not permitted inside any of the buildings. We would also love for you to share your photos. If you _____ ___, we'll send you a coupon for 20 percent off your next visit.

PART 4

UNIT 15

대화를 듣고 알맞은 답을 고르세요.

1. What is prohibited during the tour?
   (A) Leaving the group
   (B) Taking pictures
   (C) Using mobile phones
   (D) Eating food

2. What does the speaker say happened in March?
   (A) A test was carried out on the water.
   (B) Some residents were featured in a documentary.
   (C) Improvements were made to the village.
   (D) A generous donation was sent.

3. What does the speaker encourage the listeners to sign up for?
   (A) A business membership
   (B) A mailing list
   (C) A new workshop
   (D) A boat tour

4. What does the speaker explain about a trail?
   (A) How many visitors it gets
   (B) How it has been improved
   (C) How long ago it was created
   (D) How long it takes to complete

5. What does the speaker remind the listeners to do?
   (A) Bring extra water
   (B) Put their phones on silent
   (C) Check their backpacks
   (D) Carry a map

6. Why will the speaker make some stops?
   (A) To give participants a break
   (B) To take some pictures
   (C) To point out plants
   (D) To answer some questions

7. What does the speaker warn the listeners about?
   (A) An additional fee
   (B) A busy road
   (C) A refund policy
   (D) A closure time

8. What will the speaker give to the listeners?
   (A) Admission tickets
   (B) Site maps
   (C) Protective hats
   (D) Packed lunches

9. According to the speaker, what will some listeners need to do?
   (A) Find their own transportation
   (B) Pay a remaining balance
   (C) Show an identification card
   (D) Contact the hotel

10. Where is the tour taking place?
    (A) At an art museum
    (B) At a railway company
    (C) At a science museum
    (D) At a beverage factory

11. Why does the speaker apologize to the listeners?
    (A) A tour will begin late.
    (B) Some equipment is not working.
    (C) A ticketing process took a long time.
    (D) Some brochures contained an error.

12. According to the speaker, what can the listeners do at the end of the tour?
    (A) Meet some employees
    (B) Purchase some souvenirs
    (C) Try some free samples
    (D) Fill out a questionnaire

13. What does the speaker encourage the listeners to do after the tour?

(A) Watch a film
(B) View some artwork
(C) Pick up a brochure
(D) Visit a gift shop

14. What does the speaker imply when he says, "planting is going on in the rose gardens"?

(A) Some parts of the site will not be visited.
(B) A photo shoot has been moved.
(C) The listeners can watch a demonstration.
(D) Some temporary workers are needed.

15. According to the speaker, what makes the gardens popular with filmmakers?

(A) They have a wide variety of flowers.
(B) They get a lot of natural light.
(C) They are in a good location.
(D) They have a traditional design.

Section 1	Mixing
Section 2	Stretching
Section 3	Cutting
Section 4	Packaging

16. According to the speaker, what does the company focus on?

(A) Sourcing local goods
(B) Achieving steady growth
(C) Being environmentally responsible
(D) Improving customer service

17. Look at the graphic. Which area will the listeners see next?

(A) Section 1
(B) Section 2
(C) Section 3
(D) Section 4

18. Who most likely is Ashely Bowman?

(A) A factory manager
(B) A tour guide
(C) A delivery person
(D) A company founder

PART 4

UNIT 15

PART 4

Directions: You will hear some talks given by a single speaker. You will be asked to answer three questions about what the speaker says in each talk. Select the best response to each question and mark the letter (A), (B), (C), or (D) on your answer sheet. The talks will not be printed in your test book and will be spoken only one time.

71. What did the speaker do during the lunch break?

(A) He adjusted a schedule.
(B) He visited different departments.
(C) He ordered some new computers.
(D) He reviewed some meeting notes.

72. What are the listeners reminded to do?

(A) Avoid bringing food to the office
(B) Read company notices carefully
(C) Arrive for their shift on time
(D) Sign out of a software program

73. What does the speaker congratulate the listeners for?

(A) Winning an award
(B) Completing a job early
(C) Receiving good feedback
(D) Having an article published

74. Who is Frederick Bryant?

(A) An athlete
(B) A radio host
(C) A politician
(D) A teacher

75. What will Frederick Bryant talk about on the show?

(A) His retirement plan
(B) His charity work
(C) His new Web site
(D) His promotional tour

76. Why does the speaker say, "there are only a hundred"?

(A) To correct a misunderstanding
(B) To recommend going to an event early
(C) To explain why a price is high
(D) To request another order

77. Why is the speaker meeting with the listeners?

(A) To gather feedback from the listeners
(B) To introduce a machinery supplier
(C) To prepare for a relocation
(D) To show how to use some equipment

78. What does the speaker give to the listeners?

(A) A job description
(B) A set of instructions
(C) A packing checklist
(D) A product review

79. What will the listeners do at the end of the meeting?

(A) Be served a meal
(B) Receive a bonus
(C) Renew a contract
(D) Take a test

80. Who most likely is Gerald Burton?

(A) A property developer
(B) A radio host
(C) A city official
(D) A tour guide

81. What has happened recently?

(A) Some costs have increased.
(B) Some buildings failed an inspection.
(C) A site has become more popular.
(D) A local election was held.

82. What does the speaker suggest when he says, "visitor numbers won't change"?

(A) He thinks more advertising is needed.
(B) He agrees with a proposal.
(C) He is concerned about a policy.
(D) He wants a decision to be debated.

83. What is the workshop mainly about?

(A) How to invest wisely
(B) How to manage a team
(C) How to launch a product
(D) How to create a business model

84. What does the speaker advise the listeners to do?

(A) Outsource difficult tasks
(B) Spend time wisely
(C) Set clear goals
(D) Use multiple suppliers

85. What will the listeners most likely do next?

(A) Ask the speaker some questions
(B) Correct some errors in a report
(C) Watch an instructional video
(D) Have a role-play activity

86. What is the advertisement mainly about?

(A) A sports tournament
(B) An annual parade
(C) A cooking competition
(D) A grand opening

87. What does the speaker say about Carolina Department Store?

(A) It will provide free delivery for purchases.
(B) It will be closed on August 4.
(C) It will offer lower prices on some products.
(D) It will have a musical performance.

88. How can the listeners receive a discount?

(A) By completing a survey
(B) By signing up early
(C) By joining a mailing list
(D) By paying in cash

89. What event is the speaker talking about?

(A) An anniversary party
(B) A board meeting
(C) An industry trade show
(D) A community fund-raiser

90. Why does the speaker say, "It's a popular route"?

(A) To explain a price increase
(B) To warn that a train may be crowded
(C) To confirm some driving directions
(D) To suggest allowing extra travel time

91. According to the speaker, what has the management team decided to do?

(A) Cancel an order
(B) Extend a deadline
(C) Assign new teams
(D) Adjust a budget

92. According to the broadcast, what will Cantu do next month?

(A) Move to Dallas
(B) Replace its CEO
(C) Expand its service area
(D) Add children's videos

93. What unique feature does the speaker mention about Cantu?

(A) It can be used on a variety of devices.
(B) It makes recommendations for movies to watch.
(C) It lets users upload their own videos.
(D) It allows customers to pause the service.

94. What will Mary Snyder talk about?

(A) A job opening
(B) A company's history
(C) A loyalty program
(D) A project deadline

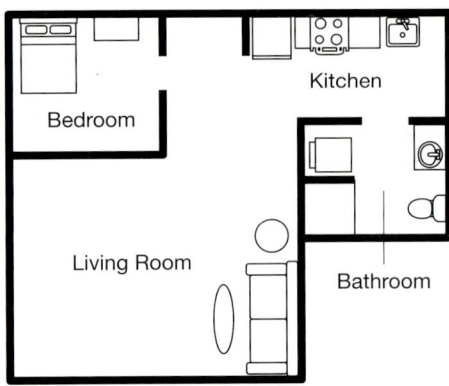

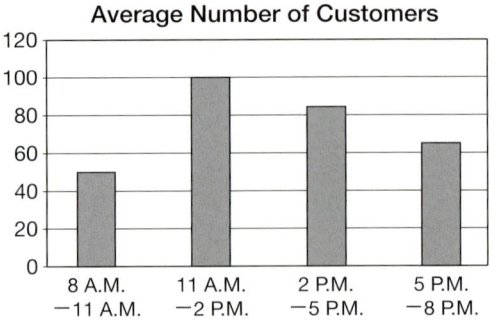

Average Number of Customers

95. Where most likely does the speaker work?

(A) At a real estate agency
(B) At a design firm
(C) At a delivery service
(D) At a cleaning company

96. Look at the graphic. Where are the listeners?

(A) In the bedroom
(B) In the kitchen
(C) In the living room
(D) In the bathroom

97. What are the listeners reminded to do?

(A) Use a parking pass
(B) Show an identification badge
(C) Wear protective gear
(D) Leave a business card

98. Who most likely is the speaker?

(A) A computer technician
(B) A store manager
(C) A financial advisor
(D) A product developer

99. Look at the graphic. When will the display be set up?

(A) From 8 A.M. to 11 A.M.
(B) From 11 A.M. to 2 P.M.
(C) From 2 P.M. to 5 P.M.
(D) From 5 P.M. to 8 P.M.

100. What will be given to employees who work extra hours?

(A) A free meal
(B) A coffee thermos
(C) A gift certificate
(D) Some time off

고난도 문제
해설 강의

실전
모의고사

ANSWER SHEET

LISTENING TEST

In the Listening test, you will be asked to demonstrate how well you understand spoken English. The entire Listening test will last approximately 45 minutes. There are four parts, and directions are given for each part. You must mark your answers on the separate answer sheet. Do not write your answers in your test book.

PART 1

Directions: For each question in this part, you will hear four statements about a picture in your test book. When you hear the statements, you must select the one statement that best describes what you see in the picture. Then find the number of the question on your answer sheet and mark your answer. The statements will not be printed in your test book and will be spoken only one time.

Statement (C), "He's making a phone call," is the best description of the picture, so you should select answer (C) and mark it on your answer sheet.

1.

2.

GO ON TO THE NEXT PAGE ➡

3.

4.

5.

6.

GO ON TO THE NEXT PAGE

PART 2

Directions: You will hear a question or statement and three responses spoken in English. They will not be printed in your test book and will be spoken only one time. Select the best response to the question or statement and mark the letter (A), (B), or (C) on your answer sheet.

7. Mark your answer on your answer sheet.

8. Mark your answer on your answer sheet.

9. Mark your answer on your answer sheet.

10. Mark your answer on your answer sheet.

11. Mark your answer on your answer sheet.

12. Mark your answer on your answer sheet.

13. Mark your answer on your answer sheet.

14. Mark your answer on your answer sheet.

15. Mark your answer on your answer sheet.

16. Mark your answer on your answer sheet.

17. Mark your answer on your answer sheet.

18. Mark your answer on your answer sheet.

19. Mark your answer on your answer sheet.

20. Mark your answer on your answer sheet.

21. Mark your answer on your answer sheet.

22. Mark your answer on your answer sheet.

23. Mark your answer on your answer sheet.

24. Mark your answer on your answer sheet.

25. Mark your answer on your answer sheet.

26. Mark your answer on your answer sheet.

27. Mark your answer on your answer sheet.

28. Mark your answer on your answer sheet.

29. Mark your answer on your answer sheet.

30. Mark your answer on your answer sheet.

31. Mark your answer on your answer sheet.

PART 3

Directions: You will hear some conversations between two or more people. You will be asked to answer three questions about what the speakers say in each conversation. Select the best response to each question and mark the letter (A), (B), (C), or (D) on your answer sheet. The conversations will not be printed in your test book and will be spoken only one time.

32. What is the woman preparing for?

(A) An international conference
(B) An office relocation
(C) A meeting with colleagues
(D) A product launch

33. Who most likely is the man?

(A) A company executive
(B) An administrative assistant
(C) A technician
(D) An event planner

34. What will the man do next?

(A) Speak with his boss
(B) Cancel a meeting
(C) Repair broken equipment
(D) Make a phone call

35. What is the man responsible for?

(A) Hiring new employees
(B) Dealing with overseas customers
(C) Outlining an annual budget
(D) Organizing company files

36. What does the woman want to do next year?

(A) Expand her team
(B) Recruit new interns
(C) Plan an event
(D) Improve customer satisfaction

37. What does the man ask the woman to do?

(A) Prepare for a conference
(B) Send him further details
(C) Write a budget proposal
(D) Set up a meeting

38. What does the man need a suit for?

(A) A job interview
(B) A photo shoot
(C) A wedding
(D) A new job

39. What does the man dislike about the suit in the window?

(A) The material
(B) The length
(C) The price
(D) The pattern

40. What does the woman say the price includes?

(A) Alterations
(B) Delivery
(C) Dress shoes
(D) Sales tax

41. What kind of company does the man most likely work for?

(A) A sporting goods retailer
(B) A food distributor
(C) A film studio
(D) A furniture company

42. What does the woman say she is worried about?

(A) The safety of the students
(B) The cleanliness of the project
(C) The cost of filming
(D) The skills of the crew

43. What does the woman agree to let the man do?

(A) Film a movie
(B) Submit a report
(C) Speak at a meeting
(D) Talk to her principal

GO ON TO THE NEXT PAGE

44. Who most likely is Francisco Zabala?

(A) An art dealer
(B) A contractor
(C) An artist
(D) A security guard

45. What renovation does the woman mention?

(A) Some windows are being replaced.
(B) Some furniture is being rearranged.
(C) Some walls are being repainted.
(S) Some restrooms are being redone.

46. What does the woman suggest the man do?

(A) Come back in the evening
(B) Go on a tour
(C) Look at some art
(D) Visit a gift shop

47. What does the speakers' company most likely sell?

(A) Automobiles
(B) Accessories
(C) Clothes
(D) Coffee beans

48. Why is the woman surprised?

(A) A new coffee shop opened.
(B) The man has finalized his report.
(C) Management asked for more information.
(D) Sales have increased greatly.

49. Why does the woman say, "Don't worry about it"?

(A) To offer some help
(B) To show she finished an assignment
(C) To suggest the man go home
(D) To take on more responsibility

50. According to the woman, what will happen at the end of the month?

(A) Research will be conducted.
(B) New products will be released.
(C) An employee will move.
(D) Executives will visit.

51. What does the man want to know?

(A) Where his new job would be
(B) Why he is being reassigned
(C) Who he would be working with
(D) When he would start the job

52. What does the woman say the company will provide?

(A) A private office
(B) A bonus
(C) Free meals
(D) Daily transportation

53. What industry do the speakers work in?

(A) Technology
(B) Law
(C) Construction
(D) Publishing

54. What does the woman say about a project?

(A) It will generate a lot of revenue.
(B) It is an important project.
(C) It is the company's first job.
(D) It will increase tourism.

55. What does Carmen say needs to be done?

(A) Workers have to be trained.
(B) Supplies have to be ordered.
(C) Schedules have to be set.
(D) A contract has to be signed.

56. What does the woman imply when she says, "I have a moment to spare"?

(A) She plans to leave soon.
(B) She is waiting for something.
(C) She has medicine to give away.
(D) She can help with a prescription.

57. What does the man realize about some medication?

(A) The supply is almost gone.
(B) It is incorrectly labeled.
(C) It will soon expire.
(D) It is missing from the shelf.

58. What does the man suggest doing in the future?

(A) Ordering more medicine
(B) Calling the doctor
(C) Finding a new supplier
(D) Giving personalized recommendations

59. Who most likely is the woman?

(A) A bank teller
(B) A lawyer
(C) A marketer
(D) A secretary

60. What kind of document are the speakers discussing?

(A) A travel itinerary
(B) A marketing strategy
(C) A user agreement
(D) A budget proposal

61. Why must the document be revised by the end of the month?

(A) To avoid a fine
(B) To correct a typo
(C) To be presented at a meeting
(D) To meet a deadline

Till's Wedding	
Service	Cost
Photography	$1,750
Catering	$9,500
Flowers	$3,765
Limo	$2,121
Total:	$17,136

62. Look at the graphic. How much did the man's company charge for its service?

(A) $1,750
(B) $9,500
(C) $3,765
(D) $2,121

63. Why does the man apologize?

(A) He overcharged the woman.
(B) He forgot some of his products.
(C) He arrived late.
(D) He gave poor service.

64. What does the woman like about the venue?

(A) It is easily accessible.
(B) It is affordable.
(C) It has a lot of space.
(D) It has a great view.

GO ON TO THE NEXT PAGE

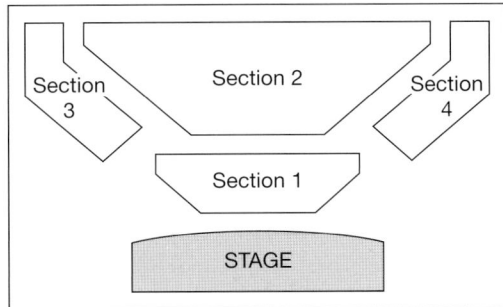

Heavenly Apartments	
242A	Tanaka
242B	Asper
243A	Kwon
243B	Singh

65. Why is the man surprised?

(A) The man's favorite band is in town.
(B) The woman met a popular musician.
(C) The tickets have not sold out.
(D) The woman got concert tickets.

66. Look at the graphic. In which section does the woman have seats?

(A) Section 1
(B) Section 2
(C) Section 3
(D) Section 4

67. What is the woman doing this weekend?

(A) Hosting a party
(B) Relocating to New York
(C) Visiting her sister
(D) Entering a raffle

68. Who most likely is the man?

(A) A property manager
(B) A company president
(C) A housekeeper
(D) A sales representative

69. Look at the graphic. Which name needs to be changed?

(A) Tanaka
(B) Asper
(C) Kwon
(D) Singh

70. What does the woman say she is going to do tomorrow?

(A) Speak to a maintenance manager
(B) Change her nameplate
(C) Move to a new apartment
(D) Have groceries delivered

Directions: You will hear some talks given by a single speaker. You will be asked to answer three questions about what the speaker says in each talk. Select the best response to each question and mark the letter (A), (B), (C), or (D) on your answer sheet. The talks will not be printed in your test book and will be spoken only one time.

71. What kind of business is the speaker most likely calling?

(A) A law firm
(B) A doctor's office
(C) A restaurant
(D) A hair salon

72. What does the speaker say about her appointment?

(A) It must be rescheduled.
(B) It is not covered by insurance.
(C) It should be an hour later.
(D) It should be at a different location.

73. What does the speaker have a question about?

(A) An insurance policy
(B) Shipping methods
(C) Payment options
(D) A warranty

74. What is the advertisement about?

(A) A photo event
(B) A new library
(C) A toy factory tour
(D) A cooking competition

75. What will visitors receive?

(A) A keychain
(B) A teddy bear
(C) A photo
(D) A free meal

76. What can the listeners get if they book a tour before 11 A.M.?

(A) A discounted price
(B) Free admission
(C) A company mug
(D) Complimentary drinks

77. Where does the announcement take place?

(A) At a university hall
(B) At a museum
(C) At a concert venue
(D) At a movie theater

78. Why does the speaker apologize?

(A) The lights are not working.
(B) The audio quality is bad.
(C) A presenter is running late.
(D) The heater is broken.

79. What is offered to the listeners?

(A) A free snack
(B) A discount coupon
(C) A parking voucher
(D) A promotional item

80. What kind of event is taking place?

(A) An athletic competition
(B) A medical workshop
(C) A charity fundraiser
(D) A business conference

81. Why does the speaker say, "And, as you can see, over 500 people are here"?

(A) To show that some advertisements were successful
(B) To imply that some people should switch venues
(C) To suggest that the space is too small
(D) To encourage people to socialize

82. What does the speaker ask the listeners to do?

(A) Visit again next year
(B) Check a schedule
(C) Form a line
(D) Fill out a questionnaire

GO ON TO THE NEXT PAGE

83. What is the goal of the plan?

(A) To raise money
(B) To decrease traffic
(C) To reduce pollution
(D) To encourage traveling

84. Who does the speaker say will receive a discount?

(A) Residents
(B) Club members
(C) Students
(D) Seniors

85. What will happen after two months?

(A) A road will be built.
(B) A program will be evaluated.
(C) A new law will be enacted.
(D) A fee will be waived.

86. What event is the speaker talking about?

(A) A farmers' market
(B) An art festival
(C) A musical performance
(D) A comedic play

87. Why does the speaker say, "the tickets are nearly sold out"?

(A) To encourage the listeners to enter a contest
(B) To point out the effectiveness of the marketing campaign
(C) To advise the listeners to arrive to the event early
(D) To warn people of large crowds

88. What will happen tomorrow morning?

(A) A fan will be a guest speaker.
(B) An interview will be conducted.
(C) A festival will begin.
(D) A new concert hall will open.

89. What type of business does the speaker work for?

(A) A jewelry company
(B) A marketing agency
(C) A clothing company
(D) An electronics company

90. What does the speaker highlight as an advantage of the material?

(A) It is affordable.
(B) It is lightweight.
(C) It is durable.
(D) It is functional.

91. What will the listeners most likely do next?

(A) Sign up for a membership
(B) Enter a contest
(C) Visit a company Web site
(D) Try on an accessory

92. Which department does the speaker work in?

(A) Information Technology
(B) Marketing
(C) Security
(D) Human Resources

93. Why does the speaker say, "there's a need for a new cybersecurity specialist in Houston"?

(A) To suggest hiring a new employee
(B) To explain that someone is retiring
(C) To approve a transfer request
(D) To highlight a security threat

94. What does the speaker want to discuss with the listener?

(A) A new proposal
(B) A moving and starting date
(C) Some constructive criticism
(D) Some research results

This Week's Guests	
Monday	Janet Greenwood
Tuesday	Marcus Crawley
Wednesday	Yukina Imano
Thursday	Leo Howe – Day 1
Friday	Leo Howe – Day 2

95. Why are guests invited on the speaker's radio show?

(A) To tell their career history
(B) To offer some advice
(C) To discuss business prospects
(D) To talk about clothes

96. What can the listeners do on a Web site?

(A) Leave feedback
(B) Sign up for a membership
(C) Buy merchandise
(D) Upload photos

97. Look at the graphic. Which day is the episode being aired?

(A) Monday
(B) Tuesday
(C) Wednesday
(D) Thursday

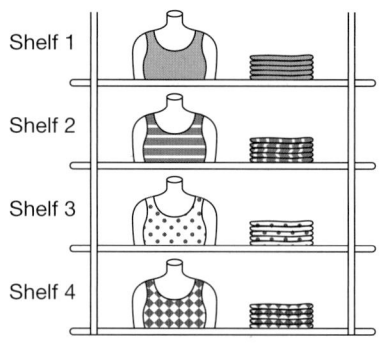

98. Look at the graphic. Where will the hats and flip-flops be displayed?

(A) On Shelf 1
(B) On Shelf 2
(C) On Shelf 3
(D) On Shelf 4

99. What will be displayed near the cash registers?

(A) Sunglasses
(B) Earrings
(C) Hats
(D) Sunscreen

100. What will the listener receive in an upcoming phone call?

(A) Shipping information
(B) Display specifications
(C) A new schedule
(D) Evaluation feedback

This is the end of the Listening test.

🎧 실전 모의고사_02 정답 및 해설 p.343

LISTENING TEST

In the Listening test, you will be asked to demonstrate how well you understand spoken English. The entire Listening test will last approximately 45 minutes. There are four parts, and directions are given for each part. You must mark your answers on the separate answer sheet. Do not write your answers in your test book.

PART 1

Directions: For each question in this part, you will hear four statements about a picture in your test book. When you hear the statements, you must select the one statement that best describes what you see in the picture. Then find the number of the question on your answer sheet and mark your answer. The statements will not be printed in your test book and will be spoken only one time.

Statement (C), "He's making a phone call," is the best description of the picture, so you should select answer (C) and mark it on your answer sheet.

1.

2.

GO ON TO THE NEXT PAGE

3.

4.

5.

6.

GO ON TO THE NEXT PAGE

PART 2

Directions: You will hear a question or statement and three responses spoken in English. They will not be printed in your test book and will be spoken only one time. Select the best response to the question or statement and mark the letter (A), (B), or (C) on your answer sheet.

7. Mark your answer on your answer sheet.

8. Mark your answer on your answer sheet.

9. Mark your answer on your answer sheet.

10. Mark your answer on your answer sheet.

11. Mark your answer on your answer sheet.

12. Mark your answer on your answer sheet.

13. Mark your answer on your answer sheet.

14. Mark your answer on your answer sheet.

15. Mark your answer on your answer sheet.

16. Mark your answer on your answer sheet.

17. Mark your answer on your answer sheet.

18. Mark your answer on your answer sheet.

19. Mark your answer on your answer sheet.

20. Mark your answer on your answer sheet.

21. Mark your answer on your answer sheet.

22. Mark your answer on your answer sheet.

23. Mark your answer on your answer sheet.

24. Mark your answer on your answer sheet.

25. Mark your answer on your answer sheet.

26. Mark your answer on your answer sheet.

27. Mark your answer on your answer sheet.

28. Mark your answer on your answer sheet.

29. Mark your answer on your answer sheet.

30. Mark your answer on your answer sheet.

31. Mark your answer on your answer sheet.

Directions: You will hear some conversations between two or more people. You will be asked to answer three questions about what the speakers say in each conversation. Select the best response to each question and mark the letter (A), (B), (C), or (D) on your answer sheet. The conversations will not be printed in your test book and will be spoken only one time.

32. Where is the conversation taking place?

(A) At a movie theater
(B) At an aquarium
(C) At an art museum
(D) At a stadium

33. What will the man most likely purchase?

(A) A group ticket
(B) A half-day ticket
(C) A season ticket
(D) A student ticket

34. What will the man do next?

(A) Complete a form
(B) Call another branch
(C) Show an ID card
(D) Make a phone call

35. Where does the man work?

(A) At a dental clinic
(B) At a business institute
(C) At a hair salon
(D) At a law firm

36. What does the woman ask about?

(A) Registration costs
(B) Transportation options
(C) An invoice date
(D) A parking fee

37. According to the man, what has the business recently done?

(A) It raised the price of its services.
(B) It updated its software.
(C) It relocated to another building.
(D) It changed a company policy.

38. Why is the man unable to use the parking area?

(A) The surface is being repaved.
(B) He does not have the correct permit.
(C) Some lines are being painted.
(D) A pipe is being repaired.

39. Who most likely is the man?

(A) A real estate agent
(B) An inspector
(C) A caterer
(D) A mechanic

40. What does the woman suggest doing?

(A) E-mailing a complaint
(B) Speaking to a manager
(C) Coming back later
(D) Checking a schedule online

41. Where is the conversation taking place?

(A) At a manufacturing facility
(B) At a restaurant
(C) At a financial institution
(D) At a flower shop

42. What does the man ask the woman to do?

(A) Refill some containers
(B) Print some signs
(C) Inspect some machinery
(D) Call a client

43. What does the man imply when he says, "I see someone at the door"?

(A) He cannot fulfill the woman's request.
(B) He wants to open the business early.
(C) The woman must clear some space.
(D) The woman should watch more carefully.

GO ON TO THE NEXT PAGE

44. What most likely is the man's profession?

    (A) Receptionist
    (B) Architect
    (C) Sales director
    (D) Journalist

45. What concern does the man express about the job?

    (A) The company is not financially stable.
    (B) His salary will not be very high.
    (C) The working hours are long.
    (D) He will have to travel frequently.

46. What will the man do on Monday?

    (A) Learn about a hiring decision
    (B) Attend a second interview
    (C) Submit a work portfolio
    (D) Take a tour of the company

47. Where are the speakers?

    (A) At an art supply store
    (B) At a computer repair shop
    (C) At an antique shop
    (D) At a clothing store

48. Why did the woman visit the business?

    (A) To apply for a job
    (B) To deliver some samples
    (C) To check an item's value
    (D) To return a faulty item

49. What will Douglas show to the woman?

    (A) A pamphlet
    (B) A business card
    (C) A furniture polish
    (D) A storage container

50. Where does the conversation take place?

    (A) At a music studio
    (B) At a travel agency
    (C) At a luggage manufacturer
    (D) At an electronics store

51. Why was the man unable to visit the business earlier?

    (A) He had to finish an urgent project.
    (B) He was out of the country.
    (C) He needed repairs on his car.
    (D) He moved to a new home.

52. What does the woman offer to do?

    (A) Issue a voucher
    (B) Exchange an item
    (C) Send a replacement part
    (D) Increase a discount

53. What have the men recently done?

    (A) Booked a stage show
    (B) Led a tour
    (C) Created a poster
    (D) Corrected an error

54. What do the men suggest doing?

    (A) Extending the business hours
    (B) Hosting a competition
    (C) Purchasing a business
    (D) Renovating a building

55. Why will Walter make some phone calls?

    (A) To research some prices
    (B) To find a guest speaker
    (C) To thank some members
    (D) To ask for donations

56. Where is the conversation most likely taking place?

(A) At a hardware store
(B) At an advertising agency
(C) At an appliance repair shop
(D) At a beverage producer

57. What does the woman say about some equipment?

(A) It needs to be cleaned frequently.
(B) It has not been delivered yet.
(C) It takes a long time to install.
(D) It has sped up a process.

58. What does the woman agree to do?

(A) Create a survey
(B) Review a manual
(C) Check a price list
(D) Renew a contract

59. Why was the woman absent from an event?

(A) She had some unexpected work.
(B) She was visiting a client.
(C) She did not register in time.
(D) She was on vacation.

60. What does the man encourage the woman to do?

(A) Hold a team meeting
(B) Set an event reminder
(C) Make a hiring request
(D) Write a press release

61. What does the man imply when he says, "I filled four pages"?

(A) He had to work additional hours.
(B) He found a talk to be useful.
(C) The number of attendees was high.
(D) A task has almost been completed.

Destination	Departure Time	Platform
London	7:31	2
Sheffield	7:50	4
Leeds	8:05	9
Birmingham	8:12	11

62. What will the speakers inquire about?

(A) A luggage policy
(B) A meal option
(C) A ticket receipt
(D) A seat upgrade

63. What will the speakers discuss on the train?

(A) A testing procedure for products
(B) A financial meeting for executives
(C) A product demonstration for investors
(D) An interview process for job candidates

64. Look at the graphic. Where do the speakers need to go?

(A) To Platform 2
(B) To Platform 4
(C) To Platform 9
(D) To Platform 11

GO ON TO THE NEXT PAGE

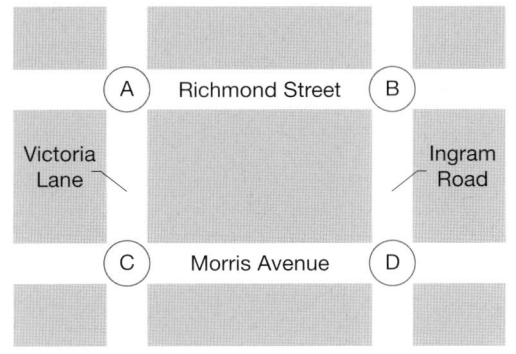

Lawn mowing: Residential, small	
Package 1: Monthly	$25
Package 2: Twice a month	$45
Package 3: Weekly	$80
Package 4: Twice a week + bush trimming	$110

65. Who most likely are the speakers?

(A) Carpenters
(B) Electricians
(C) Painters
(D) Architects

66. What will the woman do at the Kirby Building?

(A) Purchase some tools
(B) Get brochures printed
(C) Take some pictures
(D) Rent a vehicle

67. Look at the graphic. Where does the woman want to be dropped off?

(A) At Location A
(B) At Location B
(C) At Location C
(D) At Location D

68. Who recommended Gilcrest Landscaping to the man?

(A) A friend
(B) A coworker
(C) A relative
(D) A client

69. Look at the graphic. Which package does the man need?

(A) Package 1
(B) Package 2
(C) Package 3
(D) Package 4

70. What will the man most likely do next?

(A) Provide an address
(B) Make a payment
(C) Create a password
(D) Select a date

PART 4

Directions: You will hear some talks given by a single speaker. You will be asked to answer three questions about what the speaker says in each talk. Select the best response to each question and mark the letter (A), (B), (C), or (D) on your answer sheet. The talks will not be printed in your test book and will be spoken only one time.

71. What kind of business does the speaker work for?

(A) An art gallery
(B) A painting company
(C) A cleaning service
(D) A power company

72. What does the speaker say has changed?

(A) A design
(B) A delivery date
(C) A price
(D) A brand name

73. Why does the speaker want confirmation soon?

(A) A crew is busier than usual.
(B) A promotion is nearly over.
(C) A storm is approaching.
(D) A product is in high demand.

74. Who is the speaker addressing?

(A) Auto mechanics
(B) Sales representatives
(C) Job applicants
(D) Construction workers

75. What does the speaker say is important?

(A) Having good listening skills
(B) Building a large customer base
(C) Managing time effectively
(D) Keeping up with industry trends

76. According to the speaker, what has Andre Carlson recently done?

(A) Launched his own company
(B) Returned from a business trip
(C) Set a new record
(D) Received an award nomination

77. According to the broadcast, what happened in March?

(A) A road was repaired.
(B) A sports stadium opened.
(C) A city election was held.
(D) A new law was passed.

78. What have residents made complaints about?

(A) A lack of public parking
(B) An increase in traffic congestion
(C) Safety issues on roadways
(D) Noise disturbances from construction

79. Who will meet with city council members tomorrow?

(A) Transportation authorities
(B) Structural engineers
(C) Health experts
(D) Financial advisors

80. What is the purpose of the change?

(A) To comply with regulations
(B) To promote employees' health
(C) To reduce heating costs
(D) To qualify for an insurance policy

81. What does the speaker warn the listeners about?

(A) Damage to electronics
(B) Work interruptions
(C) An unexpected outage
(D) Loss of belongings

82. Why should listeners talk to Melinda?

(A) To request time off
(B) To sign up for training
(C) To reserve a workspace
(D) To get some supplies

GO ON TO THE NEXT PAGE ➡

83. Who is the speaker?

(A) A computer expert
(B) A department head
(C) A government inspector
(D) A company intern

84. What is the speech mainly about?

(A) An increase in competition
(B) A staff member's resignation
(C) A company awards dinner
(D) A fund-raising event

85. Why does the speaker say, "this is our slow season"?

(A) To reassure the listeners
(B) To extend an invitation
(C) To explain a discount
(D) To reject a proposal

86. Who most likely is the listener?

(A) A client
(B) A city official
(C) A manager
(D) A plumber

87. What will happen at the business today?

(A) A safety inspection
(B) A sales event
(C) A product recall
(D) A job interview

88. What does the speaker mean when she says, "The entrance is nearly 15 feet tall"?

(A) Some items can be loaded easily.
(B) Some different equipment is needed.
(C) She made an error in a measurement.
(D) She thinks a task is dangerous.

89. What change does the speaker mention?

(A) A phone system will be tested regularly.
(B) Meetings will be held remotely.
(C) The hours of a service will be extended.
(D) A new department manager will be selected.

90. Who most likely are the listeners?

(A) Radio station executives
(B) Call center representatives
(C) Computer sales clerks
(D) Web site developers

91. According to the speaker, what will some listeners be asked to do?

(A) Keep a record of spending
(B) Provide training to colleagues
(C) Change to a different shift
(D) Complete a detailed report

92. What kind of product is the speaker discussing?

(A) A power tool
(B) A tablet computer
(C) A mobile phone
(D) A kitchen appliance

93. What industry do the listeners probably work in?

(A) Retail
(B) Transportation
(C) Education
(D) Finance

94. What does the speaker mean when she says, "It weighs less than 200 grams"?

(A) A product can be transported easily.
(B) A shipping cost will be low.
(C) A fragile item should be treated carefully.
(D) A brochure contained an error.

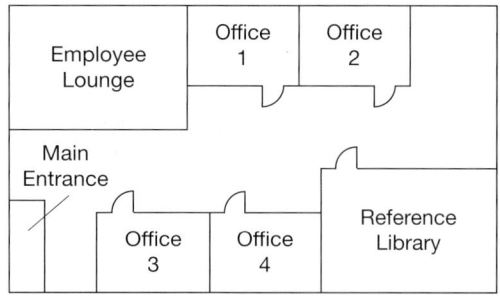

Item	Quantity
Clipboards	12
Hand sanitizer	6 bottles
Plastic gloves	15 boxes
Whiteboard markers (black)	25

95. What will be delivered to the company this afternoon?

(A) Some office chairs
(B) Some computer monitors
(C) A conference table
(D) A microwave oven

96. According to the speaker, why was a purchase necessary?

(A) A budget had a surplus.
(B) An item was recently damaged.
(C) The number of employees has grown.
(D) Some staff members made a complaint.

97. Look at the graphic. Where does Victor work?

(A) In Office 1
(B) In Office 2
(C) In Office 3
(D) In Office 4

98. What kind of business does the speaker most likely work for?

(A) A landscaping company
(B) A hospital
(C) A laundry service
(D) A factory

99. Look at the graphic. According to the speaker, which number needs to be changed?

(A) 12
(B) 6
(C) 15
(D) 25

100. What will the speaker send to the listener?

(A) A list of team members
(B) A conference registration form
(C) Some contact details
(D) Some product samples

This is the end of the Listening test.

LISTENING TEST

In the Listening test, you will be asked to demonstrate how well you understand spoken English. The entire Listening test will last approximately 45 minutes. There are four parts, and directions are given for each part. You must mark your answers on the separate answer sheet. Do not write your answers in your test book.

PART 1

Directions: For each question in this part, you will hear four statements about a picture in your test book. When you hear the statements, you must select the one statement that best describes what you see in the picture. Then find the number of the question on your answer sheet and mark your answer. The statements will not be printed in your test book and will be spoken only one time.

Statement (C), "He's making a phone call," is the best description of the picture, so you should select answer (C) and mark it on your answer sheet.

1.

2.

GO ON TO THE NEXT PAGE →

3.

4.

5.

6.

GO ON TO THE NEXT PAGE

Directions: You will hear a question or statement and three responses spoken in English. They will not be printed in your test book and will be spoken only one time. Select the best response to the question or statement and mark the letter (A), (B), or (C) on your answer sheet.

7. Mark your answer on your answer sheet.

8. Mark your answer on your answer sheet.

9. Mark your answer on your answer sheet.

10. Mark your answer on your answer sheet.

11. Mark your answer on your answer sheet.

12. Mark your answer on your answer sheet.

13. Mark your answer on your answer sheet.

14. Mark your answer on your answer sheet.

15. Mark your answer on your answer sheet.

16. Mark your answer on your answer sheet.

17. Mark your answer on your answer sheet.

18. Mark your answer on your answer sheet.

19. Mark your answer on your answer sheet.

20. Mark your answer on your answer sheet.

21. Mark your answer on your answer sheet.

22. Mark your answer on your answer sheet.

23. Mark your answer on your answer sheet.

24. Mark your answer on your answer sheet.

25. Mark your answer on your answer sheet.

26. Mark your answer on your answer sheet.

27. Mark your answer on your answer sheet.

28. Mark your answer on your answer sheet.

29. Mark your answer on your answer sheet.

30. Mark your answer on your answer sheet.

31. Mark your answer on your answer sheet.

PART 3

Directions: You will hear some conversations between two or more people. You will be asked to answer three questions about what the speakers say in each conversation. Select the best response to each question and mark the letter (A), (B), (C), or (D) on your answer sheet. The conversations will not be printed in your test book and will be spoken only one time.

32. Where does the woman work?

(A) At a television station
(B) At a travel agency
(C) At a hotel
(D) At an electronics store

33. Why is the man calling?

(A) To update payment information
(B) To ask about a policy
(C) To get an item replaced
(D) To make a reservation

34. What is the woman unsure about?

(A) When a colleague will return
(B) How much will be charged
(C) Where a file is located
(D) Who is responsible for a task

35. Where most likely are the speakers?

(A) At an art museum
(B) At a shopping mall
(C) At an aquarium
(D) At a theater

36. What is the purpose of the woman's visit?

(A) To set up a display
(B) To take some pictures
(C) To make a delivery
(D) To interview an employee

37. According to the man, why should the woman hurry?

(A) A tour group is about to depart.
(B) A line for a service is long.
(C) A business will close soon.
(D) A task will be started shortly.

38. Who is Andrea McGrath?

(A) An investor
(B) A corporate recruiter
(C) An intern
(D) A general manager

39. Where most likely are the speakers?

(A) At a pharmacy
(B) At a financial institution
(C) At an electronics store
(D) At an advertising firm

40. What does the man want Ms. McGrath to do next?

(A) Complete some paperwork
(B) Take a building tour
(C) Share a meal with her colleagues
(D) Review some safety procedures

41. Why will the company hold a party on Thursday?

(A) To say farewell to a colleague
(B) To celebrate a retirement
(C) To welcome overseas guests
(D) To acknowledge an anniversary

42. What is the woman in charge of doing?

(A) Reserving a venue
(B) Ordering some food
(C) Decorating a room
(D) Sending some invitations

43. What does the man say he is excited about?

(A) Learning useful skills
(B) Meeting new people
(C) Traveling to other countries
(D) Working flexible hours

GO ON TO THE NEXT PAGE

44. What is the problem with the woman's current file cabinet?

(A) It does not match her furniture.
(B) It takes up too much space.
(C) It cannot be secured.
(D) It makes noise when opened.

45. What does the man offer to do?

(A) Print out a coupon
(B) Give a demonstration
(C) Check a stock room
(D) Send a catalog

46. According to the man, why do people like the item?

(A) It does not scratch the floor.
(B) It is easy to assemble.
(C) It has a money-back guarantee.
(D) It is made from recycled materials.

47. What industry do the speakers most likely work in?

(A) Healthcare
(B) Magazine publishing
(C) Global finance
(D) Real estate

48. What does the woman imply when she says, "It's easy to make changes with this program"?

(A) She will not attend a training session.
(B) She wants to purchase some software.
(C) She does not need a coworker's assistance.
(D) She will assign a task to the man.

49. Why does the man thank the woman?

(A) She informed him about a promotion.
(B) She nominated him for an award.
(C) She changed an application deadline.
(D) She wrote a reference letter.

50. What are the men trying to do?

(A) Check in at a hotel
(B) Book a tour
(C) Rent a vehicle
(D) Change flight tickets

51. According to the woman, what will happen this weekend?

(A) Some fees will be increased.
(B) The city will hold a festival.
(C) A customer loyalty program will be launched.
(D) The business will extend its hours.

52. What does the woman suggest the men do in the future?

(A) Pay with a credit card
(B) Make an online reservation
(C) Sign up for a thirty-day trial
(D) Call several branches

53. Where is the conversation taking place?

(A) At a grand opening
(B) At a career fair
(C) At a farmers' market
(D) At a department store

54. What kind of business does the woman work for?

(A) A fruit orchard
(B) A beverage manufacturer
(C) A garden supply store
(D) A catering company

55. What does the woman give to the man?

(A) A product catalog
(B) A business card
(C) A site map
(D) A discount coupon

56. Who most likely are the speakers?

(A) City officials
(B) Reporters
(C) Gardeners
(D) Architects

57. Why does the woman want a decision to be made quickly?

(A) A sale period will end soon.
(B) A contract is set to expire.
(C) She is worried about a competitor.
(D) She will take a vacation.

58. Why does the man say, "Tomorrow is a national holiday"?

(A) To explain a delivery delay
(B) To request a higher pay rate
(C) To suggest doing a task earlier
(D) To ask for a deadline extension

59. Where do the speakers most likely work?

(A) At an appliance store
(B) At a bakery
(C) At a painting company
(D) At a flower shop

60. What do the speakers decide to do?

(A) Give discounts to loyal customers
(B) Launch an online ad campaign
(C) Hire some temporary workers
(D) Partner with other businesses

61. What does the woman say she will do?

(A) Get a business recommendation
(B) Share some free samples
(C) Research contact details
(D) Review some contract terms

McDowell Conference Center	
Pinedale Room	Up to 50 people
Albany Room	50–100 people
Morford Room	100–200 people
Lawson Room	200–350 people

62. What is the man preparing for?

(A) A company retreat
(B) A retirement dinner
(C) An awards ceremony
(D) A product launch

63. Look at the graphic. Which room will the man probably reserve?

(A) The Pinedale Room
(B) The Albany Room
(C) The Morford Room
(D) The Lawson Room

64. According to the woman, what is included in a fee?

(A) Lighting equipment
(B) Refreshments
(C) Live entertainment
(D) Insurance

GO ON TO THE NEXT PAGE

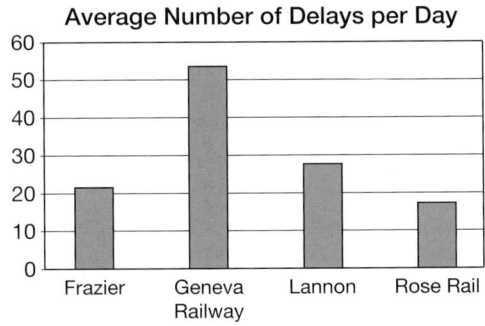

Average Number of Delays per Day

$5.00 $6.50

$2.00 $3.50

65. Who is Isabelle Randall?

(A) A train driver
(B) A tour operator
(C) A radio host
(D) A transportation expert

66. Look at the graphic. Which train station does the woman indicate?

(A) Frazier
(B) Geneva Railway
(C) Lannon
(D) Rose Rail

67. What does the woman advise the listeners to do?

(A) Arrive at the station early
(B) Purchase some insurance
(C) Check departure times online
(D) Travel during off-peak periods

68. What will take place next month?

(A) An annual festival
(B) A sports tournament
(C) A grand opening
(D) A fund-raising event

69. Look at the graphic. How much will the speakers spend per item?

(A) $5.00
(B) $6.50
(C) $2.00
(D) $3.50

70. What will the woman do next?

(A) Contact a graphic designer
(B) Print some brochures
(C) Fill out an order form
(D) Reserve a venue

Directions: You will hear some talks given by a single speaker. You will be asked to answer three questions about what the speaker says in each talk. Select the best response to each question and mark the letter (A), (B), (C), or (D) on your answer sheet. The talks will not be printed in your test book and will be spoken only one time.

71. What is being advertised?

(A) A digital camera
(B) A laptop computer
(C) A security system
(D) A power tool

72. What benefit of the product does the speaker mention?

(A) It does not need to be recharged often.
(B) It can be used with a smartphone application.
(C) It has a lightweight design.
(D) It comes with a money-back guarantee.

73. What can customers receive this week?

(A) Some coupons
(B) Free shipping
(C) A membership discount
(D) An extra battery

74. What does the company make?

(A) Office supplies
(B) Furniture
(C) Camping gear
(D) Footwear

75. According to the speaker, what is the company famous for?

(A) Its excellent customer service
(B) Its long-lasting products
(C) Its environmentally friendly materials
(D) Its wide selection

76. What will the listeners most likely do next?

(A) Collect some information
(B) Take a group photo
(C) Put on protective gear
(D) Submit their questions

77. What is the meeting mainly about?

(A) Some volunteer opportunities
(B) An industry event
(C) Some new equipment
(D) A policy change

78. According to the speaker, why will the listeners need an ID number?

(A) To sign up for a course
(B) To receive a payment
(C) To access a database
(D) To borrow an item

79. What does the speaker remind the listeners to do?

(A) Download a software program
(B) Check a schedule
(C) Express a preference
(D) Arrive early for work

80. Where does Mr. Foster work?

(A) At an airline
(B) At a fitness center
(C) At a tour company
(D) At a business institute

81. According to the speaker, what skill does Mr. Foster have?

(A) Speaking multiple languages
(B) Taking professional photographs
(C) Improving group teamwork
(D) Managing various branches

82. What does Mr. Foster plan to do after selling his business?

(A) Start his retirement
(B) Create a Web site
(C) Move abroad
(D) Take some classes

GO ON TO THE NEXT PAGE

83. Who most likely are the listeners?

(A) Accountants
(B) Reporters
(C) Salespeople
(D) Investors

84. What will the speaker send to the listeners today?

(A) An updated schedule
(B) An account password
(C) Some driving directions
(D) Some advice for taking pictures

85. Why does the speaker say, "They look forward to this every year"?

(A) To remind the listeners to ask for help
(B) To thank the listeners for their quick work
(C) To highlight a task's significance
(D) To explain why a budget was increased

86. Where most likely are the listeners?

(A) At a business institute
(B) At a recruitment agency
(C) At a bookstore
(D) At a library

87. Why does the speaker say, "some of these are hard to see"?

(A) To apologize for an inconvenience
(B) To explain the importance of an eye exam
(C) To encourage people to get a document checked
(D) To recommend changing the size of some text

88. What are the listeners invited to do now?

(A) Share their questions
(B) Watch a video
(C) Attend a talk
(D) Meet some employers

89. What is the speaker mainly discussing?

(A) Cleaning curtains
(B) Measuring curtains
(C) Selecting curtains
(D) Sewing curtains

90. What does the speaker say about silk?

(A) It is sensitive to sunlight.
(B) It can stain easily.
(C) It is lightweight.
(D) It can be very expensive.

91. What can the listeners receive from Mesa Furnishings?

(A) A fabric sample
(B) A discount code
(C) A product catalog
(D) A free consultation

92. What does the speaker thank the listener for?

(A) Giving publicity to his business
(B) Pointing out an error on a menu
(C) Investing in a restaurant
(D) Introducing a new chef

93. What does the speaker imply when he says, "This is a complex issue"?

(A) Some dishes take a long time to make.
(B) A proposed deadline is too tight.
(C) More employees may be needed.
(D) Several factors contribute to a price.

94. Why does the speaker want a return call?

(A) To recommend a colleague
(B) To provide further information
(C) To check an address
(D) To adjust an order

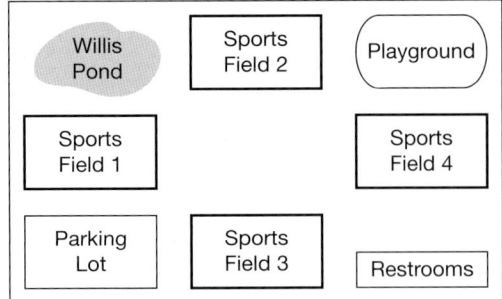

95. Who is the speaker?

(A) The city's mayor
(B) A reporter
(C) A tour guide
(D) A department head

96. Look at the graphic. Which sports field will be used for a picnic?

(A) Sports Field 1
(B) Sports Field 2
(C) Sports Field 3
(D) Sports Field 4

97. Why are volunteers needed for the site?

(A) To plan ongoing activities
(B) To clean up an area
(C) To hang up signs
(D) To take care of plants

Please check the day(s) you are available:

[ ] Tuesdays @ 3:00 P.M.

[ ] Thursdays @ 10:30 A.M.

[ ] Fridays @ 2:30 P.M.

[ ] Sundays @ 1:00 P.M.

98. Where does the speaker most likely work?

(A) At a community garden
(B) At a supermarket
(C) At a hardware store
(D) At a bakery

99. What is the speaker's goal?

(A) To cut costs
(B) To improve teamwork
(C) To encourage leadership
(D) To teach new skills

100. Look at the graphic. On which days does the speaker have a flexible schedule?

(A) Tuesdays
(B) Thursdays
(C) Fridays
(D) Sundays

This is the end of the Listening test.

ANSWER SHEET

TOEIC 실전 모의고사

응시일자	20 . .
이름	
맞은 개수	/100

LISTENING (Part I ~ IV)

(OMR answer grid, questions 1–100, each with options ⓐ ⓑ ⓒ ⓓ)

LISTENING (Part I ~ IV)

(OMR answer grid, questions 1–100, each with options ⓐ ⓑ ⓒ ⓓ)

ANSWER SHEET

TOEIC 실전 모의고사

응시일자	20 . .
이름	
맞은 개수	/100

LISTENING (Part I ~ IV)

	a b c d		a b c d		a b c d		a b c d		a b c d
1	ⓐⓑⓒⓓ	21	ⓐⓑⓒ	41	ⓐⓑⓒⓓ	61	ⓐⓑⓒⓓ	81	ⓐⓑⓒⓓ
2	ⓐⓑⓒⓓ	22	ⓐⓑⓒ	42	ⓐⓑⓒⓓ	62	ⓐⓑⓒⓓ	82	ⓐⓑⓒⓓ
3	ⓐⓑⓒⓓ	23	ⓐⓑⓒ	43	ⓐⓑⓒⓓ	63	ⓐⓑⓒⓓ	83	ⓐⓑⓒⓓ
4	ⓐⓑⓒ	24	ⓐⓑⓒ	44	ⓐⓑⓒⓓ	64	ⓐⓑⓒⓓ	84	ⓐⓑⓒⓓ
5	ⓐⓑⓒ	25	ⓐⓑⓒⓓ	45	ⓐⓑⓒⓓ	65	ⓐⓑⓒⓓ	85	ⓐⓑⓒⓓ
6	ⓐⓑⓒ	26	ⓐⓑⓒⓓ	46	ⓐⓑⓒⓓ	66	ⓐⓑⓒⓓ	86	ⓐⓑⓒⓓ
7	ⓐⓑⓒ	27	ⓐⓑⓒ	47	ⓐⓑⓒⓓ	67	ⓐⓑⓒⓓ	87	ⓐⓑⓒⓓ
8	ⓐⓑⓒ	28	ⓐⓑⓒ	48	ⓐⓑⓒⓓ	68	ⓐⓑⓒⓓ	88	ⓐⓑⓒⓓ
9	ⓐⓑⓒ	29	ⓐⓑⓒ	49	ⓐⓑⓒⓓ	69	ⓐⓑⓒⓓ	89	ⓐⓑⓒⓓ
10	ⓐⓑⓒ	30	ⓐⓑⓒ	50	ⓐⓑⓒⓓ	70	ⓐⓑⓒⓓ	90	ⓐⓑⓒⓓ
11	ⓐⓑⓒ	31	ⓐⓑⓒ	51	ⓐⓑⓒⓓ	71	ⓐⓑⓒⓓ	91	ⓐⓑⓒⓓ
12	ⓐⓑⓒ	32	ⓐⓑⓒ	52	ⓐⓑⓒⓓ	72	ⓐⓑⓒⓓ	92	ⓐⓑⓒⓓ
13	ⓐⓑⓒ	33	ⓐⓑⓒ	53	ⓐⓑⓒⓓ	73	ⓐⓑⓒⓓ	93	ⓐⓑⓒⓓ
14	ⓐⓑⓒ	34	ⓐⓑⓒ	54	ⓐⓑⓒⓓ	74	ⓐⓑⓒⓓ	94	ⓐⓑⓒⓓ
15	ⓐⓑⓒ	35	ⓐⓑⓒ	55	ⓐⓑⓒⓓ	75	ⓐⓑⓒⓓ	95	ⓐⓑⓒⓓ
16	ⓐⓑⓒ	36	ⓐⓑⓒ	56	ⓐⓑⓒⓓ	76	ⓐⓑⓒⓓ	96	ⓐⓑⓒⓓ
17	ⓐⓑⓒ	37	ⓐⓑⓒ	57	ⓐⓑⓒⓓ	77	ⓐⓑⓒⓓ	97	ⓐⓑⓒⓓ
18	ⓐⓑⓒ	38	ⓐⓑⓒ	58	ⓐⓑⓒⓓ	78	ⓐⓑⓒⓓ	98	ⓐⓑⓒⓓ
19	ⓐⓑⓒ	39	ⓐⓑⓒ	59	ⓐⓑⓒⓓ	79	ⓐⓑⓒⓓ	99	ⓐⓑⓒⓓ
20	ⓐⓑⓒ	40	ⓐⓑⓒ	60	ⓐⓑⓒⓓ	80	ⓐⓑⓒⓓ	100	ⓐⓑⓒⓓ

LISTENING (Part I ~ IV)

	a b c d		a b c d		a b c d		a b c d		a b c d
1	ⓐⓑⓒⓓ	21	ⓐⓑⓒ	41	ⓐⓑⓒⓓ	61	ⓐⓑⓒⓓ	81	ⓐⓑⓒⓓ
2	ⓐⓑⓒⓓ	22	ⓐⓑⓒ	42	ⓐⓑⓒⓓ	62	ⓐⓑⓒⓓ	82	ⓐⓑⓒⓓ
3	ⓐⓑⓒⓓ	23	ⓐⓑⓒ	43	ⓐⓑⓒⓓ	63	ⓐⓑⓒⓓ	83	ⓐⓑⓒⓓ
4	ⓐⓑⓒⓓ	24	ⓐⓑⓒ	44	ⓐⓑⓒⓓ	64	ⓐⓑⓒⓓ	84	ⓐⓑⓒⓓ
5	ⓐⓑⓒ	25	ⓐⓑⓒ	45	ⓐⓑⓒⓓ	65	ⓐⓑⓒⓓ	85	ⓐⓑⓒⓓ
6	ⓐⓑⓒ	26	ⓐⓑⓒ	46	ⓐⓑⓒⓓ	66	ⓐⓑⓒⓓ	86	ⓐⓑⓒⓓ
7	ⓐⓑⓒ	27	ⓐⓑⓒ	47	ⓐⓑⓒⓓ	67	ⓐⓑⓒⓓ	87	ⓐⓑⓒⓓ
8	ⓐⓑⓒ	28	ⓐⓑⓒ	48	ⓐⓑⓒⓓ	68	ⓐⓑⓒⓓ	88	ⓐⓑⓒⓓ
9	ⓐⓑⓒ	29	ⓐⓑⓒ	49	ⓐⓑⓒⓓ	69	ⓐⓑⓒⓓ	89	ⓐⓑⓒⓓ
10	ⓐⓑⓒ	30	ⓐⓑⓒ	50	ⓐⓑⓒⓓ	70	ⓐⓑⓒⓓ	90	ⓐⓑⓒⓓ
11	ⓐⓑⓒ	31	ⓐⓑⓒ	51	ⓐⓑⓒⓓ	71	ⓐⓑⓒⓓ	91	ⓐⓑⓒⓓ
12	ⓐⓑⓒ	32	ⓐⓑⓒ	52	ⓐⓑⓒⓓ	72	ⓐⓑⓒⓓ	92	ⓐⓑⓒⓓ
13	ⓐⓑⓒ	33	ⓐⓑⓒ	53	ⓐⓑⓒⓓ	73	ⓐⓑⓒⓓ	93	ⓐⓑⓒⓓ
14	ⓐⓑⓒ	34	ⓐⓑⓒ	54	ⓐⓑⓒⓓ	74	ⓐⓑⓒⓓ	94	ⓐⓑⓒⓓ
15	ⓐⓑⓒ	35	ⓐⓑⓒ	55	ⓐⓑⓒⓓ	75	ⓐⓑⓒⓓ	95	ⓐⓑⓒⓓ
16	ⓐⓑⓒ	36	ⓐⓑⓒ	56	ⓐⓑⓒⓓ	76	ⓐⓑⓒⓓ	96	ⓐⓑⓒⓓ
17	ⓐⓑⓒ	37	ⓐⓑⓒ	57	ⓐⓑⓒⓓ	77	ⓐⓑⓒⓓ	97	ⓐⓑⓒⓓ
18	ⓐⓑⓒ	38	ⓐⓑⓒ	58	ⓐⓑⓒⓓ	78	ⓐⓑⓒⓓ	98	ⓐⓑⓒⓓ
19	ⓐⓑⓒ	39	ⓐⓑⓒ	59	ⓐⓑⓒⓓ	79	ⓐⓑⓒⓓ	99	ⓐⓑⓒⓓ
20	ⓐⓑⓒ	40	ⓐⓑⓒ	60	ⓐⓑⓒⓓ	80	ⓐⓑⓒⓓ	100	ⓐⓑⓒⓓ

ANSWER SHEET

TOEIC 실전 모의고사

LISTENING (Part I ~ IV)

1	2	3	4	5	6	7	8	9	10	11	12	13	14	15	16	17	18	19	20
21	22	23	24	25	26	27	28	29	30	31	32	33	34	35	36	37	38	39	40
41	42	43	44	45	46	47	48	49	50	51	52	53	54	55	56	57	58	59	60
61	62	63	64	65	66	67	68	69	70	71	72	73	74	75	76	77	78	79	80
81	82	83	84	85	86	87	88	89	90	91	92	93	94	95	96	97	98	99	100

LISTENING (Part I ~ IV)

1	2	3	4	5	6	7	8	9	10	11	12	13	14	15	16	17	18	19	20
21	22	23	24	25	26	27	28	29	30	31	32	33	34	35	36	37	38	39	40
41	42	43	44	45	46	47	48	49	50	51	52	53	54	55	56	57	58	59	60
61	62	63	64	65	66	67	68	69	70	71	72	73	74	75	76	77	78	79	80
81	82	83	84	85	86	87	88	89	90	91	92	93	94	95	96	97	98	99	100

에듀윌이
너를
지지할게
ENERGY

끝이 좋아야 시작이 빛난다.

– 마리아노 리베라(Mariano Rivera)

에듀윌 토익 LISTENING LC (리스닝 종합서)

발 행 일	2022년 9월 1일 초판
편 저 자	에듀윌 어학연구소
펴 낸 이	권대호
펴 낸 곳	(주)에듀윌
등록번호	제25100-2002-000052호
주 소	08378 서울특별시 구로구 디지털로34길 55
	코오롱싸이언스밸리 2차 3층

ISBN 979-11-360-1916-5 (13740)

www.eduwill.net
대표전화 1600-6700

여러분의 작은 소리
에듀윌은 크게 듣겠습니다.

본 교재에 대한 여러분의 목소리를 들려주세요.
공부하시면서 어려웠던 점, 궁금한 점,
칭찬하고 싶은 점, 개선할 점, 어떤 것이라도 좋습니다.

에듀윌은 여러분께서 나누어 주신 의견을
통해 끊임없이 발전하고 있습니다.

에듀윌 도서몰 book.eduwill.net
- 부가학습자료 및 정오표: 에듀윌 도서몰 → 도서자료실
- 교재 문의: 에듀윌 도서몰 → 문의하기 → 교재(내용,출간) / 주문 및 배송

꿈을 현실로 만드는
에듀윌

DREAM

공무원 교육
- 선호도 1위, 신뢰도 1위! 브랜드만족도 1위!
- 합격자 수 2,100% 폭등시킨 독한 커리큘럼

자격증 교육
- 8년간 아무도 깨지 못한 기록 합격자 수 1위
- 가장 많은 합격자를 배출한 최고의 합격 시스템

직영학원
- 직영학원 수 1위
- 표준화된 커리큘럼과 호텔급 시설 자랑하는 전국 22개 학원

종합출판
- 온라인서점 베스트셀러 1위!
- 출제위원급 전문 교수진이 직접 집필한 합격 교재

어학 교육
- 토익 베스트셀러 1위
- 토익 동영상 강의 무료 제공
- 업계 최초 '토익 공식' 추천 AI 앱 서비스

콘텐츠 제휴 · B2B 교육
- 고객 맞춤형 위탁 교육 서비스 제공
- 기업, 기관, 대학 등 각 단체에 최적화된 고객 맞춤형 교육 및 제휴 서비스

부동산 아카데미
- 부동산 실무 교육 1위!
- 상위 1% 고소득 창업/취업 비법
- 부동산 실전 재테크 성공 비법

학점은행제
- 99%의 과목이수율
- 16년 연속 교육부 평가 인정 기관 선정

대학 편입
- 편입 교육 1위!
- 업계 유일 500% 환급 상품 서비스

국비무료 교육
- '5년우수훈련기관' 선정
- K-디지털, 산대특 등 특화 훈련과정
- 원격국비교육원 오픈

에듀윌 교육서비스 **공무원 교육** 9급공무원/7급공무원/경찰공무원/소방공무원/계리직공무원/기술직공무원/군무원 **자격증 교육** 공인중개사/주택관리사/감정평가사/노무사/전기기사/경비지도사/검정고시/소방설비기사/소방시설관리사/사회복지사1급/건축기사/토목기사/직업상담사/전기기능사/산업안전기사/위험물산업기사/위험물기능사/유통관리사/물류관리사/행정사/한국사능력검정/한경TESAT/매경TEST/KBS한국어능력시험/실용글쓰기/IT자격증/국제무역사/무역영어 **어학 교육** 토익 교재/토익 동영상 강의/인공지능 토익 앱 **세무/회계** 회계사/세무사/전산세무회계/ERP정보관리사/재경관리사 **대학 편입** 편입 교재/편입 영어·수학/경찰대/의치대/편입 컨설팅·면접 **직영학원** 공무원학원/경찰학원/소방학원/공인중개사 학원/주택관리사 학원/전기기사학원/세무사·회계사 학원/편입학원 **종합출판** 공무원·자격증 수험교재 및 단행본 **학점은행제** 교육부 평가인정기관 원격평생교육원(사회복지사2급/경영학/CPA)/교육부 평가인정기관 원격 사회교육원(사회복지사2급/심리학) **콘텐츠 제휴·B2B 교육** 교육 콘텐츠 제휴/기업 맞춤 자격증 교육/대학 취업역량 강화 교육 **부동산 아카데미** 부동산 창업CEO/부동산 경매 마스터/부동산 컨설팅 **국비무료 교육 (국비교육원)** 전기기능사/전기(산업)기사/소방설비(산업)기사/IT(빅데이터/자바프로그램/파이썬)/게임그래픽/3D프린터/실내건축디자인/웹퍼블리셔/그래픽디자인/영상편집(유튜브)디자인/온라인 쇼핑몰광고 및 제작(쿠팡, 스마트스토어)/전산세무회계/컴퓨터활용능력/ITQ/GTQ/직업상담사

교육문의 1600-6700 www.eduwill.net

eduwill

토익 시험 직후, 모두가 에듀윌 토익으로 몰리는 이유

가장 빠른 토익 정답
에듀윌 토익 초간단 채점

60회 이상
만점 구원

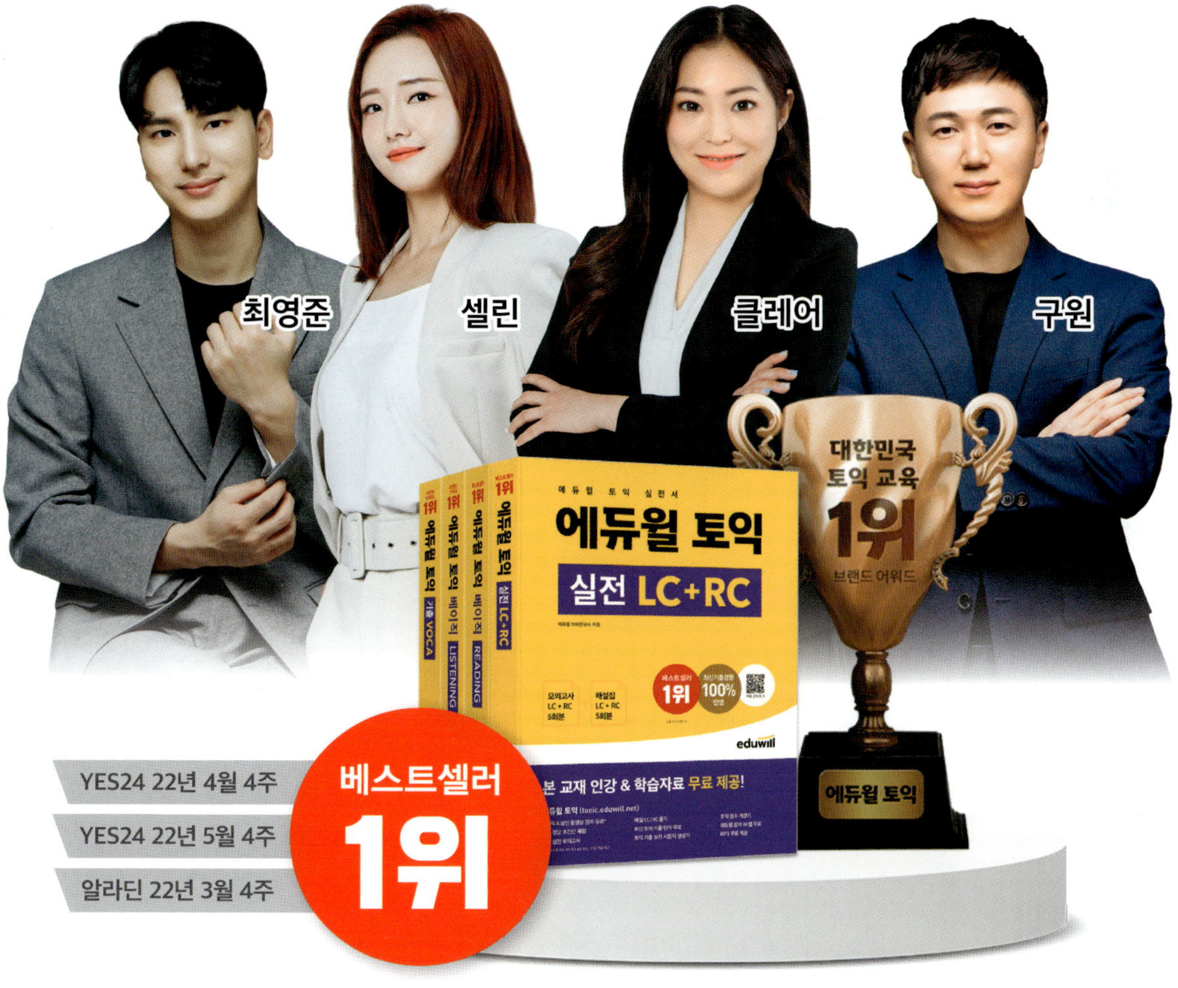

목차

머리말

If you can't measure it, you can't improve it.

"측정할 수 없으면 개선할 수 없다." 세계적인 사상가 피터 드러커가 남긴 말이다. 토익을 공부하는 데 있어서도 이 말은 매우 유용하다. 토익은 비즈니스 분야에서의 영어 능력을 측정하는 시험이며, 공정한 측정을 위해 나름의 정해진 기준을 세우고 유지한다. 그리고 그 과정에서 토익 시험은 일정한 형식을 갖추고 유형화될 수밖에 없다. 다만 그 유형들이 겉으로 드러나지 않게 순서를 뒤섞고 일련의 함정을 심어 최대한 요령이 통하지 않도록 방지할 뿐이다.

우리는 그렇게 출제자들이 공들여 만든 문제를 해체하며, 거기에서 하나하나 의미 있는 유형과 함정을 찾아 데이터화한다. 정교한 데이터 분석을 통해 어떤 유형과 함정들이 얼마나 자주 쓰였는지를 알아내고, 그 비율에 맞춰 학습 단계와 내용을 구성하여 학습자들이 하나씩 차근차근 토익을 정복해 나갈 수 있게 만든 책이 바로 '에듀윌 토익 리스닝'이다.

각각의 유형들은 파트별 유닛으로 분류하여 풀이 전략과 함께 맛보기 문제 → Check up → 빈출 표현으로 기초를 다질 수 있게 하였으며, 연습 문제 → 실전 문제 → 파트별 테스트를 거쳐 완벽하게 익힐 수 있도록 설계하였다. 기본적인 학습 체계는 토익 초보자들을 대상으로 설계하였지만 고득점을 욕심내는 학습자들을 위한 장치도 마련하였다. 파트2에서는 고난도 문제만을 영국·호주 발음으로 녹음한 별도의 파트 테스트를 제공하여 비교적 쉬운 파트에서 단기간에 점수를 올릴 수 있게 하였고, 파트4에서는 담화문 전체를 영국·호주 발음으로 재녹음하여 제공한다. 파트1과 2에서는 형식에 치우친 해설은 과감하게 걷어내고 그 대신 [기출 표현 Plus+]라는 장치를 통해 기출에서 쓰였던 다양한 표현들을 추가적으로 익힐 수 있게 하였다.

교재 끝에는 최신 기출 유형을 반영한 3회분의 모의고사를 수록하였으며, 이를 통해 전체 파트를 종합적으로 점검하고 자신의 실력을 최종적으로 정확하게 측정해 볼 수 있을 것이다.

취업에 있어서 토익 점수는 여전히 중요하며, 많은 대학생들이 취업을 위해 영어 대신 토익 '시험'을 공부한다. 하지만 토익은 어디까지나 영어 능력을 측정하는 도구이지 영어를 익히는 수단으로 자리를 잡아서는 곤란하다. 따라서, 토익을 공부하는 기간은 짧으면 짧을수록 좋다! 이 책에 담긴 빈출 유형들을 집중적으로 학습하고, 세분화된 유형들을 통해 나의 약점을 정확히 측정하고 보완해 나간다면 생각보다 빨리 내가 원하는 목표에 도달해있을 것이다.

에듀윌 어학연구소

시작하는 방법은
말을 멈추고
즉시 행동하는 것이다.

– 월트 디즈니(Walt Disney)

에듀윌 토익

LISTENING LC

독자님의 목소리에 귀 기울입니다

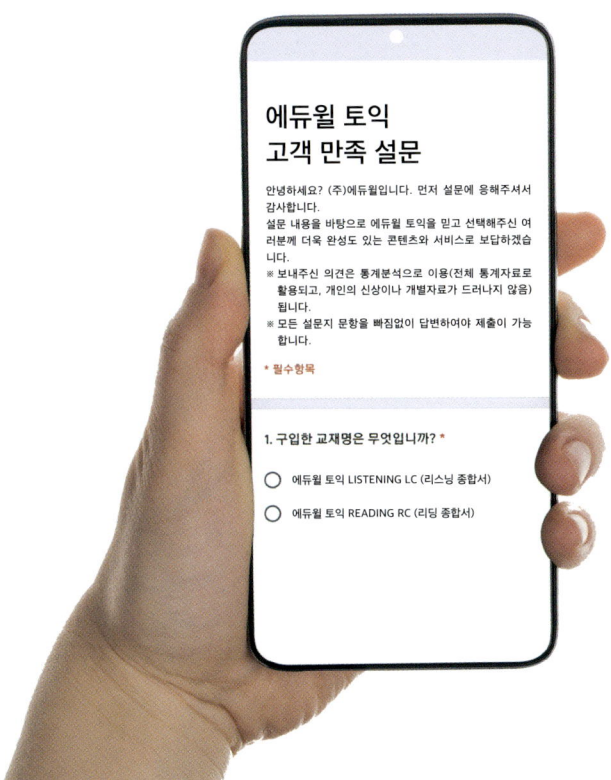

불편한 점이나
더 필요한 서비스가 있다면
말씀해 주세요.

에듀윌 토익을
믿고 선택해 주신 여러분께
더욱 완성도 있는 콘텐츠로
보답하겠습니다.

설문조사 참여 시
스타벅스 아메리카노 지급

참여 방법 QR 코드 스캔 → 설문조사 참여(1분만 투자하세요!)
추첨 방법 매월 적극적으로 의견을 주신 2분을 추첨하여 개별 연락
경 품 스타벅스 아메리카노 Tall

에듀윌 토익 설문조사
바로 가기

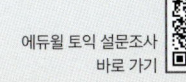

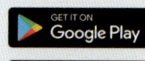
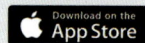

에듀윌 토익
LISTENING LC
정답 및 해설

CHAPTER 01 사진 유형별 전략

UNIT 01 1인 사진

CHECK UP
본문 p.24

1. (B) **2.** (D)

1. 미녀 🎧

(A) A man is watering a potted plant.
(B) A man is drinking from a bottle.
(C) A man is picking up a laptop.
(D) A man is plugging in a microwave oven.

해석
(A) 남자가 화분에 담긴 식물에 물을 주고 있다.
(B) 남자가 병에 든 것을 마시고 있다.
(C) 남자가 노트북 컴퓨터를 집어 들고 있다.
(D) 남자가 전자레인지의 플러그를 꽂고 있다.

어휘
potted plant 화분에 담긴 식물 pick up 집어 들다
plug in ~의 플러그를 꽂다, 전원을 연결하다

기출 표현 PLUS⁺
He's sitting at a desk. 그는 책상에 앉아 있다.
A plant has been placed on the table.
식물이 테이블 위에 놓여 있다.

2. 미녀 🎧

(A) She's placing food in a shopping basket.
(B) She's opening her bag.
(C) She's leaving a supermarket with some food.
(D) She's facing a refrigerated display case.

해석
(A) 그녀는 장바구니에 음식을 넣고 있다.
(B) 그녀는 자신의 가방을 열고 있다.
(C) 그녀는 먹을 것을 좀 가지고 슈퍼마켓을 떠나고 있다.
(D) 그녀는 냉장 진열장을 마주 보고 있다.

어휘
place 놓다, 두다 shopping basket 장바구니 leave 떠나다
face ~을 마주 보다, 향하다 refrigerated 냉장한
display case 진열 선반, 진열장

기출 표현 PLUS⁺
She's holding a shopping basket.
그녀는 장바구니를 들고 있다.
She's reaching for some food.
그녀는 음식을 향해 손을 뻗고 있다.

연습 문제
본문 p.26

1. (B) **2.** (B) **3.** (D)

1. 영녀 🎧

(A) He's pulling out a chair.
(B) He's kneeling in front of a chalkboard.
(C) He's folding an apron.
(D) He's hanging up a sign.

해석
(A) 그는 의자를 잡아당기고 있다.
(B) 그는 칠판 앞에서 무릎을 꿇고 있다.
(C) 그는 앞치마를 접고 있다.
(D) 그는 안내판을 걸고 있다.

어휘
pull out 잡아당기다 kneel 무릎을 꿇다
chalkboard (= blackboard) 칠판 hang up 걸다, 매달다

기출 표현 PLUS⁺
He's wearing an apron. 그는 앞치마를 입고 있다.
He's writing on a chalkboard.
그는 칠판에 무언가를 적고 있다.

2. 영녀 🎧

(A) She's weighing some fruit on a scale.
(B) She's holding up some fruit.
(C) She's adjusting her hat.
(D) She's chopping some vegetables.

해석
(A) 그녀는 저울에 과일의 무게를 달고 있다.
(B) 그녀는 과일을 들고 있다.
(C) 그녀는 모자를 바로잡고 있다.
(D) 그녀는 채소를 썰고 있다.

어휘
weigh 무게를 달다   scale 저울   hold up ~을 떠받치다
adjust (매무새 등을) 바로잡다, 정돈하다   chop 썰다, 다지다

기출 표현 PLUS⁺
A woman is wearing a hat. 여자가 모자를 쓰고 있다.
Some fruit has been displayed. 과일이 진열되어 있다.

3. 영녀 🎧

(A) The woman is removing an item from her
    purse.
(B) Some windows are being installed.
(C) The woman is sitting at a table.
(D) Some bags have been set on the floor.

해석
(A) 여자가 자신의 핸드백에서 물건을 꺼내고 있다.
(B) 창문이 설치되고 있다.
(C) 여자가 테이블에 앉아 있다.
(D) 몇몇 가방들이 바닥에 놓여 있다.

어휘
remove 꺼내다   purse 핸드백   install 설치하다
set (특정한 장소에) 놓다

기출 표현 PLUS⁺
She's holding a mobile phone. 그녀는 휴대폰을 들고 있다.
A cup has been placed on the table.
컵이 테이블 위에 놓여 있다.

실전 문제   본문 p.27

1. (A)   **2.** (D)   **3.** (D)   **4.** (B)   **5.** (D)
6. (C)

1. 미남 🎧

(A) She's looking into a laundry cart.
(B) She's bending down to tie her shoes.
(C) She's pressing a button on a washing machine.
(D) She's pushing a cart.

해석
(A) 그녀는 세탁물 카트 안을 살펴보고 있다.
(B) 그녀는 허리를 굽혀 신발 끈을 묶고 있다.
(C) 그녀는 세탁기의 버튼을 누르고 있다.
(D) 그녀는 카트를 밀고 있다.

어휘
look into 조사하다, 주의 깊게 살피다   laundry 세탁, 세탁물
bend down 허리를 굽히다   washing machine 세탁기

기출 표현 PLUS⁺
A woman is holding some clothes.
여자가 옷을 들고 있다.
The washing machine has been left open.
세탁기 문이 열려 있다.

2. 미녀 🎧

(A) A woman is watching a performance.
(B) A woman is carrying a music stand.
(C) A woman is putting away a violin.
(D) A woman is playing a musical instrument.

해석
(A) 여자가 공연을 관람하고 있다.
(B) 여자가 악보대를 나르고 있다.
(C) 여자가 바이올린을 치우고 있다.
(D) 여자가 악기를 연주하고 있다.

어휘
performance 공연   music stand 악보대
put away (있던 곳에) 넣다, 치우다   musical instrument 악기

A woman is wearing an ID badge.
여자가 신분증 배지를 착용하고 있다.
A woman has her chin on a violin.
여자가 바이올린을 턱에 대고 있다.

3. 영녀 🎧

(A) The man is getting in a boat.
(B) Some houses line a lake.
(C) He is securing a boat to a dock.
(D) The man is paddling a boat.

해석

(A) 남자가 배에 올라타는 중이다.
(B) 몇몇 집들이 호수를 따라 늘어서 있다.
(C) 그는 배를 부두에 고정시키고 있다.
(D) 남자가 배의 노를 젓고 있다.

어휘

line ~을 따라 늘어서다 secure (단단히) 고정시키다, 잡아매다
dock 부두 paddle 노를 젓다; 노

기출 표현 PLUS⁺

A man is holding a paddle. 남자가 노를 들고 있다.
A boat is floating on the water. 보트가 물 위에 떠 있다.

4. 호남 🎧

(A) She has set a water bottle on a lawn.
(B) She has a rolled mat under her arm.
(C) She's walking through a doorway.
(D) She's exercising on the grass.

해석

(A) 그녀는 잔디밭에 물병을 놓았다.
(B) 그녀는 겨드랑이에 돌돌 만 매트를 끼고 있다.
(C) 그녀는 출입구를 걸어서 지나가고 있다.
(D) 그녀는 잔디밭에서 운동을 하고 있다.

어휘

roll (둥글게) 말다 doorway 출입구

기출 표현 PLUS⁺

A woman is holding a water bottle. 여자가 물병을 들고 있다.

5. 미녀 🎧

(A) Some books are being arranged on a shelf.
(B) The man is putting a pen in his pocket.
(C) A lamp is being turned on.
(D) The man is bending over a desk.

해석

(A) 책 몇 권이 책꽂이에 정리되고 있다.
(B) 남자가 자신의 주머니에 펜을 넣고 있다.
(C) 전등이 켜지고 있다.
(D) 남자가 책상 위로 몸을 굽히고 있다.

어휘

arrange 정리하다, 배열하다 shelf 책꽂이, 선반
bend over 몸을 ~ 위로 굽히다

기출 표현 PLUS⁺

He's wearing glasses. 그는 안경을 쓰고 있다.
Some books have been stacked on a desk.
책들이 책상 위에 쌓여 있다.

6. 영녀 🎧

(A) He's removing his glasses.
(B) He's sipping a beverage from a cup.
(C) He's looking down at some notes.
(D) He's talking to someone on the mobile phone.

해석

(A) 그는 안경을 벗고 있다.
(B) 그는 컵으로 음료를 조금씩 마시고 있다.
(C) 그는 메모를 내려다보고 있다.
(D) 그는 휴대폰으로 누군가와 통화하고 있다.

어휘

remove (옷 등을) 벗다, 치우다 sip 홀짝이다, 조금씩 마시다
beverage 음료 look down at ~을 내려다보다

기출 표현 PLUS⁺

A man is holding a pen. 남자가 펜을 쥐고 있다.
A coffee cup has been placed on the table.
커피잔이 테이블 위에 놓여 있다.

UNIT 02 2인 이상 사진

CHECK UP   본문 p.28

1. (A)   **2.** (A)

1. 미녀 🎧

(A) They're writing some notes.
(B) They're selling some headphones.
(C) They're facing one another.
(D) They're seated in a circle.

해석
(A) 그들은 메모를 하고 있다.
(B) 그들은 헤드폰을 판매하고 있다.
(C) 그들은 서로 마주 보고 있다.
(D) 그들은 둥글게 둘러앉아 있다.

어휘
face one another 서로 마주 보다
be seated in a circle 둥글게 둘러앉아 있다

기출 표현 PLUS⁺
The people are wearing some headphones.
사람들이 헤드폰을 쓰고 있다.
A water bottle has been placed on the table.
물병이 테이블 위에 놓여 있다.

2. 미녀 🎧

(A) The women have stopped on a walkway.
(B) The women have taken off their jackets.
(C) The women are crossing a street.
(D) The women are entering a building.

해석
(A) 여자들이 보도 위에 멈춰 서 있다.
(B) 여자들은 재킷을 벗었다.
(C) 여자들이 길을 건너고 있다.
(D) 여자들이 건물에 들어가고 있다.

어휘
walkway 보도, 통로 take off (옷 등을) 벗다 enter 들어가다

기출 표현 PLUS⁺
The women are carrying some bags.
여자들이 가방을 들고 있다.
They're standing on a walkway. 그들은 보도 위에 서 있다.

연습 문제   본문 p.30

1. (B)   **2.** (C)   **3.** (C)

1. 영녀 🎧

(A) They're waiting to pay for some items.
(B) The woman is pointing at a plant.
(C) They're planting a garden.
(D) The man is watering some flowers.

해석
(A) 그들은 물건값을 지불하기 위해 기다리고 있다.
(B) 여자가 식물을 가리키고 있다.
(C) 그들은 정원에 식물을 심고 있다.
(D) 남자가 꽃에 물을 주고 있다.

어휘
pay for ~의 값을 지불하다 point at ~을 가리키다
plant 식물; 심다 water 물을 주다

기출 표현 PLUS⁺
The man is holding a potted plant.
남자가 화분에 담긴 식물을 들고 있다.
The woman is carrying a bag on her shoulder.
여자가 자신의 어깨에 가방을 메고 있다.

2. 영녀 🎧

(A) One of the men is purchasing a tire.
(B) One of the men is riding to work.
(C) The men are fixing a bicycle.
(D) The men are opening a toolbox.

해석
(A) 남자들 중 한 명이 타이어를 구매하고 있다.
(B) 남자들 중 한 명이 무언가를 타고 출근하고 있다.
(C) 남자들이 자전거를 고치고 있다.

(D) 남자들이 공구 상자를 열고 있다.

어휘

purchase 구매하다; 구매 ride (차량, 자전거 등을) 타다
fix 고치다, 수리하다 toolbox 공구 상자

기출 표현 PLUS⁺

One of the men is using a tool.
남자들 중 한 명이 공구를 사용하고 있다.
A bicycle is being repaired. 자전거가 수리되고 있다.

3. 영녀 🎧

(A) Some books are being packed into boxes.
(B) Some books are stacked on the floor.
(C) The people are visiting a library.
(D) The people are assembling some shelves.

해석

(A) 책들이 상자들에 가득 넣어지고 있다.
(B) 책들이 바닥에 쌓여 있다.
(C) 사람들이 도서관에 방문하고 있다.
(D) 사람들이 선반을 조립하고 있다.

어휘

pack (물건을) 채워 넣다, (짐을) 싸다 stack 쌓다, 포개다
assemble 조립하다 shelf 선반

기출 표현 PLUS⁺

One of the women is pointing at a book.
여자들 중 한 명이 책을 가리키고 있다.
Books are on display in a library.
책들이 도서관에 진열되어 있다.

실전 문제 · 본문 p.31

1. (B) **2.** (A) **3.** (A) **4.** (D) **5.** (D)
6. (D)

---

1. 미남 🎧

(A) The doorway has been blocked by some
    people.

**(B) Some notices have been posted to a
    bulletin board.**
(C) The woman is shaking hands with a man.
(D) One of the men is arranging papers on a table.

해석

(A) 출입구가 사람들에 의해 막혀 있다.
(B) 몇몇 공고문이 게시판에 붙어 있다.
(C) 여자가 남자와 악수하고 있다.
(D) 남자들 중 한 명이 탁자 위에 서류를 정리하고 있다.

어휘

doorway 출입구 block 막다 notice 공고, 안내; 알아차리다
post 게시[공고]하다 bulletin board 게시판
shake hands with ~와 악수하다 arrange 정리하다, 배열하다

기출 표현 PLUS⁺

Some light fixtures are mounted from the ceiling.
조명 기구들이 천장에 설치되어 있다.
Some doors are closed. 문들이 닫혀 있다.

2. 미녀 🎧

(A) The women are wearing long-sleeved shirts.
(B) The people are setting up a meeting room.
(C) Some handouts are being distributed.
(D) One of the women is typing on a computer.

해석

(A) 여자들이 긴소매 셔츠를 입고 있다.
(B) 사람들이 회의실을 준비하고 있다.
(C) 유인물이 배포되고 있다.
(D) 여자들 중 한 명이 컴퓨터로 타자를 치고 있다.

어휘

long-sleeved 긴 소매의 set up 설치하다, 마련하다
handout 유인물 distribute 배포하다, 나눠 주다
type 타자를 치다

기출 표현 PLUS⁺

The people are sitting at a table.
사람들이 테이블에 앉아 있다.
One of the women is holding a pen.
여자들 중 한 명이 펜을 쥐고 있다.

3. 영녀 🎧

(A) They're walking past a seating area.
(B) They're seated in a restaurant.
(C) One of the people is closing an umbrella.
(D) One of the people is removing a hat.

(A) 그들은 좌석이 있는 구역을 걸어 지나가고 있다.
(B) 그들은 식당에 앉아 있다.
(C) 사람들 중 한 명이 파라솔을 접고 있다.
(D) 사람들 중 한 명이 모자를 벗고 있다.

어휘

past ~을 지나서   seating 좌석, 자리   remove (옷 등을) 벗다

기출 표현 PLUS⁺

All chairs are unoccupied. 모든 의자들이 비어 있다.
A dining area has been set up outdoors.
식사 공간이 야외에 준비되어 있다.

4. 호남 🎧

(A) The woman is adjusting a mirror.
(B) The woman is getting into a vehicle.
(C) The man is rolling down a window.
(D) The man is pointing at a location on a map.

해석

(A) 여자가 거울을 조정하고 있다.
(B) 여자가 차량에 타는 중이다.
(C) 남자가 창문을 내리고 있다.
(D) 남자가 지도에서 위치를 가리키고 있다.

어휘

adjust 조정하다, 조절하다   vehicle 차량
roll down (손잡이를 돌려서) ~을 내리다[열다]
point at ~을 가리키다   location 위치, 장소

기출 표현 PLUS⁺

They're looking at a map. 그들은 지도를 보고 있다.
The man is wearing a pair of glasses.
남자가 안경을 쓰고 있다.

5. 미녀 🎧

(A) The workers are holding a clipboard.
(B) The workers are putting on a uniform.
(C) One of the people is pressing a button on the machine.
(D) The people are looking at a machine.

해석

(A) 작업자들이 클립보드를 들고 있다.
(B) 작업자들이 유니폼을 착용하는 중이다.
(C) 사람들 중 한 명이 기계의 버튼을 누르고 있다.
(D) 사람들이 기계를 바라보고 있다.

어휘

clipboard 클립보드(위에 집게가 달려 있어서 종이를 끼울 수 있는 판)

기출 표현 PLUS⁺

One of the workers is holding a clipboard.
작업자들 중 한 명이 클립보드를 들고 있다.
The people are wearing work uniforms.
사람들이 작업복을 입고 있다.

6. 영녀 🎧

(A) People are walking away from a building.
(B) Some benches are being installed.
(C) There is a car parked on the grass.
(D) Trees are lining a walkway.

해석

(A) 사람들이 건물에서 걸어 나가고 있다.
(B) 몇몇 벤치들이 설치되고 있다.
(C) 잔디 위에 주차한 차가 있다.
(D) 나무들이 보도를 따라 늘어서 있다.

어휘

install 설치하다   park 주차하다; 공원   line ~을 따라 늘어서다

기출 표현 PLUS⁺

The people are walking in a park.
사람들이 공원에서 걷고 있다.

UNIT 03 사물·풍경 사진

1. 미녀 🎧

(A) Water is flowing through a pipe.
(B) Some trees border a pond.
(C) A building overlooks a lake.
(D) Some boats are floating on the water.

해석

(A) 물이 파이프를 통과하여 흐르고 있다.
(B) 연못 가장자리를 따라 나무들이 있다.
(C) 건물이 호수를 내려다보고 있다.
(D) 배들이 물 위에 떠 있다.

어휘

border 가장자리를 이루다   overlook (건물 등이) 내려다보다
float 떠가다, 흘러가다

기출 표현 PLUS⁺

A pond is surrounded by plants.
연못이 식물들로 둘러싸여 있다.

2. 미녀 🎧

(A) A gate is blocking the road.
(B) A vehicle is parked near the curb.
(C) Lines are being painted on the street.
(D) A checkpoint barrier has been raised.

해석

(A) 차단기가 도로를 막고 있다.
(B) 차가 연석 가까이 주차되어 있다.
(C) 거리에 차선들이 그려지고 있다.
(D) 검문소의 차단기가 들어 올려져 있다.

어휘

gate 출입문, (도로의) 차단기   block 막다, 차단하다
vehicle 차량   curb 연석, 도로 경계석
checkpoint (차량, 통행인 등의) 검문소   barrier 장벽, 장애물
raise 들어 올리다

기출 표현 PLUS⁺

A barrier has been lifted. 차단기가 들어 올려져 있다.

1. 영녀 🎧

(A) All chairs are unoccupied.
(B) Napkins are being folded.
(C) Chairs have been piled next to the tables.
(D) Light fixtures are being hung over the tables.

해석

(A) 모든 의자들이 비어 있다.
(B) 냅킨을 접고 있다.
(C) 의자들이 테이블 옆에 포개져 있다.
(D) 테이블들 위로 조명들을 매달고 있다.

어휘

unoccupied 비어 있는   pile 쌓다, 포개다
light fixture 조명 기구   hang 걸다, 매달다

기출 표현 PLUS⁺

The tables have been set for a meal.
테이블들이 식사를 위해 준비되어 있다.
Light fixtures are hanging over some tables.
조명들이 테이블 위로 달려 있다.

2. 영녀 🎧

(A) Some light fixtures are mounted on the walls.
(B) Some curtains are covering the windows.
(C) Some sofas have been pushed into a corner.
(D) Some cushions have been left on the floor.

해석

(A) 일부 조명들이 벽에 고정되어 있다.
(B) 창문에 커튼이 드리워져 있다.
(C) 몇몇 소파를 구석으로 밀어 놓았다.
(D) 몇몇 쿠션이 바닥에 놓여 있다.

어휘

light fixture 조명 기구 mount 고정시키다, 설치하다

기출 표현 PLUS⁺

A rug is underneath a table. 러그가 테이블 밑에 있다.

Some cushions have been set on the sofas.
몇몇 쿠션이 소파 위에 놓여 있다.

3. 영녀 🎧

(A) A passenger is stepping through the door.
(B) A bus is being driven down a road.
(C) Some roads are closed to traffic.
(D) Some trees are being trimmed.

해석

(A) 한 승객이 문으로 걸어 들어가고 있다.
(B) 버스가 도로를 따라 운행되고 있다.
(C) 일부 도로의 교통이 폐쇄되었다.
(D) 몇몇 나무들이 다듬어지고 있다.

어휘

step (가까운 거리를) 걷다 traffic 교통(량), 차량들
trim 다듬다, 손질하다

기출 표현 PLUS⁺

Some cars have been parked near a building.
차들이 건물 가까이에 주차되어 있다.
The vehicle is next to the sidewalk. 차량이 보도 옆에 있다.

실전 문제 · 본문 p.35

1. (B)	2. (A)	3. (C)	4. (B)	5. (A)
6. (C)				

1. 미남 🎧

(A) There is a path leading to a tunnel.
(B) A car has been parked beside a building.
(C) A roof is undergoing repairs.
(D) Some bushes are planted along the curb.

해석

(A) 터널로 이어지는 길이 있다.

(B) 자동차가 건물 옆에 주차되어 있다.
(C) 지붕이 수리되고 있다.
(D) 연석을 따라 관목이 심어져 있다.

어휘

path 길 lead to ~로 이어지다 undergo (변화 등을) 겪다, 받다
repair 수리; 수리하다 bush 관목, 덤불 curb 연석, 도로 경계석

기출 표현 PLUS⁺

A walkway leads to a house. 보도가 집으로 이어져 있다.
There are some bushes in front of a house.
집 앞에 덤불이 있다.

2. 미녀 🎧

(A) Some fruit has been separated into containers.
(B) A supermarket is crowded with shoppers.
(C) Some fresh food is being transported.
(D) The aisle in a shop is being cleaned.

해석

(A) 과일이 분리되어 용기에 담겨 있다.
(B) 슈퍼마켓이 쇼핑객들로 붐빈다.
(C) 신선 식품을 운송하고 있다.
(D) 상점의 통로를 청소하고 있다.

어휘

separate 분리하다, 나누다 container 용기, 그릇, 통
be crowded with ~로 혼잡하다, 붐비다
transport 수송하다; 수송 aisle 통로

기출 표현 PLUS⁺

Some produce has been displayed in baskets.
농산물이 바구니에 진열되어 있다.

3. 영녀 🎧

(A) Some buildings are sitting along a large road.
(B) Some pots are being arranged near the houses.
(C) A big umbrella is opened next to a building.
(D) Some patio chairs are set up next to an umbrella.

(A) 몇몇 건물들이 넓은 도로를 따라 자리하고 있다.

(B) 몇몇 화분들을 주택들 근처에 정리하고 있다.

(C) 대형 파라솔이 건물 옆에 펼쳐져 있다.

(D) 몇몇 간이 의자가 파라솔 옆에 놓여 있다.

어휘

arrange 정리하다, 배열하다 umbrella 우산, 양산, 파라솔
patio chair (접을 수 있는) 간이 의자 set up 세우다, 설치하다

기출 표현 PLUS⁺

There is a large umbrella next to a building.
건물 옆에 대형 파라솔이 있다.

4. 호남 🎧

(A) Some buildings are being painted.

(B) Some flowers have been planted around a statue.

(C) There are some tents folded near a building.

(D) Some benches are being installed outside.

해석

(A) 일부 건물들을 페인트칠 하고 있다.

(B) 꽃들이 조각상 주위에 심어져 있다.

(C) 건물 근처에 일부 천막들이 접혀 있다.

(D) 벤치 몇 개가 밖에 설치되고 있다.

어휘

statue 조각상 fold 접다 install 설치하다

기출 표현 PLUS⁺

A statue is in the middle of a plaza.
조각상이 광장 한가운데에 있다.

Some people are sitting on the ground.
몇몇 사람들이 바닥에 앉아 있다.

5. 미녀 🎧

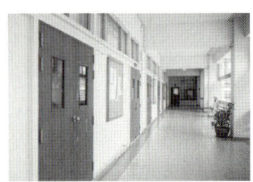

(A) Bulletin boards have been mounted on the wall.

(B) Some doors have been left open.

(C) Some floor tiles have been stacked in a pile.

(D) A potted plant has been left on a table.

해석

(A) 게시판이 벽에 고정되어 있다.

(B) 일부 문들이 열려 있다.

(C) 바닥 타일이 무더기로 쌓여 있다.

(D) 화분에 담긴 식물이 탁자 위에 놓여 있다.

어휘

bulletin board 게시판 mount 고정시키다, 설치하다
stack 쌓다, 포개다 pile 포개 놓은 것, 더미
potted plant 화분에 담긴 식물

기출 표현 PLUS⁺

Some doors are closed. 문들이 닫혀 있다.

A plant has been left on the floor. 화초가 바닥에 놓여 있다.

6. 영녀 🎧

(A) Some chairs are stored under a canopy.

(B) Some boats are floating in the water.

(C) Some furniture has been stacked near a fence.

(D) Some rocks are piled on a table.

해석

(A) 몇몇 의자들이 캐노피 아래에 보관되어 있다.

(B) 몇몇 배들이 물 위에 떠 있다.

(C) 몇몇 가구가 울타리 근처에 포개져 있다.

(D) 몇몇 돌들이 탁자 위에 쌓여 있다.

어휘

store 저장하다, 보관하다 canopy (지붕처럼 늘어뜨린) 덮개
stack 쌓다, 포개다 fence 울타리 pile 쌓다, 포개다

기출 표현 PLUS⁺

Some chairs have been stacked near a fence.
몇몇 의자들이 울타리 근처에 포개져 있다.

CHAPTER 02 사진 장소별 전략

UNIT 04 실내 업무 장소 사진

CHECK UP
본문 p.37

1. (C) **2.** (A)

1. 미녀 🎧

(A) She's unplugging a keyboard.
(B) She's tying a string around some papers.
(C) She's talking on the phone.
(D) She's wiping off a computer monitor.

해석
(A) 그녀는 키보드의 플러그를 뽑고 있다.
(B) 그녀는 서류를 줄로 묶고 있다.
(C) 그녀는 전화로 이야기하고 있다.
(D) 그녀는 컴퓨터 모니터를 닦고 있다.

어휘
unplug (전기) 플러그를 뽑다 tie a string 줄로 묶다
wipe off ~을 닦다

기출 표현 PLUS⁺
She's sitting at a desk. 그녀는 책상에 앉아 있다.
She's typing on a computer.
그녀는 컴퓨터에 타자를 치고 있다.

2. 미녀 🎧

(A) One of the people is standing by a podium.
(B) One of the people is writing on a board.
(C) One of the people is handing out brochures.
(D) One of the people is turning on a microphone.

해석
(A) 사람들 중 한 명이 연단 옆에 서 있다.
(B) 사람들 중 한 명이 보드에 무언가를 적고 있다.
(C) 사람들 중 한 명이 브로슈어를 나눠 주고 있다.
(D) 사람들 중 한 명이 마이크를 켜고 있다.

어휘
podium 연단, 연설대 hand out 나눠 주다, 배포하다
brochure 브로슈어, 소책자

기출 표현 PLUS⁺
One of the people is standing up. 사람들 중 한 명이 서 있다.

연습 문제
본문 p.38

1. (B) **2.** (C) **3.** (A)

1. 영녀 🎧

(A) The audience is receiving some handouts.
(B) The audience is facing a screen.
(C) The speaker is pointing at a chart.
(D) The speaker is turning on a computer.

해석
(A) 청중들이 유인물을 받고 있다.
(B) 청중들이 스크린을 향해 있다.
(C) 발표자가 도표를 가리키고 있다.
(D) 발표자가 컴퓨터를 켜고 있다.

어휘
audience ((집합적)) 청중, 관중 handout 인쇄물, 유인물
face ~을 마주 보다, 향하다 point at ~을 가리키다

기출 표현 PLUS⁺
The presenter is standing to one side.
발표자가 한쪽에 서 있다.
Some people are listening to a presentation.
몇몇 사람들이 발표를 듣고 있다.

2. 영녀 🎧

(A) Some shelves are being rearranged.
(B) A laptop is being plugged in.
(C) The woman is writing on a document.
(D) The woman is adjusting her glasses.

해석
(A) 몇몇 선반들이 재배열되고 있다.
(B) 노트북 컴퓨터의 플러그가 꽂히고 있다.

(C) 여자가 문서에 무언가를 쓰고 있다.
(D) 여자가 안경을 고쳐 쓰고 있다.

어휘
rearrange 재배열[배치]하다
plug in ~의 플러그를 꽂다, 전원을 연결하다
adjust one's glasses 안경을 고쳐 쓰다

기출 표현 PLUS⁺
She's holding glasses. 그녀는 안경을 들고 있다.
There is a laptop on a desk. 책상 위에 노트북 컴퓨터가 있다.

3. 영녀 🎧

(A) The man is using a microscope.
(B) The man is pointing at a screen.
(C) The man is consulting a manual.
(D) The man is looking for a pen.

해석
(A) 남자가 현미경을 사용하고 있다.
(B) 남자가 화면을 가리키고 있다.
(C) 남자가 설명서를 참고하고 있다.
(D) 남자가 펜을 찾고 있다.

어휘
microscope 현미경   point at ~을 손가락으로 가리키다
consult 참고하다; 상담하다   manual 설명서

기출 표현 PLUS⁺
The man is looking into an instrument.
남자가 기구를 들여다보고 있다.
He's using laboratory equipment.
그는 실험실 장비를 사용하고 있다.

실전 문제   본문 p.39

1. (C)   **2.** (C)   **3.** (B)   **4.** (A)   **5.** (B)
6. (A)

---

1. 미남 🎧

(A) A woman is passing a marker to a man.

(B) The people are shaking hands with one another.
(C) A man is drawing a graph on a presentation board.
(D) The people are leaving a meeting room.

해석
(A) 여자가 남자에게 마커펜을 전달하고 있다.
(B) 사람들이 서로 악수하고 있다.
(C) 남자가 발표용 보드에 그래프를 그리고 있다.
(D) 사람들이 회의실을 떠나고 있다.

어휘
marker 마커펜; 표시, 표지 shake hands with ~와 악수하다
presentation 발표, 프레젠테이션

기출 표현 PLUS⁺
Some of the people are sitting at a desk.
일부 사람들이 책상에 앉아 있다.
One of the people is drawing with a marker.
사람들 중 한 명이 마커펜으로 무언가를 그리고 있다.

2. 미녀 🎧

(A) She's exiting an office.
(B) She's lifting up a laptop.
(C) She's aiming a spray bottle at a plant.
(D) She's filling a glass with water.

해석
(A) 그녀는 사무실을 나가고 있다.
(B) 그녀는 노트북 컴퓨터를 들어 올리고 있다.
(C) 그녀는 분무기를 식물로 향하게 하고 있다.
(D) 그녀는 유리잔에 물을 채우고 있다.

어휘
exit 나가다, 떠나다 lift up 들어 올리다
aim A at B A를 B에 겨누다   fill A with B A를 B로 채우다

기출 표현 PLUS⁺
There is a glass of water on the desk.
책상 위에 물 한 컵이 있다.
A woman is using a spray bottle.
여자가 분무기를 사용하고 있다.

3. 영녀 🎧

(A) She's putting some papers down on a copier.
(B) The woman is examining a document.
(C) She is trying on eyeglasses.
(D) A copier is printing some papers.

해석

(A) 여자가 서류를 복사기에 내려놓고 있다.
(B) 여자가 문서를 살펴보고 있다.
(C) 그녀는 안경을 써 보고 있다.
(D) 복사기가 서류를 인쇄하고 있다.

어휘

put down 내려놓다   examine 조사하다, 검사하다
try on ~을 입어 보다, 써 보다

기출 표현 PLUS⁺

She's holding some papers. 그녀는 종이 몇 장을 들고 있다.
A woman is standing next to a copier.
여자가 복사기 옆에 서 있다.

4. 호남 🎧

(A) A screen has been mounted on the wall.
(B) A flower arrangement has been set on top of the table.
(C) Some chairs have been lined up along the wall.
(D) A door has been left open.

해석

(A) 스크린이 벽에 설치되어 있다.
(B) 꽃꽂이가 탁자 위에 놓여 있다.
(C) 몇몇 의자들이 벽을 따라 일렬로 놓여 있다.
(D) 문이 열려 있다.

어휘

mount 설치하다, 고정시키다   flower arrangement 꽃꽂이
line up ~을 일렬로 세우다

기출 표현 PLUS⁺

Some chairs have been set up for a meeting.
몇몇 의자들이 회의를 위해 설치되어 있다.
The room is equipped with a screen.
방에 스크린이 갖춰져 있다.

5. 미녀 🎧

(A) A woman is printing some documents.
(B) Some binders have been lined up on a shelf.
(C) A woman is walking through an office.
(D) Some papers have been left in a garbage bin.

해석

(A) 여자가 몇몇 문서를 인쇄하고 있다.
(B) 몇몇 바인더가 선반에 일렬로 세워져 있다.
(C) 여자가 사무실을 가로질러 걸어 가고 있다.
(D) 일부 서류들이 쓰레기통에 버려져 있다.

어휘

binder (종이 등을 함께 묶는) 바인더   garbage bin 쓰레기통

기출 표현 PLUS⁺

A woman is looking at some documents.
여자가 서류를 보고 있다.
Some papers have been stacked in a pile.
종이들이 더미로 쌓여 있다.

6. 영녀 🎧

(A) Some people are gathered around a desk.
(B) Some documents are being printed.
(C) Someone is clearing off a table.
(D) Some chairs are stacked by the windows.

해석

(A) 몇몇 사람들이 책상 주위에 모여 있다.
(B) 몇몇 문서가 인쇄되고 있다.
(C) 어떤 사람이 탁자를 깨끗이 치우고 있다.
(D) 몇몇 의자들이 창문 옆에 포개져 있다.

어휘

gather 모으다, 모이다   clear off 깨끗이 치우다
stack 쌓다, 포개다

기출 표현 PLUS⁺

One of the women is sitting in front of a laptop.
여자들 중 한 명이 노트북 컴퓨터 앞에 앉아 있다.

UNIT 05 야외·교통수단 사진

CHECK UP
본문 p.41

1. (D)　　**2.** (C)

1. 미녀 🎧

(A) They're making repairs to a vehicle.
(B) They're purchasing some tools.
(C) They're climbing up a ladder.
(D) They're installing a roof on a house.

해석
(A) 그들은 차량을 고치고 있다.
(B) 그들은 몇몇 도구를 구매하고 있다.
(C) 그들은 사다리를 오르고 있다.
(D) 그들은 주택에 지붕을 설치하고 있다.

어휘
make a repair 수리하다　vehicle 차량
purchase 구매하다; 구매　climb up ~에 오르다
install 설치하다

기출 표현 PLUS⁺
Some roof tiles are being installed.
지붕 타일이 설치되고 있다.
The men are doing construction work on a house.
남자들이 주택 공사를 하고 있다.

2. 미녀 🎧

(A) She's strolling across a street.
(B) She's waiting in a line.
(C) She's standing on a walkway.
(D) She's getting into a vehicle.

해석
(A) 그녀는 도로를 가로질러 거닐고 있다.
(B) 그녀는 줄을 서서 기다리고 있다.
(C) 그녀는 보도에 서 있다.
(D) 그녀는 차량에 타는 중이다.

어휘
stroll 거닐다, 산책하다　wait in (a) line 줄을 서서 기다리다

walkway 보도, 인도　get into ~에 들어가다, 타다

기출 표현 PLUS⁺
A woman is carrying a bag on her shoulder.
여자가 어깨에 가방을 메고 있다.
She's holding a cup. 그녀는 컵을 들고 있다.

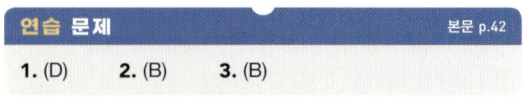

연습 문제
본문 p.42

1. (D)　　**2.** (B)　　**3.** (B)

1. 영녀 🎧

(A) Passengers are walking by a counter.
(B) A passenger is pushing a cart.
(C) A counter is being repaired.
(D) Passengers are waiting to check in.

해석
(A) 승객들이 카운터를 지나가고 있다.
(B) 한 승객이 카트를 밀고 있다.
(C) 카운터가 수리되는 중이다.
(D) 승객들이 탑승 수속을 하기 위해 기다리고 있다.

어휘
passenger 승객　walk by ~을 지나치다
counter 카운터, 계산대　repair 수리하다; 수리
check in 탑승[투숙] 수속을 밟다

기출 표현 PLUS⁺
Some people are waiting to be served.
사람들이 응대를 기다리고 있다.
Some travelers are waiting at a counter.
여행자들이 카운터에서 기다리고 있다.

2. 영녀 🎧

(A) Some crates are stacked on a walkway.
(B) Some bicycles are parked outside.
(C) A tree is being trimmed.
(D) A railing is being removed.

해석
(A) 몇몇 상자들이 보도에 쌓여 있다.

(B) 몇몇 자전거들이 옥외에 주차되어 있다.

(C) 나무를 다듬고 있다.

(D) 난간이 철거되고 있다.

어휘

crate (운송용 대형) 상자 stack 쌓다, 포개다

trim 다듬다, 손질하다 railing 난간, 울타리 remove 제거하다

기출 표현 PLUS⁺

Trees are lining both sides of a river.

나무들이 강을 두고 양쪽으로 늘어서 있다.

There are some bicycles on a bridge.

다리 위에 몇몇 자전거들이 있다.

3. 영녀 🎧

(A) There are some bottles on the ground.

(B) There's a mobile food stand on a walkway.

(C) He's washing a frying pan.

(D) He's pulling a vending cart.

해석

(A) 바닥에 병 몇 개가 있다.

(B) 보도에 이동식 음식 가판대가 있다.

(C) 그는 프라이팬을 닦고 있다.

(D) 그는 가판 카트를 끌고 있다.

어휘

mobile 이동하는, 이동식의 food stand 음식 가판대

vending cart 가판 카트

기출 표현 PLUS⁺

A man is cooking some food. 남자가 음식을 요리하고 있다.

There are some bottles on a vending cart.

가판 카트 위에 병 몇 개가 있다.

실전 문제   본문 p.43

1. (D)	2. (A)	3. (C)	4. (C)	5. (D)
6. (C)				

1. 미남 🎧

(A) The men are shaking hands.

(B) A sign has been hung from a pole.

(C) Some workers are putting on hard hats.

(D) A street lamp is being installed.

해석

(A) 남자들이 악수를 하고 있다.

(B) 표지판이 기둥에 매달려 있다.

(C) 몇몇 작업자들이 안전모를 착용하는 중이다.

(D) 가로등이 설치되고 있다.

어휘

sign 표지판, 간판 hang from ~에서 드리워지다

pole 기둥, 장대 hard hat 안전모 install 설치하다

기출 표현 PLUS⁺

The workers are wearing safety helmets.

작업자들이 안전모를 쓰고 있다.

The men are installing a street lamp.

남자들이 가로등을 설치하고 있다.

2. 영녀 🎧

(A) There's a deck overlooking a lake.

(B) Some boats are tied to a pier.

(C) Waves are crashing against the rocks.

(D) A ship is stopped at a dock.

해석

(A) 호수가 내려다보이는 갑판이 있다.

(B) 몇몇 배들이 부두에 묶여 있다.

(C) 파도가 바위에 부서지고 있다.

(D) 배가 부두에 세워져 있다.

어휘

deck 갑판 overlook (건물 등이) 바라보다, 내려다보다

tie A to B A를 B에 묶다 pier 부두

crash against ~에 충돌하다, ~와 부딪치다 dock 부두

기출 표현 PLUS⁺

There is a deck above the water. 물 위에 갑판이 있다.

3. 미녀 🎧

(A) They're measuring some packages.

(B) They're putting labels on some containers.

(C) **Some boxes have been stored inside a vehicle.**

(D) A van has been parked in a garage.

해석

(A) 그들은 몇몇 포장 상자의 치수를 재고 있다.

(B) 그들은 몇몇 용기에 라벨을 붙이고 있다.

(C) 몇몇 상자들이 차량 안에 보관되어 있다.

(D) 승합차가 차고에 주차되어 있다.

어휘

measure (치수, 양 등을) 측정하다, 재다 package 상자, 포장물 container 용기, 그릇 store 저장하다, 보관하다 van 승합차 garage 차고, 주차장

기출 표현 PLUS+

The back of a vehicle is open. 차량 뒤쪽이 열려 있다.

The men are unloading some boxes from a vehicle.

남자들이 차량에서 몇몇 상자들을 내리고 있다.

4. 호남 🎧

(A) Pedestrians are running to catch a bus.

(B) Pedestrians are boarding a bus.

(C) A man is holding onto a baby stroller.

(D) A bus is departing from a bus stop.

해석

(A) 보행자들이 버스를 잡아타려고 달리고 있다.

(B) 보행자들이 버스에 올라타는 중이다.

(C) 남자가 유모차를 붙들고 있다.

(D) 버스가 버스 정류장을 출발하고 있다.

어휘

pedestrian 보행자 board 탑승하다 hold onto ~을 꼭 잡다 baby stroller 유모차 depart from ~에서 출발하다

기출 표현 PLUS+

A child is sitting in a stroller. 아이가 유모차에 앉아 있다.

A bus is being driven down a road.

도로를 따라 버스가 운행되고 있다.

5. 미녀 🎧

(A) A man is watering the grass.

(B) A yard is covered in fallen leaves.

(C) A man is pushing a wheelbarrow.

(D) A garden has been planted outside of a building.

해석

(A) 남자가 잔디에 물을 주고 있다.

(B) 마당이 낙엽으로 덮여 있다.

(C) 남자가 손수레를 밀고 있다.

(D) 건물 밖 정원에 식물이 심어져 있다.

어휘

water 물을 주다 be covered in ~로 덮여 있다 fallen leaves 낙엽 wheelbarrow 손수레 plant (나무 등을) 심다

기출 표현 PLUS+

A man is using a shovel. 남자가 삽을 사용하고 있다.

6. 영녀 🎧

(A) Branches have fallen off some trees.

(B) Some people are removing snow from a road.

(C) There are some vehicles lining the side of a street.

(D) Some workers are pulling a car with some equipment.

해석

(A) 나뭇가지들이 나무에서 떨어져 있다.

(B) 몇몇 사람들이 도로에서 눈을 치우고 있다.

(C) 길가에 몇몇 차들이 늘어서 있다.

(D) 몇몇 작업자들이 장비로 차를 끌어당기고 있다.

어휘

fall off ~에서 떨어지다 remove 치우다, 제거하다 line ~을 따라 늘어서다 equipment ((집합적)) 장비

기출 표현 PLUS+

Some trees are covered with snow.

나무들이 눈으로 덮여 있다.

UNIT 06 여가·편의 시설 사진

1. (D)　　**2.** (A)

---

1. 미녀 🎧

(A) A cashier is folding some clothes.
(B) A cashier is hanging some items on a rack.
(C) A customer is emptying a bag.
(D) A customer is paying for a purchase.

해석
(A) 계산원이 옷을 개고 있다.
(B) 계산원이 옷걸이에 물품을 걸고 있다.
(C) 고객이 가방을 비우고 있다.
(D) 고객이 구매 대금을 치르고 있다.

어휘
cashier (상점 등의) 계산원　fold (옷 등을) 개다　empty 비우다
pay for ~의 값을 치르다　purchase 구입, 구매; 구입하다

기출 표현 PLUS⁺
Some clothes have been put on hangers.
옷들이 옷걸이에 걸려 있다.

---

2. 미녀 🎧

(A) Some people are strolling on a path.
(B) Some people are having a meal outdoors.
(C) Some people are cutting the grass.
(D) Some people are paving a road.

해석
(A) 몇몇 사람들이 길을 거닐고 있다.
(B) 몇몇 사람들이 야외에서 식사하고 있다.
(C) 몇몇 사람들이 잔디를 깎고 있다.
(D) 몇몇 사람들이 길을 포장하고 있다.

어휘
stroll 거닐다, 산책하다　outdoors 야외에서
pave (길을) 포장하다

기출 표현 PLUS⁺
Some people are walking in a park.
사람들이 공원에서 걷고 있다.

---

1. (C)　　**2.** (A)　　**3.** (C)

---

1. 영녀 🎧

(A) The diners are enjoying some food.
(B) One of the women is filling a glass.
(C) A server is taking an order.
(D) A server is collecting the menus.

해석
(A) 식사 손님들이 음식을 맛있게 먹고 있다.
(B) 여자들 중 한 명이 잔을 채우고 있다.
(C) 종업원이 주문을 받고 있다.
(D) 종업원이 메뉴판을 모으고 있다.

어휘
diner (식당에서) 식사하는 사람[손님]　server (식당의) 서버, 종업원
take an order 주문을 받다

기출 표현 PLUS⁺
A server is wearing an apron. 종업원이 앞치마를 입고 있다.
Some customers are ordering food in a restaurant.
손님들이 식당에서 음식을 주문하고 있다.

---

2. 영녀 🎧

(A) The people are looking at a menu.
(B) The woman is sipping from a glass.
(C) The man is pointing to some flowers.
(D) The people are finishing a meal.

해석
(A) 사람들이 메뉴를 보고 있다.
(B) 여자가 유리잔으로 음료를 조금씩 마시고 있다.
(C) 남자가 꽃을 가리키고 있다.
(D) 사람들이 식사를 마치는 중이다.

sip (음료를) 홀짝이다, 조금씩 마시다 point to ~을 가리키다

기출 표현 PLUS⁺

There are flowers on the railing. 난간에 꽃들이 있다.

The man is pointing at the menu.

남자가 메뉴를 가리키고 있다.

3. 영녀 🎧

(A) The people are leaving the library.

(B) One of the men is opening a bag.

(C) The people are waiting in line.

(D) The people are browsing for library books.

해석

(A) 사람들이 도서관을 떠나고 있다.

(B) 남자들 중 한 명이 가방을 열고 있다.

(C) 사람들이 줄을 서서 기다리는 중이다.

(D) 사람들이 도서관 책을 둘러보고 있다.

어휘

wait in line 줄을 서서 기다리다

기출 표현 PLUS⁺

The people are visiting a library.

사람들이 도서관에 방문하고 있다.

One of the women is handing a book to the librarian.

여자들 중 한 명이 도서관 사서에게 책을 건네고 있다.

실전 문제
본문 p.47

1. (C) **2.** (B) **3.** (D) **4.** (C) **5.** (B)

6. (A)

1. 미남 🎧

(A) A worker is pointing to a jacket.

(B) A worker is covering an item with a plastic bag.

(C) A customer is picking up some clothing at a dry cleaner's.

(D) A customer is checking a sales receipt.

해석

(A) 직원이 재킷을 가리키고 있다.

(B) 직원이 물품을 비닐봉지로 싸고 있다.

(C) 고객이 세탁소에서 옷을 찾아가고 있다.

(D) 고객이 판매 영수증을 확인하고 있다.

어휘

plastic bag 비닐봉지 clothing ((집합적)) 의류

dry cleaner's 세탁소 receipt 영수증

기출 표현 PLUS⁺

Some clothes are covered with a plastic bag.

옷들이 비닐봉지로 싸여 있다.

A worker is handing an item to the customer.

직원이 고객에게 물품을 건네고 있다.

2. 미녀 🎧

(A) An employee is stocking the shelves.

(B) Merchandise is being displayed in a case.

(C) A glass panel is being repaired.

(D) One of the women is paying for some merchandise.

해석

(A) 직원이 선반에 물건을 채우고 있다.

(B) 상품이 진열장에 진열되어 있다.

(C) 유리 패널이 수리되고 있다.

(D) 여자들 중 한 명이 물건값을 지불하고 있다.

어휘

stock (상품 등을) 들여놓다, 비축하다

merchandise ((집합적)) 상품 display 진열하다

repair 수리하다; 수리

기출 표현 PLUS⁺

Some merchandise is in a display case.

상품이 진열장에 있다.

One of the women is receiving her merchandise.

여자들 중 한 명이 상품을 받고 있다.

3. 영녀 🎧

(A) A woman is organizing some eating utensils.

(B) A woman is preparing a meal in a kitchen.

(C) A woman is washing off a plate.
(D) A woman is getting some food from a cafeteria.

해석

(A) 여자가 식기를 정리하고 있다.
(B) 여자가 부엌에서 음식을 준비하고 있다.
(C) 여자가 접시를 닦고 있다.
(D) 여자가 카페테리아에서 음식을 담고 있다.

어휘

utensil 기구 prepare (음식을) 준비하다, 마련하다
wash off 씻어내다
cafeteria 카페테리아(셀프서비스 식당), 구내식당

기출 표현 PLUS⁺

She's selecting some food in a cafeteria.
그녀는 카페테리아에서 음식을 고르고 있다.
She's holding a bowl. 그녀는 그릇을 들고 있다.

4. 호남 🎧

(A) She's cleaning the door of a display unit.
(B) She's reaching for a shopping basket.
(C) She's taking an item out of a refrigerator.
(D) She's paying for some groceries in a shop.

해석

(A) 그녀는 진열장의 문을 닦고 있다.
(B) 그녀는 장바구니를 향해 손을 뻗고 있다.
(C) 그녀는 냉장고에서 물품을 꺼내고 있다.
(D) 그녀는 상점에서 몇몇 식료품의 값을 치르고 있다.

어휘

display unit 진열장 reach for ~을 향해 손을 뻗다
refrigerator 냉장고 groceries ((보통 복수형)) 식료 잡화류

기출 표현 PLUS⁺

A woman is holding a shopping basket.
여자가 장바구니를 들고 있다.
A woman is reaching into a refrigerator.
여자가 냉장고 안으로 손을 뻗고 있다.

5. 미녀 🎧

(A) Chairs are stacked on top of one another.
(B) Sets of utensils have been arranged on napkins.
(C) Some glasses are drying on a rack.
(D) Some tablecloths are being folded.

해석

(A) 의자들이 차곡차곡 쌓여 있다.
(B) 식기들이 냅킨 위에 정돈되어 있다.
(C) 몇몇 유리잔들이 선반에서 건조되고 있다.
(D) 몇몇 테이블보를 접고 있다.

어휘

stack 쌓다, 포개다 utensil (부엌에서 쓰는) 기구, 도구, 용기
arrange 정리하다, 배열하다 rack 받침대, 선반

기출 표현 PLUS⁺

The tables have been set for a meal.
테이블들이 식사를 위해 준비되어 있다.
There are wine glasses on the table.
테이블에 와인 잔들이 있다.

6. 영녀 🎧

(A) One of the women is wearing glasses.
(B) One of the women is drinking from a straw.
(C) The man is holding up a screen.
(D) The man is wiping off a table.

해석

(A) 여자들 중 한 명이 안경을 쓰고 있다.
(B) 여자들 중 한 명이 빨대로 음료를 마시고 있다.
(C) 남자가 화면을 떠받치고 있다.
(D) 남자가 탁자를 닦고 있다.

어휘

straw 빨대 hold up ~을 떠받치다 wipe off ~을 닦아 내다

기출 표현 PLUS⁺

A laptop is on a table. 노트북 컴퓨터가 테이블 위에 있다.

UNIT 07 집·기타 장소 사진

CHECK UP   본문 p.49

1. (D)   **2.** (B)

1. 미녀 🎧

(A) There's a stool by the countertop.
(B) There's a potted plant on the windowsill.
(C) A refrigerator door is open.
(D) Some floor tiles are in a pattern.

해석

(A) 조리대 옆에 스툴이 있다.
(B) 창턱에 화분에 담긴 식물이 있다.
(C) 냉장고 문이 열려 있다.
(D) 바닥 타일 모양이 무늬를 이루고 있다.

어휘

stool (등받이와 팔걸이가 없는) 의자, 스툴
countertop (부엌의) 조리대 potted plant 화분에 담긴 식물
windowsill 창턱 pattern 무늬, 패턴

기출 표현 PLUS⁺

A flower vase has been placed on the table.
꽃병이 테이블 위에 놓여 있다.
There is a lighting fixture above the table.
테이블 위로 조명 기구가 있다.

2. 미녀 🎧

(A) He's wiping off the sink.
(B) He's washing his hands.
(C) He's refilling the soap.
(D) He's polishing the mirror.

해석

(A) 그는 세면대를 닦고 있다.
(B) 그는 손을 씻고 있다.
(C) 그는 비누를 다시 채우고 있다.
(D) 그는 거울을 닦고 있다.

어휘

wipe off 닦아 내다 refill 다시 채우다 polish 닦다, 윤을 내다

기출 표현 PLUS⁺

Water is flowing from a faucet.
수도꼭지에서 물이 흐르고 있다.

---

1. 영녀 🎧

(A) He's shopping for groceries.
(B) He's using a knife to slice some food.
(C) He's putting some utensils in the sink.
(D) He's buttoning a shirt.

해석

(A) 그는 장을 보고 있다.
(B) 그는 음식을 자르기 위해 칼을 사용하고 있다.
(C) 그는 (요리) 기구들을 싱크대에 넣고 있다.
(D) 그는 셔츠의 단추를 잠그고 있다.

어휘

shop for groceries 장을 보다 slice 얇게 썰다
utensil (부엌에서 쓰는) 기구, 도구, 용기 button 단추를 잠그다

기출 표현 PLUS⁺

Some bread is being cut with a knife.
빵이 칼로 잘리고 있다.
The refrigerator doors are closed. 냉장고 문이 닫혀 있다.

2. 영녀 🎧

(A) Some pictures are hanging on the walls.
(B) Some furniture is being cleaned.
(C) A mirror has been placed on a table.
(D) A sofa has been positioned under a window.

해석

(A) 몇몇 그림들이 벽에 걸려 있다.
(B) 몇몇 가구를 청소하는 중이다.
(C) 거울이 탁자 위에 놓여 있다.
(D) 소파가 창문 아래에 배치되어 있다.

어휘

hang 걸다, 걸리다 place 놓다, 두다 position 두다, 배치하다

기출 표현 PLUS⁺

A ceiling fan is hanging over a table.
천장용 선풍기가 테이블 위로 달려 있다.

Some curtains are open. 커튼이 열려 있다.

3. 영녀 🎧

(A) She's pouring liquid from a pitcher.
(B) She's turning on the stove.
(C) She's drinking water from a fountain.
(D) She's peeling some fruit.

해석
(A) 여자는 주전자에서 액체를 따르고 있다.
(B) 그녀는 가스레인지를 켜고 있다.
(C) 그녀는 식수대에서 물을 마시고 있다.
(D) 그녀는 과일의 껍질을 벗기고 있다.

어휘
pour (음료를) 따르다   liquid 액체
pitcher 물주전자, (음료를 따르는) 피처   fountain 분수, 식수대
peel 껍질을 벗기다

기출 표현 PLUS⁺
There is a pot on a stove. 가스레인지 위에 냄비가 있다.
A cup is being filled with water.
컵이 물로 가득 채워지고 있다.

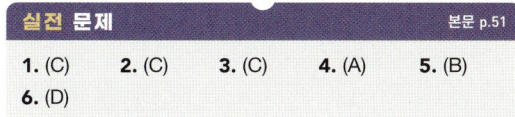

실전 문제   본문 p.51
1. (C)   **2.** (C)   **3.** (C)   **4.** (A)   **5.** (B)
6. (D)

1. 미남 🎧

(A) She's turning on a faucet.
(B) She's putting on some gloves.
(C) She's leaning over a sink.
(D) She's cleaning a mirror.

해석
(A) 그녀는 수도꼭지를 틀고 있다.
(B) 그녀는 장갑을 착용하는 중이다.
(C) 그녀는 싱크대 위로 몸을 숙이고 있다.
(D) 그녀는 거울을 닦고 있다.

어휘
faucet 수도꼭지   lean over ~ 너머로 몸을 구부리다

기출 표현 PLUS⁺
A woman is holding a spray bottle.
여자가 분무기를 들고 있다.
A sink is being cleaned. 싱크대가 청소되고 있다.

2. 미녀 🎧

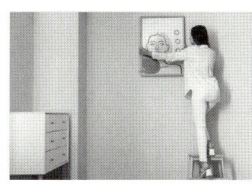

(A) The woman is clearing out a drawer.
(B) The woman is painting a wall.
(C) The woman is standing on a stepladder.
(D) The woman is buying some artwork.

해석
(A) 여자가 서랍을 청소하고 있다.
(B) 여자가 벽에 페인트칠을 하고 있다.
(C) 여자가 발판 사다리 위에 서 있다.
(D) 여자가 몇몇 미술품을 사고 있다.

어휘
clear out 청소하다   stepladder 발판 사다리   artwork 미술품

기출 표현 PLUS⁺
She's adjusting a painting.
그녀는 그림의 위치를 조절하고 있다.
A drawer is in the corner of a room.
서랍장이 방의 구석에 있다.

3. 영녀 🎧

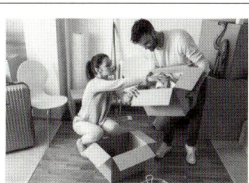

(A) Some containers are arranged in a circle.
(B) A suitcase is being zipped up.
(C) One of the people is lifting a box.
(D) One of the people is scrubbing the floor.

해석
(A) 몇몇 용기들이 원형으로 배열되어 있다.
(B) 여행 가방의 지퍼를 잠그고 있다.
(C) 사람들 중 한 명이 상자를 들어 올리고 있다.
(D) 사람들 중 한 명이 바닥을 문질러 닦고 있다.

어휘
container 용기, 그릇, 통   arrange 정리하다, 배열하다

in a circle 둥글게, 원형으로 zip up 지퍼로 잠그다
lift 들어 올리다 scrub 문질러 청소하다

기출 표현 PLUS⁺

기출 표현 PLUS+

The woman is squatting on the floor.
여자가 바닥에 쪼그리고 앉아 있다.

4. 호남 🎧

(A) Some plants have been arranged in a row.
(B) A tray of food has been left on a countertop.
(C) Plates have been stacked by a windowsill.
(D) Some dishes have been put in a sink.

해석

(A) 몇몇 식물이 나란히 배열되어 있다.
(B) 음식이 담긴 쟁반이 조리대 위에 놓여 있다.
(C) 접시들이 창턱 옆에 쌓여 있다.
(D) 그릇들이 싱크대에 놓여 있다.

어휘

in a row 잇달아, 연이어 countertop (부엌의) 조리대
windowsill 창턱

기출 표현 PLUS⁺

Some pots are suspended from the ceiling.
몇몇 냄비들이 천장에 매달려 있다.

5. 미녀 🎧

(A) A table's been covered with a cloth.
(B) A patterned rug's been placed over a floor.
(C) Some furniture is blocking a door.
(D) Some windows are being installed.

해석

(A) 탁자가 천으로 덮여 있다.
(B) 무늬가 있는 깔개가 바닥에 덮여 있다.
(C) 가구가 문을 막고 있다.
(D) 창문들이 설치되는 중이다.

어휘

be covered with ~으로 덮여 있다 patterned 무늬가 있는
place 두다, 놓다 block 막다, 차단하다 install 설치하다

기출 표현 PLUS⁺

Some doors are closed. 문들이 닫혀 있다.

6. 영녀 🎧

(A) Some lamps are mounted on the wall.
(B) Some nightstands are positioned in a row.
(C) Some bedding has been left in a basket.
(D) Some pillows have been placed on a bed.

해석

(A) 몇몇 전등들이 벽에 고정되어 있다.
(B) 몇몇 침실용 탁자들이 일렬로 배치되어 있다.
(C) 일부 침구가 바구니 안에 들어 있다.
(D) 몇몇 베개들이 침대 위에 놓여 있다.

어휘

mount 설치하다, 고정시키다 nightstand 침실용 탁자
position ~에 두다, 배치하다 in a row 연이어, 일렬로
bedding 침구 place 놓다, 두다

기출 표현 PLUS⁺

There are some lamps beside a bed.
침대 옆에 램프 몇 개가 있다.

PART TEST				본문 p.53
1. (B)	**2.** (B)	**3.** (B)	**4.** (C)	**5.** (A)
6. (B)				

1. 미남 🎧

(A) The woman is writing on a board.
(B) The woman is posting some information.
(C) The woman is printing a schedule.
(D) The woman is signing a document.

해석

(A) 여자가 게시판에 무언가를 쓰고 있다.
(B) 여자가 정보를 게시하고 있다.
(C) 여자가 일정표를 인쇄하고 있다.

(D) 여자가 문서에 서명하고 있다.

어휘

post 게시하다, 공고하다 sign 서명하다; 징후, 신호

기출 표현 PLUS⁺

She's looking at a bulletin board. 그녀는 게시판을 보고 있다.

2. 미녀

(A) He's untying a cloth apron.
(B) He's using a garden tool.
(C) He's building a greenhouse.
(D) He's watering some flowers.

해석

(A) 그는 천 앞치마를 풀고 있다.
(B) 그는 정원용 도구를 사용하고 있다.
(C) 그는 비닐하우스를 짓고 있다.
(D) 그는 꽃에 물을 주고 있다.

어휘

garden tool 정원용 도구 greenhouse 비닐하우스, 온실

기출 표현 PLUS⁺

A man is wearing a cloth apron.
남자가 천 앞치마를 입고 있다.
He's tending to some plants. 그는 식물을 손질하고 있다.

3. 영녀

(A) One of the women is walking up the steps.
(B) One of the women is tying her shoe.
(C) One of the women is putting on a hat.
(D) One of the women is holding a handbag.

해석

(A) 여자들 중 한 명이 계단을 오르고 있다.
(B) 여자들 중 한 명이 신발 끈을 묶고 있다.
(C) 여자들 중 한 명이 모자를 쓰는 중이다
(D) 여자들 중 한 명이 손가방을 들고 있다.

어휘

walk up (계단 등을) 오르다 tie 묶다, 매다

기출 표현 PLUS⁺

Some bags have been left on the ground.
가방 몇 개가 바닥에 놓여 있다.
There is a hat on top of a bag. 가방 위에 모자가 있다.

4. 호남

(A) There's a backpack sitting on the floor.
(B) A woman is washing some produce.
**(C) Some vegetables have been arranged on
shelves.**
(D) A worker is putting signs by some
merchandise.

해석

(A) 바닥에 배낭이 놓여 있다.
(B) 여자가 몇몇 농산물을 씻고 있다.
(C) 몇몇 채소가 선반에 정리되어 있다.
(D) 직원이 몇몇 상품 옆에 표지판을 놓고 있다.

어휘

produce ((집합적)) 농산물 arrange 정리하다, 배열하다
sign 표지판, 안내판 merchandise 상품

기출 표현 PLUS⁺

Some produce has been displayed in baskets.
농산물이 바구니에 진열되어 있다.

5. 미녀

(A) There are some performers on a stage.
(B) Some musicians are waving at the crowd.
(C) The audience members are leaving the venue.
(D) A technician is setting up some chairs.

해석

(A) 무대 위에 몇몇 연주자들이 있다.
(B) 몇몇 음악인들이 사람들에게 손을 흔들고 있다.
(C) 청중들이 행사장을 떠나고 있다.
(D) 기술자가 몇몇 의자들을 놓고 있다.

어휘

performer 연주자, 연기자 wave at ~을 향해 손을 흔들다
crowd 군중, 사람들 audience member 청중

venue (행사의) 장소 technician 기술자

set up ~을 놓다, 세우다, 설치하다

The audience is sitting in front of a stage.

청중이 무대 앞에 앉아 있다.

Some people are holding musical instruments.

몇몇 사람들이 악기를 들고 있다.

6. 영녀 🎧

(A) Some dishes have been spread around the table.

(B) A light fixture is hanging above a dining area.

(C) Chairs have been set up in a garden.

(D) Kitchen appliances are arranged for sale.

해석

(A) 몇몇 접시들이 탁자 주위에 흩어져 있다.

(B) 조명 기구가 식사 공간 위에 매달려 있다.

(C) 의자들이 정원에 놓여 있다.

(D) 주방용품이 판매를 위해 정리되어 있다.

어휘

spread 펼치다 light fixture 조명 기구

kitchen appliances 주방용품 arrange 정리하다, 배열하다

Some plants are on a windowsill. 식물이 창틀에 있다.

PART 2

CHAPTER 01 의문사 의문문

UNIT 01 Who 의문문

CHECK UP
본문 p.62

1. (B) **2.** (A) **3.** (B) **4.** (C)

---

1. 미남 미녀 🎧

> Who's picking up the clients at the airport?
> (A) In Terminal 1.
> **(B) Benjamin is.**
> (C) The clients are pleased.

해석

누가 공항에 고객들을 차로 마중 나갈 건가요?
(A) 1번 터미널에서요.
(B) 벤저민이요.
(C) 고객들이 기뻐해요.

어휘

pick up 자동차로 마중 나가다, 차에 태우다 pleased 기뻐하는

기출 표현 PLUS⁺

We're not sure yet. 아직은 확실하지 않아요.
Cara will pick them up. 카라가 모셔올 거예요.

---

2. 미남 미녀 🎧

> Who can open the warehouse?
> **(A) I have a key.**
> (B) I reported it to my manager.
> (C) It's out of stock.

해석

누가 창고를 열 수 있나요?
(A) 제가 열쇠를 가지고 있어요.
(B) 제 매니저에게 그것을 알렸어요.
(C) 그것은 품절입니다.

어휘

warehouse 창고 report 알리다, 보고하다
out of stock 재고가 없는

기출 표현 PLUS⁺

Michael has a key. 마이클이 열쇠를 가지고 있어요.
We have to wait for the manager.
매니저가 올 때까지 기다려야 해요.

---

3. 미남 미녀 🎧

> Who suggested the meeting with the president?
> (A) Close the door, please.
> **(B) It was my idea.**
> (C) A thirty-minute walk.

해석

누가 사장님과의 회의를 제안했나요?
(A) 문을 닫아 주시기 바랍니다.
(B) 제 생각이었어요.
(C) 걸어서 30분 거리입니다.

어휘

suggest 제안하다 president 사장, 회장

기출 표현 PLUS⁺

It was Susan's idea. 수잔의 생각이었어요.
Our manger suggested it. 저희 매니저가 제안했어요.

---

4. 미남 미녀 🎧

> Who's transferring to the Marketing team?
> (A) Yes, I am. Thank you.
> (B) Great, it's like a promotion.
> **(C) I heard it will be Ms. Stanley.**

해석

누가 마케팅팀으로 옮기나요?
(A) 네, 접니다. 감사합니다.
(B) 잘됐어요, 그건 승진인 셈이에요.
(C) 스탠리 씨라고 들었어요.

어휘

transfer to ~로 옮기다, 전근 가다 promotion 승진, 홍보

기출 표현 PLUS⁺

We haven't decided yet. 아직 결정하지 않았어요.
Mr. Pocket will be transferring. 포켓 씨가 옮길 거예요.

연습 문제
본문 p.64

1. (C) **2.** (A) **3.** (A) **4.** (B) **5.** (B)

---

1. 미남 영녀 🎧

> Who is going to be working on the city project?
> (A) I'm going into the city.
> (B) It starts this weekend.
> **(C) The sales department.**

해석

누가 시 프로젝트 작업을 할 예정인가요?

(A) 저는 시내에 갑니다.

(B) 이번 주말에 시작합니다.

(C) 영업부요.

어휘

work on ~에 대한 작업을 하다, 착수하다

sales department 영업 부서

기출 표현 PLUS⁺

Ms. Lester and her team. 레스터 씨와 그녀의 팀이요.

The whole department. 부서 전체가요.

2. 미남 영녀 🎧

Who's leading the new staff orientation?

(A) Mr. Barrera always does it.

(B) Certainly, I'd love to.

(C) How many do you need?

해석

누가 신입 직원 오리엔테이션을 진행하나요?

(A) 항상 바레라 씨가 합니다.

(B) 물론이지요, 그렇게 하고 싶어요.

(C) 몇 명이나 필요하세요?

어휘

lead 이끌다, 안내하다 the staff ((집합적)) 직원

orientation 오리엔테이션, 예비 교육

기출 표현 PLUS⁺

The CEO will do it. 대표님이 할 거예요.

Jefferson is. 제퍼슨이요.

3. 미남 영녀 🎧

Who is the best candidate for the position?

(A) There were so many impressive résumés.

(B) I'm the manager.

(C) Probably sometime next week.

해석

누가 그 자리에 최적인 후보자인가요?

(A) 인상적인 이력서들이 아주 많았어요.

(B) 제가 매니저입니다.

(C) 아마도 다음 주 언제쯤이요.

어휘

candidate 후보자, 지원자 position 일자리, 직위

impressive 인상적인, 인상 깊은 résumé 이력서

기출 표현 PLUS⁺

No one stood out. 딱히 돋보이는 사람은 없었어요.

Ms. Hamrick is. 햄릭 씨요.

4. 미남 영녀 🎧

Who needs to review this order form?

(A) Some office supplies.

(B) Nick can tell you.

(C) I ordered more.

해석

누가 이 주문서를 검토해야 합니까?

(A) 사무용품이요.

(B) 닉이 당신에게 알려 줄 거예요.

(C) 제가 더 주문했어요.

어휘

review 검토하다 order form 주문서

office supplies 사무용품

기출 표현 PLUS⁺

I can do it. 제가 할 수 있어요.

Mr. Hill can help you. 힐 씨가 도울 수 있을 거예요.

5. 미남 영녀 🎧

Who turned off the alarm?

(A) Press that red button.

(B) Jeff, the security guard.

(C) Yes, turn at the corner.

해석

누가 경보 장치를 껐나요?

(A) 빨간색 버튼을 누르세요.

(B) 보안 요원인 제프요.

(C) 네, 모퉁이에서 도세요.

어휘

alarm 경보 장치; 놀라게 하다 security guard 경비원, 보안 요원

기출 표현 PLUS⁺

I think Ruth did. 루스인 것 같아요.

Justin, the maintenance worker. 시설관리인 저스틴이요.

실전 문제 본문 p.65

1. (B)	**2.** (B)	**3.** (C)	**4.** (C)	**5.** (C)
6. (A)	**7.** (C)	**8.** (A)	**9.** (C)	**10.** (A)
11. (B)	**12.** (A)	**13.** (B)	**14.** (A)	**15.** (A)

1. 미남 영녀 🎧

Who's going out to meet with Mr. Kimmel?

(A) Before three o'clock.

(B) I think it's Jay today.

(C) On the top shelf.

해석

누가 키멜 씨와 만나러 나가나요?
(A) 3시 전에요.
(B) 오늘은 제이인 것 같아요.
(C) 맨 위 선반에요.

어휘

meet with ~와 만나다 shelf 선반, 책꽂이

기출 표현 PLUS⁺

Sally's going today. 오늘은 샐리가 갈 거예요.
We're undecided. 아직 결정 안 됐어요.

2. 미남 영녀 🎧

Who's agreed to sponsor the arts and crafts fair?
(A) No, I'm not very artistic.
(B) Didn't you hear the mayor's announcement?
(C) Here are some detailed driving directions.

해석

누가 예술 공예 박람회를 후원하기로 했나요?
(A) 아니요, 저는 예술적인 감각이 별로 없어요.
(B) 시장의 발표를 듣지 않았어요?
(C) 여기 자세한 운전 경로가 좀 있어요.

어휘

agree to do ~하기로 하다 sponsor 후원하다 craft 공예
artistic 예술적인 감각이 있는 mayor 시장
announcement 발표, 공지 detailed 상세한
directions ((보통 복수형)) 길 안내

기출 표현 PLUS⁺

Didn't you see the press release? 기사 못 보셨어요?
We're still waiting to hear back from that company.
그 회사의 답변을 기다리고 있는 중이에요.

3. 미녀 미남 🎧

Who's in charge of the training program?
(A) For job skills.
(B) Cash would be better.
(C) Ms. Kelson is.

해석

누가 교육 프로그램을 담당하나요?
(A) 직무 능력을 위해서요.
(B) 현금이 더 나을 거예요.
(C) 켈슨 씨요.

어휘

be in charge of ~을 담당하다, 책임지다 skill 기술, 기량

기출 표현 PLUS⁺

The HR department. 인사부서에서요.
Mr. Sullivan will lead it. 설리번이 진행할 거예요.

4. 미녀 미남 🎧

Who is going to introduce the speaker?
(A) About how to start a new business.
(B) In the auditorium.
(C) I believe Steven will.

해석

누가 연사를 소개할 예정인가요?
(A) 새로운 사업을 시작하는 방법에 관해서요.
(B) 강당에서요.
(C) 스티븐이 할 거라고 생각해요.

어휘

introduce 소개하다 auditorium 강당

기출 표현 PLUS⁺

George will handle that. 조지가 할 거예요.
I think Mellissa will. 멜리사가 할걸요.

5. 영녀 호남 🎧

Who's giving the welcome speech at the employee banquet?
(A) At 7 P.M. this Friday.
(B) Yes, at the Wilmont Conference Center.
(C) The office manager usually does it.

해석

누가 직원 연회에서 환영사를 하나요?
(A) 이번 주 금요일 저녁 7시에요.
(B) 네, 윌몬트 콘퍼런스 센터에서요.
(C) 보통 사무실 매니저가 합니다.

어휘

welcome speech 환영사 banquet 연회 usually 보통, 대개

기출 표현 PLUS⁺

Mr. Richards is giving it. 리처즈 씨가 할 거예요.
The head of PR usually does. 대개는 홍보팀장이 합니다.

6. 영녀 호남 🎧

Who will assign the tasks for the interns?
(A) We haven't made a decision yet.
(B) Yes, the sign looks better.
(C) They're very hard workers.

해석

누가 인턴 사원들에게 업무를 배정할 건가요?
(A) 우리는 아직 결정을 내리지 못했어요.
(B) 네, 그 표지판이 더 나아 보여요.
(C) 그들은 매우 근면한 직원들입니다.

어휘

assign 배정하다, 맡기다 task 일, 과업 sign 안내판, 표지판

기출 표현 PLUS⁺

The project manager will do it. 프로젝트 매니저가요.

Mr. White will. 화이트 씨가요.

7. 미남 미녀 🎧

> Who's responsible for the Franklin Project?
> (A) By November 15th.
> (B) Yes, that's correct.
> **(C) That's Daniel's job.**

해석

누가 프랭클린 프로젝트의 담당자입니까?
(A) 11월 15일까지요.
(B) 네, 맞습니다.
(C) 그건 다니엘의 업무예요.

어휘

be responsible for ~을 책임지다

기출 표현 PLUS⁺

That project was cancelled. 그 프로젝트는 취소됐어요.
Ms. Reyes will be leading it. 레예스 씨가 이끌게 될 겁니다.

8. 미남 미녀 🎧

> Who's going to pick up Mr. Jang at the airport?
> **(A) He cancelled the flight.**
> (B) Take the company van.
> (C) Did they come to our office?

해석

누가 공항에 차로 장 씨를 마중 나갈 건가요?
(A) 그는 항공편을 취소했습니다.
(B) 회사 승합차를 타세요.
(C) 그들이 우리 사무실에 왔나요?

어휘

cancel 취소하다 flight 항공편, 비행기 van 승합차, 밴

기출 표현 PLUS⁺

Larry can do it. 래리가 할 수 있을 거예요.
I think Mr. Kingston will take care of that.
킹스턴 씨가 할 거예요.

9. 미남 미녀 🎧

> Who notified the interns of the time and venue changes?
> (A) At the last meeting.
> (B) Just a few minor changes.
> **(C) Someone from Personnel.**

해석

누가 인턴 사원들에게 시간과 장소의 변경 사항을 알렸나요?
(A) 지난 회의에서요.
(B) 그저 몇 가지 사소한 변경입니다.
(C) 인사부의 누군가요.

어휘

notify A of B A에게 B를 알리다, 통지하다 venue (행사의) 장소
minor 사소한, 경미한 personnel 인사부

기출 표현 PLUS⁺

David, from Accounting. 회계팀의 데이비드요.
I told them yesterday morning. 제가 어제 아침에 알렸어요.

10. 미녀 호남 🎧

> Who do you think we should offer the position to?
> **(A) I'm having a hard time deciding.**
> (B) Yes, I think I should.
> (C) Leave it in that position.

해석

우리가 누구에게 그 자리를 제안해야 한다고 생각하나요?
(A) 저는 결정하느라 힘들어하고 있어요.
(B) 네, 제가 그래야 할 것 같아요.
(C) 그 위치에 두세요.

어휘

position 위치, (일)자리, 직위
have a hard time -ing ~하느라 힘든 시간을 보내다

기출 표현 PLUS⁺

I'm not sure yet. 아직 확실히 모르겠어요.
To Ms. Frankel, I think. 프랭클 씨에게요.

11. 미녀 호남 🎧

> Who can I talk to about getting a new computer monitor?
> (A) Anytime this week.
> **(B) Call the IT team.**
> (C) Alright, I'll turn it on.

해석

새 컴퓨터 모니터를 사는 것에 관해 누구에게 얘기하면 되나요?
(A) 이번 주 아무 때나요.
(B) IT 팀에 전화하세요.
(C) 좋아요, 제가 켤게요.

어휘

IT (= information technology) 정보통신 기술

기출 표현 PLUS⁺

Ask the secretary. 비서에게 물어보세요.
Ms. Harris can help you. 해리스 씨가 도와줄 수 있을 거예요.

12. 호남 영녀 🎧

> Who represented our firm at the trade fair?
> **(A) Cheryl and Matthew did.**
> (B) In San Francisco.
> (C) A large booth.

해석

무역 박람회에서 누가 우리 회사를 대표했나요?

(A) 셰릴과 매튜가 했어요.
(B) 샌프란시스코에서요.
(C) 대형 부스요.

어휘

represent 대표하다 trade fair 무역 박람회

기출 표현 PLUS⁺

The Marketing Department head did. 마케팅 부서장이요.
I think Nathan did. 네이슨이었을 거예요.

13. 호남 영녀 🎧

Who can help me access the database?
(A) That will work fine, I think.
(B) I can help you in a few minutes.
(C) The assessment went well.

해석

제가 데이터베이스에 접속하는 것을 누가 도와줄 수 있나요?
(A) 그것은 잘 될 거라고 생각해요.
(B) 몇 분 후에 제가 도와드릴게요.
(C) 평가가 잘 진행됐어요.

어휘

access 접속하다, 접근하다 work fine (일이) 잘되다
assessment 평가 go well 잘 진행되다

기출 표현 PLUS⁺

Ask someone in IT. IT 부서 직원에게 물어보세요.
I can do it. 제가 할 수 있어요.

14. 호남 영녀 🎧

Who won the Employee of the Year Award last night?
(A) Veronica Carson, from the Marketing department.
(B) I completely agree.
(C) Because of his unique ideas.

해석

누가 어젯밤에 올해의 직원 상을 수상했나요?
(A) 마케팅부의 베로니카 카슨이요.
(B) 전적으로 동의해요.
(C) 그의 독특한 아이디어 때문이에요.

어휘

completely 전적으로, 완전히 unique 독특한

기출 표현 PLUS⁺

I'm not sure. 잘 모르겠어요.
James Kilt from accounting won. 회계팀의 제임스 킬트가요.

15. 미녀 영녀 🎧

Who's selecting the venue for our product launch?
(A) Steven is touring possible sites.
(B) Of course, I'm ready for lunch.
(C) Yes, to make a good impression.

해석

누가 우리의 상품 출시 장소를 선정하나요?
(A) 스티븐이 가능한 장소들을 돌아보고 있어요.
(B) 물론이죠, 저는 점심 식사를 할 준비가 되었어요.
(C) 네, 좋은 인상을 주기 위해서요.

어휘

venue (행사의) 장소 launch 출시, 개시, 착수
tour ~을 보고 다니다, 여행하다
make a good impression 좋은 인상을 주다

기출 표현 PLUS⁺

Jessie is searching for one now. 제시가 알아보고 있어요.
We're still deciding. 아직 결정중이에요.

UNIT 02 What·Which 의문문

CHECK UP   본문 p.66

1. (A)	**2.** (B)	**3.** (C)	**4.** (B)

1. 미남 미녀 🎧

What is included in the rent?
(A) Electricity and water.
(B) On Atlantic Avenue.
(C) She lent me a bicycle.

해석

집세에는 무엇이 포함됩니까?
(A) 전기와 수도요.
(B) 애틀랜틱가에요.
(C) 그녀가 제게 자전거를 빌려주었어요.

어휘

include 포함하다 rent 집세, 임차료 electricity 전기
lend 빌려주다

기출 표현 PLUS⁺

Utilities are included. 공과금이 포함돼요.
You have to pay utilities separately.
공과금은 따로 내야 해요.

2. 미남 미녀 🎧

Which desk is yours?
(A) A comfortable chair.
(B) The one by the copy machine.
(C) Yes, I like it.

해석

어떤 책상이 당신 것인가요?
(A) 편안한 의자요.
(B) 복사기 옆에 있는 것이요.
(C) 네, 전 그것이 좋아요.

어휘

comfortable 편안한 copy machine 복사기

기출 표현 PLUS⁺

The one next to Sara's. 사라 책상 옆자리요.
The one near the window. 창가 자리요.

3. 미남 미녀 🎧

What is this sweater made of?
(A) A shopping mall.
(B) Yes, she does.
(C) Organic cotton.

해석

이 스웨터는 무엇으로 만들어졌나요?
(A) 쇼핑몰이요.
(B) 네, 그녀가 합니다.
(C) 유기농 면이요.

어휘

be made of ~으로 만들어지다 organic 유기농의 cotton 면

기출 표현 PLUS⁺

I think it's made of nylon and spandex.
나일론과 스판인 것 같아요.
It's a cotton blend. 면 혼방이에요.

4. 미남 미녀 🎧

What's the weather forecast for tomorrow?
(A) Yes, there were four available.
(B) It's going to be hot.
(C) It usually takes 4 days.

해석

내일 일기 예보는 어떤가요?
(A) 네, 4개를 이용할 수 있었습니다.
(B) 더울 거예요.
(C) 보통 4일이 걸립니다.

어휘

weather forecast 일기 예보
available 이용할 수 있는, 구할 수 있는 usually 보통, 대개

기출 표현 PLUS⁺

It's going to be cold. 추울 거예요.
I'll check. 확인해 볼게요.

연습 문제   본문 p.68

1. (B)   **2.** (C)   **3.** (A)   **4.** (B)   **5.** (A)

1. 미녀 호남 🎧

What happened to the banquet hall?
(A) The event will be held there.
(B) There was an electricity problem.
(C) Yes, it happens a lot.

해석

연회장에 무슨 일이 있었나요?
(A) 행사가 그곳에서 열릴 거예요.
(B) 전기 문제가 있었어요.
(C) 네, 자주 있는 일이에요.

어휘

banquet hall 연회장 electricity 전기

기출 표현 PLUS⁺

It's being renovated. 보수 중이에요.
It's out of business. 영업을 안 해요.

2. 미녀 호남 🎧

Which factory produces these umbrellas?
(A) Probably next year.
(B) Yes, it's going to rain.
(C) The one in Louisville.

해석

어떤 공장이 이 우산들을 생산하나요?
(A) 아마도 내년이요.
(B) 네, 비가 올 거예요.
(C) 루이스빌에 있는 거요.

어휘

produce 생산하다; 생산물, 농산물

기출 표현 PLUS⁺

The one near New York. 뉴욕 근방에 있는 공장이요.
I'm not sure. 모르겠어요.

3. 미녀 호남 🎧

Which parking lot is closest to the Macy Theater?
(A) I suggest using public transportation.
(B) The new theater in town.
(C) No, it's not sold out.

해석

어떤 주차장이 메이시 극장에서 가장 가깝습니까?

(A) 대중교통을 이용할 것을 제안합니다.

(B) 시내에 새로 생긴 극장이요.

(C) 아니요, 매진되지 않았습니다.

어휘

parking lot 주차장 close to ~에 가까운

public transportation 대중교통 sold out 다 팔린, 매진된

기출 표현 PLUS⁺

There isn't much parking over there.

그쪽에는 주차할 곳이 별로 없어요.

There's a parking lot down the street.

길 아래쪽에 주차장이 있어요.

4. 미녀 호남 🎧

> What did you think of the president's speech?
>
> (A) Sometime next month.
>
> **(B) She really inspired me.**
>
> (C) At the ceremony.

해석

사장님의 연설에 대해 어떻게 생각했어요?

(A) 다음 달 언제쯤이요.

(B) 그녀는 제게 정말 큰 영감을 주었어요.

(C) 기념식에서요.

어휘

inspire 영감을 주다, 고무하다 ceremony 의식, 식

기출 표현 PLUS⁺

It was hard to understand. 이해하기 어려웠어요.

I enjoyed listening to it. 재미있게 들었어요.

5. 미녀 호남 🎧

> What type of file cabinet do you need?
>
> **(A) A metal one.**
>
> (B) In my office.
>
> (C) Confidential documents.

해석

어떤 종류의 서류 캐비닛이 필요하신가요?

(A) 금속으로 된 것이요.

(B) 제 사무실이요.

(C) 기밀문서입니다.

어휘

metal 금속 confidential 비밀의, 기밀의

기출 표현 PLUS⁺

Any type is fine. 어떤 것이든 좋아요.

A large one would be good. 큰 게 좋을 것 같아요.

---

1. (B)	**2.** (A)	**3.** (A)	**4.** (B)	**5.** (C)
6. (C)	**7.** (B)	**8.** (C)	**9.** (B)	**10.** (C)
11. (B)	**12.** (C)	**13.** (B)	**14.** (B)	**15.** (A)

1. 미남 영녀 🎧

> What should I include in the orientation session for salespeople?
>
> (A) Yes, one of each, please.
>
> **(B) Marcy's done it a few times.**
>
> (C) Congratulations on your high sales.

해석

판매원들을 위한 오리엔테이션 시간에 무엇을 포함해야 할까요?

(A) 네, 각각 하나씩 주세요.

(B) 마시가 몇 번 해 봤어요.

(C) 당신의 높은 매출을 축하합니다.

어휘

orientation 오리엔테이션, 예비 교육

session (특정 활동을 위한) 시간, 기간 salespeople 판매원

congratulations on ~에 대한 축하

sales ((항상 복수형)) 매출(량)

기출 표현 PLUS⁺

You can ask Steven. 스티븐에게 물어보세요.

Jerry would know. 제리가 알 거예요.

2. 미남 영녀 🎧

> What's the best paint to use for patio furniture?
>
> **(A) Try the Hanley brand.**
>
> (B) Yes, it's very useful.
>
> (C) I think this metal chair is comfortable.

해석

테라스 가구에 사용하기에 가장 좋은 페인트는 무엇인가요?

(A) 핸리 브랜드를 써 보세요.

(B) 네, 그것은 아주 유용해요.

(C) 이 금속 의자가 편안한 것 같아요.

어휘

patio 파티오, (옥외) 테라스 useful 유용한 metal 금속

comfortable 편안한

기출 표현 PLUS⁺

We have many paints you can choose from.

여러 가지가 있습니다.

Home Paradise makes good paint.

홈 파라다이스 제품이 괜찮아요.

3. 미녀 미남 🎧

> What products does your company make?
> **(A) Office supplies.**
> (B) The production factory.
> (C) Yes, I tried a sample.

해석

당신의 회사는 무슨 제품을 만드나요?
(A) 사무용품이요.
(B) 생산 공장입니다.
(C) 네, 제가 샘플을 써 봤어요.

어휘

product 생산물, 제품, 상품
office supplies ((항상 복수형)) 사무용품
production 생산(량), 제작

기출 표현 PLUS+

We make medical equipment. 의료 장비요.
Baby clothing. 유아복이요.

4. 미녀 미남 🎧

> What room should we use for the staff meeting?
> (A) Yes, I was hired.
> **(B) Let's book the conference room.**
> (C) Early afternoon.

해석

우리는 직원 회의를 위해 어떤 방을 사용해야 하나요?
(A) 네, 제가 고용되었어요.
(B) 회의실을 예약합시다.
(C) 이른 오후예요.

어휘

hire 고용하다 conference room 회의실

기출 표현 PLUS+

We can use room 207. 207호요.
Let's have the meeting here. 여기에서 하죠.

5. 영녀 호남 🎧

> What time is the band scheduled to perform?
> (A) At the festival in the park.
> (B) It's a jazz concert, isn't it?
> **(C) The announcement said at 5.**

해석

그 밴드가 몇 시에 공연할 예정인가요?
(A) 공원의 축제에서요.
(B) 그것은 재즈 콘서트예요, 그렇지 않나요?
(C) 안내방송에서 5시라고 했어요.

어휘

be scheduled to do ~하기로 예정되어 있다
perform 공연하다, 연주하다 announcement 발표, 공고

기출 표현 PLUS+

I'm checking right now. 지금 확인하고 있어요.
Around 6 P.M. 오후 6시쯤이요.

6. 영녀 호남 🎧

> What date are you scheduled to leave for Dubai?
> (A) The updated itinerary.
> (B) I've been there once.
> **(C) I think August 7th.**

해석

며칠에 두바이로 떠날 예정인가요?
(A) 최신 정보가 반영된 여행 일정표입니다.
(B) 그곳에 한 번 가 봤어요.
(C) 8월 7일 같아요.

어휘

leave for ~로 떠나다 updated 최신의, 갱신된
itinerary 여행 일정표

기출 표현 PLUS+

Next Tuesday. 다음 주 화요일요.
Probably May 27th. 아마 5월 27일이요.

7. 미남 미녀 🎧

> Which software should I install to design our logo?
> (A) She's very good at designing.
> **(B) You'd better ask Jason.**
> (C) No, I'll take care of it tomorrow.

해석

로고를 디자인하려면 어떤 소프트웨어를 설치해야 하나요?
(A) 그녀는 디자인을 아주 잘해요.
(B) 제이슨에게 물어보는 게 좋겠어요.
(C) 아니요, 제가 내일 처리하겠습니다.

어휘

install 설치하다 be good at ~을 잘하다
take care of ~을 처리하다, 돌보다

기출 표현 PLUS+

You should ask Ms. Harris. 해리스 씨에게 물어보셔야 해요.
It's already installed. 벌써 설치되어 있어요.

8. 미남 미녀 🎧

> What will be discussed with the investors?
> (A) No, the weekly meeting.
> (B) That's my understanding, too.
> **(C) Didn't you receive an information packet?**

해석

투자자들과 무슨 이야기를 하게 되나요?
(A) 아니요, 주간 회의요.
(B) 저도 그렇게 알고 있어요.

(C) 자료집을 받지 않았나요?

어휘

investor 투자자 understanding 이해, 해석
information packet 자료집

기출 표현 PLUS⁺

Didn't you get the e-mail? 이메일 받지 못했나요?
I didn't get the details about it yet.
아직 세부적인 내용을 못 받았어요.

9. 미남 미녀 🎧

What was your team asked to work on this
month?
(A) Sure, I'll ask him to do it.
(B) The report on vacation pay.
(C) They were only here a month.

해석

당신의 팀은 이번 달에 무슨 작업을 해 달라고 요청받았나요?
(A) 그럼요, 제가 그에게 해 달라고 요청할게요.
(B) 휴가 수당에 대한 보고서입니다.
(C) 그들은 여기에 온 지 고작 한 달 되었어요.

어휘

work on ~을 작업하다, ~에 애쓰다 vacation pay 휴가 수당

기출 표현 PLUS⁺

Our supervisor will tell us tomorrow.
우리 상사가 내일 알려줄 거예요.
Creating more online ads. 온라인 광고를 더 만드는 일이요.

10. 미녀 호남 🎧

Which workshop session was your favorite?
(A) Registration is in the lobby.
(B) I'm looking forward to it.
(C) All of them were helpful.

해석

어떤 워크숍 시간이 좋았나요?
(A) 등록은 로비에서 합니다.
(B) 그것을 고대하고 있어요.
(C) 모든 것들이 도움이 됐어요.

어휘

favorite 매우 좋아하는; 좋아하는 것[사람] registration 등록
look forward to ~을 기대하다

기출 표현 PLUS⁺

I didn't like any of them. 다 별로였어요.
The one on marketing was great. 마케팅에 관한 게 좋았어요.

11. 미녀 호남 🎧

What did the customers say about our mobile
phone?
(A) Press 2 to speak with a representative.
(B) Most people liked the new functions.
(C) No, it was no problem.

해석

고객들이 우리 휴대폰에 대해 뭐라고 말했나요?
(A) 직원과 얘기하려면 2번을 누르세요.
(B) 대부분의 사람들이 새로운 기능들을 좋아했어요.
(C) 아니요, 문제가 되지 않았어요.

어휘

representative (판매) 대리인, 대표자, 직원 function 기능

기출 표현 PLUS⁺

They thought it was too heavy. 너무 무거웠답니다.
They liked the new features. 새 기능들을 좋아했어요.

12. 호남 영녀 🎧

Which sweater did you decide to buy for Amy's
birthday?
(A) I like your sweater.
(B) A product catalog.
(C) The one with the stripes.

해석

에이미의 생일을 위해 어떤 스웨터를 사기로 결정했나요?
(A) 저는 당신의 스웨터가 마음에 들어요.
(B) 상품 카탈로그요.
(C) 줄무늬가 있는 것이요.

어휘

product catalog 상품 카탈로그 stripe 줄무늬

기출 표현 PLUS⁺

The one from Eric's Boutique. 에릭스 부티크 걸로요.
The pink one. 핑크색으로요.

13. 호남 영녀 🎧

What did you say to Mr. Jackson yesterday?
(A) Yes, he was great.
(B) Actually, I haven't met him yet.
(C) I have an appointment with him.

해석

어제 잭슨 씨에게 뭐라고 말했어요?
(A) 네, 그는 대단했어요.
(B) 실은, 아직 그를 만나지 않았어요.
(C) 저는 그와 약속이 있어요.

어휘

actually 사실은, 실제로 appointment (업무 관련) 약속

I asked him about the merger. 합병에 대해 물어봤어요.
I just introduced myself. 그냥 제 소개를 했어요.

14. 호남 영녀 🎧

Which dates would you like to book the hotel for?
(A) I prefer non-fiction.
(B) From the 7th to the 9th, if possible.
(C) It's upstairs.

해석
어떤 날짜로 호텔을 예약하시겠어요?
(A) 저는 논픽션을 선호해요.
(B) 가능하다면, 7일에서 9일까지요.
(C) 위층입니다.

어휘
book 예약하다   non-fiction 논픽션, 실화
upstairs 위층으로, 위층에서

기출 표현 PLUS⁺
For next weekend, please. 다음 주 주말이요.
From the fifth to the eighth, please. 5일부터 8일까지요.

15. 미남 호남 🎧

Which of these designs best fits our company's image?
(A) The one that Kiko created.
(B) The computer is restarting.
(C) Around fifty new investors.

해석
이 디자인들 중 무엇이 우리 회사의 이미지에 가장 잘 맞나요?
(A) 키코가 만든 것이요.
(B) 컴퓨터가 다시 시작되는 중입니다.
(C) 약 50명의 신규 투자자들입니다.

어휘
fit ~에 맞다, 적합하다   create 만들어 내다, 창작하다
restart 다시 시작하다   investor 투자자

기출 표현 PLUS⁺
I like the classic design. 고전적인 디자인이요.
The one Joseph made is great. 조셉이 만든 게 좋아요.

UNIT 03 When 의문문

CHECK UP   본문 p.70

1. (C)   **2.** (C)   **3.** (C)   **4.** (A)

1. 미남 미녀 🎧

When should I call Dr. Pierson back?
(A) I forgot his number.
(B) There's a call for you on line 3.
(C) Anytime this afternoon.

해석
제가 언제 피어슨 박사님에게 다시 전화해야 하나요?
(A) 그의 번호를 잊어버렸어요.
(B) 3번에 당신에게 전화가 와 있어요.
(C) 오늘 오후 아무 때나요.

어휘
call back 다시 전화를 하다

기출 표현 PLUS⁺
After 1 P.M. 오후 1시 이후에요.
Before 6 P.M. 오후 6시 전에요.

2. 미남 미녀 🎧

When will you meet the marketing team?
(A) Yes, at the market.
(B) For about two hours.
(C) Right after lunch.

해석
당신은 언제 마케팅팀을 만날 건가요?
(A) 네, 시장에서요.
(B) 약 2시간 동안이요.
(C) 점심시간 직후에요.

어휘
right after ~ 직후에

기출 표현 PLUS⁺
This Friday. 이번 주 금요일요.
Next Tuesday. 다음 주 화요일요.

3. 미남 미녀 🎧

When's the art gallery's fund-raiser?
(A) Yes, a few paintings.
(B) At least a thousand dollars.
(C) Next Friday at seven.

해석
미술관의 모금 행사는 언제인가요?
(A) 네, 몇몇 그림들이요.
(B) 적어도 1,000달러입니다.
(C) 다음 주 금요일 7시에요.

어휘
art gallery 미술관, 화랑   fund-raiser 모금 행사
at least 적어도

기출 표현 PLUS⁺
Sometime next month. 다음 달쯤요.

Tonight at 6:30. 오늘밤 6시 30분요.

4. 미남 미녀 🎧

> When can we practice our sales presentation?
> **(A) I have meetings all day.**
> (B) Yes, it's an important client.
> (C) They were quite impressive.

해석

언제 우리 매출 발표를 연습할 수 있어요?
(A) 하루 종일 회의가 있어요.
(B) 네, 중요한 고객이에요.
(C) 그것들은 매우 인상적이었어요.

어휘

practice 연습하다 presentation 발표, 프레젠테이션
impressive 인상적인, 인상 깊은

기출 표현 PLUS⁺

I can do it tomorrow. 저는 내일 할 수 있어요.
Sorry, I'm busy all day. 미안하지만 저는 온종일 바빠요.

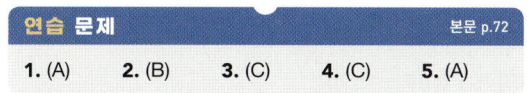

연습 문제   본문 p.72

1. (A)   **2.** (B)   **3.** (C)   **4.** (C)   **5.** (A)

1. 미남 영녀 🎧

> When did Samantha clean out the supply room?
> **(A) After we left.**
> (B) Some used boxes.
> (C) She cleaned the floor.

해석

사만다가 언제 비품실을 청소했나요?
(A) 우리가 떠난 후에요.
(B) 몇몇 쓰던 상자들이요.
(C) 그녀가 바닥을 청소했어요.

어휘

clean out 깨끗이 치우다 supply room 비품실
used 중고의, 쓰던

기출 표현 PLUS⁺

Last Friday. 지난주 금요일요.
Right after lunch. 점심시간 직후에요.

2. 미남 영녀 🎧

> When will we take inventory of our stock?
> (A) Our toasters are popular.
> **(B) Later this month.**
> (C) Yes, I stocked the shelves.

해석

언제 재고조사를 하죠?
(A) 우리 토스터들이 인기가 있어요.
(B) 이달 후반에요.
(C) 네, 제가 선반에 물건을 채웠어요.

어휘

take (an) inventory of 재고조사하다
stock (상점의) 재고품; (상품을) 비축하다, 채우다

기출 표현 PLUS⁺

In about three hours. 약 세 시간 후에요.
Next week on Monday. 다음 주 월요일에요.

3. 미남 영녀 🎧

> When do we need to meet to work on our project?
> (A) Come to my apartment.
> (B) It went very well, right?
> **(C) Let me check my calendar.**

해석

우리 프로젝트 작업을 위해 언제 만나야 할까요?
(A) 제 아파트로 오세요.
(B) 그건 아주 잘 되었죠, 맞죠?
(C) 제 일정을 확인해 볼게요.

어휘

work on ~에 대한 작업을 하다, ~에 노력을 들이다
go well 잘 되어가다

기출 표현 PLUS⁺

I'll ask when Bobby is free.
바비가 언제 시간이 되는지 물어볼게요.
In about 30 minutes. 한 30분 후에요.

4. 미남 영녀 🎧

> When will you finalize the contract?
> (A) Because he has a good reputation.
> (B) Please contact me by phone.
> **(C) By early next week.**

해석

당신은 언제 계약을 마무리 지을 건가요?
(A) 그가 평판이 좋기 때문이에요.
(B) 제게 전화로 연락 주시기 바랍니다.
(C) 다음 주 초까지요.

어휘

finalize 마무리 짓다, 완결하다 contract 계약(서)
reputation 평판, 명성

기출 표현 PLUS⁺

Probably next month. 아마 다음 달에요.
I can't say for sure. 확실하지 않아요.

5. 미남 영녀 🎧

> When can I expect the morning mail delivery?
> **(A) Around nine o'clock.**
> (B) Please put the package over there.
> (C) Thanks, but I'll copy it.

해석

오전 우편배달은 언제 오나요?
(A) 9시쯤이요.
(B) 소포를 저쪽에 두시기 바랍니다.
(C) 고맙지만, 제가 그것을 복사할게요.

어휘

expect (오기로 되어 있는 대상을) 기다리다, 예상하다
package 소포, 포장물

기출 표현 PLUS⁺

Before 10 A.M. 오전 10시 전에요.
It usually comes at 12:30. 보통 12시 30분에 와요.

실전 **문제**   본문 p.73

1. (A)	**2.** (A)	**3.** (B)	**4.** (C)	**5.** (B)
6. (B)	**7.** (B)	**8.** (C)	**9.** (C)	**10.** (C)
11. (B)	**12.** (B)	**13.** (B)	**14.** (A)	**15.** (C)

1. 미남 영녀 🎧

> When did Ms. Morgan return from her trip?
> **(A) Tuesday afternoon.**
> (B) At a travel agency.
> (C) Yes, she enjoyed it.

해석

모건 씨는 언제 여행에서 돌아왔나요?
(A) 화요일 오후요.
(B) 여행사에서요.
(C) 네, 그녀는 즐거워했어요.

어휘

travel agency 여행사

기출 표현 PLUS⁺

Just this morning. 오늘 아침에요.
Yesterday night. 어젯밤에요.

2. 미남 영녀 🎧

> When will we extend the contract with Aga Shipping?
> **(A) We're still negotiating the details.**
> (B) A large business network.
> (C) It tends to be low.

해석

우리는 아가 쉬핑 사와의 계약을 언제 연장할 건가요?
(A) 아직 세부적인 것들을 협상하고 있어요.
(B) 대규모 사업 네트워크요.
(C) 그것은 낮은 경향이 있어요.

어휘

extend 연장하다, 확대하다   contract 계약(서); 계약하다
negotiate 협상하다   details ((보통 복수형)) 세부 사항
tend to do ~하는 경향이 있다

기출 표현 PLUS⁺

Maybe next week. 아마도 다음 주에요.
We're in the middle of negotiations. 협상 중이에요.

3. 미녀 미남 🎧

> When were the batteries in these smoke detectors replaced?
> (A) They make a loud sound.
> **(B) In January, as far as I know.**
> (C) He had to charge his phone.

해석

이 연기 탐지기의 배터리들은 언제 교체되었나요?
(A) 그것들에서 큰 소리가 나요.
(B) 제가 알기로는 1월이요.
(C) 그가 전화기를 충전해야 했어요.

어휘

smoke detector 연기 탐지기   replace 교체하다, 대체하다
as far as ~하는 한   charge 충전하다, 청구하다

기출 표현 PLUS⁺

You'll have to ask William. 윌리엄에게 물어보셔야 해요.
Just last week. 지난주에요.

4. 미녀 미남 🎧

> When does the warranty on your mobile phone expire?
> (A) I met with him on Monday.
> (B) The recent software update.
> **(C) In October.**

해석

당신의 휴대폰에 대한 보증은 언제 만료되나요?
(A) 저는 그를 월요일에 만났어요.
(B) 최근의 소프트웨어 업데이트요.
(C) 10월에요.

어휘

warranty on ~에 대한 보증   expire 만료되다

기출 표현 PLUS⁺

In April, I think. 4월일 거예요.
At the end of the year. 올해 말에요.

5. 영녀 호남 🎧

> When will the employee workshop be held this year?
> (A) In Perth.
> **(B) July 6th or 7th.**
> (C) Yes, I met her then.

해석

올해 직원 워크숍은 언제 열리나요?
(A) 퍼스에서요.
(B) 7월 6일이나 7일이요.
(C) 네, 그때 그녀를 만났어요.

어휘

employee 직원 be held 개최되다, 열리다

기출 표현 PLUS⁺

The CEO will decide the date. CEO가 결정할 거예요.
Next Friday. 다음 주 금요일요.

6. 영녀 호남 🎧

> When do you expect to finish your article for the newsletter?
> (A) I'm expecting good results.
> **(B) I've just received the pictures for it.**
> (C) Please forward it to Margaret in Sales.

해석

소식지에 실을 당신의 기사를 언제 끝낼 예정이에요?
(A) 좋은 결과를 예상하고 있습니다.
(B) 방금 그것에 들어갈 사진을 받았어요.
(C) 영업부의 마거릿에게 전달해 주세요.

어휘

expect to do ~하기를 기대[예상]하다 newsletter 소식지
forward 전달하다, 보내다

기출 표현 PLUS⁺

I'm still waiting for an interview.
아직 인터뷰를 기다리는 중이에요.
By tomorrow afternoon. 내일 오후요.

7. 미남 미녀 🎧

> When do you think we'll arrive in Jakarta?
> (A) It was my first day there.
> **(B) Around midnight.**
> (C) From a city to a suburb.

해석

우리가 언제 자카르타에 도착할 것 같아요?
(A) 제가 그곳에 간 첫날이었어요.
(B) 자정쯤에요.
(C) 도시에서 교외로요.

어휘

arrive in ~에 도착하다 midnight 자정

기출 표현 PLUS⁺

In about five hours. 한 다섯 시간 후에요.
Around 3 P.M. 오후 3시쯤요.

8. 미남 미녀 🎧

> When was the last time you updated your Web site?
> (A) Use a different password.
> (B) A more modern design.
> **(C) It's been quite a while.**

해석

언제 마지막으로 웹사이트를 업데이트했나요?
(A) 다른 비밀번호를 사용하세요.
(B) 더 현대적인 디자인이요.
(C) 한참 됐어요.

어휘

update 최신의 것으로 하다, 갱신하다 modern 현대적인
quite a while 꽤 오랫동안

기출 표현 PLUS⁺

Maybe two months ago. 아마 두 달 전쯤요.
We regularly update it every month.
우린 매달 정기적으로 업데이트해요.

9. 미남 미녀 🎧

> When will construction begin?
> (A) On the south side of the building.
> (B) The new office.
> **(C) After the budget is approved.**

해석

공사가 언제 시작되나요?
(A) 건물의 남쪽에서요.
(B) 새 사무실입니다.
(C) 예산이 승인된 이후에요.

어휘

construction 건설, 공사 budget 예산
approve 승인하다, 인가하다

기출 표현 PLUS⁺

It starts next week. 다음 주에 시작해요.
We need to finalize the contract first.
먼저 계약을 마무리해야 해요.

10. 미녀 호남 🎧

> When can we take the shuttle to the city center?
> (A) Yes, it leaves in a few minutes.
> (B) The downtown area is modern.
> **(C) The hotel canceled that service.**

우리는 언제 도심으로 가는 셔틀버스를 탈 수 있나요?
(A) 네, 몇 분 후에 출발합니다.
(B) 도심 지역은 현대적이에요.
(C) 호텔이 그 서비스를 취소했어요.

어휘

shuttle 정기 왕복 버스[항공기] downtown area 도심 지역
modern 현대적인 cancel 취소하다

기출 표현 PLUS⁺

Shuttles run every 15 minutes.
셔틀 버스는 15분마다 운행해요.
The next one comes in six minutes.
다음 셔틀 버스는 6분 후에 와요.

11. 미녀 호남 🎧

> When will you replace the curtains in the
> conference room?
> (A) The second door on the left.
> **(B) I can't decide on a color.**
> (C) No, the event was fully booked.

해석

회의실의 커튼을 언제 교체할 거예요?
(A) 왼쪽 두 번째 문이요.
(B) 색상을 결정하지 못하겠어요.
(C) 아니요, 행사는 모두 예약되었어요.

어휘

replace 교체하다, 대체하다 book 예약하다

기출 표현 PLUS⁺

I'll replace them tomorrow. 내일 교체할 거예요.
I'm busy all week. 이번 주 내내 바빠요.

12. 호남 영녀 🎧

> When will you call Andrew back?
> (A) A new mobile phone.
> **(B) Probably during my lunch break.**
> (C) One of my former coworkers.

해석

언제 앤드류에게 다시 전화할 거예요?
(A) 새 휴대폰입니다.
(B) 아마도 점심시간 동안이요.
(C) 제 이전 동료들 중 한 명입니다.

어휘

call back 다시 전화하다 coworker 동료

기출 표현 PLUS⁺

After work. 일 끝나고요.
Sometime in the afternoon. 오후쯤에요.

13. 호남 영녀 🎧

> When should we renew our subscription to the
> trade magazine?
> (A) No, a used one would be cheaper.
> **(B) I don't think employees read it.**
> (C) At the national level.

해석

우리가 언제 업계 잡지의 정기 구독을 갱신해야 하나요?
(A) 아니요, 중고가 더 쌀 거예요.
(B) 직원들이 그것을 읽지 않는 것 같아요.
(C) 국가적인 차원에서요.

어휘

renew 갱신하다 subscription to ~의 정기 구독
trade magazine 업계 잡지(특정 업계나 전문 직업인 상대의 잡지)
national level 국가적인[전국적인] 차원

기출 표현 PLUS⁺

Next month, I think. 아마도 다음 달에요.
Do people still read it? 사람들이 아직 그걸 읽나요?

14. 호남 영녀 🎧

> When do you prefer to hold the training session?
> **(A) On Thursday afternoon.**
> (B) At the headquarters.
> (C) To improve on-site safety.

해석

언제 교육을 개최하는 것이 좋으세요?
(A) 목요일 오후에요.
(B) 본사에서요.
(C) 현장 안전을 개선하기 위해서요.

어휘

prefer to do ~하는 것을 선호하다 training session 교육 (과정)
headquarters 본사 improve 개선하다, 향상시키다
on-site 현장의 safety 안전

기출 표현 PLUS⁺

After lunch. 점심 시간 이후에요.
Maybe next Monday would be good.
다음 주 월요일이 좋을 것 같아요.

15. 미녀 영녀 🎧

> When did Walter transfer to the Marketing team?
> (A) Sure, that sounds perfect.
> (B) We can transfer the funds.
> **(C) I've been away all week.**

해석

월터가 언제 마케팅팀으로 옮겼나요?
(A) 물론이죠, 그거 좋겠군요.
(B) 우리는 자금을 이체할 수 있어요.
(C) 제가 일주일 내내 자리에 없었어요.

어휘

transfer 옮기다, 이동하다 fund 돈, 자금 be away 부재중이다

기출 표현 PLUS⁺

Last Tuesday, I believe. 지난 화요일에요.
I didn't know he transferred. 그가 옮긴 걸 몰랐어요.

UNIT 04 Where 의문문

CHECK UP   본문 p.74

1. (C)   **2.** (C)   **3.** (C)   **4.** (B)

1. 미남 미녀 🎧

> Where can I store my luggage?
> (A) You can check in now.
> (B) From 9 to 5.
> **(C) At the service desk over there.**

해석

제 짐을 어디에 보관하면 될까요?
(A) 지금 체크인하실 수 있습니다.
(B) 9시부터 5시까지요.
(C) 저쪽 서비스 창구에서요.

어휘

store 보관하다, 저장하다 luggage 짐, 수하물
check in 탑승[투숙] 수속을 밟다, 체크인하다

기출 표현 PLUS⁺

I can take it for you. 제가 맡아 드릴게요.
Please place it behind the counter. 카운터 뒤에 놓아주세요.

2. 미남 미녀 🎧

> Where is the closest stationery store?
> (A) It closed at 10.
> (B) We are open 24 hours.
> **(C) On Carter Avenue.**

해석

가장 가까운 문구점은 어디 있나요?
(A) 10시에 문을 닫았어요.
(B) 우리는 24시간 영업합니다.
(C) 카터 가에요.

어휘

stationery store 문구점 open 영업을 하는

기출 표현 PLUS⁺

Near the post office. 우체국 근처에요.
Next to the library. 도서관 옆에요.

3. 미남 미녀 🎧

> Where did you meet Ms. Taylor?
> (A) At 4 o'clock.
> (B) Yes, she was there.
> **(C) In the cafeteria.**

해석

테일러 씨를 어디서 만났어요?
(A) 4시에요.
(B) 네, 그녀가 거기 있었어요.
(C) 카페테리아에서요.

어휘

cafeteria 카페테리아, 구내식당

기출 표현 PLUS⁺

In the break room. 휴게실에서요.
In her office. 그녀 사무실에서요.

4. 미남 미녀 🎧

> Where can I get an employee handbook?
> (A) On the cover page.
> **(B) Let me give you one.**
> (C) Take a seat here.

해석

직원 안내서를 어디서 구할 수 있나요?
(A) 표지에서요.
(B) 제가 하나 드릴게요.
(C) 여기 앉으세요.

어휘

handbook 안내서, 편람 cover page 표지

기출 표현 PLUS⁺

Mr. Wang can give you one.
왕 씨가 한 부 드릴 수 있을 거예요.
They're in the closet. 벽장 서랍에 있어요.

연습 문제   본문 p.76

1. (C)   **2.** (B)   **3.** (C)   **4.** (B)   **5.** (B)

1. 미녀 호남 🎧

> Where is the new branch office located?
> (A) Approximately 10 years ago.
> (B) Should I trim them?
> **(C) It's just around the corner.**

해석

새 지사는 어디에 위치해 있나요?
(A) 대략 10년 전입니다.
(B) 제가 그것들을 다듬어야 할까요?

(C) 모퉁이를 돌면 바로 있어요.

어휘

branch office 지사, 지점 be located (~에) 위치하다
approximately 대략 trim 다듬다, 손질하다

기출 표현 PLUS⁺

It will be in Lisbon. 리스본에 위치할 거예요.
It's downtown. 시내에 있어요.

2. 미녀 호남 🎧

> Where are the old patient files?
> (A) Thank you for your patience.
> **(B) In the basement storage closet.**
> (C) He wasn't feeling well.

해석

예전 환자 파일은 어디에 있나요?
(A) 양해해 주셔서 감사합니다.
(B) 지하 보관 창고요.
(C) 그는 몸이 좋지 않았어요.

어휘

patience 인내심, 참을성 storage closet 보관 창고
feel well 건강 상태가 좋다

기출 표현 PLUS⁺

They should be on the computer. 컴퓨터에 있을 거예요.
In the file cabinet. 서류 캐비닛에 있어요.

3. 미녀 호남 🎧

> Where can we hold the company event?
> (A) Three hours will be enough.
> (B) There is a large turnout.
> **(C) The same place as last year.**

해석

우리가 회사 행사를 어디서 개최하면 될까요?
(A) 3시간이면 충분할 거예요.
(B) 참가자 수가 많아요.
(C) 작년과 같은 장소요.

어휘

turnout 참가자의 수

기출 표현 PLUS⁺

At the convention center. 컨벤션 센터에서요.
How about the main conference room?
대회의실은 어때요?

4. 미녀 호남 🎧

> Where can I get my ID replaced?
> (A) A few forms.
> **(B) At the security office.**
> (C) She's our new intern.

해석

제 신분증을 어디서 교체하면 되나요?
(A) 서식 몇 개입니다.
(B) 경비실에서요.
(C) 그녀는 우리의 새 인턴사원이에요.

어휘

replace 교체하다, 대체하다 security office 경비실
intern 인턴사원

기출 표현 PLUS⁺

Ask the security manager. 보안 담당자에게 물어보세요.
Go to the main office. 본사로 가세요.

5. 미녀 호남 🎧

> Where do you take clients for a meal?
> (A) No, they're still interested.
> **(B) I don't work directly with clients.**
> (C) A seven o'clock reservation.

해석

고객들과 식사할 때 어디로 가나요?
(A) 아니요, 그들은 아직 관심이 있어요.
(B) 저는 고객들과 직접적으로 일하지 않아요.
(C) 7시 예약입니다.

어휘

interested 관심이 있는 directly 직접적으로 reservation 예약

기출 표현 PLUS⁺

To the restaurant downstairs. 아래층 식당으로요.
To a fancy Mexican restaurant. 고급 멕시칸 식당으로요.

실전 문제   본문 p.77

1. (B)	**2.** (B)	**3.** (A)	**4.** (C)	**5.** (A)
6. (A)	**7.** (A)	**8.** (B)	**9.** (A)	**10.** (C)
11. (A)	**12.** (C)	**13.** (B)	**14.** (A)	**15.** (C)

1. 미남 영녀 🎧

> Where can I find Professor Mellwick's office?
> (A) Thursday between 2 and 4.
> **(B) I'm afraid he's away at a conference.**
> (C) Have you checked the lost and found?

해석

멜윅 교수님의 사무실이 어디죠?
(A) 목요일 2시에서 4시 사이예요.
(B) 유감이지만 그는 회의로 자리를 비웠어요.
(C) 분실물 취급소를 확인하셨나요?

어휘

be away 부재중이다 lost and found 분실물 취급소

기출 표현 PLUS⁺

It's down the hall, to your right. 복도 끝 오른쪽이요.
He's not in today. 오늘은 나오지 않으셨어요.

2. 미남 영녀 🎧

> Where should we hold the job applicant's interview this morning?
> (A) Yes, I'll hold it for you.
> **(B) Actually, he had to reschedule.**
> (C) No, I arrived on time.

해석

오늘 아침에 어디서 그 입사 지원자의 면접을 해야 하나요?
(A) 네, 제가 그것을 맡아 줄게요.
(B) 실은, 그가 일정을 변경해야 했어요.
(C) 아니요, 제가 시간 맞춰 도착했어요.

어휘

job applicant 입사 지원자　reschedule 일정을 변경하다
on time 시간을 어기지 않고, 정각에

기출 표현 PLUS⁺

Conference Room B should be fine.
B회의실이 괜찮을 거예요.
Actually, it's in the afternoon. 실은, 면접은 오후에 해요.

3. 미녀 미남 🎧

> Where can I get more padded envelopes?
> **(A) Actually, I don't need the rest of these.**
> (B) Before Friday afternoon.
> (C) Yes, to keep everything safe.

해석

완충재를 댄 봉투를 어디서 더 많이 구할 수 있나요?
(A) 실은, 전 이 나머지 것들(봉투)이 필요하지 않아요.
(B) 금요일 오후 이전이에요.
(C) 네, 모든 것을 안전하게 유지하기 위해서요.

어휘

padded envelope 완충재[패드]를 댄 봉투
the rest of ~의 나머지

기출 표현 PLUS⁺

You can take mine. 제걸 쓰세요.
They're in the storage closet. 물품 수납장에 있어요.

4. 미녀 미남 🎧

> Where should I put these extra file folders?
> (A) Yes, the standard size.
> (B) For confidential patient records.
> **(C) On the receptionist's desk.**

해석

이 여분의 파일 폴더를 어디에 둘까요?
(A) 네, 표준 크기입니다.
(B) 기밀 환자 기록을 위해서입니다.
(C) 접수계 책상이에요.

어휘

extra 여분의, 추가의　standard 표준의, 일반의
confidential 비밀의, 기밀의　receptionist 접수 담당자

기출 표현 PLUS⁺

In the file cabinet. 서류 캐비닛이에요.
Give them to the secretary. 비서에게 주세요.

5. 영녀 호남 🎧

> Where should I turn in my application form?
> **(A) It's written on the first page.**
> (B) Fill out the form, please.
> (C) By tomorrow at 3.

해석

어디로 제 신청서를 제출해야 하나요?
(A) 그것은 첫 번째 페이지에 쓰여 있어요.
(B) 이 서식을 기입해 주십시오.
(C) 내일 3시까지요.

어휘

turn in 제출하다　application form 신청서
fill out 기입하다, 작성하다

기출 표현 PLUS⁺

Please give it to me. 저에게 주세요.
Mr. Lamar can take it. 라마 씨가 가져갈 거예요.

6. 영녀 호남 🎧

> Where is the press conference going to be held?
> **(A) In the main hall on the first floor.**
> (B) Report to the journalists.
> (C) There aren't enough rooms.

해석

기자 회견은 어디서 열릴 예정인가요?
(A) 1층의 중앙 홀이에요.
(B) 기자들에게 알리세요.
(C) 방들이 충분하지 않습니다.

어휘

press conference 기자 회견　journalist 저널리스트, 기자

기출 표현 PLUS⁺

Just next door. 옆방에서요.
Outside the courthouse. 법원 밖에서요.

7. 미남 미녀 🎧

> Where should the new filing cabinets be placed?
> **(A) Jenice has a floor plan.**
> (B) To store packaging boxes.
> (C) I ordered it about a month ago.

해석

새로운 서류 캐비닛을 어디에 두어야 할까요?
(A) 제니스에게 평면도가 있어요.
(B) 포장 상자를 보관하기 위해서요.
(C) 제가 그것을 약 한 달 전에 주문했어요.

어휘

place 두다, 놓다 floor plan 평면도 store 보관하다
packaging 포장, 포장재

기출 표현 PLUS⁺

Next to the copiers. 복사기 옆이에요.
Ask Macy where to put them.
어디에 둬야 하는지 메이시에게 물어보세요.

8. 미남 미녀 🎧

> Where can I find paper for the copier?
> (A) No, that will be fine.
> **(B) On my desk, take two packs.**
> (C) On March 10th.

해석

복사 용지를 어디서 찾을 수 있나요?
(A) 아뇨, 그거면 될 거예요.
(B) 제 책상 위예요, 두 묶음 가져가세요.
(C) 3월 10일이에요.

어휘

copier 복사기

기출 표현 PLUS⁺

I can give you some. 제가 드릴게요.
At the end of aisle three. 3번 통로 끝에 있어요.

9. 미남 미녀 🎧

> Where did you find my briefcase?
> **(A) It was under a chair.**
> (B) In about two hours.
> (C) The meeting was brief.

해석

제 서류 가방을 어디서 찾으셨나요?
(A) 의자 밑에 있었어요.
(B) 약 두 시간 뒤에요.
(C) 회의는 간단했어요.

어휘

briefcase 서류 가방 brief (시간이) 짧은, 간단한

기출 표현 PLUS⁺

It was underneath your desk. 책상 밑에 있었어요.
It was in the break room. 휴게실에 있었어요.

10. 미녀 호남 🎧

> Where's last year's quality control report?
> (A) Not very often.
> (B) Yes, they were high-quality items.
> **(C) You can find them on the company's Web site.**

해석

작년의 품질 관리 보고서는 어디 있나요?
(A) 그리 자주는 아니에요.
(B) 네, 그것들은 고품질의 물건들이었어요.
(C) 회사의 웹사이트에서 그것들을 찾을 수 있어요.

어휘

quality control 품질 관리 high-quality 고품질의, 고급의

기출 표현 PLUS⁺

Ask Ms. Morrison. 모리슨 씨에게 물어보세요.
I saw Carol reviewing it yesterday.
캐롤이 어제 검토하고 있는 것을 봤어요.

11. 미녀 호남 🎧

> Where did the architect leave the blueprints?
> **(A) They're on the desk.**
> (B) No, that's unlikely.
> (C) It's printed in black and white.

해석

건축가가 청사진을 어디에 놔두었나요?
(A) 그것들은 책상 위에 있어요.
(B) 아니요, 그럴 리가 없어요.
(C) 그것은 흑백으로 인쇄되었어요.

어휘

architect 건축가 blueprint 청사진, 설계도
unlikely 있음 직하지 않은, 가망 없는

기출 표현 PLUS⁺

They should be on the table. 책상 위에 있을 거예요.
I'll give him a call right now. 지금 그에게 전화해 볼게요.

12. 호남 영녀 🎧

> Where is the sales report from last year?
> (A) Yes, there aren't any.
> (B) We sold them this year.
> **(C) It's in the top drawer.**

해석

작년 매출 보고서는 어디에 있나요?
(A) 네, 전혀 없어요.

(B) 우리는 올해 그것들을 팔았어요.
(C) 그것은 맨 위 서랍에 있어요.

어휘
sales 매출(량)

기출 표현 PLUS⁺
It's on my computer. 컴퓨터에 있어요.
It's on the company Web site. 회사 웹사이트에 있어요.

13. 호남 영녀 🎧

Where is the company cafeteria?
(A) No, I'm fine.
(B) On the first floor.
(C) Every morning at 10 o'clock.

해석
구내식당은 어디에 있죠?
(A) 아니요, 괜찮습니다.
(B) 1층에요.
(C) 매일 아침 10시요.

어휘
cafeteria 구내식당

기출 표현 PLUS⁺
I'll show you there. 제가 거기로 안내할게요.
Next to the main conference room. 대회의실 옆이요.

14. 호남 영녀 🎧

Where's the sports complex located?
(A) Next to the convention center.
(B) Yes, I used to play golf at school.
(C) We rented the whole complex.

해석
스포츠 종합 단지는 어디에 위치해 있나요?
(A) 컨벤션 센터 바로 옆이요.
(B) 네, 저는 학교에서 골프를 치곤 했어요.
(C) 우리는 종합 단지 전체를 빌렸어요.

어휘
be located (~에) 위치해 있다
sports complex 스포츠 종합 단지
convention center 컨벤션 센터(회의장·숙박 시설이 완비된 종합
빌딩) used to do ~하곤 했다

기출 표현 PLUS⁺
Next to the children's park. 어린이 공원 옆이요.
It's just around the corner. 모퉁이 돌면 바로요.

15. 미남 호남 🎧

Where are we supposed to store flammable
liquids?
(A) Here's a bottle of water for you.
(B) I prefer cooking with olive oil.
(C) In the shed behind the building.

해석
어디에 가연성 액체를 보관해야 하죠?
(A) 여기 물 한 병 있어요.
(B) 저는 올리브유로 요리하는 것을 좋아해요.
(C) 건물 뒤쪽 창고에요.

어휘
be supposed to do ~하기로 되어 있다
store 보관하다, 저장하다 flammable 가연성의, 불에 잘 타는
liquid 액체 shed 헛간, (간이) 창고

기출 표현 PLUS⁺
Give them to the maintenance worker.
시설관리 직원에게 주세요.
Put them away from the files.
서류에서 멀리 떨어진 곳에 두세요.

UNIT 05 How 의문문

본문 p.78

CHECK UP

1. (A)   **2.** (C)   **3.** (A)   **4.** (C)

1. 미남 미녀 🎧

How often do you give your garden tour?
(A) Usually twice a month.
(B) It starts around 6:00 P.M.
(C) You gave it to me in the garden.

해석
얼마나 자주 정원 투어를 제공하시나요?
(A) 보통 한 달에 두 번이요.
(B) 저녁 6시쯤 시작합니다.
(C) 당신은 정원에서 그것을 제게 주었어요.

어휘
give a tour 견학[구경]을 시켜 주다

기출 표현 PLUS⁺
Once a week. 일주일에 한 번이요.
Twice every Saturday. 일요일마다 두 번이요.

2. 미남 미녀 🎧

> How do you like the new payment system?
> (A) I borrowed them from the store.
> (B) I'd like to pay with my credit card.
> **(C) Actually, it's quite efficient.**

해석

새로운 결제 시스템은 어떤가요?
(A) 제가 그 가게에서 그것들을 빌렸습니다.
(B) 신용카드로 결제하겠습니다.
(C) 사실, 매우 효율적이에요.

어휘

How do you like ~? ~은 어떻습니까?
payment system 결제 시스템 efficient 효율적인

기출 표현 PLUS⁺

It's better than the old one. 예전 것보다 좋아요.
I think it needs some work. 개선이 좀 필요해 보여요.

3. 미남 미녀 🎧

> How long will it take to get to Chicago?
> **(A) Four hours by train.**
> (B) To visit my parents.
> (C) He got back yesterday.

해석

시카고에 가는 데 얼마나 걸릴까요?
(A) 기차로 4시간이요.
(B) 부모님을 뵈러 가려고요.
(C) 그는 어제 돌아왔어요.

어휘

get back 돌아오다

기출 표현 PLUS⁺

Two hours by plane. 비행기로 두 시간이요.
Six hours, if we drive. 차로 가면 6시간이요.

4. 미남 미녀 🎧

> How do I register for your class?
> (A) I didn't see it at the reception desk.
> (B) The fee is $5.
> **(C) The instructions are on our Web site.**

해석

당신의 수업에 어떻게 등록하나요?
(A) 접수처에서 그것을 못 봤어요.
(B) 수업료는 5달러입니다.
(C) 웹사이트에 안내서가 있어요.

어휘

register for ~에 등록하다, 신청하다 reception desk 접수처
fee 요금, 수수료 instructions 설명서

기출 표현 PLUS⁺

Please speak with the receptionist. 안내원에게 물어보세요.
You can register at the front desk.
프런트 데스크에서 등록하실 수 있어요.

연습 문제 본문 p.80

1. (C) **2.** (B) **3.** (B) **4.** (A) **5.** (C)

1. 미남 영녀 🎧

> How was the employee holiday party yesterday?
> (A) Yes, all week.
> (B) The Lakeline Hotel.
> **(C) It was great.**

해석

어제 직원 휴가 파티는 어땠어요?
(A) 네, 일주일 내내요.
(B) 레이크라인 호텔이요.
(C) 아주 좋았어요.

어휘

employee 직원

기출 표현

It was fun! 재미있었어요!
I had a good time. 즐거웠어요.

2. 미남 영녀 🎧

> How long have you worked at headquarters?
> (A) Long time no see.
> **(B) Since July 2014.**
> (C) During working hours.

해석

본사에서 얼마나 일했나요?
(A) 오랜만입니다.
(B) 2014년 7월 이후로요.
(C) 근무 시간 동안이요.

어휘

headquarters 본사 working hours 근무 시간

기출 표현 PLUS⁺

For almost five years. 거의 5년 동안요.
Since the merger. 합병 이후로 계속요.

3. 미남 영녀 🎧

> How can I place an order for catering?
> (A) Yes, you can.
> **(B) Just fill out this order form.**
> (C) About 70 to 100 people.

해석

출장연회 서비스 주문은 어떻게 하나요?
(A) 네, 그러시면 됩니다.
(B) 이 주문서를 작성하시면 돼요.
(C) 약 70~100명이요.

어휘

place an order for ~을 주문하다
catering 출장연회, 음식 공급(업) fill out 기입하다, 작성하다
order form 주문서

기출 표현 PLUS+

You can order on our Web site.
저희 웹사이트에서 주문하실 수 있어요.
I can help you over there. 저쪽에서 도와드릴게요.

4. 미남 영녀 🎧

How often do you go back to London to visit?
(A) Once a year.
(B) Well, I flew in last night.
(C) Yeah, it's one of my favorite cities.

해석

얼마나 자주 런던을 다시 방문하세요?
(A) 일 년에 한 번이요.
(B) 음, 저는 어젯밤에 비행기로 도착했어요.
(C) 네, 그곳은 제가 좋아하는 도시들 중 하나예요.

어휘

fly in 비행기로 도착하다 favorite 매우 좋아하는

기출 표현 PLUS+

I go during the holiday season. 휴가철에 가요.
Every other year. 격년으로요.

5. 미남 영녀 🎧

How much does this cup cost?
(A) A dozen bags.
(B) In the summer catalog.
(C) Let me check with the computer.

해석

이 컵은 얼마입니까?
(A) 가방 12개요.
(B) 여름 카탈로그에서요.
(C) 컴퓨터로 확인해 볼게요.

어휘

dozen 12개짜리 한 묶음, 다스

기출 표현 PLUS+

The price is on the tag. 상표에 써 있어요.
It's on sale for $10. 할인해서 10달러예요.

본문 p.81

실전 문제

1. (B)	2. (A)	3. (C)	4. (C)	5. (B)
6. (A)	7. (C)	8. (B)	9. (C)	10. (C)
11. (C)	12. (C)	13. (C)	14. (A)	15. (C)

1. 미남 영녀 🎧

How did the charity concert go?
(A) You might need a smaller size.
(B) We received a lot of donations.
(C) At the Cambridge Theater.

해석

자선 콘서트는 어떻게 되었나요?
(A) 더 작은 크기가 필요할지도 몰라요.
(B) 우리는 많은 기부금을 받았어요.
(C) 케임브리지 극장에서요.

어휘

charity 자선 단체, 자선 donation 기부(금), 기증(물)

기출 표현 PLUS+

It went very well. 아주 잘 됐어요.
We earned a lot of money. 많은 돈을 모았어요.

2. 미남 영녀 🎧

How can I sign up for the aerobics class?
(A) Are you a member here?
(B) She signed the contract.
(C) They're in the blue jar.

해석

어떻게 에어로빅 수업에 신청하죠?
(A) 이곳 회원이신가요?
(B) 그녀가 계약서에 사인했어요.
(C) 그것들은 파란색 병에 있어요.

어휘

sign up for ~을 신청[가입]하다 contract 계약(서)
jar 병, 단지, 항아리

기출 표현 PLUS+

You can speak to the front desk staff.
프런트 데스크 직원에게 얘기해 보세요.
Write your information down here.
여기에 정보를 적어 주세요.

3. 미녀 미남 🎧

How can we receive the fabric samples in time?
(A) Yes, in about an hour.
(B) Please sample as many as you'd like.
(C) There's an overnight delivery option.

해석

어떻게 하면 우리가 제시간에 직물 샘플을 받을 수 있나요?

(A) 네, 약 한 시간 뒤에요.

(B) 원하는 만큼 시험해 보세요.

(C) 익일 배달 옵션이 있습니다.

어휘

fabric 직물, 천 in time 제시간에

sample (견본으로) ~을 시험하다, 시식[시음]하다; 샘플, 견본

overnight delivery 익일 배달 option 선택(할 수 있는 것)

기출 표현 PLUS⁺

We'll have to get express delivery. 속달로 받아야 할 거예요.

I'll ask Louis to go pick them up.
루이스에게 받아 오라고 부탁할게요.

4. [미녀] [미남] 🎧

> How do I change the water temperature on the washing machine?
> (A) I watched it in the theater.
> (B) At least once a month, I think.
> **(C) Didn't you read the instructions?**

해석

세탁기의 물 온도를 어떻게 바꾸나요?

(A) 제가 극장에서 그것을 봤어요.

(B) 제 생각에는 적어도 한 달에 한 번이요.

(C) 설명서를 읽지 않았어요?

어휘

temperature 온도, 기온 instructions 설명서

기출 표현 PLUS⁺

Check the instructions. 설명서를 확인해 보세요.

Press this button here. 여기 이 버튼을 누르세요.

5. [영녀] [호남] 🎧

> How much will it cost to replace the old refrigerator?
> (A) I ordered 200 copies.
> **(B) It depends on the size.**
> (C) In case we are low on money.

해석

구형 냉장고를 교체하는 데 비용이 얼마나 들까요?

(A) 저는 200부를 주문했어요.

(B) 그것은 크기에 따라 달라요.

(C) 우리가 돈이 부족할 경우를 위해서요.

어휘

replace 교체하다, 대체하다 copy (책, 신문 등의) 한 부

depend on ~에 달려 있다 in case ~할 경우에 대비해서

low on ~이 부족한

기출 표현 PLUS⁺

At least $2,000. 적어도 2,000달러요.

We should check online. 온라인으로 확인해 봐야 해요.

6. [영녀] [호남] 🎧

> How do I set the security alarm?
> **(A) First, input your five-digit code.**
> (B) It's louder than I expected.
> (C) We use it throughout the day.

해석

어떻게 보안 경보를 설정하나요?

(A) 우선, 당신의 5자리 암호를 입력하세요.

(B) 제가 예상했던 것보다 소리가 더 커요.

(C) 우리는 하루 종일 그것을 사용합니다.

어휘

set 설정하다 security alarm 보안 경보 input 입력하다

digit 숫자

기출 표현 PLUS⁺

First you need to scan your ID.

먼저 신분증을 스캔하셔야 해요.

It sets itself automatically. 자동으로 설정돼요.

7. [미남] [미녀] 🎧

> How are the features of the new design software?
> (A) No, I don't like the colors.
> (B) Yes, if you'd prefer.
> **(C) I'll download it today.**

해석

새 디자인 소프트웨어의 특징들은 어떤가요?

(A) 아니요, 그 색상들이 마음에 들지 않아요.

(B) 네, 당신이 좋다면요.

(C) 전 오늘 내려받을 거예요.

어휘

feature 특징, 특색 prefer 좋아하다, 선호하다

기출 표현 PLUS⁺

They work very well. 잘 작동돼요.

I'm still getting used to it. 적응하는 중이에요.

8. [미남] [미녀] 🎧

> How will you get to the post office this afternoon?
> (A) I'll visit there tonight at the latest.
> **(B) I'll take a taxi.**
> (C) You will get plenty of rest.

해석

오늘 오후에 우체국에 어떻게 갈 거예요?

(A) 늦어도 오늘 밤에 그곳에 갈 거예요.

(B) 택시를 탈 거예요.

(C) 당신은 충분한 휴식을 취할 거예요.

어휘

at the latest 늦어도 plenty of 풍부한, 많은

기출 표현 PLUS⁺

Robert will give me a ride there.
로버트가 거기까지 태워다 주기로 했어요.
I think I'll walk there. 걸어서 가려구요.

9. 미남 미녀 🎧

> How many people visited the house for sale on Mill Street?
> (A) Let's meet at your house.
> (B) It was a good offer.
> **(C) About 25.**

해석

밀 가에 매물로 나온 그 집에 몇 명이 방문했나요?
(A) 당신 집에서 만나요.
(B) 좋은 제안이었어요.
(C) 약 25명이요.

어휘

for sale 팔려고 내놓은

기출 표현 PLUS⁺

About six or seven. 예닐곱 명쯤이요.
Only two people came. 겨우 두 명 왔어요.

10. 미녀 호남 🎧

> How quickly can you finish proofreading the manuscript?
> (A) At a publishing company.
> (B) Sign on the last page.
> **(C) I need two more hours.**

해석

당신은 얼마나 빨리 원고 교정을 끝낼 수 있나요?
(A) 출판사에서요.
(B) 마지막 페이지에 서명하세요.
(C) 두 시간 더 필요해요.

어휘

proofread 교정을 보다 manuscript 원고 publishing 출판

기출 표현 PLUS⁺

Give me two more days. 이틀 더 주세요.
Can I send it to you tomorrow? 제가 내일 보내도 될까요?

11. 미녀 호남 🎧

> How can I print on both sides of the paper?
> (A) Yes, I'd print in color.
> (B) The employee handbook.
> **(C) Press this blue button.**

해석

어떻게 하면 양면 인쇄를 할 수 있나요?
(A) 네, 제가 컬러로 인쇄하겠습니다.
(B) 직원 안내서입니다.
(C) 이 파란색 버튼을 누르세요.

어휘

in color 컬러로 handbook 안내서, 편람

기출 표현 PLUS⁺

Fix the settings on your computer. 컴퓨터 설정을 고치세요.
Press this button here. 여기 이 버튼을 누르세요.

12. 호남 영녀 🎧

> How often does the production list have to be updated?
> (A) I noticed that earlier.
> (B) They're kept in the storage room.
> **(C) Every time products are shipped abroad.**

해석

생산 품목이 얼마나 자주 업데이트되어야 하나요?
(A) 전 더 일찍 알아차렸어요.
(B) 그것들은 창고에 보관됩니다.
(C) 제품이 해외로 선적될 때마다요.

어휘

production 생산 notice 알아차리다; 통지, 주목
storage room 창고 every time ~할 때마다 ship 수송하다
abroad 해외에, 해외로

기출 표현 PLUS⁺

Twice a day. 하루에 두 번이요.
At the end of every day. 일과 끝날 때마다요.

13. 호남 영녀 🎧

> How much did sales decrease this quarter?
> (A) Because it was on sale.
> (B) I'll tell headquarters by e-mail.
> **(C) By 20 percent.**

해석

이번 분기에 매출이 얼마나 감소했나요?
(A) 세일 중이었기 때문이에요.
(B) 제가 본사에 이메일로 알릴게요.
(C) 20퍼센트요.

어휘

decrease 감소하다, 줄다 quarter 분기
on sale 할인 중인, 판매되는 headquarters 본사

기출 표현 PLUS⁺

By nearly 15 percent. 거의 15퍼센트요.
Not much. 그렇게 많이는 아니에요.

14. 호남 영녀 🎧

> How will the cleaning staff get into the building?
> **(A) The security guard can let them in.**
> (B) They're renovating the fifth floor.
> (C) The work will be done by Wednesday.

해석

청소 직원들은 어떻게 건물에 들어가나요?
(A) 보안 요원이 그들을 안으로 들여보내 주면 됩니다.
(B) 그들은 5층을 보수하고 있어요.
(C) 그 작업은 수요일까지 끝날 것입니다.

어휘

security guard 보안 요원, 경비원 renovate 개조하다, 보수하다
be done 끝나다

기출 표현 PLUS⁺

They all have ID cards. 모두 ID카드를 가지고 있어요.
The receptionist will let them in.
안내원이 들여보내 줄 거예요.

15. 미녀 영녀 🎧

> How often do you visit the manufacturing plant?
> (A) Grace Stein, the floor manager.
> (B) It's in Portland, I think.
> **(C) I haven't had a reason to lately.**

해석

얼마나 자주 제조 공장에 방문하나요?
(A) 작업장 관리자인 그레이스 스타인입니다.
(B) 포틀랜드에서인 것 같아요.
(C) 최근에는 그럴 이유가 없었어요.

어휘

manufacturing plant 제조 공장 floor (건물 내의) 작업장, 현장

기출 표현 PLUS⁺

Usually three times a year. 보통 일 년에 세 번이요.
I almost never go there. 거의 가지 않아요.

UNIT 06 Why 의문문

CHECK UP   본문 p.82

1. (B)   **2.** (C)   **3.** (A)   **4.** (A)

1. 미남 미녀 🎧

> Why was the alarm going off?
> (A) Yes, we were alarmed.
> **(B) For a system check.**
> (C) At least a few times.

해석

경보기가 왜 울렸던 거죠?
(A) 네, 우리는 놀랐어요.
(B) 시스템 점검을 위해서요.
(C) 적어도 몇 번이요.

어휘

alarm 경보, 경보기; 놀라게 하다, 경보하다
go off (경보기 등이) 울리다 at least 적어도

기출 표현 PLUS⁺

There was a fire drill. 소방 훈련이 있었어요.
It was a false alarm. 오작동이었어요.

2. 미남 미녀 🎧

> Why isn't Mr. Watson in his office?
> (A) Check on the right.
> (B) His door is closed.
> **(C) He is out sick.**

해석

왓슨 씨가 왜 그의 사무실에 없나요?
(A) 오른쪽을 확인하세요.
(B) 그의 방 문이 닫혀 있어요.
(C) 그는 아파서 결근했어요.

어휘

check on ~을 확인하다 be out sick 아파서 결근[결석]하다

기출 표현 PLUS⁺

He's on a business trip. 출장중이에요.
He's on vacation. 휴가중이에요.
He's in the cafeteria. 구내식당에 있어요.

3. 미남 미녀 🎧

> Why did the Finance department send that
> memo?
> **(A) You received a memo?**
> (B) I'm sure they can do that.
> (C) Directly to the client.

해석

회계부가 왜 회람을 보냈나요?
(A) 회람을 받으셨어요?
(B) 그들이 그렇게 할 수 있다고 확신해요.
(C) 고객에게 직접이요.

어휘

finance department 회계부, 경리부
directly to ~에게로 직접, 곧장

기출 표현 PLUS⁺

I didn't get a memo. 저는 못 받았어요.
I have no idea. 모르겠어요.

4. 미남 미녀 🎧

Why is the library closing early tonight?
(A) Because it's a holiday.
(B) A couple of librarians.
(C) This was the closest place.

해석

도서관이 왜 오늘 밤 문을 일찍 닫나요?
(A) 휴일이기 때문이에요.
(B) 사서들 두서너 명이요.
(C) 여기가 가장 가까운 곳이었어요.

어휘

librarian (도서관의) 사서

기출 표현 PLUS⁺

There is a hurricane coming tonight.
오늘 밤 허리케인이 닥칠 거예요.
It closes early on Fridays. 금요일마다 일찍 닫아요.

연습 문제   본문 p.84

1. (C)   **2.** (A)   **3.** (C)   **4.** (A)   **5.** (B)

---

1. 미녀 호남 🎧

Why did you choose Macon Airlines?
(A) Yes, I bought a ticket.
(B) An international flight.
(C) Because it's the cheapest.

해석

당신은 왜 메이컨 에어라인을 선택했나요?
(A) 네, 제가 티켓을 샀어요.
(B) 국제선입니다.
(C) 가장 싸기 때문이에요.

어휘

airline 항공사   international 국제적인   flight 항공편, 비행기

기출 표현 PLUS⁺

It has the best airline food. 기내식이 가장 훌륭해서요.
I have a rewards card with them.
그 항공사의 리워드 카드를 가지고 있어요.

2. 미녀 호남 🎧

Why haven't they received the payment?
(A) I forgot to send it.
(B) The billing department.
(C) After March 1st.

해석

그들은 왜 지급을 받지 못했나요?
(A) 제가 보내는 걸 잊었어요.

(B) 청구서 발송과예요.
(C) 3월 1일 이후예요.

어휘

payment 지불, 지급, 납입   billing department 청구서 발송과

기출 표현 PLUS⁺

The transfer takes a while. 송금하는 데 시간이 좀 걸려요.
Are you sure they didn't get it?
그들이 못 받은 게 확실한가요?

---

3. 미녀 호남 🎧

Why was the employee picnic canceled?
(A) At Burbank Park.
(B) Every summer in August.
(C) Because of bad weather.

해석

직원 야유회는 왜 취소되었나요?
(A) 버뱅크 파크에서요.
(B) 매년 여름 8월에요.
(C) 날씨가 안 좋아서요.

어휘

cancel 취소하다

기출 표현 PLUS⁺

There's a storm coming. 폭풍우가 올 거예요.
The manager is sick. 매니저가 아파서요.

---

4. 미녀 호남 🎧

Why is Mr. Gonzalo visiting our branch?
(A) To meet the staff.
(B) Next Wednesday.
(C) It's a traffic jam.

해석

곤살로 씨가 왜 우리 지사에 방문하나요?
(A) 직원들을 만나기 위해서요.
(B) 다음 주 수요일이요.
(C) 교통 체증이에요.

어휘

branch 지사, 지점   staff ((집합적)) 직원   traffic jam 교통 체증

기출 표현 PLUS⁺

To perform a safety inspection. 안전검사를 하기 위해서요.
To greet the new employees.
새 직원들에게 인사하기 위해서요.

---

5. 미녀 호남 🎧

Why has my credit card been rejected?
(A) A fuel-efficient car.
(B) You'll have to contact the company directly.
(C) The receipt can be used for returns.

실전 문제   본문 p.85

1. (B)	2. (C)	3. (C)	4. (A)	5. (C)
6. (B)	7. (C)	8. (C)	9. (C)	10. (C)
11. (B)	12. (B)	13. (A)	14. (C)	15. (B)

1. 미남 영녀 🎧

Why did you recommend taking this road instead
of the highway?
(A) Across the small bridge.
(B) Because it'll be much less crowded.
(C) You could lower it a little bit.

해석

왜 고속도로 대신 이 길로 가는 것을 추천했나요?
(A) 작은 다리를 건너서요.
(B) 훨씬 덜 혼잡하기 때문이에요.
(C) 조금 낮출 수 있습니다.

어휘

crowded 혼잡한, 붐비는 lower 낮추다, 내리다

기출 표현 PLUS+

We'll get there faster. 더 빨리 갈 수 있어요.
There's no traffic here. 이 길이 차가 안 막혀요.

2. 미남 영녀 🎧

Why did you think that I was going abroad?
(A) Just a few days, I think.
(B) It would be a good excuse.
(C) I saw a plane ticket on your desk.

해석

왜 제가 외국에 간다고 생각하셨어요?
(A) 겨우 며칠인 것 같아요.
(B) 그건 좋은 변명이 될 거예요.
(C) 당신 책상에서 비행기 티켓을 봤어요.

어휘

go abroad 외국에 가다 a good excuse 좋은 변명, 좋은 구실

기출 표현 PLUS+

I thought you said you were. 전에 얘기해 줬던 것 같아요.
Ms. Donna told me you were. 도나 씨가 알려줬어요.

3. 미녀 미남 🎧

Why didn't Ms. Granger's article appear in the
magazine?
(A) Let's order a subscription.
(B) A local newspaper.
(C) They're still fact-checking it.

해석

왜 그레인저 씨의 기사가 잡지에 실리지 않았나요?
(A) 정기 구독을 신청합시다.
(B) 지역 신문이에요.
(C) 그들이 아직 사실 확인을 하고 있어요.

어휘

subscription 정기 구독 fact-check 사실 확인을 하다

기출 표현 PLUS+

It has to be edited. 편집이 필요해서요.
We didn't have enough space. 공간이 충분하지 않았어요.

4. 미녀 미남 🎧

Why has the company picnic been postponed?
(A) Poor weather is expected.
(B) Hopefully at Columbia Park.
(C) Please bring a blanket.

해석

왜 회사 야유회가 연기되었나요?
(A) 날씨가 안 좋을 거예요.
(B) 바라건대 콜롬비아 파크에서요.
(C) 담요를 가져오세요.

어휘

postpone 연기하다, 미루다 expect 기대하다, 예상하다
hopefully 바라건대

기출 표현 PLUS+

Didn't you receive the e-mail about that?
그것에 대한 이메일 못 받았어요?
There's rain in the forecast. 비가 올 거예요.

5. 영녀 호남 🎧

Why did you place an ad in the newspaper?
(A) It will take place over three days.
(B) Which paper do you usually read?
(C) To recruit full-time staff members.

해석

왜 신문에 광고를 냈나요?
(A) 그것은 3일에 걸쳐 열릴 거예요.
(B) 당신은 보통 어떤 신문을 읽어요?
(C) 상근 직원을 모집하려고요.

어휘

place an ad 광고를 내다 take place 일어나다, 개최되다
recruit 모집하다, 뽑다 full-time 상근의, 전임의

기출 표현 PLUS⁺

We're looking for new employees.
새로운 직원들을 뽑고 있거든요.
To find new interns. 새로운 인턴을 찾으려고요.

6. 영녀 호남 🎧

Why is there a stack of reference books over here?
(A) To leave work earlier.
(B) Susan said she needed them.
(C) No, they are out of stock.

해석

왜 이쪽에 참고 도서가 쌓여 있죠?
(A) 더 일찍 퇴근하려고요.
(B) 수잔이 필요하다고 했어요.
(C) 아니요, 그것들은 품절이에요.

어휘

a stack of 한 무더기의 ~ reference book 참고 도서
out of stock 품절된

기출 표현 PLUS⁺

I forgot to put them back. 다시 가져다 놓는다는 걸 깜박했네요.
Barnie was looking at them. 바니가 보고 있었어요.

7. 미남 미녀 🎧

Why does the office look so empty this afternoon?
(A) I'll see you in the morning.
(B) Because your office is next to mine.
(C) A lot of people left early.

해석

오늘 오후에 왜 이렇게 사무실이 비어 보이죠?
(A) 아침에 봐요.
(B) 당신의 사무실이 제 사무실 바로 옆이기 때문이에요.
(C) 많은 사람들이 일찍 퇴근했어요.

어휘

empty 비어 있는

기출 표현 PLUS⁺

Some people are on vacation. 휴가중인 사람들이 있어서요.
People left early for the holiday.
휴일을 맞아 일찍 퇴근한 사람들이 있어서요.

8. 미남 미녀 🎧

Why was your business trip canceled?
(A) Yes, our business is popular.
(B) On Tuesday morning.
(C) Because the client changed his mind.

해석

당신의 출장은 왜 취소됐나요?
(A) 네, 우리 사업은 인기가 있어요.
(B) 화요일 오전에요.
(C) 고객이 생각을 바꿨기 때문이에요.

어휘

business trip 출장 change one's mind 생각[의견]을 바꾸다

기출 표현 PLUS⁺

There's a storm in the area. 그 지역에 폭풍이 와서요.
Holly will go instead. 홀리가 대신 갈 거예요.

9. 미남 미녀 🎧

Why isn't Ms. Camila in her office?
(A) Take the stairs to your right.
(B) I think it was changed to 4 o'clock.
(C) All the managers are at a staff meeting.

해석

카밀라 씨는 왜 그녀의 사무실에 없나요?
(A) 오른쪽에 있는 계단을 이용하세요.
(B) 4시 정각으로 변경된 것 같아요.
(C) 모든 관리자들이 직원 회의 중이에요.

어휘

staff meeting 직원 회의

기출 표현 PLUS⁺

She and the other interns have a meeting.
그녀랑 나머지 인턴들이 회의 중이에요.
Are you sure she's not there? 자리에 없는 게 확실해요?

10. 미녀 호남 🎧

Why are the packaging machines running so slowly?
(A) As soon as the business opens.
(B) That's a useful recommendation.
(C) Those will be inspected soon.

해석

포장 기계들이 왜 이렇게 느리게 작동하나요?
(A) 그 업체가 문을 열자마자요.
(B) 그것은 유용한 추천이에요.
(C) 그것들이 곧 점검될 거예요.

어휘

packaging 포장, 포장재 run 작동하다, 기능하다
recommendation 추천 inspect 점검하다, 검사하다

You should ask the manager. 관리자에게 물어보세요.
Maybe they need to be fixed. 수리가 필요할 거예요.

11. 미녀 호남 🎧

> Why hasn't the work schedule been posted yet?
> (A) Yes, I finished my work on time.
> **(B) I'll have to check with Samir.**
> (C) A national holiday.

해석

작업 일정이 왜 아직 게시되지 않았나요?
(A) 네, 정각에 제 일을 끝냈어요.
(B) 제가 사미르 씨에게 문의해야 할 거예요.
(C) 국경일입니다.

어휘

post 게시하다, 공고하다   on time 시간을 어기지 않고, 정각에
check with ~와 상담하다, ~에게 문의하다
national holiday 국경일

It's still uploading. 업로드 중이에요.
I'll finish it later. 이따가 마무리할게요.

12. 호남 영녀 🎧

> Why did you book a layover in Dallas?
> (A) When does your flight arrive?
> **(B) To get a better ticket price.**
> (C) Yes, I grew up there.

해석

왜 댈러스를 경유하는 것으로 예약했나요?
(A) 당신의 비행편은 언제 도착하나요?
(B) 티켓을 더 싸게 사려고요.
(C) 네, 저는 그곳에서 자랐어요.

어휘

book 예약하다
layover (= stopover) (여행 중에) 잠시 들르기, 단기 체류
flight 항공편, 비행기   grow up 성장하다

It's faster that way. 그게 더 빠르거든요.
I wanted to save some money. 돈을 절약하고 싶어서요.

13. 호남 영녀 🎧

> Why has the train been stopped so long at this station?
> **(A) Didn't you hear the announcement?**
> (B) I'll keep my bag with me.
> (C) It's not supposed to rain today.

해석

기차가 왜 이 역에 이렇게 오래 정차하나요?
(A) 안내 방송 못 들었어요?
(B) 제 가방은 제가 가지고 있을게요.
(C) 오늘은 비가 오지 않을 거예요.

어휘

announcement 안내, 공지
be supposed to do ~하기로 되어 있다

I think there was an accident. 사고가 있었던 것 같아요.
It's not the departure time yet. 아직 출발 시간이 안 됐어요.

14. 호남 영녀 🎧

> Why aren't we invited to the sales meeting?
> (A) No, I arrived on time.
> (B) The customer service procedures.
> **(C) It's only for senior staff members.**

해석

우리는 왜 영업 회의에 부르지 않나요?
(A) 아니요, 저는 정각에 도착했어요.
(B) 고객 서비스 절차입니다.
(C) 고위 직원들만을 위한 것이에요.

어휘

procedure 절차   senior staff member 고위 직원

Only managers will attend. 매니저들만 참석할 거예요.
You weren't invited? 참석 요청을 받지 않았어요?

15. 미남 호남 🎧

> Why are you taking an acting class?
> (A) A well-known movie actor apparently.
> **(B) For my own enjoyment.**
> (C) They have interesting characters.

해석

왜 연기 수업을 듣고 있나요?
(A) 듣자 하니 유명한 영화 배우예요.
(B) 제 자신의 만족을 위해서요.
(C) 그것들에는 흥미로운 등장인물들이 나와요.

어휘

well-known 잘 알려진, 유명한   apparently 듣자 하니, 보아 하니
enjoyment 즐거움, 기쁨   character 등장인물, 특징, 성격

Because it's my hobby. 제 취미라서요.
I want to become an actor. 연기자가 되고 싶어요.

UNIT 07 조동사 의문문

CHECK UP
본문 p.86

1. (C) **2.** (A) **3.** (B) **4.** (A)

1. 미남 미녀 🎧

Can I place an international call from my hotel room?
(A) No, it's at Gate 17.
(B) We're fully booked.
(C) There will be an extra fee.

해석

제 호텔 방에서 국제전화를 할 수 있나요?
(A) 아뇨, 17번 게이트입니다.
(B) 예약이 다 찼습니다.
(C) 추가 요금이 있을 것입니다.

어휘

place a call 전화를 걸다 international call 국제 전화
fully booked 예약이 다 찬 extra fee 추가 요금

기출 표현 PLUS⁺

No, sorry. 죄송합니다만 안 됩니다.
It will cost a lot of money. 돈이 많이 들 겁니다.

2. 미남 미녀 🎧

Did you park in the stadium's parking lot?
(A) I took the bus here.
(B) The championship game.
(C) The team did very well.

해석

경기장의 주차장에 주차했나요?
(A) 이곳에 버스를 타고 왔어요.
(B) 챔피언 결정전이에요.
(C) 그 팀은 아주 잘했어요.

어휘

park 주차하다 championship game 챔피언 결정전, 결승전

기출 표현 PLUS⁺

Yes, I managed to get a spot.
네, 간신히 주차 자리를 찾았어요.
No, there were too many cars. 아뇨, 차가 너무 많더라구요.

3. 미남 미녀 🎧

Do you have fresh fruits on your dessert menu?
(A) Thanks, but I'm not hungry.
(B) Yes, we have strawberries and peaches.
(C) They make these locally.

해석

디저트 메뉴에 신선한 과일이 있나요?
(A) 고맙지만, 전 배가 고프지 않아요.
(B) 네, 딸기와 복숭아가 있어요.
(C) 그들은 이것들을 현지에서 만듭니다.

어휘

locally 지역적으로, 현지에서

기출 표현 PLUS⁺

No, we only have cake. 아뇨, 케이크만 있어요.
Yes, we have seasonal fruits. 네, 제철 과일이 있어요.

4. 미남 미녀 🎧

Should we save some of these decorations for next year's party?
(A) That's a good idea.
(B) I'll invite them right away.
(C) On the laptop.

해석

내년 파티를 위해 우리가 이 장식품들 중 일부를 남겨 둬야 하나요?
(A) 그거 좋은 생각이에요.
(B) 제가 그들을 당장 초대할게요.
(C) 노트북 컴퓨터에요.

어휘

save 남겨 두다, 아끼다 decoration 장식품, 장식

기출 표현 PLUS⁺

I don't think so. 그럴 필요 없을 거예요.
We can just throw these away. 그냥 버려도 돼요.

연습 문제
본문 p.88

1. (B) **2.** (B) **3.** (B) **4.** (B) **5.** (A)

1. 미남 영녀 🎧

Should the roof be inspected for a leak?
(A) It was released last weekend.
(B) That's not a bad idea.
(C) Next to the reception desk.

해석

지붕이 새는지 점검해야 할까요?
(A) 그것은 지난 주말에 출시되었어요.
(B) 그거 괜찮은 생각이네요.

(C) 접수처 바로 옆이에요.

어휘

inspect 점검하다, 검사하다 leak 새는 곳; 새다
release 발매하다, 공개하다
reception desk 접수처, (호텔의) 프런트

기출 표현 PLUS⁺

I think that's a good idea. 좋은 생각이에요.
We just inspected it last month. 지난달에 점검했어요.

2. 미남 영녀 🎧

> Has our flight been delayed?
> (A) Has he signed off on it?
> **(B) I can look up the status on my phone.**
> (C) I was late again due to the traffic.

해석

우리 비행기가 지연되었나요?
(A) 그가 그것을 결재했나요?
(B) 제가 제 전화기로 상태를 알아볼게요.
(C) 저는 교통 체증 때문에 또 늦었어요.

어휘

flight 항공편, 항공기 delay 지연시키다; 지연, 지체
sign off (서명을 하여) ~을 승인하다 look up (정보를) 찾아보다
status 상태; 지위 traffic 차량들, 교통(량)

기출 표현 PLUS⁺

The announcement said it was.
안내방송에서 그렇게 나왔어요.
No, it's still on time. 아뇨. 제시간에 운행되고 있어요.

3. 미남 영녀 🎧

> Will Thomas join us for Friday's staff meeting?
> (A) Sure, I can help you.
> **(B) Yes, he'll be attending.**
> (C) We really enjoyed it.

해석

토마스가 우리와 같이 금요일 직원 회의를 할 건가요?
(A) 그럼요, 제가 도와드릴 수 있어요.
(B) 네, 그가 참석할 거예요.
(C) 우리는 정말 그것을 즐거워했어요.

어휘

attend 참석하다, 출석하다

기출 표현 PLUS⁺

I believe so. 그럴 거예요.
He can't make it. 그는 참석할 수 없을 거예요.

4. 미남 영녀 🎧

> Did you buy the replacement parts for the computer?
> (A) Under 50 dollars.
> **(B) They're being installed now.**
> (C) Three computers in Sales.

해석

컴퓨터의 교체 부품을 구입했나요?
(A) 50달러 미만입니다.
(B) 그것들이 지금 설치되고 있는 중이에요.
(C) 영업부의 컴퓨터 3대입니다.

어휘

replacement 교체, 대체 install 설치하다
Sales (= Sales Department) 영업부

기출 표현 PLUS⁺

Yes, I got them yesterday. 네, 어제 구입했어요.
No, not yet. 아뇨, 아직요.

5. 미남 영녀 🎧

> Have you ever managed a finance team?
> **(A) Yes, back when I worked for Fordman's.**
> (B) The bank will finance it.
> (C) The manager approved them.

해석

재무팀을 관리한 적이 있나요?
(A) 네, 예전에 제가 포드맨에서 일했을 때요.
(B) 은행이 그것에 융자를 해 줄 겁니다.
(C) 관리자가 그것들을 승인했어요.

어휘

finance 재원, 금융; 자금을 대다 approve 승인하다, 허가하다

기출 표현 PLUS⁺

No, I haven't. 아뇨.
Yes, for many years. 네, 여러 해 동안요.

실전 문제 본문 p.89

1. (C)	2. (C)	3. (C)	4. (A)	5. (C)
6. (A)	7. (C)	8. (A)	9. (A)	10. (B)
11. (A)	12. (B)	13. (A)	14. (C)	15. (B)

1. 미남 영녀 🎧

> Did you hear the news about the vacation policy?
> (A) A famous hotel.
> (B) Yes, she's my assistant.
> **(C) I wasn't in the meeting.**

해석

휴가 정책에 관한 소식을 들었어요?
(A) 유명한 호텔이에요.
(B) 네, 그녀는 제 비서예요.
(C) 저는 회의에 참석하지 않았어요.

어휘

vacation policy 휴가 정책 assistant 조수, 보조, 비서

기출 표현 PLUS⁺

What did they say? 무슨 내용이었나요?
Yes, I heard from Jarrod. 네, 재로드에게서 들었어요.

2. 미남 영녀 🎧

> Do you need a new whiteboard marker?
> (A) We'll meet in the conference room.
> (B) A discussion on policies.
> **(C) Yes, this one has dried up.**

해석

새 화이트보드 마커펜이 필요하세요?
(A) 우리는 회의실에서 만날 거예요.
(B) 정책에 관한 논의예요.
(C) 네, 이것은 다 말랐어요.

어휘

marker 마커펜, 표시를 하는 사람[도구] discussion 논의, 상의
policy 정책 dry up 바싹 마르다, 말라붙다

기출 표현 PLUS⁺

No, this one is fine. 아뇨, 쓸 만해요.
Yes, please give me one. 네, 하나만 주세요.

3. 미녀 미남 🎧

> Have you seen the play at the Three Moons
> Theater?
> (A) You did pay with a credit card.
> (B) You're right about that.
> **(C) Yes, I went there last weekend.**

해석

쓰리 문스 극장에서 하는 연극 봤어요?
(A) 당신은 신용카드로 지불했어요.
(B) 그 점에 대해서는 당신 말이 맞아요.
(C) 네, 지난 주말에 그곳에 갔었어요.

어휘

play 연극, 희곡 pay with ~으로 지불하다

기출 표현 PLUS⁺

No, I've never been there. 아뇨, 거기 가 본 적이 없어요.
I'm seeing it tonight. 오늘 밤에 볼 거예요.

4. 미녀 미남 🎧

> Have you thought about investing in a startup
> company?
> **(A) That seems like it could be risky.**
> (B) This card was issued by my bank.
> (C) I've worked here for years.

해석

스타트업 회사에 투자하는 것에 대해 생각해 봤어요?
(A) 그건 위험할 것 같아요.
(B) 이 카드는 제가 거래하는 은행에서 발급되었어요.
(C) 저는 여러 해 동안 여기서 일했어요.

어휘

invest in ~에 투자하다
startup company 신생 기업, 스타트업 회사 risky 위험한
issue 발부하다

기출 표현 PLUS⁺

I don't have the funds. 저는 투자할 돈이 없어요.
No, because it's too risky. 아뇨, 그건 너무 위험해요.

5. 영녀 호남 🎧

> Will our proposal get to the city council on time?
> (A) In the central square.
> (B) A 10% increase.
> **(C) I sent it by overnight mail.**

해석

우리의 제안서가 시간 맞춰 시 의회에 도착할까요?
(A) 중앙 광장에서요.
(B) 10% 인상이요.
(C) 제가 그걸 빠른 우편으로 보냈어요.

어휘

proposal 제안 city council 시 의회
on time 시간을 어기지 않고, 정각에
increase 증가, 인상; 증가하다
overnight mail (다음 날 배달되는) 빠른 우편

기출 표현 PLUS⁺

I hope so. 그러면 좋겠네요.
Joseph is taking it there now.
조셉이 지금 제출하러 가고 있어요.

6. 영녀 호남 🎧

> Did the food critic like the meal he had at our
> restaurant?
> **(A) Yes, he loved it.**
> (B) I go there often.
> (C) No, at his office.

해석

그 음식 비평가가 우리 식당에서 먹은 음식을 좋아했나요?

(A) 네, 그가 아주 좋아했어요.
(B) 저는 종종 그곳에 가요.
(C) 아니요, 그의 사무실에서요.

어휘
food critic 음식 비평가

기출 표현 PLUS⁺
Yes, he said it was delicious. 네, 맛있다고 했어요.
He didn't say much about it. 별말 없었어요.

7. 미남 미녀 🎧

Will the deadline be pushed back?
(A) A catalog layout.
(B) No, I've been in this line.
(C) The client has been waiting for a while.

해석
마감일이 미뤄질까요?
(A) 카탈로그 레이아웃이요.
(B) 아니요, 저는 이 줄에 있었어요.
(C) 고객이 한참을 기다려 왔어요.

해설
(C)는 고객이 오랫동안 기다려 왔으므로 마감일을 미룰 수 없을 것
이라는 우회적인 답변이다.

어휘
deadline 마감 시간, 마감일 push back 미루다
layout 레이아웃, 배치 wait for a while 한참 동안 기다리다

기출 표현 PLUS⁺
I don't think so. 그렇지 않을 거예요.
It will be pushed back two weeks. 2주 늦춰질 거예요.
I think they could extend the deadline by about two
weeks. 2주 정도 기한을 연장해 줄 수 있을 거예요.

8. 미남 미녀 🎧

Should I start working on the 23rd Street project
now?
(A) We need to hurry to meet the deadline.
(B) It has a lot of foot traffic here.
(C) I live nearby.

해석
23번가 프로젝트 작업을 지금 시작해야 하나요?
(A) 기한에 맞추려면 서둘러야 해요.
(B) 여기는 유동 인구가 많아요.
(C) 저는 근처에 살아요.

어휘
work on ~을 작업하다, ~에 노력을 들이다 foot traffic 유동 인구

기출 표현 PLUS⁺
Why don't you check your other deadlines first?
다른 마감일들을 먼저 확인해 보는 게 어때요?
There's no need to hurry. 서두를 필요 없어요.

9. 미남 미녀 🎧

Has the new business proposal been updated?
(A) We finished doing that last week.
(B) Yes, we set a date.
(C) He was on a business trip.

해석
새로운 사업 제안서가 업데이트됐나요?
(A) 우리는 지난주에 그것을 끝냈어요.
(B) 네, 날짜를 정했어요.
(C) 그는 출장 중이었어요.

어휘
business proposal 사업 제안서
update 최신의 것으로 하다, 갱신하다 business trip 출장

기출 표현 PLUS⁺
I think it should be. 업데이트되어야 할걸요.
No, we have to finish soon. 아뇨, 곧 끝내야 해요.

10. 미녀 호남 🎧

Will Mr. Foster be starting the new project
immediately?
(A) He did a great job.
(B) No, he said he was going on vacation first.
(C) It is a really good idea.

해석
포스터 씨가 즉시 새로운 프로젝트를 시작할 예정인가요?
(A) 그는 일을 잘했어요.
(B) 아니요, 그는 일단 휴가를 갈 거라고 했어요.
(C) 정말 좋은 생각이에요.

어휘
immediately 즉시 go on vacation 휴가를 가다

기출 표현 PLUS⁺
You'll have to ask him. 그에게 물어보셔야 해요.
He said he would. 그럴 거래요.

11. 미녀 호남 🎧

Do you think the new brochure gives enough
information?
(A) There should be more pictures.
(B) Thank you. I've had enough.
(C) In the company directory.

해석
새로운 안내 책자가 충분한 정보를 제공한다고 생각하나요?
(A) 사진이 더 많이 있어야 해요.
(B) 고맙습니다. 충분히 먹었습니다.
(C) 회사 인명부에서요.

어휘
brochure (안내, 광고용) 소책자, 브로슈어

directory 주소 성명록, 인명부

I think we can add more. 더 추가해도 좋을 것 같아요.
It's fine the way it is. 그대로도 괜찮아 보여요.

12. 호남 영녀 🎧

> Did Brenda call someone to fix the window?
> (A) No, I couldn't hear any noise.
> **(B) Yes, a repair crew will be here soon.**
> (C) To fix the date.

해석

브렌다가 창문을 고칠 사람을 불렀나요?
(A) 아니요, 저는 아무 소리도 못 들었어요.
(B) 네, 수리반이 곧 올 거예요.
(C) 날짜를 정하기 위해서요.

어휘

fix 고치다; (날짜·장소 등을) 정하다   repair 수리; 수리하다
crew (함께 일을 하는) 팀, 반, 조

기출 표현 PLUS+

Yes, the maintenance worker is coming.
네, 관리실 직원이 올 거예요.
No, Marcus did. 아뇨, 마커스가 불렀어요.

13. 호남 영녀 🎧

> Should we send Neon Corporation our new brochures?
> **(A) No, I've already mailed them.**
> (B) They are better than the old ones.
> (C) How many do you want?

해석

우리가 네온 사에 새 안내 책자들을 보내야 하나요?
(A) 아니요, 제가 이미 그것들을 우편으로 보냈어요.
(B) 그것들이 이전 것들보다 나아요.
(C) 얼마나 드릴까요?

어휘

mail 우편으로 보내다, 부치다

기출 표현 PLUS+

Yes, please send them. 네, 보내주세요.
No, that's already been taken care of.
아뇨, 벌써 처리했어요.

14. 호남 영녀 🎧

> Do you have a lighter printer than this one?
> (A) Hand out the brochures, please.
> (B) Yes, it was a colored one.
> **(C) No, it is the lightest one.**

해석

이것보다 더 가벼운 프린터가 있나요?
(A) 안내 책자를 나눠 주시기 바랍니다.
(B) 네, 그것은 컬러였어요.
(C) 아니요, 그게 가장 가벼운 거예요.

어휘

hand out 나눠 주다, 배포하다   colored 컬러의

기출 표현 PLUS+

Yes, we have one that's lighter. 네, 더 가벼운 게 하나 있어요.
Let me check in the back. 있는지 확인해 볼게요.

15. 미녀 영녀 🎧

> Does your team have enough people to cover Henry's absence?
> (A) The September edition.
> **(B) We've hired two more people.**
> (C) A few times a day.

해석

당신 팀에 헨리의 부재를 메울 사람들이 충분히 있나요?
(A) 9월 호요.
(B) 우리가 두 명 더 고용했어요.
(C) 하루에 몇 번이요.

어휘

cover (부재중인 사람을) 대신하다, ~의 책임을 지다
absence 결석, 결근, 부재   edition (간행물의) 판, 호

기출 표현 PLUS+

Yes, we'll be fine. 네, 괜찮을 거예요.
No, we need some extra help. 아뇨, 도움이 필요해요.

UNIT 08 Be동사 의문문

CHECK UP　　　　　　　　　본문 p.90

| **1.** (C) | **2.** (B) | **3.** (C) | **4.** (C) |

1. 미남 미녀 🎧

> Are you going to join the new gym?
> (A) It keeps me in shape.
> (B) A membership fee.
> **(C) I don't think so.**

해석

새로운 체육관에 가입할 거예요?
(A) 그것이 저를 건강하게 해줘요.
(B) 회비입니다.
(C) 그렇지는 않을 거예요.

keep in shape 건강을 유지하다 membership fee 회비

Probably not. 그러진 않을 거예요.

I'd like to look at some other places first.
먼저 다른 곳들을 알아보려고요.

2. 미남 미녀 🎧

> Are you ready to go for lunch?
> (A) I heard there's a long wait.
> **(B) I just found out I have a conference call.**
> (C) The special is $6.

해석

점심 먹으러 갈 준비 됐어요?
(A) 그곳은 오래 기다려야 한다고 들었어요.
(B) 전화 회의가 있는 걸 방금 알았어요.
(C) 특별 메뉴는 6달러입니다.

어휘

find out 알아내다, 알게 되다 conference call 전화 회의
special 특별한 것, 특별 상품

기출 표현 PLUS⁺

Yes, let's go. 네, 출발하죠.

No, give me a few minutes, please.
아뇨, 몇 분만 기다려 주세요.

3. 미남 미녀 🎧

> Is the inventory check on schedule?
> (A) The department store.
> (B) I'll put the check in the mail.
> **(C) Yes, that's what I heard.**

해석

재고 조사는 일정대로 되고 있나요?
(A) 백화점이요.
(B) 수표를 우편으로 보낼게요.
(C) 네, 그렇게 들었어요.

어휘

inventory 재고품 목록 check 확인; 수표
put ~ in the mail ~을 우편으로 보내다

기출 표현 PLUS⁺

I believe so. 그럴 거예요.
It should be. 그럴 거예요.

4. 미남 미녀 🎧

> Is Charlie attending this afternoon's meeting?
> (A) Attendance was fairly low.
> (B) The chairs are set up.
> **(C) No, he's still on vacation.**

해석

찰리가 오늘 오후 회의에 참석하나요?
(A) 출석률이 상당히 낮았어요.
(B) 의자들이 준비되었어요.
(C) 아니요, 그는 아직 휴가 중이에요.

어휘

attend 참석하다 attendance 참석, 참석률
set up 세우다, 설치하다, 준비하다 on vacation 휴가 중인

기출 표현 PLUS⁺

Yes, he'll be there. 네, 참석할 거예요.
I think you should ask him. 그에게 직접 물어보셔야 할 거예요.

연습 문제　　　　본문 p.92

| 1. (A) | 2. (B) | 3. (A) | 4. (C) | 5. (C) |

1. 미녀 호남 🎧

> Are you having a meeting today?
> **(A) Yes, around 3.**
> (B) No, not here.
> (C) I'm not very hungry.

해석

오늘 회의를 하나요?
(A) 네, 3시쯤이요.
(B) 아니요, 여기가 아니에요.
(C) 저는 그리 배고프지 않아요.

어휘

have a meeting 회의를 하다, 모임을 가지다

기출 표현 PLUS⁺

No, the meeting is tomorrow. 아뇨, 회의는 내일이에요.
Yes, in Conference Room A. 네, 회의실 A에서 해요.

2. 미녀 호남 🎧

> Were you assigned to the new advertising campaign?
> (A) Thanks for your help.
> **(B) No, I'm busy with another project.**
> (C) A magazine article.

해석

당신은 새로운 광고 캠페인에 배정되었나요?
(A) 도와줘서 고마워요.
(B) 아니요, 저는 다른 프로젝트 때문에 바빠요.
(C) 잡지 기사입니다.

어휘

assign A to B A를 B에 배정하다
be busy with ~하느라 바쁘다

Yes, I'm part of the team. 네, 팀의 일원이에요.
No, I'm helping the development team.
아뇨, 개발팀을 돕고 있어요.

3. 미녀 호남 🎧

Is this ink cartridge compatible with the printer?
(A) The model number is different.
(B) At the reception desk.
(C) Some promotional brochures.

해석
이 잉크 카트리지는 프린터와 호환이 되나요?
(A) 모델 번호가 다릅니다.
(B) 접수처에서요.
(C) 일부 홍보 책자들입니다.

어휘
be compatible with ~와 호환되다
reception desk 접수처, (호텔의) 프런트
promotional 홍보의, 판촉의

기출 표현 PLUS⁺
It doesn't look like it. 그럴 거 같지 않은데요.
It should be. 그럴 거예요.

4. 미녀 호남 🎧

Are these refreshments for everyone?
(A) I need some fresh air.
(B) I'll give them the message.
(C) Please help yourself.

해석
이 다과는 모두를 위한 것인가요?
(A) 신선한 공기를 쐬고 싶어요.
(B) 제가 그들에게 메시지를 전할게요.
(C) 마음껏 드세요.

어휘
refreshments ((항상 복수형)) 다과
Help yourself. 마음껏 드세요.

기출 표현 PLUS⁺
Yes, please take some. 네, 드셔보세요.
We prepared them for the meeting. 회의를 위해 준비했어요.

5. 미녀 호남 🎧

Is Ms. Crawford here at the office today?
(A) There are more in the stockroom.
(B) A new meeting agenda.
(C) I just saw her leave the building.

해석
크로포드 씨가 오늘 이곳 사무실에 있나요?

(A) 창고에 더 있어요.
(B) 새로운 회의 안건입니다.
(C) 방금 건물을 나가는 걸 봤어요.

어휘
stockroom 창고 agenda 의제, 안건

기출 표현 PLUS⁺
I think she's on vacation. 휴가 중일 거예요.
She called out sick today. 오늘 병가를 냈어요.

실전 문제　　　본문 p.93

1. (A)	**2.** (C)	**3.** (B)	**4.** (C)	**5.** (A)
6. (A)	**7.** (B)	**8.** (C)	**9.** (B)	**10.** (C)
11. (B)	**12.** (B)	**13.** (C)	**14.** (C)	**15.** (C)

1. 미남 영녀 🎧

Are you renewing your subscription to the magazine?
(A) I'm not sure I can afford it.
(B) It's as good as new.
(C) Thank you for the article.

해석
당신은 그 잡지의 정기 구독을 갱신할 건가요?
(A) 그럴 여유가 있는지 잘 모르겠어요.
(B) 그것은 새것이나 다름없어요.
(C) 기사에 대해 감사드립니다.

어휘
renew 갱신하다, 연장하다 subscription to ~의 정기 구독
afford (~할 금전적/시간적) 여유가 되다
as good as new 새것 같은

기출 표현 PLUS⁺
No, I'm no longer interested. 아뇨, 더 이상 관심 없어요.
I'm still thinking about it. 아직 생각 중이에요.

2. 미남 영녀 🎧

Are you going to apply for the job in Berlin?
(A) No, she doesn't work there.
(B) Yes, I'm going there now.
(C) I'm afraid the deadline was last Friday.

해석
베를린의 그 일자리에 지원할 건가요?
(A) 아니요, 그녀는 그곳에서 일하지 않아요.
(B) 네, 저는 지금 그곳에 가요.
(C) 유감스럽게도 마감일이 지난 금요일이었어요.

어휘
apply for ~에 지원하다, ~을 신청하다 deadline 마감 기한

Yes, I think it's a great opportunity.

네, 좋은 기회인 것 같아요.

No, I don't want to relocate. 아뇨, 이사하고 싶지 않아요.

3. 미녀 미남 🎧

Are there any plans to welcome our new employees?
(A) There are many new branches.
(B) We're having a party after work.
(C) That's really nice of you.

해석

우리 신입 사원들을 환영하는 무슨 계획이라도 있나요?
(A) 신규 지점들이 많이 있습니다.
(B) 우리는 퇴근 후에 파티를 할 거예요.
(C) 정말 친절하시네요.

어휘

welcome 맞이하다, 환영하다 branch 지점, 지사

기출 표현 PLUS⁺

We don't have anything planned. 아직 아무 계획 없어요.
We're discussing it at the department meeting today. 오늘 부서 회의에서 논의할 거예요.

4. 미녀 미남 🎧

Is this enough food for everyone who's coming?
(A) I brought some more chairs.
(B) That should solve the problem.
(C) Well, we ordered extra sandwiches just in case.

해석

이걸로 오시는 모든 분들에게 충분한 음식이 될까요?
(A) 제가 의자를 몇 개 더 가져왔어요.
(B) 그러면 문제가 해결될 거예요.
(C) 음, 혹시 몰라서 샌드위치를 추가로 주문했어요.

어휘

just in case 혹시 몰라서, 만약을 대비해서

기출 표현 PLUS⁺

It should be enough. 충분할 거예요.
Maybe we should order more. 더 주문해야 할지도 몰라요.

5. 영녀 호남 🎧

Are we going to need our raincoats today?
(A) Yes, it's supposed to rain.
(B) We'll run as fast as we can.
(C) To buy an umbrella.

해석

우리가 오늘 비옷이 필요할까요?

(A) 네, 비가 올 거예요.
(B) 우리는 할 수 있는 한 빨리 달릴 거예요.
(C) 우산을 사기 위해서요.

어휘

be supposed to do ~하기로 되어 있다

기출 표현 PLUS⁺

No, the sky is clear. 아뇨, 하늘이 맑은걸요.
No, it's not going to rain. 아뇨, 비는 안 올 거예요.

6. 영녀 호남 🎧

Are you sure we can fit everything in the van?
(A) Yes, I believe so.
(B) Excuse me, what time is it?
(C) The moving company.

해석

우리가 모든 걸 승합차에 실을 수 있는 것이 확실해요?
(A) 네, 그렇다고 생각해요.
(B) 실례지만, 몇 시인가요?
(C) 이사 회사입니다.

어휘

fit ~을 (…에) 맞추다, 끼우다 van 밴, 승합차

기출 표현 PLUS⁺

We might need another van.
승합차가 하나 더 필요할지 몰라요.
No, I think we need more space.
아뇨, 공간이 부족할 거예요.

7. 미남 미녀 🎧

Is there a dressing room where I can try these shirts on?
(A) The store opened at 11 A.M.
(B) You can follow me.
(C) She's out of the office today.

해석

이 셔츠를 입어 볼 수 있는 탈의실이 있나요?
(A) 그 상점은 오전 11시에 문을 열었습니다.
(B) 저를 따라오세요.
(C) 그녀는 오늘 사무실에 없습니다.

어휘

dressing room 탈의실 try on ~을 입어 보다

기출 표현 PLUS⁺

It's at the back of the store. 가게 뒤쪽에 있어요.
Sorry, we don't have a dressing room.
죄송합니다만 저희는 탈의실이 없습니다.

8. 미남 미녀 🎧

> Are you interested in taking an online Italian class?
> (A) Lots of interesting articles.
> (B) It took longer than expected.
> **(C) No, I'm very busy these days.**

해석

온라인으로 이탈리아어 수업을 듣는 데 관심 있어요?
(A) 많은 흥미로운 기사들입니다.
(B) 예상보다 더 오래 걸렸어요.
(C) 아니요, 저는 요즘 매우 바빠요.

어휘

be interested in ~에 관심[흥미]가 있다   take a class 수강하다
than expected 예상했던 것보다

기출 표현 PLUS⁺

Yes, I would love to. 네, 듣고 싶어요.
I'm not sure I have time. 시간이 될지 모르겠어요.

9. 미남 미녀 🎧

> Is the security team going to issue new ID badges?
> (A) No, we secured the labels.
> **(B) That happens every January.**
> (C) They'll sue the company.

해석

보안팀이 새 신분증을 발급할 예정인가요?
(A) 아니요, 라벨들을 안 떨어지게 단단히 붙였어요.
(B) 그건 매년 1월에 해요.
(C) 그들은 그 회사를 고소할 거예요.

어휘

security 보안, 경비 issue 발급하다; 안건, 문제
ID badge 신분증 secure (단단히) 고정시키다 sue 고소하다

기출 표현 PLUS⁺

I believe they will. 그럴 거예요.
You should ask the security manager.
보안 담당자에게 물어보세요.

10. 미녀 호남 🎧

> Are you responsible for subscription renewals?
> (A) Where's the waiting room?
> (B) A two-year subscription.
> **(C) I work in research and development.**

해석

정기 구독 갱신을 담당하시나요?
(A) 대기실은 어디인가요?
(B) 2년 정기 구독입니다.
(C) 저는 연구 개발팀에서 일해요.

어휘

be responsible for ~의 책임이 있다, ~을 담당하다
subscription 정기 구독 renewal 갱신, (기한) 연장
research and development (= R&D) (기업 등의) 연구 개발

기출 표현 PLUS⁺

No, I'm in marketing. 아뇨, 저는 마케팅 부서에 근무해요.
Yes, do you need help with something?
네, 도움이 필요하세요?

11. 미녀 호남 🎧

> Was Jackie able to negotiate a landscaping contract?
> (A) During Monday's budget meeting.
> **(B) The terms are still being discussed.**
> (C) It's in a good location.

해석

재키가 조경 계약을 협상할 수 있었나요?
(A) 월요일 예산 회의 동안이요.
(B) 계약 조항이 여전히 논의되는 중입니다.
(C) 그것은 좋은 위치에 있어요.

어휘

negotiate 협상하다 landscaping 조경 contract 계약(서)
budget 예산 terms ((항상 복수형)) (합의·계약 등의) 조건
location 위치, 장소

기출 표현 PLUS⁺

She's still in negotiations now. 아직 협상 중이에요.
Yes, she did a great job. 네, 그녀가 잘 해냈어요.

12. 호남 영녀 🎧

> Are you sure we can finish the design on time?
> (A) The clock on the wall.
> **(B) Yes, I think so.**
> (C) Where's the finish line?

해석

우리가 시간에 맞춰 디자인을 마칠 수 있는 것이 확실해요?
(A) 벽에 걸린 시계요.
(B) 네, 그렇게 생각해요.
(C) 결승선이 어디예요?

어휘

on time 시간에 맞춰, 정각에 finish line 결승선

기출 표현 PLUS⁺

If we hurry. 서두른다면요.
We need to ask them to extend the deadline.
그들에게 마감일을 연장해 달라고 요청할 필요가 있어요.

13. 호남 영녀 🎧

> Is Mr. Baek participating in the writing workshop tomorrow?
> (A) Because his clients are overseas.
> (B) Across from the elevators.
> **(C) Adam has the guest list.**

해석

백 씨가 내일 글쓰기 워크숍에 참가하나요?
(A) 그의 고객들이 해외에 있기 때문이에요.
(B) 엘리베이터 맞은편이에요.
(C) 애덤에게 손님 명단이 있어요.

어휘

participate in ~에 참가[참여]하다 overseas 해외에, 외국으로
across from ~의 바로 맞은편에

기출 표현 PLUS+

Yes, he should be. 네, 그럴 거예요.
Ask the receptionist for the guest list.
안내원에게 손님 명단을 요청하세요.

14. 호남 영녀 🎧

> Was the manuscript checked by the editing team?
> (A) No, I transferred departments.
> (B) To get a clear description.
> **(C) We're waiting for two more chapters.**

해석

편집팀에서 그 원고를 검토했나요?
(A) 아니요, 저는 부서를 옮겼어요.
(B) 명확한 설명을 듣기 위해서요.
(C) 아직 두 챕터 남았어요.

어휘

manuscript 원고 editing 편집 transfer 옮기다, 이동하다
description 서술, 묘사

기출 표현 PLUS+

They're checking it right now. 지금 검토 중이에요.
They finished checking last week. 지난주에 끝냈어요.

15. 미남 호남 🎧

> Was the café busy yesterday?
> (A) A lunch special.
> (B) With experienced servers.
> **(C) Not particularly.**

해석

어제 그 카페가 붐볐나요?
(A) 점심 특선입니다.
(B) 숙련된 종업원들과 함께요.
(C) 특별히 그렇지는 않았어요.

어휘

special 특별한 것, 특별 상품; 특별한
experienced 경험이 있는, 능숙한
server (식당에서) 서빙하는 사람, 종업원 particularly 특별히

기출 표현 PLUS+

Just a little. 조금요.
It was very crowded. 무척 붐볐어요.

UNIT 09 부정 의문문

CHECK UP 본문 p.94

1. (A)	2. (B)	3. (A)	4. (B)

1. 미남 미녀 🎧

> Doesn't your boss usually leave at 5?
> **(A) Yes, but he's working late tonight.**
> (B) Actually, I have to leave now.
> (C) It shouldn't take long.

해석

당신의 상사는 보통 5시에 퇴근하지 않나요?
(A) 네, 하지만 오늘 밤엔 늦게까지 일할 거예요.
(B) 사실, 전 지금 출발해야 해요.
(C) 오래 걸리지 않을 거예요.

어휘

usually 보통, 대개 work late 늦게까지 일하다

기출 표현 PLUS+

No, he leaves around six. 아뇨, 그는 6시경에 퇴근해요.
Sometimes he leaves earlier. 때로는 더 일찍 퇴근해요.

2. 미남 미녀 🎧

> Won't the staff meeting finish by 6?
> (A) Attendance at the meeting is compulsory.
> **(B) I'm afraid not.**
> (C) I'll be on time tomorrow.

해석

직원 회의가 6시까지 끝나지 않을까요?
(A) 그 회의 참석은 의무예요.
(B) 유감스럽게도 아니에요.
(C) 제가 내일 시간 맞춰 올게요.

어휘

compulsory 의무의 on time 시간에 맞춰, 정각에

기출 표현 PLUS+

I don't believe so. 그렇지 않을 거예요.
It should be done by then. 그때까지는 끝날 거예요.

3. 미남 미녀 🎧

> Aren't we taking the same train?
> **(A) No, mine leaves later.**
> (B) The dining car is at the back.
> (C) You can take some of these.

해석

우리가 같은 기차를 타지 않나요?
(A) 아니요, 제 기차는 더 늦게 출발해요.
(B) 식당차는 뒤쪽에 있어요.
(C) 이것들 일부를 가져가셔도 돼요.

어휘

dining car (기차의) 식당차

기출 표현 PLUS⁺

I thought so. 그렇다고 생각했어요.
No, I'm going in the other direction.
아뇨, 저는 다른 방향이에요.

4. 미남 미녀 🎧

> Aren't you leaving for London this afternoon?
> (A) Leave it on my desk.
> **(B) No, I'm going tomorrow.**
> (C) They'll be arriving tonight.

해석

오늘 오후에 런던으로 떠나지 않나요?
(A) 제 책상 위에 두세요.
(B) 아니요, 내일 가요.
(C) 그들이 오늘 밤에 도착할 거예요.

어휘

leave 떠나다; ~을 두고 오다[가다]

기출 표현 PLUS⁺

Yes, my flight is at three. 네, 3시 비행기예요.
My flight was cancelled. 비행기가 취소되었어요.

연습 문제　　　　　본문 p.96

1. (A)　**2.** (B)　**3.** (B)　**4.** (A)　**5.** (C)

1. 미남 영녀 🎧

> Didn't you go to the festival yesterday?
> **(A) I don't like crowds.**
> (B) All big name bands line up.
> (C) When does it start?

해석

어제 축제에 가지 않았나요?
(A) 저는 사람들이 많은 곳을 좋아하지 않아요.
(B) 유명한 밴드들이 모두 나와요.
(C) 몇 시에 시작하나요?

어휘

crowd 사람들, 군중　big name 유명한, 일류의
line up 줄을 서다; 준비[마련]하다

기출 표현 PLUS⁺

Yes, I had a great time. 네, 정말 즐거웠어요.
No, but I wish I had. 아뇨, 갔었으면 좋았을 텐데 말이에요.

2. 미남 영녀 🎧

> Aren't the instructors coming today?
> (A) I'd like to introduce myself.
> **(B) Class was canceled.**
> (C) I will leave by 4:00 P.M.

해석

오늘 강사들이 오지 않나요?
(A) 제 소개를 하려고 합니다.
(B) 수업이 취소되었어요.
(C) 저는 오후 4시까지 떠납니다.

어휘

instructor 강사, 교사　cancel 취소하다

기출 표현 PLUS⁺

They'll be here soon. 곧 도착할 거예요.
I thought the class was tomorrow.
수업이 내일이라고 생각했어요.

3. 미남 영녀 🎧

> Hasn't the architect finished the drawings?
> (A) I took a tour.
> **(B) Yes, we received them today.**
> (C) You may win a prize.

해석

건축가가 스케치를 마치지 않았나요?
(A) 제가 둘러봤어요.
(B) 네, 우리가 오늘 그것들을 받았어요.
(C) 당신이 상을 탈지도 몰라요.

어휘

architect 건축가　drawing (색칠을 하지 않은) 그림, 스케치
take a tour 둘러보다, 견학하다

기출 표현 PLUS⁺

No, we're still waiting for them. 아뇨, 아직 기다리고 있어요.
He's almost finished. 그가 거의 끝냈어요.

4. 미남 영녀 🎧

> Isn't the bridge still closed?
> **(A) I think it's been repaired.**
> (B) It's not far from here.
> (C) The store closes at 9.

해석

다리가 여전히 폐쇄되어 있지 않나요?

(A) 수리된 것 같아요.

(B) 여기서 멀지 않아요.

(C) 그 상점은 9시에 문을 닫아요.

어휘

repair 수리하다; 수리

기출 표현 PLUS⁺

I'm afraid it's still closed. 여전히 폐쇄되어 있어요.

No, it should be open now. 아뇨, 지금은 열었을 거예요.

---

5. 미남 영녀 🎧

> Shouldn't we ask for help from management?
> (A) He was just trying to help.
> (B) No, I don't have any.
> **(C) That might make it easier.**

해석

경영진의 도움을 요청해야 하지 않나요?

(A) 그는 도우려고 했을 뿐이에요.

(B) 아니요, 제게는 전혀 없어요.

(C) 그렇게 하면 더 수월해질 거예요.

어휘

ask for ~를 요청하다   management 경영(진), 운영(진)

기출 표현 PLUS⁺

That's a good idea. 좋은 생각이네요.

They should be able to help us.
그들이 우리를 도울 수 있을 거예요.

실전 문제				본문 p.97
1. (A)	**2.** (B)	**3.** (B)	**4.** (A)	**5.** (C)
6. (B)	**7.** (C)	**8.** (A)	**9.** (A)	**10.** (A)
11. (A)	**12.** (B)	**13.** (A)	**14.** (B)	**15.** (B)

---

1. 미남 영녀 🎧

> Isn't the vice president attending the conference?
> **(A) Yes, he promised to come.**
> (B) I have business to attend to.
> (C) I'll get you the form.

해석

부사장이 회의에 참석하지 않나요?

(A) 네, 그가 오겠다고 약속했어요.

(B) 제가 처리해야 할 업무가 있어요.

(C) 제가 서식을 가져다 드릴게요.

어휘

vice president 부사장   promise to do ~하기로 약속하다

attend to ~을 처리하다, 돌보다   form 서식

기출 표현 PLUS⁺

Yes, he'll be here soon. 네, 곧 올 거예요.

No, he had another appointment.
아뇨, 그는 다른 약속이 있었어요.

---

2. 미남 영녀 🎧

> Don't you sell ink cartridges for the Bassell-5
> printer?
> (A) Yes, I drove my car here.
> **(B) They were discontinued last year.**
> (C) It leaked onto the table.

해석

바셀-5 프린터용 잉크 카트리지를 파시지 않나요?

(A) 네, 제가 차를 운전해서 여기에 왔어요.

(B) 그것들은 작년에 단종되었어요.

(C) 탁자 위로 새어 나왔어요.

어휘

discontinue (생산을) 중단하다

leak (액체, 기체가) 새다, 새게 하다

기출 표현 PLUS⁺

Yes, how many do you need? 네, 얼마나 필요하세요?

We just sold out. 방금 다 팔렸어요.

---

3. 미녀 미남 🎧

> Doesn't the public library close at five o'clock?
> (A) A table for four, please.
> **(B) They have extended hours on Saturdays.**
> (C) I'll close the door behind me.

해석

공립 도서관은 5시 정각에 문을 닫지 않나요?

(A) 네 명이 앉을 수 있는 자리로 부탁합니다.

(B) 토요일에는 연장 운영을 해요.

(C) 제가 나가면서 문을 닫을게요.

어휘

public 공공의, 일반의; 일반 사람들, 대중

extend 연장하다, 확대하다

기출 표현 PLUS⁺

No, they close at six o'clock. 아뇨, 6시에 닫아요.

They aren't open on Mondays. 월요일은 문을 열지 않아요.

---

4. 미녀 미남 🎧

> Aren't we allowed to park near the side entrance?
> **(A) Actually, that area is for customers.**
> (B) The button is on the side.
> (C) I don't mind covering your shift.

해석

우리가 옆문 근처에 주차하는 것이 허용되지 않나요?

(A) 사실, 그 구역은 고객들을 위한 곳이에요.

(B) 옆면에 버튼이 있어요.

(C) 당신 대신 근무할 수 있어요.

어휘

allow to do ~하도록 허락[허용]하다 side entrance 옆문
cover one's shift ~ 대신 근무하다

기출 표현 PLUS⁺

Yes, anyone can park there. 네, 아무나 그곳에 주차 가능해요.
No, that's for employees. 아뇨, 그곳은 직원 전용이에요.

---

5. 영녀 호남 🎧

> Isn't Arturo taking the blueprints to the client's office?
> (A) It only took me an hour.
> (B) I prefer the blue curtains.
> **(C) Yes, tomorrow morning.**

해석

아르투로가 고객 사무실에 청사진을 가져가지 않나요?

(A) 딱 한 시간 걸렸어요.

(B) 저는 파란색 커튼이 더 좋아요.

(C) 네, 내일 아침이요.

어휘

blueprint 청사진 prefer ~을 (더) 좋아하다, 선호하다

기출 표현 PLUS⁺

No, Harold will do that. 아뇨, 해럴드가 할 거예요.
He already took them. 벌써 가져갔어요.

---

6. 영녀 호남 🎧

> Doesn't this wall paint need to dry for twenty-four hours?
> (A) Just a two-hour drive.
> **(B) I decided on a different brand.**
> (C) Light blue would look better.

해석

이 벽 페인트는 24시간 동안 건조해야 하지 않나요?

(A) 겨우 자동차로 2시간이에요.

(B) 다른 브랜드로 결정했습니다.

(C) 밝은 파란색이 더 나아 보여요.

해설

(B) 해당 페인트는 건조하는 데 시간이 오래 걸려서 다른 브랜드의 페인트를 사기로 했다는 우회적 답변이다.

어휘

decide on ~으로 정하다

기출 표현 PLUS⁺

Yes, so please be careful. 네, 그러니 조심해 주세요.
No, it doesn't take that long.
아뇨, 그렇게 오래 걸리지는 않아요.

---

7. 미남 미녀 🎧

> Doesn't your hotel have any rooms available?
> (A) No, there's not enough room for that big TV set.
> (B) Yes, I can tell you where the hotel is.
> **(C) No, we're fully booked until next month.**

해석

당신의 호텔에 방이 있지 않나요?

(A) 아니요, 그렇게 큰 TV를 위한 공간이 충분하지 않아요.

(B) 네, 제가 그 호텔이 어디 있는지 알려 드릴게요.

(C) 아니요, 저희는 다음 달까지 모두 예약되었습니다.

어휘

room 방; 자리, 공간 fully booked 모두 예약된

기출 표현 PLUS⁺

Yes, would you like to book one? 네, 예약하시겠어요?
We only have the executive suite available.
특실만 남아 있습니다.

---

8. 미남 미녀 🎧

> Didn't Jayden use to work in the warehouse?
> **(A) Yes, but he was transferred.**
> (B) I sent it to his house.
> (C) No, I didn't work there.

해석

제이든이 창고에서 일하지 않았었나요?

(A) 네, 하지만 옮겼어요.

(B) 제가 그것을 그의 집에 보냈어요.

(C) 아니요, 전 그곳에서 일하지 않았어요.

어휘

used to do ~하곤 했다, 한때는 ~했다 (부정: didn't use to do)
transfer 옮기다, 이동시키다

기출 표현 PLUS⁺

No, he's an office worker. 아뇨, 그는 사무직이에요.
Yes, but he retired. 네, 하지만 퇴직했어요.

---

9. 미남 미녀 🎧

> Wasn't the sale supposed to start this week?
> **(A) No, I postponed it.**
> (B) Profits were up 20%.
> (C) Yes, she started it last year.

해석

이번 주부터 세일 아니었나요?

(A) 아니요, 제가 그것을 연기했어요.

(B) 수익이 20% 증가했어요.

(C) 네, 그녀가 작년에 그것을 시작했어요.

어휘

sale 할인판매 be supposed to do ~하기로 되어 있다

postpone 연기하다, 미루다 profit 수익, 이익

기출 표현 PLUS⁺

Yes, it starts tomorrow. 네, 내일 시작해요.
No, it starts next week. 아뇨, 다음 주에 시작해요.

10. 미녀 호남 🎧

> Couldn't we postpone the conference until
> February?
> **(A) The hotel charges a cancellation fee.**
> (B) The nearest post office.
> (C) Yes, that was a great conference.

해석

우리가 2월로 회의를 연기할 수 없을까요?
(A) 그 호텔은 취소 수수료를 부과해요.
(B) 가장 가까운 우체국이요.
(C) 네, 그것은 훌륭한 회의였어요.

어휘

charge 청구하다; 요금 cancellation 취소 fee 요금, 수수료

기출 표현 PLUS⁺

That's an option. 그것도 방법이긴 해요.
I don't think the guest would like that.
손님들이 좋아하지 않을 것 같아요.

11. 미녀 호남 🎧

> Didn't Ruth say there were extra notepads in the
> cabinet?
> **(A) They're in the box next to the copier.**
> (B) I'll take the notes.
> (C) I bought them online.

해석

루스가 캐비닛에 여분의 메모지가 있다고 말하지 않았나요?
(A) 그것들은 복사기 바로 옆 상자 안에 있어요.
(B) 제가 메모할게요.
(C) 전 그것들을 인터넷으로 샀어요.

어휘

extra 여분의, 추가의 notepad 메모지
take notes 메모하다, 받아 적다

기출 표현 PLUS⁺

They're actually in the closet. 서랍장에 있어요.
They should be next to the pens. 펜 옆에 있을 거예요.

12. 호남 영녀 🎧

> Shouldn't we buy tickets for the movie in
> advance?
> (A) I don't think I saw it.
> **(B) Yes, it is quite popular.**
> (C) Let's move to a coffee shop.

해석

우리가 미리 그 영화의 티켓을 사야 하지 않나요?
(A) 저는 그것을 본 것 같지 않아요.
(B) 네, 그것은 아주 인기 있어요.
(C) 커피숍으로 이동합시다.

어휘

in advance 미리, 사전에

기출 표현 PLUS⁺

No, it will be fine. 아뇨, 괜찮을 거예요.
I already bought the tickets from the Web site.
이미 웹사이트에서 표를 샀어요.

13. 호남 영녀 🎧

> Wasn't the budget report supposed to be finished
> this morning?
> **(A) There was an error on page two.**
> (B) I suppose it'll work.
> (C) No, by the director's office.

해석

예산 보고서가 오늘 아침에 완료될 예정 아니었나요?
(A) 2페이지에 오류가 있었어요.
(B) 그것이 효과가 있을 거라고 생각해요.
(C) 아니요, 부장실 옆이요.

어휘

budget 예산 be supposed to do ~하기로 되어 있다
suppose 생각하다, 추측하다 work 효과가 있다

기출 표현 PLUS⁺

Yes, I just submitted it. 네, 방금 제출했어요.
Yes, but I'm still working on it.
네, 하지만 아직 작업하고 있는 중이에요.

14. 호남 영녀 🎧

> Isn't the stage manager bringing another
> microphone?
> (A) Oh, do we?
> **(B) No, there's only one presenter.**
> (C) It's a popular play.

해석

무대 감독이 또 다른 마이크를 가져오지 않나요?
(A) 아, 우리가요?
(B) 아니요, 발표자는 한 사람뿐이에요.
(C) 그것은 인기 있는 연극이에요.

어휘

stage manager 무대 감독 presenter 발표자

기출 표현 PLUS⁺

We only need one microphone. 마이크는 하나만 필요해요.
Yes, she's coming right now. 네, 지금 오고 있어요.

15. 미녀 영녀 🎧

> Haven't we started advertising the orchestra concert yet?
> (A) The auditorium is large.
> **(B) The tour dates aren't finalized.**
> (C) A talented musician.

해석

우리가 아직 오케스트라 연주회 광고를 시작하지 않았나요?
(A) 객석이 넓어요.
(B) 투어 일자가 확정되지 않았어요.
(C) 재능 있는 음악인입니다.

어휘

advertise 광고하다　auditorium 객석, 강당
finalize 마무리 짓다, 완결하다　talented 재능이 있는

기출 표현 PLUS⁺

No, we're starting next month. 아뇨, 다음 달에 시작해요.
No, not yet. 아뇨, 아직요.

UNIT 10 제안·요청 의문문

CHECK UP　　　　　　　　　본문 p.98

1. (A)　　**2.** (C)　　**3.** (A)　　**4.** (A)

1. 미남 미녀 🎧

> Would you like to talk before me?
> **(A) I don't have much to say.**
> (B) Our plans for the coming year.
> (C) Yes, you did.

해석

먼저 말씀하시겠어요?
(A) 저는 할 말이 별로 없어요.
(B) 우리의 내년 계획입니다.
(C) 네, 당신이 했어요.

어휘

coming year 다가오는 해

기출 표현 PLUS⁺

No, you can go first. 아뇨, 먼저 하세요.
If you don't mind. 괜찮으시다면요.

2. 미남 미녀 🎧

> Can you hand me the scissors, please?
> (A) Sure, I'll have some.
> (B) It's a new fabric.
> **(C) Yes, here they are.**

해석

가위 좀 건네주시겠어요?
(A) 물론이죠, 좀 먹을게요.
(B) 그것은 새로운 직물이에요.
(C) 네, 여기 있어요.

어휘

fabric 천, 직물

기출 표현 PLUS⁺

Here you go. 여기 있어요.
I'm still using them. 아직 제가 쓰고 있어요.

3. 미남 미녀 🎧

> Why don't we drive separately to the stadium?
> **(A) Sounds good to me.**
> (B) Replace the hard drive.
> (C) The tickets are on sale.

해석

경기장까지 따로 운전해서 가는 것이 어때요?
(A) 좋은 생각이에요.
(B) 하드 드라이브를 교체하세요.
(C) 티켓들이 판매되고 있어요.

어휘

separately 따로, 별도로　replace 교체하다, 대체하다

기출 표현 PLUS⁺

That's a good idea. 좋은 생각이에요.
It's easier if we go together. 함께 가면 더 편할 거예요.

4. 미남 미녀 🎧

> Would you care to go to a movie with us tonight?
> **(A) Sorry, I have other plans.**
> (B) He moved to a new apartment.
> (C) Please take a seat.

해석

오늘 밤 저희와 함께 영화를 보러 가시겠어요?
(A) 죄송해요, 다른 계획이 있어요.
(B) 그는 새 아파트로 이사했어요.
(C) 앉으시기 바랍니다.

어휘

Would you care to do ~? (정중하게) ~하시겠어요?

기출 표현 PLUS⁺

I'd love to. 좋습니다.
What kind of movie will you see? 어떤 영화를 보실 건데요?

연습 문제　　　　　　　　　본문 p.100

1. (C)　　**2.** (C)　　**3.** (A)　　**4.** (A)　　**5.** (C)

1. 미녀 호남 🎧

Would you like to sit in the front row?
(A) No, he's standing over there.
(B) The national concert hall.
(C) Of course, that would be great.

해석

앞줄에 앉으시겠어요?
(A) 아니요, 그는 저쪽에 서 있어요.
(B) 국립 콘서트홀이요.
(C) 물론이죠, 그러면 좋겠어요.

어휘

front row 앞줄   national 국가의, 국립의

기출 표현 PLUS⁺

That sounds lovely. 좋습니다.
I'd prefer to be in the middle. 저는 중간이 좋아요.

2. 미녀 호남 🎧

Why don't we take a 20-minute break?
(A) I think it's broken.
(B) Don't we already have one of them?
(C) How about half an hour?

해석

20분간 휴식을 취하는 게 어때요?
(A) 그것은 고장 난 것 같아요.
(B) 우리가 이미 그것들 중 하나를 가지고 있지 않나요?
(C) 30분은 어때요?

어휘

How about ~? ~은 어때요?

기출 표현 PLUS⁺

That's a great idea. 좋습니다.
Can we make it 10 minutes? 10분이면 안 될까요?

3. 미녀 호남 🎧

Could you pick up the party decorations?
(A) Sure, on my way home.
(B) The shopping mall.
(C) I had a great time.

해석

파티 장식품들을 찾아와 주시겠어요?
(A) 물론이죠, 집에 오는 길에 그렇게 할게요.
(B) 쇼핑몰이요.
(C) 매우 즐거운 시간을 보냈어요.

어휘

pick up (산 물건 등을) 들고 오다   decoration 장식, 장식품

기출 표현 PLUS⁺

Sorry, I'm busy today. 죄송한데, 저는 오늘 바빠요.
I can get them after work. 퇴근 후에 찾아올 수 있어요.

4. 미녀 호남 🎧

Would you mind reviewing these design portfolios?
(A) Sure, give me a few minutes.
(B) The bold colors.
(C) Some job openings.

해석

이 디자인 포트폴리오를 검토해 주시겠어요?
(A) 물론이죠, 잠시만요.
(B) 선명한 색상이요.
(C) 일부 공석인 일자리들이요.

어휘

review 검토하다, 비평하다; 검토, 비평
portfolio 작품집, 포트폴리오   bold 선명한, 굵은
job opening 공석인 일자리

기출 표현 PLUS⁺

Chris would be better at that. 그건 크리스가 더 잘 할 거예요.
Sure, please give them to me. 물론이죠, 제게 주세요.

5. 미녀 호남 🎧

Can you get some more vitamins at the pharmacy?
(A) Take three pills after a meal.
(B) Yes, a dairy farm.
(C) I think they close at five.

해석

약국에서 비타민을 좀 더 사다 주시겠어요?
(A) 식후 세 알씩 드세요.
(B) 네, 낙농장입니다.
(C) 그들은 5시에 문을 닫는 것 같아요.

어휘

pharmacy 약국   pill 알약   dairy farm 낙농장

기출 표현 PLUS⁺

I don't think they're open on Sundays.
일요일에는 문을 안 여는 것 같아요.
Sure, what kind do you need?
물론이죠. 어떤 종류가 필요하세요?

실전 문제 본문 p.101

1. (C)	**2.** (B)	**3.** (C)	**4.** (C)	**5.** (B)
6. (A)	**7.** (C)	**8.** (C)	**9.** (C)	**10.** (B)
11. (A)	**12.** (B)	**13.** (A)	**14.** (A)	**15.** (A)

1. [미남] [영녀] 🎧

Would you be interested in signing up for the 5km race with me?
(A) The sign says they're open.
(B) It's across the street.
(C) Yes, that sounds like fun!

해석

저와 함께 5킬로미터 경주에 신청하는 데 관심 있으세요?
(A) 표지판에 영업 중이라고 쓰여 있어요.
(B) 길 건너편에 있어요.
(C) 네, 그거 재미있겠어요!

어휘

be interested in ~에 관심[흥미]이 있다
sign up for ~을 신청[가입]하다

기출 표현 PLUS⁺

I'm not sure I can do that. 제가 할 수 있을지 모르겠네요.
When is it? 언제인데요?

2. [미남] [영녀] 🎧

Can you look up the restaurant's opening times online?
(A) I'll take mine to go.
(B) My computer's just crashed.
(C) The tall building on Bruce Street.

해석

그 식당의 영업시간을 인터넷으로 찾아봐 주시겠어요?
(A) 제 것은 가져갈게요.
(B) 제 컴퓨터가 방금 먹통이 돼 버렸어요.
(C) 브루스 거리에 있는 높은 건물입니다.

어휘

look up (정보를) 찾아보다 opening time 영업시간
crash (컴퓨터가) 갑자기 고장 나다

기출 표현 PLUS⁺

Sure, let me check now. 물론이죠. 지금 확인해 볼게요.
My cellphone isn't working. 제 휴대폰이 작동을 안 해요.

3. [미녀] [미남] 🎧

Why don't you take next week off?
(A) They are selling spa packages.
(B) The others are cheaper.
(C) I'd rather finish my work.

해석

다음 주에 쉬는 게 어때요?
(A) 그들은 온천 패키지 여행 상품을 판매하고 있어요.
(B) 나머지 것들이 더 싸요.
(C) 일을 먼저 끝내야 해요.

어휘

take off ~(동안)을 쉬다 spa 온천
package (여행사의) 패키지 여행; 포장, 소포

기출 표현 PLUS⁺

No, this isn't the best time. 아뇨, 지금은 때가 아니에요.
I think one day would be enough. 하루면 될 것 같아요.

4. [미녀] [미남] 🎧

Why don't we send the whole team to the conference?
(A) He has a business network.
(B) Thanks, I enjoyed it a lot.
(C) It's being held overseas.

해석

팀 전체를 콘퍼런스에 보내는 게 어때요?
(A) 그는 사업상의 인맥이 있어요.
(B) 고마워요, 아주 재미있었어요.
(C) 해외에서 개최될 거예요.

해설

해외에서 개최되는 콘퍼런스이기 때문에 팀 전체가 참여하기에는 비용이 너무 많이 들 것이라는 우회적인 답변이다.

어휘

conference (대규모로 열리는) 회의, 학회
overseas 해외에서, 해외로

기출 표현 PLUS⁺

It would be too expensive. 비용이 너무 많이 들 거예요.
I don't think it's necessary. 그럴 필요까지는 없을 것 같아요.

5. [영녀] [호남] 🎧

Could you please include Maria in the group e-mails you send out?
(A) Several days ago.
(B) I'll add her to the list.
(C) In the attachment.

해석

당신이 발송하는 단체 이메일에 마리아를 포함시켜 주시겠어요?
(A) 며칠 전에요.
(B) 제가 그녀를 명단에 추가할게요.
(C) 첨부 파일이에요.

어휘

send out 발송하다
attachment (이메일의) 첨부 파일; 부착, 부속물

기출 표현 PLUS⁺

I don't have her e-mail address.
그녀의 이메일 주소를 몰라요.
Sorry, I didn't know she needed it.
죄송해요, 그녀가 필요로 하는지 몰랐어요.

6. 영녀 호남 🎧

> Could you recommend some good restaurants in this town?
> **(A) I know several places you'll like.**
> (B) There are several banks.
> (C) I recommend James for security.

해석

이 동네의 괜찮은 식당들을 좀 추천해 주시겠어요?
(A) 당신이 좋아할 만한 몇 곳을 알아요.
(B) 몇몇 은행들이 있어요.
(C) 보안 담당으로 제임스를 추천합니다.

어휘

security 보안, 경비, 안보

기출 표현 PLUS⁺

The restaurant down the road is great.
길 끝에 있는 식당이 괜찮아요.
I'm not too familiar with the restaurants here.
저도 여기 식당들을 그다지 잘 알지는 못해요.

7. 미남 미녀 🎧

> Could you set up the chairs in the conference room?
> (A) Yes, I enjoyed the conference.
> (B) At the Hickory Center.
> **(C) Kelly said she'd take care of it.**

해석

회의실에 의자를 준비해 주시겠어요?
(A) 네, 콘퍼런스는 아주 좋았어요.
(B) 히코리 센터에서요.
(C) 켈리가 자신이 처리하겠다고 말했어요.

어휘

set up 세우다, 설치하다 take care of ~을 처리하다, ~을 돌보다

기출 표현 PLUS⁺

Sure, I'll get started right now. 물론이죠, 당장 시작할게요.
I thought Katie was setting them up.
케이티가 설치하고 있는 줄 알았어요.

8. 미남 미녀 🎧

> Would you like help moving the boxes of supplies?
> (A) Please write it carefully.
> (B) Everyone was quite surprised.
> **(C) There are still quite a few.**

해석

용품 상자들을 옮기는 것을 도와드릴까요?
(A) 주의 깊게 작성해 주시기 바랍니다.
(B) 모든 사람들이 매우 놀랐습니다.

(C) 아직 꽤 많이 있네요.

어휘

supplies 용품, 비품

기출 표현 PLUS⁺

If you don't mind. 괜찮으시다면요.
I can do it on my own. 혼자 할 수 있어요.

9. 미남 미녀 🎧

> Could you help me connect my laptop to the internet?
> (A) No, I work remotely.
> (B) Please make that a priority.
> **(C) Why don't you contact technical support?**

해석

제 노트북을 인터넷에 연결하는 것 좀 도와주실 수 있으세요?
(A) 아뇨, 저는 재택근무해요.
(B) 그걸 우선순위로 하세요.
(C) 기술 지원 팀에 연락해 보는 게 어때요?

어휘

work remotely 재택근무하다 priority 우선순위
contact ~에게 연락하다

기출 표현 PLUS⁺

Sorry, I have to go see my clients now.
죄송한데, 제가 지금 고객을 만나러 가야 해서요.
Sorry, I'm not very good with computers.
죄송합니다만, 제가 컴퓨터를 잘 못 다루거든요.

10. 미녀 호남 🎧

> Why don't you help Kyle sort the résumés?
> (A) For a junior accountant.
> **(B) Yes, he's falling behind.**
> (C) I hope you get the job.

해석

카일이 이력서를 분류하는 것을 도와주는 게 어때요?
(A) 하급 회계사를 위해서요.
(B) 네, 그의 일이 뒤처지고 있네요.
(C) 그 직장에 취직하기를 바랍니다.

어휘

sort 분류하다, 구분하다 junior accountant 하급 회계사
fall behind 늦어지다, 낙오하다

기출 표현 PLUS⁺

Sure, I don't mind. 네, 물론이죠.
I have a few minutes to spare. 잠시 시간이 있어요.

11. 미녀 호남 🎧

> Would you hang up these posters in the hallways?
> **(A) Sure, I can handle that.**
> (B) How many people will attend?
> (C) His office is upstairs.

해석

복도에 이 포스터들을 걸어 주시겠어요?
(A) 물론이죠, 제가 처리할게요.
(B) 몇 명이 참석할 건가요?
(C) 그의 사무실은 위층에 있어요.

어휘

hang up 걸다 hallway 복도 handle 다루다, 처리하다

기출 표현 PLUS⁺

In a few minutes. 잠시 후에요.
I'm too busy today. 오늘은 너무 바빠요.

12. 호남 영녀 🎧

> Can you install the software before lunch?
> (A) The temporary password.
> **(B) Okay, what's your computer model?**
> (C) I brought one from home.

해석

점심 식사 전에 소프트웨어를 설치해 줄 수 있나요?
(A) 임시 비밀번호입니다.
(B) 알겠어요, 당신의 컴퓨터 모델은 무엇인가요?
(C) 제가 집에서 하나 가져왔어요.

어휘

install 설치하다 temporary 임시의, 일시적인

기출 표현 PLUS⁺

I think so. 할 수 있을 것 같아요.
No, it will take some time. 아뇨, 그건 시간이 꽤 걸릴 거예요.

13. 호남 영녀 🎧

> Would you mind picking up the client at the airport?
> **(A) Her flight's tomorrow morning, right?**
> (B) Funding has increased.
> (C) It's in the blue folder.

해석

공항에서 고객을 모셔와 주시겠어요?
(A) 그녀의 항공편이 내일 아침 맞죠?
(B) 자금이 증가했어요.
(C) 파란색 폴더 안에 있어요.

어휘

flight 항공편, 비행기 funding 자금, 자금 제공

기출 표현 PLUS⁺

She's coming in tonight, right? 그녀는 오늘 도착하죠, 그렇죠?
Which airport will she arrive in? 그녀는 어떤 공항으로 도착하죠?

14. 호남 영녀 🎧

> Can I carry some of these boxes for you?
> **(A) I'd appreciate that.**
> (B) A late shipment of samples.
> (C) Some packaging materials.

해석

이 상자들을 좀 들어 드릴까요?
(A) 그래 주시면 감사하겠습니다.
(B) 샘플 배송이 늦어져서요.
(C) 일부 포장 재료입니다.

어휘

appreciate 고마워하다 shipment 수송(품)
packaging 포장, 포장재 material 재료, 자료

기출 표현 PLUS⁺

Yes, thank you so much. 네, 정말 고마워요.
That would be helpful. 그러면 도움이 될 것 같습니다.

15. 미남 호남 🎧

> How about hiring an event planner to organize the staff party?
> **(A) Our budget's much smaller than last year's.**
> (B) Sure, thanks for inviting me.
> (C) You should check the file cabinet.

해석

직원 파티를 준비하기 위해 행사 기획자를 고용하는 게 어때요?
(A) 우리 예산이 작년보다 많이 적어요.
(B) 물론이에요, 초대해 주셔서 감사해요.
(C) 서류 캐비닛을 확인하셔야 합니다.

어휘

organize 준비하다, 조직하다 budget 예산

기출 표현 PLUS⁺

Do you think we can afford one? 그럴 예산이 될까요?
I don't think that's necessary. 그럴 필요 있을지 모르겠어요.

UNIT 11 부가 의문문

CHECK UP 본문 p.102

1. (B)	**2.** (C)	**3.** (C)	**4.** (B)

1. 미남 미녀 🎧

This meal comes with a beverage, doesn't it?
(A) I'd like to come with you.
(B) Any soft drink or juice.
(C) It was delicious.

해석

이 식사는 음료와 함께 나오죠, 그렇지 않나요?
(A) 당신과 함께 가고 싶어요.
(B) 청량음료나 주스가 함께 나옵니다.
(C) 맛있었어요.

어휘

beverage 음료 soft drink 청량음료 delicious 맛있는

기출 표현 PLUS⁺

Yes, it does. 네, 그렇습니다.
No, the beverage is separate. 아뇨, 음료는 별도입니다.

2. 미남 미녀 🎧

You are planning to visit Dr. Schmidt today, aren't you?
(A) Let's sit together.
(B) I have a rash on my arm.
(C) Yes, later today.

해석

오늘 슈미트 박사를 방문할 계획이죠, 그렇지 않나요?
(A) 함께 앉아요.
(B) 팔에 발진이 생겼어요.
(C) 네, 오늘 늦게요.

어휘

be planning to do ~할 계획이다 rash 발진

기출 표현 PLUS⁺

Yes, in the evening. 네, 저녁에요.
No, that's tomorrow. 아뇨, 내일이에요.

3. 미남 미녀 🎧

This is our last box of paper, isn't it?
(A) The new employee manuals.
(B) Press the red button.
(C) Gina orders the supplies.

해석

이것이 우리에게 마지막 남은 종이 상자예요, 그렇지 않나요?
(A) 신입 직원 안내서입니다.
(B) 빨간색 버튼을 누르세요.
(C) 지나가 비품을 주문합니다.

해설

(C)는 지나가 비품 주문을 담당하므로 그녀에게 물어보라는 의미이다.

어휘

manual 안내서, 설명서 order 주문하다; 주문
supplies 용품, 비품

기출 표현 PLUS⁺

Yes, we need to order more. 네, 더 주문을 해야 해요.
There should be more in the supply cabinet.
비품 캐비닛에 더 있을 거예요.

4. 미남 미녀 🎧

You've sent the package to Mr. Olsen, haven't you?
(A) Where does he live?
(B) I just did it an hour ago.
(C) It costs 25 dollars.

해석

당신이 올슨 씨에게 소포를 보냈죠, 그렇지 않나요?
(A) 어디에 사세요?
(B) 제가 한 시간 전에 그렇게 했어요.
(C) 25달러입니다.

어휘

package 소포, 포장물 cost (비용이) ~이다, 들다

기출 표현 PLUS⁺

No, I'll send it tomorrow. 아뇨, 내일 보낼 거예요.
Yes, but he hasn't received it yet.
네, 하지만 그가 아직 받지 않았어요.

연습 문제   본문 p.104

1. (A)   **2.** (C)   **3.** (A)   **4.** (B)   **5.** (B)

1. 미남 영녀 🎧

Their plane is half an hour late, isn't it?
(A) Yes, I just heard.
(B) They have a plan.
(C) To avoid being late.

해석

그들의 비행기가 30분 연착하죠, 그렇지 않나요?
(A) 네, 방금 들었어요.
(B) 그들은 계획이 있어요.
(C) 늦지 않기 위해서요.

어휘

avoid 피하다, 방지하다

기출 표현 PLUS⁺

It seems like it. 그런 것 같아요.
I can look up the status on my phone.
제 핸드폰으로 상태를 확인해 볼 수 있어요.

2. 미남 영녀 🎧

> You ordered the new business cards, didn't you?
> (A) Please see the information on the back.
> (B) A small law firm.
> **(C) I'm still waiting for mine.**

해석

당신은 새 명함을 주문했지요, 그렇지 않나요?
(A) 뒤쪽의 정보를 확인하시기 바랍니다.
(B) 작은 법률 회사예요.
(C) 아직 제 것을 기다리고 있어요.

어휘

business card 명함 law firm 법률 회사

기출 표현 PLUS⁺

Yes, but they didn't arrive yet.
네, 하지만 아직 도착하지 않았어요.
No, I don't need any more. 아뇨, 더 필요하지 않아요.

3. 미남 영녀 🎧

> The new Italian restaurant opens in June, doesn't it?
> **(A) No, not until July.**
> (B) Here's the new version.
> (C) At the entrance.

해석

새로운 이탈리아 식당이 6월에 문을 열어요, 그렇지 않나요?
(A) 아니요, 7월이나 되어야 해요.
(B) 여기 새로운 버전이 있습니다.
(C) 입구에서요.

어휘

version – 판, 형태, 버전 entrance (출)입구, 문

기출 표현 PLUS⁺

Yes, that's what I heard. 네, 그렇게 들었어요.
I thought it opens in May. 5월에 오픈하는 줄 알았어요.

4. 미남 영녀 🎧

> You're going to be free this afternoon, aren't you?
> (A) No, it costs 20 dollars.
> **(B) Yes, I will be.**
> (C) Yes, to the railway station.

해석

오늘 오후에 한가하지요, 그렇지 않나요?
(A) 아니요, 그건 20달러입니다.
(B) 네, 그럴 거예요.
(C) 네, 철도역으로요.

어휘

railway station 철도역

기출 표현 PLUS⁺

Yes, I'll have time. 네, 시간이 될 거예요.
No, I have another appointment. 아뇨, 약속이 있어요.

5. 미남 영녀 🎧

> You only design women's clothing, right?
> (A) OK. We'll check if it's in stock.
> **(B) No, I have a men's line as well.**
> (C) Just sign at the bottom.

해석

당신은 여성 의류만 디자인하지요, 맞죠?
(A) 좋아요. 재고가 있는지 저희가 확인할게요.
(B) 아니요, 남성복 라인도 있어요.
(C) 아래에 서명만 하세요.

어휘

clothing ((집합적)) 의류 in stock 재고가 있는
line (상품의) 종류

기출 표현 PLUS⁺

Yes, especially shirts and skirts. 네, 특히 셔츠와 치마요.
No, I design baby clothing too. 아뇨, 유아복도 디자인해요.

실전 문제 본문 p.105

1. (C)	**2.** (A)	**3.** (C)	**4.** (A)	**5.** (B)
6. (B)	**7.** (C)	**8.** (C)	**9.** (C)	**10.** (A)
11. (B)	**12.** (A)	**13.** (C)	**14.** (A)	**15.** (A)

1. 미남 영녀 🎧

> This coffee machine makes excellent coffee, doesn't it?
> (A) The instructions for cleaning.
> (B) Maybe the button is broken.
> **(C) It brews quickly, too.**

해석

이 커피 기계는 커피 맛이 훌륭해요, 그렇지 않나요?
(A) 세척을 위한 지침입니다.
(B) 아마도 버튼이 고장 난 것 같아요.
(C) 빨리 만들기도 해요.

어휘

instructions 설명서 broken 고장 난
brew (커피, 차를) 끓이다, 만들다

기출 표현 PLUS⁺

Yes, it's quite amazing. 네, 정말 대단해요.
I think it's just average. 그냥 보통인 것 같아요.

2. 미남 영녀 🎧

> You haven't hired an assistant manager yet, have you?
> **(A) No, we're still holding interviews.**
> (B) It's higher than I expected.
> (C) A full-time position.

해석
당신은 아직 부지배인을 고용하지 않았군요, 그렇죠?
(A) 네, 우리는 아직 면접을 진행하고 있어요.
(B) 예상했던 것보다 높아요.
(C) 정규직이에요.

어휘
hire 고용하다 assistant manager 부지배인, 부팀장
full-time position 정규직

기출 표현 PLUS⁺
No, I'm waiting for the right person.
네, 아직 적임자를 기다리고 있어요.
Yes, he'll be starting tomorrow. 내일부터 출근할 거예요.

3. 미녀 미남 🎧

> There isn't a pharmacy in this neighborhood, is there?
> (A) Because I wasn't feeling well.
> (B) How many do you have?
> **(C) No, not within walking distance.**

해석
이 근처에는 약국이 없죠, 그렇죠?
(A) 제가 몸이 안 좋았기 때문이에요.
(B) 몇 개가 있어요?
(C) 네, 걸어서 갈 수 있는 거리에는 없어요.

어휘
pharmacy 약국 neighborhood 근처, 인근, 이웃
within walking distance 걸어서 갈 수 있는 거리에

기출 표현 PLUS⁺
Actually, there's one near the hospital.
사실, 병원 근처에 한 군데 있어요.
I saw one behind the hospital. 병원 뒤쪽에서 한 군데 봤어요.

4. 미녀 미남 🎧

> The pool is open today until seven, right?
> **(A) I'm afraid there's a class in there now.**
> (B) No, it's six dollars.
> (C) Press this button to open the case.

해석
오늘 수영장이 7시까지 열지요, 맞죠?
(A) 유감스럽지만 지금 그 안에서 수업이 있어요.
(B) 아니요, 6달러입니다.

(C) 용기를 열려면 이 버튼을 누르세요.

어휘
press 누르다 case 용기, 상자

기출 표현 PLUS⁺
It's open until nine actually. 실은 9시까지 해요.
Yes, but they're cleaning it now.
네, 그런데 지금은 청소 중이에요.

5. 영녀 호남 🎧

> The presenter is difficult to hear, isn't she?
> (A) For an important lecture series.
> **(B) We could move closer to the stage.**
> (C) I think it looks good on you.

해석
발표자의 말을 알아듣기가 힘들어요, 그렇지 않나요?
(A) 중요한 강연 시리즈를 위해서요.
(B) 무대 쪽으로 더 가까이 이동하면 될 것 같아요.
(C) 그것은 당신에게 잘 어울리는 것 같아요.

어휘
presenter 발표자 lecture 강연
look good on ~에게 잘 어울리다

기출 표현 PLUS⁺
Let's try to get better seats next time.
다음에는 더 좋은 자리를 맡도록 하죠.
I can hear her just fine. 전 잘 들려요.

6. 영녀 호남 🎧

> The package is insured for free, isn't it?
> (A) I haven't packed my suitcase.
> **(B) No, that's charged separately.**
> (C) We often drive to work.

해석
이 소포는 무료로 보험에 가입되죠, 그렇지 않나요?
(A) 제 여행 가방을 싸지 않았어요.
(B) 아니요, 별도로 요금이 부과돼요.
(C) 우리는 종종 운전해서 출근해요.

어휘
package 소포, 포장물 insure 보험에 들다[가입하다]
pack 짐을 싸다[챙기다] suitcase 여행 가방
charge (요금을) 청구하다; 요금 separately 별도로, 따로따로

기출 표현 PLUS⁺
Yes, up to $50. 네, 50달러까지요.
No, that costs extra. 아뇨, 비용이 별도예요.

7. 미남 미녀 🎧

> You transferred to this branch recently, didn't you?
> (A) My trip to South America.
> (B) It's the largest one.
> **(C) No, I've worked here for years.**

해석

최근에 이 지점으로 옮기셨죠, 그렇지 않나요?
(A) 저의 남아메리카 여행이요.
(B) 그게 가장 큰 것입니다.
(C) 아니요, 이곳에서 여러 해 동안 일해 왔어요.

어휘

transfer to ~로 옮기다, 이동하다 branch 지점, 지사

기출 표현 PLUS⁺

Yes, just last week. 네, 지난주에 왔어요.
Yes, I'm new here. 네, 이곳에 새로 왔어요.

8. 미남 미녀 🎧

> We should report all damage to the manufacturer, shouldn't we?
> (A) The factory is hiring.
> (B) A range of kitchen appliances.
> **(C) No, it depends on the problem.**

해석

우리가 모든 피해를 제조사에 알려야 하죠, 그렇지 않나요?
(A) 공장이 채용 중이에요.
(B) 다양한 주방용품들이에요.
(C) 아니요, 문제에 따라 달라요.

어휘

damage 피해 manufacturer 제조사, 생산 회사
a range of 다양한 kitchen appliance 주방용품
depend on ~에 달려 있다

기출 표현 PLUS⁺

Let me check the damage first. 먼저 피해를 확인해 볼게요.
Yes, so we can get someone to come fix them.
네, 와서 수리해 달라고 하면 돼요.

9. 미남 미녀 🎧

> This badge should be returned to the reception desk, right?
> (A) Around fifty applications.
> (B) Turn at the stop sign.
> **(C) Nicholas knows the procedure.**

해석

이 배지를 접수처에 반납해야 하지요, 맞죠?
(A) 약 50개의 신청서입니다.
(B) 정지 신호에서 방향을 전환하세요.
(C) 니콜라스가 절차를 알고 있어요.

어휘

badge 배지, 신분증 reception desk 접수처
application 지원(서), 신청(서) procedure 절차, 방법

기출 표현 PLUS⁺

You can actually hand it to me. 저에게 주시면 돼요.
You'd better ask the security guard.
경비원에게 물어보는 게 좋겠어요.

10. 미녀 호남 🎧

> You accept submissions from freelance writers, don't you?
> **(A) Not at the moment.**
> (B) A small application fee.
> (C) He's an editorial assistant.

해석

프리랜서 작가의 투고를 받으시죠, 그렇지 않나요?
(A) 지금은 아니에요.
(B) 소액의 신청 수수료입니다.
(C) 그는 편집 보조원입니다.

어휘

submission (서류·제안서 등의) 제출(물)
freelance writer 프리랜서 작가 application fee 신청 수수료
editorial 편집의 assistant 보조, 조수

기출 표현 PLUS⁺

Yes, we welcome all submissions.
네, 어떤 원고든 환영합니다.
Yes, the instructions are on our Web site.
네, 저희 웹사이트에 투고 방법이 나와 있어요.

11. 미녀 호남 🎧

> The landlord will make the repairs, won't he?
> (A) A two-bedroom unit, please.
> **(B) Yes, he will.**
> (C) An outdoor balcony.

해석

집주인이 수리할 거예요, 그렇지 않나요?
(A) 침실이 두 개인 세대로 부탁드립니다.
(B) 네, 그럴 거예요.
(C) 옥외 발코니입니다.

어휘

landlord 집주인 make a repair 수리하다
unit (공동 주택 내의) 한 가구 outdoor 야외의

기출 표현 PLUS⁺

He said he would. 그런다고 했어요.
No, I don't think so. 아뇨, 아닐걸요.

12. 호남 영녀 🎧

> Rex, you've come up with new proposals before, haven't you?
> **(A) Yes, I've done it many times.**
> (B) No, they haven't arrived here yet.
> (C) I don't think we've met before.

해석

렉스, 이전에 새로운 제안을 한 적이 있지요, 그렇지 않나요?
(A) 네, 여러 번 해 봤어요.
(B) 아니요, 그들이 아직 여기 도착하지 않았어요.
(C) 우리는 이전에 만난 적이 없는 것 같아요.

어휘

come up with ~을 제시하다, 내놓다 proposal 제안, 제의

기출 표현 PLUS⁺

No, this is my first time. 아뇨, 이번이 처음이에요.
Of course I have. 물론이죠.

13. 호남 영녀 🎧

> Gabriel requested the floor plan for the lobby, didn't he?
> (A) My new laptop.
> (B) He accepted the job offer.
> **(C) I'll ask him.**

해석

가브리엘이 로비의 평면도를 요청했지요, 그렇지 않나요?
(A) 제 새 노트북 컴퓨터예요.
(B) 그가 일자리 제의를 받아들였어요.
(C) 제가 그에게 물어볼게요.

어휘

floor plan (건물의) 평면도

기출 표현 PLUS⁺

I believe he did. 그랬을 거예요.
No, that was George. 아뇨, 그건 조지였어요.

14. 호남 영녀 🎧

> You've seen the new company trademark, haven't you?
> **(A) Yes, it's very simple and clean.**
> (B) Yes, he will check it out tomorrow.
> (C) No, I don't work for a trading company.

해석

새로운 회사 상표를 봤지요, 그렇지 않나요?
(A) 네, 아주 간결하고 명확해요.
(B) 네, 그가 내일 확인할 거예요.
(C) 아니요, 저는 무역회사에서 일하지 않아요.

어휘

trademark (등록) 상표, 트레이드마크 check out 확인하다

trading 거래, 교역, 무역

기출 표현 PLUS⁺

No, not yet. 아뇨, 아직요.
Yes, I really like it. 네, 아주 좋던걸요.

15. 미녀 영녀 🎧

> It would be best to call a taxi, don't you think?
> **(A) The subway would be faster.**
> (B) I updated the tax form.
> (C) A two-door vehicle.

해석

택시를 부르는 게 좋겠어요, 그렇게 생각하지 않아요?
(A) 지하철이 더 빠를 거예요.
(B) 납세 신고서를 업데이트했어요.
(C) 문이 두 개인 차량입니다.

어휘

update 최신의 것으로 하다, 갱신하다
tax form 납세 신고서, 세금 서식 vehicle 차량, 탈것

기출 표현 PLUS⁺

Yes, let's call one now. 네, 지금 부르죠.
No, we can actually walk there faster.
아뇨, 걸어가는 게 더 빨라요.

UNIT 12 선택 의문문

CHECK UP　　　　　　　　　本문 p.106

1. (A)　　**2.** (C)　　**3.** (B)　　**4.** (A)

1. 미남 미녀 🎧

> Do you want to practice the speech here or in my office?
> **(A) Let's go through it here.**
> (B) Yes, I saw him.
> (C) He spoke about it on Tuesday.

해석

연설 연습을 여기서 하고 싶으세요, 아니면 제 사무실에서 하고 싶으세요?
(A) 여기서 검토하죠.
(B) 네, 그를 봤어요.
(C) 그가 화요일에 그것에 대해 이야기했어요.

어휘

practice 연습하다 speech 연설, 담화
go through ~을 검토하다, 살펴보다

기출 표현 PLUS⁺

Your office would be good. 당신 사무실이 좋을 것 같아요.
Whichever you prefer. 편한 대로 하세요.

2. [미남] [미녀] 🎧

> Should I turn at this light or the next one?
> (A) There's always so much traffic.
> (B) My seat belt is too tight.
> **(C) I can't remember, actually.**

해석

이번 신호등에서 방향을 바꿔야 하나요, 아니면 다음 신호등에서 바꿔야 하나요?
(A) 항상 차들이 너무 많아요.
(B) 제 안전벨트가 너무 조여요.
(C) 사실, 기억나지 않아요.

어휘

traffic 차량들, 교통(량) seat belt 안전벨트, 안전띠
tight 꼭 조이는, 딱 붙는

기출 표현 PLUS⁺

Turn at this one. 이번에 바꾸세요.
Turn at the next one. 다음 신호등에서 바꾸세요.

3. [미남] [미녀] 🎧

> Is this the line for making purchases or returning merchandise?
> (A) Where's the men's department?
> **(B) It's for returning items.**
> (C) No, not that much.

해석

이것이 구매하는 줄인가요, 아니면 반품하는 줄인가요?
(A) 남성복 매장은 어디인가요?
(B) 반품 줄입니다.
(C) 아니요, 그렇게 많이는 아니에요.

어휘

make a purchase 구매하다 return 돌려주다, 반납하다
merchandise 상품 men's department 남성복 매장

기출 표현 PLUS⁺

This line is for getting information. 문의하는 줄이에요.
You can make purchases here. 이 줄에서 구매하시면 돼요.

4. [미남] [미녀] 🎧

> Should I return her call, or should I just wait?
> **(A) She said she would call back later.**
> (B) There's no turning back now.
> (C) She called about the boiler.

해석

그녀에게 회신 전화를 해야 하나요, 아니면 그냥 기다려야 하나요?
(A) 그녀가 나중에 다시 전화하겠다고 했어요.
(B) 지금은 돌아갈 수 없어요.
(C) 그녀가 보일러에 관해서 전화했어요.

어휘

return one's call 답례 전화를 하다
There is no -ing ~할 수 없다
turn back 되돌아오다, ~을 되돌리다

기출 표현 PLUS⁺

I think you should call her back. 전화하셔야 할 것 같은데요.
Waiting is best. 기다리는 게 최선이에요.

연습 문제 본문 p.108

1. (C)	**2.** (B)	**3.** (B)	**4.** (A)	**5.** (B)

1. [미녀] [호남] 🎧

> Will you check out on Sunday or Monday?
> (A) Of course, here you are.
> (B) A domestic airline.
> **(C) Monday after breakfast.**

해석

일요일에 퇴실하시나요, 아니면 월요일에 하시나요?
(A) 물론입니다, 여기 있어요.
(B) 국내선입니다.
(C) 월요일 아침 식사 후예요.

어휘

check out (호텔 등에서) 체크아웃하다, 퇴실하다
domestic 국내의, 가정의 airline 항공사

기출 표현 PLUS⁺

I'm leaving on Sunday. 일요일에 떠납니다.
I'm actually staying until Tuesday.
사실 화요일까지 머물러요.

2. [미녀] [호남] 🎧

> Should I send you a copy or give you the original?
> (A) It was essential.
> **(B) I'll need the original.**
> (C) With milk and sugar, please.

해석

사본을 보내야 하나요, 아니면 원본을 드려야 하나요?
(A) 그것은 필수적이었어요.
(B) 원본이 필요할 거예요.
(C) 우유와 설탕을 넣어 주시기 바랍니다.

어휘

copy 복사본, (책, 신문 등의) 한 부 original 원본; 원래의
essential 필수적인, 극히 중요한

기출 표현 PLUS⁺

A copy would be fine. 사본이면 돼요.
I need the original, please. 원본이 필요해요.

3. [미녀] [호남] 🎧

> Do you prefer to work in a team, or work independently?
> (A) It's quite comfortable.
> **(B) I'm OK with either.**
> (C) I walk to work.

해석

팀으로 일하는 걸 선호하세요, 아니면 혼자 일하는 걸 선호하세요?
(A) 그것은 매우 편안합니다.
(B) 둘 다 괜찮아요.
(C) 저는 걸어서 출근해요.

어휘

independently 독립적으로 comfortable 편한, 편안한
either (둘 중의) 어느 쪽도

기출 표현 PLUS⁺

I work best alone. 혼자 일할 때가 제일 잘 돼요.
I enjoy working in a group. 함께 일하는 걸 좋아해요.

4. [미녀] [호남] 🎧

> Can I pay by credit card, or do I have to pay in cash?
> **(A) We only take cash.**
> (B) Yes, that's the right price.
> (C) No, it's not on sale.

해석

신용카드로 지불해야 하나요, 아니면 현금으로 지불해야 하나요?
(A) 저희는 현금만 받습니다.
(B) 네, 그것이 적정 가격입니다.
(C) 아니요, 그것은 세일 중이 아닙니다.

어휘

in cash 현금으로 right price 적정 가격
on sale 판매되는, 할인[세일] 중인

기출 표현 PLUS⁺

Credit card is fine. 신용카드도 괜찮습니다.
Cash is preferable. 현금이 좋습니다.

5. [미녀] [호남] 🎧

> Are you ready to leave or are you still packing?
> (A) The package will arrive tomorrow.
> **(B) I need a few more minutes.**
> (C) Is Samuel coming here?

해석

출발할 준비가 되었나요, 아니면 아직도 짐을 싸고 있나요?
(A) 그 소포는 내일 도착할 것입니다.
(B) 몇 분 더 필요해요.
(C) 새뮤얼이 이리로 오고 있어요?

어휘

be ready to do ~할 준비가 되다 pack (짐을) 싸다, 챙기다

기출 표현 PLUS⁺

I'll be ready soon. 곧 준비돼요.
I need to pack one more bag. 가방 하나 더 싸야 해요.

실전 문제   본문 p.109

1. (A)	**2.** (B)	**3.** (B)	**4.** (C)	**5.** (C)
6. (A)	**7.** (C)	**8.** (A)	**9.** (C)	**10.** (B)
11. (A)	**12.** (B)	**13.** (B)	**14.** (B)	**15.** (A)

1. [미남] [영녀] 🎧

> Would you like your items shipped in the same box or separately?
> **(A) I want them all together.**
> (B) A cargo ship.
> (C) A reasonable fee.

해석

당신의 물건들을 같은 상자에 넣어 운송할까요, 아니면 따로 할까요?
(A) 그것들을 모두 한꺼번에 해 주세요.
(B) 화물선입니다.
(C) 적당한 요금이에요.

어휘

ship 수송[운송]하다 separately 별도로, 따로따로
all together 다 함께 cargo ship 화물선
reasonable 적정한, 너무 비싸지 않은

기출 표현 PLUS⁺

Separately, please. 따로 해 주세요.
Please ship them all together. 한꺼번에 배송해 주세요.

2. [미남] [영녀] 🎧

> Should we take our lunch break now or finish up these files first?
> (A) A few days later.
> **(B) I had a big breakfast.**
> (C) They're in alphabetical order.

해석

지금 점심시간을 가져야 하나요, 아니면 일단 이 파일들을 모두 끝내야 하나요?
(A) 며칠 후에요.
(B) 아침을 푸짐하게 먹었어요.
(C) 그것들은 알파벳 순으로 되어 있어요.

해설

(B)는 아침을 푸짐하게 먹었으니 점심은 나중에 먹고 일을 먼저 하자는 의미이므로 적절한 대답이다.

어휘

lunch break 점심시간 in alphabetical order 알파벳 순으로

기출 표현 PLUS⁺

The files are more important. 파일이 더 중요해요.
We can eat lunch quickly. 점심을 빨리 먹을 수 있을 거예요.

3. 미녀 미남 🎧

Will this interview be in the newspaper or just on
your Web site?
(A) The questions were difficult to answer.
(B) We'll print it in tomorrow's paper.
(C) They were pleased with the news.

해석

이번 인터뷰는 신문에 실리나요, 아니면 그냥 웹사이트에 올라가나
요?
(A) 그 질문들은 대답하기 어려웠습니다.
(B) 저희가 내일 신문에 실을 거예요.
(C) 그들은 그 소식에 기뻐했어요.

어휘

print (인쇄 매체에) 싣다, 게재하다; 인쇄하다

기출 표현 PLUS⁺

It'll be on the Web site. 웹사이트에 올라갈 거예요.
It will appear in both. 두 곳에 모두 실릴 거예요.

4. 미녀 미남 🎧

Would you like to sit at a booth or a regular table?
(A) I'll try the chef's special.
(B) For Friday at seven o'clock.
(C) We called ahead with a takeout order.

해석

칸막이가 있는 자리에 앉으시겠어요, 아니면 일반 테이블에 앉으시겠
어요?
(A) 주방장 특선 요리를 먹어 볼게요.
(B) 금요일 7시로 해 주세요.
(C) 저희는 전화로 미리 테이크아웃 주문을 했어요.

어휘

booth 칸막이가 있는 자리
regular 일반적인, 보통의; 규칙적인, 정기적인
special 특별한 것, 특별 상품 call ahead 미리 전화하다

기출 표현 PLUS⁺

Can I get my order to go? 테이크아웃 할 수 있나요?
I'd prefer a booth, thanks. 칸막이가 있는 곳으로 할게요.

5. 영녀 호남 🎧

Would you rather register for the three or six-
month membership to our gym?
(A) At the registration window over there.
(B) Charles Avenue and Baker Street.
(C) I think the shorter one is better.

해석

저희 체육관에 3개월 회원 가입 신청을 하시겠어요, 아니면 6개월
회원 가입 신청을 하시겠어요?
(A) 저쪽의 등록 창구에서요.
(B) 찰스 가와 베이커 도로입니다.
(C) 짧은 것이 더 나은 것 같아요.

어휘

register for ~에 등록하다, 신청하다
membership 회원 (자격, 신분) registration 등록

기출 표현 PLUS⁺

Six months would be perfect. 6개월이 좋습니다.
Three months would be too short.
3개월은 너무 짧은 것 같네요.

6. 영녀 호남 🎧

Would you rather lead the younger ones or the
older ones?
(A) It doesn't matter to me.
(B) At the community center.
(C) He's quite old.

해석

나이가 더 적은 사람들을 안내하시겠어요, 아니면 더 많은 사람들을
안내하시겠어요?
(A) 어느 그룹이든 상관없어요.
(B) 지역 문화 센터에서요.
(C) 그는 꽤 나이가 들었어요.

어휘

lead 이끌다, 안내하다

기출 표현 PLUS⁺

I'll lead the first group this time.
이번에는 첫 번째 그룹을 안내할게요.
I think I can handle the younger ones.
젊은 사람들을 맡을 수 있을 것 같아요.

7. 미남 미녀 🎧

Do we have to order four or five tickets for the
movie?
(A) One time, I saw a movie star.
(B) It's in alphabetical order.
(C) Sandra said she has an appointment then.

해석

우리가 그 영화의 티켓을 4장 주문해야 하나요, 아니면 5장 주문해야 하나요?

(A) 한 번 영화배우를 봤어요.
(B) 알파벳 순으로 되어 있어요.
(C) 산드라가 그때 약속이 있다고 했어요.

어휘

in alphabetical order 알파벳 순으로

기출 표현 PLUS⁺

Let's see how many are going.
몇 명이 가는지 확인 좀 해 보고요.
Maybe order five, just in case.
혹시 모르니 다섯 장을 주문해 주세요.

8. 미남 미녀 🎧

Do you like driving your motorcycle or your car to work?
(A) I prefer my motorcycle.
(B) I drove him there.
(C) Experienced marketing executives.

해석

오토바이로 출근하는 걸 좋아하세요, 차를 타고 출근하는 걸 좋아하세요?

(A) 오토바이 타고 출근하는 게 더 좋아요.
(B) 제가 그를 거기까지 태워다 줬어요.
(C) 경험이 풍부한 마케팅 중역들이에요.

어휘

motorcycle 오토바이 experienced 경험이 있는, 능숙한
executive (기업이나 조직의) 임원, 중역

기출 표현 PLUS⁺

It's too far to go by motorcycle.
오토바이를 타고 가기에는 너무 멀어요.
It's much faster to go by car. 차로 가는 게 훨씬 빨라요.

9. 미남 미녀 🎧

Do you think we should leave now, or can we wait a bit?
(A) I'll have a little bit.
(B) You can leave it here, thanks.
(C) What's traffic like this time of day?

해석

우리가 지금 출발해야 한다고 생각해요, 아니면 조금 기다려도 될까요?

(A) 조금만 먹을게요.
(B) 여기 두시면 돼요, 감사합니다.
(C) 하루 중 이 시간에는 교통량이 어때요?

어휘

traffic 차량들, 교통(량)

기출 표현 PLUS⁺

There's no rush now. 지금 막히지는 않아요.
We have plenty of time. 시간이 충분해요.

10. 미녀 호남 🎧

Should we design the book cover in-house, or do we have to hire someone?
(A) It's higher than expected.
(B) Our team can handle it.
(C) No, I read nonfiction.

해석

우리가 책 표지 디자인을 내부에서 해야 할까요, 아니면 누군가를 고용해야 할까요?

(A) 예상보다 높아요.
(B) 저희 팀이 처리할 수 있어요.
(C) 아니요, 저는 논픽션을 읽어요.

어휘

in-house (회사·조직) 내부에서 handle 처리하다, 다루다
nonfiction 논픽션(소설·이야기 외의 산문 문학)

기출 표현 PLUS⁺

We need to cut costs. 비용을 절감할 필요가 있어요.
Can you recommend a good freelance designer?
괜찮은 프리랜서 디자이너를 추천해 줄 수 있어요?

11. 미녀 호남 🎧

Should I attend the meeting, or is it only for managers?
(A) You should be there.
(B) A few hours.
(C) Okay, on the agenda.

해석

제가 회의에 참석해야 하나요, 아니면 관리자들만을 위한 것인가요?

(A) 당신도 참석해야 해요.
(B) 몇 시간이요.
(C) 좋아요, 안건으로 넘어가죠.

어휘

attend 참석하다 agenda 안건, 의제

기출 표현 PLUS⁺

Everyone must be there. 모두 참석해야 해요.
It's only for upper management. 고위 관리자 회의예요.

12. 호남 영녀 🎧

Did you make this yourself, or did you ask someone for help?
(A) Sure, I'll make it for you.
(B) Raymond was a big help.
(C) I asked him to do that.

해석

이것을 직접 만들었나요, 아니면 누군가에게 도움을 요청했나요?
(A) 물론이죠, 제가 만들어 드릴게요.
(B) 레이먼드가 큰 도움이 되었어요.
(C) 그에게 그렇게 해 달라고 요청했어요.

어휘

oneself 직접

기출 표현 PLUS⁺

I made it myself. 제가 직접 했어요.
Janice helped me make it. 제니스가 만드는 걸 도와줬어요.

13. 호남 영녀 🎧

> Should we take the 3 o'clock bus or the 4
> o'clock?
> (A) Yes, it goes fast.
> **(B) Wouldn't it be better to take the later one?**
> (C) I prefer to go there.

해석

우리가 3시 버스를 타야 하나요, 아니면 4시 버스를 타야 하나요?
(A) 네, 그것은 빨리 가요.
(B) 나중 것을 타는 게 낫지 않을까요?
(C) 저는 그곳에 가는 걸 좋아해요.

어휘

later 뒤의, 나중의; 나중에 prefer (더) 좋아하다, 선호하다

기출 표현 PLUS⁺

I don't think it matters. 상관없을 거예요.
Let's take the earlier one. 더 빨리 출발하는 걸 타죠.

14. 호남 영녀 🎧

> Do you think customers like the new flavor or
> prefer the old one?
> (A) No, a used one is cheaper.
> **(B) The survey is still being distributed.**
> (C) Do me a favor.

해석

고객들이 새로운 맛을 좋아하는 것 같나요, 아니면 기존 맛을 더 좋아하는 것 같나요?
(A) 아니요, 중고가 더 싸요.
(B) 설문지가 여전히 배포되는 중이에요.
(C) 부탁 좀 할게요.

어휘

flavor 맛, 풍미 used 중고의 survey (설문) 조사
distribute 나누어 주다, 배포하다 favor 호의, 부탁

기출 표현 PLUS⁺

I think they like the new one better.
새것을 더 좋아할 거예요.
They keep asking about the old one.
고객들이 옛날 것에 대해 계속 물어봐요.

15. 미남 호남 🎧

> Are you going to the eye doctor today or
> tomorrow?
> **(A) I still have to make an appointment.**
> (B) He went to medical school.
> (C) Probably at the hospital.

해석

안과에 오늘 가요, 아니면 내일 가요?
(A) 아직 예약해야 해요.
(B) 그는 의대에 갔어요.
(C) 아마도 병원에서요.

어휘

make an appointment 만날 약속을 하다, 예약하다
medical school 의과 대학

기출 표현 PLUS⁺

I'm going today after work. 오늘 퇴근 후에 가려고요.
Tomorrow afternoon. 내일 오후에요.

UNIT 13 간접 의문문

CHECK UP
본문 p.110

1. (A) **2.** (B) **3.** (B) **4.** (A)

1. 미남 미녀 🎧

> Can you tell me where the employee lounge is?
> **(A) Tina is going there now.**
> (B) Yes, she is.
> (C) For lunch breaks.

해석

직원 휴게실이 어디인지 알려 주시겠어요?
(A) 티나가 지금 그곳으로 가고 있어요.
(B) 네, 그래요.
(C) 점심 휴식을 위해서요.

어휘

employee lounge 직원 휴게실

기출 표현 PLUS⁺

It's next to the restroom. 화장실 옆이에요.
It's on the second floor. 2층에 있어요.

2. 미남 미녀 🎧

> Who can show me how to set up the projector?
> (A) I just saw this month's figures.
> **(B) I can in a few minutes.**
> (C) Due to a new project.

해석

누가 저에게 프로젝터를 설치하는 방법을 알려 줄 수 있나요?
(A) 제가 방금 이번 달의 수치를 봤어요.
(B) 몇 분 뒤에 제가 알려 드릴게요.
(C) 새로운 프로젝트 때문이에요.

어휘

set up 설치하다, 세우다 projector 프로젝터, 영사기
figures 수치

기출 표현 PLUS⁺

Kevin can do it. 케빈이 알려 줄 수 있어요.
I'm not sure how to use it.
저도 어떻게 사용하는지 잘 모르겠어요.

3. 미남 미녀 🎧

Can you check to see when the restaurant closes?
(A) The food was delicious.
(B) I can't connect to the Internet.
(C) Near the shopping mall.

해석

그 식당이 언제 문을 닫는지 확인해 주시겠어요?
(A) 음식이 맛있었어요.
(B) 인터넷에 접속할 수 없어요.
(C) 쇼핑몰 근처에요.

어휘

check to see 확인하다 connect to ~에 접속하다

기출 표현 PLUS⁺

Sure, I'll check with my cellphone.
물론이죠. 휴대폰으로 확인해 볼게요.
I think it's open until 9. 아홉 시까지 열 거예요.

4. 미남 미녀 🎧

Do you know which customer ordered a coffee refill?
(A) The woman by the window.
(B) I prefer coffee.
(C) Take as much as you want.

해석

어떤 고객이 커피 리필을 주문했는지 아세요?
(A) 창가의 여자분이요.
(B) 저는 커피를 더 좋아해요.
(C) 원하는 만큼 가져가세요.

어휘

order 주문하다; 주문 refill 다시 채운 것; 다시 채우다

기출 표현 PLUS⁺

The man sitting in the booth.
칸막이 좌석에 앉아 있는 남자분이요.
Laura took the order. 로라가 그 주문을 받았어요.

---

1. (C)　　**2.** (A)　　**3.** (C)　　**4.** (B)　　**5.** (B)

1. 미남 영녀 🎧

Can I ask where the nearest dry cleaner is?
(A) It's open on weekends.
(B) Yes, I believe so.
(C) It's just around the corner.

해석

가장 가까운 세탁소가 어디 있는지 여쭤봐도 될까요?
(A) 주말에 문을 열어요.
(B) 네, 그렇게 생각해요.
(C) 모퉁이를 돌면 바로 있어요.

어휘

dry cleaner 세탁소 around the corner 길모퉁이를 돌아

기출 표현 PLUS⁺

It's a few miles away. 몇 마일 가야 해요.
I'm not sure where it is. 어디 있는지 모르겠어요.

2. 미남 영녀 🎧

Do you know who has a key to room 3?
(A) It's open now.
(B) Here is a room directory.
(C) It is ready for the next meeting.

해석

누가 3번 방 열쇠를 가지고 있는지 아나요?
(A) 지금 열려 있어요.
(B) 여기 객실 안내 책자가 있어요.
(C) 다음 회의를 위한 준비가 되었어요.

어휘

room directory 객실 안내 책자 ready for ~을 위해 준비된

기출 표현 PLUS⁺

The director should have one.
부장님이 하나 가지고 있을 거예요.
You can ask the security guard. 경비원에게 물어보세요.

3. 미남 영녀 🎧

Can you explain how to operate this ticket machine?
(A) I booked a first-class seat.
(B) Ten by five inches.
(C) Yes, just a moment, please.

해석

이 승차권 발매기를 작동하는 방법을 설명해 주시겠어요?
(A) 제가 일등석을 예약했어요.
(B) 10X5인치요.

(C) 네, 잠깐만 기다려 주세요.

어휘
어휘
operate 작동하다, 작동되다 book 예약하다

기출 표현 PLUS⁺
기출 표현 PLUS⁺
Give me one minute. 잠시만요.
I don't know how to work it either.
저도 어떻게 하는지 모르겠어요.

---

4. 미남 영녀 🎧

> Do you know what the price of this carpet is?
> (A) The carpet is soft.
> **(B) You'll need to check the tag.**
> (C) Yes, she's a sales representative.

해석
이 카펫의 가격이 얼마인지 아시나요?
(A) 그 카펫은 부드러워요.
(B) 가격표를 확인해 보셔야 합니다.
(C) 네, 그녀는 판매 직원이에요.

어휘
tag 꼬리표, 가격표 representative (판매) 대리인, 대표(자)

기출 표현 PLUS⁺
I can scan the barcode for you. 바코드를 스캔해 볼게요.
Let me ask my manager. 매니저에게 물어볼게요.

---

5. 미남 영녀 🎧

> Do you know where the art museum is?
> (A) Have you met the artist?
> **(B) Yes, I go there regularly.**
> (C) A modern art exhibit.

해석
미술관이 어디 있는지 아세요?
(A) 그 화가를 만난 적이 있어요?
(B) 네, 저는 그곳에 자주 가요.
(C) 현대미술 전시입니다.

어휘
regularly 정기적으로, 자주 exhibit 전시(품); 전시하다

기출 표현 PLUS⁺
Yes, it's just around the corner.
네, 모퉁이를 돌면 바로 있어요.
No, I've never been there before. 아뇨, 전 가 본 적이 없어요.

실전 문제   본문 p.113

1. (C)	**2.** (A)	**3.** (B)	**4.** (A)	**5.** (C)
6. (B)	**7.** (A)	**8.** (B)	**9.** (B)	**10.** (C)
11. (A)	**12.** (C)	**13.** (B)	**14.** (B)	**15.** (A)

---

1. 미남 영녀 🎧

> Do you know who is going to be the keynote speaker for the conference?
> (A) Certainly, at a hotel next door.
> (B) No, I couldn't make it.
> **(C) The same speaker as last year.**

해석
누가 콘퍼런스의 기조 연설자가 될 예정인지 아세요?
(A) 물론이죠, 바로 옆에 있는 호텔에서요.
(B) 아니요, 저는 참석하지 못했어요.
(C) 작년과 같은 연설자예요.

어휘
keynote speaker 기조 연설자
certainly 그럼요, 물론이지요; 틀림없이

기출 표현 PLUS⁺
I have no idea. 모르겠어요.
I heard Mr. Harris will be the speaker.
해리스 씨라고 들었어요.

---

2. 미남 영녀 🎧

> Did you find out when the anniversary party will be held?
> **(A) The planning committee is still discussing it.**
> (B) Twenty-five years in business.
> (C) At the Palace Hotel.

해석
기념 파티가 언제 열리는지 알아냈어요?
(A) 기획 위원회가 아직 논의하는 중이에요.
(B) 25년간 운영해 왔어요.
(C) 팰리스 호텔에서요.

어휘
find out 알아내다, 알게 되다 anniversary 기념일
committee 위원회

기출 표현 PLUS⁺
We're still not sure yet. 아직 확실하지 않아요.
Next Friday. 다음 주 금요일요.

---

3. 미녀 미남 🎧

> Could you explain how to use this software?
> (A) Ms. MacNeil usually wears it.
> **(B) Actually, it's new to me, too.**
> (C) To design a new logo.

해석
이 소프트웨어를 사용하는 방법을 설명해 주시겠어요?
(A) 맥닐 씨가 보통 그것을 착용해요.
(B) 실은, 그것은 제게도 낯설어요.

(C) 새로운 로고를 디자인 하기 위해서요.

usually 보통, 대개 logo 로고, 상징

Let's ask the IT department. IT 부서에 물어봅시다.
I can show you in just a moment. 잠시 후에 보여드릴게요.

4. 미녀 미남 🎧

Do you know what the criteria are for the monthly bonus?
(A) Mary should know.
(B) I think she's qualified.
(C) The salary is competitive.

해석

월별 보너스의 기준이 무엇인지 아세요?
(A) 메리가 알 거예요.
(B) 그녀가 자격이 있다고 생각해요.
(C) 급여가 높아요.

어휘

criteria ((criterion의 복수형)) 규준, 표준, 기준
qualified 자격(증)이 있는
competitive 경쟁력 있는, 뒤지지 않는; 경쟁의

기출 표현 PLUS⁺

You can check the employee manual.
직원 매뉴얼을 확인해 보세요.
I think Lisa knows. 리사가 알 거예요.

5. 영녀 호남 🎧

Can you show me how to organize the old patient files?
(A) Thank you for waiting.
(B) In the basement, I think.
(C) I'm busy until the afternoon.

해석

오래된 환자 파일을 정리하는 법을 알려 주시겠어요?
(A) 기다려 주셔서 감사해요.
(B) 지하인 것 같아요.
(C) 제가 오후까지 바빠요.

어휘

organize 준비하다, 정리하다 basement 지하층

기출 표현 PLUS⁺

I can show you tomorrow. 내일 알려드릴게요.
Sure, in a few minutes, please. 그럼요. 잠시만요.

6. 영녀 호남 🎧

Do you know why Ms. Lee extended the enrollment deadline?
(A) By visiting the Web site.
(B) Few people have signed up.
(C) A business writing class.

해석

이 씨가 왜 등록 마감을 연장했는지 아세요?
(A) 웹사이트를 방문함으로써요.
(B) 등록한 사람이 거의 없었어요.
(C) 비즈니스 글쓰기 수업이에요.

어휘

extend 연장하다, 확대하다 enrollment 등록
deadline 마감 기한 sign up 등록하다, 신청하다

기출 표현 PLUS⁺

You'll have to ask her. 그녀에게 물어보세요.
I believe more people showed interest.
더 많은 사람들이 관심을 보였어요.

7. 미남 미녀 🎧

Have you heard who's replacing the CEO after he retires?
(A) I have no idea.
(B) On the top floor.
(C) It was too small.

해석

CEO가 은퇴한 뒤 누가 그 자리를 대신하는지 들었어요?
(A) 전혀 몰라요.
(B) 꼭대기 층에서요.
(C) 그건 너무 작았어요.

어휘

replace 대신하다, 대체하다, 교체하다
CEO (= chief executive officer) 최고 경영자
top floor 꼭대기 층

기출 표현 PLUS⁺

I'm not sure. 잘 모르겠어요.
I think it will be Ms. Clarkson. 클락슨 씨일 것 같아요.

8. 미남 미녀 🎧

Do you know when I can get a parking permit?
(A) Yes, thanks. I like it, too.
(B) You can pick it up tomorrow morning.
(C) There are many shops near the park.

해석

제가 언제 주차증을 받을 수 있는지 아세요?
(A) 네, 고마워요. 저도 좋아해요.
(B) 내일 아침에 받을 수 있어요.

(C) 공원 주변에 상점들이 많이 있어요.

어휘

parking permit 주차증

기출 표현 PLUS⁺

After working here for one month.
여기에서 한 달 일한 후에요.
I'm not really sure. 잘 모르겠어요.

9. 미남 미녀 🎧

Has the manager told you what is due by Friday?
(A) That would be fine with me.
(B) Check the list posted online.
(C) Before the industry convention.

해석

금요일까지 무엇을 해야 하는지 매니저가 당신에게 말했나요?
(A) 저는 좋아요.
(B) 인터넷에 게시된 목록을 확인하세요.
(C) 산업 컨벤션 전에요.

어휘

due ~하기로 되어 있는[예정된] post 게시하다, 공고하다
convention (정치·종교·교육·산업 따위의) 대회, 총회

기출 표현 PLUS⁺

No, he hasn't. 아뇨, 얘기 안 해 줬어요.
No, I should go ask her. 아뇨, 가서 물어봐야 해요.

10. 미녀 호남 🎧

Could you tell me why I was charged an additional fifty dollars?
(A) Yes, you can borrow mine.
(B) Four times is enough.
(C) That's the sales tax.

해석

왜 제게 추가로 50달러가 청구되었는지 알려 주시겠어요?
(A) 네, 제 것을 빌려 드릴게요.
(B) 네 번이면 충분합니다.
(C) 그것은 판매세예요.

어휘

charge (요금을) 청구하다; 요금 additional 추가의
sales tax 판매세

기출 표현 PLUS⁺

I'm sorry, that was a mistake. 죄송하지만, 그건 실수였어요.
Let me check your bill right now.
지금 청구서를 확인해 볼게요.

11. 미녀 호남 🎧

Do you know who this briefcase belongs to?
(A) It belongs to Nicholas.
(B) The speech was brief.
(C) Yes, I'll look for it.

해석

이 서류 가방이 누구의 것인지 아세요?
(A) 니콜라스 거예요.
(B) 연설이 간단했어요.
(C) 네, 제가 그것을 찾아볼게요.

어휘

briefcase 서류 가방 belong to ~의 것이다 brief 짧은, 간단한

기출 표현 PLUS⁺

I think that's the manger's briefcase.
매니저의 가방일 거예요.
I have no idea. 모르겠어요.

12. 호남 영녀 🎧

Do you know who's coming to the party?
(A) The cake looks delicious.
(B) I don't know how to do that.
(C) Everyone from our team.

해석

파티에 누가 오는지 아세요?
(A) 그 케이크는 맛있어 보여요.
(B) 그것을 어떻게 하는지 몰라요.
(C) 우리 팀 모두요.

기출 표현 PLUS⁺

The whole company is invited. 전 직원이 초대됩니다.
Everyone except Beatrice. 베아트리체를 제외하고 모두요.

13. 호남 영녀 🎧

Did you see what the announcement on the company Web site said?
(A) Yes, I have design skills.
(B) I haven't logged in yet.
(C) Sorry to keep you waiting.

해석

회사 웹사이트의 공지에서 뭐라고 했는지 봤어요?
(A) 네, 저는 디자인 기술이 있어요.
(B) 아직 접속하지 않았어요.
(C) 기다리게 해서 죄송해요.

어휘

announcement 공고, 발표
log in (컴퓨터에) 접속하다, 로그인하다

No, what did it say? 아뇨, 뭐라고 했던가요?
Yes, I read the whole thing. 네, 다 읽어 봤어요.

14. 호남 영녀 🎧

Can you remember where the performance
evaluations were saved?
(A) I appreciate your honest feedback.
(B) Yes, there's a special folder.
(C) You can begin anytime.

해석

업무 평가가 어디에 저장됐는지 기억나요?
(A) 당신의 솔직한 의견에 감사드립니다.
(B) 네, 특별 폴더에 있어요.
(C) 언제든 시작하시면 됩니다.

어휘

performance 수행, 성과; 공연 evaluation 평가
save 저장하다 appreciate 고마워하다 feedback 의견, 피드백

기출 표현 PLUS⁺

I'm not sure where they are. 저도 어디 있는지 모르겠어요.
They're on the CEO's computer. 대표님 컴퓨터에 있어요.

15. 미녀 영녀 🎧

Have you decided how the tables should be
arranged for the workshop?
(A) We'll use the same layout as last time.
(B) Sure, I decided to sign up.
(C) It's about team cooperation.

해석

워크숍을 위해 테이블을 어떻게 배열할지 결정했어요?
(A) 우리는 지난번과 똑같은 배치를 이용할 거예요.
(B) 그럼요, 신청하기로 결정했어요.
(C) 팀 협동에 관한 것이에요.

어휘

arrange 정리하다, 배열하다 layout 배치, 레이아웃
sign up 신청하다, 등록하다 cooperation 협력, 협동

기출 표현 PLUS⁺

The tables are fine as they are. 지금 그대로도 좋아요.
I'm still thinking about it. 아직 고민중이에요.

UNIT 14 평서문

CHECK UP   본문 p.114

1. (B)   **2.** (A)   **3.** (C)   **4.** (B)

1. 미남 미녀 🎧

Thank you for coming all this way to see me.
(A) I'll see you later.
(B) No problem at all.
(C) I saw him coming this way.

해석

저를 만나러 이렇게 먼 길을 와 주셔서 감사합니다.
(A) 나중에 만나요.
(B) 천만에요.
(C) 그가 이쪽으로 오는 걸 봤어요.

어휘

later 나중에

기출 표현 PLUS⁺

Of course! 천만에요!
I don't mind. 천만에요.

2. 미남 미녀 🎧

The training session lasted about two months.
(A) Isn't that too long?
(B) No, it's our first choice.
(C) The train's just arrived.

해석

교육이 약 두 달 동안 계속되었어요.
(A) 그건 너무 길지 않아요?
(B) 아니요, 그것은 우리의 첫 번째 선택이에요.
(C) 기차가 방금 도착했어요.

어휘

training session 교육 (과정) last 계속되다

기출 표현 PLUS⁺

That seems pretty short. 상당히 짧은 것 같은데요.
That's a long time. 꽤 길었네요.

3. 미남 미녀 🎧

I left my umbrella at the hotel.
(A) It's actually a right turn.
(B) I'm going to book a room there.
(C) It's going to be sunny today anyway.

해석

제 우산을 호텔에 두고 왔어요.
(A) 사실 우회전했어야 해요.
(B) 제가 거기에 방을 예약할 거예요.
(C) 어쨌든 오늘은 화창할 거예요.

어휘

leave ~을 두고 오다[가다], 떠나다 book 예약하다

기출 표현 PLUS⁺

Let's go back and get it. 돌아가서 가져오죠.
I don't think it'll rain today. 오늘은 비가 안 올 거예요.

4. 미남 미녀 🎧

> This restaurant would be a good place to bring
> clients.
> (A) I think it's Bill.
> **(B) Yes, it would.**
> (C) The lunch menu.

해석

이 식당은 고객들을 데려오기에 좋은 곳일 거예요.
(A) 빌인 것 같아요.
(B) 네, 그럴 거예요.
(C) 점심 메뉴입니다.

어휘

place 장소, 곳 client 고객, 의뢰인

기출 표현 PLUS⁺

Yes, I agree. 네, 같은 생각이에요.
That's a good point. 그러게 말이에요.

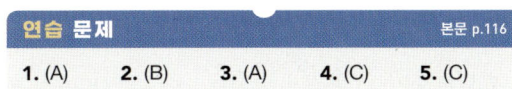

연습 문제   본문 p.116

1. (A)   **2.** (B)   **3.** (A)   **4.** (C)   **5.** (C)

1. 미녀 호남 🎧

> The new backpacks aren't selling well.
> **(A) Yeah, there are a lot left.**
> (B) Please show your receipt.
> (C) I'm hiking back in the afternoon.

해석

새로운 배낭들이 잘 팔리지 않고 있어요.
(A) 맞아요, 많이 남아 있어요.
(B) 영수증을 보여 주세요.
(C) 오늘 오후에 하이킹해서 돌아올 거예요.

어휘

backpack 배낭, 백팩 hike 하이킹[도보 여행]을 가다

기출 표현 PLUS⁺

I can see that. 그러게요.
Unfortunately, you're right. 안타깝지만 그렇네요.

2. 미녀 호남 🎧

> I'm sorry, your table isn't ready yet.
> (A) Around seven o'clock.
> **(B) I'm not in a hurry.**
> (C) That's a fantastic idea.

해석

죄송하지만 아직 당신의 테이블이 준비되지 않았어요.
(A) 7시쯤에요.
(B) 저는 급하지 않아요.

(C) 그거 멋진 생각이에요.

어휘

in a hurry 서둘러, 급히 fantastic 기막히게 좋은, 환상적인

기출 표현 PLUS⁺

Oh, that's too bad. 이런, 낭패인데요.
When will it be ready? 언제 준비되죠?

3. 미녀 호남 🎧

> That was an amazing orchestra concert.
> **(A) The violin soloist is talented.**
> (B) Sorry, I'm working that day.
> (C) How did the audition go?

해석

그것은 놀라운 오케스트라 연주회였어요.
(A) 그 바이올린 독주자가 재능이 있네요.
(B) 미안해요, 그날 일해요.
(C) 오디션은 어떻게 됐어요?

어휘

amazing 놀라운 soloist 독주자 talented 재능이 있는

기출 표현 PLUS⁺

I was really impressed. 정말 감명받았어요.
Yeah, I'd like to see another one soon.
네, 또 구경하고 싶어요.

4. 미녀 호남 🎧

> Let's move to a quieter location.
> (A) They moved to Singapore last year.
> (B) A new apartment building.
> **(C) Room 503 is empty.**

해석

더 조용한 장소로 옮깁시다.
(A) 그들은 작년에 싱가포르로 이사했어요.
(B) 새로운 아파트 건물입니다.
(C) 503호가 비어 있어요.

어휘

location 장소, 위치 empty 비어 있는

기출 표현 PLUS⁺

I think my office would be better.
제 사무실이 괜찮을 것 같아요.
The conference room is probably empty.
회의실이 아마 비어 있을 거예요.

5. 미녀 호남 🎧

> The copier in the meeting room is broken.
> (A) It's in the manager's room.
> (B) Let's meet up at 3.
> **(C) Please contact the maintenance team.**

해석

회의실의 복사기가 고장 났어요.
(A) 그것은 관리인실에 있어요.
(B) 3시에 만나죠.
(C) 관리팀에 연락하세요.

어휘

copier 복사기 broken 고장 난 maintenance 유지, 보수, 관리

기출 표현 PLUS+

I think I can fix it. 제가 고칠 수 있을 거예요.
Let's call a technician. 기술자에게 전화해 보죠.

실전 문제
본문 p.117

1. (A)	**2.** (C)	**3.** (B)	**4.** (A)	**5.** (B)
6. (A)	**7.** (B)	**8.** (A)	**9.** (A)	**10.** (C)
11. (B)	**12.** (C)	**13.** (B)	**14.** (A)	**15.** (B)

1. 미남 영녀 🎧

I don't mind giving you a ride home from work.
(A) Thanks, but I'm staying late.
(B) She's getting a larger apartment.
(C) Please find it soon.

해석

퇴근하고 집에 가면서 당신을 태워 줄게요.
(A) 고맙지만 전 늦게까지 있을 거예요.
(B) 그녀는 더 넓은 아파트를 살 거예요.
(C) 빨리 그것을 찾으세요.

어휘

not mind -ing 기꺼이 ~을 하다 give a ride (차를) 태워주다

기출 표현 PLUS+

Thanks, I appreciate it. 감사합니다.
Oh, you don't have to. 그러실 필요 없어요.

2. 미남 영녀 🎧

The bookstore seems much more crowded than usual today.
(A) It's in the non-fiction section.
(B) Within a few weeks.
(C) They're holding a special event.

해석

그 서점은 오늘 평소보다 훨씬 더 붐비는 것 같아요.
(A) 논픽션 코너에 있습니다.
(B) 몇 주 이내에요.
(C) 특별한 행사를 개최하고 있어요.

어휘

crowded 붐비는, 혼잡한 than usual 평소보다
non-fiction 논픽션, 실화 section 부분, 부문

기출 표현 PLUS+

A new book was just released. 신간이 방금 출시됐어요.
I think that's because it's a holiday. 휴일이라 그럴 거예요.

3. 미녀 미남 🎧

I left my key in my office and locked myself out.
(A) Where were you going?
(B) I'll call a manager.
(C) I can close the window for you.

해석

열쇠를 사무실 안에 두고 문을 잠갔지 뭐예요.
(A) 어디에 가고 있었어요?
(B) 관리인에게 전화할게요.
(C) 창문을 닫아 드릴게요.

어휘

lock ~ out ~가 들어가지 못하게 문을 잠그다

기출 표현 PLUS+

I can call security for you. 경비실에 연락해 드릴게요.
You can use my key. 제 열쇠를 사용하세요.

4. 미녀 미남 🎧

There's a table full of refreshments in the lobby.
(A) What's the occasion?
(B) Would you prefer a table by the window?
(C) It's too heavy for me to move.

해석

로비 테이블에 다과가 가득해요.
(A) 무슨 행사라도 있나요?
(B) 창가 테이블로 하시겠어요?
(C) 제가 옮기기에는 너무 무거워요.

어휘

refreshments ((항상 복수형)) 다과, 음식물
occasion 특별한 행사[의식/축하]

기출 표현 PLUS+

I'll go get something to eat. 가서 먹을 것 좀 가져올게요.
I've just finished eating lunch. 저는 방금 점심을 먹었어요.

5. 영녀 호남 🎧

I don't think the banquet hall is big enough for the event.
(A) The third door down the hallway.
(B) Then we will hold the event outside.
(C) They reserved more seats.

해석

연회장이 행사를 하기에 충분히 큰 것 같지 않아요.
(A) 복도를 따라가다가 세 번째 문이에요.
(B) 그러면 행사를 외부에서 개최하죠.

(C) 그들이 더 많은 자리를 예약했어요.

어휘

banquet hall 연회장 hallway 복도 reserve 예약하다

기출 표현 PLUS⁺

Maybe we can rent a different place.
다른 장소를 대여해야 할까봐요.

How about we use the banquet hall and the lobby?
연회장과 로비를 함께 이용하면 어떨까요?

---

6. 영녀 호남 🎧

I think Sarah can handle the budget forecast report.
(A) She's only worked here a few weeks.
(B) It's supposed to rain.
(C) Salaries are outlined in the contract.

해석

사라가 예산 예측 보고를 처리할 수 있다고 생각해요.
(A) 그녀는 이곳에서 겨우 몇 주 일했을 뿐이에요.
(B) 비가 올 거예요.
(C) 급여는 계약서에 개략적으로 나와 있어요.

어휘

handle 처리하다, 다루다 budget 예산 forecast 예측, 예보
be supposed to do ~하기로 되어 있다
outline 개요를 서술하다 contract 계약(서)

기출 표현 PLUS⁺

I think so too. 저도 그렇게 생각해요.
Yes, Sarah is good with numbers. 네, 사라가 계산을 잘해요.

---

7. 미남 미녀 🎧

Maybe we should get a backup generator for the building.
(A) He'll be back shortly.
(B) That's not a bad idea.
(C) Do you live near here?

해석

아마도 건물을 위해 예비 발전기를 마련해야겠어요.
(A) 그가 곧 돌아올 거예요.
(B) 괜찮은 생각인데요.
(C) 이 근처에 사세요?

어휘

backup 지원, 예비 generator 발전기 shortly 곧, 얼마 안 되어

기출 표현 PLUS⁺

I like that idea. 괜찮은 생각이네요.
It might be too expensive. 너무 비쌀 수도 있어요.

---

8. 미남 미녀 🎧

Please let me know when you're done using this laptop.
(A) Sure, it'll be just a few minutes.
(B) For the new filing cabinet.
(C) No, they're in a different folder.

해석

이 노트북 컴퓨터를 다 사용하시면 알려 주세요.
(A) 그럴게요, 몇 분이면 될 거예요.
(B) 새로운 서류 캐비닛을 위해서요.
(C) 아니요, 그것들은 다른 폴더에 들어 있어요.

기출 표현 PLUS⁺

I need just a couple of minutes. 몇 분이면 돼요.
I'll be using it all day. 하루 종일 쓸 거예요.

---

9. 미남 미녀 🎧

The wool sweaters from Truby Fashions are popular.
(A) Great, I'll restock that shelf.
(B) I think it looks great on you.
(C) No, I didn't sweat after my workout.

해석

트루비 패션의 울 스웨터가 인기가 많아요.
(A) 잘됐네요, 제가 선반에 다시 채워 넣을게요.
(B) 그것은 당신에게 아주 잘 어울리는 것 같아요.
(C) 아니요, 저는 운동 후에 땀을 흘리지 않았어요.

어휘

restock 다시 채우다, 보충하다
look great on ~에게 잘 어울리다 sweat 땀; 땀을 흘리다
workout 운동

기출 표현 PLUS⁺

They sold out quickly. 그것들은 금세 매진됐어요.
I think we'll have to restock them soon.
곧 다시 채워 넣어야 할 거예요.

---

10. 미녀 호남 🎧

I wonder if this sequel will be as good as the original.
(A) Yes, we originally booked for yesterday.
(B) There are a few more tasks.
(C) The director is very talented.

해석

이번 속편이 원작만큼 괜찮을지 궁금해요.
(A) 네, 우리는 원래 어제로 예약했어요.
(B) 일이 몇 가지 더 있어요.
(C) 감독이 아주 재능이 있어요.

어휘

sequel (책, 영화 등의) 속편 original 원본; 원본의, 원래의
book 예약하다 task 일, 과업 talented 재능 있는

기출 표현 PLUS+

The reviews are good. 평들이 좋아요.
I hope it is. 그러면 좋겠어요.

11. 미녀 호남 🎧

I think we'd better ask Mr. Stark for his opinion
right now.
(A) I think I lost my glasses.
(B) The managers are still in a meeting.
(C) I'll download it now.

해석

지금 당장 스타크 씨에게 그의 의견을 물어보는 게 좋을 것 같아요.
(A) 안경을 잃어버린 것 같아요.
(B) 관리자들이 아직 회의 중이에요.
(C) 지금 그것을 내려받을게요.

어휘

opinion 의견 right now 지금 당장

기출 표현 PLUS+

We'll have to wait until he comes back.
그가 돌아올 때까지 기다려야 해요.
He's on vacation right now. 그는 지금 휴가중이에요.

12. 호남 영녀 🎧

There isn't any more space in the storeroom on
the 2nd floor.
(A) Just a few kilometers down the main highway.
(B) Yes, we'll make a delivery on Friday.
**(C) I actually asked about the one on the 3rd
floor.**

해석

2층의 저장실에는 더 이상 공간이 없어요.
(A) 주 고속도로를 따라 몇 킬로미터만 가면 돼요.
(B) 네, 우리가 금요일에 배달할 거예요.
(C) 실은 제가 3층 저장실에 대해 물어봤어요.

어휘

storeroom 저장실 make a delivery 배달하다

기출 표현 PLUS+

So let's use the basement. 그럼 지하실을 사용합시다.
Can you double-check? 다시 한번 더 확인해 주실래요?

13. 호남 영녀 🎧

I'm afraid we don't have enough printed materials
for the workshop.
(A) It was very informative and interesting.
(B) I will call the printer's immediately.
(C) I'll practice my speech for the event.

해석

워크숍에 쓸 인쇄물이 충분하지 않아요.
(A) 그것은 매우 유익하고 흥미로웠어요.
(B) 즉시 인쇄소에 전화할게요.
(C) 행사를 위해 제 연설을 연습할 거예요.

어휘

material 재료, 자료 informative 유익한
printer 인쇄업자, 인쇄소, 프린터 immediately 즉시
practice 연습하다

기출 표현 PLUS+

I'll go print some more brochures.
제가 가서 브로슈어를 더 인쇄해 올게요.
I'll let the secretary know. 비서에게 얘기할게요.

14. 호남 영녀 🎧

I heard you finished installing the new software on
all the computers.
(A) Yes, the system is working better now.
(B) It will take about 10 minutes.
(C) He's a technology consultant.

해석

당신이 모든 컴퓨터에 새로운 소프트웨어 설치를 끝냈다고 들었어요.
(A) 네, 시스템이 이제 더 잘 작동하고 있어요.
(B) 약 10분 걸릴 겁니다.
(C) 그는 기술 자문 위원이에요.

어휘

install 설치하다 technology 기술
consultant 상담가, 자문 위원, 컨설턴트

기출 표현 PLUS+

Yes, it took all day. 네, 하루 종일 걸렸어요.
Actually, I still have a few more left. 사실 몇 대 더 남았어요.

15. 미남 호남 🎧

I would like some information on your upcoming
tours.
(A) Last November with three companies.
(B) Sure, here are a few brochures.
(C) Eight round-trip tickets.

해석

곧 있을 여행에 대한 정보를 좀 원합니다.
(A) 3개 회사와 함께 지난 11월에요.

(B) 물론이죠, 안내 책자 몇 개가 여기 있습니다.
(C) 왕복 여행 티켓 8장입니다.

어휘

upcoming 다가오는, 곧 있을 brochure 안내 책자, 브로슈어
round-trip 왕복 여행의

기출 표현 PLUS+

You can check out our Web site.
저희 웹사이트에서 확인해 보시면 됩니다.
Which tours are you interested in?
어떤 여행에 관심이 있으세요?

PART TEST 1

본문 p.118

7. (C)	**8.** (B)	**9.** (A)	**10.** (A)	**11.** (A)
12. (C)	**13.** (B)	**14.** (C)	**15.** (B)	**16.** (B)
17. (B)	**18.** (A)	**19.** (C)	**20.** (C)	**21.** (C)
22. (B)	**23.** (C)	**24.** (A)	**25.** (C)	**26.** (C)
27. (C)	**28.** (B)	**29.** (C)	**30.** (C)	**31.** (B)

7. 미남 영녀 🎧

What is the period for returns?
(A) Sale items.
(B) In the department store.
(C) Thirty days.

해석

반품 기간은 어떻게 되나요?
(A) 할인 품목입니다.
(B) 백화점에서요.
(C) 30일입니다.

어휘

period 기간 return 반품

기출 표현 PLUS+

These shirts are non-returnable.
이 셔츠들은 반품이 안 됩니다.
This item isn't returnable. 이 상품은 반품이 안 됩니다.

8. 호남 영녀 🎧

Should I schedule the interview for Thursday or
Friday?
(A) The junior accountant.
(B) I prefer Thursday.
(C) He's very experienced.

해석

면접 일정을 목요일로 잡아야 하나요, 아니면 금요일로 잡아야 하나
요?

(A) 하급 회계원입니다.
(B) 저는 목요일이 더 좋아요.
(C) 그는 매우 능숙해요

어휘

schedule 일정을 잡다; 일정 junior 하급의
accountant 회계원, 회계사 experienced 경험이 있는, 능숙한

기출 표현 PLUS+

Friday would be better. 금요일이 좋을 것 같아요.
Either day is fine. 둘 다 괜찮아요.

9. 미녀 미남 🎧

Where are the vouchers for Customer
Appreciation Day?
(A) I think there's nothing left.
(B) Yes, we are very thankful.
(C) It is a good bargain.

해석

'고객 감사의 날' 상품권들이 어디 있나요?
(A) 남은 게 없을걸요.
(B) 네, 우리는 매우 감사해요.
(C) 싸게 주고 샀네요.

어휘

voucher 상품권, 할인권 appreciation 감사; 감상
thankful 고맙게 생각하는, 감사하는 good bargain 싸게 산 물건

기출 표현 PLUS+

They're in the supply closet. 비품 창고에 있어요.
They should be next to the register.
금전 등록기 옆에 있을 거예요.

10. 미녀 미남 🎧

Didn't the restaurant launch a catering service?
(A) Yes, a few weeks ago.
(B) A table on the patio.
(C) I enjoyed the lunch.

해석

그 식당이 출장연회 서비스를 시작하지 않았나요?
(A) 네, 몇 주 전에요.
(B) 테라스의 테이블로요.
(C) 점심을 맛있게 먹었어요.

어휘

launch 시작하다, 출시하다
catering 출장연회, 음식 공급(업) patio (옥외) 테라스, 안뜰

기출 표현 PLUS+

No, not yet. 아뇨, 아직요.
The owner is still considering it. 주인이 아직 고민중이에요.

11. 영녀 호남 🎧

> This coupon can be used for all accessories,
> right?
> **(A) Yes, anything in our collection.**
> (B) It's a formal dress code.
> (C) The necklace looks great on you.

해석

이 쿠폰은 모든 액세서리에 사용할 수 있지요, 맞죠?
(A) 네, 저희 컬렉션에 있는 어떤 것이든요.
(B) 정장을 착용하는 복장 규정입니다.
(C) 목걸이가 당신에게 잘 어울려요.

어휘

accessories ((보통 복수형)) 액세서리, 장신구, 부대용품
collection 컬렉션, 모음집 formal 격식을 차린, 정중한
dress code 복장 규정 look great on ~에게 잘 어울리다

기출 표현 PLUS⁺

It's only for non-sale items. 할인하지 않는 품목에 한해서요.
Yes, it works for accessories and shoes.
네, 액세서리랑 신발에 사용할 수 있어요.

12. 영녀 호남 🎧

> This novel has really interesting characters.
> (A) Yes, at the local bookstore.
> (B) Congratulations on your award.
> **(C) I don't read very much sci-fi.**

해석

이 소설에는 정말 흥미로운 인물들이 등장합니다.
(A) 네, 지역 서점에서요.
(B) 수상을 축하드립니다.
(C) 전 공상 과학 소설을 그리 많이 읽지 않아요.

어휘

character (책·영화 등의) 등장인물, 성격, 특성
congratulations on ~에 대한 축하
sci-fi (= science fiction) 공상 과학 소설

기출 표현 PLUS⁺

I don't enjoy reading very much.
저는 독서를 그다지 좋아하지 않아요.
What's so interesting about them? 어떤 부분이 흥미롭죠?

13. 미남 미녀 🎧

> When will the prototype be ready for testing?
> (A) On the third floor.
> **(B) By Thursday morning.**
> (C) Just a few components.

해석

견본이 언제 테스트를 위해 준비될까요?
(A) 3층에서요.

(B) 목요일 아침까지요.
(C) 그저 몇 가지 부품입니다.

어휘

prototype 원형, 견본, 모델 component (구성) 요소, 부품

기출 표현 PLUS⁺

Maybe next month. 다음 달쯤요.
By next Friday. 다음 주 금요일까지요.

14. 미남 미녀 🎧

> Why did the ambassador cut the meeting short?
> (A) The main conference room.
> (B) I've never traveled overseas.
> **(C) Because of an urgent call.**

해석

왜 대사가 회의를 갑자기 끝냈나요?
(A) 주 회의실입니다.
(B) 저는 해외 여행을 해 본 적이 없어요.
(C) 긴급한 전화 때문입니다.

어휘

ambassador 대사 cut ~ short ~을 갑자기 끝내다, 가로막다
overseas 해외에서, 해외로 urgent 긴급한

기출 표현 PLUS⁺

He has important business to attend to.
처리해야 할 중요한 일이 있어서요.
His flight time suddenly changed.
비행기 시간이 갑자기 변경됐어요.

15. 미남 영녀 🎧

> Will you attend the summer music festival?
> (A) Singers from across the country.
> **(B) I'm working overtime this weekend.**
> (C) It was a festive atmosphere.

해석

여름 음악 축제에 참석할 거예요?
(A) 전국에서 온 가수들이에요.
(B) 이번 주말에 초과근무를 해요.
(C) 축제 분위기였어요.

어휘

work overtime 초과근무를 하다 festive 축제의, 축하하는
atmosphere 분위기, 대기

기출 표현 PLUS⁺

No, I don't like festivals. 아뇨, 저는 축제를 안 좋아해요.
Yes, I can't wait to go! 그럼요, 벌써부터 기다려지네요!

16. 미녀 호남 🎧

> When will the bank make a decision about the loan?
> (A) A business expansion.
> **(B) By March 31.**
> (C) She did it alone.

해석

언제 은행에서 대출에 관한 결정을 내릴 건가요?
(A) 사업 확장입니다.
(B) 3월 31일까지요.
(C) 그녀가 혼자서 그것을 했어요.

어휘

make a decision 결정을 하다 loan 대출, 융자
expansion 확장, 확대, 팽창

기출 표현 PLUS⁺

I'm not sure. 잘 모르겠어요.
Probably by the end of this week.
아마도 이번 주 말까지는 결정할 거예요.

17. 미녀 호남 🎧

> Can I book a direct flight instead of having a layover?
> (A) No, a mobile phone.
> **(B) We don't have enough money in the budget.**
> (C) I have three vacation days.

해석

경유하는 대신 직항편을 예약할 수 있나요?
(A) 아니요, 휴대폰이요.
(B) 예산이 충분하지 않아요.
(C) 저는 사흘간 휴가입니다.

어휘

book 예약하다 direct flight 직항편
have a layover 경유하다

기출 표현 PLUS⁺

Your ticket price will be more expensive.
표 가격이 더 비싸질 거예요.
No, there aren't any direct flights. 아뇨, 직항은 없어요.

18. 호남 영녀 🎧

> Your furniture store is open on Sundays, right?
> **(A) Yes, from nine to six.**
> (B) No, I decided to return it.
> (C) That's a very comfortable sofa.

해석

당신의 가구점은 일요일에 문을 열지요, 맞죠?
(A) 네, 9시부터 6시까지입니다.
(B) 아니요, 그것을 반품하기로 결정했습니다.
(C) 그것은 아주 편안한 소파네요.

어휘

return 반환하다, 돌려주다 comfortable 편한, 편안한

기출 표현 PLUS⁺

No, we're closed on Sundays. 아뇨, 일요일에는 문을 닫아요.
Yes, until seven o'clock. 네, 7시까지요.

19. 호남 영녀 🎧

> How many customers completed the questionnaire?
> (A) Did we get a good score?
> (B) No, I'm busy this week.
> **(C) I haven't seen them yet.**

해석

몇 명의 고객이 설문지를 작성했나요?
(A) 우리가 좋은 점수를 받았나요?
(B) 아니요, 이번 주에는 바빠요.
(C) 아직 확인하지 않았어요.

어휘

complete 기입하다, 작성하다 questionnaire 설문지

기출 표현 PLUS⁺

I didn't check. 확인 안 했어요.
About 45. 45명 정도요.

20. 영녀 미녀 🎧

> When will the Internet be working again?
> (A) Yes, it was unfortunate.
> (B) I work on weekdays.
> **(C) By noon.**

해석

언제 인터넷이 다시 작동될까요?
(A) 네, 그 점은 유감이었어요.
(B) 저는 평일에 일합니다.
(C) 정오까지는요.

어휘

work 작동되다, 기능하다 unfortunate 유감스러운, 불행한
weekday 평일

기출 표현 PLUS⁺

Hopefully by the end of the day. 오늘 안에는 되지 않을까요.
Probably tomorrow morning. 아마도 내일 아침에요.

21. 미남 영녀 🎧

> Where should we examine these product samples?
> (A) I doubt it.
> (B) A well-known manufacturer.
> **(C) No one is in the conference room.**

해석

어디서 우리가 이 제품 샘플을 검사해야 하나요?

(A) 그렇지 않을 거예요.

(B) 유명한 제조업체입니다.

(C) 회의실에 아무도 없어요.

어휘

examine 조사하다, 검토하다 doubt 믿지 않다, 의심하다

well-known 잘 알려진, 유명한 manufacturer 제조사, 제조업체

기출 표현 PLUS⁺

The break room should be fine. 휴게실이 괜찮을 거예요.

I think Conference Room 2 is empty.

2번 회의실이 비어 있을 거예요.

---

22. 미남 영녀 🎧

> Who turned off the copy machine?
> (A) One more cup, please.
> **(B) Well, I thought everyone had gone home.**
> (C) It's for ten percent off.

해석

누가 복사기를 껐나요?

(A) 한 잔 더 부탁합니다.

(B) 음, 모두 집에 갔다고 생각했어요.

(C) 10% 할인된 것입니다.

어휘

turn off 끄다 copy machine 복사기(copier, photocopier)

기출 표현 PLUS⁺

Sorry, I thought you left. 죄송해요, 가신 줄 알았어요.

The copier is broken. 그 복사기는 고장 났어요.

---

23. 미녀 미남 🎧

> It's nice to have the option to work from home.
> (A) Sometime last month.
> (B) A three-bedroom apartment.
> **(C) Yes, I know what you mean.**

해석

재택근무를 할 수 있는 선택권이 있어서 좋아요.

(A) 지난달 언젠가에요.

(B) 침실이 3개인 아파트입니다.

(C) 네, 무슨 말인지 알아요.

어휘

option 선택, 선택권 work from home 재택근무를 하다

기출 표현 PLUS⁺

Yes, it's much better than commuting.

네, 출퇴근하는 것보다 훨씬 좋아요.

Right, I much prefer it. 네, 저도 재택이 훨씬 좋아요.

---

24. 미녀 미남 🎧

> Do you need a copy of the manager's memo?
> **(A) No, I've already received one.**
> (B) A security upgrade.
> (C) The address is wrong.

해석

매니저의 회람이 한 부 필요하세요?

(A) 아니요, 이미 받았어요.

(B) 보안 업그레이드입니다.

(C) 주소가 틀렸어요.

어휘

copy (책, 신문 등의) 한 부, 복사본 security 보안, 안보

기출 표현 PLUS⁺

Yes, can you send it to me? 네, 저한테 보내주시겠어요?

No, I already spoke with him. 아뇨, 이미 그와 얘기했어요.

---

25. 영녀 호남 🎧

> Aren't there a lot of technology firms in this area?
> (A) Please close it firmly.
> (B) I've read the instructions.
> **(C) Yes, it's attracting a lot of talent.**

해석

이 지역에 기술 회사가 많이 있지 않나요?

(A) 꼭 닫아 주시기 바랍니다.

(B) 제가 설명서를 읽어 봤어요.

(C) 네, 덕분에 인재들이 몰려들고 있어요.

어휘

technology 기술 firmly 단단하게, 견고하게

instructions 설명서 attract 끌어들이다, 끌어모으다

talent 재능, 인재

기출 표현 PLUS⁺

No, not really. 아뇨, 그렇지 않아요.

This area is well-known for finance companies.

이 지역은 금융 회사들로 유명해요.

---

26. 영녀 호남 🎧

> May I book an appointment with Ms. Vincent?
> (A) In our most recent catalog.
> (B) I'll point it out to you.
> **(C) What is this regarding?**

해석

빈센트 씨와 약속을 잡을 수 있을까요?

(A) 저희의 가장 최근 카탈로그에서요.

(B) 제가 그것을 당신에게 알려 줄게요.

(C) 무슨 용건이시죠?

어휘

book 예약하다 appointment (업무 관련) 약속

point A out to B B에게 A를 가리켜 보이다[알려 주다]
regarding ~에 관하여

May I ask who is calling? 성함이 어떻게 되시죠?
What is this in reference to? 어떤 일로 그러시죠?

27. 미남 미녀 🎧

> Why were these boxes left in the hallway?
> (A) Yes, turn left at the corner.
> (B) The office at the end.
> **(C) Because the storage closet was full.**

해석

왜 이 상자들이 복도에 있죠?
(A) 네, 모퉁이에서 좌회전하세요.
(B) 맨 끝에 있는 사무실입니다.
(C) 수납장이 가득 찼기 때문이에요.

어휘

hallway 복도 storage closet 수납장, 보관용 캐비닛

기출 표현 PLUS⁺

There's no space in the shed. 창고에는 공간이 없어요.
We're still moving them to the new office.
새 사무실로 옮기는 중이었어요.

28. 미남 미녀 🎧

> I need help getting these crates labeled before two o'clock.
> (A) Fragile glass dishes.
> **(B) I'm not doing anything now.**
> (C) The press conference was helpful.

해석

저는 2시 전에 이 상자들에 라벨을 붙이기 위해 도움이 필요해요.
(A) 깨지기 쉬운 유리그릇들입니다.
(B) 전 지금 손이 비었어요.
(C) 기자회견이 도움이 됐어요.

어휘

crate (운송용) 상자 label 라벨을 붙이다; 라벨, 표
fragile 깨지기[부서지기] 쉬운 press conference 기자회견

기출 표현 PLUS⁺

I have some time to help you. 네, 시간 가능해요.
Sorry, I'm busy at the moment.
죄송해요, 제가 지금 좀 바빠서요.

29. 미녀 호남 🎧

> Who would like my extra ticket to tomorrow's baseball game?
> (A) The local champions.
> (B) Extra paper is in the cabinet.
> **(C) I'm going to the opera.**

해석

제게 남은 내일 야구 경기 티켓을 누가 가질래요?
(A) 지역 챔피언들입니다.
(B) 여분의 종이는 캐비닛 안에 있어요.
(C) 전 오페라 공연에 가요.

어휘

extra 여분의, 추가의 champion 챔피언, 우승자

기출 표현 PLUS⁺

I would, but I already have plans.
갖고는 싶은데 이미 계획이 있어요.
Maybe Jessica would like it. 제시카가 원할걸요.

30. 미녀 호남 🎧

> Could you set up the table for the catered lunch?
> (A) Thanks, I'm quite hungry.
> (B) The Italian place is nice.
> **(C) But it's only nine-thirty.**

해석

업체에 주문한 점심 식사를 위해 테이블을 준비해 주시겠어요?
(A) 고마워요, 전 몹시 배가 고파요.
(B) 이탈리아 식당이 좋아요.
(C) 하지만 겨우 9시 30분인걸요.

어휘

set up 세우다, 설치하다, 준비하다 cater (행사에) 음식을 공급하다

기출 표현 PLUS⁺

I think it's a bit early for that. 그러기엔 좀 이른데요.
I can set it up in about an hour.
한 시간 뒤쯤 준비해 놓을게요.

31. 호남 미남 🎧

> What's the average commute for our team members?
> (A) I renewed my membership.
> **(B) Around half an hour.**
> (C) One of the suburbs.

해석

우리 팀원들의 평균 통근 시간은 어떻게 되나요?
(A) 제가 회원권을 갱신했어요.
(B) 약 30분입니다.
(C) 교외의 한 곳이요.

어휘

average 평균의; 평균 commute 통근 (시간); 통근하다
renew 갱신하다 suburb 교외

기출 표현 PLUS⁺

It won't be more than half an hour.
30분 이상 걸리지는 않을 거예요.
Almost one hour. 거의 한 시간이요.

7. (C)	**8.** (B)	**9.** (A)	**10.** (C)	**11.** (C)
12. (C)	**13.** (A)	**14.** (B)	**15.** (C)	**16.** (B)
17. (B)	**18.** (C)	**19.** (C)	**20.** (A)	**21.** (A)
22. (B)	**23.** (B)	**24.** (A)	**25.** (B)	**26.** (B)
27. (B)	**28.** (A)	**29.** (C)	**30.** (C)	**31.** (A)

7. 영녀 호남 🎧

Who's doing the orientation for the new recruits tomorrow?
(A) A recent college graduate.
(B) I can show you some.
(C) I'm leaving for a business trip tonight.

해석
내일 신규 직원들을 위해 누가 오리엔테이션을 하죠?
(A) 최근에 대학을 졸업한 사람입니다.
(B) 일부 보여 드릴 수 있어요.
(C) 저는 오늘밤 출장을 떠나요.

어휘
recruit 직원　a business trip 출장

8. 영녀 호남 🎧

Maybe you should include more evidence in your paper.
(A) Was Kevin invited?
(B) I was thinking the same thing.
(C) You can store the photos on the computer.

해석
보고서에 증거를 더 많이 포함해야 할 것 같군요.
(A) 케빈이 초대되었나요?
(B) 저도 같은 생각이었어요.
(C) 컴퓨터에 사진을 저장할 수 있습니다.

어휘
invite 초대하다　store 저장하다

9. 영녀 호남 🎧

When will the copier be fixed?
(A) Didn't you read the notice?
(B) Down the hall to the right.
(C) I don't have a fixed schedule this week.

해석
언제 복사기가 수리될까요?
(A) 공지 못 보셨어요?
(B) 복도 따라가다 오른쪽이요.
(C) 저는 이번 주에는 정해진 일정이 없어요.

어휘
copier 복사기　fix 고치다, 확정하다

10. 영녀 호남 🎧

Should we open the store at nine or ten tomorrow?
(A) There's a sign on the door.
(B) I've never seen this before.
(C) Let me check when the festival starts.

해석
내일 가게를 9시에 열어야 하나요, 10시에 열어야 하나요?
(A) 문에 표지판이 있어요.
(B) 전에 이걸 본 적이 없어요.
(C) 축제가 언제 시작하는지 확인해 볼게요.

11. 영녀 호남 🎧

We should leave early for lunch with our clients.
(A) The menu was recently updated.
(B) Yes, I've met them before.
(C) I haven't finished my work.

해석
우리는 고객과의 점심을 위해 일찍 나가야 해요.
(A) 메뉴가 최근 업데이트되었어요.
(B) 네, 전에 그들을 만난 적 있어요.
(C) 제 일을 아직 못 끝냈어요.

12. 영녀 호남 🎧

Shouldn't we request permission from the CEO?
(A) No, a previous submission.
(B) The decision hasn't been finalized.
(C) This is an exception.

해석
대표님의 승인을 얻어야 하지 않나요?
(A) 아뇨, 이전에 제출한 거요.
(B) 결정이 확정되지 않았어요.
(C) 이건 예외예요.

어휘
request 요구하다　permission 승인　exception 예외

13. 영녀 호남 🎧

Can you forward the e-mail Mr. Cunningham sent yesterday to me?
(A) I didn't receive it.
(B) It should be at the post office.
(C) I sent it via express shipping.

해석
커닝햄 씨가 어제 보낸 이메일을 제게 전달해 주시겠어요?

(A) 전 못 받았어요.

(B) 우체국에 있을 거예요.

(C) 특급 배송으로 보냈어요.

14. 영녀 호남 🎧

Where should I park when I go to the conference?

(A) For people in the sales industry.

(B) It's better to take a taxi.

(C) There are a lot of trees here.

해석

콘퍼런스에 가면 어디에 주차해야 하죠?

(A) 판매업에 종사하는 사람들을 위해서요.

(B) 택시를 타는 게 나아요.

(C) 여기 나무가 많아요.

15. 영녀 호남 🎧

How can we lower our restaurant expenses?

(A) It's very crowded today.

(B) A new menu item.

(C) We give a lot of free refills for drinks.

해석

우리 식당의 비용을 어떻게 낮출 수 있을까요?

(A) 오늘은 무척 붐비네요.

(B) 신메뉴.

(C) 우린 음료 리필을 너무 많이 해 주고 있어요.

16. 영녀 호남 🎧

Isn't the head of human resources visiting today?

(A) I'm looking for the source of the problem.

(B) I have to check the schedule.

(C) I have a map you can use.

해석

인사부서장이 오늘 방문하지 않나요?

(A) 문제의 원인을 찾아보고 있어요.

(B) 일정을 확인해 봐야 해요.

(C) 당신이 사용할 수 있는 지도가 있어요.

17. 영녀 호남 🎧

Are you going to print more flyers for the festival?

(A) About three hours.

(B) We have more than enough.

(C) Keep the posters in the office next door.

해석

축제를 위해 전단지를 더 인쇄할 건가요?

(A) 세 시간 정도요.

(B) 충분하고도 남아요.

(C) 포스터들을 옆 사무실에 보관해 놓으세요.

18. 영녀 호남 🎧

Isn't Charlie going to drive the CEO to the airport?

(A) An extra charge for luggage.

(B) My hard drive is missing.

(C) The trip was cancelled.

해석

찰리가 대표님을 공항에 모시고 가지 않나요?

(A) 수하물에 대한 추가 비용입니다.

(B) 제 하드 드라이브가 없어졌어요.

(C) 출장이 취소되었어요.

19. 영녀 호남 🎧

Don't you carry this laptop in silver?

(A) I need some help lifting it.

(B) Put it on top of the file cabinet.

(C) We're getting a new shipment next week.

해석

이 노트북 은색도 파나요?

(A) 그걸 드는 데 도움이 좀 필요해요.

(B) 서류함 위에 올려놓으세요.

(C) 다음 주에 물품 배송이 와요.

20. 영녀 호남 🎧

Why don't we use a freelance designer instead of hiring a new employee?

(A) I don't see why not.

(B) A complicated hiring process.

(C) They employ a lot of experienced workers.

해석

신규 직원을 고용하는 대신 프리랜서 디자이너를 쓰는 게 어때요?

(A) 안 될 거 없죠.

(B) 복잡한 고용 절차입니다.

(C) 그들은 경력자들을 많이 고용하고 있어요.

어휘

hire 고용하다   process 절차

experienced 경험이 있는, 경험이 풍부한

21. 영녀 호남 🎧

I can purchase a yearly gym membership, right?

(A) You should ask the front desk.

(B) You can change your order.

(C) The fitness room is on the left.

해석

헬스클럽 1년 회원권을 구매할 수 있죠, 그렇죠?

(A) 프런트 데스크에 물어보셔야 해요.

(B) 주문을 변경하실 수 있습니다.

(C) 헬스장은 왼쪽에 있습니다.

어휘

purchase 구매하다   yearly 연간의

22. 영녀 호남 🎧

We reserved tickets for the conference, didn't we?

(A) That price seems fair.

(B) Yes, Susan did it last month.

(C) I'd like a one-way flight to Bangkok, please.

해석

콘퍼런스 표를 예매했죠, 그렇지 않나요?

(A) 가격이 적절해 보여요.

(B) 네, 수잔이 지난달에 예매했어요.

(C) 방콕행 편도 한 장이요.

어휘

reserve 예약하다   fair 타당한, 온당한   one-way 편도의

23. 영녀 호남 🎧

What's the total cost for my order?

(A) In a couple of days.

(B) You can find the price on your receipt.

(C) I have some boxes you can use.

해석

총 주문 가격이 얼마죠?

(A) 이삼일 후에요.

(B) 영수증에 가격이 나와 있어요.

(C) 당신이 사용할 수 있는 상자들이 있어요.

어휘

a couple of 둘의, 두서너 개의

24. 영녀 호남 🎧

I need to update this software, right?

(A) The IT team can help you.

(B) No, it's a bit hard.

(C) It came from the warehouse.

해석

이 소프트웨어를 업데이트해야죠, 그렇죠?

(A) IT 팀에서 도와줄 거예요.

(B) 아뇨, 그건 좀 힘들어요.

(C) 그건 창고에서 왔어요.

25. 영녀 호남 🎧

Do you want to meet outside in the park or inside the restaurant?

(A) The weather is terrible.

(B) The parking lot is behind the building.

(C) Monday, the sixteenth.

해석

야외 공원에서 만날까요, 식당 안에서 볼까요?

(A) 날씨가 너무 안 좋아요.

(B) 주차장은 건물 뒤에 있어요.

(C) 16일 월요일이요.

26. 영녀 호남 🎧

Is there any construction going on downstairs?

(A) He prefers to take the stairs.

(B) Is the noise too loud?

(C) I don't think that idea will work.

해석

아래층에서 공사가 진행 중인가요?

(A) 그는 계단을 이용하는 걸 좋아해요.

(B) 소음이 너무 큰가요?

(C) 그 아이디어는 안 될 것 같아요.

어휘

go on 진행되다   take the stairs 계단을 이용하다

27. 영녀 호남 🎧

Mr. Garrison will be absent from the meeting today.

(A) In Room 207.

(B) I'll take notes for him.

(C) I was late for work yesterday.

해석

개리슨 씨가 오늘 회의에 참석하지 못할 거예요.

(A) 207호실이에요.

(B) 제가 그를 대신해 회의록을 쓸게요.

(C) 저는 어제 회사에 지각했어요.

어휘

be absent from ~에 결석하다, ~에 불참하다
take notes 메모하다, 필기를 하다

28. 영녀 호남 🎧

> Don't you want to come to the movie premiere with us tonight?
> **(A) I don't like horror films.**
> (B) The mall is in a prime location in the city center.
> (C) Is Martha coming to the party next week?

해석

오늘 밤 우리와 함께 영화 시사회에 가지 않을래요?
(A) 저는 공포 영화를 좋아하지 않아요.
(B) 그 쇼핑몰은 도심에서 가장 좋은 위치에 있어요.
(C) 마사는 다음 주에 파티에 오나요?

어휘

premiere 개봉, 초연 prime 주된, 뛰어난, 최고의

29. 영녀 호남 🎧

> Stacey is the best department leader we have.
> (A) No, I just need a part of it.
> (B) Who will lead the team?
> **(C) She always brings out the best in people.**

해석

스테이시는 최고의 부서장입니다.
(A) 아뇨, 저는 그것의 일부만 필요합니다.
(B) 누가 그 팀을 이끌 거죠?
(C) 그녀는 늘 직원들이 최고의 기량을 발휘하게 해요.

어휘

bring out ~을 끌어내다

30. 영녀 호남 🎧

> Excuse me, the store is closing in ten minutes.
> (A) There are some in the storage closet.
> (B) I bought it yesterday.
> **(C) I thought you were open until 10.**

해석

실례합니다만, 10분 후에 가게 문을 닫습니다.
(A) 수납장에 조금 있어요.
(B) 어제 샀어요.
(C) 10시까지 영업하는 줄 알았어요.

어휘

storage closet 수납장, 벽장

31. 영녀 호남 🎧

> Where's the main entrance to the library?
> **(A) There's a pretty long line over there.**
> (B) A special poetry collection.
> (C) I think it'll rain later.

해석

도서관 정문이 어디죠?
(A) 저기 엄청 긴 줄이 늘어서 있어요.
(B) 특별 시집이요.
(C) 이따가 비가 올 거 같아요.

어휘

main entrance 정문 poetry collection 시집

PART 3

UNIT 01 주제·목적 문제

CHECK UP   本文 p.124

1. (B)   **2.** (C)

[1] 미남 미녀 🎧

Question 1 refers to the following conversation.

> **M** Hello, this is Calvin Hector. I've recently sent an invoice for a picture I took for your community newspaper. Could you tell me when I will receive payment for it?
>
> **W** Well, it depends on when you sent the invoice to us. Just a moment, please. Hmm… I can't seem to find your name in the system. When did you send us the invoice?
>
> **M** I posted it last Tuesday, so it should've arrived by Friday at the latest.
>
> **W** Oh, I'm sorry. Our office was closed on Friday for repairs. I will talk to the mail carrier and then give you a call back.

해석

1번은 다음 대화에 관한 문제입니다.

남 안녕하세요, 저는 캘빈 헥터입니다. 제가 당신의 지역신문을 위해 촬영한 사진에 대한 청구서를 최근에 보냈습니다. **그것에 대해 언제 지급받게 될지 알려 주시겠어요?**

여 음, 언제 저희에게 그 청구서를 보내셨는지에 따라 달라요. 잠시만 기다려주세요. 흠… 시스템에서 당신의 이름을 찾을 수 없을 것 같아요. 언제 저희에게 청구서를 보내셨지요?

남 지난 화요일에 우편으로 부쳤으니까, 늦어도 금요일까지는 도착했어야 해요.

여 아, 죄송합니다. 저희 사무실이 수리를 위해 금요일에 문을 닫았어요. 제가 우편 배달원과 얘기한 다음에 다시 전화를 드릴게요.

어휘

invoice 청구서, 송장 payment 지불, 지급
depend on ~에 달려 있다 post (우편물을) 발송하다
at the latest 늦어도 repair 수리, 보수; 수리하다
mail carrier 우편 배달원

1.

남자는 왜 전화하고 있는가?

(A) 연락처를 갱신하기 위해

(B) 대금 지급에 관해 문의하기 위해

(C) 계약서 사본을 요청하기 위해

(D) 청구서의 오류를 정정하기 위해

어휘

update 갱신하다 contact information 연락처
contract 계약(서) correct 정정하다, 바로잡다

[2] 미녀 미남 🎧

Question 2 refers to the following conversation.

> **W** Frank, we need to come up with some ideas about what to add to our inventory. I've heard that our competitor, Simon's, only sells domestic products, which are quite popular. What do you think?
>
> **M** I heard about that too. We will have to do some research and see if we can find some vendors who sell the things we need at a good price.
>
> **W** Great. I will assign some staff to help you find the information. Let's have a meeting next Tuesday about this.
>
> **M** Thanks! But could we try for Thursday instead? I've got a doctor's appointment on Tuesday.

해석

2번은 다음 대화에 관한 문제입니다.

여 프랭크, **우리의 재고 품목에 무엇을 추가해야 하는지에 관해 아이디어를 좀 내야 해요.** 우리 경쟁사인 시몬스는 국산 제품만 판매하는데, 그것이 꽤 인기가 있다고 들었어요. 어떻게 생각해요?

남 저도 그것에 관해 들었어요. 우리는 조사를 좀 해서 우리가 필요한 물건들을 괜찮은 가격에 파는 판매 회사들을 좀 찾을 수 있는지 알아봐야 할 거예요.

여 좋아요. 제가 몇몇 직원을 배정해서 당신이 그 정보를 찾는 것을 돕도록 할게요. 이 건에 관해 다음 주 화요일에 회의를 하죠.

남 감사해요! 그런데 대신 목요일로 해도 될까요? 제가 화요일에는 병원 예약이 돼 있어서요.

어휘

come up with ~을 생각해내다 inventory 재고(품)
competitor 경쟁사, 경쟁자 domestic 국산의, 국내의
research 연구, 조사 vendor 판매 회사
assign (일 등을) 맡기다, 배정하다 appointment 예약, 약속

2.

화자들은 무엇에 관해 이야기하고 있는가?

(A) 설문 조사 결과

(B) 채용 공고

(C) 신제품 아이디어

(D) 마케팅 계획

survey (설문) 조사 job opening 채용 공고, 일자리 공석

패러프레이징

ideas about what to add to our inventory
→ Some new product ideas

패러프레이징 연습　　　　　　　　　　본문 p.126

1-4. 스크립트 참조　　**5.** (B)　　**6.** (A)

1.

Q 대화의 주제는 무엇인가?

A 단체 관광을 준비하는 것

[미녀] [미남] 🎧

> **W** I need a team-building activity for the members of my department, so I'm planning a group activity.
> **M** No problem. We offer a variety of tours to suit any budget.

해석

여　제 부서원들을 위한 팀워크 활동이 필요해서, **단체 활동을 계획하고 있어요.**

남　문제없어요. **저희는 어떤 예산에도 맞출 수 있는 다양한 관광들을 제공합니다.**

어휘

arrange 마련하다, 준비하다 offer 제공하다
a variety of 다양한 suit ~에 잘 맞다 budget 예산

패러프레이징

planning a group activity → Arranging a group tour

2.

Q 남자는 왜 전화하고 있는가?

A 임시 직원을 요청하기 위해

[미남] [미녀] 🎧

> **M** Hello. This is Alan from Ingram Accounting. We need to hire a temporary worker for our busy season, which starts in January.
> **W** I can help you with that. What kind of duties do you need covered?

해석

남　안녕하세요. 저는 인그램 회계법인의 앨런입니다. **저희가 성수기를 위해 임시 직원을 고용해야 하는데요,** 1월부터 시작합니다.

여　제가 도와드리겠습니다. 어떤 종류의 업무를 맡기셔야 하나요?

어휘

temporary 임시의, 일시적인 accounting 회계 (업무)
busy season 성수기 duty 업무, 직무
cover 떠맡다, ~의 책임을 지다

패러프레이징

worker → staff

3.

Q 대화는 주로 무엇에 관한 것인가?

A 건물을 수리하는 것

[미녀] [미남] 🎧

> **W** I've got great news, Naveen! We were approved for a grant from the federal government. Now we have enough to repair the historic Westbury Chapel. This will be an exciting project for our town.
> **M** I'm so glad to hear that we'll finally be able to make the necessary repairs. It'll look so much better once the work is all finished.

해석

여　아주 좋은 소식이 있어요, 나빈! 우리가 연방 정부로부터 보조금을 승인받았어요. 이제 우리는 **역사적으로 중요한 웨스트베리 예배당을 보수하기에** 충분해요. 우리 동네를 위한 흥미로운 프로젝트가 될 거예요.

남　우리가 마침내 **필요한 수리를 할 수 있을** 것이라니 아주 기뻐요. 작업이 모두 끝나면 그곳은 훨씬 더 나아 보일 거예요.

어휘

renovate 수리하다, 개조하다 approve 승인하다 grant 보조금
federal government 연방 정부 repair 수리하다; 수리
historic 역사적으로 중요한, 역사적인 chapel 예배당

패러프레이징

repair the historic Westbury Chapel
→ Renovating a building

4.

Q 여자의 전화 목적은 무엇인가?

A 채용 면접 일정을 잡기 위해

[미녀] [미남] 🎧

> **W** Good morning. I'm calling from Cruz Recruitment. You applied for a position at BC Sales, and I'd like you to come in next week for an interview.
> **M** That's great. I'm free on Thursday and Friday.
> **W** Alright. How about Thursday at 9:30 A.M.?

해석

여　안녕하세요. 크루즈 채용사에서 전화드립니다. **BC 세일즈의 일자리에 지원하셨는데요, 다음 주에 면접을 위해 오셨으면 합니다.**

남　좋습니다. 저는 목요일과 금요일에 시간이 됩니다.

여　알겠습니다. 목요일 오전 9시 30분은 어떠세요?

어휘

apply for ~에 지원하다, ~을 신청하다 position (일)자리, 직위

패러프레이징

applied for a position ~ come in next week for an
interview → arrange a job interview

5.

화자들은 무엇에 관해 이야기하고 있는가?

(A) 직원들을 교육하는 것

(B) 기계를 구입하는 것

미녀 미남 🎧

> W Antonio, do you have a minute? I got a call
> from a salesperson who would like to give us a
> demonstration of some machines his company
> has designed.
> M Well, we are looking to get some new
> equipment.

해석

여 안토니오, 시간 좀 있어요? 우리에게 자사에서 설계한 **기계를** 시
연하고 싶어 하는 판매원으로부터 전화를 받았어요.

남 음, 우리는 새 장비를 좀 들이려고 생각하고 있긴 해요.

어휘

staff member 직원 purchase 구입하다; 구매
salesperson 판매원 give a demonstration 시연하다
look to ~하는 것을 고려하다, 생각하다 equipment 장비

패러프레이징

get some new equipment
→ Purchasing some machines

6.

여자는 왜 남자에게 전화하고 있는가?

(A) 예약을 하기 위해

(B) 청구 대금을 지불하기 위해

미녀 미남 🎧

> W Hi, I'd like to schedule a checkup with
> Dr. Desousa. My name is Sarah Lomax, and
> I was last there in April.
> M Let's see… yes, you're in our system,
> Ms. Lomax. Could you come on June 8 at 11
> o'clock?

해석

여 안녕하세요, 드수자 박사님과의 건강검진 일정을 잡고 싶어요.
제 이름은 사라 로맥스이고, 4월에 마지막으로 갔었어요.

남 어디 볼게요... 네, 저희 시스템에 있네요, 로맥스 씨. 6월 8일
11시에 오실 수 있나요?

어휘

appointment 예약, 약속 bill 청구서
schedule 일정을 잡다, 예정하다 checkup (건강)검진

패러프레이징

schedule a checkup with Dr. Desousa
→ make an appointment

연습 문제   본문 p.127

1. (A)	**2.** (A)	**3.** (D)	**4.** (B)	**5.** (D)

[1] 영녀 미남 🎧

Question 1 refers to the following conversation.

> W Brandon, I just got off the phone with Margaret
> in Houston. I can't come back Tuesday
> morning from Houston because of a meeting
> that the marketing team has scheduled.
> M Okay, would you like me to look for a flight
> returning on Tuesday afternoon?
> W Yes, and make sure it is a direct flight. I want to
> spend as little time as possible traveling.
> M No problem.

해석

1번은 다음 대화에 관한 문제입니다.

여 브랜든, 방금 휴스턴에 있는 마거릿과 통화했어요. 마케팅팀이
잡아 놓은 회의 때문에 **제가 화요일 오전에 휴스턴에서 돌아올
수 없어요.**

남 알겠습니다, 화요일 오후에 돌아오는 항공편을 알아봐 드릴까
요?

여 네, 그리고 반드시 직항편으로 해 주세요. 이동하는 데 가급적 시
간을 덜 쓰고 싶어요.

남 문제없습니다.

어휘

get off the phone 전화를 끊다 schedule 일정을 잡다
make sure 반드시 ~하다, ~을 확실히 하다 direct flight 직항편

1.

여자는 왜 남자에게 전화하고 있는가?

(A) 일정 변경을 논의하기 위해

(B) 회의를 취소하기 위해

(C) 휴스턴에서 호텔을 찾기 위해

(D) 항공편의 가격을 확인하기 위해

어휘

cancel 취소하다 confirm 확인하다

[2-3] 영녀 미남 🎧

Questions 2-3 refer to the following conversation.

> W ²Did you hear that Tyson has been promoted
> to marketing team leader? All the senior
> executives agreed to promote him out of the
> three candidates.

M That was fast! Wasn't he just transferred to the marketing team? I guess the senior executives all valued his leadership and commitment. He deserves it.

W I agree with that. Anyway, ³I'm going to prepare a party for him to celebrate this achievement. Would you like to help me out with it?

해석

2–3번은 다음 대화에 관한 문제입니다.

여 ²타이슨이 마케팅 팀장으로 승진됐다는 것 들었어요? 모든 고위 간부들이 세 명의 후보 중에서 그를 승진시키는 데 동의했어요.

남 그거 빠르네요! 그는 마케팅팀으로 옮긴 지 얼마 되지 않았잖아요? 고위 간부들 모두 그의 리더십과 헌신을 높이 평가한 것 같아요. 그는 그럴 자격이 있어요.

여 그 말에 동의해요. 어쨌든, ³이번 성취를 축하하기 위해 그를 위한 파티를 준비하려고 해요. 저를 도와주시겠어요?

어휘

promote 승진시키다 senior executive 최고 중역, 고위 간부
candidate 후보자, 지원자 transfer 옮기다, 이전하다
value 평가하다 commitment 헌신, 전념
deserve ~할 자격이 있다 prepare 준비하다
celebrate 축하하다 achievement 업적, 성취
help out 도와주다

2.

대화는 주로 무엇에 관한 것인가?
(A) 동료의 승진
(B) 신입 직원
(C) 마케팅 전략
(D) 사업 회의

어휘

colleague (직장) 동료 promotion 승진

3.

여자는 무엇을 할 것이라고 말하는가?
(A) 신임 마케팅 팀장 교육하기
(B) 고위 간부들에게 연락하기
(C) 프로젝트를 위해 초과근무 하기
(D) 동료를 위해 행사 준비하기

어휘

work overtime 초과근무를 하다

패러프레이징

a party → an event

[4-5] 영녀 미남 🎧

Questions 4-5 refer to the following conversation.

W Hello, my name is Diane Madsen. ⁴I'm looking for studio space for my art class. Are you renting out units at Rossline Studios on 5th Street?

M Yes, we are. Could you tell me when you are planning to move in?

W Well, August would be perfect, as I want to get everything ready before I open my class in September.

M ⁵I'm afraid all studios are leased until August or later. However, that may change. Why don't I talk to the tenants first and I'll let you know later?

해석

4–5번은 다음 대화에 관한 문제입니다.

여 안녕하세요, 제 이름은 다이앤 매드슨입니다. ⁴제 미술 수업을 위해서 작업실 공간을 찾고 있어요. 5번가에 있는 로슬린 스튜디오의 세대들을 임대하고 계시나요?

남 네, 그렇습니다. 언제 이사 들어오실 계획인지 알려 주시겠어요?

여 음, 8월이면 딱 좋겠어요, 9월에 제 수업을 열기 전에 모든 것이 준비되게 하고 싶거든요.

남 ⁵죄송하지만 모든 작업실이 8월이나 그 이후까지 임대된 상태예요. 하지만, 바뀔 수도 있어요. 제가 일단 세입자들과 얘기해 보고 나중에 알려 드리는 게 어떨까요?

어휘

studio 작업실, 강습소 rent out ~을 임대하다
unit (공동주택 내의) 한 가구 lease 임대하다
tenant 세입자, 임차인

4.

여자는 왜 전화하고 있는가?
(A) 새 집을 사기 위해
(B) 사업을 위한 공간을 찾기 위해
(C) 미술 수업을 듣기 위해
(D) 일부 세입자들에 관해 불만을 제기하기 위해

어휘

complain 불만을 제기하다

패러프레이징

looking for studio space for my art class
→ find a space for her business

5.

남자는 어떤 문제를 언급하는가?
(A) 건물이 편리한 위치에 있지 않다.
(B) 부지가 예상했던 것보다 더 작다.
(C) 임대료가 여자의 예산보다 비싸다.
(D) 모든 작업실이 현재 이용할 수 없다.

어휘

favorable 편리한, 호의적인 budget 예산 currently 현재
unavailable 이용할 수 없는

패러프레이징

all studios are leased until August or later
→ All studios are currently unavailable

실전 문제				본문 p.128
1. (C)	**2.** (A)	**3.** (B)	**4.** (B)	**5.** (B)
6. (C)	**7.** (C)	**8.** (B)	**9.** (B)	**10.** (B)
11. (B)	**12.** (B)	**13.** (D)	**14.** (A)	**15.** (C)
16. (D)	**17.** (D)	**18.** (B)		

[1-3] 미녀 미남 🎧

Questions 1-3 refer to the following conversation.

> W Hello. I'm here about solar panels for a
> residential property. **¹I heard that you give a**
> **free consultation to potential customers, so I'd**
> **like to make an appointment for one of those.**
> My name is Christine Arnold, and I live at 935
> Roane Avenue.
>
> M Thanks for coming. Let's see... are you
> available this Saturday at 2 P.M.?
>
> W Yes, that would be great, thanks. Actually, **²my**
> **neighbor used your services last year, and he**
> **suggested that I get my panels from you.** But
> I'm a little worried they'll be too expensive for
> me.
>
> M If that's your concern, **³you could make the**
> **payments in several installments to spread out**
> **the cost.**

해석

1-3번은 다음 대화에 관한 문제입니다.

여 안녕하세요. 주택용 태양 전지판 관련해서 왔어요. **¹당신이 잠재
고객들에게 무료 상담을 해 주신다고 들었어요, 그래서 그런 상
담들 중 하나를 예약하고 싶습니다.** 제 이름은 크리스틴 아널드
이고, 론가 935번지에 삽니다.

남 와 주셔서 감사합니다. 어디 볼게요... 이번 토요일 오후 2시에
시간 되시나요?

여 네, 그때면 좋아요, 감사합니다. 사실, **²제 이웃이 작년에 당신의
서비스를 이용했는데, 그가 제게 당신으로부터 전지판을 구매하
라고 제안했어요.** 하지만 제게는 너무 비쌀까 봐 조금 걱정이 됩
니다.

남 그 점이 걱정이시면, **³비용이 분산되도록 여러 번 분납하는 식으
로 지불하실 수 있어요.**

어휘

solar panel 태양 전지판 residential 주거의
property 부동산, 재산 consultation 상담, 협의
potential 잠재적인 expensive 비싼, 돈이 많이 드는

concern 걱정, 우려 make a payment 지불하다
in installments 분납으로 spread out 분산하다

1.

여자의 방문 목적은 무엇인가?
(A) 주소를 갱신하기 위해
(B) 일자리에 지원하기 위해
(C) 상담을 예약하기 위해
(D) 불만을 제기하기 위해

어휘

apply for ~에 지원하다 book 예약하다
make a complaint 불만을 제기하다

패러프레이징

make an appointment → book

2.

여자는 이웃에 대해 무엇이라고 말하는가?
(A) 그가 업체를 추천했다.
(B) 그는 기술자로 일한다.
(C) 그는 서비스에 실망했다.
(D) 그는 최근에 이사했다.

어휘

technician 기술자 be disappointed with ~에 실망하다

패러프레이징

used your services ~ suggested that I get my panels
from you → recommended a business

3.

남자는 여자에게 무엇을 하라고 제안하는가?
(A) 다른 지점에 전화하기
(B) 분할하여 납부하기
(C) 팸플릿을 읽기
(D) 보험 상품 구매하기

어휘

insurance 보험

패러프레이징

make the payments in several installments
→ Pay in installments

[4-6] 미남 영녀 🎧

Questions 4-6 refer to the following conversation.

> M Ms. Gunderson, **⁴did you have a chance to**
> **look over the profit summary for this past**
> **quarter?**
>
> W Yes. I knew we were facing tough competition
> from DC Rentals, but these profit figures were
> even worse than I expected.
>
> M Right. **⁵I think adjusting our business model**
> **might be necessary.** We need to look for new
> revenue streams.

W In that case... ⁶we need to make sure we have an expert who can guide us through that process. I'll see if Ruth Castro is available. She's helped a lot of local companies.

PART 3

UNIT 01

해석

4-6번은 다음 대화에 관한 문제입니다.

남 건더슨 씨, ⁴지난 분기의 수익 요약을 훑어볼 기회가 있었나요?

여 네. 우리가 DC 렌털과의 힘든 경쟁에 직면하고 있다는 걸 알고 있었지만, 이 수익 수치는 제가 예상한 것보다 훨씬 더 심각했어요.

남 맞아요. ⁵저는 우리의 사업 모델을 조정하는 것이 필요할지도 모른다고 생각해요. 우리는 새로운 수입원을 찾아야 해요.

여 그렇다면... ⁶우리에게 그러한 과정을 안내해 줄 수 있는 전문가를 반드시 확보해야 해요. 제가 루스 카스트로가 시간이 되는지 알아볼게요. 그녀는 지역의 많은 회사들을 도왔어요.

어휘

look over ~을 훑어보다 profit 이익, 수익
summary 요약, 개요 quarter 4분기 face 직면하다
competition 경쟁 figures 수치 adjust 조정하다
revenue stream 수입원 in that case 그런 경우에는
make sure 반드시 ~하도록 하다 expert 전문가
guide A through B A에게 B를 안내하다

4.

대화의 주제는 무엇인가?

(A) 고용 정책
(B) 분기별 이익
(C) 임대료
(D) 배송 일정

어휘

policy 정책 quarterly 분기별의 rental 임대의

패러프레이징

the profit summary for this past quarter
→ Quarterly profits

5.

남자는 무엇을 할 것을 제안하는가?

(A) 설문 조사를 시행하는 것
(B) 사업 모델을 바꾸는 것
(C) 웹사이트를 개편하는 것
(D) 더 많은 광고를 내는 것

어휘

conduct (특정한 활동을) 하다 survey (설문) 조사
run an advertisement 광고를 내다

패러프레이징

adjusting → Changing

6.

루스 카스트로는 누구인 것 같은가?

(A) 건물주

(B) 컴퓨터 기술자
(C) 사업 컨설턴트
(D) 공장 직원

패러프레이징

an expert who can guide us ~ helped a lot of local companies → A business consultant

[7-9] 호남 미녀 🎧

Questions 7-9 refer to the following conversation.

M Good morning, Dove Botanical Gardens.

W Hello. I recently learned that you hold weddings at your site. I've just started planning my wedding, and I'm looking for a venue... um... ⁷I'm wondering how much it would cost to hold the event there.

M Well, it depends on the duration of the event. I can e-mail you an information packet, if you'd like.

W That would be wonderful. ⁸I saw the photo gallery on your Web site, and everything looks so beautiful. And I love that it's a remote setting.

M Oh, about that... ⁹We are no longer running our shuttle service from Renwick Subway Station. So, make sure to take that into consideration.

해석

7-9번은 다음 대화에 관한 문제입니다.

남 안녕하세요, 도브 식물원입니다.

여 안녕하세요. 그곳에서 결혼식을 열기도 한다는 걸 최근에 알게 되었어요. 제가 막 결혼 계획을 세우기 시작했거든요, 그래서 장소를 찾고 있는데... 음... ⁷그곳에서 행사를 열려면 비용이 얼마나 드는지 궁금합니다.

남 음, 행사의 기간에 따라 달라요. 원하시면 제가 자료집을 이메일로 보내 드릴 수 있어요.

여 그래 주시면 정말 좋겠어요. ⁸그곳의 웹사이트에서 사진 갤러리를 보았는데, 모든 것이 정말 아름다워 보여요. 그리고 외진 장소라는 점이 아주 마음에 들어요.

남 아, 그것에 관해서는... ⁹저희가 더 이상 렌윅 지하철역에서 셔틀 서비스를 운행하지 않아요. 그러니, 반드시 그 점을 고려해 주세요.

어휘

hold (행사를) 열다, 개최하다 venue (행사의) 장소
depend on ~에 달려 있다, 의존하다 duration 지속, 기간
information packet 자료 묶음 remote 외진, 외딴
setting 환경, 장소 take ~ into consideration ~을 고려하다

7.

여자는 왜 도브 식물원에 전화하고 있는가?

(A) 견학을 신청하기 위해
(B) 예약을 취소하기 위해
(C) 요금에 관해 문의하기 위해

(D) 입장권을 구매하기 위해

어휘
reservation 예약 inquire 문의하다

패러프레이징
I'm wondering how much it would cost
→ inquire about fees

8.
여자는 웹사이트에서 무엇을 보았는가?
(A) 몇몇 후기들
(B) 몇몇 이미지들
(C) 운전해서 오는 방법
(D) 영업 시간

어휘
directions 길 안내

패러프레이징
the photo gallery → Some images

9.
남자는 무엇을 더 이상 이용할 수 없다고 말하는가?
(A) 단체 할인
(B) 교통 서비스
(C) 식사 선택
(D) 전액 환불

어휘
transportation 교통, 운송 refund 환불; 환불하다

패러프레이징
shuttle service → A transportation service

[10-12] 호남 영녀 🎧
Questions 10-12 refer to the following conversation.

M Shari, ¹⁰I'm going to the international food festival at Simpson Park this Saturday. ¹¹How about joining me? I think it would be a lot of fun.
W Oh... um... I'm moving to a new apartment this weekend. I went last year, though, and I had a lot of fun.
M Well, I hope everything goes well. I think the event will be really useful because I can get some new ideas for our restaurant's menu. ¹²I'll be sure to take a lot of pictures, and maybe we can talk about it next week.

해석
10-12번은 다음 대화에 관한 문제입니다.
남 샤리, ¹⁰저는 이번 토요일에 심슨 파크에서 있을 국제 음식 축제에 갈 거예요. ¹¹저와 같이 가는 게 어때요? 아주 재미있을 것 같아요.
여 아... 음... 제가 이번 주말에 새 아파트로 이사해요. 근데 작년에

가긴 했어요. 그리고 아주 재미있었어요.
남 음, 모든 것이 순조롭게 진행되기를 바라요. 제가 우리 식당의 메뉴를 위한 몇몇 새로운 아이디어를 얻을 수 있기 때문에 그 행사는 정말 유익할 거라고 생각해요. ¹²제가 꼭 사진을 많이 찍을게요. 그리고 아마도 우리가 다음 주에 그것에 관해 얘기할 수 있을 거예요.

어휘
international 국제의 be sure to 꼭 ~하다

10.
화자들은 어떤 행사에 관해 이야기하고 있는가?
(A) 채용 박람회
(B) 음식 축제
(C) 모금 행사
(D) 영화 상영

어휘
fund-raiser 모금 행사 screening 상영, 방영

11.
여자는 왜 "제가 이번 주말에 새 아파트로 이사해요"라고 말하는가?
(A) 일부 잘못된 정보를 정정하기 위해
(B) 제안을 거절하기 위해
(C) 주소를 새로 알려 주기 위해
(D) 도움을 요청하기 위해

어휘
correct 바로잡다, 정정하다 misinformation 잘못된 정보
reject 거절하다 invitation 제안, 초대 ask for ~을 요청하다
assistance 도움, 원조

12.
남자는 무엇을 할 것이라고 말하는가?
(A) 다른 행사 찾기
(B) 사진 찍기
(C) 광고 책자 가져오기
(D) 여자의 근무 대신하기

어휘
cover (일을) 대신하다 shift 교대 근무

[13-15] 미녀 호남 영녀 🎧
Questions 13-15 refer to the following conversation with three speakers.

W1 ¹³I just came back from my business trip, and I think I spent a lot on parking. Do either of you know if we can get reimbursed for parking while on company business?
M I know your rental car fees are definitely reimbursed, but I'm not sure about parking. Do you know, Susan?
W2 ¹⁴It used to be, but the policy changed a few months ago. So, I'm not quite sure, either.

W1 I think parking should be included because it's an extension of transportation needs.
M Exactly. Well, hold on. ¹⁵I just remembered I have the list of everything that's reimbursed on my computer. I'll send it to you.
W1 That'd be great. Thanks!
W2 ¹⁵Please let me have it too, just in case.
M Sure thing.

해석

13-15번은 다음 세 명의 대화에 관한 문제입니다.

여1 ¹³제가 방금 출장에서 돌아왔어요. 그런데 주차에 돈을 많이 쓴 것 같아요. 우리가 회사 업무 중의 주차에 대해 환급받을 수 있는지 두 사람 중 누구라도 알고 있나요?

남 렌터카 요금은 분명히 환급되는 걸로 알지만, 주차에 관해서는 잘 모르겠어요. 당신은 알아요, 수잔?

여2 ¹⁴예전에는 그랬지만, 몇 달 전에 정책이 바뀌었어요. 그래서 저도 확실히 모르겠어요.

여1 전 주차가 포함되어야 한다고 생각해요, 그것도 교통에 필요한 것의 연장이니까요.

남 맞아요. 음, 잠시만요. ¹⁵제 컴퓨터에 환급되는 모든 것의 목록이 있는 게 방금 기억났어요. 그걸 당신에게 보내 줄게요.

여1 그래 주면 좋죠. 고마워요!

여2 ¹⁵만약을 위해서 저한테도 주세요.

남 물론이죠.

어휘

reimburse 상환하다, 변상하다 rental 임대의
definitely 분명히, 확실히 used to (예전에는) ~했다, ~하곤 했다
policy 정책, 방침 extension 확대, 연장
transportation 교통, 운송 needs 필요한 것, 요구
just in case 만약을 위해서

13.

대화의 주제는 무엇인가?
(A) 회사의 초과 근무 정책
(B) 출장의 불편함
(C) 주차장의 위치
(D) 여행 경비의 환급

어휘

overtime 초과 근무 inconvenience 불편
reimbursement 상환, 변상

14.

수잔은 회사의 정책에 대해 무엇이라고 말하는가?
(A) 그것은 최근에 변경되었다.
(B) 그것은 많은 항목을 다루지 않는다.
(C) 그것은 주차를 포함하지 않는다.
(D) 그것은 개정되어야 한다.

어휘

cover 다루다, 포함하다

패러프레이징

the policy changed a few months ago
→ It has recently changed

15.

남자는 아마도 다음에 무엇을 할 것인가?
(A) 정책에 관해 불만 제기하기
(B) 자신의 컴퓨터에 있는 일부 소프트웨어 업데이트하기
(C) 여자들에게 정보 보내기
(D) 직원 명단 인쇄하기

패러프레이징

the list of everything that's reimbursed → information

[16-18] 미남 미녀 🎧

Questions 16-18 refer to the following conversation and list.

M Thanks for visiting the Midlands Natural History Museum. Is there anything I can help you with?
W Hi. ¹⁶I'm making a Web site about local attractions, and I'd like to take some pictures of your exhibits. I'm particularly interested in the fossils you have on display.
M ¹⁷I'm afraid visitors are not currently allowed to go into the room where we keep the fossils. It's undergoing some repairs with the electrical system.
W Oh, that's a shame. Do you know when it will be open again?
M Probably within a few days. ¹⁸I suggest you leave your name and phone number, and then someone can call you when it's available for visiting.

해석

16-18번은 다음 대화와 목록에 관한 문제입니다.

남 미들랜드 자연사 박물관에 방문해 주셔서 감사합니다. 제가 도와 드릴 것이 있나요?

여 안녕하세요. ¹⁶제가 지역의 관광명소에 관한 웹사이트를 만들고 있는데, 이곳의 전시품 일부를 촬영하고 싶습니다. 저는 전시되어 있는 화석들에 특히 관심이 있습니다.

남 ¹⁷죄송하지만 현재 방문객은 저희가 화석을 보관하고 있는 전시실에 입장이 허용되지 않습니다. 전기 시스템과 관련된 수리 중이에요.

여 아, 그거 안타깝네요. 언제 다시 개방되는지 아시나요?

남 아마도 며칠 이내예요. ¹⁸성함과 전화번호를 남기시는 것을 추천 드려요, 그러면 방문이 가능할 때 누군가 전화를 드릴 수 있습니다.

어휘

local 지역의 attraction 명소, 명물 exhibit 전시(품); 전시하다
particularly 특히 be interested in ~에 관심이 있다
fossil 화석 on display 전시된 currently 현재
be allowed to ~하도록 허용되다 undergo 겪다, 받다
electrical 전기의

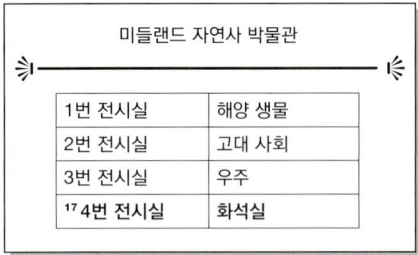

미들랜드 자연사 박물관

1번 전시실	해양 생물
2번 전시실	고대 사회
3번 전시실	우주
¹⁷ 4번 전시실	화석실

16.

여자의 방문 목적은 무엇인가?
(A) 웹사이트를 홍보하기 위해
(B) 견학을 이끌기 위해
(C) 일자리에 지원하기 위해
(D) 사진을 찍기 위해

어휘

promote 홍보하다 apply for ~에 지원하다

패러프레이징

take some pictures of your exhibits
→ take some photographs

17.

시각 자료를 보시오. 어느 전시실이 현재 이용 불가능한가?
(A) 1번 전시실
(B) 2번 전시실
(C) 3번 전시실
(D) 4번 전시실

패러프레이징

not currently allowed to go into the room
→ currently not available

18.

남자는 무엇을 할 것을 추천하는가?
(A) 다른 지점을 방문하는 것
(B) 연락처를 제공하는 것
(C) 정보 책자를 가져가는 것
(D) 관리자에게 이야기하는 것

어휘

branch 지점 contact information 연락처
informational 정보의

패러프레이징

leave your name and phone number
→ Providing some contact information

UNIT 02 화자·장소 문제

CHECK UP

본문 p.130

1. (C) **2.** (C)

[1] 미녀 미남 🎧
Question 1 refers to the following conversation.

> W Hi, I'm looking for a beginner guitar that's not very expensive. Do you have something like that?
>
> M We do. But the guitars at lower prices are usually hard to tune.
>
> W I see. Well, my brother is familiar with tuning methods, so it's OK. I just want to learn some easy songs and play around a bit.
>
> M In that case, the guitar you should look at is downstairs. This way, please.
>
> W Do you sell music books as well?
>
> M Yes, we have many books for beginners to get you started with your new guitar.

해석

1번은 다음 대화에 관한 문제입니다.
여 안녕하세요, 저는 그리 비싸지 않은 초보자용 기타를 찾고 있어요. 그런 것이 있나요?
남 있습니다. 하지만 저의 기타들은 보통 튜닝하기가 힘들어요.
여 그렇군요. 음, 제 남동생이 튜닝 방법을 잘 아니까 그건 괜찮아요. 저는 그냥 쉬운 곡들을 좀 배워서 재미 삼아 치고 싶어요.
남 그렇다면, 당신이 보실 만한 기타가 아래층에 있어요. 이쪽으로 오세요.
여 악보집도 판매하시나요?
남 네, 당신이 새 기타로 연주를 시작하게 해 줄 초보자용 악보집이 많이 있어요.

어휘

beginner 초보자, 초심자 expensive 비싼, 돈이 많이 드는
tune (악기의) 음을 맞추다 be familiar with ~을 잘 알다, 정통하다
play around 가지고 놀다

1.

화자들은 어디에 있는가?
(A) 서점에
(B) 콘서트장에
(C) 악기 상점에
(D) 미술 학교에

어휘

musical instrument 악기

패러프레이징

guitar → musical instrument

[2] 미녀 미남 🎧

Question 2 refers to the following conversation.

> **W** I'm glad the company bought these new laptops for our presentation at the workshop.
> **M** Yeah, it's convenient to have so many features. I especially like the long battery life.
> **W** Me, too. Anyway, um… is there anything else we need to review before the talk?
> **M** I feel like we've practiced enough. I'll start by explaining the tips for taking photos for property listings. After that, you can cover how to attract potential home buyers.
> **W** Perfect. And when it comes to questions from the participants, I think either of us can answer them, depending on the topic.

해석

2번은 다음 대화에 관한 문제입니다.

여 워크숍에서 할 우리의 발표를 위해 회사에서 새 노트북들을 사주어서 기뻐요.

남 네, 아주 많은 기능이 있어서 편리해요. 저는 특히 배터리가 오래 가는 것이 마음에 들어요.

여 저도요. 그건 그렇고, 음… 연설 전에 우리가 검토해야 하는 게 더 있나요?

남 우리는 충분히 연습한 것 같아요. **제가 부동산 목록을 위해 사진을 찍는 요령을 설명하는 것으로 시작할게요. 그 후에, 당신이 잠재적 주택 구매자를 끌어모으는 방법을 다루면 돼요.**

여 완벽해요. 그리고 참가자들의 질문에 관해서는, 주제에 따라서 우리 둘 중 한 사람이 답변할 수 있을 것 같아요.

어휘

presentation 발표, 프레젠테이션 convenient 편리한
feature 기능, 특징 especially 특별히, 특히
practice 연습하다; 연습 property 건물, 부동산 listing 목록
cover 다루다, 포함하다 attract 끌어모으다, 끌어들이다
potential 잠재적인 when it comes to ~에 관한 한
participant 참가자 depending on ~에 따라

2.

화자들은 어떤 업계에서 일하는 것 같은가?
(A) 언론
(B) 의료
(C) 부동산
(D) 기술

패러프레이징 **연습**		본문 p.132
1-4. 스크립트 참조	**5.** (A)	**6.** (A)

1.

Q 남자는 누구인가?
A 시 공무원

미녀 미남 🎧

> **W** I'm pleased to welcome to the studio our special guest today, Mr. Joseph Warren. He's the director of the city's department of transportation.
> **M** Thanks for inviting me, Cecilia.

해석

여 오늘 특별 손님인 조지프 워런 씨를 스튜디오로 모시게 되어 기쁩니다. 그는 시의 **교통부 국장**입니다.

남 초대해 주셔서 감사합니다, 세실리아.

어휘

city official 시 공무원 be pleased to ~해서 기쁘다
director 책임자, 감독 transportation 교통, 운송

패러프레이징

the director of the city's department of transportation
→ A city official

2.

Q 대화는 어디에서 일어나는 것 같은가?
A 기차에서

미남 미녀 🎧

> **M** Ms. Santos, I've checked the platform of the station, and there are no other passengers trying to board the passenger cars.
> **W** Great. The luggage has been secured in the cargo car. So, we're ready to announce to the passengers that we'll be departing the station shortly.

해석

남 산토스 씨, 제가 **역의 플랫폼**을 확인했고, **객차**에 탑승하려고 하는 다른 승객들은 없어요.

여 좋습니다. 수하물은 화물칸에 단단히 고정되어 있어요. 그러니, 우리는 승객들에게 곧 역을 출발한다고 알릴 준비가 되었네요.

어휘

board 탑승하다 passenger car (기차의) 객차
luggage (여행용) 짐, 수하물
secure (단단히) 고정시키다, 잡아매다 cargo car (기차의) 화물칸
be ready to ~할 준비가 되다 announce 알리다, 발표하다
depart 출발하다 shortly 곧

3.

Q 대화는 어디에서 일어나는가?
A 식당에서

> **M** Alice, could you help me change the tablecloths on the tables in our dining area? The wait staff will be arriving soon to serve our diners.
>
> **W** Sure, I can help with that.
>
> **M** Thanks! And I've ordered a new oven, so that should arrive later this week.

해석

남 앨리스, 우리 식사 공간에 있는 식탁들 위의 식탁보를 교체하는 것을 도와주시겠어요? 식사 손님들에게 서빙할 종업원들이 곧 도착할 거예요.

여 그럼요, 제가 도와드릴게요.

남 고마워요! 그리고 제가 새 오븐을 주문했어요, 그래서 그것이 이번 주 후반에 도착할 거예요.

어휘

dining area 식사 구역 wait staff (식당 등의) 종업원, 웨이터
serve (음식을) 차려 주다, 내다 diner (식당에서) 식사하는 사람
order 주문하다; 주문

4.

Q 남자는 어디에서 일하는가?

A 가전제품 제조사에서

미남 미녀 🎧

> **M** Thanks for agreeing to take on this consulting job, Ms. Lucas. We recently released new refrigerator and air conditioner models. However, we've been getting bad reviews, which is affecting our company's reputation.
>
> **W** Don't worry. I'll devise some strategies to help improve your image.

해석

남 이번 컨설팅 일을 맡기로 해 주셔서 감사합니다, 루카스 씨. 저희가 최근 새로운 냉장고와 에어컨 모델을 출시했습니다. 하지만, 안 좋은 후기들을 받고 있고, 그것이 저희 회사의 평판에 영향을 주고 있어요.

여 걱정하지 마세요. 제가 당신의 회사 이미지를 개선하도록 도와줄 몇몇 전략을 고안하겠습니다.

어휘

appliance (가정용) 전자 제품 manufacturer 제조사, 생산 회사
take on ~을 떠맡다 release 출시하다, 공개하다
affect 영향을 미치다 reputation 평판, 명성 devise 고안하다
strategy 전략, 계획 improve 개선하다, 향상시키다

패러프레이징

refrigerator and air conditioner → appliance

5.

화자들은 어떤 종류의 회사에서 일하는 것 같은가?

(A) 광고

(B) 금융

미녀 미남 🎧

> **W** Pedro, I really enjoyed the ad campaign presentation you gave at the meeting. The representatives from Kenwood Enterprise were impressed with our agency's creative designs.
>
> **M** I'm glad to hear that.

해석

여 페드로, 회의에서 당신이 한 광고 캠페인 발표는 정말 좋았어요. 켄우드 사의 대표들이 우리 대행사의 창의적인 디자인에 깊은 인상을 받았어요.

남 그 말을 들으니 기쁘네요.

어휘

presentation 발표, 프레젠테이션 representative 대표, 대리인
be impressed with ~에 깊은 인상을 받다 agency 대행사
creative 창의적인

패러프레이징

ad campaign → Advertising

6.

화자들은 어디에 있는 것 같은가?

(A) 철물점에

(B) 공사 현장에

미녀 미남 🎧

> **W** Good morning, sir. Can I help you find any tools or supplies?
>
> **M** Actually, I'm planning to do a painting project at my home. I'm looking for house paint that can last a long time. I'll be using it on the exterior and don't want to do the job again soon.

해석

여 안녕하세요, 손님. 찾으시는 공구나 용품이 있으면 도와드릴까요?

남 실은, 저희 집에 페인트 작업을 할 계획이에요. 오래갈 수 있는 가정용 페인트를 찾고 있어요. 외부에 사용할 것이고 가까운 시일 내에 이 일을 또 하고 싶지 않아요.

어휘

hardware store 철물점 construction 공사, 건설
tool 공구, 도구 supplies 용품, 비품 last 오래가다, 지속되다
exterior 외부; 외부의

패러프레이징

tools or supplies → hardware

연습 문제

본문 p.133

1. (D) **2.** (D) **3.** (B) **4.** (C) **5.** (B)

[1] 미녀 호남 🎧

Question 1 refers to the following conversation.

> W How are the trainees in your department doing?
> M You mean the new bank cashiers? They're doing really well. In fact, I plan to promote all of them to full-time cashiers.
> W That's great news. I wonder if some of them could work with us as loan officers. We're short-staffed again.
> M Well, after the training is completed, I'll send you the names of those who may be interested in changing departments.

해석

1번은 다음 대화에 관한 문제입니다.

여 당신 부서의 수습 직원들은 어때요?
남 **출납계 신규 직원들 말하는 거예요?** 그들은 정말 잘하고 있어요. 사실, 저는 그들 모두를 정규직으로 승진시킬 계획이에요.
여 그거 아주 좋은 소식이네요. **그들 중 몇 명이 대출 담당 직원으로 우리와 같이 일할 수 있는지 궁금해요.** 우리가 또 직원이 부족하거든요.
남 음, 교육이 완료된 후에, 부서를 바꾸는 데 관심이 있을지도 모르는 사람들의 명단을 보내 드릴게요.

어휘

trainee 교육을 받는 사람, 수습 (직원) cashier (은행 등의) 출납원
promote 승진시키다 full-time 상근의, 풀타임의
loan officer 대출 담당 직원 short-staffed 직원이 부족한
complete 완료하다, 끝마치다 be interested in ~에 관심이 있다

1.

화자들은 어디에서 일하는가?
(A) 음식점에서
(B) 백화점에서
(C) 부동산 중개소에서
(D) 은행에서

어휘

real estate 부동산

[2-3] 미녀 호남 🎧

Questions 2-3 refer to the following conversation.

> W Alex, I heard you did a great job leading the meeting with Allstar Autos. ²They really liked the new advertising campaign you proposed. You're setting up more meetings with new clients this month, right?
> M Yes, but I've been thinking of doing video conferences rather than meeting face to face.
> W Aren't there always problems with the video conference system?
> M Well… I've just read an article about a new system that we might want to purchase. ³I'll send some details about it to you when I get back to my desk.

해석

2-3번은 다음 대화에 관한 문제입니다.

여 알렉스, 당신이 올스타 오토 사와의 회의를 잘 이끌었다고 들었어요. ²그들이 당신이 제안한 새로운 광고 캠페인을 정말 좋아했어요. 당신은 이번 달에 새로운 의뢰인들과 더 많은 회의를 준비하고 있죠, 맞죠?
남 네, 하지만 대면 회의보다는 화상 회의를 고려 중이에요.
여 화상 회의 시스템에는 항상 문제가 있지 않나요?
남 음… 제가 방금 우리가 구매하면 어떨까 하는 새로운 시스템에 관한 기사를 읽었어요. ³제 자리로 돌아가면 그것에 관한 몇 가지 정보를 당신에게 보내 줄게요.

어휘

propose 제안하다 set up 준비하다, 설치하다
face to face 마주보고, 대면하여 details 정보

2.

화자들은 어떤 분야에서 일하는 것 같은가?
(A) 통신
(B) 연예
(C) 관광
(D) 광고

3.

남자는 무엇을 할 것이라고 말하는가?
(A) 일부 장비 반납하기
(B) 여자에게 정보 제공하기
(C) 의뢰인과 회의 참석하기
(D) 구매한 제품 교환하기

어휘

equipment 장비

패러프레이징

send some details about it to you
→ Provide information to the woman

[4-5] 호남 미녀 🎧

Questions 4-5 refer to the following conversation.

> M Good morning. What can I do for you?
> W Hi, ⁴I'm here to make a change to my wedding invitation. The order is under my fiancé's name. His last name is Monfort.

M OK… let's see… Oh, here's the order. [4]It looks like we haven't started printing it yet, so it'll be no problem to adjust it. What change would you like to make?

W [5]We've decided to use a different hotel—The Golden Lodge, not The Rose Inn.

해석

4-5번은 다음 대화에 관한 문제입니다.

남 안녕하세요. 무엇을 도와드릴까요?

여 안녕하세요. [4]제 결혼 초대장을 변경하려고 왔어요. 주문은 제 약혼자 이름으로 되어 있어요. 그의 성은 몬포트입니다.

남 알겠습니다... 어디 볼게요... 아, 여기 주문 내역이 있네요. [4]저희가 아직 인쇄를 시작하지 않은 것으로 보여요, 그러니 그것을 조정하는 건 아무 문제 없을 거예요. 어떻게 변경하고 싶으세요?

여 [5]저희가 다른 호텔을 이용하기로 결정했어요, 로즈 인이 아니라 골든 로지요.

어휘

make a change 변경하다 invitation 초대(장) fiancé 약혼자
adjust 조정하다

4.
화자들은 어디에 있는 것 같은가?
(A) 케이터링 업체에
(B) 사무용품점에
(C) 인쇄소에
(D) 호텔에

5.
여자에 따르면, 행사에 대해 무엇이 바뀌었는가?
(A) 시간
(B) 장소
(C) 후원자
(D) 날짜

패러프레이징

hotel → The venue

실전 문제
본문 p.134

1. (C)	2. (A)	3. (C)	4. (C)	5. (C)
6. (D)	7. (B)	8. (B)	9. (A)	10. (A)
11. (B)	12. (D)	13. (B)	14. (C)	15. (A)
16. (C)	17. (D)	18. (C)		

[1-3] 미녀 미남 🎧
Questions 1-3 refer to the following conversation.

W Thank you for visiting Everton's. How may I help you?

M Hi. I own an Everton spinner [1]suitcase. Uh… [2]the last time I went traveling, one of the wheels broke.

W Under the warranty, you can get free replacement parts within the first year.

M Unfortunately, I bought it three years ago, but I don't mind paying for the wheel.

W All right… but [1]we don't keep those items in stock.

M What would I need to do to get one?

W [3]If you tell me the model number, I can put in a special order for you. It would arrive by early next week.

해석

1-3번은 다음 대화에 관한 문제입니다.

여 에버튼을 방문해 주셔서 감사합니다. 어떻게 도와드릴까요?

남 안녕하세요. 저는 에버튼 스피너 [1]여행 가방을 가지고 있어요. 어… [2]지난번에 제가 여행을 갔을 때, 바퀴 중 하나가 망가졌어요.

여 보증 기간이라면, 첫 1년 동안은 부품 교체를 무료로 받으실 수 있어요.

남 안타깝게도, 저는 그걸 3년 전에 샀어요, 하지만 바퀴 비용을 지불하는 것은 개의치 않습니다.

여 알겠습니다... 하지만 [1]저희에게 그 품목의 재고가 없어요.

남 그것을 구하려면 제가 어떻게 해야 할까요?

여 [3]제게 모델 번호를 말씀해 주시면, 특별 주문을 넣어 드릴 수 있습니다. 다음 주 초까지 도착할 거예요.

어휘

suitcase 여행 가방 under the warranty 보증 기간 중인
replacement 교체, 대체 unfortunately 안타깝게도, 불행하게도
not mind -ing ~하는 것을 신경 쓰지 않다
keep ~ in stock ~의 재고가 있다 put in an order 주문하다

1.
대화는 어디에서 일어나고 있는가?
(A) 여행사에서
(B) 공항에서
(C) 여행 가방 상점에서
(D) 버스 정류장에서

2.
남자는 어떤 문제를 언급하는가?
(A) 부품이 망가졌다.
(B) 요금이 인상되었다.
(C) 가방이 너무 무겁다.
(D) 카탈로그에 오류가 있었다.

어휘

fee 요금

패러프레이징

one of the wheels broke → A part is broken

3.

여자는 무엇을 해 주겠다고 제안하는가?

(A) 환불하기
(B) 보증 기간 연장하기
(C) 주문하기
(D) 관리자에게 연락하기

어휘

extend 연장하다

패러프레이징

put in a special order → Place an order

[4-6] 미남 영녀 🎧

Questions 4-6 refer to the following conversation.

> M Hello, ⁴I'm checking in for flight 471 to Dallas. Here's my passport.
>
> W All right, sir. Let's see... we have seat 42C reserved for you. There is a 25-dollar charge for checking a bag. But... um... ⁵it looks like you haven't made the payment for that yet.
>
> M Oh, I didn't realize there was a charge. This trip was booked by my company.
>
> W You can make the payment here. It only takes a moment to process it.
>
> M I'd need to put it on the company card. ⁶But I'd better call my office first to make sure that's okay.
>
> W Of course.

해석

4-6번은 다음 대화에 관한 문제입니다.

남 안녕하세요, ⁴댈러스행 471 항공편 탑승 수속을 하려고요. 여기 제 여권입니다.

여 알겠습니다, 고객님. 어디 볼게요... 저희가 42C 좌석을 예약해 드렸습니다. 가방을 부치시려면 25달러의 요금이 있습니다. 그런데... 음... ⁵아직 요금을 지불하시지 않은 것 같아요.

남 아, 요금이 있다는 걸 몰랐어요. 이번 여행은 제 회사에서 예약했거든요.

여 여기서 지불하시면 됩니다. 그것을 처리하는 것은 잠깐이면 됩니다.

남 저는 그것을 회사 카드로 청구해야 할 거예요. ⁶하지만 그렇게 해도 괜찮다는 것을 확실히 하기 위해 우선 제 사무실에 전화해 보는 게 낫겠어요.

여 그러시지요.

어휘

check in 탑승 수속을 밟다   reserve 예약하다   charge 요금
make a payment 지불하다   book 예약하다
process 처리하다

4.

대화는 어디에서 일어나는가?

(A) 백화점에서

(B) 호텔에서
(C) 공항에서
(D) 버스 정류장에서

5.

여자는 어떤 문제를 언급하는가?

(A) 서비스가 중단되었다.
(B) 여권이 만료되었다.
(C) 요금이 지불되지 않았다.
(D) 예약이 되지 않았다.

어휘

discontinue 중단하다   expire 만료되다

패러프레이징

you haven't made the payment for that yet
→ A fee has not been paid

6.

남자는 다음에 무엇을 할 것 같은가?

(A) 서식 작성하기
(B) 확인 코드 제공하기
(C) 여행 일정표 인쇄하기
(D) 전화 통화하기

어휘

confirmation 확인   itinerary 여행 일정표

패러프레이징

call my office → Make a phone call

[7-9] 영녀 호남 미남 🎧

Questions 7-9 refer to the following conversation with three speakers.

> W Excuse me, ⁷I was here for this afternoon's baseball game. I took a ticket when I entered the stadium's parking lot, but now the machine won't take it.
>
> M1 We haven't been having any problems with the machine... Oh, I see what happened. ⁸Your ticket is torn at the corner, so the machine can't read it. My colleague, Gilbert, can help you with that.
>
> M2 Sorry you're having trouble, ma'am. I can process the ticket manually. ⁹Then I'll print you a receipt.
>
> W Thank you.

해석

7-9번은 다음 세 명의 대화에 관한 문제입니다.

여 실례합니다, ⁷오늘 오후 야구 경기 때문에 이곳에 왔어요. 경기장 주차장에 들어올 때 표를 끊었지만, 지금 기계가 그것을 받지 않아요.

남1 기계에는 아무 문제가 없었는데요... 아, 어떻게 된 건지 알겠어요. ⁸당신의 표는 모서리가 찢어져서, 기계가 그것을 읽지 못해

요. 제 동료 길버트가 그 문제를 도와드릴 수 있어요.

남2 불편을 끼쳐 드려 죄송합니다, 부인. 수동으로 표를 처리하겠습니다. ⁹ 그런 다음 영수증을 출력해 드릴게요.

여 감사합니다.

어휘

have trouble 애를 먹다, 고생하다 process 처리하다
manually 손으로, 수동으로 receipt 영수증

7.

대화는 어디에서 일어나는가?

(A) 쇼핑센터에서
(B) 운동 경기장에서
(C) 콘서트장에서
(D) 버스 터미널에서

8.

여자는 왜 티켓을 이용할 수 없는가?

(A) 그것은 만료되었다.
(B) 그것은 손상되었다.
(C) 그것은 잘못된 날짜의 것이다.
(D) 그것은 일부 정보가 빠졌다.

어휘

expire 만료되다 damage 손상시키다

패러프레이징

Your ticket is torn at the corner
→ It has been damaged

9.

길버트는 여자에게 무엇을 줄 것인가?

(A) 영수증
(B) 지도
(C) 주차권
(D) 잔돈

[10-12] 미녀 호남 🎧

Questions 10-12 refer to the following conversation.

W Good morning, Mr. Leon. ¹⁰ Welcome to your first day at Oakridge Insurance. I'm Victoria.

M Nice to meet you. I'm so pleased to be here. But... um... when I arrived this morning, I wasn't sure where to park. I used the visitor area.

W That's fine for today. I'm going to show you around the office soon, but we'll drop by the HR team first, and ¹¹ you'll get a pass for your assigned spot there.

M That's great. Actually, I used to take the subway to commute before, but... it takes much more time than driving to work here.

W I understand. ¹² We used to run a shuttle bus through your area, but now there are few employees living there.

해석

10-12번은 다음 대화에 관한 문제입니다.

여 안녕하세요, 레온 씨. ¹⁰ 오크리지 보험사에서의 첫날을 환영합니다. 저는 빅토리아예요.

남 만나서 반갑습니다. 이곳에 오게 되어 매우 기뻐요. 그런데... 음... 제가 오늘 아침에 도착했을 때, 어디에 주차를 해야 하는지 잘 모르겠더라고요. 방문객 구역을 이용했어요.

여 오늘은 그렇게 하셔도 괜찮아요. 제가 곧 사무실을 구경시켜 드릴 테지만, 우리는 우선 인사팀에 들를 거예요, 그리고 그곳에서 ¹¹ 당신에게 배정된 자리에 대한 주차권을 받게 될 겁니다.

남 잘됐네요. 사실, 전에는 지하철을 타고 출근했어요, 그런데... 운전해서 이곳으로 출근하는 것보다 훨씬 더 시간이 많이 걸려요.

여 이해해요. ¹² 우리가 전에는 당신이 사는 지역을 지나는 셔틀버스를 운행했지만, 지금은 그곳에 사는 직원들이 거의 없어요.

어휘

show A around B A에게 B를 둘러보도록 안내하다
drop by 잠깐 들르다 pass 출입증, 통행증
assign 배정하다, 맡기다

10.

화자들은 어떤 업계에서 일하는 것 같은가?

(A) 보험
(B) 출판
(C) 연예
(D) 금융

11.

여자는 주차장에 대해 무엇이라고 말하는가?

(A) 그것은 편리한 위치에 있다.
(B) 그것은 직원들을 위한 특정 자리가 있다.
(C) 그것은 수리를 위해 일시적으로 폐쇄되었다.
(D) 그것은 소정의 요금을 내고 이용할 수 있다.

어휘

conveniently 편리하게 locate 위치하다
specific 특정한, 구체적인 temporarily 일시적으로

패러프레이징

your assigned spot → specific spots for employees

12.

여자는 "그곳에 사는 직원들이 거의 없어요"라고 말할 때 무엇을 암시하는가?

(A) 버스 여행은 시간이 오래 걸린다.
(B) 사무실 이전이 취소되었다.
(C) 지하철역이 폐쇄되었다.
(D) 더 이상 서비스를 이용할 수 없다.

어휘

journey 여행 relocation 재배치, 이전
available 이용할 수 있는

[13-15] 영녀 호남 🎧

Questions 13-15 refer to the following conversation.

> **W** Hi, may I speak to Rupert Warren?
> **M** This is Rupert.
> **W** Hi, my name is Diana Holt, and I'm a freelance writer. I'm working on a children's book, and **13 I'd love to have you do the illustrations for my book. 14 I saw your drawings in a book I bought for my nephew,** and I was really impressed.
> **M** Thank you. What is your book about?
> **W** Well... it's about a boy who finds a magical key.
> **M** That sounds like a lot of fun. **15 Could you send me a bit of what you've written so far?**

해석

13-15번은 다음 대화에 관한 문제입니다.

여 안녕하세요, 루퍼트 워런 씨와 통화할 수 있을까요?
남 제가 루퍼트입니다.
여 안녕하세요, 제 이름은 다이애나 홀트이고, 프리랜서 작가입니다. 제가 어린이 책을 작업하고 있는데, **13 당신이 제 책에 삽화를 그려 주셨으면 합니다. 14 제 조카를 위해 산 책에서 당신의 그림을 보았는데,** 정말 인상 깊었어요.
남 감사합니다. 무엇에 관한 책인가요?
여 음... 마법 열쇠를 발견한 소년에 관한 것이에요.
남 아주 재미있을 것 같아요. **15 지금까지 쓰신 것 일부를 조금 보내 주실 수 있나요?**

어휘

freelance 프리랜서로 일하는 illustration 삽화, 도해
impress 깊은 인상을 주다

13.

남자는 누구인 것 같은가?
(A) 컴퓨터 프로그래머
(B) 삽화가
(C) 음악가
(D) 영화감독

14.

여자는 남자의 작업물에 대해 어떻게 알게 되었는가?
(A) 웹사이트를 방문함으로써
(B) 그의 이력서를 읽음으로써
(C) 그의 작품 중 하나를 구매함으로써
(D) 학회에 참석함으로써

어휘

résumé 이력서 attend 참석하다

패러프레이징

drawings in a book I bought
→ purchasing one of his projects

15.

남자는 무엇을 요청하는가?
(A) 본문 샘플
(B) 입사 지원서
(C) 명함
(D) 계약서

어휘

text 본문, 원문

패러프레이징

a bit of what you've written so far → A sample text

[16-18] 미남 미녀 🎧

Questions 16-18 refer to the following conversation and price list.

> **M** **16 I received the file for our bakery's new brochure.** I like the design you created. Now we just have to figure out what kind of order to place with the printer.
> **W** Well, I've got the price list here for one thousand brochures, which is what we want. Do you think we should get standard paper or glossy paper?
> **M** **17 Glossy paper is more expensive, but it's well worth it. It's a lot stronger, so it doesn't tear easily.** To save money, we wouldn't have to get the largest size.
> **W** Okay, **18 then let's get the glossy paper in the medium size.**

해석

16-18번은 다음 대화와 가격표에 관한 문제입니다.

남 **16 우리 제과점의 새 광고 책자에 관한 파일을 받았어요.** 당신이 만든 디자인이 마음에 들어요. 이제 우리는 인쇄소에 어떤 주문을 할지만 생각하면 돼요.
여 음, 우리가 원하는 광고 책자 1,000부에 대한 가격표가 여기 있어요. 일반 용지로 해야 한다고 생각해요, 아니면 광택지로 해야 한다고 생각해요?
남 **17 광택지가 더 비싸지만, 그만한 가치가 충분히 있어요. 훨씬 튼튼해서 쉽게 찢어지지 않아요.** 돈을 절약하기 위해서는, 가장 큰 크기로 하지 않아도 될 거예요.
여 좋아요, **18 그럼 중간 크기의 광택지로 하죠.**

어휘

brochure (안내·광고용) 책자 figure out 생각해내다, 이해하다
place an order 주문하다 standard 일반적인, 표준 규격에 맞춘
glossy 광이 나는 well worth ~의 가치가 충분한

인쇄 요금 (1,000장당)		
크기	일반 용지	**18 광택지**
소형	90달러	100달러
18 중형	110달러	**130달러**
대형	145달러	150달러

16.

화자들은 어떤 종류의 업체에서 일하는가?

(A) 도서관

(B) 자동차 정비소

(C) 제과점

(D) 인쇄소

17.

남자는 광택지에 대해 무엇이라고 말하는가?

(A) 그것은 일반 용지보다 접기 쉽다.

(B) 그것은 예산에 비해 너무 비싸다.

(C) 그것은 색상을 더 밝아 보이게 한다.

(D) 그것은 일반 용지보다 내구성이 더 좋다.

어휘

fold 접다 budget 예산 durable 내구성이 있는, 오래가는

패러프레이징

a lot stronger ~ doesn't tear easily → more durable

18.

시각 자료를 보시오. 화자들에게 얼마가 청구될 것 같은가?

(A) 100달러

(B) 110달러

(C) 130달러

(D) 150달러

어휘

rate 요금

UNIT 03 문제점·이유 문제

CHECK UP   본문 p.136

1. (B)   **2.** (B)

[1] 미남 미녀 🎧

Question 1 refers to the following conversation.

M I just got off the phone with Nancy Glover, and I'm afraid I have some bad news.

W Oh, no. What's happened?

M She can't speak at the workshop tomorrow.

W That's very short notice. Did she tell you why?

M A client just canceled a meeting and has asked to reschedule it for tomorrow morning. She had no choice but to make the client a priority. So… uh… should I try to find someone to fill her spot?

W No, that's all right. The workshop will just have to be a little shorter than we planned.

해석

1번은 다음 대화에 관한 문제입니다.

남 제가 방금 낸시 글로버와 통화했는데, 유감스럽게도 나쁜 소식이 좀 있어요.

여 아, 이런. 무슨 일이에요?

남 그녀가 내일 워크숍에서 발표를 할 수 없어요.

여 그건 너무 촉박한 통보예요. 그녀가 이유를 말해 주었나요?

남 한 고객이 방금 회의를 취소하고 내일 아침으로 일정을 변경해 달라고 요청했어요. 그녀는 고객을 최우선으로 생각할 수밖에 없었고요. 그래서… 어… 제가 그녀의 자리를 메울 누군가를 찾아봐야 할까요?

여 아니요, 괜찮아요. 그저 워크숍이 우리가 계획한 것보다 조금 더 짧아지겠네요.

어휘

get off the phone 전화를 끊다 short notice 촉박한 통보

reschedule 일정을 변경하다

have no choice but to ~할 수밖에 없다 priority 우선 사항

1.

남자는 어떤 문제를 언급하는가?

(A) 고객이 계약을 취소했다.

(B) 연설자가 행사에 올 수 없다.

(C) 이사회가 연기되었다.

(D) 워크숍이 초과 예약되었다.

어휘

contract 계약(서) make it to ~에 이르다, 도착하다

board meeting 이사회 postpone 연기하다

overbook 예약을 너무 많이 받다

패러프레이징

can't speak at the workshop

→ cannot make it to an event

[2] 미녀 미남 🎧

Question 2 refers to the following conversation.

W Hi, Martin. I'm in charge of planning the company retreat this year. I know that you were part of the team who worked on it last year, so I'd like you to join me.

M Sure, I can do that. Have you selected a date yet?

W Not yet. I thought it would be best to find an impressive venue first. Then we can see what kind of availability the site has.

M That's a good idea. I could do some research and recommend a few places.

W Thanks! I would really appreciate that. I'll send you some information about the budget.

해석
2번은 다음 대화에 관한 문제입니다.

여 안녕하세요, 마틴. 제가 올해 회사 야유회 기획 담당이에요. **당신이 작년에 그 일을 했던 팀의 일원이었던 것으로 알아요, 그래서 당신이 나와 함께해 줬으면 좋겠어요.**

남 물론이죠, 그렇게 할 수 있어요. 벌써 날짜를 골랐나요?

여 아직 아니에요. 일단 인상적인 장소를 찾는 것이 가장 좋겠다고 생각했어요. 그런 다음 그 장소에 이용할 수 있는 것이 뭐가 있는지 알아보면 돼요.

남 그거 좋은 생각이에요. 제가 조사를 좀 해서 몇 군데 추천할 수 있어요.

여 고마워요! 그렇게 해 주시면 정말 감사하겠어요. 제가 예산에 관한 정보를 당신에게 보내 줄게요.

어휘
be in charge of ~을 담당하다 company retreat 회사 야유회
impressive 인상적인 venue (행사의) 장소
availability 유용성, 이용할 수 있음 appreciate 고맙게 여기다
budget 예산

2.
여자는 왜 프로젝트를 위해 남자를 선택했는가?
(A) 그가 최근에 다른 업무를 끝냈다.
(B) 그가 작년에 같은 행사를 도왔다.
(C) 그가 사업 계약의 거대한 네트워크를 갖추고 있다.
(D) 그가 인상적인 학력을 지니고 있다.

어휘
duty 임무, 직무 assist with ~을 돕다
educational background 교육적 배경, 학력

패러프레이징
you were part of the team who worked on it
→ assisted with the same event

패러프레이징 **연습**
본문 p.138

1-4. 스크립트 참조   **5.** (B)   **6.** (A)

1.
Q 여자는 어떤 문제를 언급하는가?
A 전자제품에 누수가 있다.

🔲미남 🔲미녀 🎧

M Welcome to the Clearview Towers property management office. How may I help you?

W My name is Justine Romo, and I live in unit 433. I was running my dishwasher this morning, but it seems there's a leak. After it had been running for a while, I saw water all over the floor.

해석
남 클리어뷰 타워 부동산 관리소에 오신 것을 환영합니다. 어떻게 도와드릴까요?

여 제 이름은 저스틴 로모이고, 433호에 삽니다. **오늘 아침에 식기 세척기를 돌리고 있었는데, 물이 새는 것 같아요.** 잠시 동안 작동한 후에 보니, 바닥이 온통 물바다였어요.

어휘
appliance (가정용) 전자기기 leak (물·가스 등이) 새다; 누출
property 부동산, 재산 management 관리, 운영
unit (공동주택의) 한 가구 run 작동시키다, 작동하다

패러프레이징
dishwasher ~ there's a leak
→ An appliance has leaked

2.
Q 남자는 어떤 문제를 언급하는가?
A 일부 비용이 처리되지 않는다.

🔲미녀 🔲미남 🎧

W Good morning, Mr. Ennis. You said you had a concern about the contract?

M Yes. There's no provision for our travel expenses. This is important, as our band is coming from out of town.

해석
여 안녕하세요, 에니스 씨. 계약에 대해 우려되는 것이 있다고 말씀하셨죠?

남 네. **우리의 여행 경비에 대한 조항이 없어요.** 이것은 중요해요, 우리 밴드는 다른 지역에서 가니까요.

어휘
expense 비용, 경비 cover 다루다, 포함시키다
concern 우려, 걱정 contract 계약(서) provision 조항, 규정
from out of town 다른 곳에서 온

패러프레이징
There's no provision for our travel expenses
→ Some expenses are not covered

3.
Q 남자는 왜 그의 새 아파트에 대해 들떠 있는가?
A 그곳은 공원에서 가깝다.

🔲미녀 🔲미남 🎧

W I heard you are moving to the Victoria neighborhood.

M Yes, to an apartment on Dayton Street. It's located near Spruce Park, so I'm excited to move there.

해석

여 당신이 빅토리아 근처로 이사한다고 들었어요.

남 맞아요, 데이턴 거리에 있는 아파트로요. **스프루스 공원 근처에 있어서, 그곳으로 이사하게 되어 신나요.**

어휘

excited about ~에 관해 들뜬, 흥분한 close to ~에 가까운
neighborhood 근처, 인근, 이웃 be located (~에) 위치해 있다

패러프레이징

located near Spruce Park → close to a park

4.

Q 남자는 왜 여자를 도울 수 없는가?

A 그는 전화를 받아야 한다.

미녀 미남 🎧

W Now that I'm checked in, would you mind showing me how to get to your on-site gym?

M I can in a moment, but my phone's ringing and I need to take this call.

해석

여 이제 체크인했으니, 건물 내의 헬스장에 가는 법을 알려 주시겠어요?

남 곧 해 드릴게요, 그런데 제 전화벨이 울리고 있어서 이 전화를 받아야 해요.

어휘

now that ~이므로, ~이기 때문에
be checked in (= check in) 체크인하다, 탑승 수속을 하다
would you mind -ing? ~해 주시겠습니까?
on-site 현장의, 건물 내의 in a moment 곧, 바로

패러프레이징

take this call → answer a phone call

5.

남자는 왜 걱정하는가?

(A) 고객이 화가 났다.

(B) 위치가 외지다.

미녀 미남 🎧

W What did you think of the properties the real estate agent showed us? The one on Holford Street is spacious and has low rent.

M That's true, but it's on the city outskirts. I think we'd have a hard time attracting people there.

해석

여 부동산 중개인이 우리에게 보여 준 건물들을 어떻게 생각해요? 홀퍼드 거리에 있는 것은 널찍하고 임대료가 저렴해요.

남 맞아요, 하지만 **도시 외곽에 있어요.** 우리가 그곳으로 사람들을 끌어들이기가 힘들 것 같아요.

어휘

location 위치, 장소 remote 외진, 외딴 property 건물, 부동산
real estate agent 부동산 중개인 spacious 널찍한
rent 집세, 임차료 outskirt 변두리, 교외
have a hard time -ing ~하는 데 어려움이 있다
attract 끌어들이다, 끌어모으다

패러프레이징

it's on the city outskirts → A location is remote

6.

문제는 무엇인가?

(A) 일부 장비가 제대로 작동하지 않는다.

(B) 승객이 시간에 맞춰 도착하지 않았다.

미남 미녀 🎧

M We're set to begin boarding in 25 minutes. How are the pre-flight checks going?

W Well, I've checked our intercom system. No matter what I tried, the sound volume was still really low.

해석

남 우리는 25분 후에 탑승을 시작할 예정이에요. 비행 전 점검은 어떻게 되어 가고 있죠?

여 음, 우리 구내방송 시스템을 확인했는데요. 아무리 해봐도 음량이 여전히 너무 낮았어요.

어휘

equipment 장비 work (기계 등이) 작동되다
properly 제대로, 적절히 on time 시간에 맞춰
be set to ~하도록 예정되어 있다 board 탑승하다
pre-flight 비행 전의, 비행에 대비한 intercom 구내방송
no matter what 아무리 ~해도

패러프레이징

our intercom system ~ the sound volume was still
really low → Some equipment is not working properly

연습 문제 본문 p.139

1. (C) **2.** (D) **3.** (C) **4.** (A) **5.** (D)

[1] 영녀 미남 🎧

Question 1 refers to the following conversation.

W Excuse me, could you check the refrigerator in the staff lounge when you're finished here?

M Another employee already told me about that, so I checked it a little while ago. The fan in the back is starting to make a humming sound again, it seems.

W How soon can you fix it? The noise is quite distracting.

M I'll need to get a replacement part, so I'll fix it tomorrow.

해석

1번은 다음 대화에 관한 문제입니다.

여 실례합니다, 이곳 일을 끝내시면 직원 휴게실의 냉장고를 확인해 주시겠어요?

남 다른 직원분이 이미 그것에 관해 제게 말씀하셔서, 조금 전에 확인했어요. 뒤쪽의 팬에서 다시 윙윙거리는 소리가 나기 시작하는 것 같더라고요.

여 얼마나 빨리 고치실 수 있어요? 소음 때문에 너무 집중이 안 돼요.

남 대체 부품을 구해야 할 거예요, 그러니 내일 고치겠습니다.

어휘

staff lounge 직원 휴게실 a little while ago 조금 전에
humming 윙윙거리는 fix 수리하다
distracting 마음을 산란하게 하는 replacement part 대체 부품

1.

문제는 무엇인가?
(A) 조명이 작동하지 않는다.
(B) 일부 서류가 분실되었다.
(C) 전자기기가 소음이 심하다.
(D) 직원 휴게실이 너무 덥다.

어휘

appliance (가정용) 기기

패러프레이징

refrigerator → appliance /
The noise is quite distracting → too noisy

[2-3] 미남 영녀 🎧

Questions 2-3 refer to the following conversation.

M Excuse me, ²I just moved here, and I'd like to sign up for a library card to check out some books. How can I do that?

W First, you'll need to fill out the application form. Then you'll need to show your driver's license and proof of address, such as your credit card statement or utility bill.

M Well, ³I have my driver's license with me, but I'll have to come back tomorrow with my utility bill.

W That's fine. ²Once you do that, we can issue the library card.

해석

2-3번은 다음 대화에 관한 문제입니다.

남 실례합니다, ²제가 막 여기로 이사 왔는데요, 책을 좀 대출하기 위해 도서관 대출증을 신청하고 싶습니다. 어떻게 하면 되나요?

여 우선, 신청서를 작성하셔야 할 거예요. 그런 다음 운전면허증과 신용카드 명세서나 공과금 고지서 같은 주소 증빙 서류를 보여주셔야 합니다.

남 음, ³운전면허증은 가지고 있지만, 공과금 고지서를 가지고 내일 다시 와야겠습니다.

여 좋습니다. ²그렇게 하시면 저희가 도서관 대출증을 발급해 드릴 수 있습니다.

어휘

sign up for ~을 신청하다 check out (도서관 등에서) 대출하다
fill out 작성하다, 기입하다 application form 신청서, 지원서
proof 증거(물) credit card statement 신용카드 명세서
utility bill 공과금 고지서 issue 발부하다

2.

여자는 어디에서 일하는 것 같은가?
(A) 은행에서
(B) 서점에서
(C) 운전면허 발급 센터에서
(D) 공공 도서관에서

3.

남자는 왜 내일 다시 올 것인가?
(A) 신청서를 받기 위해
(B) 무료 행사에 참석하기 위해
(C) 추가 서류를 제공하기 위해
(D) 새 신용카드를 요청하기 위해

어휘

extra 추가의, 가외의

패러프레이징

come back ~ with my utility bill
→ provide an extra document

[4-5] 영녀 미남 🎧

Questions 4-5 refer to the following conversation.

W Hi, my name is Kendra Wood. I just opened a business account here. However, ⁴I haven't received my debit card from you yet.

M Sorry. Let me look up your information. Hmm… It says it was delivered on Monday and signed for by Mr. Kahleem.

W Oh, really? I didn't ask him. I'm glad it arrived. ⁵I need to go shopping for some office supplies tomorrow with it. I guess I should have checked around the office before coming here.

해석

4-5번은 다음 대화에 관한 문제입니다.

여 안녕하세요, 제 이름은 켄드라 우드입니다. 제가 막 이곳에서 기업 계좌를 개설했습니다. 하지만, ⁴아직 직불 카드를 받지 못했어요.

남 죄송합니다. 당신의 정보를 찾아볼게요. 흠... 월요일에 배송되었고 칼림 씨가 서명하신 것으로 되어 있는데요.

여 아, 정말요? 그에게 물어보지 않았어요. 도착했다니 다행이네요. ⁵그것을 가지고 내일 사무용품을 좀 사러 가야 하거든요. 여기 오기 전에 사무실 주변을 확인해 봤어야 했나 봐요.

어휘

account 계좌, 계정 debit card 직불 카드
look up (정보를) 찾아보다 shop for ~을 사다
office supply 사무용품

4.

여자는 어떤 문제를 언급하는가?
(A) 물품을 수령하지 못했다.
(B) 계좌 비밀번호가 안 맞는다.
(C) 카드가 만료되었다.
(D) 일부 정보가 삭제되었다.

어휘

expire 만료되다 delete 삭제하다

패러프레이징

I haven't received my debit card
→ An item was never received

5.

여자는 내일 무엇을 할 것 같은가?
(A) 장비 수리하기
(B) 서류 배달하기
(C) 또 다른 카드 신청하기
(D) 비품 구매하기

어휘

equipment 장비 document 서류, 문서
apply for ~을 신청하다

패러프레이징

go shopping for some office supplies
→ Shop for supplies

실전 문제 본문 p.140

1. (C)	2. (C)	3. (B)	4. (B)	5. (C)
6. (B)	7. (A)	8. (B)	9. (C)	10. (B)
11. (A)	12. (D)	13. (C)	14. (D)	15. (D)
16. (D)	17. (D)	18. (A)		

[1-3] 미남 미녀 🎧

Questions 1-3 refer to the following conversation.

M Hi, Tammy. You look really busy. Is that some paperwork for a client?

W No, ¹I wanted to nominate Crystal for the Teamwork Award. I'm filling out the form now, but there are a lot of details to include.

M Oh, right. It's nice that employees can support their coworkers like that.

W Yeah, but the deadline is today at noon. ²I'm worried that I'm not going to get it finished in time.

M Didn't you read the memo from this morning? ³They've extended the deadline to Friday.

W Oh, that's great news! ³Thanks for letting me know.

해석

1-3번은 다음 대화에 관한 문제입니다.

남 안녕하세요, 태미. 정말 바빠 보여요. 그건 고객을 위한 서류 작업이에요?

여 아니요, ¹팀워크 상에 크리스털을 후보로 추천하고 싶었어요. 지금 양식을 작성하는 중인데, 포함시킬 세부 사항이 많이 있어요.

남 아, 맞아요. 직원들이 그런 식으로 동료들을 지지할 수 있어서 좋아요.

여 네, 하지만 마감 시한이 오늘 정오예요. ²시간 맞춰 끝내지 못할까 봐 걱정이에요.

남 오늘 아침에 온 회람 안 읽었어요? ³마감 시한을 금요일로 연장했어요.

여 아, 그거 아주 좋은 소식이네요! ³알려 줘서 고마워요.

어휘

paperwork 서류 작업 nominate (후보자로) 추천하다, 지명하다
fill out 기입하다, 작성하다 detail 세부 사항 deadline 마감 시간
in time 시간 맞춰 extend 연장하다

1.

여자는 무엇을 준비하고 있는가?
(A) 회의 안건
(B) 기조 연설
(C) 추천서
(D) 학회 등록

어휘

agenda 안건 keynote speech 기조 연설
nomination 지명, 추천

2.

여자는 무엇에 대해 걱정하는가?
(A) 서류를 분실하는 것
(B) 장시간 일하는 것
(C) 마감 시한을 놓치는 것
(D) 예산을 초과하는 것

어휘

exceed 넘다, 초과하다

패러프레이징

I'm not going to get it finished in time
→ Missing a deadline

3.

여자는 왜 남자에게 고마워하는가?

(A) 그가 늦게까지 일하는 데 동의했다.

(B) 그가 그녀에게 정보를 주었다.

(C) 그가 문서를 교정하겠다고 제안했다.

(D) 그가 그녀를 고객에게 소개시킬 것이다.

어휘

proofread 교정을 보다

패러프레이징

letting me know → gave her some information

[4-6] 영녀 미남 🎧

Questions 4-6 refer to the following conversation.

> W ⁴I just got a call from Hartford Bank, and they have approved our application for a business loan. I'm thrilled.
> M That's wonderful!
> W Indeed. Now we can finally renovate our store. ⁵We should get started as soon as possible.
> M Well... um... it's good to have the funding, but we're in the middle of our peak season.
> W Good point. ⁵We don't want that to get interrupted.
> M However, we could research contractors and choose one now. ⁶My friend works in the construction industry, so he can probably give us some advice.

해석

4-6번은 다음 대화에 관한 문제입니다.

여 ⁴제가 방금 하트퍼드 은행으로부터 전화를 받았어요, 그들이 우리의 사업 대출 신청을 승인했어요. 신나요.

남 정말 잘됐어요!

여 정말로요. 이제 우리가 드디어 가게를 보수할 수 있어요. ⁵우리는 가능한 한 빨리 시작해야 해요.

남 글쎄요... 음... 자금을 확보한 것은 기쁘지만, 우리는 한창 성수기예요.

여 좋은 지적이에요. ⁵우리는 그게 방해받는 걸 원치 않아요.

남 하지만, 우리가 지금 도급업체들을 조사해서 한 곳을 고를 수 있어요. ⁶제 친구가 건설업에서 일하니, 그가 아마도 우리에게 조언을 좀 해 줄 수 있을 거예요.

어휘

approve 승인하다, 인가하다 application 지원(서), 신청(서)
business loan 기업 대출 thrilled 아주 흥분한, 신이 난
indeed 정말, 확실히 renovate 개조하다, 보수하다
get started (어떤 일을 하기) 시작하다 funding 자금, 자금 제공
in the middle of ~의 도중에 peak season 성수기
good point 좋은 지적 get interrupted 방해받다
contractor 계약자, 도급업자 construction 건설, 공사

4.

여자는 왜 기뻐하는가?

(A) 은행이 영업시간을 연장할 것이다.

(B) 대출 신청이 승인되었다.

(C) 그녀는 승진을 제안받았다.

(D) 그녀는 새로운 지점으로 전근 갈 것이다.

어휘

extend 연장하다, 확대하다 promotion 승진, 홍보, 판촉

패러프레이징

they have approved our application for a business loan → A loan application was approved

5.

남자는 "우리는 한창 성수기예요"라고 말할 때 무엇을 의미하는가?

(A) 그는 여자를 도와줄 시간이 없다.

(B) 프로젝트에 쓸 여윳돈이 있다.

(C) 제안한 일정은 문제가 될 것이다.

(D) 사업이 잘 되고 있다.

어휘

extra money 여분의 돈 timeline 시간표, 연대표

6.

남자는 그의 친구에 대해 무엇이라고 말하는가?

(A) 그는 현재 직장을 구하고 있다.

(B) 그는 결정에 대해 그들에게 조언해 줄 수 있다.

(C) 그는 곧 이 업체를 방문할 것이다.

(D) 그는 업계 학회에 참석했다.

어휘

currently 현재 advise A on B A에게 B에 대해 충고하다
attend 참석하다

패러프레이징

give us some advice → advise them on a decision

[7-9] 미녀 호남 🎧

Questions 7-9 refer to the following conversation.

> W Excuse me, ⁷I purchased this shirt here yesterday, but there was a problem when I tried it on. I noticed there was a small hole in it. ⁷I would like to exchange it for another one.
> M ⁸I apologize for that, but we are sold out of that particular shirt. You may return it for store credit and purchase something else if you'd like.
> W I was really quite pleased with this shirt, so I'd like to wait until it comes back in and exchange it later. Do you know when you'll be getting more?
> M Unfortunately, I'm not sure. However, ⁹I'll let you know once they come in. May I have your number, please?

해석

패러프레이징
let you know → contact the woman

7-9번은 다음 대화에 관한 문제입니다.

여 실례합니다, **7제가 어제 여기서 이 셔츠를 샀어요. 그런데 입어 봤더니 문제가 있었어요. 셔츠에 작은 구멍이 하나 있는 걸 발견했어요. 7다른 것으로 교환하고 싶어요.**

남 **8그 점에 대해 사과드립니다, 하지만 그 특정 셔츠는 재고가 없어요.** 원하시면 상점 포인트로 환불받으시고 다른 것을 구매하셔도 돼요.

여 저는 이 셔츠에 정말 만족해요, 그래서 다시 입고될 때까지 기다렸다가 나중에 교환하고 싶어요. 언제 더 들어오는지 아세요?

남 안타깝지만, 확실하지 않아요. 하지만, **9일단 입고되면 알려 드릴게요. 전화번호를 알려 주시겠어요?**

어휘
try on 입어 보다 notice 알아채다, 주목하다
apologize for ~에 대해 사과하다
sold out 재고가 없는, 다 팔린 particular 특정한
store credit 물건 값을 상점의 채무로 처리하는 것
be pleased with ~에 만족하다

7.
여자는 무엇을 하기를 원하는가?
(A) 물품 교환하기
(B) 긴급 주문하기
(C) 상품권 구매하기
(D) 환불받기

어휘
place an order 주문하다 refund 환불; 환불하다

패러프레이징
shirt → an item

8.
남자는 어떤 문제를 언급하는가?
(A) 상점이 막 문을 닫으려던 참이다.
(B) 물품이 재고가 없다.
(C) 가격이 최근에 올랐다.
(D) 쿠폰이 더 이상 유효하지 않다.

어휘
be about to 막 ~하려고 하다 out of stock 품절인
valid 유효한, 정당한

패러프레이징
we are sold out of that particular shirt
→ An item is out of stock

9.
남자는 무엇을 할 것이라고 말하는가?
(A) 그는 여자에게 상점 포인트를 줄 것이다.
(B) 그는 창고에 전화할 것이다.
(C) 그는 여자에게 연락할 것이다.
(D) 그는 상점의 웹사이트를 확인할 것이다.

[10-12] 영녀 호남 🎧
Questions 10-12 refer to the following conversation.

> W Hi, Bryan. I'm wondering if you know which bus goes to Montana Avenue, and where the nearest bus stop is. **10I'm meeting a friend who lives there.**
>
> M Oh, sure. **11The bus stop is not far from here. You can see it right across from the pharmacy over there, at the corner of Ken and Shinewood.** It's the number 34 that you want to take. But… uh… what happened to your car? Don't you usually drive?
>
> W **12The last time I visited my friend's neighborhood, I was not able to find any parking.** So, I thought taking the bus this time would be easier.

해석

10-12번은 다음 대화에 관한 문제입니다.

여 안녕하세요, 브라이언. 어떤 버스가 몬태나 가로 가는지와, 가장 가까운 버스 정류장이 어디인지 당신이 아는지 궁금해요. **10그곳에 사는 친구를 만날 거예요.**

남 아, 물론이죠. **11버스 정류장은 여기서 멀지 않아요. 저쪽에 있는 약국 바로 맞은편에 보여요, 켄과 샤인우드의 모퉁이예요.** 당신이 타야 하는 건 34번이에요. 그런데… 어… 당신 차에 무슨 일이 있어요? 보통 운전하지 않아요?

여 **12지난번에 제 친구 동네를 방문했을 때, 주차 공간을 전혀 찾을 수가 없었어요.** 그래서 이번에는 버스를 타는 것이 더 편하겠다고 생각했어요.

어휘
right across from ~의 바로 맞은편에 pharmacy 약국
neighborhood 근처, 이웃 parking 주차 공간

10.
여자는 무엇을 하려고 계획하고 있는가?
(A) 저녁 회식에 참석하기
(B) 친구 방문하기
(C) 차 찾아오기
(D) 새 가전제품 사기

어휘
business dinner 회식 home appliance 가정용 전자기기

패러프레이징
meeting → Visit

11.
남자는 어떤 정보를 제공하는가?
(A) 어디서 버스를 타는지
(B) 어디서 표를 사는지

(C) 어떻게 택시를 찾는지
(D) 어떻게 주차 비용을 지불하는지

12.

여자의 문제는 무엇인가?
(A) 그녀는 돈을 충분히 갖고 있지 않다.
(B) 그녀의 차가 수리되는 중이다.
(C) 그녀는 회의에 늦었다.
(D) 주차 공간이 없다.

패러프레이징

I was not able to find any parking
→ There are no parking spaces

[13-15] 영녀 미녀 호남 🎧
Questions 13-15 refer to the following conversation with three speakers.

> W1 Joanna, I had a missed call from the director. Is there a problem?
> W2 Yes, ¹³ in examination room 3. ¹⁴ The heater started blowing out only cold air. Tom said there weren't any problems with that when he used the room the other day.
> W1 Alright. Stuart, I need your help. Could you please check out room 3? ¹⁴ The heating system is running, but the air coming out isn't warm.
> M Okay. It might be an issue with the filter. I'll try replacing it to see if that helps.
> W1 I hope it does. ^{13, 15} We have an important patient getting a check-up in an hour, and I really want to make a good impression.

해석
13-15번은 다음 세 명의 대화에 관한 문제입니다.
여1 조애나, 제가 원장님의 전화를 못 받았어요. 무슨 문제가 있나요?
여2 네, ¹³ 3번 검사실이요. ¹⁴ 난방기에서 찬 바람만 나오기 시작했어요. 톰이 며칠 전에 그 방을 사용했을 때는 난방기에 아무 문제가 없었다고 했어요.
여1 알겠어요. 스튜어트, 당신의 도움이 필요해요. 3번 방을 확인해 주시겠어요? ¹⁴ 난방 시스템이 돌아가지만, 나오는 바람이 따뜻하지 않아요.
남 알겠어요. 아마도 필터 문제일 거예요. 제가 그것을 교체해 보고 그게 도움이 되는지 알아볼게요.
여1 그랬으면 좋겠네요. ^{13, 15} 한 시간 뒤에 검진을 받을 중요한 환자가 있는데, 정말 좋은 인상을 주고 싶어요.

어휘
director 책임자, 관리자 examination 검사, 조사
blow out (가스 등을) 내뿜다 check out 확인하다, 조사하다
run (기계 등이) 돌아가다, 움직이다 issue (걱정거리가 되는) 문제
replace 바꾸다, 교체하다 check-up 검진
make a good impression 좋은 인상을 주다

13.

대화는 어디에서 일어나고 있는 것 같은가?
(A) 경영 연구소에서
(B) 슈퍼마켓에서
(C) 병원에서
(D) 제조 시설에서

어휘
institute 협회, 연구소 manufacturing 제조(업); 제조(업)의

14.

여자들은 어떤 문제에 관해 이야기하고 있는가?
(A) 전등이 켜지지 않는다.
(B) 배송품이 늦게 도착할 것이다.
(C) 문이 열리지 않는다.
(D) 난방기가 고장 났다.

어휘
malfunction (기계 등이) 제대로 작동하지 않다

패러프레이징

The heater started blowing out only cold air
→ A heater has malfunctioned

15.

한 시간 뒤에 무슨 일이 일어날 것인가?
(A) 업체가 문을 닫을 것이다.
(B) 교육이 시작될 것이다.
(C) 방이 청소될 것이다.
(D) 환자가 예약되어 있을 것이다.

어휘
close for the day 폐점하다 training session 교육 (과정)
appointment 예약, 약속

패러프레이징

We have an important patient getting a check-up
→ A patient will have an appointment

[16-18] 미남 미녀 🎧
Questions 16-18 refer to the following conversation and schedule.

> M Hi, Victoria. You wanted to talk about the work schedule for next week?
> W Yes, that's right.
> M What's going on?
> W ¹⁶ There's a writing seminar at the Finwood Community Center that I'd really like to attend. I'm wondering if I can skip my dinner shift.
> M Well… we'll still need a head server on duty. That's the only way to keep the restaurant running smoothly. ¹⁷ Why don't you find out who is working the Wednesday lunch shift? Maybe that person would be willing to work a double shift.

W Okay, I'll do that. ¹⁸I'll call you later today to let you know if there will be a change.

M Thanks.

해석

16–18번은 다음 대화와 일정표에 관한 문제입니다.

남 안녕하세요, 빅토리아. 다음 주 근무 일정에 관해 얘기하길 원하셨죠?

여 네, 맞아요.

남 무슨 일인데요?

여 ¹⁶핀우드 커뮤니티 센터에서 글쓰기 세미나가 있는데 정말 참석하고 싶어요. 저녁 근무에서 빠질 수 있는지 궁금해요.

남 음... 우리는 아직 책임 서버가 계속해서 근무해야 해요. 그것이 식당이 순조롭게 돌아가도록 하는 유일한 방법이에요. ¹⁷누가 수요일 점심 근무를 하는지 알아보는 게 어때요? 아마도 그 사람이 기꺼이 이중 근무를 할지도 몰라요.

여 알겠어요, 그렇게 할게요. ¹⁸오늘 이따가 당신에게 전화해서 변경이 있을지 알려 드릴게요.

남 고마워요.

어휘

skip (일을) 거르다, 건너뛰다 shift 교대 근무 (시간)
head (단체·조직의) 책임자 server 서빙하는 사람
on duty 근무 중인, 일하고 있는 find out 발견하다, 생각해내다
be willing to 기꺼이 ~하다

	¹⁷점심 근무	저녁 근무
월요일	빅토리아	니콜
화요일	테레사	가브리엘
¹⁷수요일	키노카	빅토리아
목요일	공휴일 휴점	

16.

여자는 왜 휴가 내기를 원하는가?
(A) 가족들을 방문하기 위해
(B) 여행을 떠나기 위해
(C) 병원에 가기 위해
(D) 세미나에 참석하기 위해

어휘

take time off 휴가를 내다

17.

시각 자료를 보시오. 여자는 누구에게 말할 것 같은가?
(A) 니콜
(B) 테레사
(C) 가브리엘
(D) 키노카

18.

여자는 오늘 나중에 무엇을 할 것이라고 말하는가?
(A) 남자에게 전화하기
(B) 새 일정표 출력하기

(C) 식당에 들르기
(D) 추가 근무하기

패러프레이징

call you → Give the man a call

UNIT O4 세부사항 문제

CHECK UP 본문 p.142

1. (D) **2.** (A)

[1] 미남 미녀 🎧

Question 1 refers to the following conversation.

M Hey, Sally, you're the one handling the book launch event, right? I heard the customer wanted the event to be held outside next Thursday.

W Right. Why? Is something wrong?

M Well, I have the weather forecast here, and it says they expect rain from Wednesday through the weekend. I think it's best we move up the event to Monday or Tuesday.

W Monday won't do. Catering has an event on that day. I'll e-mail the client and ask if they would be okay with changing the schedule to another day.

해석

1번은 다음 대화에 관한 문제입니다.

남 이봐요, 샐리, 당신이 도서 출간 행사를 담당하는 사람이죠, 맞죠? 고객이 그 행사를 다음 주 목요일 야외에서 진행되길 원한다고 들었어요.

여 맞아요. 왜요? 뭐가 잘못됐어요?

남 음, 여기 일기예보가 있는데, 수요일에서 주말까지 내내 비가 예상된다고 해요. 우리가 월요일이나 화요일로 행사를 앞당기는 게 최선일 것 같아요.

여 월요일은 안 돼요. 케이터링 업체가 그날 행사가 있어요. 제가 고객에게 이메일을 보내서 일정을 다른 날로 바꾸어도 괜찮은지 물어볼게요.

어휘

handle 다루다, 처리하다 launch 출시, 출간; 출시하다, 출간하다
be held (행사가) 열리다 weather forecast 일기예보
expect 예상하다, 기대하다 move up (날짜를) 앞당기다
catering 케이터링, 음식 공급(업)

1.

여자는 무엇에 대해 책임이 있는가?
(A) 저녁 식사에 음식을 제공하는 것
(B) 책을 출판하는 것
(C) 모든 손님들에게 전화하는 것

(D) 행사를 조정하는 것

어휘

be responsible for ~에 책임이 있다 publish 출판하다
coordinate 조정하다

패러프레이징

handling the book launch event
→ Coordinating an event

[2] 미남 미녀 🎧

Question 2 refers to the following conversation.

> M Hi, I'm sorry I'm late. It took such a long time to find a parking spot.
> W No problem. I've just arrived as well. There were hardly any spots left. Where did you park your car?
> M I parked one block away from here. But the parking meter was acting strange.
> W What do you mean?
> M When I tried to put in a quarter, it got stuck.
> W Why don't you go move your car somewhere else after ordering your meal? It'll take some time for the food to come out. You don't want to risk getting a fine.

해석

2번은 다음 대화에 관한 문제입니다.
남 안녕하세요, 늦어서 미안해요. 주차 공간을 찾는 데 너무 오래 걸렸어요.
여 괜찮아요. 저도 방금 도착했어요. 남은 자리가 거의 없더라구요. 당신의 차를 어디에 주차했나요?
남 저는 여기서 한 블록 떨어진 곳에 주차했어요. **그런데 주차 요금 징수기 작동이 이상했어요.**
여 무슨 말이에요?
남 **제가 25센트를 넣으려고 하자 끼어 버렸거든요.**
여 당신의 식사를 주문한 후에 차를 어디 다른 곳으로 옮기는 게 어때요? 음식이 나오려면 시간이 좀 걸릴 거예요. 벌금을 낼 위험을 감수할 필요는 없잖아요.

어휘

parking spot 주차 공간 hardly any 거의 없는
parking meter 주차 요금 징수기 quarter 25센트짜리 동전
get stuck 꼼짝 못하게 되다 order 주문하다
risk -ing ~하는 위험을 무릅쓰다 fine 벌금

2.

남자는 주차 요금 징수기에 대해 무엇이라고 말하는가?
(A) 그것은 고장 났다.
(B) 그것은 편리하다.
(C) 그것은 곧 만료될 것이다.
(D) 그것은 요금이 비싸다.

어휘

out of order 고장 난 convenient 편리한 expire 만료되다

패러프레이징

acting strange → out of order

패러프레이징 연습   본문 p.144

1-4. 스크립트 참조   **5.** (A)   **6.** (B)

1.

Q 여자는 자문 프로그램에 대해 무엇이라고 말하는가?
A 그것은 매우 인기 있었다.

미남 미녀 🎧

> M Erica, you're planning the office's Health Week this year, right?
> W Yes, I had a personal trainer offer consultations with employees about workouts. A lot of people signed up. It was very well received.

해석

남 에리카, 당신이 올해 사무실의 건강 주간을 계획하고 있죠, 맞죠?
여 네, 개인 트레이너가 운동에 관한 직원들과의 상담을 제공하게 했어요. 많은 사람들이 신청했어요. **그것은 아주 호평을 받았어요.**

어휘

consultation 상담, 상의 personal trainer 개인 트레이너
workout 운동 sign up 신청하다, 등록하다
be well received 호평을 받다

패러프레이징

well received → popular

2.

Q 여자는 다음에 어디에 갈 것 같은가?
A 은행에

미녀 미남 🎧

> W We've just received the new electric mixers from Davis Manufacturing, so we need to set up a display.
> M I can start working on that now.
> W Thank you. I'll help you when I get back, but first I need to go and deposit yesterday's cash.

해석

여 우리가 방금 데이비스 제조사로부터 새 전기 믹서를 받아서, 진열을 해야 해요.
남 제가 지금 그 작업을 시작할 수 있어요.
여 고마워요. 제가 돌아오면 도와줄게요. **하지만 먼저 어제의 현금을 예금하러 가야 해요.**

어휘

electric 전기의 set up 설치하다, 세우다 display 진열, 전시

work on ~을 작업하다 deposit 예금하다; 예금

3.

Q 여자는 어떻게 포스터를 바꾸라고 제안하는가?

A 서체를 덜 사용함으로써

미남 미녀 🎧

> **M** I sent you the first draft of the poster to advertise our new theater show. Did you get a chance to look at it yet? I'd like your opinion.
>
> **W** Well, I like the combination of colors, but having so many different fonts is distracting. I think you'd better just use one or two.

해석

남 제가 당신에게 우리의 새 연극 공연을 광고하기 위한 포스터의 초안을 보냈어요. 그것을 볼 기회가 있었나요? 당신의 의견을 듣고 싶어요.

여 음, 색상의 조합은 마음에 들지만, **서체가 너무 여러 가지여서 산만합니다. 한두 개만 사용하는 게 나을 것 같아요.**

어휘

font 서체, 폰트 draft 초안, 초고 advertise 광고하다
opinion 의견, 견해 combination 조합, 결합
distract 산만하게 하다

패러프레이징

many different fonts ~ just use one or two
→ using fewer fonts

4.

Q 여자는 어떤 제품 특성에 대해 우려하는가?

A 내구성

미남 미녀 🎧

> **M** I'm excited about the new hiking boots we'll be releasing this spring. I think a lot of our customers will be interested in them.
>
> **W** Yes, I agree. However, we have to make sure we don't rush the testing process. It's important for the boots to be durable enough for long hikes on rough trails.

해석

남 저는 우리가 올봄에 출시할 예정인 새로운 등산화가 기대돼요. 많은 고객들이 그것에 관심을 가질 것 같아요.

여 네, 저도 그렇게 생각해요. 하지만, 우리는 절대 시험 과정을 서두르지 말아야 해요. **등산화가 험한 산길에서 긴 시간 하이킹을 하기에 충분히 내구성이 있는지가 중요해요.**

어휘

product feature 제품 특성 durability 내구성
hiking boots 등산화, 하이킹용 부츠 release 출시하다, 공개하다
be interested in ~에 관심을 갖다 rush 급히 서두르다
durable 내구성이 있는, 오래가는

hike 도보 여행, 하이킹 trail 산길, 시골길

패러프레이징

durable enough → Durability

5.

여자는 무엇을 해야 한다고 말하는가?

(A) 밴드 멤버에게 이야기하기

(B) 운전해서 가는 길 안내받기

미남 미녀 🎧

> **M** Hi, Caroline. This is Nigel calling from the Sparkle Café. Everyone loved the performance your band gave last weekend. I'm wondering if you can give another show on April 10.
>
> **W** That would be great, but I need to ask my drummer first. Can I call you back shortly?

해석

남 안녕하세요, 캐롤라인. 저는 스파클 카페의 나이젤입니다. 모든 사람들이 지난 주말 당신의 밴드가 했던 공연을 정말 좋아했어요. 4월 10일에 한 번 더 공연해 주실 수 있는지 궁금합니다.

여 그러면 좋죠, 하지만 **일단 저희 드러머에게 물어봐야 해요.** 곧 다시 전화드려도 될까요?

어휘

bandmate 밴드 멤버 directions 길 안내
performance 공연, 연주 shortly 곧

패러프레이징

ask my drummer → Speak to a bandmate

6.

남자는 여자에게 무엇에 관해 주의를 주는가?

(A) 그의 차에 문제가 있다.

(B) 다른 사람들이 동행할 것이다.

미녀 미남 🎧

> **W** Hi, Victor. I'm wondering if I could get a ride to work tomorrow. My car's in the shop.
>
> **M** Yes, that's no problem. I'll stop by your apartment around 7:45. Just to warn you, it might be a little crowded. I'm carpooling with Amanda and Walter.

해석

여 안녕하세요, 빅터. 내일 출근할 때 제가 차를 얻어 탈 수 있는지 궁금해요. 제 차가 정비소에 있어요.

남 네, 문제없어요. 7시 45분쯤 당신의 아파트에 들를게요. **다만 주의를 주자면, 조금 복잡할지도 몰라요. 제가 아만다와 월터와 카풀을 하고 있거든요.**

어휘

warn 경고하다, 주의를 주다 get a ride 차를 얻어 타다
shop 공장, 수선소 stop by ~에 들르다
crowded 복잡한, 혼잡한

carpool 카풀(승용차 함께 타기)을 하다

패러프레이징

패러프레이징

I'm carpooling with Amanda and Walter
→ Other people will be with him

연습 문제　　　　　　　　　본문 p.145

1. (A)　　2. (C)　　3. (A)　　4. (C)　　5. (A)

[1] 미녀 호남 🎧
Question 1 refers to the following conversation.

> W　I have only half an hour, so I'd like to order something that can be made quickly. Will the salad take long?
> M　Not at all. Plus, today we have a special on the ricotta cheese salad.
> W　Sounds good. My friend asked me to order for her, since she'll be here in a few minutes. So, can I get two special salads and two coffees, please?
> M　Okay, I'll be back shortly.

해석
1번은 다음 대화에 관한 문제입니다.
여　제가 30분밖에 없어서 빨리 만들 수 있는 것을 주문하려고 해요. 샐러드가 오래 걸릴까요?
남　전혀 그렇지 않습니다. 게다가, 오늘 저희는 리코타 치즈 샐러드를 특별 메뉴로 제공합니다.
여　잘됐네요. **제 친구가 제게 대신 주문해 달라고 부탁했어요, 그녀가 몇 분 뒤에 올 거라서요.** 그럼, 스페셜 샐러드 두 개와 커피 두 잔 주시겠어요?
남　알겠습니다, 곧 다시 오겠습니다.

어휘
order 주문하다　plus 더욱이, 게다가
special 특별한 것, 특별 상품; 특별한　shortly 곧, 얼마 지나지 않아

1.
여자에 따르면, 누가 곧 도착할 것인가?
(A) 친구
(B) 동료
(C) 상사
(D) 고객

[2-3] 미녀 호남 🎧
Questions 2-3 refer to the following conversation.

> W　Excuse me. ²I'd like to apply for a passport. I'll be doing some international travel. I was told it normally takes about a week to receive a passport, but is there any way I can get it sooner?

> M　Yes, there's an option for the express service, but you will need to pay an additional fee of 30 dollars. It takes about two business days.
> W　That's fine. I'll apply for the express service. ³Can I do that here?
> M　³Sorry, you should go downstairs to the express service counter.

해석
2-3번은 다음 대화에 관한 문제입니다.
여　실례합니다. ²**여권을 신청하고 싶습니다.** 해외여행을 좀 할 예정입니다. 여권을 받는 데 보통 일주일쯤 걸린다고 들었지만, 더 빨리 받을 수 있는 어떤 방법이 있나요?
남　네, 신속 서비스를 선택할 수 있어요, 하지만 추가 요금 30달러를 내셔야 할 거예요. 대략 2영업일이 걸립니다.
여　그건 괜찮아요. 신속 서비스를 신청할게요. ³**여기서 하면 되나요?**
남　³**죄송하지만, 아래층의 신속 서비스 창구로 가셔야 해요.**

어휘
apply for ~을 신청하다, ~에 지원하다　passport 여권
normally 보통　option 선택(할 수 있는 것)
express 급행의, 신속한　additional fee 추가 요금
business day 영업일, 평일

2.
여자는 무엇을 하기를 원하는가?
(A) 해외 일자리에 지원하기
(B) 대출 신청하기
(C) 공문서 받기
(D) 구입한 제품 교환하기

어휘
loan 대출　official document 공문서

패러프레이징
apply for a passport → Get an official document

3.
여자는 아마도 다음에 어디로 갈 것인가?
(A) 다른 창구로
(B) 자신의 사무실로
(C) 다른 지점으로
(D) 아래층 카페로

어휘
branch 지점

패러프레이징
to the express service counter
→ To a different counter

Questions 4-5 refer to the following conversation.

> M Maria, ⁴have you heard that the company has decided to extend our customer service hours starting from next week?
>
> W Yes, it'll be great for business. ⁵But now we need to re-record our voicemail greeting right away to include our new schedule.
>
> M Right, I forgot about that. You know, the sound quality isn't very good. ⁵I'm wondering how much a professional recording service would cost.
>
> W One of my friends recently hired someone to do that for her company. I'll call her and find out how much she paid.

해석

4-5번은 다음 대화에 관한 문제입니다.

남 마리아, ⁴회사에서 다음 주부터 우리 고객 서비스 시간을 연장하기로 결정했다는 걸 들었어요?

여 네, 그러면 사업에 매우 좋을 거예요. ⁵하지만 이제 새 일정을 포함하도록 즉시 우리 음성 메일 인사말을 다시 녹음해야 해요.

남 맞아요, 제가 그것에 관해서는 잊어버렸네요. 있잖아요, 그 음질이 그리 좋지 않아요. ⁵전문 녹음 서비스는 비용이 얼마나 드는지 궁금해요.

여 제 친구 중 한 명이 최근에 자신의 회사를 위해 그 일을 할 사람을 고용했어요. 제가 그녀에게 전화해서 얼마를 지불했는지 알아볼게요.

어휘

extend 연장하다 voicemail 음성 메일 greeting 인사
sound quality 음질 professional 전문적인, 직업의
hire 고용하다

4.

업체는 언제 서비스 시간을 변경할 것인가?

(A) 오늘
(B) 내일
(C) 다음 주에
(D) 다음 달에

5.

남자는 음성 메일을 어떻게 하고 싶어 하는가?

(A) 전문 서비스 고용하기
(B) 메시지를 짧게 줄이기
(C) 고객들로부터 의견 받기
(D) 보안 기능 추가하기

어휘

shorten 짧게 하다, 단축하다 feedback 피드백, 의견
security 보안, 안보 feature 특징, 기능

1. (C)	**2.** (C)	**3.** (A)	**4.** (D)	**5.** (C)
6. (B)	**7.** (C)	**8.** (C)	**9.** (A)	**10.** (B)
11. (B)	**12.** (A)	**13.** (B)	**14.** (D)	**15.** (B)
16. (A)	**17.** (B)	**18.** (B)		

Questions 1-3 refer to the following conversation.

> W Thank you for calling Spangler's. How can I help you?
>
> M Good morning. ¹I purchased an electric mixer from your online shop, and it just arrived today. ²It was supposed to come with three attachments, but there was only one in the box.
>
> W ²I'm very sorry about that, sir. Could you tell me the model number, please?
>
> M Yes, it's R745. And the main mixer blade is the only one that came with it.
>
> W All right. I'll send the other two blades today, um... that's the small-sized blade and the shredder.
>
> M Thanks. ³And I don't have to pay for delivery, right?
>
> W That's right, because it was our fault. Could you please give me your preferred mailing address?

해석

1-3번은 다음 대화에 관한 문제입니다.

여 스팽글러 사에 전화 주셔서 감사합니다. 어떻게 도와드릴까요?

남 안녕하세요. ¹제가 귀사의 온라인 상점에서 전기 믹서기를 구매했고, 오늘 막 도착했어요. ²부속품 세 개가 딸려 있는 걸로 되어 있었는데, 상자 안에는 한 개만 있었어요.

여 ²그 점에 대해 대단히 죄송합니다, 고객님. 모델 번호를 알려주시겠습니까?

남 네, R745예요. 그리고 본품 믹서 날이 딸려 온 유일한 것이에요.

여 알겠습니다. 제가 오늘 나머지 날 두 개를 보내 드릴게요, 음... 소형 날과 분쇄기요.

남 고맙습니다. ³그리고 제가 배송비를 지불할 필요는 없죠, 맞죠?

여 맞습니다, 저희 잘못이니까요. 선호하시는 우편물 발송 주소를 알려 주시겠어요?

어휘

electric 전기의 be supposed to ~하기로 되어 있다
come with ~이 딸려 있다 attachment 부속물
blade (칼·도구 등의) 날 shredder 분쇄기 fault 잘못
preferred 선호되는 mailing address 우편물 발송 주소

1.

여자의 회사는 무엇을 생산하는 것 같은가?

(A) 컴퓨터 주변기기

(B) 원예용품
(C) 주방용품
(D) 운동 장비

어휘

accessory 부대용품, 액세서리 appliance (가정용) 기기
equipment 장비

패러프레이징

an electric mixer → Kitchen appliances

2.

여자는 왜 사과하는가?
(A) 기기가 켜지지 않는다.
(B) 물품이 크기가 잘못됐다.
(C) 일부 구성 요소가 누락되었다.
(D) 남자에게 과잉 청구되었다.

어휘

device 장치, 기구 component (구성) 요소, 부품
overcharge (금액을 너무) 많이 청구하다

패러프레이징

there was only one in the box
→ Some components were missing

3.

남자는 무엇에 대해 질문하는가?
(A) 배송 요금
(B) 반품 정책
(C) 상품 카탈로그
(D) 우편물 발송 목록

어휘

charge 요금; 청구하다

패러프레이징

pay for delivery → A delivery charge

[4-6] 영녀 미남 🎧

Questions 4-6 refer to the following conversation.

W Good morning, and welcome to Sunburg
   Community Center. How may I help you?
M Hello. I'm interested in finding a place to play
   racquetball. **⁴,⁵ I just moved to this town for a
   new job, and someone at work recommended
   this place.**
W Great! We have four racquetball courts, but
   you have to be a member to use them.
M Okay. Would it be possible to see your
   facilities?
W Of course. **⁶ I'll ask my coworker, Amy, to show
   you around.** Wait here just a moment, please.

해석

4-6번은 다음 대화에 관한 문제입니다.

여 안녕하세요, 선버그 커뮤니티 센터에 오신 것을 환영합니다. 어
   떻게 도와드릴까요?
남 안녕하세요. 저는 라켓볼을 할 곳을 찾는 데 관심이 있습니다.
   **⁴,⁵ 새 직장 때문에 이 동네로 막 이사 왔는데, 직장의 어떤 사람
   이 이곳을 추천했어요.**
여 잘됐네요! 저희는 라켓볼 코트가 4개 있습니다만, 그것들을 이용
   하기 위해서는 회원이 되셔야 해요.
남 알겠습니다. 이곳의 시설들을 볼 수 있을까요?
여 물론이죠. **⁶ 제 동료 에이미에게 당신이 둘러보시도록 안내해 드
   리라고 요청할게요.** 잠시만 여기서 기다려 주세요.

어휘

be interested in ~에 관심이 있다
Would it be possible to ~? ~하는 것이 가능할까요?
facility 시설 show ~ around ~에게 둘러보도록 안내하다

4.

남자는 업체에 대해 어떻게 알게 되었는가?
(A) 밖에 있는 간판을 읽음으로써
(B) 이메일을 받음으로써
(C) 온라인 검색을 함으로써
(D) 동료와 이야기함으로써

어휘

sign 게시, 간판 perform 수행하다, 실시하다

패러프레이징

someone at work recommended this place
→ speaking to a coworker

5.

남자는 최근에 무엇을 했는가?
(A) 학위를 이수했다
(B) 사업체를 열었다
(C) 이 지역으로 이사 왔다
(D) 대회에서 우승했다

어휘

complete 완료하다, 끝마치다 degree 학위
competition (경연) 대회, 시합

패러프레이징

moved to this town → Moved into the area

6.

여자는 동료에게 무엇을 해 달라고 요청할 것인가?
(A) 주차증 발급하기
(B) 남자에게 구경시켜 주기
(C) 일부 서류 가져오기
(D) 회원 가입비 조정하기

어휘

issue 발급하다 give ~ a tour ~에게 구경시켜 주다
adjust 조정하다

패러프레이징

show you around → Give the man a tour

Questions 7-9 refer to the following conversation.

> **W** Hello, my name is Patty York, and I live at 782 Caldwell Street. **7** I received a notice saying my payment for June is overdue. However, I paid that bill by bank transfer last week, so there must be some kind of mistake.
>
> **M** Let me check on that, Ms. York. Hmm... there isn't any record of a payment on our system. **8** However, we've just upgraded our software. Maybe that's causing some problems.
>
> **W** Alright, then... what do I need to do?
>
> **M** Let's see if the payment shows up within a few days. **9** If not, you may have to give us a copy of your bank statement proving the payment.

해석

7-9번은 다음 대화에 관한 문제입니다.

여 안녕하세요, 제 이름은 패티 요크이고, 콜드웰 도로 782번지에 살아요. **7** 6월분 납부 기한이 지났다는 공지를 받았어요. 하지만, 저는 지난주에 계좌 이체로 공과금을 지불했어요, 그러니 무슨 착오가 있는 게 틀림없어요.

남 그것을 확인해 볼게요, 요크 씨. 흠... 저희 시스템에는 납부 기록이 전혀 없어요. **8** 그런데 저희가 막 소프트웨어를 업그레이드했거든요. 아마도 그게 문제를 좀 일으키고 있는지도 몰라요.

여 알겠습니다, 그럼... 제가 어떻게 해야 하나요?

남 며칠 안에 납부했다고 뜨는지 보죠. **9** 그렇지 않으면, 저희에게 납부를 입증하는 입출금 내역서 사본을 주셔야 할지도 몰라요.

어휘

notice 공고문, 안내문 payment 지불, 납입
overdue (지불·반납 등의) 기한이 지난 bill 고지서, 청구서
bank transfer 계좌 이체 cause 야기하다, 초래하다
show up 나타나다 bank statement 입출금 내역서
prove 입증하다, 증명하다

7.

여자는 왜 전화하고 있는가?
(A) 납부를 하기 위해
(B) 서비스를 신청하기 위해
(C) 오류를 보고하기 위해
(D) 수리를 요청하기 위해

어휘

sign up for ~을 신청하다 repair 수리; 수리하다

패러프레이징

some kind of mistake → an error

8.

남자는 소프트웨어 프로그램에 대해 무엇이라고 말하는가?
(A) 그것은 곧 교체될 것이다.
(B) 그것은 암호가 필요하다.
(C) 그것은 최근에 업그레이드되었다.

(D) 그것은 자동으로 다시 시작한다.

어휘

replace 교체하다, 대체하다 automatically 자동적으로

패러프레이징

we've just upgraded our software
→ It has recently been upgraded

9.

남자는 무엇이 필요할지도 모른다고 말하는가?
(A) 서류를 제출하는 것
(B) 사무실을 방문하는 것
(C) 계좌를 해지하는 것
(D) 관리자에게 연락하는 것

어휘

submit 제출하다

패러프레이징

give us a copy of your bank statement
→ Submitting a document

Questions 10-12 refer to the following conversation with three speakers.

> **M** Good morning. My name is Cory, and **10** I'll be leading this training for your safety inspector certification. How about you introduce yourselves?
>
> **W1** Hi, I'm Marcy. I'm currently working in retail, but I'd like something with a little more variety.
>
> **W2** I'm Fernanda. I'd like to get a government job after I complete my certification.
>
> **M** Well, I'm glad you're both here. Now, at the end of this training, you have to pass a test. **11** Unfortunately, we're currently having some problems with our software program. So, you might have to take a paper-based test instead. **12** Yes, Marcy?
>
> **W1** **12** I'm wondering if there will be a break for lunch.
>
> **M** Yes, from noon to one.

해석

10-12번은 다음 세 명의 대화에 관한 문제입니다.

남 안녕하세요. 제 이름은 코리이고, **10** 제가 여러분의 안전 검사관 인증을 위한 이번 교육을 진행할 것입니다. 자기소개를 하는 게 어떨까요?

여1 안녕하세요, 저는 마시예요. 현재는 소매업에서 일하지만, 좀 더 다양한 무언가를 하고 싶어요.

여2 저는 페르난다예요. 저는 인증 과정을 수료한 후에 공무원으로 일하고 싶어요.

남 음, 두 분 모두 함께해서 기쁩니다. 자, 이 교육이 끝날 때, 여러분은 시험을 통과해야 합니다. **11** 안타깝지만, 현재 저희 소프트

웨어 프로그램에 문제가 좀 있습니다. 그래서, 대신 서면으로 시험을 치러야 할 수도 있습니다. ¹²네, 마시?

여1 ¹²점심 식사를 위한 휴식 시간이 있는지 궁금합니다.

남 네, 정오부터 1시까지입니다.

어휘

lead 안내하다, 이끌다 safety inspector 안전 검사관
certification 증명(서) currently 현재, 지금 retail 소매, 소매상
with more variety 더 다양한 complete 마치다, 완료하다
paper-based 종이를 바탕으로 한 break 휴식 (시간)

10.

여자들은 어떤 종류의 직업을 위해 교육받고 있는가?

(A) 전기 기술자
(B) 안전 검사관
(C) 건축가
(D) 부동산 중개인

어휘

train 교육받다, 교육시키다 real estate 부동산

11.

남자는 여자들에게 무엇에 대해 주의를 주는가?

(A) 일손 부족
(B) 소프트웨어 문제
(C) 추가 요금
(D) 대기 명단

어휘

labor 노동 shortage 부족 issue (걱정거리가 되는) 문제
additional 추가적인

패러프레이징

some problems with our software program
→ A software issue

12.

마시는 무엇에 대해 질문하는가?

(A) 식사 시간
(B) 교재
(C) 견학
(D) 비밀번호

패러프레이징

a break for lunch → A meal break

[13-15] 호남 영녀 🎧

Questions 13-15 refer to the following conversation.

M Look at this! ¹³The report on Lenox is due this Friday.

W I didn't realize the management team was still interested in Lenox. Well, maybe it's because they failed to get the contract with Keystone Corporation.

M ¹⁴I don't think I can finish it on time. What am I supposed to do?

W Don't worry. It's only Tuesday. That's plenty of time to finish it.

M ¹⁴But I'm leaving for a business trip in Washington this evening, and I won't be back until Thursday.

W ¹⁵In that case, you have a good reason to ask the manager to extend the deadline.

해석

13-15번은 다음 대화에 관한 문제입니다.

남 이것 보세요! ¹³레녹스에 대한 보고서가 이번 금요일에 마감이에요.

여 경영팀이 여전히 레녹스에 관심이 있었다는 걸 몰랐어요. 음, 아마도 그들이 키스톤 사와 계약을 체결하는 데 실패했기 때문일 거예요.

남 ¹⁴전 시간 맞춰 끝낼 수 있을 것 같지 않아요. 어떻게 해야 하죠?

여 걱정 말아요. 이제 겨우 화요일이잖아요. 그것을 끝낼 시간은 많아요.

남 ¹⁴하지만 전 오늘 저녁에 워싱턴 출장을 떠나요, 그리고 목요일이나 되어야 돌아올 거예요.

여 ¹⁵그런 경우라면, 관리자에게 마감일을 연장해 달라고 요청할 좋은 이유가 있네요.

어휘

be due ~에 마감이다 fail to ~하는 데 실패하다
get the contract with ~와 계약을 맺다
on time 시간을 어기지 않고, 정각에
be supposed to ~하기로 되어 있다 plenty of 많은
in that case 그런 경우에는 extend 연장하다, 확대하다

13.

남자는 금요일까지 무엇을 해야 하는가?

(A) 팀장과 만나기
(B) 보고서 제출하기
(C) 계약서에 서명하기
(D) 고객들과 협상하기

어휘

submit 제출하다 negotiate 협상하다

14.

남자는 "목요일이나 되어야 돌아올 거예요"라고 말할 때 무엇을 암시하는가?

(A) 그는 계약이 완료되었다고 생각한다.
(B) 그는 여자와의 회의를 연기하기를 원한다.
(C) 그는 예기치 못하게 항공편을 변경했다.
(D) 그는 일을 마칠 시간이 없다.

어휘

complete 끝마치다, 완료하다 postpone 연기하다
unexpectedly 예기치 못하게 task 직무, 과업

15.

여자는 남자에게 무엇을 하라고 제안하는가?

(A) 조수 고용하기

(B) 연장 요청하기

(C) 출장 취소하기

(D) 담당자에게 전화하기

어휘

assistant 조수, 보조원 ask for ~을 요청하다

extension 연장, 확대 representative 대표자, 대리인

패러프레이징

ask the manager to extend the deadline

→ Ask for an extension

[16-18] 미남 미녀 🎧

Questions 16-18 refer to the following conversation and chart.

> M Thanks for meeting with me, Ms. Malcolm. ¹⁶I've just compiled the data from the customer survey for our wireless headphones. Overall, the ratings were favorable. Here's a chart of the most highly rated features.
>
> W Those figures are better than I expected. ¹⁷And I'm especially pleased that people liked the packaging so much. The team really worked hard on that.
>
> M I agree. So, we've obviously got a good product here. What should we do next?
>
> W Uh... ¹⁸We need to film a commercial. I'd love to get a famous musician to star in it.

해석

16-18번은 다음 대화와 표에 관한 문제입니다.

남 저를 만나 주어서 고마워요, 맬컴 씨. ¹⁶제가 방금 우리 무선 헤드폰에 대한 고객 설문 조사 자료를 모았어요. 전반적으로, 평가가 호의적이었어요. 여기 가장 높은 평가를 받은 특징들의 표입니다.

여 그 수치들은 제가 예상했던 것보다 더 좋네요. ¹⁷그리고 사람들이 포장을 많이 좋아했다는 점이 특히 기뻐요. 그 팀은 그것에 정말 열심히 노력을 기울였어요.

남 동의해요. 그럼, 우리에게 좋은 제품이 있다는 것이 확실하네요. 다음에 우리는 무엇을 해야 할까요?

여 어... ¹⁸광고를 촬영해야 해요. 그것에 유명한 음악인을 출연시키고 싶어요.

어휘

compile (자료를) 모으다, 편집하다

customer survey 고객 설문 조사 wireless 무선의

overall 전반적으로 rating 평가, 순위 favorable 호의적인

rate 평가하다 feature 특징 especially 특별히

packaging 포장, 포장재 work on ~에 노력을 들이다

obviously 확실히, 분명히 commercial 광고 (방송)

star in ~에 주연을 맡다

특징	평가 (10점 만점)
스타일	9.9
¹⁷포장	9.8
내구성	9.1
사용 편의성	8.7

16.

화자들은 어떤 종류의 제품에 관해 이야기하고 있는가?

(A) 헤드폰

(B) 태블릿 컴퓨터

(C) 프린터

(D) 스마트폰

17.

시각 자료를 보시오. 여자는 특히 어떤 평가에 대해 기뻐하는가?

(A) 9.9

(B) 9.8

(C) 9.1

(D) 8.7

어휘

durability 내구성

18.

여자는 무엇을 하기를 바라는가?

(A) 제품의 에너지 효율성 향상시키기

(B) 광고를 위해 유명인 고용하기

(C) 음악 축제에서 제품 홍보하기

(D) 웹사이트 개선하기

어휘

improve 개선하다, 향상시키다 efficiency 효율(성)

celebrity 유명 인사 promote 홍보하다

make improvements 개선하다

패러프레이징

commercial ~ get a famous musician to star in it

→ Hire a celebrity for an advertisement

UNIT O5 제안·요청사항 문제

CHECK UP 본문 p.148

1. (C) **2.** (A)

[1] 미남 미녀 🎧

Question 1 refers to the following conversation.

> M Camilla, I'm organizing the company anniversary dinner next week. I need some volunteers to help set the tables and clean up after the event. Are you interested?

W Oh, sorry… uh… I'm really busy with monthly sales reports. I'm sure you can find help if you let people know that you still need volunteers.

M You know, I was thinking about sending an e-mail, but the last time I did that, I didn't get many responses.

W Well, then, why don't you bring this issue up at the staff meeting this afternoon? You can talk about it and ask our colleagues in person to sign up to volunteer.

해석

1번은 다음 대화에 관한 문제입니다.

남 카밀라, 제가 다음 주에 있을 회사 기념일 만찬을 준비하고 있어요. 테이블을 세팅하고 행사 후에 치우는 것을 도울 지원자가 좀 필요해요. 관심 있어요?

여 아, 미안해요… 어… 제가 월 매출 보고서 때문에 정말 바빠요. 사람들에게 당신이 아직 지원자를 필요로 한다고 알리면 분명 도움을 구할 수 있을 거예요.

남 있잖아요, 이메일을 보낼 생각을 하고 있었지만, 지난번에 그렇게 했을 때 회신을 많이 못 받았어요.

여 음, 그러면, 오늘 오후에 직원 회의에서 이 안건을 꺼내는 게 어때요? 당신이 그것에 대해 얘기하고 우리 동료들에게 지원 신청을 해 달라고 직접 부탁할 수 있어요.

어휘

organize 준비하다, 조직하다 anniversary 기념일
volunteer 지원자, 자원봉사자; 자원하다 response 응답, 회신
bring up (화제를) 꺼내다 issue 주제, 안건 in person 직접
sign up 신청하다, 등록하다

1.
여자는 남자에게 무엇을 하라고 추천하는가?
(A) 기념 파티 참석하기
(B) 행사에서 발표하기
(C) 회의에서 직원들에게 도움 요청하기
(D) 직원들의 연락처 업데이트하기

어휘
give a presentation 발표하다

패러프레이징
ask our colleagues in person to sign up to volunteer
→ Ask employees for help

[2] 미남 미녀 🎧
Question 2 refers to the following conversation.

M Sharon, I was really impressed with the way you managed your team for the renovations at the Chestnut Hotel. Not only did you finish ahead of schedule, but you also came in under budget.

W I'm pleased with the final result. I hope the clients were happy.

M They certainly were. That's why I'd like you to supervise the construction of the new Purcell Bank building. It's a big job, but I'm confident that you'll handle it well.

W Thank you. I appreciate the opportunity to take on more responsibility.

M Let's meet next week to discuss the details further.

해석

2번은 다음 대화에 관한 문제입니다.

남 샤론, 당신이 체스넛 호텔 개조를 위해 당신 팀을 운영한 방식에 정말 깊은 인상을 받았어요. 당신은 일정을 앞당겨 끝냈을 뿐만 아니라 예산보다 비용을 적게 썼어요.

여 최종 결과에 만족합니다. 고객들이 좋아했기를 바라요.

남 그들은 틀림없이 그랬어요. 그래서 당신이 새로운 퍼셀 은행 건물의 공사를 감독했으면 하는 거예요. 큰일이지만 당신이 잘 처리할 거라고 확신해요.

여 감사합니다. 더 많은 책임을 맡을 기회를 주신 것에 대해 감사하게 생각해요.

남 다음 주에 만나서 자세한 내용을 더 이야기합시다.

어휘

be impressed with ~에 깊은 인상을 받다
renovation 수리, 수선
not only A but also B A뿐만 아니라 B도
ahead of schedule 예정보다 먼저
come in under budget 예산보다 비용이 적게 들다
certainly 틀림없이, 분명히 supervise 감독하다
construction 건설, 공사 confident (전적으로) 확신하는
handle 처리하다, 다루다 appreciate 고마워하다
take on (일 등을) 맡다 responsibility 책임, 책무

2.
남자는 여자에게 무엇을 해 달라고 요청하는가?
(A) 프로젝트 감독하기
(B) 의견 제공하기
(C) 일정 확인하기
(D) 고객에게 전화하기

어휘
oversee 감독하다 confirm 확인하다

패러프레이징
supervise the construction of the new Purcell Bank building → Oversee a project

패러프레이징 연습   본문 p.150
1-4. 스크립트 참조   **5.** (B)   **6.** (B)

1.
Q 남자는 무엇을 해 주겠다고 제안하는가?
A 제안 목록 보내기

W I'm excited about my business trip to Berlin. It'll be my first time visiting Germany. You used to work in Berlin, right?

M Yes, for two years. I can e-mail you some recommendations for places to go in your free time.

해석

여 저는 베를린 출장에 대한 기대로 들떠 있어요. 독일을 방문하는 건 처음이에요. 당신은 베를린에서 일한 적이 있죠, 맞죠?

남 네, 2년 동안요. **자유 시간에 갈 만한 곳으로 추천하는 장소들을 당신에게 이메일로 보내 줄 수 있어요.**

어휘

suggestion 제안, 제의 business trip 출장
recommendation 추천, 권고

패러프레이징

e-mail you some recommendations for places to go
→ Send a list of suggestions

2.

Q 남자는 무엇을 할 것을 제안하는가?

A 다양한 물품들을 사는 것

M Here is our section of camping lanterns. All of them are lightweight as well as water-resistant. Will you be camping by yourself or in a group?

W There will be about 10 of us.

M In that case, I suggest getting more than one. Our store has a variety of options to choose from.

해석

남 여기는 캠핑용 랜턴 구역입니다. 이것들 모두 어느 정도 방수가 될 뿐만 아니라 가벼워요. 혼자서 캠핑을 하실 건가요, 아니면 여럿이서 하실 건가요?

여 저희는 10명 정도 될 거예요.

남 **그렇다면, 하나 이상 구매하시는 것을 제안합니다.** 저희 상점은 고를 수 있는 다양한 것들이 있습니다.

어휘

multiple 많은, 다수의 lantern 랜턴, 손전등
lightweight 가벼운 water-resistant 물이 잘 스며들지 않는
by oneself 혼자서 in a group 한 무리를 이루어
a variety of 다양한

패러프레이징

getting more than one → Buying multiple items

3.

Q 남자는 여자에게 무엇을 해 달라고 요청하는가?

A 직물 공급 업체 찾기

W I love the designs you've created for our new trousers, Liam. However, the linen supplier we currently use doesn't have a wide range of colors.

M We'll need to find a new one then. Could you please do some research about this?

해석

여 우리의 새 바지를 위해 당신이 만든 디자인이 아주 마음에 들어요, 리암. 하지만, 우리가 현재 이용하는 **리넨 제품 공급 업체**는 색상이 다양하지 않아요.

남 그러면 우리가 새 공급 업체를 찾아야 할 거예요. 이에 관해 조사를 좀 해 주시겠어요?

어휘

fabric 직물, 천 supplier 공급자, 공급 회사
trousers ((항상 복수형)) 바지 linen 리넨 제품
currently 현재, 지금 a wide range of 다양한, 광범위한
do research 조사를 하다

패러프레이징

the linen supplier, find a new one
→ Find a fabric supplier

4.

Q 여자는 남자에게 어떤 일을 해 달라고 요청하는가?

A 공지하기

W Brian, please announce to everyone that we'll begin boarding in about five minutes. I'd like passengers to start getting their IDs ready.

M Alright, I'll do that right now.

해석

여 브라이언, **모든 사람들에게 우리가 약 5분 뒤에 탑승을 시작할 거라고 알려 주세요.** 승객들이 신분증을 준비하기 시작했으면 해요.

남 알겠습니다, 지금 바로 그렇게 하겠습니다.

어휘

task 일, 과업 make an announcement 공표하다, 발표하다
announce 발표하다, 알리다 board 탑승하다

패러프레이징

announce to everyone → Make an announcement

5.

여자는 남자에게 무엇을 해 달라고 요청하는가?

(A) 식당에 물품 가져오기

(B) 동료를 대신하기

> **W** Hi, Mario. It's Nora. I know you're not scheduled to work at the restaurant today. However, Kristin just called and said she won't be able to make it. Could you please take her place today?
> **M** That depends. What time does the shift start?

해석

여 안녕하세요, 마리오. 저 노라예요. 오늘은 당신이 식당에서 근무하는 날이 아니라는 걸 알아요. 하지만, 크리스틴이 방금 전화해서 못 온다고 했어요. **오늘 그녀를 대신해 줄 수 있어요?**

남 상황에 따라 달라요. 근무가 몇 시에 시작하나요?

어휘

supply 용품, 물품 substitute for ~을 대신하게 되다
be scheduled to ~할 예정이다 make it 가다, 참석하다
take one's place ~를 대신하다 shift 교대 근무 (시간)

패러프레이징

take her place → Substitute for a coworker

6.

남자는 여자에게 무엇을 하라고 제안하는가?

(A) 청구서 확인하기
(B) 다른 일 먼저 하기

> **W** Ted, I've got some cleaning supplies to drop off. Do you know if anyone is at Gate 24?
> **M** Let's see… that flight was delayed, so there aren't any employees there yet. You'd better make your next delivery first.

해석

여 테드, 제게 내려놓을 청소용품이 좀 있어요. 24번 게이트에 누군가가 있는지 아시나요?

남 어디 볼게요... 항공편이 지연되어서 아직 그곳에 직원들이 아무도 없어요. **다음 배달을 먼저 하는 게 좋겠어요.**

어휘

invoice 청구서, 송장 perform 수행하다
cleaning supplies 청소용품 drop off ~을 내려놓다
flight 항공편, 비행기 delay 미루다, 연기하다
make a delivery 배달하다

패러프레이징

make your next delivery first
→ Perform another task first

연습 문제 본문 p.151

1. (A) **2.** (B) **3.** (D) **4.** (A) **5.** (C)

---

[1] 미남 영녀 🎧

Question 1 refers to the following conversation.

> **M** Thanks for coming out to today's sales meeting, everyone. What are your thoughts on the quarterly profit report?
> **W** I was quite surprised. I didn't realize how popular our tablets are.
> **M** Yes, we've sold a lot. But I think we should focus on the products that aren't selling well.
> **W** Hmm… maybe the marketing department should start a new campaign. Will you make a list of customer comments to share with them?

해석

1번은 다음 대화에 관한 문제입니다.

남 모두들 오늘 매출 회의에 와 주셔서 감사합니다. 분기 이익 보고에 대한 여러분의 생각은 어떤가요?

여 저는 상당히 놀랐어요. 우리의 태블릿 컴퓨터가 얼마나 인기 있는지 몰랐거든요.

남 네, 많이 팔았어요. 하지만 저는 잘 팔리지 않는 제품들에 집중해야 한다고 생각해요.

여 흠... 아마도 마케팅 부서가 새 캠페인을 시작해야 할 거예요. 당신이 고객 의견 목록을 작성해서 그들과 공유해 주시겠어요?

어휘

quarterly 분기의 profit 이익 tablet 태블릿 컴퓨터
focus on ~에 주력하다, 초점을 맞추다 sell well 잘 팔리다
make a list of ~의 목록을 만들다 share with ~와 공유하다

1.

여자는 남자에게 무엇을 해 달라고 요청하는가?

(A) 의견 목록 작성하기
(B) 또 다른 회의 일정 잡기
(C) 제품 시연하기
(D) 보고서의 일부 수치 확인하기

어휘

schedule 일정을 잡다 demonstrate 보여주다, 설명하다
figures ((보통 복수형)) 수치

[2-3] 미남 영녀 🎧

Questions 2-3 refer to the following conversation.

> **M** ²Have you heard about Lighthouse Publishing Company? One of their books is ranked second on the bestseller's list.
> **W** Really? I heard they have just brought in Erik Benson. His designs are great, which will contribute further to their success.
> **M** But they're not doing well overseas.
> **W** Well, once their commercials begin, I know they will succeed there, too. We don't want to lose market share to them, so ³we'd better call in some talented book designers.

해석

2-3번은 다음 대화에 관한 문제입니다.

남 ²라이트하우스 출판사에 대해 들었어요? 그들의 책 중 하나가 베스트셀러 목록 2위에 올랐어요.

여 정말요? 그들이 막 에릭 벤슨을 데려왔다고 들었어요. 그의 디자인은 훌륭해요, 이 점이 그들의 성공에 더욱 기여할 거예요.

남 하지만 그들은 해외에서는 잘 되지 않고 있어요.

여 음, 일단 그들의 광고가 시작되면, 거기서도 성공할 거라고 생각해요. 우리는 그들에게 시장 점유율을 잃고 싶지 않아요, 그러니 ³재능 있는 도서 디자이너를 영입하는 게 좋겠어요.

어휘

rank (등급·순위를) 매기다, 평가하다 bring in ~을 들여오다
contribute to ~에 기여하다 overseas 해외에, 해외로
commercial 광고 market share 시장 점유율
call in ~을 불러들이다 talented 재능이 있는

2.

화자들은 무엇에 관해 이야기하고 있는가?

(A) 사업체 이전
(B) 경쟁 회사
(C) 창고 정리 판매
(D) 일자리 공석

어휘

relocation 이전, 재배치 rival 경쟁자, 경쟁 상대

3.

여자는 무엇을 하자고 제안하는가?

(A) 해외 지점 열기
(B) 대상 독자 변경하기
(C) 해외 도서 번역하기
(D) 실력 있는 도서 디자이너 고용하기

어휘

target 목표, 대상 translate 번역하다 skilled 숙련된, 노련한

패러프레이징

call in some talented book designers
→ Hire skilled book designers

[4-5] 영녀 미남 🎧
Questions 4-5 refer to the following conversation.

W You said you needed to talk to me.
M That's right. ⁴I talked to accounting, and they said we need to cut the budget for Mr. Jeong's office by 250 dollars.
W I see. Well, we could use that extra table in my office instead of buying a new one. And he can probably use just one filing cabinet instead of two.
M Good idea. ⁵Please adjust the purchase list so accounting can sign off on it.

해석

4-5번은 다음 대화에 관한 문제입니다.

여 저와 이야기할 게 있다고 하셨죠.

남 맞아요. ⁴회계 부서와 이야기했는데, 우리가 정 씨의 사무실을 위한 예산을 250달러로 삭감해야 한다고 했어요.

여 알겠어요. 음, 새 탁자를 사는 대신 제 사무실의 여분의 탁자를 이용하면 되겠어요. 그리고 아마도 그가 서류 캐비닛을 두 개 대신 하나만 사용하면 될 거예요.

남 좋은 생각이에요. ⁵회계 부서에서 그에 대해 승인할 수 있도록 구매 목록을 수정해 주세요.

어휘

accounting 회계 (업무) budget 예산 extra 여분의, 추가의
filing cabinet 서류 캐비닛 adjust 조정하다, 조절하다
sign off ~을 승인하다

4.

남자는 어떤 문제를 언급하는가?

(A) 예산이 삭감되어야 한다.
(B) 직원이 이동할 것이다.
(C) 사무실을 이용할 수 없게 되었다.
(D) 물품이 재고가 없다.

어휘

reduce 줄이다, 삭감하다 relocate 이전하다, 이동시키다
out of stock 재고가 없는

패러프레이징

we need to cut the budget
→ A budget must be reduced

5.

여자는 무엇을 하도록 요청받는가?

(A) 사무실 설계하기
(B) 일부 장비 주문하기
(C) 문서 조정하기
(D) 치수 재기

어휘

equipment 장비 take measurements 치수를 재다

패러프레이징

the purchase list → a document

실전 문제				본문 p.152
1. (A)	**2.** (D)	**3.** (C)	**4.** (B)	**5.** (C)
6. (A)	**7.** (D)	**8.** (C)	**9.** (B)	**10.** (B)
11. (D)	**12.** (C)	**13.** (C)	**14.** (B)	**15.** (B)
16. (A)	**17.** (B)	**18.** (B)		

[1-3] 미남 미녀 🎧
Questions 1-3 refer to the following conversation.

M [1]Daniela, the Interior Design Fair in Portland is next week. I'm planning on driving there. Do you want to come with me?

W I knew that was coming up, but I'm completely booked next week.

M Oh... are you working on a new project?

W I have a few projects in progress, and [2]I'm meeting with a new client, Marcus Turner. He's redoing his office and needs some advice about what color to have the walls painted. But, uh... [3]if you see brochures for any interesting products at the fair, can you grab them for me?

M Of course.

해석

1-3번은 다음 대화에 관한 문제입니다.

남 ¹다니엘라, 포틀랜드에서 열리는 인테리어 디자인 박람회가 다음 주예요. 저는 운전해서 그곳에 갈 계획이에요. 저와 함께 갈래요?

여 박람회가 다가오고 있는 건 알았지만, 제가 다음 주에는 일정이 완전히 다 찼어요.

남 아... 새 프로젝트에 착수하나요?

여 진행 중인 몇 개의 프로젝트가 있어요, 그리고 ²새 고객인 마커스 터너 씨를 만날 예정이에요. 그가 자신의 사무실을 개조하는데 벽을 무슨 색으로 칠해야 하는지에 관해 조언을 좀 필요로 해요. 하지만, 어... ³만약 당신이 박람회에서 무엇이든 흥미로운 제품의 책자를 본다면, 저를 위해 가져와 줄 수 있나요?

남 물론이죠.

어휘

plan on ~할 계획이다 come up 다가오다
completely 완전히, 전적으로 be booked 일정이 차다
work on ~에 노력을 들이다, 착수하다 in progress 진행 중인
redo 개조하다, 다시 하다 grab 붙잡다

1.

여자는 "제가 다음 주에는 일정이 완전히 다 찼어요"라고 말할 때 무엇을 의미하는가?

(A) 그녀는 행사에 참석할 수 없다.
(B) 그녀는 남자의 도움이 필요하다.
(C) 그녀는 약속을 취소하고 싶다.
(D) 그녀는 포틀랜드에 머물러야 한다.

2.

터너 씨는 무엇에 관해 이야기하기를 원하는가?

(A) 카펫
(B) 가구
(C) 조명
(D) 벽 색상

패러프레이징

what color to have the walls painted → Wall colors

3.

여자는 남자에게 무엇을 해 달라고 요청하는가?

(A) 신제품 테스트하기
(B) 고객에게 자신을 소개하기
(C) 책자 가져오기
(D) 일부 샘플 제공하기

패러프레이징

grab → Pick up

[4-6] 영녀 미남 🎧

Questions 4-6 refer to the following conversation.

W Jason, [4]I've been reading the most recent reviews for our city tours, and I'm afraid we've been getting a lot of negative ones.

M Oh, really? But we spent so much time planning exciting activities.

W Well... it seems that the issue is with the tour guides. People are saying they aren't very good at answering questions. [5]Maybe we should hold some training sessions for guides.

M That's a good idea, but... our office wouldn't be large enough to do that. [6]I can call a few meeting venues to check on prices.

W That'd be helpful.

해석

4-6번은 다음 대화에 관한 문제입니다.

여 제이슨, ⁴제가 우리의 도시 관광에 대한 가장 최근의 후기를 읽고 있는데, 유감스럽게도 부정적인 후기들을 많이 받고 있어요.

남 아, 정말요? 하지만 우리는 재미있는 활동들을 기획하는 데 매우 많은 시간을 쏟았잖아요.

여 음... 문제는 여행 가이드들과 관련이 있는 것 같아요. 사람들이 말하기로는 그들이 질문에 답변하는 데 그다지 능숙하지 않대요. ⁵아마도 우리가 가이드들을 위해 교육을 좀 주최해야 할 것 같아요.

남 좋은 생각이에요, 하지만... 그러기에는 우리 사무실이 충분히 크지 않아요. ⁶제가 몇몇 모임 장소에 전화해서 비용을 확인할게요.

여 그게 도움이 되겠네요.

어휘

negative 부정적인 be good at ~에 능숙하다
training session 교육 (과정) venue (행사의) 장소
check on ~을 확인하다

4.

화자들은 주로 어떤 문제에 관해 이야기하고 있는가?

(A) 공급업체가 가격을 인상했다.
(B) 회사가 좋지 않은 후기들을 받았다.
(C) 도시 축제가 취소되었다.
(D) 업계의 경쟁이 심해졌다.

supplier 공급업체 raise 올리다, 인상하다 competition 경쟁

reviews ~ getting a lot of negative ones
→ received poor reviews

5.

여자는 무엇을 제안하는가?
(A) 행사 날짜를 바꾸는 것
(B) 컨설턴트를 고용하는 것
(C) 교육을 제공하는 것
(D) 홍보를 하는 것

consultant 컨설턴트, 상담가 promotion 홍보, 판촉

hold some training sessions
→ Providing some training

6.

남자는 무엇을 해 주겠다고 제안하는가?
(A) 일부 업체들에게 연락하기
(B) 계약서 수정하기
(C) 추가 근무하기
(D) 회의 안건 준비하기

revise 수정하다 additional 추가의 prepare 준비하다
agenda 안건, 의제

call a few meeting venues
→ Contact some businesses

[7-9] 호남 미녀 🎧
Questions 7-9 refer to the following conversation.

> M ⁷On tonight's show, I'm pleased to welcome Colleen Jordan as my guest. She's the founder of Hartway Tech. Thanks for being here, Colleen.
> W Thanks for inviting me on your show.
> M My pleasure. Now, your company's Web design software is a top seller. But you've just confirmed in a press conference that you're branching out in your business?
> W That's right. ⁸We're going to start a program to teach people about coding.
> M Will it be classroom-based?
> W It will be entirely online, so people can do it from anywhere. ⁹There's a video on our Web site explaining more. You and your viewers should check it out.

7-9번은 다음 대화에 관한 문제입니다.

남 ⁷오늘 밤 쇼에서, 콜린 조던을 초대 손님으로 맞이하게 되어 기쁩니다. 그녀는 하트웨이 테크 사의 창립자입니다. 자리해 주셔서 감사합니다, 콜린 씨.
여 당신의 쇼에 초대해 주셔서 감사합니다.
남 천만에요. 자, 당신 회사의 웹디자인 소프트웨어는 가장 많이 팔리고 있습니다. 하지만 당신은 방금 기자 회견에서 새로운 사업을 시작할 것임을 확정하셨다죠?
여 맞습니다. ⁸저희는 사람들에게 코딩에 관해 가르치는 프로그램을 시작할 예정입니다.
남 그것은 교실 기반이 될 것인가요?
여 전적으로 온라인이 될 것이므로 사람들이 어디서든 그것을 할 수 있습니다. ⁹저희 웹사이트에 좀 더 자세히 설명하는 동영상이 있습니다. 당신과 시청자들이 확인해 보셨으면 합니다.

be pleased to ~해서 기쁘다 founder 창립자
top seller 가장 잘 팔리는 것 confirm 확인하다, 확정하다
press conference 기자 회견
branch out (새로운 사업을) 시작하다 entirely 전적으로, 완전히
viewer 시청자, 보는 사람 check out 확인하다

7.

남자는 누구인 것 같은가?
(A) 웹디자이너
(B) 잡지 기자
(C) 마케팅 컨설턴트
(D) 토크쇼 진행자

journalist 기자, 저널리스트 host 진행자

8.

하트웨이 테크 사는 최근에 무엇을 확정했는가?
(A) 고객들을 위한 경연 대회
(B) 경영진 교체
(C) 교육 프로그램 출시
(D) 다른 회사와의 제휴

competition (경연) 대회, 시합 replacement 교체, 대체
executive 경영진 launch 출시, 개시 educational 교육의
partnership 제휴

start a program to teach people
→ The launch of an educational program

9.

여자는 남자에게 무엇을 하라고 권하는가?
(A) 일자리에 지원하기
(B) 동영상 시청하기
(C) 우편물 발송 목록에 가입하기
(D) 몇몇 차트를 검토하기

어휘

review 검토하다

패러프레이징

a video ~ check it out → Watch a video

[10-12] 영녀 호남 🎧

Questions 10-12 refer to the following conversation.

> **W** Hi, I've purchased a ticket for your special exhibit of contemporary art. **¹⁰**I'd like to take some pictures of the paintings. Is that allowed?
> **M** Yes, um... but please make sure you turn off your flash first.
> **W** Okay, great. I'm looking forward to this exhibit.
> **M** I hope you enjoy it. **¹¹**And here's a brochure of our future events that you might be interested in.
> **W** Thanks. I'll give that a look.
> **M** **¹²**Also, I suggest you hold onto your ticket. You can show it at the café to get a discount.

해석

10-12번은 다음 대화에 관한 문제입니다.

여 안녕하세요, 제가 이곳의 현대 미술 특별전 입장권을 구매했어요. **¹⁰**그림들의 사진을 좀 찍고 싶어요. 그래도 되나요?

남 네, 음... 하지만 반드시 먼저 플래시를 끄도록 해 주세요.

여 네, 좋습니다. 전 이번 전시가 기대돼요.

남 재미있게 보시길 바랍니다. **¹¹**그리고 앞으로 있을 저희 행사에 대한 책자가 여기 있는데 관심이 있으실지도 모르겠네요.

여 감사합니다. 한번 볼게요.

남 **¹²**또한, 입장권을 가지고 계시기를 추천합니다. 카페에서 보여주고 할인을 받으실 수 있습니다.

어휘

exhibit 전시; 전시하다 contemporary 현대의, 동시대의
allow 허락하다, 용납하다 look forward to ~을 고대하다
hold onto ~을 꼭 잡다 get a discount 할인을 받다

10.

여자는 무엇을 하고 싶다고 말하는가?

(A) 강의 참석하기
(B) 사진 찍기
(C) 여행 떠나기
(D) 기념품 사기

어휘

souvenir 기념품

패러프레이징

pictures of the paintings → photographs

11.

남자는 여자에게 무엇에 관한 정보를 주는가?

(A) 예술가들의 배경
(B) 결제 방법

(C) 회원제 프로그램
(D) 다가오는 행사

어휘

payment 지불, 납입 option 선택(권)
upcoming 다가오는, 곧 있을

패러프레이징

our future events → Upcoming events

12.

남자는 무엇을 할 것을 제안하는가?

(A) 새로운 음식을 먹어 보는 것
(B) 웹사이트에 방문하는 것
(C) 입장권을 가지고 있는 것
(D) 단체 예약을 하는 것

어휘

make a reservation 예약하다

패러프레이징

hold onto → Keeping

[13-15] 호남 미녀 영녀 🎧

Questions 13-15 refer to the following conversation with three speakers.

> **M** Hello, **¹³**I'm here to do some research for an article for *Science* magazine.
> **W1** Mr. Hayes? We've been expecting you. I'll tell Ms. Finn you are here.
> **M** Ms. Finn? **¹⁴**I had an appointment with Mr. Johnson, the public relations manager.
> **W1** **¹⁴**I know, but he's running late this morning due to car trouble. So, his assistant will help you. Here she comes.
> **W2** Hello, I'm Amanda Finn, Mr. Johnson's assistant. I'll show you around the museum.
> **M** Thank you. I was actually hoping to speak to some of the employees.
> **W2** I'm way ahead of you. I've already arranged for several people to answer your questions. **¹⁵**Oh, and don't forget your temporary security pass.

해석

13-15번은 다음 세 명의 대화에 관한 문제입니다.

남 안녕하세요, **¹³**〈사이언스〉지에 실을 기사를 위해 조사를 좀 하려고 왔어요.

여1 헤이스 씨죠? 저희가 당신을 기다리고 있었어요. 제가 핀 씨에게 당신이 오셨다고 얘기할게요.

남 핀 씨요? **¹⁴**전 홍보 매니저인 존슨 씨와 약속을 했는데요.

여1 **¹⁴**알고 있어요, 하지만 그는 차가 고장 나서 오늘 아침에 늦을 거예요. 그래서 그의 보조원이 당신을 도와드릴 거예요. 여기 그녀가 오네요.

여2 안녕하세요, 저는 존슨 씨의 보조원인 아만다 핀입니다. 제가 박물관을 안내해 드릴게요.

남 감사합니다. 실은 직원 몇 분과 얘기하기를 바라고 있었어요.

여2 제가 당신보다 훨씬 빨랐네요. 제가 이미 당신의 질문에 답변할 몇 명을 준비해 두었어요. **15** 아, 그리고 임시 **보안 출입증**을 잊지 마세요.

어휘

research 조사, 연구 article 기사, 글
expect 기다리다, 예상하다 appointment 약속
public relations 홍보 (활동) run late 늦다 due to ~ 때문에
car trouble 차량의 고장 assistant 조수, 보조원
show A around B A에게 B를 둘러보도록 안내하다
way ahead of ~보다 훨씬 앞선 arrange for ~을 준비하다
temporary 임시의 security pass 보안 출입증

13.

남자는 누구인 것 같은가?
(A) 여행 가이드
(B) 마케팅 관리자
(C) 기자
(D) 비서

14.

존슨 씨는 왜 부재중인가?
(A) 그는 다른 회의가 있다.
(B) 그는 교통 문제를 겪고 있다.
(C) 그는 전시회에 가고 있다.
(D) 그는 약속에 대해 잊었다.

어휘

transportation 교통, 운송

패러프레이징

running late ~ due to car trouble
→ having transportation issues

15.

남자는 무엇을 지참하도록 요청받는가?
(A) 전시회 책자
(B) 보안 배지
(C) 운전면허증
(D) 작업 포트폴리오

어휘

exhibition 전시(회) brochure (안내·광고용) 책자
badge 배지, 표

패러프레이징

temporary security pass → A security badge

[16-18] 미녀 미남 🎧

Questions 16-18 refer to the following conversation and map.

> W Thanks for calling Pearl Salon. How may I help you?

M Hi, this is Larry Norton. **16** I was supposed to get a haircut this morning, but a pipe in my kitchen burst. I have to wait for the plumber to come and fix it, so I'll have to reschedule.

W How about tomorrow at noon?

M That's fine. And I can park in the city's lot, right?

W Oh, actually, we're at a new location now. **17** The building is on the corner of Harrison Street and Lemay Avenue. It's right across from the Keller Gallery. You can use the underground parking garage for free for two hours.

M Okay, thanks.

W **18** Also, please bring some pictures of the hairstyle you have in mind.

해석

16–18번은 다음 대화와 지도에 관한 문제입니다.

여 펄 살롱에 전화해 주셔서 감사합니다. 어떻게 도와드릴까요?

남 안녕하세요, 저는 래리 노턴입니다. **16** 오늘 오전에 머리를 자르기로 되어 있었지만, 제 부엌의 파이프가 터졌어요. 배관공이 와서 고치는 걸 기다려야 해서 일정을 다시 잡아야겠어요.

여 내일 정오는 어떠세요?

남 좋아요. 그리고 공영 주차장에 주차하면 되죠, 맞죠?

여 아, 실은, 지금 저희가 새로운 장소에 있어요. **17** 건물이 해리슨 가와 르메이 가의 모퉁이에 있어요. 켈러 미술관 바로 맞은편이에요. 2시간 동안 무료로 지하 주차장을 이용하실 수 있습니다.

남 알겠어요, 감사해요.

여 **18** 또한, 생각해 두신 머리 모양의 사진을 몇 장 가져와 주세요.

어휘

be supposed to ~하기로 되어 있다 burst 터지다
plumber 배관공 fix 고치다 reschedule 일정을 다시 잡다
lot (= parking lot) 주차장 location 장소, 위치
right across from ~의 바로 맞은편에 parking garage 주차장
have ~ in mind ~을 생각하다, 염두에 두다

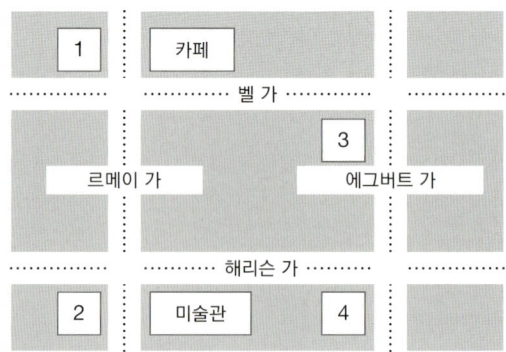

16.

남자는 왜 원래 약속에 참석할 수 없는가?
(A) 그는 집에서 수리를 받아야 한다.

(B) 그는 긴급한 업무가 있다.
(C) 그는 출장을 간다.
(D) 그는 공항에 친구를 데리러 간다.

어휘

repair 수리, 수선   urgent 긴급한

패러프레이징

have to wait for the plumber to come and fix it
→ needs a repair done at his home

17.

시각 자료를 보시오. 여자는 어디에서 일하는가?
(A) 1번 장소에서
(B) 2번 장소에서
(C) 3번 장소에서
(D) 4번 장소에서

18.

여자는 무엇을 요청하는가?
(A) 모발 관리 제품
(B) 사진
(C) 신분증
(D) 확인 번호

어휘

confirmation 확인

패러프레이징

pictures → photographs

UNIT 06 다음에 할·일어날 일 문제

CHECK UP   본문 p.154

1. (B)   **2.** (C)

[1] 미남 미녀 🎧
Question 1 refers to the following conversation.

> M Hello, my name is Carl Schein, and I'm from Children's Shelter Home. I'm calling to see if you are interested in supporting our organization. We're collecting gently used books from the public.
> W Oh, I have some that I could donate. What do I need to do?
> M Just drop the books you want to donate into a box at one of our collection points around town.
> W I work on Martin Luther Street, and I'm wondering which site is nearest to me.
> M Well, I can text you the address for each site.

해석

1번은 다음 대화에 관한 문제입니다.
남 안녕하세요, 제 이름은 칼 샤인이고, 어린이 보호소 소속입니다. 저희 단체를 후원하는 데 관심이 있으신지 알아보려고 전화드렸습니다. 저희는 사람들로부터 깨끗이 사용한 도서를 모으고 있습니다.
여 아, 제게 기증할 수 있는 것들이 좀 있어요. 어떻게 하면 되나요?
남 기증하고 싶은 책들을 동네 주변의 저희 수거 지점 중 하나에 있는 함에 넣기만 하면 됩니다.
여 저는 마틴 루터 가에서 근무하는데, 어느 장소가 저한테 가장 가까운지 궁금합니다.
남 음, 제가 각 장소의 주소를 문자로 보내드리겠습니다.

어휘

shelter 쉼터, 보호소   be interested in ~에 관심이 있다
support 후원하다, 지원하다   organization 단체, 조직
collect 모으다   gently used 깨끗하게 사용된
the public 일반 사람들, 대중   donate 기부하다, 기증하다
collection 수거, 수집   site 위치, 장소

1.

남자는 다음에 무엇을 할 것 같은가?
(A) 책 추천하기
(B) 주소 정보 제공하기
(C) 여자의 전화 돌려주기
(D) 지불 처리하기

어휘

transfer a call 전화를 다른 사람 번호로 돌려주다
payment 지불, 납입

패러프레이징

text you the address for each site
→ Provide address information

[2] 미남 미녀 🎧
Question 2 refers to the following conversation.

> M Jane, I'd like to talk about the Robinson ad campaign, since the meeting with the client is tomorrow afternoon.
> W I've finished the assignment, but while creating the designs, I realized this budget is too small for what they need.
> M I see what you're saying. But they made it clear that they don't want to spend any more than what they told us.
> W What if we made two versions of the campaign? Then we could present both versions to them to demonstrate what's possible with a little more funding.
> M That's not a bad idea. We'll just have to work late tonight to put something together in time.

2번은 다음 대화에 관한 문제입니다.

남 제인, 로빈슨 광고 캠페인에 대해 얘기하고 싶어요, **고객과의 회의가 내일 오후에 있거든요.**

여 맡은 일은 끝냈어요, 하지만 디자인을 만들면서, 이 예산이 그들에게 필요한 것에는 너무 적다는 것을 알게 되었어요.

남 무슨 말인지 알겠어요. 하지만 그들은 우리에게 말한 것 이상은 조금도 지출하고 싶지 않다는 것을 명확히 했어요.

여 우리가 두 가지 버전의 캠페인을 만들면 어떨까요? 그러면 우리가 그들에게 두 버전을 모두 보여 주고 자금을 조금 더 들이면 가능한 것을 설명할 수 있어요.

남 그건 나쁘지 않은 생각이에요. 시간 맞춰 준비하려면 우리가 오늘 밤늦게까지 일해야 할 뿐이겠네요.

어휘

ad (= advertisement) 광고 assignment 임무, 과제
create 만들다, 창작하다 budget 예산
make clear 명료하게 하다 version 판, 형태
present 제시하다, 보여 주다 demonstrate 설명하다
funding 자금 put together 만들다, 준비하다
in time 시간 맞춰

2.

내일 무슨 일이 일어날 것인가?
(A) 고객이 대금을 보낼 것이다.
(B) 고객이 계약을 갱신할 것이다.
(C) 화자들이 발표할 것이다.
(D) 화자들이 제품을 출시할 것이다.

어휘

payment 지불, 납입 renew 갱신하다 launch 출시하다

패러프레이징

present both versions to them → give a presentation

패러프레이징 **연습** 본문 p.156

1-4. 스크립트 참조 **5.** (A) **6.** (B)

1.

Q 여자는 다음에 무엇을 할 것이라고 말하는가?
A 가격 계산하기

미남 미녀 🎧

> M Hmm... I like the layout of the kitchen you've designed, but I'm not sure about the material for the countertops. Would it be possible to get marble countertops instead of granite?
> W Of course, let me figure out the final cost.

해석

남 흠... 당신이 디자인한 주방의 배치가 마음에 들어요, 하지만 조리대의 재질에 대해서는 잘 모르겠어요. 화강암 대신 대리석 조리대로 하는 것이 가능할까요?

여 물론이죠, **최종 비용을 계산해 볼게요.**

어휘

calculate 계산하다 layout 배치 material 재료, 자재
countertop (주방의) 조리대 marble 대리석 granite 화강암
figure out 계산해 내다, 생각해 내다

패러프레이징

figure out the final cost → Calculate a price

2.

Q 남자는 이번 주에 무슨 일이 일어날 것이라고 말하는가?
A 구매 시 무료 상품을 받을 수 있다.

미녀 미남 🎧

> W Hi. I need a coffee machine, but I'm not sure which brand is best.
> M Well, Ellison is a popular choice. And this week the store is offering a free coffee mug with every purchase of an Ellison product.

해석

여 안녕하세요. 저는 커피 기계가 필요해요, 하지만 어떤 브랜드가 가장 좋은지 잘 모르겠어요.

남 음, 많은 사람들이 엘리슨을 선택해요. 그리고 **이번 주는 엘리슨 제품을 구매하면 상점에서 무료로 커피 머그잔을 줘요.**

어휘

available 이용할 수 있는, 구할 수 있는 purchase 구매; 구매하다

패러프레이징

offering a free coffee mug with every purchase
→ A free item is available with purchase

3.

Q 여자는 다음에 무엇을 할 것 같은가?
A 문서 출력하기

미녀 미남 🎧

> W The number of tourists visiting the area has been declining steadily. You can see on this graph how this year compares to previous years. This is part of the reason our hotel chain has been struggling.
> M I'd like to share this with the board of directors. Please get me a printout of this information right away.

해석

여 이 지역을 방문하는 관광객들의 수가 꾸준히 줄고 있어요. 올해가 이전 해들과 어떻게 비교되는지 이 그래프에서 보실 수 있어요. 이것이 우리 호텔 체인점들이 고군분투하고 있는 이유 중 일부예요.

남 이것을 이사회와 공유하고 싶어요. **제게 즉시 이 정보의 인쇄물을 갖다주세요.**

어휘

decline 줄어들다, 감소하다　steadily 꾸준히
compare to ~와 비교가 되다　previous 이전의
struggle 투쟁하다, 몸부림치다　board of directors 이사회
printout 인쇄물

패러프레이징

get me a printout of this information
→ Print a document

4.

Q 금요일에 무슨 일이 일어날 것인가?
A 사무실 수리

미남 미녀 🎧

> **M** Thanks for getting back to me. I wanted you to know that there's going to be repair work in our office on Friday. So, we need to find a different place to meet.
> **W** That's fine with me. Why don't we reserve a table at the Indigo Restaurant, as it's conveniently located for both of us?

해석

남 회신 주셔서 고마워요. **금요일에 저희 사무실에 보수 공사가 있을 예정이라는 걸 알려 드리려고 했어요.** 그래서 우리가 만날 다른 장소를 찾아야 해요.
여 전 괜찮아요. 인디고 레스토랑이 우리 둘 모두에게 편리한 위치에 있으니까, 거기에 자리를 예약하는 것은 어때요?

어휘

repair 수리; 수리하다　get back to ~에게 다시 연락하다
reserve 예약하다　conveniently 편리하게
be located (~에) 위치하다

패러프레이징

repair work in our office → Some office repairs

5.

여자는 다음에 무엇을 할 것인가?
(A) 공지하기
(B) 일기 예보 확인하기

미남 미녀 🎧

> **M** The snowstorm hasn't cleared up as quickly as we had expected. We're going to have to delay the flight to Chicago.
> **W** Alright. Let me get on the intercom system and tell our passengers about it. We can offer some snacks at the gate while people wait.

해석

남 눈보라가 우리가 예상했던 것만큼 빨리 걷히지 않고 있어요. 시카고행 비행기를 연기해야 할 거예요.
여 알겠어요. **제가 구내방송 시스템에 접속해서 우리 승객들에게 그**

것에 대해 말할게요. 사람들이 기다리는 동안 우리가 탑승구에서 간식을 좀 제공할 수 있어요.

어휘

weather forecast 일기 예보　clear up (날씨가) 개다
delay 미루다, 연기하다　flight 항공편, 비행기
get on (인터넷 등에) 접속하다　intercom 구내방송

패러프레이징

get on the intercom system and tell our passengers about it → Make an announcement

6.

남자에 따르면, 다음 주 수요일에 무슨 일이 일어날 것인가?
(A) 교육 프로그램이 시작될 것이다.
(B) 한 집단이 건물을 방문할 것이다.

미남 미녀 🎧

> **M** I'm looking for volunteers because next Wednesday we'll have a high school group coming to take a tour of the library. You would just need to answer their questions.
> **W** That sounds like fun. I'm happy to help. Should I prepare anything in advance?

해석

남 다음 주 수요일에 고등학교에서 단체로 도서관을 견학하러 올 예정이기 때문에 자원봉사자를 찾고 있어요. 그들의 질문에 답변만 하면 될 거예요.
여 그거 재미있겠어요. 제가 기꺼이 도울게요. 미리 준비해야 하는 것이라도 있나요?

어휘

volunteer 자원봉사자; 자원봉사를 하다
take a tour of ~을 견학하다, 둘러보다　in advance 사전에, 미리

패러프레이징

a high school group coming to take a tour of the library → A group will visit a building

연습 문제				본문 p.157
1. (C)	**2.** (D)	**3.** (A)	**4.** (A)	**5.** (C)

[1] 호남 미녀 🎧
Question 1 refers to the following conversation.

> **M** I just finished checking in for our flight. We're departing from Gate 52.
> **W** Okay. I hope this meeting goes well. I'm a bit nervous. The client is very demanding.

M It'll be fine. The last time we were in Vancouver, they were very happy with your designs. Now… um… we still have about 40 minutes left before the flight. Let's relax and grab a bite to eat.

W Sounds great.

해석

1번은 다음 대화에 관한 문제입니다.

남 제가 막 우리 항공편 탑승 수속을 끝냈어요. 우리는 52번 탑승구에서 출발해요.

여 좋아요. 이번 회의가 잘 되기를 바라요. 전 조금 긴장돼요. 고객이 아주 요구가 많아요.

남 괜찮을 거예요. 지난번에 우리가 밴쿠버에 갔을 때 그들이 당신의 디자인을 아주 마음에 들어 했어요. 이제... 음... 비행 전에 아직 40분 정도 남아 있어요. **느긋이 쉬면서 뭘 좀 간단히 먹죠.**

여 그게 좋겠어요.

어휘

check in 탑승 수속을 밟다 flight 비행, 항공편 depart 출발하다 go well 잘 되어 가다 nervous 불안해하는, 초조해하는 demanding 요구가 많은 grab a bite to eat 간단히 먹다

1.

화자들은 다음에 무엇을 할 것인가?
(A) 새로운 좌석 요청하기
(B) 기념품 사기
(C) 무언가를 먹기
(D) 고객에게 연락하기

어휘

souvenir 기념품

패러프레이징

grab a bite to eat → Have something to eat

[2-3] 미녀 호남 🎧

Questions 2-3 refer to the following conversation.

W Mr. Howard, ²I haven't received your article on your trip to Brussels yet.

M Well, I e-mailed it to Eric Rivers for editing, and I'm waiting for his comments.

W Okay, I'll ask him to forward it to me as soon as possible. The article also needs to be done by tomorrow because I have to send it to the printer then.

M Actually, ³I'm going to see Eric in the board meeting in a few minutes. Would you like me to ask him to stop by your desk as soon as the meeting ends?

해석

2-3번은 다음 대화에 관한 문제입니다.

여 하워드 씨, ²**브뤼셀 여행에 대한 당신의 기사를 아직 받지 못했어요.**

남 음, 편집을 위해 이메일로 에릭 리버스에게 보냈고, 그의 의견을 기다리는 중이에요.

여 알겠어요, 제가 그에게 가능한 한 빨리 제게 전달해 달라고 요청할게요. 그 기사는 또한 내일까지 완료되어야 해요. 그때 인쇄소에 보내야 하거든요.

남 사실, ³**몇 분 뒤에 이사회 회의에서 에릭을 만날 거예요.** 그에게 회의가 끝나는 대로 당신의 자리에 들르라고 요청할까요?

어휘

edit 편집하다 comment 논평, 언급 forward 보내다, 전달하다 board meeting 이사회 회의 stop by ~에 들르다

2.

화자들은 주로 무엇에 관해 이야기하고 있는가?
(A) 새 책
(B) 출장
(C) 직원
(D) 기사

3.

남자는 무엇을 할 것이라고 말하는가?
(A) 회의 참석하기
(B) 또 다른 기사 보내기
(C) 자신의 직원에게 전화하기
(D) 자신의 동료 사무실에 들르기

패러프레이징

see Eric in the board meeting → Attend a meeting

[4-5] 미녀 호남 🎧

Questions 4-5 refer to the following conversation.

W Hi, Daniel. ⁵I wanted to let you know that Mr. Baldwin from All-Tech is interested in our catering service. However, he said there wasn't enough information on our Web site. I'd send him a brochure, but we've run out.

M Don't worry. I called the print shop yesterday and asked them to reprint more as soon as possible. ⁴They promised to send more brochures to us tomorrow morning.

W Great. Thanks. ⁵I'll call Mr. Baldwin to get his mailing address.

해석

4-5번은 다음 대화에 관한 문제입니다.

여 안녕하세요, 대니얼. ⁵**올테크 사의 볼드윈 씨가 우리 케이터링 서비스에 관심이 있다는 걸 당신에게 알려 주고 싶었어요.** 하지만, 그가 말하길 우리 웹사이트에 정보가 충분하지 않았대요. 제가 그에게 안내 책자를 보내려고 했지만, 다 떨어졌어요.

남 걱정 말아요. 제가 어제 인쇄소에 전화해서 가능한 한 빨리 재쇄를 더 찍어 달라고 요청했어요. ⁴**그들이 내일 아침 우리에게 안내 책자를 더 보내 준다고 약속했어요.**

여 잘됐네요. 고마워요. ⁵**제가 볼드윈 씨에게 전화해서 그의 우편물 수령 주소를 받을게요.**

어휘

brochure (안내·광고) 책자 run out 다 쓰다, 다 떨어지다
reprint (책 등의) 재쇄를 찍다 promise to ~하기로 약속하다

4.

남자는 내일 아침에 무슨 일이 일어날 것이라고 말하는가?
(A) 새로운 안내 책자가 배송될 것이다.
(B) 일부 케이터링 음식이 준비될 것이다.
(C) 신규 고객이 회사를 방문할 것이다.
(D) 여자가 인쇄소에 전화할 것이다.

어휘

print shop 인쇄소

패러프레이징

promised to send more brochures to us
→ New brochures will be delivered

5.

여자는 다음에 무엇을 할 것 같은가?
(A) 회의 참석하기
(B) 웹사이트 업데이트하기
(C) 잠재 고객에게 전화하기
(D) 안내 책자 교정하기

어휘

potential 잠재적인 proofread 교정을 보다

패러프레이징

interested in our catering service
→ a potential customer

실전 문제
본문 p.158

1. (B)	**2.** (C)	**3.** (D)	**4.** (C)	**5.** (A)
6. (D)	**7.** (A)	**8.** (D)	**9.** (B)	**10.** (B)
11. (C)	**12.** (A)	**13.** (B)	**14.** (B)	**15.** (C)
16. (B)	**17.** (D)	**18.** (A)		

[1-3] 미남 미녀 🎧

Questions 1-3 refer to the following conversation.

M ¹The new billboard for our gym went up
yesterday. I think it's going to be a great way to
advertise our business.
W ¹I saw it as I was driving to work this morning.
It looks great.
M Yeah, and I'm glad it's on such a busy road.
W Right. Many people will see it, so we'll
probably get a lot of new members this month.
²We should make sure all employees know
how to register new members.
M That's a good point. ³I'll e-mail everyone now
with a reminder of how to do it.

해석

1-3번은 다음 대화에 관한 문제입니다.
남 ¹우리 체육관을 위한 새로운 옥외 광고판이 어제 올라갔어요. 우
리 업체를 광고하는 훌륭한 방법이 될 것 같아요.
여 ¹오늘 아침 차로 출근하는 중에 그걸 봤어요. 아주 멋있더라고
요.
남 네, 그리고 그렇게 붐비는 도로에 있어서 다행이에요.
여 맞아요. 많은 사람이 그것을 볼 테니, 아마도 우리가 이번 달에
많은 신규 회원들을 모으게 될 거예요. ²반드시 모든 직원들이
신규 회원을 등록시키는 방법을 숙지하도록 해야 해요.
남 좋은 지적이에요. ³제가 지금 모든 사람들에게 그렇게 하는 방법
을 상기시키는 메모와 함께 이메일을 보낼게요.

어휘

billboard 옥외 광고판, 게시판 advertise 광고하다
register 등록하다 good point 좋은 지적
reminder 상기시켜 주는 편지, 메모

1.

여자는 오늘 아침에 무엇을 했는가?
(A) 그녀는 신문을 샀다.
(B) 그녀는 광고를 봤다.
(C) 그녀는 체육관에서 운동했다.
(D) 그녀는 일부 용품을 가지러 갔다.

어휘

work out 운동하다 supplies ((보통 복수형)) 용품

패러프레이징

The new billboard → an advertisement

2.

여자는 업체가 무엇을 준비해야 한다고 생각하는가?
(A) 다른 업체들과의 경쟁에 직면하는 것
(B) 시설 점검을 받는 것
(C) 더 많은 회원이 등록하게 하는 것
(D) 가격 인상을 위한 자금 계획을 세우는 것

어휘

face 직면하다 competition 경쟁, (경연) 대회
undergo 받다, 겪다 facility 시설 inspection 점검, 검사
sign up 신청하다, 등록하다 budget 자금 계획을 세우다; 예산

패러프레이징

register new members
→ Having more members sign up

3.

남자는 무엇을 할 것이라고 말하는가?
(A) 일정 조정하기
(B) 웹사이트 확인하기
(C) 계약서 출력하기
(D) 메시지 보내기

어휘

adjust 조정하다, 조절하다

패러프레이징

e-mail → Send a message

[4-6] 미남 영녀 🎧

Questions 4-6 refer to the following conversation.

> **M** Wendy, did you hear about the change planned for ⁴our movie theater? ⁵We'll give a 20 percent discount to groups of five or more people.
>
> **W** ⁵Yeah, I heard about that. It starts from next week, right? Well... um... I wonder if it will help us to sell more tickets.
>
> **M** I think it will. People will want to take advantage of the offer. And, actually... uh... ⁶I suppose we'll need an adjusted price list to show the new costs. Can you print one out and post it at the ticket counter?
>
> **W** ⁶Sure, I'll do that now.

해석

4-6번은 다음 대화에 관한 문제입니다.

남 웬디, ⁴우리 영화관에 계획된 변경 사항에 대해 들었어요? ⁵우리는 5인 이상 단체에 20% 할인을 해 줄 거예요.

여 ⁵네, 그것에 대해 들었어요. 다음 주부터 시작하죠, 맞죠? 글쎄요... 음... 우리가 티켓을 더 많이 파는 데 그게 도움이 될지 궁금해요.

남 그럴 거라고 생각해요. 사람들이 이 할인 혜택을 이용하고 싶어 할 거예요. 그리고, 실은... 어... ⁶제 생각에는 새로운 가격을 안내하기 위해 조정된 가격표가 필요할 것 같아요. 하나 출력해서 매표소에 게시해 주시겠어요?

여 ⁶물론이죠, 제가 지금 그렇게 할게요.

어휘

discount 할인 take advantage of ~을 이용하다 offer 할인
suppose 생각하다, 추측하다 adjusted 조정된
price list 가격표 print out 출력하다 post 게시하다, 공고하다

4.

화자들은 어디에서 일하는 것 같은가?

(A) 놀이공원에서

(B) 운동 경기장에서

(C) 영화관에서

(D) 수족관에서

5.

다음 주에 무슨 일이 일어날 예정인가?

(A) 단체 할인을 이용할 수 있을 것이다.

(B) 운영 시간이 변경될 것이다.

(C) 새로운 웹사이트가 출시될 것이다.

(D) 업체의 또 다른 지점이 문을 열 것이다.

어휘

available 이용할 수 있는 hours of operation 운영 시간
launch 시작하다, 출시하다

패러프레이징

give a 20 percent discount to groups of five or more people → Group discounts will become available

6.

여자는 다음에 무엇을 할 것 같은가?

(A) 주문하기

(B) 포스터 디자인하기

(C) 근무 일정 조정하기

(D) 가격표 인쇄하기

[7-9] 미녀 호남 🎧

Questions 7-9 refer to the following conversation.

> **W** Good afternoon. ⁷You've reached the Maintenance Department. How may I help you?
>
> **M** Hi, this is Patrick Morelli, from office 307. My door won't close all the way. I'm wondering if someone can come and repair it.
>
> **W** Well... um... ⁸unless it's an emergency, like a water leak, we require employees to give 24 hours' notice for repairs.
>
> **M** 24 hours? But some clients are meeting me in half an hour. We'll need the door closed for privacy.
>
> **W** Hmm... let me see if someone is available now. ⁹I'll call you back in a few minutes.
>
> **M** Thank you so much. I really appreciate it.

해석

7-9번은 다음 대화에 관한 문제입니다.

여 안녕하세요. ⁷유지보수 부서에 연결되셨습니다. 어떻게 도와드릴까요?

남 안녕하세요, 저는 307호 사무실의 패트릭 모렐리입니다. 제 사무실 문이 줄곧 닫히지 않아요. 누가 와서 그것을 고쳐 줄 수 있는지 궁금합니다.

여 글쎄요... 음... ⁸누수 같은 긴급한 상황이 아닌 한, 저희는 직원들에게 24시간 전에 수리 요청 통보를 할 것을 요구합니다.

남 24시간이요? 하지만 고객 몇 분과 30분 뒤에 만날 예정입니다. 프라이버시를 위해 문을 닫아야 하고요.

여 흠... 누가 지금 시간이 되는지 확인해 볼게요. ⁹몇 분 뒤에 다시 전화드릴게요.

남 대단히 고맙습니다. 정말 감사드려요.

어휘

reach (전화로) 연락하다 maintenance 유지, 보수
repair 고치다, 수리하다; 수리 emergency 긴급 사태
water leak 누수 require 요구하다 give a notice 통보하다
privacy 사생활, 프라이버시 appreciate 고마워하다

7.

여자는 누구인 것 같은가?

(A) 유지보수 직원

(B) 사업주
(C) 경비원
(D) 컴퓨터 기술자

어휘

security 보안, 경비 technician 기술자, 기사

8.

남자는 왜 "고객 몇 분과 30분 뒤에 만날 예정입니다"라고 말하는가?
(A) 요청을 취소하기 위해
(B) 신남을 표현하기 위해
(C) 허락하기 위해
(D) 예외를 요청하기 위해

어휘

excitement 흥분, 신남 permission 허락, 허가
exception 예외

9.

여자는 무엇을 할 것이라고 말하는가?
(A) 남자의 사무실 방문하기
(B) 남자에게 다시 전화하기
(C) 문서 인쇄하기
(D) 정책 확인하기

[10-12] 미남 호남 영녀 🎧
Questions 10-12 refer to the following conversation with three speakers.

> M1 ¹⁰ I've posted the signs telling people to come to the back of the store to get their books signed.
> M2 ¹⁰ I've set up the table, and we have plenty of copies available. ¹¹ Ms. Ferguson, I think your book will sell well. People are worried about their finances these days, so they'll want to learn from your experience.
> W I hope people find it helpful. I tried to avoid using too much technical language.
> M1 You did a great job. And we really appreciate your taking part in this event. ¹² Are we all set, Ted?
> M2 ¹² I just need to make the tea and coffee. I'll do that now.

해석

10-12번은 다음 세 명의 대화에 관한 문제입니다.
남1 ¹⁰ 제가 사람들에게 책에 사인을 받기 위해 상점 뒤쪽으로 오라고 알리는 게시물을 붙였어요.
남2 ¹⁰ 전 테이블을 설치했고, 판매 가능한 책을 충분히 가져다 놓았어요. ¹¹ 퍼거슨 씨, 전 당신의 책이 잘 팔릴 것이라고 생각해요. 사람들은 요즘 자신의 재정에 관해 걱정하고 있어요, 그러니 당신의 경험으로부터 배우고 싶을 거예요.
여 사람들에게 도움이 되길 바라요. 전문용어를 너무 많이 쓰지 않

으려고 노력했어요.
남1 정말 잘하셨어요. 그리고 저희는 당신이 이번 행사에 참여해 주셔서 정말 감사드려요. ¹² 우리 준비 다 됐나요, 테드?
남2 ¹² 제가 차와 커피만 준비하면 돼요. 지금 그렇게 할게요.

어휘

post 게시하다 sign 게시, 표지; 서명하다, 사인하다
set up 설치하다, 세우다 plenty of 많은 copy 한 부
available 이용할 수 있는 finance 재정, 재무
avoid -ing ~하는 것을 피하다 technical language 전문용어
take part in ~에 참여하다

10.

남자들은 무엇을 준비하고 있는가?
(A) 글쓰기 대회
(B) 도서 사인회
(C) 미술 수업
(D) 음악 공연

어휘

competition (경연) 대회 performance 공연, 연주

11.

퍼거슨 씨는 누구인 것 같은가?
(A) 음악 강사
(B) 신문 기자
(C) 재정 전문가
(D) 건물주

어휘

instructor 강사, 교사 financial 재정의 expert 전문가

12.

테드는 다음에 무엇을 할 것 같은가?
(A) 음료 만들기
(B) 게시물 인쇄하기
(C) 관리자에게 전화하기
(D) 휴식 취하기

어휘

beverage 음료 supervisor 감독관, 관리자

패러프레이징

the tea and coffee → some beverages

[13-15] 영녀 호남 🎧
Questions 13-15 refer to the following conversation.

> W Excuse me. ¹³ Is this the luggage counter?
> M ¹³ Yes, for Palazzo Airlines. Did you take one of our flights?
> W I did, and there's a problem with my suitcase. I've just picked it up, but, as you can see, ¹⁴ the retractable handle has been broken off. I think I should be financially compensated for this.

M Let me take a look… yes, this would be covered under our policy. If it cannot be repaired, we will either replace it with a similar bag or provide payment to purchase a new one.

W Great. What do I need to do?

M [15] You'll need to complete this claim form describing the problem. You can borrow my pen.

해석

13-15번은 다음 대화에 관한 문제입니다.

여 실례합니다. [13] 여기가 수하물 창구인가요?

남 [13] 네, 팔라초 항공 전용입니다. 저희 항공편 중 하나를 이용하셨나요?

여 그렇습니다, 그런데 제 여행 가방에 문제가 있습니다. 제가 방금 그것을 찾아왔어요, 하지만 보시다시피, [14] 집어넣는 손잡이가 떨어졌어요. 이에 대해서 금전적으로 보상을 받아야 할 것 같아요.

남 제가 한번 볼게요… 네, 이것은 저희 정책에 적용될 겁니다. 수리할 수 없다면, 저희가 비슷한 가방으로 교체해 드리거나 새것을 구매하시도록 대금을 지불하겠습니다.

여 다행이네요. 제가 어떻게 하면 되죠?

남 [15] 문제에 대해 서술하는 이 청구 양식을 작성하셔야 합니다. 제 펜을 빌려 드릴게요.

어휘

luggage 짐, 수하물 flight 항공편, 비행
retractable (속으로) 집어넣을 수 있는 break off ~을 분리시키다
financially 재정적으로 compensate for ~에 대해 보상하다
cover 다루다, 포함시키다 policy 정책
replace A with B A를 B로 교체하다
complete 기입하다, 작성하다 claim form 청구 양식
describe 서술하다, 말하다

13.

화자들은 어디에 있는 것 같은가?
(A) 백화점에
(B) 공항에
(C) 호텔에
(D) 버스 정류장에

14.

여자는 무엇을 하기를 원하는가?
(A) 음식을 먹을 장소 찾기
(B) 피해에 대해 보상받기
(C) 일부 수하물의 무게 확인하기
(D) 자신의 표 교환하기

어휘

compensation 보상(금) damage 손상, 피해

패러프레이징

broken off ~ be financially compensated for this
→ Receive compensation for damage

15.

여자는 다음에 무엇을 할 것 같은가?
(A) 여권 보여주기
(B) 관리자에게 이야기하기
(C) 서식 기입하기
(D) 지도 보기

어휘

passport 여권 fill out 기입하다

패러프레이징

complete this claim form → Fill out a form

[16-18] 미남 미녀 🎧

Questions 16-18 refer to the following conversation and order list.

M Hi, I'm from Atlanta Enterprises. One of my coworkers placed an order. His name is Gary Kimmel.

W Oh, it looks like our new employee didn't write down any names, only the order numbers. Do you have that? It should be a three-digit number, like 7-1-1.

M Sorry, but I don't have that. [16] I just know it's a small bouquet wrapped in paper.

W Wait… I think it's this one.

M That looks right. [17] We're holding our annual awards banquet tonight, and that will go to the winner.

W How lovely.

M [18] Do I need to store it in water?

W Yes, that would be best.

해석

16-18번은 다음 대화와 주문 목록에 관한 문제입니다.

남 안녕하세요, 애틀랜타 산업에서 왔어요. 제 동료 중 한 명이 주문을 했어요. 그의 이름은 게리 키멜이에요.

여 아, 저희 신입 직원이 이름들을 전혀 적어 놓지 않은 것 같아요, 주문번호들뿐이네요. 주문번호가 있으신가요? 7-1-1 같은 세 자리 숫자여야 해요.

남 죄송합니다만, 가지고 있지 않아요. [16] 종이로 포장한 작은 꽃다발이라는 것만 알아요.

여 잠시만요… 이것 같아요.

남 그게 맞는 것 같아요. [17] 저희는 오늘 밤에 연례 시상 축하연을 개최할 거예요, 그리고 그건 수상자에게 줄 거고요.

여 정말 아름답네요.

남 [18] 물속에 보관해야 할까요?

여 네, 그게 가장 좋을 거예요.

어휘

place an order 주문하다 write down 적어 놓다 digit 숫자
bouquet 꽃다발, 부케 wrap 싸다, 포장하다
hold 열다, 개최하다 annual 매년의, 연례의
banquet 연회 store 보관하다, 저장하다

711번 ¹⁶718번

720번 725번

16.
시각 자료를 보시오. 남자는 어떤 주문을 찾아갈 것인가?
(A) 711번
(B) 718번
(C) 720번
(D) 725번

17.
남자에 따르면, 오늘 무슨 행사가 열릴 것인가?
(A) 교육 워크숍
(B) 기념일 파티
(C) 환영회
(D) 시상식 만찬

어휘
take place 개최되다, 일어나다 anniversary 기념일
reception 환영회, 리셉션

패러프레이징
annual awards banquet → An awards dinner

18.
남자는 무엇에 관해 문의하는가?
(A) 물품을 보관하는 것
(B) 하나 더 주문하는 것
(C) 대금을 지불하는 것
(D) 카드를 추가하는 것

어휘
inquire about ~에 관하여 묻다

UNIT 07 화자의 의도 파악 문제

CHECK UP   본문 p.160

1. (B)   **2.** (C)

[1] 미녀 미남 🎧
Question 1 refers to the following conversation.

W Thank you for calling Lab Suppliers Incorporated. How can I help you?
M Hello, I'd like to order four of your standard microscopes. I'm wondering if they're currently available.
W Yes, we have plenty of those in stock at the moment. I can set four aside for you to pick up. We close at five today.
M I work until 6 o'clock.
W That's no problem at all. You can have them delivered for free. Let me just grab a form so I can get the necessary details from you. Please wait a moment.

해석
1번은 다음 대화에 관한 문제입니다.
여 랩 서플라이어즈 주식회사에 전화 주셔서 감사합니다. 어떻게 도와드릴까요?
남 안녕하세요, 귀사의 표준 현미경 4대를 주문하고 싶습니다. 그것들을 지금 구매할 수 있는지 궁금합니다.
여 네, 지금 재고가 많이 있습니다. **가져가시도록 4대를 따로 준비해 두겠습니다.** 저희는 오늘 5시에 문을 닫습니다.
남 제가 6시까지 일해요.
여 전혀 문제없습니다. 무료로 배달받으실 수 있습니다. 당신의 필수 정보를 기입할 수 있도록 서식을 가져오겠습니다. 잠시 기다려 주세요.

어휘
incorporated 주식회사 order 주문하다 microscope 현미경
currently 현재, 지금 plenty of 많은, 풍부한
in stock 재고가 있는 at the moment 바로 지금
set ~ aside 따로 떼어 두다 details 세부 정보

1.
남자는 "제가 6시까지 일해요"라고 말할 때 무엇을 암시하는가?
(A) 그는 나중에 여자를 만날 것이다.
(B) 그는 상점에 갈 수 없다.
(C) 그는 마감 기한이 빠듯하다.
(D) 그는 곧 현미경을 확인할 것이다.

[2] 미녀 미남 🎧
Question 2 refers to the following conversation.

W It's wonderful that Justine Hammond has agreed to join this year's Summer Music Festival.
M Yes, her music is very popular. And, since she grew up here in Mapleville, I think a lot of people will be interested in seeing her perform.
W I hope that's true. I was just viewing the figures for our ticket sales this morning, and they're a lot lower than expected. I'm getting worried about that.

M You know, we just announced it two days ago.

W That's true. I shouldn't expect the news to have an effect right away.

M Exactly. I'm sure we'll be able to meet our goal for attendance.

해석

2번은 다음 대화에 관한 문제입니다.

여 저스틴 해먼드가 올해의 여름 음악 축제에 합류하기로 했다니 멋져요.

남 네, 그녀의 음악은 인기가 아주 많아요. 그리고 그녀는 이곳 메이플빌에서 자랐기 때문에, 많은 사람들이 그녀의 공연을 보는 데 관심이 있을 거라고 생각해요.

여 그 말이 맞길 바라요. 마침 오늘 아침에 우리의 티켓 판매 수치를 살펴보고 있었는데, 예상보다 훨씬 적더라고요. 그 점이 걱정돼요.

남 알잖아요, 우리는 겨우 이틀 전에 그것을 알렸어요.

여 맞아요. 이 소식이 즉시 효과가 있을 거라고 기대해선 안 돼요.

남 바로 그거예요. 저는 우리가 목표로 하는 참석자 수를 달성할 수 있을 거라고 확신해요.

어휘

perform 공연하다, 연주하다 view 보다
figures ((보통 복수형)) 수치 than expected 기대했던 것보다
have an effect 효과가 있다 meet a goal 목표를 달성하다
attendance 참석자 수, 출석률

2.

남자는 왜 "우리는 겨우 이틀 전에 그것을 알렸어요"라고 말하는가?
(A) 여자에게 마감 기한을 상기시키기 위해
(B) 제안을 거절하기 위해
(C) 여자를 안심시키기 위해
(D) 요청하기 위해

어휘

remind A of B A에게 B를 상기시키다
decline 거절하다, 감소하다 reassure 안심시키다

연습 문제　　　　본문 p.163

1. (D)　　**2.** (A)　　**3.** (D)　　**4.** (D)　　**5.** (C)

[1] 미남 영녀 🎧

Question 1 refers to the following conversation.

M Francesca, I'm wondering if you are still working on the invitation.

W You mean the one for the awards ceremony?

M That's right. Could you add some driving directions? I think a lot of people have never been to that venue before.

W I sent it to the printer this morning. I guess people will need to just look up the directions online if they need them.

해석

1번은 다음 대화에 관한 문제입니다.

남 프란체스카, 당신이 아직 초대장 작업을 하고 있는지 궁금해요.

여 시상식을 위한 것 말이에요?

남 맞아요. 운전해서 오는 길을 좀 추가해 주실 수 있나요? 많은 사람들이 전에 그 장소에 가 본 적이 전혀 없는 것 같아요.

여 제가 오늘 아침에 그것을 인쇄소에 보냈어요. 필요하다면 사람들이 그냥 인터넷에서 길 안내를 찾아봐야 할 것 같아요.

어휘

invitation 초대(장) awards ceremony 시상식
directions ((보통 복수형)) 길 안내 venue ((행사의)) 장소
look up 찾아보다

1.

여자는 "제가 오늘 아침에 그것을 인쇄소에 보냈어요"라고 말할 때 무엇을 의미하는가?
(A) 그녀는 그 장소에 가는 방법을 안다.
(B) 그녀는 지정된 마감 기한을 놓쳤다.
(C) 그녀는 너무 바빠서 메시지를 읽지 못했다.
(D) 그녀는 변경을 할 수 없다.

어휘

site 장소, 위치 assigned 지정된, 할당된
make a change 변경하다

[2-3] 미남 영녀 🎧

Questions 2-3 refer to the following conversation.

M Hello, Ms. Hodge? This is Tony from Fremont Furniture. ²I'm calling about your order of three leather sofas for your hotel's lobby. They were supposed to be delivered today, but I'm afraid there's going to be a delay.

W We're shooting the commercial on Friday. ²Our site needs to look its best.

M I'm very sorry for the inconvenience. Our supplier is having some distribution issues, but I think we can still get the sofas to you within a few days. ³I'll call you tomorrow to confirm the new delivery date.

해석

2-3번은 다음 대화에 관한 문제입니다.

남 여보세요, 하지 씨? 저는 프레몬트 가구사의 토니입니다. ²당신이 호텔 로비용으로 가죽 소파 세 개를 주문하신 건에 관해 전화 드립니다. ²그것들이 오늘 배달되기로 되어 있었으나, 유감스럽게도 지연이 있겠습니다.

여 저희가 금요일에 그 광고를 촬영해요. ²저희 장소가 가장 좋게 보여야 하는데요.

남 불편을 끼쳐 드려 대단히 죄송합니다. 저희 공급업체가 유통 문

제를 좀 겪고 있지만, 그래도 며칠 내로 받게 해드릴 수 있을 것 같습니다. ³내일 전화드려서 새로운 배송 날짜를 확정하겠습니다.

2.
여자는 왜 "저희가 금요일에 그 광고를 촬영해요"라고 말하는가?
(A) 우려를 나타내기 위해
(B) 도움을 요청하기 위해
(C) 일자리를 제안하기 위해
(D) 제안을 거절하기 위해

3.
남자는 내일 무엇을 할 계획인가?
(A) 가구 트럭에서 짐 내리기
(B) 부분 환불액 지급하기
(C) 업데이트된 카탈로그 보내기
(D) 배송 일정 확정하기

패러프레이징

the new delivery date → a delivery schedule

[4-5] 영녀 미남 🎧
Questions 4-5 refer to the following conversation.

> W Victor, ⁴did you hear that the charity will hold a special dinner for volunteers next weekend? It's a way to show appreciation for the work we've been doing.
> M I must have missed the e-mail about that. Do you know when and where it will take place?
> W Yes, it's at the Lakeside Restaurant on Saturday at 7 P.M. ⁵If you'd like, I can give you a ride.
> M I live within walking distance. But thanks for letting me know.

해석

4-5번은 다음 대화에 관한 문제입니다.
여 빅터, ⁴자선 단체가 다음 주말에 자원봉사자들을 위해 특별 만찬을 연다는 걸 들었어요? 그건 우리가 해오고 있는 일에 대해 감사를 표하기 위한 **방법**이에요.

남 제가 그것에 관한 이메일을 지나친 게 틀림없어요. 언제 어디서 열리는지 알아요?
여 네, 토요일 저녁 7시에 레이크사이드 레스토랑에서 열려요. ⁵원하시면 제가 차를 태워 드릴게요.
남 전 걸어서 갈 수 있는 거리에 살아요. 하지만 알려 줘서 고마워요.

4.
화자들은 어떻게 서로 만났을 것 같은가?
(A) 그들은 같은 동네에 산다.
(B) 그들은 같은 대학을 다녔다.
(C) 그들은 같은 식당에 고용되었다.
(D) 그들은 같은 자선 단체에서 자원봉사를 한다.

5.
남자는 왜 "전 걸어서 갈 수 있는 거리에 살아요"라고 말하는가?
(A) 안도감을 표하기 위해
(B) 음식을 먹을 곳을 제안하기 위해
(C) 제안을 거절하기 위해
(D) 일정을 조정하기 위해

실전 문제 본문 p.164

1. (A)	**2.** (B)	**3.** (C)	**4.** (C)	**5.** (A)
6. (D)	**7.** (B)	**8.** (D)	**9.** (A)	**10.** (B)
11. (D)	**12.** (C)	**13.** (C)	**14.** (D)	**15.** (B)
16. (D)	**17.** (C)	**18.** (B)		

[1-3] 미남 미녀 🎧
Questions 1-3 refer to the following conversation.

> M Josephine, ²Ms. Harper and Mr. Estrada are stopping by at 11. ¹They are considering having us take photos at their wedding. It's going to be quite a special event. There will be a lot of influential people there, so it might also help us to get more business.
> W Oh, but Nicholas is in Los Angeles. ²His flight was delayed.
> M That's alright. ²,³Nicholas already prepared the slide show. He has it saved on his work computer, and he told me where to find it.

W	Do you have a key to his office?
M	Yes, ³so I'll go download what I need now. Could you please set up some chairs for our visitors?
W	Sure.

해석

1–3번은 다음 대화에 관한 문제입니다.

남 조세핀, ²하퍼 씨와 에스트라다 씨가 11시에 들를 거예요. ¹그들이 우리에게 결혼식 사진 촬영을 맡기는 것을 고려하고 있어요. 그건 아주 특별한 행사가 될 거예요. 영향력 있는 사람들이 많이 올 것이니, 우리가 더 많은 사업을 확보하는 데도 도움이 될 거예요.

여 아, 하지만 니콜라스가 로스앤젤레스에 있는데요. ²그의 항공편이 지연되었거든요.

남 괜찮아요. ², ³니콜라스가 이미 슬라이드쇼를 준비했어요. 그가 그것을 자신의 작업 컴퓨터에 저장해 두었고, 어디서 찾으면 되는지 제게 알려 주었어요.

여 당신에게 그의 사무실 열쇠가 있어요?

남 네, ³그래서 지금 제가 필요한 것을 다운로드하러 갈 거예요. 당신은 우리 방문객들을 위해 의자를 좀 준비해 주시겠어요?

여 물론이죠.

어휘

stop by ~에 들르다   consider -ing ~하는 것을 고려하다
influential 영향력 있는   flight 항공편, 비행
be delayed 지연되다   prepare 준비하다   save 저장하다
set up 설치하다

1.

화자들은 어떤 종류의 업체에서 일하는 것 같은가?

(A) 사진 촬영 스튜디오
(B) 잡지 출판사
(C) 케이터링 회사
(D) 여행사

어휘

photography 사진 촬영   publisher 출판사

2.

여자는 왜 "니콜라스가 로스앤젤레스에 있는데요"라고 말하는가?

(A) 직원을 칭찬하기 위해
(B) 놀라움을 표현하기 위해
(C) 도움을 거절하기 위해
(D) 결정을 밝히기 위해

어휘

reject 거절하다   assistance 도움, 지원   clarify 명확하게 하다
decision 결정

3.

남자는 왜 니콜라스의 사무실에 갈 것인가?

(A) 항공편 정보를 찾기 위해
(B) 회의를 위한 의자를 구하기 위해
(C) 컴퓨터에서 파일을 다운로드하기 위해

(D) 일부 장비를 설치하기 위해

패러프레이징

the slide show → a file

[4-6] 영녀 호남 🎧

Questions 4-6 refer to the following conversation.

W	⁴Welcome to Renwick Studio. I'm Vanessa, one of the photographers.
M	Hi. I'd like to get some professional portraits taken of my family to include with our holiday cards. Would you be able to visit us at my home?
W	Yes, of course. Let's see… it looks like the next available appointment is in three weeks.
M	Three weeks? ⁵I didn't realize it would be that long.
W	Well, we've got the lowest prices in the region. ⁵And I think you'll agree that you won't find better quality anywhere else. ⁶Let me get a brochure for you so you can see some of our previous work.
M	Okay.

해석

4–6번은 다음 대화에 관한 문제입니다.

여 ⁴렌윅 스튜디오에 오신 것을 환영합니다. 저는 촬영기사 중 한 명인 바네사입니다.

남 안녕하세요. 저희 가족의 인물 사진을 좀 전문적으로 찍어서 저희 연하장에 넣고 싶습니다. 저희 집으로 방문해 주실 수 있으신가요?

여 네, 그럼요. 한번 볼게요... 다음 예약은 3주 뒤에 가능할 것 같아요.

남 3주요? ⁵그렇게 오래 걸릴 줄은 몰랐어요.

여 음, 저희는 지역에서 가장 저렴한 가격을 받아요. ⁵그리고 다른 어느 곳에서도 더 좋은 품질을 찾지 못하실 거라는 데 당신도 동의하게 될 거라고 생각해요. ⁶저희의 이전 작업 일부를 보실 수 있도록 안내 책자를 가져다드릴게요.

남 좋습니다.

어휘

photographer 사진작가, 사진사
professional 전문적인, 전문가의   portrait 인물 사진, 초상화
include 포함시키다   available 이용할 수 있는
appointment 예약, 약속   quality 품질, 우수함   brochure 책자
previous 이전의

4.

화자들은 어디에 있는가?

(A) 기업 연구소에
(B) 헬스장에
(C) 사진 촬영 스튜디오에
(D) 미술관에

어휘

institute 협회, 연구 기관

5.

여자는 왜 "저희는 지역에서 가장 저렴한 가격을 받아요"라고 말하는가?

(A) 대기 시간을 정당화하기 위해
(B) 웹사이트 오류를 정정하기 위해
(C) 실수에 대해 사과하기 위해
(D) 요청을 거절하기 위해

어휘

justify 정당화시키다, 해명하다   correct 바로잡다, 정정하다
apologize for ~에 대해 사과하다   reject 거절하다

6.

여자는 남자에게 무엇을 줄 것인가?
(A) 쿠폰
(B) 명함
(C) 지도
(D) 안내 책자

[7-9] 미녀 호남 🎧

Questions 7-9 refer to the following conversation.

> W ⁷,⁸ Did you take a look at the new design I made for the interior of the bowling alley?
> M I just got in.
> W Well, I have it with me here, so let me show you. What do you think?
> M Hmm… It's quite bright and flashy. And the owner wanted a more retro style. This is a bit too modern.
> W But you said to use striking colors.
> M This isn't what I meant. ⁹ Let me find my notes from the client meeting, and I will explain further.

해석

7-9번은 다음 대화에 관한 문제입니다.

여 ⁷,⁸ 볼링장 내부를 위해 제가 한 새 디자인을 보셨나요?
남 제가 방금 들어왔어요.
여 음, 제가 여기 가지고 있으니 보여 드릴게요. 어떻게 생각하세요?
남 흠… 아주 밝고 화려하네요. 그런데 소유주가 좀 더 복고풍을 원했어요. 이건 너무 현대적이에요.
여 하지만 눈에 띄는 색상을 쓰라고 하셨잖아요.
남 이건 제가 뜻한 게 아니에요. ⁹ 고객 미팅 내용을 적어 둔 것을 찾아볼게요, 그리고 더 설명할게요.

어휘

take a look at ~을 한 번 보다   interior 내부; 내부의
bowling alley 볼링장   flashy 호화로운, 화려한   retro 복고풍의
modern 현대적인   striking 눈에 띄는, 두드러진   further 더

7.

화자들은 주로 무엇에 관해 이야기하고 있는가?
(A) 이메일
(B) 인테리어 디자인
(C) 고객
(D) 광고

8.

남자는 "제가 방금 들어왔어요"라고 말할 때 무엇을 의미하는가?
(A) 그는 방금 고객의 사무실에서 돌아왔다.
(B) 그는 방금 이메일을 받았다.
(C) 그는 소포를 찾으러 갔었다.
(D) 그는 무언가를 검토할 기회가 없었다.

어휘

package 소포, 포장물   look over 검토하다

9.

남자는 다음에 무엇을 할 것 같은가?
(A) 메모 찾기
(B) 디자인에 대해서 누군가에게 전화하기
(C) 평면도 인쇄하기
(D) 고객과 만나기

어휘

floor plan 평면도

패러프레이징

find my notes from the client meeting
→ Look for some notes

[10-12] 영녀 호남 🎧

Questions 10-12 refer to the following conversation.

> W Good morning, Amir. ¹⁰ Henry extended his business trip in Singapore, so I need a second person to interview some job candidates with me today. Could you do it?
> M Sure, I've got some time.
> W Thanks! ¹¹ Here are the résumés to read through. The first interview is at 10.
> M Hmm… ¹¹ there are a lot of pages here, and it's nearly 10 now.
> W I understand. Just do your best. I'll be asking most of the questions.
> M All right. Will Henry be back by Friday? He's supposed to give the welcome speech at the employee dinner.
> W ¹² I'm going to call Henry tomorrow to get an update.

해석

10-12번은 다음 대화에 관한 문제입니다.

여 안녕하세요, 아미르. ¹⁰ 헨리가 싱가포르 출장을 연장했어요, 그래서 오늘 저와 함께 몇몇 입사 지원자들을 면접할 다른 사람이

필요해요. 당신이 할 수 있나요?

남 그럼요, 제가 시간이 좀 있어요.

여 고마워요! **¹¹여기 읽어 봐야 할 이력서들이에요. 첫 번째 면접은 10시예요.**

남 흠... **¹¹페이지가 많네요.** 그리고 **지금 10시가 다 되어 가요.**

여 이해해요. 그냥 할 수 있는 만큼만 하세요. 질문은 대부분 제가 할게요.

남 좋아요. 헨리가 금요일까지 돌아올까요? 그가 직원 회식에서 환영사를 하기로 되어 있어요.

여 **¹²제가 내일 헨리에게 전화해서 새로운 소식을 알아볼게요.**

어휘

extend 연장하다 business trip 출장
job candidate 입사 지원자 résumé 이력서 nearly 거의
do one's best 최선을 다하다 welcome speech 환영사
update 최신 정보

10.

여자는 무엇을 하는 데 도움이 필요한가?
(A) 몇몇 투자자들과 만나는 것
(B) 면접을 실시하는 것
(C) 발표하는 것
(D) 제품을 테스트하는 것

어휘

investor 투자자 conduct 실시하다, 수행하다

패러프레이징

interview some job candidates
→ Conducting some interviews

11.

남자는 왜 "지금 10시가 다 되어 가요"라고 말하는가?
(A) 직원의 노고를 치하하기 위해
(B) 지연에 대해 불만을 제기하기 위해
(C) 휴식을 취하자고 제안하기 위해
(D) 그가 준비되지 않을 것임을 설명하기 위해

어휘

complain 불평하다, 항의하다 delay 지연; 지연시키다

12.

여자는 내일 무엇을 할 것이라고 말하는가?
(A) 방문객 맞이하기
(B) 연설하기
(C) 동료에게 연락하기
(D) 계약 마무리하기

어휘

finalize 마무리 짓다, 완결하다

패러프레이징

call Henry → Contact a colleague

[13-15] 미녀 미남 🎧

Questions 13-15 refer to the following conversation.

W Raj, **¹³I'm ordering some refreshments for the company retreat. Any suggestions?**

M Well... last time, the cupcakes were gone in the first 20 minutes.

W Oh, great. **¹³I'll make sure to get plenty of those. Thanks. ¹⁴And what about something special for the new marketing consultant to welcome her to the team? I was thinking... um... maybe a box of chocolates.**

M Actually, **¹⁵it's possible she's allergic to nuts or something like that, so you'd better avoid a food gift.** How about a bouquet of flowers?

W Good idea. Thanks for your advice!

해석

13-15번은 다음 대화에 관한 문제입니다.

여 라지, **¹³회사 야유회를 위해 다과를 좀 주문하려고요. 뭐든 제안할 것이 있나요?**

남 음... 지난번에, 컵케이크가 첫 20분 만에 사라졌어요.

여 아, 좋아요. **¹³제가 꼭 그것들을 많이 살게요.** 고마워요. **¹⁴그리고 새로운 마케팅 컨설턴트를 위한 특별한 것을 준비해서 그녀가 팀에 들어온 것을 환영하는 건 어때요?** 제가 생각해 봤는데요... 음... 초콜릿 상자 같은 것이요.

남 사실, **¹⁵그녀가 견과류나 뭐 그런 것에 대해 알레르기가 있을 수 있으니 음식 선물은 피하는 게 나아요.** 꽃다발은 어때요?

여 좋은 생각이에요. 조언 고마워요!

어휘

order 주문하다; 주문 refreshments ((항상 복수형)) 다과, 음식물
company retreat 회사 야유회 suggestion 제안
make sure to 반드시 ~하다 plenty of 많은
consultant 컨설턴트, 자문가 allergic to ~에 알레르기가 있는
avoid 피하다 How about ~? ~하는 게 어때요?
bouquet of flowers 꽃다발 advice 충고, 조언

13.

남자는 "컵케이크가 첫 20분 만에 사라졌어요"라고 말할 때 무엇을 의미하는가?
(A) 여자는 분실물을 찾아야 한다.
(B) 그는 늦게 도착한 것에 실망했다.
(C) 여자는 컵케이크를 많이 주문해야 한다.
(D) 그는 휴식 시간이 너무 짧았다고 생각한다.

어휘

disappointed 실망한

14.

누가 최근에 회사에 합류했는가?
(A) 선임 회계사
(B) 판매 관리자
(C) 그래픽 디자이너
(D) 마케팅 컨설턴트

15.

남자는 여자에게 무엇에 대해 경고하는가?

(A) 폐업

(B) 음식 알레르기

(C) 처리 시간

(D) 다가오는 마감 기한

어휘

process 처리하다; 과정 approach 다가오다, 다가가다

패러프레이징

allergic to nuts or something like that → A food allergy

[16-18] 영녀 미남 🎧

Questions 16-18 refer to the following conversation.

> W Hi, Albert. ¹⁶This is Sonia from the Human Resources department.
>
> M Hi, Sonia. What can I help you with?
>
> W Well, we've decided that we need to start recognizing employees for their hard work. So, ¹⁷we're going to launch an Employee of the Month Award.
>
> M That would be great.
>
> W I'm glad you like the idea. ¹⁸I know that you have all the quarterly performance evaluations written by the managers. I'm wondering if you could print copies of those for me.
>
> M Actually… uh… I uploaded the files to the database.
>
> W Oh, that's great. I'll view them there. Thanks.

해석

16–18번은 다음 대화에 관한 문제입니다.

여 안녕하세요, 앨버트. ¹⁶저는 인사부의 소니아예요.

남 안녕하세요, 소니아. 무엇을 도와드릴까요?

여 음, 저희는 직원들의 노고를 인정하기 시작해야 한다고 결정했어요. 그래서 ¹⁷저희가 '이달의 직원 상'을 시작하려고 해요.

남 그거 정말 좋겠어요.

여 당신이 이 아이디어를 좋아하니 기뻐요. ¹⁸당신에게 관리자들이 작성한 모든 분기별 직무 평가가 있다고 알고 있어요. 그것들의 사본을 인쇄해 주실 수 있는지 궁금합니다.

남 실은… 어… 제가 데이터베이스에 그 파일들을 업로드했어요.

여 아, 잘됐네요. 제가 거기서 볼게요. 고마워요.

어휘

Human Resources department 인사부
recognize 인정하다 hard work 노고, 열심히 한 일
launch 시작하다 quarterly 분기별의
performance evaluations 직무 평가 copy 복사본

16.

여자는 어떤 부서에서 일하는가?

(A) 제품 개발

(B) 기술 지원

(C) 회계

(D) 인사

17.

여자는 무엇을 준비하고 있는가?

(A) 기자 회견

(B) 이사회 회의

(C) 직원 상

(D) 채용 박람회

패러프레이징

an Employee of the Month Award → A staff award

18.

남자는 "제가 데이터베이스에 그 파일들을 업로드했어요"라고 말할 때 무엇을 암시하는가?

(A) 여자는 접속 코드를 변경해야 한다.

(B) 여자는 도움이 필요하지 않을 것이다.

(C) 그는 파일 몇 개를 잃어버렸다.

(D) 그는 시스템이 왜 느리게 작동하는지 안다.

어휘

access 접속, 접근 assistance 도움, 지원

UNIT O8 시각 자료 연계 문제

연습 문제		본문 p.169
1. (C)	**2.** (C)	**3.** (D)

[1] 미녀 호남 🎧

Question 1 refers to the following conversation and employee directory.

> W Jason, have you had a chance to try out the new software yet? It has a lot of nice new features, but it doesn't run very fast.
>
> M Are the other team members experiencing the same problem?
>
> W Yeah. Many of my team members have said the same thing. I think we should report it to someone in charge.
>
> M I'll call the IT department and ask them to look into this issue.

해석

1번은 다음 대화와 직원 명부에 관한 문제입니다.

여 제이슨, 새로운 소프트웨어를 시험적으로 사용해 볼 기회가 있었어요? 좋고 새로운 기능이 많이 있지만, 그다지 빨리 작동하지는 않아요.

남 나머지 팀원들도 같은 문제를 겪고 있나요?

여 네. 저희 팀원들 다수가 같은 얘기를 했어요. 우리가 그것을 담당자에게 보고해야 할 것 같아요.

남 제가 IT 부서에 전화해서 그들에게 이 문제를 조사해 달라고 요청할게요.

내선 번호	직함
567	회계 부장
569	인사 부장
573	**IT 부장**
575	총무 부장

1.

시각 자료를 보시오. 남자는 어느 내선 번호로 전화할 것 같은가?
(A) 567
(B) 569
(C) 573
(D) 575

[2-3] 호남 미녀 🎧

Questions 2-3 refer to the following conversation and floor plan.

> M Hello, could you please let me know where I can find Tiffany Henson's office? ²My name is Ross Preston, and I'm here to show Ms. Henson how to use my company's new wireless projector.
>
> W Her office is number 304, but she doesn't usually get to the office until nine.
>
> M That's fine. I'm quite early because traffic was light. I'll just get a snack while I wait.
>
> W Oh… um… in that case, ³don't use the machine closest to the elevator. It's been malfunctioning all morning.

해석

2-3번은 다음 대화와 평면도에 관한 문제입니다.

남 안녕하세요, 티파니 헨슨의 사무실을 어디서 찾을 수 있는지 알려 주시겠어요? ²제 이름은 로스 프레스턴이고, 헨슨 씨에게 저희 회사의 새로운 무선 프로젝터 사용법을 알려 드리려고 왔습니다.

여 그녀의 사무실은 304호지만, 그녀는 보통 9시는 되어야 사무실에 옵니다.

남 그건 괜찮습니다. 차가 안 막혀서 제가 좀 일찍 왔어요. 기다리는 동안 그냥 뭘 좀 먹고 있을게요.

여 아… 음… 그러시다면, ³엘리베이터에서 가장 가까운 기계는 사용하지 마세요. 그건 아침 내내 제대로 작동하지 않고 있어요.

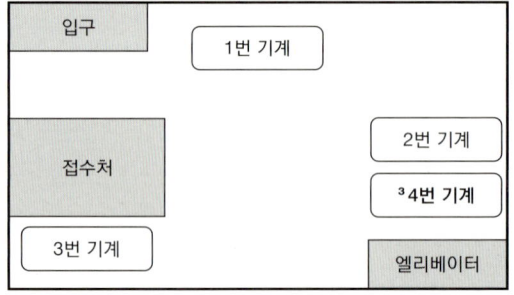

2.

남자는 왜 이 장소를 방문했는가?
(A) 조사를 하기 위해
(B) 문서를 배달하기 위해
(C) 시연을 하기 위해
(D) 채용 면접에 참석하기 위해

패러프레이징

show ~ how to use my company's new wireless projector → give a demonstration

3.

시각 자료를 보시오. 어떤 기계가 작동하지 않고 있는가?
(A) 1번 기계
(B) 2번 기계
(C) 3번 기계
(D) 4번 기계

실전 문제 본문 p.170

1. (A)	2. (C)	3. (B)	4. (B)	5. (C)
6. (D)	7. (C)	8. (C)	9. (D)	10. (B)
11. (C)	12. (A)			

[1-3] 미녀 미남 🎧

Questions 1-3 refer to the following conversation and graph.

W **¹Jerald, thanks for helping me with the preparations for next week's job fair.** I hope we find some talented salespeople.

M So do I. We need to find a way to boost sales. Have you seen the latest figures? **²We're struggling to hit the targets for several products, especially this one here. 5,000 units are not enough.**

W With the right staff, we can correct that problem. But maybe we should think about dropping the lower-performing products from our line.

M Um... that may be something to consider in the future, but not in the short-term. **³I've just renewed the distribution contracts for several of these items.**

W I understand.

해석

1–3번은 다음 대화와 그래프에 관한 문제입니다.

여 **¹제럴드, 다음 주에 있을 채용 박람회 준비를 도와줘서 고마워요.** 우리가 유능한 판매원들을 찾을 수 있길 바라요.

남 저도요. 우리는 판매를 증가시킬 방법을 찾아야 해요. 가장 최근의 수치 봤어요? **²우리는 몇 가지 제품에 대해서는 목표액을 맞추느라 고전하고 있어요. 특히 여기 이것이요. 5천 개는 충분하지 않아요.**

여 적임의 직원들이 있다면, 우리가 그 문제를 해결할 수 있어요. 하지만 아마도 우리 제품 라인에서 실적이 저조한 제품들을 빼는 것에 대해 생각해 봐야 해요.

남 음... 그건 나중에는 고려해야 할 것일 수도 있지만, 단기적으로는 아니에요. **³제가 막 이 품목들 몇몇에 대한 유통 계약을 갱신했어요.**

여 알겠어요.

어휘

preparation for ~에 대한 준비   job fair 채용 박람회
talented 재능이 있는   boost 신장시키다, 북돋우다
struggle to ~하려고 분투하다, 애쓰다
hit the target 목표액에 달하다   unit 한 개
correct 바로잡다, 정정하다   drop A from B B에서 A를 빼다
lower-performing 성과가 낮은   consider 고려하다
in the short-term 단기적으로   renew 갱신하다
distribution 유통, 분배   contract 계약(서)

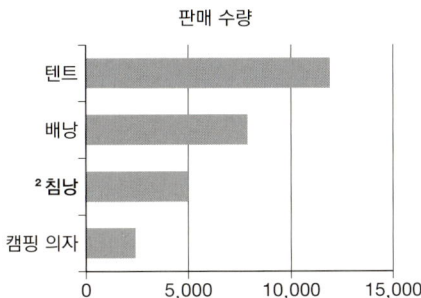

판매 수량

1.

화자들은 무엇을 준비하고 있는가?
(A) 취업 박람회
(B) 제품 출시
(C) 이사회 회의
(D) 정치 토론

어휘

launch 출시, 개시   political 정치의   debate 토론

패러프레이징

next week's job fair → A career fair

2.

시각 자료를 보시오. 남자는 어떤 제품을 언급하는가?
(A) 텐트
(B) 배낭
(C) 침낭
(D) 캠핑 의자

3.

남자는 최근에 무엇을 했는가?
(A) 그는 본사를 방문했다.
(B) 그는 몇몇 계약을 갱신했다.
(C) 그는 워크숍에 참석했다.
(D) 그는 사무 공간을 임대했다.

어휘

headquarters 본사, 본부
rent 임차하다, 임대하다

[4-6] 영녀 미남 🎧

Questions 4-6 refer to the following conversation and order form.

W Jin, **⁴I'm ordering the new uniforms for the regular staff and managers in the bakery department of our grocery store.** Do you have a minute to look it over to make sure it's alright?

M Sure, I can do that now. **⁵Um... the trousers for the uniform aren't changing, so we'll only need two of those... uh... for the two new employees.**

W Oh, I had forgotten about that. Thanks.

M Everything else looks fine. If you have any other questions, **⁶I'll be in the back. One of the trucks arrived early, and the team needs help unloading it.**

W Okay. I can help with that, too, after I submit this order.

해석

4–6번은 다음 대화와 주문서에 관한 문제입니다.

여 진, **⁴우리 식료품점 제빵 코너의 정규 직원들과 관리자들을 위한**

새 유니폼을 주문하려고요. 괜찮은지 확인하기 위해 훑어볼 시간 있으세요?

남 그럼요, 지금 할 수 있어요. **⁵음... 유니폼의 바지는 바뀌지 않을 거예요. 그러니 그것들은 두 개만 필요해요... 어... 두 명의 신입 직원을 위해서요.**

여 아, 제가 그것에 대해 잊고 있었네요. 고마워요.

남 다른 모든 것들은 괜찮아 보여요. 질문이 더 있으시면, **⁶전 뒤쪽에 있을 거예요.** 트럭 하나가 일찍 도착해서, 팀에서 물건을 내리는 데 도움이 필요해요.

여 알겠어요. 이 주문서를 제출한 뒤에 저도 도와드릴게요.

어휘

order 주문하다; 주문 regular staff 정규 직원
look over 훑어보다, 살펴보다 trousers ((항상 복수형)) 바지
unload (짐을) 내리다 submit 제출하다

주문서		
품목	수량	총액
조끼	24	180달러
모자	4	40달러
⁵바지	12	150달러
셔츠	36	360달러

4.
화자들은 어디에서 일하는 것 같은가?
(A) 광고 대행사에서
(B) 슈퍼마켓에서
(C) 회계 사무소에서
(D) 음료 제조사에서

어휘

advertising 광고 accounting 회계 (업무)
manufacturer 제조사, 생산 회사

패러프레이징

our grocery store → a supermarket

5.
시각 자료를 보시오. 남자는 어떤 수량이 바뀌어야 한다고 말하는가?
(A) 24
(B) 4
(C) 12
(D) 36

6.
남자는 다음에 무엇을 할 계획인가?
(A) 일정 업데이트하기
(B) 몇몇 가격 확인하기
(C) 일부 고객과 이야기하기
(D) 트럭에서 짐 내리기

Questions 7-9 refer to the following conversation and price list.

W Well, of all the shops we've visited, I think this one has the best selection. I'm glad we're finally buying reusable cups to serve drinks at ⁷our law firm. It's much better for the environment.

M I agree. ⁸I like the style of these mugs, and they're a good price. Let's get 30 of them.

W All right. You brought the company card to pay for them, right?

M Yes, I've got it right here.

W You know... these are going to be quite heavy. ⁹How about I bring the car right to the entrance so they don't have to be carried very far?

해석

7-9번은 다음 대화와 가격표에 관한 문제입니다.

여 음, 우리가 방문했던 모든 상점들 중에서, 이곳에 가장 좋은 제품들이 있는 것 같아요. 드디어 **⁷우리 법률 사무소에서 음료 접대를 위해 재사용할 수 있는 컵을 구매하게 되어 기뻐요. 그것이 환경을 위해 훨씬 더 좋아요.**

남 동의해요. **⁸전 이 머그잔들의 스타일이 마음에 들어요, 가격도 괜찮고요. 그것들 30개를 사요.**

여 좋아요. 당신이 비용을 결제할 회사 카드를 가지고 왔죠, 그렇죠?

남 네, 지금 여기 가지고 있어요.

여 있잖아요... 이것들은 꽤 무거울 거예요. **⁹그것들을 멀리까지 들고 갈 필요 없도록 제가 입구 바로 앞으로 차를 가져오는 게 어떨까요?**

어휘

selection 선택 가능한 것들 reusable 재사용할 수 있는
serve (음식을) 차려주다, 내다 law firm 법률 사무소
environment 환경 entrance 입구, 문
carry 나르다, 가지고 다니다

판매용 컵

와인 잔 12달러	유리잔 8달러
⁸커피 머그잔 5달러	피처 20달러

7.
화자들은 어떤 종류의 업체에서 일하는가?
(A) 커피숍
(B) 환경 단체
(C) 법률 회사

(D) 케이터링 회사

environmental 환경의

8.
시각 자료를 보시오. 화자들은 품목당 얼마를 지불할 것인가?
(A) 12달러
(B) 8달러
(C) 5달러
(D) 20달러

9.
여자는 무엇을 해 주겠다고 제안하는가?
(A) 영수증 기록하기
(B) 자신의 신용카드 사용하기
(C) 출입문 열기
(D) 차량 옮기기

어휘
keep track of ~을 기록하다 receipt 영수증 unlock 열다

패러프레이징
bring the car right to the entrance → Move a vehicle

[10-12] 영녀 호남 🎧
Questions 10-12 refer to the following conversation and request form.

> W Jimmy, I didn't see Mr. Norton on the list of new members. ¹⁰I know he was excited about taking lessons here at our golf club. Did he change his mind?
> M He hasn't paid yet. Actually, I called him this morning, and it seems there was an error in filling out his bank transfer form.
> W Let's see... here's the form.
> M Right. ¹¹He wrote the wrong branch number. I've corrected it now.
> W Great. I suppose that may take a few days to process. ¹²I'll call down to reception and ask them to prepare a pass for Mr. Norton in case he wants to visit the site sooner than that.
> M Thanks. I'll let him know.

해석
10-12번은 다음 대화와 신청서에 관한 문제입니다.
여 지미, 신규 회원 명단에 노턴 씨가 보이지 않았어요. ¹⁰그가 이곳 우리 골프 클럽에서 강습을 듣게 되어 신나 했던 것으로 알아요. 그가 마음을 바꾸었나요?
남 그가 아직 요금을 지불하지 않았어요. 실은, 제가 오늘 아침에 그에게 전화했는데, 그의 계좌 이체 서식을 기입하는 데 오류가 있었던 것 같아요.
여 어디 볼게요... 여기 서식이 있어요.
남 맞네요. ¹¹그가 다른 지점 번호를 적었어요. 제가 지금 그것을 고

쳤어요.
여 잘하셨어요. 그것은 처리되는 데 며칠 걸릴 수도 있을 것 같아요. 노턴 씨가 그것보다 빨리 현장을 방문하기를 원할 경우에 대비해서, ¹²제가 접수처를 불러서 노턴 씨를 위한 출입증을 준비하라고 요청할게요.
남 고마워요. 제가 그에게 알려 줄게요.

어휘
take a lesson 수업을 받다
change one's mind 생각을 바꾸다 fill out 기입하다, 작성하다
bank transfer 계좌 이체 branch 지점, 지사
correct 바로잡다, 정정하다 suppose 생각하다, 추측하다
process 처리하다 call down 부르다 reception 접수처
pass 출입증 in case ~할 경우에 대비해서

계좌 이체 신청서:
송금자 정보

1. 이름 조지 노턴

2. 주소 워커 가 181번지, 디트로이트, 미시건 주 48219

3. 은행명 오세오 은행

¹¹4. 지점 번호 054

5. 계좌 번호 420532947

10.
여자에 따르면, 노턴 씨는 무엇을 하는 것에 관해 신나 하는가?
(A) 새 일을 시작하는 것
(B) 골프 강습을 받는 것
(C) 토너먼트 대회에 나가는 것
(D) 새로운 사람들을 만나는 것

어휘
tournament 토너먼트, 승자 진출전

11.
시각 자료를 보시오. 어느 줄에 오류가 있는가?
(A) 2행
(B) 3행
(C) 4행
(D) 5행

12.
여자는 왜 접수처를 부를 계획인가?
(A) 노턴 씨를 위한 출입증을 요청하기 위해
(B) 노턴 씨의 연락처를 얻기 위해
(C) 컴퓨터 오류를 보고하기 위해
(D) 견학 일정을 잡기 위해

어휘
contact details 연락처 schedule 일정을 잡다

CHAPTER 02 대화 주제별 전략

UNIT 09 회사 업무·인사 관련 대화

CHECK UP
본문 p.172

1. (A)　　**2.** (C)　　**3.** (B)

[1-3] 미녀 미남 🎧

Questions 1-3 refer to the following conversation.

> **W** Hi, this is Ava Schaffer from the personnel department at Soul Food Incorporated. ¹I'm calling to confirm that Monday will be your first day with us.
>
> **M** Yes. Is there anything I have to do before then?
>
> **W** Not really. I'll meet you at the security office first to get you an employee badge. ²Don't forget to bring a photo identification card.
>
> **M** I'll be sure to have that. By the way, ³did you get my signed employment contract that I sent by e-mail yesterday?
>
> **W** ³Yes, I read it this morning.
>
> **M** Oh, okay. Have a nice weekend, and I'll see you on Monday. Thank you for the call.

해석

1–3번은 다음 대화에 관한 문제입니다.

여 안녕하세요, 소울 푸드 주식회사 인사부의 에바 셰퍼입니다. ¹월요일이 당신이 이곳에서 근무하는 첫날임을 확인하기 위해 전화 드립니다.

남 네. 제가 그 전에 해야 할 일이라도 있나요?

여 그렇지는 않습니다. 사원증을 드리기 위해 제가 제일 먼저 경비실에서 당신을 만날 것입니다. ²사진이 부착된 신분증을 가져오시는 것을 잊지 마세요.

남 꼭 그렇게 하겠습니다. 그런데, ³제가 어제 이메일로 보내 드린, 제 서명을 한 고용 계약서를 받으셨나요?

여 ³네, 오늘 아침에 그것을 읽었습니다.

남 아, 알겠습니다. 즐거운 주말 보내시고, 월요일에 뵙겠습니다. 전화 주셔서 감사합니다.

어휘

personnel department 인사부　incorporated 주식회사
confirm 확인하다, 확정하다　security office 경비실
badge 표, 배지　identification card 신분증
be sure to 꼭 ~하다　signed 서명이 있는
employment contract 고용 계약서

1.

남자는 월요일에 무엇을 할 것인가?

(A) 새로운 일 시작하기
(B) 면접 보기
(C) 견학 이끌기
(D) 교육에 참가하기

어휘

participate in ~에 참가하다

패러프레이징

your first day with us → Start a new job

2.

여자는 남자에게 무엇을 해 달라고 요청하는가?

(A) 서식 제출하기
(B) 보고서 준비하기
(C) 신분증 가져오기
(D) 이력서 업데이트하기

어휘

submit 제출하다

3.

여자는 남자로부터 무엇을 받았는가?

(A) 일부 작업 샘플
(B) 서명한 계약서
(C) 추천서
(D) 회원증

패러프레이징

my signed employment contract → A signed contract

패러프레이징 연습
본문 p.174

1-4. 스크립트 참조　　**5.** (A)　　**6.** (A)

1.

Q 화자들은 어떤 자리를 채우려고 하고 있는가?

A 소프트웨어 개발자

미남 미녀 🎧

> **M** We have a lot of great candidates for the open position, don't you think?
>
> **W** Definitely. I'm confident that we'll find the right person to work on developing our new software.
>
> **M** Shall we meet tomorrow to discuss the decision further?

해석

남 그 공석에 지원한 훌륭한 후보자들이 많아요, 그렇게 생각하지 않아요?

여 물론입니다. 우리의 새 소프트웨어를 개발하는 작업을 하기에 적합한 사람을 찾을 거라고 확신해요.

남 내일 만나서 결정에 대해 더 논의할까요?

어휘

fill a position 자리를 채우다 developer 개발자, 개발업자
candidate 후보자, 지원자 definitely 분명히, 확실히
confident 확신하는, 자신감 있는 develop 개발하다 further 더

패러프레이징

the right person to work on developing our new
software → Software developer

2.

Q 여자는 어떤 문제를 언급하는가?
A 일부 설정이 변경하기 어렵다.

미남 미녀 🎧

> **M** How have the reviews for our new copy
>   machine been so far?
> **W** Most people are satisfied with it. However,
>   several reviewers reported that they had
>   trouble adjusting the settings.
> **M** Hmm… we'd better make the R&D team aware
>   of this issue.

해석

남 지금까지 우리 새 복사기에 대한 리뷰들은 어떤가요?
여 대부분의 사람들이 그것에 만족스러워해요. **하지만, 몇몇 사용자**
  들은 설정을 조정하느라 힘들었다고 전했어요.
남 흠... 연구개발팀에 이 문제를 알리는 게 좋겠어요.

어휘

setting 설정 review 평가, 리뷰
be satisfied with ~에 만족하다
have trouble -ing ~하느라 힘들어하다
adjust 조정하다, 조절하다 aware of ~을 알고 있는

패러프레이징

had trouble adjusting the settings
→ Some settings are difficult to change

3.

Q 남자는 여자에게 무엇을 해 달라고 요청하는가?
A 기사 제출하기

미남 미녀 🎧

> **M** Your blog is very impressive, Ms. Stewart.
>   Would you be willing to write a special article
>   on summer fashion trends? You can e-mail me
>   the draft as soon as it's ready.
> **W** Sure, I'm highly interested in contributing to
>   your magazine.

해석

남 당신의 블로그는 매우 인상적이에요, 스튜어트 씨. **여름 패션 동**
  향에 대해 특별 기사를 쓸 의향이 있나요? 준비되는 대로 제게
  초고를 이메일로 보내 주면 돼요.

여 물론이죠, 저는 당신의 잡지에 기고하는 데 아주 관심이 많아요.

어휘

submit 제출하다 article 글, 기사 impressive 인상적인
be willing to 기꺼이 ~하다 trend 동향, 추세
draft 초고, 초안 highly 대단히, 매우
contribute to a magazine 잡지에 기고하다

패러프레이징

write a special article on summer fashion trends ~
e-mail me the draft → Submit an article

4.

Q 남자는 회사에 대해 무엇이 좋다고 말하는가?
A 그곳은 성장할 기회들을 제공한다.

미녀 미남 🎧

> **W** Thank you for attending this interview,
>   Mr. Jones. It seems that you have a lot of
>   experience in the field. Why did you decide to
>   apply for this role?
> **M** Well, I know that this firm provides good
>   opportunities for training and education. I can
>   picture myself being here for the long term.

해석

여 이번 면접에 참석해 주셔서 감사합니다, 존스 씨. 당신은 이 분야
  에 많은 경험이 있는 것 같아요. 왜 이 역할에 지원하기로 결정하
  셨죠?
남 음, **이 회사는 연수 및 교육을 위한 좋은 기회들을 제공하는 걸로**
  알고 있습니다. 제가 오랜 기간 동안 여기 있는 것을 상상할 수
  있습니다.

어휘

opportunity 기회 growth 성장 attend 참석하다, 출석하다
field 분야 apply for ~에 지원하다 role 역할, 임무
training 교육, 연수 education 교육
picture 상상하다, 마음속에 그리다 long term 장기간

패러프레이징

provides good opportunities for training and
education → offers opportunities for growth

5.

여자는 남자에게 무엇을 제안하는가?
(A) 승진
(B) 행사 초대

미녀 미남 🎧

> **W** Eric, because of your hard work, we would like
>   you to take over Victoria's position when she
>   leaves. This promotion would be a great use of
>   your skills.
> **M** Thank you. I didn't expect an offer to move up.
>   I would happily accept the opportunity.

해석

여 에릭, 당신의 노고를 보아, **우리는 빅토리아가 떠나면 당신이 그녀의 자리를 인계받았으면 합니다.** 이번 승진으로 당신의 기량을 충분히 발휘하게 될 것입니다.

남 고맙습니다. 승진 제안을 받을 줄은 예상하지 못했어요. 기꺼이 이 기회를 받아들이겠습니다.

어휘

job promotion 승진 invitation 초대(장)
hard work 노력, 노고 take over 인계받다
position 일자리, 직위 skill 기량, 기술
expect 기대하다, 예상하다 move up 승진하다

패러프레이징

take over Victoria's position → A job promotion

6.

여자는 신제품에 대해 무엇이라고 말하는가?
(A) 그것은 에너지 효율이 좋다.
(B) 그것은 비싸지 않다.

미녀 미남 🎧

> W Hi, Jeffery. Thanks for sending me the press release for the company's new dishwasher. I like how you emphasized that it received the highest ranking for energy efficiency.
>
> M Yes, I think that's a feature that a lot of consumers will find appealing.

해석

여 안녕하세요, 제프리. 제게 회사의 새 식기세척기에 대한 보도 자료를 보내 줘서 고마워요. 그것이 에너지 효율 최고 등급을 받았다는 것을 강조한 방식이 마음에 들어요.

남 네, 그 점이 많은 소비자들이 매력적이라고 생각할 특징인 것 같아요.

어휘

energy efficient 에너지 효율이 좋은 inexpensive 비싸지 않은
press release 보도 자료 emphasize 강조하다
ranking 등급 매기기 energy efficiency 에너지 효율
feature 특징 consumer 소비자
appealing 매력적인, 호소하는

패러프레이징

received the highest ranking for energy efficiency
→ energy efficient

연습 문제   본문 p.175

1. (C)   **2.** (D)   **3.** (A)   **4.** (B)   **5.** (D)

[1] 영녀 미남 🎧

Question 1 refers to the following conversation.

> W Harvey, you've just completed your certification for performing financial audits, right?
>
> M Yes. I was taking courses on the weekend. Why do you ask?
>
> W Well, there's an opening for a full-time auditor at our Worthington branch. It has a competitive salary and excellent benefits. I think you'd do a great job. Would you consider submitting an application?
>
> M That's a great opportunity. I'll do that.

해석

1번은 다음 대화에 관한 문제입니다.

여 하비, 당신은 막 회계감사 수행을 위한 인증 과정을 이수했죠, 맞죠?

남 네. 주말에 강의를 들었어요. 무슨 일로 물어보시나요?

여 음, 우리 워딩턴 지점에 정규직 회계감사 자리가 비었어요. 급여가 높고 혜택도 아주 많아요. 당신이라면 일을 잘할 것 같아요. 지원서 제출을 고려해 보시겠어요?

남 그건 아주 좋은 기회예요. 그렇게 할게요.

어휘

complete 완료하다, 끝마치다 certification 증명, 증명서
perform 수행하다, 실시하다 financial audit 재무감사, 회계감사
take a course 강의를 듣다 opening 빈자리, 공석
full-time 정규직의 auditor 회계감사원
competitive 경쟁력 있는, 뒤지지 않는
benefits ((보통 복수형)) 특전, 수당
consider -ing ~하는 것을 고려하다 submit 제출하다
application 지원서, 신청서

1.

여자는 남자가 무엇을 해야 한다고 생각하는가?
(A) 일부 신입 직원 교육하기
(B) 수강 신청하기
(C) 새로운 일자리에 지원하기
(D) 행사의 예산 점검하기

어휘

sign up for ~을 신청하다 apply for ~에 지원하다
budget 예산

패러프레이징

an opening for a full-time auditor ~ submitting an application → Apply for a new position

[2-3] 미남 영녀 🎧

Questions 2-3 refer to the following conversation.

> M I had a meeting with Mr. Rentz at Amvac Chemicals yesterday. I'm not sure if he'll use our service or not. He likes our approach to international companies. ²However, he's very worried about spending too much.

W That must be why he wasn't interested in our proposal last time.

M Well, this time, he asked me to send him more details. ³We should start working on the timeline for the project right away.

W That's fine with me.

해석
2-3번은 다음 대화에 관한 문제입니다.

남 어제 암바크 화학의 렌츠 씨와 회의를 했어요. 그가 우리 서비스를 이용할지 말지 잘 모르겠어요. 그는 국제적 기업들에 대한 우리의 접근 방식을 좋아해요. ²하지만, 너무 많은 비용을 쓰는 것에 대해 매우 우려해요.

여 틀림없이 그게 그가 지난번 우리의 제안에 관심이 없었던 이유겠네요.

남 음, 이번에는, 그가 제게 더 많은 세부 정보를 보내 달라고 요청했어요. ³우리는 당장 그 프로젝트를 위한 일정표 작업을 시작해야 해요.

여 전 좋아요.

어휘
approach 접근법, 처리 방법; 다가가다 international 국제적인
be worried about ~에 대해서 걱정하다
be interested in ~에 관심이 있다 proposal 제안
work on ~에 착수하다, 노력을 들이다 timeline 일정표, 연대기

2.
남자는 렌츠 씨에 대해 무엇이라고 말하는가?
(A) 그는 계약을 연장하기를 원한다.
(B) 그는 새 프로젝트를 좋아하지 않는다.
(C) 그는 새로운 제안서를 보냈다.
(D) 그는 예산에 관해 우려한다.

어휘
extend 연장하다, 확대하다
be concerned about ~에 관해 걱정하다

패러프레이징
very worried about spending too much
→ concerned about a budget

3.
화자들은 다음에 무엇을 할 것 같은가?
(A) 자세한 일정 세우기
(B) 렌츠 씨의 사무실 방문하기
(C) 두 번째 발표하기
(D) 직원들에게 팀에 합류해 달라고 요청하기

어휘
detailed 자세한 give a presentation 발표하다

패러프레이징
start working on the timeline for the project
→ Make a detailed schedule

[4-5] 영녀 미남 🎧
Questions 4-5 refer to the following conversation.

W Good morning. I'm Audrey Coolidge from CPA Accounting Firm. I have an appointment at 1 o'clock with the manager, Mr. Johnson, to confirm the contract details.

M ⁴Actually, Mr. Johnson is scheduled for a meeting with you at 2 P.M., not 1 P.M.

W ⁴Oh, I must have misunderstood. Well, is he available now by any chance?

M Unfortunately, he's at a business luncheon. ⁵Why don't you meet with our assistant manager instead? He's familiar with all the details of the contract.

해석
4-5번은 다음 대화에 관한 문제입니다.

여 안녕하세요. 저는 CPA 회계 법인의 오드리 쿨리지입니다. 계약 세부 사항을 확정하기 위해, 1시에 매니저이신 존슨 씨와 약속이 되어 있습니다.

남 ⁴실은, 존슨 씨는 오후 1시가 아니라 2시에 당신과 회의가 잡혀 있어요.

여 ⁴아, 제가 잘못 알았던 모양이에요. 그럼, 혹시라도 그분이 지금 시간이 되실까요?

남 유감스럽게도, 오찬 회의 중이에요. ⁵대신 저희 부매니저를 만나시는 건 어떠세요? 그는 그 계약의 모든 세부 사항에 대해 잘 알고 있습니다.

어휘
accounting firm 회계 법인, 회계 사무소
confirm 확정하다, 확인하다 contract details 계약 세부 사항
available (만날) 시간이 있는 by any chance 혹시라도
luncheon 오찬 모임, 점심
be familiar with ~을 잘 알다, ~에 익숙하다

4.
여자는 무엇을 잘못 알았는가?
(A) 매니저의 이름
(B) 회의 시간
(C) 회의 장소
(D) 점심 메뉴

어휘
venue (행사의) 장소

5.
남자는 여자에게 무엇을 하라고 제안하는가?
(A) 더 많은 세부 사항 제공하기
(B) 점심시간 이후에 다시 오기
(C) 로비에서 기다리기
(D) 다른 사람 만나기

meet with our assistant manager instead
→ Meet another person

본문 p.176

실전 문제

1. (B)	**2.** (C)	**3.** (D)	**4.** (A)	**5.** (D)
6. (C)	**7.** (D)	**8.** (B)	**9.** (C)	**10.** (B)
11. (C)	**12.** (C)	**13.** (A)	**14.** (B)	**15.** (B)
16. (B)	**17.** (C)	**18.** (A)		

[1-3] 미남 미녀 🎧

Questions 1-3 refer to the following conversation.

> **M** Hi, Sohee. Do you have a minute? **¹I was looking over the form you sent here to the finance department for some business expenses.** Let's see... booking some hotel rooms. But you forgot to list the reason.
>
> **W** Oh, I'm sorry about that. **²We have some potential investors from London visiting our firm next month,** and we're providing accommodations for them.
>
> **M** Okay, please e-mail me their names, and I'll add that information to the form. Also, do I need to prepare financial statements for them like last time?
>
> **W** Thanks, but **³I've already received the necessary financial reports and e-mailed them to the investors.**

해석

1-3번은 다음 대화에 관한 문제입니다.

남 안녕하세요, 소희 씨. 시간 좀 있어요? **¹당신이 일부 업무 비용에 대해 저희 회계부에 보낸 서식을 살펴보고 있었어요.** 어디 볼게요... 호텔 객실 예약 건이고요. 그런데 당신이 사유를 작성하는 것을 잊었어요.

여 아, 그 점은 미안해요. **²다음 달에 런던에서 우리 회사를 방문하는 몇몇 잠재 투자자들이 있어서 저희가 그들에게 숙소를 제공하려고 해요.**

남 알겠어요, 그들의 명단을 제게 이메일로 보내 주세요, 그러면 제가 그 정보를 서식에 추가할게요. 또, 제가 지난번처럼 그들을 위해 재무제표를 준비해야 하나요?

여 고마워요, 하지만 **³제가 이미 필요한 재무 보고서를 받아서 투자자들에게 이메일로 보냈어요.**

어휘

look over 훑어보다, 살펴보다
finance department 회계부, 경리부 expense 돈, 비용
book 예약하다 list 목록을 작성하다, 열거하다
potential 잠재적인 investor 투자자
accommodations ((항상 복수형)) 숙박시설
financial statements 재무제표

1.

남자는 어느 부서에서 일하는가?
(A) 영업
(B) 회계
(C) 그래픽 디자인
(D) 제품 개발

2.

여자는 다음 달에 무슨 일이 일어날 것이라고 말하는가?
(A) 직원 축하 행사가 열릴 것이다.
(B) 새로운 규제가 시행될 것이다.
(C) 어떤 사람들이 회사를 방문할 것이다.
(D) 몇몇 신입 직원들이 채용될 것이다.

어휘

celebration 기념 (행사) regulation 규제, 규정
go into effect 효력이 발생되다 hire 고용하다

패러프레이징

some potential investors from London visiting our firm → Some people will visit the company

3.

여자는 왜 남자의 제안을 거절하는가?
(A) 관리자의 승인이 필요하다.
(B) 곧 마감 기한이 다가온다.
(C) 예산에 여유가 충분하지 않다.
(D) 일이 이미 완료되었다.

어휘

supervisor 관리자, 감독관 approval 승인, 인정
require 요구하다, 필요로 하다 room 여지, 여유 budget 예산

패러프레이징

already received ~ and e-mailed them
→ A task has already been completed

[4-6] 영녀 미남 🎧

Questions 4-6 refer to the following conversation.

> **W** Hello, Mr. Kendrick? My name is Courtney Rush. **⁴I'm calling about your job advertisement on the Internet. I'm wondering if the market researcher position is still available.**
>
> **M** Yes, you're not too late. We're not closing recruitment until the end of this week. So, you can still send your résumé if you're interested.
>
> **W** Thank you. **⁵I'm glad I called. I was afraid I'd be too late.** One more thing, I wasn't sure if you wanted me to provide my references.
>
> **M** Yes, **⁶we'll need three different references and their contact information.** Should you pass the first round of interviews, we will contact them with a few questions.

4-6번은 다음 대화에 관한 문제입니다.

여 여보세요, 켄드릭 씨죠? 저는 코트니 러시라고 합니다. **⁴인터넷의 구인 광고에 관해 전화드립니다. 시장 조사원 자리가 아직 비어 있는지 궁금합니다.**

남 네, 그리 늦지는 않으셨어요. 이번 주말에 채용을 마감할 예정입니다. 그러니, 관심이 있으시면 아직 이력서를 보내셔도 됩니다.

여 감사합니다. **⁵전화드리길 잘했네요.** 너무 늦었을까 봐 걱정했거든요. 한 가지 더요, 제가 추천서를 제출해야 하는지 궁금했습니다.

남 네, **⁶저희는 서로 다른 추천서 세 통과 추천인들의 연락처가 필요합니다.** 만약 당신이 1차 면접을 통과하면, 저희가 그분들에게 연락해서 몇 가지 질문을 할 것입니다.

어휘

job advertisement 구인 광고
market researcher 시장 조사원 recruitment 채용, 신규 모집
résumé 이력서 interested 관심 있어 하는 reference 추천서
contact information 연락처 round (장기적인 일의) 한 차례

4.

여자는 누구인가?
(A) 입사 지원자
(B) 면접관
(C) 행정 보조
(D) 광고 책임자

어휘

administrative 행정의, 관리의 assistant 조수, 보조원
executive 경영 간부, 임원

5.

여자는 왜 기뻐하는가?
(A) 그녀는 직위가 마음에 든다.
(B) 그녀는 추천서를 충분히 가지고 있다.
(C) 그녀는 일자리를 제안받았다.
(D) 그녀는 마감 기한을 놓치지 않았다.

어휘

job position 직위 miss a deadline 기한을 놓치다

패러프레이징

too late → missed a deadline

6.

남자는 여자에게 무엇을 해 달라고 요청하는가?
(A) 급여 협상하기
(B) 오늘 이력서 보내기
(C) 추천서 제공하기
(D) 면접 일정 잡기

어휘

negotiate 협상하다 schedule 일정을 잡다

패러프레이징

need three different references and their contact
information → Provide some references

[7-9] 미녀 호남 🎧

Questions 7-9 refer to the following conversation.

W **⁷Thanks for helping me with the hiring process for a new architect.** Here are the résumés we've received.

M Hmm... **⁷It seems that we had a good response to our job posting.** Is there anyone you think stands out?

W Well, **⁸I was impressed with Marie Solomon's résumé since she graduated from such a prestigious university.**

M That's great. Then we should definitely offer her an interview. **⁹I'll look over these résumés this afternoon.** After we have a list of potential candidates, we can start booking interviews next week.

해석

7-9번은 다음 대화에 관한 문제입니다.

여 **⁷신입 건축가를 위한 채용 과정을 도와주셔서 고마워요.** 이것은 우리가 받은 이력서들이에요.

남 흠... **⁷우리의 채용 공고가 좋은 반응을 얻은 것 같군요.** 당신이 생각하기에 눈에 띄는 사람이라도 있나요?

여 음, **⁸마리 솔로몬의 이력서가 인상 깊었는데, 그녀가 명문 대학교를 졸업했기 때문이에요.**

남 잘됐네요. 그러면 우리가 반드시 그녀에게 면접 제안을 해야겠군요. **⁹제가 오늘 오후에 이 이력서들을 살펴볼게요.** 유력한 후보자들의 명단을 작성한 후에, 다음 주 면접 일정을 잡기 시작하면 돼요.

어휘

hire 채용하다 architect 건축가 résumé 이력서
response to ~에 대한 반응, 응답 job posting 채용 공고
stand out 눈에 띄다, 빼어나다
be impressed with ~에 깊은 인상을 받다
graduate from ~을 졸업하다 prestigious 명망 있는, 일류의
definitely 분명히, 틀림없이 look over 살펴보다, 훑어보다
potential 가능성이 있는, 잠재적인 candidate 후보자, 지원자
book 예약하다

7.

대화는 주로 무엇에 관한 것인가?
(A) 새로운 투자자를 찾는 것
(B) 직원 불만에 대응하는 것
(C) 교육 프로그램을 개발하는 것
(D) 일자리 공석을 채우는 것

어휘

investor 투자자 respond to ~에 대응하다
complaint 불평, 항의

패러프레이징

the hiring process for a new architect
→ Filling a job opening

8.

무엇이 여자에게 솔로몬 씨에 관해 깊은 인상을 주었는가?

(A) 그녀의 사업상의 인맥

(B) 그녀의 학력

(C) 그녀의 커뮤니케이션 능력

(D) 그녀의 오랜 경력

어휘

educational 교육의 skill 기능, 기술 career history 경력

패러프레이징

graduated from such a prestigious university
→ educational background

9.

남자는 오늘 오후에 무엇을 할 계획인가?

(A) 안내서 만들기

(B) 공지하기

(C) 몇몇 문서 검토하기

(D) 면접 참석하기

어휘

handbook 안내서 announcement 발표, 공지

패러프레이징

look over these résumés → Review some documents

[10-12] 미남 미녀 🎧

Questions 10-12 refer to the following conversation.

M　Mimi, ¹⁰ have you received the box of new books for the library yet?

W　Yes. ¹¹ I've already put our stickers on them and put up a display near the entrance.

M　Thank you. And... uh... don't forget that at 2 o'clock there's a lecture by Professor Kirkland. We need to start setting up the room.

W　We can't do that now. There's a book club group holding a meeting in there. They won't be finished until 1:45.

M　¹² That won't give us enough time.

W　¹² Don't worry. Professor Kirkland won't use a projector. Anyway, I'll come and get you when that group is finished.

해석

10-12번은 다음 대화에 관한 문제입니다.

남　미미, ¹⁰ 도서관 앞으로 온 신간 도서 상자를 벌써 받았나요?

여　네. ¹¹ 제가 이미 그것들에 우리 스티커를 붙여서 입구 근처에 진열했어요.

남　고마워요. 그리고... 어... 2시에 커클랜드 교수님의 강연이 있다는 걸 잊지 말아요. 우리가 그 방을 준비하기 시작해야 해요.

여　지금은 못 해요. 그곳에서 독서 클럽 사람들이 모임을 갖고 있어요. 그들은 1시 45분이 되어야 끝날 거예요.

남　¹² 그러면 우리에게 시간이 충분하지 않네요.

여　¹² 걱정 말아요. 커클랜드 교수님은 프로젝터를 사용하지 않을 거

예요. 어쨌든, 그 사람들이 마무리하면 제가 와서 당신에게 알려줄게요.

어휘

put up 내붙이다, 게시하다 display 전시, 진열
entrance 입구 set up 준비하다, 설치하다

10.

화자들은 누구인 것 같은가?

(A) 투자자들

(B) 사서들

(C) 부동산 중개인들

(D) 유지 보수 직원들

어휘

real estate 부동산 maintenance 유지 보수

11.

여자는 무엇을 했다고 말하는가?

(A) 소포를 보냈다

(B) 발표를 연습했다

(C) 진열을 했다

(D) 책을 읽었다

어휘

package 소포, 포장 presentation 발표

패러프레이징

put up → Set up

12.

여자는 "커클랜드 교수님은 프로젝터를 사용하지 않을 거예요"라고 말할 때 무엇을 암시하는가?

(A) 그녀는 결정에 놀랐다.

(B) 그녀는 스크린을 제거할 것이다.

(C) 작업이 오래 걸리지 않을 것이다.

(D) 주문이 취소되어야 한다.

어휘

remove 제거하다 task 일, 과업 cancel 취소하다

[13-15] 영녀 호남 미녀 🎧

Questions 13-15 refer to the following conversation with three speakers.

W1　Thanks for joining us, Travis.

M　My pleasure. ¹³ Actually, this is my first time here. I've read a lot of positive comments about their coffee online. I'm looking forward to trying it.

W1　Well, before we order our drinks, we want to talk to you about something, right, Beth?

W2　That's right. You've been doing a great job as the assistant director. So, ¹⁴ we have chosen you to be the new director of the sales department.

M Wow, that's great news! ¹⁴ Thank you so much!

W2 ¹⁵ I'll work out the contract details this week and send you a copy to review.

M Perfect.

해석

13-15번은 다음 세 명의 대화에 관한 문제입니다.

여1 우리와 함께해 주어서 고마워요, 트래비스.

남 별말씀을요. ¹³실은, 전 이번에 이곳에 처음 왔어요. 온라인에서 이곳의 커피에 대해 긍정적인 의견들을 많이 읽었어요. 한번 마셔 보기를 고대했어요.

여1 음, 음료를 주문하기 전에, 우리가 당신에게 하고 싶은 얘기가 있어요, 맞죠, 베스?

여2 맞아요. 당신은 차장으로서 일을 아주 잘해오고 있어요. 그래서, ¹⁴우리가 당신을 영업부의 새로운 부장으로 선택했어요.

남 우와, 그거 굉장한 소식이네요! ¹⁴정말 감사해요!

여2 ¹⁵제가 이번 주에 계약 세부 사항을 만들어서 당신이 검토하도록 사본을 보낼게요.

남 아주 좋아요.

어휘

positive 긍정적인 comment 논평, 언급
look forward to ~을 기대하다 order 주문하다
director 임원, 책임자 work out 만들어내다, 생각해내다
contract 계약(서) copy 사본 review 검토하다

13.

화자들은 어디에 있는 것 같은가?

(A) 커피숍에
(B) 기술 회사에
(C) 체육관에
(D) 신문 가판대에

14.

남자는 왜 여자들에게 고마워하는가?

(A) 그들이 그에게 새로운 장비를 주겠다고 제안했다.
(B) 그들이 그를 승진 대상자로 선택했다.
(C) 그들이 그의 휴가 신청을 승인했다.
(D) 그들이 그에게 강연을 해 달라고 요청했다.

어휘

equipment 장비 promotion 승진, 홍보 approve 승인하다
give a talk 강연하다

패러프레이징

chosen you to be the new director of the sales department → selected him for a promotion

15.

베스는 이번 주에 무엇을 할 것이라고 말하는가?

(A) 고객 만나기
(B) 계약서 준비하기
(C) 공지하기
(D) 제품 테스트하기

패러프레이징

work out the contract details → Prepare a contract

[16-18] 영녀 호남 🎧

Questions 16-18 refer to the following conversation and business analysis chart.

W ¹⁶ Our business has been struggling ever since more dry cleaner's opened in the area. It's important for us to find a way to stand out.

M I've been working on this exact problem. I've made a chart to compare our services to those of Wexford Dry Cleaner's, the one that's nearest to us. This might give us some insight.

W Great idea. Hmm... well, ¹⁷ one of our services isn't offered by Wexford. I'd like us to concentrate our efforts on that.

M Okay. And we could advertise the service, too. ¹⁸ I'll call the local newspaper to find out their current advertising rates.

해석

16-18번은 다음 대화와 업체 분석표에 관한 문제입니다.

여 ¹⁶이 지역에 더 많은 세탁소들이 문을 연 이후로 줄곧 우리 사업이 고전 중이에요. 우리가 돋보일 방법을 찾는 것이 중요해요.

남 제가 바로 이 문제로 애쓰고 있어요. 우리와 가장 가까운 곳인 웩스퍼드 세탁소와 우리의 서비스를 비교하기 위해 표를 만들었어요. 이것이 우리에게 어떤 통찰을 줄지도 몰라요.

여 좋은 생각이에요. 흠... 저, ¹⁷우리 서비스 중 하나를 웩스퍼드에서는 제공하지 않아요. 우리가 그 부분에 노력을 집중하는 것이 좋겠어요.

남 알겠어요. 그리고 우리가 그 서비스를 광고할 수도 있어요. ¹⁸제가 지역 신문사에 전화해서 그들의 현재 광고 요금을 알아볼게요.

어휘

struggle 분투하다 ever since ~ 이후로 줄곧
dry cleaner's 세탁소 stand out 두드러지다, 뛰어나다
work on ~에 노력을 들이다 exact 정확한 compare 비교하다
insight 통찰, 간파 concentrate A on B A를 B에 집중시키다
effort 수고, 노력 current 현재의 rate 요금

	에코	웩스퍼드
당일 수령		✔
배달	✔	✔
¹⁷ 의류 개조	✔	
수선	✔	✔

16.

여자에 따르면, 무엇이 문제를 일으켰는가?

(A) 공급업체가 믿을만하지 않다.
(B) 경쟁이 심해졌다.
(C) 숙련된 직원을 찾기 힘들다.
(D) 일부 기계가 교체되어야 한다.

supplier 공급자, 공급회사 unreliable 믿을 수 없는
competition 경쟁 skilled 숙련된, 노련한 replace 교체하다

more dry cleaner's opened in the area
→ Competition has increased

17.
시각 자료를 보시오. 여자는 어떤 서비스에 집중하기를 원하는가?
(A) 당일 수령
(B) 배달
(C) 의류 개조
(D) 수선

alteration 변경, 개조 repair 수선, 수리

18.
남자는 아마도 다음에 무엇을 할 것인가?
(A) 업체에 연락하기
(B) 광고 디자인하기
(C) 신문 기사 읽기
(D) 가격표 조정하기

adjust 조정하다, 조절하다

call the local newspaper → Contact a business

UNIT 10 사내 행사·시설 관련 대화

CHECK UP 본문 p.178

1. (A) **2.** (B) **3.** (C)

[1-3] 미남 미녀 🎧
Questions 1-3 refer to the following conversation.

> M Hi, Joanne. ¹I'm wondering if I can get your advice about next week's orientation session, since you have a lot of experience with it.
> W Sure. ¹You're in charge of training the staff this time, right?
> M Yes, but there is a lot of material to go through. ²I'm worried that the participants will be bored. Is there any way to prevent that?
> W Well, in my experience, ³you should put people in small groups rather than one large audience. This facilitates discussions and it helps people get to know each other.
> M I hadn't considered that. I'll give it a try.

1-3번은 다음 대화에 관한 문제입니다.
남 안녕하세요, 조앤. ¹제가 다음 주의 오리엔테이션에 관해 당신의 조언을 얻을 수 있는지 궁금해요, 당신은 그에 관한 경험이 풍부하니까요.
여 그럼요. ¹당신이 이번에 직원 교육을 담당하는군요, 맞죠?
남 네, 하지만 살펴볼 자료가 많아요. ²참가자들이 지루해할까 봐 걱정이에요. 그런 일을 막을 무슨 방법이 있나요?
여 음, 제 경험상, ³사람들을 하나의 대규모 청중보다는 소그룹으로 묶어야 해요. 이것이 토론을 용이하게 하고, 사람들이 서로 친해지도록 도와줘요.
남 제가 그 점을 고려하지 않았어요. 한번 그렇게 해 볼게요.

session 시간, 기간 experience 경험
be in charge of ~을 담당하다 material 재료, 자료
go through 살펴보다, 검토하다 participant 참가자
prevent 막다, 예방하다 audience 청중, 관객
facilitate 용이하게 하다 get to know 알게 되다
consider 고려하다 give ~ a try ~을 한번 해 보다

1.
대화는 주로 무엇에 관한 것인가?
(A) 교육
(B) 정책 변경
(C) 산업 학회
(D) 출장

orientation session → A training session

2.
남자는 무엇을 하기를 원하는가?
(A) 비용 절감하기
(B) 활동을 더욱 흥미롭게 만들기
(C) 휴가 내기
(D) 등록자 수 증대시키기

expense 비용 activity 활동 take time off 휴가를 내다
enrollment figures 등록자 수

3.
여자는 무엇을 할 것을 제안하는가?
(A) 떨어진 공간을 예약하는 것
(B) 컨설턴트를 고용하는 것
(C) 참가자들을 그룹에 배정하는 것
(D) 설문지를 준비하는 것

reserve 예약하다 off-site (~에서) 떨어진, 부지 밖의
consultant 컨설턴트, 상담가 assign 배치하다
questionnaire 설문지

다고 생각할까 봐 걱정이에요.

put people in small groups
→ Assigning participants to groups

패러프레이징 연습 본문 p.180

1-4. 스크립트 참조 **5.** (B) **6.** (A)

1.

Q 남자는 왜 걱정하는가?
A 공간이 너무 작을지도 모른다.

미남 미녀 🎧

> **M** Which venue are you considering for the upcoming social media marketing workshop?
> **W** Last time we rented the Concord Center. I was thinking about doing that again.
> **M** Hmm… we're expecting a lot of attendees, so maybe it won't fit everyone.

해석

남 다가오는 소셜 미디어 마케팅 워크숍에 어느 장소를 고려하고 있나요?
여 우리가 지난번에는 콩코드 센터를 빌렸어요. 또 그렇게 할 생각이었어요.
남 흠… 참석자들이 많을 것으로 예상돼요, 그래서 아마도 그곳은 모두가 들어가기에는 적합하지 않을 거예요.

어휘

venue (행사의) 장소 consider 고려하다
upcoming 다가오는, 곧 있을 rent 임차하다, 임대하다
attendee 참석자 fit ~에 적합하다, 알맞다

패러프레이징

maybe it won't fit everyone
→ A space may be too small

2.

Q 화자들은 어디에서 일하는가?
A 호텔에서

미녀 미남 🎧

> **W** Did you hear that we're removing all of the carpets in the guest rooms? We're going with wooden flooring instead.
> **M** That'll look great, and it will be easier to clean each hotel room. But I'm worried some people will think the atmosphere is not very cozy.

해석

여 우리가 객실의 모든 카펫을 없앨 거라는 얘기 들었어요? 목재 바닥으로 대신할 거예요.
남 그러면 멋져 보이겠네요, 그리고 각 호텔 객실을 청소하기가 더 쉬울 거예요. 하지만 일부 사람들이 분위기가 그리 아늑하지 않

어휘

remove 치우다, 없애다 wooden 목재의, 나무로 된
flooring 바닥재 atmosphere 분위기, 기운 cozy 아늑한

패러프레이징

the guest rooms, hotel room → At a hotel

3.

Q 남자는 여자에게 무엇에 대해 상기시키는가?
A 은퇴 축하 파티

미남 미녀 🎧

> **M** Do you want to walk to the conference room together, Katelyn? Ravi's retirement celebration is starting soon.
> **W** Oh, I had forgotten that was today!
> **M** Then I guess it's a good thing I stopped by. You might have missed it.

해석

남 회의실까지 함께 걸어갈래요, 케이틀린? 라비의 은퇴 기념 행사가 곧 시작해요.
여 아, 그게 오늘인 걸 잊고 있었어요!
남 그럼 제가 들르길 잘한 것 같네요. 당신이 그걸 놓쳤을지도 몰라요.

어휘

remind 상기시키다 retirement 은퇴, 퇴직
celebration 기념 행사
it is a good thing (that) ~이어서 다행이다
stop by ~에 들르다 might have p.p. ~했을지도 모른다

패러프레이징

Ravi's retirement celebration → A retirement party

4.

Q 남자는 누구에게 발표할 것인가?
A 잠재적 투자자들

미녀 미남 🎧

> **W** Hi, David. I got your message about needing someone from IT to set up a projector and screen.
> **M** Yes, thanks. My team has got a meeting in the conference room at 2 P.M. for some people we hope will become investors.

해석

여 안녕하세요, 데이비드. 프로젝터와 스크린을 설치하기 위해 IT 팀의 누군가가 필요하다는 당신의 메시지를 받았어요.
남 네, 고마워요. 저희 팀은 오후 2시에 회의실에서 우리가 투자자가 되기를 바라는 몇몇 사람들을 위한 회의가 있어요.

어휘

give a presentation 발표하다 potential 잠재적인

investor 투자자 set up 설치하다

some people we hope will become investors
→ Potential investors

5.
어떤 문제가 논의되고 있는가?
(A) 동료가 중요한 마감 기한을 놓쳤다.
(B) 이메일 시스템이 제대로 작동하지 않는다.

[미녀] [미남] 🎧

> W Hmm… this is running very slow. Have you been experiencing long delays with your e-mail, Jun?
> M Yes. Ben said he sent me something 20 minutes ago, but it still hasn't shown up in my inbox. There must be some kind of problem.

해석

여 흠… 이거 속도가 아주 느리네요. 당신의 이메일도 오래 지연되고 있어요, 준?
남 네. 벤이 20분 전에 제게 뭘 보냈다고 했는데, 제 메일함에는 여전히 보이지 않아요. 무슨 문제가 있는 게 틀림없어요.

어휘

deadline 마감 기한 function 기능하다, 작용하다
properly 제대로, 적절히 run 작동하다 delay 지연, 지체
show up 눈에 띄다, 나타나다 inbox 받은 편지함

패러프레이징

experiencing long delays with your e-mail, it still hasn't shown up in my inbox
→ An e-mail system is not functioning properly

6.
여자는 왜 행사에 들떠 있는가?
(A) 초청 연사가 평판이 매우 좋다.
(B) 참석자들이 전문 자격증을 받을 수 있다.

[미남] [미녀] 🎧

> M Are you planning to attend Thursday's lecture at the Somerton Business Institute?
> W Yes. I signed up a few weeks ago. I'm really looking forward to it. Jessica Elkins is an outstanding presenter. I think everyone will learn a lot.

해석

남 서머턴 경영 연구소에서 목요일에 있을 강연에 참석할 계획인가요?
여 네. 몇 주 전에 신청했어요. 정말 기대돼요. **제시카 엘킨스는 뛰어난 발표자예요.** 모두들 많이 배울 거라고 생각해요.

어휘

guest speaker 초청 연사 reputation 명성, 평판

attendee 참석자 professional certification 전문 자격증
institute 연구소, 기관, 협회 sign up 신청하다, 등록하다
look forward to ~을 고대하다 outstanding 뛰어난, 걸출한
presenter 발표자

패러프레이징

Jessica Elkins is an outstanding presenter
→ The guest speaker has an excellent reputation

연습 문제   본문 p.181

1. (B)   **2.** (A)   **3.** (C)   **4.** (D)   **5.** (C)

[1] [호남] [미녀] 🎧
Question 1 refers to the following conversation.

> M Hello, Ms. Clayton? I'm calling from Sedalia Swimwear. We're planning to introduce our new line of swimsuits on May 25. Since you're a well-known local athlete, we were wondering if you would like to help promote the product and attend our launch celebration.
> W Well, I'd have to try the swimsuit myself first.
> M Of course. I can send you a sample so you can see how great the quality is.

해석

1번은 다음 대화에 관한 문제입니다.

남 여보세요, 클레이턴 씨죠? 시데일리아 수영복에서 전화드립니다. **저희가 5월 25일에 저희 수영복 신제품 라인을 소개할 계획입니다.** 당신은 지역에서 유명한 운동선수이시니, 그 제품을 홍보하는 것을 도와주시고 **저희의 출시 기념 행사에 참석하실 의향이 있으신지 궁금합니다.**
여 음, 일단 제가 직접 수영복을 입어 봐야겠어요.
남 물론입니다. 품질이 얼마나 우수한지 확인하실 수 있도록 제가 샘플을 보내드리겠습니다.

어휘

swimsuit 수영복 well-known 잘 알려진, 유명한
athlete 운동선수 promote 홍보하다 launch 출시, 개시
celebration 기념 행사 quality 품질

1.
남자는 어떤 종류의 행사를 계획하고 있는가?
(A) 모금 행사
(B) 출시 기념 파티
(C) 경품 추첨
(D) 운동 시합

어휘

fund-raising 모금 draw 뽑다, 추첨하다
competition 시합, 대회

패러프레이징

our launch celebration → A launch party

[2-3] 미녀 호남 🎧

Questions 2-3 refer to the following conversation.

> **W** Do you have a minute, Mr. McGuire? ² I've just realized that when we were making the purchases for the new conference room, we forgot to include a conference phone.
> **M** That was a huge oversight. Have you looked into our options?
> **W** ³ Well, I don't think we should purchase another Digicom product. Their warranty is too limited.
> **M** Okay. Order whatever you think is best. Just don't spend over 200 dollars. That should be plenty to get something suitable.

해석

2-3번은 다음 대화에 관한 문제입니다.

여 시간 좀 있어요, 맥과이어 씨? ² 우리가 새 회의실을 위해 물건들을 샀을 때 회의용 전화를 포함시키는 것을 잊어버렸다는 걸 방금 깨달았어요.

남 그건 엄청난 실수예요. 우리가 선택할 만한 것들을 살펴보셨어요?

여 ³ 음, 디지콤 제품은 더는 사지 말아야 할 것 같아요. 그들의 품질 보증은 너무 제한적이에요.

남 알았어요. 당신이 가장 좋다고 생각하는 것으로 아무거나 주문하세요. 200달러 넘게 지출하지만 마세요. 그러면 적절한 것을 사기에 충분할 거예요.

어휘

make a purchase 구매하다 conference (대규모) 회의
oversight 실수, 간과 look into 조사하다, 주의 깊게 살피다
option 선택(할 수 있는 것) warranty 보증, 보증서
limited 제한된, 한정된 plenty 충분한 양
suitable 적합한, 적절한

2.

여자는 어떤 문제를 언급하는가?

(A) 물품이 주문되지 않았다.
(B) 행사가 연기되었다.
(C) 계약이 최근에 만료되었다.
(D) 보증이 취소되었다.

어휘

postpone 연기하다 expire 만료되다 cancel 취소하다

패러프레이징

making the purchases ~ forgot to include a conference phone → An item wasn't ordered

3.

여자는 디지콤 제품들에 대해 무엇이라고 말하는가?
(A) 그것들은 작동하기 쉽다.
(B) 그것들은 경쟁사의 제품들보다 더 비싸다.
(C) 그것들은 보증 범위가 제한적이다.
(D) 그것들은 후기가 매우 좋다.

어휘

operate 작동하다, 작동되다 competitor 경쟁자, 경쟁사
coverage 적용 범위 restrictive 제한하는

패러프레이징

warranty is too limited
→ warranty coverage is restrictive

[4-5] 미녀 호남 🎧

Questions 4-5 refer to the following conversation.

> **W** Hello. I'm Clair Appaw from Merits. ⁴ I need a photographer for our corporate banquet on May 27th. One of my colleagues recommended you, so I'm wondering if you're available.
> **M** Let's see… Yes, my calendar is clear on that day. How long do you think the event will last?
> **W** We're planning to take group pictures right after lunch. It shouldn't take more than two hours.
> **M** That's fine. ⁵ I'll send you a contract to go over. Can I have your e-mail address, please?

해석

4-5번은 다음 대화에 관한 문제입니다.

여 안녕하세요. 저는 메리츠 사의 클레어 어포입니다. ⁴ 5월 27일에 있을 저희 회사의 연회를 위해 사진사가 필요합니다. 제 동료 중 한 명이 당신을 추천했어요, 그래서 시간이 되시는지 궁금합니다.

남 어디 볼게요... 네, 그날 제 일정표가 비어 있네요. 행사가 얼마 동안 진행될 것 같으세요?

여 저희는 점심 식사 직후에 단체 사진을 찍을 계획입니다. 2시간 이상 걸리지 않을 거예요.

남 좋습니다. ⁵ 검토하실 계약서를 보내 드리겠습니다. 이메일 주소를 알려 주시겠습니까?

어휘

photographer 사진사 corporate 기업의, 회사의
banquet 연회, 만찬 available 시간이 있는, 이용할 수 있는
last 계속되다 contract 계약(서) go over 검토하다, 조사하다

4.

여자는 무엇을 하기를 원하는가?
(A) 워크숍 참석하기
(B) 일자리에 지원하기
(C) 발표하기
(D) 사진사 고용하기

5.

남자는 여자에게 무엇을 보낼 것이라고 말하는가?
(A) 주소
(B) 포트폴리오
(C) 계약서
(D) 사진

1. (D)	**2.** (C)	**3.** (B)	**4.** (A)	**5.** (B)
6. (B)	**7.** (C)	**8.** (B)	**9.** (D)	**10.** (B)
11. (C)	**12.** (A)	**13.** (A)	**14.** (D)	**15.** (C)
16. (D)	**17.** (B)	**18.** (A)		

[1-3] 미녀 미남 🎧

Questions 1-3 refer to the following conversation.

> W   Hiroshi, I got your message saying you were worried about having the company picnic at Collins Park.
>
> M   Yes... well, ¹the picnic area there isn't covered. If it starts to rain, there won't be anywhere for people to go. How about holding it at Staten Park instead?
>
> W   I wish we could use Staten Park. It does have a large covered area with picnic tables. ²However, we have to think about how far away it is. A lot of our employees don't have cars. Any ideas?
>
> M   The company could rent a shuttle for employees. ³I'll call Foley Incorporated and reserve a shuttle bus for that day.

해석

1–3번은 다음 대화에 관한 문제입니다.

여   히로시, 콜린스 파크에서 회사 야유회를 하는 것에 걱정하는 당신의 메시지를 받았어요.

남   네... 음, ¹그곳의 피크닉 구역은 지붕이 없어요. 비가 오기 시작하면, 사람들이 갈 만한 곳이 어디에도 없을 거예요. 대신 스테이튼 파크에서 하는 건 어때요?

여   우리가 스테이튼 파크를 이용할 수 있으면 좋겠어요. 피크닉 테이블이 있고 지붕이 덮여 있는 넓은 구역이 있어요. ²하지만, 얼마나 먼지에 대해 생각해 봐야 해요. 우리 직원 다수가 차가 없어요. 무슨 아이디어 있나요?

남   회사가 직원들을 위해 셔틀버스를 임대하면 돼요. ³제가 폴리 사에 전화해서 그날 셔틀버스를 예약할게요.

어휘

covered 지붕이 덮인   rent 임대하다, 임차하다
reserve 예약하다

1.

남자는 왜 콜린스 파크에서 행사를 여는 것에 대해 우려하는가?
(A) 그곳은 피크닉 구역이 없다.
(B) 그곳은 주차 공간이 많지 않다.
(C) 그곳은 보통 매우 혼잡하다.
(D) 그곳은 비가 오는 날씨에 부적합하다.

어휘

limited 제한된, 많지 않은   crowded 붐비는, 복잡한
suitable 적합한, 적절한

패러프레이징

If it starts to rain, there won't be anywhere for people to go → not suitable in rainy weather

2.

여자는 그들이 무엇을 고려해야 한다고 말하는가?
(A) 시작 시간
(B) 메뉴 품목
(C) 여행 거리
(D) 총비용

어휘

overall 종합적인, 전체의   expense 비용

패러프레이징

how far away it is → The travel distance

3.

남자는 왜 폴리 사에 연락할 것인가?
(A) 정책을 확인하기 위해
(B) 교통편을 준비하기 위해
(C) 직원을 모집하기 위해
(D) 음식을 주문하기 위해

어휘

arrange 마련하다, 정리하다   transportation 운송, 수송
recruit 모집하다

패러프레이징

reserve a shuttle bus → To arrange transportation

[4-6] 미남 영녀 🎧

Questions 4-6 refer to the following conversation.

> M   Sonya, ⁴, ⁵we're going to have to cancel the 3 o'clock aerobics class. I was just in classroom 2, and it's really hot in there. It seems that the air conditioner is broken.
>
> W   Oh, that's a shame! And we can't move it to classroom 1 because of the yoga class. We need to get this fixed as soon as possible. ⁶I think I still have the business card from the repairperson we used last time. He was able to get here quickly.
>
> M   ⁶Could you try to find it? I don't want to cancel any more classes than we have to.

해석

4–6번은 다음 대화에 관한 문제입니다.

남   소냐, ⁴, ⁵우리는 3시의 에어로빅 강습을 취소해야 할 거예요. 제가 방금 2번 강의실에 있었는데 그 안이 정말 더워요. 에어컨이 고장 난 것 같아요.

여   아, 유감이네요! 그리고 요가 강습 때문에 1번 강의실로 옮길 수는 없어요. 가능한 한 빨리 이것을 고쳐야 해요. 우리가 지난번에 불렀던 수리공의 ⁶명함을 제가 아직 가지고 있는 것 같아요. 그는 여기에 빨리 올 수 있었어요.

남 ⁶그것을 찾아봐 주시겠어요? 전 필요 이상으로 강습을 취소하고 싶지 않아요.

cancel 취소하다 aerobics 에어로빅 broken 고장 난, 깨진
That's a shame. 유감이다. business card 명함
repairperson 수리공

4.

대화는 어디에서 일어나고 있는 것 같은가?
(A) 피트니스 센터에서
(B) 경영 연구소에서
(C) 전자제품 매장에서
(D) 도서관에서

어휘

institute 협회, 연구소 appliance (가정용) 기기, 전자제품

5.

남자는 어떤 문제를 설명하는가?
(A) 문이 잠겼다.
(B) 방이 너무 덥다.
(C) 직원이 결근했다.
(D) 공간이 이중으로 예약되었다.

어휘

absent 결석한, 결근한 double-book 이중으로 예약을 받다

패러프레이징

classroom ~ it's really hot in there
→ A room is too hot

6.

남자는 여자에게 무엇을 해 달라고 요청하는가?
(A) 공고문 게시하기
(B) 명함 찾기
(C) 환불금 지급하기
(D) 수리공에게 대금 지불하기

어휘

post 게시하다 notice 공고문, 안내문
issue a refund 환불금을 지급하다, 환불해 주다

패러프레이징

find → Look for

[7-9] 호남 미녀 🎧
Questions 7-9 refer to the following conversation.

M Thank you for calling IT support. This is Vincent.
W Hi, this is Coleen Williams from the R&D department. ⁷I tried to use my username and password to get into the database this morning. However, I keep getting an error message.

M Have you reset your password? ⁸We recently made our security procedures stricter. So, you'll have to create a stronger password.
W I see. How do I do that?
M ⁹There's a page on the company Web site with all the steps in the process. I'll send you a link. Should I send it to your company account?
W Yes, please. Thanks for the help.

해석

7-9번은 다음 대화에 관한 문제입니다.
남 IT 지원팀에 전화해 주셔서 감사합니다. 저는 빈센트입니다.
여 안녕하세요, 저는 연구 개발 부서의 콜린 윌리엄스입니다. ⁷제가 오늘 아침에 사용자 이름과 비밀번호를 이용해서 데이터베이스에 들어가려고 했어요. 그런데, 계속해서 오류 메시지가 뜹니다.
남 비밀번호를 재설정하셨나요? ⁸저희가 최근 보안 절차를 더욱 엄격하게 만들었습니다. 그래서 더 강력한 비밀번호를 만드셔야 할 겁니다.
여 그렇군요. 그건 어떻게 하는 거죠?
남 ⁹회사 웹사이트에 그 과정의 모든 단계가 있는 페이지가 있어요. 제가 링크를 보내 드릴게요. 당신의 회사 계정으로 보내 드릴까요?
여 네, 그렇게 해 주세요. 도와주셔서 감사합니다.

어휘

support 지원, 지지
R&D (= research & development) 연구 개발
username 사용자 명 reset 재설정하다 recently 최근에
security 보안, 안보 procedure 절차 strict 엄격한
process 과정 account 계정, 계좌

7.

여자에 따르면, 무엇이 문제인가?
(A) 그녀의 주차권이 만료되었다.
(B) 그녀의 컴퓨터가 켜지지 않는다.
(C) 그녀가 데이터베이스에 접속할 수 없다.
(D) 그녀가 회의에 빠질 것이다.

어휘

parking pass 주차권 expire 만료되다
access 접속하다, 접근하다 be absent from ~에 결석하다

패러프레이징

get into the database → access a database

8.

이 업체는 최근에 무엇을 했는가?
(A) 새로운 웹사이트를 출시했다
(B) 보안 조치를 강화했다
(C) 새 건물로 이전했다
(D) 관리팀을 확장했다

어휘

launch 개시하다, 출시하다 measure 조치, 정책
relocate to ~로 이전하다 expand 확대하다

management 관리, 경영

패러프레이징
made our security procedures stricter
→ Increased its security measures

9.
남자에 따르면, 웹사이트에서 무엇을 찾을 수 있는가?
(A) 사진
(B) 업데이트된 일정
(C) 이메일 주소
(D) 지시 사항

어휘
instructions ((보통 복수형)) 지시, 설명서

패러프레이징
all the steps in the process → Some instructions

[10-12] 호남 영녀 미녀 🎧
Questions 10-12 refer to the following conversation with three speakers.

> M ¹⁰Palak and Minhee, I've just received an e-mail about signing up for this year's publishing trade fair. I was thinking... uh... maybe we shouldn't have a booth to promote our books there this year.
> W1 Really? But all of the major companies will be there.
> M That's true, ¹¹but the event is attracting fewer and fewer people every year. I don't think it's worth it.
> W2 Hmm... that's a good point. Maybe we'd be better off spending that money elsewhere.
> W1 Well, ¹²we do have plans to make upgrades to our Web site next month. We could increase the budget for that. Let's talk about this more at the meeting.

해석
10-12번은 다음 세 명의 대화에 관한 문제입니다.
남 ¹⁰팔락, 민희, 제가 방금 올해의 출판 산업 박람회 신청에 관한 이메일을 받았어요. 어... 아마도 올해는 그곳에 우리 책을 홍보하는 부스를 마련하지 말아야 할 것 같아요.
여1 정말요? 하지만 모든 주요 기업들이 올 텐데요.
남 맞아요, ¹¹하지만 매년 이 행사가 끌어모으는 사람들이 점점 줄고 있어요. 그만한 가치가 있는 것 같지 않아요.
여2 흠... 좋은 지적이에요. 아마도 그 돈을 다른 곳에 쓰는 편이 나을 거예요.
여1 음, ¹²다음 달에 우리 웹사이트를 업그레이드할 계획이에요. 그것을 위한 예산을 늘릴 수 있겠어요. 회의에서 이것에 대해 더 얘기해 봐요.

어휘
sign up for ~을 신청하다 publishing 출판

trade fair 산업 박람회 promote 홍보하다
attract 끌어들이다, 끌어모으다 worth ~할 가치가 있는
would be better off ~하는 편이 더 낫다 budget 예산

10.
화자들은 어떤 유형의 업체에서 일하는 것 같은가?
(A) 광고 대행사
(B) 출판사
(C) 텔레비전 스튜디오
(D) 법률 회사

11.
남자는 산업 박람회의 어떤 문제를 언급하는가?
(A) 그것의 부스들이 모두 예약되었다.
(B) 그것의 요금이 계획된 예산을 초과한다.
(C) 그것의 참석자 수가 줄고 있다.
(D) 그것의 장소가 너무 멀다.

어휘
fully booked 모두 예약된 fee 수수료, 요금 exceed 초과하다
attendance 출석, 참석자 수 decline 감소하다

패러프레이징
the event is attracting fewer and fewer people
→ Its attendance has been declining

12.
화자들의 회사는 다음 달에 무엇을 할 것인가?
(A) 웹사이트 업그레이드하기
(B) 계약 갱신하기
(C) 더 많은 직원 채용하기
(D) 새 사무실로 옮기기

어휘
renew 갱신하다

패러프레이징
make upgrades to our Web site
→ Upgrade a Web site

[13-15] 미녀 미남 🎧
Questions 13-15 refer to the following conversation.

> W Anthony, ¹³I'm working on the ceremony for presenting employee awards in December. You've planned big events before, right?
> M Yes, a few times. There's quite a lot to do, isn't there? Do you need help with something?
> W Yes, it's more work than I expected. ¹⁴For example, I have to find a caterer, but there are so many. I have no idea where to start.
> M I usually hire Pomona Catering. The food from Mr. Snyder's retirement party was from there.
> W ¹⁵I'll give them a call after lunch to see if they are available for our desired date. Do you

happen to have their phone number?

M No, but I'm sure you can find their details online easily.

해석

13-15번은 다음 대화에 관한 문제입니다.

여 앤서니, ¹³제가 12월에 있을 직원상 수여식에 관한 업무를 하고 있어요. 당신은 전에 큰 행사들을 기획해 보았죠, 맞죠?

남 네, 몇 번이요. 할 일이 꽤 많아요, 그렇지 않나요? 도움이 좀 필요한가요?

여 네, 제가 예상했던 것보다 일이 더 많아요. ¹⁴예를 들면, 케이터링 업체를 찾아야 하는데, 너무 많아요. 어디서부터 시작해야 할지 전혀 모르겠어요.

남 저는 보통 포모나 케이터링을 고용해요. 스나이더 씨의 은퇴 기념 파티 음식이 그곳 음식이었어요.

여 ¹⁵점심시간 이후에 그들에게 전화해서 우리가 희망하는 날짜에 시간이 되는지 알아볼게요. 혹시 그들의 전화번호를 가지고 있나요?

남 아니요, 하지만 분명히 온라인에서 그들의 정보를 쉽게 찾을 수 있을 거예요.

어휘

ceremony 의식, 식　present 주다, 수여하다
caterer (행사의) 음식 공급 업체　hire 고용하다
retirement 은퇴, 퇴직　available 시간이 있는
desire 바라다, 희망하다　happen to 우연히 ~하다

13.

어떤 종류의 행사가 12월에 일어날 것인가?

(A) 시상식
(B) 미술관 개관
(C) 은퇴 기념 파티
(D) 무역 박람회

패러프레이징

the ceremony for presenting employee awards
→ An awards ceremony

14.

남자는 왜 "저는 보통 포모나 케이터링을 고용해요"라고 말하는가?

(A) 놀람을 표현하기 위해
(B) 오해를 바로잡기 위해
(C) 제안을 거절하기 위해
(D) 제안하기 위해

어휘

correct 바로잡다, 정정하다　misunderstanding 오해, 착오
reject 거절하다　proposal 제안　suggestion 제안, 의견

15.

여자는 오늘 오후에 무엇을 할 것인가?

(A) 샘플 맛보기
(B) 초대장 보내기
(C) 업체에 연락하기
(D) 행사 장소 방문하기

어휘

invitation 초대(장)　venue (행사의) 장소

패러프레이징

give them a call → Contact a business

[16-18] 호남 영녀 🎧

Questions 16-18 refer to the following conversation and layout.

M Hi, Rebecca. This delivery just arrived from Lancaster Appliances. It must be the new water cooler for our waiting room.

W Yes, you're right. ¹⁶I chose this model because it won't take up much space compared to other models.

M That's great. ¹⁷But... uh... wouldn't the motor be too noisy if we put it next to the sofa? People usually read while they're waiting.

W It's fairly quiet, but I wasn't going to put it there anyway. ¹⁸I think it would be best by the door, right under the light switch.

해석

16-18번은 다음 대화와 배치도에 관한 문제입니다.

남 안녕하세요, 레베카. 방금 랭커스터 가전제품점에서 이 배달이 도착했어요. 우리 대기실을 위한 새로운 냉수기인 게 분명해요.

여 네, 맞아요. ¹⁶다른 모델들에 비해 공간을 많이 차지하지 않을 거라서 제가 이 모델을 골랐어요.

남 잘했네요. ¹⁷하지만... 어... 우리가 그것을 소파 바로 옆에 두면 모터가 너무 시끄럽지 않을까요? 사람들이 기다리는 동안 보통 뭘 읽잖아요.

여 그건 꽤 조용해요, 하지만 어쨌든 거기에 두려고 하지는 않았어요. ¹⁸제 생각엔 문 옆이 가장 좋을 것 같아요, 전등 스위치 바로 아래예요.

어휘

delivery 배달, 배달물　appliance (가정용) 기기, 전기 제품
water cooler 냉수기　waiting room 대기실
take up 차지하다　compared to ~와 비교하여
fairly 상당히, 꽤　light switch 전등 스위치

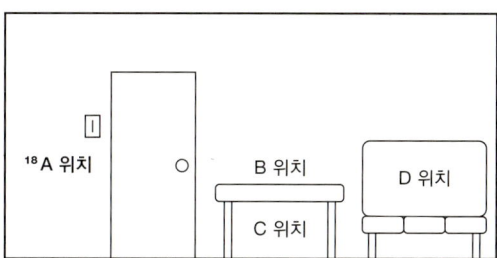

16.

무엇이 여자가 이 기기를 사게 만들었는가?

(A) 그것은 여러 색상으로 나왔다.

(B) 그것은 에너지를 많이 사용하지 않는다.

(C) 그것은 설정이 다양하다.

(D) 그것은 소형이다.

어휘

a variety of 여러 가지의, 다양한 setting 설정

패러프레이징

it won't take up much space → It is a compact size

17.

남자는 무엇에 대해 걱정하는가?

(A) 기기가 사용하기 헷갈릴 수 있다.

(B) 기기가 소음이 심할지도 모른다.

(C) 기기가 청소하기 어려울 것이다.

(D) 기기의 전원 코드가 짧다.

어휘

confusing 헷갈리는, 혼란스러운

18.

시각 자료를 보시오. 여자는 어디에 이 기기를 놓을 것을 제안하는가?

(A) A 위치에

(B) B 위치에

(C) C 위치에

(D) D 위치에

어휘

place 놓다, 두다 location 위치, 장소

UNIT 11 쇼핑·여가·일상 관련 대화

CHECK UP   본문 p.184

1. (C)	2. (B)	3. (B)

[1-3] 미남 미녀 🎧

Questions 1-3 refer to the following conversation.

> M Hi, this is James Abel calling. ¹I was in your store yesterday to have my pants hemmed. I was told to call back today to check if they are ready.
>
> W Hello, Mr. Abel. Let's see... they'll be ready for you later today. You can come in anytime after 4 o'clock to pick them up.
>
> M Okay, great. ²I can stop by at around 5. Could you tell me how much it will cost? ³I got a text from your store with a discount coupon last week.

> W Well, it's 20 dollars, but you can use the coupon as long as it's not expired. Just present it when you pay.

해석

1-3번은 다음 대화에 관한 문제입니다.

남 안녕하세요, 저는 제임스 아벨입니다. ¹제가 어제 바지의 단을 줄이려고 당신의 가게에 갔었어요. 제게 오늘 다시 전화해서 다 됐는지 확인하라고 하셨고요.

여 안녕하세요, 아벨 씨. 어디 볼게요... 오늘 늦게 준비가 될 거예요. 4시 이후에 아무 때나 오셔서 찾아가시면 됩니다.

남 알겠어요, 잘됐네요. ²5시쯤 들르겠습니다. 비용이 얼마나 될지 알려 주시겠어요? ³지난주에 당신의 가게에서 할인 쿠폰이 포함된 문자를 받았어요.

여 음, 20달러이지만, 기한이 만료되지 않았다면 그 쿠폰을 사용하실 수 있어요. 결제하실 때 보여 주시기만 하세요.

어휘

hem (옷 등의) 단을 올리다; 단 stop by ~에 들르다

discount coupon 할인 쿠폰 as long as ~하는 한

expire 만료되다 present 제시하다, 보여 주다

1.

남자는 왜 전화하고 있는가?

(A) 신제품을 사기 위해

(B) 할인 쿠폰을 얻기 위해

(C) 주문 처리 상황을 확인하기 위해

(D) 배송비에 관해 항의하기 위해

어휘

status 상황 complain about ~에 대해 항의하다

패러프레이징

check if they are ready → check his order's status

2.

남자는 무엇을 할 것이라고 말하는가?

(A) 주문 취소하기

(B) 업체 방문하기

(C) 연체료 지불하기

(D) 이메일 보내기

어휘

late fee 연체료

패러프레이징

stop by → Visit

3.

남자는 지난주에 무엇을 받았는가?

(A) 영수증

(B) 쿠폰

(C) 상품 카탈로그

(D) 의견 설문 조사

어휘

feedback 피드백, 의견 survey (설문) 조사

1.

Q 남자는 왜 도움을 요청하는가?
A 그는 면허가 없다.

미녀 미남 🎧

> W Hi. I have a business account here, but I'm thinking of moving some of the funds into a different investment type, like stocks.
> M I'm not qualified to give financial advice, but I can get one of our advisors to help you.

해석

여 안녕하세요. 제가 이곳에 사업용 계좌가 있어요. 하지만 자금 중 일부를 주식 같은 다른 투자 유형으로 옮길까 생각 중이에요.
남 **저는 금융 관련 조언을 해 드릴 수 있는 면허가 없어요**, 하지만 저희 상담원 중 한 명이 도와드리게 하겠습니다.

어휘

ask for ~을 요청하다 assistance 도움, 지원
qualification 자격, 면허 business account 사업용 계좌
fund 기금, 자금 investment 투자 stock 주식
qualified 면허가 있는 financial 금융의 advisor 조언자, 고문

패러프레이징

qualified to → have a qualification

2.

Q 고객들은 상점에서 무엇을 할 수 있는가?
A 자신만의 상품 디자인하기

미녀 미남 🎧

> W Thank you for visiting Rivera Jewelry. Can I help you find anything?
> M Actually, I heard that you allow customers to design their own jewelry. I'd like to make a unique ring as a gift.
> W Of course. What did you have in mind?

해석

여 리베라 주얼리에 방문해 주셔서 감사합니다. 찾으시는 게 있나요?
남 실은, **이곳에서 고객들에게 자신만의 액세서리를 디자인하게 해 준다고 들었어요**. 선물로 독특한 반지를 만들고 싶어요.
여 물론입니다. 어떤 걸 생각하셨나요?

어휘

allow 허용하다 jewelry 보석류, 장신구류 unique 독특한
have ~ in mind ~을 염두에 두다, 생각하다

패러프레이징

jewelry → products

3.

Q 남자는 무엇을 제안하는가?
A 재사용할 수 있는 물품을 구매하는 것

미녀 미남 🎧

> W Hi. I'd like to order a drink to-go. A large latte with caramel syrup, please.
> M Alright. And we've just started selling reusable cups. If you buy the cup, you can get 25 cents off every time you use it.

해석

여 안녕하세요, 테이크아웃 음료를 주문할게요. 캐러멜 시럽을 넣은 라테 큰 것으로 주세요.
남 알겠습니다. 그리고 저희가 이제 막 재사용할 수 있는 컵을 판매하기 시작했어요. 만약 그 컵을 사시면, 그것을 사용할 때마다 25센트씩 할인받으실 수 있어요.

어휘

reusable 재사용할 수 있는 to-go 가지고 갈

패러프레이징

cup → item

4.

Q 여자는 남자에게 어떤 새로운 정책에 대해 말하는가?
A 그는 예약할 필요가 없다.

미남 미녀 🎧

> M Hi, my name is Terry Williams, and I'm calling to make an appointment with Dr. Lee. I need to get a flu shot. Do you have any openings this week?
> W Actually, our policy has changed. Patients no longer need to see the doctor to get a flu shot. You can just come in anytime during the clinic's opening hours.

해석

남 안녕하세요, 제 이름은 테리 윌리엄스이고, 이 박사님께 예약하려고 전화드렸습니다. 전 독감 예방 주사를 맞아야 해요. 이번 주에 비어 있는 시간이 있나요?
여 실은, 저희 정책이 변경되었어요. **환자들은 더 이상 독감 예방 주사를 맞기 위해 의사의 진찰을 받을 필요가 없습니다.** 그냥 병원 운영 시간 중에 아무 때나 오시면 됩니다.

어휘

policy 정책, 방침 make an appointment 예약을 하다
flu shot 독감 예방 주사 no longer 더 이상 ~ 아닌
opening hours 영업시간

패러프레이징

no longer need to see the doctor
→ does not need an appointment

5.

여자는 어떤 서비스를 언급하는가?

(A) 무제한 수리

(B) 무료 설치

미남 미녀 🎧

> M Thanks for explaining the features. I'd like to buy this washing machine.
> W That's great. And, just so you know, we offer a free lifetime repair service for this brand.
> M Wow! That's a fantastic deal!

해석

남 기능을 설명해 주셔서 감사합니다. 이 세탁기를 사겠어요.

여 좋습니다. 그리고 참고로 말씀드리면, **저희가 이 브랜드에 대해 평생 무상 수리 서비스를 제공합니다.**

남 우와! 그거 아주 좋은 조건이네요!

어휘

unlimited 무제한의 repair 수리 installation 설치
feature 특징, 기능
just so you know 그냥 말하자면, 참고로 말하자면
lifetime 평생, 일생 fantastic 기막히게 좋은, 환상적인 deal 거래

패러프레이징

a free lifetime repair service → Unlimited repairs

6.

여자는 남자에게 무엇을 하라고 제안하는가?

(A) 다른 지점 방문하기

(B) 온라인 수단 이용하기

미남 미녀 🎧

> M My friend attended one of your writing workshops recently and highly recommended it. I'm wondering how to sign up for one.
> W Actually, we don't have anything new on the schedule. However, there is an online service called Portal Instruction. You can use it to participate in workshops virtually.

해석

남 제 친구가 당신의 글쓰기 워크숍 중 하나에 최근 참석하고는 적극 추천했어요. 워크숍을 신청하는 방법이 궁금해요.

여 사실, 새로 잡힌 일정이 전혀 없어요. 하지만, **포털 인스트럭션이라는 온라인 서비스가 있어요. 그것을 이용해서 가상으로 워크숍에 참석하시면 됩니다.**

어휘

resource 수단, 방편 highly 대단히, 매우
sign up for ~을 신청하다 participate in ~에 참가하다
virtually 가상으로

패러프레이징

service → resource

본문 p.187

연습 문제

1. (B)	2. (D)	3. (C)	4. (B)	5. (A)

[1] 영녀 미남 🎧

Question 1 refers to the following conversation.

> W Would you like me to bring the dessert menu, sir? We're running a special today. If you order a slice of our raspberry cheesecake, you can get a free cup of coffee.
> M Thanks, but the lunch portion was more than enough. I'd just like the bill. That was an excellent meal, though.
> W The chef will be glad to hear that. I'll be back in just a moment.

해석

1번은 다음 대화에 관한 문제입니다.

여 디저트 메뉴를 가져다드릴까요, 손님? 오늘은 특별 할인가로 제공합니다. 저희 라즈베리 치즈케이크 한 조각을 주문하시면, 커피 한 잔을 무료로 드실 수 있습니다.

남 고맙지만, 점심 양이 충분하고도 남았어요. 그냥 계산서만 주세요. 그렇지만 훌륭한 식사였어요.

여 주방장이 그 얘기를 들으면 기뻐할 거예요. 잠시 후에 다시 오겠습니다.

어휘

run (서비스 등을) 제공하다 special 특별 할인가 portion 1인분
more than enough 너무 많은 bill 청구서, 계산서

1.

여자는 누구인 것 같은가?

(A) 호텔 관리자

(B) 식당 종업원

(C) 전문 요리사

(D) 슈퍼마켓 직원

어휘

professional 전문적인

[2-3] 영녀 미남 🎧

Questions 2-3 refer to the following conversation.

> W ²I can't wait for this Saturday. Lena invited me to go to the opera. It's been a long time since I went to one.
> M Really? I hope you have a good time. I've never been to the opera, but I'd like to see one sometime.
> W I think some of her friends said they probably won't be able to make it. They might want to sell their tickets.

M That sounds great. ³Please let her know I'm interested in buying a ticket if one is available.

해석
2–3번은 다음 대화에 관한 문제입니다.
여 ²전 이번 토요일이 몹시 기다려져요. 레나가 제게 오페라에 가자고 했거든요. 오페라에 가 본 지 오래됐어요.
남 정말요? 좋은 시간 보내길 바라요. 전 오페라에 가 본 적이 없지만, 언젠가는 보고 싶어요.
여 아마도 그녀의 친구 중 몇 명이 못 간다고 말했다는 것 같아요. 자신들의 티켓을 팔고 싶어 할지도 몰라요.
남 그거 잘됐네요. ³하나 구할 수 있으면 제가 티켓을 사는 데 관심 있다고 그녀에게 알려 주세요.

어휘
can't wait for/to 너무 ~하고 싶다 invite 청하다, 요청하다
make it 시간 맞춰 가다 be interested in ~에 관심이 있다
available 구할 수 있는, 이용할 수 있는

2.
화자들은 어떤 행사에 대해 이야기하고 있는가?
(A) 재즈 콘서트
(B) 미술 전시
(C) 새 영화
(D) 오페라

어휘
exhibition 전시(회)

3.
남자는 무엇을 하기를 원하는가?
(A) 극장에 전화하기
(B) 다른 행사에 대해 알아보기
(C) 누군가에게서 티켓 사기
(D) 웹사이트 확인하기

[4-5] 영녀 미남 🎧
Questions 4-5 refer to the following conversation.

W Excuse me. ⁴Do you have any cotton material in this color? I need it for a garment I'm working on.
M Hmm... I'm afraid we're out of that particular color at the moment. ⁵Why don't you try Martin's down the street? They might sell it.
W Thanks for the tip, but I have a gift certificate for your store. I'd prefer to make use of that. I'm not in any rush anyway. I can come back another time.

해석
4–5번은 다음 대화에 관한 문제입니다.
여 실례합니다. ⁴이 색상으로 면직물이 있나요? 제가 지금 작업하고 있는 옷에 그것이 필요해요.
남 흠... 유감스럽지만 지금 그 색상은 다 떨어졌어요. ⁵길 아래 마

틴스에 가 보시는 것은 어때요? 그들이 그걸 팔지도 몰라요.
여 조언 감사해요, 하지만 제게 이 가게의 상품권이 있어요. 그걸 이용하는 게 좋겠어요. 게다가 전혀 급하지 않아요. 다음에 다시 올게요.

어휘
cotton material 면직물 garment 의복, 옷
be out of ~이 떨어지다, 바닥나다 particular 특정한
at the moment 바로 지금 tip 조언, 정보
gift certificate 상품권 prefer 선호하다
make use of ~을 이용하다 be in a rush 정신없을 정도로 바쁘다

4.
화자들은 어디에 있는 것 같은가?
(A) 의류 공장에
(B) 직물 가게에
(C) 인테리어 디자인 회사에
(D) 식당에

어휘
clothing 의류 fabric 직물, 천

패러프레이징
cotton material → fabric

5.
남자는 여자에게 무엇을 하라고 제안하는가?
(A) 다른 상점에 가기
(B) 웹사이트 검색하기
(C) 다음 주에 다시 오기
(D) 창고 확인하기

어휘
stock room 창고

패러프레이징
try Martin's down the street → Go to another shop

실전 문제
본문 p.188

1. (C)	2. (B)	3. (D)	4. (A)	5. (B)
6. (D)	7. (C)	8. (B)	9. (D)	10. (B)
11. (D)	12. (A)	13. (C)	14. (B)	15. (B)
16. (A)	17. (D)	18. (D)		

[1-3] 미녀 미남 🎧
Questions 1-3 refer to the following conversation.

W I saw this scarf in the window and was wondering if you had more of them. It would be a perfect present for my boss.
M Let me check. Hmm... We just ran out this morning. That scarf is one of our most popular items right now. ¹That is the last one in the whole store.

W Well, is there a way to order more? What about in a different color?

M Unfortunately, not. That's it. ²We could offer you a 20 percent discount on the display item, though. Would that work for you?

W That's perfect. Also, could you gift wrap it for me? ³I need it for a retirement party tomorrow evening.

해석

1-3번은 다음 대화에 관한 문제입니다.

여 진열창에서 이 스카프를 봤는데 그것들이 더 있는지 궁금해요. 제 상사를 위한 완벽한 선물이 될 거예요.

남 확인해 볼게요. 흠... 오늘 아침에 막 다 나갔어요. 그 스카프가 지금 저희의 가장 인기 있는 제품 중 하나거든요. ¹**그것은 매장 전체에서 마지막 남은 하나예요.**

여 음, 더 주문하는 방법이 있나요? 다른 색상은요?

남 안타깝지만, 없어요. 그것이 전부예요. ²**하지만 진열 제품에 대하여 20% 할인해 드릴 수 있어요.** 괜찮으세요?

여 그러면 딱 좋겠네요. 그리고, 선물 포장을 해 주시겠어요? ³**내일 저녁 은퇴 기념 파티를 위해 필요해요.**

어휘

run out 다 떨어지다 whole 전체의 order 주문하다; 주문
unfortunately 불행하게도, 유감스럽게도
discount 할인; 할인하다 display 전시, 진열
work for ~에게 효과가 있다 gift wrap 선물용으로 포장하다
retirement 퇴직, 은퇴

1.

스카프에 대해 무엇이 언급되는가?
(A) 그것은 여러 색상으로 나온다.
(B) 그것은 신제품 라인의 일부이다.
(C) 그것은 단 하나만 남았다.
(D) 그것은 아침에 도착했다.

패러프레이징

That is the last one in the whole store
→ There is just one left

2.

남자는 무엇을 해 주겠다고 제안하는가?
(A) 선물 포장하기
(B) 물품 할인하기
(C) 다른 가게에 전화하기
(D) 제품 주문하기

패러프레이징

offer you a 20 percent discount on the display item
→ Discount an item

3.

내일 어떤 행사가 열릴 것인가?
(A) 직원 야유회
(B) 자선 모금 행사

(C) 개업식
(D) 은퇴 기념 파티

어휘

charity 자선 단체, 자선 fund-raiser 모금 행사

[4-6] 미남 영녀 🎧

Questions 4-6 refer to the following conversation.

M Hello, and welcome to the Winnipeg Public Library. How can I help you?

W Hi. ⁴I moved from Winkler here to Winnipeg last month, and ⁵I'd like to register for a library card.

M All right. It's free to anyone living in Winnipeg. ⁵You'll need to fill out this form and provide proof of your address. For example, you can show a signed lease or a utility bill.

W Hmm… I didn't bring anything like that with me. Are you open on weekends?

M Yes, and ⁶you can check the library's Web site to see a full list of our hours.

해석

4-6번은 다음 대화에 관한 문제입니다.

남 안녕하세요, 위니펙 공립 도서관에 오신 것을 환영합니다. 어떻게 도와드릴까요?

여 안녕하세요. ⁴**제가 지난달에 윈클러에서 이곳 위니펙으로 이사 했어요,** 그래서 ⁵**도서 대출증을 신청하고 싶어요.**

남 좋습니다. 위니펙에 살면 누구든 무료입니다. ⁵**이 서식을 기입하 시고 주소를 증명할 만한 것을 제출하셔야 합니다.** 예를 들면, 서 명이 있는 임대차 계약서나 공과금 고지서를 보여 주시면 됩니 다.

여 흠... 제가 그런 것을 하나도 가져오지 않았어요. 주말에도 운영 하시나요?

남 네, 그리고 ⁶**저희의 전체 운영 시간을 알아보시려면 도서관의 웹 사이트를 확인하시면 됩니다.**

어휘

register for ~을 신청하다 fill out 기입하다 proof 증거, 증명
signed 서명이 있는 lease 임대차 계약 utility bill 공과금 고지서
hours 근무 시간, 영업시간

4.

여자는 지난달에 무엇을 했는가?
(A) 그녀는 새로운 도시로 이사했다.
(B) 그녀는 대학을 졸업했다.
(C) 그녀는 도서관 책을 잃어버렸다.
(D) 그녀는 지역 행사에 참석했다.

어휘

graduate from ~을 졸업하다

패러프레이징

moved from Winkler here to Winnipeg
→ moved to a new city

5.

대화는 주로 무엇에 관한 것인가?

(A) 일자리 공석
(B) 등록 절차
(C) 전문 개발 워크숍
(D) 아파트 임대 조건

어휘

registration 등록 procedure 절차, 수순
professional 전문적인 terms 조건

6.

남자에 따르면, 웹사이트에서 무엇을 찾을 수 있는가?

(A) 사진 갤러리
(B) 다가오는 행사
(C) 계정 상태
(D) 운영 시간

어휘

upcoming 다가오는 account 계정, 계좌 status 상태, 상황

패러프레이징

a full list of our hours → Operating hours

[7-9] 미녀 호남 🎧

Questions 7-9 refer to the following conversation.

W EXP Courier Services, this is Marcia speaking. How may I help you?

M Good afternoon. ⁷I have a package that needs to be at the Bravatti Art Gallery on 428 Belmar Avenue by 3 P.M. I'm at 16 West 24th right now.

W I will send a courier to you within the hour, then. ⁸Please have the form filled out upon the courier's arrival.

M Also, please let your employee know that ⁹the box is heavy, but extremely fragile. So, it must be handled very carefully.

해석

7-9번은 다음 대화에 관한 문제입니다.

여 EXP 택배 서비스, 마샤입니다. 어떻게 도와드릴까요?

남 안녕하세요. ⁷오후 3시까지 벨마 가 428번지 브라바티 미술관에 도착해야 하는 포장물이 있습니다. 저는 지금 웨스트 24번가 16번지에 있습니다.

여 그러면 제가 한 시간 이내에 배송 기사를 보내 드리겠습니다. ⁸배송 기사가 도착하는 대로 서식을 기입하시기 바랍니다.

남 그리고, 직원에게 ⁹상자가 무겁지만 깨지기 아주 쉽다고 알려 주시기 바랍니다. ⁹그래서 아주 조심스럽게 다뤄야 합니다.

어휘

courier 택배 회사, 배달원 package 소포, 포장물
fill out 기입하다, 작성하다 upon arrival 도착하자마자
extremely 극도로, 극히 fragile 깨지기 쉬운
handle 다루다, 처리하다

7.

남자는 포장물을 어디로 보내야 하는가?

(A) 호텔로
(B) 아파트로
(C) 미술관으로
(D) 사무실 건물로

8.

여자는 남자에게 무엇을 해 달라고 요청하는가?

(A) 여자에게 주소 주기
(B) 서식 기입하기
(C) 택배 기사에게 지불하기
(D) 상자 들어 올리기

어휘

complete 기입하다, 작성하다

패러프레이징

have the form filled out → Complete a form

9.

남자는 상자에 대해 무엇이라고 말하는가?

(A) 그것은 작고 비싸다.
(B) 그것은 환불이 불가능한 물품들이 들어 있다.
(C) 그것은 분실되었다.
(D) 그것은 특별한 주의가 필요하다.

어휘

expensive 비싼 non-refundable 환불이 안 되는
care 조심, 주의

패러프레이징

must be handled very carefully → needs special care

[10-12] 미남 미녀 🎧

Questions 10-12 refer to the following conversation.

M Hello. I heard from my friend that your enrollment period for new classes has just started. Do I need previous experience?

W The classes are aimed at complete beginners, so it's no problem even if you've never cooked a dish.

M That's great. ¹⁰I'd really like to start making meals at home.

W ¹¹If you register early, anytime this week, you'll get 15 percent off the class fee. The first class will be at 4 P.M. on Wednesday, March 13.

M ¹²Oh, 4 P.M.? I work until 6 on weekdays.

W Well, our schedule will change in the summer.

M I see. ¹²I'll be sure to check back for the new classes then. Thanks.

해석

10-12번은 다음 대화에 관한 문제입니다.

남 안녕하세요. 제 친구에게서 새로운 강좌들의 등록 기간이 막 시

작되었다고 들었습니다. 이전의 경험이 필요한가요?

여 강좌들은 완전 초보자들을 대상으로 하므로 요리를 해 본 적이 없더라도 전혀 문제 되지 않습니다.

남 잘됐군요. **¹⁰** 전 정말 집에서 음식을 만들기 시작하고 싶어요.

여 **¹¹** 이번 주 아무 때라도 일찍 등록하시면 수강료를 15% 할인받으실 수 있습니다. 첫 강좌는 3월 13일 수요일 오후 4시입니다.

남 **¹²** 아, 오후 4시요? 저는 주중에는 6시까지 일해요.

여 음, 저희 시간표는 여름에 바뀔 거예요.

남 알겠습니다. **¹²** 그때 꼭 새로운 강좌들에 대해 다시 확인해 보겠습니다. 감사합니다.

어휘

enrollment 등록, 가입 period 기간, 시기 previous 이전의
experience 경험 be aimed at ~을 대상으로 하다
complete 완전한 beginner 초보자
register 등록하다, 신청하다 fee 요금, 수수료

10.

남자는 어떤 종류의 강좌에 관심이 있는가?
(A) 사진 촬영
(B) 요리
(C) 미술
(D) 음악

11.

여자는 왜 일찍 등록할 것을 제안하는가?
(A) 상품권을 받기 위해
(B) 시간을 절약하기 위해
(C) 이용 가능성을 보장하기 위해
(D) 할인을 받기 위해

어휘

voucher 상품권, 할인권 ensure 보장하다
availability 가능성, 유효성

패러프레이징

get 15 percent off the class fee → get a discount

12.

여자는 왜 "저희 시간표는 여름에 바뀔 거예요"라고 말하는가?
(A) 가능한 해결책을 제안하기 위해
(B) 실망감을 드러내기 위해
(C) 지연에 대해 사과하기 위해
(D) 비용을 정당화하기 위해

어휘

propose 제안하다 solution 해결책
disappointment 실망, 낙심 apologize for ~에 대해 사과하다
delay 지연, 지체 justify 정당화시키다, 해명하다

[13-15] 영녀 호남 미녀 🎧

Questions 13-15 refer to the following conversation with three speakers.

W1 **¹³** Thanks for visiting Spirit Shoes. Is there anything specific I can help you find?

M **¹⁴** I've just been hired at an accounting firm, and I'm starting on Monday. The dress code there is formal, so... uh... I need some dress shoes that will go well with a suit.

W1 I'd recommend the Concord brand. Their designs look great, and they're very comfortable. My colleague, Hannah, can show you our selection.

W2 Hi, I'm Hannah. **¹⁵** Do you know your size, or would you like me to measure your foot?

M **¹⁵** I'd better get measured to make sure I get the perfect fit.

해석

13-15번은 다음 세 명의 대화에 관한 문제입니다.

여 **¹³** 스피릿 슈즈에 방문해 주셔서 감사합니다. 특별히 찾으시는 것이라도 있나요?

남 **¹⁴** 제가 막 회계 법인에 취직이 되어서 월요일에 일을 시작해요. 그곳의 복장 규정이 정장이에요, 그래서... 어... 정장과 잘 어울리는 정장 구두가 좀 필요해요.

여1 콩코드 브랜드를 추천합니다. 디자인이 훌륭하고 아주 편해요. 제 동료 한나가 저희 상품들을 보여 드릴게요.

여2 안녕하세요, 한나입니다. **¹⁵** 사이즈를 알고 계시나요, 아니면 발 치수를 재 드릴까요?

남 확실히 딱 맞게 하려면 **¹⁵** 치수를 재는 게 좋겠어요.

어휘

specific 구체적인, 특정한 hire 고용하다
accounting firm 회계 법인, 회계 사무소 dress code 복장 규정
formal 격식을 차린, 정중한 dress shoes 예복용 구두
go well with ~와 잘 어울리다 comfortable 편안한
selection 선택 가능한 것들 measure 측정하다, 재다
perfect fit 딱 맞는 것

13.

여자들은 어디에서 일하는가?
(A) 구내식당에서
(B) 귀금속점에서
(C) 신발 가게에서
(D) 지역 문화 센터에서

14.

남자는 왜 물건을 사기를 원하는가?
(A) 그는 선물을 줄 것이다.
(B) 그는 새로운 일을 시작할 것이다.
(C) 그는 결혼식에 참석할 것이다.
(D) 그는 여행을 떠날 것이다.

어휘

make a purchase 물건을 사다 take a trip 여행하다

패러프레이징

been hired at an accounting firm, and I'm starting on Monday → start a new job

15.

남자는 한나가 무엇을 하기를 원하는가?

(A) 브랜드 추천하기
(B) 치수 재기
(C) 정책 설명하기
(D) 창고 확인하기

어휘

take a measurement 치수를 재다 policy 정책
stock room 창고, 보관소

패러프레이징

get measured → Take some measurements

[16-18] 호남 영녀 🎧

Questions 16-18 refer to the following conversation and schedule.

M ¹⁶Thank you for calling Star Salon. This is Doug. How can I help you?

W Hi, I'd like to schedule a haircut for this Thursday. Becky is usually the one who does my hair, so I'd like an appointment with her, if possible.

M ¹⁷Unfortunately, Becky doesn't work here anymore. She moved to Dallas a couple of weeks ago.

W Oh, I didn't realize that. ¹⁸In that case, is there someone else available on Thursday? I could come any time after 4 o'clock.

M I'll check the schedule to see who is available at that time. Could you please hold?

해석

16-18번은 다음 대화와 일정표에 관한 문제입니다.

남 ¹⁶스타 살롱에 전화 주셔서 감사합니다. 저는 더그입니다. 어떻게 도와드릴까요?

여 안녕하세요, 이번 주 목요일로 커트 날짜를 잡고 싶습니다. 베키 씨가 보통 제 머리를 손질해 주시는 분이니, 가능하다면 그녀와 예약하고 싶습니다.

남 ¹⁷안타깝게도, 베키는 더 이상 여기서 일하지 않아요. 2주 전쯤 댈러스로 이사했어요.

여 아, 그건 몰랐어요. ¹⁸그렇다면, 목요일에 시간이 되시는 다른 분이 있나요? 전 4시 이후면 아무 때나 갈 수 있어요.

남 일정표를 확인해서 그때 누가 시간이 되는지 알아볼게요. 잠시 기다려 주시겠어요?

어휘

schedule 일정을 잡다; 일정 do one's hair 머리를 손질하다
available 시간이 있는, 이용할 수 있는

목요일 일정표	
오전 9시 – 오전 11시	더그
오전 11시 – 오후 1시	바이올렛
오후 1시 – 오후 3시	제임스
¹⁸오후 3시 – 오후 5시	캐럴

16.

남자는 어디에서 일하는가?

(A) 미용실에서
(B) 치과에서
(C) 영화관에서
(D) 금융 기관에서

어휘

financial 금융의, 재정의 institution 기관, 단체, 협회

17.

남자는 어떤 문제를 언급하는가?

(A) 제시간에 배달이 되지 않았다.
(B) 업체가 곧 문을 닫을 것이다.
(C) 일정표에 착오가 있었다.
(D) 직원이 동네를 떠났다.

어휘

make a delivery 배달하다 on time 제시간에, 정각에

패러프레이징

moved to Dallas → moved out of town

18.

시각 자료를 보시오. 누가 여자를 도울 것 같은가?

(A) 더그
(B) 바이올렛
(C) 제임스
(D) 캐럴

UNIT 12 교통·여행·주거 관련 대화

CHECK UP 본문 p.190

1. (B) **2.** (C) **3.** (D)

[1-3] 미녀 미남 🎧

Questions 1-3 refer to the following conversation.

W Excuse me, ¹I'm considering going to Miami on vacation in July, and one of my coworkers recommended your agency.

M Miami is a wonderful destination, but everyone goes there at this time of year. I'd like to suggest Houston instead. It also has nearby beaches, great food, and modern facilities.

---

²And you could save quite a bit of money with discounted hotel charges and airfares available only this month.

W Hmm… that sounds really good. I guess I need a little bit more time to think about it before I decide anything.

M That's fine. ³Why don't you take a look at our Web site? It has a lot of useful information.

해석

1-3번은 다음 대화에 관한 문제입니다.

여 실례합니다, ¹저는 7월에 휴가로 마이애미에 가는 것을 고려 중인데요, 제 동료 중 한 명이 이곳 대행사를 추천했어요.

남 마이애미는 멋진 여행지예요, 하지만 모두가 매년 이맘때 그곳에 가요. 저는 대신 휴스턴을 제안하고 싶어요. 그곳 역시 가까운 해변, 훌륭한 음식, 현대적인 편의시설이 있어요. ²그리고 이번 달에 한해 할인된 호텔 요금과 항공 요금을 이용할 수 있어서 상당한 돈을 절약할 수 있어요.

여 흠… 정말 괜찮은데요. 어느 쪽으로든 결정하기 전에 생각할 시간이 조금 더 필요할 것 같아요.

남 좋습니다. ³저희 웹사이트를 한번 보시는 게 어때요? 유용한 정보들이 많습니다.

어휘

consider -ing ~하는 것을 고려하다 on vacation 휴가로
agency 대리점, 대행사 destination 목적지, 도착지
nearby 인근의 modern 현대적인
facilities ((보통 복수형)) 편의 시설 quite a bit of 많은
discounted 할인된 charge 요금; 청구하다 airfare 항공 요금
available 이용할 수 있는 useful 유용한

1.

여자는 이 대행사에 대해 어떻게 알게 되었는가?
(A) 그녀는 온라인에서 후기를 읽었다.
(B) 동료가 그곳에 대해 말해 주었다.
(C) 그녀는 상점 진열창에서 전단을 보았다.
(D) 그녀의 회사가 출장을 위해 그곳을 이용한다.

어휘

flyer (광고·안내용) 전단

패러프레이징

one of my coworkers recommended your agency
→ A coworker told her about it

2.

남자에 따르면, 이번 달에 무엇을 이용할 수 있는가?
(A) 무료 업그레이드
(B) 새로운 숙박 시설
(C) 저렴한 가격
(D) 가이드가 있는 관광

어휘

accommodations 숙박 시설 guided 가이드가 안내하는

패러프레이징

discounted hotel charges and airfares → Lower prices

3.

남자는 여자에게 무엇을 하라고 말하는가?
(A) 홍보 영상 보기
(B) 지도 구매하기
(C) 여권 신청서 기입하기
(D) 웹사이트 확인하기

어휘

promotional 홍보의 purchase 구매하다
fill out 기입하다, 작성하다 passport 여권
application 신청(서)

패러프레이징

take a look at → Check

패러프레이징 연습　　　　　　　　본문 p.192

1-4. 스크립트 참조　　　**5.** (B)　　**6.** (B)

1.

Q 여자는 왜 시애틀에 갈 것인가?
A 발표하기 위해

〔미녀〕〔미남〕🎧

W Hi, Omar. It's Lori. I'm wondering if you've booked my plane tickets for Seattle yet.

M You mean for your business trip to present at the conference? I was going to choose the flights today.

해석

여 안녕하세요, 오마르. 로리예요. 당신이 이미 제 시애틀행 비행기 티켓을 예약했는지 궁금해요.

남 학회 발표를 위한 출장 말씀하시는 거죠? 오늘 항공편을 선택하려고 했어요.

어휘

book 예약하다 business trip 출장
present 발표하다, 보여 주다 conference 학회
flight 항공편, 비행기

패러프레이징

present → give a presentation

2.

Q 남자는 두 달 후에 무엇을 할 계획인가?
A 사업체 열기

미녀 미남 🎧

> **W** Hi, Mr. Baek. This is Vivian from Jackson Realty. There's a commercial space that I think would be perfect for your accounting firm. Do you have time to look at it this week?
>
> **M** Sure! I hope to get my business up and running in two months, so I need to find somewhere soon so I can open on time.

해석

여 안녕하세요, 백 씨. 저는 잭슨 부동산의 비비언이에요. 당신의 회계 법인에 딱 맞을 것 같은 상업 공간이 있어요. 이번 주에 둘러볼 시간 있으세요?

남 그럼요! 저는 두 달 후에 제 사업이 운영되기를 바라요, 그래서 제때에 문을 열 수 있도록 빨리 공간을 찾아야 해요.

어휘

realty 부동산 commercial 상업적인
accounting firm 회계 법인, 회계 사무소
up and running 정상적으로 돌아가는, 본격적으로 운영되는
on time 제때에, 정각에

패러프레이징

get my business up and running → Open a business

3.

Q 도로는 왜 차단되었는가?

A 일부 충전소가 설치되고 있는 중이다.

미남 미녀 🎧

> **M** Excuse me. I saw the sign saying this road is temporarily closed. I'm wondering what's going on. Are you part of the construction team?
>
> **W** Yes. The road has to stay closed while we put in some charging stations for electric cars. You'll have to use another route.

해석

남 실례합니다. 이 도로가 임시로 폐쇄되었다는 표지를 봤습니다. 무슨 일이 있는지 궁금합니다. 당신은 공사팀의 일원이신가요?

여 네. 그 도로는 저희가 전기 자동차 충전소를 설치하는 동안 폐쇄되어야 합니다. 당신은 다른 길을 이용해야 할 거예요.

어휘

block off 막다, 차단하다
charging station 전기 자동차가 배터리를 충전하는 장소
install 설치하다 sign 표지판, 간판
temporarily 임시로, 일시적으로 construction 공사, 건설
put in 설치하다, 들여놓다 electric 전기의 route 길, 경로

패러프레이징

put in some charging stations for electric cars
→ Some charging stations are being installed

4.

Q 여자는 여행 가방에 대해 무엇을 알리는가?

A 그것은 중량 제한을 초과했다.

미녀 미남 🎧

> **W** You're all checked in for your flight, Mr. Hubbard, but… um… it seems that your suitcase is five kilograms over the airline's baggage allowance. You'll have to pay an additional fee.
>
> **M** Oh, I didn't realize that. Do you take credit cards?

해석

여 당신은 항공편에 대한 탑승 수속을 모두 완료했습니다, 허버드 씨. 하지만… 음… 당신의 여행 가방이 항공사의 수하물 허용량을 5킬로그램 초과한 것 같아요. 추가 요금을 지불하셔야 할 겁니다.

남 아, 그건 몰랐어요. 신용카드 받으시나요?

어휘

notice 통지하다, 알리다 suitcase 여행 가방
weight limit 중량 제한 airline 항공사 baggage 수하물
allowance 허용량 additional fee 추가 요금

패러프레이징

five kilograms over the airline's baggage allowance
→ over a weight limit

5.

남자는 기차 승차권에 대해 무엇이라고 말하는가?

(A) 그것은 최근에 가격이 인상되었다.

(B) 그것은 여행 전에 구매하는 것이 더 저렴하다.

미남 미녀 🎧

> **M** I've booked the hotel and flight for your trip to Europe, Ms. Davis. However, I'm wondering if you plan to do some traveling by train while you're there.
>
> **W** Yes, I do. Why do you ask?
>
> **M** In that case, I'd suggest buying a train pass now. You only get the tourist discount if you buy it before you go.

해석

남 제가 당신의 유럽 여행을 위한 호텔과 항공편을 예약했어요, 데이비스 씨. 하지만, 당신이 그곳에 있는 동안 기차로 여행을 좀 할 계획인지 궁금해요.

여 네, 그래요. 왜 물어보시는데요?

남 그렇다면, 지금 기차 승차권을 살 것을 제안합니다. 가시기 전에 승차권을 사실 경우에만 여행자 할인을 받을 수 있습니다.

어휘

train pass 기차 승차권 price increase 가격 인상
purchase 구매하다 book 예약하다

패러프레이징

get the tourist discount if you buy it before you go
→ It is cheaper to purchase before a trip

6.

여자는 누구인 것 같은가?
(A) 공사 인부
(B) 부동산 관리인

미녀 미남 🎧

> W Good morning, Saginaw Apartments management office. How may I help you?
> M Hello, this is Edward Durham from unit 409. I'm having some issues with my air conditioning.
> W I can send one of our technicians to check it out today.

해석

여 안녕하세요, **새기노 아파트 관리사무소입니다. 어떻게 도와드릴까요?**
남 안녕하세요, 저는 409호의 에드워드 더럼입니다. 제 에어컨에 문제가 좀 있어요.
여 오늘 그것을 점검하도록 저희 기술자 중 한 명을 보내드릴 수 있습니다.

어휘

construction 공사 property 부동산, 재산
management 관리, 운영 unit (공동 주택의) 한 가구
issue 문제, 안건 technician 기술자

패러프레이징

Saginaw Apartments management office
→ A property manager

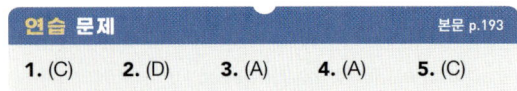

연습 문제 본문 p.193

1. (C) **2.** (D) **3.** (A) **4.** (A) **5.** (C)

[1] 호남 미녀 🎧

Question 1 refers to the following conversation.

> M Jaime, I noticed you weren't at the meeting this morning. Is everything okay?
> W Yes, I just got held up in traffic on Hershey Street.
> M There always seems to be heavy congestion there. Why don't you take South Street instead?
> W Actually, I have to take Hershey Street to drop my son off at school. I'll just have to leave home a little earlier from now on.

해석

1번은 다음 대화에 관한 문제입니다.
남 제이미, 오늘 아침 회의에 당신이 없는 것을 알았어요. 별문제 아

니죠?
여 네, 그저 허시 거리에서 차가 막혀 꼼짝할 수 없었어요.
남 그곳은 항상 교통 정체가 심한 것 같아요. 대신 사우스 거리로 가는 게 어때요?
여 실은, 제 아들을 학교에 내려 주려면 허시 거리로 가야 해요. 이제부터는 그냥 집에서 좀 더 일찍 출발해야겠어요.

어휘

notice 알아채다, 주의하다 hold ~ up ~을 지연시키다, 방해하다
traffic 차량들, 교통(량) congestion 교통 정체
drop ~ off ~을 내려 주다 from now on 이제부터

1.

제이미는 왜 회의에 빠졌는가?
(A) 그녀는 일정표를 가지고 있지 않았다.
(B) 그녀는 새 학교를 구경했다.
(C) 그녀는 교통 체증으로 꼼짝 못 했다.
(D) 그녀는 다른 경로로 갔다.

어휘

tour 견학하다, 둘러보다 be stuck 꼼짝도 못 하다
alternate route 대체 도로

패러프레이징

got held up in traffic on Hershey Street
→ was stuck on a road

[2-3] 미녀 호남 🎧

Questions 2-3 refer to the following conversation.

> W Hi, there. I saw your leaflet for moving services. I'm planning on moving my store to a larger space in another city. Could you help?
> M Of course! Which city are you moving to, and on what date would you prefer? We're booked up quite a bit for March, and we are closed on Wednesdays.
> W We're moving to Atlanta. ² How is the 15th of April?
> M Perfect! ³ But we need to know what kind of breakable things we will be transporting. We want to prepare the packaging in advance.

해석

2-3번은 다음 대화에 관한 문제입니다.
여 안녕하세요. 이곳의 이사 서비스 전단지를 보았어요. 제 가게를 다른 도시의 더 큰 공간으로 옮길 계획입니다. 도와주실 수 있나요?
남 물론입니다! 어떤 도시로 옮기시고, 어느 날짜가 좋으시겠어요? 저희가 3월에는 상당히 많이 바빠요, 그리고 수요일에는 문을 닫습니다.
여 저희는 애틀랜타로 옮겨요. ² **4월 15일은 어떠세요?**
남 딱 좋아요! ³ 그런데 저희가 어떤 종류의 깨지기 쉬운 물건들을 **운송할지 알아야 해요.** 미리 포장재를 준비하고자 하거든요.

어휘

leaflet (광고용) 전단　be booked up 몹시 바쁘다, 예약이 끝나다
quite a bit 꽤 많이, 상당히　breakable 깨지기 쉬운
transport 수송하다　packaging 포장재, 포장
in advance 사전에, 미리

2.

이사는 언제 일어날 것인가?
(A) 3월 14일에
(B) 3월 15일에
(C) 4월 14일에
(D) 4월 15일에

3.

남자는 무엇에 대해 물어보는가?
(A) 깨지기 쉬운 물건들
(B) 특별 할인
(C) 회사 정책
(D) 배달 요금

어휘

fragile 깨지기 쉬운　policy 정책　fee 요금, 수수료

패러프레이징

breakable things → Fragile items

[4-5] 미녀 호남 🎧

Questions 4-5 refer to the following conversation.

> **W** Excuse me. ⁴I'm booked on the 12:15 flight to Chicago, but I'm not sure which gate it's departing from.
> **M** Let's see… according to my computer, that flight is boarding at Gate 23. It's in Terminal 3.
> **W** Isn't that quite a long walk from here?
> **M** Yes, ⁵so you should take the free airport shuttle to save time. There's no charge for it, and it departs from right over there. The next one should be here in just a few minutes.

해석

4-5번은 다음 대화에 관한 문제입니다.
여 실례합니다. ⁴저는 시카고행 12시 15분 항공편에 예약되어 있지만, 어떤 게이트에서 출발하는지 잘 모르겠어요.
남 어디 볼게요… 제 컴퓨터에 따르면, 그 항공편은 23번 게이트에서 탑승해요. 3번 터미널에 있어요.
여 여기서 꽤 오래 걸어야 하지 않나요?
남 네, ⁵그러니까 시간을 절약하려면 무료 공항 셔틀버스를 타야 해요. 요금이 들지 않고, 바로 저쪽에서 출발해요. 몇 분만 있으면 다음 버스가 여기로 와요.

어휘

flight 항공편, 비행　depart from ~에서 출발하다
board (비행기·배가) 탑승에 들어가다　save 절약하다
charge 요금; 청구하다

4.

여자는 어떤 문제를 언급하는가?
(A) 그녀는 어디로 가야 하는지 모른다.
(B) 그녀는 자신의 여행 가방을 망가뜨렸다.
(C) 그녀는 더 늦은 항공편이 필요하다.
(D) 그녀는 티켓을 잃어버렸다.

어휘

damage 손상을 주다, 피해를 입히다　suitcase 여행 가방

패러프레이징

I'm not sure which gate it's departing from
→ She does not know where to go

5.

남자는 무엇을 할 것을 제안하는가?
(A) 물품을 교체하는 것
(B) 공지를 하는 것
(C) 셔틀버스를 이용하는 것
(D) 업그레이드 비용을 지불하는 것

어휘

replace 교체하다, 대체하다　announcement 발표, 공고

패러프레이징

take the free airport shuttle → Using a shuttle

실전 문제　　　　본문 p.194

1. (D)	**2.** (B)	**3.** (C)	**4.** (B)	**5.** (C)
6. (B)	**7.** (D)	**8.** (C)	**9.** (A)	**10.** (D)
11. (B)	**12.** (A)	**13.** (A)	**14.** (D)	**15.** (C)
16. (B)	**17.** (D)	**18.** (B)		

[1-3] 미남 미녀 🎧

Questions 1-3 refer to the following conversation.

> **M** Excuse me. ¹Are you also waiting for bus number 45? I've been waiting for almost an hour. Do you know what's going on by any chance?
> **W** Actually, I'm taking bus 11, ²but number 45 is probably running late because of the music festival downtown this weekend. More people are riding than usual.
> **M** Oh, I see. I guess I'd better take the subway or a cab now instead of the bus.
> **W** ³If I were you, I'd take a cab. The nearest subway station is on Martin Street, which is about a mile away from here.

해석

1-3번은 다음 대화에 관한 문제입니다.
남 실례합니다. ¹당신도 45번 버스를 기다리고 있나요? 전 거의 한 시간 동안 기다리고 있어요. 혹시 무슨 일인지 아시나요?

여 실은, 전 11번 버스를 타요, ² 하지만 45번은 아마도 이번 주말 시내에서 열리는 음악 축제 때문에 늦을 거예요. 평소보다 더 많은 사람들이 타고 있어요.

남 아, 그렇군요. 지금은 버스 대신 지하철이나 택시를 타는 게 나을 것 같네요.

여 ³ 제가 당신이라면 택시를 타겠어요. 가장 가까운 지하철역이 마틴 거리에 있는데, 여기서 약 1마일 떨어져 있어요.

어휘

by any chance 혹시라도 probably 아마도 run late 늦다
downtown 시내에 than usual 평소보다

1.

화자들은 어디에 있는 것 같은가?
(A) 음악 축제에
(B) 지하철역에
(C) 매표소에
(D) 버스 정류장에

2.

여자는 무엇이 지연을 일으켰다고 생각하는가?
(A) 버스 기사들의 부족
(B) 시내의 행사
(C) 마틴 거리의 공사
(D) 험한 날씨

어휘

shortage 부족 construction 공사, 건설
severe 극심한, 심각한

패러프레이징

the music festival → An event

3.

여자는 무엇을 할 것을 제안하는가?
(A) 다음 버스를 기다리는 것
(B) 행사에 참석하는 것
(C) 다른 교통편을 이용하는 것
(D) 온라인으로 일정을 확인하는 것

어휘

alternate 대체의, 교대의 transportation 교통, 운송

패러프레이징

take a cab → Taking alternate transportation

[4-6] 미남 영녀 🎧

Questions 4-6 refer to the following conversation.

> M Hello, I'd like to take the next train to Cornwall this afternoon. Are there any seats still available?
>
> W I'm sorry. ⁴The next train is completely booked due to a bike race in Bristol tomorrow.

M Oh, no. I have to be there by noon tomorrow. Are there any other options that will get me there by tomorrow morning?

W ⁵,⁶Well, there is a train at midnight that still has a few seats available. How does that sound?

M Well, what else can I do? ⁶One ticket, please.

해석

4-6번은 다음 대화에 관한 문제입니다.

남 안녕하세요, 오늘 오후에 콘월로 가는 다음 기차를 타려고 합니다. 아직 이용할 수 있는 좌석이 있나요?

여 죄송합니다. ⁴다음 열차는 내일 브리스틀에서 열리는 자전거 경주 때문에 예약이 꽉 찼어요.

남 아, 이런. 저는 내일 정오까지 그곳에 가야 해요. 제가 내일 아침까지 그곳에 도착하게 해 줄 다른 방법이 있나요?

여 ⁵,⁶음, 아직 이용할 수 있는 좌석이 몇 개 있는 자정 기차가 있어요. 그건 어떠세요?

남 음, 달리 제가 뭘 할 수 있겠어요? ⁶티켓 한 장 주세요.

어휘

available 구할 수 있는, 이용할 수 있는 completely 완전히
book 예약하다 due to ~ 때문에
option 선택(할 수 있는 것), 선택권 what else 다른 무엇

4.

여자에 따르면, 내일 브리스틀에서 어떤 행사가 개최되는가?
(A) 마라톤
(B) 자전거 경주
(C) 채용 박람회
(D) 학회

5.

여자는 남자에게 무엇을 하라고 추천하는가?
(A) 비행기 티켓 예약하기
(B) 브리스틀 곳곳을 여행하기
(C) 다른 기차 타기
(D) 환불 신청하기

어휘

request 요청하다 refund 환불; 환불하다

패러프레이징

a train at midnight → another train

6.

남자는 "달리 제가 뭘 할 수 있겠어요"라고 말할 때 무엇을 암시하는가?
(A) 그는 또 다른 아이디어를 듣고 싶다.
(B) 그는 자정에 기차를 타야 한다.
(C) 그는 콘월에 갈 수 없다.
(D) 그는 다른 기차의 시간표를 확인할 것이다.

[7-9] 호남 미녀 🎧

Questions 7-9 refer to the following conversation.

M Hi, Stephanie. Do you have a moment to talk about my business trip to Toronto?

W Sure. Is there a problem with the schedule?

M ⁷Well, the conference ends on Thursday morning, but the return flight is booked for Friday evening. Could it be changed to Thursday evening instead?

W Of course. But… um... I thought you said you'd like to have an extra day in the city to do some sightseeing.

M Sorry, I had forgotten about that. ⁸Now there's a workshop on Friday that I need to attend here.

W No problem. I can take care of that right away. ⁹I'll e-mail you the updated itinerary shortly.

해석

7-9번은 다음 대화에 관한 문제입니다.

남 안녕하세요, 스테파니. 제 토론토 출장에 관해 잠시 얘기할 시간 있어요?

여 그럼요. 일정에 문제가 있나요?

남 ⁷음, 회의가 목요일 아침에 끝나는데, 돌아오는 비행편이 금요일 저녁으로 예약되어 있어요. 대신 목요일 저녁으로 바꿀 수 있을까요?

여 물론이죠. 그런데… 음... 당신이 관광을 좀 하기 위해 그 도시에서 하루 더 있고 싶다고 했던 것 같은데요.

남 미안해요, 그걸 잊고 있었어요. ⁸제가 이곳에서 참가해야 하는 워크숍이 금요일에 있어요.

여 문제없어요. 즉시 처리하겠습니다. ⁹업데이트된 여행 일정표를 이메일로 곧 보내 드릴게요.

어휘

conference (대규모) 회의, 학회 flight 비행기, 항공편
book 예약하다 instead 대신에 extra 추가의, 가외의
sightseeing 관광 take care of ~을 처리하다
updated 최신의, 업데이트된 itinerary 여행 일정표 shortly 곧

7.

남자는 무엇에 관해 물어보는가?
(A) 회의에서 강연하는 것
(B) 토론토에서 고객을 만나는 것
(C) 업무 경비에 대해 환급받는 것
(D) 여행 준비를 일부 변경하는 것

어휘

give a talk 강연하다 get reimbursed for ~을 환급받다
expense 비용, 경비 travel arrangement 여행 준비

패러프레이징

be changed to Thursday evening instead
→ Changing some travel arrangements

8.

남자는 금요일에 무엇을 할 계획인가?

(A) 몇몇 친구들 만나기
(B) 도시의 유명한 장소들 구경하기
(C) 워크숍에 참석하기
(D) 결정 확정하기

9.

남자에게 무엇이 보내질 것인가?
(A) 여행 일정표
(B) 주소
(C) 접속 코드
(D) 신청서

[10-12] 미남 미녀 🎧

Questions 10-12 refer to the following conversation.

M Hello, I'm looking for some activities to do. ¹⁰Are there any tour package deals at this hotel?

W What kind of tours are you interested in?

M I'd like to do some water activities on the beach.

W ¹¹In that case, I recommend Towson Travel. They offer quite a few different excursions that you might find enjoyable.

M Thank you. Do you have any pamphlets I can take to review?

W Sure. Here you are. When you make up your mind, just let me know. ¹²I can get you some discounts since you are a hotel guest.

해석

10-12번은 다음 대화에 관한 문제입니다.

남 안녕하세요, 제가 할 만한 활동을 좀 찾고 있어요. ¹⁰이 호텔에 관광 패키지 상품이 있나요?

여 어떤 관광에 관심이 있으세요?

남 해변에서 수상 활동을 좀 하고 싶어요.

여 ¹¹그렇다면, 타운슨 트래블을 추천합니다. 당신이 즐거워하실 만한 꽤 다양한 당일 여행을 제공해요.

남 고맙습니다. 제가 가져가서 검토할 수 있는 팸플릿이라도 있나요?

여 물론입니다. 여기 있어요. 결정하시면, 제게 알려 주세요. ¹²호텔 고객이시니 할인해 드리겠습니다.

어휘

package deal 일괄 거래 상품
be interested in ~에 관심이 있다
quite a few 상당한 수(의)
excursion (보통 단체로 짧게 하는) 여행 enjoyable 즐거운
pamphlet 팸플릿 review 검토하다
make up one's mind 결심하다 discount 할인

10.

대화는 어디에서 일어나고 있는가?
(A) 공항에서

(B) 여행사에서
(C) 매표소에서
(D) 호텔에서

11.
여자는 타운슨 트래블에 대해 무엇이라고 말하는가?
(A) 그곳은 바다 근처에 위치해 있다.
(B) 그곳은 선택 범위가 다양한 활동들이 있다.
(C) 그곳은 도시 곳곳에서 무료 관광을 제공한다.
(D) 그곳은 그 지역에서 가격이 가장 적당하다.

어휘
be located (~에) 위치해 있다
a large selection of 선택 범위가 다양한
affordable (가격이) 알맞은

패러프레이징
offer quite a few different excursions
→ has a large selection of activities

12.
여자는 무엇을 해 주겠다고 제안하는가?
(A) 특가 제공하기
(B) 남자에게 티켓 보내기
(C) 남자에게 장비 빌려주기
(D) 무료 식사 제공하기

어휘
special price 특별 할인가   equipment 장비
complimentary 무료의

패러프레이징
get you some discounts → Give a special price

[13-15] 영녀 호남 미남 🎧
Questions 13-15 refer to the following conversation
with three speakers.

W **13** Thanks for stopping by the apartment
complex to sign the lease, Mr. Ortiz.

M1 It's no problem. I was in the neighborhood
anyway.

W **14** Your move-in date is scheduled for June 4.

M1 Is there anything special I need to do?

W **14** Just come to the office here to pick up your
keys. A staff member will join you for a walk-
through to make sure everything's okay.

M1 Okay. And would it be possible to get the exact
measurements of the rooms in advance?

W I'm just on my way out, but Kevin can help you
with that. **15** Kevin, could you get a copy of the
layout of unit 203 for Mr. Ortiz?

M2 **15** Of course. Let me print that for you, Mr. Ortiz.

해석
13-15번은 다음 세 명의 대화에 관한 문제입니다.

여 **13** 임대차 계약에 서명하기 위해 아파트 단지에 들러 주셔서 고맙습니다, 오르티스 씨.

남1 별일도 아닌데요. 어쨌든 근처에 있었어요.

여 **14** 당신의 입주 날짜는 6월 4일로 잡혀 있습니다.

남1 제가 뭐 특별히 해야 하는 것이라도 있나요?

여 **14** 그냥 이곳 사무실로 오셔서 열쇠를 받아 가세요. 모든 것에 이상이 없는지 확인하기 위해 저희 직원이 동행하여 자세히 설명할 것입니다.

남1 알겠습니다. 그리고 사전에 정확한 방 치수를 재는 것이 가능할까요?

여 제가 막 나가는 길이라서요, 하지만 케빈이 도와드릴 거예요. **15** 케빈, 오르티스 씨에게 203호 배치도 사본을 갖다 드리겠어요?

남2 **15** 물론입니다. 제가 출력해 드릴게요, 오르티스 씨.

어휘
stop by ~에 들르다   complex 복합 건물, (건물) 단지
lease 임대차 계약   neighborhood 근처, 인근, 이웃
move-in 입주   staff member 직원
walk-through (단계적인) 자세한 설명   exact 정확한
measurements ((보통 복수형)) 치수   in advance 사전에, 미리
on one's way out 나가는 중인   layout 배치(도)

13.
대화는 어디에서 일어나고 있는가?
(A) 아파트 건물에서
(B) 창고에서
(C) 백화점에서
(D) 금융 기관에서

어휘
financial 금융의, 재정의   institution 기관, 협회, 연구소

패러프레이징
complex → building

14.
여자는 오르티스 씨에게 무엇에 대해 말하는가?
(A) 환불 정책
(B) 미지불 청구서
(C) 일정상의 문제
(D) 입주 절차

어휘
outstanding 미지불된, 미해결된   procedure 절차

15.
케빈은 오르티스 씨를 위해 무엇을 할 것인가?
(A) 그에게 건물 구경시켜 주기
(B) 그에게 주차권 주기
(C) 평면도 출력하기
(D) 열쇠가 작동하는지 확인하기

어휘
parking pass 주차권   floor layout 평면도

[16-18] 영녀 호남 🎧

Questions 16-18 refer to the following conversation and schedule.

> W Hello, ¹⁶I'm Dianne Liebold from City Hall. Can I speak to the building manager, please?
>
> M This is Jeremy Kaur, the manager. What is this regarding?
>
> W I'm calling to notify you of some re-pavement work in front of your building starting next week.
>
> M Oh, thanks for letting me know. ¹⁷Which days exactly is the work scheduled for?
>
> W ¹⁷Monday and Tuesday. This means your tenants won't be able to access the building through the main entrance.
>
> M ¹⁸I'll put a notice about the road work in the lobby today. Thank you again for the advanced warning.

해석

16-18번은 다음 대화와 일정표에 관한 문제입니다.

여 안녕하세요, ¹⁶저는 **시청의 다이앤 리볼드**입니다. 건물 관리인과 통화할 수 있을까요?

남 제가 관리인인 제레미 카우르입니다. 무슨 일 때문에 그러시죠?

여 다음 주부터 당신의 건물 앞에서 일부 도로 재포장 작업이 있다고 알려드리려 전화했습니다.

남 아, 알려 주셔서 감사합니다. ¹⁷정확히 어느 날에 작업이 예정되어 있나요?

여 ¹⁷**월요일과 화요일**입니다. 이것은 세입자들이 정문을 통해서 건물에 들어갈 수 없을 것이라는 뜻입니다.

남 ¹⁸오늘 로비에 도로 공사에 관한 공고문을 붙일게요. 미리 경고해 주셔서 다시 한번 감사드립니다.

어휘

What is this regarding? 무슨 일 때문에 그러시죠?
notify A of B A에게 B를 통보하다
re-pavement (도로의) 재포장 starting ~부터
tenant 세입자 access 접근하다; 접근
main entrance 정문, 중앙 출입구 notice 공고문, 안내문
advanced warning 사전 경고

도로 재포장 일정	
7월 1-2일 (금 - 토)	그랜트 가
7월 7-8일 (목 - 금)	시어스 가
7월 13 - 14일 (수 - 목)	파커 가
¹⁷7월 18 - 19일 (월 - 화)	보더 가

16.

여자는 누구인 것 같은가?

(A) 건물 세입자
(B) 공무원
(C) 현장 관리자
(D) 공사 인부

어휘

field 현장 construction 건설, 공사

17.

시각 자료를 보시오. 남자의 건물은 어디에 위치해 있는 것 같은가?

(A) 그랜트 가에
(B) 시어스 가에
(C) 파커 가에
(D) 보더 가에

18.

남자는 이 전화 후에 무엇을 할 것인가?

(A) 시청에 전화하기
(B) 게시물 붙이기
(C) 그의 차 이동하기
(D) 그의 근무 일정 변경하기

어휘

post 게시하다, 공고하다 sign 표지, 게시

패러프레이징

put a notice → Post a sign

PART **TEST**				본문 p.196
32. (A)	**33.** (D)	**34.** (C)	**35.** (A)	**36.** (C)
37. (C)	**38.** (C)	**39.** (A)	**40.** (B)	**41.** (B)
42. (A)	**43.** (C)	**44.** (B)	**45.** (C)	**46.** (A)
47. (D)	**48.** (D)	**49.** (B)	**50.** (D)	**51.** (B)
52. (C)	**53.** (A)	**54.** (B)	**55.** (C)	**56.** (C)
57. (A)	**58.** (D)	**59.** (C)	**60.** (D)	**61.** (D)
62. (B)	**63.** (D)	**64.** (A)	**65.** (C)	**66.** (D)
67. (B)	**68.** (C)	**69.** (B)	**70.** (B)	

[32-34] 영녀 미남 🎧

Questions 32-34 refer to the following conversation.

> W Hi, Mr. Caspar. Are you busy right now?
>
> M Not really. Can I help you with something?
>
> W Well... uh... ³²I was wondering if I can use three of my vacation days next week, Monday through Wednesday. ³³Our team has been so busy because Benjamin got transferred unexpectedly, so I'd like some time to relax.
>
> M That shouldn't be a problem since we've finished the project now.
>
> W Thanks. That's what I was thinking.

M ³⁴Make sure you complete the request form on the company's Web site.

W I'll get right to it.

해석

32-34번은 다음 대화에 관한 문제입니다.

여 안녕하세요. 캐스파 씨. 지금 바쁘신가요?

남 괜찮아요. 뭘 좀 도와드릴까요?

여 그게... 어... ³²제가 다음 주에 3일간 휴가를 사용할 수 있는지 궁금해서요. 월요일부터 수요일까지요. ³³벤자민이 갑자기 전근을 가는 바람에 저희 팀이 그동안 너무 바빠서, 좀 쉬고 싶네요.

남 이제 프로젝트가 끝났으니 문제 될 게 없죠.

여 고마워요. 저도 그렇게 생각했어요.

남 ³⁴회사 웹사이트에서 반드시 신청서를 작성하세요.

여 바로 그렇게 할게요.

어휘

transfer 옮기다; 이동 unexpectedly 갑자기, 예치기 못하게 complete 작성하다, 완료하다 request form 신청서

32.

여자는 무엇을 요청하는가?

(A) 잠시 쉬는 것

(B) 임금을 인상받는 것

(C) 더 큰 사무실로 이전하는 것

(D) 회의 시간을 변경하는 것

어휘

pay raise 임금 인상

패러프레이징

use three of my vacation days → Taking some time off

33.

팀은 왜 평소보다 바빴는가?

(A) 일부 장비가 작동을 멈추었다.

(B) 일부 중요한 파일이 분실되었다.

(C) 고객이 마감일을 변경했다.

(D) 동료가 전근을 갔다.

어휘

equipment 장비, 용품 colleague 동료

패러프레이징

Benjamin → A colleague

34.

여자는 다음에 무엇을 할 것 같은가?

(A) 휴게실에 공지사항 게시하기

(B) 몇 가지 수치 확인하기

(C) 웹사이트 방문하기

(D) 인사 담당자와 상담하기

어휘

post 게시하다 notice 공고문, 안내문

---

representative 대리인, 대표자

패러프레이징

complete the request form on the company's Web site → Visit a Web site

[35-37] 미녀 호남 🎧

Questions 35-37 refer to the following conversation.

W I've finished taking the photos at the property on Vasquez Street.

M Thank you. ³⁵I hope they'll attract a lot of people to Saturday's open house.

W Me, too. This house really is amazing. And… um… ³⁶since it overlooks the coast, I think visitors will love the view. It's stunning.

M I agree. I think that will help us get a good price for the buyer.

W Should I just send the photos by e-mail?

M Yes, please. ³⁷I'll design the brochures today, and then I can get them printed tomorrow.

해석

35-37번은 다음 대화에 관한 문제입니다.

여 바스케스 거리의 부동산 매물에서 촬영을 끝냈습니다.

남 고맙습니다. ³⁵토요일 공개일에 많은 사람들이 모였으면 좋겠네요.

여 저도요. 이 집은 정말 놀랍네요. 그리고... 음... ³⁶해안이 내려다 보이기 때문에 방문객들이 경치를 좋아할 거라고 생각해요. 정말 근사해요.

남 동의해요. 저는 그 점이 구매자에게 좋은 가격을 받는 데 도움이 될 거라고 생각해요.

여 사진들을 이메일로 보내면 되나요?

남 네, 부탁해요. ³⁷소책자는 오늘 디자인해서 내일 인쇄할 수 있어요.

어휘

property 건물, 부동산 attract 끌어모으다
open house (사람들이 부동산을 둘러볼 수 있게 하는) 공개일
overlook 내려다보다, 바라보다 coast 해안
stunning 굉장히 멋진 brochure 소책자, 브로슈어

35.

토요일에 무슨 일이 일어날 것인가?

(A) 부동산 공개일

(B) 사진 수업

(C) 도시 관광

(D) 제품 출시

어휘

launch 출시; 출시하다

36.

여자는 참가자들이 무엇에 관심을 가질 것이라고 생각하는가?

(A) 전문가의 조언

(B) 합리적인 가격
(C) 아름다운 경관
(D) 보안 장치

어휘

participant 참가자 expert 전문가
reasonable 합리적인, 타당한 security 보안, 경비

패러프레이징

overlooks the coast ~ visitors will love the view ~
stunning → A beautiful view

37.

남자는 내일 무엇을 할 계획인가?
(A) 일정표 업데이트하기
(B) 재무 보고서 제출하기
(C) 소책자 인쇄하기
(D) 컨설턴트에게 말하기

어휘

consultant 컨설턴트, 상담가

패러프레이징

get them printed → Print some brochures

[38-40] 호남 미녀 🎧

Questions 38-40 refer to the following conversation.

> **M** Hi, Harumi. ³⁸ I've been reading some of the reviews for our vitamin supplements. There are complaints about the packaging. People say it's difficult to get the cap off the bottle. Maybe we should change it.
>
> **W** Well... uh... ³⁹ that was designed on purpose as a safety feature. If it's easy to get the cap off, there could be a problem with children getting to the bottle's contents.
>
> **M** Maybe we could have two different bottle styles.
>
> **W** Do any of our competitors do that?
>
> **M** I'm not sure. ⁴⁰ I'll research what others are doing and get back to you.

해석

38-40번은 다음 대화에 관한 문제입니다.
남 안녕하세요. 하루미. ³⁸ 우리 비타민 보충제에 관련된 후기들을 읽고 있었는데요. 포장에 대한 불만이 있네요. 사람들이 병뚜껑을 열기가 힘들다고 해요. 아마도 바꿔야 할 것 같아요.
여 음... 어... ³⁹ 그건 안전을 위해 의도적으로 디자인된 거예요. 만일 뚜껑이 쉽게 열리면, 아이들이 병의 내용물을 접하게 될 문제가 생길 수 있어요.
남 어쩌면 두 가지 다른 병 모양으로 갈 수도 있겠네요.
여 경쟁사 중에 그런 곳이 있나요?
남 잘 모르겠어요. ⁴⁰ 다른 회사들은 어떻게 하는지 조사해 보고 다시 답변드릴게요.

어휘

supplement 보충, 추가 complaint 불만, 불평
on purpose 의도적으로, 일부러 feature 특징
contents 내용물, 속에 든 것 competitor 경쟁자, 참가자

38.

화자들의 회사는 어떤 유형의 제품을 만드는가?
(A) 건강에 좋은 간식
(B) 핸드 로션
(C) 비타민 보충제
(D) 에너지 드링크

어휘

healthy 건강에 좋은, 건강한

39.

여자는 무엇에 대해 걱정하는가?
(A) 안전 문제
(B) 나쁜 후기
(C) 증가된 비용
(D) 환경 문제

어휘

issue (걱정거리가 되는) 문제

패러프레이징

there could be a problem with children getting to the
bottle's contents → A safety issue

40.

남자는 무엇을 할 것이라고 말하는가?
(A) 공급업체 변경하기
(B) 몇몇 조사 수행하기
(C) 몇몇 포장재 테스트하기
(D) 주문하기

어휘

supplier 공급자, 공급 회사 conduct 수행하다, 처리하다

패러프레이징

research what others are doing
→ Conduct some research

[41-43] 미남 미녀 🎧

Questions 41-43 refer to the following conversation.

> **M** Hello. My name is Thomas Lee. I'm here to have a job interview with Ms. Mitchell. ⁴¹ She said I should pick up a temporary ID card here first.
>
> **W** Let's see... ⁴² It looks like your name isn't on our visitor list.
>
> **M** Oh, really? ⁴² Ms. Mitchell told me it would be added. I'm sure she tried to do so.

W You know, we've changed our software recently. ⁴³My manager can issue a special pass for you. Let me ask him. Just a moment, please.

해석

41-43번은 다음 대화에 관한 문제입니다.

남 안녕하세요. 제 이름은 토머스 리입니다. 미첼 씨와 채용 면접을 보러 이곳에 왔습니다. ⁴¹그분이 제가 먼저 여기서 임시 신분증을 찾아와야 한다고 하셨습니다.

여 어디 볼게요... ⁴²저희 방문객 명단에 당신의 이름이 없는 것 같네요.

남 아, 정말요? ⁴²미첼 씨가 추가되었을 거라고 말씀하셨는데요. 분명히 그렇게 하려고 하셨을 거예요.

여 그게, 저희가 최근에 소프트웨어를 변경했어요. ⁴³저희 관리자가 당신께 특별 출입증을 발급해 드릴 수 있어요. 제가 물어볼게요. 잠시만 기다려 주세요.

어휘

pick up ~을 찾다, 찾아오다 temporary 임시의, 일시적인
issue 발급하다

41.

남자는 무엇을 요청하는가?

(A) 주차권
(B) 신분증
(C) 업무 일정표
(D) 건물 안내도

어휘

identification 신원 확인, 신분 증명

패러프레이징

a temporary ID card → An identification card

42.

여자는 왜 "저희가 최근에 소프트웨어를 변경했어요"라고 말하는가?

(A) 문제를 설명하기 위해
(B) 제품을 추천하기 위해
(C) 대안을 제시하기 위해
(D) 동의를 나타내기 위해

어휘

alternative 대안, 다른 방도

43.

여자는 다음에 무엇을 할 것 같은가?

(A) 양식 확인하기
(B) 수리 기사 부르기
(C) 관리자에게 말하기
(D) 문서 출력하기

어휘

supervisor 감독, 관리자

패러프레이징

My manager ~ ask him → Speak to a supervisor

[44-46] 영녀 미남 호남 🎧

Questions 44-46 refer to the following conversation with three speakers.

W Hi, Ben and Leo. I heard an advertisement on the radio promoting Summit Theater's new screen. It's the largest one in town now. ⁴⁴That's going to make it even more difficult for our movie theater to stay competitive.

M1 That's not our only problem. ⁴⁵We've been getting a lot of bad reviews online from customers.

M2 ⁴⁵I'm worried about that, too. Most of them mention our uncomfortable seats.

W I know that's been an ongoing problem. Fortunately, we have room in the budget to replace them. ⁴⁶That's why I contacted Sinclair Interiors this morning. They'll be able to fit our project in right away even though it was a last-minute request. We can then advertise the seating upgrade after it's finished.

해석

44-46번은 다음 세 명의 대화에 관한 문제입니다.

여 벤, 레오, 안녕하세요. 제가 서밋 극장의 새 스크린을 홍보하는 라디오 광고를 들었는데요. 지금 이 동네에서 가장 크네요. ⁴⁴그건 우리 영화관이 경쟁력을 유지하는 걸 훨씬 더 어렵게 할 거예요.

남1 그게 우리의 유일한 문제가 아니에요. ⁴⁵우리는 고객들로부터 온라인에서 나쁜 평가를 많이 받고 있어요.

남2 ⁴⁵저도 그게 걱정이에요. 그들 대부분은 우리의 불편한 좌석을 언급하네요.

여 그게 지속적인 문제라는 걸 알아요. 다행히도, 그것들을 교체할 예산이 좀 있어요. ⁴⁶그래서 오늘 아침에 싱클레어 인테리어에 연락했어요. 막바지 요청이었지만 그들은 우리 프로젝트를 바로 맞춰 넣을 수 있을 거예요. 그러면 좌석 업그레이드가 완료된 후에 광고를 할 수 있어요.

어휘

promote 홍보하다 competitive 경쟁력 있는, 뒤지지 않는
mention 말하다; 언급, 거론 uncomfortable 불편한
ongoing 계속 진행 중인 fortunately 다행스럽게도
budget 예산 last-minute 마지막 순간의, 막바지의

44.

화자들은 어떤 종류의 업체에서 일하는가?

(A) 라디오 방송국
(B) 영화관
(C) 전자제품 매장
(D) 가구 제조사

어휘

electronics ((항상 복수형)) 전자제품

45.

남자들은 무엇에 대해 걱정을 나타내는가?

(A) 경쟁사의 낮은 가격

(B) 규정 변경

(C) 몇몇 좋지 않은 평가

(D) 몇몇 결근한 직원

어휘

competitor 경쟁자 regulation 규정, 단속

absent 결석한, 결근한; 결석하다

패러프레이징

bad → poor

46.

여자는 싱클레어 인테리어에 대해 무엇이라고 말하는가?

(A) 그곳은 촉박한 통보에도 작업할 수 있다.

(B) 그곳은 고품질 서비스를 제공한다.

(C) 그곳은 전에도 업체를 도와주었다.

(D) 그곳은 가장 저렴한 서비스를 제공한다.

어휘

short notice 촉박한 통보

패러프레이징

fit our project ~ a last-minute request

→ work on short notice

[47-49] 호남 영녀 🎧

Questions 47-49 refer to the following conversation.

> M Good morning. 47 I'm scheduled to meet Sandra Abbot, the factory manager.
>
> W That's me. You must be Matthew Dawson. I heard someone from the main office was coming for an inspection.
>
> M 48 I need to confirm that the machinery has been upgraded as required. Have you completed everything?
>
> W Yes. In fact, our crew got it done earlier than expected. We had planned for some obstacles, but the process went quite smoothly this time. 47 I can show you to the production floor.
>
> M Thank you. 49 I'll be turning in my report on Wednesday. I'll be sure to send you a copy as well for your records.

해석

47-49번은 다음 대화에 관한 문제입니다.

남 좋은 아침입니다. 47 공장장이신 샌드라 애벗 씨를 뵙기로 했습니다.

여 저예요. 매튜 도슨 씨군요. 본사에서 누군가가 시찰하러 오실 거라고 들었습니다.

남 48 기계가 필요에 따라 업그레이드되었는지 확인해야 합니다. 모두 완료하셨나요?

여 네. 사실 저희 직원들이 예상보다 일찍 일을 끝냈습니다. 저희는 몇 가지 장애에 대한 계획을 세웠지만, 이번에 그 과정이 상당히 순조롭게 진행되었습니다. 47 생산 현장까지 안내해 드릴 수 있습니다.

남 고맙습니다. 49 수요일에 보고서를 제출하겠습니다. 기록을 위해서 사본을 꼭 보내드리겠습니다.

어휘

be scheduled to ~할 예정이다 inspection 시찰, 검사

confirm 확인하다 machinery 기계, 기계류

as required 필요한 만큼 complete 완료하다, 마치다

obstacle 장애, 장애물 turn in ~을 제출하다

47.

화자들은 어디에 있는 것 같은가?

(A) 자동차 정비소에

(B) 진료소에

(C) 이사 업체에

(D) 제조 시설에

어휘

repair 수리; 수리하다 manufacture 제조하다; 제조

facility 시설

48.

남자는 무엇에 대해 질문하는가?

(A) 몇몇 직원들은 어디에서 찾을 수 있는지

(B) 몇몇 기계는 어떻게 조립되어야 하는지

(C) 주문은 언제 배송될 것인지

(D) 몇몇 업그레이드가 완료되었는지

어휘

assemble 조립하다, 모으다

패러프레이징

the machinery has been upgraded as required

→ some upgrades have been completed

49.

남자는 수요일에 무엇을 할 것인가?

(A) 설문지 작성하기

(B) 보고서 제출하기

(C) 시연하기

(D) 몇 개의 상자를 풀기

어휘

questionnaire 설문지 demonstration 실물 설명, 실연

unpack (짐을) 풀다, 꺼내다

패러프레이징

be turning in → Submit

[50-52] 미녀 미남 🎧

Questions 50-52 refer to the following conversation.

W Excuse me. ⁵⁰Do you happen to know if Bus 413 goes to Salinas Park?

M Yes, it stops right in front of the main entrance. You've just missed the bus, but another one will be along in about 15 minutes or so.

W Thank you. I've heard that Salinas Park has beautiful flower gardens, so I'd like to take some pictures there.

M Oh, but it'll be rainy all afternoon. ^{51, 52}If you don't want to get your equipment wet, you could check out the Newport Art Gallery instead.

W That might be better. I've never been there before.

M It's on Barron Street, about a five-minute walk north of the park.

W Thanks a lot.

해석

50-52번은 다음 대화에 관한 문제입니다.

여 실례합니다. ⁵⁰혹시 413번 버스가 샐리너스 공원에 가는지 아세요?

남 네, 그 버스는 정문 바로 앞에 정차합니다. 방금 버스를 놓치셨는데, 15분 정도 뒤에 다른 버스가 올 거예요.

여 고맙습니다. 샐리너스 공원에 아름다운 꽃밭이 있다고 해서, 거기서 사진을 좀 찍고 싶어요.

남 아, 그런데 오후 내내 비가 올 거예요. ^{51, 52}장비를 적시고 싶지 않으시다면, 대신에 뉴포트 미술관을 둘러보세요.

여 그게 더 낫겠네요. 저는 전에 거기에 가본 적이 한 번도 없거든요.

남 그곳은 공원에서 북쪽으로 5분 정도 걸어가면 되는 배론 가에 있어요.

여 정말 감사합니다.

어휘

in front of ~의 앞에 entrance 입구, 문
equipment 장비, 용품 check out 확인하다

50.

여자는 남자에게 무엇에 관해 묻는가?
(A) 지불 방법
(B) 입장료
(C) 폐점 시간
(D) 버스 노선

어휘

route 노선, 경로

패러프레이징

if Bus 413 goes to Salinas Park → A bus route

51.

남자는 "오후 내내 비가 올 거예요"라고 말할 때 무엇을 의미하는가?
(A) 평소보다 대기 시간이 더 길어질 수 있다.

(B) 여자는 계획을 바꿔야 할지도 모른다.
(C) 행사가 지연될 가능성이 있다.
(D) 그는 우산을 잃어버려서 실망했다.

어휘

disappointed 실망한, 낙담한

52.

남자는 어디로 갈 것을 추천하는가?
(A) 골동품 가게로
(B) 쇼핑센터로
(C) 미술관으로
(D) 극장으로

어휘

antique 골동품

[53-55] 미녀 호남 🎧

Questions 53-55 refer to the following conversation.

W Excuse me. I just saw a sign about an interior design service at the entrance. ⁵³I am particularly interested in doing some remodeling in my kitchen. Could you help me with that?

M Yes, of course. ⁵⁴I can set up an appointment with one of our designers who can visit your place.

W Great! My budget isn't very big, but I hope it will be enough for the project.

M Fortunately, this is the perfect time to book a service. ⁵⁵We are offering 15 percent off on any home improvement purchases this month.

W Sounds good. Please let me know when I can book the service. I'm free any weekday morning or anytime during the weekend.

해석

53-55번은 다음 대화에 관한 문제입니다.

여 실례합니다. 방금 입구에서 인테리어 디자인 서비스 안내판을 봤는데요. ⁵³저는 특히 주방 리모델링에 관심이 있어요. 그걸 도와주시겠어요?

남 네, 그럼요. ⁵⁴제가 고객님 댁을 방문할 수 있는 저희 디자이너 중 한 명과 약속을 잡아드릴 수 있습니다.

여 좋네요! 제 예산이 그리 크지 않지만, 그 프로젝트에 충분했으면 좋겠네요.

남 다행히, 지금이 서비스 예약에 최적의 시기입니다. ⁵⁵이번 달에 저희는 모든 주택 개조 서비스 구매에 대해 15% 할인을 제공합니다.

여 좋군요. 언제 서비스를 예약할 수 있는지 알려주세요. 저는 평일 오전이나 주말 아무 때나 괜찮습니다.

어휘

particularly 특히, 특별히 set up 잡다, 마련하다
budget 예산, 비용 book 예약하다 improvement 개량, 개선

purchase 구입, 구매

53.

여자는 무엇을 할 계획인가?

(A) 공간 개조하기
(B) 가전제품 구입하기
(C) 디자인 수업에 등록하기
(D) 새집으로 이사하기

어휘

renovate 개조하다   appliance 가전제품
enroll 등록하다, 입학하다

패러프레이징

doing some remodeling in my kitchen
→ Have a room renovated

54.

남자에 따르면, 여자는 무엇을 받을 수 있는가?

(A) 온라인 도구
(B) 현장 방문 상담
(C) 무료 샘플
(D) 연장된 보증

어휘

on-site 현장의, 현지의   consultation 상담, 상의
extended (기한을) 연장한   warranty 보증, 보증서

패러프레이징

an appointment with one of our designers who can
visit your place → An on-site consultation

55.

월말까지 무엇을 이용할 수 있는가?

(A) 고객 우대 카드
(B) 할부 제도
(C) 할인된 가격
(D) 특정 브랜드

어휘

installment 할부, 할부금   particular 특정한, 특별한

패러프레이징

offering 15 percent off → A discounted price

[56-58] 미남 영녀 호남 🎧

Questions 56-58 refer to the following conversation
with three speakers.

M1 We're excited to have you on our team,
Christine.
W Thanks! ⁵⁶ I enjoyed the tour of the orchard,
and I'm excited to learn about how the apples
are processed into cider.
M1 Scott and I will be showing you all of the steps
in the cider-making process today. ⁵⁷ It's very
important that our machines are kept clean.

We'll show you how to do that now. Right,
Scott?
M2 Yes, that's right. ⁵⁸ But I think it will be easier if
you take a look at the instruction manual first.
Here you are.
W Thanks.

해석

56-58번은 다음 세 명의 대화에 관한 문제입니다.
남1 크리스틴, 당신이 우리 팀에 합류하게 되어서 기뻐요.
여 고마워요! ⁵⁶ 과수원 견학은 즐거웠고, 사과가 어떻게 사이다로
가공되는지 알게 되어 신나요.
남1 스콧과 제가 오늘 사이다 제조 과정의 모든 단계를 보여드릴 거
예요. ⁵⁷ 기계를 깨끗하게 유지하는 게 매우 중요해요. 그 방법을
지금 보여드릴게요. 그렇죠, 스콧?
남2 네, 맞습니다. ⁵⁸ 하지만 사용 설명서를 먼저 보시면 더 쉬울 거라
생각합니다. 여기 있습니다.
여 고맙습니다.

어휘

orchard 과수원   process 가공하다, 처리하다
instruction manual 사용 설명서

56.

화자들은 어디에 있는 것 같은가?

(A) 식당에
(B) 실험실에
(C) 과수원에
(D) 여행사에

어휘

laboratory 실험실

57.

남자들은 여자에게 먼저 무엇을 하는 법을 가르칠 것인가?

(A) 기계 청소하기
(B) 소프트웨어 프로그램 사용하기
(C) 수리하기
(D) 결제 처리하기

패러프레이징

our machines are kept clean
→ Clean some machinery

58.

스콧은 여자에게 무엇을 주는가?

(A) 명함
(B) 보호 장비
(C) 명찰
(D) 사용자 설명서

어휘

protective gear 보호 장비

패러프레이징

the instruction manual → A user manual

Questions 59-61 refer to the following conversation.

> **M** Hello. ⁵⁹ I would like to reserve a table at your restaurant for four, tomorrow at 7 in the evening. Can we be seated with a view of the lake?
>
> **W** ⁵⁹ I'm sorry, but those tables are all booked up. You usually need to call at least a week in advance to reserve them. If you prefer, ⁶⁰ we do have rooms for you to dine in privacy at an additional charge of 25 dollars.
>
> **M** That is also a good idea. By the way, ⁶¹ do you have vegetarian-friendly options? It's for my coworker who can't eat meat.
>
> **W** There are three vegetarian pasta dishes, and we do also have a vegetarian burger called Granny's Burger.

해석

59-61번은 다음 대화에 관한 문제입니다.

남 안녕하세요. 내일 저녁 7시 ⁵⁹당신의 식당에 4인 테이블을 예약하고 싶은데요. 호수가 보이는 자리에 앉을 수 있을까요?

여 ⁵⁹죄송합니다만, 그 테이블은 모두 예약이 되어 있습니다. 보통 그 자리를 예약하시려면 적어도 일주일 전에는 연락하셔야 합니다. 원하시면, ⁶⁰25달러 추가 요금에 다른 사람들 없이 식사하실 수 있는 방이 있습니다.

남 그것도 좋네요. 그런데, ⁶¹채식주의자를 위한 메뉴가 있나요? 고기를 못 먹는 제 직장 동료를 위해서요.

여 채식 파스타 요리는 세 가지가 있고요, 그래니스 버거라는 채식 버거도 있습니다.

어휘

reserve 예약하다 be booked up 전부 예약되다
in advance 미리, 전부터 in privacy 비밀리에
additional charge 추가 요금
vegetarian-friendly 채식주의자에게 적합한
coworker 동료, 같이 일하는 사람

59.

여자는 누구인 것 같은가?
(A) 호텔 주인
(B) 유명한 요리사
(C) 식당 직원
(D) 행사 기획자

60.

남자는 분리된 방을 쓰려면 무엇을 해야 하는가?
(A) 멤버십 가입하기
(B) 적어도 일주일 전에 예약하기
(C) 단체로 업체 방문하기
(D) 추가 요금 지불하기

어휘

separate 분리된, 따로 떨어진 sign up for ~에 가입하다

패러프레이징

at an additional charge of 25 dollars
→ Pay an extra fee

61.

남자는 왜 메뉴에 관해 문의하고 있는가?
(A) 그는 온라인에서 메뉴를 찾을 수 없다.
(B) 그는 음식의 양에 대해 걱정하고 있다.
(C) 그가 가진 예산이 한정되어 있다.
(D) 그의 일행 중 누군가에게 식단 제약이 있다.

어휘

party 일행, 무리 dietary 식사의, 음식의 restriction 제한, 제약

패러프레이징

vegetarian-friendly options → dietary restrictions

Questions 62-64 refer to the following conversation and price list.

> **W** Hello. I'm looking to get a new cell phone plan. ⁶² I currently have the plan with 50 minutes. But I sometimes run out of minutes, so ⁶² I'd like the next level up.
>
> **M** ⁶² Are you sure you don't need unlimited minutes? Then you would never run out.
>
> **W** ⁶² That won't be necessary, thanks. It's already quite pricey for me. Also, I need to replace my phone, too. ⁶³ It stopped working yesterday, and I need it for my business.
>
> **M** Sure. Follow me to the display case. You're in luck. ⁶⁴ We just got a brand-new phone in today.

해석

62-64번은 다음 대화와 가격표에 관한 문제입니다.

여 안녕하세요. 저는 새로운 휴대폰 요금제를 찾고 있어요. ⁶²현재 50분 요금제를 사용 중이에요. 그런데 종종 시간이 소진되어서, ⁶²그다음 단계 요금제로 올리고 싶어요.

남 ⁶²무제한 시간이 필요하진 않으신가요? 그러면 소진될 일이 없거든요.

여 고맙지만, ⁶²그건 필요하지 않을 것 같아요. 이미 저한테 상당히 비싸거든요. 또한, 저는 휴대폰도 교체해야 해요. ⁶³어제 작동을 멈췄는데, 저는 업무를 위해 전화가 필요해요.

남 알겠습니다. 진열장까지 저를 따라오세요. 운이 좋으시네요. ⁶⁴오늘 막 신상 휴대폰이 들어왔어요.

어휘

currently 현재 run out of ~을 다 써버리다
unlimited 무제한의, 무한정의 pricey 값비싼
replace 교체하다, 대체하다
brand-new 완전 새것인, 아주 새로운

브론즈 요금제	50분	50달러
⁶² 실버 요금제	**100분**	**75달러**
골드 요금제	150분	85달러
플래티넘 요금제	무제한	100달러

62.

시각 자료를 보시오. 여자는 어떤 요금제에 가입할 것 같은가?

(A) 브론즈 요금제
(B) 실버 요금제
(C) 골드 요금제
(D) 플래티넘 요금제

63.

여자는 현재 휴대폰에 대해 무엇이라고 말하는가?

(A) 그것은 매우 비싸다.
(B) 그것은 사용하기 어렵다.
(C) 그것은 예상했던 것보다 크다.
(D) 그것은 제대로 작동하지 않는다.

어휘

function 작동하다; 기능 properly 제대로, 적절히

패러프레이징

stopped working → not functioning properly

64.

남자에 따르면, 오늘 일찍 가게에 무슨 일이 일어났는가?

(A) 새 모델이 배달되었다.
(B) 진열장이 파손되었다.
(C) 정책이 변경되었다.
(D) 기기가 반환되었다.

어휘

device 기기, 장치

패러프레이징

got a brand-new phone in
→ A new model was delivered

[65-67] 미녀 미남 🎧

Questions 65-67 refer to the following conversation and schedule.

> W ⁶⁵ We've run into a problem on the factory floor.
> M That's the last thing we need—the clients are going to be here in 10 minutes. What happened?
> W ⁶⁶ The wrapping machine has blown a belt and it's caused the whole line to shut down. It's going to take at least half an hour to fix it.
> M All right. ⁶⁷ Let Margaret know that we'll have to do the presentation right after the greetings and introductions. The facility tour can be later. That should give them enough time to fix it.

> W Sure. I'll talk to her now.
> M Thanks. And please tell me the minute the line starts back up.

해석

65-67번은 다음 대화와 일정표에 관한 문제입니다.

여 ⁶⁵공장 현장이 문제에 부딪쳤어요.

남 그건 우리가 원치 않는 일인데요. 고객들이 10분 뒤에 여기로 올 거예요. 무슨 일이죠?

여 ⁶⁶포장 기계의 벨트가 끊어져서 전체 라인이 중단되었어요. 고치는 데 적어도 30분은 걸릴 거예요.

남 알겠어요. ⁶⁷마거릿에게 인사와 소개가 끝나면 바로 발표를 해야 한다고 전해 주세요. 시설 견학은 나중에 해도 돼요. 그래야 고칠 시간이 충분할 거예요.

여 그렇죠. 지금 그녀에게 얘기할게요.

남 고마워요. 그리고 라인이 복구되면 즉시 저한테 알려주세요.

어휘

run into (문제 등에) 부딪치다 factory floor (공장의) 작업 현장
wrapping machine 포장 기계 cause ~을 야기하다
shut down 멈추다, 정지하다 presentation 발표
greetings 안부의 말, 인사 facility 시설

고객 방문 및 견학	
활동	시간
인사와 소개	오후 2시
공장 견학	**⁶⁷오후 2시 15분**
발표: 회사 역사	오후 2시 45분
커피와 디저트	오후 3시 15분

65.

이 대화는 어디에서 일어나고 있는 것 같은가?

(A) 대학교에서
(B) 채용 대행사에서
(C) 제조 공장에서
(D) 부동산 사무소에서

어휘

recruiting 채용 활동, 구인 활동 real estate 부동산

패러프레이징

the factory floor → a manufacturing plant

66.

여자는 어떤 문제를 언급하는가?

(A) 고객 방문이 연기되었다.
(B) 전기 문이 오작동한다.
(C) 판매 영수증이 분실되었다.
(D) 장비 하나가 고장 났다.

어휘

postpone 연기하다, 미루다 electric 전기의
malfunction 제대로 작동하지 않다 receipt 영수증

The wrapping machine has blown a belt
→ A piece of equipment has broken down

67.

시각 자료를 보시오. 발표는 언제 있을 것인가?

(A) 오후 2시에
(B) 오후 2시 15분에
(C) 오후 2시 45분에
(D) 오후 3시 15분에

[68-70] 미남 영녀 🎧

Questions 68-70 refer to the following conversation and floor plan.

> M Hi, Suzanne. I'm running a bit late, but I'm getting on the subway now. I'll be at McKinley Station by 10:30.
> W No problem. ⁶⁸ We can get to our 11 o'clock appointment with the real estate agent on time. I'm looking forward to looking around the office unit she suggested for us.
> M Me, too. I hope it will suit our business well. Where should I meet you?
> W ⁶⁹ I'll be waiting at the exit near the restrooms.
> M Okay, see you in about 15 minutes. Sorry to make you wait.
> W That's fine. ⁷⁰ I'd like to grab a coffee at the café first anyway.

해석

68-70번은 다음 대화와 평면도에 관한 문제입니다.

남 안녕하세요, 수잔. 좀 늦었지만, 지금 지하철을 타고 있어요. 저는 10시 30분까지 맥킨리역에 갈 거예요.
여 문제없어요. **⁶⁸ 우리는 부동산 중개인과의 11시 약속에 맞춰서 갈 수 있어요. 그녀가 우리에게 제안한 사무실 세대를 둘러보는 게 기대되네요.**
남 저도요. 그곳이 우리 사업과 잘 맞기를 바라요. 당신을 어디서 만나야 할까요?
여 **⁶⁹ 화장실 근처 출구에서 기다리고 있을게요.**
남 알겠어요. 약 15분 후에 봐요. 기다리게 해서 미안해요.
여 괜찮아요. **⁷⁰ 어차피 저는 먼저 카페에서 커피를 마시고 싶어요.**

어휘

run late 늦다 appointment (업무 관련) 약속
real estate 부동산 look forward to -ing ~하는 것을 기대하다

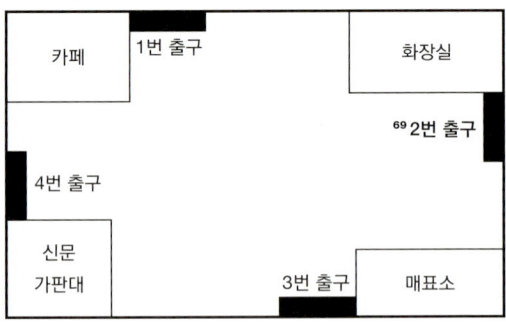

68.

화자들은 11시에 무엇을 할 계획인가?

(A) 비즈니스 과정에 참가하기
(B) 세미나 이끌기
(C) 상업용 부동산 둘러보기
(D) 투자자 만나기

어휘

participate in ~에 참가하다

패러프레이징

looking around the office unit
→ Tour a commercial property

69.

시각 자료를 보시오. 화자들은 어디에서 만날 것인가?

(A) 1번 출구에서
(B) 2번 출구에서
(C) 3번 출구에서
(D) 4번 출구에서

70.

여자는 무엇을 하고 싶다고 말하는가?

(A) 약속 일정 변경하기
(B) 음료 구입하기
(C) 주소 확인하기
(D) 선물 찾기

어휘

reschedule 일정을 변경하다 confirm 확인하다, 확정하다

패러프레이징

grab a coffee at the café → Purchase a beverage

PART 4

CHAPTER 01 문제 유형별 전략

UNIT 01 주제·목적 문제

CHECK UP
본문 p.204

1. (A) **2.** (C)

[1] 미남 🎧

Question 1 refers to the following announcement.

> **M** I want to remind you that there will be a short session on how to use the new internal phone system. We will meet in the conference room, and I will explain all of the new features to you. It took me longer than I expected to figure them all out. A member of the IT Department will also be on hand. So... uh... come prepared with any questions you might have. The session will take place on July 6th, at 2:30 P.M. I expect all employees to attend the session.

해석

1번은 다음 공지에 관한 문제입니다.

남 여러분에게 새로운 내부 전화 시스템을 사용하는 방법에 관한 짧은 시간을 가질 것임을 알려드리고자 합니다. 우리는 회의실에서 모일 것이고, 제가 여러분에게 모든 새로운 기능들을 설명할 것입니다. 제가 그 모든 걸 이해하는 데 예상보다 더 오래 걸렸습니다. IT 부서의 일원 한 명 역시 참석할 것입니다. 그러니... 어... 무슨 질문이든 있으시면 준비해 오시기 바랍니다. 이 시간은 7월 6일 오후 2시 30분에 열릴 것입니다. 모든 직원들이 이 시간에 참석하기를 기대합니다.

어휘

remind 알려 주다, 상기시키다
session (특정 활동을 위한) 시간, 회의 internal 내부의
feature 특징, 기능 figure out 이해하다
be on hand 참가하다 come prepared with ~을 준비해 오다
take place 개최되다, 일어나다 attend 참석하다

1.
화자는 무엇에 관해 이야기하고 있는가?
(A) 교육 시간
(B) 소프트웨어 오류
(C) 산업 학회
(D) 안내서

어휘

educational 교육의

패러프레이징

a short session on how to use the new internal phone system → An educational session

[2] 미녀 🎧

Question 2 refers to the following talk.

> **W** It's a pleasure to be here at this year's National Hospitality Trade Fair. My company produces environmentally friendly cleaning supplies for the hotel industry. Today I'd like to present our newest carpet cleaner. It's very effective, so it will save your housekeeping staff a lot of time. In addition, it has a pleasant smell and is made from all-natural ingredients. I'll be showing you how it can fight even the toughest stains. And don't forget to pick up a coupon for 25 percent off before you leave. Those are being distributed at our booth.

해석

2번은 다음 담화에 관한 문제입니다.

여 올해의 전국 접객 산업 박람회에 참석하게 되어 기쁩니다. 저희 회사는 호텔 산업을 위한 친환경 청소용품을 생산합니다. **오늘 저희의 최신 카펫 세척제를 보여 드리려고 합니다.** 매우 효과가 좋아서, 객실 관리 직원들의 시간을 상당히 절약해 줄 것입니다. 게다가, 냄새가 상쾌하고 천연 성분으로만 만들어졌습니다. 그것이 어떻게 잘 빠지지 않는 얼룩까지도 없앨 수 있는지 제가 여러분에게 보여 드리겠습니다. 그리고 나가시기 전에 25% 할인 쿠폰을 가져가시는 것을 잊지 마세요. 그것들은 저희 부스에서 배포되고 있습니다.

어휘

hospitality 접대, 환대 trade fair 산업 박람회
environmentally friendly 환경친화적인
cleaning supplies 청소용품 present 보여 주다, 제시하다
effective 효과적인 housekeeping 살림살이, 가사
pleasant 쾌적한, 즐거운 be made from ~으로 만들어지다
ingredient 재료, 성분 stain 얼룩
distribute 나누어 주다, 분배하다

2.
담화의 목적은 무엇인가?
(A) 직원들을 모집하기 위해
(B) 승진을 알리기 위해
(C) 제품을 소개하기 위해
(D) 고객 리뷰를 평가하기 위해

어휘

recruit (신입 사원 등을) 모집하다, 뽑다

job promotion 승진 assess 평가하다

패러프레이징

present our newest carpet cleaner
→ introduce a product

패러프레이징 **연습**	본문 p.206
1-4. 스크립트 참조 **5.** (A) **6.** (B)	

1.

Q 방송은 무엇에 관한 것인가?

A 보수 공사

미녀 🎧

> **W** At a press conference yesterday, city officials announced that renovations to the swimming facilities at the Filbert Recreation Center will begin in August. The interior of the pool will be retiled, and the filter system will be upgraded.

해석

여 어제 기자 회견에서, **시 공무원들은 필버트 레크리에이션 센터의 수영 시설에 대한 보수가 8월에 시작된다고 발표했습니다.** 수영장의 내부에 타일을 다시 깔고, 필터 시스템을 업그레이드할 것입니다.

어휘

renovation 수리, 보수 press conference 기자 회견
city official 시 공무원 facilities ((보통 복수형)) 편의 시설
interior 내부 retile 타일을 다시 깔다

패러프레이징

renovations to the swimming facilities at the Filbert Recreation Center → A renovation project

2.

Q 화자는 왜 청자들과 만나고 있는가?

A 서비스를 홍보하기 위해

미남 🎧

> **M** Hello, everyone, and thanks for attending this meeting. I appreciate this opportunity to tell you about Eastland Accounting. At Eastland Accounting, we provide bookkeeping services to small businesses in a variety of fields.

해석

남 안녕하세요, 여러분, 이번 모임에 참석해 주셔서 감사합니다. 이렇게 여러분에게 **이스트랜드 회계사무소에 대해 말씀드릴 기회**를 가지게 되어 감사하게 생각합니다. 이스트랜드 회계사무소에서는, 다양한 분야의 소기업들에게 **회계 장부 정리 서비스를 제공합니다.**

어휘

promote 홍보하다, 승진시키다 attend 참석하다
appreciate 고맙게 여기다 opportunity 기회
accounting 회계 bookkeeping 회계 장부 정리
field 분야

패러프레이징

tell you about ~ bookkeeping services
→ promote a service

3.

Q 무엇이 광고되고 있는 것 같은가?

A 상업용 부동산 중개 서비스

미녀 🎧

> **W** Are you hoping to find the perfect office space for a new business or looking to expand and need an additional location? Whatever you require, officesearch.com is the solution.

해석

여 새로운 사업체에 완벽한 사무 공간을 찾기를 바라시나요? 혹은 확장하거나 추가적인 장소가 필요할 예정인가요? 무엇이 필요하시든 officesearch.com이 해결책입니다.

어휘

commercial 상업의 real estate 부동산 (중개업)
look to ~할 예정이다, ~하기를 바라다 expand 확장하다
additional 추가적인 location 장소, 위치
require 필요하다, 요구하다 solution 해결책

패러프레이징

office space for a new business
→ commercial real estate

4.

Q 화자는 무엇에 관해 이야기하고 있는가?

A 웹사이트 업데이트

미남 🎧

> **M** Last on today's agenda, I wanted to let you know about some updates to the company's internal Web site. You can now track your working hours, request time off, and give feedback all in the same place.

해석

남 오늘 마지막 안건으로, **여러분에게 회사 내부 웹사이트의 일부 업데이트에 대해 알려드리고 싶습니다.** 여러분은 이제 근무 시간을 기록하고, 휴가를 신청하고, 의견을 제시하는 일 모두를 같은 곳에서 할 수 있습니다.

어휘

agenda 의제, 안건 internal 내부의 track 추적하다, 기록하다
time off 휴식 feedback 피드백, 의견

패러프레이징

some updates to the company's internal Web site
→ A Web site update

5.

화자는 왜 전화하고 있는가?

(A) 청자에게 함께 이동하자고 청하기 위해

(B) 청자에게 워크숍을 진행해 달라고 요청하기 위해

미남 🎧

> **M** Hello, Ms. Burke. This is Jack Kircher from the Oakland branch. I wanted to ask you if you'd like to carpool with me to this year's technology workshop in Los Angeles on the first weekend in June.

해석

남 안녕하세요, 버크 씨. 저는 오클랜드 지점의 잭 키르처입니다. 6월 첫째 주말에 로스앤젤레스에서 열리는 올해의 기술 워크숍에 저와 차를 같이 타고 가고 싶으신지 여쭤보고 싶습니다.

어휘

conduct (특정한 활동을) 하다, 지휘하다

패러프레이징

carpool with me to this year's technology workshop in Los Angeles → travel with him

6.

방송의 주제는 무엇인가?

(A) 두 사업체의 합병

(B) 회사의 지도부 변화

미녀 🎧

> **W** And now for the local news on Radio 107. Beverage producer Spritz Drinks confirmed that it has chosen Byungmin Lee to take over as CEO. Mr. Lee will contribute more than three decades of leadership experience to this role.

해석

여 라디오 107의 지역 뉴스 시간입니다. 음료 생산 회사인 스프리츠 드링크는 CEO 자리를 인계받을 사람으로 이병민 씨를 선택했다고 확인해 주었습니다. 이 씨는 30년 이상의 지도자 경험을 이 역할에 바칠 것입니다.

어휘

merger 합병 leadership (조직의) 지도부 beverage 음료 producer 생산자, 생산 회사 confirm 확인해 주다, 확정하다 take over as ~의 자리를 이어받다 contribute to ~에 기여하다 decade 10년

패러프레이징

it has chosen Byungmin Lee to take over as CEO
→ A leadership change

---

1. (D)	**2.** (C)	**3.** (C)	**4.** (A)	**5.** (B)

[1] 미남 🎧

Question 1 refers to the following broadcast.

> **M** Good morning. You're listening to KWRP's morning business report. Brook Services announced today that it will now be known as Brook Equity Research. The company has been the industry's leading provider of investment research for the last 32 years. The reason for the change is that its name should accurately reflect its services. President Donald Vance states that the company will grow by nearly 10 percent in the coming year. Investors are looking forward to this growth.

해석

1번은 다음 방송에 관한 문제입니다.

남 안녕하세요. 여러분은 KWRP의 아침 경제 보도를 듣고 계십니다. 브룩 서비스가 이제 브룩 자산 연구로 알려지게 될 것이라고 오늘 발표했습니다. 이 회사는 지난 32년간 투자 연구 업계의 선도적인 공급 업체였습니다. 변화의 이유는 회사의 이름이 회사의 서비스를 정확하게 반영해야 하기 때문입니다. 도널드 밴스 회장은 회사가 다가오는 해에 거의 10%까지 성장할 것이라고 말합니다. 투자자들은 이 같은 성장을 고대하고 있습니다.

어휘

be known as ~로 알려지다 equity 자산, 지분 leading 선도적인, 이끄는 provider 공급자 investment 투자 accurately 정확히 reflect 반영하다 state 말하다 look forward to ~을 기대하다 growth 성장

1.

뉴스 보도는 주로 무엇에 관한 것인가?

(A) 회사의 인수

(B) 신규 공장

(C) 제품 리뷰

(D) 회사 이름 변경

어휘

acquisition (기업) 인수

패러프레이징

it will now be known as Brook Equity Research
→ A company's name change

[2-3] 미녀 🎧

Questions 2-3 refer to the following advertisement.

W Are you planning to get away for a relaxing weekend? Well, now is your chance to go at a great price. ²Luxurious Skytop Grounds is offering 40 percent off all room rates through the end of March. We've never offered such great prices. ²Choose from our many daily activities, or simply lounge by one of our pools. And, speaking of pools, ³we've just finished upgrading our outdoor Olympic-size pool. Every night is filled with entertainment to please all ages at Skytop Grounds. Visit our Web site today at www.skytopgrounds.com.

해석

2-3번은 다음 광고에 관한 문제입니다.

여 느긋한 주말을 위해 휴가를 갈 계획이신가요? 그렇다면, 지금이 아주 좋은 가격에 가실 기회입니다. ²럭셔리어스 스카이탑 그라운드 사가 3월 말까지 모든 객실 요금을 40% 할인해 드립니다. 저희는 이렇게 좋은 가격을 제공한 적이 없습니다. ²저희의 여러 가지 일일 활동 중에서 고르시거나 그저 저희 수영장 중 하나에서 느긋하게 쉬세요. 그리고, 수영장으로 말하자면, ³저희가 막 올림픽 규격의 야외 수영장의 업그레이드를 마쳤습니다. 매일 밤 스카이탑 그라운드에 머무시는 모든 연령층을 기쁘게 해 드릴 오락 거리가 가득합니다. www.skytopgrounds.com으로 오늘 저희 웹사이트를 방문하세요.

어휘

get away 휴가를 가다 relaxing 마음을 느긋하게 해 주는, 편한
rate 요금 daily 매일 일어나는 activity 활동
lounge 느긋하게 있다 outdoor 야외의
Olympic-size 올림픽 규격의 be filled with ~으로 가득 차다
entertainment 오락, 여흥

2.
무엇이 광고되고 있는가?
(A) 도보 여행
(B) 유람선 여행
(C) 휴양지 여행 상품
(D) 항공편

3.
이 업체에 최근에 어떤 변화가 일어났는가?
(A) 부지가 확장되었다.
(B) 일부 식사 메뉴가 개선되었다.
(C) 수영장이 보수되었다.
(D) 야외 활동이 추가되었다.

어휘

improve 개선하다, 향상시키다 renovate 수리하다

패러프레이징

finished upgrading our outdoor Olympic-size pool → A pool was renovated

[4-5] 미남 🎧

Questions 4-5 refer to the following telephone message.

M Hello, this is Travis Kurowski. In March, ⁴I hired your company to replace my gravel driveway with a paved one. ⁵It looked great when you finished, but now it's cracking and there are some holes forming. It's only been two months, so... this is distressing. According to your policy on your Web site, you guarantee a response to any complaints within 24 hours. Please call me as soon as you get this. My number's 555-2289. Thank you.

해석

4-5번은 다음 전화 메시지에 관한 문제입니다.

남 안녕하세요, 저는 트레비스 쿠로스키입니다. 3월에, ⁴제 자갈 진입로를 포장 진입로로 교체하기 위해 귀사를 고용했습니다. ⁵작업을 끝냈을 때는 아주 좋아 보였지만, 지금은 금이 가고 구멍들이 좀 생겼습니다. 고작 2개월 됐는데 말이죠, 그래서... 이것 때문에 몹시 신경이 쓰입니다. 귀사의 웹사이트상의 정책에 따르면, 어떤 불만 사항이든 24시간 이내에 응대할 것을 보장하고 있습니다. 이것을 들으시는 대로 제게 전화 주시기 바랍니다. 제 번호는 555-2289입니다. 감사합니다.

어휘

hire 고용하다 replace A with B A를 B로 교체하다
gravel 자갈 driveway 진입로 paved (도로가) 포장된
crack 갈라지다, 금이 가다 form 형성되다, 형성시키다
distressing 괴로움을 주는, 고통스러운
guarantee 보장하다, 약속하다 response 응답, 회신
complaint 항의, 불만

4.
화자는 어떤 종류의 업체에 전화하고 있는가?
(A) 주택 개조 회사
(B) 자동차 대리점
(C) 통신 회사
(D) 배관 서비스

어휘

home improvement 주택 개조 dealership (승용차) 대리점
telecommunication 통신 plumbing 배관 작업

패러프레이징

company to replace my gravel driveway with a paved one → A home improvement company

5.
화자는 왜 전화하고 있는가?
(A) 공석인 일자리에 관해 문의하기 위해
(B) 항의를 제기하기 위해
(C) 배송지를 변경하기 위해
(D) 제품 가격을 알아보기 위해

어휘

inquire about ~에 관해 문의하다

file a complaint 항의를 제기하다 find out ~을 알아내다

본문 p.208

실전 문제

1. (D)	**2.** (B)	**3.** (D)	**4.** (C)	**5.** (C)
6. (A)	**7.** (B)	**8.** (D)	**9.** (C)	**10.** (D)
11. (A)	**12.** (C)	**13.** (B)	**14.** (B)	**15.** (C)
16. (D)	**17.** (C)	**18.** (A)		

[1-3] 미녀 🎧

Questions 1-3 refer to the following advertisement.

W Are you looking for a way to make household chores easier? ¹Do you want to help Rigby Incorporated improve our vacuum cleaner? ²Then why not sign up to become a product tester? If you're currently running your own blog, you're eligible to join the campaign. Just use our new vacuum at home and give us feedback. ²You can sign up at our Web site, www.rigbyinc.net. You'll get to keep the device, and you'll also get a voucher to use toward your next purchase. ³This will be sent by e-mail and can be used instantly.

해석

1-3번은 다음 광고에 관한 문제입니다.

여 집안일을 더 쉽게 하는 방법을 찾고 계시나요? ¹릭비 사가 진공청소기를 개선하는 것을 돕고 싶으신가요? ²그렇다면 제품 테스터가 되기 위해 신청하시는 게 어떠세요? 현재 자신의 블로그를 운영하고 계시다면, 이 캠페인에 참여할 자격이 있습니다. 그저 집에서 새 진공청소기를 써 보시고 의견을 주시면 됩니다. ²저희 웹사이트 www.rigbyinc.net에서 신청하실 수 있습니다. 이 기기는 계속 가지시게 되며, 다음 번 구입 시 이용할 수 있도록 상품권도 받으시게 됩니다. ³이것은 이메일로 발송될 것이고 즉시 사용할 수 있습니다.

어휘

household chores 집안일 improve 개선하다, 향상시키다
vacuum cleaner 진공청소기 sign up 가입하다, 신청하다
tester 시험하는 사람 currently 현재 run 운영하다, 경영하다
be eligible to ~할 자격이 있다 device 장치, 기구
voucher 상품권, 할인권 instantly 즉시

1.

광고는 무엇에 관한 것인가?
(A) 에어컨
(B) 냉장고
(C) 식기세척기
(D) 진공청소기

2.

청자들은 왜 이 회사의 웹사이트를 방문해야 하는가?
(A) 영상을 시청하기 위해
(B) 제품 테스터가 되기 위해
(C) 의견을 남기기 위해
(D) 매장 목록을 보기 위해

3.

상품권에 대해 무엇이 언급되는가?
(A) 어떻게 생겼는지
(B) 얼마의 가치가 있는지
(C) 언제 만료될지
(D) 어떻게 발송될지

어휘

worth ~의 가치가 있는 expire 만료되다

[4-6] 영녀 🎧

Questions 4-6 refer to the following excerpt from a meeting.

W Good afternoon, everyone. ⁴I'm happy to announce that we've just received confirmation that the merger between our company and Cervantes Industries has been finalized. A representative from Cervantes Industries will visit our office on April 7 to find out more about each person's role. ⁵He will be asking for a lot of details, but don't think this means he is doubting your abilities. Um... He doesn't know much about our operations. I'll send you an e-mail with more information, but I'm afraid I can't stay to answer questions. ⁶I have to leave before the meeting is over to have a conference call.

해석

4-6번은 다음 회의 발췌록에 관한 문제입니다.

여 안녕하세요, 여러분. ⁴우리 회사와 세르반테스 인더스트리 사의 합병이 마무리되었다는 확인을 받았음을 알려 드리게 되어 기쁩니다. 세르반테스 인더스트리 사의 대표가 4월 7일 우리 사무실을 방문하여 각자의 역할에 대해 더 많이 알아볼 것입니다. ⁵그가 많은 세부 정보들을 요청하겠지만, 이것이 여러분의 기량을 의심하고 있다는 뜻이라고 생각하지 마세요. 음... 그는 우리 사업에 대해 많이 알지 못합니다. 제가 더 많은 정보가 담긴 이메일을 보내 드리겠지만, 유감스럽게도 질문에 대답하기 위해 여기에 있을 수가 없습니다. ⁶전화 회의를 하기 위해 이 회의가 끝나기 전에 떠나야 합니다.

어휘

confirmation 확인 merger (기업의) 합병
finalize 마무리 짓다, 완결하다 representative 대표(자), 대리인
ability 재능, 기량 operation 사업, 영업
conference call 전화 회의

4.

회의의 주제는 무엇인가?

(A) 사생활 보호 정책

(B) 일자리 공석

(C) 기업 합병

(D) 자금 삭감

privacy 사생활, 프라이버시 corporate 기업의, 회사의

reduction 축소, 삭감

패러프레이징

the merger between our company and Cervantes
Industries → A corporate merger

5.

화자는 왜 "그는 우리 사업에 대해 많이 알지 못합니다"라고 말하는가?

(A) 오류를 설명하기 위해

(B) 시간을 더 요청하기 위해

(C) 안심시키기 위해

(D) 결정을 비판하기 위해

어휘

reassurance 안심시킴, 안도 criticize 비판하다

6.

화자는 왜 지금 질문에 대답할 수 없는가?

(A) 그녀는 일찍 회의에서 나와야 한다.

(B) 그녀는 일부 정보가 기밀이라고 생각한다.

(C) 그녀는 교육 프로그램을 이수해야 한다.

(D) 그녀는 고객으로부터 답장을 기다리고 있다.

어휘

confidential 기밀의, 비밀의 complete 완료하다, 끝마치다

reply 대답, 답장

패러프레이징

leave before the meeting is over
→ leave the meeting early

[7-9] 미남 🎧

Questions 7-9 refer to the following excerpt from a
meeting.

> M **7** Next on our agenda is to let you know who
> has been selected as our new marketing
> director. We're pleased to promote Arthur Allen
> to this position, and we are confident that he
> will do an excellent job. **8** He has been working
> in this industry for a long time. To celebrate
> Mr. Allen's achievement, we're going to have
> **9** a company lunch tomorrow at the Beluga
> Restaurant. **9** If you'd like to join in, please
> e-mail me by the end of the day so I can
> reserve the right number of seats.

해석

7-9번은 다음 회의 발췌록에 관한 문제입니다.

남 **7** 다음 안건으로 여러분에게 우리의 신임 마케팅부장으로 누가 선발되었는지 알려 드리겠습니다. 우리는 이 자리에 아서 앨런을 승진시키게 되어 기쁘며, 그가 훌륭히 직무를 수행할 것이라고 확신합니다. **8** 그는 오랜 시간 이 업계에서 일해 왔습니다. 앨런 씨의 성취를 축하하기 위해, 내일 벨루가 레스토랑에서 **9** 점심 회식을 하려고 합니다. **9** 함께하시고 싶으시면, 제가 정확한 좌석 수를 예약할 수 있도록 오늘 업무를 마칠 때까지 **9** 제게 이메일을 보내 주세요.

어휘

agenda 안건, 의제 promote 승진시키다, 홍보하다

confident 확신하는 celebrate 기념하다, 축하하다

achievement 업적, 성취한 것 join in 함께 ~을 하다

reserve 예약하다

7.

담화의 목적은 무엇인가?

(A) 상을 수여하기 위해

(B) 승진을 알리기 위해

(C) 마케팅 캠페인을 소개하기 위해

(D) 일부 팀원들에게 감사하기 위해

어휘

promotion 승진, 홍보

패러프레이징

let you know who has been selected as our new
marketing director → announce a promotion

8.

화자는 앨런 씨에 대해 무엇이라고 말하는가?

(A) 그는 회사의 창립 멤버였다.

(B) 그는 다른 지점에서 옮겨 올 것이다.

(C) 그는 최근에 책을 출판했다.

(D) 그는 경험이 많다.

어휘

founding member 창립 멤버

transfer from ~에서 옮기다, 옮겨지다 publish 출판하다

패러프레이징

has been working in this industry for a long time
→ has a lot of experience

9.

청자들은 왜 화자에게 이메일을 보내야 하는가?

(A) 교육을 신청하기 위해

(B) 행사 장소를 제안하기 위해

(C) 식사에 참여하기 위해

(D) 질문을 공유하기 위해

어휘

sign up for ~을 신청하다 training session 교육 (과정)

venue (행사의) 장소 participate in ~에 참가하다

패러프레이징

a company lunch ~ join in → participate in a meal

[10-12] 호남 🎧

Questions 10-12 refer to the following broadcast.

> M Thanks for tuning in to Radio 92.4. ¹⁰In local news, yesterday, the city held its annual volunteer event to pick up trash at Raeford Beach. Nearly one hundred people donated their time. ¹¹Participants received a free ticket to an upcoming Lexington Bobcats baseball game. ¹²Some of the trash will be made into sculptures by Layla Fenbury to raise awareness about the problem. These sculptures will be exhibited at the Goldpoint Museum later this summer.

해석

10-12번은 다음 방송에 관한 문제입니다.

남 라디오 92.4를 청취해 주셔서 감사합니다. ¹⁰지역 뉴스를 전해 드리겠습니다. 어제, 시는 래포드 해변에서 쓰레기를 줍는 연례 자원봉사 행사를 개최했습니다. 거의 100명의 사람들이 그들의 시간을 기부했습니다. ¹¹참가자들은 다가오는 렉싱턴 보브캣츠 야구 경기의 무료 티켓을 받았습니다. ¹²문제에 대한 인식을 높이기 위해 쓰레기의 일부는 라일라 펜버리에 의해 조각품들로 만들어질 것입니다. 이 조각품들은 올여름 늦게 골드포인트 박물관에서 전시될 것입니다.

어휘

annual 연례의 donate 기부하다, 기증하다 participant 참가자
upcoming 다가오는, 곧 있을 sculpture 조각(품)
raise awareness 의식을 고취시키다 exhibit 전시하다; 전시

10.

방송은 주로 무엇에 관한 것인가?
(A) 노래 경연 대회
(B) 지역사회 모금 행사
(C) 개업식
(D) 해변 대청소 프로젝트

어휘

fund-raiser 모금 행사 grand opening 개장, 개점
cleanup 대청소

패러프레이징

its annual volunteer event to pick up trash at Raeford Beach → A beach cleanup project

11.

무엇이 참가자들에게 주어졌는가?
(A) 경기 티켓
(B) 가방
(C) 물병
(D) 상점 쿠폰

패러프레이징

a free ticket to an upcoming Lexington Bobcats baseball game → A game ticket

12.

화자에 따르면, 펜버리 씨는 무엇을 준비할 것인가?
(A) 온라인 워크숍
(B) 음악 공연
(C) 박물관 전시
(D) 사진 모음집

패러프레이징

be exhibited at the Goldpoint Museum
→ A museum exhibit

[13-15] 미남 🎧

Questions 13-15 refer to the following excerpt from a meeting.

> M Good morning, everyone. ¹³I called this meeting because there is an urgent need for us to change the way our commissions are paid to salespeople. ¹⁴Gene Richmond, who is in charge of hiring at our company, has reported that he is having a lot of trouble recruiting skilled salespeople. That's... uh... that's because our compensation package is not competitive compared to other companies in our industry. Now, you may think we're spending enough already, but the sales process is quite involved. ¹⁵I've invited our sales director, John Norris, to give a brief explanation of each step. I hope that will give you some insight into how hard his team is working.

해석

13-15번은 다음 회의 발췌록에 관한 문제입니다.

남 안녕하세요, 여러분. ¹³우리의 수수료가 판매원들에게 지급되는 방식을 변경해야 한다는 긴급한 요구가 있어서 이번 회의를 소집했습니다. ¹⁴우리 회사에서 고용을 담당하고 있는 진 리치먼드가 숙련된 판매원들을 모집하는 데 많은 어려움을 겪고 있다고 알려 왔습니다. 그것은... 어... 그것은 우리의 보수가 우리 업계의 다른 회사들과 비교해 경쟁력이 없기 때문입니다. 자, 여러분은 우리가 이미 충분히 지출하고 있다고 생각하실 수도 있지만, 판매 과정이 상당히 복잡합니다. ¹⁵제가 우리 영업 부장인 존 노리스에게 각 단계를 간단히 설명해 달라고 부탁했습니다. 이것이 그의 팀이 얼마나 힘들게 일하고 있는지에 대해 여러분이 이해할 수 있게 해 줄 것으로 기대합니다.

어휘

call a meeting 회의를 소집하다 urgent 긴급한
commission 수수료, 커미션 be in charge of ~을 담당하다
have trouble -ing ~하는 데 어려움을 겪다
recruit (신입 사원 등을) 모집하다 skilled 숙련된, 노련한

compensation package (급여와 복리후생을 포함한) 보수
competitive 경쟁력 있는 involved 복잡한, 뒤얽힌
insight into ~에 관한 통찰력, 이해

13.

회의의 목적은 무엇인가?

(A) 광고 전략을 기획하기 위해

(B) 수수료 구조를 조정하기 위해

(C) 고객 의견을 분석하기 위해

(D) 신입 직원을 교육하기 위해

어휘

strategy 전략 adjust 조정하다, 조절하다 structure 구조
analyze 분석하다

패러프레이징

change the way our commissions are paid
→ adjust a commission structure

14.

진 리치먼드는 누구인 것 같은가?

(A) 사업주

(B) 고용 담당자

(C) 프리랜서 작가

(D) 판매원

패러프레이징

in charge of hiring → A hiring manager

15.

청자들은 다음에 무엇을 할 것 같은가?

(A) 계약서 검토하기

(B) 투표하기

(C) 담화 듣기

(D) 시장 동향에 대해 이야기하기

어휘

contract 계약(서)

[16-18] 영녀 🎧

Questions 16-18 refer to the following telephone message and map.

> W Hi, Mr. Lowry. This is Kimberly from Valley Landscaping. **16 I wanted to let you know that I've finished assessing the flower beds at your property.** The good news is that most of them are healthy. However, **17 the rose bushes planted in the bed closest to the entrance of your building have an issue.** There are black spots on the leaves. They will need a special treatment to prevent further damage. **18 There are some products that you can spray on them yourself. I'll e-mail you a list of those after lunch.** If you need any further help, just let me know.

해석

16-18번은 다음 전화 메시지와 지도에 관한 문제입니다.

여 안녕하세요, 로리 씨. 저는 밸리 조경의 킴벌리입니다. **16 당신이 소유하신 건물의 화단들을 평가하는 일을 마쳤음을 알려 드리고자 합니다.** 좋은 소식은 그것들 대부분이 건강하다는 것입니다. 하지만, **17 건물 입구에서 가장 가까운 화단에 심은 장미 관목은 문제가 있습니다.** 잎들에 검은 점들이 있습니다. 더 이상의 손상을 막기 위해 특별한 처치가 필요할 것입니다. **18 직접 잎에 뿌리실 수 있는 몇몇 제품들이 있습니다.** 제가 점심시간 이후에 그것들의 목록을 이메일로 보내 드리겠습니다. 도움이 더 필요하시면, 알려 주세요.

어휘

landscaping 조경 assess 평가하다 bed 화단, 모판
property 부동산, 건물 bush 관목, 덤불 entrance 입구, 문
treatment 처치, 치료 prevent 막다, 예방하다
damage 손상, 피해 spray 뿌리다, 살포하다

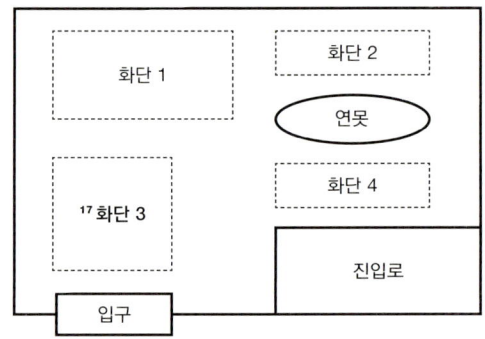

로리 씨의 정원

16.

화자는 왜 전화하고 있는가?

(A) 후기에 대해 청자에게 감사하기 위해

(B) 새로운 서비스를 소개하기 위해

(C) 업무 지연에 대해 사과하기 위해

(D) 평가 결과를 알려 주기 위해

어휘

assessment 평가

패러프레이징

let you know that I've finished assessing the flower beds → give the results of an assessment

17.

시각 자료를 보시오. 화자는 어떤 화단에 대해 우려하는가?

(A) 화단 1

(B) 화단 2

(C) 화단 3

(D) 화단 4

어휘

driveway 진입로

18.

화자는 오늘 오후에 무엇을 할 것인가?

(A) 제품 목록 보내기
(B) 사진 찍기
(C) 꽃 주문하기
(D) 청자 방문하기

패러프레이징

some products that you can spray on them ~ e-mail you a list of those → Send a product list

UNIT 02 화자·청자·장소 문제

CHECK UP
본문 p.210

1. (D)   **2.** (C)

[1] 미녀 🎧

Question 1 refers to the following announcement.

> **W** For those of you who had planned to pay for your appointment by credit card, please note that we are having some issues with our machine. You can still see the dentist as usual. However, we may have to send you a bill later for the service you receive today. If your treatment is covered by insurance, it will be processed as usual. We apologize for any inconvenience this may cause. If you have any questions, please talk to someone in reception. Thank you.

해석

1번은 다음 공지에 관한 문제입니다.

여 진료비를 신용카드로 결제하실 계획이었던 분들은 저희 기계에 문제가 좀 있다는 점을 유념해 주시기 바랍니다. **평소처럼 치과 진료를 받을 수는 있습니다.** 하지만, 오늘 받으시는 진료 서비스에 대한 청구서를 나중에 보내 드려야 할 수도 있습니다. 만약 치료가 보험으로 처리된다면, 평소처럼 처리될 것입니다. 이로 인한 모든 불편에 사과드립니다. 질문이 있으시면, 접수 담당자에게 말씀하시기 바랍니다. 감사합니다

어휘

note ~에 주목하다, 주의하다 dentist 치과 의사
as usual 평소대로 bill 청구서 treatment 치료
covered by insurance 보험에 들어 있는 process 처리하다
apologize for ~에 대해 사과하다 inconvenience 불편
reception 접수처

1.

청자들은 어디에 있는 것 같은가?

(A) 연구소에
(B) 미용실에
(C) 헬스장에
(D) 치과에

어휘

research laboratory 연구소

[2] 미남 🎧

Question 2 refers to the following radio broadcast.

> **M** Good afternoon. I'm Christopher Boden, host of the *Garden Corner* show here on WTTR Radio. Today I'm going to talk to you about caring for your outdoor plants in the summer. It all starts with good planning. Certain plants simply cannot stand a lot of direct sunlight, so you need to plant your garden accordingly. During the show, I'll tell you the best plants for sunny areas as well as those that love the shade. I'll also give you tips on keeping the soil moist enough in dry weather. There's plenty to learn, so stay tuned.

해석

2번은 다음 라디오 방송에 관한 문제입니다.

남 안녕하세요. **저는 이곳 WTTR 라디오의 〈가든 코너〉 진행자인 크리스토퍼 보덴입니다.** 오늘 저는 여름철 옥외 식물들을 관리하는 법에 관해 얘기하려고 합니다. 이 모든 것은 올바른 계획으로 시작됩니다. 어떤 식물은 다량의 직사광선조차 견딜 수 없기 때문에, 그에 맞춰 정원에 식물을 심어야 합니다. 프로그램이 진행되는 동안, 음지를 좋아하는 식물들은 물론 양지에 가장 적합한 식물들도 알려 드리겠습니다. 또한 건조한 날씨에 토양을 충분히 촉촉하게 유지하는 비법도 전해 드리겠습니다. 배울 것들이 많으니 채널 고정해 주세요.

어휘

care for ~를 보살피다 stand 견뎌내다
direct sunlight 태양 직사광
accordingly (상황에) 부응해서, 그에 맞춰 tip on ~의 비결, 비법
moist 촉촉한 plenty 풍부한 양

2.

화자는 누구인가?

(A) 텔레비전 연출자
(B) 정부 공무원
(C) 라디오 진행자
(D) 부동산 관리인

어휘

official 공무원, 관리 property 부동산, 재산

패러프레이징 연습
본문 p.212

1-4. 스크립트 참조   **5.** (B)   **6.** (A)

1.

Q 청자들은 어디에 있는가?

A 요리 교실에

미녀 🎧

> **W** Welcome, everyone, to Home Italian. I'm Gina, and I'm looking forward to teaching you how to make delicious dishes in this cooking series. For our first class, you'll learn how to make a simple tomato-based sauce that tastes great on pasta.

해석

여 홈 이탈리안에 오신 모든 분들을 환영합니다. 저는 지나이고, **이 요리 시리즈에서 맛있는 요리를 만드는 법을 가르치기를 고대하고 있습니다.** 우리의 첫 번째 수업에서는, 파스타와 먹으면 맛이 아주 좋은, 토마토를 베이스로 한 간단한 소스를 만드는 법을 배우게 됩니다.

어휘

look forward to ~을 기대하다 dish 요리, 접시

패러프레이징

teaching you how to make delicious dishes
→ a cooking class

2.

Q 청자들은 누구인 것 같은가?

A 판매원

미남 🎧

> **M** You're all doing a great job with appliance sales, and this is our best month so far. Now, you should know that we're offering a great deal on Omaha brand dishwashers. When customers ask you for suggestions, please be sure to mention this promotion.

해석

남 **여러분 모두 전자제품 판매를 잘 해주고 계시며,** 지금은 이제껏 실적이 가장 좋은 달입니다. 이제, 우리가 오마하 브랜드의 식기세척기를 아주 싼 가격에 제공한다는 것을 숙지하셔야 합니다. 고객들이 추천을 해 달라고 하면, 반드시 이번 판촉 행사를 언급하시기 바랍니다.

어휘

appliance (가정용) 기기
offer a great deal on ~을 아주 싼 가격에 제공하다
mention 언급하다 promotion 판촉

3.

Q 화자는 누구인가?

A 회사 회장

미녀 🎧

> **W** Good afternoon. As president of Macon Technology, I'm delighted to be presenting at this shareholder's meeting. We have a lot of exciting news about projects for the upcoming year that I'm going to share with you today.

해석

여 안녕하세요, 메이컨 테크놀로지 사의 회장으로서, 저는 이번 주주 회의에서 발표하게 되어 매우 기쁩니다. 오늘 여러분과 함께 나눌, 다가오는 해의 프로젝트에 관한 흥미로운 소식들이 많습니다.

어휘

delighted 아주 기뻐하는 present 발표하다, 보여 주다
shareholder 주주 upcoming 다가오는, 곧 있을

패러프레이징

president of Macon Technology
→ A company president

4.

Q 견학은 어디에서 이루어지고 있는가?

A 도자기 공장에서

미남 🎧

> **M** It is my pleasure to welcome you all to Layton Manufacturing. Our town is known for the beautiful ceramics produced by its factories. The tradition has been carried on for over a hundred years.

해석

남 여러분 모두를 레이턴 제조사에 모시게 되어 기쁩니다. 저희 마을은 이곳의 공장들에서 생산하는 아름다운 도자기로 유명합니다. 이 전통은 100년 이상 계속되어 왔습니다.

어휘

ceramics ((항상 복수형)) 도예, 도자기류
manufacturing 제조업 be known for ~로 알려져 있다
tradition 전통 carry on ~을 계속하다

5.

화자는 어떤 종류의 회사에서 일하는가?

(A) 광고 대행사

(B) 법률 회사

미녀 🎧

> **W** Hi, Mr. Schriver. This is Crystal Miller from Denby Attorneys. I wanted to give you an update about the proposed purchase of your competitor's Web site. Our legal team has made some suggested changes to the contract to better protect your interests.

해석

여 안녕하세요, 슈라이버 씨. **저는 덴비 변호사 사무실의 크리스털 밀러입니다.** 경쟁사 웹사이트 구매 제안에 관한 최신 소식을 전해 드리고 싶었습니다. 당신의 이익을 좀 더 잘 보호하기 위해 저희 법률팀이 일부 변경 제안사항을 만들었습니다.

어휘

attorney 변호사 give an update 최신 소식을 전하다
proposed 제안된 competitor 경쟁사, 경쟁자 legal 법의
contract 계약(서) interests ((보통 복수형)) 이익

패러프레이징

Denby Attorneys → A law firm

6.
공지는 어디에서 이루어지고 있는가?
(A) 식료품점에서
(B) 식당에서

미남 🎧

> M Attention, all Rubio Supermarket shoppers. We have just found a phone near the baked goods section. If it is yours, please come to the customer service area to identify it. Thank you.

해석

남 **모든 루비오 슈퍼마켓 고객들에게 알려 드립니다.** 저희가 방금 제빵 코너 근처에서 전화기를 발견했습니다. 자신의 것이라면, 고객 서비스 구역으로 오셔서 확인하시기 바랍니다. 감사합니다.

어휘

baked goods 제빵류 section 부분, 부문 identify 확인하다

패러프레이징

Rubio Supermarket → a grocery store

연습 문제 본문 p.213

1. (B) **2.** (D) **3.** (A) **4.** (A) **5.** (D)

[1] 호남 🎧
Question 1 refers to the following announcement.

> M Hello and thank you for attending the North Star Business Conference. Before we begin today's events, I have two announcements. First, the men's room on the first floor is currently under construction, so we ask that you use the one on the second floor. And the second announcement is about Emmanuel Durand. Due to a scheduling conflict, he will be our first presenter of the day, as he must head out immediately after.

해석

1번은 다음 공지에 관한 문제입니다.

남 **안녕하세요, 노스 스타 비즈니스 학회에 참석해 주셔서 감사합니다.** 오늘의 행사를 시작하기 전에, 두 가지 공지 사항이 있습니다. 첫째, 1층 남자 화장실이 현재 공사 중이므로 2층 화장실을 사용하실 것을 부탁드립니다. 그리고 두 번째 공지 사항은 에마누엘 듀랜드에 관한 것입니다. 일정이 겹쳐서, 그가 오늘의 첫 번째 발표자가 될 것인데요, 그는 끝나면 바로 출발해야 하기 때문입니다.

어휘

attend 참석하다 under construction 공사 중인
scheduling conflict 일정 충돌, 겹치는 일정
presenter 발표자 head out (~로) 향하다, 출발하다
immediately after 곧, 뒤따라

1.
화자는 어디에 있는 것 같은가?
(A) 무역 박람회에
(B) 비즈니스 학회에
(C) 집단 면접에
(D) 직원 오리엔테이션에

[2-3] 영녀 🎧
Questions 2-3 refer to the following excerpt from a meeting.

> W Hello, everyone. I'd like to take this time to introduce our newest employee. ²Regina Glover is joining the lawyers here at Hart & Collins. While she won't be spending any time in court, she will be a vital member of our team. She is filling the position of Human Resources Manager. I was thrilled when I heard the news that she accepted our offer last week. We are very lucky to have her. ³Please take the time to introduce yourself and make her feel at home here.

해석

2-3번은 다음 회의 발췌록에 관한 문제입니다.

여 안녕하세요, 여러분. 이 시간을 빌어 새로운 직원을 소개하려고 합니다. **²레지나 글로버가 이곳 하트 앤 콜린스의 변호사들과 함께하게 되었습니다.** 그녀가 법정에서 보내는 시간은 전혀 없겠지만, 우리 팀의 중요한 일원이 될 것입니다. 그녀는 인사부장의 자리를 채울 것입니다. 지난주에 그녀가 우리의 제안을 수락했다는 소식을 들었을 때 저는 몹시 기뻤습니다. 그녀가 있는 것은 우리에게 큰 행운입니다. **³시간을 내서 자기소개를 하시고, 그녀가 이곳에서 편안하게 느끼게 해 주시기를 바랍니다.**

어휘

court 법정, 법원 vital 필수적인 fill a position 자리를 채우다
Human Resources 인사부 thrilled 아주 흥분한
make ~ feel at home ~를 편안하게 느끼게 해 주다

2.

화자는 어떤 종류의 업체에서 일하는 것 같은가?

(A) 회계 법인
(B) 배송 회사
(C) 제조 시설
(D) 법률 회사

어휘

manufacturing 제조업 facility 시설

3.

청자들은 무엇을 하라고 조언받는가?

(A) 신입 직원 환영하기
(B) 관리자에게 보고하기
(C) 환영회에 참석하기
(D) 자신의 업무 평가하기

어휘

reception 환영 연회, 접수처 evaluate 평가하다

패러프레이징

take the time to introduce yourself and make her feel at home → Welcome a new employee

[4-5] 호남 🎧

Questions 4-5 refer to the following talk.

> M It's wonderful to see so many people here for today's lecture. Thanks for coming. ⁴A lot has changed in the industry since I first started my architecture firm. One of the popular trends these days is to incorporate recycled goods into the design. I'll tell you all about the advantages and disadvantages of various building materials during this talk. However, ⁵first I'd like to discuss the charts that were distributed to you when you arrived. Please take a moment to familiarize yourself with them.

해석

4-5번은 다음 담화에 관한 문제입니다.

남 오늘 강의에서 이렇게 많은 분들을 뵙게 되어 기쁩니다. 와 주셔서 감사합니다. ⁴제가 처음 제 건축 회사를 시작한 이후로 업계에서 많은 것이 달라졌습니다. 요즘 인기 있는 트렌드 중 하나는 재활용품을 디자인에 통합시키는 것입니다. 이 강연 동안 다양한 건축 자재의 장단점에 대해 모두 알려 드리겠습니다. 하지만, ⁵우선 도착하셨을 때 여러분에게 나눠 드린 도표에 대해 이야기하고 싶습니다. 잠시 시간을 내어 그것을 숙지하시기 바랍니다.

어휘

industry 산업 architecture 건축 trend 추세, 동향
incorporate A into B A를 B에 통합시키다
recycled goods 재활용품
advantages and disadvantages 장단점, 이해득실
building material 건축 자재 distribute 나누어 주다, 분배하다

take a moment to ~할 시간을 잠시 가지다
familiarize oneself with ~에 정통하다

4.

화자는 누구인 것 같은가?

(A) 건축가
(B) 은행원
(C) 변호사
(D) 기자

5.

청자들은 다음에 무엇을 할 것인가?

(A) 영상 시청하기
(B) 샘플 써 보기
(C) 자기소개하기
(D) 인쇄물 읽기

어휘

handout 인쇄물, 유인물

패러프레이징

the charts that were distributed ~ familiarize yourself with them → Read some handouts

실전 문제				본문 p.214
1. (D)	**2.** (A)	**3.** (B)	**4.** (D)	**5.** (A)
6. (B)	**7.** (D)	**8.** (B)	**9.** (B)	**10.** (B)
11. (C)	**12.** (A)	**13.** (C)	**14.** (A)	**15.** (B)
16. (A)	**17.** (C)	**18.** (B)		

[1-3] 미남 🎧

Questions 1-3 refer to the following announcement.

> M As many of you know, the construction of the Starcity Mall right next to our building will be completed next month, and ¹some coffee shops that are larger than us will open on the first floor of the building. ²You can find a list of them in the handout I've just passed out.
> I expect the new mall will bring a lot of customers to the area. But... uh... as many of you have already expressed concern about losing our business to the mall, we need to prepare ourselves for the fierce competition. ³So, I want you to come up with some ideas for unique sales promotions and ways we can get customers to notice our business.

해석

1-3번은 다음 공지에 관한 문제입니다.

남 여러분들이 아시다시피, 우리 건물 바로 옆 스타시티 몰의 건설이 다음 달에 완공될 것이고, ¹우리보다 더 큰 일부 커피숍들이

건물 1층에 문을 열 것입니다. ²제가 방금 나눠 드린 인쇄물에서 이들의 목록을 찾으실 수 있습니다. 새로운 쇼핑몰이 이 지역에 많은 고객들을 데려올 것으로 기대합니다. 하지만... 어... 많은 분들이 우리 거래를 그 쇼핑몰에 빼앗기게 되는 것에 대한 우려를 표하셨듯이, 우리는 심한 경쟁에 대비해야 합니다. ³따라서 독특한 판매 홍보 아이디어와 고객들이 우리 업체에 주목하게 할 수 있는 방법들을 제안해 주셨으면 합니다.

어휘

construction 건설, 공사 complete 완료하다, 끝마치다
handout 인쇄물, 유인물 pass out 나눠 주다
lose A to B A를 B에게 잃다, 빼앗기다
fierce competition 심한 경쟁
come up with ~을 생각하다, 제안하다 unique 독특한
promotion 홍보 (활동) notice 주목하다, 관심을 기울이다

1.
화자는 어떤 종류의 업체에서 일하는가?
(A) 건설 회사
(B) 부동산 중개소
(C) 광고 대행사
(D) 커피숍

2.
화자에 따르면, 청자들은 일부 커피숍에 대해 어떻게 알 수 있는가?
(A) 인쇄물을 읽음으로써
(B) 회의에 참석함으로써
(C) 화자와 이야기함으로써
(D) 이메일을 받음으로써

3.
화자는 청자들에게 무엇을 해 달라고 요청하는가?
(A) 직원 교육에 참석하기
(B) 업체를 홍보할 방법 생각해 내기
(C) 경쟁사의 메뉴 조사하기
(D) 공석인 일자리에 관해 사람들에게 말하기

어휘

training session 교육 (과정) promote 홍보하다
competitor 경쟁자, 경쟁사

패러프레이징

come up with some ideas for unique sales promotions and ways we can get customers to notice our business → Think of ways to promote the business

[4-6] 영녀 🎧
Questions 4-6 refer to the following excerpt from a meeting.

> **W** To begin this meeting, I have some exciting news about Charles Kent. ^{4, 5}This month, he sold 35 vehicles from our lot. ⁵That's the most anyone has ever sold. The previous record was 28. Great job, Charles! This month, we're going to hold a contest to keep all of the sales staff motivated. The group that has the highest sales will win a prize. ⁶I'll put you in your groups now, and then we can discuss the details.

해석

4-6번은 다음 회의 발췌록에 관한 문제입니다.

여 찰스 켄트에 관한 흥분되는 소식으로 이번 회의를 시작하겠습니다. ^{4, 5}이번 달에 그가 우리 지구에서 35대의 차량을 판매했습니다. ⁵그것은 지금까지 누군가가 판매한 수량 중 가장 많은 수치입니다. 이전 기록은 28대였습니다. 잘했어요, 찰스! 이번 달에, 모든 판매 직원들의 동기를 부여하기 위해 대회를 열 것입니다. 판매 실적이 가장 높은 그룹이 상을 타게 될 것입니다. ⁶제가 지금 여러분을 그룹으로 묶고, 그런 다음 세부 정보에 대해 이야기하겠습니다.

어휘

vehicle 차량 lot 지역, 부지 previous 이전의
contest 대회, 시합 keep ~ motivated ~에게 동기를 부여하다
win a prize 상을 타다

4.
청자들은 어디에서 일하는 것 같은가?
(A) 옷 가게에서
(B) 전자제품 제조업체에서
(C) 제약회사에서
(D) 자동차 대리점에서

어휘

electronics ((항상 복수형)) 전자 기기
pharmaceutical 약학의, 제약의 dealership 대리점

5.
찰스 켄트는 최근에 무엇을 했는가?
(A) 그는 새로운 판매 기록을 세웠다.
(B) 그는 다른 지점에서 옮겨 왔다.
(C) 그는 승진했다.
(D) 그는 뉴스에 등장했다.

어휘

set a record 기록을 세우다 job promotion 승진
feature ~을 특집 기사로 다루다

패러프레이징

sold ~ the most anyone has ever sold
→ set a new sales record

6.
화자는 다음에 무엇을 할 것인가?
(A) 일부 우려에 대응하기
(B) 청자들을 그룹에 배치하기
(C) 매출액 보여 주기
(D) 상 수여하기

respond to ~에 대응하다 assign (사람을) 배치하다
sales figures 매출액 award 수여하다

패러프레이징

put you in your groups
→ Assign the listeners to groups

[7-9] 미녀 🎧

Questions 7-9 refer to the following telephone message.

> W Hi, this message is for Hank Howard. ⁷ This is Tonya from the Jacobson Appliance Store. You stopped by yesterday and placed an order for one of our compact ovens. They're currently on sale, but ⁸ I believe one of our cashiers charged you incorrectly. She wasn't aware that the six-piece oven accessory set is included with all oven purchases during the promotion. ⁹ If you have time, could you please stop by our store so we can correct your receipt? If not, we can do this over the phone. Thank you for your understanding, and we apologize for the inconvenience.

해석

7-9번은 다음 전화 메시지에 관한 문제입니다.

여 안녕하세요, 이 메시지는 행크 하워드에게 전하는 것입니다. ⁷ 저는 제이콥슨 가전 매장의 토냐입니다. 어제 당신이 들르셔서 저희 소형 오븐 중 하나를 주문하셨습니다. 그것들이 현재 세일 중인데, ⁸ 저희 계산원 중 한 명이 당신에게 잘못 청구한 것 같습니다. 그녀는 판촉 기간 동안 모든 오븐 구매에 6개들이 오븐 부대용품 세트가 포함된다는 것을 모르고 있었습니다. ⁹ 시간이 되시면, 저희가 영수증을 정정할 수 있도록 저희 매장에 들러 주시겠습니까? 그렇지 않으시면, 전화로 그렇게 하겠습니다. 양해해 주셔서 감사드리며, 불편을 드려 죄송합니다.

어휘

appliance (가정용) 기기 stop by ~에 들르다
place an order for ~을 주문하다 compact 소형의
on sale 세일 중인, 판매되는 charge (요금을) 청구하다
incorrectly 부정확하게, 맞지 않게
accessory 부대용품, 액세서리 promotion 홍보, 판촉
correct 바로잡다, 정정하다 inconvenience 불편

7.

화자는 어디에서 일하는 것 같은가?
(A) 호텔에서
(B) 식당에서
(C) 제과점에서
(D) 상점에서

8.

메시지의 목적은 무엇인가?

(A) 세일을 광고하기 위해
(B) 실수를 바로잡기 위해
(C) 환불 정책을 설명하기 위해
(D) 결제를 요청하기 위해

어휘

return policy 환불 정책 payment 지불, 납입

패러프레이징

one of our cashiers charged you incorrectly
→ a mistake

9.

화자는 청자에게 무엇을 해 달라고 요청하는가?
(A) 일부 정보를 이메일로 보내기
(B) 업체 방문하기
(C) 서비스 후기 남기기
(D) 배달 시간 예약하기

어휘

book 예약하다

패러프레이징

stop by our store → Visit the business

[10-12] 호남 🎧

Questions 10-12 refer to the following talk.

> M Welcome to Yorkshire National Park. I'm Michael, and ¹⁰ I'll be leading you on today's hike. We'll stop at some of the most popular parts of the park. However, we won't visit Eagle Peak, as the trail is closed due to heavy rains making it too wet. ¹¹ We try to let people know about these kinds of cancellations in advance, but the storm was last night. We'll be heading out soon, but first ¹² I'd like to pass out the packed lunches that are included in the tour's fee.

해석

10-12번은 다음 담화에 관한 문제입니다.

남 요크셔 국립 공원에 오신 것을 환영합니다. 저는 마이클이고, ¹⁰ 오늘의 하이킹에서 여러분을 인솔할 것입니다. 우리는 공원의 가장 인기 있는 구역들 중 몇 곳에서 멈출 것입니다. 하지만, 이글 피크에는 방문하지 않을 것인데, 폭우로 산길이 너무 질퍽거려서 폐쇄되었기 때문입니다. ¹¹ 저희가 미리 이 같은 취소 사항에 대해서 알려 드리려고 노력하지만, 폭풍우가 내린 것은 어젯밤이었습니다. 곧 출발하겠지만, 먼저 투어 요금에 포함된 ¹² 점심 도시락을 나눠 드리겠습니다.

어휘

lead 안내하다, 이끌다 hike 하이킹, 도보 여행 trail 산길, 오솔길
cancellation 취소(된 것) in advance 사전에, 미리
head out 출발하다, 향하다 pass out 나눠 주다
packed lunch 도시락

10.

담화는 어디에서 이루어지는 것 같은가?

(A) 보트 투어에서

(B) 단체 하이킹에서

(C) 스포츠 토너먼트에서

(D) 휴일 축제에서

어휘

tournament 토너먼트, 승자 진출전

11.

화자는 "폭풍우가 내린 것은 어젯밤이었습니다"라고 말할 때 무엇을 암시하는가?

(A) 현장이 평소처럼 혼잡하지 않다.

(B) 화자의 동료가 늦을 것이다.

(C) 변화를 예측할 수 없었다.

(D) 일기 예보가 부정확했다.

어휘

as usual 평소대로 predict 예측하다 inaccurate 부정확한

12.

화자는 청자들에게 무엇을 줄 것인가?

(A) 음식

(B) 옷

(C) 입장권

(D) 지도

어휘

admission 입장, 입학

패러프레이징

the packed lunches → Some food

[13-15] 미남 🎧

Questions 13-15 refer to the following excerpt from a meeting.

> **M** Good morning, everyone. ¹³I'd like to let you know about a change at our restaurant that will affect your deliveries. ¹⁴Starting from next week, customers will be able to place food orders using our new smartphone application. When you leave the restaurant with the food to be delivered, they'll be able to track your progress along the route. ¹⁵I think this will cut down on the transaction time because... uh... customers will know exactly when to expect you, and they can be ready to answer the door quickly. I'll be showing you how to use all of the app's features later in this meeting. Thanks.

해석

13-15번은 다음 회의 발췌록에 관한 문제입니다.

남 안녕하세요, 여러분. ¹³여러분의 배달에 영향을 미칠 우리 식당의 변경 사항에 대해 알려 드리고 싶습니다. ¹⁴다음 주부터, 고객

들이 우리의 새로운 스마트폰 앱을 이용해 음식을 주문할 수 있게 됩니다. 여러분이 배달될 음식을 가지고 식당을 출발할 때, 고객들은 경로를 따라 여러분이 얼마나 왔는지 추적할 수 있게 됩니다. ¹⁵이것이 거래 시간을 줄여줄 것이라고 생각하는데요, 왜냐하면... 어... 고객들은 정확히 언제 여러분이 오는지 알게 되어 빨리 문을 열러 나갈 준비를 할 수 있기 때문입니다. 이번 회의 후반에 앱의 모든 기능을 사용하는 법을 보여드리겠습니다. 감사합니다.

어휘

application (= app) 앱, 응용 프로그램

progress 진척, 진행 route 경로, 길 cut down on ~을 줄이다

transaction 거래, 매매

answer the door 문을 열러 나가다 feature 특징, 기능

13.

청자들은 누구인 것 같은가?

(A) 위생 검사관

(B) 음식 비평가

(C) 배달 기사

(D) 주방 직원

어휘

inspector 조사관, 감독관 critic 비평가, 평론가

14.

화자에 따르면, 고객들은 다음 주부터 무엇을 할 수 있는가?

(A) 모바일 앱을 통해 주문하기

(B) 대량 주문에 대해 할인받기

(C) 고객 보상 프로그램에 가입하기

(D) 채식주의 메뉴 즐기기

어휘

bulk order 대량 주문 loyalty program 고객 보상 프로그램

vegetarian 채식주의자(의)

패러프레이징

place food orders using our new smartphone application → Order through a mobile app

15.

화자는 어떤 이점을 언급하는가?

(A) 비용을 절감하는 것

(B) 시간을 절약하는 것

(C) 안전을 개선하는 것

(D) 일자리를 창출하는 것

어휘

benefit 이익, 혜택

패러프레이징

cut down on the transaction time → Saving time

[16-18] 영녀 🎧

Questions 16-18 refer to the following talk and task list.

> **W** Before we start today's shift, I'd like to thank everyone for your hard work during yesterday's clearance sale. ¹⁶We sold a record number of power tools, and we also exceeded our goal for selling floor tiles. Because we got rid of so many items, we have plenty of room now to set up the display area to ¹⁷demonstrate the features of our new table saw. That will be done at ten, noon, two, and four today. One more thing, ¹⁸Ricardo called in sick, so Jessica has agreed to cover his duties today.

해석

16-18번은 다음 담화와 업무 목록에 관한 문제입니다.

여 오늘 근무를 시작하기 전에, 어제의 창고 정리 판매 동안 모든 분들의 노고에 대해 감사드리고 싶습니다. ¹⁶**우리는 기록적인 수량의 전동 공구를 판매했으며, 바닥 타일 판매에 대해서도 목표를 초과했습니다.** 우리가 아주 많은 품목들을 처분했기 때문에 이제 ¹⁷**새로운 테이블톱의 기능을 시연하기 위한 진열 구역을 설치할** 공간이 많아졌습니다. ¹⁷**그것은 오늘 10시, 12시, 2시, 4시에 진행될 것입니다.** 한 가지 더 말씀드리자면, ¹⁸**리카도가 병가를 내서 제시카가 오늘 그의 업무를 대신 하기로 했습니다.**

어휘

shift 교대 근무 (시간) clearance sale 창고 정리 판매
record number 기록적인 수치 power tool 전동 공구
exceed 초과하다 get rid of ~을 처리하다, 없애다
room 자리, 공간 set up 세우다, 설치하다
feature 특징, 기능 call in sick 전화로 병결을 알리다
cover (일을) 대신하다 duties ((보통 복수형)) 업무

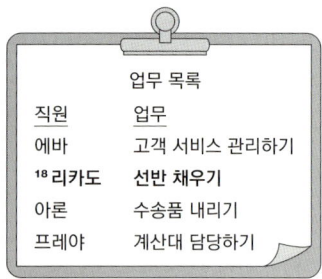

업무 목록	
직원	**업무**
에바	고객 서비스 관리하기
¹⁸**리카도**	**선반 채우기**
아론	수송품 내리기
프레야	계산대 담당하기

16.

담화는 어디에서 일어나고 있는 것 같은가?
(A) 철물점에서
(B) 신발 가게에서
(C) 서점에서
(D) 가구점에서

어휘

hardware 철물, 장비

패러프레이징

power tools, floor tiles → hardware

17.

화자는 오늘 무슨 일이 일어날 것이라고 말하는가?
(A) 재고 정리 세일이 열릴 것이다.
(B) 몇몇 신상품이 디자인될 것이다.
(C) 시연이 진행될 것이다.
(D) 교육을 위해 업체가 문을 닫을 것이다.

어휘

merchandise 상품

패러프레이징

demonstrate the features of our new table saw
→ Some demonstrations will be given

18.

시각 자료를 보시오. 제시카는 오늘 어떤 업무를 할 것인가?
(A) 고객 서비스 관리하기
(B) 선반 채우기
(C) 수송품 내리기
(D) 계산대 담당하기

어휘

restock 다시 채우다 unload (짐을) 내리다
shipment 수송(품), 적하물 cash register 금전 등록기

UNIT 03 문제점·이유 문제

CHECK UP　　　　　　　　　　　본문 p.216

1. (D)　　**2.** (C)

[1] 미남 🎧

Question 1 refers to the following telephone message.

> **M** Hi, this is Robert Sinclair. I bought four tickets to the basketball tournament at the Ashburn Arena. I paid extra to have them mailed to me. However, it's been over a week, and I still don't have them yet. The event is coming up soon, so I want to make sure there isn't a problem. Could you please check on this and call me back? My number is 555-8453, and I'll be available for the rest of the day. Thank you.

해석

1번은 다음 전화 메시지에 관한 문제입니다.

남 안녕하세요, 저는 로버트 싱클레어입니다. 애시번 아레나에서 열리는 **농구 토너먼트 대회 티켓 4장을 샀습니다.** 그것들이 제게 우편으로 배송되도록 별도로 요금을 지불했습니다. **하지만, 일주**

일 넘게 지났는데도 여전히 티켓들을 받지 못했습니다. 경기가 곧 다가오므로 문제가 있는 게 아니라는 걸 확인하고 싶습니다. 이것을 확인하시고 제게 전화 주시겠습니까? 제 번호는 555-84553이고, 오늘 남은 시간 계속 연락받을 수 있습니다. 감사합니다.

어휘
tournament 토너먼트, 승자 진출전
pay extra 별도로 값을 치르다   mail 우편으로 보내다
the rest of ~의 나머지

1.
화자는 어떤 문제를 언급하는가?
(A) 일부 대금이 지불되지 않았다.
(B) 주소가 틀렸다.
(C) 그는 웹사이트에 접속할 수 없다.
(D) 그는 자신의 티켓을 받지 못했다.

어휘
make a payment 지불하다   incorrect 틀린
log on to (인터넷 등에) 접속하다

패러프레이징
bought four tickets ~ still don't have them yet
→ has not received his tickets

[2] 미녀 🎧
Question 2 refers to the following radio broadcast.

> **W** Welcome back, Radio ARJ listeners. For those who missed our announcement earlier, we will be having a sweepstakes to celebrate our Schoolhouse Quiz series' 10th anniversary. We have prepared gift packs filled with over 100 dollars worth of merchandise from our online store. They will be given away at random to 50 lucky listeners. Winners will be announced on July 31st, and prizes will be sent out on August 15th. For your chance to win, visit our Web site at www.radioarj.com and click the banner for the event. Don't let this opportunity pass you by!

해석
2번은 다음 라디오 방송에 관한 문제입니다.
여 어서 오세요, ARJ 라디오 청취자 여러분. 저희의 이전 안내 방송을 놓치신 분들께 알려 드리자면, 저희 스쿨하우스 퀴즈 시리즈 10주년을 기념하기 위해 경품 행사를 엽니다. 100달러 상당 이상의 저희 온라인 상점의 상품으로 채워진 선물 꾸러미들을 준비했습니다. 그것들을 행운의 청취자 50분에게 무작위로 드릴 것입니다. 당첨자는 7월 31일에 발표될 것이며, 상품은 8월 15일에 발송될 것입니다. **당첨을 원하시면, 저희 웹사이트 www.radioarj.com을 방문하시어 이벤트 배너를 클릭하세요.** 이 기회를 그냥 지나치지 마세요!

어휘
sweepstakes (상금을 건) 경쟁, 복권   celebrate 축하하다
anniversary 기념일   gift pack 선물 꾸러미
filled with ~로 채워진   worth of ~의 값어치만큼의 양
merchandise 상품   at random 무작위로, 임의로
banner 배너, 현수막   opportunity 기회   pass by 지나치다

2.
청자들은 왜 웹사이트를 방문하라고 요청받는가?
(A) 일련의 규칙을 검토하기 위해
(B) 당첨자 명단을 찾기 위해
(C) 행사에 등록하기 위해
(D) 상품을 고르기 위해

어휘
register for ~에 등록하다   pick out 선택하다, 뽑다

패러프레이징
click the banner for the event → register for an event

패러프레이징 연습   본문 p.218
1-4. 스크립트 참조   **5.** (B)   **6.** (B)

1.
Q 화자는 상품에 있는 어떤 문제를 언급하는가?
A 그것은 소음이 너무 많이 난다.

미남 🎧

> **M** Good afternoon, everyone. To begin today's meeting, I'd like to address an issue with our recently released washing machine. A lot of customers have complained that it is noisier than expected. As we want to ensure the best experience for people using our products, we need to find a way to resolve this problem.

해석
남 안녕하세요, 여러분. 오늘 회의를 시작하기 위해, 우리가 최근 출시한 세탁기에 관한 문제를 다루려고 합니다. **많은 고객들이 예상보다 더 시끄럽다고 불평했습니다.** 우리는 우리 제품을 사용하는 사람들에게 최고의 경험을 보장하고 싶기 때문에, 이 문제를 해결하기 위한 방법을 찾아야 합니다.

어휘
address (문제 등을) 다루다, 고심하다   issue 문제, 안건
release 출시하다, 공개하다   complain 불평하다, 항의하다
ensure 반드시 ~하게 하다, 보장하다   resolve 해결하다

패러프레이징
noisier than expected → makes too much noise

2.
Q 화자는 왜 청자들에게 일찍 도착하라고 요청하는가?

A 옷을 받기 위해

> W I'd just like to remind everyone that we'll start offering our new menu from Monday. This is also the day that we will change our uniforms to complement the rebranding of our restaurant. Please come for your shift a bit earlier than usual to pick up the new shirt and apron set. Thank you.

해석

여 모든 분들에게 월요일부터 우리가 새로운 메뉴를 제공하기 시작할 것임을 알려 드리고 싶습니다. 이날은 또한 우리 식당의 이미지 쇄신을 보완하기 위해 우리 유니폼을 교체하는 날이기도 합니다. 새로운 셔츠와 앞치마 세트를 가져가기 위해 평소보다 조금 더 일찍 출근하시기 바랍니다. 감사합니다.

어휘

remind 상기시키다, 알려 주다　complement 보완하다
rebrand 브랜드 이미지를 새롭게 하다　shift 교대 근무 (시간)

패러프레이징

pick up the new shirt and apron set
→ receive some clothing

3.

Q 화자는 왜 사과하는가?
A 이용할 수 있는 의자가 충분하지 않다.

> M Thank you for being here for this morning's staff meeting. I'm sorry that there are not enough chairs set up. We usually don't meet with all of the departments together, so I hope some of you don't mind standing.

해석

남 오늘 아침 직원 회의에 참석해 주셔서 감사합니다. 준비된 의자가 충분하지 않아서 죄송합니다. 우리는 보통 모든 부서가 다 같이 모이지 않아요, 그래서 몇몇 분은 서 계시는 걸 개의치 않아 하셨으면 합니다.

어휘

available 이용할 수 있는
mind -ing ~하는 것을 신경 쓰다, 꺼리다

패러프레이징

there are not enough chairs set up
→ Not enough chairs are available

4.

Q 업계는 어떤 문제를 겪고 있는가?
A 수익 손실

> W In national news, an analysis of hundreds of trucking companies has revealed an alarming trend in the industry. Price increases have caused companies to lose thousands of dollars each year. The lost revenue comes mostly from the rising cost of gasoline.

해석

여 국내 뉴스입니다. 운송 회사 수백 곳에 대한 분석으로 업계의 놀라운 동향이 드러났습니다. 가격 인상 때문에 회사들이 매해 수천 달러의 손실을 입어 왔습니다. 손실된 수익은 대부분 휘발유 가격의 인상에서 비롯된 것입니다.

어휘

industry 산업, 업계　revenue 수익, 수입　analysis 분석
trucking company 운송 회사　reveal 드러내다
alarming 놀라운　trend 동향, 추세
price increase 가격 인상　gasoline 휘발유

패러프레이징

lose thousands of dollars → A loss of revenue

5.

화자는 왜 전화로 연락 달라고 요청하는가?
(A) 그가 사무실에서 나와 있다.
(B) 그의 컴퓨터가 작동하지 않는다.

> M Hi, Ms. Everson. This is Ronald. I'd like to talk to you about the job candidates we interviewed earlier this week, so let's set up a time to meet. But… um… I'm having some problems with my computer, so I can't access my e-mail. I'd appreciate a call instead.

해석

남 안녕하세요, 에버슨 씨. 로널드예요. 이번 주 초에 우리가 면접했던 입사 지원자들에 관해 얘기하고 싶어요, 그러니 만날 시간을 정하죠. 하지만… 음… 제 컴퓨터에 문제가 좀 있어서 제 이메일에 접속할 수가 없어요. 그러니 대신 전화 주시면 고맙겠어요.

어휘

job candidate 입사 지원자　set up 정하다
access 접속하다; 접속　appreciate 고마워하다, 환영하다

패러프레이징

having some problems with my computer
→ computer is not working

6.

화자는 어떤 문제를 언급하는가?
(A) 오케스트라 단원 몇 명이 결석했다.
(B) 참석자 수가 저조했다.

> **W** I'd like to speak to all of the orchestra members before this rehearsal begins. This concert series is usually a popular event with locals and tourists alike. However, so far, we've sold fewer tickets than usual, so I'm looking for strategies to improve our attendance for the remaining shows.

해석

여 이번 리허설이 시작되기 전에, 모든 오케스트라 단원들에게 드릴 말씀이 있습니다. 이번 콘서트 시리즈는 보통 지역 주민들과 관광객에게 똑같이 인기가 있는 행사입니다. **하지만 지금까지, 평소보다 티켓이 덜 팔렸어요, 그래서 제가 남은 공연의 참석자 수를 높이기 위한 전략을 찾고 있습니다.**

어휘

attendance 참석자 수, 참석률 local 주민; 지역의
alike 둘 다, 똑같이 strategy 전략
improve 개선하다, 향상시키다 remaining 남아있는

패러프레이징

we've sold fewer tickets than usual
→ Attendance has been poor

연습 문제 본문 p.219

1. (D) **2.** (A) **3.** (C) **4.** (B) **5.** (C)

---

[1] 미녀 🎧

Question 1 refers to the following announcement.

> **W** Thanks, everyone, for volunteering to work for the company picnic. As you know, this is the largest event organized by our company, so your help means a lot. Unfortunately, we have to make a slight change to our schedule. The food has already arrived, but we can't start setting up yet since the truck of plates and glasses broke down. So, while waiting for the truck, I'd like some of you to help me with decorating the tables.

해석

1번은 다음 공지에 관한 문제입니다.

여 회사 야유회를 위해 자원해서 일해 주신 모든 분들께 감사드립니다. 아시다시피, 이것은 우리 회사에서 준비하는 가장 큰 행사이므로 여러분의 도움은 큰 의미가 있습니다. 안타깝게도, 우리 일정을 조금 바꿔야 합니다. **음식은 이미 도착했지만, 접시와 유리잔을 실은 트럭이 고장 나서 아직 세팅을 시작할 수 없습니다.** 따라서, 트럭을 기다리는 동안, 여러분 중 몇 분이 저를 도와 테이블을 장식해 주셨으면 합니다.

어휘

volunteer to 자원해서 ~하다 organize 조직하다, 준비하다
make a change to ~을 바꾸다 break down 고장 나다
decorate 장식하다

1.

화자에 따르면, 무엇이 문제인가?
(A) 일부 직원들이 늦게 출근했다.
(B) 장소가 변경되었다.
(C) 행사에 너무 많은 사람들이 왔다.
(D) 일부 용품이 아직 준비되지 않았다.

어휘

venue (행사의) 장소 supplies ((보통 복수형)) 용품, 비품

패러프레이징

plates and glasses → Some supplies

[2-3] 미남 🎧

Questions 2-3 refer to the following telephone message.

> **M** Hello, this message is for Mr. Donald Jeffrey. This is Andrew Harris. ²I received your e-mail regarding the catering of your parents' 50th wedding anniversary on June 10th. Unfortunately, some of the food options aren't available at the prices you mentioned. I think you must have been looking at an older version of our brochure. ³Prices have risen drastically since that was printed. So, the new total is higher than the budget you proposed. But, we have several other options I'd love to discuss with you. Please call me back.

해석

2-3번은 다음 전화 메시지에 관한 문제입니다.

남 안녕하세요, 이 메시지는 도널드 제프리 씨에게 전하는 것입니다. 저는 앤드루 해리스입니다. ²6월 10일 부모님의 50주년 결혼기념일의 케이터링에 관한 당신의 이메일을 받았습니다. 안타깝게도, 선택하신 음식 일부는 언급하신 가격에 이용하실 수 없습니다. 저희 안내 책자의 예전 버전을 보시고 계신 게 틀림없는 듯합니다. ³그것이 인쇄된 이후로 가격이 대폭 인상되었습니다. 따라서, 새 총액은 제안하신 예산보다 더 높습니다. 하지만, 당신과 논의하고 싶은 몇 가지 다른 선택할 만한 것들이 있습니다. 다시 전화 주시기 바랍니다.

어휘

regarding ~에 관하여 brochure 소책자, 브로슈어
drastically 급격히, 대폭 budget 예산 propose 제안하다

2.

화자는 어떤 종류의 업체에서 일하는 것 같은가?
(A) 케이터링 회사
(B) 통신사

(C) 은행
(D) 인쇄소

3.
화자는 어떤 문제를 언급하는가?
(A) 일부 직원들이 미숙하다.
(B) 이메일 시스템이 작동하지 않는다.
(C) 일부 품목의 가격이 올랐다.
(D) 업체가 그날 초과 예약된 상태이다.

어휘
inexperienced 경험이 부족한, 미숙한
overbooked 초과 예약된

패러프레이징
Prices have risen drastically
→ The price of some items has risen

[4-5] 미녀 🎧
Questions 4-5 refer to the following advertisement.

> W When it comes to traveling abroad, Fly4you takes you to more cities around the world than any other airline. And, ⁴starting in January, we'll be adding more frequent service to 10 destinations in Europe to make your travel even easier and faster. Our fares are usually two-thirds of the price of other airlines. In addition, all of our flights are equipped with spacious and comfortable seating. ⁵To see the timetables of our new flights, visit our Web site at www.Fly4youair.com. We hope you travel with us soon.

해석
4-5번은 다음 광고에 관한 문제입니다.
여 해외여행에 관한 한, 플라이포유는 그 어느 항공사보다도 전 세계의 더 많은 도시로 여러분을 모셔다드립니다. 그리고, ⁴1월부터 유럽의 10개 목적지에 더 잦은 운항 서비스를 추가하여 여러분의 여행을 훨씬 더 쉽고 빠르게 해 드릴 것입니다. 저희 요금은 보통 다른 항공사들의 3분의 2입니다. 게다가, 저희의 모든 비행기에는 넓고 편안한 좌석이 갖춰져 있습니다. ⁵저희의 새로운 항공편의 시간표를 확인하시려면, 저희 웹사이트 www.Fly4youair.com을 방문하세요. 곧 저희와 함께 여행하시기를 바랍니다.

어휘
when it comes to ~에 관한 한 airline 항공사
frequent 잦은, 빈번한 destination 목적지, 도착지
fare (교통) 요금 be equipped with ~을 갖추고 있다
spacious 넓찍한 seating 좌석, 자리

4.
플라이포유는 1월에 무엇을 할 계획인가?
(A) 좌석 업그레이드하기
(B) 더 잦은 서비스 추가하기

(C) 무료 시간표 제공하기
(D) 티켓 가격 인하하기

5.
청자들은 왜 웹사이트에 방문하도록 권장받는가?
(A) 지도를 요청하기 위해
(B) 티켓을 구매하기 위해
(C) 수정된 시간표를 보기 위해
(D) 여행 보험을 신청하기 위해

어휘
encourage to ~하도록 권장하다 revised 수정된
register for ~을 신청하다 insurance 보험

패러프레이징
see the timetables of our new flights
→ view a revised schedule

실전 문제   본문 p.220

1. (A)	**2.** (B)	**3.** (C)	**4.** (D)	**5.** (C)
6. (A)	**7.** (D)	**8.** (A)	**9.** (C)	**10.** (A)
11. (A)	**12.** (C)	**13.** (B)	**14.** (B)	**15.** (C)
16. (C)	**17.** (C)	**18.** (D)		

[1-3] 미녀 🎧
Questions 1-3 refer to the following announcement.

> W ¹I'd like to make a quick announcement before we open the gym. Unfortunately, classroom 2 will be unavailable today. As you know, there is construction going on at the building next door. ²One of their workers accidentally hit the window with a crane, breaking the glass. So, that room will be too cold to use until a repair is made. ³I'll print a notice and hang it on the door to let people know that classes in that room are canceled today.

해석
1-3번은 다음 공지에 관한 문제입니다.
여 ¹우리가 체육관 문을 열기 전에 간단한 공지를 하려고 합니다. 안타깝게도, 오늘 2번 강습실을 사용할 수 없을 것입니다. 아시다시피, 바로 옆 건물에서 공사가 진행 중입니다. ²그들의 인부 한 명이 의도치 않게 크레인으로 창문을 쳐서, 유리가 깨졌습니다. 따라서 그 방은 수리가 될 때까지 너무 추워서 사용할 수 없을 것입니다. ³사람들에게 오늘 그 방의 수업들이 취소되었다는 걸 알리기 위해 제가 안내문을 인쇄해서 문에 걸겠습니다.

어휘
make an announcement 공지하다, 발표하다
unavailable 이용할 수 없는 construction 공사, 건설
accidentally 우연히, 뜻하지 않게 crane 기중기, 크레인
make a repair 수리하다 notice 공고문, 안내문
cancel 취소하다

1.

청자들은 누구인가?

(A) 체육관 직원
(B) 미술 강사
(C) 식당 종업원
(D) 공장 노동자

어휘

instructor 강사, 교사   server 서빙하는 사람

2.

화자에 따르면, 무엇이 문제를 일으켰는가?

(A) 배송품이 늦게 도착했다.
(B) 창문이 깨졌다.
(C) 일부 공사 작업이 시끄럽다.
(D) 일부 제품이 생산 중단되었다.

어휘

shipment 배송품   discontinue (생산을) 중단하다

패러프레이징

breaking the glass → A window has been broken

3.

화자는 무엇을 할 것이라고 말하는가?

(A) 요금 면제하기
(B) 수리공에게 전화하기
(C) 공지 게시하기
(D) 관리자에게 말하기

어휘

waive a fee 요금을 면제하다   put up 내붙이다, 게시하다
supervisor 감독관, 관리자

패러프레이징

print a notice and hang it on the door
→ Put up a notice

[4-6] 호남 🎧

Questions 4-6 refer to the following announcement.

> **M** This is an announcement for Foxtrot passengers to Manhattan, scheduled for 4:30. Due to the local festival on Main Street, there is heavy traffic, so we are still waiting for the bus. It will be arriving in about 20 minutes. ⁴We apologize for this delay. Once the bus has arrived, we're going to clean and refuel it, so ⁵we expect to depart in about half an hour. In the meantime, ⁶we're offering a complimentary voucher for a free coffee or soft drink at the cafeteria next to Gate 10. Please go there and show your bus ticket or confirmation number on your mobile phone at the counter. Thank you for your patience.

해석

4–6번은 다음 공지에 관한 문제입니다.

남 이것은 4시 30분으로 예정된 맨해튼행 폭스트롯 승객들을 위한 안내 방송입니다. 메인가의 지역 축제로 인해 교통이 혼잡하여 저희가 아직도 버스를 기다리고 있는 중입니다. 약 20분 뒤에 도착할 것입니다. ⁴이 지연에 사과드립니다. 일단 버스가 도착하면 청소를 하고 연료를 재급유할 것이므로 ⁵약 30분 뒤에 출발할 것으로 예상됩니다. 그러는 동안에, ⁶10번 탑승구 옆 카페테리아에서 무료로 커피나 탄산음료를 드실 수 있는 무료 교환권을 드리겠습니다. 그곳에 가셔서 계산대에 버스 티켓이나 휴대폰의 확인 번호를 제시하시기 바랍니다. 양해해 주셔서 감사합니다.

어휘

scheduled for ~로 일정이 잡힌   heavy traffic 교통 정체
apologize for ~에 대해 사과하다   delay 지연, 지체
refuel 연료를 재급유하다   depart 출발하다
in the meantime 그러는 동안에   complimentary 무료의
voucher 교환권, 상품권   cafeteria 카페테리아, 구내식당
confirmation 확인   patience 인내력, 참을성

4.

화자는 왜 사과하는가?

(A) 일부 좌석이 불편하다.
(B) 한 구역이 청소가 되지 않았다.
(C) 티켓이 다 팔렸다.
(D) 서비스가 예정보다 늦다.

어휘

uncomfortable 불편한   sold out 매진된
behind schedule 예정보다 늦게

패러프레이징

delay → behind schedule

5.

화자에 따르면, 버스는 맨해튼으로 언제 출발할 것 같은가?

(A) 10분 뒤에
(B) 20분 뒤에
(C) 30분 뒤에
(D) 1시간 뒤에

6.

어떤 종류의 시설이 10번 탑승구 옆에 있는가?

(A) 카페테리아
(B) 전화 부스
(C) 매표소
(D) 자동판매기

어휘

facility 시설

[7-9] 미녀 🎧

Questions 7-9 refer to the following talk.

W I'm glad everyone got the message that I had changed our classroom to this one. ⁷It's larger and can fit everyone, including the extra students who joined the class late. Anyway, ⁸today in our Web design workshop, I'll be teaching you how to resize photos and other graphics on a Web site. Before we begin, up on the screen there's a code that I'd like you all to write down. ⁹You can use it to sign into the software we're using today. This can be done from anywhere, so you can keep working on your project after you leave the workshop.

해석

7-9번은 다음 담화에 관한 문제입니다.

여 모든 분들이 제가 교실을 이곳으로 바꾸었다는 메시지를 받으셔서 다행입니다. ⁷이곳이 더 커서 수업에 늦게 신청한 추가 학생들을 포함한 모든 분들을 수용할 수 있거든요. 그건 그렇고, ⁸오늘 우리 웹디자인 워크숍에서는, 제가 여러분에게 웹사이트에서 사진 및 기타 그래픽들의 크기를 조절하는 법을 가르쳐 드릴 것입니다. 시작하기 전에, 여러분 모두 적어 두셨으면 하는 코드가 화면에 띄워져 있습니다. ⁹그것을 이용해서 우리가 오늘 사용하는 소프트웨어에 로그인할 수 있습니다. 이것은 어디서든 가능하니 워크숍을 마친 후에도 여러분의 프로젝트를 계속 작업하실 수 있습니다.

어휘

fit ~에 맞다 resize 크기를 조절하다
up on the screen 화면에 나타난 code 암호, 부호
write down 적어 두다 sign into 로그인하다

7.

화자는 왜 교실을 바꾸었는가?
(A) 그곳이 더 조용한 환경을 제공한다.
(B) 그곳이 더 편리한 위치에 있다.
(C) 그곳에 새로 구입한 장비가 있다.
(D) 그곳이 더 많은 학생들을 수용할 수 있다.

어휘

environment 환경 equipment 장비
accommodate 수용하다, 충분한 공간을 제공하다

패러프레이징

fit everyone, including the extra students
→ accommodate more students

8.

청자들은 오늘 워크숍에서 무엇을 하는 것을 배울 것인가?
(A) 이미지 크기 조절하기
(B) 검색창 만들기
(C) 배너 추가하기
(D) 글자 색깔 바꾸기

어휘

search bar 검색창 banner 배너, 현수막

패러프레이징

photos and other graphics → images

9.

화자에 따르면, 청자들은 코드로 무엇을 할 수 있는가?
(A) 피드백 주기
(B) 할인받기
(C) 소프트웨어 프로그램에 접속하기
(D) 다른 수업에 등록하기

어휘

access 접속하다; 접속 enroll in ~에 등록하다

패러프레이징

sign into the software → Access a software program

[10-12] 호남 🎧

Questions 10-12 refer to the following broadcast.

M It's time for the *Burlington Local Events Calendar*. ¹⁰Vargas Community Theater is holding a fund-raiser this Saturday, June 10, starting at 7 P.M. It will be a performance from the Seattle Dance Troupe, which specializes in modern dance. ¹¹All proceeds from the ticket sales will go toward buying a new lighting system for the theater's stage. This will greatly improve the viewing experience for audience members. The theater's director is asking for help in promoting the fund-raising show. ¹²If you would like to volunteer to distribute promotional flyers on Friday, please call the theater at 555-4116.

해석

10-12번은 다음 방송에 관한 문제입니다.

남 〈벌링턴 지역 행사 일정〉 시간입니다. ¹⁰바르가스 커뮤니티 극장은 이번 주 토요일인 6월 10일 저녁 7시부터 모금 행사를 개최합니다. 그것은 시애틀 무용단의 공연이 될 것인데, 이들은 현대 무용을 전문으로 합니다. ¹¹티켓 판매 수익은 모두 극장의 무대를 위한 새로운 조명 시스템을 구입하는 데 쓰일 것입니다. 이것은 관객들의 관람 경험을 크게 개선해 줄 것입니다. 극장의 감독은 모금 공연 홍보에 대한 도움을 요청하고 있습니다. ¹²금요일에 자진해서 홍보 전단을 배포하고 싶으시면, 555-4116으로 극장에 전화하시기 바랍니다.

어휘

fund-raiser 모금 행사 performance 공연, 연주
dance troupe 무용단 specialize in ~을 전문으로 하다
proceeds 수익금 go toward ~의 값으로 들어가다, ~에 바쳐지다
lighting 조명 improve 개선하다, 향상시키다 audience 관람객
promote 홍보하다 volunteer to 자진해서 ~하다
distribute 나누어 주다 promotional flyer 홍보용 전단

10.

6월 10일 행사에서 누가 공연할 것인가?

(A) 무용수
(B) 코미디언
(C) 가수
(D) 배우

패러프레이징

Seattle Dance Troupe → Dancers

11.

모금 행사는 왜 열릴 것인가?

(A) 새 장비를 구입하기 위해
(B) 건물 수리를 완료하기 위해
(C) 무대를 더 크게 만들기 위해
(D) 직원을 더 고용하기 위해

어휘

complete 완료하다, 끝마치다

패러프레이징

buying a new lighting system
→ purchase new equipment

12.

지원자들은 금요일에 무엇을 할 것인가?

(A) 주차장 관리하기
(B) 좌석 배열하기
(C) 전단 나눠 주기
(D) 공연 티켓 팔기

어휘

arrange 정리하다, 배열하다 pass out 나눠 주다

패러프레이징

distribute promotional flyers → Pass out flyers

[13-15] 미녀 🎧

Questions 13-15 refer to the following advertisement.

> W Are you tired of being stuck in an office or retail shop all day? Do you have a valid driver's license and your own car? ¹³ Why not become a delivery driver for Maria's Laundry? ¹⁴ We've just launched a home-delivery service for our customers' convenience. So, we need drivers who can do both pick-ups and drop-offs. ¹⁵ The number of hours is dependent on the demand. However, a lot of customers have shown interest. To find out more, stop by in person and ask for a manager.

해석

13-15번은 다음 광고에 관한 문제입니다.

여 하루 종일 사무실이나 소매점에 박혀 있기 지겨우신가요? 유효한 운전면허증과 본인 소유의 자동차를 갖고 계시나요? ¹³ 마리아 세탁소의 배달 기사가 되는 것이 어떠세요? ¹⁴ 저희는 고객들의 편의를 위해 가정배달 서비스를 시작했습니다. 그래서 세탁물을 가져오고 가져다주는 일 둘 다 할 수 있는 기사들이 필요합니다. ¹⁵ 근로 시간은 수요에 달려 있습니다. 그러나, 많은 고객들이 관심을 보였습니다. 더 많이 알고 싶으시면, 직접 들러서 매니저에게 물어보세요.

어휘

be stuck in ~에서 꼼짝 못 하다, 박혀 있다 retail shop 소매점
valid 유효한 launch 시작하다 convenience 편의, 편리한 것
pick-up 수집, 수거 drop-off 내려주기, 내려주는 곳
dependent on ~에 의존하는 demand 수요 stop by 들르다
in person 직접

13.

어떤 종류의 업체가 이야기되고 있는가?

(A) 가구점
(B) 세탁 시설
(C) 식당
(D) 공장

14.

광고에 따르면, 이 업체는 왜 직원들을 모집하는가?

(A) 그곳은 새로운 파트너를 확보했다.
(B) 그곳은 새로운 서비스를 시작했다.
(C) 그곳은 두 번째 지점을 열었다.
(D) 그곳은 영업시간을 연장했다.

어휘

recruit 모집하다, 뽑다 secure 획득하다 location 장소, 위치
extend 연장하다, 확대하다

패러프레이징

a home-delivery service → a new service

15.

화자는 "많은 고객들이 관심을 보였습니다"라고 말할 때 무엇을 의미하는가?

(A) 광고 캠페인이 효과가 있었다.
(B) 상품이 곧 매진될 것이다.
(C) 직원들이 일을 많이 할 것 같다.
(D) 관리팀이 유능하다.

어휘

work 효과가 있다 sell out 다 팔리다
be likely to do ~할 것 같다 effective 효과적인, 유능한

[16-18] 영녀 🎧

Questions 16-18 refer to the following telephone message and review.

> W Hi, Michael. It's Liz. I've confirmed a meeting with Ms. Baldwin for October 9. ¹⁶ She's considering hiring our business to handle all of her company's legal matters, so this would be a major account for us. After the meeting, I'm taking her to dinner and then a show. ¹⁷ There's

a three-star show playing at the theater right by the restaurant, so I bought tickets for that. I want to make sure I'm fully prepared, so [18]do you have some time to meet tomorrow? I'd like to go over the quarterly reports together with you. Thanks.

해석

16–18번은 다음 전화 메시지와 평가에 관한 문제입니다.

여 안녕하세요, 마이클. 리즈예요. 제가 10월 9일 볼드윈 씨와의 회의를 확정했어요. [16]그녀는 회사의 모든 법적인 문제들을 처리하기 위해 우리 회사를 고용하는 걸 고려하고 있어요, 따라서 이곳은 우리에게 주요 거래처가 될 거예요. 회의 후에, 제가 그녀에게 저녁 식사를 대접하고, 그런 다음 공연을 보여 줄 거예요. [17]그 식당 바로 옆 극장에서 별 세 개짜리 공연을 하고 있어요, 그래서 제가 그 티켓을 샀어요. 저는 제가 충분히 준비가 되었는지 확인하고 싶어요, 그러니 [18]내일 만날 시간이 좀 있어요? 당신과 함께 분기별 보고서를 검토했으면 해요. 고마워요.

어휘

confirm 확인하다 consider -ing ~하는 것을 고려하다
handle 처리하다, 다루다 legal 법률과 관련된
major account 주요 거래처 fully prepared 완전히 준비된
go over ~을 검토하다 quarterly 분기별의

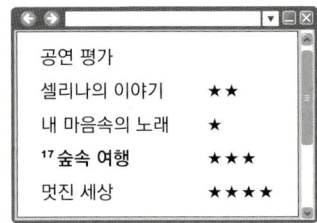

공연 평가	
셀리나의 이야기	★★
내 마음속의 노래	★
[17]숲속 여행	★★★
멋진 세상	★★★★

16.

화자는 어떤 종류의 업체에서 일하는 것 같은가?
(A) 회계 법인
(B) 직업소개소
(C) 법률 회사
(D) 금융 기관

어휘

employment 고용 financial 재정의, 금융의
institution 기관, 단체, 협회

17.

시각 자료를 보시오. 화자는 어떤 공연의 티켓을 샀는가?
(A) 셀리나의 이야기
(B) 내 마음속의 노래
(C) 숲속 여행
(D) 멋진 세상

18.

화자는 왜 내일 청자와 만나고 싶어 하는가?

(A) 고객을 소개하기 위해
(B) 발표 슬라이드를 만들기 위해
(C) 식당을 고르기 위해
(D) 몇몇 보고서를 검토하기 위해

패러프레이징

go over the quarterly reports → review some reports

UNIT 04 세부사항 문제

CHECK UP 본문 p.222

1. (B) **2.** (A)

[1] 미남 🎧

Question 1 refers to the following introduction.

M Ladies and gentlemen, it is now time for the main event, the announcement of the winner of this year's Music Education Award. It is given to someone in the community who has helped others learn about and enjoy music. The recipient will receive this beautiful trophy, along with a cash prize. But before we find out the winner, I'd like to welcome Gabriela Rowan to the stage. She is the one who has generously donated the funds for the cash prize, and she will be presenting the award. Let's give her a round of applause as she comes forward.

해석

1번은 다음 소개에 관한 문제입니다.

남 신사 숙녀 여러분, 이제 본 행사인 올해의 음악 교육상의 수상자 발표 시간입니다. 이것은 다른 사람들이 음악에 관해 배우고 음악을 즐기도록 도와준 지역사회의 인물에게 주어집니다. 수상자는 상금과 함께 이 아름다운 트로피를 받게 됩니다. 하지만 수상자를 알아보기 전에, 가브리엘라 로언 씨를 무대로 모시겠습니다. 그녀는 상금으로 쓰일 자금을 후하게 기부하신 분이며, 그녀가 이 상을 수여하겠습니다. 그녀가 앞으로 나오는 동안 박수를 보내 주세요.

어휘

community 지역사회 recipient 받는 사람, 수령인
along with ~와 함께 cash prize 상금
generously 후하게, 넉넉하게 donate 기부하다, 기증하다
fund 기금, 자금 a round of applause 한차례의 박수 (갈채)

1.

가브리엘라 로언은 누구인가?
(A) 전문 음악인
(B) 재정 기부자
(C) 시 공무원
(D) 행사 기획자

어휘

financial 재정의, 금융의 donor 기부자

패러프레이징

the one who has generously donated the funds
→ A financial donor

[2] 미녀 🎧

Question 2 refers to the following announcement.

> **W** I'd like to make a quick announcement, everyone. Saturday, February 8, will be our bank's free financial planning seminar. Every year, we invite community members to come and learn about the best ways to plan for major events in their lives such as… um… retirement or buying a house. We need some volunteers to assist with the event. You would set up equipment, sign people in, and do other tasks throughout the seminar. Since we know your weekends are valuable, everyone who volunteers will be given a gift certificate for the Fulton Department Store as a token of our gratitude.

해석

2번은 다음 공지에 관한 문제입니다.

여 여러분, 간단히 안내 말씀 드리겠습니다. 2월 8일 토요일에 우리 은행의 무료 재무 설계 세미나가 있습니다. 매해, 우리는 지역 주민들을 모셔서 인생에서 중요한 일들, 그러니까… 음… 은퇴나 주택 구매 같은 것들을 위한 계획을 세우는 가장 좋은 방법들에 대해 배우게 해 드립니다. 우리는 이 행사를 도와줄 자원봉사자 몇 명이 필요합니다. 여러분은 장비를 설치하고, 명부에 사람들의 이름을 적고, 그 밖의 다른 일들을 세미나 동안 하게 됩니다. 우리는 여러분의 주말이 얼마나 소중한지 알고 있으므로 자원봉사하시는 모든 분들에게는 감사의 표시로 풀턴 백화점 상품권을 드릴 것입니다.

어휘

financial 재정의, 금융의 retirement 은퇴
assist with ~을 돕다 set up 설치하다, 세우다
equipment 장비 sign in 명부에 기록하다 task 일, 과업
valuable 소중한 gift certificate 상품권 token 표시, 증거
gratitude 고마움, 감사

2.

청자들은 자원봉사의 대가로 무엇을 받을 것인가?
(A) 상품권
(B) 현금 보너스
(C) 티셔츠
(D) 하루 휴가

본문 p.224

패러프레이징 연습

1-4. 스크립트 참조   **5.** (A)   **6.** (A)

1.

Q 승무원들이 무엇을 도와줄 수 있는가?
A 서식을 기입하는 것

미남 🎧

> **M** Good morning, passengers. We are on schedule for our arrival in New York and will be landing in approximately half an hour. If you are having any difficulty filling out your customs or immigration forms, please notify one of our flight attendants to receive assistance.

해석

남 안녕하세요, 승객 여러분. 우리는 뉴욕에 예정대로 도착할 예정이며, 대략 30분 후에 착륙할 것입니다. 세관 신고서나 출입국 신고서 기입에 어려움이 있으시면, 저희 승무원 중 한 명에게 알리시고 도움을 받으시기 바랍니다.

어휘

flight attendant 승무원 on schedule 시간표대로, 예정대로
arrival 도착 land 착륙하다 approximately 대략, 거의
have difficulty -ing ~하는 데 어려움을 겪다
fill out 작성하다, 기입하다 customs 세관
immigration 출입국 assistance 도움, 지원

패러프레이징

filling out your customs or immigration forms
→ Completing a form

2.

Q 회사는 작년에 무엇을 했는가?
A 광고 전략을 바꾸었다.

미녀 🎧

> **W** I'd like to give you an update on our exercise bikes. Last year, we switched our advertising to include targeted ads on popular blogs. This has been a great move. The new strategy has led to a 30 percent increase in sales.

해석

여 우리의 실내 운동용 자전거에 대한 최신 소식을 알려드리고 싶습니다. 작년에 우리는 인기 있는 블로그에 타깃 광고를 포함시키는 것으로 우리 광고를 전환했습니다. 이것은 중요한 움직임이었습니다. 새로운 전략은 매출 30% 증가를 이끌었습니다.

어휘

strategy 전략 give an update 최신 소식을 알려주다
exercise bike 실내 운동용 자전거 switch 전환하다, 바꾸다
lead to ~로 이어지다

패러프레이징

switched our advertising to include targeted ads on popular blogs → changed an advertising strategy

3.

Q 화자는 책을 쓰기 위한 영감을 언제 처음 받았는가?
A 해외여행을 하는 동안

미남 🎧

> **M** It is an honor to speak here today at the Southfield Public Library. I'd like to thank everyone who has come to listen to this talk about my recently published book. I actually first got the idea for the plot when I was on vacation overseas in Singapore.

해석

남 오늘 이곳 사우스필드 공립 도서관에서 연설하게 되어 영광입니다. 제가 최근 출간한 책에 관한 이번 강연을 들으러 와 주신 모든 분들께 감사드리고 싶습니다. **사실 제가 처음 줄거리에 대한 아이디어를 얻은 것은 싱가포르에서 해외 휴가 중일 때였습니다.**

어휘

inspire to ~하도록 고무하다, 영감을 주다
travel abroad 해외여행을 하다
it's an honor to ~하게 되어 영광이다
publish 출판하다, 출간하다　plot 구성, 줄거리
on vacation 휴가로, 휴가 중인　overseas 해외에; 해외의

패러프레이징

when I was on vacation overseas in Singapore → While traveling abroad

4.

Q 크레스트뷰 지역은 무엇으로 유명한가?
A 그곳의 긴 역사

미녀 🎧

> **W** The next stop on our tour will be the Crestview neighborhood. I think you'll all enjoy exploring this area. It is known for having the oldest homes in the city. Many of them were built over 300 years ago.

해석

여 우리 관광의 다음 목적지는 크레스트뷰 지역이 되겠습니다. 여러분 모두 이 지역을 즐겁게 둘러보시리라 생각합니다. **이곳은 이 도시에서 가장 오래된 주택들이 있는 것으로 유명합니다. 그중 많은 것들이 300여 년 전에 지어졌습니다.**

어휘

be known for ~로 알려져 있다, 유명하다
neighborhood 인근, 지역　explore 답사하다

패러프레이징

the oldest homes ~ built over 300 years ago

→ long history

5.

청자들은 어떻게 할인을 받을 수 있는가?
(A) 온라인으로 구매함으로써
(B) 단체로 티켓을 구매함으로써

미녀 🎧

> **W** The Sunrise Theater has announced that it has added a second performance for the Amsterdam Dance Troupe on July 10. This is because the first performance is nearly sold out. Some tickets may be available at the door. However, those who go online and buy them will get 15 percent off.

해석

여 선라이즈 극장은 7월 10일 암스테르담 무용단의 두 번째 공연을 추가했다고 발표했습니다. 이것은 첫 번째 공연이 거의 매진되었기 때문입니다. 일부 티켓은 입구에서 구입하실 수도 있습니다. **하지만, 온라인에 접속해 티켓을 구매하시는 분들은 15% 할인 받게 됩니다.**

어휘

discount 할인　make a purchase 구매하다
performance 공연, 연주　dance troupe 무용단
sold out 매진된　available 이용할 수 있는, 구할 수 있는

패러프레이징

go online and buy them → making a purchase online

6.

화자는 건물에 대해 무엇이라고 말하는가?
(A) 그곳은 출입 코드가 필요하다.
(B) 그곳은 주차장이 없다.

미남 🎧

> **M** I will send you a list of all the documents you should bring to the interview. Please make sure you prepare everything. In addition, visitors need to enter a special code in the keypad to unlock the front door of our building. It's 3225. If you have any questions, please e-mail me.

해석

남 당신이 면접에 가져와야 할 모든 서류 목록을 보내드리겠습니다. 반드시 모든 것을 준비하시기 바랍니다. 또한, **방문객들이 저희 건물의 정문을 열려면 키패드에 특별 코드를 입력해야 합니다.** 그것은 3225입니다. 질문이 있으시면, 제게 이메일을 보내 주세요.

어휘

require 필요하다, 요구하다　entry 들어감, 출입
parking area 주차장　enter 들어가다, 입력하다
unlock 열다

need to enter a special code to unlock the front door
→ requires an entry code

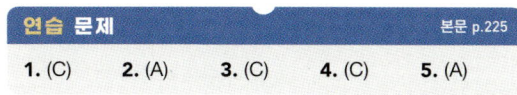

1. (C)   **2.** (A)   **3.** (C)   **4.** (C)   **5.** (A)

[1] 영녀 🎧

Question 1 refers to the following telephone message.

> W   This is a message for Dan White. I'm Michelle from Hampton Computer Services. I'm calling about the monitor you dropped off to be repaired last Thursday. I told you we'd be able to have it back to you by tomorrow. Unfortunately, we are still waiting for a part to arrive. It's supposed to be delivered on Monday, so I'll call you back then when I know more. I'm sorry for the inconvenience caused.

해석

1번은 다음 전화 메시지에 관한 문제입니다.

여   이것은 댄 화이트에게 전하는 메시지입니다. 저는 햄턴 컴퓨터 서비스의 미셸입니다. 당신이 지난 목요일 수리를 위해 맡기신 모니터에 관해 전화드립니다. **제가 내일까지 돌려받으실 수 있게 하겠다고 말씀드렸죠. 안타깝게도, 저희는 아직 부품 하나가 도착하기를 기다리는 중입니다. 그것이 월요일에 배달될 예정이에요,** 그러니 제가 더 자세히 알게 되면 그때 다시 전화드리도록 하겠습니다. 이로 인한 불편에 사과드립니다.

어휘

drop off 내려놓다, 내려 주다   repair 수리하다; 수리
inconvenience 불편   cause 초래하다, 야기하다

1.

화자는 수리에 관해 무엇이라고 말하는가?
(A) 그것은 전문가에 의해 진행될 수 있다.
(B) 그것은 예상보다 비용이 더 많이 들 것이다.
(C) 그것은 지연되었다.
(D) 그것은 많은 단계를 거치지 않을 것이다.

어휘

expert 전문가   involve 수반하다, 관련시키다

[2-3] 호남 🎧

Questions 2-3 refer to the following advertisement.

> M   Are you looking for an easy way to move your furniture and belongings? Well, Top Movers is here for you. One of our qualified and professional employees can visit your house to offer you a price quotation. Plus, ²you can

save up to 20 percent on our price quote just by answering a few simple questions on your move at our Web site, www.topmovers.com. Remember, ³if you are not satisfied with our service for any reason, we will return 100 percent of your money, no questions asked.

해석

2-3번은 다음 광고에 관한 문제입니다.

남   가구와 소유물을 옮기는 쉬운 방법을 찾고 계시나요? 음, 당신을 위해 탑 이삿짐 운송업체가 있습니다. 자격을 갖춘 전문적인 저희 직원 중 한 명이 당신의 집을 방문하여 비용 견적을 내드릴 수 있습니다. 게다가, **²저희 웹사이트 www.topmovers.com에서 당신의 이사에 관한 몇 가지 간단한 질문에 응답하시기만 하면, 비용 견적에서 최대 20%까지 할인받으실 수 있습니다.** 기억하세요, **³무슨 이유로든 저희 서비스에 만족하지 않으면 어떤 질문도 없이 돈을 100% 환불해 드립니다.**

어휘

belongings ((항상 복수형)) 소유물   qualified 자격이 있는
professional 전문적인   price quotation 비용 견적
price quote 비용 견적, 견적서   be satisfied with ~에 만족하다

2.

청자들은 회사 웹사이트에서 무엇을 하도록 요청받는가?
(A) 설문지 작성하기
(B) 주택 사진 제공하기
(C) 팔려고 내놓은 주택들 비교하기
(D) 고객 의견 읽기

어휘

fill out 기입하다, 작성하다   questionnaire 설문지
compare 비교하다

패러프레이징

answering a few simple questions
→ Fill out a questionnaire

3.

고객들이 서비스에 만족하지 않으면 무엇을 받을 수 있는가?
(A) 청소 서비스
(B) 할인 쿠폰
(C) 전액 환불
(D) 상점 상품권

어휘

refund 환불; 환불해 주다   voucher 상품권, 할인권

패러프레이징

return 100 percent of your money → A full refund

[4-5] 영녀 🎧

Questions 4-5 refer to the following talk.

> W   I'm delighted to share with you our most recent invention. The T17 Electric Drone is everything

that has been missing in drone technology. Moreover, ⁴it has a battery life about 10 times longer than any drone out there. Members of our design team are here to walk you through the process we took to create it. Just a reminder, ⁵please write down a few of your thoughts in the space provided on the back of the brochure. That way, you'll have them fresh in your mind during the feedback session.

해석

4-5번은 다음 담화에 관한 문제입니다.

여 우리의 가장 최근 발명품을 공유하게 되어 기쁩니다. T17 전기 드론에는 드론 기술에서 빠졌던 모든 것이 있습니다. 게다가, ⁴시중의 어떤 드론보다도 약 10배 긴 배터리 수명을 가지고 있습니다. 우리 설계팀의 팀원들이 그것을 만들기 위해 우리가 거쳤던 과정을 여러분에게 차근차근 설명해 드리기 위해 이곳에 자리했습니다. 다시 한번 알려 드리자면, ⁵책자 뒤에 제공된 공간에 여러분의 생각을 몇 가지 적어 두시기 바랍니다. 그렇게 하면, 피드백 시간 동안 그것들이 생생하게 기억날 것입니다.

어휘

invention 발명품, 발명 electric 전기의 missing 없어진, 빠진
walk ~ through ~에게 차근차근 알려 주다, 자세하게 설명해 주다
process 과정, 절차 reminder 상기시키는 것
brochure 안내 책자 have ~ in mind ~에 관해 생각하고 있다

4.

제품의 특징은 무엇인가?
(A) 경량
(B) 경쟁력 있는 가격
(C) 긴 배터리 수명
(D) 소형 크기

어휘

feature 특징, 특색 competitive 경쟁력 있는
compact 소형의

패러프레이징

a battery life about 10 times longer than any drone
→ A long battery life

5.

청자들은 무엇을 하도록 권고받는가?
(A) 자신의 생각 적어 두기
(B) 전시 부스 방문하기
(C) 디자인에 투표하기
(D) 앞쪽으로 이동하기

어휘

display 전시, 진열 vote on ~에 대해 투표하다

패러프레이징

a few of your thoughts → ideas

본문 p.226

실전 문제

1. (C)	2. (A)	3. (B)	4. (C)	5. (B)
6. (A)	7. (D)	8. (B)	9. (C)	10. (C)
11. (B)	12. (A)	13. (B)	14. (B)	15. (C)
16. (C)	17. (B)	18. (A)		

[1-3] 미남 🎧

Questions 1-3 refer to the following telephone message.

M Hi, Nicola. It's Kai. ¹I'm working on the new clothing designs for the upcoming runway show. I've been having some difficulty getting the fabrics that I need. So, ²if you don't mind, I'd like to change our supplier. I think we could get better variety as well as better service that way. Also, ³I saw your drawing with the changes you suggested making to the denim jacket. Unfortunately... um... it's similar to the Pacifica brand. ³I think we'd better try to make our look stand out.

해석

1-3번은 다음 전화 메시지에 관한 문제입니다.

남 안녕하세요, 니콜라. 카이예요. ¹다가오는 패션쇼를 위해 새로운 의상 디자인 작업을 하는 중이에요. 제게 필요한 직물을 구하는 데 어려움을 좀 겪고 있어요. 그래서, ²당신이 괜찮다면 우리 공급업체를 바꾸고 싶어요. 그렇게 하면 더 나은 서비스뿐만 아니라 더 나은 다양성을 얻을 수 있을 것 같아요. 또한, ³당신이 청재킷에 제안한 수정 사항이 담긴 당신의 그림을 봤어요. 안타깝게도... 음... 그건 퍼시피아 브랜드와 유사해요. ³우리의 스타일이 돋보이게 하려고 노력하는 게 좋을 것 같아요.

어휘

work on ~에 노력을 들이다, ~을 작업하다 clothing 옷, 의류
upcoming 다가오는, 곧 있을 runway show 패션쇼
have difficulty -ing ~하는 데 어려움을 겪다 fabric 직물, 천
supplier 공급자, 공급 회사 variety 다양성
similar to ~와 비슷한 stand out 눈에 띄다, 돋보이다

1.

화자는 무엇을 전문으로 하는 것 같은가?
(A) 소프트웨어 개발
(B) 식품 생산
(C) 패션 디자인
(D) 부동산

어휘

development 개발 production 생산

패러프레이징

clothing designs → Fashion design

2.
화자는 무엇을 하고 싶어 하는가?
(A) 다른 공급업체 이용하기
(B) 조수 고용하기
(C) 색상 바꾸기
(D) 테스트 더 많이 하기

assistant 조수, 보조원 perform 수행하다, 실시하다

패러프레이징

change our supplier → Use a different supplier

3.
화자는 왜 "그건 퍼시피아 브랜드와 유사해요"라고 말하는가?
(A) 칭찬하기 위해
(B) 제안을 거절하기 위해
(C) 전략을 확인하기 위해
(D) 업체를 추천하기 위해

어휘

compliment 칭찬 reject 거절하다 suggestion 제안
confirm 확인하다 strategy 전략

[4-6] 영녀 🎧
Questions 4-6 refer to the following broadcast.

> **W** And now for news from the publishing world. Deanna Caruso's new cookbook has made the top of the best-seller list again this week. ⁴While most of you know her for her successful swimming career, she is now showing off her talents for cooking. ⁵The cookbook, *Deanna at Home*, has been selling so well because each recipe gives you different options to change ingredients. It's perfect for people with allergies or those on special diets. Last Friday, Ms. Caruso announced that she is also launching ⁶a Web site with cooking videos and more. That goes live tomorrow, so don't miss it!

해석

4-6번은 다음 방송에 관한 문제입니다.

여 이제 출판계 뉴스 시간입니다. 디애나 카루소의 새 요리책이 이번 주에 또다시 베스트셀러 1위 자리에 올랐습니다. ⁴여러분 대부분은 그녀를 그녀의 성공적인 수영 경력으로 알고 계시지만, 이제 그녀는 요리에 대한 재능을 뽐내고 있습니다. ⁵요리책 〈디애나 앳 홈〉이 아주 잘 팔리고 있는데, 각 조리법이 재료를 바꿀 수 있는 다양한 선택권을 주기 때문입니다. 알레르기가 있는 사람들이나 특별 규정식을 하는 사람들에게 딱입니다. 지난 금요일, 카루소 씨는 또한 ⁶요리 영상 등이 있는 웹사이트를 출시한다고 발표했습니다. ⁶내일 가동되니, 놓치지 마세요!

어휘

publishing 출판 cookbook 요리책 career 경력, 이력
show off ~을 자랑하다 talents for ~의 재능 recipe 조리법

---

ingredient 재료, 성분 special diet 특별 규정식
launch 시작하다, 개시하다 go live 가동 준비가 되다

4.
디애나 카루소는 누구인가?
(A) 라디오 진행자
(B) 기자
(C) 프로 운동선수
(D) 식당 주인

어휘

professional 직업의, 전문적인

패러프레이징

successful swimming career → A professional athlete

5.
이 요리책은 왜 인기가 있는가?
(A) 그것은 건강식에 관한 아이디어가 많다.
(B) 그것은 재료를 대체하는 것을 쉽게 해 준다.
(C) 그것은 사진이 많이 들어 있다.
(D) 그것의 조리법은 많은 단계를 요구하지 않는다.

어휘

substitute 대체하다, 대신하다 require 요구하다, 필요하다

패러프레이징

gives you different options to change ingredients
→ makes it easy to substitute ingredients

6.
화자에 따르면, 웹사이트는 언제 출시될 것인가?
(A) 내일
(B) 이번 금요일에
(C) 다음 주에
(D) 다음 달에

[7-9] 미남 🎧
Questions 7-9 refer to the following announcement.

> **M** ⁷Attention visitors to the City Art Museum. We are thrilled to announce that the construction of the garden on our property is complete. ⁸Just like the museum, there will be no admission fee. We have outdoor chairs so visitors can relax among beautiful flowers and plants. ⁹Originally, we had planned to close the garden at 6 P.M. daily. However, we've now decided to give it the same closing time as our building, which is 8 P.M.

해석

7-9번은 다음 공지에 관한 문제입니다.

남 ⁷시립 미술관 방문객들에게 알립니다. 저희 건물 구내의 정원 공사가 완료되었음을 알려 드리게 되어 기쁩니다. ⁸미술관과 마찬가지로, 입장료는 없습니다. 방문객들이 아름다운 꽃과 나무들

사이에서 편안히 쉬실 수 있도록 야외용 의자를 비치해 두었습니다. **⁹원래는, 매일 저녁 6시에 정원을 폐장할 계획이었습니다.** 하지만, 지금은 저희 건물과 같은 똑같은 폐장 시간인 저녁 8시를 적용하기로 결정하였습니다.

어휘

thrilled 아주 흥분한, 신나는 construction 건설, 공사
property 건물, 건물 구매 complete 완료된
admission fee 입장료 relax 휴식을 취하다 originally 원래

7.

공지는 어디에서 이루어지고 있는가?
(A) 사무용 건물에서
(B) 공원에서
(C) 호텔에서
(D) 미술관에서

8.

화자는 정원에 대해 무엇이라고 말하는가?
(A) 그곳은 곧 새로운 식물들을 받을 것이다.
(B) 그곳은 무료로 방문할 수 있다.
(C) 그곳은 야외 미술 전시를 할 것이다.
(D) 그곳은 비공개 파티를 위한 공간을 제공할 수 있다.

어휘

feature 특별히 포함하다, 특징으로 삼다
exhibit 전시(품); 전시하다
accommodate 공간을 제공하다, 수용하다
private 사적인, 비공개의

패러프레이징

there will be no admission fee
→ It can be visited for free

9.

원래 계획에 대해 무엇이 변경되었는가?
(A) 공사 예산
(B) 좌석 배치
(C) 폐장 시간
(D) 방문객 수

어휘

original 원래의; 원본 budget 예산 layout 레이아웃, 배치

[10-12] 영녀 🎧

Questions 10-12 refer to the following excerpt from a meeting.

> W Good morning, everyone. To begin today's meeting, I'd like to congratulate the entire team. **¹⁰Because of the ad campaign you developed for our new sofa, we have seen record sales for this item.** I'm happy to say that the figures are even better than we expected. Now, some of you may have heard that Clair Yates plans to transfer to another branch at

the end of the month. That means... um... **¹¹one of you will have the opportunity to be promoted to team leader. If you're interested, ¹²please visit the company's internal Web site to read a description of the role.**

해석

10-12번은 다음 회의 발췌록에 관한 문제입니다.

여 안녕하세요, 여러분. 팀 전체를 축하하는 것으로 오늘 회의를 시작하려고 합니다. **¹⁰여러분이 우리의 새 소파를 위해 개발한 광고 캠페인 덕분에, 우리는 이 품목에 대해 기록적인 매출을 냈습니다.** 그 수치가 우리가 예상한 것보다 훨씬 더 좋다고 말씀드리게 되어 기쁩니다. 자, 여러분 중 몇 사람은 클레어 예이츠가 이달 말에 다른 지점으로 옮길 계획이라는 걸 들었을지도 모릅니다. 이것은... 음... **¹¹여러분 중 한 명에게 팀장으로 승진될 기회가 주어질 것이라는 의미입니다. 관심이 있으면, ¹²회사의 내부 웹사이트에 방문하여 역할에 대한 설명을 읽어 보기 바랍니다.**

어휘

congratulate 축하하다 entire 전체의 record 기록적인
figures ((보통 복수형)) 수치 opportunity 기회
promote 승진시키다 description 서술, 설명

10.

화자는 왜 청자들을 축하하는가?
(A) 회사가 수상 후보로 지명되었다.
(B) 고객들이 긍정적인 평가를 했다.
(C) 신상품이 잘 팔리고 있다.
(D) 프로젝트가 일찍 완료되었다.

어휘

be nominated for ~의 후보로 지명되다 positive 긍정적인
review 검토, 비평 complete 완료하다, 마치다

패러프레이징

our new sofa, we have seen record sales for this item
→ A new product is selling well

11.

화자에 따르면, 청자들 중 한 명은 무엇을 할 수 있을 것인가?
(A) 발표하기
(B) 승진하기
(C) 팀 임무 선택하기
(D) 출장 가기

어휘

promotion 승진 assignment 과제, 임무

패러프레이징

be promoted to team leader → Get a promotion

12.

화자는 웹사이트에서 무엇을 할 것을 제안하는가?
(A) 직무 설명을 읽는 것
(B) 계정을 만드는 것
(C) 서식을 다운로드하는 것

(D) 행사에 등록하는 것

어휘

account 계정, 계좌 register for ~에 등록하다

패러프레이징

a description of the role → a job description

[13-15] 미녀 🎧

Questions 13-15 refer to the following advertisement.

> **W** Do you want to get premium-brand products at a great price? With a little help from Coupon Spotter, you'll never miss another sale again. **13** We send text alerts directly to your phone, notifying you about special offers in your area. **14** To sign up, simply visit our Web site at www.couponspotter.net and enter your phone number. You can choose between daily, weekly, or monthly messages. And, **15** if you sign up this month, by August 31, you'll get a free adjustable cell phone stand. Join Coupon Spotter today and start saving!

해석

13-15번은 다음 광고에 관한 문제입니다.

여 저렴한 가격에 고급 브랜드 제품을 구매하고 싶으세요? 쿠폰 스포터로부터 약간의 도움을 받으면, 또 다른 세일을 놓치는 일이 다시는 없을 것입니다. **13** 저희가 여러분의 전화로 바로 문자 알림을 보내서 지역의 특가 판매에 대해 알려 드립니다. **14** 신청하시려면, 그저 저희 웹사이트 www.couponspotter.net에 방문하셔서 전화번호를 입력하세요. 일일, 주간, 혹은 월간 메시지 중에서 고르시면 됩니다. 그리고, **15** 이번 달, 그러니까 8월 31일까지 신청하시면, 조절 가능한 휴대폰 거치대를 무료로 받게 됩니다. 오늘 쿠폰 스포터에 등록하시고 절약을 시작하세요!

어휘

premium 아주 높은, 고급의 text alert 문자 알림
directly 곧장, 똑바로 notify 알리다, 통지하다
special offer 특가 판매 sign up 신청하다, 등록하다
enter 입력하다 adjustable 조절 가능한 stand 스탠드, 거치대
join 가입하다 save 절약하다, 아끼다

13.

이 서비스는 무엇을 제공하는가?

(A) 무료 배달

(B) 할인에 대한 알림

(C) 모바일 은행 업무

(D) 지역 뉴스

어휘

banking 은행 업무

패러프레이징

text alerts ~ notifying you about special offers
→ Alerts on discounts

14.

사람들은 웹사이트에서 무엇을 제공해야 하는가?

(A) 선호하는 브랜드

(B) 전화번호

(C) 이메일 주소

(D) 신용카드 번호

어휘

preference 선호, 선호되는 것

패러프레이징

enter → provide

15.

청자들은 어떻게 무료 선물을 받을 수 있는가?

(A) 일정 금액을 지출함으로써

(B) 친구를 추천함으로써

(C) 8월에 신청함으로써

(D) 설문 조사를 작성함으로써

어휘

amount 액수, 총액 complete 기입하다, 작성하다
survey 설문 조사

패러프레이징

a free adjustable cell phone stand → a free gift

[16-18] 영녀 🎧

Questions 16-18 refer to the following telephone message and work schedule.

> **W** Hi, Kenny. **16** It's Debra Rooney from Yorkshire Pharmaceuticals. I've been looking at the results for our new allergy medication. I'm pleased with the figures so far, but **17** I think we'd better do further testing before moving forward with the project. I'd like to talk to you about this, so let's schedule a meeting. I want to make sure we aren't missing anything important. **18** I'm wondering if you're free tomorrow morning, March 9, at 9 o'clock. Something on my schedule got canceled, so I'm available then. Please call me back at 555-0037. Thank you.

해석

16-18번은 다음 전화 메시지와 업무 일정표에 관한 문제입니다.

여 안녕하세요, 케니. **16** 요크셔 제약의 데브라 루니예요. 우리의 새로운 알레르기 약의 결과를 살펴보고 있었어요. 지금까지의 수치에는 만족하지만, **17** 이 프로젝트를 추진하기 전에 추가 테스트를 하는 게 좋을 것 같아요. 이에 대해 당신과 이야기하고 싶으니 회의 일정을 잡도록 하죠. 저는 우리가 중요한 것을 하나도 놓치지 않았음을 확실히 하고 싶어요. **18** 당신이 내일 아침, 그러니까 3월 9일 9시에 시간이 있는지 궁금해요. 제 일정 중 어떤 것이 취소되어서 전 그때 시간이 돼요. 555-0037로 다시 전화 주세요. 고마워요.

어휘

pharmaceuticals 약, 제약 medication 약, 약물
figures ((보통 복수형)) 수치 further 추가의
move forward 전진하다 get canceled 취소되다
available (만날) 시간이 있는

데브라 루니: 3월 9일 일정	
¹⁸ 오전 9시	디자인팀 브리핑
오전 9시 30분	신문사 전화 인터뷰
오전 10시	경영진 회의
오전 11시	온라인 교육

16.

화자는 어떤 종류의 업체에서 일하는가?

(A) 회계 기관
(B) 우체국
(C) 제약 회사
(D) 금융 기관

어휘

accounting 회계 financial 금융의, 재정의
institution 기관, 단체, 협회

17.

화자는 회의에서 무엇에 대해 이야기하기를 원하는가?

(A) 프로젝트를 취소하는 것
(B) 더 많은 실험을 하는 것
(C) 비용을 절감하는 것
(D) 투자자를 찾는 것

어휘

run (테스트·검사 등을) 하다 expense 비용 investor 투자자

패러프레이징

do further testing → Running more tests

18.

시각 자료를 보시오. 화자의 일정에서 어떤 활동이 취소되었는가?

(A) 디자인팀 브리핑
(B) 신문사 전화 인터뷰
(C) 경영진 회의
(D) 온라인 교육

UNIT 05 제안·요청사항 문제

CHECK UP

본문 p.228

1. (C)　　**2.** (A)

---

[1] 미녀 🎧

Question 1 refers to the following announcement.

> W Attention, please. As you know, we've decided to begin selling men's clothes in our store to expand our business, starting next month. Our sales from women's clothes have been great, so we expect this new business to increase profits. Before we start selling the new products, we will have to take inventory of all lines of clothes in our warehouse. It must be done by this weekend to ensure we have space for the deliveries of the new stock. Also, we'll be getting our new uniforms next week. Those will be passed out by your supervisor.

해석

1번은 다음 공지에 관한 문제입니다.

여 주목해 주세요. 아시다피, 다음 달부터 사업을 확장하기 위해 매장에서 남성복 판매를 시작하기로 결정했습니다. 여성복 매출이 아주 좋았기 때문에 이번 신규 사업도 수익을 증가시킬 것으로 기대하고 있습니다. **신제품을 판매하기 전에, 우리 창고에 있는 모든 의류 라인의 재고 조사를 해야 할 것입니다. 새 재고가 배송될 공간을 확보하기 위해 조사는 이번 주말까지 완료되어야 합니다.** 또한, 우리는 다음 주에 새로운 유니폼을 받게 될 겁니다. 여러분의 관리자가 그것들을 나누어 드릴 겁니다.

어휘

expand 확장하다 take inventory 재고 조사를 하다
warehouse 창고 ensure 확보하다, 확실하게 하다
stock 재고, 재고품 pass out 나누어 주다
supervisor 상사, 관리자

1.

청자들은 이번 주말까지 무엇을 하도록 요청받는가?

(A) 신제품 들여놓기
(B) 창고 청소하기
(C) 재고 파악하기
(D) 새 유니폼 입기

어휘

stock (물품을) 들여놓다

[2] 미남 🎧

Question 2 refers to the following broadcast.

> M It's 10 o'clock, time for the traffic update on Radio 105. Anyone taking Route 32 can enjoy an easy commute, as traffic is flowing smoothly in both directions. A work crew is painting lines on Austin Street, so there have been reports of some delays in the area. Also, if you're traveling in the Warson neighborhood, there is construction on Glenn Street. This project will be ongoing for a few weeks, so look for

해석

2번은 다음 방송에 관한 문제입니다.

남 10시 정각, 라디오 105 교통 정보 업데이트 시간입니다. 32번 국도를 이용하시는 분들은 양방향 교통 흐름이 원활하므로 수월하게 통근하실 수 있습니다. 작업자들이 오스틴가에서 차선 페인트 작업 중이라, 그 지역에 일부 정체가 있다는 보고가 있습니다. 또한, 워슨 지역을 이동 중이시라면, 글렌가에 공사가 있습니다. 이 프로젝트는 몇 주 동안 계속될 예정이므로 **발생할 수 있는 통행 지장 상황을 더 알아보시려면 시의 웹페이지에서 최신 정보를 찾아보십시오.** 다음은 조너선 라크의 스포츠 요약입니다.

어휘

commute 통근; 통근하다 flow 흘러가다, 이동하다
smoothly 원활하게, 순조롭게 direction 방향 delay 정체, 지연
ongoing 진행 중인 disruption 지장, 중단, 방해
recap (= recapitulation) 요약

2.

청자들은 무엇을 하도록 권고받는가?
(A) 웹사이트 확인하기
(B) 매니저에게 연락하기
(C) 문자 경보 알림 받기
(D) 다른 경로로 이동하기

어휘

alert 경계 경보

패러프레이징

look for updates on the city's Web page
→ Check a Web site

패러프레이징 연습
본문 p.230

1-4. 스크립트 참조   **5.** (B)   **6.** (A)

1.

Q 화자는 청자에게 무엇을 해 달라고 요청하는가?
A 서식 작성하기

미남 🎧

M Our customers' opinions matter to us, and we
use their feedback to make improvements. So,
I hope you fill out the customer satisfaction
survey that was sent to you by e-mail.

해석

남 고객님들의 의견은 저희에게 중요하고, 저희는 개선을 위해 고객님들의 피드백을 활용합니다. 그러니, **여러분에게 이메일로 전송된 고객 만족도 설문 조사를 기입해 주시면 좋겠습니다.**

어휘

fill out 기입하다, 작성하다 matter 중요하다, 문제되다; 문제
feedback 피드백, 의견, 반응
make an improvement 개선하다, 향상시키다
customer satisfaction 고객 만족 survey (설문) 조사

패러프레이징

fill out the customer satisfaction survey
→ Fill out a form

2.

Q 청자들은 무엇을 하도록 요청받는가?
A 교육 과정에 등록하기

미녀 🎧

W You cannot use the new machinery until you
have been certified. Therefore, training
sessions will be held throughout the week.
Please sign up for one that suits your
schedule. The sign-up sheet is in the break
room.

해석

여 여러분은 자격증을 받을 때까지 새 기계를 사용할 수 없습니다. 따라서, **한 주 내내 교육이 열릴 것입니다. 여러분의 일정에 맞는 것을 신청하시기 바랍니다.** 신청서는 휴게실에 있습니다.

어휘

register for ~에 등록하다 machinery 기계(류)
certify 증명하다, 자격증을 교부하다 sign up for ~을 신청하다
suit (~에게) 맞다 sign-up sheet 참가 신청서
break room 휴게실

패러프레이징

sign up for one → Register for a training session

3.

Q 화자는 청자들에게 무엇을 하라고 제안하는가?
A 셔틀버스 타기

미남 🎧

M This weekend, the city's annual Independence
Day parade will be held in downtown area. The
city center will be crowded, and parking will be
very limited. So, I recommend taking one of
the hotel's complimentary shuttle buses if you
plan to attend this event.

해석

남 이번 주말, 시의 연례 독립 기념일 퍼레이드가 도심 지역에서 열립니다. 도시가 붐빌 것이고, 주차 공간은 매우 제한적일 것입니다. 따라서, **이 행사에 참석하실 계획이라면 호텔의 무료 셔틀버스 중 하나를 이용하시길 추천합니다.**

어휘

annual 매년의, 연례의

Independence Day (미국의) 독립 기념일
parade 퍼레이드, 가두 행진 downtown area 도심 지역
limited 제한된, 한정된 complimentary 무료의
attend 참석하다

taking one of the hotel's complimentary shuttle buses
→ Take a shuttle bus

4.

Q 청자들은 5월에 무엇을 하도록 권장받는가?
A 시험 삼아 타 보기

미녀 🎧

> **W** Our new bicycle folds into a compact size for easy storage. Nevertheless, it has the excellent performance you would expect from a standard bicycle. Stop by any Coney's retail location during the month of May to take a free spin on one and try it out.

해석

여 우리의 새로운 자전거는 쉬운 보관을 위해 소형 크기로 접힙니다. 그럼에도 불구하고, 표준 규격의 자전거에서 기대할 수 있는 우수한 성능을 가지고 있습니다. **5월에 아무 코니 판매점에 들러서 무료로 하나 타 보시고 시험해 보세요.**

어휘

take a test ride 시험 삼아 타다 fold 접다 compact 소형의
storage 저장, 보관 nevertheless 그럼에도 불구하고
performance 성능, 효율 take a spin 타러 가다
try out 시험 삼아 해 보다

패러프레이징
take a free spin on one and try it out
→ Take a test ride

5.

화자는 무엇을 제안하는가?
(A) 새 분석가를 고용하는 것
(B) 일부 고객들을 대상으로 설문 조사를 하는 것

미녀 🎧

> **W** Unfortunately, my analysis shows that there has been a steady decline in our footwear sales. We need to find out why this is happening. So, I think we should e-mail a questionnaire to some of our customers. I believe that this will give us some insight into the issue.

해석

여 안타깝게도, 제 분석은 우리 신발의 매출이 꾸준히 감소하고 있음을 보여 줍니다. 우리는 왜 이러한 일이 일어나는지 알아내야 합니다. 따라서, **우리가 일부 고객들에게 이메일로 설문지를 보**

내야 한다고 생각합니다. 이것이 우리에게 이 문제에 대한 통찰을 줄 것이라고 생각합니다.

어휘

analyst 분석가 survey (설문) 조사하다; (설문) 조사
analysis 분석 steady 꾸준한 decline 감소, 하락; 감소하다
footwear 신발(류) questionnaire 설문지
insight 이해, 간파, 통찰력

패러프레이징
e-mail a questionnaire to some of our customers
→ Surveying some customers

6.

화자는 청자들에게 무엇을 하라고 요청하는가?
(A) 다과 먹기
(B) 그들의 제안 공유하기

미남 🎧

> **M** Finally on today's agenda, I'd like to recognize Lawrence for the hard work he did on the contract negotiations. Great job, Lawrence! And to celebrate getting this contract, we've got cookies and coffee at the back. Don't forget to grab some before you leave.

해석

남 오늘의 마지막 안건으로, 로렌스가 계약 협상에 들인 공로를 인정하고 싶습니다. 잘했어요, 로렌스! 그리고 이번 계약을 따낸 것을 축하하기 위해, **뒤쪽에 과자와 커피를 준비했습니다. 떠나기 전에 잊지 말고 드세요.**

어휘

refreshments ((항상 복수형)) 다과, 음식물 agenda 의제, 안건
recognize 인정하다, 알아보다 negotiation 협상
get a contract 계약을 따내다 grab 재빨리 먹다, 이용하다

패러프레이징
cookies and coffee ~ grab some
→ Have some refreshments

연습 문제   본문 p.231

1. (A)   **2.** (C)   **3.** (B)   **4.** (B)   **5.** (A)

[1] 미남 🎧
Question 1 refers to the following tour information.

> **M** Good morning, everyone. My name is Kyle, and I'll be leading you on today's hike. We'll be taking the Eagleview Trail. It is one of the most difficult trails in the park, so that's why we only offer it to experienced hikers. We'll start our hike at 9 o'clock, which is in about 10 minutes. Before then, feel free to give your backpack

and other equipment one last look to make
sure it is in good condition.

해석
1번은 다음 관광 정보에 관한 문제입니다.

남 안녕하세요, 여러분. 제 이름은 카일이고, 오늘 하이킹에서 여러분을 안내해 드릴 겁니다. 우리는 이글뷰 트레일을 갈 건데요. 공원에서 가장 힘든 산길 중 하나이기 때문에 숙련된 등산객들에게만 제공하고 있습니다. **우리는 대략 10분 뒤인 9시 정각에 하이킹을 시작할 겁니다. 그전에, 여러분의 배낭과 다른 장비가 좋은 상태인지 확실히 하기 위해 마지막으로 한번 더 확인하세요.**

어휘
lead 안내하다, 이끌다 hike 하이킹, 도보 여행; 하이킹하다
trail 산길, 시골길 equipment 장비

1.
화자는 청자들에게 9시 전에 무엇을 하라고 제안하는가?
(A) 일부 장비들 점검하기
(B) 지도 내려받기
(C) 물 마시기
(D) 사진 몇 장 찍기

패러프레이징
give your backpack and other equipment one last
look → Check some equipment

[2-3] 미남 🎧
Questions 2-3 refer to the following telephone
message.

M Hello, Gary. This is Stanley. ²I just got the
results from the survey on where to go for the
company retreat this year. We really wanted
everyone's opinion this year, and, thankfully,
everyone participated. Unfortunately, the
beach you suggested was the least popular.
But don't worry, the other places we are
looking at apparently have a lot to do. I'll
e-mail you the results in a minute. ³Please look
up the rates and specifics of the top two
places. We can choose one after we know a
bit more.

해석
2-3번은 다음 전화 메시지에 관한 문제입니다.

남 안녕하세요, 게리. 저는 스탠리입니다. **²올해 회사 야유회를 어디로 갈지에 관한 설문 조사 결과를 방금 받았습니다. 우리는 올해 정말 모두의 의견을 원했고, 감사하게도 모두가 참여했습니다.** 안타깝게도, 당신이 제안한 해변은 가장 인기가 없었습니다. 하지만 걱정하지 마세요, 우리가 검토하고 있는 다른 장소들엔 할 일이 많아 보입니다. 잠시 후에 결과를 이메일로 보내드리겠습니다. **³상위 두 곳의 요금과 세부 사항을 찾아봐 주세요.** 조금 더 알아보고 하나를 고를 수 있습니다.

어휘
company retreat 회사 야유회 opinion 의견, 생각
participate 참여하다 apparently 보기에
look up ~을 찾아보다 specifics 세부 사항

2.
화자는 설문 조사에 대해 무엇이라고 말하는가?
(A) 그것은 너무 빨리 실시되었다.
(B) 그것은 참가자들을 혼란스럽게 했다.
(C) 그것은 모두의 의견을 반영한다.
(D) 그것은 게리에 의해 만들어질 것이다.

어휘
confuse 혼란시키다 participant 참가자, 참여자
reflect 반영하다, 나타내다

패러프레이징
everyone participated → reflects everyone's opinion

3.
청자는 무엇을 하도록 요청받는가?
(A) 화자에게 전화하기
(B) 자세한 정보 알아보기
(C) 예약하기
(D) 다른 설문 조사 수행하기

어휘
detailed 자세한, 상세한 conduct 수행하다

패러프레이징
look up the rates and specifics
→ Find detailed information

[4-5] 미녀 🎧
Questions 4-5 refer to the following talk.

W Thank you all for coming in on a Saturday
morning. Our insurance company has asked
for some additions to our driving safety policy,
so that is the reason for this class. ⁴At the end
of the class, everyone is required to watch a
short film provided by the insurance company.
It covers a few tips on how to avoid road
accidents. Also, ⁵you should include your
signature on the back of the handout before
turning it in, to verify you've seen and
understood the film.

해석
4-5번은 다음 담화에 관한 문제입니다.

여 토요일 아침인데도 와 주신 모든 분들께 감사드립니다. 우리 보험사가 주행 안전 정책에 몇 가지 추가 사항을 요청해서 이 수업이 열리게 되었습니다. **⁴수업 마지막에 모든 분들은 보험 회사에서 제공한 짧은 영상을 시청하셔야 합니다.** 영상은 도로 사고를 피하기 위한 방법에 관한 몇 가지 요령을 다룹니다. 또한, 그 영상을 보고 이해했는지 확인하기 위해 **⁵유인물을 제출하시기 전**

에 그 뒤에 여러분의 서명을 하셔야 합니다.

어휘
insurance 보험 be required to ~하도록 요구되다
cover 다루다 avoid 피하다 accident 사고 signature 서명
handout 유인물, 인쇄물 turn in ~을 제출하다
verify 확인하다, 증명하다

4.
마지막 활동은 무엇이 될 것인가?
(A) 시험에 응시하는 것
(B) 영상을 시청하는 것
(C) 정책을 검토하는 것
(D) 토론을 하는 것

어휘
review 검토하다; 검토 discussion 토론, 논의

패러프레이징
a short film → a video

5.
화자는 청자들에게 무엇을 해 달라고 요청하는가?
(A) 서류에 서명하기
(B) 조사 수행하기
(C) 질문 적기
(D) 소그룹에 참여하기

어휘
perform 수행하다, 실시하다 inspection 조사, 점검
write down 적다, 기록하다

패러프레이징
include your signature on the back of the handout
→ Sign a document

실전 문제
본문 p.232

1. (D)	2. (D)	3. (B)	4. (C)	5. (B)
6. (B)	7. (C)	8. (B)	9. (B)	10. (D)
11. (A)	12. (B)	13. (C)	14. (A)	15. (B)
16. (B)	17. (D)	18. (C)		

[1-3] 미낭
Questions 1-3 refer to the following talk.

M ¹It's wonderful to see so many people here for this fund-raiser for Hilltop Park. Your generous donations will help us build an outdoor stage for the community park. I hope you have all enjoyed tonight's performance by Alice Miramar. ²There are free posters signed by Ms. Miramar as a thank-you gift. Don't forget to get yours on the way out. Also, ³all the pictures from tonight's event will be in the photo gallery on our Web site, so you can check them out.

해석
1-3번은 다음 담화에 관한 문제입니다.
남 ¹힐탑 파크를 위한 이번 모금 행사에 이렇게 많은 분들을 여기서 뵙게 되어 기쁩니다. 여러분의 후한 기부가 근린공원에 야외무대를 짓는 데 도움이 될 것입니다. 오늘 밤 앨리스 미라마의 공연을 모두가 즐기셨길 바랍니다. ²감사 선물로 미라마 씨가 사인한 무료 포스터가 있습니다. 나가실 때 잊지 말고 챙기세요. 또한, ³오늘 밤 행사의 모든 사진은 저희 웹사이트 사진 갤러리에 올라올 것이므로 그곳에서 확인하실 수 있습니다.

어휘
fund-raiser 모금 행사 generous 아끼지 않는, 후한
donation 기부, 기증 outdoor 야외의
performance 공연, 연주회 on the way out 나가는 길에

1.
청자들은 어떤 행사에 참여하고 있는가?
(A) 음악 수업
(B) 시상식
(C) 회사 야유회
(D) 지역 모금 행사

어휘
community 지역 사회, 공동체

패러프레이징
fund-raiser for Hilltop Park
→ A community fund-raiser

2.
화자는 청자들에게 무엇을 하라고 상기시키는가?
(A) 신분증 보여주기
(B) 메일 수신자 명단에 가입하기
(C) 티켓 보관하기
(D) 선물 가져가기

어휘
remind 상기시키다, 생각나게 하다 identification 신분증

패러프레이징
a thank-you gift ~ get yours → Pick up a gift

3.
화자에 따르면, 청자들은 왜 웹사이트를 방문해야 하는가?
(A) 행사에 등록하기 위해
(B) 이미지를 보기 위해
(C) 디자인을 고르기 위해
(D) 우승자를 알아보기 위해

어휘
register for ~에 등록하다 find out ~을 알아보다

패러프레이징
all the pictures from tonight's event → some images

[4-6] 영녀 🎧

Questions 4-6 refer to the following announcement.

> W ⁴Attention, all passengers at Barnett Bus Terminal. We are pleased to announce that, starting from next week, crews will be working to upgrade our facility. ⁵We will be expanding our food court, making it easier for travelers to find something to eat that suits their tastes. During the project, ⁶some of the existing stalls will be shut down temporarily. These are listed on our Web site, so I suggest you look them over before making any plans.

해석

4-6번은 다음 공지에 관한 문제입니다.

여 ⁴바넷 버스 터미널의 모든 승객 여러분, 주목해 주세요. 다음 주부터 직원들이 시설 업그레이드를 위해 작업할 것임을 알려 드리게 되어 기쁩니다. ⁵저희는 푸드코트를 확장하여, 여행객들이 입맛에 맞는 음식을 더 쉽게 찾을 수 있도록 하겠습니다. 이 프로젝트 기간 동안, ⁶기존 노점들 중 일부가 일시적으로 문을 닫게 될 것입니다. 이들은 저희 웹사이트에 올라와 있으니, 계획을 세우기 전에 살펴보시길 권합니다.

어휘

be pleased to ~해서 기쁘다 facility 시설 expand 확장하다
suit ~에 맞다 taste 입맛, 맛 stall 노점, 가판대
shut down 문을 닫다 temporarily 일시적으로
look over ~을 살펴보다

4.

공지는 어디에서 일어나고 있는가?
(A) 유람선에서
(B) 호텔 셔틀버스에서
(C) 버스 터미널에서
(D) 공항에서

5.

화자에 따르면, 프로젝트는 어떻게 여행객들을 도울 것인가?
(A) 티켓 가격을 낮춤으로써
(B) 더 많은 음식 선택 메뉴를 추가함으로써
(C) 이동 시간을 단축함으로써
(D) 주차장을 확장함으로써

어휘

reduce 낮추다, 할인하다 journey 이동, 여행
expand 확장하다, 넓히다

패러프레이징

expanding our food court
→ adding more food options

6.

화자는 청자들에게 무엇을 하라고 권하는가?
(A) 수하물 점검하기

(B) 휴업 확인하기
(C) 티켓 일찍 구매하기
(D) 다른 출입구로 가기

어휘

inspect 점검하다, 조사하다 luggage 수하물, 짐
closure 휴업, 폐점

패러프레이징

shut down → closures

[7-9] 호남 🎧

Questions 7-9 refer to the following telephone message.

> M Hi, Amelie. It's Ikumu. ⁷I've just reviewed the new security system you designed for our building. I'm really happy with how it turned out. The next step is to write a user manual to explain all the features. ⁸When it's finished, I'd be happy to check it for errors if you'd like. Also, ⁹I know that you scheduled a training session to teach everyone how to use the system, but... um... a detailed manual will work.

해석

7-9번은 다음 전화 메시지에 관한 문제입니다.

남 안녕하세요, 아멜리에. 이쿠무입니다. ⁷당신이 우리 건물을 위해 설계한 새로운 보안 시스템을 방금 검토했습니다. 그것이 잘 나와서 정말 기쁩니다. 다음 단계는 모든 특징을 설명하는 사용 설명서를 작성하는 것입니다. ⁸작업이 완료되면, 원하실 경우, 오류가 있는지 확인하겠습니다. 또한, ⁹저는 당신이 모두에게 시스템 사용법을 가르치기 위해 교육 시간을 예약하신 걸 알고 있지만, 음... 자세한 설명서 하나면 될 겁니다.

어휘

security 보안, 경비 turn out (특정한 결과가) 나오다
feature 특징, 특색

7.

청자는 무엇을 설계했는가?
(A) 비디오 게임
(B) 디지털 온도계
(C) 보안 시스템
(D) 스마트폰 앱

어휘

thermometer 온도계, 체온계

8.

화자는 무엇을 해 주겠다고 제안하는가?
(A) 동료 소개하기
(B) 설명서 교정하기
(C) 일부 서류 인쇄하기
(D) 기술자 호출하기

colleague 동료 proofread 교정을 보다

check it for errors → Proofread

9.

화자는 왜 "자세한 설명서 하나면 될 겁니다"라고 말하는가?
(A) 보증을 제공하기 위해
(B) 교육 시간 취소를 제안하기 위해
(C) 새 디자인을 홍보하기 위해
(D) 비싼 요금을 정당화하기 위해

guarantee 보증, 보장 justify 정당화하다

[10-12] 미녀 🎧

Questions 10-12 refer to the following telephone message.

> W ¹⁰ Hi, this is Morena from the Purchasing Office. I'm calling because we have to make a change in our production schedule for your factory. ¹¹ This morning, our supplier informed me that they can't deliver the packaging boxes until this Friday. Those were supposed to arrive today. I know all of your workers have worked hard to meet the deadline and most products are now ready for packaging. But, due to this unexpected problem, ¹² I need you to check which workers from your team are willing to work overtime this weekend so we can catch up with our schedule. It's really important that we still meet the deadline despite this issue. Thank you.

10-12번은 다음 전화 메시지에 관한 문제입니다.

여 ¹⁰ **안녕하세요, 저는 구매부의 모레나입니다.** 당신의 공장 생산 일정을 변경해야 해서 연락드렸습니다. ¹¹ **오늘 아침, 우리 공급 업체가 이번 주 금요일까지 포장 상자를 납품할 수 없다고 알려 왔습니다.** 그것들은 오늘 도착하기로 되어 있었습니다. 당신의 모든 직원들이 마감일을 맞추기 위해 열심히 근무했고, 이제 대부분의 상품이 포장 준비가 되었다는 걸 압니다. 하지만, 이 예상치 못한 문제로 인해, 일정을 따라잡을 수 있게 ¹² **당신 팀의 어떤 직원들이 이번 주말에 초과 근무할 의사가 있는지 확인해 주셔야 겠습니다.** 이 문제에도 불구하고 마감일을 지키는 게 정말 중요합니다. 고맙습니다.

supplier 공급 업체 inform 알리다, 통지하다
be supposed to ~하기로 되어 있다 unexpected 예기치 않은
be willing to 기꺼이 ~하다 catch up with ~을 따라잡다
despite ~에도 불구하고

10.

화자는 어떤 부서에서 근무하는가?
(A) 영업
(B) 회계
(C) 인사
(D) 구매

11.

화자에 따르면, 무엇이 문제를 일으켰는가?
(A) 일부 물품이 제때 배달되지 않았다.
(B) 공급 업체가 가격을 올렸다.
(C) 몇몇 작업자들이 경험이 부족하다.
(D) 장비가 고장 났다.

inexperienced 경험이 부족한

they can't deliver the packaging boxes until this Friday → Some items were not delivered on time

12.

화자는 청자에게 무엇을 해 달라고 요청하는가?
(A) 포장 디자인 변경하기
(B) 주말 근무자 찾기
(C) 직원 회의 참석하기
(D) 생산 목표 검토하기

check which workers ~ willing to work overtime this weekend → Find workers for the weekend

[13-15] 미남 🎧

Questions 13-15 refer to the following announcement.

> M This is an announcement for all warehouse supervisors. ¹³ An inspector from the fire department will visit and check the premises from 8 to 9 A.M. tomorrow. We want a clean report, so we're counting on each supervisor to take responsibility for his or her respective shop area. ¹⁴ Please make sure all production floor pathways and fire exits are clear of any obstructions. More detailed information has been added to our company Web site. Or, if you have a question, please call ¹⁵ the general manager, Mr. Firth, at extension 301. Thank you for your cooperation.

13-15번은 다음 공지에 관한 문제입니다.

남 모든 창고 관리자들을 위한 공지입니다. ¹³ **내일 오전 8시부터 9시까지 소방서의 조사관이 구내를 방문하여 점검할 예정입니다.** 우리는 결점 없는 보고를 원하므로 각 감독자가 각자의 구역을

책임져 주리라 믿습니다. **¹⁴모든 생산 현장 통로와 비상구에 장애물이 없는지 확인해 주세요.** 더 자세한 정보는 우리 회사 웹사이트에 추가되었습니다. 혹은 질문이 있을 경우, 내선 301번으로 **¹⁵총괄 관리자 퍼스 씨에게 전화해 주세요.** 협조해 주셔서 감사합니다.

어휘

warehouse 창고 supervisor 관리자, 감독관
inspector 조사관 premises ((항상 복수형)) 구내, 부지
count on ~을 믿다, 확신하다
take responsibility for ~을 책임지다
respective 각자의, 각각의 pathway 통로, 길
obstruction 장애물, 방해물 cooperation 협조, 협력

13.
담화의 목적은 무엇인가?
(A) 새로운 직원을 소개하기 위해
(B) 변경한 절차를 시연하기 위해
(C) 곧 있을 점검을 알리기 위해
(D) 생산 증가를 보고하기 위해

어휘
demonstrate 시연하다, 보여 주다 revised 변경한, 수정한
procedure 절차 upcoming 곧 있을, 다가오는

패러프레이징
An inspector ~ will visit and check ~ tomorrow
→ an upcoming inspection

14.
청자들은 무엇을 하도록 요청받는가?
(A) 막혀 있는 모든 출구 치우기
(B) 소화기 점검하기
(C) 화재경보기 테스트하기
(D) 비상조치 절차 검토하기

어휘
extinguisher 소화기

패러프레이징
all production floor pathways and fire exits are clear
of any obstructions → Clear any blocked exits

15.
퍼스 씨는 누구인가?
(A) 조사관
(B) 관리자
(C) 소방관
(D) 의뢰인

어휘
firefighter 소방관

[16-18] 영녀 🎧
Questions 16-18 refer to the following telephone
message and invoice.

W Hi, Brian. It's Alicia. **¹⁶I'm calling from Tokyo. I just wanted to let you know I'm taking a late flight right after my speech at the International Tech Convention**, so I'll be back in the office tomorrow. However, I forgot that I ordered a piece of furniture. **¹⁷A metal file cabinet will be delivered today.** It can just be left in the hallway for now, but please check that the invoice has the right reference number. Oh, and if you're not busy, **¹⁸you're welcome to join me on Thursday to visit some commercial buildings that are possible sites for our new location.**

해석
16-18번은 다음 전화 메시지와 청구서에 관한 문제입니다.
여 안녕하세요, 브라이언. 알리시아입니다. **¹⁶도쿄에서 연락드립니다. 국제 기술 회의에서 연설이 끝나고 바로 늦은 비행기를 탄다는 걸 알려드리려고요.** 그래서 내일 사무실에 돌아갈 예정입니다. 그런데 제가 가구 한 점을 주문했던 걸 깜빡했습니다. **¹⁷철제 파일 캐비닛이 오늘 배송될 예정입니다.** 지금은 일단 복도에 두면 되지만, 송장에 있는 참조 번호가 맞는지 확인 부탁드립니다. 아, 그리고 바쁘지 않으시다면, **¹⁸목요일에 저와 함께 우리 새로운 장소로 쓸 수 있는 몇몇 상업용 건물을 방문하셔도 좋습니다.**

어휘
hallway 복도 invoice 송장, 청구서 reference 참조, 참고
commercial 상업적인 site 부지, 현장, 장소

물품	참조 번호
테이블 램프	48-J
나무 책상	60-P
책상 의자	72-W
¹⁷파일 캐비닛	**91-C**

16.
화자는 왜 도쿄에 갔는가?
(A) 워크숍을 이끌기 위해
(B) 연설을 하기 위해
(C) 시설을 점검하기 위해
(D) 수상을 하기 위해

17.
시각 자료를 보시오. 어떤 참조 번호가 오늘 도착할 것인가?
(A) 48-J
(B) 60-P
(C) 72-W
(D) 91-C

패러프레이징
be delivered → arrive

18.

화자는 청자에게 목요일에 무엇을 해 달라고 요청하는가?

(A) 회의 참석하기
(B) 몇 가지 제품 샘플 사용해 보기
(C) 몇몇 건물 살펴보기
(D) 입사 지원자 만나기

어휘

conference 회의 property 건물 job candidate 입사 지원자

패러프레이징

visit some commercial buildings
→ Look at some properties

UNIT 06 다음에 할·일어날 일 문제

CHECK UP
본문 p.234

1. (D)   **2.** (C)

[1] 미남 🎧

Question 1 refers to the following speech.

> M It's wonderful to see so many people here for
> the opening of this new branch of the
> Clarksville Public Library. I think our residents
> will especially like the spacious reading area in
> the lobby, which has lots of natural light due to
> the glass roof. As the city's mayor, I am proud
> that the community has worked so hard to
> support this important project, and I'd like to
> thank those of you who made private
> donations. Alright, well… now it's time to show
> you around the building. Please follow me.

해석

1번은 다음 연설에 관한 문제입니다.

남 클라크스빌 공립 도서관의 이번 새로운 분관의 개관식에 이렇게
많은 분들이 자리하신 걸 보니 기쁩니다. 우리 주민 분들께서 특
히 로비에 있는 널찍한 열람실을 좋아하실 것 같은데요, 그곳은
유리 지붕 덕분에 풍부한 자연광이 듭니다. 시장으로서 저는 지
역 주민이 이 중요한 프로젝트를 지원하기 위해 애써 주신 것이
자랑스러우며, 개인적인 기부를 해 주신 분들께 감사드립니다.
좋습니다, 음... **이제 건물을 구경시켜 드릴 시간입니다. 저를 따
라오시기 바랍니다.**

어휘

resident 주민 especially 특히 spacious 널찍한
natural light 자연광 mayor 시장 support 지지하다, 지원하다
make a donation 기부를 하다 private 사적인
show around ~을 구경시켜 주다

1.

화자는 다음에 무엇을 할 것 같은가?

(A) 상을 수여하기
(B) 단체 사진 찍기
(C) 몇몇 기부자들 소개하기
(D) 견학 인솔하기

어휘

present 주다, 수여하다 donor 기부자
conduct a tour 견학을 인솔하다

패러프레이징

show you around the building → Conduct a tour

[2] 미녀 🎧

Question 2 refers to the following advertisement.

> W Do you want your garden to look its best? Are
> you too busy to take care of your yard
> yourself? Then you need help from Meadow
> Landscaping! We can plant flower beds, mow
> the grass, trim trees, and so much more. We
> have been in business for over 25 years, and
> all of our employees are highly experienced.
> And, we're currently offering a 20 percent
> discount to new customers who sign up for
> our monthly service. But you'd better act fast.
> That special price is only available if you sign
> up before August 11.

해석

2번은 다음 광고에 관한 문제입니다.

여 당신의 정원이 가장 좋게 보이길 원하시나요? 너무 바빠서 직접
정원을 돌볼 수 없으신가요? 그렇다면 메도우 조경의 도움이 필
요합니다! 저희는 화단을 만들고, 잔디를 깎고, 나무를 다듬는 등
여러 일을 합니다. 저희는 25년 이상 영업해 왔으며, 저희 직원
모두 대단히 경험이 풍부합니다. 그리고, 저희는 현재 월간 서비
스에 신청하시는 신규 고객들에게 20% 할인을 해 드리고 있습
니다. 하지만 빨리 신청하시는 게 좋습니다. **그 특별 가격은 8월
11일 이전에 신청하신 경우에만 이용할 수 있습니다.**

어휘

look one's best 가장 좋게 보이다 take care of ~을 돌보다
meadow 목초지 landscaping 조경 plant (나무 등을) 심다
flower bed 화단 mow 깎다 trim 다듬다, 손질하다
highly 대단히, 매우 experienced 경험이 있는, 능숙한
currently 현재, 지금

2.

8월 11일에 무슨 일이 일어날 것인가?

(A) 단체 면접이 있을 것이다.
(B) 계약이 갱신될 것이다.
(C) 특별 판매가 종료될 것이다.
(D) 새로운 지점이 문을 열 것이다.

어휘

contract 계약(서) renew 갱신하다 special offer 특별 판매

패러프레이징

That special price is only available ~ before
→ A special offer will end

패러프레이징 **연습**　　　　　　　본문 p.236

1-4. 스크립트 참조　　**5.** (A)　　**6.** (B)

1.

Q 청자들은 다음에 무엇을 할 것 같은가?

A 또 다른 영상 시청하기

미녀 🎧

> **W** So, whenever you receive a customer complaint, please transfer the call to a supervisor right away. The next video in this training session will show you how to do so on our phone system. It will load automatically in just a moment.

해석

여 따라서, 고객 불만을 받을 때마다 즉시 전화를 감독관에게 돌려 주시기 바랍니다. **이번 교육의 다음 영상에서 여러분에게 우리 전화 시스템으로 그렇게 하는 방법을 보여드리겠습니다.** 영상은 잠시 후 자동으로 로딩될 것입니다.

어휘

customer complaint 고객 불만 transfer 옮기다, 이동하다
supervisor 감독관, 관리자 training session 교육 (과정)
automatically 자동적으로

패러프레이징

next video ~ will show you → Watch another video

2.

Q 화자는 다음에 무엇을 할 것인가?

A 시연하기

미남 🎧

> **M** Before the items are packaged, they must be weighed carefully on our scale, which is by the entrance. Let me take you there now to show you the features of the scale and how to reset it before each weighing session. There are just a few steps, so I don't think you'll have any issues with it.

해석

남 물품들은 포장되기 전에 저울로 세심하게 무게가 측정되어야 하며, 저울은 입구 옆에 있습니다. **제가 지금 여러분을 그곳으로 데려가서 저울의 기능과 매번 무게를 달기 전에 저울을 맞추는 방**

법을 보여 드리겠습니다. 몇 단계 되지 않아서 여러분이 배우는 데 아무 문제도 없을 것이라고 생각합니다.

어휘

give a demonstration 시연하다 package 포장하다
weigh 무게를 달다 scale 저울 entrance (출)입구, 문
feature 특징, 기능 reset 다시 맞추다

패러프레이징

show you the features of the scale and how to reset it
→ Give a demonstration

3.

Q 월요일에 무슨 일이 일어날 것인가?

A 새 라벨들이 사용될 것이다.

미녀 🎧

> **W** We have recently partnered with Brenson Couriers to improve the speed of our deliveries. We will be adopting their tracking system, so we must use their labels on the packages we are processing. Therefore, on Monday morning, every workstation will need to be restocked with their labels.

해석

여 우리는 최근에 우리의 배달 속도를 개선하기 위해 브렌슨 택배 회사와 협약을 맺었습니다. 우리는 그들의 추적 시스템을 쓸 것이므로 우리가 처리하는 포장물에 그들의 라벨을 사용해야 합니다. **따라서, 월요일 아침에 모든 작업장이 그들의 라벨을 붙여 다시 채워져야 할 것입니다.**

어휘

label 라벨, 표 partner with ~와 협력하다
courier 운반원, 택배 회사 adopt 쓰다, 채택하다 track 추적하다
package 포장(물) process 처리하다; 처리, 과정
restock (물건 등을) 다시 채우다

패러프레이징

be restocked with their labels
→ New labels will be used

4.

Q 청자들은 다음에 무엇을 할 것 같은가?

A 둘러보기

미남 🎧

> **M** Our firm has been growing rapidly, so it's great to welcome you all to the team. Now, a lot of new employees find the layout of this building to be very confusing. So, let's start by showing you around the different rooms that you'll need to be familiar with.

해석

남 우리 회사가 급속도로 성장하고 있으므로 여러분 모두 팀에 합류

하게 된 것을 환영하게 되어 기쁩니다. 자, 많은 신입 직원들이 이 건물의 구조가 매우 헷갈린다고 생각합니다. 따라서, **여러분이 익숙해져야 할 여러 공간들을 구경시켜 드리는 것으로 시작합시다.**

어휘

go on a tour 둘러보다, 여행을 떠나다 rapidly 급속히
layout 배치, 설계 confusing 혼란시키는, 헷갈리는
be familiar with ~에 익숙하다

패러프레이징

showing you around → Go on a tour

5.

다음에 무슨 일이 일어날 것인가?
(A) 상품이 나눠질 것이다.
(B) 서류 작업이 완료될 것이다.

🔲미남 🎧

M You've all done a great job in the first session of the workshop, so I'd like to have a quick, fun activity. I've put everyone's name on a slip of paper. I'll be drawing them at random from the bowl, and if your name is called, you'll get to choose a prize.

해석

남 여러분 모두 워크숍의 첫 번째 세션을 잘 해내셨으니 간단하고 재미있는 활동을 하겠습니다. 제가 쪽지에 모든 사람의 이름을 적었습니다. 제가 통에서 무작위로 쪽지를 뽑을 것이고, 이름이 불리면 상품을 고르게 됩니다.

어휘

give out ~을 나눠 주다 paperwork 서류 작업
complete 마치다, 완료하다 slip 작은 종이 조각, 쪽지
draw (제비를) 뽑다 at random 무작위로

패러프레이징

you'll get to choose a prize
→ Some prizes will be given out

6.

화자는 다음에 무엇을 할 것인가?
(A) 설문조사 문항 만들기
(B) 정보 나눠 주기

🔲미녀 🎧

W We've analyzed the survey results, which show that recycling rates have not improved despite our recent campaign. I'd like us to discuss this issue. So, I've put those results and more data about similar programs in a summary that I'll be handing out now.

해석

여 우리가 설문조사 결과를 분석했는데, 이것은 우리의 최근 캠페인

에도 불구하고 재활용률이 개선되지 않았음을 보여줍니다. 우리가 이 문제에 대해서 논의했으면 합니다. 따라서, **제가 지금 나눠 드릴 요약서에 그 결과와 비슷한 프로그램에 대한 더 많은 데이터를 담았습니다.**

어휘

create 만들어 내다, 창작하다 survey 설문조사
distribute 나눠 주다, 배부하다 analyze 분석하다
recycling 재활용 rate 속도, 비율 despite ~에도 불구하고
summary 요약, 개요 hand out 나눠 주다, 배포하다

패러프레이징

those results and more data ~ handing out
→ Distribute information

연습 문제 · 본문 p.237

1. (A)	2. (B)	3. (C)	4. (D)	5. (C)

[1] 🔲호남 🎧

Question 1 refers to the following talk.

M My name is Joshua Ellis, and I'm a market analyst from Conway Analytics. I've been researching the possible reasons for the slow sales of your new line of low-fat yogurts. Although people enjoy the taste, it seems that there are not very many flavor options. That's why consumers are choosing other brands. So, I'd like us to make a list of suggested flavors that you think would be popular. Then we'll see how those compare to what's currently available.

해석

1번은 다음 담화에 관한 문제입니다.
남 제 이름은 조슈아 엘리스이고, 콘웨이 분석 회사의 시장 분석가입니다. 제가 여러분 회사의 저지방 요구르트 신제품 라인의 지지부진한 판매에 대해 납득 가능한 이유를 조사하고 있습니다. 비록 사람들이 그 맛을 좋아하기는 하지만 선택할 수 있는 맛이 그리 많지 않아 보입니다. 그것이 고객들이 다른 브랜드를 선택하는 이유입니다. 따라서 우리가 인기 있을 것으로 생각하는 맛의 추천 목록을 만들었으면 합니다. 그러면 그것들이 현재 이용할 수 있는 것들과 비교하여 어떠한지 알게 될 것입니다.

어휘

analyst 분석가 research 연구하다, 조사하다 line (상품의) 종류
low-fat 저지방의 flavor 풍미, 향미, 맛
compare to ~와 비교가 되다 currently 현재, 지금
available 이용할 수 있는

1.

청자들은 다음에 무엇을 하도록 요청받는가?
(A) 아이디어 제시하기

(B) 판매 보고서 읽기
(C) 일부 샘플 맛보기
(D) 도표 보기

어휘
come up with ~을 생각해 내다, 제시하다 sample 맛보다; 샘플

패러프레이징
make a list of suggested flavors
→ Come up with some ideas

[2-3] 영녀 🎧
Questions 2-3 refer to the following speech.

> W [2] I think this is one of the best meetings I've ever had with distinguished scientists like you. Before we end this meeting, I want to mention a few things. First, our next meeting will be held at the Grand Convention Center on Parker Street on Friday, September 21, which is two days later than what we had originally planned. So, don't forget to update your calendars. Also, [3] remember that we need some volunteers for our annual membership dinner next month. Please visit our Web site for more details.

해석
2-3번은 다음 연설에 관한 문제입니다.
여 [2] 이번 회의는 여러분과 같은 뛰어난 과학자들과 가졌던 최고의 회의 중 하나라고 생각합니다. 이번 회의를 마치기 전에 몇 가지 사항을 언급하고 싶습니다. 첫째로 우리의 다음 회의는 9월 21일 금요일에 파커가에 있는 그랜드 컨벤션 센터에서 열릴 것이며, 이것은 우리가 원래 계획했던 것보다 이틀 뒤입니다. 따라서 잊지 말고 여러분의 일정표를 업데이트하세요. 또한, [3] 다음 달에 있을 우리의 연례 회원 만찬을 위해 자원봉사자들이 필요하다는 것도 기억하십시오. 더 자세한 정보를 원하시면 저희 웹사이트를 방문해 주세요.

어휘
distinguished 뛰어난, 빼어난 originally 원래 annual 연례의
membership 회원 (자격)

2.
청자들은 누구인 것 같은가?
(A) 행사 기획자
(B) 과학 전문가
(C) 소프트웨어 개발자
(D) 기자

패러프레이징
scientists → Science experts

3.
화자는 다음 달에 무슨 일이 일어날 것이라고 말하는가?
(A) 건물이 보수될 것이다.

(B) 신제품이 출시될 것이다.
(C) 회원들이 모여서 식사를 할 것이다.
(D) 웹사이트가 출시될 것이다.

어휘
undergo 겪다, 받다 renovation 수리, 보수
release 출시하다, 발표하다 launch 시작하다, 출시하다

패러프레이징
our annual membership dinner
→ Members will gather for a meal

[4-5] 호남 🎧
Questions 4-5 refer to the following telephone message.

> M Hi, this message is for Stella Weiss. This is Gerald from the animal rescue shelter. I want to thank you so much for volunteering at our adoption event last Saturday. [4] Since we were so understaffed, your presence really meant a lot. You expressed interest in coming in a few mornings a week, right? I think we can find a regular task for you. [5] I'll e-mail you a schedule of what needs to be done. Call me back and let me know which one you'd like to sign up for. Thanks!

해석
4-5번은 다음 전화 메시지에 관한 문제입니다.
남 안녕하세요, 이 메시지는 스텔라 바이스에게 전하는 것입니다. 저는 동물 구호 보호소의 제럴드입니다. 지난 토요일 저희의 입양 행사에서 자원봉사를 해 주셔서 대단히 감사드립니다. [4] 저희가 인원이 너무 부족했기 때문에, 당신의 참석은 정말 큰 의미가 있었습니다. 일주일에 몇 번 아침에 오시는 데 관심이 있다고 하셨죠, 맞죠? 저희가 당신을 위한 정기적인 업무를 찾을 수 있을 것 같습니다. [5] 해야 하는 일의 일정표를 이메일로 보내 드리겠습니다. 제게 다시 전화 주셔서 어떤 것에 신청하시고 싶은지 알려 주세요. 고맙습니다!

어휘
rescue 구출, 구조; 구조하다 shelter 대피처, 피신처
adoption 입양, 채택 understaffed 인원이 부족한
presence 있음, 존재, 참석 regular 정기적인, 규칙적인
task 일, 과업

4.
화자는 지난 토요일에 대해 무엇이라고 말하는가?
(A) 행사가 취소되어야 했다.
(B) 아침에 현장이 폐쇄되었다.
(C) 그들은 소개를 받았다.
(D) 자원봉사자들이 충분하지 않았다.

어휘
referral 소개, 위탁

패러프레이징

we were so understaffed
→ There weren't enough volunteers

5.

화자는 다음에 무엇을 할 것 같은가?
(A) 정책 확인하기
(B) 직원에게 전화하기
(C) 문서 보내기
(D) 등록 신청서 작성하기

어휘

complete 기입하다, 작성하다 registration 등록

패러프레이징

e-mail you a schedule → Send a document

실전 문제   본문 p.238

1. (C)	**2.** (C)	**3.** (D)	**4.** (A)	**5.** (D)
6. (C)	**7.** (B)	**8.** (D)	**9.** (C)	**10.** (C)
11. (A)	**12.** (C)	**13.** (C)	**14.** (B)	**15.** (B)
16. (B)	**17.** (B)	**18.** (B)		

[1-3] 미남 🎧

Questions 1-3 refer to the following telephone message.

> M Hi, Rita. It's Thomas. I hope you got my earlier message about having to stay an extra night in Chicago. I've just left the hotel, and I'm in a taxi on the way to the airport now. My flight lands at noon, so I'm going to miss **¹the press conference that's scheduled for 11 o'clock.** **²I know I was supposed to explain the new photo editing software,** but... um... that won't be possible. Diana worked on the project. **³Could you please talk to her?**

해석

1-3번은 다음 전화 메시지에 관한 문제입니다.
남 안녕하세요, 리타. 토마스예요. 시카고에서 하룻밤 더 머물러야 한다고 한, 제가 이전에 보낸 메시지를 받으셨길 바랍니다. 저는 방금 호텔을 나와서 지금 공항으로 가는 택시 안에 있어요. 제 비행기가 정오에 도착하기 때문에 **¹11시 정각으로 예정되어 있는 기자회견에 빠지게 될 거예요. ²제가 새로운 사진 편집 소프트웨어에 대해 설명하기로 되어 있는 걸 알아요,** 하지만... 음... 그건 가능하지 않을 거예요. 다이애나가 그 프로젝트에 참여했어요. **³그녀에게 얘기해 보시겠어요?**

어휘

on the way to ~로 가는 도중에 land 착륙하다, 도착하다
press conference 기자회견
be supposed to ~하기로 되어 있다 editing 편집

1.

11시에 무슨 일이 일어날 것인가?
(A) 채용 면접이 있을 것이다.
(B) 수상자가 발표될 것이다.
(C) 기자회견이 열릴 것이다.
(D) 시카고발 항공편이 출발할 것이다.

어휘

take place 개최되다, 일어나다 depart 출발하다

패러프레이징

the press conference that's scheduled
→ A press conference will be held

2.

화자는 무엇을 하기로 되어 있었는가?
(A) 돈 기부하기
(B) 경연 대회 참가하기
(C) 회의에서 발표하기
(D) 면접 실시하기

어휘

donate 기부하다 competition (경연) 대회, 시합
conduct 실시하다

패러프레이징

explain → Present

3.

화자는 왜 "다이애나가 그 프로젝트에 참여했어요"라고 말하는가?
(A) 동료의 비판을 거부하기 위해
(B) 오해를 바로잡기 위해
(C) 도움에 감사를 표하기 위해
(D) 대신할 사람을 추천하기 위해

어휘

reject 거부하다 criticism 비판, 비난
correct 바로잡다, 정정하다 misunderstanding 오해, 착오
appreciation 감사 replacement 대체(물), 대신할 사람

[4-6] 영녀 🎧

Questions 4-6 refer to the following broadcast.

> W Thanks for tuning in to *Entrepreneur's Corner*, the show that gives you tips on starting your own business. **⁴Today we're talking about building a social media presence.** My guest is Pamela Abbott. **⁵After attending a workshop on social media management in February,** she started to use the techniques to promote her accounting firm. Since then, she has built a solid client base of more than 100 companies. In fact, she has been so successful that she's been nominated for a Local Entrepreneur Award. **⁶That award will be presented at a ceremony tonight.** Let's hear how Pamela got started.

해석

4-6번은 다음 방송에 관한 문제입니다.

여 개인 사업을 시작하는 것에 관해 조언해 드리는 프로그램인 〈기업가 코너〉를 들어 주셔서 감사합니다. **4오늘 우리는 소셜 미디어 입지를 구축하는 것에 관해 얘기할 것입니다.** 게스트는 파멜라 애벗입니다. **5 2월에 소셜 미디어 운영에 관한 워크숍에 참석한 후에,** 그녀는 자신의 회계 법인을 홍보하기 위해 이 기법들을 사용하기 시작했습니다. 그때 이후로, 그녀는 100개가 넘는 기업으로 이뤄진 탄탄한 고객 기반을 구축했습니다. 사실, 그녀는 매우 성공해서 지역 기업가상의 후보로 지명되었습니다. **6 그 상은 오늘 밤 시상식에서 수여될 것입니다.** 파멜라가 어떻게 시작했는지 들어보시죠.

어휘

entrepreneur 기업가 tip 조언, 정보 presence 존재, 영향력
technique 기법, 기술 promote 홍보하다
accounting firm 회계 법인, 회계 사무소 solid 단단한
client base 고객 기반, 고객층
be nominated for ~의 후보로 지명되다 present 주다, 수여하다

4.
방송은 무엇에 관한 것인가?
(A) 소셜 미디어
(B) 이력서 작성
(C) 진로 수업
(D) 인터넷 보안

어휘
security 보안, 안보

5.
파멜라 애벗은 2월에 무엇을 했는가?
(A) 그녀는 해외여행을 했다.
(B) 그녀는 책을 출간했다.
(C) 그녀는 웹사이트를 개설했다.
(D) 그녀는 워크숍에 참석했다.

어휘
launch 시작하다, 출시하다

6.
화자에 따르면, 오늘 밤 무슨 일이 일어날 것인가?
(A) 협약이 체결될 것이다.
(B) 등록 기간이 시작될 것이다.
(C) 수상자가 발표될 것이다.
(D) 영상이 업로드될 것이다.

어휘
agreement 협정, 계약 registration 등록

패러프레이징
That award will be presented
→ An award winner will be announced

[7-9] 호남 🎧
Questions 7-9 refer to the following talk.

M **7 Just up here is one of the most popular artifacts in our exhibit,** a metal tool that is over 2,000 years old. Now, you'll see that the label says it is from France. **8 However, some recent tests have revealed that it was actually made much further north, in Denmark.** Many items in our collection cannot **9 be photographed** because they are sensitive to light, but this one can. **9 So, please take advantage of this opportunity.**

해석
7-9번은 다음 담화에 관한 문제입니다.

남 **7 바로 여기에 저희 전시에서 가장 인기 있는 공예품 중 하나인,** 2천 년 이상 된 금속 도구가 있습니다. 자, **8 표찰에 프랑스산이라고 쓰여 있는 게 보이실 겁니다.** 하지만, 몇몇 최근 검사는 그것이 사실 훨씬 더 북쪽인 덴마크에서 만들어졌다는 것을 밝혀냈습니다. 저희 소장품 중 상당수가 빛에 민감하기 때문에 **9 촬영할 수 없지만,** 이것은 가능합니다. **9 그러니 이번 기회를 활용하시기 바랍니다.**

어휘
artifact 공예품, 인공물 exhibit 전시(품); 전시하다
label 라벨, 표 reveal 드러내다, 밝히다
collection 소장품, 수집품 photograph 사진을 찍다; 사진
sensitive to ~에 민감한 take advantage of ~을 이용하다

7.
청자들은 어디에 있는 것 같은가?
(A) 미술 협회에
(B) 박물관에
(C) 연구소에
(D) 원예용품 상점에

어휘
institute 기관, 협회 laboratory 실험실
gardening 정원 가꾸기, 원예

8.
화자에 따르면, 표찰의 어떤 정보가 틀렸는가?
(A) 재료
(B) 무게
(C) 만든 날짜
(D) 만들어진 국가

어휘
creation 창조, 창작 origin 기원, 근원

9.
청자들은 다음에 무엇을 할 것인가?
(A) 다과 먹기
(B) 질문 적어 놓기
(C) 사진 찍기
(D) 기념품 가게 방문하기

어휘

refreshments ((항상 복수형)) 다과, 음식물

write down 적어 놓다

패러프레이징

be photographed → Take some pictures

[10-12] 미녀 🎧

Questions 10-12 refer to the following announcement.

> **W** Thanks for attending this meeting before your shift begins. I wanted to remind you all about ¹⁰the regional marathon, which is scheduled for next week… uh…. on Saturday, the 11th of June. This event always draws a lot of people. And because of the increase in tourists, ¹¹our taxi service will be busier than ever. That's why we're hoping to expand our usual service on that day. ¹²If you have the day off and are able to work, or if you would like to work an additional shift to what you're scheduled for, let me know after this meeting. Thanks.

해석

10-12번은 다음 공지에 관한 문제입니다.

여 교대 근무를 시작하기 전에, 이번 회의에 참석해 주신 데 감사드립니다. 여러분 모두에게 다음 주… 어… ¹⁰6월 11일 토요일로 예정된 지역 마라톤에 대해 상기시켜 드리고 싶었습니다. 이 행사는 항상 많은 사람들을 끌어모읍니다. 그리고 관광객 증가로 인해 ¹¹우리의 택시 영업은 그 어느 때보다 바쁠 것입니다. 그래서 우리는 그날 정상 영업을 확대했으면 하고 있습니다. ¹²휴가인데 일할 수 있거나, 예정된 데 더해 추가 근무를 하고 싶다면 이 회의가 끝난 뒤 알려 주세요. 감사합니다.

어휘

shift 교대 근무 (시간) remind 상기시키다, 다시 한번 알려 주다

regional 지역의 be scheduled for ~로 예정되어 있다

draw (남의 마음 또는 손님을) 끌다 increase 증가; 증가하다

tourists 관광객 expand 확대하다, 확대되다

day off (근무를) 쉬는 날 additional 추가의

10.

화자에 따르면, 다음 주에 무슨 일이 일어날 것인가?

(A) 음악 축제

(B) 취업 박람회

(C) 스포츠 대회

(D) 기념일 파티

어휘

competition (경연) 대회, 경쟁 anniversary 기념일

패러프레이징

the regional marathon → A sports competition

11.

화자는 어떤 업계에서 일하는 것 같은가?

(A) 교통

(B) 금융

(C) 기술

(D) 의료

패러프레이징

our taxi service → Transportation

12.

청자들은 왜 화자에게 말해야 하는가?

(A) 정책에 관해 질문하기 위해

(B) 몇 가지 개선을 제안하기 위해

(C) 추가 근무에 자원하기 위해

(D) 교육 일정을 잡기 위해

어휘

improvement 향상, 개선 volunteer for ~에 자원하다

extra 추가의, 가외의

패러프레이징

work an additional shift → volunteer for an extra shift

[13-15] 미남 🎧

Questions 13-15 refer to the following excerpt from a meeting.

> **M** Thanks for being here, everyone. ¹³I scheduled this meeting to tell you about a change in the vacation policy. Employees will still need to get approval from a supervisor to take time off. However, starting from next week, this will all be done through the company Web site. Um… You simply submit your request, and you'll get a reply by e-mail. ¹⁴It's great because you'll no longer have to spend a lot of time filling out long forms. ¹⁵Bernard will tell you the steps for signing in, so please give him your full attention.

해석

13-15번은 다음 회의 발췌록에 관한 문제입니다.

남 자리해 주셔서 감사합니다, 여러분. ¹³저는 여러분에게 휴가 정책의 변경에 관해 말씀드리기 위해 이번 회의 일정을 잡았습니다. 직원들이 휴가를 내려면 여전히 관리자의 승인을 받아야 합니다. 하지만, 다음 주부터, 이것이 모두 회사 웹사이트를 통해 이루어질 것입니다. 음… 여러분은 신청서만 제출하면 이메일로 답신을 받게 될 것입니다. ¹⁴더 이상 긴 양식을 작성하는 데 많은 시간을 들일 필요가 없어서 좋습니다. ¹⁵버나드가 접수하는 단계를 설명해 드릴 테니 경청해 주시기 바랍니다.

어휘

vacation policy 휴가 정책 approval 승인, 허가

supervisor 감독관, 관리자 take time off 휴가를 내다

submit 제출하다 reply 답장, 답신 fill out 기입하다, 작성하다

give attention 주의를 기울이다

13.
화자는 왜 회의를 소집했는가?
(A) 자원봉사를 요청하기 위해
(B) 회의를 준비하기 위해
(C) 휴가 정책에 대해 이야기하기 위해
(D) 신제품을 소개하기 위해

어휘
call a meeting 회의를 소집하다

패러프레이징
tell you about a change → discuss

14.
화자는 어떤 이점에 대해 언급하는가?
(A) 몇몇 서식들이 읽기가 더 쉽다.
(B) 직원들이 많은 시간을 절약할 수 있다.
(C) 회사가 수익을 더 많이 낼 것이다.
(D) 고객들이 더욱 만족할 것이다.

어휘
benefit 혜택, 이득 paper form 서식 save 절약하다, 저축하다
profitable 이익이 되는 be satisfied 만족하다

패러프레이징
you'll no longer have to spend a lot of time
→ Employees can save a lot of time

15.
버나드는 다음에 무엇을 할 것인가?
(A) 유인물 나눠 주기
(B) 접수 절차 설명하기
(C) 재무 보고서 제출하기
(D) 화자 소개하기

어휘
distribute 나눠 주다, 분배하다 handout 유인물
financial 재정의, 금융의

패러프레이징
tell you the steps for signing in
→ Explain a sign-in process

[16-18] 호남 🎧
Questions 16-18 refer to the following talk and chart.

> **M** Good afternoon. ¹⁶I'm Roy Sandberg, the consultant in charge of assisting you with the expansion of your chain of ice cream shops. To help more people get to know your brand, I recommend opening another small stand at a tourist destination, like the one you have at the Bloom Theater. This will help to keep overhead costs down. Here I have a chart of the attractions people mentioned in a recent

> survey. You're already operating at all but one of them. Look at this... ¹⁷21 percent of people mentioned this site, and you don't have a stand there. ¹⁸I'll contact the manager there to find out if they have booths available and whether you could choose the location.

해석
16-18번은 다음 담화와 도표에 관한 문제입니다.
남 안녕하세요. **¹⁶저는 당신의 아이스크림 매장 체인의 확장을 돕는 일을 맡은 컨설턴트 로이 샌드버그입니다.** 더 많은 사람들이 당신의 브랜드를 알게 되도록 돕기 위해서, 관광지에 작은 가판대를 하나 더 여는 것을 추천합니다. 블룸 극장에 가지고 계신 것처럼 말이죠. 이렇게 하면 간접비를 낮추는 데 도움이 될 것입니다. 여기 최근 설문조사에서 사람들이 언급한 관광 명소들의 도표가 있습니다. 당신은 이미 그것들 중 하나를 제외하고 모든 곳에서 영업을 하고 있습니다. 이것을 보세요... **¹⁷21%의 사람들이 이 장소를 언급했는데, 그곳에는 가판대가 없습니다. ¹⁸이용할 수 있는 부스가 있는지, 그리고 당신이 장소를 선택할 수 있는지 알아보기 위해 제가 그곳 관리자에게 연락해 보겠습니다.**

어휘
consultant 상담가, 컨설턴트 in charge of ~을 담당하는
assist A with B A가 B 하는 것을 돕다 expansion 확대, 확장
stand 가판대, 좌판 tourist destination 관광지
keep ~ down ~을 낮추다, 억제하다 overhead cost 간접비
attraction 명소, 명물 operate 영업하다, 운영하다
available 이용할 수 있는 location 위치, 장소

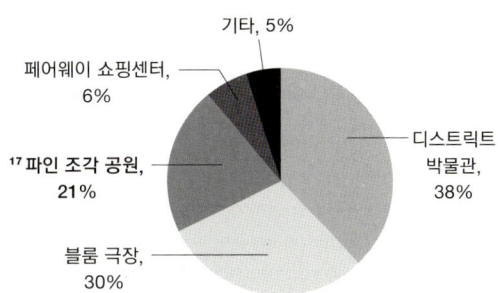

16.
화자는 누구인가?
(A) 음식 노점상
(B) 사업 컨설턴트
(C) 시 공무원
(D) 행사 진행자

어휘
vendor 노점상, 판매 회사 coordinator 조정자, 진행자

패러프레이징
the consultant in charge of assisting you with the expansion of your chain of ice cream shops
→ A business consultant

17.

시각 자료를 보시오. 어느 장소에 아이스크림 매장이 없는가?

(A) 페어웨이 쇼핑센터

(B) 파인 조각 공원

(C) 블룸 극장

(D) 디스트릭트 박물관

18.

화자는 무엇을 할 계획인가?

(A) 또 다른 설문조사 실시하기

(B) 임대 옵션 검토하기

(C) 새로운 맛 소개하기

(D) 가격 조정하기

어휘

conduct 실시하다, 수행하다 assess 가늠하다, 평가하다

flavor 맛, 풍미 adjust 조정하다, 조절하다

패러프레이징

find out if they have booths available and whether you could choose the location

→ Assess rental options

UNIT 07 화자의 의도 파악 문제

CHECK UP

본문 p.240

1. (D)   **2.** (C)

[1] 미녀 🎧

Question 1 refers to the following talk.

> W Good evening, and thank you for being here for tonight's exhibition of landscape art by Felix Stone. We appreciate your support. There are 25 oil paintings on display. The catalog you received when you arrived tells you more about each one in detail. And, of course, all of the paintings are available for sale. You don't have to make a purchase tonight, but… um… this artist is very popular. I'm sure you'll want to avoid disappointment. If you have any questions, please speak to a member of staff.

해석

1번은 다음 담화에 관한 문제입니다.

여 안녕하세요, 오늘 밤 펠릭스 스톤의 풍경화 전시에 와 주셔서 감사합니다. 여러분의 후원을 감사하게 생각합니다. 유화 25점이 전시되고 있습니다. 여러분이 도착하셨을 때 받으신 카탈로그에 각 그림에 대해 좀 더 자세히 설명되어 있습니다. 그리고 물론 모든 그림은 판매 가능합니다. 오늘 밤에 구매하실 필요는 없지만… 음… **이 화가는 인기가 아주 많습니다.** 분명 실망하고 싶지 않으실 겁니다. 질문이 있으시면 직원에게 말씀하시기 바랍니다.

어휘

exhibition 전시회, 전시 landscape art 풍경화

appreciate 고마워하다, 감사하다 support 지원, 후원

oil painting 유화 on display 전시된 in detail 상세하게

available for sale 판매 가능한 make a purchase 구매하다

avoid 방지하다, 피하다 disappointment 실망, 낙심

1.

화자는 "이 화가는 인기가 아주 많습니다"라고 할 때 무엇을 의미하는가?

(A) 행사가 혼잡할 것으로 예상된다.

(B) 일부 미술작품은 가치가 올라갈 것이다.

(C) 제시된 가격은 타당하다.

(D) 일부 작품들은 아마도 빨리 팔릴 것이다.

어휘

proposed 제안된 fair 타당한, 공정한

[2] 미남 🎧

Question 2 refers to the following telephone message.

> M Hi, Erica. It's Calvin. I got your message about cutting operating costs at the office. You mentioned that we could get an automated phone system to handle incoming calls. While it would be efficient, and we wouldn't need to have more than one receptionist working at any given time, what people like about our business is the friendly service. How about we meet sometime tomorrow to discuss the matter further? I'm free for most of the day, so please let me know what time works best for you. Thanks.

해석

2번은 다음 전화 메시지에 관한 문제입니다.

남 안녕하세요, 에리카. 캘빈이에요. 사무실의 운영비 삭감에 관한 당신의 메시지를 받았어요. **걸려오는 전화를 처리하기 위해 자동 전화 시스템을 갖출 수 있다고 언급하셨죠.** 그것이 효율적이고, 우리가 언제가 되었든 근무하는 접수 담당자를 여러 명 둘 필요도 없는 반면, **사람들이 우리 사업에 대해 좋아하는 점은 친절한 서비스입니다.** 우리가 내일 만나서 이 문제를 더 얘기하는 게 어떨까요? 저는 거의 하루 종일 한가하므로 몇 시가 당신에게 가장 좋은지 알려 주시기 바랍니다. 고맙습니다.

어휘

operating cost 운영비, 영업 경비

automated 자동화된, 자동의 handle 처리하다, 다루다

incoming 도착하는, 들어오는 efficient 효율적인

receptionist 접수 담당자 friendly 친절한, 다정한

matter 문제, 일 work for ~에게 효과가 나타나다

2.

화자는 왜 "사람들이 우리 사업에 대해 좋아하는 점은 친절한 서비

스입니다"라고 말하는가?
(A) 가격을 정당화하기 위해
(B) 안심시키기 위해
(C) 제안을 거절하기 위해
(D) 청자를 칭찬하기 위해

어휘

justify 정당화하다, 해명하다 reassurance 안심시키기
reject 거절하다, 거부하다

연습 문제 본문 p.243

1. (B) **2.** (B) **3.** (A) **4.** (D) **5.** (C)

---

[1] 미남 🎧

Question 1 refers to the following broadcast.

> M Welcome, everyone, to the semi-final round of our televised baking contest. We have just five bakers left in our competition, and after today, it will be four. These bakers have really shown their talent throughout the competition. Now, a lot of people think that our judges may have a favorite participant. But don't forget, when they taste the food, they don't know who made it. That way, they can judge fairly at all times.

해석

1번은 다음 방송에 관한 문제입니다.

남 TV로 방송되는 저희 제빵 경연 대회의 준결승전을 시청하시는 모든 분들을 환영합니다. 저희는 단 5명의 제빵사만 경연에 남겨 두고 있고, 오늘이 지나면 4명이 될 것입니다. 이 제빵사들은 경연 내내 자신의 재능을 정말 많이 보여 주었습니다. 자, 많은 분들이 저희 심사위원단이 편애하는 참가자가 있을지도 모른다고 생각하십니다. 하지만 잊지 마세요, 그들이 음식을 맛볼 때는 누가 만들었는지 모릅니다. 그렇게 하면, 항상 공정하게 심사할 수 있습니다.

어휘

semi-final 준결승전 televised TV로 방송되는 baker 제빵사
competition 경연 대회, 경쟁 talent 재능
judge 심사위원, 심판; 판정하다 participant 참가자
fairly 공정하게, 상당히

1.

화자는 왜 "누가 만들었는지 모릅니다"라고 말하는가?
(A) 정정을 요청하기 위해
(B) 오해를 바로잡기 위해
(C) 다른 과정을 추천하기 위해
(D) 몇 가지 정보를 요청하기 위해

어휘

correction 정정, 수정 correct 바로잡다, 고치다
misunderstanding 오해

[2-3] 미녀 🎧

Questions 2-3 refer to the following talk.

> W Welcome to today's walking tour of historical Bristol. We're here on Luther Avenue. Now, I know what you're thinking, ²the buildings on your left are clearly older than the buildings on your right. Actually, there used to be a wall here, and these buildings were built at different times. Due to population growth, the wall was knocked down to make room for new housing. At the end of this tour, ³we'll visit the history museum, where we can see a model that shows what the old city looked like.

해석

2-3번은 다음 담화에 관한 문제입니다.

여 오늘 역사적으로 유명한 브리스틀 도보 여행에 오신 것을 환영합니다. 우리는 이곳 루터가에 있습니다. 자, 여러분이 무슨 생각을 하시는지 압니다, ²왼쪽에 있는 건물들이 오른쪽에 있는 건물들보다 확연히 낡았죠. 사실, 이곳에는 담이 있었고, 이 건물들은 다른 시대에 지어졌습니다. 인구 증가 때문에, 새로운 주택을 위한 공간을 마련하기 위해 담이 철거되었습니다. 이번 여행의 마지막에, ³우리는 역사 박물관에 방문할 것인데, 그곳에서 오래된 도시의 모습이 어떠했는지 보여주는 모델을 볼 수 있습니다.

어휘

historical 역사상의 clearly 분명히, 또렷하게
used to ~하곤 했다 population growth 인구 증가
knock down 철거하다, 부수다 housing 주택 (공급)

2.

화자는 왜 "여러분이 무슨 생각을 하시는지 압니다"라고 말하는가?
(A) 불만을 제기하기 위해
(B) 혼란을 해결하기 위해
(C) 지연에 대해 설명하기 위해
(D) 제안을 거절하기 위해

어휘

complaint 불만, 항의 address (문제 등을) 다루다
confusion 혼란, 혼동

3.

청자들은 박물관에서 무엇을 할 수 있는가?
(A) 오래된 도시의 복제본 보기
(B) 역사 강연에 참석하기
(C) 브리스틀에 대한 영상 시청하기
(D) 오래전 사진 구매하기

어휘

reproduction 복사, 복제

패러프레이징

a model that shows what the old city looked like
→ a reproduction of the old city

Questions 4-5 refer to the following excerpt from a meeting.

> **W** ⁴Here you go. These are all the brochures I could find for things to do in the Chicago area. We need to build a strong relationship with our clients through a special activity. So far, we've spent all of our time in meetings, so we haven't been able to get any closer to them. Thankfully, ⁵I think it's not going to rain next weekend, so we can do an outdoor activity if we want. Just in case, I'll double-check that. Please let me know what you might prefer.

해석

4-5번은 다음 회의 발췌록에 관한 문제입니다.

여 ⁴여기 있습니다. 이것들은 모두 제가 시카고 지역에서 할 만한 것들을 위해 찾은 안내 책자입니다. 우리는 특별한 활동을 통해 우리 고객들과 공고한 관계를 쌓아야 합니다. 지금까지, 우리는 모든 시간을 회의하는 데 썼기에 그들에게 가까이 갈 수 없었습니다. 다행스럽게도, ⁵다음 주말에 비가 오지 않을 것 같으니, 우리가 원한다면 야외 활동을 할 수 있습니다. 만약을 위해 제가 그것을 다시 한번 확인하겠습니다. 여러분이 무엇을 선호하는지 알려 주시기 바랍니다.

어휘

relationship 관계 thankfully 고맙게도, 다행스럽게도
outdoor activity 야외 활동 just in case 만약을 위해서
double-check 재확인하다 prefer (더) 좋아하다, 선호하다

4.

화자는 청자들에게 무엇을 주는가?
(A) 여행 일정표
(B) 방문증
(C) 건물 지도
(D) 광고 팸플릿

패러프레이징

brochures I could find for things to do
→ Advertising pamphlets

5.

화자는 "제가 그것을 다시 한번 확인하겠습니다"라고 말할 때 무엇을 암시하는가?
(A) 그녀는 일부 재무 수치가 부정확하다고 생각한다.
(B) 그녀는 고객들의 관심사를 모른다.
(C) 그녀는 날씨가 좋을 것임을 확인할 것이다.
(D) 그녀는 일부 계약 조건이 걱정된다.

어휘

financial 금융의, 재정의 figures ((보통 복수형)) 수치
incorrect 부정확한, 맞지 않는 interest 관심사, 관심
verify 확인하다 contract terms 계약 조건

실전 문제 본문 p.244

1. (C)	**2.** (B)	**3.** (C)	**4.** (A)	**5.** (B)
6. (D)	**7.** (A)	**8.** (C)	**9.** (A)	**10.** (C)
11. (B)	**12.** (A)	**13.** (B)	**14.** (C)	**15.** (B)
16. (C)	**17.** (D)	**18.** (B)		

Questions 1-3 refer to the following excerpt from a meeting.

> **M** Let's get this planning meeting started. ¹The art festival at Conifer Park will be held on August 8. ²Our goal is to sell 3,000 tickets in advance. Well... I just found out that, there is another major event that day, and ²it'll be much bigger than ours. We just need to do our best. We'll start hanging up posters next week to promote the event. ³I have some sample designs here, so let's talk about what you like and dislike about each one.

해석

1-3번은 다음 회의 발췌록에 관한 문제입니다.

남 이번 기획 회의를 시작하겠습니다. ¹예술 축제가 코니퍼 파크에서 8월 8일에 열릴 것입니다. ²우리의 목표는 사전에 티켓 3천 장을 판매하는 것입니다. 음... 제가 방금 그날 또 다른 주요 행사가 있다는 것을 알게 되었는데요, ²그것이 우리 행사보다 규모가 훨씬 더 클 것입니다. 우리는 그저 최선을 다하기만 하면 됩니다. 행사를 홍보하기 위해 다음 주에 포스터를 걸기 시작할 것입니다. ³여기 몇몇 샘플 디자인이 있으니 각각에 대해 무엇이 좋고 무엇이 싫은지 얘기합시다.

어휘

get started 시작하다 planning meeting 기획 회의
be held (행사가) 열리다, 개최되다 goal 목표
in advance 미리, 사전에 find out 알아내다, 알게 되다
do one's best 최선을 다하다 hang up 걸다
promote 홍보하다

1.

8월에 어떤 행사가 개최될 것인가?
(A) 연례 퍼레이드
(B) 공원 대청소 프로젝트
(C) 예술 축제
(D) 모금 만찬

어휘

take place 개최되다 cleanup 대청소, 재고 정리

fund-raising 모금

2.
화자는 "그날 또 다른 주요 행사가 있다"라고 말할 때 무엇을 의미하는가?
(A) 장소를 이용할 수 없다.
(B) 목표를 달성하지 못할 수도 있다.
(C) 행사 날짜가 변경될 것이다.
(D) 교통 혼잡이 예상된다.

site 현장, 장소 reach a goal 목표를 달성하다
traffic congestion 교통 혼잡

3.
청자들은 다음에 무엇을 할 것인가?
(A) 지도 보기
(B) 행사 장소 고르기
(C) 몇몇 포스터에 대해 이야기하기
(D) 다과 먹기

venue (행사의) 장소 refreshments ((항상 복수형)) 음식물, 다과

talk about what you like and dislike → Discuss

[4-6] 호남 🎧
Questions 4-6 refer to the following telephone message.

> M Hi, Ms. Garcia. This is Antonio Maynard. [4] I've just been looking over your reimbursement request for your recent business trip. I'd like to process the payment as soon as possible. Um... I see from your note that [5] you didn't keep your receipt for the business dinner with Ms. Beasley. We can work around that. [5] For example, if you paid by credit card, we could look at that statement. Please let me know if that's possible. Also, [6] I've e-mailed you the details about the reimbursement policy so you'll know what to do next time.

4-6번은 다음 전화 메시지에 관한 문제입니다.
남 안녕하세요, 가르시아 씨. 저는 안토니오 메이나드입니다. [4] 제가 방금 당신의 최근 출장에 대한 환급 신청을 살펴보고 있었습니다. 최대한 빨리 지급 처리를 하려고 합니다. 음... 당신의 메모를 보니 [5] 비슬리 씨와 했던 업무상 저녁 식사의 영수증을 보관하지 않으셨더군요. 저희가 해결할 수 있습니다. [5] 예를 들어, 신용카드로 지불하셨다면, 저희가 내역서를 보면 됩니다. 그것이 가능한지 저에게 알려 주세요. 또한, [6] 환급 정책에 관한 세부 내용을 이메일로 보내 드렸으니 다음번에는 어떻게 해야 하는지 아시게 될 겁니다.

look over ~을 살펴보다 reimbursement 상환, 변제, 환급
business trip 출장 process 처리하다 payment 지불, 지급
note 메모, 쪽지 receipt 영수증 statement 입출금 내역서
policy 정책, 방침

4.
화자는 어느 부서에서 일하는 것 같은가?
(A) 재무
(B) 그래픽 디자인
(C) 관리
(D) 홍보

5.
화자는 "저희가 해결할 수 있습니다"라고 말할 때 무엇을 암시하는가?
(A) 출장이 승인되었다.
(B) 영수증이 항상 필수는 아니다.
(C) 근무 일정이 유동적이다.
(D) 예산이 충분히 많다.

approve 승인하다, 허가하다 be required 요구되다
flexible 유동적인 budget 예산

6.
화자는 이메일로 무엇을 보냈는가?
(A) 곧 있을 행사
(B) 새로운 과제
(C) 신용카드 신청서
(D) 회사 정책

upcoming 다가오는, 곧 있을 application 신청(서), 지원(서)

the details about the reimbursement policy
→ A company policy

[7-9] 미녀 🎧
Questions 7-9 refer to the following excerpt from a meeting.

> W The last thing on the agenda is some exciting news. [7] We got the contract for the Haymond Incorporated headquarters building! Their representatives loved our designs, and we finalized the contract terms this morning. [7] We'll begin its construction shortly. [8] I know that preparing the proposal wasn't easy. The office was full every weekend. Thank you so much! Now, [9] don't forget that this information is confidential. So, don't post about it on social media, discuss it with people outside our staff, uh... things like that. Haymond Incorporated

wants to make the announcement themselves in their own time.

해석

7-9번은 다음 회의 발췌록에 관한 문제입니다.

여 마지막 안건은 신나는 소식입니다. **7 우리가 헤이먼드 사 본사 건물에 대한 계약을 따냈습니다!** 그쪽 대표들이 우리의 설계를 매우 좋아했고, 오늘 아침에 계약 조건을 마무리 지었습니다. **7 우리는 곧 그곳의 건설을 시작할 것입니다. 8 제안서를 준비하는 일이 쉽지 않았다는 것을 알고 있습니다.** 사무실이 매 주말마다 꽉 차 있었어요. 대단히 고맙습니다! 자, **9 이 정보는 기밀이라는 것**을 잊지 마세요. 그러니 소셜미디어에 이에 대해 게시하거나, 직원 이외의 사람들과 이에 대해 이야기하거나, 어... 그런 일들을 하지 마세요. 헤이먼드 사는 적절한 시기에 직접 발표하기를 원합니다.

어휘

agenda 안건, 의제 get the contract 계약을 따내다
headquarters 본사, 본부 representative 대표(자), 대리인
finalize 마무리 짓다, 완결하다 contract terms 계약 조건
construction 공사, 건설 shortly 곧 proposal 제안
confidential 기밀의, 비밀의
in one's own time 형편이 좋을 때에

7.

화자는 어디에서 일하는 것 같은가?

(A) 건축 회사에서
(B) 출판사에서
(C) 실험실에서
(D) 백화점에서

어휘

architecture 건축, 건축학

패러프레이징

construction → architecture

8.

화자는 왜 "사무실이 매 주말마다 꽉 차 있었어요"라고 말하는가?
(A) 주차 문제에 대해 항의하기 위해
(B) 새로운 건물로 이사할 것을 제안하기 위해
(C) 청자들의 노고를 강조하기 위해
(D) 참석자 명단을 확인하기 위해

어휘

complain 불평하다, 항의하다 emphasize 강조하다
confirm 확인하다 attendance list 참석자 명단

9.

화자는 청자들에게 무엇에 대해 상기시키는가?
(A) 어떻게 민감한 정보를 다루는지
(B) 어디서 회사 웹사이트를 찾는지
(C) 누가 프로젝트에 대한 자격이 있는지
(D) 언제 양식을 제출하는지

어휘

sensitive 민감한, 세심한 be eligible for ~에 자격이 있다
turn in 제출하다

패러프레이징

this information is confidential → sensitive information

[10-12] 영녀 🎧

Questions 10-12 refer to the following telephone message.

W **10 This is Belkin Laundry calling about the dress you dropped off here this morning. We were able to remove the large stain and clean it. It didn't take long, and now it looks as good as new. 11 You'll be able to wear it with confidence at the event this evening.** You can pick it up whenever you would like. **11 However, you mentioned that you had a busy schedule today** and, it's already 4:30. **12 So we would be happy to deliver it to you.** We have two addresses on file for you. One appears to be your office and the other is your apartment. Please contact us if you'd like to arrange for us to do that.

해석

10-12번은 다음 전화 메시지에 관한 문제입니다.

여 **10 벨킨 세탁소에서 당신이 오늘 아침 저희에게 맡기신 드레스에 관해 전화드립니다.** 저희는 커다란 얼룩을 제거하고 드레스를 세탁할 수 있었어요. 오래 걸리지 않았고, 이제는 새것이나 다름없어 보입니다. **11 오늘 저녁 행사에서 자신 있게 입으실 수 있을 거예요.** 편한 시간에 아무 때나 찾아가시면 됩니다. **11 하지만, 오늘 바쁜 일정이 있다고 말씀하셨고,** 벌써 4시 30분이네요. **12 따라서 저희가 기꺼이 배달해 드리겠습니다.** 당신의 파일에 주소가 두 개 있어요. 하나는 당신의 사무실로 보이고 나머지 하나는 당신의 아파트 주소입니다. 저희가 그렇게 하도록 처리하고 싶으시면 연락 주시기 바랍니다.

어휘

drop off 내려 주다, 내려놓다, 맡기다 remove 제거하다, 없애다
stain 얼룩 as good as new 새것이나 다름없는
with confidence 자신을 가지고 appear ~인 것 같다
arrange to ~하도록 처리하다

10.

화자는 청자를 위해 무엇을 했는가?
(A) 문서 보내기
(B) 상점 추천하기
(C) 옷 세탁하기
(D) 환불해 주기

어휘

garment 의복, 옷 issue 발부하다, 지급하다
refund 환불; 환불하다

패러프레이징

the dress → a garment

11.

화자는 "벌써 4시 30분이네요"라고 말할 때 무엇을 의미하는가?

(A) 작업이 예상했던 것보다 오래 걸렸다.

(B) 행사 전까지 시간이 많이 남아 있지 않다.

(C) 그녀는 만남을 연기하고 싶다.

(D) 그녀는 약속에 늦었다.

어휘

task 일, 과업 anticipate 기대하다, 예상하다

postpone 연기하다

12.

화자는 무엇을 해 주겠다고 제안하는가?

(A) 물품 배달하기

(B) 견적 제공하기

(C) 고객에게 연락하기

(D) 예약 취소하기

어휘

supply 공급하다, 제공하다 estimate 견적(서)

reservation 예약

[13-15] 미남 🎧

Questions 13-15 refer to the following talk.

> M ¹³Thanks for coming to this VG Sports managers' meeting. I'm excited that we'll be the exclusive retailer of a line of running shoes from Andrus. We'll be closing off the northwest corner of the store for two days to set up a display to feature the shoes. ¹⁴I know it may seem like a long time, but this is not our usual display. There will be lights, moving parts, sounds… uh… it's really going to attract shoppers. In fact, ¹⁵a reporter from the *Bloomfield Tribune* is coming on Friday to write an article about the launch.

해석

13-15번은 다음 담화에 관한 문제입니다.

남 ¹³이번 VG 스포츠 매니저 회의에 참석해 주셔서 감사합니다. 저는 우리가 앤드러스의 운동화 라인의 독점 소매업자가 될 예정이라는 사실에 흥분됩니다. 우리는 이 신발들을 선보일 진열을 설치하기 위해 이틀 동안 매장의 북서쪽 코너를 막아 놓을 것입니다. ¹⁴긴 시간처럼 보일 수도 있다는 것을 알지만, 이것은 우리의 통상적인 진열이 아닙니다. 조명과 움직이는 부품들, 음향 시스템이 있을 거예요... 어... 그것은 정말 쇼핑객들의 관심을 끌 것입니다. 사실, ¹⁵〈블룸필드 트리뷴〉의 기자가 출시에 대한 기사를 쓰기 위해 금요일에 올 것입니다.

어휘

exclusive 독점적인 retailer 소매업자

close off 폐쇄시키다, 차단하다 set up 설치하다, 세우다, 준비하다

display 진열, 전시 feature 특별히 포함하다, 특징으로 삼다

usual 평상시의, 보통의 attract 마음을 끌다, 끌어들이다

launch 출시; 출시하다

13.

화자는 어디에서 일하는가?

(A) 소프트웨어 회사에서

(B) 스포츠용품 매장에서

(C) 병원에서

(D) 제조 시설에서

어휘

sporting goods 스포츠용품 manufacturing 제조(업)

패러프레이징

running shoes → sporting goods

14.

화자는 왜 "이것은 우리의 통상적인 진열이 아닙니다"라고 말하는가?

(A) 청자들에게 감사하기 위해

(B) 실수를 비판하기 위해

(C) 일정이 타당함을 보여주기 위해

(D) 요청을 거절하기 위해

어휘

criticize 비판하다, 비난하다 justify 정당화시키다, 해명하다

timeline 연대표, 시간표 reject 거절하다

15.

화자는 금요일에 무슨 일이 일어날 것이라고 말하는가?

(A) 유명 인사가 사인을 할 것이다.

(B) 기자가 업체를 방문할 것이다.

(C) 할인이 실시될 것이다.

(D) TV 광고가 촬영될 것이다.

어휘

celebrity 유명 인사 autograph 사인; 사인을 해 주다

journalist 기자 go into effect 효력이 발생되다, 실시되다

commercial 광고 (방송)

패러프레이징

a reporter ~ is coming

→ A journalist will visit the business

[16-18] 영녀 🎧

Questions 16-18 refer to the following advertisement.

> W ¹⁶Sunshine Cleaners can handle all of your cleaning needs. We never miss a detail, and we put a ray of sunshine into even the most difficult spaces. ¹⁷We are now offering six free weeks of our service to any business that signs a one-year contract. This never happens in the industry. When you work with us, you are

guaranteed the highest level of service. It's this dedication to perfection that separates us from our competition. [18] Visit our Web site to read honest reviews from a wide range of commercial customers. And contact us today to set up an initial meeting. We can't wait to work with you!

해석

16-18번은 다음 광고에 관한 문제입니다.

여 [16] 선샤인 청소 회사는 여러분의 모든 청소 요구를 처리해 드릴 수 있습니다. 저희는 세세한 부분을 결코 놓치지 않으며, 심지어 청소하기 가장 힘든 공간에도 한 줄기 빛을 비추어 드립니다. [17] 지금 1년 계약을 맺는 모든 업체에게 6주간 무료로 저희 서비스를 제공해 드리고 있습니다. 이것은 업계에서 절대 없는 일입니다. 저희와 함께 일하시면, 최고 수준의 서비스를 보장받으시게 됩니다. 저희를 경쟁자와 구분 짓는 것이 바로 완벽에 대한 이러한 헌신입니다. [18] 저희 웹사이트를 방문하시어 다양한 기업 고객들의 솔직한 평가를 읽어 보세요. 그리고 첫 회의를 잡으시려면 오늘 저희에게 연락하세요. 빨리 여러분과 일하고 싶습니다!

어휘

handle 다루다, 처리하다　needs ((보통 복수형)) 요구
sign a contract 계약을 맺다, 계약서에 서명하다
guarantee 보장하다　dedication 전념, 헌신
perfection 완벽, 완전
separate A from B B에서 A를 분리시키다
competition 경쟁, 경쟁자　a wide range of 광범위한, 다양한
commercial 기업의　initial 처음의

16.

무엇이 광고되고 있는가?
(A) 유니폼 제조업체
(B) 세탁 서비스
(C) 청소 회사
(D) 조경 회사

어휘

manufacturer 제조사, 제조업체　laundry 세탁, 세탁업
landscaping 조경

17.

화자는 "이것은 업계에서 절대 없는 일입니다"라고 말할 때 무엇을 암시하는가?
(A) 서비스가 구식이었다.
(B) 정보가 부정확할지도 모른다.
(C) 고객들이 많다.
(D) 이 특별 할인은 엄청난 것이다.

어휘

out of date 구식의, 시대에 뒤떨어진
incorrect 부정확한, 맞지 않는
special offer 특별 할인, 특가 판매
impressive 강한 인상을 주는, 훌륭한

18.

화자에 따르면, 웹사이트에서 무엇을 찾을 수 있는가?
(A) 지점들의 지도
(B) 고객들의 반응
(C) 직원 명부
(D) 홍보 물품

어휘

feedback 반응, 의견　directory 주소 성명록, 인명부
promotional 홍보의

패러프레이징

reviews from a wide range of commercial customers
→ Feedback from customers

UNIT 08 시각 자료 연계 문제

연습 문제			본문 p.249
1. (D)	**2.** (B)	**3.** (C)	

[1] 미남 🎧

Question 1 refers to the following announcement and chart.

M I have some good news, everyone. We had some surplus funds in the budget, so I was able to buy some new accounting software for our company. I looked into several programs. In the end, I decided to buy the one with the highest rating. It had a lot of additional features that I think we will find useful. I'll start inputting our financial records into the new software from tomorrow.

해석

1번은 다음 공지와 도표에 관한 문제입니다.

남 여러분, 좋은 소식이 있습니다. 예산에 잉여 자금이 있어서 우리 회사를 위해 새로운 회계 소프트웨어를 구매할 수 있게 되었습니다. 제가 몇 가지 프로그램을 조사했습니다. 결국, 가장 높은 평가를 받은 것을 구매하기로 결정했습니다. 그것에는 우리가 유용하다고 생각할 만한 많은 추가 기능이 있었습니다. 제가 내일부터 새로운 소프트웨어에 우리 재무 기록 입력을 시작하겠습니다.

어휘

surplus 과잉의, 잉여의　fund 돈, 자금　budget 예산
accounting 회계 (업무)　in the end 마침내, 결국
rating 순위, 평가, 등급　additional 추가의　feature 특징, 기능
useful 유용한　input 입력하다　financial 금융의, 재정의

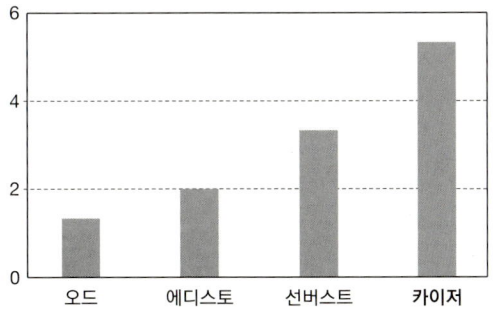

소프트웨어 평가

1.
시각 자료를 보시오. 화자는 어떤 회계 소프트웨어를 구매했는가?
(A) 오드
(B) 에디스토
(C) 선버스트
(D) 카이저

패러프레이징
buy → purchase

[2-3] 미남 🎧
Questions 2-3 refer to the following telephone message and price list.

> M Hello, Mr. Walker. This is Victor from Blake Hardware. I just spoke to our supplier, and the paint you ordered this morning is going to come in later than expected. We would deliver it on Wednesday instead of Monday. ²As an apology, I'll cancel your delivery charge. I understand if you want to cancel your order instead. However, ³Smith-Wright does have the best quality in paint, so I think it's well worth the wait. If you have any questions, please call me back at 555-3574. Thank you.

해석
2-3번은 다음 전화 메시지와 가격표에 관한 문제입니다.
남 안녕하세요, 워커 씨. 저는 블레이크 철물점의 빅터입니다. 방금 저희 공급업체와 얘기했는데요, 당신이 오늘 아침에 주문한 페인트가 예상보다 늦게 도착할 것입니다. 저희가 월요일 대신 수요일에 그것을 배달해 드리겠습니다. **²사과의 의미로, 배달료를 취소해 드리겠습니다.** 이것 대신 주문을 취소하길 원하시더라도 이해합니다. 하지만, **³스미스라이트는 정말 최고 품질의 페인트를 보유하고 있으니 기다릴 만한 가치가 충분히 있다고 생각합니다.** 질문이 있으시면, 555-3574로 답신 전화 주시기 바랍니다. 감사합니다.

어휘
supplier 공급자, 공급 회사 apology 사과
charge 요금; 청구하다 quality 질, 우수함
well worth ~의 가치가 충분히 있는

인테리어 페인트

페인트 브랜드	가격
블레이크 인테리어 라텍스	29.99달러
스트룹 인테리어 라텍스	31.99달러
³스미스라이트 인테리어 라텍스	32.99달러
랜스 페인트 아크릴 라텍스	34.99달러

2.
화자는 무엇을 해 주겠다고 제안하는가?
(A) 공급업체에게 연락하기
(B) 요금 취소하기
(C) 청구서 보내기
(D) 제품 추천하기

어휘
fee 요금, 수수료 invoice 청구서, 송장

패러프레이징
delivery charge → a fee

3.
시각 자료를 보시오. 워커 씨는 자신의 주문에 대해 얼마를 지불할 것인가?
(A) 29.99달러
(B) 31.99달러
(C) 32.99달러
(D) 34.99달러

실전 문제   본문 p.250

1. (D)	**2.** (B)	**3.** (B)	**4.** (A)	**5.** (C)
6. (D)	**7.** (B)	**8.** (C)	**9.** (A)	**10.** (A)
11. (C)	**12.** (D)			

[1-3] 미녀 🎧
Questions 1-3 refer to the following telephone message and map.

> W Hi, Mr. Davis. It's Cynthia O'Neal from Athens Incorporated. ¹I'm sorry that I'm just calling now after such a long time. Actually, I never got your first telephone message about confirming my visit. So… um… yes, I'm still interested in finding out more about your jewelry company's products. ²The bracelets and necklaces would be particularly interesting to my customers. ³You said you are available at two on Wednesday, and I can be there then. I understand that I should meet you at the tower with the administration offices. See you soon!

해석

1-3번은 다음 전화 메시지와 지도에 관한 문제입니다.

여 안녕하세요, 데이비스 씨. 아테네 주식회사의 신시아 오닐입니다. **¹이렇게 한참 뒤에 이제야 전화드려서 죄송합니다. 사실, 제 방문을 확인해 주신 첫 번째 전화 메시지를 받은 적이 없습니다.** 그래서... 음... 네, 당신의 귀금속 회사 제품에 관해 더 많이 알아보는 데 여전히 관심이 있습니다. **²팔찌와 목걸이가 제 고객들에게 특히 흥미로울 것 같습니다. ³수요일에 2시에 시간이 되신다고 하셨지요, 그때 갈 수 있습니다. 총무부가 있는 건물에서 당신을 만나야 한다는 것을 알고 있습니다.** 곧 뵙겠습니다!

어휘

confirm 확인하다, 확정하다 particularly 특히, 특별히
available (만날) 시간이 있는, 이용할 수 있는
administration office 총무부, 행정실

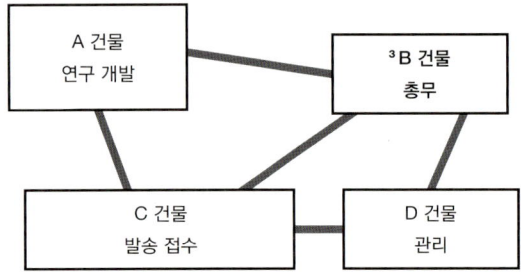

렌웨이 비즈니스 복합 단지

1.

화자는 왜 회신하는 데 오랜 시간이 걸렸는가?
(A) 그녀는 업무 회의가 많았다.
(B) 그녀는 자신의 일정에 대해 확실히 몰랐다.
(C) 그녀는 청자의 연락처를 잃어버렸다.
(D) 그녀는 메시지를 받지 못했다.

어휘

reply 답장을 보내다; 답장 unsure 확신하지 못하는
contact details 연락처

패러프레이징

never got your first telephone message
→ did not get a message

2.

청자의 회사는 어떤 제품을 판매하는가?
(A) 가구
(B) 귀금속
(C) 주방용품
(D) 화장품

패러프레이징

bracelets and necklaces → Jewelry

3.

시각 자료를 보시오. 화자는 수요일에 어디에서 청자를 만날 것인가?

(A) A 건물에서
(B) B 건물에서
(C) C 건물에서
(D) D 건물에서

[4-6] 호남 🎧

Questions 4-6 refer to the following talk and schedule.

M Thanks for being here today. ⁴We wanted to have everyone meet at the same time to learn how to operate the different functions of the new system for voicemail messages. That way, we can all be on the same page as we move forward. Before we get started, I'd like to tell you a few things. ⁵Could everyone please fill out the survey after the class is finished? It will help us be more effective in the future. Um... the other thing is... ⁶the last presenter on our schedule had to be out of the office today, so Mr. Thomas will cover her material. That's it. I hope you all find this as informative as we planned it to be.

해석

4-6번은 다음 담화와 일정표에 관한 문제입니다.

남 오늘 이 자리에 와 주셔서 감사합니다. **⁴우리는 새로운 음성 메시지 시스템의 여러 가지 기능을 작동하는 방법을 배우기 위해 모든 사람이 같은 시간에 모이게 하고 싶었습니다.** 그렇게 하면, 우리가 진도를 나갈 때 모두 똑같이 이해할 수 있습니다. 시작하기 전에, 몇 가지 말씀을 드리겠습니다. **⁵강의가 끝난 후에 모두 설문 조사를 작성해 주시겠습니까?** 그것은 앞으로 우리가 더욱 효과적으로 일하는 데 도움이 될 것입니다. 음... 다른 한 가지는... **⁶우리 일정표 상의 마지막 발표자가 오늘 사무실을 비워야 했기 때문에 토마스 씨가 그녀의 주제를 담당할 것입니다.** 이상입니다. 여러분 모두 이것이 우리가 계획했던 만큼 유익하다고 느끼길 바랍니다.

어휘

operate 작동하다; 작동되다 function 기능
be on the same page 이해하고 있는 내용이 같다
move forward 전진하다, (일이) 순조롭게 진행되다
fill out 기입하다, 작성하다 survey 설문 조사
effective 효과적인, 유능한 presenter 발표자
cover (다른 사람의 일을) 대신하다, 담당하다 material 자료, 재료
informative 유익한

교육 일정표	
시간	발표자 및 주제
8:00-8:15	리이언스 씨: 소개하는 말
8:15-8:45	스콧 씨: 시작하기
8:45-9:30	벤 씨: 고급 기능
⁶9:30-10:00	**록하트 씨: 사용자화**

4.

청자들은 무엇에 대해 배울 것인가?

(A) 메시지 전송 시스템
(B) 연구 데이터베이스
(C) 시각 디자인 프로그램
(D) 보안 경고

어휘

security 보안, 경비 alarm 경보(음)

패러프레이징

the new system for voicemail messages
→ A messaging system

5.

청자들은 무엇을 하도록 요청받는가?

(A) 시스템 사용 연습하기
(B) 설명서 검토하기
(C) 설문 조사 기입하기
(D) 환영회 참석하기

어휘

review 검토하다 manual 설명서
complete 기입하다, 작성하다 reception 환영회

패러프레이징

fill out → Complete

6.

시각 자료를 보시오. 토마스 씨는 무슨 주제를 맡을 것인가?

(A) 소개하는 말
(B) 시작하기
(C) 고급 기능
(D) 사용자화

어휘

introduction 소개, 도입 advanced 고급의
feature 특징, 기능 personalization 사용자화

[7-9] 영녀 🎧

Questions 7-9 refer to the following talk and chart.

> **W** Good morning, everyone. I'd like to start today's staff meeting by introducing a new organizational structure. As you know, we've been having a problem with communication these days. ⁷That's because we've all taken on more assignments due to the increase in demand. So, ⁸we've added a position under the general manager to help out with that issue. We will be hiring in-house to fill these roles and begin interviews next week. ⁹After this meeting, I will place the sign-up sheet in the company cafeteria. Please take a look at the sheet carefully to see if you'd like to apply.

해석

7-9번은 다음 담화와 도표에 관한 문제입니다.

여 안녕하세요, 여러분. 새로운 조직 구조를 소개하는 것으로 오늘의 직원 회의를 시작하겠습니다. 아시다시피, 우리가 요즘 의사소통에 문제를 겪고 있습니다. ⁷그것은 수요 증가로 인해 우리 모두가 더 많은 업무를 맡았기 때문입니다. 따라서, ⁸그 문제의 해결을 돕기 위해 총괄 매니저 아래에 직위를 추가했습니다. 우리는 이 역할을 채우기 위해 내부 채용을 할 것이며 다음 주에 면접을 시작할 것입니다. ⁹이 회의 후에, 제가 회사 카페테리아에 신청서를 비치할 것입니다. 신청서를 주의 깊게 살펴보시고 지원 여부를 결정해 주시기 바랍니다.

어휘

organizational 조직(상)의 structure 구조
communication 의사소통 take on (일 등을) 맡다
assignment 임무, 과제 demand 수요
position (일)자리, 직위 help out with ~을 돕다
in-house 조직 내에서 place 놓다, 두다
sign-up sheet 신청서 apply 지원하다, 신청하다

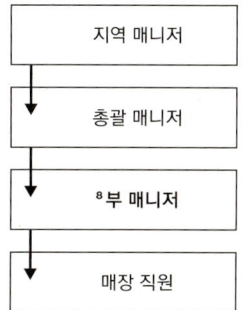

지역 매니저

↓

총괄 매니저

↓

⁸부 매니저

↓

매장 직원

7.

화자에 따르면, 무엇이 문제를 일으켰는가?

(A) 지원자 부족
(B) 더 많은 업무량
(C) 훈련되어 있지 않은 직원들
(D) 시대에 뒤진 기술

어휘

lack 부족 applicant 지원자 workload 업무량, 작업량
outdated 구식인, 시대에 뒤진

패러프레이징

taken on more assignments → Heavier workload

8.

시각 자료를 보시오. 최근에 어떤 직위가 추가되었는가?

(A) 지역 매니저
(B) 총괄 매니저
(C) 부 매니저
(D) 매장 직원

9.

화자는 회의 후에 무엇을 할 것인가?

(A) 문서 게시하기
(B) 이메일 보내기
(C) 프로그램에 지원하기
(D) 웹사이트 업데이트하기

어휘

post 게시하다, 공고하다

패러프레이징

place the sign-up sheet → Post a document

[10-12] 미녀 🎧

Questions 10-12 refer to the following telephone
message and layout.

> W Hi, Sam. It's Marcia. I got your message about
> room assignments, but I think someone made
> a mistake. The manager's office is currently
> assigned to one of the rooms next to the
> conference room. ¹⁰But he wanted a room that
> was quieter, away from the conference room
> and copy room. So, that will need to be
> changed. ¹¹Also, I called the furniture company
> and asked them to refund our order of lamps.
> ¹²We've decided to get skylights instead, as
> the cost of lighting was much too high. Those
> will be delivered and installed next Wednesday.

해석

10-12번은 다음 전화 메시지와 배치도에 관한 문제입니다.

여 안녕하세요, 샘. 마샤예요. 방 배정에 관한 당신의 메시지를 받았
지만, 누군가 실수를 한 것 같아요. 매니저의 사무실이 현재 회의
실 바로 옆에 있는 방들 중 하나에 배정되어 있어요. ¹⁰하지만 그
는 더 조용하고, 회의실과 복사실에서 떨어져 있는 방을 원했어
요. 따라서, 그것은 바뀌어야 할 거예요. ¹¹또한, 제가 가구 회사
에 전화해서 우리가 주문한 전등을 환불해 달라고 요청했어요.
¹²대신 채광창을 내기로 결정했는데요, 조명의 비용이 지나치게
높았기 때문이에요. 그것들은 다음 주 수요일에 배달 및 설치될
거예요.

어휘

assignment 배정, 배치 make a mistake 실수하다
currently 현재, 지금 assign to ~에 배정하다
refund 환불; 환불하다 skylight (천장의) 채광창 lighting 조명
install 설치하다

2번 사무실	¹⁰1번 사무실	창고
회의실		4번 사무실
3번 사무실		복사실

10.

시각 자료를 보시오. 매니저는 어떤 사무실을 받을 것 같은가?
(A) 1번 사무실
(B) 2번 사무실
(C) 3번 사무실
(D) 4번 사무실

11.

화자는 왜 가구 회사에 전화했는가?
(A) 불만을 제기하기 위해
(B) 전등을 추가로 주문하기 위해
(C) 환불을 요청하기 위해
(D) 주소를 변경하기 위해

어휘

address 제기하다, 제출하다 complaint 불평, 항의
extra 추가의, 가외의

패러프레이징

asked them to refund our order of lamps
→ ask for a refund

12.

화자는 조명에 대해 무엇이라고 말하는가?
(A) 크기를 잘못 골랐다.
(B) 스타일이 방에 딱 맞았다.
(C) 너무 많은 품목을 주문했다.
(D) 가격이 적당하지 않았다.

어휘

affordable (가격 등이) 알맞은

패러프레이징

the cost of lighting was much too high
→ The price was not affordable

UNIT O9 전화 메시지

CHECK UP   본문 p.252

1. (B)   **2.** (A)   **3.** (C)

[1-3] 미남 🎧

Questions 1-3 refer to the following telephone message.

> **M** Good morning, Ms. Simpson. This is Carl from Galligan Incorporated. ¹I'm returning your call about the chairs and tables you're renting for your upcoming event. You asked if we could change the delivery time from 10 A.M. to 9 A.M. tomorrow. Unfortunately, ²one of our delivery trucks broke down, and our other truck has a delivery at that time, so we cannot accommodate your request. However, if you can accept the items at 8 A.M., ³I could start work earlier than usual to get those to you. Please call me back at 555-7711.

해석

1-3번은 다음 전화 메시지에 관한 문제입니다.

남 안녕하세요, 심슨 씨. 저는 걸리건 주식회사의 칼입니다. ¹곧 있을 행사를 위해 빌리실 예정인 의자와 테이블에 관해 주신 전화에 회신드립니다. 저희가 배달 시간을 내일 오전 10시에서 9시로 바꿀 수 있는지 물어보셨죠. 안타깝게도, ²저희 배달 트럭 중 하나가 고장 났고 다른 트럭은 그 시간에 배달이 있어서 요청을 들어 드릴 수가 없습니다. 하지만, 물건들을 오전 8시에 받으실 수 있다면, ³제가 평소보다 더 일찍 근무를 시작해서 그것들을 당신에게 가져다 드리겠습니다. 555-7711로 제게 다시 전화 주시기 바랍니다.

어휘

return a call 답신 전화를 하다 rent 빌리다, 임대하다
upcoming 다가오는, 곧 있을 break down 고장 나다
accommodate 협조하다, 수용하다 accept 받아들이다
than usual 평소보다

1.

화자의 회사는 어떤 서비스를 제공하는가?
(A) 가전제품 수리
(B) 가구 임대
(C) 음악회
(D) 기업 회계

어휘

appliance (가정용) 기기 repair 수리 rental 임대
entertainment 오락, 연예 accounting 회계

패러프레이징

chairs and tables → Furniture

2.

화자는 왜 요청을 들어줄 수 없는가?
(A) 차량이 작동하지 않는다.
(B) 직원이 결근했다.
(C) 일부 용품이 품절이다.
(D) 일부 지시사항이 명확하지 않았다.

어휘

fulfill 이행하다, 수행하다 absent 결석한, 결근한
supplies ((보통 복수형)) 용품, 비품 sold out 품절의, 매진된
instructions ((보통 복수형)) 지시, 명령, 설명서

패러프레이징

one of our delivery trucks broke down
→ A vehicle is not working

3.

화자는 무엇을 해 주겠다고 제안하는가?
(A) 환불해 주기
(B) 시연하기
(C) 일찍 출근하기
(D) 할인 제공하기

어휘

issue 발부하다, 지급하다 refund 환불; 환불하다

패러프레이징

start work earlier than usual → Come to work early

패러프레이징 연습   본문 p.254

1-4. 스크립트 참조   **5.** (A)   **6.** (A)

1.

Q 화자는 청자에게 무엇을 해 달라고 요청하는가?
A 작업 할당 바꾸기

미녀 🎧

> **W** I've just received a report about a water leak in the employee kitchen. Could you schedule the maintenance team to work on that for a few hours today instead of painting the hallway on the second floor?

해석

여 제가 방금 탕비실에 물이 샌다는 얘기를 전달받았습니다. 유지 보수팀이 오늘 몇 시간 동안 2층 복도에 페인트칠을 하지 않고 그 작업을 하도록 일정을 잡아 주시겠어요?

어휘

task 직무, 과업 assignment 배정, 배치 water leak 누수
maintenance 유지, 보수 관리

패러프레이징

schedule the maintenance team to work on that ~
instead of ~ → Change a task assignment

2.

Q 화자는 센터에 대해 무엇이 마음에 든다고 말하는가?

A 기술 지원

미녀 🎧

> **W** Thank you for giving me a tour of your convention center yesterday. I would like to go forward with the booking, as your site seems perfect for us. I was especially interested in the option to use your technical staff. This will make it much easier to set up for our video presentations.

해석

여 어제 컨벤션 센터를 안내해 주셔서 감사합니다. 그쪽 장소가 저희에게 딱 알맞아 보이므로 예약을 진행하고 싶습니다. **저는 특히 기술 직원들을 이용할 수 있는 옵션에 관심이 있었어요.** 이렇게 하면 저희의 화상 발표를 준비하기가 훨씬 쉬워질 것입니다.

어휘

technical support 기술 지원
give a tour of ~을 구경시켜 주다, ~에 대해 안내하다
go forward with ~을 진행시키다 booking 예약
set up for ~을 준비하다 presentation 발표

패러프레이징

use your technical staff → The technical support

3.

Q 화자는 무엇을 알리게 되어 기뻐하는가?

A 모금 목표가 달성되었다.

미남 🎧

> **M** Hi, Christine. This is Douglas Conway from the Nashville Art Museum. I've got some exciting news for you. We reached our goal of raising ten thousand dollars to make upgrades to the community garden on our property. I'm wondering if you could write a press release about this.

해석

남 안녕하세요, 크리스틴. 저는 내슈빌 미술관의 더글러스 콘웨이입니다. 당신을 위한 신나는 소식이 좀 있습니다. **우리 건물 구내의 공동체 텃밭을 정비하기 위해 1만 달러를 모으는 목표를 달성했습니다.** 당신이 이에 대한 보도 자료를 작성해 줄 수 있는지 궁금합니다.

어휘

fund-raising 모금 활동; 모금 활동의
reach a goal 목표를 달성하다

make an upgrade to ~을 개선하다, 업그레이드하다
property 부동산, 건물 press release 보도 자료

패러프레이징

reached our goal of raising ten thousand dollars
→ A fund-raising goal was met

4.

Q 메시지는 주로 무엇에 관한 것인가?

A 도로 보수 작업 프로젝트

미남 🎧

> **M** Hi, this is Juan Rodriguez, the head of the state's transportation department. I'm calling about our proposed highway expansion project. I would like to discuss the preliminary designs at your earliest convenience.

해석

남 안녕하세요, 주의 교통부 책임자 후안 로드리게스입니다. **저희가 제안 드린 고속도로 확장 프로젝트 때문에 전화드렸습니다.** 가급적 빨리 예비 설계에 관해 논의하고 싶습니다.

어휘

roadwork 도로 보수 작업 head 책임자
transportation 교통, 운송, 수송 proposed 제안된
expansion 확장, 확대 preliminary 예비의
at your earliest convenience 가급적 빨리

패러프레이징

highway expansion → roadwork

5.

전화의 목적은 무엇인가?

(A) 늦는 이유를 설명하기 위해

(B) 주문하기 위해

미녀 🎧

> **W** Hi, this is Jiwon Kim. I'm really sorry about my order of cupcakes. I just looked at the clock and realized I'm behind schedule. I was supposed to come pick up my order at 3 o'clock. It's nearly three now, and it will take me at least 40 minutes to get there. I was in the middle of a work assignment, so I totally forgot about it. I'm headed there now.

해석

여 안녕하세요, 저는 김지원입니다. 제 컵케이크 주문 건에 대해서는 정말 죄송해요. **제가 방금 시계를 보고 늦었다는 것을 깨달았습니다.** 3시에 제 주문을 찾으러 가기로 되어 있었어요. 지금 거의 3시고, 제가 그곳에 도착하는 데 적어도 40분이 걸립니다. **제가 한창 맡은 일을 하던 중이라서 그것에 대해 완전히 잊어버렸어요.** 지금 그곳으로 가고 있습니다.

어휘

place an order 주문하다 behind schedule 예정보다 늦게
be supposed to ~하기로 되어 있다
be in the middle of 한창 (바쁘게) ~하는 중이다 totally 완전히
be headed ~로 향하여 가다

패러프레이징

behind schedule → delay

6.

스타버스트 카페는 일주일 내내 무엇을 제공하는가?
(A) 할인된 식사
(B) 무료 음료

미남 🎧

> M Thanks for calling the Starburst Café. We are currently closed. We're open daily from 6 A.M. to 9 P.M. You can call back during those times or send us a message on our social media page anytime. This week is our 10-year anniversary. So, we're offering 10 percent off our breakfast plates all week. We hope to see you soon at the Starburst Café!

해석

남 스타버스트 카페에 전화 주셔서 감사합니다. 저희는 현재 영업을 종료했습니다. 저희는 매일 오전 6시부터 저녁 9시까지 영업합니다. 이 시간에 다시 전화 주시거나 저희 소셜미디어 페이지로 언제든 메시지를 보내 주시면 됩니다. 이번 주에는 저희의 10주년을 기념합니다. 따라서, 일주일 내내 아침 식사 요리를 10% 할인해 드립니다. 조만간 스타버스트 카페에서 뵙기를 바랍니다!

어휘

discounted 할인된 beverage 음료 currently 현재, 지금
anniversary 기념일 plate 요리

패러프레이징

10 percent off our breakfast plates
→ Discounted meals

연습 문제				본문 p.255
1. (C)	**2.** (D)	**3.** (C)	**4.** (A)	**5.** (B)

[1] 미녀 🎧
Question 1 refers to the following telephone message.

> W Hello, Mr. Daniels. This is Liz Marrota, the manager of Benson Tech. I'm calling to tell you about the laptop you dropped off at our shop for repairs yesterday. I'm afraid I have bad news. While we were able to retrieve the data from your hard drive, the mainboard is too

broken to save. Please call me back at 555-4638 to plan the next step. Thank you.

해석

1번은 다음 전화 메시지에 관한 문제입니다.

여 안녕하세요, 대니얼스 씨. 저는 벤슨 테크 사의 매니저, 리즈 마로타입니다. 당신이 어제 수리를 위해 저희 가게에 맡기신 노트북 컴퓨터에 관해 말씀드리려고 전화했습니다. 유감스럽게도 나쁜 소식이 있습니다. 저희 기술자들이 당신의 하드 드라이브에서 데이터를 복구할 수는 있었지만, 메인보드는 너무 손상되어 살릴 수가 없습니다. 다음 단계를 계획하도록 555-4638로 제게 다시 전화 주시기 바랍니다. 감사합니다.

어휘

drop off ~을 맡기다 retrieve 되찾다, 복구하다

1.

화자는 어디에서 일하는가?
(A) 자동차 대여소에서
(B) 재활용 센터에서
(C) 컴퓨터 수리점에서
(D) 회계 법인에서

어휘

rental agency 대여소 recycling 재활용 accounting 회계

패러프레이징

the laptop you dropped off at our shop for repairs
→ a computer repair shop

[2-3] 미남 🎧
Questions 2-3 refer to the following telephone message.

> M This is a message for Mr. Baker. This is Dan from Lansing Books. ²The book you ordered… um… *Structures of Europe*, is currently out of stock. We won't be able to deliver it on Friday as originally planned. Unfortunately, we are unsure how long it will be before we get more. ³If you would like to cancel this order, please call us at your earliest convenience. You would receive a full refund, of course. The number is on your order form. We apologize for the inconvenience this may cause.

해석

2-3번은 다음 전화 메시지에 관한 문제입니다.

남 이것은 베이커 씨에게 전하는 메시지입니다. 저는 랜싱 북스의 댄입니다. ²당신이 주문하신 책인… 음… 〈유럽의 구조〉가 현재 품절입니다. 저희는 원래 계획대로 금요일에 배달할 수 없을 것입니다. 안타깝게도, 더 들어오기까지 얼마나 오래 걸릴지 확실하지 않습니다. ³이 주문을 취소하고 싶으시면, 가급적 빨리 저희에게 전화 주시기 바랍니다. 물론, 전액 환불받으시게 됩니다. 번호는 주문서에 있습니다. 이로 인한 불편에 사과드립니다.

structure 구조 currently 현재, 지금 out of stock 품절된
originally 원래, 본래 unsure 확신하지 못하는
at your earliest convenience 가급적 빨리
full refund 전액 환불 order form 주문서
apologize for ~에 대해 사과하다 inconvenience 불편

2.
화자는 주문에 대해 무엇이라고 말하는가?
(A) 그것은 예상보다 비용이 더 많이 들 것이다.
(B) 그것은 잘못된 주소로 배송되었다.
(C) 그것은 운송 중에 손상되었다.
(D) 그것은 현재 이용할 수 없다.

어휘

ship 운송하다 damage 손상을 주다 in transit 수송 중에
unavailable 이용할 수 없는, 무효의

패러프레이징

out of stock → unavailable

3.
청자는 어떻게 주문을 취소할 수 있는가?
(A) 직접 업체에 방문함으로써
(B) 영수증 사본을 보냄으로써
(C) 상점에 직접 전화함으로써
(D) 신청서를 작성함으로써

어휘

in person 직접 copy 사본 directly 곧장, 똑바로
complete 기입하다, 작성하다

[4-5] 미남
Questions 4-5 refer to the following recorded message.

M Hello. You've reached the voicemail of Brian Baldwin of Hillside Incorporated. **⁴We are proud to be the area's top-rated company for constructing commercial buildings.** I'm sorry I am unable to take your call at this time. I will be out of town for the rest of the week due to an industry event. I will return on Monday, June 7. In the meantime, **⁵if you need immediate assistance, please direct your questions to Lilian Meyer at extension number 21.** Thank you.

해석

4-5번은 다음 녹음 메시지에 관한 문제입니다.
남 안녕하세요. 힐사이드 주식회사의 브라이언 볼드윈의 음성 메일입니다. ⁴저희는 상업용 건물을 건설하는 이 지역 최고의 기업임을 자랑스럽게 생각합니다. 죄송하지만 지금은 전화를 받을 수 없습니다. 업계 행사 때문에 이번 주 남은 기간 동안 이 지역을 떠나 있을 것입니다. 저는 6월 7일 월요일에 돌아올 것입니다.

그동안에, ⁵즉각적인 도움이 필요하시면, 내선번호 21번으로 릴리언 마이어에게 질문하시기 바랍니다. 감사합니다.

어휘

be proud to ~하는 것을 자랑스러워하다
top-rated 가장 인기 있는, 최고 순위에 올라 있는
construct 건설하다 commercial 상업의
be unable to ~할 수 없다 in the meantime 그러는 사이에
immediate 즉각적인 assistance 도움, 지원
direct a question to ~에게 질문하다
extension 내선, 구내전화

4.
화자는 어디에서 일하는가?
(A) 건설 회사에서
(B) 전자기기 제조업체에서
(C) 부동산 중개소에서
(D) 인테리어 디자인 회사에서

어휘

construction 건설, 공사 electronics ((항상 복수형)) 전자기기
manufacturer 제조업체 real estate 부동산

패러프레이징

company for constructing commercial buildings
→ a construction firm

5.
화자는 릴리언 마이어에 대해 무엇이라고 말하는가?
(A) 그녀는 업계 행사에 참석할 것이다.
(B) 그녀는 질문에 답할 시간이 된다.
(C) 그녀는 회의 일정을 잡을 계획이다.
(D) 그녀는 회사의 신입사원이다.

어휘

be available to ~할 시간이 있다

실전 문제 본문 p.256

1. (B)	**2.** (A)	**3.** (B)	**4.** (D)	**5.** (C)
6. (C)	**7.** (C)	**8.** (D)	**9.** (D)	**10.** (D)
11. (B)	**12.** (A)	**13.** (A)	**14.** (B)	**15.** (B)
16. (A)	**17.** (B)	**18.** (C)		

[1-3] 미남
Questions 1-3 refer to the following telephone message.

M Hello, Mr. Mills. This is Edgar Polanco, the owner of the apartment building on Wellington Street. **¹You seemed to be impressed by the one-bedroom apartment I showed you yesterday.** I know you said that you need a little more time to decide, but I have another person who is interested. However, he wants to rent the apartment for only six months, so ²I prefer that you lease it since you said you were willing to rent it for more than two years. Well, ³if I don't hear from you by tomorrow morning, I'm going to have to offer it to the other person. Please think about it and let me know your decision. Thank you.

해석

1-3번은 다음 전화 메시지에 관한 문제입니다.

남 안녕하세요, 밀스 씨. 저는 웰링턴 가에 있는 아파트 건물의 소유주인 에드거 폴란코입니다. ¹제가 어제 당신에게 보여 드린 침실 1개짜리 아파트에 좋은 인상을 받으신 것 같았어요. 결정하는 데 시간이 좀 더 필요하다고 말씀하신 걸 알지만, 관심 있어 하는 다른 사람이 있어요. 하지만 그는 6개월 동안만 아파트를 빌리고 싶어 하므로 ²저는 당신이 임차하시는 것이 더 좋아요, 당신은 2년 이상 임차하실 의향이 있다고 말씀하셨으니까요. 음, ³내일 아침까지 아무 연락 없으시면, 다른 사람에게 넘겨야 할 겁니다. 이에 대해 생각해 보시고 당신의 결정을 알려 주세요. 감사합니다.

어휘

be impressed by ~에 깊은 인상을 받다, 감동을 받다
rent 임대하다 prefer ~을 (더) 좋아하다
lease 임대하다; 임대차 계약 be willing to 기꺼이 ~하다
decision 결정

1.

메시지는 무엇에 관한 것인가?
(A) 새 집을 짓는 것
(B) 아파트를 임대하는 것
(C) 시내로 이사하는 것
(D) 외국에서 사는 것

어휘

abroad 해외에서, 해외로

2.

화자에 따르면, 청자는 왜 선호되는가?
(A) 그는 장기 임대를 원한다.
(B) 그는 믿을만한 사람이다.
(C) 그는 대출을 승인받았다.
(D) 그는 전문가의 추천을 받았다.

어휘

long-term 장기적인 reliable 믿을 수 있는 approve 승인하다
loan 대출, 융자 professional 전문가의, 전문직에 종사하는

패러프레이징

you were willing to rent it for more than two years
→ He wants a long-term lease

3.

청자가 결정해야 하는 기한은 언제인가?

(A) 오늘 오후
(B) 내일 오전
(C) 이번 주말
(D) 내일모레

[4-6] 영녀 🎧

Questions 4-6 refer to the following recorded message.

W You've reached Highland Communications. ⁴We are currently experiencing some service outages for our Internet customers in the northwest region. Our team is working to resolve the issue as quickly as possible. ⁵This issue occurred because of an upgrade to our distribution network. Please keep in mind that you may be eligible for credit, depending on the length of the outage. ⁶Once the service is resumed, you should sign into your account on our Web site to check your status.

해석

4-6번은 다음 녹음 메시지에 관한 문제입니다.

여 하이랜드 커뮤니케이션 사에 연락하셨습니다. ⁴현재 북서부 지역의 저희 인터넷 고객들에게 일부 서비스가 중단된 상태입니다. 저희 팀이 최대한 빨리 이 문제를 해결하기 위해 작업 중입니다. ⁵이 문제는 저희 배분망 업그레이드로 인해 발생했습니다. 중단 기간에 따라 공제를 받을 자격이 될 수도 있다는 점을 기억해 두세요. ⁶일단 서비스가 재개되면, 여러분의 상태를 확인하기 위해 저희 웹사이트에서 여러분의 계정에 로그인하셔야 합니다.

어휘

outage 사용 불능, 공급 정지 resolve 해결하다
occur 일어나다, 발생하다 distribution network 유통망, 배전망
keep in mind 명심하다, ~을 기억해 두다
be eligible for ~에 대한 자격이 있다
credit 신용, 공제액 depending on ~에 따라
resume 재개하다, 다시 시작하다 account 계정, 계좌
status 상태, 지위

4.

메시지는 주로 무엇에 관한 것인가?
(A) 소유권 변경
(B) 월 청구서 오류
(C) 새로운 통신 패키지 상품
(D) 인터넷 서비스 장애

어휘

ownership 소유(권) bill 고지서, 청구서 package 일괄 계약
loss 손실, 손해

패러프레이징

some service outages for our Internet customers
→ A loss of Internet service

5.

화자에 따르면, 무엇이 문제를 일으켰는가?

(A) 직원 부족

(B) 심한 폭풍

(C) 기술 업그레이드

(D) 규정 변경

어휘

shortage 부족 regulation 규정

패러프레이징

an upgrade to our distribution network
→ A technology upgrade

6.

청자들은 무엇을 하도록 권장받는가?

(A) 설문지 작성하기

(B) 회사에 문제 보고하기

(C) 계정에 접속하기

(D) 지불 승인하기

어휘

complete 기입하다, 작성하다 questionnaire 설문지

log into ~에 접속하다 authorize 허가하다

패러프레이징

sign into → Log into

[7-9] 호남 🎧

Questions 7-9 refer to the following telephone message.

> **M** Hello, this is Leonard from the Millington Hotel. **7 You booked a suite for July 7th to 9th. Unfortunately, we had an issue with our system, and the hotel is actually fully booked for those nights.** However, there is another possible option. There's space at our partner hotel, the Lindale Hotel. It's just five minutes from our hotel. **8 You could take our shuttle bus between hotels at no cost.** Or you can cancel for a full refund. Please call me back at 555-4747 once you decide what you'd like to do. **9 I can hold this room for you for now, but…** um… we expect a lot of interest in it. Thanks.

해석

7-9번은 다음 전화 메시지에 관한 문제입니다.

남 안녕하세요, 저는 밀링턴 호텔의 레너드입니다. **7 당신은 7월 7일부터 9일까지 스위트룸을 예약하셨습니다.** 유감스럽게도, 저희 시스템에 문제가 있었고, 실은 호텔이 그날 모두 예약이 된 상태입니다. 하지만, 다른 가능한 선택이 있습니다. 저희의 협력 호텔인 린데일 호텔에 빈방이 있습니다. 저희 호텔에서 겨우 5분 거리입니다. **8 호텔들 사이를 오가는 셔틀버스를 무료로 이용하실 수도 있습니다.** 아니면, 취소하시고 전액 환불받으실 수도 있습니다. 어떻게 하시고 싶은지 결정하시는 대로 555-4747로 다

시 전화 주시기 바랍니다. **9 우선은 당신을 위해 이 방을 잡아 두겠지만… 음… 많이들 관심 있어 할 것으로 예상합니다.** 감사합니다.

어휘

book 예약하다 have an issue with ~와 문제가 있다

at no cost 무료로 cancel 취소하다 full refund 전액 환불

for now 우선은, 당분간은

7.

전화의 목적은 무엇인가?

(A) 마감 기한을 확인하기 위해

(B) 지연에 대해 설명하기 위해

(C) 예약에 관해 이야기하기 위해

(D) 지불을 요청하기 위해

어휘

confirm 확인하다 deadline 마감 기한 reservation 예약

패러프레이징

booked a suite → reservation

8.

화자에 따르면, 청자는 무료로 무엇을 할 수 있는가?

(A) 업그레이드 받기

(B) 식사하기

(C) 공연에 참석하기

(D) 셔틀버스 타기

패러프레이징

take → Ride

9.

화자는 "많이들 관심 있어 할 것으로 예상합니다"라고 말할 때 무엇을 암시하는가?

(A) 그는 행사를 위해 시간을 낼 것이다.

(B) 가격이 곧 인상될 것 같다.

(C) 청자가 좋은 제안을 했다.

(D) 청자가 빨리 행동해야 한다.

어휘

make time for ~을 위해 시간을 내다 be likely to ~할 것 같다

[10-12] 미녀 🎧

Questions 10-12 refer to the following telephone message.

> **W** **10 Thank you for calling MJ Carpeting.** We have closed for the day. We will reopen tomorrow at 9 A.M. **11 Please note that we are scheduled to close at 4 P.M. instead of 7 P.M. this Friday, October 7,** for an employee training event. And don't forget our special event this week. **12 Customers who make a purchase of 40 dollars and over will receive a bottle of complimentary carpet cleaner and a stain**

remover stick. Together, they have a value of over 30 dollars. We are looking forward to serving you soon.

해석

10-12번은 다음 전화 메시지에 관한 문제입니다.

여 **¹⁰엠제이 카페팅에 전화 주셔서 감사합니다.** 오늘 영업은 종료되었습니다. 내일 오전 9시에 다시 문을 엽니다. **¹¹저희가 이번 주 금요일인 10월 7일에는 직원 교육 행사 때문에 ¹¹오후 7시가 아닌 4시에 문을 닫을 예정임을 알아 두시기 바랍니다.** 그리고 이번 주 저희의 특별 행사를 잊지 마세요. **¹²40달러 이상 구매 고객들은 카펫 세척제 한 병과 얼룩 제거 스틱을 무료로 받게 됩니다.** 그것들은 합쳐서 30달러 이상의 가치가 있습니다. 곧 여러분에게 서비스하게 되기를 기대합니다.

어휘

make a purchase 구매하다 complimentary 무료의
stain remover 얼룩 제거제 value 가치
look forward to ~을 기대하다

10.

화자는 어디에서 일하는 것 같은가?
(A) 철물점에서
(B) 의류 제조업체에서
(C) 운송 회사에서
(D) 카펫 상점에서

어휘

manufacturer 제조업체 shipping 운송, 선적

11.

화자는 이번 주 금요일에 대해 무엇이라고 말하는가?
(A) 연례 세일이 시작될 것이다.
(B) 업체가 일찍 문을 닫을 것이다.
(C) 신상품이 도착할 것이다.
(D) 업체가 평소보다 더 바쁠지도 모른다.

어휘

annual 연례의 than usual 평소보다

패러프레이징

close at 4 P.M. instead of 7 P.M. → close early

12.

고객들은 이번 주에 무엇을 받을 수 있는가?
(A) 무료 세척용품
(B) 익일 배송
(C) 연장된 보증
(D) 상점 상품권

어휘

supplies ((보통 복수형)) 용품, 비품 warranty 품질 보증(서)
voucher 상품권, 할인권, 쿠폰

패러프레이징

complimentary carpet cleaner and a stain remover
stick → Free cleaning supplies

[13-15] 미녀 🎧
Questions 13-15 refer to the following telephone message.

> W Dennis? It's Caroline. I was wondering if you have time tomorrow to help me with ¹³some of the designs for the Gottlieb Cosmetics ad campaign. ¹⁴I just received the flyers from the printing company, but the colors aren't quite what we had in mind. So, I'd like a second opinion about them. Let me know when we can set up a time to discuss this. Oh, and the new forms for reporting business trip expenditures have come in. I've sent copies to your inbox. ¹⁵I will go over those with you tomorrow. Talk to you soon.

해석

13-15번은 다음 전화 메시지에 관한 문제입니다.

여 데니스? 캐롤라인이에요. 내일 **¹³고틀리브 화장품 회사의 광고 캠페인을 위한 디자인을 좀 도와줄 시간이 있는지 궁금해서요.** **¹⁴제가 방금 인쇄소에서 전단지를 받았는데, 색상이 우리가 생각했던 것과 달라요.** 그래서, 그것들에 관해 다른 사람의 의견을 듣고 싶어요. 이 얘기를 할 시간을 언제로 잡으면 될지 알려 주세요. 아, 그리고 출장 경비 보고를 위한 새로운 양식이 나왔어요. 제가 사본을 당신의 메일로 보냈어요. **¹⁵내일 당신과 함께 그것들을 검토할 거예요.** 곧 다시 통화해요.

어휘

cosmetics 화장품 flyer (광고용) 전단
have in mind ~에 관해 생각하고 있다, ~을 염두에 두다
second opinion 다른 사람의 의견 set up 정하다
expenditure 지출, 경비 come in 받게 되다, 도착하다
inbox 받은 편지함 go over 검토하다, 점검하다

13.

화자는 어디에서 일하는가?
(A) 광고 회사에서
(B) 식료품점에서
(C) 인쇄소에서
(D) 미용실에서

패러프레이징

ad campaign → advertising

14.

화자는 전단지에 대해 무엇이라고 말하는가?
(A) 그녀는 그래픽을 더 추가하고 싶다.
(B) 그녀는 다른 색상을 기대했다.
(C) 그녀는 충분하지 않을 거라고 생각한다.
(D) 그녀는 크기를 바꾸는 것을 고려하고 있다.

어휘

consider -ing ~하는 것을 고려하다

15.

내일 무슨 일이 일어날 것인가?
(A) 여행 티켓을 구매할 것이다.
(B) 몇몇 새로운 서식이 검토될 것이다.
(C) 고객과의 회의가 있을 것이다.
(D) 문서가 온라인으로 게시될 것이다.

어휘

purchase 구매하다; 구매   review 검토하다
post 게시하다, 올리다

패러프레이징

go over → be reviewed

[16-18] 영녀 🎧

Questions 16-18 refer to the following telephone message and schedule.

> W Hi, Ms. Castillas. It's Charlene from *Quest Magazine*. ¹⁶Thanks again for agreeing to meet with me tomorrow and be interviewed about your spa's unique services. I know we arranged for a meeting at Mountain Coffee Shop… uh… at 8 A.M. However, they've made a change to their hours, and, according to their sign, ¹⁷they won't open until nine tomorrow. How about going to Bluebell Diner instead? ¹⁸It has a large dining area, so I'm sure we'll have no problem getting a table right away. Please let me know if that is convenient for you. Thanks!

해석

16-18번은 다음 전화 메시지와 일정표에 관한 문제입니다.
여 안녕하세요, 카스티야스 씨. 〈퀘스트 매거진〉의 살린이에요. ¹⁶내일 저와 만나서 당신의 스파의 독특한 서비스에 대해 인터뷰하기로 해 주셔서 다시 한번 감사드립니다. 우리가 마운틴 커피숍에서… 어… 오전 8시에 만나기로 약속을 잡은 것으로 알고 있어요. 하지만, 그곳이 영업시간을 변경했어요, 그들의 안내판에 따르면 ¹⁷내일 9시가 되어야 문을 열 거예요. 대신 블루벨 다이너로 가는 것이 어떨까요? ¹⁸식사 공간이 넓어서 바로 테이블을 잡는 데 아무 문제가 없을 거예요. 그렇게 하는 것이 편할지 저에게 알려주세요. 감사해요!

어휘

spa 스파, 온천   unique 독특한
arrange for ~을 준비하다, ~에 대한 계획을 짜다
make a change to ~을 변경하다   sign 표지판, 안내판
instead 대신에   dining area 식사 공간   convenient 편리한

마운틴 커피숍	
일요일	오전 8시–오후 4시
월요일–수요일	휴점
¹⁷목요일	오전 9시–오후 6시
금요일	오전 8시–오후 9시
토요일	오전 7시–오후 8시

16.

화자는 왜 청자와 만날 것인가?
(A) 인터뷰를 하기 위해
(B) 계약을 체결하기 위해
(C) 구독을 갱신하기 위해
(D) 일부 샘플들을 공유하기 위해

어휘

conduct 실시하다, 행하다   sign a contract 계약을 맺다
renew 갱신하다   subscription 정기 구독

패러프레이징

meet with me ~ and be interviewed
→ conduct an interview

17.

시각 자료를 보시오. 화자는 어느 요일에 청자를 만날 계획인가?
(A) 일요일
(B) 목요일
(C) 금요일
(D) 토요일

18.

화자는 블루벨 다이너에 대해 무엇이라고 말하는가?
(A) 그곳은 무료 주차를 제공한다.
(B) 그곳은 시외에 위치하고 있다.
(C) 그곳은 공간이 많이 있다.
(D) 그곳은 최근에 메뉴를 변경했다.

어휘

be located 위치해 있다

패러프레이징

a large dining area → a lot of space

UNIT 10 사내 공지

CHECK UP   본문 p.258

1. (C)   **2.** (B)   **3.** (A)

[1-3] 미녀 🎧

Questions 1-3 refer to the following excerpt from a meeting.

> W Good afternoon, everyone. ¹I'd like to start with an update on our branch in Laurelville. It's only been open for a week, but we are feeling optimistic about this expansion. ²To bring attention to our tax preparation service there, we are holding a special event on January 20. I need one person to volunteer to make arrangements for refreshments for this event. ³The employee who does so will receive a gift voucher as a thank-you. Please speak to me after the meeting if you are interested. Thanks.

해석

1-3번은 다음 회의 발췌록에 관한 문제입니다.

여 안녕하세요, 여러분. ¹로렐빌에 있는 우리 지점에 대한 최근 소식으로 시작하겠습니다. 문을 연 지 겨우 일주일 되었지만, 우리는 이번 확장에 관해 낙관적으로 느끼고 있습니다. ²그곳에서 우리 세무 대행 서비스에 대한 관심을 모으기 위해서, 1월 20일에 특별한 행사를 개최할 것입니다. 저는 이 행사를 위해 자원해서 다과 준비를 해 줄 사람이 한 명 필요합니다. ³그 일을 하는 직원은 감사의 의미로 상품권을 받게 됩니다. 관심이 있으면 회의 후에 저에게 얘기해 주세요. 감사합니다.

어휘

optimistic 낙관적인 expansion 확대, 확장
bring attention to ~에 관심을 가져오다
tax preparation service 세무대리업
make an arrangement ~을 준비하다
refreshments ((항상 복수형)) 다과, 음식물 gift voucher 상품권

1.

회사는 최근에 무엇을 했는가?
(A) 제품 라인을 출시했다
(B) 수상 후보로 지명되었다
(C) 새로운 지점을 열었다
(D) 컨설턴트를 고용했다

어휘

launch 출시하다, 시작하다 line (상품의) 종류
nomination 지명, 추천 consultant 컨설턴트, 자문 위원, 상담가

패러프레이징

It's only been open for a week
→ Opened a new branch

2.

화자에 따르면, 회사는 왜 특별 행사를 개최할 것인가?
(A) 직원을 소개하기 위해
(B) 서비스를 홍보하기 위해
(C) 직원들을 모집하기 위해
(D) 기념일을 축하하기 위해

어휘

promote 홍보하다 recruit 모집하다, 뽑다
celebrate 축하하다, 기념하다 anniversary 기념일

패러프레이징

bring attention to our tax preparation service
→ promote a service

3.

청자들 중 한 명에게 무엇이 주어질 것인가?
(A) 상품권
(B) 추가 휴가
(C) 무료 식사
(D) 일부 사무용품

패러프레이징 **연습**		본문 p.260
1-4. 스크립트 참조	5. (A)	6. (B)

1.

Q 넬슨 씨는 내일 무엇을 할 것인가?
A 발표하기

미남 🎧

> M I've invited Sandra Nelson, our senior technician, to today's meeting. She'll go over her research with our team before sharing it formally at a conference tomorrow. This will help you become familiar with the main findings.

해석

남 제가 오늘 회의에 우리 선임 기술자인 샌드라 넬슨을 초대했습니다. 그녀는 내일 학회에서 공식적으로 자신의 연구를 공유하기 전에 우리 팀과 함께 검토할 것입니다. 이는 여러분이 주요 조사 결과에 대해 익숙해지는 데 도움이 될 것입니다.

어휘

senior 선임의, 상급자인 technician 기술자
go over 검토하다, 조사하다 formally 공식적으로, 정중하게
familiar with ~에 익숙한, 친숙한
findings ((보통 복수형)) 조사 결과

패러프레이징

sharing it formally at a conference
→ Give a presentation

2.

Q 청자들은 다음에 무엇을 하기로 되어 있는가?
A 웹사이트에 접속하기

미녀 🎧

> W Welcome, everyone, and thank you for coming to this orientation. Let's begin by activating

your accounts on our employee Web site. There you will see links to things like your work assignments, time-off requests, and payment summaries.

해석
여 모든 분들을 환영하며, 이번 오리엔테이션에 와 주셔서 감사합니다. 우리 **직원 웹사이트에서 여러분의 계정을 활성화하는 것으로 시작하겠습니다.** 그곳에서 여러분의 업무, 휴가 신청서, 지급 내역 같은 것들로 연결되는 링크를 보게 될 것입니다.

어휘
be supposed to ~하기로 되어 있다
activate 활성화시키다, 작동시키다 account 계정, 계좌
assignment 임무, 과제 time-off 휴식 payment 지불, 지급
summary 요약, 개요

패러프레이징
activating your accounts on our employee Web site → Log into a Web site

3.
Q 청자들은 오늘까지 무엇을 작성하라고 요청받았는가?
A 직무 기술서

미남 🎧

> M At the end of our last meeting, I asked everyone to submit a detailed description of your work responsibilities by today. These will help me to make sure that all responsibilities are covered and that there are no overlapping duties.

해석
남 지난번 회의 마지막에, **제가 여러분에게 자신의 업무에 대한 상세한 기술서를 오늘까지 제출하라고 요청했습니다.** 이것은 해야 할 일들이 모두 처리되고 중복되는 업무가 없도록 하는 데 도움이 될 것입니다.

어휘
draft 초안을 작성하다; 원고 job description 직무 기술서
submit 제출하다 detailed 상세한 responsibility 책무, 책임
overlapping 중복되는 duties ((보통 복수형)) 업무

패러프레이징
detailed description of your work responsibilities → Job descriptions

4.
Q 화자는 청자들에게 무엇에 대해 상기시키는가?
A 예산 제한

미녀 🎧

> W I think a gift for each employee would help to show our appreciation for everything they've done this year. I know that concert tickets are

a popular option. But don't forget that our budget is only 50 dollars per employee.

해석
여 직원 한 명 한 명에게 선물을 하는 것이 올해 그들이 해 준 모든 것에 대한 우리의 감사를 표하는 데 도움이 될 것이라고 생각해요. 콘서트 티켓이 인기 있는 선택 방안이라는 걸 알아요. **하지만 우리 예산은 직원 한 명당 50달러밖에 되지 않는다는 것을 잊지 마세요.**

어휘
remind 상기시키다, 다시 한번 알려 주다 budget 예산
limit 제한 appreciation 감사

패러프레이징
only 50 dollars per employee → A budget limit

5.
어떤 종류의 제품이 논의되고 있는가?
(A) 음료
(B) 의류

미남 🎧

> M We're thinking of changing the design of the bottle to make it easier to use. A lot of people consume our sports drink while on the go. That's why I think it's important to make the cap easy to open. I've brought some examples of designs that I think would work well.

해석
남 우리는 사용하기 더 쉽게 하기 위해 병의 디자인을 변경하는 것을 고려하고 있습니다. **많은 사람들이 이동하면서 우리 스포츠음료를 마십니다.** 그래서 제가 뚜껑을 열기 쉽게 만드는 것이 중요하다고 생각하는 것입니다. 아주 효과가 좋을 것으로 생각하는 몇몇 디자인 예시를 가져왔습니다.

어휘
beverage 음료 clothing 의류 consume 먹다, 마시다
on the go 이동하면서, 움직이면서

패러프레이징
our sports drink → A beverage

6.
화자는 무엇을 할 것이라고 말하는가?
(A) 제품의 가격 조정하기
(B) 더 많은 직원들을 프로젝트에 배정하기

미녀 🎧

> W It is essential that we release the new cordless headphones before the holiday shopping season. Therefore, I'll temporarily reassign some of the team members currently working on the smartphone charger to the headphones to ensure we get everything done on time.

해석

여 우리가 연휴 쇼핑 시즌 전에 새로운 무선 헤드폰을 출시하는 것이 아주 중요합니다. 따라서, **반드시 우리가 모든 일을 시간에 맞춰 끝내기 위해서, 현재 스마트폰 충전기 작업을 하는 일부 팀원들을 헤드폰 프로젝트에 일시적으로 재배정할 것입니다.**

어휘

adjust 조정하다 assign (일 등을) 배정하다, 맡기다
essential 필수적인, 극히 중요한 release 출시하다, 공개하다
cordless 무선의 temporarily 일시적으로, 임시로
charger 충전기 on time 시간을 어기지 않고, 정각에

패러프레이징

reassign some of the team members ~ to the headphones
→ Assign more staff members to a project

연습 문제
본문 p.261

1. (A) **2.** (A) **3.** (C) **4.** (D) **5.** (B)

---

[1] 호남 🎧

Questions 1 refers to the following announcement.

> M I hope everyone got a good night's sleep. Today should be a lot of fun. It will also hopefully bring us closer together and allow us to work better as a team. Okay then... ah, I have an announcement as you finish your breakfast. Please put your bags in the company vans as soon as you check out of the hotel. We'll be taking the vans to the horse-riding sessions, so we want to make sure we have everything.

해석

1번은 다음 공지에 관한 문제입니다.

남 모든 분들이 밤새 잘 주무셨기를 바랍니다. 오늘은 아주 재미있을 겁니다. 또한 바라건대 우리를 더욱 돈독하게 해주고 팀으로 일을 더 잘하게 해줄 것입니다. 좋아요, 그러면... 아, 여러분이 아침 식사를 마치시는 동안 알려 드릴 것이 있습니다. **호텔에서 체크아웃을 하시자마자 회사 승합차에 가방을 두시기 바랍니다.** 우리는 그 승합차를 타고 승마를 하러 갈 것이므로 반드시 모든 것을 다 챙겨야 합니다.

어휘

hopefully 바라건대 van 밴, 승합차
check out of ~에서 체크아웃하다 horse-riding 승마

1.
청자들은 무엇을 하도록 요청받는가?
(A) 소지품을 차량 안에 두기
(B) 점심 식사를 위해 호텔에서 만나기
(C) 활동 중에 주의하기

(D) 모든 시간에 참여하기

어휘

belongings ((항상 복수형)) 소유물, 재산
cautious 조심스러운, 신중한 activity 활동
participate in ~에 참여하다

패러프레이징

put your bags in the company vans
→ Place their belongings in a vehicle

[2-3] 호남 🎧

Questions 2-3 refer to the following excerpt from a meeting.

> M ²Thanks for coming to the managers meeting today. We have a lot to cover, so let's get started right away. I'd like to touch on page 6 of the packet I gave you. As you can see from the profit chart, it could've been a lot worse. We anticipated negative feedback following the product reviews, but in-store profits have been surprisingly positive. Therefore, we would like to launch a new advertising campaign. ³I'd like you all to generate an idea for the campaign by tomorrow.

해석

2-3번은 다음 회의 발췌록에 관한 문제입니다.

남 ²오늘 매니저 회의에 와 주셔서 감사합니다. 다룰 것들이 많으므로 바로 시작하죠. 제가 여러분에게 드린 자료집의 6쪽을 보겠습니다. 수익 도표에서 보실 수 있이, 이 정도로 끝나서 다행입니다. 우리는 제품 평가 뒤에 부정적인 반응을 예상했지만, 매장 내 수익이 놀라울 정도로 긍정적이었습니다. 따라서, 새로운 광고 캠페인을 시작하려고 합니다. ³여러분 모두 내일까지 캠페인을 위한 아이디어를 내기 바랍니다.

어휘

right away 바로, 즉시 packet 다발, 묶음 profit 이익, 수익
anticipate 예상하다, 기대하다 negative 부정적인
following ~ 후에 review 검토, 평가; 검토하다
in-store 매장 내의 surprisingly 놀랍게도 positive 긍정적인
launch 출시하다, 시작하다 generate 발생시키다, 만들어 내다

2.
청자들은 누구인 것 같은가?
(A) 매니저
(B) 고객
(C) 입사 지원자
(D) 주주

3.
화자는 청자들에게 무엇을 해 달라고 요청하는가?
(A) 제품 평가 발송하기
(B) 매니저와 만나기

(C) 광고 아이디어 만들어 내기

(D) 몇몇 잠재 고객 방문하기

어휘

create 만들어 내다, 창작하다 advertisement 광고
potential 잠재적인

패러프레이징

generate → Create

[4-5] 영녀 🎧

Questions 4-5 refer to the following announcement.

> **W** I have some good news, everyone. We found a site for another store in the southern region. ⁴More people are getting interested in the shovels and rakes that we sell, as well as our seeds, soil, and plants. This new store will help us keep up with demand. ⁵The main reason that our business is so popular is because of you. Our staff knows a lot about the products and can answer questions. So, I just want you to know that I appreciate your hard work and dedication.

해석

4-5번은 다음 공지에 관한 문제입니다.

여 여러분, 좋은 소식이 있습니다. 우리가 남부 지역에서 또 다른 매장을 위한 부지를 찾았습니다. ⁴더 많은 사람들이 우리의 씨앗, 토양, 식물뿐만 아니라 우리가 파는 삽과 갈퀴에도 관심을 갖고 있습니다. 이번 새 매장은 우리가 수요를 따라잡도록 도와줄 것입니다. ⁵우리 사업이 이렇게 인기 있는 주된 이유는 여러분 덕분입니다. 우리 직원들은 제품에 대해 많이 알고 있고 질문에 답할 수 있습니다. 따라서, 그저 제가 여러분의 노고와 헌신에 고마워한다는 것을 알아주셨으면 합니다.

어휘

site 장소, 현장 rake 갈퀴 plant 식물
keep up with ~에 뒤지지 않다 demand 요구, 수요
appreciate 고마워하다 hard work 노고, 고된 일
dedication 헌신, 전념

4.

화자의 업체는 어떤 종류의 제품을 판매하는가?

(A) 자동차 부품

(B) 목재 가구

(C) 가전제품

(D) 정원용품

어휘

automotive 자동차의 wooden 나무로 된
appliance (가정용) 기기 gardening 정원 가꾸기

패러프레이징

shovels and rakes → Gardening supplies

5.

화자에 따르면, 이 업체는 왜 인기가 있는가?

(A) 그곳은 품질 보증 기간을 길게 제공한다.

(B) 그곳은 아는 것이 많은 직원들이 있다.

(C) 그곳은 가격이 저렴하다.

(D) 그곳은 영업시간을 연장하여 운영한다.

어휘

warranty 품질 보증(서) knowledgeable 아는 것이 많은
extended 연장한

패러프레이징

Our staff knows a lot about the products
→ has knowledgeable employees

실전 문제 본문 p.262

1. (D)	**2.** (B)	**3.** (B)	**4.** (B)	**5.** (D)
6. (A)	**7.** (A)	**8.** (A)	**9.** (D)	**10.** (C)
11. (A)	**12.** (C)	**13.** (B)	**14.** (D)	**15.** (A)
16. (B)	**17.** (B)	**18.** (C)		

[1-3] 미남 🎧

Questions 1-3 refer to the following excerpt from a meeting.

> **M** First on today's staff meeting agenda, ¹I want to discuss a possible new product you'll be developing. This could really help to set our business apart. ²Now, normally, when a foam mattress wears out, there isn't much use for it. But what if we could replace only the parts that aren't performing well anymore? We could create a mattress that has sections that could be removed and replaced. Now more than ever, ³consumers are purchasing products that are good for the environment, so they'll love how this mattress heavily reduces waste.

해석

1-3번은 다음 회의 발췌록에 관한 문제입니다.

남 오늘 직원 회의 안건의 첫 번째로, ¹여러분이 개발할 가능성이 있는 신제품에 관해 얘기하고 싶습니다. 이것은 정말 우리 사업을 돋보이게 해 줄 것입니다. ²자, 보통은 폼 매트리스가 낡아서 떨어지면 쓸모가 별로 없습니다. 하지만 더 이상 제대로 기능하지 않는 부품만 교체할 수 있다면 어떻게 될까요? 우리는 제거 및 교체할 수 있는 부분이 있는 매트리스를 만들 수 있습니다. 지금 그 어느 때보다도, ³소비자들이 환경에 좋은 제품을 구매하고 있으므로 그들은 이 매트리스가 쓰레기를 대폭 줄이는 방식을 매우 좋아할 것입니다.

어휘

agenda 안건, 의제 possible 가능한 develop 개발하다
normally 보통, 정상적으로 wear out 낡아서 떨어지다

replace 교체하다, 대체하다 perform 작동하다, 기능하다
create 만들어 내다 remove 제거하다 consumer 소비자
environment 환경 heavily 심하게, 아주 많이
waste 쓰레기, 폐기물

1.

청자들은 누구인 것 같은가?
(A) 소규모 자영업자
(B) 잠재적 투자자
(C) 판매원
(D) 제품 개발자

prospective 장래의, 유망한 investor 투자자

2.

화자는 주로 무엇에 관해 이야기하고 있는가?
(A) 저장 용기
(B) 폼 매트리스
(C) 전동 공구
(D) 보호 케이스

어휘

storage 보관, 저장 container 용기, 그릇
protective 보호하는, 보호용의

3.

화자는 왜 제품이 잘 팔릴 것이라고 생각하는가?
(A) 그것은 다양한 색상으로 나올 것이다.
(B) 그것은 환경친화적인 디자인일 것이다.
(C) 그것은 지역에서 만들어질 것이다.
(D) 그것은 현대적으로 보일 것이다.

어휘

a variety of 다양한 eco-friendly 환경친화적인
locally 지역에서, 현지에서 modern 현대적인

패러프레이징

heavily reduces waste → have an eco-friendly design

[4-6] 영녀 🎧

Questions 4-6 refer to the following announcement.

W Good morning, everyone. ⁴Please be aware
that an inspector will visit our facility this
Thursday morning. He will need access to all
parts of the building, so ⁵please do not lock
your office when you are not there. Also, I'd
like to remind everyone that the company
picnic is this Friday at Sunrise Park. We've
reserved the clubhouse there. So, ⁶even if it is
rainy or cold, the event won't be canceled. I'm
looking forward to seeing you all there!

해석

4-6번은 다음 공지에 관한 문제입니다.

여 안녕하세요, 여러분. ⁴이번 주 목요일 오전에 조사관이 우리 시
설에 방문할 것임을 알아 두시기 바랍니다. 그는 건물의 모든 부
분에 접근할 수 있어야 할 것이므로 ⁵여러분이 사무실을 비울 때
문을 잠그지 마시기 바랍니다. 또한, 여러분에게 이번 주 금요일
선라이즈 파크에서 회사 야유회가 있다는 것을 다시 한번 알려
드립니다. 우리가 그곳의 클럽 하우스를 예약했습니다. 따라서
⁶비가 오거나 춥더라도 행사는 취소되지 않을 것입니다. 여러분
모두 그곳에서 만나기를 기대합니다!

어휘

inspector 조사관, 감독관 facility 시설 access to ~로의 접근
reserve 예약하다 look forward to ~을 기대하다

4.

목요일에 무슨 일이 일어날 것인가?
(A) 교육 과정
(B) 현장 점검
(C) 기자 회견
(D) 기업 합병

어휘

inspection 점검, 검사 corporate 기업의, 회사의
merger 합병

패러프레이징

an inspector will visit our facility → A site inspection

5.

화자는 청자들에게 무엇을 해 달라고 요청하는가?
(A) 참석 가능 여부 확정하기
(B) 이메일로 질문 제출하기
(C) 설명서를 주의 깊게 읽기
(D) 방을 잠그지 않은 상태로 두기

어휘

confirm 확인하다 availability 이용 가능성 submit 제출하다
manual 설명서 unlocked 잠겨 있지 않은

패러프레이징

do not lock your office
→ Leave some rooms unlocked

6.

화자는 회사 야유회에 관해 무엇이라고 말하는가?
(A) 그것은 날씨의 영향을 받지 않을 것이다.
(B) 참석자들이 음식을 가져와야 한다.
(C) 그것은 원래 계획보다 더 일찍 시작할 것이다.
(D) 가족이 손님으로 참여하는 것이 허용된다.

어휘

affect 영향을 미치다 attendee 참석자 originally 원래, 본래
be allowed to ~하는 것이 허용되다 participate 참가하다

패러프레이징

even if it is rainy or cold, the event won't be canceled
→ not be affected by the weather

Questions 7-9 refer to the following announcement.

> M Before you begin your shifts, I'd like to make an announcement. As you know, ⁷our goal is to provide reliable and affordable care to our patients. In order to accomplish this, we need to purchase new equipment, such as machines for x-rays and blood testing. ⁸I will be working on applying for a federal grant for this purpose. I know you all need me for other matters, but the form is brief. And to keep us all better informed, ⁹I'm going to e-mail you all a report each month that summarizes our budget situation.

해석

7-9번은 다음 공지에 관한 문제입니다.

남 교대 근무를 시작하기 전에, 공지 사항을 전달하겠습니다. 아시다시피, ⁷우리 목표는 우리 환자들에게 믿을 수 있고 저렴한 치료를 제공하는 것입니다. 이를 완수하기 위해서, 우리는 엑스레이나 혈액 검사용 기계 같은 새로운 장비를 구매해야 합니다. ⁸이것을 위해 저는 연방 정부의 보조금 신청에 착수할 것입니다. 여러분 모두 다른 문제들로 제 도움이 필요하다는 건 알지만, 양식은 간단합니다. 그리고 계속해서 우리 모두 더 잘 숙지하도록, ⁹제가 매달 여러분 모두에게 우리의 예산 상황을 요약한 보고서를 이메일로 보내드리겠습니다.

어휘

shift 교대 근무 (시간) reliable 믿을 수 있는
affordable (가격이) 알맞은 care 돌봄, 보살핌
accomplish 완수하다, 성취하다 federal 연방 정부의
grant 보조금 purpose 목적 brief 짧은, 간단한
keep ~ informed ~에게 계속해서 알려 주다
summarize 요약하다 budget 예산

7.

청자들은 어떤 업계에서 일하는 것 같은가?
(A) 보건 의료
(B) 교통
(C) 교육
(D) 금융

패러프레이징

care to our patients → Healthcare

8.

화자는 "양식은 간단합니다"라고 말할 때 무엇을 의미하는가?
(A) 일을 빨리 끝낼 수 있다.
(B) 몇몇 질문이 추가되어야 한다.
(C) 서류가 완전하게 인쇄되지 않았다.
(D) 제안된 마감 기한이 타당하다.

어휘

task 일, 과업 completely 완전히, 전적으로

proposed 제안된 reasonable 타당한, 합당한

9.

화자는 청자들에게 매달 무엇을 보낼 것인가?
(A) 팀 과제
(B) 고객 명단
(C) 작업 일정
(D) 예산 요약

어휘

assignment 과제, 임무 summary 요약, 개요

패러프레이징

a report ~ that summarizes our budget situation
→ A budget summary

Questions 10-12 refer to the following excerpt from a meeting.

> W I called this meeting because I wanted to let you know about ¹⁰the most recent customer feedback. I'm very pleased because customers love our translation service, and they have great things to say about it in their reviews. To help expand our business further, ¹¹we have decided to partner with an international law firm. We would assist with translating contracts and other legal documents. ¹²I have to thank Vanna DeRose, as she's looking into which firm would be the best fit for us. If this works well, we may do the same with other companies.

해석

10-12번은 다음 회의 발췌록에 관한 문제입니다.

여 ¹⁰가장 최근의 고객 피드백에 관해 알려 드리고 싶어서 이번 회의를 소집했습니다. ¹⁰고객들이 우리 번역 서비스를 아주 마음에 들어 하고, 그들의 후기에서 그에 관해 좋은 말들을 해서 매우 기쁩니다. 우리 사업을 더욱 확장하기 위해, ¹¹우리는 국제적인 법률 회사와 협력하기로 결정했습니다. 우리가 계약서 및 기타 법률 관련 문서의 번역을 도울 것입니다. ¹²바나 드로제에게 감사해야 하는데요, 그녀가 우리에게 어떤 회사가 최적일지 조사하고 있기 때문입니다. 이것이 잘 되면, 우리는 다른 회사들과도 똑같이 할 수 있습니다.

어휘

translation 번역, 통역 expand 확장하다, 확대하다
partner with ~와 협력하다 international 국제적인
assist with ~을 돕다 translate 번역하다 contract 계약(서)
legal 법률과 관련된, 합법적인 look into ~을 조사하다
fit for ~에게 적합한, 알맞은

10.

최근에 무슨 일이 일어났는가?
(A) 새로운 규정이 통과되었다.

(B) 공급업체가 계약서에 서명했다.
(C) 서비스가 긍정적인 평가를 받았다.
(D) 공석인 자리가 채워졌다.

어휘

regulation 규정 supplier 공급업체
sign a contract 계약을 맺다 positive 긍정적인

패러프레이징

customers ~ have great things to say about it in their
reviews → A service received positive reviews

11.

회사는 무엇을 할 계획인가?
(A) 업무 제휴 맺기
(B) 직원 설문 조사 실시하기
(C) 본사 이전하기
(D) 수수료 구조 변경하기

어휘

form a partnership 제휴를 맺다 conduct 실시하다, 행하다
relocate 이전하다 headquarters 본사
commission 수수료, 커미션

패러프레이징

partner with an international law firm
→ Form a business partnership

12.

화자는 왜 바나 드로제에게 고마워하는가?
(A) 그녀가 몇몇 직원을 채용했다.
(B) 그녀가 출장을 갈 것이다.
(C) 그녀가 조사를 하고 있다.
(D) 그녀가 계약 협상을 하고 있다.

어휘

negotiate 협상하다

패러프레이징

looking into → doing some research

[13-15] 미남 🎧
Questions 13-15 refer to the following
announcement.

> **M** Before we finish this meeting, ¹³I have an
> update on our new insurance package, which
> covers all ages at comparably cheaper prices
> than our competition. We are estimating that
> sales will double in comparison to last quarter.
> Already our revenue has increased by 15
> percent, and ¹⁴we took second place in the
> financial and insurance market last month. I'm
> very grateful to you all for the hard work you've
> done and also want you to keep up the good
> work. To show my appreciation, I have
> arranged a 10 percent bonus to be given with

> your paycheck at the end of this month. ¹⁵For
> more details, check the notification section on
> our company Web site or ask your managers.
> Thank you again.

해석

13-15번은 다음 공지에 관한 문제입니다.

남 이번 회의를 마치기 전에, **¹³우리의 새로운 보험 패키지에 대한
최신 정보가 있는데요, 이것은 우리 경쟁사보다 비교적 더 저렴
한 가격에 모든 연령을 보장합니다.** 우리는 지난 분기와 비교해
매출이 두 배 늘어날 것으로 추정합니다. 이미 수익이 15% 증가
했고, **¹⁴지난달에 금융 및 보험 시장에서 2위를 차지했습니다.**
애써 주신 데 대해 여러분 모두에게 매우 감사하며 또한 앞으로
도 계속해서 잘해 주시기를 바랍니다. 감사를 표하기 위해서, 제
가 이번 달 말에 여러분의 급여와 함께 보너스 10%가 지급되도
록 처리했습니다. **¹⁵더 자세한 정보를 원하시면, 우리 회사 웹사
이트의 공지 섹션을 확인하시거나 여러분의 매니저들에게 물어
보세요.** 거듭 감사드립니다.

어휘

insurance 보험 cover 보장하다
comparably 비교할 수 있을 만큼, 동등하게
competition 경쟁, 경쟁자 estimate 추산하다, 추정하다
in comparison to ~와 비교할 때 revenue 수익
financial 금융의, 재정의 grateful 고마워하는, 감사하는
appreciation 감사 paycheck 급여 notification 통지, 공고

13.

새로운 보험 패키지에 관해 무엇이 언급되는가?
(A) 그것은 매년 갱신될 것이다.
(B) 그것은 경쟁사의 것보다 덜 비싸다.
(C) 그것은 15% 할인하여 제공될 것이다.
(D) 그것은 오직 노년층을 대상으로 한다.

어휘

competitor 경쟁자 intend for ~을 위해 만들다
senior citizen 어르신

패러프레이징

comparably cheaper prices than our competition
→ less expensive than those of competitors

14.

지난달에 무슨 일이 일어났는가?
(A) 직원들이 그들의 노고에 대해 보상을 받았다.
(B) 형편없는 서비스에 대해 항의가 제기되었다.
(C) 직무 교육 워크숍이 열렸다.
(D) 회사가 시장에서 2위를 차지했다.

어휘

reward for ~에 대해 보상하다 complaint 불만, 항의
job training 직무 교육 rank 매기다, 평가하다

패러프레이징

took second place in the financial and insurance
market → was ranked second in the market

15.

청자들은 왜 웹사이트를 방문해야 하는가?

(A) 더 많은 정보를 얻기 위해
(B) 공고를 게시하기 위해
(C) 쿠폰을 다운로드하기 위해
(D) 일정을 확인하기 위해

어휘

post 게시하다 notice 공고, 통지

패러프레이징

For more details → To get more information

[16-18] 영녀 🎧

Questions 16-18 refer to the following announcement and flow chart.

> W After much thought, ¹⁶I have decided that a new strategy is needed at our factory. From now on, each shift will include two managers. One will focus on safety, while the other will focus on quality control. This is because we've been having some issues with our plastic packaging. ¹⁷The color is coming out too dark. It's probably an issue with one of our main mixers. We'll need to investigate further to be sure. So, ¹⁸the first thing to do is run some tests with the machinery at that stage. I'll take care of that right after this meeting. Hopefully, we can resolve the issue quickly.

해석

16-18번은 다음 공지와 순서도에 관한 문제입니다.

여 숙고 끝에, ¹⁶저는 우리 공장에 새로운 전략이 필요하다고 결정을 내렸습니다. 지금부터, 각 교대 조에 두 명의 관리자가 포함될 것입니다. 한 명은 안전에 초점을 맞추는 반면, 다른 한 명은 품질 관리에 주력할 것입니다. 이것은 우리 플라스틱 포장에 문제가 좀 있기 때문입니다. ¹⁷색상이 너무 어둡게 나오고 있습니다. 아마도 중앙 혼합기 중 하나와 관련된 문제인 듯합니다. 확실히 하기 위하여 우리가 좀 더 조사해야 할 것입니다. 따라서 ¹⁸가장 먼저 할 일은 그 단계의 기계를 검사하는 것입니다. 이 회의 직후에 제가 그것을 처리하겠습니다. 우리가 이 문제를 빨리 해결할 수 있기를 바랍니다.

어휘

strategy 전략, 계획 focus on ~에 주력하다, 초점을 맞추다
safety 안전(성) quality control 품질 관리
packaging 포장, 포장재 mixer 혼합기 investigate 조사하다
run a test 검사를 하다 machinery 기계(류)
hopefully 바라건대 resolve 해결하다

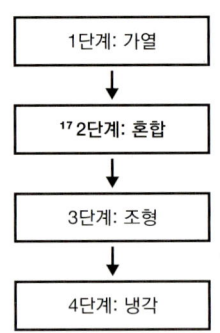

1단계: 가열
↓
¹⁷ 2단계: 혼합
↓
3단계: 조형
↓
4단계: 냉각

16.

화자는 어떤 결정을 내렸는가?
(A) 안전 규약이 업데이트되어야 한다.
(B) 두 명의 관리자가 각 교대 조에 배정되어야 한다.
(C) 야간 근무가 일정에 추가되어야 한다.
(D) 임시 직원들이 채용되어야 한다.

어휘

protocol 규약, 프로토콜 assign to ~에 배정하다
temporary 임시의, 일시적인

패러프레이징

each shift will include two managers
→ Two managers should be assigned to each shift

17.

시각 자료를 보시오. 화자는 어떤 단계에서 문제가 발생했다고 생각하는가?
(A) 1단계
(B) 2단계
(C) 3단계
(D) 4단계

어휘

occur 일어나다, 발생하다

18.

화자는 회의 후에 무엇을 할 것인가?
(A) 몇 가지 부품 주문하기
(B) 수리공에게 전화하기
(C) 테스트 실시하기
(D) 수송품 내리기

어휘

unload (짐을) 내리다 shipment 수송품, 적하물

패러프레이징

run → Conduct

UNIT 11 공공장소 안내

[1-3] 미녀 🎧

Questions 1-3 refer to the following announcement.

> W ¹Welcome to Bentley Concert Hall. Today's performance was scheduled to begin at 7:30, but unfortunately, we are having an issue with our sound system. ²We expect to resolve the issue by 8 o'clock. In the meantime, the café is open until 10. Our employees would be happy to serve you. ³And don't forget to keep your admission ticket. You can use it to get a 10 percent discount in the gift shop, which is located near the main entrance. We apologize for the inconvenience, and we thank you for your understanding.

해석

1-3번은 다음 공지에 관한 문제입니다.

여 ¹벤틀리 콘서트홀에 오신 것을 환영합니다. 오늘 공연은 7시 30분에 시작될 예정이었지만, 유감스럽게도 음향 시스템에 문제가 있습니다. ²저희는 8시 정각까지 문제를 해결할 것으로 예상합니다. 그동안에, 카페가 10시까지 운영합니다. 저희 직원들이 기쁜 마음으로 여러분을 모실 것입니다. ³그리고 잊지 말고 입장권을 가지고 계세요. 그것을 이용해 기념품점에서 10% 할인받으실 수 있는데, 그곳은 중앙 출입구 근처에 위치해 있습니다. 불편을 끼쳐 사과드리며, 양해해 주셔서 감사합니다.

어휘

performance 공연, 연주회
have an issue with ~와 문제가 있다 resolve 해결하다
in the meantime 그동안에, 그 사이에
admission ticket 입장권 be located (~에) 위치하다
entrance 입구 apologize for ~에 대해 사과하다
inconvenience 불편

1.

공지는 어디에서 이루어지고 있는가?
(A) 스포츠 시설에서
(B) 콘서트장에서
(C) 미술관에서
(D) 공원에서

어휘

facility 시설

2.

화자는 왜 "카페가 10시까지 운영합니다"라고 말하는가?
(A) 예약을 변경하기 위해
(B) 식사 초대를 거절하기 위해

(C) 오해를 바로잡기 위해
(D) 다과를 먹을 것을 권하기 위해

어휘

reservation 예약 reject 거절하다, 거부하다
correct 고치다, 바로잡다 misunderstanding 오해, 착오
refreshments ((항상 복수형)) 다과, 음식물

3.

화자에 따르면, 청자들은 왜 티켓을 가지고 있어야 하는가?
(A) 할인을 받기 위해
(B) 환불을 받기 위해
(C) 경품 추첨에 응모하기 위해
(D) 고객 보상 프로그램에 등록하기 위해

어휘

issue a refund 환불해 주다 enter (대회 등에) 출전하다
drawing 제비뽑기 enroll in ~에 등록하다
loyalty program 고객 보상 프로그램

1.

Q 화자는 일부 청자들에게 웹사이트에서 무엇을 하라고 말하는가?
A 서식 작성하기

미남 🎧

> M You can pick up your conference packet at the table right outside the main auditorium. And if you have not completed the registration forms yet, please visit our Web site and fill them out before you go to the table. You can use your smartphone or borrow a tablet from one of our staff members.

해석

남 대강당 바로 밖 테이블에서 학회 패킷을 가져가실 수 있습니다. 그리고 여러분이 아직 신청서를 작성하지 않았다면, 테이블로 가시기 전에 저희 웹사이트에 방문하여 신청서를 작성하시기 바랍니다. 여러분의 스마트폰을 사용하시거나 저희 직원들 중 한 명에게서 태블릿 PC를 빌리셔도 됩니다.

어휘

complete 기입하다, 작성하다 packet 다발, 묶음
auditorium 강당, 객석 registration form 신청서
staff member 직원

패러프레이징

registration forms ~ fill them out
→ Complete some forms

2.

Q 화자는 화요일 저녁 영화에 대해 무엇이라고 말하는가?

A 티켓 가격이 인하되었다.

미녀 🎧

> **W** Attention, Summit Cinema patrons. Tickets for the 7 P.M. screening of *The Mountaineers* are nearly sold out. You can reserve tickets online for future movies on our Web site. And don't forget that tickets are half price for the movie screening on Tuesday evening. Visit our Web site for more information.

해석

여 서밋 영화관 고객 여러분 주목해 주세요. 〈등산가들〉의 저녁 7시 상영 티켓이 거의 매진되었습니다. 앞으로 상영될 영화들은 저희 웹사이트에서 온라인으로 예매하실 수 있습니다. 그리고 화요일 저녁에 상영하는 영화에 대해서는 티켓이 반값이라는 것을 잊지 마세요. 더 많은 정보를 원하시면 저희 웹사이트를 방문하세요.

어휘

reduce (가격 등을) 낮추다 patron 고객 screening (영화) 상영
mountaineer 등산가, 등산객 sold out 표가 매진된
reserve 예약하다 half price 반값

패러프레이징

tickets are half price → Ticket prices are reduced

3.

Q 화자는 왜 청자들에게 사과하는가?

A 지연이 있었다.

미남 🎧

> **M** Good afternoon, everyone, and welcome aboard this flight to Atlanta. We apologize for the delay at takeoff. We had an issue with the meals for our in-flight service, but the problem has been resolved.

해석

남 안녕하세요, 여러분, 애틀랜타행 항공편에 탑승하신 것을 환영합니다. 이륙이 지연된 데 사과드립니다. 기내 서비스를 위한 음식에 문제가 있었지만, 해결되었습니다.

어휘

apologize 사과하다 delay 지연, 지체 aboard 탑승한
flight 항공편, 비행기 takeoff 이륙
have an issue with ~와 문제가 있다
in-flight 기내의, 운항 중의 resolve 해결하다

패러프레이징

the delay at takeoff → There was a delay

4.

Q 화자는 무도회장에 대해 무엇이라고 말하는가?

A 입장하려면 초대장이 필요하다.

미녀 🎧

> **W** Attention, visitors to Alvarez Convention Center. The ballroom is now open for entry for the Carlyle Incorporated Awards Dinner. For those attending the event, please make sure that you have your invitation with you.

해석

여 앨버레즈 컨벤션 센터 방문객들께서는 주목해 주세요. 이제 칼라일 주식회사 시상식 만찬 입장을 위한 무도회장이 열렸습니다. 행사에 참석하시는 분들께서는, 반드시 초대장을 지참하시기 바랍니다.

어휘

ballroom 무도회장 invitation 초대(장) entry 입장
attend 참석하다

패러프레이징

make sure that you have your invitation with you
→ An invitation is needed

5.

화자는 이제 무엇을 이용할 수 있다고 말하는가?

(A) 무료 인터넷 서비스

(B) 등받이가 뒤로 넘어가는 좌석

미남 🎧

> **M** The upgrades to the trains on the Horizon Railways will be completed this weekend. We hope our customers will enjoy the expanded luggage area and comfortable seats. In addition, complimentary wireless Internet is now offered in all cars of the train for your convenience.

해석

남 호라이즌 철도의 열차들에 대한 개선 작업이 이번 주말에 완료될 예정입니다. 저희는 고객들이 넓어진 짐칸과 편안한 좌석을 좋아하시길 기대합니다. 또한, 여러분의 편의를 위해 이제 열차의 모든 객차에 무료 무선 인터넷이 제공됩니다.

어휘

available 이용할 수 있는 complete 완료하다, 마치다
expanded 넓어진, 확대된 luggage area 짐칸
comfortable 편안한 complimentary 무료의
convenience 편의, 편리

패러프레이징

complimentary wireless Internet
→ Free Internet service

6.

화자는 최근에 무슨 일이 일어났다고 말하는가?

(A) 직원들이 교육을 받았다.

(B) 줄이 길어졌다.

> **W** Welcome to the Department of Transportation. There have been longer lines of people than usual recently. To help us serve you more quickly, please make sure your paperwork is completed before your number is called. If you need a pen, you can find them at the table near the entrance.

해석

여 교통부에 오신 것을 환영합니다. **최근 평소보다 사람들의 줄이 더 길어졌습니다.** 저희가 더 신속하게 여러분을 응대하는 데 도움이 되도록, 반드시 번호가 불리기 전에 서류 작업을 마쳐 주시기 바랍니다. 펜이 필요하시면, 입구 근처의 테이블에서 찾으실 수 있습니다.

어휘

Department of Transportation 교통부
serve 응대하다, 봉사하다 paperwork 서류 작업
entrance 입구

패러프레이징

There have been longer lines of people than usual → Lines have grown

---

연습 문제 본문 p.267

1. (C) **2.** (B) **3.** (A) **4.** (C) **5.** (A)

---

[1] 미남 🎧

Question 1 refers to the following announcement.

> **M** May I have your attention for the following announcement? We regret to inform you that the 4:15 train to Boston has been delayed due to a mechanical issue. We have called a technician and hope to fix the problem quickly. However, we do not know how long this process will take. Passengers are invited to take the 4:40 train instead. A new ticket will not be required. Simply show your ticket to a staff member. Thank you for your patience.

해석

1번은 다음 공지에 관한 문제입니다.

남 다음 공지에 주목해 주시겠습니까? 유감스럽게도 보스턴행 4시 15분 열차가 기계적인 문제로 인해 지연되었음을 알려 드립니다. 저희는 기술자를 불렀고 신속히 문제를 해결하기를 바랍니다. 하지만, 이 과정이 얼마나 걸릴지 모릅니다. 승객들께 대신 4시 40분 기차를 이용하시기를 청합니다. 새로운 티켓은 필요하지 않을 것입니다. 그저 직원에게 가지고 계신 티켓을 보여주세요. 양해해 주셔서 감사합니다.

어휘

attention 주의, 주목 regret 유감스럽게 생각하다, 후회하다
mechanical 기계적인 technician 기술자
process 과정, 절차 invite 요청하다, 청하다
require 필요로 하다, 요구하다 patience 참을성, 인내력

1.

열차는 왜 지연되었는가?
(A) 그것은 추가 연료가 필요하다.
(B) 그것은 다른 운전자가 필요하다.
(C) 그것은 기계적인 문제가 있다.
(D) 그것은 초과 예약을 받았다.

어휘

additional 추가의 overbook 예약을 한도 이상으로 받다

패러프레이징

issue → problem

[2-3] 미녀 🎧

Questions 2-3 refer to the following announcement.

> **W** Attention, Mapleton Supermarket shoppers. ²A customer has found a handbag and turned it in to our staff. Please take a moment to see if you are missing it. ³If so, please come to the express check-out counter, which is located near Aisle 18. We will hold the bag securely until it has been claimed. It will need to be properly identified to be released. Thank you for shopping with us today. It is our pleasure to serve you.

해석

2-3번은 다음 공지에 관한 문제입니다.

여 메이플턴 슈퍼마켓 고객분들은 주목해 주세요. ²**한 고객이 핸드백을 발견하여 저희 직원에게 가져다주었습니다.** 잠시 시간을 내어 여러분이 잃어버린 것인지 여부를 확인해 주시기 바랍니다. ³**만일 그렇다면, 18번 통로 근처의 빠른 계산대로 와 주시기 바랍니다.** 찾으러 오실 때까지 저희가 안전하게 가방을 보관하겠습니다. 그것이 내보내지려면 제대로 확인되어야 할 것입니다. 오늘 저희와 함께 쇼핑해 주셔서 감사합니다. 여러분을 모시게 되어 기쁩니다.

어휘

turn in ~을 돌려주다, 제출하다 take a moment 시간을 내다
express check-out counter 빠른 계산대
be located (~에) 위치하다 aisle 통로
securely 안전하게, 튼튼하게 claim 요구하다, 청구하다
properly 올바로, 적절히 identify 확인하다
release 놓아 주다, 방출하다 serve (손님을) 응대하다

2.

공지의 목적은 무엇인가?
(A) 청자들에게 폐점을 알리기 위해

(B) 발견된 물건을 알리기 위해
(C) 배송 지연에 대해 사과하기 위해
(D) 새로운 서비스를 소개하기 위해

어휘

closure 폐쇄, 종료 apologize for ~에 대해 사과하다
shipment 수송품, 선적물

패러프레이징

handbag → item

3.
일부 청자들은 어디로 가야 하는가?
(A) 계산대로
(B) 정문으로
(C) 매니저의 사무실로
(D) 주차장으로

어휘

front entrance 정문, 현관

[4-5] 미남 🎧
Questions 4-5 refer to the following announcement.

> M Attention, all passengers. The northern wing of the facility is temporarily closed due to repairs. Visitors are prohibited from entering the area. Thank you for your compliance. ⁴For the next few weeks, buses to Jacksonville, Wrightham, and Tawney City will leave from Gate Area C instead. ⁵To find your exact gate number, we recommend checking the departure boards about 20 to 30 minutes before your scheduled departure time. We wish you a safe and comfortable journey, and thank you for traveling with us today.

해석

4-5번은 다음 공지에 관한 문제입니다.
남 모든 승객들은 주목해 주세요. 이 시설의 북쪽 부속 건물이 보수로 인해 임시로 폐쇄되었습니다. 방문객들에게는 이 구역 출입을 금지합니다. 준수해 주셔서 감사합니다. ⁴다음 몇 주 동안은 잭슨빌, 라이트햄, 그리고 토니 시티로 가는 버스들이 대신 C 탑승구 구역에서 출발할 것입니다. ⁵정확한 탑승구 번호를 아시려면, 예정된 출발 시간보다 약 20분에서 30분 전에 출발 안내 전광판을 확인하실 것을 권장합니다. 안전하고 편안하게 여행하시길 기원하며, 오늘 저희와 함께 여행해 주셔서 감사합니다.

어휘

northern 북쪽의 wing 부속 건물 facility 시설
temporarily 일시적으로, 임시로
prohibit from ~을 금지하다 compliance 준수, 따름
gate 탑승구, 게이트 exact 정확한
departure board 출발 안내 전광판 scheduled 예정된

4.
청자들은 어디에 있는 것 같은가?
(A) 여객선 터미널에
(B) 공항에
(C) 버스 터미널에
(D) 기차역에

5.
화자는 무엇을 할 것을 권장하는가?
(A) 미리 정보를 확인하는 것
(B) 계정을 신청하는 것
(C) 여행 일정표 사본을 인쇄하는 것
(D) 문자 알림 시스템을 이용하는 것

어휘

in advance 미리, 사전에 sign up for ~을 신청하다
account 계정, 계좌 itinerary 여행 일정표 alert 경보, 경계

패러프레이징

about 20 to 30 minutes before → in advance

실전 문제   본문 p.268

1. (B)	**2.** (C)	**3.** (D)	**4.** (C)	**5.** (D)
6. (D)	**7.** (B)	**8.** (A)	**9.** (D)	**10.** (D)
11. (B)	**12.** (C)	**13.** (C)	**14.** (D)	**15.** (B)
16. (C)	**17.** (B)	**18.** (C)		

[1-3] 미녀 🎧
Questions 1-3 refer to the following announcement.

> W Attention, Appleton Bookstore patrons. ¹In about 20 minutes, writer Yadira Blake will be reading some of her poems in our event room at the rear of the store. Anyone can get free admission to this event. After the session, Ms. Blake will be signing autographs. ²We expect long lines for her books after the session, so we advise you to buy yours in advance to reduce your wait time. ³And don't forget to visit our Web site at www.appletonbooks.com. There you can sign up for our mailing list so you can be informed about future events at our store.

해석

1-3번은 다음 공지에 관한 문제입니다.
여 애플턴 서점 고객들은 주목해 주세요. ¹약 20분 뒤에, 야디라 블레이크 작가가 매장 뒤쪽에 있는 저희 행사장에서 그녀의 시 일부를 낭독할 것입니다. 누구든 이 행사에 무료로 입장하실 수 있습니다. 그 시간이 끝나면, 블레이크 씨가 사인을 해 줄 것입니다. ²그 시간 이후에는 그녀의 책을 사려고 길게 줄을 설 것으로 예상되므로, 대기 시간을 줄이기 위해 미리 구매하실 것을 권합니다. ³그리고 잊지 말고 저희 웹사이트 www.appletonbooks.

com에 방문하세요. 그곳에서 앞으로 저희 서점에서 있을 행사에 대해 정보를 받으실 수 있도록 ³우편물 수신자 명단에 가입하실 수 있습니다.

1.
화자는 주로 무엇에 관해 이야기하고 있는가?
(A) 창고 정리 판매
(B) 시 낭독
(C) 지역사회 모금 행사
(D) 글쓰기 워크숍

어휘

clearance sale 창고 정리 판매 poetry 시
fund-raiser 기금 모금 행사

패러프레이징

reading some of her poems → A poetry reading

2.
화자는 무엇을 할 것을 제안하는가?
(A) 앞쪽 가까이 앉는 것
(B) 시작 시간을 확인하는 것
(C) 미리 구매하는 것
(D) 질문을 서면으로 제출하는 것

어휘

front 앞쪽 make a purchase 구매하다 submit 제출하다
in writing 서면으로

패러프레이징

buy → Making a purchase

3.
화자에 따르면, 청자들은 왜 웹사이트에 방문해야 하는가?
(A) 의견을 공유하기 위해
(B) 신상품에 대해 알아보기 위해
(C) 행사 티켓을 구매하기 위해
(D) 우편물 수신자 명단에 가입하기 위해

패러프레이징

sign up for → join

[4-6] 호남 🎧
Questions 4-6 refer to the following announcement.

M ⁴I'd like to make an announcement about the 12:15 train to Liverpool. Unfortunately, we're still waiting for the train to arrive at Platform 7. ⁵This delay is due to some signaling lights that are not functioning properly. Our team is working to address the situation, and we expect the train to arrive shortly. ⁶To reduce boarding time, please keep your ticket out so you can show it to the staff quickly. Thank you for your compliance.

해석

4~6번은 다음 공지에 관한 문제입니다.

남 ⁴리버풀행 12시 15분 열차에 대해 안내 말씀드리겠습니다. 유감스럽게도, 아직 7번 플랫폼에 열차가 도착하기를 기다리는 중입니다. ⁵이번 지연은 제대로 작동하지 않고 있는 일부 신호등 때문입니다. 저희 팀이 이 상황을 처리하기 위해 작업 중이고, 열차가 곧 도착할 것으로 예상합니다. ⁶탑승 시간을 단축하기 위해, 티켓을 직원에게 빨리 보여줄 수 있도록 밖에 꺼내 놓으시기 바랍니다. 지시에 따라 주셔서 감사합니다.

어휘

platform 플랫폼, 승강장 signaling 신호 표시
function 기능하다, 작용하다 properly 제대로
address 다루다, 처리하다 shortly 곧 board 탑승하다
compliance 준수, 따름

4.
공지는 어디에서 이루어지고 있는 것 같은가?
(A) 자동차 정비소에서
(B) 여행사에서
(C) 기차역에서
(D) 버스 정류장에서

5.
화자에 따르면, 지연의 원인은 무엇이었는가?
(A) 매표 오류
(B) 나쁜 기상 조건
(C) 수송 지연
(D) 결함이 있는 장비

어휘

cause 원인 shipment 수송, 수송품 faulty 결함이 있는
equipment 장비, 용품

패러프레이징

signaling lights that are not functioning properly
→ faulty equipment

6.
청자들은 무엇을 하도록 요청받는가?
(A) 화자에게 문제점 알리기
(B) 개인 소지품을 잘 가지고 다니기
(C) 다른 구역으로 이동하기
(D) 티켓을 보여 줄 준비하기

어휘

personal 개인의, 개인적인
belongings ((항상 복수형)) 재산, 소유물
present 보여 주다, 제시하다

패러프레이징

keep your ticket out so you can show it to the staff
quickly → Have their ticket ready to present

[7-9] 미남 🎧

Questions 7-9 refer to the following announcement.

> **M** Welcome aboard flight 406 to Vancouver. **⁷We
> apologize for the delay. Unfortunately, we had
> to wait for the severe snowstorm to pass.**
> However, we are now ready to depart. As we
> prepare for takeoff, **⁸please remember to place
> your bags under the seat in front of you or in
> the overhead compartments. We must keep
> the aisles clear.** If you are interested in signing
> up for the Ashford Airlines Loyalty Program,
> please speak to one of our flight attendants.
> **⁹All new members will receive a voucher for a
> seat upgrade on a future flight.**

해석

7-9번은 다음 공지에 관한 문제입니다.

남 밴쿠버행 406 항공편에 탑승하신 것을 환영합니다. **⁷항공편 지
연에 대해 사과드립니다. 유감스럽게도, 저희는 심한 눈보라가
지나가기를 기다려야 했습니다.** 하지만, 이제 출발할 준비가 되
었습니다. 저희가 이륙을 준비하는 동안, **⁸여러분 앞 좌석 아래
나 머리 위 짐칸에 가방을 두시는 것을 명심하시기 바랍니다. 통
로를 비워 두어야 합니다.** 애시포드 에어라인 고객 보상 프로그
램에 신청하는 데 관심이 있으시면, 저희 승무원들 중 한 명에게
말씀하시기 바랍니다. **⁹모든 신입 회원들은 향후 비행 시 좌석을
업그레이드할 수 있는 상품권을 받게 됩니다.**

어휘

aboard 탑승하여 flight 항공편, 비행기
apologize for ~에 대해 사과하다 severe 극심한, 심각한
depart 출발하다 takeoff 이륙 place 두다, 놓다
overhead compartment 머리 위 짐칸 aisle 통로
loyalty program 고객 보상 프로그램 flight attendant 승무원
voucher 상품권, 할인권

7.

무엇이 지연을 일으켰는가?
(A) 일부 티켓이 잘못됐다.
(B) 기상 상태가 나빴다.
(C) 기술적인 문제가 좀 있었다.
(D) 직원이 늦게 도착했다.

어휘

cause 야기하다, 초래하다 incorrect 부정확한, 맞지 않는
technical 기술적인

패러프레이징

severe snowstorm → Weather conditions were bad

8.

화자는 청자들에게 무엇에 관해 상기시키는가?
(A) 가방을 치우는 것
(B) 탑승권을 보여 주는 것
(C) 안전벨트를 착용하는 것
(D) 기내 테이블의 위치를 되돌려 놓는 것

어휘

put away 치우다 boarding pass 탑승권
fasten the seat belt 안전벨트를 착용하다
reposition ~의 위치를 바꾸다 tray table 기내 테이블

패러프레이징

keep the aisles clear → Putting away their bags

9.

청자들은 고객 보상 프로그램에 가입하면 무엇을 받을 수 있는가?
(A) 개인 라운지 이용권
(B) 무료 음료
(C) 추가 고객 보상 포인트
(D) 업그레이드용 상품권

어휘

private 개인의, 사적인 complimentary 무료의
additional 추가의

[10-12] 영녀 🎧

Questions 10-12 refer to the following
announcement.

> **W** Good evening, and **¹⁰welcome to tonight's
> performance of the Berlin Orchestra.** Before
> you hear this group's beautiful music, **¹¹I'd like
> to inform you that everyone is entitled to
> receive a free poster signed by the orchestra
> members. You can pick it up at the ticket
> counter after the show.** Additionally, we have
> recently completed renovations at our site.
> **¹²We hope you enjoy the new seats that have
> replaced our uncomfortable and outdated
> ones.** Enjoy the show and thank you for your
> patronage!

해석

10-12번은 다음 공지에 관한 문제입니다.

여 안녕하세요, **¹⁰오늘 밤 베를린 오케스트라의 공연에 오신 걸 환
영합니다.** 이 연주단의 아름다운 음악을 듣기 전에, **¹¹여러분 모
두 오케스트라 단원들이 사인한 무료 포스터를 받을 수 있음을
알려 드립니다. 공연이 끝난 후 매표소에서 찾아가시면 됩니다.**
또한, 저희가 최근 이곳의 보수를 마쳤습니다. **¹²불편하고 낡은
좌석들을 새 좌석으로 교체했으니 맘껏 즐기시기를 바랍니다.** 공
연을 즐겁게 감상하시고 후원해 주셔서 감사합니다!

어휘

performance 공연, 연주회 inform 알리다, 통보하다
be entitled to ~할 자격이 있다 complete 완료하다, 마치다

renovation 보수, 수리 site 장소, 현장 replace 교체하다
uncomfortable 불편한 outdated 구식의, 낡은
patronage 애용, 후원

10.
공지는 어디서 이루어지는가?
(A) 쇼핑센터에서
(B) 도서관에서
(C) 호텔에서
(D) 콘서트장에서

11.
화자에 따르면, 매표소에서 무엇을 구할 수 있을 것인가?
(A) 음료
(B) 포스터
(C) 쿠폰
(D) 카탈로그

12.
최근에 이 장소에 무엇이 행해졌는가?
(A) 일부 주차장이 재포장되었다.
(B) 매표 시스템이 업그레이드되었다.
(C) 일부 좌석이 교체되었다.
(D) 건물이 확장되었다.

어휘
repave (길을) 다시 포장하다 expand 확장하다, 확대하다

[13-15] 영녀 🎧
Questions 13-15 refer to the following announcement.

> W ¹³Thank you for visiting Joywood Food Market today. We appreciate you shopping with us, and we would like to ask you for your feedback on your shopping experience. We are asking all visitors to the Joywood Food Market this week to fill out a form about their trip. ¹⁴Survey forms can be picked up at the customer service desk or any cash register. For all those who participate, we are offering a gift certificate to use at our store. Don't be shy. ¹⁵Any and all feedback is welcome. Once again, we'd like to thank you for shopping at Joywood Food Market and hope you have a pleasant day.

해석
13-15번은 다음 공지에 관한 문제입니다.
여 ¹³오늘 조이우드 푸드 마켓을 방문해 주셔서 감사합니다. 저희와 함께 쇼핑해 주셔서 감사드리며, 여러분의 쇼핑 경험에 대한 의견을 요청드리고 싶습니다. 저희는 이번 주에 조이우드 푸드 마켓의 모든 방문객들에게 그들의 쇼핑 나들이에 관한 설문지를 작성해 주실 것을 요청하고 있습니다. ¹⁴설문지는 고객 서비스 창

구나 모든 계산대에서 수령하실 수 있습니다. 참가하시는 모든 분들께는 저희 매장에서 사용할 수 있는 상품권을 드립니다. 부끄러워하지 마세요. ¹⁵어떤 의견이든 모두 환영합니다. 다시 한 번, 조이우드 푸드 마켓에서 쇼핑해 주셔서 감사드리며 즐거운 하루를 보내시기를 바랍니다.

어휘
appreciate 고마워하다, 인정하다 experience 경험
fill out 기입하다, 작성하다 survey 설문 조사
cash register 금전 등록기, 계산대 participate 참가하다
gift certificate 상품권 pleasant 즐거운

13.
공지는 어디에서 이루어지고 있는가?
(A) 농장에서
(B) 옷 가게에서
(C) 식료품점에서
(D) 전자제품 매장에서

어휘
clothing 의류 electronics ((항상 복수형)) 전자제품

패러프레이징
Food Market → a grocery store

14.
화자에 따르면, 계산대에서 무엇을 찾을 수 있는가?
(A) 메뉴
(B) 상품권
(C) 쇼핑백
(D) 설문지

패러프레이징
Survey forms → Questionnaires

15.
화자가 "부끄러워하지 마세요"라고 말할 때 무엇을 암시하는가?
(A) 그녀는 모든 사람이 신제품을 써 보아야 한다고 생각한다.
(B) 그녀는 사람들이 자유롭게 의견을 공유하기를 원한다.
(C) 그녀는 청자들이 자주 다시 찾아오기를 바란다.
(D) 그녀는 상품권 사용을 권장한다.

어휘
frequently 자주, 흔히 encourage 권장하다, 장려하다

[16-18] 미녀 🎧
Questions 16-18 refer to the following announcement and map.

> W Attention, shoppers. ¹⁶Elkview Shopping Mall has extended its hours of operation. We are now open from 8 A.M. to 8 P.M. daily. Don't miss this opportunity to explore our unique stores. Additionally, please note that we are still running our free shuttle service to the Rhoden Convention Center. ¹⁷You can board

the shuttle at the parking area between Molly's Shoes and Yorkshire Avenue. ¹⁸And tomorrow, at 10 A.M., chef Elizabeth Lewis will demonstrate some cooking techniques in the central atrium.

해석

16-18번은 다음 공지와 지도에 관한 문제입니다.

여 쇼핑객 여러분 주목해 주세요. ¹⁶엘크뷰 쇼핑몰이 운영 시간을 연장했습니다. 저희는 이제 매일 오전 8시부터 저녁 8시까지 문을 엽니다. 저희의 독특한 매장들을 살펴볼 이번 기회를 놓치지 마세요. 또한, 저희가 아직 로덴 컨벤션 센터까지 무료 셔틀버스 서비스를 운영한다는 것도 알아 두시기 바랍니다. ¹⁷셔틀버스는 몰리스 신발과 요크셔 거리 사이의 주차장에서 탑승하실 수 있습니다. ¹⁸그리고 내일 오전 10시에 요리사 엘리자베스 루이스가 중앙 아트리움에서 요리 비법을 시연할 것입니다.

어휘

extend 연장하다, 확대하다 hours of operation 운영 시간 opportunity 기회 explore 탐험하다 unique 독특한 note 주목하다 run 운영하다 board 탑승하다 demonstrate 보여 주다, 시연하다 technique 기법, 기술

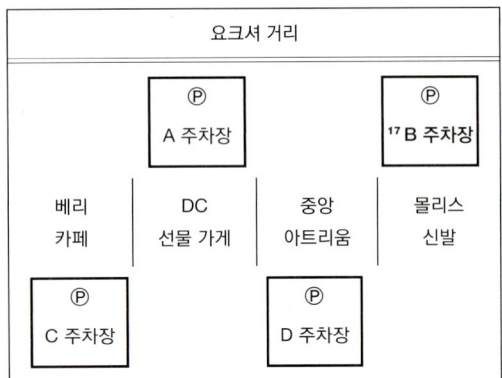

요크셔 거리

16.

화자는 어떤 변화에 대해 공지하는가?
(A) 다양한 음악 공연들
(B) 주차 요금 취소
(C) 영업시간 연장
(D) 식품 판매대 추가

어휘

performance 공연, 연주회 cancellation 취소, 무효화 vendor 노점상, 판매 회사

패러프레이징

extended its hours of operation
→ Longer business hours

17.

시각 자료를 보시오. 청자들은 어디에서 셔틀버스를 탈 수 있는가?
(A) A 주차장에서

(B) B 주차장에서
(C) C 주차장에서
(D) D 주차장에서

18.

내일 어떤 행사가 열릴 것인가?
(A) 지역사회 축제
(B) 개점 행사
(C) 요리 시연
(D) 패션쇼

어휘

demonstration 시연, 시범 설명

패러프레이징

demonstrate some cooking techniques
→ A cooking demonstration

UNIT 12 연설·강연·소개

CHECK UP   본문 p.270

1. (A)   **2.** (C)   **3.** (D)

[1-3] 미녀 🎧

Questions 1-3 refer to the following talk.

W ¹Welcome to the annual Software Developers Trade Show. First of all, thank you for letting us attend this event and show you our latest application. I'm looking forward to the honest feedback we can get before officially releasing it. ²As I go through the presentation, you can practice using the application on the mobile phones displayed on the tables. But first, ³I need to ask you to enter your name in the password box to access the system. I am happy to answer any questions you may have.

해석

1-3번은 다음 담화에 관한 문제입니다.

여 ¹연례 소프트웨어 개발자 무역 박람회에 오신 것을 환영합니다. 무엇보다도 먼저, 저희가 이 행사에 참석하여 저희의 최신 애플리케이션을 선보일 수 있게 해 주셔서 감사드립니다. 공식적으로 출시하기 전에 가장 솔직한 피드백을 받을 수 있기를 고대하고 있습니다. ²제가 발표를 진행하는 동안 여러분은 테이블 위에 전시된 휴대폰으로 애플리케이션 사용법을 익히실 수 있습니다. 하지만 우선, ³시스템에 접속하기 위해 비밀번호 칸에 이름을 입력하실 것을 요청드립니다. 어떤 질문을 하시든 기꺼이 답변하겠습니다.

어휘

annual 연례의 developer 개발자 trade show 무역 박람회 latest 최신의 application (= app) 애플리케이션, 응용 프로그램

look forward to ~을 기대하다 officially 공식적으로
release 출시하다, 공개하다
go through (행동·절차를) 거치다, ~을 살펴보다
display 전시하다, 진열하다 enter 입력하다
access 접속하다, 이용하다

1.
어떤 행사가 개최되고 있는가?
(A) 무역 박람회
(B) 운동 경기
(C) 취업 박람회
(D) 시상식

어휘
competition 경쟁, (경연) 대회

2.
청자들은 발표 동안 무엇을 할 수 있는가?
(A) 카탈로그 훑어보기
(B) 서식 작성하기
(C) 새로운 애플리케이션 사용해 보기
(D) 영상 시청하기

어휘
browse 훑어보다, 둘러보다 complete 기입하다, 작성하다

패러프레이징
practice using the application → Try a new application

3.
화자는 청자들에게 무엇을 해 달라고 요청하는가?
(A) 그룹 만들기
(B) 헤드폰 쓰기
(C) 설명서 읽기
(D) 이름 입력하기

어휘
manual 설명서

패러프레이징 연습   본문 p.272

1-4. 스크립트 참조   5. (B)   6. (B)

1.
Q 청자들은 어떤 종류의 행사에 참석하고 있는가?
A 산업 학회

미녀 🎧

> W I'd like to welcome you all to the annual
> conference on wastewater management. Our
> first speaker today is Carl Armstrong, the head
> of Goodwin Industries. He'll be discussing the
> best ways to reuse wastewater and the
> systems needed to do so.

해석
여 폐수 관리에 관한 연례 학회에 오신 여러분 모두를 환영합니다.
오늘 우리의 첫 번째 연사는 굿윈 인더스트리의 대표인 칼 암스
트롱입니다. 그는 폐수를 재사용하는 가장 좋은 방법과 그렇게
하기 위해 필요한 시스템에 대해 얘기할 것입니다.

어휘
industry 산업 conference 회의, 학회 annual 연례의
wastewater 폐수, 하수 management 운영, 관리
head 책임자, 대표 reuse 재사용하다

패러프레이징
the annual conference on wastewater management
→ An industry conference

2.
Q 화자는 쇼베 서비스 사에 무엇에 대해 감사하는가?
A 울타리를 설치한 것

미남 🎧

> M It is a pleasure to welcome you all to the
> opening of Fairview Park. We hope everyone in
> the community will enjoy this outdoor space. I
> would especially like to thank Shobe Services,
> who put up the wooden fence at the south end
> of the park.

해석
남 페어뷰 파크의 개장식에 여러분 모두를 모시게 되어 기쁩니다.
저희는 지역 사회의 모든 분들이 이 야외 공간에서 즐거운 시간
을 보내시길 바랍니다. 저는 특히 공원의 남쪽 끝에 나무 울타리
를 세운 쇼베 서비스 사에 감사드리고 싶습니다.

어휘
opening 개장식 outdoor 야외의 put up 설치하다
fence 울타리

패러프레이징
put up the wooden fence → Installing a fence

3.
Q 화자는 청자들에게 무엇을 하라고 권장하는가?
A 특별 행사에 등록하기

미녀 🎧

> W I hope everyone is enjoying the conference so
> far. Please note that the closing dinner led by
> Joe Thorson is not included with the event
> registration. We still have spots available for
> that. If you don't have a ticket and would like
> to attend, please sign up. There's a registration
> table near the rear entrance.

해석
여 지금까지 모든 분들이 학회에서 즐거운 시간을 보내고 계시기를
바랍니다. 조 토르손이 이끄는 폐회 만찬은 등록하신 행사에 포

함되지 않는다는 것을 알아 두시기 바랍니다. 아직 그 만찬의 자리가 남아 있습니다. 티켓이 없는데 참석하고 싶으시면, 신청하시기 바랍니다. 뒤쪽 출입구 근처에 등록 테이블이 있습니다.

어휘

registration 등록 spot (특정한) 자리, 장소
available 이용할 수 있는 entrance (출)입구

패러프레이징

the closing dinner lead by Joe Thorson
→ a special event

4.

Q 화자에 따르면, 누가 워크웰을 창안했는가?
A 의사

미남 🎧

> **M** Thank you all for attending this press conference. We are excited to introduce Work-Well, a well-being program designed to help office workers minimize their stress through a series of targeted stretches. Dr. Aubrey Ramirez, a physician who is a leading expert in health and wellness, developed the program last year.

해석

남 이번 기자회견에 참석해 주신 여러분 모두에게 감사드립니다. 일련의 부분 스트레칭을 통해 사무직 근로자들이 스트레스를 최소화하는 것을 돕기 위해 고안된 웰빙 프로그램인 워크웰을 소개하게 되어 대단히 기쁩니다. 건강 분야의 선두적인 전문가인 내과 의사 오브리 라미레즈 박사가 작년에 이 프로그램을 개발했습니다.

어휘

create 만들어내다, 창안하다 medical 의학의
press conference 기자회견 well-being 행복, 안녕, 웰빙
minimize 최소화하다 a series of 일련의 targeted 목표가 된
physician 의사, 내과 의사 leading 선두적인, 가장 중요한
expert 전문가 wellness 건강(함)

패러프레이징

a physician → A medical doctor

5.

회기 동안 무엇이 논의될 것인가?
(A) 시의회 의원 선거
(B) 새로운 법에 대한 제안

미녀 🎧

> **W** During this session of the Bradford City Council, we will talk about a proposed local law that would lower the speed limit to 20 miles per hour in residential zones. Many residents have asked for a change to improve

the safety of their neighborhoods, especially for pedestrians.

해석

여 브래드포드 시의회의 이번 회기 동안, 우리는 주택가에서 속도 제한을 시속 20마일로 낮출 것을 제안하는 지방 법에 관해 이야기할 것입니다. 많은 주민들이 이웃 주민, 특히 보행자들의 안전을 개선하기 위해서 변경을 요청했습니다.

어휘

session (의회 등의) 회기 election 선거 city council 시의회
proposal 제안, 제의 proposed 제안된 lower 낮추다
speed limit 제한 속도 residential zone 주택 지대
resident 주민, 거주자 improve 개선하다, 향상하다
safety 안전 pedestrian 보행자

패러프레이징

a proposed local law → A proposal for a new law

6.

화자는 자신의 직업의 어떤 측면을 좋아하는가?
(A) 승진 기회
(B) 자신만의 프로젝트를 선택할 수 있음

미녀 🎧

> **W** I was ready for a career change, so I studied to become a chemical engineer specializing in scents. I'm currently working for a perfume company. What I really like about my job is the amount of freedom I've had to pursue the work projects I'm most interested in. It helps to keep me motivated and engaged.

해석

여 저는 다른 일을 할 준비가 되어 있었고, 그래서 향을 전문으로 하는 화학 공학 기술자가 되기 위해 공부했습니다. 저는 현재 향수 회사에서 일하고 있습니다. 제가 제 일에 대해 정말 좋아하는 점은 제가 가장 흥미를 가진 프로젝트를 수행할 수 있도록 제게 주어진 자유입니다. 그것이 계속하여 제게 동기부여가 되고 몰입하게 도와줍니다.

어휘

aspect 측면, 양상 job promotion 승진
ability (~을) 할 수 있음, 능력 career 직업, 경력
chemical 화학의 specialize in ~을 전문으로 하다 scent 향기
perfume 향수 amount (무엇의) 양
have freedom to ~할 자유가 있다 pursue 추구하다, 수행하다
motivated 동기부여가 되는 engaged 바쁜, 열심인

패러프레이징

freedom ~ to pursue the work projects
→ The ability to choose her own projects

1. (B)   **2.** (D)   **3.** (C)   **4.** (B)   **5.** (B)

[1] 호남 🎧

Question 1 refers to the following introduction.

> M Good morning, and welcome to this annual gathering. It's wonderful to see so many aviation engineers here to learn more about the field. Our keynote speaker will be Megan Frazier, an industry specialist who will be talking about communications technology. Ms. Frazier has been in the field for decades, and she started her own company a few years ago to develop new strategies for dealing with increasingly crowded airspace. After the talk, you will have the opportunity to ask questions.

해석

1번은 다음 소개에 관한 문제입니다.

남 안녕하세요, 이번 연례 모임에 오신 것을 환영합니다. **이 분야에 관해 더 많이 배우기 위해 이렇게 많은 항공 기술자들이 자리하신 것을 보니 기쁩니다.** 우리의 기조연설자는 메건 프레이저로, 통신 기술에 관해 얘기할 업계 전문가입니다. 프레이저 씨는 수십 년간 이 분야에 종사해 왔으며, 점점 더 붐비는 영공을 해결하기 위한 새로운 전략들을 개발하기 위해 몇 년 전에 자신의 사업을 시작했습니다. 담화 후에, 여러분이 질문할 기회가 있을 것입니다.

어휘

annual 연례의   gathering 모임
aviation engineer 항공 기술자   field 분야
keynote speaker 기조연설자   industry 산업, 업
specialist 전문가   communications technology 통신 기술
decade 10년   strategy 전략   deal with ~을 다루다, 처리하다
increasingly 점점 더   crowded 붐비는, 복잡한
airspace 영공

1.

청자들은 어떤 업계에서 일하는가?
(A) 보험
(B) 항공
(C) 의료
(D) 자동차

[2-3] 영녀 🎧

Questions 2-3 refer to the following instruction.

> W ²This is an instructional video to help you install your new NCY accounting program onto your computer. As the instructions play, you can click the pause button at any time. The installation process will take approximately

seven minutes, so please make sure you are available for the entire time. ³At the end of the process, you will be asked to restart your computer to complete the installation. Now, let's begin by double-clicking the blue start icon on top of your screen.

해석

2-3번은 다음 설명에 관한 문제입니다.

여 ²**이것은 여러분의 컴퓨터에 새로운 NCY 회계 프로그램을 설치하는 것을 돕는 교육용 영상입니다.** 설명이 재생되는 동안 언제라도 일시 정지 버튼을 클릭하실 수 있습니다. 설치 과정에는 대략 7분이 소요될 것이니 이 시간 내내 반드시 자리를 지키시기 바랍니다. ³**과정이 끝날 때, 설치를 완료하기 위해 컴퓨터를 재시작하라는 요청을 받게 될 것입니다.** 자, 화면 상단에 있는 파란색 아이콘을 더블클릭하는 것으로 시작하겠습니다.

어휘

instructional 교육의   install 설치하다   accounting 회계
instruction 설명, 지시   pause 멈춤, 정지 (버튼)
installation 설치   process 과정, 절차
approximately 대략, 거의   available for ~을 위한 시간이 있는
entire 전체의   restart 다시 시작하다
complete 완료하다, 끝마치다

2.

설명은 무엇을 위한 것인가?
(A) 영상을 편집하는 것
(B) 은행 계좌를 개설하는 것
(C) 보안 카메라를 사용하는 것
(D) 소프트웨어를 설치하는 것

어휘

edit 편집하다   account 계좌, 계정   security 보안, 경비

3.

청자들은 과정이 끝날 때 무엇을 하도록 요청받는가?
(A) 시작 아이콘 더블클릭하기
(B) 일시 정지 버튼 사용하기
(C) 컴퓨터 재시작하기
(D) 응용 프로그램 내려받기

어휘

application (= app) 응용 프로그램

[4-5] 호남 🎧

Questions 4-5 refer to the following talk.

> M I'd like to welcome you all to this appreciation dinner. ⁴The city holds the International Food Festival every year, and it would not be possible without volunteers like you. We want to thank you for your hard work and commitment. Please enjoy your meal and the live music. ⁵And don't forget to sign up for the

free raffle. There are a number of exciting prizes to be given away, and we will announce the winners at the end of the event. Have a wonderful evening!

해석

4-5번은 다음 담화에 관한 문제입니다.

남 이번 감사 만찬에 오신 여러분 모두를 환영합니다. **4**시는 매년 국제 음식 축제를 개최하고 있고, 이것은 여러분 같은 자원봉사자들 없이는 가능하지 않을 것입니다. 저희는 여러분의 노고와 헌신에 감사드리고자 합니다. 식사와 라이브 음악을 즐겨 주시길 바랍니다. **5**그리고 잊지 말고 무료 추첨에 신청하세요. 나눠 드릴 흥미로운 상품들이 많이 있으며, 행사가 끝날 때 당첨자를 발표할 것입니다. 멋진 저녁 보내세요!

어휘

appreciation 감사 hold (행사를) 개최하다, 열다
volunteer 자원봉사자; 자원봉사 하다 hard work 고된 일, 노력
commitment 헌신, 전념 raffle 제비뽑기, 복권 판매
give away ~을 선물로 주다 announce 발표하다, 알리다
winner 당첨자, 우승자

4.
청자들은 누구인 것 같은가?
(A) 직업 요리사
(B) 축제 자원봉사자
(C) 선출 공무원
(D) 입사 지원자

어휘

professional 직업의, 전문적인 elected 선출된
official 공무원, 관리 applicant 지원자, 신청자

5.
화자는 청자들에게 무엇에 관해 상기시키는가?
(A) 설문 조사 결과가 발표될 것이다.
(B) 경품 추첨 행사가 열릴 것이다.
(C) 특별한 초대 손님이 강연을 할 것이다.
(D) 식사를 미리 주문해야 한다.

어휘

survey (설문) 조사 prize drawing 경품 추첨
give a talk 강연하다 in advance 사전에, 미리

패러프레이징

the free raffle → A prize drawing

실전 문제
본문 p.274

1. (A)	**2.** (D)	**3.** (B)	**4.** (C)	**5.** (D)
6. (B)	**7.** (C)	**8.** (D)	**9.** (C)	**10.** (B)
11. (C)	**12.** (A)	**13.** (D)	**14.** (C)	**15.** (B)
16. (B)	**17.** (C)	**18.** (D)		

[1-3] 미녀 🎧
Questions 1-3 refer to the following talk.

> W I'd like to introduce myself. **1**I'm Linda Webster, the museum's head archivist. As I'm sure you're aware, **2**we need to regularly clean the artifacts in our collection to keep them in good condition. Today, this training session will teach you the proper way to do that so you don't cause any damage. It's important to be both gentle and thorough. Now, **3**as far as I know, you'll be working in small groups after the training, but you should speak with Adam. Now, let me just pass out the supplies.

해석

1-3번은 다음 담화에 관한 문제입니다.

여 제 소개를 하겠습니다. **1**저는 박물관의 자료 보관 책임자인 린다 웹스터입니다. 다들 아시다시피, **2**우리는 소장 중인 공예품들을 좋은 상태로 유지하기 위해서 정기적으로 세척해야 합니다. 오늘 이 교육 과정에서 여러분에게 그렇게 하는 적절한 방법을 가르쳐 드릴 텐데요, 여러분이 아무런 손상도 입히지 않도록 하기 위해서입니다. 조심스러움과 꼼꼼함 모두 중요합니다. 자, **3**제가 알기로는 교육 후에 여러분은 소그룹으로 작업하게 되는데요, 하지만 여러분은 애덤과 이야기해야 합니다. 이제, 용품들을 나눠 드리겠습니다.

어휘

head (단체·조직의) 책임자 archivist 기록 보관 담당자
aware (~을) 알고 있는 regularly 정기적으로 artifact 공예품
collection 수집품, 소장품
keep ~ in good condition ~을 좋은 상태로 유지하다
proper 적절한 damage 피해, 손상 gentle 온화한, 조심스러운
thorough 빈틈없는, 철저한 as far as ~하는 한

1.
청자들은 어디에서 일하는 것 같은가?
(A) 박물관에서
(B) 우체국에서
(C) 제과점에서
(D) 서점에서

2.
청자들은 오늘 무엇에 대해 배울 것인가?
(A) 안전 수칙
(B) 안내 책자 디자인
(C) 고객 불만
(D) 청소 기법

어휘

safety 안전 guideline 지침, 가이드라인
brochure 안내 책자, 브로슈어 complaint 항의, 불만
technique 기법, 기술

clean the artifacts ~ the proper way to do
→ Cleaning techniques

3.

화자는 "여러분은 애덤과 이야기해야 합니다"라고 말할 때 무엇을 암시하는가?
(A) 애덤에게 필요한 용품이 있다.
(B) 애덤이 그룹 과제를 확정할 것이다.
(C) 그녀는 일정상의 오류를 바로잡고 있다.
(D) 그녀는 애덤의 시연을 지켜볼 계획이다.

어휘

confirm 확인하다, 확정하다 assignment 과제, 임무
correct 고치다, 바로잡다

[4-6] 호남 🎧

Questions 4-6 refer to the following talk.

M In today's workshop, you'll learn how to improve communication in the workplace. ⁴We'll have three speakers here today, and we'd like to get your feedback at the end of the workshop. Any suggestions or comments are welcome and will be very helpful for us in organizing our next event. ⁵You'll be receiving an evaluation form by e-mail later today. Please complete it and return it to us. ⁶Don't worry, your name, contact information, and comments will be confidential and will not be used for any other purpose other than our survey. We are looking forward to your responses and thank you again for coming to this workshop.

해석

4-6번은 다음 담화에 관한 문제입니다.

남 오늘 워크숍에서, 여러분은 직장에서 의사소통을 개선하는 방법을 배우게 됩니다. ⁴**오늘 세 분의 연사를 모실 것이고, 워크숍이 끝날 때 여러분의 의견을 받고자 합니다.** 어떤 제안이나 의견이든 환영하며 저희가 다음 행사를 준비하는 데 매우 도움이 될 것입니다. ⁵**여러분은 오늘 나중에 이메일로 평가서를 받게 되실 겁니다.** 작성하셔서 저희에게 돌려주시기 바랍니다. ⁶**걱정하지 마세요, 여러분의 이름, 연락처, 의견은 기밀이고 설문 조사 이외의** 다른 목적으로는 사용되지 않을 것입니다. 여러분의 응답을 기대하며 다시 한번 이번 워크숍에 와 주셔서 감사드립니다.

어휘

improve 개선하다, 향상하다 communication 의사소통, 통신
workplace 직장, 업무 현장 comment 의견, 논평
organize 조직하다, 준비하다 evaluation form 평가서
complete 작성하다, 기입하다 contact information 연락처
confidential 비밀의, 기밀의 purpose 목적
look forward to ~을 기대하다 response 응답, 회신

4.

담화의 목적은 무엇인가?
(A) 워크숍을 취소하기 위해
(B) 직원에게 경의를 표하기 위해
(C) 의견을 모으기 위해
(D) 신제품을 출시하기 위해

어휘

honor 경의를 표하다, 명예를 주다 gather 모으다, 모이다
launch 출시하다, 시작하다

패러프레이징

get your feedback → gather feedback

5.

청자들은 오늘 나중에 무엇을 받을 것인가?
(A) 행사 기념품
(B) 업무 보고
(C) 계약서
(D) 설문 조사서

어휘

souvenir 기념품, 선물

패러프레이징

an evaluation form → A survey form

6.

화자는 무엇에 대해 청자들을 안심시키는가?
(A) 그들은 다음 행사에 참석할 수 있다.
(B) 그들의 정보는 공개되지 않을 것이다.
(C) 그들의 일정은 변경되지 않을 것이다.
(D) 그들은 발표를 기록할 수 있다.

어휘

reassure 안심시키다 reveal 밝히다, 드러내다

패러프레이징

your name, contact information, and comments will be confidential
→ Their information will not be revealed

[7-9] 미남 🎧

Questions 7-9 refer to the following talk.

M Thank you all for attending this press conference. ⁷My name is Isaac Beckman, and I'm the head of the city's Parks and Recreation Department. ⁸I'm happy to announce that funding has been approved to add more trails to the city's bicycle path. Most of the changes will be in the northern part of the city. Construction will start next month and will take approximately three months. ⁹After this project is finished, we hope that more people will be motivated to use the path to work out more. This is essential for good health.

해석

7-9번은 다음 담화에 관한 문제입니다.

남 이번 기자회견에 참석해 주신 모든 분들께 감사드립니다. **⁷제 이름은 아이작 베크먼이고, 시의 공원 및 위락 시설 관리국의 책임자입니다.** **⁸시의 자전거 도로에 코스를 더 많이 추가하기 위한 자금이 승인되었다는 것을 알려 드리게 되어서 기쁩니다.** 대부분의 변화는 시의 북쪽 부분에서 이루어질 것입니다. 공사는 다음 달에 시작되어 대략 3개월이 소요될 것입니다. **⁹이 프로젝트가 완료되고 나면, 더 많은 사람들이 자전거 도로를 이용해 더 많이 운동하도록 동기부여가 되기를 바랍니다.** 이것은 좋은 건강에 꼭 필요한 것입니다.

어휘

press conference 기자회견
recreation 휴양, 레크리에이션, 기분 전환 funding 자금
approve 승인하다 trail 코스, 산길 bicycle path 자전거 도로
construction 공사, 건설 approximately 대략, 거의
motivate to ~하도록 동기를 유발하다 work out 운동하다
essential 필수적인, 극히 중요한

7.

화자는 누구인가?
(A) 운동 강사
(B) 안전 조사관
(C) 정부 공무원
(D) 건축 설계사

어휘

instructor 강사, 교사 inspector 조사관 government 정부
official 공무원, 관리

패러프레이징

the head of the city's Parks and Recreation
Department → A government official

8.

담화는 주로 무엇에 관한 것인가?
(A) 야외 축제를 위한 장소
(B) 경기장의 건설
(C) 일부 공공 재산의 판매
(D) 자전거 도로 확장

어휘

venue (행사의) 장소 stadium 경기장, 스타디움
property 재산, 부동산 expansion 확대, 확장 path 길, 도로

패러프레이징

add more trails to the city's bicycle path
→ The expansion of a bicycle path

9.

화자에 따르면, 프로젝트의 목적은 무엇인가?
(A) 세수를 창출하기 위해
(B) 교통량을 줄이기 위해
(C) 사람들이 운동하도록 장려하기 위해
(D) 이 지역에 관광객들을 유치하기 위해

어휘

generate 발생시키다, 만들어 내다 revenue 수익, 수입
exercise 운동하다; 운동 attract 끌어모으다

패러프레이징

more people will be motivated to use the path to
work out more → encourage people to exercise

[10-12] 영녀 🎧

Questions 10-12 refer to the following introduction.

W Attention, please. Before we end this staff meeting, I want to introduce our new translator, Lino Wilder. **¹⁰He will be working full time with our chief editor, John Cooper.** **¹¹He majored in German Literature and lived overseas in Germany for five years**, working at Die Zeit. After returning home, he specialized in Social Media Literature at Olsen University. **¹⁰Now he's here to help us with his extraordinary expertise in the European book market.** Please make him feel welcome. One more thing, **¹²our next meeting will be next Thursday, not Friday, due to the Internet cable replacement work that's scheduled that day**, which is why we need to leave the office before three next Friday.

해석

10-12번은 다음 소개에 관한 문제입니다.

여 주목해 주시기 바랍니다. 이번 직원 회의를 마치기 전에, 우리의 새 번역가인 리노 와일더를 소개하고자 합니다. **¹⁰그는 우리 편집장 존 쿠퍼와 정규직으로 근무할 것입니다.** **¹¹그는 독문학을 전공했으며 5년간 독일에서 해외 거주했고, 디 차이트에서 근무했습니다.** 귀국한 후에는, 올센 대학교에서 소셜미디어 문학을 전공했습니다. **¹⁰이제 그는 이곳에서 유럽 도서 시장에 대한 놀랄 만한 전문 지식으로 우리를 도울 것입니다.** 그를 환영해 주시기 바랍니다. 한 가지 더 말씀드리면, **¹²다음 회의는 금요일이 아니라 목요일이 될 것인데요, 그날 예정되어 있는 인터넷 케이블 교체 작업 때문이며, 이로 인해 우리는 다음 주 금요일에 3시 이전에 퇴근해야 합니다.**

어휘

translator 번역가, 통역사 work full time 전임으로 일하다
chief editor 편집장 major in ~을 전공하다 literature 문학
overseas 해외에; 해외의
specialize in ~을 전문으로 하다, 전공하다
extraordinary 비범한, 대단한 expertise 전문 지식
make ~ feel welcome ~를 환영하다
replacement 교체, 대체 scheduled 예정된

10.

화자는 어디에서 일하는 것 같은가?
(A) 대학교에서
(B) 출판사에서

(C) 인터넷 서비스 공급업체에서
(D) 인테리어 디자인 회사에서

어휘

provider 공급자

11.

화자는 와일더 씨에 대해 무엇이라고 말하는가?
(A) 그는 발표를 할 것이다.
(B) 그는 쿠퍼 씨를 대신할 것이다.
(C) 그는 해외에서 살았다.
(D) 그는 상을 받았다.

어휘

replace 대신하다, 대체하다   win an award 상을 타다

패러프레이징

overseas → abroad

12.

다음 주 금요일에 무슨 일이 일어날 것인가?
(A) 정비 작업
(B) 교육
(C) 직원 회의
(D) 환영 파티

어휘

maintenance 유지, 보수, 정비

패러프레이징

the Internet cable replacement work
→ Some maintenance work

[13-15] 호남 🎧

Questions 13-15 refer to the following introduction.

> M Good evening, everyone. ¹³It is my pleasure to present the Innovation Award to Heather Flynn. Congratulations! It is well deserved. Heather and her team did a great job developing plastic-free packaging for our folders. ¹⁴This is especially important because young professionals these days want to reduce their environmental impact. While Ms. Flynn comes forward, I'd like to let you all know that, going forward, the management team wants to hear from you about these awards. ¹⁵You can nominate one of your coworkers by e-mailing the head of HR. We hope you'll all consider doing so.

해석

13-15번은 다음 소개에 관한 문제입니다.

남 안녕하세요, 여러분. ¹³헤더 플린에게 혁신상을 수여하게 되어 기쁩니다. 축하합니다! 충분히 받을 만합니다. 헤더와 그녀의 팀은 우리 서류 폴더를 위해 플라스틱이 없는 포장재를 개발하는 일을 훌륭하게 해냈습니다. ¹⁴요즘 젊은 전문직 종사자들은 환경

에 미치는 영향을 줄이고 싶어 하기 때문에 이것은 특히 중요합니다. 플린 씨가 앞으로 나오는 동안, 여러분 모두에게 앞으로 관리팀은 이 상에 관해 여러분의 의견을 듣고자 한다는 것을 알려 드리고 싶습니다. ¹⁵여러분은 인사부장에게 이메일을 보내서 동료들 중 한 명을 후보로 추천할 수 있습니다. 여러분 모두 그렇게 하는 것을 고려해 주시기 바랍니다.

어휘

innovation 혁신   well deserved 충분한 자격이 있는
plastic-free 플라스틱이 없는   packaging 포장재, 포장
folder 서류철, 폴더   especially 특히
professional 전문직 종사자; 전문적인
environmental impact 환경에 미치는 영향
come forward 앞으로 나오다   going forward 앞으로(의)
management 경영, 관리   nominate (후보자로) 지명하다
consider -ing ~하는 것을 고려하다

13.

화자는 어디에 있는가?
(A) 개장식에
(B) 집단 면접에
(C) 무역 박람회에
(D) 시상식에

14.

화자는 젊은 전문직 종사자들에 대해 무엇이라고 말하는가?
(A) 그들은 과학 기술 장치에 능숙하다.
(B) 그들은 자기 사업을 시작하고 싶어 한다.
(C) 그들은 환경에 대해 우려한다.
(D) 그들은 충분한 경험을 갖고 있지 않다.

어휘

be skilled with ~에 능숙하다   technical 과학 기술의
device 장치, 기구   be concerned about ~을 걱정하다
environment 환경

패러프레이징

want to reduce their environmental impact
→ concerned about the environment

15.

화자에 따르면, 직원들은 이제 무엇을 할 수 있을 것인가?
(A) 이메일 백업하기
(B) 후보 추천서 제출하기
(C) 재택근무 하기
(D) 새로 계좌 만들기

어휘

nomination 지명, 추천   account 계좌, 계정

패러프레이징

nominate one of your coworkers
→ Submit nominations

Questions 16-18 refer to the following talk and prop designs.

> W Good afternoon. I'm here to talk about the props in the film *Shining River*. ¹⁶This was a particularly exciting project for me because my friend, Daniel Troy, wrote the script. As a leading expert in antiques, I gathered the film's props. ¹⁷In fact, the mirror in the main character's bedroom came from my home! In addition, I made some of the props myself. ¹⁸Let me show you some before and after photos. Afterward, you can see a clip from the film.

해석

16-18번은 다음 담화와 소품 디자인에 관한 문제입니다.

여 안녕하세요. 영화 〈반짝이는 강물〉의 소품에 관해 얘기하려고 왔습니다. ¹⁶제 친구 대니얼 트로이가 대본을 썼기 때문에 이것은 저에게 특히 흥미로운 프로젝트였습니다. 손꼽히는 골동품 전문가로서, 제가 이 영화의 소품들을 골라 모았습니다. ¹⁷실은 주인공의 침실 거울은 저희 집에서 가져온 것이었습니다! 또한, 일부 소품들은 제가 직접 만들었습니다. ¹⁸제가 전후 사진을 몇 장 보여 드리겠습니다. 그 후에, 여러분은 영화 속 한 장면을 보실 수 있습니다.

어휘

prop (연극·영화에 쓰이는) 소품 particularly 특히, 특별히 script 대본 leading 가장 중요한, 선두적인 expert 전문가 antique 골동품 gather 모으다, 챙기다 character 등장인물 afterward 후에, 나중에

16.

영화는 왜 화자에게 특별했는가?
(A) 그것의 예산이 매우 컸다.
(B) 그것의 대본이 친구에 의해 쓰였다.
(C) 그것은 흥미로운 장소에서 촬영되었다.
(D) 그것에 유명한 배우가 출연했다.

어휘

budget 예산 location 장소, 위치 star 주연을 맡다

패러프레이징

my friend ~ wrote the script
→ Its script was written by a friend

17.

시각 자료를 보시오. 화자는 어떤 물품을 언급하는가?
(A) 물품 1
(B) 물품 2
(C) 물품 3
(D) 물품 4

18.

화자는 다음에 무엇을 할 것 같은가?
(A) 인쇄물 나눠 주기
(B) 질문에 답하기
(C) 동료 소개하기
(D) 이미지 보여 주기

어휘

distribute 나누어 주다, 배부하다 handout 인쇄물, 유인물

패러프레이징

before and after photos → images

UNIT 13 광고

> **CHECK UP** 본문 p.276
>
> **1.** (A) **2.** (D) **3.** (C)

Questions 1-3 refer to the following advertisement.

> M Do you want to improve your business skills? ¹The Edison Business Institute will run a new course about giving effective presentations. No matter what field you work in, being able to communicate effectively will always be useful. ²And our classes are unique because, at the end of the course, you can give your final presentation to a panel of specialists and hear their comments on how to improve. ³If you're interested in finding out more, complete an information request form on our Web site.

해석

1-3번은 다음 광고에 관한 문제입니다.

남 당신의 업무 능력을 향상시키고 싶으신가요? ¹에디슨 비즈니스 협회는 효과적인 발표를 하는 것에 관한 새로운 과정을 운영할 것입니다. 당신이 어떤 분야에서 일하든지, 효과적으로 의사소통

하는 능력은 언제나 유용할 것입니다. ² 그리고 저희 수업의 독특한 점은 과정이 끝날 때 전문가단에게 최종 발표를 하고 개선 방법에 관한 그들의 의견을 들을 수 있다는 것입니다. ³ 더 많이 알고 싶으시면, 저희 웹사이트에서 정보 문의 신청 양식을 작성하세요.

어휘

improve 개선하다, 향상시키다 skill 기술, 능력
institute 기관, 협회 run 운영하다 effective 효과적인
no matter what 비록 무엇이 ~한다 하더라도 field 분야
communicate 의사소통을 하다 unique 독특한
panel (공개 토론회의) 패널, 전문 위원회 specialist 전문가
comment 논평, 의견

1.

어떤 종류의 수업이 광고되고 있는가?
(A) 발표
(B) 업무용 글쓰기
(C) 회계
(D) 컴퓨터 프로그래밍

2.

화자에 따르면, 수업들은 왜 독특한가?
(A) 수업료가 비슷한 과정들보다 저렴하다.
(B) 마지막에 자격증이 발급될 것이다.
(C) 그것들은 대면으로도, 온라인으로도 이용할 수 있다.
(D) 그것들은 전문가들의 의견을 포함한다.

어휘

fee 수수료, 요금 certificate 증명서, 자격증
issue 발부하다 in person 직접 expert 전문가

패러프레이징

a panel of specialists ~ their comments on how to
improve → feedback from experts

3.

청자들은 어떻게 추가 정보를 얻을 수 있는가?
(A) 행사에 참석함으로써
(B) 이메일을 보냄으로써
(C) 웹사이트에 방문함으로써
(D) 기관에 전화함으로써

패러프레이징

complete an information request form on our Web
site → visiting a Web site

패러프레이징 연습 본문 p.278

1-4. 스크립트 참조 **5.** (A) **6.** (A)

1.

Q 광고는 무엇에 관한 것인가?
A 스포츠 음료

미녀 🎧

W Do you work out regularly? Then you need a way to keep your body hydrated and fueled. Fire-Flex is a new line of performance beverages that will surely quench your thirst when you're working out. They also deliver a targeted combination of vitamins to nourish your muscles and reduce fatigue.

해석

여 규칙적으로 운동하시나요? 그렇다면 신체에 수분과 열량을 꾸준히 공급할 방법이 필요합니다. 파이어플렉스는 운동할 때 확실하게 갈증을 해소해 줄 신제품 기능성 음료입니다. 이것은 또한 근육에 영양분을 공급하고 피로를 줄여 주기 위해 선별하고 조합한 비타민들을 몸에 전달합니다.

어휘

regularly 규칙적으로, 정기적으로 hydrate 수분을 공급하다
fuel 연료를 공급하다 line (상품의) 종류
performance 실행, 수행 beverage 음료
surely 확실히, 분명히 quench (갈증을) 풀다 thirst 갈증
targeted 목표 대상으로 하는, 겨냥하는 combination 조합
nourish 영양분을 공급하다 fatigue 피로

패러프레이징

performance beverages → A sports drink

2.

Q 신규 고객들에게 무엇이 제공되고 있는가?
A 무료 상담

미남 🎧

M It's time to start planning for your future with help from Vernon Investments. If you've never used our services before, sign up today to get a complimentary consultation with one of our investment advisors.

해석

남 버논 투자사의 도움을 받아 여러분의 미래를 계획하기 시작할 때입니다. 전에 저희 서비스를 전혀 이용해 보신 적이 없다면, 오늘 신청하시고 저희 투자 자문가들 중 한 명과 무료 상담을 받으세요.

어휘

consultation 상담 it's time to ~할 시간이다
investment 투자 complimentary 무료의
advisor (= adviser) 고문, 조언자

패러프레이징

complimentary → free

3.

Q 청자들은 어떻게 무료 선물을 받을 수 있는가?
A 계정을 등록함으로써

> **W** We're pleased to introduce our new loyalty program where you can earn points on every purchase at Tino's Department Store. Anyone who registers for a customer account with our store will receive a free tote bag with the Tino's logo. More information is available at our customer service desk.

해석

여 티노 백화점에서 구매할 때마다 포인트를 적립할 수 있는 저희의 새로운 고객 보상 프로그램을 소개하게 되어 기쁩니다. **저희 매장에 고객 계정을 등록하는 분은 누구나 티노의 로고가 있는 무료 토트백을 받으실 겁니다.** 더 많은 정보는 저희 고객 서비스 창구에서 이용하실 수 있습니다.

어휘

account 계정, 계좌 loyalty program 고객 보상 프로그램
earn 얻다, (돈을) 벌다 purchase 구매; 구매하다
register for ~에 등록하다 available 이용할 수 있는

패러프레이징

registers for → signing up for

4.

Q 고객들은 4월 30일 이전에 구매하면 무엇을 받을 수 있는가?
A 교육

> **M** Our photo editing software will help to make all of your projects look as if they were created by a professional. And, if you purchase the software before April 30th, we'll give you a free instructional session. This will help you to become familiar with all of the features.

해석

남 저희 사진 편집 소프트웨어는 여러분의 모든 프로젝트가 마치 전문가에 의해 만들어진 것처럼 보이게 하도록 도와줄 것입니다. **그리고, 4월 30일 이전에 소프트웨어를 구매하시면 무료로 교육 세션을 제공해 드립니다.** 이것은 여러분이 모든 기능에 익숙해지도록 도와줄 것입니다.

어휘

make a purchase 구매하다 training 교육, 훈련
editing 편집 professional 전문가; 전문적인
instructional 교육용의
become familiar with ~에 익숙해지다 feature 기능, 특징

패러프레이징

instructional session → training

5.

화자에 따르면, 업체는 최근에 무엇을 했는가?
(A) 그곳은 보수 공사를 마쳤다.

(B) 그곳은 주방장을 새로 고용했다.

> **W** Enjoy authentic Italian food made with fresh ingredients at Valentina's. We offer a wide range of pasta dishes and pizza. And we've just finished remodeling the dining area. It now has additional seating and plenty of space for large groups. We hope to see you at Valentina's soon.

해석

여 발렌티나스에서 신선한 재료로 만든 정통 이탈리아 음식을 즐기세요. 저희는 다양한 종류의 파스타 요리와 피자를 제공합니다. **그리고 저희가 막 식사 공간 리모델링을 마쳤습니다.** 이제 좌석이 추가되었으며 대규모 단체 손님들을 위한 충분한 공간이 있습니다. 발렌티나스에서 곧 뵙기를 바랍니다.

어휘

complete 완료하다, 마치다 renovation 수리, 보수, 혁신
authentic 진짜의, 진정한 ingredient 재료
a wide range of 다양한, 광범위한
remodeling 주택 개보수, 리모델링 dining area 식사 공간
additional 추가의 seating 좌석, 자리 plenty of 많은

패러프레이징

finished remodeling the dining area
→ completed a renovation project

6.

화자는 청자들에게 무엇을 하라고 권장하는가?
(A) 미리 주문하기
(B) 평가 남기기

> **M** If you're a music lover, you'll love the Briscoe noise-canceling headphones. They are specially designed to be comfortable as well as providing the best audio quality on the market. So, preorder these amazing headphones and take your music to the next level. Visit www.briscoe.com.

해석

남 음악 애호가시라면, 브리스코 소음 차단 헤드폰을 정말 마음에 들어 하실 겁니다. 시중에서 가장 좋은 음질을 제공할 뿐만 아니라 특별히 편안하게 디자인되었습니다. 따라서, **이 놀라운 헤드폰을 선주문하시고 당신의 음악 수준을 한 차원 높여 보세요.** www.briscoe.com을 방문하세요.

어휘

in advance 미리, 사전에 review 평가, 검토
noise-canceling 소음을 차단하는 quality 품질, 질
on the market 시장에 나와 있는 preorder 선주문하다

preorder → Order in advance

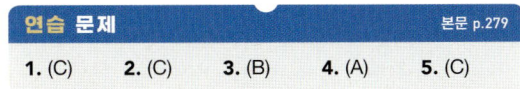

[1] 미녀 🎧
Question 1 refers to the following advertisement.

> **W** If you're having trouble getting motivated about going to work every day, it might be time for a change. At Utica Automotive Company, you can have an exciting as well as lucrative career in car sales. You'll get to meet lots of people while working in a supportive environment. We're currently hiring people with great communication skills, even those who are not experienced in sales. To find out more, call us anytime from 8 A.M. to 6 P.M. at 555-1212.

해석
1번은 다음 광고에 관한 문제입니다.
여 매일 출근할 의욕을 다지기가 힘들다면, 변화가 필요한 때일지도 모릅니다. 유티카 자동차 회사에서, 여러분은 자동차 영업 분야에서 재미도 있고 수익도 높은 일을 할 수 있습니다. 지원을 아끼지 않는 환경에서 근무하면서 많은 사람들을 만나게 될 것입니다. 저희는 현재 뛰어난 의사소통 능력을 지닌 사람들, 심지어 판매 경험이 없는 분들도 채용하고 있습니다. 더 많이 알고 싶으시면, 오전 8시부터 저녁 6시까지 555-1212로 언제든 전화 주세요.

어휘
have trouble -ing ~하느라 힘들다
get motivated 동기를 부여받다, 의욕을 가지다
automotive 자동차의 lucrative 수익성이 좋은
supportive 지원하는, 도와주는 environment 환경
currently 현재, 지금 communication skill 의사소통 기술
experienced 경험이 있는, 능숙한

1.
청자들은 어떻게 더 많은 정보를 얻을 수 있는가?
(A) 웹사이트를 방문함으로써
(B) 관리자에게 이메일을 보냄으로써
(C) 회사에 전화함으로써
(D) 영상을 시청함으로써

[2-3] 미남 🎧
Questions 2-3 refer to the following advertisement.

> **M** In today's fast-paced world, no one can afford to lag behind. ²That's why Rapid Express offers the fastest parcel service on the market today. We will deliver packages 15 percent faster than any other company working today. We guarantee that all international packages will be delivered within 48 hours and all domestic packages within 24 hours. ³Contact us now to see how affordable our services can be for your specific package. Call us at 555-0147. We'll save you time and help you deliver results.

해석
2-3번은 다음 광고에 관한 문제입니다.
남 오늘날의 빠르게 돌아가는 세상에서는, 아무도 뒤처질 여유가 없습니다. ²그것이 래피드 익스프레스가 현재 시중에서 가장 빠른 택배 서비스를 제공하는 이유입니다. 저희는 현재 영업 중인 어떤 다른 회사보다 15% 더 빨리 소포가 도착하도록 할 것입니다. 모든 국제 소포는 48시간 이내에 배송되고, 모든 국내 소포는 24시간 이내에 배송될 것을 보장합니다. ³지금 저희에게 연락하셔서 특정 소포에 대해 저희 서비스가 얼마나 저렴할 수 있는지 확인해 보세요. 555-0147로 전화 주세요. 여러분의 시간을 절약해 드리고, 결과물이 전달되도록 돕겠습니다.

어휘
fast-paced 빠르게 진행되는 afford to ~할 여유가 있다
lag behind 뒤처지다 parcel 소포, 꾸러미
package 소포, 포장물 guarantee 보장하다; 보장
international 국제적인 domestic 국내의
affordable (가격이) 알맞은 specific 구체적인, 특정한

2.
무엇이 광고되고 있는가?
(A) 리모델링 회사
(B) 마케팅 회사
(C) 배송 회사
(D) 인스턴트 메신저 서비스

패러프레이징
offers the fastest parcel service
→ A delivery company

3.
화자에 따르면, 청자들은 왜 이 업체에 연락해야 하는가?
(A) 할인을 요청하기 위해
(B) 가격을 확인하기 위해
(C) 계좌를 개설하기 위해
(D) 입사 지원을 하기 위해

패러프레이징
see how affordable our services can be
→ check a price

[4-5] 미녀 🎧
Questions 4-5 refer to the following advertisement.

W 4Brooklyn Botanical Garden is proud to announce the 35th anniversary of our Spring and Sunshine Festival. This weekend, we will offer over 60 events celebrating the gorgeous trees and the return of spring. The two-day festival will begin next Saturday, the 30th of April. Bring your whole family. In fact, 5you can download a special discount coupon from our Web site. It will give your whole family, up to two adults and two children, admission to the gardens for the price of two adult tickets. Come celebrate spring with Brooklyn Botanical Gardens.

해석
4-5번은 다음 광고에 관한 문제입니다.

여 4브루클린 식물원은 저희 봄 햇살 축제의 35주년 기념일을 알려 드리게 되어 영광입니다. 이번 주말, 저희는 아주 멋진 나무들과 봄의 도래를 축하하는 60개 이상의 행사를 제공할 것입니다. 이틀간의 축제는 4월 30일, 다음 주 토요일에 시작될 것입니다. 온 가족을 모시고 오세요. 실은, 5저희 웹사이트에서 특별 할인 쿠폰을 다운로드하실 수 있습니다. 그것은 성인 2명의 티켓 가격으로 성인 2명과 어린이 2명까지를 포함하는 여러분의 가족 모두가 식물원에 입장하게 해 드릴 것입니다. 브루클린 식물원과 함께 봄을 축하하러 오세요.

어휘
botanical garden 식물원 anniversary 기념일
celebrate 축하하다, 기념하다 gorgeous 아주 멋진, 아름다운
up to ~까지 admission 입장, 입학

4.
어떤 종류의 행사가 광고되고 있는가?
(A) 연례 축제
(B) 대형 식물 판매
(C) 놀이공원 개장
(D) 원예용품 박람회

어휘
amusement park 놀이공원 gardening supply 원예용품
exposition 전시회, 박람회

패러프레이징
the 35th anniversary of our Spring and Sunshine Festival → An annual festival

5.
화자에 따르면, 웹사이트에서 무엇을 이용할 수 있는가?
(A) 운영시간
(B) 행사 목록
(C) 할인권
(D) 행사 장소

어휘
voucher 상품권, 할인권, 쿠폰

패러프레이징
a special discount coupon → A discount voucher

실전 문제   본문 p.280

1. (B)	2. (C)	3. (B)	4. (B)	5. (A)
6. (C)	7. (B)	8. (A)	9. (D)	10. (A)
11. (C)	12. (D)	13. (D)	14. (B)	15. (A)
16. (D)	17. (B)	18. (A)		

[1-3] 미남 🎧
Questions 1-3 refer to the following advertisement.

M Do you need to cut growing business costs? Travel is becoming more and more expensive. 1That's why you should try Keyser, the videoconferencing software that keeps you connected with your clients without visiting them face to face. 2Similar programs have complicated sign-in processes and require you to read a long manual. Not Keyser. Scheduling and accessing meetings only take a few seconds. Why not give Keyser a try? 3You can use it at no cost throughout the month of January to see if you like it. Find out more at www.keyseroffer.com.

해석
1-3번은 다음 광고에 관한 문제입니다.

남 증가하는 업무 비용을 줄여야 하나요? 이동하는 데는 점점 더 많은 비용이 듭니다. 1그래서 대면 방문 없이도 여러분을 고객들과 연결해 주는 화상 회의 소프트웨어인 카이저를 이용해 보셔야 하는 것입니다. 2비슷한 프로그램들은 가입 절차가 복잡하고, 긴 설명서를 읽어야 합니다. 카이저는 그렇지 않습니다. 일정을 잡고 회의에 참석하는 데 겨우 몇 초 걸릴 뿐입니다. 카이저를 이용해 보는 게 어떻습니까? 3마음에 드실지 알아볼 수 있도록 1월 내내 무료로 이용하실 수 있습니다. www.keyseroffer.com에서 더 알아보세요.

어휘
cut cost 비용을 줄이다 expensive 비싼, 돈이 많이 드는
videoconferencing 화상 회의
face to face 서로 얼굴을 맞대고 similar 비슷한
complicated 복잡한 sign-in 서명, 가입, 참가 신청
require 요구하다, 필요하다 manual 설명서
access 접근하다, 들어가다 give a try 한번 해 보다
at no cost 무료로

1.
무엇이 광고되고 있는가?
(A) 사무실 보안 시스템
(B) 화상 회의 소프트웨어 프로그램
(C) 인터넷 서비스 공급업체

(D) 새로운 버전의 스마트폰

어휘

security 보안, 경비 videoconference 화상 회의

2.

화자는 제품의 어떤 이점을 언급하는가?
(A) 그것은 저렴하다.
(B) 그것은 많은 기능이 있다.
(C) 그것은 사용하기 쉽다.
(D) 그것은 품질 보증이 된다.

어휘

benefit 이익, 혜택 affordable (가격이) 알맞은
feature 특징, 기능 guarantee 품질 보증서, 보장

3.

화자에 따르면, 청자들은 1월에 무엇을 할 수 있는가?
(A) 대리인이 방문하게 하기
(B) 무료로 제품 사용해 보기
(C) 경품 추첨 행사에 응모하기
(D) 시연 보기

어휘

representative 대표, 대리인 prize drawing 경품 추첨
demonstration 시범 설명, 시연

패러프레이징

use it at no cost → Try a product for free

[4-6] 영녀 🎧

Questions 4-6 refer to the following advertisement.

> **W** It's time for a unique experience during your next visit to Elmhurst! Sign up for a guided tour at Hickman Pottery Factory. You'll learn all the steps of the pottery-making process. ⁴And at the end of the tour, you can even paint your own vase, which you can take home. ⁵We also recommend stopping by the gift shop to purchase beautiful plates at wholesale prices. ⁶And don't forget to wear comfortable shoes, as the tour includes a lot of walking. Tours are offered daily. We hope to see you soon!

해석

4-6번은 다음 광고에 관한 문제입니다.

여 다음번에 엘름허스트를 방문할 때는 독특한 경험을 위한 시간을 가져 보세요! 히크먼 도자기 공장의 가이드가 안내하는 견학을 신청하세요. 도자기 제조 과정의 모든 단계에 대해서 알게 되실 겁니다. ⁴그리고 견학 마지막에는 자신의 화병에 그림도 그릴 수 있는데, 그것을 집에 가져가셔도 됩니다. ⁵저희는 또한 기념품 가게에 들르셔서 도매가격으로 아름다운 접시들을 구매하실 것을 추천합니다. ⁶그리고 편한 신발을 신는 것을 잊지 마세요, 견학하면서 많이 걷게 되기 때문입니다. 견학은 매일 제공됩니다. 곧 뵙기를 바랍니다!

unique 독특한, 특별한 guided tour 가이드가 딸린 여행
pottery 도자기류 stop by ~에 들르다
wholesale 도매의, 대량의 comfortable 편안한
include ~을 포함하다

4.

공장 견학은 어떻게 끝나는가?
(A) 카탈로그들이 배포된다.
(B) 참가자들이 물건에 그림을 그린다.
(C) 단체 사진을 찍는다.
(D) 직원들이 질문에 응답한다.

어휘

distribute 나눠 주다, 배부하다 participant 참가자
respond to ~에 대응하다

패러프레이징

paint your own vase → paint an item

5.

화자에 따르면, 기념품 가게에서 무엇이 판매되는가?
(A) 접시
(B) 간식
(C) 지도
(D) 옷

패러프레이징

beautiful plates → Dishes

6.

화자는 청자들에게 무엇에 관해 상기시키는가?
(A) 누구에게 연락할지
(B) 언제 장소가 문을 닫는지
(C) 어떤 신발을 이용할지
(D) 어디에 소지품을 두고 갈지

어휘

footwear 신발류 belongings ((항상 복수형)) 재산, 소유물

패러프레이징

shoes → footwear

[7-9] 미녀 🎧

Questions 7-9 refer to the following advertisement.

> **W** ⁷If you're tired of having your food cooked unevenly, it's time to get a new microwave! ⁸The R-60 microwave from Quarry Electronics uses less energy than other appliances of its kind. So, you can rest assured that you're doing your part to help the environment. ⁹There are numerous settings on this device, so why not stop by our display at any Quarry Electronics store to check out all the features? You can't miss it.

해석

7-9번은 다음 광고에 관한 문제입니다.

여 **7**음식이 고르게 익지 않아 진절머리가 난다면, 전자레인지를 새로 구매할 때입니다! **8**쿼리 전자의 R-60 전자레인지는 같은 종류의 다른 전자제품들보다 에너지를 덜 사용합니다. 따라서, 환경을 돕기 위한 당신의 역할을 다하게 될 테니 안심하세요. **9**이 기기에는 여러 가지 설정이 있으므로 아무 쿼리 전자 매장의 저희 진열대에 들르셔서 모든 특징들을 확인해 보시는 게 어떨까요? 그것은 그냥 지나칠 수 없을 겁니다.

어휘

be tired of ~하는 데 넌더리 나다 unevenly 고르지 않게
microwave 전자레인지 electronics ((항상 복수형)) 전자 기기
appliance (가정용) 기기
you can rest assured (that) ~이니 안심해도 좋다
do one's part ~의 자신의 몫을 다하다 environment 환경
device 장치, 기구 stop by ~에 들르다
display 전시, 진열, 진열품 feature 특색, 특징

7.

어떤 종류의 제품이 광고되고 있는가?
(A) 믹서기
(B) 전자레인지
(C) 커피 기계
(D) 냉장고

8.

화자는 R-60의 어떤 특징을 강조하는가?
(A) 그것은 에너지 효율이 좋다.
(B) 그것은 가격이 저렴하다.
(C) 그것은 소형이다.
(D) 그것은 내구성이 좋다.

어휘

highlight 강조하다 energy efficient 에너지 효율이 좋은
affordable (가격 등이) 알맞은, 감당할 수 있는
compact 소형의, 간편한 durable 내구성이 있는, 오래가는

패러프레이징

uses less energy than other appliances
→ energy efficient

9.

화자는 "그것은 그냥 지나칠 수 없을 겁니다"라고 말할 때 무엇을 암시하는가?
(A) 청자들이 주의해야 한다.
(B) 참석이 의무이다.
(C) 특별 할인이 곧 끝난다.
(D) 전시품을 찾기 쉽다.

어휘

attendance 출석, 참석 mandatory 의무적인
special offer 특가 판매, 특별 할인

[10-12] 호남 🎧

Questions 10-12 refer to the following advertisement.

> M **10**Don't miss this weekend's most exciting activity, the release of the highly anticipated documentary *Sands of Time* by director Harold Gilmore. The Trombly Theater is holding an event to show this movie for the first time on Saturday at 7 P.M. **11**Visit the theater's Web site to make a reservation for your preferred seat. **12**After the movie, Mr. Gilmore will be signing copies of the movie poster, so you won't want to miss that. Visit www.tromblyevents.com for more information.

해석

10-12번은 다음 광고에 관한 문제입니다.

남 **10**이번 주의 가장 흥미로운 행사, 많은 기대를 받은 해럴드 길모어 감독의 다큐멘터리 〈시간의 모래〉의 개봉을 놓치지 마세요. 트롬블리 극장은 이 영화를 토요일 저녁 7시에 최초로 상영하는 행사를 개최합니다. **11**극장 웹사이트에 방문하여 선호하는 좌석을 예약하세요. **12**영화가 끝난 후에, 길모어 씨가 영화 포스터에 사인을 할 것이므로 이를 놓치고 싶지 않으실 겁니다. 더 많은 정보를 원하시면 www.tromblyevents.com을 방문하세요.

어휘

release 개봉, 발표; 개봉하다, 발표하다 highly 대단히, 매우
anticipate 기대하다, 고대하다
documentary 다큐멘터리, 기록물 for the first time 처음으로
make a reservation 예약하다 preferred 선호하는

10.

무엇이 광고되고 있는가?
(A) 영화 상영
(B) 예술 축제
(C) 스포츠 경기
(D) 도서 판매

어휘

competition 경쟁, (경연) 대회, 시합

패러프레이징

the release of the highly anticipated documentary
→ A film screening

11.

화자에 따르면, 청자들은 온라인으로 무엇을 할 수 있는가?
(A) 환불 신청하기
(B) 운전해서 가는 길 알아내기
(C) 좌석 예약하기
(D) 기부하기

어휘

refund 환불; 환불하다 reserve 예약하다 donation 기부, 기증

패러프레이징

make a reservation for your preferred seat

→ Reserve a seat

12.
행사 마지막에 무슨 일이 일어날 것인가?
(A) 상이 수여될 것이다.
(B) 경품 추첨 행사가 열릴 것이다.
(C) 기자가 인터뷰를 촬영할 것이다.
(D) 어떤 사람이 사인을 해 줄 것이다.

[13-15] 영녀 🎧
Questions 13-15 refer to the following advertisement.

> W Do you have customers visit your business in person? It's important to make a good impression with a modern-looking office space. ¹³ That's why you should consider moving to the Doyle Business Complex. ¹⁴ We're close to Newport subway station and several bus stops, so it is easy for your employees and customers to get here, even if they don't drive. We have a wide variety of unit sizes available, ¹⁵ e-mail our property manager at inquiries@doylebusiness.com to find out more. We guarantee that we'll get back to you within two business days.

해석

13−15번은 다음 광고에 관한 문제입니다.

여 고객들이 직접 여러분의 업체를 방문하게 하시나요? 현대식 사무 공간으로 좋은 인상을 주는 것은 중요합니다. ¹³ 그래서 도일 비즈니스 복합 단지로 이사하는 것을 고려해야 하는 것입니다. ¹⁴ 저희는 뉴포트 지하철역 및 여러 버스 정류장과 가까워서, 운전을 하지 않더라도 직원들이나 고객들이 오기 편합니다. 저희는 다양한 크기의 세대를 보유하고 있으니, ¹⁵ 더 많이 알아보시려면 inquiries @doylebusiness.com으로 저희 건물 관리자에게 이메일을 보내세요. 영업일로 이틀 이내에 회신드릴 것을 약속합니다.

13.
무엇이 광고되고 있는가?

(A) 아파트 건물
(B) 스포츠 경기장
(C) 음악 공연장
(D) 사무 복합 단지

14.
화자는 장소의 어떤 이점을 강조하는가?
(A) 새로운 전자제품
(B) 대중교통 접근성
(C) 널찍한 주차장
(D) 야외 휴양 공간

15.
화자에 따르면, 청자들은 어떻게 더 많은 정보를 얻을 수 있는가?
(A) 이메일을 보냄으로써
(B) 웹사이트를 검색함으로써
(C) 견학을 함으로써
(D) 업체에 전화함으로써

[16-18] 미남 🎧
Questions 16-18 refer to the following advertisement and price list.

> M Little Italy Buffet serves delicious food at a reasonable price. We offer some of the best Italian dishes you can find outside of Italy. ¹⁶ Have you been to our third Little Italy Buffet we just opened on Court Street? Well, if you haven't, now is the time, because we have a special offer. ¹⁷ Throughout April, adults can get the lunch buffet at the child's buffet price. That's right! This offer is available for a limited time, so don't miss it. ¹⁸ Call us now and ask us to save you a table for tonight. You'll be glad you did. Little Italy Buffet is open from 9 A.M. to 11 P.M. daily.

16-18번은 다음 광고와 가격표에 관한 문제입니다.

남 리틀 이태리 뷔페는 합리적인 가격에 맛있는 음식을 제공합니다. 저희는 이탈리아 밖에서 찾을 수 있는 최고의 이탈리아 요리들을 제공합니다. **¹⁶ 저희가 코트 가에 막 개점한 리틀 이태리 뷔페 3호 점에 가 보셨나요?** 음, 가 보시지 못했다면, 지금이 절호의 기회인데요, 저희가 특별 할인을 해드리기 때문입니다. **¹⁷ 4월 내내 성인들이 점심 뷔페를 어린이 뷔페 가격에 이용하실 수 있습니다.** 그렇습니다! 이번 할인은 한정된 시간 동안만 이용할 수 있으니 놓치지 마세요. **¹⁸ 지금 저희에게 전화하셔서 오늘 밤 테이블을 남겨 두어 달라고 요청하세요.** 그렇게 하길 잘했다고 생각하게 될 겁니다. 리틀 이태리 뷔페는 매일 오전 9시부터 저녁 11시까지 영업합니다.

어휘

reasonable price 적정 가격 dish 요리
special offer 특가 판매, 특별 할인 throughout ~ 동안 쭉, 내내
available 이용할 수 있는 limited 제한된, 한정된 daily 매일

리틀 이태리 뷔페	
뷔페 식사	가격
무제한 점심 식사: 성인	11.99달러
¹⁷ 무제한 점심 식사: 어린이	**9.99달러**
무제한 저녁 식사: 성인	12.99달러
무제한 저녁 식사: 어린이	10.99달러

16.

이 업체는 최근 무엇을 했는가?
(A) 그곳은 메뉴를 늘렸다.
(B) 그곳은 야외 좌석을 추가했다.
(C) 그곳은 영업시간을 연장했다.
(D) 그곳은 새로운 장소에 문을 열었다.

어휘

expand 확대하다 extend 연장하다 operation 영업, 운영
location 장소, 위치

패러프레이징

our third Little Italy Buffet we just opened on Court Street → opened a new location

17.

시각 자료를 보시오. 4월에 성인 점심 뷔페는 얼마인가?
(A) 11.99달러
(B) 9.99달러
(C) 12.99달러
(D) 10.99달러

18.

청자들은 왜 업체에 전화하도록 요청받는가?
(A) 예약하기 위해
(B) 집으로 음식을 배달시키기 위해

(C) 평가를 남기기 위해
(D) 식사 제한을 알리기 위해

패러프레이징

ask us to save you a table → make a reservation

UNIT 14 방송

CHECK UP   본문 p.282

1. (C)   **2.** (A)   **3.** (B)

[1-3] 미녀

Questions 1-3 refer to the following radio broadcast.

> W This is the technology news update on Channel 8. **¹ A spokesperson for software developer Sutton Tech announced today that the company has launched a new program called Elite Talk, which helps people to learn a foreign language.** It currently offers French, Spanish, and Mandarin, but other languages will be added later. So far, **² the program is getting great reviews. You can read them for yourself on the company's Web site at www.suttontech. com.** We have Elite Talk's creator, James Duncan, here with us in the studio today. **³ But before we get to the interview, let's take a look at the traffic conditions in the area.**

해석

1-3번은 다음 라디오 방송에 관한 문제입니다.

여 채널 8의 최신 과학 기술 뉴스입니다. **¹ 소프트웨어 개발 업체인 서튼 테크의 대변인은 사람들이 외국어를 배우는 것을 돕는 새로운 프로그램인 엘리트 토크를 자사에서 출시했다고 오늘 발표했습니다.** 현재 프랑스어, 스페인어, 표준 중국어를 제공하지만, 다른 언어들도 나중에 추가될 것입니다. 지금까지, **² 이 프로그램은 아주 좋은 평가를 받고 있습니다. 회사 웹사이트 www.suttontech. com에서 직접 읽어 보실 수 있습니다.** 저희는 오늘 엘리트 토크의 창안자인 제임스 덩컨을 이곳 스튜디오에 모셨습니다. **³ 하지만 인터뷰를 하기 전에 지역 교통 상황을 살펴보겠습니다.**

어휘

technology 과학 기술 news update 최신 뉴스
spokesperson 대변인 developer 개발자
launch 출시하다, 개시하다 foreign language 외국어
currently 지금, 현재 Mandarin 표준 중국어 review 평가
for oneself 혼자 힘으로 creator 창안자, 창작자
take a look at ~을 (한번) 보다 traffic 교통(량)

1.

방송은 무엇에 관한 것인가?
(A) 산업 학회

(B) 경력 개발 워크숍
(C) 소프트웨어 프로그램
(D) 일자리 공석

2.
화자에 따르면, 청자들은 왜 웹사이트를 방문해야 하는가?
(A) 일부 평가를 읽기 위해
(B) 쿠폰을 내려받기 위해
(C) 무료 체험을 신청하기 위해
(D) 일정표를 보기 위해

어휘
trial 시험, 실험

3.
청자들은 다음에 무엇을 들을 것인가?
(A) 광고
(B) 교통 방송
(C) 정치 토론
(D) 일기 예보

어휘
political 정치와 관련된

패러프레이징 **연습**		본문 p.284
1-4. 스크립트 참조	**5.** (A)	**6.** (B)

1.
Q 월스턴 사는 다음 달에 무엇을 할 것인가?
A 인턴십 프로그램 시작하기

미남 🎧

> **M** At a press conference this morning, a representative from Walston Enterprises announced that the company will launch an internship program next month. Walston is the leading provider of marketing services in the technology sector. It is seeking to help the next generation of marketers as well as identifying potential employees.

해석
남 오늘 아침 기자 회견에서, **월스턴 사의 대표는 자사가 다음 달에 인턴십 프로그램을 시작할 것이라고 발표했습니다.** 월스턴은 과학 기술 분야의 선두적인 마케팅 서비스 공급업체입니다. 이 회사는 잠재적인 직원들을 찾아낼 뿐만 아니라 차세대 마케터들을 돕고자 합니다.

어휘
internship 인턴사원 근무 (기간) press conference 기자 회견
representative 대표, 대리인 launch 시작하다, 출시하다
leading 선두적인 provider 공급자 technology 과학 기술
sector 부문, 분야 seek to ~하도록 추구하다 generation 세대

identify 확인하다, 찾다 potential 가능성이 있는, 잠재적인

패러프레이징
launch → Start

2.
Q 화자에 따르면, 업체는 왜 성공했는가?
A 그곳은 폭넓은 선택권을 제공한다.

미녀 🎧

> **W** Thanks for tuning in to *City Life*, the show about what to do in and around Lexington. Today we're looking at Carson Resort. This is one of the most visited attractions in Lexington. Its popularity is due largely to the variety of activities it provides.

해석
여 렉싱턴 주변에서 무엇을 해야 하는지에 관한 프로그램인 〈시티 라이프〉를 들어 주셔서 감사합니다. 오늘 우리는 카슨 리조트를 살펴보겠습니다. 이곳은 렉싱턴에서 가장 많이 방문하는 명소들 중 하나입니다. **그 인기는 주로 그곳에서 제공하는 다양한 활동들 때문입니다.**

어휘
a wide selection 폭넓은 선택 attraction 명소, 명물
popularity 인기 largely 대체로, 주로 a variety of 다양한

패러프레이징
the variety of activities it provides
→ It offers a wide selection

3.
Q 9월에 로지빌에서 무슨 일이 일어날 것인가?
A 스포츠 행사

미남 🎧

> **M** Event planners in Lodgeville are still looking for volunteers to assist with the annual marathon in September. The race is expected to attract visitors from across the state as people come to watch the athletes compete.

해석
남 로지빌의 행사 기획자들은 9월에 있을 연례 마라톤을 도울 자원봉사자들을 여전히 찾고 있습니다. 사람들이 선수들이 경쟁하는 것을 보러 오면서 이 경주는 주 전역에서 방문객들을 끌어모을 것으로 예상됩니다.

어휘
take place 일어나다, 개최되다 volunteer 자원봉사자
assist with ~을 돕다, 지원하다 annual 연례의
attract 끌어들이다, 끌어모으다
compete 경쟁하다, (시합 등에) 참가하다

패러프레이징

the annual marathon → A sporting event

4.

Q 최근에 받은 기부금은 어떻게 사용될 것인가?
A 번역가들에게 지불하기 위해

미녀 🎧

> **W** You're listening to *Nature News* on Radio 103.4 FM. Our guest today is Patrick Miller, head of the National Parks Service. He'll be discussing a Web site upgrade aimed at attracting international visitors to the parks. For example, thanks to a recent private donation, the department will be able to hire translators for the Web site's contents.

해석

여 여러분은 103.4 FM 라디오의 〈네이처 뉴스〉를 듣고 계십니다. 오늘 초대 손님은 패트릭 밀러로, 국립 공원 관리청의 책임자입니다. 그는 해외 방문객들을 공원으로 유치하는 것을 목표로 한 웹사이트 업그레이드에 대해 얘기할 것입니다. 예를 들면, 최근에 받은 개인 기부금 덕분에 이 부서는 웹사이트 내용을 위한 번역가들을 고용할 수 있을 것입니다.

어휘

donation 기부, 기증 translator 번역가, 통역가
head (조직의) 책임자 aimed at ~을 목표로 한
international 국제적인 private 개인의, 사적인
contents 내용물

패러프레이징

hire → pay for

5.

화자에 따르면, 전문가들은 무엇을 예상하고 있는가?
(A) 가격 인상
(B) 다양성 강화

미남 🎧

> **M** Unfortunately, the cold weather has damaged many of the locally grown flowers. With fewer flowers available, market specialists anticipate an increase in prices of as much as 20 percent. Consumers will probably notice the change soon at local flower shops.

해석

남 유감스럽게도, 추운 날씨가 지역에서 재배되는 꽃의 상당수에 피해를 입혔습니다. 공급할 수 있는 꽃이 적어져서, 시장 전문가들은 많게는 20%까지 가격이 상승할 것으로 예상합니다. 소비자들은 아마도 지역 꽃 가게에서 곧 변화를 알아차리게 될 것입니다.

어휘

anticipate 예상하다 variety 여러 가지, 다양성
damage 손상을 주다, 피해를 입히다 locally 지역에서, 현지에서
specialist 전문가 consumer 소비자
notice 알아차리다, 주목하다

패러프레이징

an increase in prices → Higher prices

6.

화자는 어떤 문제를 언급하는가?
(A) 재료비 인상
(B) 숙련된 직원들의 부족

미녀 🎧

> **W** In business news, the manufacturing industry is facing a crisis as more sophisticated machinery is installed in factories. That has made it harder to find the skilled workers required to keep the factories running.

해석

여 경제 뉴스입니다. 더 복잡한 기계가 공장에 설치되면서 제조업이 위기를 맞고 있습니다. 이는 계속하여 공장을 가동하기 위해 필요한 숙련된 직원들을 찾는 것을 더 어렵게 만들었습니다.

어휘

material 재료 shortage 부족 skilled 숙련된, 노련한
manufacturing 제조업 face 마주 보다, 직면하다 crisis 위기
sophisticated 정교한, 복잡한 machinery 기계류
install 설치하다 require 필요로 하다

패러프레이징

made it harder to find the skilled workers
→ A shortage of skilled employees

연습 문제   본문 p.285

1. (C) **2.** (B) **3.** (D) **4.** (C) **5.** (B)

[1] 영녀 🎧

Question 1 refers to the following broadcast.

> **W** Now let's take a look at what's in the forecast for this weekend. Both Saturday and Sunday will be cool and sunny with no chance of rain. That's perfect weather for the Summer Festival at Camden Park. The New York Dance Group will be giving an outdoor show, so I'm really looking forward to that. I'm glad we'll have nice weather for it. Remember, you don't need tickets for the festival. However, you may want to bring your own chairs.

해석

1번은 다음 방송에 관한 문제입니다.

여 이제 이번 주말 일기 예보가 어떤지 보겠습니다. 토요일과 일요일 모두 비가 올 가능성은 없으며 시원하고 화창하겠습니다. 캠든 파크에서 열리는 여름 축제에 딱 맞는 날씨입니다. **뉴욕 댄스 팀이 야외 공연을 할 예정이어서 몹시 기대가 됩니다.** 이를 위해서도 좋은 날씨가 될 것이니 기쁩니다. 축제에는 티켓이 필요 없다는 것을 기억하세요. 하지만, 자신의 의자를 가져오는 것이 좋을 겁니다.

어휘

forecast 예측, 예보 outdoor 야외의
look forward to ~을 기대하다

1.

화자는 무엇에 관해 들떠 있다고 말하는가?
(A) 스포츠 토너먼트
(B) 미술 전시
(C) 댄스 공연
(D) 노래 경연 대회

어휘

tournament 토너먼트, 승자 진출전 exhibition 전시(회)

패러프레이징

an outdoor show → performance

[2-3] 호남 🎧

Questions 2-3 refer to the following broadcast.

M This is *Fresh Horizons*, and I'm Steven Shapiro. On today's episode, Olivia Mann will be joining us. She is a professor of Psychology at Pearfield University. ²She will be telling us about her book, *How We Think*, which just came out in paperback. But, before we get to Ms. Mann, let's look at the weather report. Tonight and tomorrow, we have a slight chance of precipitation. Then, on Sunday it's going to clear up. ³Now, we will be right back with Olivia Mann after a short commercial break.

해석

2-3번은 다음 방송에 관한 문제입니다.

남 이것은 〈프레시 호라이즌〉, 저는 스티븐 샤피로입니다. 오늘 방송에서는, 올리비아 만이 우리와 함께하겠습니다. 그녀는 페어필드 대학의 심리학 교수입니다. ²그녀가 막 종이책으로 출간된 자신의 책 〈우리는 어떻게 사고하는가〉에 대해서 얘기할 것입니다. 하지만 만 씨와 만나기 전에, 일기예보를 확인하겠습니다. 오늘 밤과 내일은, 강수 확률이 조금 있습니다. 그런 후에, 일요일에는 날씨가 개겠습니다. ³자, 짧은 광고 뒤에 올리비아 만과 함께 돌아오겠습니다.

어휘

psychology 심리학 paperback 페이퍼백, 종이 표지의 책
slight 약간의, 조금의 precipitation 강수(량)

clear up (날씨가) 개다 commercial break 광고 시간

2.

누가 인터뷰될 것인가?
(A) 의사
(B) 작가
(C) 정치가
(D) 기자

3.

청자들은 다음에 무엇을 들을 것인가?
(A) 뉴스 보도
(B) 스포츠 최신 소식
(C) 교통 방송
(D) 광고

어휘

traffic 교통(량) commercial 광고 (방송); 상업의

패러프레이징

a short commercial break → Some commercials

[4-5] 영녀 🎧

Questions 4-5 refer to the following report.

W ⁴Let's take a look at the rush hour traffic. As usual, traffic is very heavy on all routes headed into the city center. This has been an ongoing problem and a source of stress for commuters. Most experts say that it is unlikely to change without adding a carpool lane. If you think this is a good idea and would like to voice your opinion, ⁵you should come to next Tuesday's city council meeting to join in the debate.

해석

4-5번은 다음 보도에 관한 문제입니다.

여 ⁴혼잡 시간대 교통 상황을 살펴보겠습니다. 평소와 마찬가지로, 도심으로 향하는 모든 길에 교통이 매우 혼잡합니다. 이것은 계속 진행 중인 문제이자 통근자들이 받는 스트레스의 근원입니다. 대부분의 전문가들은 카풀 차로를 추가하지 않으면 바뀔 것 같지 않다고 말합니다. 이것이 좋은 생각이라고 생각하여 여러분의 의견을 말하고 싶으시면, ⁵다음 주 화요일의 시 의회 회의에 오셔서 함께 토론하십시오.

어휘

rush hour (출퇴근) 혼잡 시간대, 러시아워 traffic 교통(량)
as usual 평상시처럼 route 길, 노선 head into ~로 들어가다
ongoing 계속 진행 중인 source (문제의) 근원
commuter 통근자 expert 전문가
unlikely to ~할 것 같지 않은
voice one's opinion 의견을 말하다 city council 시 의회
join in 함께 ~을 하다 debate 토론

4.

화자는 무엇에 관해 이야기하고 있는가?

(A) 도로 파손
(B) 버스 운행
(C) 교통 혼잡
(D) 주차 문제

어휘

damage 피해, 손상 issue 문제, 안건

패러프레이징

traffic is very heavy → Heavy traffic

5.

화자는 무엇을 할 것을 추천하는가?

(A) 추가 시간을 허용하는 것
(B) 회의에 참석하는 것
(C) 도로 사고를 알리는 것
(D) 주택가를 이용하는 것

어휘

extra 추가의, 가외의 residential 주거의, 주택용의

패러프레이징

come to next Tuesday's city council meeting
→ Attending a meeting

실전 문제

본문 p.286

1. (C)	**2.** (D)	**3.** (A)	**4.** (C)	**5.** (C)
6. (A)	**7.** (A)	**8.** (A)	**9.** (B)	**10.** (D)
11. (B)	**12.** (C)	**13.** (C)	**14.** (A)	**15.** (B)
16. (D)	**17.** (C)	**18.** (B)		

[1-3] 미남 🎧

Questions 1-3 refer to the following broadcast.

M Thanks for tuning in to *Art Corner* on Radio 3. Our special guest today is world-renowned nature photographer Richard Kirwin. [1]This summer, he's volunteering his time and talents to be a photography instructor at the Rubin Community Center. [2]But today, he'll be telling us all about his special exhibit at the Everton Art Gallery. It is focused on the seasonal changes of certain wildlife populations. [3]If you have questions that you'd like Mr. Kirwin to answer on the show, please call the radio station at 555-1188. We'll try to get to as many questions as possible.

해석

1-3번은 다음 방송에 관한 문제입니다.

남 라디오 3의 〈아트 코너〉를 들어 주셔서 감사합니다. 오늘 저희의 특별 초대 손님은 세계적으로 유명한 자연 사진작가인 리처드 커

원입니다. [1]이번 여름, 그는 자신의 시간과 재능을 자발적으로 제공하여 루빈 지역 문화 센터에서 사진 촬영 강사가 됩니다. [2]하지만 오늘 그는 우리에게 에버튼 미술관에서 있는 자신의 특별 전시에 대한 모든 것을 얘기해 줄 것입니다. 전시는 특정 야생 생물 개체군의 계절적 변화에 초점을 맞추었습니다. [3]커윈이 이 프로그램에서 답해 주었으면 하는 질문이 있으시다면, 555-1188로 라디오 방송국에 전화 주시기 바랍니다. 가능한 한 많은 질문을 받도록 노력하겠습니다.

어휘

world-renowned 세계적으로 유명한 photography 사진술
instructor 강사, 교사 exhibit 전시품; 전시하다
focus on ~에 주력하다, 초점을 맞추다 seasonal 계절적인
certain 특정한, 일정한 wildlife 야생 생물
population 개체군, 집단 radio station 라디오 방송국

1.

화자에 따르면, 커윈 씨는 이번 여름에 무엇을 할 것인가?

(A) 사업에 투자하기
(B) 세계 여행하기
(C) 수업 가르치기
(D) 제품 라인 공개하기

어휘

invest in ~에 투자하다 release 공개하다

패러프레이징

be a photography instructor → Teach a class

2.

커윈 씨는 오늘 프로그램에서 무엇에 대해 이야기할 것인가?

(A) 그의 이력
(B) 그의 새 책
(C) 그의 교육 목표
(D) 그의 미술 전시

어휘

educational 교육의, 교육적인

패러프레이징

special exhibit at the Everton Art Gallery → art exhibit

3.

청자들은 무엇을 하라고 권장받는가?

(A) 전화해서 질문하기
(B) 경연 대회에 참가하기
(C) 티켓 미리 구매하기
(D) 우편물 수신자 명단에 가입하기

어휘

enter (대회 등에) 참가하다 in advance 사전에, 미리
mailing list 우편물 수신자 명단

패러프레이징

If you have questions ~ please call the radio station
→ Call with questions

[4-6] 영녀 🎧

Questions 4-6 refer to the following radio broadcast.

> **W** You're listening to *Food Fun*, a show about unusual and interesting foods. ⁴Today we're going to talk about pomegranates, a fruit that is commonly grown in the Middle East and the Mediterranean. On the show today, I'll conduct an interview with Gina Diaz, an expert in nutrition. ⁵She'll explain how eating pomegranates can be good for your health. And, if you want to try this fruit at home but are not sure how to add it to your diet, ⁶visit our Web site. There you can download recipes that are delicious as well as easy to make.

해석

4-6번은 다음 라디오 방송에 관한 문제입니다.

여 여러분은 색다르고 흥미로운 식품에 관한 프로그램인 〈푸드 펀〉을 듣고 계십니다. ⁴오늘 우리는 일반적으로 중동과 지중해에서 재배되는 과일인 석류에 대해 얘기할 것입니다. 오늘 프로그램에서는 영양학 전문가인 지나 디아즈를 인터뷰하겠습니다. ⁵그녀가 석류를 먹는 것이 어떻게 건강에 좋은지 설명할 것입니다. 그리고, 집에서 이 과일을 먹어 보고 싶지만 식단에 넣는 방법을 잘 모르신다면, ⁶저희 웹사이트를 방문하세요. 만들기 쉬울 뿐만 아니라 맛도 좋은 조리법을 그곳에서 다운로드하실 수 있습니다.

어휘

unusual 특이한, 색다른 pomegranate 석류
commonly 흔히, 보통 the Middle East 중동
the Mediterranean 지중해 conduct 수행하다, 실시하다
expert 전문가 nutrition 영양, 영양학 diet 식단, 음식
recipe 조리법

4.

라디오 프로그램은 어떤 종류의 식품에 관한 것인가?
(A) 유제품
(B) 음료
(C) 과일
(D) 채소

어휘

dairy 유제품의, 낙농(업)의

5.

지나 디아즈는 식품에 관해 무슨 이야기를 할 것인가?
(A) 그것의 생산
(B) 그것의 높아지는 인기
(C) 그것의 건강상의 이점
(D) 그것의 가격

어휘

production 생산 popularity 인기 benefit 이익, 혜택

패러프레이징

how eating pomegranates can be good for your
health → health benefits

6.

청자들은 왜 웹사이트에 방문해야 하는가?
(A) 조리법을 얻기 위해
(B) 의견을 게시하기 위해
(C) 일정을 확인하기 위해
(D) 매장을 찾기 위해

어휘

post 게시하다, 공고하다 search for ~을 찾다

패러프레이징

download → get

[7-9] 호남 🎧

Questions 7-9 refer to the following report.

> **M** This is an alert for drivers in the Lakeland district. There is a significant delay on Highway 15. ⁷This is because the northbound lanes are entirely closed due to the construction of a new lane. There is traffic congestion as drivers headed that way are being redirected to another route. ⁸They should follow the detour signs. ⁹You can find out more about planned closures such as this by getting the Department of Transportation smartphone application. Download it for free from the department's Web site.

해석

7-9번은 다음 보도에 관한 문제입니다.

남 레이크랜드 지역의 운전자들에게 알립니다. 15번 고속도로가 상당히 지체되고 있습니다. ⁷이것은 새로운 차로 공사 때문에 북쪽 방향 차로가 완전히 폐쇄되었기 때문입니다. 그 방향으로 가던 운전자들이 다른 길로 방향을 바꾸게 되면서 교통이 혼잡합니다. ⁸운전자들은 우회로 표지를 따라야 합니다. ⁹교통부의 스마트폰 애플리케이션을 받아서 이 같은 예정된 폐쇄에 대해 더 알아볼 수 있습니다. 교통부 웹사이트에서 무료로 다운로드하세요.

어휘

alert 경보, 경계 district 지구, 구역 significant 상당한, 현저한
northbound 북쪽으로 향하는 entirely 완전히
construction 건설, 공사 traffic congestion 교통 혼잡
redirect (다른 방향으로) 다시 보내다 route 경로, 길
detour 우회로 transportation 교통, 수송

7.

지체의 원인은 무엇인가?
(A) 도로 공사가 진행 중이다.
(B) 차가 고장 났다.
(C) 고속도로에 차선을 그리고 있다.
(D) 날씨가 좋지 않다.

제기했습니다. 채널 고정해 주세요.

in progress 진행 중인 break down 고장 나다
inclement (날씨가) 좋지 못한, 궂은

패러프레이징

due to the construction of a new lane
→ Road construction is in progress

8.

일부 운전자들은 무엇을 해야 할 것인가?
(A) 우회하기
(B) 대중교통 이용하기
(C) 다른 곳에 주차하기
(D) 통행료 내기

어휘

public transportation 대중교통 toll 통행료

패러프레이징

follow the detour signs → Take a detour

9.

화자에 따르면, 청자들은 어떻게 더 많은 정보를 얻을 수 있는가?
(A) 라디오 방송국에 전화함으로써
(B) 모바일 애플리케이션을 다운로드함으로써
(C) 안내 책자를 읽음으로써
(D) 다른 방송을 청취함으로써

패러프레이징

getting the Department of Transportation smartphone
application → downloading a mobile application

[10-12] 미녀 🎧

Questions 10-12 refer to the following business
report.

> W Good evening, here's the latest news. ¹⁰The
> governor announced that a new public library
> will be built in Nicholas County. ¹¹The governor
> has emphasized that the project will create
> over 200 jobs, helping to boost the local
> employment rate. ¹²After the break, I'll talk with
> some local citizens living in Nicholas County.
> They've raised concerns that the proposed site
> for the project will have a negative impact on
> wildlife in the area. Stay tuned.

해석

10-12번은 다음 경제 보도에 관한 문제입니다.
여 안녕하십니까, 최신 뉴스입니다. ¹⁰주지사가 니콜라스 카운티에
새로운 공립 도서관이 건설될 것이라고 발표했습니다. ¹¹주지사
는 이 프로젝트가 200개 이상의 일자리를 창출해, 지역 고용률
을 증대시키는 데 도움이 될 것이라고 강조했습니다. ¹²광고를
듣고 잠시 후에 니콜라스 카운티에 거주하는 몇몇 지역 주민들과
이야기를 나누겠습니다. 그들은 이 프로젝트를 위해 제안된 부지
가 이 지역 야생 생물에게 부정적인 영향을 끼칠 거라는 우려를

어휘

governor 주지사 emphasize 강조하다
create 창출하다, 창작하다 boost 신장시키다, 북돋우다
employment rate 취업률, 고용률
raise concerns 우려를 제기하다 proposed 제안된
have a negative impact on ~에 부정적인 영향을 끼치다

10.

지역 사회에 무엇이 건설될 것인가?
(A) 지역 문화 센터
(B) 공원
(C) 병원
(D) 도서관

11.

프로젝트의 어떤 이점이 언급되는가?
(A) 그것은 야생 생물을 보호할 것이다.
(B) 그것은 고용률을 개선할 것이다.
(C) 그것은 관광업을 증진시킬 것이다.
(D) 그것은 인구 증가를 확대시킬 것이다.

어휘

benefit 이득, 혜택 conserve 보호하다, 보존하다
tourism 관광 사업 population growth 인구 증가

패러프레이징

boost → improve

12.

잠시 뒤에 누가 인터뷰될 것인가?
(A) 주지사
(B) 강사
(C) 지역 주민들
(D) 야생 생물 전문가들

패러프레이징

some local citizens living in Nicholas County
→ Community residents

[13-15] 영녀 🎧

Questions 13-15 refer to the following news report.

> W ¹³This is Diana Donahue with the regional
> business news. Today we'll be talking about
> Dinner-Box, a company that was founded by
> Shane Evans. The company delivers pre-
> packaged ingredients to make it easy for
> people to cook fresh meals at home. Mr. Evans
> gave out hundreds of free meals as a way to
> get people interested in his business. ¹⁴He
> started with just one delivery van a year ago.
> Well, 10 more vans were recently added. Now
> Mr. Evans wants to expand to retail locations
> so people can pick up a single meal without an

account. ¹⁵He'll meet several supermarket owners next week to try to set up a business arrangement.

해석

13-15번은 다음 뉴스 보도에 관한 문제입니다.

여 ¹³지역 경제 뉴스를 전해 드릴 다이애나 도너휴입니다. 오늘 우리는 셰인 에번스가 설립한 회사인 디너 박스에 대해 얘기할 것입니다. 이 회사는 사람들이 가정에서 쉽게 집밥을 요리할 수 있도록 미리 포장해 놓은 재료를 배송합니다. 에번스 씨는 사람들이 자신의 사업에 관심을 가지게 하기 위한 방법으로 무료 식사 수백 회분을 나눠 주었습니다. ¹⁴그는 1년 전에 배달용 밴 단 한 대로 시작했습니다. 음, 최근에 밴 10대가 더 추가되었습니다. 이제 에번스 씨는 사람들이 디너 박스 계정 없이도 한 끼의 식사를 들고 올 수 있도록 소매점으로 확장하기를 원합니다. ¹⁵그는 사업 약정을 맺는 시도를 하기 위해 다음 주에 몇몇 슈퍼마켓 소유주들을 만날 것입니다.

어휘

regional 지역의 found 설립하다 pre-packaged 사전 포장된
ingredient 재료, 성분 cook a meal 식사 준비를 하다
expand 확장시키다 retail location 소매점
account 계정, 계좌 set up an arrangement 협정을 맺다

13.

뉴스 보도는 주로 무엇에 관한 것인가?
(A) 지역사회에서 주는 상
(B) 기업 합병
(C) 지역 업체
(D) 상품 리콜

어휘

corporate 기업의 merger 합병 recall 회수, 리콜

패러프레이징

regional → local

14.

화자는 "최근에 밴 10대가 더 추가되었습니다"라고 말할 때 무엇을 암시하는가?
(A) 서비스가 인기가 많아지고 있다.
(B) 주문에 착오가 있었다.
(C) 업체에 정보가 더 필요하다.
(D) 새로운 투자자들이 필요하다.

어휘

investor 투자자

15.

에번스 씨는 다음 주에 누구와 만날 것인가?
(A) 마케팅 전문가들
(B) 상점 주인들
(C) 지역 의사들
(D) 시 공무원들

어휘

expert 전문가 official 공무원, 관리

패러프레이징

supermarket → Store

[16-18] 미남 🎧

Questions 16-18 refer to the following broadcast and forecast.

M This is the local events calendar on Radio WPLB. ¹⁶Officials at Valley Amusement Park are preparing for their grand opening event this week. According to the weather forecast, this Friday is going to be the coldest day of the week. However, residents and tourists alike are excited about the opening, so it will likely be crowded. ¹⁷The park features rides for all ages, including the vintage Wethersfield Roller Coaster, which was disassembled at its original home at Wethersfield Beach and moved to the new park. The park covers over 500 acres, so ¹⁸visitors are advised to wear comfortable shoes or boots because there will be a lot of walking! You can view pictures of the park at www.valleyfun.com.

해석

16-18번은 다음 방송과 일기 예보에 관한 문제입니다.

남 라디오 WPLB의 지역 행사 일정입니다. ¹⁶밸리 놀이공원의 관계자들이 이번 주에 있을 개장 행사를 준비하고 있습니다. 일기 예보에 따르면, 이번 주 금요일은 주중 가장 추운 날이 될 것입니다. 하지만, 주민들과 관광객들 모두 개장에 대해 신나 있어서 공원이 붐빌 것 같습니다. ¹⁷공원은 유서 깊은 웨더스필드 롤러코스터를 포함하여 모든 연령대를 위한 탈것들이 있는데요, 그것은 원래 웨더스필드 비치에 있던 것을 해체하여 새로운 공원으로 옮겨온 것입니다. 공원은 500여 에이커에 걸쳐 있어서 많이 걷게 될 것이므로 ¹⁸방문객들은 편한 신발이나 부츠를 신을 것을 권합니다! www.valleyfun.com에서 공원 사진을 보실 수 있습니다.

어휘

official 관계자, 공무원 amusement park 놀이공원
grand opening 개장, 개점 weather forecast 일기 예보
alike 둘 다, 똑같이 crowded 붐비는, 혼잡한
feature 특별히 포함하다, ~의 특징을 이루다
vintage 유서 깊은, 전통 있는 disassemble 분해하다, 해체하다
cover (~에) 걸치다 advise to ~하라고 충고하다
comfortable 편한, 편안한

날짜	기온	강수 가능성
4월 7일	11°C	25%
4월 8일	15°C	20%
4월 9일	12°C	5%
4월 10일	14°C	10%
16 4월 11일	9°C	15%

16.

시각 자료를 보시오. 개장 행사는 언제 열릴 것인가?

(A) 4월 8일
(B) 4월 9일
(C) 4월 10일
(D) 4월 11일

어휘

temperature 온도, 기온 chance 가능성, 기회

17.

무엇이 밸리 놀이공원으로 이전되었는가?

(A) 해변가의 집
(B) 유명한 조각상
(C) 롤러코스터
(D) 야외 무대

어휘

relocate 이전하다

패러프레이징

moved → relocated

18.

공원 방문객들은 무엇을 하라고 조언받는가?

(A) 자신의 점심 식사 가져오기
(B) 편한 신발 신기
(C) 우산 챙기기
(D) 단체 티켓 구매하기

어휘

footwear 신발 pack (짐을) 싸다, 챙기다

패러프레이징

shoes or boots → footwear

UNIT 15 관광·견학

CHECK UP 본문 p.288

1. (C)　　**2.** (B)　　**3.** (A)

[1-3] 미남 🎧

Questions 1-3 refer to the following talk.

M Alright, everyone. I hope you had a nice time exploring Anaheim Market. **¹**I double-checked your bicycles while you were shopping, and everything is in order. So, we are ready to start the next part of the tour, the village of Pendleton. It's about a 10-mile ride from here. **²**Pendleton is best known for its unique homes and other building structures, which have been built right into the hillside. **³**It wasn't cold this morning, so I know that some of you packed away your jackets, but... um... the forecast said it will be windy.

해석

1-3번은 다음 담화에 관한 문제입니다.

남 좋습니다, 여러분. 애너하임 마켓을 돌아보면서 즐거운 시간을 보내셨기를 바랍니다. **¹**여러분이 쇼핑하는 동안 제가 여러분의 자전거를 재확인했는데 모든 것이 정상입니다. 따라서, 우리는 여행의 다음 부분인 펜들턴 마을에서 시작할 준비가 되었습니다. 여기서 자전거로 약 10마일 거리입니다. **²**펜들턴은 독특한 주택들과 다른 건축 구조물들로 가장 잘 알려져 있는데요, 이것들은 언덕 비탈 바로 위에 지어져 있습니다. **³**오늘 아침은 춥지 않았기에 여러분 중 몇 분은 재킷을 치워 놓으신 걸로 아는데요... 그렇지만... 음... 일기 예보에서 바람이 불 거라고 했습니다.

어휘

explore 답사하다 double-check 재확인하다
in order 제대로 된, 적절한 be known for ~로 알려져 있다
unique 독특한 structure 구조물, 건축물
hillside (작은 산·언덕의) 비탈 pack away 챙겨서 치워 놓다
forecast (일기) 예보

1.

화자는 어떤 종류의 여행을 인솔하고 있는가?

(A) 보트 여행
(B) 기차 여행
(C) 자전거 여행
(D) 도보 여행

2.

펜들턴 마을은 무엇으로 유명한가?

(A) 다양한 야생 생물
(B) 독특한 건축
(C) 수제 귀금속
(D) 전통 음악

어휘

diverse 다양한 architecture 건축(술) traditional 전통적인

패러프레이징

homes and other building structures → architecture

3.

화자는 "일기 예보에서 바람이 불 거라고 했습니다"라고 말할 때 무

엇을 암시하는가?

(A) 청자들은 따뜻한 옷을 준비해야 한다.

(B) 여행이 평소보다 더 오래 걸릴지도 모른다.

(C) 안전 규칙을 준수해야 한다.

(D) 이전의 보도가 정확하지 않았다.

어휘

than usual 평소보다   previous 이전의

incorrect 부정확한, 맞지 않는

| 패러프레이징 **연습** | 본문 p.290 |

1-4. 스크립트 참조   5. (B)   6. (A)

1.

Q 청자들은 여행에서 무엇을 할 기회가 있을 것인가?

A 집에 대해 알아보기

미남 🎧

> **M** I hope you will all enjoy this tour of the historic Terrick Mansion, which was built in the 1700s. Our tour today will cover just the mansion itself. I would be happy to answer any questions you may have along the way.

해석

남 여러분 모두 1700년대에 지어진 역사적인 테릭 맨션에 대한 이번 관광을 즐기시길 바랍니다. 오늘 관광에는 맨션 자체만 포함될 것입니다. 그 과정에서 질문이 있으시면 무엇이든 기꺼이 답변드리겠습니다.

어휘

opportunity 기회   historic 역사적으로 중요한, 역사적인

mansion 대저택   cover 다루다, 포함시키다

along the way 그 과정에서

패러프레이징

cover just the mansion → Learn about a house

2.

Q 화자는 왜 주기적으로 멈출 계획인가?

A 무리를 한데 모으기 위해

미녀 🎧

> **W** As we go higher on the hiking trail, you'll begin to get an amazing view of the valley below. You are welcome to hike at your own pace. However, please don't lose sight of the group as we go. I'll stop regularly to let people catch up and make sure we're all still together.

해석

여 우리가 등산로를 타고 더 높이 올라감에 따라, 아래로 계곡의 놀라운 경관이 보이기 시작할 것입니다. 여러분만의 속도로 산을

올라도 됩니다. 하지만, 가는 동안 무리를 놓치지 마시기 바랍니다. 사람들이 따라잡을 수 있게 하고 우리 모두가 계속해서 함께 있음을 확인하기 위해 주기적으로 멈출 것입니다.

어휘

regularly 정기적으로, 규칙적으로

hiking trail 등산로, 하이킹 코스   view 경관, 전망

hike 하이킹을 가다   pace 속도

lose sight of ~을 잃다, 안 보이다

catch up (with) (~을) 따라잡다

패러프레이징

let people catch up and make sure we're all still together → keep the group together

3.

Q 화자에 따르면, 휴이트 사유지는 무엇으로 유명한가?

A 영화 촬영지로 사용된 것

미남 🎧

> **M** The pillars at the front of the historic Hewitt Estate are made from marble that was imported from Italy. The home is well-known for being the filming location of the movie *The Queen's Secret*, so it will probably look familiar to you.

해석

남 역사적인 휴이트 에스테이트의 정면 기둥들은 이탈리아에서 수입한 대리석으로 만들어졌습니다. 이 집은 영화 〈여왕의 비밀〉의 촬영 장소로 잘 알려져 있어서 아마도 여러분에게 익숙하게 보일 것입니다.

어휘

be famous for ~로 유명하다   location (영화의) 촬영지, 장소

pillar 기둥   historic 역사적으로 중요한, 역사적인

be made from ~으로 만들어지다   marble 대리석

import 수입하다   well-known for ~으로 잘 알려진

familiar 익숙한, 친숙한

패러프레이징

the filming location of the movie → a film location

4.

Q 청자들은 어디에 있는가?

A 도자기 공장에

미녀 🎧

> **W** We hope you will all enjoy this tour of our ceramics manufacturing plant. At Wayfair Ceramics, we are dedicated to creating stylish designs that will look great in your home. And we make our products to last for a long time.

해석

여 이번 저희 도자기 제조 공장 견학을 즐겨 주시기를 바랍니다. 웨

이페어 도자기에서는 여러분의 가정에 잘 어울릴 멋진 디자인을 만들어 내는 데 전념하고 있습니다. 그리고 저희는 오래가는 제품을 만듭니다.

어휘
ceramics ((항상 복수형)) 도예, 도자기류
manufacturing 제조(업) be dedicated to ~에 전념하다
stylish 멋진, 우아한 last 계속되다, 지속되다

패러프레이징
manufacturing plant → factory

5.
화자는 회사에 대해 무엇이라고 말하는가?
(A) 그곳은 두 번째 지점을 열었다.
(B) 그곳은 가족 경영 업체이다.

미남 🎧

> **M** Thank you for visiting the Hartley Factory. This company was founded nearly 60 years ago by my grandfather, James Hartley. It remains a family-owned and operated business today. During the tour, I'll be showing you each step in the process of making our popular light fixtures.

해석
남 하틀리 공장에 방문해 주셔서 감사합니다. 이 회사는 거의 60년 전에 저희 할아버지이신 제임스 하틀리께서 설립하셨습니다. **현재까지 계속하여 가족 소유 기업으로 운영되고 있습니다.** 견학하는 동안, 제가 저희의 인기 있는 조명 기구를 만드는 각 단계를 보여 드리겠습니다.

어휘
family-run 가족 경영의 operation 기업, 사업체
found 설립하다 remain 계속 ~이다 process 과정, 절차
light fixture 조명 기구

패러프레이징
a family-owned and operated business
→ a family-run operation

6.
화자에 따르면, 사람들은 왜 전시를 좋아하는가?
(A) 그것은 자주 업데이트된다.
(B) 그것은 매우 교육적이다.

미녀 🎧

> **W** Welcome to the Langford Museum of Modern Art. The first stop on the tour is our gallery of local artists. Visitors like this exhibit because it features work by a different artist every three months. So, art lovers keep returning so they can see new artwork.

해석
여 랭퍼드 현대미술관에 오신 것을 환영합니다. 첫 번째로 관람할 곳은 우리 지역 미술가들의 전시장입니다. **3개월 단위로 다른 미술가들의 작품을 선보이기 때문에 방문객들은 이 전시를 좋아합니다.** 그래서, 미술 애호가들이 새로운 미술품을 보기 위해 계속 다시 찾아옵니다.

어휘
exhibit 전시품; 전시하다 frequently 자주, 흔히
educational 교육적인
feature 특별히 포함하다, (~의) 특징을 이루다 artwork 미술품

패러프레이징
it features work by a different artist every three months → It is updated frequently

---

연습 문제
본문 p.291

1. (B) **2.** (A) **3.** (C) **4.** (C) **5.** (C)

[1] 미녀 🎧
Question 1 refers to the following tour information.

> **W** As we tour the Crescent Museum today, you'll see a wide range of artifacts from the Middle Ages. Our permanent exhibit is one of the nation's largest collections of sculptures, mosaics, and tapestries from this period. The tour will last approximately one hour. After that, we are holding a workshop in which you can make a craft using a book-binding technique from the 10th century. We invite you to attend. The event is available at no additional cost.

해석
1번은 다음 견학 정보에 관한 문제입니다.
여 오늘 우리가 크레센트 박물관을 견학하는 동안, 여러분은 중세 시대의 다양한 유물들을 보게 될 것입니다. 저희 상설 전시는 이 시기의 조각, 모자이크, 태피스트리로 구성된 국내 최대의 소장품 중 하나입니다. 견학은 1시간가량 계속될 것입니다. 그 후에, **10세기의 제본 기법을 사용하여 공예품을 만드는 워크숍을 개최할 것입니다. 여러분에게 참석해 주실 것을 청합니다.** 이 행사는 추가 비용 없이 이용할 수 있습니다.

어휘
a wide range of 광범위한, 다양한 artifact 공예품, 유물
the Middle Ages 중세 시대 permanent 영구적인
exhibit 전시품; 전시하다 collection 수집품, 소장품
sculpture 조각(품) last 계속되다 craft 공예, 수예
book-binding 장정, 제본 technique 기법, 기술
invite 청하다, 권하다 additional cost 추가 비용

1.
화자는 청자들에게 무엇을 해 달라고 요청하는가?

(A) 현장 카페 방문하기
(B) 워크숍 참석하기
(C) 고객 보상 프로그램 가입하기
(D) 모금 행사 참여하기

어휘

on-site 현장의, 현지의 loyalty program 고객 보상 프로그램
participate in ~에 참여하다 fund-raiser 모금 행사

[2-3] 미남 🎧

Questions 2-3 refer to the following talk.

> M Now, we are approaching the last stop on this tour. On your right, you'll notice an old red brick building. ²This is the first bank in our country, designed by Italian architect Christian Maggio and built in the early 18th century. Construction of this bank took much longer than expected due to the unusually cold weather that winter. ³Before we finish our tour, let's go into the bank and have a look at the mint, where you can see the entire process of making coins and bills.

해석

2-3번은 다음 담화에 관한 문제입니다.

남 이제, 우리는 이번 관광에서 마지막으로 들를 곳에 다다르고 있습니다. 여러분의 오른쪽으로, 오래된 붉은 벽돌 건물이 보이실 겁니다. ²이것은 우리나라 최초의 은행으로, 이탈리아 건축가 크리스티안 마지오가 설계했으며 18세기에 초에 지어졌습니다. 이 은행의 건설은 그해 겨울 유독 추웠던 날씨 때문에 예상보다 훨씬 더 오래 걸렸습니다. ³관광을 마치기 전에, 은행 안으로 들어가서 조폐국을 둘러보시죠. 그곳에서 동전과 지폐를 만드는 전체 과정을 볼 수 있습니다.

어휘

approach ~에 다가가다 notice ~을 알아차리다
architect 건축가 construction 건설, 공사
than expected 예상보다 unusually 몹시, 평소와 달리
mint 화폐 주조소, 조폐국 entire 전체의

2.

화자는 크리스티안 마지오에 대해 무엇이라고 말하는가?
(A) 그는 은행을 설계했다.
(B) 그는 최초의 은행원이었다.
(C) 그는 그 장소를 구경시켜 줄 것이다.
(D) 그는 동전과 지폐를 만들었다.

어휘

bank teller 은행원 show ~ around ~에게 구경시켜 주다

3.

청자들은 다음에 무엇을 할 것인가?
(A) 영상 시청하기
(B) 기념품 구매하기

(C) 관광 명소 방문하기
(D) 다과 먹기

어휘

souvenir 기념품 tourist attraction 관광 명소
refreshments ((항상 복수형)) 다과, 음식물

패러프레이징

go into the bank and have a look at the mint
→ Visit a tourist attraction

[4-5] 미녀 🎧

Questions 4-5 refer to the following talk.

> W I'd like to welcome you all to the Guildford Zoo. ⁴On our tour today, you'll have the opportunity to see a wide variety of exotic creatures such as lions, flamingos, and giraffes. Please feel free to take as many pictures as you like, but remember that flash photography is not permitted inside any of the buildings. We would also love for you to share your photos. ⁵If you post a picture on our Web site, we'll send you a coupon for 20 percent off your next visit.

해석

4-5번은 다음 담화에 관한 문제입니다.

여 길포드 동물원에 오신 여러분 모두를 환영합니다. ⁴오늘 관람 중에 여러분은 사자, 홍학, 기린 같은 매우 다양한 이국적인 생물들을 보실 기회가 있을 겁니다. 자유롭게 원하시는 만큼 사진을 찍으시기 바라지만, 플래시를 사용한 사진 촬영은 모든 건물 내부에서 허용되지 않는다는 것을 기억하세요. 저희는 또한 여러분의 사진을 공유해 주셨으면 합니다. ⁵저희 웹사이트에 사진을 올리시면, 다음 방문 때 20% 할인받을 수 있는 쿠폰을 보내 드리겠습니다.

어휘

a wide variety of 매우 다양한 exotic 이국적인
creature 생물 flamingo 홍학, 플라밍고
feel free to 마음대로 ~하다 photography 사진 촬영
permit 허용하다; 허가증 post 올리다, 게시하다

4.

청자들은 관람 중에 무엇을 볼 것인가?
(A) 현대식 기계
(B) 유명한 그림
(C) 이국적인 동물
(D) 역사적인 건축 양식

어휘

machinery 기계류 historic 역사적인
architecture 건축, 건축술

패러프레이징

creatures → animals

5.

청자들은 어떻게 쿠폰을 받을 수 있는가?
(A) 기념품점에서 구매함으로써
(B) 단체와 계약함으로써
(C) 온라인으로 사진을 게시함으로써
(D) 설문 조사를 작성함으로써

어휘

sign up with ~와 계약하다 fill out 기입하다, 작성하다
survey (설문) 조사

패러프레이징

on our Web site → online

실전 문제 본문 p.292

1. (D)	**2.** (B)	**3.** (C)	**4.** (B)	**5.** (A)
6. (C)	**7.** (B)	**8.** (A)	**9.** (A)	**10.** (D)
11. (B)	**12.** (B)	**13.** (B)	**14.** (A)	**15.** (D)
16. (C)	**17.** (C)	**18.** (A)		

[1-3] 미녀 🎧

Questions 1-3 refer to the following tour information.

W Welcome to this tour of the Walden fishing village. I'm Ava, your tour guide. **¹As we walk through the village today, please remember that you are not allowed to eat anything while on the tour.** This is because the packaging can be dropped and get into the water. The village is starting to gain attention nationally. **²For example, in March, some of the boat operators who live here were featured in a documentary.** If you would like to learn some traditional fishing methods, you're in luck. **³We've just launched a workshop on Saturdays, and I highly recommend signing up for it.**

해석

1-3번은 다음 관광 정보에 관한 문제입니다.

여 이번 월든 어촌 관광에 오신 것을 환영합니다. 저는 여러분의 가이드 에이바입니다. **¹오늘 마을을 지나실 때, 관광 중에는 아무것도 드실 수 없다는 걸 기억해 주세요.** 포장지가 떨어져 물에 들어갈 수 있기 때문입니다. 마을은 전국적으로 주목을 받기 시작했습니다. **²예를 들면, 3월에, 이곳에 사는 보트 운영자들 중 몇몇이 다큐멘터리에 출연했습니다.** 만약 전통적인 낚시 방법을 배우고 싶으시다면, 여러분은 운이 좋으십니다. **³토요일마다 하는 워크숍을 막 시작했는데, 거기에 등록하시는 걸 적극 추천합니다.**

어휘

through ~을 지나서 be allowed to ~하는 것이 허용되다
packaging 포장지 drop 떨어지다 gain 얻다
attention 주목, 관심 nationally 전국적으로 operator 운영자
feature 출연시키다; 특징, 특색 launch 시작하다

1.

관광 중에 무엇이 금지되는가?
(A) 그룹을 이탈하는 것
(B) 사진을 찍는 것
(C) 휴대전화를 사용하는 것
(D) 음식을 먹는 것

어휘

prohibit 금지하다 leave 떠나다

패러프레이징

not allowed → prohibited

2.

화자는 3월에 무슨 일이 일어났다고 말하는가?
(A) 물 위에서 시험이 수행되었다.
(B) 몇몇 주민들이 다큐멘터리에 출연했다.
(C) 마을이 개선되었다.
(D) 후한 기부금이 보내졌다.

어휘

carry out ~을 수행하다 improvement 개선, 개량
generous 후한, 넉넉한 donation 기부금

패러프레이징

some of the boat operators who live here
→ Some residents

3.

화자는 청자들에게 무엇에 등록하라고 권하는가?
(A) 비즈니스 멤버십
(B) 우편물 수신자 명단
(C) 새로운 워크숍
(D) 보트 여행

패러프레이징

just launched a workshop → A new workshop

[4-6] 호남 🎧

Questions 4-6 refer to the following talk.

M Hello, everyone. My name is Scott, and I'll be leading today's hike along the Cheriton Trail. If you hiked this trail last year, you'll notice some differences. **⁴Park rangers have added wood chips to make the surface easier to walk on. They've also added railings to some of the steeper parts.** We'll leave in about 10 minutes. **⁵It's going to be really hot today, so don't forget to bring more water than usual.** I have extra bottles if you need them. **⁶There are some rare flowers and shrubs along the trail. When I see them, I'll make sure to stop and bring your attention to them.**

해석

4-6번은 다음 담화에 관한 문제입니다.

남 여러분, 안녕하세요. 제 이름은 스콧이고, 오늘 체리턴 트레일을 따라 하이킹을 인솔할 것입니다. 작년에 이 산길을 하이킹하셨다면, 몇 가지 차이점들을 알아채실 겁니다. **⁴공원 관리인들이 지면을 걷기 쉽게 만들기 위해 나뭇조각을 추가했습니다.** 그들은 또한 일부 더 가파른 부분에 난간을 추가했습니다. 약 10분 뒤에 출발하겠습니다. **⁵오늘은 정말 더울 테니, 평소보다 더 많은 물을 가져오시는 걸 잊지 마세요.** 필요하시다면 제게 여분의 병이 있습니다. **⁶산길을 따라 희귀한 꽃과 관목들이 있습니다. 제가 그것들을 보면, 멈춰서 여러분께 알려드리겠습니다.**

어휘
lead 이끌다, 안내하다 trail 산길, 오솔길 notice 알아채다
ranger 관리인 wood chip 나뭇조각 surface 표면, 지면
railing 난간 steep 가파른 extra 여분의, 추가의
rare 희귀한, 진귀한 shrub (= bush) 관목

4.
화자는 산길에 대해 무엇을 설명하는가?
(A) 얼마나 많은 방문객이 오는지
(B) 어떻게 개선되었는지
(C) 얼마나 오래전에 만들어졌는지
(D) 완료하는 데 얼마나 걸리는지

5.
화자는 청자들에게 무엇을 하도록 상기시키는가?
(A) 여분의 물 가져오기
(B) 전화기를 무음으로 설정하기
(C) 배낭 점검하기
(D) 지도 휴대하기

어휘
put ~ on silent ~을 무음으로 설정하다

패러프레이징
more → extra

6.
화자는 왜 잠시 멈출 것인가?
(A) 참가자들에게 휴식을 주기 위해
(B) 사진을 몇 장 찍기 위해
(C) 식물들을 지목하기 위해
(D) 몇 가지 질문에 답하기 위해

어휘
participant 참가자 point out 지목하다, 가리키다

패러프레이징
rare flowers and shrubs ~ bring your attention
→ point out plants

[7-9] 미남 🎧
Questions 7-9 refer to the following talk.

> M The final stop on our tour is Terrington Park. **⁷As you are leaving the tour bus, please be careful, as this road has a lot of traffic.** We'll visit the famous Stone Fountain at this site. **⁸You'll need a ticket to get into the park, so I'll hand those out before you get off the bus.** The bus will return to the hotel at 6 P.M. There are several nice restaurants within walking distance from here. **⁹So, those of you who prefer to have dinner here will have to arrange a taxi back to the hotel.**

해석
7-9번은 다음 담화에 관한 문제입니다.
남 우리 여행의 마지막 목적지는 테링턴 파크입니다. **⁷이곳 도로는 교통량이 많으니 관광버스에서 내리실 때 조심하시기 바랍니다.** 우리는 이 장소에서 유명한 스톤 파운틴을 방문할 겁니다. **⁸공원에 들어가려면 표가 필요하므로 버스에서 내리시기 전에 표를 나눠 드리겠습니다.** 버스는 오후 6시에 호텔로 돌아갈 것입니다. 여기서 걸어서 갈 수 있는 거리에 여러 멋진 식당들이 있습니다. **⁹그러니, 여기서 저녁을 드시고 싶으신 분은 호텔로 돌아가는 택시를 예약하셔야 할 겁니다.**

어휘
traffic 교통량, 교통 site 장소, 위치 hand out 나누어 주다
get off (탈것에서) 내리다 return 돌아가다
walking distance 걸어서 갈 수 있는 거리
prefer ~을 원하다 arrange 정하다, 준비하다

7.
화자는 청자들에게 무엇에 대해 조심하라고 하는가?
(A) 추가 요금
(B) 혼잡한 도로
(C) 환불 정책
(D) 폐점 시간

어휘
warn 조심하라고 하다, 경고하다 refund 환불; 환불하다
policy 정책, 방침 closure 폐점

패러프레이징
this road has a lot of traffic → A busy road

8.
화자는 청자들에게 무엇을 줄 것인가?
(A) 입장권
(B) 현장 지도
(C) 안전모
(D) 도시락

어휘
admission 입장 protective 보호하는 packed lunch 도시락

패러프레이징
a ticket to get into the park → Admission tickets

9.
화자에 따르면, 몇몇 청자들은 무엇을 해야 할 것인가?
(A) 자신의 교통수단 찾기

(B) 잔액 지급하기
(C) 신분증 제시하기
(D) 호텔에 연락하기

어휘

transportation 교통수단, 탈것 remaining balance 잔액

패러프레이징

arrange a taxi → Find their own transportation

[10-12] 영녀 🎧

Questions 10-12 refer to the following tour information.

> W ¹⁰Welcome to Bella Beverage Company. I'm Tina, your guide for this tour. Now, we would usually begin with a video about the company's history, but ¹¹I'm sorry our projector is not working. I'll send you all a link so you can watch it on our Web site later. ¹²And at the end of the tour, we'll stop by the gift shop. There you can buy items with our logo such as T-shirts, tote bags, and calendars as a reminder of your visit today. As we get started, please stay with the group at all times, as machinery is currently in operation.

해석

10-12번은 다음 견학 정보에 관한 문제입니다.

여 ¹⁰벨라 음료 회사에 오신 것을 환영합니다. 저는 이 견학의 가이드인 티나입니다. 자, 보통은 회사의 역사에 관한 영상으로 시작하는데, ¹¹죄송하지만 프로젝터가 작동하지 않습니다. 나중에 저희 웹사이트에서 보실 수 있도록 여러분 모두에게 링크를 보내드리겠습니다. ¹²그리고 견학이 끝나면, 기념품 가게에 들를 겁니다. 그곳에서 오늘 방문을 기념하는 티셔츠, 토트백, 그리고 달력 등과 같은 저희 회사의 로고가 새겨진 물건들을 구입하실 수 있습니다. 현재 기계가 작동 중이므로, 시작할 때 항상 그룹과 함께 있어 주시기 바랍니다.

어휘

beverage 음료, 마실 것 stop by ~에 들르다
reminder 생각나게 하는 것 at all times 항상, 언제나
machinery 기계 currently 현재, 지금
in operation 작동 중인

10.

견학은 어디에서 일어나고 있는가?
(A) 미술관에서
(B) 철도 회사에서
(D) 과학박물관에서
(D) 음료 공장에서

패러프레이징

Bella Beverage Company → a beverage factory

11.

화자는 왜 청자들에게 사과하는가?
(A) 견학이 늦게 시작될 것이다.
(B) 일부 장비가 작동하지 않는다.
(C) 발권 과정이 오래 걸렸다.
(D) 일부 안내 책자에 오류가 있다.

패러프레이징

our projector → Some equipment

12.

화자에 따르면, 청자들은 견학이 끝날 때 무엇을 할 수 있는가?
(A) 몇몇 직원들 만나기
(B) 기념품 구입하기
(C) 무료 샘플 사용해 보기
(D) 설문지 작성하기

어휘

purchase 구입하다; 구입 souvenir 기념품
questionnaire 설문지

패러프레이징

buy items with our logo such as T-shirts, tote bags, and calendars → Purchase some souvenirs

[13-15] 호남 🎧

Questions 13-15 refer to the following tour information.

> M Welcome to the historic Hargreaves Estate and Gardens. A local artist has painted some of the garden's flowers, and ¹³those paintings are on display in Britford Hall. I recommend viewing them after the tour. Now, ¹⁴you would get access to all parts of the garden. But unfortunately, planting is going on in the rose gardens. You'll still get to see everything else though. After nearly 300 years, ¹⁵the garden still maintains a design that is traditional to the era in which it was built. In fact, that's exactly why it is so popular with filmmakers.

해석

13-15번은 다음 관광 정보에 관한 문제입니다.

남 역사적으로 중요한 하그리브스 정원 단지에 오신 것을 환영합니다. 한 지역 미술가가 이 정원의 꽃들을 그렸는데, ¹³그 그림들이 브릿퍼드홀에서 전시되고 있습니다. 관광 후에 그것들을 관람하실 것을 추천합니다. 자, ¹⁴여러분은 정원의 모든 구역에 접근하실 수 있어야 할 것입니다. 하지만 유감스럽게도, 장미 정원에서 나무 심기가 진행되고 있습니다. 그래도 그 외의 모든 것들을 보시게 될 겁니다. 거의 300년이 지났지만, ¹⁵정원은 여전히 그것이 지어졌던 시대의 전통적인 디자인을 유지하고 있습니다. 실은, 정확히 그 이유로 영화 제작자들에게 그렇게 인기가 있는 것입니다.

어휘

historic 역사적인, 역사적으로 중요한 on display 전시된
get access to ~에 접근하다 planting 나무 심기, 식재
maintain 유지하다 traditional 전통적인 era 시대
filmmaker 영화 제작자

13.

화자는 청자들에게 관광 후에 무엇을 하라고 권장하는가?
(A) 영화 보기
(B) 미술품 보기
(C) 안내 책자 가져가기
(D) 기념품 가게 방문하기

패러프레이징

paintings → some artwork

14.

화자는 "장미 정원에서 나무 심기가 진행되고 있습니다"라고 말할
때 무엇을 암시하는가?
(A) 일부 장소에는 방문하지 않을 것이다.
(B) 사진 촬영 시간이 옮겨졌다.
(C) 청자들이 시연을 볼 수 있다.
(D) 임시 직원들이 좀 필요하다.

어휘

photo shoot 사진 촬영 demonstration 시연, 시범 설명
temporary 일시적인, 임시의

15.

화자에 따르면, 무엇이 정원을 영화 제작자들에게 인기 있게 만드는
가?
(A) 그곳은 매우 다양한 꽃들이 있다.
(B) 그곳은 자연광이 많이 든다.
(C) 그곳은 좋은 위치에 있다.
(D) 그곳은 전통적인 디자인을 가지고 있다.

어휘

a wide variety of 매우 다양한 natural light 자연광
location 위치, 장소

패러프레이징

maintains a design that is traditional
→ have a traditional design

[16-18] 미녀 🎧

Questions 16-18 refer to the following tour
information and layout.

W Welcome to the Osborne Candy Factory, which
was founded by Dylan Osborne over 50 years
ago. ¹⁶We are a family-owned and operated
business, with a focus on making sure our
practices do not harm the environment. For
example, we use recycled materials in our
packaging, and we operate our machinery with
sustainable energy. If you look around this
section, you'll see the candy mixture being
stretched on the cooling tables. ¹⁷The next
step is to cut the candy into the correct size.
Let's move on to that section now. ¹⁸There you
will also meet Ashley Bowman, who is in
charge of the operations at the site. You'll be
able to ask her questions.

해석

16-18번은 다음 견학 정보와 배치도에 관한 문제입니다.

여 오스본 사탕 공장에 오신 것을 환영합니다. 이곳은 50여 년 전에
딜런 오스본에 의해 설립되었습니다. ¹⁶저희는 가족 소유 기업으
로 운영되고 있으며, 저희의 관행이 환경에 해를 끼치지 않도록
하는데 중점을 둡니다. 예를 들면, 포장에 재활용 재료를 사용하
며, 지속 가능한 에너지로 기계를 작동합니다. 이 구역을 둘러보
시면, 사탕 혼합물을 냉각 테이블에 늘여 놓은 것이 보이실 겁니
다. ¹⁷다음 단계는 사탕을 정확한 크기로 자르는 것입니다. 이제
그 구역으로 이동하겠습니다. ¹⁸그곳에서는 또한 현장에서 운영
을 담당하는 애슐리 보먼을 만나실 겁니다. 그녀에게 질문을 하
실 수 있습니다.

어휘

found 설립하다
family-owned and operated 가족이 소유하고 운영하는
practice 관행, 관례 harm 해를 끼치다
recycled material 재활용 재료 packaging 포장재, 포장
machinery 기계류 sustainable 지속 가능한
section 부분, 부문 mixture 혼합물 stretch 늘이다, 늘어지다
in charge of ~을 맡아서, 담당해서

1구역	혼합하기
2구역	늘이기
¹⁷3구역	자르기
4구역	포장하기

16.

화자에 따르면, 회사는 무엇에 중점을 두는가?
(A) 현지 제품을 공급받는 것
(B) 꾸준한 성장을 이루는 것
(C) 환경적으로 책임감을 갖는 것
(D) 고객 서비스를 개선하는 것

어휘

source ~을 얻다, 공급자를 찾다
environmentally 환경적으로 responsible 책임이 있는

17.

시각 자료를 보시오. 청자들은 다음에 어느 구역을 볼 것인가?
(A) 1구역
(B) 2구역
(C) 3구역
(D) 4구역

18.

애슐리 보먼은 누구인 것 같은가?

(A) 공장 관리자
(B) 여행 가이드
(C) 배달원
(D) 회사 설립자

패러프레이징

who is in charge of the operations at the site
→ A factory manager

PART TEST   본문 p.294

71. (B)	**72.** (D)	**73.** (C)	**74.** (A)	**75.** (B)
76. (B)	**77.** (D)	**78.** (B)	**79.** (D)	**80.** (C)
81. (A)	**82.** (B)	**83.** (B)	**84.** (C)	**85.** (D)
86. (C)	**87.** (C)	**88.** (B)	**89.** (C)	**90.** (B)
91. (B)	**92.** (C)	**93.** (D)	**94.** (B)	**95.** (D)
96. (C)	**97.** (C)	**98.** (B)	**99.** (A)	**100.** (C)

[71-73] 미남 🎧

Questions 71-73 refer to the following excerpt from a meeting.

> **M** As you all know, it's important for our company to keep records confidential. **71** During today's lunch break, I went to all of the departments, and I noticed a problem. A lot of employees were still signed into our secure database. **72** Please remember to sign out of this program every time you leave your desk. Otherwise, anyone could access it. Now on to some good news… uh… **73** our firm has been getting excellent reviews from customers. Great job, everyone!

해석

71-73번은 다음 회의 발췌록에 관한 문제입니다.

남 모두 아시다시피, 우리 회사는 기록을 기밀로 유지하는 게 중요합니다. **71 오늘 점심시간 동안, 저는 모든 부서를 다니며 문제점을 발견했습니다.** 많은 직원들이 여전히 우리 보안 데이터베이스에 로그인되어 있었습니다. **72 자리를 비울 때마다 이 프로그램에서 로그아웃하는 걸 명심해 주세요.** 그렇지 않으면 누구나 그것에 접속할 수 있습니다. 이제 좀 좋은 소식인데요… 어… **73 우리 회사가 고객들로부터 우수한 평가를 받고 있습니다.** 모두 수고하셨습니다!

어휘

confidential 기밀의, 비밀의   notice 알아채다, 인지하다
sign into ~에 로그인하다   secure 안전한, 보안이 철저한
sign out (= log out) ~에서 로그아웃하다
otherwise 그렇지 않으면   access 접속하다

---

excellent 우수한, 훌륭한

71.

화자는 점심시간 동안 무엇을 했는가?

(A) 그는 일정을 조정했다.
(B) 그는 다른 부서들을 방문했다.
(C) 그는 새 컴퓨터 몇 대를 주문했다.
(D) 그는 회의록 몇 개를 검토했다.

어휘

adjust 조정하다   visit 방문하다; 방문   order 주문하다

패러프레이징

went to all of the departments
→ visited different departments

72.

청자들은 무엇을 하도록 상기되는가?

(A) 사무실에 음식을 가져오는 것 피하기
(B) 회사 공지 주의 깊게 읽기
(C) 교대 시간에 맞춰서 도착하기
(D) 소프트웨어 프로그램에서 로그아웃하기

어휘

avoid 피하다, 방지하다   carefully 주의 깊게   shift 교대 근무
on time 시간에 맞추어서, 정각에

73.

화자는 무엇에 대해 청자들을 축하하는가?

(A) 상을 받은 것
(B) 작업을 일찍 끝낸 것
(C) 좋은 피드백을 받은 것
(D) 기사가 게재된 것

어휘

win (상품 등을) 타다, 얻다   complete 완료하다   receive 받다
publish 게재하다, 싣다

패러프레이징

getting excellent reviews → Receiving good feedback

[74-76] 영녀 🎧

Questions 74-76 refer to the following broadcast.

> **W** Thanks for tuning in to *The Knoxville Review*. I'm honored to have Frederick Bryant as my guest today. **74** Frederick grew up here in Knoxville, and I'm sure you all know him from his professional basketball career. Well, now he is looking for a way to give back to the community. **75** He has launched his own charity, which will provide educational programs for low-income neighborhoods. He'll tell us more about that on the show. Also, he'll be signing autographs at the Timpson Mall tomorrow starting from 9 A.M. **76** He'll also be selling

limited edition basketballs until they run out, but… um… there are only a hundred, ⁷⁶so don't miss out.

해석

74-76번은 다음 방송에 관한 문제입니다.

여 〈녹스빌 리뷰〉를 청취해 주셔서 감사합니다. 오늘 프레데릭 브라이언트를 초대 손님으로 모시게 되어 영광입니다. ⁷⁴프레데릭은 여기 녹스빌에서 성장했고, 여러분 모두 그의 프로 농구 경력을 통해 그를 아실 거라고 확신합니다. 자, 이제 그는 지역 사회에 환원할 방법을 찾고 있습니다. ⁷⁵그는 저소득층 주민을 위해 교육 프로그램을 제공하는 자선 단체를 설립했습니다. 그는 이 프로그램에서 그것에 대해 더 자세히 이야기할 것입니다. 그리고 그는 내일 오전 9시부터 팀프스 몰에서 사인회를 가질 예정입니다. ⁷⁶그는 또한 한정판 농구공이 소진될 때까지 판매할 예정이지만, 음… 100개밖에 없으니 ⁷⁶놓치지 마세요.

어휘

be honored to ~을 하게 되어 영광이다 grow up 성장하다
professional 프로의 career 경력, 이력
give back 환원하다, 되돌려주다 community 지역 사회, 주민
launch 시작하다, 착수하다 charity 자선 단체
low-income 저소득의 autograph 사인; 사인하다
limited edition 한정판 run out 다 떨어지다

74.

프레데릭 브라이언트는 누구인가?
(A) 운동선수
(B) 라디오 진행자
(C) 정치인
(D) 교사

어휘

athlete 운동선수 politician 정치인, 정치가

패러프레이징

professional basketball career → athlete

75.

프레데릭 브라이언트는 프로그램에서 무엇에 관해 이야기할 것인가?
(A) 그의 은퇴 계획
(B) 그의 자선 사업
(C) 그의 새로운 웹사이트
(D) 그의 홍보 투어

어휘

retirement 은퇴, 퇴직 promotional 홍보의, 판촉의

패러프레이징

educational programs for low-income neighborhoods → charity work

76.

화자는 왜 "100개밖에 없으니"라고 말하는가?
(A) 오해를 바로잡기 위해

(B) 행사에 일찍 가는 것을 추천하기 위해
(C) 가격이 비싼 이유를 설명하기 위해
(D) 다른 주문을 요청하기 위해

어휘

correct 바로잡다, 정정하다 misunderstanding 오해, 착오
request 요청하다; 요구

[77-79] 미녀 🎧

Questions 77-79 refer to the following excerpt from a meeting.

W ⁷⁷Today I'm going to demonstrate how to use the new forklift. It's not much different from our current one, but there are a few things to keep in mind when checking the machine. ⁷⁸I'm passing out the handout now, which has a list of each step in order. Please listen carefully, as, ⁷⁹at the end of the meeting, you'll have to take a brief test about what was covered today. You must pass it in order to operate the forklift.

해석

77-79번은 다음 회의 발췌록에 관한 문제입니다.

여 ⁷⁷오늘 저는 새로운 지게차 사용법을 보여드리려고 합니다. 현재 것과 크게 다르지 않지만, 기계를 점검할 때 유의해야 할 사항이 몇 가지 있습니다. ⁷⁸제가 지금 각 단계별 목록이 순서대로 나와 있는 유인물을 나눠 드릴 겁니다. ⁷⁹회의 마지막에 여러분은 오늘 다룬 것에 대한 간단한 테스트를 치러야 하므로 주의 깊게 들어주시기 바랍니다. 지게차를 운전하기 위해선 이 시험을 통과해야 합니다.

어휘

demonstrate (사용법을) 보여주다, 설명하다
forklift 지게차, 포크리프트 current 현재의, 지금의
keep in mind ~을 유의하다 pass out 나누어 주다
handout 유인물, 인쇄물 cover 다루다
in order to ~하기 위해 operate 운전하다, 조종하다

77.

화자는 왜 청자들을 만나고 있는가?
(A) 청자들로부터 피드백을 수집하기 위해
(B) 기계 공급 업체를 소개하기 위해
(C) 이전을 준비하기 위해
(D) 장비 사용법을 보여주기 위해

어휘

gather (정보를) 수집하다, 모으다 supplier 공급자, 공급 회사
relocation 이전, 재배치

패러프레이징

demonstrate how to use the new forklift
→ show how to use some equipment

78.

화자는 청자들에게 무엇을 주는가?

(A) 직무 기술서
(B) 일련의 사용 설명서
(C) 포장 체크 리스트
(D) 제품 리뷰

description 기술, 서술
instructions ((보통 복수형)) 사용 설명서

the handout ~ which has a list of each step in order
→ A set of instructions

79.

청자들은 회의 마지막에 무엇을 할 것인가?

(A) 식사 제공받기
(B) 보너스 받기
(C) 계약 갱신하기
(D) 시험 치르기

serve (음식을) 제공하다 meal 식사, 끼니
renew 갱신하다, 연장하다

[80-82] 호남 🎧

Questions 80-82 refer to the following broadcast.

M You're listening to the local news report on 102.1 FM. The city council is discussing plans to increase the parking fees at the lot near Ezna Beach. ⁸⁰ Gerald Burton, a city council member, said that the rates have remained the same for several years. However, ⁸¹ expenses for maintaining the lot have gone up recently, so something had to be done. Residents who often visit the beach believe the fees are already too high. ⁸² But Mr. Burton and others say the small increase will not discourage people from going to the beach. And I think visitor numbers won't change.

80-82번은 다음 방송에 관한 문제입니다.

남 여러분은 102.1 FM에서 지역 뉴스 보도를 청취하고 계십니다. 시의회는 에즈나 해변 인근 지역의 주차 요금을 인상하는 방안을 논의하고 있습니다. ⁸⁰ 시의회 의원인 제럴드 버턴은 요금이 몇 년 동안 동일하게 유지되었다고 말했습니다. 그러나 ⁸¹ 최근 부지 유지비가 올라서 조치를 취해야 했습니다. 해변을 자주 찾는 주민들은 요금이 이미 너무 높다고 생각하는데요. ⁸² 하지만 버턴 씨와 다른 사람들은 소폭 인상이 사람들이 해변에 가는 것을 단념시키지는 않을 거라고 말합니다. 그리고 저는 방문객 수가 변하지 않을 것이라고 생각합니다.

city council 시의회 discuss 논의하다 lot 지역, 부지
rate 요금 remain 여전히 ~이다
expenses ((보통 복수형)) 비용, 소요 경비 maintain 유지하다
discourage 단념시키다

80.

제럴드 버턴은 누구인 것 같은가?

(A) 부동산 개발업자
(B) 라디오 진행자
(C) 시 공무원
(D) 여행 가이드

property 부동산 developer 개발업자

a city council member → A city official

81.

최근에 무슨 일이 일어났는가?

(A) 일부 비용이 증가했다.
(B) 몇몇 건물이 검사에 불합격했다.
(C) 장소가 더 유명해졌다.
(D) 지방 선거가 열렸다.

fail 불합격하다, 낙제하다 inspection 검사, 점검 site 부지, 용지
election 선거

expenses for maintaining the lot have gone up
→ Some costs have increased

82.

화자는 "방문객 수가 변하지 않을 것"이라고 말할 때 무엇을 암시하는가?

(A) 그는 더 많은 광고가 필요하다고 생각한다.
(B) 그는 제안에 동의한다.
(C) 그는 정책에 대해 걱정한다.
(D) 그는 결정이 논의되기를 원한다.

advertising 광고 proposal 제안 policy 정책, 방침
decision 결정, 판단 debate 논의하다; 토론

[83-85] 영녀 🎧

Questions 83-85 refer to the following talk.

W It's wonderful to see that so many people signed up for this workshop. ⁸³ Today I'm going to teach you some effective methods for managing your team members. One reason that groups struggle is that they're not sure what end result they are trying to achieve. ⁸⁴ When it comes to goals, make sure they are well defined and easy to understand. But before we talk about that, we'll work on one of the hardest tasks you'll have… um… giving negative feedback. 85 There's a right way and a wrong way to do this, so we're going to get into small groups and role-play some situations.

해석

83-85번은 다음 담화에 관한 문제입니다.

여 이번 워크숍에 이렇게 많은 분들이 참가 신청을 해 주신 걸 보니 좋습니다. 83 오늘 저는 팀원들을 관리하는 몇 가지 효과적인 방법을 알려 드리겠습니다. 집단이 고전하는 한 가지 이유는 어떤 최종 결과를 이루어 내고자 하는지 확실히 알지 못하기 때문입니다. 84 목표에 관한 한, 그것은 반드시 명확하고 이해하기 쉽게 하세요. 하지만 그것에 대해 이야기하기 전에, 여러분이 수행할 가장 어려운 과제 중 하나를 다룰 것인데요… 음… 부정적인 피드백을 주는 것입니다. 85 이렇게 하는 데는 올바른 방법과 잘못된 방법이 있습니다. 따라서 우리는 소그룹으로 나눠서 몇 가지 상황을 역할극으로 해 볼 예정입니다.

어휘

sign up for ~을 신청하다 effective 효과적인 method 방법
struggle 고전하다, 애쓰다 end result 최종 결과
achieve 달성하다, 성취하다 when it comes to ~에 관한 한
well defined 명확한 negative 부정적인, 나쁜
role-play ~의 역할을 하다; 역할극

83.

워크숍은 주로 무엇에 관한 것인가?
(A) 현명하게 투자하는 방법
(B) 팀을 관리하는 방법
(C) 제품을 출시하는 방법
(D) 비즈니스 모델을 만드는 방법

어휘

invest 투자하다 wisely 현명하게

패러프레이징

some effective methods for managing your team members → How to manage a team

84.

화자는 청자들에게 무엇을 하라고 조언하는가?
(A) 어려운 업무 외주 맡기기
(B) 시간 현명하게 사용하기
(C) 명확한 목표 세우기
(D) 여러 공급 업체 이용하기

어휘

outsource 외주 제작하다 multiple 많은, 다수의

패러프레이징

goals, make sure they are well defined and easy to understand → Set clear goals

85.

청자들은 다음에 무엇을 할 것 같은가?
(A) 화자에게 몇 가지 질문하기
(B) 보고서에 있는 일부 오류 수정하기
(C) 교육용 비디오 시청하기
(D) 역할극 활동하기

어휘

instructional 교육용의 activity 활동

패러프레이징

role-play some situations → Have a role-play activity

[86-88] 미남 🎧

Questions 86-88 refer to the following advertisement.

M Do you love creating tasty dishes with your own recipes? Do you want to show off your skills? 86 Then sign up for the Milbridge Cooking Contest, taking place on August 4. Our judging panel will select winners in a variety of categories, and we're offering fabulous prizes. The public is also welcome to attend the event, try delicious samples of food, and 87 take advantage of discounts on cookware from Carolina Department Store. Registration begins today and ends on July 31. 88 But everyone who signs up in the first week will receive 25 percent off the participation fee.

해석

86-88번은 다음 광고에 관한 문제입니다.

남 당신만의 고유 레시피로 맛있는 요리를 만드는 걸 좋아하십니까? 당신의 기술을 뽐내고 싶으십니까? 86 그렇다면 8월 4일에 열리는 밀브리지 요리 대회에 등록하십시오. 우리 심사위원단이 다양한 부문에서 우승자를 가리고, 저희가 멋진 상품을 제공할 것입니다. 일반인도 행사에 참석해서 맛있는 음식을 시식하고, 87 캐롤라이나 백화점에서 조리 기구 할인 혜택을 누리는 걸 환영합니다. 참가 신청은 오늘 시작되어 7월 31일에 종료됩니다. 88 하지만 첫 주에 등록하시는 모든 분들은 참가비를 25퍼센트 할인받으실 겁니다.

어휘

tasty 맛있는 dish 요리 recipe 요리법, 조리법
take place 열리다, 일어나다 judging panel 심사위원단
a variety of 다양한, 여러 가지의 category 부문, 범주
fabulous 멋진, 굉장한 cookware 조리 기구
registration 등록 participation 참가, 참여

86.

광고는 주로 무엇에 관한 것인가?
(A) 스포츠 토너먼트
(B) 연례 퍼레이드
(C) 요리 대회
(D) 개업식

어휘

tournament 토너먼트, 시합 parade 퍼레이드, 행진
competition 대회, 시합

패러프레이징

the Milbridge Cooking Contest
→ A cooking competition

87.

화자는 캐롤리나 백화점에 대해 무엇이라고 말하는가?
(A) 그곳은 구매에 대해 무료 배송을 제공할 것이다.
(B) 그곳은 8월 4일에 문을 닫을 것이다.
(C) 그곳은 일부 제품을 더 낮은 가격에 제공할 것이다.
(D) 그곳에서 음악 공연을 할 것이다.

패러프레이징

take advantage of discounts on cookware
→ offer lower prices on some products

88.

청자들은 어떻게 할인을 받을 수 있는가?
(A) 설문 조사를 완료함으로써
(B) 일찍 등록함으로써
(C) 우편물 발송 명단에 가입함으로써
(D) 현금으로 지불함으로써

어휘

in cash 현금으로

패러프레이징

signs up in the first week → signing up early

[89-91] 호남 🎧

Questions 89-91 refer to the following excerpt from a meeting.

> M **89** In today's meeting, we'll be discussing the upcoming Interior Design Trade Show in Baltimore. Regarding travel, if possible, I encourage you to drive to the event, as this would be a relaxing way to get to Baltimore. The company will pay for your fuel costs. Alternatively, we can purchase you a train ticket, but **90** we can't guarantee that you would have a seat. It's a popular route. Also, to help you focus on this event, **91** the management team has decided that the due date for your quarterly reports will be October 10th instead of October 5th.

해석

89-91번은 다음 회의 발췌록에 관한 문제입니다.
남 **89** 오늘 회의에서 우리는 볼티모어에서 곧 있을 인테리어 디자인 무역 박람회에 대해 논의할 것입니다. 출장과 관련해서, 가능하다면 행사장까지 운전해서 가는 것을 권장합니다. 이 방법이 볼티모어까지 가는 편한 방법일 것이기 때문입니다. 회사가 여러분

의 연료비를 지불할 것입니다. 그렇지 않으면, 저희가 기차표를 구매해 드릴 수 있지만 **90** 좌석이 있다고 보장할 수는 없습니다. 그것은 인기 있는 노선입니다. 또한, 여러분이 이 행사에 집중할 수 있도록, **91** 경영진은 분기 보고서의 마감일을 10월 5일 대신에 10월 10일로 결정했습니다.

어휘

upcoming 곧 있을, 다가오는 regarding ~에 관하여
relaxing 편한 fuel cost 연료비
alternatively 그렇지 않으면, 그 대신에 guarantee 보장하다
route 노선, 길 due date 마감일 quarterly 분기별의

89.

화자는 어떤 행사에 대해 이야기하고 있는가?
(A) 기념일 파티
(B) 이사회
(C) 산업 무역 박람회
(D) 지역 모금 행사

어휘

anniversary 기념일 industry 산업 community 지역 사회
fund-raiser 모금 행사

패러프레이징

Interior Design → industry

90.

화자는 왜 "그것은 인기 있는 노선입니다"라고 말하는가?
(A) 가격 인상을 설명하기 위해
(B) 기차가 혼잡할 수 있음을 경고하기 위해
(C) 주행 경로를 확인하기 위해
(D) 추가 여행 시간 허용을 제안하기 위해

어휘

warn 경고하다, 주의를 주다 crowded 혼잡한, 붐비는
confirm 확인하다 direction 경로, 방향

91.

화자에 따르면, 경영진은 무엇을 하기로 결정했는가?
(A) 주문 취소하기
(B) 기한 연장하기
(C) 새로운 팀 배정하기
(D) 예산 조정하기

어휘

extend 연장하다 assign 할당하다 adjust 조정하다
budget 예산

패러프레이징

the due date ~ will be October 10th instead of October 5th → Extend a deadline

[92-94] 미남 🎧

Questions 92-94 refer to the following broadcast.

> M Now let's check in with business news. **92** Cantu, the online video streaming service

based in Dallas, has announced that beginning next month, viewers in Canada and some parts of Europe will be able to access the platform. Cantu has been growing in popularity not only thanks to its large collection of movies and television shows but also because ⁹³it is the only video-streaming service that lets customers pause their subscription. Today we have Mary Snyder, Cantu's CEO, on the line. ⁹⁴She'll talk about how the business got started and the important steps it took to become a market leader.

해석

92-94번은 다음 방송에 관한 문제입니다.

남 이제 경제 뉴스를 확인해 보겠습니다. ⁹²댈러스에 기반을 둔 온라인 비디오 스트리밍 서비스인 칸투는 다음 달부터 캐나다와 유럽 일부 지역의 시청자들이 이 플랫폼에 접속할 수 있을 것이라고 발표했습니다. 칸투는 방대한 영화와 텔레비전 프로그램 컬렉션 때문뿐만 아니라 ⁹³고객들이 구독을 일시 중단하는 것을 허용하는 유일한 비디오 스트리밍 서비스이기 때문에 인기를 얻고 있습니다. 오늘 우리는 칸투의 대표이사인 메리 스나이더와 전화 연결이 되어 있습니다. ⁹⁴그녀는 사업을 어떻게 시작했는지와, 시장의 선두 주자가 되기까지 밟아 온 중요한 단계에 대해 이야기할 것입니다.

어휘

popularity 인기 pause 잠시 멈추다 subscription 구독

92.

방송에 따르면, 칸투는 다음 달에 무엇을 할 것인가?
(A) 댈러스로 이전하기
(B) 대표이사 교체하기
(C) 서비스 지역 확장하기
(D) 어린이용 영상 추가하기

어휘

replace 바꾸다, 교체하다 expand 확장하다

패러프레이징

viewers in Canada and some parts of Europe will be able to access the platform → Expand its service area

93.

화자는 칸투에 대해 어떤 독특한 특징을 언급하는가?
(A) 그것은 다양한 기기에서 사용할 수 있다.
(B) 그것은 볼 만한 영화를 추천해 준다.
(C) 그것은 사용자가 자신의 동영상을 업로드할 수 있게 한다.
(D) 그것은 고객들이 서비스를 일시 정지하는 것을 허용한다.

어휘

device 기기, 장치 recommendation 추천

패러프레이징

lets customers pause their subscription
→ allows customers to pause the service

94.

메리 스나이더는 무엇에 대해 이야기할 것인가?
(A) 채용 공고
(B) 회사 연혁
(C) 고객 보상 프로그램
(D) 프로젝트 마감일

어휘

job opening 채용 공고

패러프레이징

how the business got started and the important steps it took to become a market leader
→ A company's history

[95-97] 호남 🎧

Questions 95-97 refer to the following talk and floor plan.

M All right, everyone. ⁹⁵We've been hired to clean all of the apartments in this building before its grand opening tomorrow. I'll show you everything that needs to be done. For example, ⁹⁶here in the largest room… uh… where we are now, you'll need to vacuum and clean the windows. The sinks in the bathroom and kitchen are new, but the client still wants them to be scrubbed thoroughly. ⁹⁷Don't forget to wear a pair of gloves to protect your hands while you're doing it. If you have any questions, just let me know.

해석

95-97번은 다음 담화와 평면도에 관한 문제입니다.

남 좋습니다, 여러분. ⁹⁵우리는 내일 개장식 전에 이 건물의 모든 아파트를 청소하도록 고용되었습니다. 제가 여러분께 해야 할 모든 것들을 보여드리겠습니다. 예를 들면, ⁹⁶우리가 지금 있는 곳인… 어… 여기 가장 큰 방은 진공청소기로 청소하고 창문을 닦아야 할 것입니다. 욕실과 주방의 개수대는 새것이지만, 고객은 여전히 그것을 철저히 문질러 닦아 주기를 원합니다. ⁹⁷청소하는 동안 손을 보호하기 위해 장갑을 착용하는 것을 잊지 마세요. 질문이 있으시면, 알려 주세요.

어휘

hire 고용하다 vacuum 진공청소기로 청소하다
sink 싱크대, 개수대 scrub 문질러 청소하다
thoroughly 철저히, 완전히 a pair of gloves 장갑 한 켤레
protect 보호하다

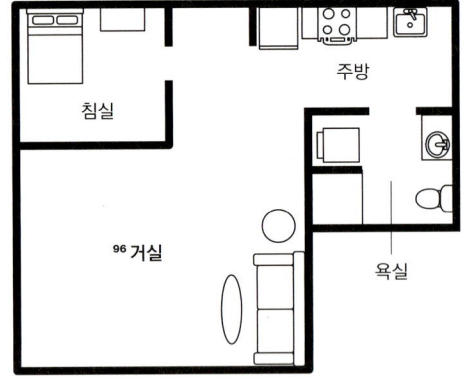

95.

화자는 어디에서 일하는 것 같은가?

(A) 부동산 중개업소에서
(B) 디자인 회사에서
(C) 배달 업체에서
(D) 청소 회사에서

어휘

real estate 부동산

96.

시각 자료를 보시오. 청자들은 어디에 있는가?

(A) 침실에
(B) 주방에
(C) 거실에
(D) 욕실에

97.

청자들은 무엇을 하도록 상기되는가?

(A) 주차권 사용하기
(B) 신분 확인 명찰 제시하기
(C) 보호 장비 착용하기
(D) 명함 남기기

어휘

identification badge 신분 확인 명찰 protective 보호하는
gear 장비

패러프레이징

a pair of gloves to protect your hands
→ protective gear

[98-100] 미녀 🎧

Questions 98-100 refer to the following instruction and chart.

> W ⁹⁸I'd like to let you know that I've finalized the plans for the holiday display at our store. It's going to take a lot of work to set it up because we need to move some of our current shelving out of the way. The set-up day will be November 15. If you're not scheduled to work that day and you can help with the display, please let me know. ⁹⁹We need to work on it when the store has the least amount of customers, as this will minimize disruptions. ¹⁰⁰All employees who work extra hours on that day will be given a gift certificate for 50 dollars, which can be used at the coffee shop next door.

해석

98-100번은 다음 설명과 도표에 관한 문제입니다.

여 ⁹⁸우리 매장의 휴가철 진열 계획을 확정하였음을 알려 드립니다. 현재의 선반 일부를 치워야 하기 때문에 설치하는 데 많은 작업이 필요할 겁니다. 설치 날짜는 11월 15일입니다. 그날 근무 예정이 아니고 진열을 도와줄 수 있다면 제게 알려 주세요. ⁹⁹매장에 고객이 가장 적을 때 이 작업을 해야 하는데요, 그래야 지장을 최소로 할 것이기 때문입니다. ¹⁰⁰그날 시간 외 근무를 하는 모든 직원에게는 옆 커피숍에서 사용할 수 있는 50달러 상당의 상품권이 지급될 것입니다.

어휘

finalize 완성하다, 끝내다 current 현재의, 지금의
shelving 선반 work on ~에 착수하다 minimize 최소화하다
disruption 중단, 혼란 gift certificate 상품권

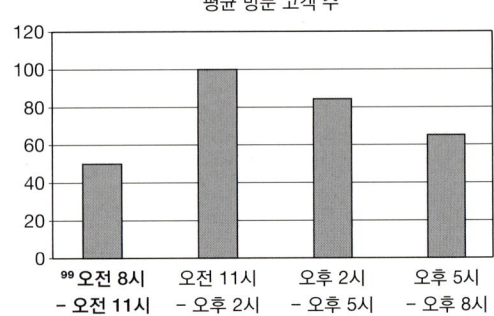

평균 방문 고객 수

98.

화자는 누구인 것 같은가?

(A) 컴퓨터 기술자
(B) 매장 관리자
(C) 재정 고문
(D) 제품 개발자

어휘

technician 기술자 financial 재정의, 금융의
advisor 고문, 조언자 developer 개발자

99.

시각 자료를 보시오. 진열은 언제 설치될 것인가?

(A) 오전 8시부터 오전 11시까지
(B) 오전 11시부터 오후 2시까지
(C) 오후 2시부터 오후 5시까지
(D) 오후 5시부터 오후 8시까지

100.

추가 근무를 하는 직원들에게는 무엇이 지급될 것인가?

(A) 무료 식사

(B) 커피 보온병

(C) 상품권

(D) 얼마간의 휴가

어휘

meal 식사 thermos 보온병 time off 휴가, 휴식

실전 모의고사 1회

본문 p.300

1. (C)	2. (A)	3. (B)	4. (A)	5. (C)
6. (D)	7. (A)	8. (B)	9. (B)	10. (B)
11. (B)	12. (C)	13. (C)	14. (B)	15. (A)
16. (C)	17. (A)	18. (C)	19. (B)	20. (B)
21. (A)	22. (B)	23. (C)	24. (A)	25. (B)
26. (A)	27. (C)	28. (A)	29. (C)	30. (B)
31. (A)	32. (C)	33. (B)	34. (D)	35. (C)
36. (A)	37. (B)	38. (D)	39. (D)	40. (B)
41. (C)	42. (B)	43. (C)	44. (C)	45. (A)
46. (C)	47. (D)	48. (B)	49. (A)	50. (C)
51. (D)	52. (B)	53. (C)	54. (B)	55. (D)
56. (D)	57. (A)	58. (A)	59. (B)	60. (C)
61. (A)	62. (C)	63. (C)	64. (B)	65. (D)
66. (B)	67. (C)	68. (C)	69. (B)	70. (A)
71. (B)	72. (A)	73. (A)	74. (C)	75. (C)
76. (A)	77. (C)	78. (A)	79. (B)	80. (D)
81. (A)	82. (B)	83. (B)	84. (A)	85. (B)
86. (B)	87. (A)	88. (B)	89. (A)	90. (C)
91. (D)	92. (D)	93. (C)	94. (B)	95. (A)
96. (C)	97. (A)	98. (C)	99. (B)	100. (A)

1. 호남 🎧

(A) They're sitting on a couch.
(B) They're looking out the window.
(C) They're lifting some furniture.
(D) They're closing the curtains.

해석
(A) 그들은 소파에 앉아있다.
(B) 그들은 창밖을 바라보고 있다.
(C) 그들은 가구를 들어 올리고 있다.
(D) 그들은 커튼을 닫고 있다.

어휘
couch 긴 의자, 소파 lift ~을 들어 올리다

2. 영녀 🎧

(A) The man is taking notes.
(B) The man is typing on a laptop.
(C) The man is drinking from a coffee cup.
(D) The man is watering a plant.

해석
(A) 남자가 메모하고 있다.
(B) 남자가 노트북 컴퓨터에 입력하고 있다.
(C) 남자가 커피잔으로 무언가를 마시고 있다.
(D) 남자가 화초에 물을 주고 있다.

어휘
take notes 메모[기록]하다 type 입력하다, 타자 치다
water 물을 주다

3. 미남 🎧

(A) They are standing in front of a desk.
(B) The woman is holding a mug.
(C) The man is looking at some pictures.
(D) They are using their cellphones.

해석
(A) 그들은 책상 앞에 앉아 있다.
(B) 여자가 머그잔을 들고 있다.
(C) 남자가 몇몇 사진을 보고 있다.
(D) 그들은 휴대폰을 사용하고 있다.

어휘
mug 머그잔

4. 미녀 🎧

(A) The man is bending over an engine.
(B) A car is being driven.
(C) The man is wearing a lab coat.
(D) A tire is being replaced.

해석

(A) 남자가 엔진 위로 몸을 굽히고 있다.
(B) 차를 운전하고 있다.
(C) 남자가 실험 가운을 입고 있다.
(D) 타이어가 교체되고 있다.

어휘

bend over 몸을 ~위로 굽히다   lab coat 실험 가운
replace 교체하다, 바꾸다

5. 호남 🎧

(A) A sofa is beneath a picture.
(B) Some books are stacked on the ground.
(C) A picture is hanging on the wall.
(D) There is a basket on a dresser.

해석

(A) 소파가 그림 아래에 있다.
(B) 책들이 바닥에 쌓여 있다.
(C) 사진이 벽에 걸려 있다.
(D) 장롱 위에 바구니가 있다.

어휘

stack 쌓다   dresser 장롱

6. 영녀 🎧

(A) She's sitting on a bench.
(B) She's holding her bag.
(C) She's reading a book.
(D) She's looking at her laptop.

해석

(A) 그녀는 벤치에 앉아 있다.
(B) 그녀는 가방을 들고 있다.
(C) 그녀는 책을 읽고 있다.
(D) 그녀는 그녀의 노트북을 보고 있다.

7. 호남 영녀 🎧

Why was the meeting rescheduled?
(A) Because the project leader is sick.
(B) In the conference room.
(C) Let's meet next Tuesday.

해석

왜 회의 일정이 변경되었나요?
(A) 프로젝트 리더가 아프기 때문이에요.
(B) 회의실에서요.
(C) 다음 주 화요일에 만나요.

어휘

reschedule 일정을 변경하다

8. 영녀 미남 🎧

You visit this shop for iced coffee often, don't you?
(A) Please add extra sugar.
(B) Yes, almost every day.
(C) Be careful not to slip on the ice outside.

해석

당신은 아이스 커피를 마시러 이 가게에 자주 방문하죠, 그렇지 않나요?
(A) 설탕을 더 넣어 주시기 바랍니다.
(B) 네, 거의 매일이요.
(C) 밖에서 얼음에 미끄러져 넘어지지 않도록 조심하세요.

어휘

extra 추가의, 가외의
slip on the ice 얼음 위에서 미끄러져 넘어지다

9. 미녀 호남 🎧

Do you have the photos from the design department?
(A) An instant camera.
(B) No, they'll be ready tomorrow.
(C) Sure, that's fine.

해석

디자인 부서에서 받은 사진이 있나요?
(A) 즉석카메라입니다.
(B) 아니요, 그것들은 내일 준비될 거예요.
(C) 그럼요, 괜찮습니다.

어휘

instant 즉각적인, 인스턴트의

10. 미남 미녀 🎧

When are you moving to the Stockholm office?
(A) The office fax machine.
(B) The schedule is being decided.
(C) Competition is tough this quarter.

해석

언제 스톡홀름 사무소로 옮기세요?
(A) 사무실 팩스기입니다.
(B) 일정을 정하는 중이에요.
(C) 이번 분기는 경쟁이 심해요.

어휘

competition 경쟁, 경연 대회   quarter 분기

11. 미녀 호남 🎧

Would you like to join our rewards program?
(A) You can get this one for free.
(B) Sure, sign me up.
(C) Can I join the meeting?

해석

저희의 보상 프로그램에 가입하시겠어요?
(A) 이것을 무료로 받으실 수 있어요.
(B) 그럼요, 저를 가입시켜 주세요.
(C) 제가 회의에 참석해도 될까요?

어휘

reward 보상; 보상하다   for free 무료로
sign ~ up ~를 가입[등록]시켜 주다

12. 미남 영녀 🎧

How often do we have company retreats?
(A) The company president is coming.
(B) I'll treat you to some tea.
(C) Twice a year.

해석

우리는 얼마나 자주 회사 야유회를 가나요?
(A) 사장님이 오고 계세요.
(B) 제가 차를 좀 대접할게요.
(C) 1년에 두 번이요.

어휘

company retreat 회사 야유회
treat A to B A에게 B를 대접하다, 한턱내다

13. 영녀 미남 🎧

I can use the hotel gym, right?
(A) A trendy exercise routine.
(B) Feel free to use the towels by the pool.
(C) Yes, it's right down the hall.

해석

제가 호텔 헬스장을 이용할 수 있죠, 맞죠?
(A) 최신 유행하는 운동 순서예요.
(B) 수영장 근처의 수건을 마음대로 사용하세요.
(C) 네, 복도를 따라가면 바로 있어요.

어휘

trendy 최신 유행의
routine 루틴(규칙적으로 하는 일의 통상적인 순서와 방법)
feel free to 마음대로 ~하다

14. 호남 미녀 🎧

Have you e-mailed Mr. Garrison about the merger?
(A) Can you help me send this package?
(B) Yes, he already replied.
(C) Be careful when merging into traffic.

해석

개리슨 씨에게 합병에 대해 이메일을 보냈나요?
(A) 제가 이 소포를 보내는 것을 도와주시겠어요?
(B) 네, 그가 벌써 답장을 보냈어요.
(C) 차량들에 합류할 때는 조심하세요.

어휘

merger (기업의) 합병   package 소포, 꾸러미   reply 답장하다
merge into traffic 차량들에 합류하다

15. 영녀 미남 🎧

Don't we have to finalize the project today?
(A) No, we already finished it.
(B) A new high-definition projector.
(C) This is my final week working here.

해석

우리가 오늘 프로젝트를 마무리 지어야 하지 않나요?
(A) 아니요, 우리는 이미 그것을 마쳤습니다.
(B) 새로운 고화질 프로젝터입니다.
(C) 이번 주가 제가 이곳에서 일하는 마지막 주입니다.

어휘

finalize 마무리 짓다, 완결하다   high-definition 고화질의

16. 영녀 미녀 🎧

What's the cost for the restaurant's renovation?
(A) In a few weeks.
(B) I think we should rest a bit.
(C) It's about $6,000.

해석

식당 보수 비용은 얼마입니까?
(A) 몇 주 후에요.
(B) 우리가 조금 쉬어야 할 것 같아요.
(C) 약 6천 달러입니다.

어휘

renovation 보수, 수리, 혁신 rest 쉬다; 휴식

17. 미녀 호남 🎧

> Where can I get a new monitor for my desktop?
> **(A) You have to submit an official request.**
> (B) A mechanical pencil.
> (C) Your new desk will arrive soon.

해석

제 데스크톱 컴퓨터를 위한 새 모니터를 어디서 받을 수 있나요?
(A) 공식 요청서를 제출해야 합니다.
(B) 샤프펜슬입니다.
(C) 당신의 새 책상이 곧 도착할 거예요.

어휘

submit 제출하다 official request 공식 요청(서)
mechanical pencil 샤프펜슬

18. 미남 미녀 🎧

> How do I get to the park?
> (A) By the end of the week.
> (B) The parking lot is nearby.
> **(C) You should make a right at the corner.**

해석

그 공원에 어떻게 가나요?
(A) 주말까지요.
(B) 주차장이 인근에 있습니다.
(C) 모퉁이에서 오른쪽으로 돌아야 합니다.

어휘

parking lot 주차장 nearby 인근의, 인근에
make a right 우회전하다

19. 호남 미남 🎧

> Could you check to see if the computer is plugged in?
> (A) A better power cord.
> **(B) That's the first thing I did.**
> (C) I don't know the answer.

해석

컴퓨터가 전원에 연결되어 있는지 확인해 주시겠어요?
(A) 더 나은 전선입니다.
(B) 맨 먼저 그것부터 했어요.
(C) 답을 모르겠어요.

어휘

plug in 전원을 연결하다, ~의 플러그를 꽂다 power cord 전선

20. 미남 영녀 🎧

> Is the new data entry process more efficient?
> (A) Yes, he's a new hire.
> **(B) It only took me twenty minutes.**
> (C) Enter the access code.

해석

새로운 데이터 입력 과정이 더 효율적인가요?
(A) 네, 그는 신입사원입니다.
(B) 저는 겨우 20분 걸렸어요.
(C) 접속 코드를 입력하세요.

어휘

entry (컴퓨터의) 입력, 입장 efficient 효율적인
new hire 신입 사원

21. 호남 미녀 🎧

> Would you like the black pants or the blue pants?
> **(A) I'll take the blue.**
> (B) I drink my coffee black.
> (C) My shoes are at the cleaner's.

해석

검은색 바지로 하시겠어요, 파란색 바지로 하시겠습니까?
(A) 파란색으로 하겠습니다.
(B) 저는 블랙 커피로 마십니다.
(C) 제 신발이 세탁소에 있어요.

어휘

cleaner's 세탁소

22. 영녀 호남 🎧

> Who's leading this afternoon's marketing strategy meeting?
> (A) Ms. Parley is a great leader.
> **(B) I have a different meeting to attend.**
> (C) Let me tell you where to meet.

해석

오늘 오후의 마케팅 전략 회의를 누가 진행하나요?
(A) 팔리 씨는 훌륭한 리더입니다.
(B) 저는 참석해야 할 다른 회의가 있어요.
(C) 어디서 만날지 말씀드릴게요.

어휘

lead 이끌다, 안내하다 strategy 전략, 계획 attend 참석하다

23. 미남 영녀 🎧

> Your budget proposal's being reviewed during today's meeting.
> (A) That movie has bad reviews.
> (B) About $2000.
> **(C) I didn't get to work on it much.**

당신의 예산 제안서가 오늘 회의 중에 검토될 거예요.
(A) 그 영화는 평이 나빠요.
(B) 약 2천 달러입니다.
(C) 제가 그 일을 많이 못 했어요.

어휘

budget proposal 예산 제안서, 예산안
review 검토하다; 검토, 평가
work on ~을 작업하다, ~에 노력을 들이다

24. 영녀 호남 🎧

Don't you serve vegetarian dishes here?
(A) Of course we do.
(B) Our vegetables are always fresh.
(C) I'll read the message now.

해석

이곳에서는 채식 요리를 제공하지 않나요?
(A) 물론 합니다.
(B) 저희 채소는 항상 신선합니다.
(C) 지금 그 메시지를 읽겠습니다.

어휘

serve (식당 등에서 음식을) 제공하다   vegetarian dish 채식 요리

25. 미녀 미남 🎧

Would you like to have dinner with our client?
(A) About two hours left.
(B) Sure, let's try the restaurant downstairs.
(C) The project is nearly finished.

해석

우리 고객과 저녁 식사를 하시겠어요?
(A) 약 2시간 남았습니다.
(B) 물론이에요, 아래층 식당에 가 보죠.
(C) 그 프로젝트는 거의 완료되었어요.

어휘

try ~을 해 보다   nearly 거의

26. 호남 영녀 🎧

How about we hire an event planner for the company party?
(A) Our budget won't allow it.
(B) Sure, I'd love to go.
(C) Our company is developing new products.

해석

우리가 회사 파티를 위해 행사 기획자를 고용하는 게 어때요?
(A) 우리 예산이 허락하지 않을 거예요.
(B) 그럼요, 가고 싶어요.
(C) 우리 회사가 신제품을 개발하고 있어요.

어휘

event planner 행사 기획자   budget 예산
allow 허락[허용]하다

27. 미남 미녀 🎧

Isn't that electronics company planning to develop its own semiconductors soon?
(A) Congratulations on the new job!
(B) I have a business trip coming up.
(C) Yes, that's what I heard.

해석

그 전자 회사는 곧 자체적으로 반도체를 개발할 계획이지 않나요?
(A) 새 직장을 얻은 것을 축하해요!
(B) 저는 출장을 앞두고 있어요.
(C) 네, 제가 들은 바로는 그래요.

어휘

electronics company 전자 회사
be planning to ~할 계획이다   semiconductor 반도체
congratulations on ~을 축합니다

28. 미녀 미남 🎧

Susan came up with the idea for the new ad campaign, didn't she?
(A) Actually, it was Jessica.
(B) In department stores.
(C) I think we should add more color to the poster.

해석

수잔이 새로운 광고 캠페인을 위한 아이디어를 제시했죠, 그렇지 않나요?
(A) 실은, 제시카였어요.
(B) 백화점에서요.
(C) 우리가 포스터에 색깔을 더 추가해야 한다고 생각해요.

어휘

come up with ~을 생각해 내다, 제시하다

29. 호남 영녀 🎧

Who is in charge of doing market research in the Philippines?
(A) They sell many fruits and vegetables there.
(B) Yes, it's on South Street.
(C) Martin is heading up that team.

해석

누가 필리핀의 시장 조사를 하는 일을 담당하나요?
(A) 그곳에서는 과일과 채소를 많이 팔아요.
(B) 네, 그것은 사우스 거리에 있습니다.
(C) 마틴이 그 팀을 이끌 거예요.

어휘

in charge of ~을 담당하는, 책임지는   head up 이끌다

30. 미녀 호남 🎧

> Have you purchased the plane tickets for the convention, or should I?
> (A) Unfortunately, this bag will cost extra.
> **(B) I don't have the company credit card.**
> (C) We also accept checks.

해석

컨벤션을 위한 비행기 티켓을 구매했나요, 아니면 제가 할까요?
(A) 유감스럽게도, 이 가방은 추가로 비용이 듭니다.
(B) 저는 법인카드를 갖고 있지 않아요.
(C) 저희는 또한 수표도 받습니다.

어휘

convention 컨벤션, 총회 cost extra 추가로 비용이 들다

31. 미남 영녀 🎧

> These reports should have been entered into the computer yesterday.
> **(A) I thought the deadline was Thursday.**
> (B) Please report this to your department manager.
> (C) The entrance is right next door.

해석

이 보고서들은 어제 컴퓨터에 입력되었어야 해요.
(A) 마감일이 목요일이라고 생각했어요.
(B) 이것을 당신의 부서장에게 보고하시기 바랍니다.
(C) 입구는 바로 옆문입니다.

어휘

enter into ~에 입력하다 entrance (출)입구

[32-34] 영녀 미남 🎧

Questions 32-34 refer to the following conversation.

> W Hi, this is Stacey from Marketing. Do you think I can reserve Conference Room B on Monday? ³²My staff needs to have a quick meeting about recent sales figures.
> M ³³Sure, that shouldn't be a problem. When is the meeting?
> W The meeting is from 11 A.M. to noon.
> M Got it. ³³I'll set aside that time slot for you. Do you need anything else?
> W Actually, I think a few of the lights in that room are broken. Do you think you can get someone to fix them before Monday?
> M Sure. ³⁴I'll call the technician now and he'll come fix them.

해석

32-34번은 다음 대화에 관한 문제입니다.
여 안녕하세요, 저는 마케팅부의 스테이시예요. 제가 월요일에 B 회의실을 예약할 수 있을까요? ³²저희 부서원들이 최근 판매 수치

에 관해서 간단한 회의를 해야 해요.
남 ³³네, 문제없어요. 회의가 언제인가요?
여 회의는 오전 11시부터 정오까지예요.
남 알겠습니다. ³³당신을 위해 그 시간대를 비워 두겠습니다. 그 밖에 다른 것이 필요하신가요?
여 실은, 그 방의 전등 몇 개가 고장 났어요. 월요일 전에 누군가를 시켜서 그걸 고치게 할 수 있을까요?
남 물론입니다. ³⁴제가 지금 기술자에게 전화해서 그것들을 고치러 와 달라고 할게요.

어휘

reserve 예약하다 staff ((집합적)) 직원, 부원
sales figures 매출 수치 set aside (돈·시간을) 따로 떼어 두다
time slot 시간대 broken 고장 난 fix 수리하다, 바로잡다
technician 기술자

32.

여자는 무엇을 준비하고 있는가?
(A) 국제 콘퍼런스
(B) 사무실 이전
(C) 동료들과의 회의
(D) 제품 출시

어휘

relocation 재배치, 이전 launch 출시, 개시; 출시하다; 시작하다

패러프레이징

staff → colleagues

33.

남자는 누구인 것 같은가?
(A) 회사 임원
(B) 관리 보조원
(C) 기술자
(D) 행사 기획자

어휘

executive (기업 등의) 임원, 간부
administrative 관리[행정]상의 assistant 조수, 보조원

34.

남자는 다음에 무엇을 할 것인가?
(A) 상사와 얘기하기
(B) 회의 취소하기
(C) 고장 난 장비 수리하기
(D) 전화하기

어휘

repair 수리하다; 수리 equipment ((집합적)) 장비

패러프레이징

call → Make a phone call

[35-37] 미녀 호남 🎧

Questions 35-37 refer to the following conversation.

W Matthew, ³⁵ have you started working on next year's budget proposal?

M No, I haven't. ³⁵ I was planning on starting tomorrow.

W That's perfect. If the company has funds for them, ³⁶ I'd like to add some new marketing specialists to my team next year. I thought two would be enough, but I think we'll need at least four because we are planning to expand to the overseas market.

M Not a problem. I should be able to add that to the budget. ³⁷ Can you send me details about job expectations and pay ranges when you get the chance?

해석

35-37번은 다음 대화에 관한 문제입니다.

여 매튜, ³⁵ 내년 예산 제안서 작업을 시작했어요?

남 아니요, 아직이요. ³⁵ 내일 시작할 계획이었어요.

여 잘됐네요. 만약 회사가 그럴 자금이 있다면, ³⁶ 내년에 우리 팀에 **신규 마케팅 전문가 몇 명을 추가하고 싶어요**. 두 명이면 충분할 거라고 생각했지만, 해외 시장으로 확장할 계획이기 때문에 적어도 네 명이 필요할 것 같아요.

남 문제없어요. 제가 예산에 그걸 추가할 수 있을 거예요. ³⁷ 기회가 되시면 직무 기대와 급여 범위에 대한 자세한 내용을 제게 보내 주실 수 있나요?

어휘

budget proposal 예산안, 예산 제안서
plan on ~할 계획[예정]이다 fund 자금, 돈 specialist 전문가
at least 적어도 expand to ~로 확장하다
overseas 해외의; 해외에서 details 세부 정보
expectations ((보통 복수형)) 기대되는 것 pay range 급여 범위

35.

남자는 무엇에 대한 책임이 있는가?
(A) 신규 직원을 채용하는 것
(B) 해외 고객을 상대하는 것
(C) 연간 예산 개요를 작성하는 것
(D) 회사 파일을 정리하는 것

어휘

be responsible for ~에 책임이 있다
deal with ~을 다루다, 처리하다 outline ~의 개요를 서술하다
organize 정리하다, 체계화하다

패러프레이징

working on next year's budget proposal
→ Outlining an annual budget

36.

여자는 내년에 무엇을 하기를 원하는가?
(A) 팀 확장하기
(B) 신규 인턴사원 모집하기

(C) 행사 기획하기
(D) 고객 만족도 높이기

어휘

recruit 모집하다, 뽑다 customer satisfaction 고객 만족

패러프레이징

add some new marketing specialists to my team
→ Expand her team

37.

남자는 여자에게 무엇을 해 달라고 요청하는가?
(A) 회의 준비하기
(B) 남자에게 더욱 자세한 내용 보내 주기
(C) 예산안 작성하기
(D) 회의 잡기

어휘

prepare for ~을 준비하다

패러프레이징

details about job expectations and pay ranges
→ further details

[38-40] 영녀 미남 🎧

Questions 38-40 refer to the following conversation.

W Welcome to Bargain Business Suits. What can I do for you?

M Hi. ³⁸ I wanted to buy a couple of suits for my new job.

W Oh, congratulations! What kind of suits are you looking for?

M ³⁹ I really like the one in your display window, but I'm not a fan of the pattern...

W Unfortunately, that suit only comes in that pattern. Maybe you'd like to see our other suits that have different styles.

M Great. My budget is about 200 dollars for each suit. Please find me some suits that are similar to the one in the window.

W I can show you some suits that are around that price. Just so you know, if you need your suits altered, there is a small fee, ⁴⁰ but delivery is included in your purchase.

해석

38-40번은 다음 대화에 관한 문제입니다.

여 바겐 비즈니스 정장에 오신 것을 환영합니다. 무엇을 도와드릴까요?

남 안녕하세요. ³⁸ 새 직장 출근을 위해 정장 몇 벌을 사고 싶습니다.

여 아, 축하합니다! 어떤 종류의 정장을 찾고 계세요?

남 ³⁹ 진열창에 있는 게 마음에 들기는 한데, 저런 무늬를 좋아하지 않아서.

여 유감스럽게도, 저 정장은 저 무늬로만 나와요. 다양한 스타일이 있는 저희의 다른 정장들을 보시고 싶을 것 같은데요.

남 좋습니다. 제 예산은 정장 한 벌당 약 200달러예요. 진열창에 있는 것과 비슷한 정장들로 좀 찾아 주세요.

여 그 가격대의 정장들을 좀 보여 드릴게요. 참고로 말씀드리면, 정장을 수선해야 한다면 소정의 요금이 있어요, **⁴⁰하지만 배송이 구매에 포함됩니다.**

어휘

suit 정장, 옷 (한 벌) Congratulations! 축하합니다!
display window 진열창, 쇼윈도
not a fan of ~을 좋아하는 편은 아닌 pattern 무늬, 패턴
unfortunately 안타깝게도 budget 예산 similar ~와 비슷한
alter (옷을) 고치다, 바꾸다 fee 요금, 수수료

38.

남자는 무엇을 위해 정장이 필요한가?
(A) 면접
(B) 사진 촬영
(C) 결혼식
(D) 새 직장

39.

남자는 진열창에 있는 정장에 대해 무엇을 싫어하는가?
(A) 재질
(B) 길이
(C) 가격
(D) 무늬

40.

여자는 가격에 무엇이 포함된다고 말하는가?
(A) 수선
(B) 배달
(C) 정장 구두
(D) 판매세

어휘

alteration 개조, 고침

[41-43] 영녀 미남 🎧

Questions 41-43 refer to the following conversation.

W Weston Private School. How may I help you?
M Hello, ⁴¹I'm calling on behalf of Fabulous Films. We would like to film a scene at the main entrance of your school. We need to do a flashback for one of our movie's characters.
W Actually, there was a film shoot at our school last year. It was mostly fine, but ⁴²the problem was the company made a complete mess for us to clean up afterward. I'm worried that might happen again.
M I understand your concern, but we promise to maintain the school's cleanliness.
W Hmm. Well, ⁴³there's a board meeting here next week. You can have 5 minutes at the

beginning of it to give us details about the project.

해석

41-43번은 다음 대화에 관한 문제입니다.
여 웨스턴 사립학교입니다. 어떻게 도와드릴까요?
남 안녕하세요. ⁴¹패뷸러스 필름을 대표해서 전화드립니다. 저희는 그 학교의 정문에서 영화 장면을 촬영하고 싶어요. 저희 영화 속 등장인물 중 한 명의 회상 장면을 찍어야 해요.
여 실은 작년에 저희 학교에서 영화 촬영을 했었어요. 대체로 괜찮았지만, ⁴²문제는 회사가 완전히 엉망으로 만들어 놓아서 저희가 뒷정리를 했던 거예요. 그런 일이 다시 일어날까 봐 걱정스럽습니다.
남 당신의 염려를 이해합니다, 하지만 저희가 학교를 깨끗한 상태로 유지할 것을 약속드립니다.
여 흠. 음, ⁴³다음 주에 이사회가 있어요. 저희에게 프로젝트에 대해 상세히 설명하실 수 있게 시작할 때 5분을 드리겠습니다.

어휘

private 사적인, 사립의 on behalf of ~을 대신[대표]하여
flashback (영화·연극 등에서) 회상 장면 character 등장인물
film shoot 영화 촬영 mostly 대체로
make a mess 뒤범벅을 만들다 complete 완전한
afterward 나중에 concern 걱정, 염려
promise to ~하기로 약속하다 cleanliness 청결, 깨끗함
board meeting 이사회 give details 상세히 설명하다

41.

남자는 어떤 종류의 회사에서 일하는 것 같은가?
(A) 스포츠 용품 소매업
(B) 식품 유통업체
(C) 영화사
(D) 가구 회사

어휘

retailer 소매업, 소매상 distributor 유통업자

42.

여자는 무엇에 대해 걱정한다고 말하는가?
(A) 학생들의 안전
(B) 프로젝트의 깨끗함
(C) 영화 촬영 비용
(D) 작업 팀의 기량

어휘

safety 안전 crew (함께 일하는) 팀, 반, 조

패러프레이징

clean up → cleanliness

43.

여자는 남자가 무엇을 하게 해 주는 데 동의하는가?
(A) 영화 촬영하기
(B) 보고서 제출하기
(C) 회의에서 이야기하기

(D) 그녀의 교장에게 말하기

어휘
어휘

principal 교장, 학장, 총장; 주요한

패러프레이징

give us details / board meeting → Speak at a meeting

[44-46] 호남 미녀 🎧
Questions 44-46 refer to the following conversation.

> M Pardon me, but ⁴⁴I'm looking for Francisco Zabala's sculpture called *The Canyon*.
> W Sorry, but his sculptures aren't on display at the moment. Thankfully, it's only temporary though. ⁴⁵We're installing new windows in that part of the museum. If you come back in about a month, the installation will be done and you can see all of Zabala's artwork.
> M I'm sorry to hear that. I'm here on a business trip so I only have a few days left in town.
> W I apologize, sir. ⁴⁶But if you're interested in that artist, you can see some of his paintings on the second floor.

해석

44-46번은 다음 대화에 관한 문제입니다.

남 실례합니다만, ⁴⁴저는 〈협곡〉이라는 프란시스코 자발라의 조각품을 찾고 있어요.

여 죄송하지만, 그의 조각품들은 지금 전시 중이 아니에요. 다행히도 일시적인 것이긴 하지만요. ⁴⁵저희가 박물관의 그 부분에 진열창을 새로 설치하고 있어요. 한 달쯤 뒤에 다시 오시면, 설치가 완료되어서 자발라의 미술품을 모두 보실 수 있어요.

남 그렇다니 유감이네요. 제가 이곳에서 출장 중이어서 이 도시에 머물 날이 며칠 안 남았어요.

여 죄송합니다, 손님. ⁴⁶하지만 그 미술가에 관심이 있으시다면, 2층에서 그의 그림들 중 일부를 보실 수 있습니다.

어휘

sculpture 조각품, 조각 canyon 협곡
on display 전시[진열]된 at the moment 바로 지금
thankfully 고맙게도, 다행스럽게도 temporary 일시적인, 임시의
install 설치하다 installation 설치 artwork 미술품
apologize 사과하다 be interested in ~에 관심이 있다

44.

프란시스코 자발라는 누구인 것 같은가?
(A) 미술품 중개인
(B) 도급업자
(C) 예술가
(D) 보안 요원

어휘

dealer 딜러, 중개인 contractor 도급업자, 계약자

45.

여자는 어떤 보수를 언급하는가?
(A) 진열창이 교체되고 있다.
(B) 가구가 재배치되고 있다.
(C) 벽에 다시 페인트칠을 하고 있다.
(D) 화장실이 개조되고 있다.

어휘

renovation 보수, 수리 replace 교체하다
rearrange 재배열하다 redo 개조하다

패러프레이징

installing new windows
→ Some windows are being replaced

46.

여자는 남자에게 무엇을 하라고 제안하는가?
(A) 저녁에 다시 오기
(B) 여행 떠나기
(C) 일부 미술품 보기
(D) 기념품 가게에 방문하기

패러프레이징

see some of his paintings → Look at some art

[47-49] 영녀 호남 🎧
Questions 47-49 refer to the following conversation.

> W Hi, Lawrence. How is your sales report going? Organizing data from the cafés in my region is taking a really long time for me. ⁴⁷Management wants additional information on coffee bean purchases, delivery times, and things like that, so it's taking longer than usual.
> M Have you tried creating a spreadsheet? That's what I did, and it didn't take too long.
> W ⁴⁸Really? Did you finish already?
> M ⁴⁸I finished gathering and analyzing the data, but I'm not so confident about the presentation. We don't have any guidelines for it.
> W Don't worry about it. ⁴⁹I'm great with that sort of thing. If you help me with my data, I'll help you with your presentation.

해석

47-49번은 다음 대화에 관한 문제입니다.

여 안녕하세요, 로렌스. 판매 보고서는 어떻게 되어 가고 있어요? 제 지역 카페들의 데이터를 정리하는 일이 제게 정말 오래 걸리고 있어요. ⁴⁷경영진이 커피 콩 구매, 배달 시간 같은 것들에 대한 추가 정보를 원해서 평소보다 시간이 더 오래 걸리고 있어요.

남 스프레드시트를 만들어 보셨어요? 제가 바로 그렇게 했어요, 그랬더니 그리 오래 걸리지 않았어요.

여 ⁴⁸정말요? 당신은 이미 끝났어요?

남 ⁴⁸데이터를 모아서 분석하는 것은 끝냈지만, 발표에 대해서는 그

다지 자신이 없어요. 우리에겐 그에 대한 가이드라인이 전혀 없어요.

여 그것에 대해선 걱정하지 말아요. **⁴⁹제가 그런 것은 잘해요.** 당신이 제 데이터를 도와주면, 제가 당신의 발표를 도와줄게요.

어휘

organize 정리하다, 체계화하다 management 경영, 운영, 관리
additional 추가적인 than usual 평소보다 create 만들어 내다
gather (정보를) 모으다, 수집하다 analyze 분석하다
confident 자신감 있는 presentation 발표, 프레젠테이션
guideline 가이드라인, 지침 sort 종류

47.

화자의 회사는 무엇을 판매하는 것 같은가?
(A) 자동차
(B) 액세서리
(C) 옷
(D) 커피 콩

48.

여자는 왜 놀라는가?
(A) 커피숍이 새로 문을 열었다.
(B) 남자가 자신의 보고서를 마무리 지었다.
(C) 경영진이 더 많은 정보를 요청했다.
(D) 매출이 크게 증가했다.

어휘

finalize 마무리 짓다 greatly 대단히, 크게

패러프레이징

finished → finalized

49.

여자는 왜 "그것에 대해선 걱정하지 말아요"라고 말하는가?
(A) 도움을 제안하기 위해
(B) 그녀가 업무를 끝냈다는 것을 보여 주기 위해
(C) 남자에게 집에 가라고 제안하기 위해
(D) 더 많은 책임을 떠맡기 위해

어휘

assignment 임무, 과제 take on ~을 떠맡다
responsibility 책임

[50-52] 미녀 미남 🎧

Questions 50-52 refer to the following conversation.

W Thanks for coming, Kenny. Have you heard the news? **⁵⁰Joyce Davidson is moving out of the country at the end of the month.** That means her position as head of international marketing in Nepal will be open. I was wondering if you are interested in taking her place.

M Wow! That would be a huge promotion for me. Hmm. I think I'll need some time to talk it over with my family. **⁵¹When would I start working?**

W Ideally, the first week of July. **⁵²The company**

would also give you a relocation bonus if you decide to accept the offer.

해석

50-52번은 다음 대화에 관한 문제입니다.

여 와 주셔서 고마워요, 케니. 소식 들었어요? **⁵⁰조이스 데이비드슨이 이달 말에 국외로 이주해요.** 그 말은 네팔의 해외 마케팅 책임자인 그녀의 자리가 공석이 될 거라는 거예요. 당신이 그녀의 자리를 맡는 데 관심이 있는지 궁금해요.

남 와! 그건 제게 엄청난 승진이 되겠네요. 제 가족과 그것에 대해 얘기할 시간이 좀 필요할 거예요. **⁵¹제가 언제 일을 시작하게 되나요?**

여 이상적으로는, 7월 첫째 주예요. **⁵²또한, 당신이 제안을 받아들이기로 결정하면 회사에서 전근 보너스를 지급할 거예요.**

어휘

position (일)자리, 직위 head (조직의) 책임자
huge 엄청난, 거대한 promotion 승진
talk over ~에 대해 이야기를 나누다 ideally 이상적으로
relocation 이전, 전근, 재배치 accept 받아들이다

50.

여자에 따르면, 이달 말에 무슨 일이 일어날 것인가?
(A) 조사가 실시될 것이다.
(B) 신상품이 출시될 것이다.
(C) 직원이 이사할 것이다.
(D) 임원진이 방문할 것이다.

어휘

conduct 실시하다, 행하다 release 출시하다, 발표하다
executive (기업 등의) 간부, 임원, 이사

패러프레이징

is moving out of → will move

51.

남자는 무엇을 알고 싶어 하는가?
(A) 새 직장이 어디에 있을지
(B) 왜 그에게 다른 임무가 맡겨지는지
(C) 그가 누구와 함께 일하게 될지
(D) 그가 언제 일을 시작할지

어휘

reassign (임무·직책 등을) 다시 배정하다

패러프레이징

start working → start the job

52.

여자는 회사가 무엇을 제공할 것이라고 말하는가?
(A) 개인 사무실
(B) 보너스
(C) 무료 식사
(D) 일일 교통편

어휘

private 개인적인, 사적인 transportation 교통, 운송

패러프레이징

a relocation bonus → A bonus

[53-55] 미남 영녀 미녀 🎧

Questions 53-55 refer to the following conversation with three speakers.

> **M** Lucy, ⁵³ I just found out our construction company won the bid to build the bridge over Garret River.
>
> **W1** Me too! It's great news. ⁵⁴ The bridge is the biggest project we've had in a while.
>
> **M** Exactly. Do you happen to know when construction will begin?
>
> **W1** I don't, but the project manager is coming. Let's ask her... Carmen, have you heard any updates on the bridge construction?
>
> **W2** ⁵⁵ First, we have to wait until the contract is officially signed. It will be a while before we actually get started.

해석

53-55번은 다음 세 명의 대화에 관한 문제입니다.

남 루시, ⁵³ 제가 방금 우리 건설 회사가 개럿 강 위에 다리를 건설하는 입찰을 따냈다는 것을 알았어요.

여1 저도요! 굉장한 소식이에요. ⁵⁴ 그 다리는 우리가 한동안 해왔던 것 중 가장 큰 프로젝트예요.

남 맞아요. 언제 공사가 시작되는지 혹시 알아요?

여1 아니요, 하지만 프로젝트 매니저가 오고 있어요. 그녀에게 물어보죠... 카먼, 다리 건설에 대한 최신 정보 좀 들었어요?

여2 ⁵⁵ 일단, 우리는 계약이 공식적으로 체결될 때까지 기다려야 해요. 우리가 실제로 시작하기 전까지 시간이 좀 걸릴 거예요.

어휘

find out ~을 알아내다, 알게 되다 construction 건설, 공사
win the bid 입찰을 따다 in a while 한동안, 일정 기간
exactly ((맞장구치는 말로)) 맞아, 바로 그거야; 정확히, 틀림없이
happen to 우연히 ~하다 update 최신 정보
sign a contract 계약을 맺다, 계약서에 서명하다
officially 공식적으로 actually 실제로 get started 시작하다

53.

화자들은 어떤 업계에서 일하는가?
(A) 과학 기술
(B) 법률
(C) 건설
(D) 출판

54.

여자는 프로젝트에 대해서 무엇이라고 말하는가?
(A) 그것은 많은 수익을 발생시킬 것이다.
(B) 그것은 중요한 프로젝트이다.

(C) 그것은 회사의 첫 번째 작업이다.
(D) 그것은 관광업을 증진시킬 것이다.

어휘

generate 발생시키다, 만들어 내다 revenue 수익, 수입
tourism 관광업, ((집합적)) 관광객

패러프레이징

the biggest project → an important project

55.

카먼은 무슨 일이 행해져야 한다고 말하는가?
(A) 직원들이 훈련을 받아야 한다.
(B) 용품이 주문되어야 한다.
(C) 일정이 잡혀야 한다.
(D) 계약서가 서명되어야 한다.

어휘

supplies ((주로 복수형)) 용품, 비품 set 정하다, 결정하다

[56-58] 호남 미녀 🎧

Questions 56-58 refer to the following conversation.

> **M** ⁵⁶ I have a question about a customer's prescription. He... oh, sorry! You look busy.
>
> **W** I have a moment to spare.
>
> **M** Great. ⁵⁷ His doctor prescribed a 30-day supply of this medication, but I realized we only have enough in stock for 15 days.
>
> **W** We're getting a shipment tomorrow morning. You can give the customer 15 pills and ask him to come back later for the rest. It's flu season, so we'll be selling a lot of that medicine.
>
> **M** ⁵⁸ If that's the case, maybe we should request more bottles from our supplier for our next order.

해석

56-58번은 다음 대화에 관한 문제입니다.

남 ⁵⁶ 한 고객의 처방에 대해 질문이 있어요. 그가... 오, 죄송해요! 바빠 보이세요.

여 제가 잠깐 시간이 나요.

남 잘됐네요. ⁵⁷ 그의 의사가 이 약을 30일 분량 처방했는데, 우리에겐 재고가 15일 분량밖에 없다는 것을 깨달았어요.

여 내일 아침에 배송품을 받을 거예요. 그 고객에게 15알을 드리고, 나머지는 나중에 다시 와서 받으시라고 요청하면 돼요. 독감 유행철이어서 그 약이 많이 팔릴 거예요.

남 ⁵⁸ 그렇다면, 아마도 다음 주문을 대비해서 공급업체에 더 많은 약병을 요청해야겠어요.

어휘

prescription 처방전 spare (시간·돈 등을) 할애하다
prescribe 처방을 내리다 medication 약, 약물
in stock 재고가 있는 shipment 수송품, 배송품 pill 알약, 정제
flu 독감 medicine 의학, 약 supplier 공급업체

56.

여자는 "제가 잠깐 시간이 나요"라고 말할 때 무엇을 암시하는가?

(A) 그녀는 곧 떠날 계획이다.

(B) 그녀는 무언가를 기다리고 있다.

(C) 그녀는 나눠 줄 약이 있다.

(D) 그녀는 처방을 도와줄 수 있다.

어휘

give away 거저 주다, 나누어 주다 help with ~을 돕다

57.

남자는 일부 약품에 대해 무엇을 깨닫는가?

(A) 공급품이 거의 떨어졌다.

(B) 그것은 라벨이 잘못 붙여졌다.

(C) 그것은 곧 유통 기한이 만료될 것이다.

(D) 그것이 선반에서 누락되었다.

어휘

incorrectly 부정확하게 label 라벨을 붙이다 expire 만료되다
missing from ~에서 빠진

패러프레이징

we only have enough in stock for 15 days
→ The supply is almost gone

58.

남자는 앞으로 무엇을 할 것을 제안하는가?

(A) 약을 더 많이 주문하는 것

(B) 의사에게 전화하는 것

(C) 새로운 공급업체를 찾는 것

(D) 개인별 맞춤형 추천을 하는 것

어휘

personalized 개인이 원하는 대로 할 수 있는

패러프레이징

request more bottles from our supplier
→ Ordering more medicine

[59-61] 미남 호남 미녀 🎧

Questions 59-61 refer to the following conversation
with three speakers.

> **M1** Good Morning, Ms. Jackman. ⁵⁹, ⁶⁰ We just
> heard back from your legal team about the
> terms and agreements for the new platinum
> card that we issued.
>
> **M2** What revisions do we need to make to be in
> compliance with the law?
>
> **W** ⁶⁰ The problem with the agreement is that it
> doesn't disclose to customers that if the card
> is used overseas, an extra fee will be charged.
>
> **M1** That's a big oversight on our part. We're glad
> you were able to catch it.
>
> **W** ⁶¹ We should notify all cardholders about the
> rule by the end of the month to avoid being
> fined by banking regulators.

해석

59-61번은 다음 세 명의 대화에 관한 문제입니다.

남1 안녕하세요, 잭맨 씨. ⁵⁹, ⁶⁰ 방금 당신의 법률팀으로부터 저희가
발급한 새로운 플래티넘 카드의 조건과 계약에 관하여 회신을 받
았습니다.

남2 법을 준수하려면 저희가 어떻게 수정을 해야 하나요?

여 ⁶⁰ 계약과 관련된 문제는 카드가 해외에서 사용될 경우에 추가 수
수료가 청구된다는 것을 고객들에게 밝히지 않은 것입니다.

남1 그건 저희 측의 큰 실수예요. 당신이 그것을 잡아낼 수 있었기에
다행이에요.

여 ⁶¹ 은행 감독 기관에서 벌금을 부과받지 않으려면 이달 말까지
그 규정에 관해 모든 카드 소지자들에게 통보해야 해요.

어휘

legal 법률의, 법률에 관한 terms ((항상 복수형)) (계약 등의) 조건
agreement 협정, 합의, 계약 issue 발부하다
revision 수정, 변경 in compliance with ~에 따라, ~에 응하여
disclose 밝히다, 드러내다 overseas 해외에서
extra fee 추가 수수료 charge 부과하다, 청구하다
oversight 실수, 간과 catch 알아채다, 포착하다 notify 알리다
cardholder 카드 소지자 fine 벌금; 벌금을 부과하다
banking regulator 은행 감독 기관

59.

여자는 누구인 것 같은가?

(A) 은행원

(B) 변호사

(C) 마케팅 담당자

(D) 비서

패러프레이징

your legal team → A lawyer

60.

화자들은 어떤 종류의 문서에 대해 이야기하고 있는가?

(A) 여행 일정표

(B) 마케팅 전략

(C) 사용자 계약서

(D) 예산 제안서

어휘

itinerary 여행 일정표 strategy 전략, 계획

패러프레이징

customers → user

61.

문서는 왜 월 말까지 수정되어야 하는가?

(A) 벌금을 피하기 위해

(B) 오자를 바로잡기 위해

(C) 회의에서 발표되기 위해

(D) 마감 시한을 맞추기 위해

어휘

fine 벌금 correct 바로잡다, 고치다 typo 오자

being fined → a fine

[62-64] 호남 영녀 🎧

Questions 62-64 refer to the following conversation and list.

M Ms. Till, I believe the last wedding guests have left the venue. My staff's going to start packing and loading our things into the van.

W That sounds fine. ⁶²The plants you set up were amazing. My son and his new wife were pleased with your work.

M I'm glad we could be of service today. And, again, ⁶³I apologize for arriving late. I drove right past the turnoff when coming here.

W I understand. This place is difficult to see from the road. ⁶⁴Still, I really like the location because of its reasonable price.

해석

62-64번은 다음 대화와 목록에 관한 문제입니다.

남 틸 씨, 결혼식의 마지막 하객들이 행사장을 떠났어요. 저희 직원들이 물건들을 챙겨서 밴에 싣기 시작할 거예요.

여 그게 좋겠군요. ⁶²당신이 준비한 식물들이 멋졌어요. 제 아들과 그의 신부가 당신의 작업을 마음에 들어 했어요.

남 저희가 오늘 도움이 되었다니 기뻐요. 그리고, 다시 한번 ⁶³늦게 도착한 데 대해 사과드립니다. 이쪽으로 올 때 운전하면서 분기점을 그냥 지나쳐 버렸어요.

여 이해해요. 이곳은 도로에서 잘 보이지 않아요. ⁶⁴그래도, 합리적인 가격 때문에 저는 이 장소가 정말 마음에 들어요.

틸 결혼식	
서비스	가격
사진 촬영	1,750달러
케이터링	9,500달러
⁶²꽃	**3,765달러**
리무진	2,121달러
합계:	17,136달러

어휘

venue (행사의) 장소 pack (짐을) 싸다, 챙기다 load (짐을) 싣다 set up 설치하다, 준비하다 be of service 유용하다, 도움이 되다 apologize for ~에 대해 사과하다 turnoff 분기점, 갈림길 location 위치, 장소 reasonable 합리적인, 타당한 catering 음식 공급(업)

62.

시각 자료를 보시오. 남자의 회사는 서비스에 대해 얼마를 청구했는가?

(A) 1,750달러
(B) 9,500달러
(C) 3,765달러

(D) 2,121달러

어휘

charge (비용을) 청구하다; 요금

63.

남자는 왜 사과하는가?

(A) 그는 여자에게 과잉 청구했다.
(B) 그는 자신의 제품 일부를 잊어버렸다.
(C) 그는 늦게 도착했다.
(D) 그는 형편없는 서비스를 했다.

어휘

overcharge (금액을) 너무 많이 청구하다

64.

여자는 행사 장소에 대해 무엇을 좋아하는가?

(A) 그곳은 쉽게 접근할 수 있다.
(B) 그곳은 가격이 적당하다.
(C) 그곳은 공간이 넓다.
(D) 그곳은 전망이 아주 좋다.

어휘

accessible 접근 가능한 affordable (가격이) 적당한

패러프레이징

reasonable → affordable

[65-67] 미녀 호남 🎧

Questions 65-67 refer to the following conversation and seating chart.

W Hey, Raphael? You like music, right? A local band is having a concert this weekend, and I have two tickets that I don't need. Do you want them?

M Are you serious? ⁶⁵You got tickets to that concert? I'm shocked! The tickets sold out within a few hours.

W That's true, but I won these tickets in a raffle, which is why I'm giving them away. ⁶⁶The seats aren't bad. They're a bit far from the stage, but they're right in the middle.

M I'll take them! Thanks a lot! But why can't you go?

W ⁶⁷This weekend is my sister's birthday. I'm planning to go to New York to visit her.

해석

65-67번은 다음 대화와 좌석 배치도에 관한 문제입니다.

여 이봐요, 라파엘? 당신 음악 좋아하죠, 맞죠? 지역 밴드가 이번 주말에 콘서트를 하는데, 저한테 필요 없는 표가 두 장 있어요. 당신이 가질래요?

남 진심이에요? ⁶⁵당신이 그 콘서트 티켓을 구했다고요? 깜짝 놀랐어요! 그 티켓은 몇 시간 만에 다 팔렸어요.

여 맞아요, 하지만 전 추첨으로 이 티켓들을 받았어요, 그래서 그걸

주려는 거예요. **66** 좌석은 나쁘지 않아요. 무대에서는 조금 멀지만 한가운데예요.

남 제가 가질게요! 정말 고마워요! 그런데 당신은 왜 못 가요?

여 **67** 이번 주말이 제 여동생 생일이에요. 그 애를 만나러 뉴욕에 갈 계획이에요.

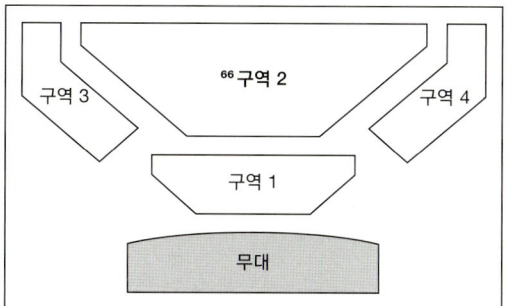

65.
남자는 왜 놀라워하는가?
(A) 남자가 가장 좋아하는 밴드가 동네에 왔다.
(B) 여자가 인기 있는 음악가를 만났다.
(C) 티켓이 매진되지 않았다.
(D) 여자가 콘서트 티켓을 구했다.

66.
시각 자료를 보시오. 여자는 어떤 구역에 좌석이 있는가?
(A) 1구역
(B) 2구역
(C) 3구역
(D) 4구역

67.
여자는 이번 주말에 무엇을 할 것인가?
(A) 파티를 열 것
(B) 뉴욕으로 이사할 것
(C) 여동생을 방문할 것
(D) 추첨에 응모할 것

[68-70] 미남 미녀 🎧
Questions 68-70 refer to the following conversation and list.

M Hello. **68** Heavenly Apartments management office. How can I help you?

W Hi. **69** I'm Lauren Aspers. I live in Unit 242B. I'm a new tenant here.

M Are you enjoying your new apartment?

W Yes, I love it. However... **69** my last name is spelled incorrectly on the directory. Can you fix that?

M I'm so sorry about the mistake, ma'am. I can send someone over in about an hour. Unit 242B, you said?

W Yes. Also, **70** I'd like to talk to you about repainting my walls tomorrow evening after grocery shopping.

M Okay. I'll see you then.

해석
68-70번은 다음 대화에 관한 문제입니다.

남 안녕하세요. **68** 헤븐리 아파트 관리사무소입니다. 어떻게 도와드릴까요?

여 안녕하세요. **69** 저는 로렌 애스퍼스예요. 242B호에 살아요. 이곳에 새로 온 세입자예요.

남 새 아파트는 마음에 드시나요?

여 네, 아주 좋아요. 하지만... **69** 호수 안내판에 제 성의 철자가 잘못 쓰여 있어요. 그것을 고쳐 주시겠어요?

남 실수에 대해 정말 죄송합니다, 부인. 한 시간쯤 뒤에 사람을 보낼게요. 242B호라고 하셨죠?

여 네. 그리고, **70** 제가 내일 저녁 장을 본 뒤에 벽 페인트 칠을 다시 하는 것에 대해 말씀드리고 싶어요.

남 알겠습니다. 그때 뵙겠습니다.

헤븐리 아파트	
242A	다나카
69 242B	애스퍼
243A	권
243B	싱

68.
남자는 누구인 것 같은가?
(A) 건물 관리인
(B) 회사 대표
(C) 가정부
(D) 판매 직원

어휘

property 부동산, 건물 representative 대표(자), (판매) 대리인

패러프레이징

Apartments management office → property manager

69.

시각 자료를 보시오. 어떤 이름이 변경되어야 하는가?

(A) 다나카
(B) 애스퍼
(C) 권
(D) 싱

70.

여자는 내일 무엇을 할 것이라고 말하는가?

(A) 관리실 직원에게 말하기
(B) 문패 바꾸기
(C) 새 아파트로 이사하기
(D) 식료품 배달받기

어휘

nameplate 문패, 명패

패러프레이징

talk to → speak to

[71-73] 미녀 🎧

Questions 71-73 refer to the following telephone message.

> W Hello, this is Chloe Goodman. ⁷¹On Wednesday, I have an appointment with Dr. Washington for a health checkup. Unfortunately, ⁷²I won't be able to make it to the appointment. I just found out I have to go on a business trip, and I'm not exactly sure how long I'll be gone. ⁷³I also had a question about your updated insurance policy, so please call me back at 555-0128. Thank you!

해석

71-73번은 다음 전화 메시지에 관한 문제입니다.

여 안녕하세요, 저는 클로에 굿맨입니다. **⁷¹수요일에, 건강검진을 위해 워싱턴 박사님과 예약이 되어 있습니다.** 유감스럽게도, **⁷²예약에 맞춰 갈 수 없어요.** 출장을 가야 한다는 걸 막 알았는데, 얼마나 가 있을지 정확히 몰라요. **⁷³그리고 최신 정보가 반영된 보험 약관에 관해 질문이 있으니 555-0128로 제게 회신 전화 주시기 바랍니다.** 감사합니다.

어휘

appointment (만날) 약속, 예약 health checkup 건강 검진
unfortunately 유감스럽게도 make it to ~에 이르다, 도착하다
find out 알아내다, 알게 되다 exactly 정확히 updated 최신의
insurance policy 보험 약관

71.

화자는 어떤 종류의 업체에게 전화하고 있는 것 같은가?

(A) 법률 회사
(B) 병원
(C) 식당
(D) 미용실

72.

화자는 그녀의 예약에 대해 무엇이라고 말하는가?

(A) 그것은 일정이 변경되어야 한다.
(B) 그것은 보험에 적용되지 않는다.
(C) 그것은 한 시간 늦춰져야 한다.
(D) 그것은 다른 장소로 바뀌어야 한다.

어휘

reschedule 일정을 변경하다 cover 다루다, 포함시키다

73.

화자는 무엇에 대해 질문이 있는가?

(A) 보험 약관
(B) 배송 방법
(C) 결제 방법
(D) 품질 보증서

어휘

shipping 운송, 배송 payment 지불, 납입
warranty 품질 보증(서)

[74-76] 미남 🎧

Questions 74-76 refer to the following advertisement.

> M ⁷⁴Ever wonder how teddy bears are made? If so, come visit us at Terrific Teddy's Factory! We promise you'll have an excellent experience. Our factory is located right next to the Johnston City Library, and we offer guided tours every Saturday and Sunday. During your hour-long visit, you'll be able to see exactly how we create and package our famous teddy bears. As part of the tour, you'll be able to meet Tommy the Teddy, our beloved mascot. ⁷⁵You can even take home a professionally-shot photo with Tommy as a souvenir. ⁷⁶And if you book a tour before 11 A.M., you qualify for a special 25 percent off discount.

해석

74-76번은 다음 광고에 관한 문제입니다.

남 **⁷⁴곰 인형이 어떻게 만들어지는지 궁금했던 적 있나요?** 그렇다면, 저희 테리픽 테디스 팩토리에 방문하세요! 멋진 경험을 하시게 될 것을 약속합니다. 저희 공장은 존슨 시립 도서관 바로 옆에 위치하고 있으며, 매주 토요일과 일요일에 가이드가 안내하는 견학을 제공합니다. 한 시간 동안 방문하시면서, 여러분은 정확히 어떻게 저희가 저희의 유명한 곰 인형을 만들고 포장하는지 보실 수 있습니다. 견학의 일부로, 저희의 사랑스러운 마스코트인 토

미 더 테디를 만날 수 있습니다. **75**심지어 기념품으로 전문가가 토미와 함께 찍어 준 사진을 집에 가져가실 수 있습니다. **76**그리고 오전 11시 전 견학을 예약하시면, 25% 특별 할인을 받을 자격이 되십니다.

어휘

teddy bear (봉제) 곰 인형 be located (~에) 위치하다
guided 가이드가 안내하는 exactly 정확하게
create 만들어 내다, 창작하다 package 포장하다; 포장물
beloved 사랑스러운, 가장 사랑하는
professionally-shot 전문적으로 촬영된 souvenir 기념품
book 예약하다 qualify for ~의 자격을 얻다

74.

광고는 무엇에 관한 것인가?
(A) 사진 행사
(B) 새 도서관
(C) 장난감 공장 견학
(D) 요리 경연 대회

어휘

competition 경쟁, (경연) 대회

패러프레이징

Terrific Teddy's Factory → A toy factory

75.

방문객들은 무엇을 받을 것인가?
(A) 열쇠고리
(B) 곰 인형
(C) 사진
(D) 무료 식사

76.

청자들은 오전 11시 전 견학을 예약하면 무엇을 얻을 수 있는가?
(A) 할인 가격
(B) 무료 입장
(C) 회사 머그잔
(D) 무료 음료

어휘

admission 입장, 입학 complimentary 무료의; 칭찬하는

패러프레이징

a special 25 percent off discount
→ A discounted price

[77-79] 영녀 🎧

Questions 77-79 refer to the following announcement.

W Attention, everyone. **77**Unfortunately, we've had to stop the performance. As you can see, **78**we're having technical difficulties with the band's lighting. We are extremely sorry about this. We take the quality of our lighting seriously and will have specialists working on the issue as soon as possible. **79**When you leave, please head to the customer service desk to pick up a coupon for an extra 20 dollars off your next ticket purchase. Again, we apologize for the inconvenience.

해석

77-79번은 다음 안내 방송에 관한 문제입니다.

여 모든 분들께 알립니다. **77**유감스럽게도, 저희가 공연을 중단해야 했습니다. 보시다시피, **78**밴드의 조명에 기술적인 문제가 있습니다. 이 점에 대해 정말 죄송하게 생각합니다. 저희는 조명의 질을 중요하게 생각하며, 최대한 빨리 전문가들이 이 문제에 착수하도록 할 것입니다. **79**나가실 때 고객 서비스 창구로 가셔서 다음번 티켓 구매 시 추가로 20달러 할인해 드리는 쿠폰을 받아 가세요. 다시 한번, 불편을 끼쳐 사과드립니다.

어휘

performance 공연, 연주회 technical difficulty 기술상의 곤란
lighting 조명 extremely 극도로, 극히
take ~ seriously ~을 심각하게[중요하게] 여기다
quality 질, 우수함 work on ~에 노력을 들이다, 착수하다
issue 문제, 안건 head (특정 방향으로) 가다, 향하다
extra 추가의, 가외의 apologize for ~에 대해 사과하다
inconvenience 불편

77.

안내방송은 어디에서 이루어지고 있는가?
(A) 대학교 강당에서
(B) 박물관에서
(C) 콘서트 장소에서
(D) 영화관에서

어휘

venue (행사의) 장소

78.

화자는 왜 사과하는가?
(A) 조명이 작동하지 않는다.
(B) 음질이 나쁘다.
(C) 진행자가 늦는다.
(D) 난방기가 고장 났다.

어휘

presenter 진행자, 발표자
run late (예정보다) 늦게 출발[도착]하다 broken 고장 난

패러프레이징

technical difficulties with the band's lighting
→ lights are not working

79.

청자들에게 무엇이 제공되는가?
(A) 무료 간식
(B) 할인 쿠폰

(C) 주차권
(D) 홍보물

어휘
voucher 상품권, 할인권, 쿠폰 promotional 홍보의, 판촉의

패러프레이징
a coupon for an extra 20 dollars off
→ A discount coupon

[80-82] 미녀 🎧
Questions 80-82 refer to the following talk.

> **W** Hello, everyone. ⁸⁰ Welcome to Harper Company's third annual conference on international business. Our company decided to try something new to publicize this event. ⁸¹ We advertised through personalized advertisements and e-mails rather than posting ads online. And, as you can see, over 500 people are here! The first presentation will begin in about 10 minutes. We have various talks going on throughout the conference area, ⁸² so please refer to your programs for more details.

해석
80-82번은 다음 담화에 관한 문제입니다.
여 안녕하세요, 여러분. ⁸⁰ 하퍼 컴퍼니의 제3회 국제 비즈니스에 관한 연례 회의에 오신 것을 환영합니다. 저희 회사는 이번 행사를 홍보하기 위해 새로운 것을 시도하기로 결정했습니다. ⁸¹ 저희는 온라인에 광고를 게시하기보다 개인 맞춤 광고와 이메일을 통해 광고했습니다. 그리고, 보시다시피 500명이 넘는 분들이 여기 오셨습니다! 첫 번째 발표는 약 10분 뒤에 시작하겠습니다. 회의장 곳곳에서 다양한 담화가 진행되고 있으니, ⁸² 더 자세한 내용은 여러분이 가지고 계신 프로그램을 참고하시기 바랍니다.

어휘
annual 연례의 publicize 알리다, 광고[홍보]하다
advertise 광고하다
personalized 개인이 원하는 대로 할 수 있는
advertisement (= ad) 광고 post 공고하다, 게시하다
presentation 발표, 프레젠테이션 go on 계속되다
throughout 도처에, ~동안 내내
refer to (정보를 알아내기 위해) ~을 보다, ~에게 문의하다
details 세부 정보

80.
어떤 종류의 행사가 개최되고 있는가?
(A) 운동 경기
(B) 의학 워크숍
(C) 자선 모금 행사
(D) 비즈니스 회의

어휘
athletic 운동 경기의 competition 경쟁, 대회 medical 의학의

charity 자선 fundraiser 모금 행사

패러프레이징
Harper Company's third annual conference on international business → A business conference

81.
화자는 왜 "그리고, 보시다시피 500명이 넘는 분들이 여기 오셨습니다"라고 말하는가?
(A) 광고가 성공적이었다는 것을 보여 주기 위해
(B) 몇몇 사람들이 장소를 옮겨야 한다고 암시하기 위해
(C) 공간이 너무 좁다는 것을 시사하기 위해
(D) 사람들에게 서로 어울리도록 권장하기 위해

어휘
switch 전환하다, 바꾸다 venue (행사의) 장소
encourage 권장하다, 장려하다 socialize 사귀다, 어울리다

82.
화자는 청자들에게 무엇을 해 달라고 요청하는가?
(A) 내년에 다시 방문하기
(B) 일정표 확인하기
(C) 줄 서기
(D) 설문지 작성하기

어휘
fill out 작성하다, 기입하다 questionnaire 설문지

패러프레이징
refer to your programs → Check a schedule

[83-85] 호남 🎧
Questions 83-85 refer to the following talk.

> **M** On behalf of the Central City Department of Transportation, ⁸³ I would like to alert drivers in the area about a new experimental program to reduce traffic. Beginning next month, there will be an eight-dollar fee for each vehicle that enters our city. ⁸⁴ Central City residents, however, will only have to pay half of that price to enter the city. This means they will pay four dollars instead of the full eight dollars. The point of this experiment is to discourage people from driving into this overcrowded area. ⁸⁵ This program will be in effect for two months. Following that, the Department of Transportation will decide if traffic congestion has decreased enough to make the program permanent.

해석
83-85번은 다음 담화에 관한 문제입니다.
남 센트럴 시티 교통부를 대표해서, ⁸³ 이 지역 운전자들에게 교통량을 줄이기 위한 새로운 실험적인 프로그램에 대해 알려 드립니다. 다음 달부터, 우리 시에 들어오는 차량 한 대당 8달러의 요금

이 부과될 것입니다. **84** 그러나 센트럴 시티 주민들은 단지 금액의 절반만 지불하시고 시로 들어오시면 됩니다. 8달러 전액 대신 4달러를 지불하시게 된다는 뜻입니다. 이 실험의 요점은 사람들이 이 초만원인 구역으로 차를 가져오는 것을 막는 것입니다. **85** 이 프로그램은 두 달간 시행될 것입니다. 그 후에, 프로그램을 계속 유지할 만큼 충분히 교통 혼잡이 줄었는지 교통부가 결정할 것입니다.

어휘

on behalf of ~을 대신[대표]하여 transportation 교통, 수송
alert (위험 등을) 알리다 experimental 실험적인
traffic 교통(량), 차량들 fee 요금, 수수료
enter 들어가다, 들어오다 only have to 단지 ~하기만 하면 된다
experiment 실험 discourage 막다, 말리다
overcrowded 너무 붐비는, 초만원의 be in effect 시행되다
traffic congestion 교통 혼잡 permanent 영구적인

83.

계획의 목적은 무엇인가?
(A) 돈을 마련하기 위해
(B) 교통량을 줄이기 위해
(C) 오염을 줄이기 위해
(D) 여행을 장려하기 위해

어휘

raise (자금·사람 등을) 모으다 pollution 오염, 공해

패러프레이징

reduce traffic → decrease traffic

84.

화자는 누가 할인을 받을 것이라고 말하는가?
(A) 주민들
(B) 클럽 회원들
(C) 학생들
(D) 어르신들

패러프레이징

Central City residents → Residents

85.

두 달 뒤에 무슨 일이 일어날 것인가?
(A) 도로가 건설될 것이다.
(B) 프로그램이 평가될 것이다.
(C) 새로운 법이 제정될 것이다.
(D) 요금이 면제될 것이다.

어휘

evaluate 평가하다 enact (법을) 제정하다
waive (규칙 등을) 적용하지 않다

패러프레이징

decide if traffic congestion has decreased
→ A program will be evaluated

[86-88] 영녀 🎧

Questions 86-88 refer to the following broadcast.

> W You're listening to *All About Art* on Rockin' Radio. **86** I'd like to remind you that the Contemporary Art Festival is this weekend. **87** Rockin' Radio is offering one lucky listener the chance to win a pair of tickets by entering our art contest. In order to enter the contest, visit our Web site and join our online mailing list. And, just so you know, the tickets are nearly sold out. This year, we have a very special guest coming to the event: famous painter Jesse Greens. **88** Tomorrow morning, join us for an exclusive interview with Mr. Greens about some of his famous artwork. You won't want to miss it!

해석

86~88번은 다음 방송에 관한 문제입니다.

여 여러분은 로킨 라디오의 〈예술에 대한 모든 것〉을 듣고 계십니다. **86** 이번 주말에 현대 미술 축제가 있다는 것을 상기시켜 드립니다. **87** 로킨 라디오는 행운의 청취자 한 분에게 저희 미술 대회에 참가해서 티켓 두 장을 상품으로 받으실 기회를 드립니다. 경연 대회에 참가하시려면, 저희 웹사이트에 방문하셔서 온라인 메일링 리스트에 가입하세요. 그리고, 참고로 말씀드리면, 티켓은 거의 매진되었습니다. 올해, 아주 특별한 초대 손님을 행사에 모시는데요, 유명 화가인 제시 그린즈입니다. **88** 내일 아침, 그의 유명한 미술품 일부에 관한 그린즈 씨와의 독점 인터뷰를 함께해 주세요. 놓치고 싶지 않으실 거예요!

어휘

remind 상기시키다 contemporary 현대의, 동시대의
enter (대회 등에) 참가하다
mailing list 메일링 리스트, 우편물 수신자 명단
just so you know 참고로 말하면 nearly 거의
sold out 매진된 exclusive 독점적인 artwork 미술품

86.

화자는 어떤 행사에 대해 이야기하고 있는가?
(A) 농산물 시장
(B) 미술 축제
(C) 음악 공연
(D) 코미디 연극

어휘

comedic 희극(풍)의

패러프레이징

the Contemporary Art Festival → An art festival

87.

화자는 왜 "티켓은 거의 매진되었습니다"라고 말하는가?
(A) 청자들이 경연대회에 참가하도록 권장하기 위해
(B) 마케팅 캠페인의 효과를 언급하기 위해

(C) 청자들에게 행사에 일찍 오라고 조언하기 위해
(D) 사람들에게 많은 군중들에 대해 경고하기 위해

어휘

encourage 권장[장려]하다 point out 가리키다, 지적하다
effectiveness 효과성 advise 조언하다 warn 경고하다

88.

내일 아침에 무슨 일이 일어날 것인가?
(A) 한 팬이 초청 연사가 될 것이다.
(B) 인터뷰가 진행될 것이다.
(C) 축제가 시작될 것이다.
(D) 새로운 콘서트장이 개장할 것이다.

[89-91] 미녀 🎧
Questions 89-91 refer to the following talk.

> W Thank you for visiting our booth here at the craft fair. You might be familiar with **89 our necklaces and earrings**, but we've recently expanded our collection to include other items. We're delighted to show you **89, 90 our new bracelet selection**, made with a unique material. **90 These pieces are all gorgeous and long-lasting. They are durable and require only light maintenance. 91 I'll let you try on one of our bracelets for yourself.** Feel free to take a picture of yourself wearing our jewelry to see how great it looks in photos.

해석

89-91번은 다음 담화에 관한 문제입니다.
여 공예 박람회의 이곳 저희 부스에 방문해 주셔서 감사합니다. 여러분은 **89 저희 목걸이와 귀걸이에** 익숙하시겠지만, 다른 품목들을 포함시키기 위해 최근에 컬렉션을 확장했습니다. 여러분에게 독특한 재료로 만들어진, **89, 90 엄선한 저희의 새로운 팔찌들을** 보여 드리게 되어 기쁩니다. **90 이것들은 모두 아주 아름답고 오래갑니다. 내구성이 좋고 가벼운 관리만 요구합니다. 91 저희 팔찌 중 하나를 직접 착용해 보시게 해 드리겠습니다.** 주얼리를 착용하신 여러분 자신의 사진을 자유롭게 찍으시고 사진에서 그것이 얼마나 멋지게 보이는지 확인하세요.

어휘

craft 공예 be familiar with ~에 익숙[친숙]하다
expand 확장[확대]하다 collection 컬렉션, 소장품
be delighted to ~하게 되어 기쁘다 selection 선정된 것들
unique 독특한 material 재료
piece (하나의 세트를 이루는 일부가 되는) 하나
gorgeous 아주 멋진, 아름다운 long-lasting 오래가는, 지속적인
durable 내구성이 있는, 오래가는 maintenance 유지, 관리
try on 입어[신어] 보다 feel free to 마음대로 ~하다
jewelry 보석류, 장신구

89.

화자는 어떤 종류의 업체에서 일하는가?

(A) 주얼리 회사
(B) 마케팅 대행사
(C) 의류 회사
(D) 전자제품 회사

어휘

electronics ((항상 복수형)) 전자 기기

패러프레이징

necklaces and earrings / bracelet → jewelry

90.

화자는 재료의 장점으로 무엇을 강조하는가?
(A) 그것은 가격이 적당하다.
(B) 그것은 가볍다.
(C) 그것은 내구성이 있다.
(D) 그것은 기능적이다.

어휘

highlight 강조하다 advantage 이점, 장점
functional 기능적인, 실용적인

패러프레이징

long-lasting → durable

91.

청자들은 다음에 무엇을 할 것 같은가?
(A) 회원 가입 신청하기
(B) 경연 대회에 참가하기
(C) 회사 웹사이트에 방문하기
(D) 액세서리 착용해 보기

어휘

sign up for ~에 신청[등록]하다 membership 회원 (자격)
accessory 액세서리, 장신구

패러프레이징

bracelets → accessory

[92-94] 영녀 🎧
Questions 92-94 refer to the following telephone message.

> W **92 This is Angela, Director of Human Resources here in San Diego. 93 I'm calling in reference to your transfer request to our branch in Houston.** I know you're feeling a bit homesick and would prefer to live near your family, so I spoke with the manager at that location. Thankfully, there's a need for a new cybersecurity specialist in Houston. There are a few forms you'll need to fill out before I can process your request though. **94 After that, we'll have to talk about your moving and start date.** Please call me back when you get the chance.

92-94번은 다음 전화 메시지에 관한 문제입니다.

여 ⁹²저는 이곳 샌디에이고의 인사부장 앤절라예요. ⁹³우리 휴스턴 지점으로의 당신의 전근 요청에 관하여 전화드립니다. 당신이 향수병이 좀 있고 가족 곁에서 살고 싶어 하는 것을 알아요. 그래서 그곳의 매니저와 얘기했어요. 다행히, 휴스턴에 새로운 사이버 보안 전문가가 필요해요. 제가 당신의 요청을 처리하기 전에 당신이 작성해야 할 양식이 몇 가지 있긴 하지만요. ⁹⁴그 후에 당신의 이사와 근무 시작일에 대해 얘기해야 할 거예요. 기회가 되시면 제게 답신 전화 주세요.

어휘

Human Resources 인사부 in reference to ~에 관하여
transfer request 전근 요청 branch 지점, 지사
feel homesick 향수병에 걸리다 location 장소, 위치
thankfully 고맙게도, 다행스럽게도 cybersecurity 사이버 보안
specialist 전문가 fill out 기입하다, 작성하다
process 처리하다; 과정, 절차

92.

화자는 어떤 부서에서 일하는가?
(A) 정보 통신 기술
(B) 마케팅
(C) 보안
(D) 인사부

93.

화자는 왜 "휴스턴에 새로운 사이버 보안 전문가가 필요해요"라고 말하는가?
(A) 신규 직원 고용을 제안하기 위해
(B) 누군가 은퇴한다고 설명하기 위해
(C) 전근 요청을 승인하기 위해
(D) 보안 위협을 강조하기 위해

어휘

approve 승인하다 highlight 강조하다 threat 위협, 협박

94.

화자는 청자와 무엇에 관해 이야기하고 싶어 하는가?
(A) 새로운 제안
(B) 이사 및 근무 시작일
(C) 건설적인 비판
(D) 조사 결과

어휘

constructive 건설적인 criticism 비판, 비평

패러프레이징

your start date → starting date

[95-97] 미남 🎧

Questions 95-97 refer to the following broadcast and list.

M You're listening to *How I Became a Pro Athlete* with Kurt Rodriguez. In each episode of this series, ⁹⁵I invite professional athletes from across the country to talk about how they started their careers. To celebrate our radio show's five-year anniversary, ⁹⁶we have launched a Web site that now sells official merchandise. We have hoodies, shirts, socks, hats, and more. Now you can show some love for our radio show while looking stylish at the same time! On that note, ⁹⁷let's welcome Janet Greenwood to the show. Ms. Greenwood is happy to be here today.

해석

95-97번은 다음 방송과 목록에 관한 문제입니다.

남 여러분은 커트 로드리게스와 함께하는 〈나는 어떻게 프로 선수가 되었는가〉를 듣고 계십니다. 이 시리즈의 각 회차에서, ⁹⁵제가 전국의 직업 선수들을 초대하여 그들이 어떻게 경력을 시작했는지에 대해 얘기 나눌 것입니다. 저희 라디오 프로그램의 5주년 기념을 축하하기 위해서, ⁹⁶공식 상품을 판매하는 웹사이트를 개설했습니다. 후드 티, 셔츠, 양말, 모자 등이 있습니다. 이제 저희 라디오 프로그램을 위한 사랑을 보여 주시면서 동시에 멋지게 보이실 수 있습니다! 이쯤에서, ⁹⁷프로그램에 재닛 그린우드를 모시겠습니다. 그린우드 씨가 기꺼이 오늘 자리해 주셨습니다.

이번 주 초대 손님	
⁹⁷월요일	재닛 그린우드
화요일	마커스 크롤리
수요일	유키나 이마노
목요일	레오 하우 – 첫째 날
금요일	레오 하우 – 둘째 날

어휘

episode 1회 방송분, 사건, 에피소드
professional 직업의, 전문적인 career 직업, 경력
celebrate 기념하다, 축하하다 anniversary 기념일
launch 시작하다, 출시하다 official 공식적인
merchandise 물품, 상품 hoodie 모자 달린 옷
stylish 멋진, 유행을 따른 on that note 그런 의미에서, 이쯤에서

95.

초대 손님들은 왜 화자의 라디오 프로그램에 초대받는가?
(A) 그들의 이력에 대해 말하기 위해
(B) 조언을 해 주기 위해
(C) 사업 전망에 대해 이야기하기 위해
(D) 옷에 대해 얘기 나누기 위해

어휘

career history 이력 prospects ((항상 복수형)) 전망

패러프레이징

talk about how they started their careers

→ tell their career history

96.

청자들은 웹사이트에서 무엇을 할 수 있는가?

(A) 의견 남기기
(B) 회원 가입 신청하기
(C) 상품 구매하기
(D) 사진 업로드하기

어휘

sign up for ~에 신청[가입]하다 membership 회원(자격)

97.

시각 자료를 보시오. 이 회차는 어느 요일에 방송되고 있는가?

(A) 월요일
(B) 화요일
(C) 수요일
(D) 목요일

[98-100] 호남 🎧

Questions 98-100 refer to the following telephone message and store shelf.

> M Hi, it's Finlay. I'm calling from the company's headquarters. The merchandising team wants to make a change to the summer display stands. **98** They want all stores to hang the polka dot women's bathing suits instead of having them folded on the shelf. We'll showcase some of our accessories, such as hats and flip-flops, in that area instead. Also, **99** please display the earrings on the shelves next to the cash registers. People will grab them as they're waiting in line. The sunglasses you requested will be shipped to you shortly. **100** I'll give you another call and let you know about the delivery date.

해석

98-100번은 다음 전화 메시지와 매장 선반에 관한 문제입니다.

남 안녕하세요, 핀레이예요. 본사에서 전화드립니다. 판촉팀이 여름 진열대를 변경하고 싶어 해요. **98** 그들은 모든 매장이 물방울무늬 여성 수영복을 선반에 접어 놓는 것보다 걸어 놓기를 원해요. 대신 우리가 그 공간에 모자나 플립플롭 샌들 같은 우리 부대용품 일부를 진열할 거예요. 또한, **99** 귀걸이는 계산대 바로 옆 선반에 진열하시기 바랍니다. 사람들이 줄을 서 있을 때 그것들을 손쉽게 구매할 거예요. 당신이 요청한 선글라스는 곧 배송될 거예요. **100** 제가 또 전화해서 배송 날짜에 대해 알려 드릴게요.

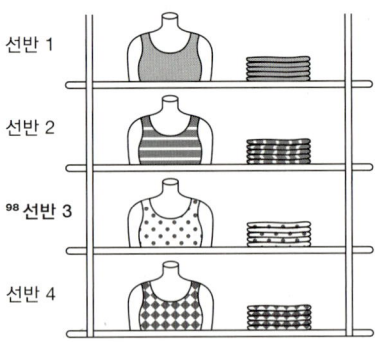

선반 1
선반 2
98 선반 3
선반 4

어휘

headquarters ((항상 복수형)) 본사, 본부
merchandising 판매 계획, 판촉
make a change to ~을 바꾸다 display stand 진열대
polka dot 물방울무늬 bathing suit 수영복
showcase 진열[전시]하다 accessory 부대용품, 액세서리
flip-flop (발가락 사이로) 끈을 끼워서 신는 샌들[슬리퍼]
cash registers 계산대, 현금 등록기
grab 꽉 잡다, 재빨리 손에 넣다 wait in line 줄을 서서 기다리다
ship 수송[운송]하다 shortly 곧

98.

시각 자료를 보시오. 모자와 플립플롭 샌들은 어디에 진열될 것인가?

(A) 선반 1에
(B) 선반 2에
(C) 선반 3에
(D) 선반 4에

99.

계산대 근처에 무엇이 진열될 것인가?

(A) 선글라스
(B) 귀걸이
(C) 모자
(D) 자외선 차단제

패러프레이징

next to → near

100.

청자는 다음 전화 통화에서 무엇을 받을 것인가?

(A) 배송 정보
(B) 상세한 진열 설명
(C) 새로운 일정
(D) 평가 의견

어휘

shipping 운송 specification (자세한) 설명서
evaluation 평가

패러프레이징

the delivery date → Shipping information

1. (D)	2. (A)	3. (B)	4. (C)	5. (B)
6. (D)	7. (B)	8. (B)	9. (C)	10. (C)
11. (A)	12. (B)	13. (A)	14. (C)	15. (B)
16. (A)	17. (B)	18. (C)	19. (C)	20. (B)
21. (C)	22. (C)	23. (A)	24. (B)	25. (C)
26. (B)	27. (C)	28. (C)	29. (C)	30. (B)
31. (A)	32. (B)	33. (C)	34. (A)	35. (A)
36. (D)	37. (B)	38. (D)	39. (C)	40. (B)
41. (D)	42. (A)	43. (B)	44. (B)	45. (C)
46. (A)	47. (C)	48. (C)	49. (C)	50. (D)
51. (B)	52. (A)	53. (C)	54. (B)	55. (D)
56. (D)	57. (A)	58. (A)	59. (A)	60. (C)
61. (B)	62. (D)	63. (C)	64. (C)	65. (B)
66. (C)	67. (A)	68. (C)	69. (B)	70. (A)
71. (B)	72. (C)	73. (D)	74. (C)	75. (A)
76. (C)	77. (B)	78. (B)	79. (D)	80. (C)
81. (A)	82. (D)	83. (B)	84. (B)	85. (A)
86. (C)	87. (B)	88. (D)	89. (C)	90. (B)
91. (B)	92. (B)	93. (A)	94. (A)	95. (B)
96. (C)	97. (A)	98. (B)	99. (C)	100. (C)

1. 호남 🎧

(A) The people are decorating a wall.
(B) The man is using a napkin.
(C) One of the women is serving food.
(D) The people are looking at some menus.

해석

(A) 사람들이 벽을 장식하고 있다.
(B) 남자가 냅킨을 사용하고 있다.
(C) 여자들 중 한 명이 음식을 서빙하고 있다.
(D) 사람들이 메뉴판을 보고 있다.

2. 영녀 🎧

(A) The woman is standing on a stool.
(B) The woman is replacing a lightbulb.
(C) The woman is installing a bookshelf.
(D) The woman is climbing a staircase.

해석

(A) 여자가 의자 위에 서 있다.
(B) 여자가 전구를 교체하고 있다.
(C) 여자가 책장을 설치하고 있다.
(D) 여자가 계단을 올라가고 있다.

3. 미녀 🎧

(A) Some people are planting some trees.
(B) Some people are strolling on a path.
(C) Some people are getting on a train.
(D) Some people are jogging on a beach.

해석

(A) 사람들이 나무를 심고 있다.
(B) 사람들이 오솔길을 걷고 있다.
(C) 사람들이 기차를 타고 있다.
(D) 사람들이 해변에서 달리고 있다.

4. 미남 🎧

(A) The men are facing each other.
(B) The men are crossing a street.
(C) The men have stopped on a walkway.
(D) The men have left their suitcases open.

해석

(A) 남자들이 서로를 바라보고 있다.
(B) 남자들이 길을 건너고 있다.
(C) 남자들이 인도 위에 멈춰 서 있다.
(D) 남자들이 여행가방을 열어 놓았다.

5. 영녀 🎧

(A) Some leaves have been swept into a pile.
**(B) Some furniture has been stacked near a
　 fence.**

(C) An umbrella has fallen on the ground.

(D) A bicycle has been chained to a pole.

(A) 나뭇잎들이 무더기로 모여 있다.

(B) 가구가 담장 가까이 쌓여 있다.

(C) 우산이 땅에 떨어졌다.

(D) 자전거가 기둥에 사슬로 묶여 있다.

6. 호남 🎧

(A) Some office workers are sitting in a circle.

(B) One of the men is writing on a notepad.

(C) One of the women is wiping a whiteboard.

(D) Some notices have been posted to a bulletin board.

해석

(A) 몇몇 사무직원들이 빙 둘러 앉아 있다.

(B) 남자들 중 한 명이 메모장에 필기하고 있다.

(C) 여자들 중 한 명이 화이트보드를 지우고 있다.

(D) 쪽지들이 게시판에 붙어 있다.

7. 호남 미녀 🎧

Who is in charge of cleaning the display case?

(A) Use a soft cloth.

(B) Jonathan said he'd do it.

(C) Yes, five feet wide.

해석

누가 진열장 청소를 담당하죠?

(A) 부드러운 천을 사용하세요.

(B) 조나단이 하겠다고 했어요.

(C) 네, 5피트 넓이예요.

어휘

be in charge of ~을 담당하다 display case 진열장 cloth 천

8. 영녀 미남 🎧

Would you like to see the proposed cover designs?

(A) The print shop nearby.

(B) Sure, I'm free after lunch.

(C) It's for the travel industry.

해석

제안받은 표지 디자인을 보시겠어요?

(A) 근처 인쇄소요.

(B) 물론이죠, 점심 이후에 시간 있어요.

(C) 관광 산업을 위한 거예요.

어휘

propose 제안하다 cover 표지 nearby 근처, 인근의

9. 영녀 미녀 🎧

Here are the staff evaluations.

(A) Congratulations to everyone.

(B) Within a few days.

(C) Thanks, please set them on my desk.

해석

여기 직원 평가서를 드릴게요.

(A) 모두 축하해요.

(B) 며칠 안에요.

(C) 고맙습니다, 제 책상 위에 두세요.

어휘

staff 직원 evaluation 평가(서)

10. 미남 호남 🎧

Should we unload the truck from the front or side entrance?

(A) The figure is quite low.

(B) Some crates of produce.

(C) There are wide doors at the side.

해석

트럭에서 짐을 정문으로 내릴까요, 옆문으로 내릴까요?

(A) 수치가 꽤 낮아요.

(B) 농작물 상자들이요.

(C) 옆문이 넓어요.

어휘

unload 내리다, 하역하다 figure 수치, 숫자 crate 상자
produce 농작물, 농산물

11. 영녀 미남 🎧

Why was the location of the workshop changed?

(A) Because a lot of people signed up.

(B) I live on Franklin Avenue.

(C) It was held last weekend.

해석

워크숍 장소가 왜 바뀌었나요?

(A) 많은 사람이 신청했기 때문이에요.

(B) 저는 프랭클린 애비뉴에 살아요.

(C) 그건 지난주에 했어요.

어휘

location 장소 sign up 신청하다

12. 영녀 미남 🎧

I'm looking forward to the basketball tournament, aren't you?
(A) A colorful uniform.
(B) I don't really follow sports.
(C) Over 1,000 people.

해석

농구 대회가 기대되네요, 안 그래요?
(A) 화려한 유니폼이요.
(B) 저는 스포츠에 딱히 관심 없어요.
(C) 1,000명 이상이요.

어휘

look forward to ~를 기대하다 follow 따르다, 관심을 가지다

13. 미남 미녀 🎧

Are you going to apply for the management role?
(A) No, I don't think I'm qualified.
(B) She's an expert in her field.
(C) Please apply one thin coat.

해석

관리자 직책에 지원하시나요?
(A) 아니요, 저는 자격이 안 되는 것 같아요.
(B) 그녀는 자기 분야에서 전문가예요.
(C) 얇게 코팅을 한 겹 해주세요.

어휘

management 관리 role 역할, 직책
qualify 자격이 있다, 자격을 얻다 field 분야

14. 미녀 미남 🎧

Could you e-mail me a copy of the guest list?
(A) No, she'll be absent.
(B) You are welcome to come.
(C) Sure, that's no problem.

해석

손님 명단의 사본을 메일로 보내줄 수 있어요?
(A) 아니요, 그녀는 불참할 거예요.
(B) 당신이 오는 건 환영입니다.
(C) 그럼요, 문제없어요.

어휘

absent 결석한, 불참한

15. 호남 영녀 🎧

Doesn't the courier offer an express shipping service?
(A) It's a box of product samples.
(B) Yes, but only to certain countries.
(C) He expressed his appreciation.

해석

그 택배 회사는 속달 배송 서비스를 제공하지 않나요?
(A) 제품 샘플 상자예요.
(B) 네, 하지만 특정 나라에만요.
(C) 그는 감사를 표했어요.

어휘

courier 택배 회사, 운반원 shipping 운송, 배송
certain 특정한 express one's appreciation 감사를 표하다

16. 미남 미녀 🎧

I need to go to the post office on my lunch break.
(A) Would you mind buying me some stamps?
(B) No thanks, I'm not hungry.
(C) Sure, but I would need directions.

해석

전 점심시간에 우체국에 가야 해요.
(A) 우표 몇 개 사줄 수 있나요?
(B) 괜찮아요, 배고프지 않아요.
(C) 물론이죠, 하지만 방향을 알려주셔야 해요.

어휘

stamp 우표 direction 방향

17. 영녀 호남 🎧

Why is such a long session booked for the software training?
(A) I hope you can come along.
(B) Have you seen its list of features?
(C) Thursday in Room 205.

해석

소프트웨어 교육에 왜 이렇게 긴 세션이 예약된 거예요?
(A) 당신이 함께 올 수 있었으면 좋겠어요.
(B) 기능 목록을 확인해 보셨나요?
(C) 목요일, 205호에서요

해설

(B) 설명해야 할 소프트웨어의 기능들이 많아서 교육 세션이 길 수밖에 없다는 응답이다.

어휘

book 예약하다 come along 함께 오다 feature 특징

18. 미남 미녀 🎧

Who's going to pick you up at the airport?
(A) They picked the most expensive one.
(B) Yes, it's easy to drive.
(C) I'm taking the shuttle bus.

해석

공항에 누가 당신을 태우러 가죠?
(A) 그들은 가장 비싼 것을 골랐어요.

(B) 네, 그건 운전하기 쉬워요.

(C) 저는 셔틀버스를 탈 거예요.

어휘

pick ~ up ~을 태우다

19. 영녀 호남 🎧

> How do I get added to the mailing list?
> (A) No, last month's newsletter.
> (B) I made a small error.
> **(C) Let Benjamin know you're interested.**

해석

수신자 명단에 어떻게 추가될 수 있나요?

(A) 아니요, 지난달의 소식지예요.

(B) 제가 작은 실수를 했어요.

(C) 당신이 관심이 있다고 벤저민에게 알려주세요.

어휘

mailing list (우편물) 수신자 명단 newsletter 소식지

20. 미녀 미남 🎧

> What kind of flowers should we buy for the reception?
> (A) A surprising reaction.
> **(B) The venue will provide them.**
> (C) Yes, to welcome new employees.

해석

연회를 위해 어떤 꽃을 사야 할까요?

(A) 놀라운 반응이에요.

(B) 행사장에서 제공할 거예요.

(C) 네, 새로운 직원을 환영하려고요.

어휘

reception 접수처 venue (행사의) 장소

21. 영녀 호남 🎧

> Where did the building manager leave the extra keys?
> (A) For minor repairs and maintenance.
> (B) Actually, I need to leave early.
> **(C) They're at the front desk.**

해석

건물 관리자가 여분의 열쇠를 어디에 두었나요?

(A) 소규모 수리와 유지 보수를 위해서요

(B) 사실, 일찍 떠나야 해요.

(C) 접수처에 있어요.

어휘

minor 작은, 가벼운 maintenance 관리, 유지보수

22. 미남 미녀 🎧

> How much longer do you think the managers will be using the room?
> (A) No, that sounds too expensive.
> (B) It was for planning the upcoming year.
> **(C) I can call you when they're finished.**

해석

관리자들이 저 방을 얼마나 더 쓸 거 같아요?

(A) 아니요, 그건 너무 비싼 것 같아요.

(B) 내년을 계획하기 위해서였어요.

(C) 그들이 끝났을 때 전화할게요.

어휘

upcoming 곧 있을, 다가오는

23. 호남 영녀 🎧

> When are employees receiving their bonuses?
> **(A) Probably on the last day of the month.**
> (B) For meeting sales targets.
> (C) The receipt is in the bag.

해석

직원들은 언제 상여금을 받나요?

(A) 아마 월말일 거예요.

(B) 판매 목표를 달성하기 위해서요.

(C) 영수증은 가방 안에 있어요.

어휘

employee 직원 meet a target 목표를 달성하다

receipt 영수증

24. 미녀 호남 🎧

> Would you like to try our new banana nut muffins?
> (A) Please let her know.
> **(B) I have a nut allergy.**
> (C) The hotel's breakfast is included.

해석

새로운 바나나 견과류 머핀을 드셔보시겠어요?

(A) 그녀에게 알려주세요.

(B) 저는 견과류 알러지가 있어요.

(C) 호텔 조식이 포함되어 있습니다.

어휘

nut 견과류 allergy 알러지 include 포함하다

25. 미녀 미남 🎧

> These packages need to be shipped today, don't they?
> (A) Please update my e-mail address.
> (B) The new line of wool sweaters.
> **(C) I'm sure the crew won't forget.**

해석

이 상자들은 오늘 배송되어야 해요, 안 그래요?

(A) 내 이메일 주소를 업데이트해주세요.

(B) 새로운 울 스웨터 라인이요.

(C) 직원들이 잊지 않을 거라 확신해요.

어휘

package 소포

26. 호남 미녀 🎧

> Should we leave for the theater at 6 or 6:30?
> (A) A musical performance.
> **(B) Because of traffic, earlier would be better.**
> (C) Please leave them on my desk.

해석

극장에 6시에 갈까요, 6시 반에 갈까요?

(A) 뮤지컬 공연이요.

(B) 교통 체증 때문에 더 빨리 가는 게 좋을 거예요.

(C) 제 책상 위에 놔주세요.

어휘

theater 극장 performance 공연 traffic 교통 체증

27. 영녀 호남 🎧

> What kind of restaurants do you usually go to?
> (A) Your reservation has been confirmed.
> (B) Mainly on weekends or holidays.
> **(C) I'm a big fan of Italian cuisine.**

해석

보통 어떤 종류의 식당에 가시나요?

(A) 예약이 확인되었습니다.

(B) 주로 주말이나 휴일이에요.

(C) 저는 이탈리아 요리를 매우 좋아해요.

어휘

confirm 확인하다, 확정하다 mainly 주로

big fan of ~를 매우 좋아하다 cuisine 요리

28. 미녀 호남 🎧

> How long do I need to wait to hear about my business loan?
> (A) It's a new photography business.
> (B) That's what I heard as well.
> **(C) A decision will be made sometime this week.**

해석

제 사업 대출에 관해 들으려면 얼마나 기다려야 하나요?

(A) 새로운 사진 촬영 사업이에요.

(B) 제가 들은 바도 마찬가지예요.

(C) 이번 주 안으로 결정될 거예요.

어휘

business loan 사업 대출 photography 사진 decision 결정

29. 영녀 호남 🎧

> Where should the management trainees go first?
> (A) It had a lot of valuable information.
> (B) No later than 10 o'clock.
> **(C) I'll prepare a detailed schedule.**

해석

관리자 교육을 받는 사람들은 먼저 어디로 가야 하나요?

(A) 유익한 정보가 많았어요.

(B) 늦어도 10시까지요.

(C) 제가 세부 일정을 준비할게요.

어휘

management 관리, 경영 trainee 교육을 받는 사람, 수습 직원

valuable 소중한, 유익한 detailed 상세한

30. 미남 영녀 🎧

> Would keeping our pharmacy open later be worthwhile?
> (A) This coupon is worth 10 percent off.
> **(B) The shifts are already too long.**
> (C) Thanks, but I'm feeling better now.

해석

약국을 더 늦은 시간까지 운영하는 게 가치가 있을까요?

(A) 이 쿠폰으로 10% 할인받을 수 있습니다.

(B) 이미 교대 근무 시간이 너무 길어요.

(C) 고맙지만 이제 좀 나아졌어요.

어휘

pharmacy 약국 worthwhile 가치 있는 shift 교대 근무 (시간)

31. 미남 미녀 🎧

> Who's giving the first part of the sales pitch?
> **(A) I'm handling the presentation on my own.**
> (B) It's for a prospective client.
> (C) That would be really helpful.

해석

누가 세일즈 피치의 첫 부분을 담당하나요?

(A) 이 발표는 저 혼자 처리할 거예요.

(B) 예상 고객을 위한 거예요.

(C) 매우 도움이 되겠네요.

어휘

sales pitch 판매 권유, 홍보 handle 처리하다

prospective 예상되는, 가망 있는

Questions 32-34 refer to the following conversation.

W	³²Thank you for visiting the Kaysville Aquarium. How may I help you?
M	I'd like an admission ticket, please.
W	The regular ticket is 22 dollars. However, ³³you can get a season ticket for just 75 dollars. That allows you to visit our site as many times as you want for one year.
M	³³Hmm … you know, since I live locally, I'll probably come back many times. I guess I'll take that.
W	Great! ³⁴All I need is for you to fill out this application form.
M	Of course.

해석

32-34번은 다음 대화에 관한 문제입니다.

여 ³²케이스빌 수족관에 방문해주셔서 감사합니다. 어떻게 도와드릴까요?

남 입장권을 사고 싶어요.

여 일반 표는 $22입니다. 근데, ³³시즌권을 단 $75로 **구매하실 수 있으세요.** 이걸로 1년 동안 원하시는 만큼 저희 지점을 방문하실 수 있습니다.

남 ³³흠... 사실 제가 이 지역에 살아서 아마 자주 방문할 것 같아요. 그걸로 해야겠네요.

여 좋아요! ³⁴이 신청서만 작성해주시면 됩니다.

남 물론이죠.

어휘

aquarium 수족관 admission 입장, 입학 regular 일반
locally 현지에서, 지역에서 fill out 작성하다
application form 신청서

32.

대화는 어디에서 일어나고 있는가?

(A) 영화관에서

(B) 수족관에서

(C) 미술관에서

(D) 경기장에서

어휘

movie theater 영화관 aquarium 수족관
art museum 미술관 stadium 경기장

33.

남자는 다음에 무엇을 살 것 같은가?

(A) 단체 입장권

(B) 반나절 입장권

(C) 시즌 입장권

(D) 학생 입장권

어휘

half-day 반나절

34.

남자는 다음에 무엇을 할 것인가?

(A) 서식 작성하기

(B) 다른 지점 전화하기

(C) 신분증 보여주기

(D) 전화 통화하기

어휘

complete 완료하다, 작성하다 branch 지점 ID card 신분증

패러프레이징

fill out this application form → complete a form

Questions 35-37 refer to the following conversation.

M	Good morning. ³⁵I'm calling from the Paradise Dental Clinic. I just wanted to remind you that you're booked for an examination on Thursday at 9:30 A.M.
W	Oh, that's right. I was actually going to call you today because I'm going out of town unexpectedly. I need to reschedule my appointment for next week.
M	That's no problem. How about next Tuesday at 10 A.M.?
W	That works for me. ³⁶And is there a cost to park at your site?
M	No, it's free. Let me take care of the change, but please wait a moment while I do so. ³⁷We just got new software, so I'm still getting used to it.

해석

35-37번은 다음 대화에 관한 문제입니다.

남 안녕하세요. ³⁵파라다이스 치과입니다. 목요일 오전 9시 반에 검진 예약이 있다는 것을 다시 알려드리려고 전화했습니다.

여 아, 맞아요. 제가 갑자기 시외에 나갈 일이 생겨서 사실 오늘 전화하려고 했어요. 예약을 다음주로 변경해야 할 것 같아요.

남 괜찮습니다. 다음주 화요일 오전 10시 어떠세요?

여 좋아요. ³⁶그리고 거기 주차비를 따로 받나요?

남 아뇨, 무료예요. 예약 변경하는 동안 잠시 기다려주세요. ³⁷최근에 새로운 소프트웨어를 설치해서 아직 익숙하지 않아서요.

어휘

remind 상기시키다, 다시 한번 알려주다 examination 검사, 검진
be out of town 부재중이다 unexpectedly 갑자기
appointment 예약, 약속 get used to ~에 익숙해지다

35.

남자는 어디에서 일하는가?

(A) 치과에서

(B) 경영 기관에서

(C) 미용실에서

(D) 법률 사무소에서

물건들을 멀리까지 들고 가지 않아도 될 거예요.

어휘
institution 기관

36.

여자는 무엇에 관해 질문하는가?
(A) 등록비
(B) 교통수단
(C) 청구서 날짜
(D) 주차비

패러프레이징

a cost to park → a parking fee

37.

남자에 따르면, 그의 사업장은 최근에 무엇을 했는가?
(A) 제공하는 서비스의 가격을 인상했다.
(B) 소프트웨어를 업데이트했다.
(C) 다른 건물로 이전했다.
(D) 회사 정책을 수정했다.

어휘

raise 올리다 relocate 이전하다 policy 정책

패러프레이징

got new software → updated its software

[38-40] 미남 미녀 🎧

Questions 38-40 refer to the following conversation.

M Excuse me, ³⁸ do you know why the parking area is closed? Are you a member of the work crew?

W Yes, our firm is carrying out this project. ³⁸ A pipe under the parking lot has burst, so we're fixing it now. It should be done in about 3 hours.

M Oh, I see. Well, ³⁹ I'm dropping off the catered food my company made for an event here in the Kent Building. There's quite a lot, so I wanted to park near the entrance.

W ⁴⁰ If you speak to the manager, he can probably unlock the rear entrance for you. Then you wouldn't have to carry your items very far.

해석

38-40번은 다음 대화에 관한 문제입니다.
남 실례합니다, ³⁸ 주차 공간이 왜 닫혀 있는지 아세요? 작업팀의 일원이신가요?
여 네, 우리 회사에서 이 프로젝트를 진행하고 있습니다. ³⁸ 주차장 아래에 있는 배관이 터져서 저희가 지금 고치고 있어요. 약 3시간 안에 끝날 거예요.
남 아, 알겠습니다. 그, ³⁹ 저희 회사에서 만든 요리를 여기 켄트 건물에서 진행하는 행사를 위해 배달하려고요. 꽤 많아서 입구 근처에 주차하고 싶었어요.
여 ⁴⁰ 매니저에게 말하면 아마 뒷문을 열어줄 수도 있어요. 그러면

어휘

burst 터지다 drop off 내려주다, 전해주다
catered food (행사, 파티 등을 위한) 출장 음식 rear 뒤쪽, 뒤쪽의

38.

남자는 왜 주차 공간을 사용할 수 없는가?
(A) 표면이 재포장되고 있다.
(B) 그는 적절한 허가증이 없다.
(C) 주차선이 페인트칠 되고 있다.
(D) 파이프가 수리되고 있다.

어휘

surface 표면 repave 재포장하다 permit 허가증

패러프레이징

A pipe ~ fixing it → A pipe is being repaired

39.

남자는 누구일 것 같은가?
(A) 부동산 업자
(B) 조사관
(C) 출장 음식 공급업자
(D) 정비공

어휘

real estate 부동산

패러프레이징

the catered food my company made → A caterer

40.

여자는 무엇을 할 것을 제안하는가?
(A) 불만 사항을 이메일로 보내는 것
(B) 매니저에게 이야기하는 것
(C) 나중에 돌아오는 것
(D) 온라인에서 일정을 확인하는 것

어휘

complaint 불평, 불만

[41-43] 영녀 호남 🎧

Questions 41-43 refer to the following conversation.

W Good morning, Mr. Burke. Since I got here a bit early, I wiped down the ⁴¹ display cases of the fresh-cut flowers, and I've put up the signs about ⁴¹ our new prices on bouquets. Is there anything else I should do before the ⁴¹ shop opens?

M ⁴² Could you refill the water in the vases? Some of them were looking empty.

W Of course. I'll take care of that now. ⁴³ We open in 10 minutes, right?

M Yes, but … um … I see someone at the door.

W ⁴³ I don't mind unlocking it now.

41-43번은 다음 대화에 관한 문제입니다.

여 안녕하세요, 버크 씨. 제가 좀 일찍 와서 **41** 갓 다듬은 꽃이 있는 진열장을 닦고, **41** 부케의 새로 책정된 가격 표지판을 세워 두었어요. **41** 가게를 열기 전에 다른 해야 할 일이 있을까요?

남 **42** 꽃병에 있는 물을 다시 채워 줄 수 있나요? 몇 개는 비어있는 것 같아 보였어요.

여 물론이죠. 지금 처리할게요. **43** 10분 안에 열죠?

남 네, 근데... 음... 문 앞에 누가 있네요.

여 **43** 지금 열어도 저는 괜찮아요.

어휘

wipe 닦다 display case 진열장 take care of ~를 처리하다
unlock 열다

41.

대화는 어디에서 일어나고 있는가?
(A) 제조 시설에서
(B) 식당에서
(C) 금융 기관에서
(D) 꽃집에서

어휘

manufacture 제조 facility 시설 financial 금융의

패러프레이징

fresh-cut flowers / new prices on bouquets / shop
→ a flower shop

42.

남자는 여자에게 무엇을 하라고 요청하는가?
(A) 몇몇 용기 채우기
(B) 몇몇 표지판을 인쇄하기
(C) 몇몇 기계 점검하기
(D) 고객에게 전화하기

어휘

container 용기, 그릇 inspect 점검하다, 검사하다
machinery 기계

패러프레이징

refill the water in the vases → Refill some containers

43.

남자가 "문 앞에 누가 있네요"라고 말할 때 암시하는 것은 무엇인가?
(A) 그는 여자의 요청을 들어줄 수 없다.
(B) 그는 가게를 더 일찍 열고 싶어한다.
(C) 여자는 어느 공간을 치워야 한다.
(D) 여자는 더 주의 깊게 살펴봐야 한다.

어휘

fulfill 수행하다, 성취하다 request 요청

[44-46] 영녀 미남 🎧

Questions 44-46 refer to the following conversation.

> W Minjun, how was your interview for **44** the junior architect position at Larimore Incorporated?
>
> M It went well. The interviewers said I was among the top people they are considering.
>
> W That's fantastic! Would you accept the job if they made you an offer?
>
> M I'm not sure. The salary's attractive, but according to the job description, **45** I'd have to take a lot of business trips.
>
> W Well, you have some time to think about it.
>
> M Yes, but not much. **46** They're going to call me on Monday to let me know what has been decided.

해석

44-46번은 다음 대화에 관한 문제입니다.

여 민준, 당신이 본 라리모어 사의 **44** 하급 건축가 면접은 어땠나요?

남 잘했어요. 면접관들이 우선순위로 생각하는 사람 중에 제가 포함된다고 했어요.

여 멋지네요! 만약 제안이 들어온다면, 수락할 건가요?

남 잘 모르겠어요. 급여 조건은 매력적인데, 직무 기술서에 따르면 **45** 출장을 많이 가야 할 것 같아요.

여 뭐, 생각해 볼 시간은 있으니까요.

남 네, 근데 많지는 않아요. **46** 결정된 것을 알려주려고 월요일에 연락이 올 거예요.

어휘

architect 건축가 consider 고려하다
attractive 매력적인, 멋진 job description 직무 기술서
business trip 출장

44.

남자의 직업은 무엇일 것 같은가?
(A) 접수 담당자
(B) 건축가
(C) 판매 책임자
(D) 기자

45.

남자는 직업에 관해 무슨 걱정을 표현하는가?
(A) 회사가 재정적으로 안정적이지 않다.
(B) 급여가 매우 높지는 않다.
(C) 업무 시간이 길다.
(D) 그는 자주 여행을 해야 할 것이다.

어휘

financially 금전적으로 stable 안정적인
working hour 업무 시간 frequently 자주

패러프레이징

take a lot of business trips → travel frequently

46.

남자는 월요일에 무엇을 할 것인가?

(A) 채용 결정에 대해 알게 될 것이다
(B) 두 번째 면접에 참석할 것이다
(C) 작업 포트폴리오를 제출할 것이다
(D) 회사를 탐방할 것이다

어휘

hiring 채용 decision 결정 submit 제출하다

패러프레이징

let me know what has been decided
→ Learn about a hiring decision

[47-49] 호남 미녀 미남 🎧

Questions 47-49 refer to the following conversation
with three speakers.

> M1 ⁴⁷Welcome to Simpson Antiques. How may I
> help you?
> W Hi. ⁴⁸I heard that you do free appraisals. I
> brought in this wooden jewelry box from the
> Victorian Era, and ⁴⁸I'd like to find out how
> much it is worth.
> M1 ⁴⁷The store manager, Douglas, can assist you
> with that.
> M2 Hi, I'm Douglas. Let's see, based on the
> markings, I can identify the approximate age,
> but I'll do a little research to get an accurate
> value. Do you keep this item in storage?
> W No, I usually have it sitting on a shelf in my
> living room.
> M2 In that case, ⁴⁹you should use a special
> furniture polish to protect the exterior. I'll show
> you the one we recommend.

해석

47-49번은 다음 세 명의 대화에 관한 문제입니다.

남1 ⁴⁷심슨 골동품에 오신 것을 환영합니다. 어떻게 도와드릴까요?
여 안녕하세요. ⁴⁸무료 감정을 하신다고 들었습니다. 빅토리아 시대
의 목재 보석함을 가져왔는데, ⁴⁸이게 얼마의 가치가 있을지 알
고 싶습니다.
남1 그건 ⁴⁷우리 상점의 매니저, 더글러스가 도와드릴 겁니다.
남2 안녕하세요, 더글러스입니다. 한번 볼게요, 이 무늬를 기반으로
거의 정확한 생산 연도를 확인할 수 있지만 정확한 가치를 알기
위해 간단한 조사를 할 겁니다. 이 물품을 창고에 보관하시나요?
여 아니요, 보통 저희 거실에 있는 선반에 놓여 있어요.
남2 그 경우에, ⁴⁹외관을 보호하기 위해 특수 가구 광택제를 사용하
셔야 해요. 저희가 추천하는 것을 보여드리죠.

어휘

appraisal 감정, 평가 worth 가치가 있는 assist 돕다
base on ~를 기반으로 approximate 거의 정확한
accurate 정확한 storage 창고 polish 광택제 exterior 외관
recommend 추천하다

47.

화자들은 어디에 있는가?

(A) 미술 용품 상점에
(B) 컴퓨터 수리점에
(C) 골동품 상점에
(D) 의류 상점에

어휘

art supply 미술 용품

48.

여자는 왜 업체를 방문했는가?

(A) 취업 지원을 위해
(B) 몇몇 샘플을 전달하기 위해
(C) 물품의 가치를 확인하기 위해
(D) 하자가 있는 물품을 반품하기 위해

어휘

apply 지원하다 value 가치 faulty 결함이 있는

패러프레이징

find out how much it is worth → check an item's value

49.

더글러스는 여자에게 무엇을 보여줄 것인가?

(A) 팸플릿
(B) 명함
(C) 가구 광택제
(D) 보관 용기

[50-52] 호남 미녀 🎧

Questions 50-52 refer to the following conversation.

> M Hi. ⁵⁰I bought these headphones here last
> month, and I'd like to return them for a refund.
> Here is the original receipt.
> W Hmm … I'm sorry, but we do not accept
> returns on electronic devices after 30 days.
> M Oh, I didn't realize that. ⁵¹I would have returned
> them sooner, but I was on an overseas
> business trip for the past month. Is there
> anything I can do?
> W Well, since they're still in the original
> packaging, ⁵²I can give you a voucher for store
> credit in the amount you spent on them.
> M I suppose that will have to do.

해석

50-52번은 다음 대화에 관한 문제입니다.

남 안녕하세요. ⁵⁰지난달에 여기에서 이 헤드폰을 샀는데, 환불받고
싶습니다. 여기 원본 영수증이요.
여 흠... 죄송하지만, 30일 이후엔 전자 기기 환불 신청을 받지 않습
니다.
남 아, 그건 몰랐어요. ⁵¹더 일찍 환불하려 했는데, 지난달 동안 해
외 출장 중이었어요. 제가 할 수 있는 게 있을까요?

여 음, 기존 포장 상태 그대로이니까 쓰신 금액만큼 ⁵² 저희 매장 적립금으로 전환한 상품권을 드릴 수 있어요.

남 그거면 될 것 같네요.

어휘

refund 환불 receipt 영수증 device 기기
realize 깨닫다, 알다 overseas 해외의 voucher 상품권

50.

대화는 어디에서 이루어지고 있는가?

(A) 음악 스튜디오에서
(B) 여행사에서
(C) 수화물 제조사에서
(D) 전자 제품 상점에서

어휘

manufacturer 제조사

패러프레이징

headphones → electronics

51.

남자는 왜 업체를 더 일찍 방문하지 못했는가?

(A) 그는 급한 프로젝트를 끝내야 했다.
(B) 그는 국내에 없었다.
(C) 그는 차를 수리해야 했다.
(D) 그는 새로운 집으로 이사했다.

어휘

urgent 급한 be out of ~에 없다

패러프레이징

I was on an overseas business trip
→ He was out of the country

52.

여자는 무엇을 해주겠다고 제안하는가?

(A) 상품권 발급하기
(B) 상품 교환해주기
(C) 교체 부품 보내주기
(D) 할인율 높여주기

어휘

issue 발급하다 voucher 상품권 exchange 교환하다
replacement 교체

패러프레이징

give you a voucher → Issue a voucher

[53-55] 영녀 호남 미남 🎧

Questions 53-55 refer to the following conversation
with three speakers.

W ⁵³ I wanted to thank both of you for your work
on the poster you designed for our theater's
new show. We need to get more attention for
our theater's events.

M1 Actually, ⁵⁵ Walter and I were just talking about
an idea for that. ⁵⁴ How about holding a singing
contest? People would invite their friends and
family, so that would boost ticket sales.

M2 Right. And some ⁵⁵ local businesses could
donate some prizes for the event in exchange
for publicity. ⁵⁵ I'll call around to see if I can find
some business owners who are willing to do
so.

해석

53-55번은 다음 세 명의 대화에 관한 문제입니다.

여 우리 극장의 새로운 공연을 위해 ⁵³ 두 분께서 디자인한 포스터 작업에 대해 감사드리고 싶어요. 극장 행사에 더 많은 이목을 끌어야 해요.

남1 사실 ⁵⁵ 월터와 제가 방금 그걸 위한 아이디어에 관해 이야기하고 있었어요. ⁵⁴ 노래 경연을 주최하는 게 어떨까요? 사람들이 자기 친구와 가족을 초대하면 표 판매량이 증가할 거예요.

남2 맞아요. 그리고 몇몇 ⁵⁵ 지역 업체들이 홍보를 대가로 행사를 위해 ⁵⁵ 상품을 기부할 수도 있어요. 그러길 바라는 업체가 있는지 확인하기 위해 여러 곳에 전화해볼게요.

어휘

attention 관심, 이목 boost 증가하다, 올리다 local 지역의
donate 기부하다, 기증하다 in exchange for ~를 대가로
publicity 홍보 call around 여러 곳에 전화하다

53.

남자들은 최근에 무엇을 했는가?

(A) 무대 공연 예약하기
(B) 관광 주관하기
(C) 포스터 제작하기
(D) 오류 수정하기

어휘

book 예약하다

패러프레이징

the poster you designed → Created a poster

54.

남자들은 무엇을 할 것을 제안하는가?

(A) 영업 시간을 연장하는 것
(B) 대회를 주최하는 것
(C) 사업체를 인수하는 것
(D) 건물을 개조하는 것

어휘

extend 연장하다, 늘리다 business hours 영업 시간
host 주최하다 competition 대회, 경쟁 renovate 개조하다

패러프레이징

holding a singing contest → Hosting a competition

55.

월터는 왜 전화를 할 것인가?

(A) 가격을 조사하기 위해
(B) 초청 연사를 구하기 위해
(C) 몇몇 회원들에게 감사를 표하기 위해
(D) 기부를 부탁하기 위해

어휘

guest speaker 초청 연사 donation 기부, 기증

패러프레이징

donate some prizes → To ask for donations

[56-58] 미남 영녀 🎧

Questions 56-58 refer to the following conversation.

> M Good morning, Emily. Have you seen the latest figures for ⁵⁶ our line of energy drinks?
> W Yes, it looks like supermarkets are starting to place larger orders.
> M Right. It's great news for us. How are things going with the new ⁵⁷ machinery on the production line?
> W Well, the employees were able to learn how to use it quickly. However, ⁵⁷ it has to be cleaned every 2 hours, much more often than before.
> M Hmm … I'd like to know what the staff thinks. ⁵⁸ Could you make a survey for the workers? Their feedback could help improve our productivity.
> W Of course.

해석

56-58번은 다음 대화에 관한 문제입니다.

남 좋은 아침이에요, 에밀리. ⁵⁶ **저희 에너지 음료 라인의 최근 매출량을 봤나요?**

여 네, 슈퍼마켓들이 대량 주문을 하기 시작한 것 같아요.

남 맞아요. 저희에게는 좋은 소식이죠. 생산 설비에 새로 온 ⁵⁷ **기계는 어떤가요?**

여 음, 사용하는 법을 직원들이 빨리 익힐 수 있었어요. 하지만 ⁵⁷ **이건 2시간마다 세척되어야 해요, 전보다 훨씬 자주 해야 하는 거죠.**

남 흠… 직원들이 어떻게 생각하는지 알고 싶네요. ⁵⁸ **직원들을 대상으로 한 설문지를 만들어 줄 수 있나요?** 생산성을 개선하는 것에 그들의 피드백이 도움이 될 수 있을 거예요.

여 물론이죠.

어휘

latest 최신 figure 수치 machinery 기계
production 생산, 생산량 survey 설문(지), 설문 조사
improve 개선하다 productivity 생산성

56.

대화는 어디에서 일어나고 있는 것 같은가?
(A) 철물점에서
(B) 광고 회사에서
(C) 가전제품 수리점에서

(D) 음료 생산 회사에서

어휘

hardware 철물 appliance 가전제품 beverage 음료

패러프레이징

our line of energy drinks → beverage producer

57.

여자는 장비에 대해 무엇이라고 말하는가?
(A) 그것은 자주 세척되어야 한다.
(B) 그것은 아직 배송이 되지 않았다.
(C) 그것은 설치하는 데 오랜 시간이 걸린다.
(D) 그것은 과정의 속도를 올렸다.

어휘

frequently 자주 install 설치하다 speed up 속도를 올리다
process 과정

패러프레이징

cleaned every 2 hours, much more often
→ cleaned frequently

58.

여자는 무엇을 하기로 동의하는가?
(A) 설문지 작성하기
(B) 설명서 검토하기
(C) 가격표 확인하기
(D) 계약서 갱신하기

어휘

manual 설명서 renew 갱신하다 contract 계약서

패러프레이징

make a survey → Create a survey

[59-61] 미녀 호남 🎧

Questions 59-61 refer to the following conversation.

> W Hi, Rishi. Sorry I missed the sustainable energy conference. I wish I could have gone, but ⁵⁹ I got a last-minute work assignment that I had to deal with.
> M It seems that you're always working overtime. ⁶⁰ You should talk to someone in HR to ask if they would be willing to hire a part-time worker for your team.
> W Hmm … that would take off a lot of pressure. Thanks for the tip.
> M My pleasure.
> W So, how was the trade show? I know you were planning on ⁶¹ attending a talk on wind turbines. Did you learn anything new?
> M ⁶¹ I took notes, which I'll share with you. In fact, I filled four pages.
> W Wow, that sounds great!

59-61번은 다음 대화에 관한 문제입니다.

여 안녕하세요, 리쉬. 지속 가능한 에너지 콘퍼런스에 참여하지 못해서 미안해요. 갈 수 있었으면 좋았겠지만 **⁵⁹제가 처리해야 하는 막바지 업무 과제**가 있었어요.

남 당신은 늘 초과근무 하는 것 같아요. **⁶⁰인사팀의 누군가와 이야기해서 당신의 팀에 ⁶⁰시간제 직원을 채용할 생각이 있는지 물어봐야 해요.**

여 음... 그게 부담을 많이 줄여주겠네요. 조언 감사해요.

남 도움이 되어 저도 기쁘네요.

여 그래서, 무역 박람회는 어땠나요? 풍력 원동기에 대한 **⁶¹연설에 참석할 계획**이 있었다고 알고 있어요. 새로운 게 있었나요?

남 **⁶¹필기해왔어요**, 공유해 드릴게요. 사실, 4페이지나 채웠어요.

여 우와, 그거 좋네요!

어휘

sustainable 지속 가능한 last-minute 막바지의
assignment 과제 work overtime 초과 근무하다
pressure 부담 take note 필기하다, 주목하다

59.

여자는 왜 행사에 불참했는가?

(A) 그녀는 예기치 않은 업무가 있었다.
(B) 그녀는 고객을 방문 중이었다.
(C) 그녀는 제시간에 등록하지 않았다.
(D) 그녀는 휴가 중이었다.

어휘

unexpected 예기치 못한 register 등록하다
in time 제시간에 be on vacation 휴가 중이다

패러프레이징

a last-minute work assignment → unexpected work

60.

남자는 여자에게 무엇을 하기를 권유하는가?

(A) 팀 회의하기
(B) 행사 알림을 설정하기
(C) 채용 요청하기
(D) 보도 자료를 쓰기

어휘

reminder 알림 press release 보도자료

패러프레이징

talk to ~ hire a part-time worker
→ make a hiring request

61.

남자가 "4페이지나 채웠어요"라고 말할 때 암시하는 것은 무엇인가?

(A) 그는 추가 근무를 해야 했다.
(B) 그는 연설이 유용하다고 느꼈다.
(C) 참석자가 많았다.
(D) 업무가 거의 완료됐다.

어휘

additional 추가의 attendee 참석자

[62-64] 미남 영녀 🎧

Questions 62-64 refer to the following conversation and train schedule.

> M Hannah, I know we had originally bought standard class seats for the train, ⁶²but why don't we upgrade to first class? With a little more space, I think we can work on the train.
>
> W I agree. I wanted to use this time on the train to go over ⁶³which parts of the software each of us will demonstrate at the investors' meeting.
>
> M Right, let me go ask a ticket agent right away.
>
> W Wait, let's see … we don't have much time. ⁶⁴Our train's supposed to depart at 8:05. We should probably just head to the platform now. I think we can change our tickets on the train.
>
> M Okay.

해석

62-64번은 다음 대화와 기차 일정표에 관한 문제입니다.

남 한나, 우리가 원래는 일반 등급 좌석을 산 걸로 알고 있는데, **⁶²일등석으로 업그레이드하는 건 어때요?** 공간이 조금 더 있으면, 기차에서 일할 수 있을 것 같아요.

여 동의해요. 기차에 있는 시간을 활용해서 **⁶³투자자 회의에서 우리가 각각 소프트웨어의 어느 부분을 시연할 것인지 검토하고 싶었어요.**

남 맞아요, 지금 당장 매표원에게 물어볼게요.

여 잠깐만요, 어디 보자... 시간이 많이 없어요. **⁶⁴기차가 8시 5분에 떠나요.** 지금은 아마도 그냥 승강장으로 가야 할 것 같아요. 표는 기차 안에서 바꿀 수 있을 것 같아요.

남 알겠어요.

어휘

originally 원래, 본래 space 공간 demonstrate 시연하다
investor 투자자 ticket agent 매표원 depart 떠나다

도착지	출발 시간	승강장
런던	7:31	2
셰필드	7:50	4
리즈	⁶⁴8:05	⁶⁴9
버밍햄	8:12	11

62.

화자들은 무엇에 관해 물어볼 것인가?

(A) 수화물 정책
(B) 식사 종류
(C) 표 영수증
(D) 좌석 업그레이드

어휘

luggage 짐, 수화물 policy 정책

패러프레이징

upgrade to first class → A seat upgrade

63.

화자들은 기차에서 무엇을 논의할 것인가?
(A) 제품에 대한 점검 절차
(B) 경영진을 위한 재무 회의
(C) 투자자를 위한 제품 시연
(D) 입사 지원자를 위한 면접 절차

어휘

procedure 절차, 방법   executive 경영진
job candidate 입사 지원자

패러프레이징

parts of the software ~ demonstrate at the investors
meeting → A product demonstration for investors

64.

시각 자료를 보시오. 화자들은 어디로 가야 하는가?
(A) 승강장 2로
(B) 승강장 4로
(C) 승강장 9로
(D) 승강장 11로

[65-67] 미녀 호남 🎧

Questions 65-67 refer to the following conversation
and map.

> W Alright, Jesse. ⁶⁵That was the last exterior light
> that needed to be rewired. Now we just need
> to ⁶⁵turn the electricity back on and make sure
> everything is working.
> M That's great. We'll be able to head back to the
> office early then.
> W Actually, ⁶⁶I need to go to the Kirby Building to
> take some pictures of a job we did there. The
> owner said we could highlight the work in our
> brochure.
> M Oh, I see.
> W Would you mind giving me a ride there?
> There's nowhere to park, but ⁶⁷you could drop
> me off at the corner of Richmond Street and
> Victoria Lane.
> M No problem.

해석

65-67번은 다음 대화와 지도에 관한 문제입니다.
여 좋아요, 제시. ⁶⁵그게 배선을 교체해야 했던 마지막 외관 조명이
   었어요. 이제 ⁶⁵다시 불을 켜보고 잘 작동하는지 확인만 하면 돼
   요.
남 훌륭해요. 그럼 사무실로 일찍 돌아갈 수 있겠네요.
여 사실, ⁶⁶저는 커비 건물에 저희가 거기에서 작업한 것들 사진을
   좀 찍으러 가야 해요. 거기 주인이 그 작업물을 우리 책자에 내도
   된다고 했어요.

남 아, 그렇군요.
여 거기까지 데려다 줄 수 있나요? 주차할 곳이 없지만, ⁶⁷리치먼드
   가와 빅토리아 길 사이의 모퉁이에 내려줘도 돼요.
남 그럼요.

어휘

rewire 배선을 교체하다   electricity 전력, 전기
give a ride 태워주다   drop off 내려주다

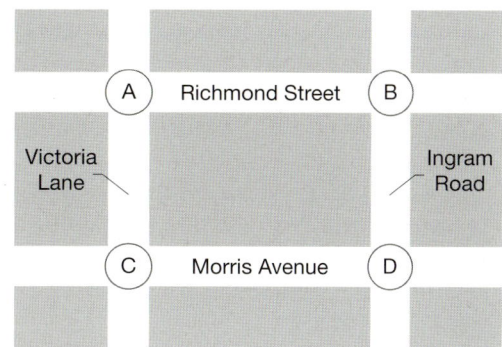

65.

화자들은 누구일 것 같은가?
(A) 목수
(B) 전기 기사
(C) 화가
(D) 건축가

66.

여자는 커비 건물에서 무엇을 할 것인가?
(A) 도구 구매하기
(B) 책자 인쇄하기
(C) 사진 찍기
(D) 차량 대여하기

어휘

tool 도구   brochure 책자   vehicle 차량

67.

시각 자료를 보시오. 여자는 어디에 내리기 원하는가?
(A) 장소 A에
(B) 장소 B에
(C) 장소 C에
(D) 장소 D에

[68-70] 영녀 호남 🎧

Questions 68-70 refer to the following conversation
and price list.

> W Thank you for calling Gilcrest Landscaping.
> How may I help you?
> M Hello. I just moved into a new house, and I'm
> looking for someone to do lawn mowing

services. **68** My cousin uses your company, and he told me that it's great.

W Oh, I'm glad to hear that he is pleased with our service. What size is your lawn?

M It's quite small. **69** I'd like someone to visit just twice every month. I don't mind if the grass gets a little long in between.

W Alright. I need to make an account for you. **70** Could you please tell me where you live?

해석

68-70번은 다음 대화와 가격표에 관한 문제입니다.

여 길크레스트 조경에 전화 주셔서 감사합니다. 어떻게 도와드릴까요?

남 안녕하세요. 저는 막 새집으로 이사 와서 예초 서비스를 제공하는 사람을 찾고 있어요. **68** 제 사촌이 당신의 회사를 이용하는데, **훌륭하다고 이야기 들었어요.**

여 아, 그가 저희 서비스에 만족 하신다는 걸 들으니 기쁘네요. 잔디밭의 크기가 어떻게 되나요?

남 꽤 작아요. **69** 매달 두 번만 방문해주면 좋을 것 같아요. 그 사이에 잔디가 좀 자라는 것은 괜찮아요.

여 알겠습니다. 계정을 만들어 드릴게요. **70** 어디 사시는지 알려주시겠어요?

어휘

landscaping 조경 lawn mowing 잔디를 깎다
account 계정, 계좌

잔디 손질: 주택, 작은 크기	
상품 1: 한 달에 한 번	$25
69 상품 2: 한 달에 두 번	$45
상품 3: 한 주에 한 번	$80
상품 4: 한 주에 두 번 + 덤불 정리	$110

68.

남자에게 누가 길크레스트 조경을 추천했는가?
(A) 친구
(B) 동료
(C) 친척
(D) 고객

패러프레이징

My cousin → A relative

69.

시각 자료를 보시오. 남자는 어떤 상품을 필요로 하는가?
(A) 상품 1
(B) 상품 2
(C) 상품 3
(D) 상품 4

70.

남자는 다음에 무엇을 할 것 같은가?
(A) 주소 알려주기
(B) 요금 지불하기
(C) 비밀번호 생성하기
(D) 날짜 선택하기

어휘

payment 지불, 지급

패러프레이징

tell me where you live → Provide an address

[71-73] 미녀 🎧

Questions 71-73 refer to the following telephone message.

W Hi, **71** this is Robin from Elliot Painting. I've checked on the paint that you wanted for the exterior of your home. **72** Originally, I told you it would cost 24 pounds per can. However, I've just found out from the supplier that it has recently increased to 28. I think this is still worth it, though, as it's the best quality on the market. Please call me back to let me know whether you still want to go forward with the project. **73** I'd like to get confirmation as soon as possible so I can place the order. This paint is very popular, so it could sell out quickly.

해석

71-73번은 다음 전화 메시지에 관한 문제입니다.

여 안녕하세요. **71** 엘리엇 페인트 시공업체의 로빈입니다. 당신이 집의 외벽에 칠하기를 원했던 페인트를 확인해봤습니다. **72** 원래 한 캔당 £24라고 말씀드렸죠. 근데 방금 공급처로부터 그것이 28로 인상됐다는 것을 알게 됐어요. 시중에 있는 것 중에 품질이 최고이니까 저는 그래도 가치가 있다고 생각해요. 이 프로젝트를 계속 진행하길 원하시는지 다시 전화해서 알려주세요. **73** 주문할 수 있게 최대한 빨리 확인 부탁드려요. 이 페인트는 매우 인기가 많아서 빨리 품절될 수 있어요.

어휘

exterior 외관 supplier 공급자, 공급처 quality 품질
go forward 진행하다 sell out 품절되다

71.

화자는 어떤 종류의 업체에서 근무하는가?
(A) 미술관
(B) 페인트 시공업체
(C) 청소 업체
(D) 전력 회사

72.

화자는 무엇이 변했다고 하는가?
(A) 디자인

(B) 배송 날짜
(C) 가격
(D) 브랜드 명

패러프레이징
cost → price

73.

화자는 왜 확인을 빨리 받고 싶어 하는가?
(A) 작업반이 평소보다 바쁘다.
(B) 할인이 거의 끝나간다.
(C) 폭풍우가 다가온다.
(D) 제품의 수요가 높다.

어휘
usual 평소 approach 다가오다 demand 수요

패러프레이징
This paint is very popular
→ A product is in high demand

[74-76] 미남 🎧

Questions 74-76 refer to the following talk.

M Thank you all for being here for this ⁷⁴ workshop for salespeople. As you begin your career with us, we want to give you the tools to be successful. When selling our line of vehicles, ⁷⁵ your ability to listen to customers is really important. That way, you can make suitable recommendations for them. I've invited ⁷⁶ Andre Carlson to lead the first part of this workshop. Just last month, ⁷⁶ he beat our company's record for most cars sold in a month. So, there's a lot that you can learn from his strategy. I encourage you to pay attention.

해석
74-76번은 다음 담화에 관한 문제입니다.
남 ⁷⁴ 판매원들을 위한 워크숍에 와주셔서 모두 감사합니다. 저희와 함께 일을 하게 되었으니, 성공하기 위한 방법들을 제시해 드리고 싶습니다. 저희 자동차 라인을 판매할 때는 ⁷⁵ 고객의 이야기를 듣는 능력이 매우 중요합니다. 그렇게 하면 고객에게 적절한 추천을 할 수 있죠. ⁷⁶ 안드레 칼슨을 이 워크숍의 첫 부분을 이끌어 주실 수 있도록 초청했습니다. 바로 지난달 그가 한 달 동안 가장 많이 차를 판 것으로 ⁷⁶ 우리 회사의 기록을 경신했죠. 그렇기 때문에 여러분은 그의 전략으로부터 배울 수 있는 것이 많을 거예요. 집중하시길 바랍니다.

어휘
sales person 판매원 successful 성공한
suitable 적절한, 알맞은 recommendation 추천
beat a record 기록을 깨다, 기록을 경신하다 strategy 전략
pay attention 집중하다

74.

화자는 누구에게 연설하는가?
(A) 자동차 정비공
(B) 판매 대리인
(C) 취업 지원자
(D) 공사 현장 인부

패러프레이징
salespeople → Sales representatives

75.

화자는 무엇이 중요하다고 하는가?
(A) 경청하는 능력을 갖추는 것
(B) 큰 고객 기반을 쌓는 것
(C) 시간을 효과적으로 관리하는 것
(D) 업계 동향에 따르는 것

어휘
keep up with (유행을) 따르다

패러프레이징
your ability to listen to customers
→ Having good listening skills

76.

화자에 따르면 안드레 칼슨은 최근에 무엇을 했는가?
(A) 그의 회사를 시작했다
(B) 출장에서 돌아왔다
(C) 새로운 기록을 세웠다
(D) 수상자 후보가 되었다

어휘
nomination 추천, 임명

패러프레이징
beat our company's record → Set a new record

[77-79] 영녀 🎧

Questions 77-79 refer to the following broadcast.

W Now for your local news report. After receiving a lot of pressure from the public, city council members are finally starting to address the traffic issues in the Englewood neighborhood. ⁷⁷ Since the new athletic stadium opened there in March, there has been an increase in visitors to the area. ⁷⁸ Residents have complained that traffic jams and delays have become more frequent, especially on Redmond Road. The ⁷⁹ city council is looking into adding another lane to the road. ⁷⁹ They will meet with financial consultants tomorrow to examine whether or not this is possible with the current budget. This is a closed meeting, but residents are encouraged to express their opinions on the city's online feedback forum.

해석

77-79번은 다음 방송에 관한 문제입니다.

여 지역 뉴스 보도를 시작하겠습니다. 대중으로부터 많은 압력을 받은 후, 시의회는 드디어 잉글우드 근교의 교통 문제에 대처하기 시작했습니다. **77 새로운 체육 경기장이 3월에 개장된 이후로, 그 지역의 방문객이 증가했습니다. 78 주민들은** 특히 레드먼드 도로를 중심으로 **교통 체증과 지연이 잦아졌다고** 불평했습니다. **79 시의회는** 도로에 다른 차선을 추가하는 것을 검토하고 있습니다. 그들은 현재 예산으로 이것이 가능할지 검토하기 위해 **79 내일 재무 자문위원을 만날 것입니다.** 이것은 비공개회의지만, 주민들이 온라인 피드백 포럼에 의견을 표명하는 것은 권장되고 있습니다.

어휘

pressure 압박, 압력 public 대중 city council 시의회
address 대처하다, 착수하다 traffic jam 교통 체증
lane 차선, 도로 consultant 상담가, 자문위원
examine 검토하다, 검사하다 closed 닫은, 비공개의

77.

방송에 따르면, 3월에 무슨 일이 일어났는가?
(A) 도로가 수리되었다.
(B) 경기장이 개장했다.
(C) 시 선거가 있었다.
(D) 새로운 법이 통과되었다.

어휘

election 투표

패러프레이징

athletic stadium → sports stadium

78.

주민들은 무엇에 대한 불평을 했는가?
(A) 공영 주차 공간 부족
(B) 교통체증 증가
(C) 도로 안전 문제
(D) 공사로 인한 소음 공해

어휘

lack 부족 congestion 혼잡 safety 안전성, 안전
disturbance 방해, 소란

패러프레이징

traffic jams and delays → traffic congestion

79.

누가 내일 시의회를 만날 것인가?
(A) 교통 당국
(B) 구조 공학자
(C) 건강 전문가
(D) 재무 자문가

어휘

authorities 당국, 관계자 advisor 자문가, 고문

패러프레이징

financial consultant → financial advisor

[80-82] 호남 🎧

Questions 80-82 refer to the following excerpt from a meeting.

> M Finally, I'd like to let you all know about some upcoming building work. We will be having the windows replaced this weekend. **80 This project is to cut down on heating expenses,** as the new windows will be much better insulated. Now, this work creates a lot of dust, **81 which can be harmful to electronic devices.** So, please be sure to move smaller items into your desk drawers and cover your computer before you leave the office on Friday. **82 If you need boxes, tape, or sheets of plastic to protect your belongings, talk to Melinda** in the administration office.

해석

80-82번은 다음 회의 발췌록에 관한 문제입니다.

남 마지막으로, 곧 있을 건축 작업에 대해 알려드리고자 합니다. 이번 주말에는 창문을 교체할 예정입니다. **80 이 프로젝트는** 새로운 창문의 단열효과로부터 비롯될 **80 난방비 절감을 위한 것입니다.** 이 작업은 많은 먼지를 발생시키며, **81 이것은 전자 기기에 해로울 수 있습니다.** 그러니 금요일 퇴근하기 전에 작은 물건들은 책상 서랍에 넣고 컴퓨터를 덮으세요. **82 여러분의 소지품을 보호하기 위해 상자나 테이프, 플라스틱 시트가 필요하다면,** 행정실의 **82 멜린다에게 이야기하세요.**

어휘

cut down on ~를 줄이다, ~를 절감하다
insulate 단열 처리를 하다 harmful 해롭다
belongings 소유물, 소지품

80.

변경의 목적은 무엇인가?
(A) 법규에 따르기 위해
(B) 직원의 건강을 증진하기 위해
(C) 난방 비용을 줄이기 위해
(D) 보험 정책 자격을 얻기 위해

어휘

comply 따르다, 순응하다 regulation 법규, 규칙

패러프레이징

to cut down on heating expenses
→ To reduce heating costs

81.

화자는 청자들에게 무엇을 경고하는가?
(A) 전자 기기 손상
(B) 업무 방해
(C) 예정에 없는 정전
(D) 소지품 분실

harmful to electronic devices
→ damage to electronics

82.

청자들은 왜 멜린다에게 이야기해야 하는가?
(A) 휴가를 요청하기 위해
(B) 교육을 신청하기 위해
(C) 작업 공간을 예약하기 위해
(D) 보급품을 받기 위해

어휘

time off 휴가 sign up 신청하다 workspace 작업 공간

패러프레이징

If you need boxes, tape, or sheets of plastic
→ To get some supplies

[83-85] 미남 🎧

Questions 83-85 refer to the following speech.

M Good afternoon. 83 As the accounting director, it is important that I keep you informed about what's going on. I wanted to let you know that I had a meeting with Ashley White this morning. 84 She informed me that she has decided to leave the company. This decision was made for personal reasons and is effective immediately. Of course, it will take some time to find and train her replacement, so 85 you may be worrying that this will significantly increase your workload. Well, this is our slow season. In fact, if this had to happen, the timing couldn't have been better.

해석

83-85번은 다음 연설에 관한 문제입니다.
남 안녕하세요. 83 **회계팀장으로서**, 무슨 일이 일어나고 있는지 계속 알려드리는 것은 중요합니다. 오늘 아침에 애슐리 화이트와 미팅이 있었다는 것을 알려드리고 싶었습니다. 84 **그녀는 저에게 회사를 그만두기로 했다고 알려주었습니다.** 이 결정은 개인적인 이유로 내려졌으며 즉시 시행될 것입니다. 물론 그녀의 후임자를 찾고 교육하는 데 시간이 좀 걸릴 것이기 때문에 85 **여러분의 업무량이 크게 증가할 것이라고 걱정할 수도 있습니다.** 근데, 지금은 비수기예요. 사실 이런 일이 있기에 가장 좋은 시기라고 할 수 있습니다.

어휘

inform 알리다 decision 결정 effective 시행되는
replacement 후임자, 교체 significantly 크게
workload 업무량

83.

화자는 누구인가?
(A) 컴퓨터 전문가

(B) 부서장
(C) 정부 조사관
(D) 회사 인턴

패러프레이징

the accounting director → A department head

84.

연설은 주로 무엇에 관한 것인가?
(A) 경쟁의 증가
(B) 직원의 사직
(C) 사내 시상식 만찬
(D) 모금 행사

어휘

resignation 사직 fund-raising 모금

패러프레이징

she has decided to leave the company
→ A staff member's resignation

85.

화자는 왜 "지금은 비수기예요"라고 말하는가?
(A) 청자들을 안심시키기 위해
(B) 초대를 확대시키기 위해
(C) 할인을 설명하기 위해
(D) 제안을 거절하기 위해

어휘

reassure 안심시키다 extend 연장하다, 확대하다
reject 거절하다, 거부하다

[86-88] 미녀 🎧

Questions 86-88 refer to the following telephone message.

W Hi, Mr. Mendez. 86 This is Carla from the store's Sierra Street branch. We'll be opening shortly, and I'm making sure everything is ready for 87 our annual clearance sale today. I see that you had requested that we hang up a large banner above the front entrance. Well, 88 the winds are really strong right now, so I'm not sure I should be sending someone up on a ladder. The entrance is nearly 15 feet tall. 86 I'd like your advice on what to do, so please call me back when you get this message. Thanks a lot.

해석

86-88번은 다음 전화 메세지에 관한 문제입니다.
여 안녕하세요, 멘데즈 씨. 86 **저는 시에라 거리 지점 매장의 칼라입니다.** 곧 매장을 열 것이며, 87 **오늘 있을 연간 재고 정리 할인에** 모든 것이 준비되도록 확인하고 있습니다. 정문 위에 큰 현수막을 걸어달라고 요청하신 것 같은데요. 음, 88 **지금은 바람이 너무 강해서 사다리 위로 누군가를 보내도 될지 잘 모르겠어요.** 입구

는 거의 15피트 높이예요. **86** 어떻게 해야 할지 당신의 조언이 필요하니, 이 메시지를 받으면 다시 전화해 주세요. 감사합니다.

어휘

shortly 곧 make sure 확인하다 request 요청하다
ladder 사다리 advice 조언, 충고

86.

청자는 누구일 것 같은가?

(A) 고객
(B) 시 공무원
(C) 매니저
(D) 배관공

87.

오늘 영업시간에 무슨 일이 일어날 것인가?

(A) 안전 검사
(B) 할인 행사
(C) 제품 회수
(D) 채용 면접

패러프레이징

our annual clearance sale → A sales event

88.

화자가 "입구는 거의 15피트 높이예요"라고 말할 때 그녀가 의미하는 것은 무엇인가?

(A) 몇몇 제품은 쉽게 실을 수 있다.
(B) 몇몇 다른 도구가 필요하다.
(C) 그녀는 치수를 잘못 쟀다.
(D) 그녀는 업무가 위험하다고 생각한다.

어휘

load 싣다, 적재하다 equipment 도구
measurement 측정, 치수

[89-91] 호남 🎧

Questions 89-91 refer to the following excerpt from a meeting.

M I'd like to update you on some changes ahead at the company. When customers experience a technical issue, **89** our helpline is a great tool for resolving the problem. For our customers' convenience, **89** we have decided to start offering this service 24 hours a day instead of just between 9 and 6. Your schedules will remain the same, and **90** you will continue in your role of assisting customers. We plan to outsource the overnight hours to a different company. However, **91** I'll need some of you to help train those new workers so that our service is consistent. I'll discuss that with you on an individual basis later.

해석

89-91번은 다음 회의 발췌록에 관한 문제입니다.

남 앞으로 있을 회사의 몇 가지 변경 사항을 업데이트하고 싶습니다. 고객이 기술적 문제를 겪고 있을 때, **89** 당사의 도움 라인은 이 문제를 해결하기 위한 훌륭한 도구입니다. 고객의 편의를 위해 **89** 이 서비스를 9시부터 6시가 아닌, **89** 하루 24시간 동안 제공하도록 결정했습니다. 여러분의 일정은 그대로일 것이며, **90** 고객을 지원하는 업무를 계속할 것입니다. 야간 업무는 다른 회사의 인력을 활용할 계획입니다. 어찌 됐든, 저희 서비스가 일관되게 유지되도록 **91** 이 새로운 업무 교육을 도와주실 몇 분이 필요할 겁니다. 그건 나중에 개인적으로 상의하도록 하겠습니다.

어휘

technical 기술적인 resolve 해결하다 convenience 편의
assist 돕다, 지원하다 overnight 야간의 consistent 일관된

89.

화자는 무슨 변화를 언급하는가?

(A) 전화 시스템이 정기적으로 점검될 것이다.
(B) 회의가 원격으로 진행될 것이다.
(C) 서비스 제공 시간이 연장될 것이다.
(D) 새로운 부서장이 선발될 것이다.

어휘

regularly 정기적으로, 규칙적으로 remotely 원격으로
extend 연장하다, 확대하다

패러프레이징

start offering this service 24 hours ~ between 9 and 6
→ The hours of a service will be extended.

90.

청자는 누구일 것 같은가?

(A) 라디오 방송국 경영진
(B) 전화 상담실 직원들
(C) 컴퓨터 판매원들
(D) 웹사이트 개발자들

어휘

executives 경영진 representative 대리인, 외판원
sales clerk 판매원 developer 개발자

패러프레이징

your role of assisting customers
→ call center representatives

91.

화자에 따르면, 청자들은 무엇을 할 것을 요청받는가?

(A) 소비를 기록하기
(B) 동료에게 교육하기
(C) 다른 업무 시간대로 전환하기
(D) 자세한 보고서 작성하기

어휘

spending 소비 shift 변화, 교대 근무 detailed 자세한, 상세한

패러프레이징

help train those new workers
→ Provide training to colleagues

[92-94] 미녀 🎧

Questions 92-94 refer to the following talk.

> W Thanks for stopping by the Memphis Technology booth here at this year's trade show. I'd like to take this opportunity to tell you about my company's newest ⁹²tablet device. It's a powerful computer designed to help you ⁹³track inventory at your store effortlessly. We understand the importance of having up-to-the-minute information about what's going on at your business. ⁹⁴That's why we've designed this device to be carried anywhere. It weighs less than 200 grams. We're so sure that you'll love this device that we're offering a money-back guarantee on any purchase made at today's event.

해석

92-94번은 다음 담화에 관한 문제입니다.

여 올해 무역 박람회에 멤피스 기술 부스를 방문해주셔서 감사합니다. 이번 기회에 우리 회사의 최신 ⁹²태블릿 기기에 관해 설명하고 싶습니다. ⁹³여러분 상품의 재고를 쉽게 추적할 수 있도록 설계된 강력한 컴퓨터입니다. 매장에서 발생하는 일에 대한 실시간 정보를 가지는 게 얼마나 중요한지 저희는 알고 있습니다. ⁹⁴그렇기 때문에 이 장치는 어디든지 가지고 다닐 수 있게 디자인되었습니다. 200그램도 안 되는 무게입니다. 이 장치가 마음에 드실 것이라고 확신하기 때문에 오늘 행사에서 구매하시는 모든 제품에 대해 환불 보증을 해드리고 있습니다.

어휘

trade show 무역 박람회 track 추적하다 inventory 재고
effortlessly 쉽게 up-to-the-minute 최첨단의, 가장 최근의
device 기기

92.

화자는 어떤 종류의 제품에 관해 논의하고 있는가?
(A) 전동 공구
(B) 태블릿 컴퓨터
(C) 휴대전화
(D) 주방 가전

패러프레이징

tablet device → tablet computer

93.

청자들은 어떤 업계에서 일하는 것 같은가?
(A) 소매
(B) 운송
(C) 교육
(D) 금융

패러프레이징

track inventory at your store → retail

94.

화자가 "200그램도 안 되는 무게입니다"라고 말할 때 의미하는 것은 무엇인가?
(A) 제품은 쉽게 이동될 수 있다.
(B) 배송비가 낮을 것이다.
(C) 깨지기 쉬운 물품은 주의해서 취급해야 한다.
(D) 책자에 오류가 있다.

어휘

shipping cost 배송비 fragile 깨지기 쉬운 contain 포함하다

패러프레이징

device to be carried anywhere
→ product can be transported easily

[95-97] 미남 🎧

Questions 95-97 refer to the following announcement and layout.

> M I'd like to make a quick announcement, everyone. This ⁹⁵afternoon, our company is going to receive a delivery of 10 computer monitors. They are needed because ⁹⁶we've recently hired 10 new salespeople. They'll be training off-site while the renovations to their offices on the third floor are completed. In the meantime, we've decided to store the devices in ⁹⁷Victor's office, since he's out of town at the moment. So, when the items arrive, I need a few people to help me ⁹⁷move them to the office next to the employee lounge. If you're willing to help, please let me know. Thank you.

해석

95-97번은 다음 공지와 배치도에 관한 문제입니다.

남 여러분, 간단한 공지를 하고 싶습니다. 오늘 ⁹⁵오후에 회사로 컴퓨터 모니터 10대를 배송받을 예정입니다. ⁹⁶최근에 10명의 새로운 영업 사원들을 채용했기 때문에 필요한 것들입니다. 그들은 3층 사무실 개조가 완료되는 동안 외부에서 교육받을 예정입니다. 그동안 현재 출장 중인 ⁹⁷빅터의 사무실에 기기들을 보관하기로 했습니다. 그러니 물품이 도착하면 ⁹⁷직원 휴게실 옆에 있는 사무실로 옮기는 것을 도와줄 사람이 몇 명 필요합니다. 도와줄 의향이 있다면, 저에게 알려주세요. 감사합니다.

어휘

announcement 발표 hire 채용하다 salespeople 영업 사원
in the meantime 그동안에 at the moment 지금

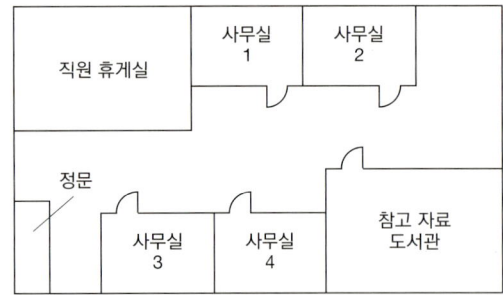

95.
오늘 오후에 회사로 무엇이 배달될 것인가?
(A) 몇몇 사무실 의자
(B) 몇몇 컴퓨터 모니터
(C) 회의 책상
(D) 전자레인지

96.
화자에 따르면, 왜 구매가 필수적이었는가?
(A) 예산이 남았다.
(B) 물품이 최근에 손상되었다.
(C) 직원의 수가 늘었다.
(D) 일부 직원의 불만이 있었다.

어휘
budget 예산 surplus 과잉의 complaint 불평, 불만

패러프레이징
we've recently hired 10 new salespeople
→ The number of employees has grown

97.
시각 자료를 보시오. 빅터는 어디에서 일하는가?
(A) 사무실 1에서
(B) 사무실 2에서
(C) 사무실 3에서
(D) 사무실 4에서

[98-100] 영녀 🎧
Questions 98-100 refer to the following telephone message and order form.

> **W** Hi, Corey. This is Emma from the ⁹⁸radiology department. I was going to call you sooner, but some of ⁹⁸the patient appointments took longer than expected. I wanted to let you know that I've double-checked our inventory, and ⁹⁹we only need 8 boxes of gloves. I hope it's not too late to make a change to the order form I gave you. Also, I'll be traveling to Denver for a conference this afternoon, so Laura Kaspar will be in charge for a few days. ¹⁰⁰I'll e-mail you her phone number and e-mail address just in case. Thanks!

해석
98-100번은 다음 전화 메시지와 주문서에 관한 문제입니다.
여 안녕하세요, 코리. ⁹⁸**방사선과**의 엠마예요. 더 일찍 전화하려고 했는데, 일부 ⁹⁸**환자 진료 예약**이 생각보다 오래 걸렸어요. 재고를 다시 확인했는데 ⁹⁹**장갑은 8박스만 있으면 됩니다**. 제가 드린 주문서를 변경하기에 늦지 않았기를 바랍니다. 또한, 오늘 오후에 덴버로 회의차 여행을 갈 예정이라, 로라 카스파가 며칠 동안 담당하게 될 겁니다. 혹시 모르니 ¹⁰⁰**그녀의 전화번호와 이메일 주소를 메일로 보내드리겠습니다**. 감사합니다!

어휘
radiology 방사선학 patient 환자
double-check 재확인하다, 다시 확인하다 inventory 재고
order form 주문서 be in charge 담당하다
just in case 만약을 위해서

품목	수량
클립보드	12
손 세정제	6병
⁹⁹비닐 장갑	⁹⁹15상자
화이트보드 마커(검정색)	25

98.
화자는 어떤 종류의 업체에서 일하는 것 같은가?
(A) 조경 회사
(B) 병원
(C) 세탁 서비스 제공 회사
(D) 공장

99.
시각 자료를 보시오. 화자에 따르면 어느 숫자가 수정되어야 하는가?
(A) 12
(B) 6
(C) 15
(D) 25

패러프레이징
8 boxes of gloves → Plastic gloves

100.
화자는 청자에게 무엇을 보낼 것인가?
(A) 팀원 명단
(B) 콘퍼런스 등록 서식
(C) 연락 정보
(D) 제품 샘플

어휘
registration 등록, 신청

패러프레이징
her phone number and e-mail address
→ Some contact details

1. (C)	2. (D)	3. (B)	4. (A)	5. (D)
6. (B)	7. (A)	8. (B)	9. (A)	10. (B)
11. (A)	12. (C)	13. (A)	14. (C)	15. (C)
16. (C)	17. (B)	18. (A)	19. (C)	20. (A)
21. (B)	22. (B)	23. (A)	24. (A)	25. (B)
26. (A)	27. (C)	28. (B)	29. (C)	30. (C)
31. (B)	32. (C)	33. (C)	34. (A)	35. (C)
36. (B)	37. (D)	38. (C)	39. (D)	40. (A)
41. (A)	42. (B)	43. (D)	44. (C)	45. (B)
46. (D)	47. (B)	48. (C)	49. (D)	50. (C)
51. (B)	52. (B)	53. (C)	54. (A)	55. (A)
56. (C)	57. (A)	58. (C)	59. (B)	60. (D)
61. (C)	62. (D)	63. (D)	64. (C)	65. (D)
66. (B)	67. (B)	68. (C)	69. (A)	70. (A)
71. (A)	72. (D)	73. (D)	74. (D)	75. (B)
76. (C)	77. (C)	78. (D)	79. (C)	80. (C)
81. (A)	82. (B)	83. (B)	84. (C)	85. (C)
86. (D)	87. (C)	88. (C)	89. (C)	90. (A)
91. (D)	92. (A)	93. (D)	94. (B)	95. (D)
96. (B)	97. (B)	98. (C)	99. (D)	100. (B)

1. 호남 🎧

(A) He's untying a cloth apron.
(B) He's holding a frying pan.
(C) He's using a knife to slice some food.
(D) He's putting some groceries in a drawer.

해석
(A) 그는 천 앞치마를 풀고 있다.
(B) 그는 프라이팬을 들고 있다.
(C) 그는 칼로 음식을 썰고 있다.
(D) 그는 식료품을 서랍에 넣고 있다.

2. 미녀 🎧

(A) She's fixing her sunglasses.
(B) She's resting her hand on a bench.
(C) She's reaching into a handbag.
(D) She's talking on the phone.

해석
(A) 그녀는 선글라스를 고치고 있다.
(B) 그녀는 벤치에 손을 얹고 있다.
(C) 그녀는 핸드백에 손을 넣고 있다.
(D) 그녀는 전화 통화를 하고 있다.

3. 미남 🎧

(A) One of the women is leaning over a trash can.
(B) One of the women is pointing at a post on a bulletin board.
(C) One of the women is standing next to an entrance.
(D) One of the women is counting money from a machine.

해석
(A) 여자들 중 한 명이 쓰레기통 위로 몸을 구부리고 있다.
(B) 여자들 중 한 명이 게시판의 게시물을 가리키고 있다.
(C) 여자들 중 한 명이 입구 옆에 서 있다.
(D) 여자들 중 한 명이 현금인출기에서 나온 돈을 세고 있다.

4. 미녀 🎧

(A) A car has been parked beside a building.
(B) A door has been propped open.
(C) There's a sign posted on a fence.
(D) Some plants have been arranged in a row.

해석
(A) 차가 건물 옆에 주차되어 있다.
(B) 문이 열린 채 고정되어 있다.
(C) 울타리에 표지판이 붙어 있다.
(D) 식물들이 일렬로 놓여 있다.

5. 영녀 🎧

(A) Some light fixtures are being installed.
(B) A display case is being wiped.
(C) A server is distributing menus.
(D) A server is taking an order.

6. 호남 🎧

(A) A vehicle is covered with cloth.
(B) Some equipment has been placed inside a truck.
(C) He's driving a vehicle into a parking garage.
(D) He's stacking some crates.

7. 미녀 호남 🎧

Why did this film get good reviews?
(A) Because the acting was excellent.
(B) At the Central Theater.
(C) Tickets for the afternoon show, please.

8. 미남 영녀 🎧

When does the grocery store open?
(A) He's the marketing director.
(B) Daily at seven o'clock.
(C) I left the door open.

9. 호남 영녀 🎧

Which building did Brian move his office to?
(A) The tall one on the corner.
(B) Thanks, I appreciate that.
(C) Show the parking pass at the gate.

10. 미녀 미남 🎧

Excuse me, how do I get to Terminal 3?
(A) Renovations to the airport.
(B) There's a shuttle bus over there.
(C) Because my flight will depart soon.

11. 미남 영녀 🎧

Who's giving the tour to the new employees?
(A) That's Maggie's responsibility.
(B) About half an hour ago.
(C) Two or three is enough.

어휘

new employee 신입 사원 responsibility 책임, 책무

12. 미녀 호남 🎧

What's the problem with the elevator?
(A) Yes, for the top floor.
(B) On the west side of the lobby.
(C) The maintenance manager e-mailed you.

해석

엘리베이터에 무슨 문제가 있나요?
(A) 네, 꼭대기 층이요.
(B) 로비의 서쪽에요.
(C) 유지 보수 관리자가 당신에게 이메일을 보냈어요.

어휘

maintenance 유지 보수 manager 관리자

13. 호남 영녀 🎧

You need to pay a penalty to cancel the contract.
(A) I'm aware of that.
(B) A business arrangement.
(C) You can borrow my pen.

해석

계약을 취소하시려면 위약금을 내셔야 합니다.
(A) 저도 알아요.
(B) 사업상의 계약이에요.
(C) 제 펜을 빌려도 돼요.

어휘

penalty 벌금, 위약금 cancel 취소하다 contract 계약(서)
be aware of ~을 알다 arrangement 배열, 협정

14. 영녀 미남 🎧

Why didn't you sign up for the business writing
workshop?
(A) Whenever we have a new client.
(B) Here is a sample.
(C) Because I'll be out of town.

해석

왜 비즈니스 글쓰기 워크숍에 등록하지 않으셨어요?
(A) 새로운 고객이 생길 때마다요.
(B) 여기 견본이 있어요.
(C) 제가 출장을 갈 거라서요.

어휘

sign up for ~에 등록하다 workshop 워크숍 client 고객
be out of town (출장 등으로) 도시를 떠나 있다

15. 미녀 영녀 🎧

You're here for the hotel manager interview, right?
(A) Sorry, we are fully booked.
(B) It's a lovely view from here.
(C) Yes, I hope I'm in the right place.

해석

호텔 지배인 면접을 보러 여기 오신 거죠, 그렇죠?
(A) 죄송합니다, 예약이 꽉 찼습니다.
(B) 여기서 보면 경치가 아주 좋아요.
(C) 네, 제가 제대로 온 것이면 좋겠네요.

어휘

fully booked 예약이 꽉 찬 lovely 아주 좋은, 멋진
view 경치, 관점

16. 영녀 호남 🎧

Are you still working at the department store on
Saturdays?
(A) Yes, my apartment is very new.
(B) It might be cheaper online.
(C) I'm the weekend manager.

해석

아직도 토요일에 백화점에서 일하세요?
(A) 네, 제 아파트는 아주 새로운 아파트예요.
(B) 온라인으로는 더 저렴할 거예요.
(C) 저는 주말 매니저예요.

어휘

department store 백화점

17. 미남 영녀 🎧

When could I borrow a copy of the manual?
(A) In chapter three.
(B) Actually, there's an updated version online.
(C) I prefer tea to coffee.

해석

제가 언제 설명서 한 부를 빌릴 수 있을까요?
(A) 3장에요.
(B) 사실, 온라인에 업데이트된 버전이 있어요.
(C) 저는 커피보다 차를 더 좋아해요.

어휘

a copy of ~ 한 부 manual 설명서, 안내서 actually 사실은
version 버전, ~판
prefer A to B B보다 A를 더 좋아하다[선호하다]

18. 미남 호남 🎧

Where can I find a vacation request form?
(A) On the company Web site.
(B) Yes, I agree with you.
(C) In about two weeks.

해석

휴가 신청서는 어디에서 찾을 수 있나요?
(A) 회사 웹사이트에서요.
(B) 네, 저도 당신 말에 동의해요.
(C) 약 2주 후에요.

어휘

request form 휴가 신청서 agree with ~에 동의하다

19. 미녀 미남 🎧

It's too late to get a laptop from the IT department, isn't it?
(A) Sure, Kevin knows the software.
(B) On the second floor.
(C) I'm not using mine right now.

해석

IT 부서에서 노트북을 받기에는 너무 늦었죠, 그렇지 않나요?
(A) 물론이죠, 케빈이 그 소프트웨어를 알아요.
(B) 2층에요.
(C) 저는 제 것을 지금은 안 써요.

해설

(C) 지금 자신의 노트북을 사용하지 않으므로 빌려줄 수 있다는 의미이다.

어휘

laptop 노트북 컴퓨터 department 부서 software 소프트웨어
right now 지금은, 지금 당장

20. 호남 미녀 🎧

How many of the restaurant's tables were empty at lunchtime?
(A) No more than three.
(B) I emptied all of the crates.
(C) It shouldn't take very long.

해석

점심시간에 식당의 테이블 중 몇 개가 비어 있었나요?
(A) 3개 만요.
(B) 제가 상자를 모두 비웠어요.
(C) 그리 오래 걸리지 않을 거예요.

어휘

empty 비어 있는; 비우다
no more than 단지 ~에 지나지 않다, ~일 뿐 crate 상자

21. 영녀 미남 🎧

Should we upgrade the copy machine on the second floor?
(A) Well, I like the phone's features.
(B) No, it's not that old.
(C) I'll be moving to a different floor.

해석

2층에 있는 복사기를 업그레이드해야 할까요?
(A) 음, 저는 전화기의 기능이 마음에 들어요.
(B) 아니요, 그건 그다지 오래되지 않았어요.
(C) 저는 다른 층으로 이동할 거예요.

어휘

upgrade 업그레이드하다, ~의 등급을 올리다
copy machine 복사기 feature 특징, 기능

22. 호남 미녀 🎧

Do we need to put the trade show banners in our car?
(A) Our company is growing.
(B) No, the manager offered to bring them.
(C) Could I try your product?

해석

우리 차에 무역 박람회 플래카드를 넣어야 할까요?
(A) 우리 회사는 성장하고 있어요.
(B) 아니요, 매니저가 그걸 가져오겠다고 했어요.
(C) 제가 귀사의 제품을 사용해 봐도 될까요?

어휘

banner 플래카드, 현수막
offer to do (~하겠다고) 말하다, ~을 제안하다 product 제품

23. 미녀 미남 🎧

Has Melanie completed her performance reviews yet?
(A) She just came back from her trip.
(B) No, we finished everything early.
(C) The restaurant got great reviews.

해석

멜라니가 업무 평가를 마쳤나요?
(A) 그녀는 막 출장에서 돌아왔어요.
(B) 아니요, 우리는 모든 걸 일찍 끝냈어요.
(C) 그 식당은 좋은 평가를 받았어요.

어휘

complete 완료하다, 끝마치다
performance review 업무 평가, 인사 고과

24. 미남 영녀 🎧

Did you replace the light bulb in the conference room?
(A) Actually, a few of them were out.
(B) Everyone is welcome to attend.
(C) That's the perfect place.

해석

회의실에 있는 전구를 교체했나요?
(A) 사실, 그것들 중 몇 개가 나갔더라고요.
(B) 누구나 참석할 수 있어요.
(C) 그곳은 완벽한 장소예요.

어휘

replace 교체하다 light bulb 백열전구
conference room 회의실 attend 참석하다

25. 미녀 미남 🎧

Don't you want to join us for the music festival on Saturday?
(A) The list of songs is online.
(B) I'll be visiting my parents.
(C) We really enjoyed it.

해석

토요일에 열리는 음악 축제에 우리와 함께 가고 싶지 않으세요?
(A) 노래 목록은 온라인에 있어요.
(B) 저는 부모님을 뵈러 갈 거예요.
(C) 정말 즐거웠어요.

어휘

festival 축제 list 목록 visit 방문하다, 찾아가다
enjoy 즐거워하다

26. 영녀 호남 🎧

Does the cream pasta come with chicken or seafood?
(A) It's a chicken dish.
(B) Yes, for the lunch special.
(C) I'd prefer to have it for take-out.

해석

크림 파스타에 닭고기나 해산물도 함께 나오나요?
(A) 그건 닭고기 요리입니다.
(B) 네, 점심 특선 메뉴로요.
(C) 테이크아웃으로 먹고 싶어요.

어휘

dish 요리 take-out 테이크아웃, 가지고 가는 음식

27. 미남 영녀 🎧

Who chooses the site for the company retreat?
(A) No, I couldn't go last year.
(B) Usually at a nearby luxury hotel.
(C) Ask someone on the planning committee.

해석

회사 야유회 장소는 누가 정하나요?
(A) 아니요, 저는 작년에 못 갔어요.
(B) 보통 근처의 고급 호텔에서요.
(C) 기획 위원회에 있는 사람에게 물어보세요.

어휘

choose 선택하다, 고르다 site 장소, 현장
retreat 후퇴, 휴양지; 후퇴하다 nearby 근처의 luxury 고급의
committee 위원회

28. 호남 미녀 🎧

Could you check to see if I've set up the projector correctly?
(A) She finished the project yesterday.
(B) I do have experience in IT.
(C) An important sales presentation.

해석

제가 프로젝터를 바르게 설치했는지 확인해 주시겠어요?
(A) 그녀는 어제 프로젝트를 끝냈어요.
(B) 저는 IT 관련 경험이 있어요.
(C) 중요한 영업 프레젠테이션이에요.

어휘

set up ~을 설치하다 projector 프로젝터, 영사기
correctly 올바르게, 제대로 presentation 프레젠테이션, 발표

29. 미녀 호남 🎧

Let me proofread the product descriptions for the catalog.
(A) Our new line of summer footwear.
(B) Put the extra boxes in the storage room.
(C) Thanks, I'd appreciate that.

해석

제가 카탈로그의 제품 설명을 교정해 드릴게요.
(A) 여름 신발 신제품입니다.
(B) 여분의 상자는 창고에 두세요.
(C) 고마워요, 그래 주시면 고맙죠.

어휘

proofread 교정하다 description 설명, 묘사
catalog 카탈로그 line (상품의) 종류 footwear 신발
extra 여분의 storage room 창고

30. 미남 미녀 🎧

> Will the sales charts be ready for this afternoon's presentation?
> (A) On sale for fifty percent off.
> (B) At the company's headquarters, I think.
> **(C) Nicholas added them yesterday.**

해석

오늘 오후 발표에 판매 도표가 준비될까요?
(A) 50% 할인 중입니다.
(B) 본사에서 일 거예요.
(C) 니콜라스가 어제 추가했어요.

어휘

chart 차트, 도표 on sale 할인 중인 headquarters 본사
add 추가하다

31. 호남 영녀 🎧

> Would you like to have a seat in the waiting area?
> (A) Yes, for my annual checkup.
> **(B) Can I use free Wi-Fi here?**
> (C) No, I haven't met him.

해석

대기실에 앉으시겠어요?
(A) 네, 연례 건강 검진을 위해서요.
(B) 여기서 무료 와이파이를 사용할 수 있나요?
(C) 아니요, 저는 그를 만난 적이 없어요.

어휘

have a seat (자리에) 앉다 waiting area 대기실
annual 연례의, 매년의 checkup 검사, 건강 진단

[32-34] 미녀 호남 🎧

Questions 32-34 refer to the following conversation.

> W ³²Marion Hotel front desk. How may I help you?
> M Hello. I'm staying in room 407. ³³My remote control isn't working. I'd like a new one.
> W I can bring one up to you, but ³⁴I'll have to wait until my colleague gets back. He's making some copies, so ³⁴I'm not sure how long it will take. Or, you can come down to the front desk if you prefer.
> M I'll come down right now.
> W Okay. See you shortly.

해석

32-34번은 다음 대화에 관한 문제입니다.
여 ³²매리온 호텔 프런트입니다. 무엇을 도와드릴까요?
남 안녕하세요. 저는 407호에 묵고 있습니다. ³³제 리모컨이 작동하지 않아요. 새걸로 주세요.
여 가져다드릴 수는 있지만, ³⁴동료가 돌아올 때까지 기다려야 할

것 같아요. 그가 복사를 하고 있어서 ³⁴얼마나 걸릴지 모르겠어요. 아니면, 원하시면 프런트로 내려오셔도 됩니다.
남 지금 바로 내려갈게요.
여 알겠습니다. 곧 뵙겠습니다.

어휘

front desk (호텔 등의) 프런트[안내 데스크]
remote control 리모컨 work 작동하다 colleague 동료
get back 돌아오다 make a copy 복사하다, 사본을 만들다
come down 내려오다 shortly 얼마 안 되어, 곧

32.

여자가 일하는 곳은 어디인가?
(A) 텔레비전 방송국
(B) 여행사
(C) 호텔
(D) 전자 제품 매장

33.

남자가 전화를 건 이유는 무엇인가?
(A) 결제 정보를 업데이트하기 위해
(B) 정책에 대해 문의하기 위해
(C) 물건을 교체하기 위해
(D) 예약을 하기 위해

어휘

payment 지불, 결제 policy 정책, 방침
make a reservation 예약하다

34.

여자는 무엇에 대해 확신이 없는가?
(A) 동료가 돌아올 시기
(B) 요금이 얼마나 나올지
(C) 파일이 있는 위치
(D) 업무를 담당하는 사람

어휘

charge (요금·값을) 청구하다 be locate 위치해 있다
be responsible for ~을 맡다[담당하다] task 과제, 업무

패러프레이징

my colleague gets back → a colleague will return

[35-37] 미남 영녀 🎧

Questions 35-37 refer to the following conversation.

> M Alright, that's fourteen ninety-nine for one adult ticket. Please note that some of ³⁵the tropical fish tanks are currently closed for repairs.
> W Oh, I wish I had known that. ³⁶I came here to take some photographs of the angelfish for an art project that I'm working on.
> M That tank is still in operation. Actually, ³⁷one of our employees is going to feed the angelfish soon, so you might get some interesting shots.

해석

35-37번은 다음 대화에 관한 문제입니다.

남 알겠습니다, 성인 티켓 한 장에 14달러 99센트입니다. 일부 **35 열대어 어항**은 현재 수리를 위해 폐쇄되어 있는 걸 알아 두시기 바랍니다.

여 아, 제가 그걸 알았더라면 좋았을 텐데요. **36 제가 작업 중인 예술 프로젝트를 위해 에인절피시 사진을 찍으러 왔거든요.**

남 그 어항은 아직 가동 중이에요. 사실, **37 우리 직원들 중 한 명이 곧 에인절피시에게 먹이를 줄 것이니, 재미있는 사진을 얻을 수 있을지도 몰라요.** 그래도 서두르시는 게 좋을 거예요. 5분 정도 후에 시작할 거거든요.

어휘

note (~이라는 것에) 주의하다, ~에 주목하다 tropical fish 열대어 tank (물·기름·가스 등의) 탱크, 수조, 어항 currently 현재, 지금 repair 수리 work on ~을 작업하다 in operation 가동 중인 feed 먹이를 주다 shot 사진, 장면

35.

화자들이 있을 것 같은 곳은 어디인가?
(A) 미술관
(B) 쇼핑몰
(C) 수족관
(D) 극장

36.

여자의 방문 목적은 무엇인가?
(A) 전시를 준비하기 위해
(B) 사진을 찍기 위해
(C) 배달을 하기 위해
(D) 직원을 인터뷰하기 위해

어휘

display 전시, 진열 make a delivery 배달하다

37.

남자에 따르면, 여자가 서둘러야 하는 이유는 무엇인가?
(A) 관광단이 막 출발하려고 한다.
(B) 서비스를 받기 위한 줄이 길다.
(C) 업체가 곧 문을 닫을 것이다.
(D) 작업이 곧 시작될 것이다.

어휘

be about to do 막 ~하려고 하다

패러프레이징

one of our employees is going to feed the angelfish soon → A task will be started soon.

[38-40] 미남 미녀 영녀 🎧

Questions 38-40 refer to the following conversation with three speakers.

M Good morning, Stacey. I'd like to introduce you to **38 Andrea McGrath, our new intern.**

W1 It's nice to meet you, Andrea. So, **39 you're interested in learning more about the field of advertising?**

W2 That's right. **39 I'm particularly interested in creating digital ads.**

W1 That's great. **39 I hope you'll learn a lot during your time here at our firm.**

W2 Thank you. I'm really looking forward to it.

M Well, we'd better go. **40 I'd like Andrea to fill out her HR forms** before I go over her job duties. Talk to you later.

해석

38-40번은 다음 3명의 대화에 관한 문제입니다.

남 안녕하세요, 스테이시. **38 새로 온 인턴 안드레아 맥그라스 씨를 소개해 드릴게요.**

여1 만나서 반가워요, 안드레아 씨. 그래서, **39 광고 분야에 대해 더 알고 싶으신가요?**

여2 맞아요. **39 저는 특히 디지털 광고를 만드는 것에 관심이 있어요.**

여1 잘됐네요. **39 우리 회사에서 일하는 동안 많은 것을 배우시길 바랍니다.**

여2 감사합니다. 정말 기대가 됩니다.

남 자, 우리는 가는 게 좋겠어요. 제가 그녀의 직무를 검토하기 전에 **40 안드레아 씨가 인사 서류를 작성하면 좋겠어요.** 나중에 이야기합시다.

어휘

introduce 소개하다 intern 인턴사원 field 들판, 분야 advertising 광고(업) particularly 특히 firm 회사 look forward to ~을 기대[고대]하다 fill out 작성하다 go over 검토하다 job duties 직무

38.

안드레아 맥그라스는 누구인가?
(A) 투자자
(B) 기업 채용 담당자
(C) 인턴
(D) 총지배인

어휘

investor 투자자 corporate 기업[회사]의 recruiter 신병[신인] 모집자

39.

화자들이 있을 것 같은 곳은 어디인가?
(A) 약국
(B) 금융 기관
(C) 전자 제품 매장
(D) 광고 회사

어휘

pharmacy 약국 financial 금융[재정]의 institution 기관, 협회

40.

남자는 맥그라스 씨가 다음에 무엇을 하기를 원하는가?

(A) 몇 가지 서류 작성하기
(B) 건물 견학하기
(C) 동료들과 식사하기
(D) 일부 안전 수칙 검토하기

어휘

paperwork 서류 작업, 서류 safety procedure 안전 수칙

패러프레이징

fill out her HR forms → Complete some paperwork

[41-43] 미녀 호남 🎧

Questions 41-43 refer to the following conversation.

> W Hi, Nicholas. ⁴¹Your going away party on Thursday will be fun, but we'll all miss you after you transfer to the Scranton branch.
> M I'll miss this place, too.
> W ⁴²Is there any particular cuisine you'd like me to order from the caterer?
> M Hmm … I like spicy food.
> W I'll keep that in mind. Will your role at the Scranton branch be the same?
> M I will have a lot of the same duties, but ⁴³the schedule is flexible. I'm excited about choosing my own hours.
> W That sounds great.

해석

41-43번은 다음 대화에 관한 문제입니다.

여 안녕하세요, 니콜라스. **⁴¹목요일에 있을 송별회는** 재미있겠지만, 당신이 스크랜턴 지점으로 전근 가시면 우리 모두 당신이 그리울 거예요.
남 저도 이곳이 그리울 거예요.
여 **⁴²출장 요리업자에게 특별히 주문했으면 하는 요리가 있나요?**
남 음... 저는 매운 음식을 좋아해요.
여 기억해 둘게요. 스크랜턴 지점에서의 당신의 역할은 똑같을까요?
남 같은 업무가 많겠지만, **⁴³일정은 유동적이에요. 제 시간을 정할 수 있어서 신나요.**
여 그거 좋은데요.

어휘

transfer 옮기다, 전근[전학] 가다 branch 나뭇가지, 지점
particular 특정한, 특별한 cuisine 요리 caterer 출장 요리업자
keep ~ in mind ~을 명심하다 role 역할, 임무
flexible 유동적인, 유연한

41.

회사가 목요일에 파티를 여는 이유는 무엇인가?

(A) 동료에게 작별 인사를 하기 위해
(B) 은퇴를 축하하기 위해
(C) 해외 손님을 맞이하기 위해

(D) 기념일을 승인하기 위해

어휘

say farewell 고별인사를 하다 celebrate 축하하다, 기념하다
retirement 은퇴 overseas 해외의
acknowledge 승인하다, 인정하다 anniversary 기념일

42.

여자가 담당하는 것은 무엇인가?

(A) 장소 예약하기
(B) 음식 주문하기
(C) 방 꾸미기
(D) 초대장 보내기

어휘

be in charge of ~을 담당하다 venue 장소
decorate 장식하다, 꾸미다 invitation 초대장, 초대

43.

남자는 무엇에 대해 신난다고 하는가?

(A) 유용한 기술을 배우는 것
(B) 새로운 사람들을 만나는 것
(C) 다른 나라로 여행하는 것
(D) 유연 근무 시간제로 일하는 것

패러프레이징

choosing my own hours → Working flexible hours

[44-46] 영녀 호남 🎧

Questions 44-46 refer to the following conversation.

> W Excuse me. I'm trying to decide which of these file cabinets would be best for me. ⁴⁴I already have a file cabinet in my office, but it doesn't have a lock on it. I have some important confidential documents in there, so I don't want anyone to be able to open it.
> M This model here can be locked, and it is fire-resistant as well. There is a double-locking system. ⁴⁵I'd be happy to show you how easy it is to use.
> W Thanks. That looks to be about the right size.
> M And ⁴⁶this item is very popular with our customers because it's made from recycled steel. So, it's environmentally responsible.

해석

44-46번은 다음 대화에 관한 문제입니다.

여 실례합니다. 저는 이 서류 캐비닛들 중 어떤 게 저한테 가장 좋을지 결정하려고 하고 있어요. **⁴⁴제 사무실에 이미 서류 캐비닛이 하나 있는데, 자물쇠가 달려 있지 않아요. 그 안에 중요한 기밀 문서가 있어서 아무도 그걸 열어 볼 수 있게 하고 싶지 않아요.**
남 여기 이 모델은 잠글 수 있고 화재에도 끄떡없어요. 이중 잠금 장치가 있거든요. **⁴⁵사용하기에 얼마나 쉬운지 기꺼이 보여 드리겠습니다.**

여 고맙습니다. 그것은 거의 적당한 크기인 것 같아요.

남 그리고 ⁴⁶이 제품은 재활용된 강철로 만들어져서 고객들에게 매우 인기가 있습니다. 그러니까, 그건 환경에 책임질 수 있답니다.

어휘

file cabinet 서류 캐비닛 lock 자물쇠; 잠그다
confidential 기밀의 document 서류, 문서
fire-resistant 내화성의, 불에 잘 타지 않는
double-lock 이중으로 자물쇠를 채우다 recycle 재활용하다
steel 강철 environmentally 환경적으로
responsible 책임이 있는

44.

여자의 현재 서류 캐비닛에 있는 문제는 무엇인가?

(A) 그녀의 가구와 어울리지 않는다.
(B) 공간을 너무 많이 차지한다.
(C) 보호될 수 없다.
(D) 열었을 때 소리가 난다.

어휘

take up 차지하다 secure 보호하다, 지키다

패러프레이징

it doesn't have a lock on it → It cannot be secured.

45.

남자가 제안하는 것은 무엇인가?

(A) 쿠폰 출력하기
(B) 제품 시연하기
(C) 창고 확인하기
(D) 카탈로그 보내기

어휘

print out (프린터로) 출력하다
give a demonstration 시연하다 stock room 창고

패러프레이징

show you how easy it is to use
→ Give a demonstration

46.

남자에 따르면, 사람들이 그 제품을 좋아하는 이유는 무엇인가?

(A) 바닥을 긁지 않는다.
(B) 조립하기 쉽다.
(C) 환불 보증이 되어 있다.
(D) 재활용 재료로 만들어진다.

어휘

scratch 긁다 assemble 조립하다
money-back guarantee 환불 보증
be made from ~으로 만들어지다 material 재료, 자료

패러프레이징

steel → materials

[47-49] 미남 영녀 🎧

Questions 47-49 refer to the following conversation.

M Ming, have you finished ⁴⁷the cover design for the April issue yet?

W I have ⁴⁷the magazine's layout done, but I want to make some adjustments to ⁴⁷the font sizes.

M ⁴⁸Maybe Nigel could help you with that. I think his team is not very busy today.

W It's easy to make changes with this program.

M Okay, great. Oh, by the way, ⁴⁹thanks for writing a letter of reference for my application for a promotion. I think it will really help me to stand out.

W My pleasure. I hope you get it. You would do a great job in that role.

해석

47-49번은 다음 대화에 관한 문제입니다.

남 밍, ⁴⁷4월호 표지 디자인은 이제 다 하셨나요?

여 ⁴⁷잡지 레이아웃은 다 했는데, ⁴⁷글자 크기를 좀 조정하고 싶어요.

남 ⁴⁸아마 나이젤이 그걸 도와줄 수 있을 거예요. 그의 팀이 오늘 별로 바쁘지 않은 것 같거든요.

여 이 프로그램으로 변경하면 쉬워요.

남 좋아요. 아, 그건 그렇고 승진 신청서에 ⁴⁹추천서를 써 주셔서 감사합니다. 제가 눈에 띄는 데 정말 도움이 될 것 같아요.

여 천만에요. 승진하시면 좋겠네요. 그 역할을 훌륭히 해내실 거예요.

어휘

issue (정기 간행물의) 호 magazine 잡지
layout 레이아웃[배치] make an adjustment 조정하다
font 폰트, 글꼴 make a change ~을 변경하다
by the way 그런데, 그건 그렇고 letter of reference 추천서
application 신청(서) promotion 승진, 촉진
stand out 눈에 띄다

47.

화자들이 근무할 것 같은 업계는 무엇인가?

(A) 보건 의료
(B) 잡지 출판
(C) 국제 금융
(D) 부동산

어휘

healthcare 보건 의료 (서비스), 건강 관리 real estate 부동산

48.

여자가 "이 프로그램으로 변경하면 쉬워요"라고 말한 의도는 무엇인가?

(A) 그녀는 교육 과정에 참석하지 않을 것이다.
(B) 그녀는 소프트웨어를 구매하고 싶어 한다.
(C) 그녀는 동료의 도움이 필요하지 않다.
(D) 그녀는 남자에게 업무를 할당할 것이다.

attend 참석하다 training session 교육 (과정)
purchase 구매하다 coworker 동료 assistance 도움, 원조
assign 할당하다

Nigel could help you with that
→ coworker's assistance

49.

남자가 여자에게 고마워하는 이유는 무엇인가?
(A) 그녀는 그에게 승진을 알렸다.
(B) 그녀는 그를 상의 후보로 지명했다.
(C) 그녀는 신청 기한을 변경했다.
(D) 그녀는 추천서를 썼다.

어휘

inform 알리다 nominate for ~에 지명하다
award 상 deadline 기한

패러프레이징

writing a letter of reference → wrote a reference letter

[50-52] 미녀 미남 호남 🎧
Questions 50-52 refer to the following conversation
with three speakers.

> W Welcome to Junction Rentals. How may I help
>   you?
> M1 Hi. ⁵⁰We'd like to rent a car.
> M2 ⁵⁰Right. For three days. We're interested in a
>   car that's fuel efficient, if possible.
> W I'm sorry, but we're all out of our small vehicles
>   at the moment.
> M1 Oh, really? I thought you had a big fleet.
> W We do, but ⁵¹the city's summer music festival
>   is this weekend. There's a much higher
>   demand than usual.
> M2 Then we'll just take whatever you have
>   available.
> W Okay. And ⁵²next time, you should reserve the
>   vehicle you want on our Web site. You can do
>   it up to thirty days in advance.

해석

50-52번은 다음 3명의 대화에 관한 문제입니다.
여 정션 렌탈즈에 오신 것을 환영합니다. 무엇을 도와드릴까요?
남1 안녕하세요. ⁵⁰차를 빌리고 싶은데요.
남2 ⁵⁰맞아요. 3일 동안이요. 가능하다면 연비가 좋은 차에 관심이
    있습니다.
여 죄송하지만 소형차는 현재 모두 매진되었어요.
남1 아, 정말요? 차가 많은 줄 알았는데요.
여 그렇긴 한데, ⁵¹시의 여름 음악제가 이번 주말이라서요. 평소보
    다 훨씬 더 수요가 많아요.
남2 그럼 그냥 이용할 수 있는 아무거나 가져갈게요.

여 좋아요. 그리고 ⁵²다음 번에는 저희 웹사이트에서 원하시는 차량
    을 예약하셔야 해요. 그건 30일 전까지 미리 할 수 있어요.

어휘

rent 빌리다 fuel efficient 연료 효율이 좋은 vehicle 차량
at the moment 현재는, 지금은 fleet (한 회사 소유의) 전 차량
demand 수요, 요구 (사항) than usual 평소보다
available 구할[이용할] 수 있는, 시간이 있는 reserve 예약하다
up to ~까지 in advance 미리, 사전에

50.

남자들이 하려고 하는 것은 무엇인가?
(A) 호텔에 체크인하기
(B) 관광 예약하기
(C) 차량 빌리기
(D) 항공권 변경하기

어휘

check in 체크인하다 book 예약하다

51.

여자에 따르면, 이번 주말에 일어날 일은 무엇인가?
(A) 일부 수수료가 인상될 것이다.
(B) 시에서 축제를 열 것이다.
(C) 고객 보상 프로그램이 시작될 것이다.
(D) 그 업체가 영업시간을 연장할 것이다.

어휘

fee 수수료, 요금 increase 증가하다, 인상되다
hold 열다, 개최하다 loyalty 충성, 성실
launch 시작하다, 착수하다 extend 연장하다

패러프레이징

the city's summer music festival
→ The city will hold a festival.

52.

여자가 남자들에게 앞으로 하도록 제안하는 것은 무엇인가?
(A) 신용 카드로 결제하기
(B) 온라인 예약하기
(C) 30일 체험 등록하기
(D) 여러 지점에 전화하기

어휘

credit card 신용 카드 make a reservation 예약하다
trial 시험, 시도

패러프레이징

reserve the vehicle you want on our Web site
→ Make an online reservation

[53-55] 호남 영녀 🎧
Questions 53-55 refer to the following conversation.

> M Prairie Fields? I've never heard of your
>   business before. ⁵³Is this your first time
>   participating in the farmers' market?

W Yes. We've been in business for several years, but we're just starting to attend events like this. **54** Our orchard specializes in producing jam with no added sugar. And we are a local business.

M Oh, the peach jam looks good. I run a small inn, and we serve a free breakfast to guests. I'm always looking for locally made products.

W Well, **55** here's a catalog with the full range of flavors we offer.

해석

53-55번은 다음 대화에 관한 문제입니다.

남 프레리 필즈요? 귀하의 사업체에 대해 들어 본 적이 없어요. **53** 농산물 직거래 장터 참여는 이번이 처음인가요?

여 네. 우리는 수년간 사업을 했지만, 이제 막 이런 행사에 참여하기 시작했어요. **54** 우리 과수원은 무가당 잼을 전문적으로 생산해요. 그리고 우리는 지역 사업체입니다.

남 아, 복숭아 잼이 맛있어 보이네요. 저는 작은 여관을 운영하는데, 손님들에게 무료 조식을 제공해요. 저는 항상 현지 생산 제품을 찾고 있어요.

여 음, **55** 여기 우리가 제공하는 모든 종류의 맛이 담긴 카탈로그가 있습니다.

어휘

participate in ~에 참여하다 farmers' market 농산물 직판장
orchard 과수원 specialize in ~을 전문으로 하다
produce 생산하다 local 지역의, 현지의 run 운영하다 inn 여관
serve 제공하다 locally 가까이에, 근처에 range 범위, 종류
offer 제공하다

53.

대화가 일어나고 있는 곳은 어디인가?
(A) 개업식
(B) 취업 박람회
(C) 농산물 직판장
(D) 백화점

어휘

grand opening 개점, 개장 career fair 취업 박람회
department store 백화점

54.

여자가 일하는 사업체의 종류는?
(A) 과수원
(B) 음료 제조업체
(C) 원예용품점
(D) 출장 요리 업체

어휘

beverage 음료 manufacturer 제조업체

패러프레이징

Our orchard → A fruit orchard

55.

여자가 남자에게 주는 것은 무엇인가?
(A) 제품 카탈로그
(B) 명함
(C) 사이트 맵
(D) 할인 쿠폰

어휘

business card 명함

패러프레이징

a catalog with the full range of flavors we offer
→ A product catalog

[56-58] 미남 영녀 🎧

Questions 56-58 refer to the following conversation.

M Hi, Colleen. I'm wondering about **56** the garden we're planting in front of City Hall. Has anyone confirmed what kind of flowers they want?

W No, not yet. And they need to decide soon. **57** I have to place the order with the nursery this week. Otherwise, we can't take advantage of the annual sale. **58** I was going to call tomorrow to finalize the details.

M Tomorrow is a national holiday.

W Oh, that's right! They'll be closed. **58** I'd better call now instead.

해석

56-58번은 다음 대화에 관한 문제입니다.

남 안녕하세요, Colleen. **56** 우리가 시청 앞에 가꾸고 있는 정원에 대해 궁금해서 그러는데, 어떤 종류의 꽃을 원하는지 확인해 준 사람이 있나요?

여 아니요, 아직이요. 그리고 그들은 곧 결정해야 해요. **57** 제가 이번 주에 묘목장에 주문을 해야 하거든요. 그렇지 않으면 우리는 연간 세일을 이용할 수 없어요. **58** 내일 전화해서 세부 사항을 확정하려고 했어요.

남 내일은 국경일이에요.

여 아, 맞아요! 그들은 문을 닫을 거예요. **58** 대신 지금 전화하는 게 낫겠어요.

어휘

confirm 확인해 주다 place an order 주문하다
nursery 묘목장, 보육원 otherwise 그렇지 않으면
take advantage of ~을 이용하다 annual 연례의, 연간의
finalize 마무리 짓다, 완결하다 detail 세부 사항
national holiday 국경일

56.

화자들은 누구일 것 같은가?
(A) 시 공무원
(B) 기자
(C) 정원사
(D) 건축가

57.

여자가 결정이 빨리 내려지길 원하는 이유는 무엇인가?
(A) 세일 기간이 곧 끝날 것이다.
(B) 계약이 만료될 예정이다.
(C) 그녀는 경쟁업체에 대해 걱정한다.
(D) 그녀는 휴가를 갈 것이다.

58.

남자가 "내일은 국경일이에요"라고 말한 이유는 무엇인가?
(A) 배송 지연을 설명하기 위해
(B) 더 높은 급여율을 요청하기 위해
(C) 작업을 더 일찍 행할 것을 제안하기 위해
(D) 기한 연장을 요청하기 위해

[59-61] 미녀 호남 🎧

Questions 59-61 refer to the following conversation.

> W Salvador, sales have been going well so far, but I think we should look for ways to sell 59 our custom cakes at large events.
> M That's a good idea. You know, a lot of caterers 59 outsource baked goods to businesses like ours. 60 We should make a business arrangement with local caterers. They could recommend us to clients and earn a commission.
> W 60 Alright. 61 I'll make a list of the local caterers and their phone numbers today, and then we can start calling them tomorrow to share our ideas.

해석

59-61번은 다음 대화에 관한 문제입니다.
여 살바도르, 지금까지 판매가 잘 되고 있지만, 대규모 행사에서 59우리 주문 케이크를 판매할 수 있는 방법을 찾아야 할 것 같아요.
남 좋은 생각이에요. 알다시피, 많은 음식 공급업체에서 59우리 같은 업체에 제과류 외주를 줘요. 60우리는 지역 음식 공급업체들과 사업 계약을 해야 해요. 그들은 고객에게 우리를 추천하고 수수료를 벌 수도 있어요.
여 60알았어요. 61제가 오늘 지역 음식 공급업체와 전화번호 목록을

만들고 나서, 내일 그들에게 전화해서 우리 생각을 공유할 수 있어요.

59.

화자들이 일할 것 같은 곳은 어디인가?
(A) 가전제품 매장
(B) 제과점
(C) 도장 회사
(D) 꽃집

60.

화자들이 하기로 결정한 것은 무엇인가?
(A) 단골 고객에게 할인 제공하기
(B) 온라인 광고 캠페인 시작하기
(C) 임시 직원 고용하기
(D) 다른 업체와 협력 관계 맺기

61.

여자가 할 것이라고 하는 것은 무엇인가?
(A) 사업 추천받기
(B) 무료 샘플 공유하기
(C) 연락처 조사하기
(D) 일부 계약 조건 검토하기

[62-64] 미녀 미남 🎧

Questions 62-64 refer to the following conversation and list.

> W Thanks for calling the McDowell Conference Center. How may I help you?
> M Hi. I'm calling from Irving Tech. 62 We're launching a new smartphone on July 9, and we'd like to hold our event at your venue.

W That's great! How many people are you anticipating?

M There will be around 250 guests.

W Alright. ⁶³ We have an event room that accommodates between 200 and 300 people.

M That sounds great. And we're going to set up a small stage, so we'll need lights for that.

W No problem. ⁶⁴ We have the necessary equipment on hand, and it's all part of the rental fee.

해석

62-64번은 다음 대화와 표에 관한 문제입니다.

여 맥다웰 컨퍼런스 센터에 전화해 주셔서 감사합니다. 무엇을 도와 드릴까요?

남 안녕하세요. 어빙 테크에서 전화드렸습니다. ⁶² 우리가 7월 9일에 새로운 스마트폰을 출시할 예정인데, 귀사의 행사장에서 행사를 열고자 합니다.

여 잘됐네요! 몇 명이나 오실 걸로 예상하시나요?

남 약 250명의 손님이 오실 거예요.

여 알았어요. ⁶³ 200명에서 300명 사이의 사람들을 수용하는 행사실이 있어요.

남 그거 좋은데요. 그리고 우리는 작은 무대를 설치할 예정이니, 그러기 위해서 조명이 필요할 거예요.

여 문제없습니다. ⁶⁴ 저희는 필요한 장비를 보유하고 있으며, 모두 대여료에 포함됩니다.

어휘

anticipate 예상하다, 기대하다   accommodate 수용하다
equipment 장비   on hand 소유하여, 수중에

맥다웰 컨퍼런스 센터	
파인데일 룸	50명까지
올버니 룸	50-100명
모포드 룸	100-200명
⁶³ 로슨 룸	200-350명

62.

남자가 준비하고 있는 것은 무엇인가?

(A) 회사 야유회
(B) 은퇴 만찬
(C) 시상식
(D) 제품 출시

어휘

awards ceremony 시상식

패러프레이징

launching a new smartphone → A product launch

63.

시각 자료를 보시오. 남자는 어느 방을 예약할 것 같은가?

(A) 파인데일 룸
(B) 올버니 룸

(C) 모포드 룸
(D) 로슨 룸

64.

여자에 따르면, 요금에 포함된 것은 무엇인가?

(A) 조명 장비
(B) 다과
(C) 라이브 공연
(D) 보험

어휘

refreshments 다과   entertainment 오락(물), 접대
insurance 보험

[65-67] 호남 미녀

Questions 65-67 refer to the following conversation and chart.

M On this evening's edition of *Travel Time*, we have ⁶⁵ Isabell Randall as our guest. ⁶⁵ She's an expert in the field of transportation. Welcome, Isabelle.

W Thanks, Henry.

M We've been seeing an increase in train delays. Why is this happening?

W Well, the railway equipment is outdated. So, things like signal failures can cause delays.

M Are all companies affected?

W On this graph, you'll see that the average number of daily delays can differ significantly. Some are lower than thirty, but ⁶⁶ this company here had an average over fifty.

M Is there anything travelers can do?

W ⁶⁷ It's a good idea to buy travel insurance. That way, you can get compensated for financial losses caused by a delay.

해석

65-67번은 다음 대화와 그래프에 관한 문제입니다.

남 〈트래블 타임〉 오늘 저녁 방송분에서 ⁶⁵ 이사벨 랜덜 씨를 게스트로 모셨습니다. ⁶⁵ 그녀는 교통 기관 분야의 전문가이십니다. 어서 오세요, 이사벨.

여 고마워요, 헨리.

남 열차 지연이 증가하고 있습니다. 왜 이런 일이 생기는 건가요?

여 음, 철도 설비가 구식이에요. 그래서 신호 오류와 같은 일들이 지연을 일으킬 수 있죠.

남 모든 회사가 영향을 받나요?

여 이 그래프에서, 일일 평균 지연 횟수가 크게 다를 수 있음을 알 수 있습니다. 일부는 30회 미만이지만, ⁶⁶ 여기 이 회사는 평균 50회가 넘었습니다.

남 여행객들이 할 수 있는 일이 있나요?

여 ⁶⁷ 여행 보험 가입을 생각해 볼 수 있습니다. 그렇게 하면 지연으로 인한 재정적 손실을 보상받을 수 있습니다.

edition (시리즈 간행물·방송물의 특정) 호[회] **expert** 전문가
transportation 교통 기관 **increase** 증가; 증가하다
railway 철도 **outdated** 구식의 **signal** 신호
failure 실패, 고장 **cause** 일으키다 **affect** 영향을 주다
average 평균의 **differ** 다르다 **significantly** 상당히[크게]
insurance 보험 **compensated for** 보상하다 **loss** 손실

일일 평균 지연 횟수

(막대 그래프: Frazier 약 22, ⁶⁶Geneva Railway 약 54, Lannon 약 28, Rose Rail 약 18, y축 0~60)

65.
이사벨 랜덜은 누구인가?
(A) 기관사
(B) 관광업자
(C) 라디오 진행자
(D) 교통 전문가

패러프레이징

an expert in the field of transportation
→ A transportation expert

66.
시각 자료를 보시오. 여자는 어느 기차역을 가리키는가?
(A) Frazier
(B) Geneva Railway
(C) Lannon
(D) Rose Rail

67.
여자가 청자들에게 하도록 조언하는 것은 무엇인가?
(A) 역에 일찍 도착하기
(B) 보험에 가입하기
(C) 온라인으로 출발 시간 확인하기
(D) 비수기에 여행하기

어휘

departure 출발 **off-peak period** 비수기

패러프레이징

buy travel insurance → Purchase some insurance

[68-70] 미남 미녀 🎧
Questions 68-70 refer to the following conversation
and promotional items.

M Marlena, we still need to figure out what kind
of gift to give away to customers during ⁶⁸our
store's grand opening event next month.
W Yes, we can get our logo printed on certain
promotional items. Here are the options.
M Hmm … ⁶⁹I think the tote bag would be best.
Then we wouldn't have to worry about sizes
like we would with the shirts.
W That's a good point. ⁷⁰I'll call the person
designing our logo now and ask him to send
the file we'll need for the printing.

해석
68-70번은 다음 대화와 판촉물에 관한 문제입니다.
남 말리나, ⁶⁸다음 달 우리 매장 개업 행사 때 손님들에게 어떤 선물
을 나눠 드릴지 생각해 내야 해요.
여 네, 특정 판촉물에 우리 로고를 인쇄할 수 있어요. 여기 옵션이
있습니다.
남 음... ⁶⁹토트백이 가장 좋을 것 같아요. 그럼 셔츠처럼 사이즈 걱
정은 안 해도 될 거예요.
여 좋은 지적입니다. ⁷⁰지금 우리 로고를 디자인하는 분께 전화해서
인쇄에 필요한 파일을 보내 달라고 요청할게요.

어휘
figure out 생각해 내다, 알아내다 **give away** 나누어 주다
promotional 홍보[판촉]의

68.
다음 달에 일어날 일은 무엇인가?
(A) 연례 축제
(B) 스포츠 토너먼트
(C) 개업식
(D) 모금 행사

어휘
fund-raising 모금

69.
시각 자료를 보시오. 화자들은 한 품목당 얼마를 쓸 것인가?
(A) 5.00달러
(B) 6.50달러

(C) 2.00달러
(D) 3.50달러

70.

여자가 다음에 할 일은 무엇인가?

(A) 그래픽 디자이너에게 연락하기
(B) 안내 책자 인쇄하기
(C) 주문서 작성하기
(D) 장소 예약하기

어휘

contact 연락하다   brochure 안내 책자   fill out 작성하다

패러프레이징

call the person designing our logo
→ Contact a graphic designer

[71-73] 미남 🎧

Questions 71-73 refer to the following advertisement.

> M Are you looking for an affordable way to take high-quality pictures? Whether you're an amateur or a professional photographer, you'll love ⁷¹the new Nexson-7 digital camera from Harmon Tech. Our customers have consistently given the product excellent reviews. And we're so sure that you'll love it that ⁷²if you're not fully satisfied for any reason, you can get a full refund. That's our promise to you. We're also running a limited-time offer. ⁷³Customers who buy the camera this week can get a free spare battery!

해석

71-73번은 다음 광고에 관한 문제입니다.

남 고품질의 사진을 저렴하게 찍을 수 있는 방법을 찾고 계십니까? 여러분이 아마추어 사진작가든 전문 사진작가든, 하몬 테크의 ⁷¹**새로운 Nexson-7 디지털 카메라**가 마음에 드실 겁니다. 저희 고객들은 그 제품에 일관되게 좋은 평가를 해 오셨습니다. 그리고 그 제품을 여러분이 사랑하실 거라고 확신하는 바, ⁷²**어떤 이유로든 만족스럽지 않으시면 전액 환불 가능합니다.** 그게 여러분께 저희가 드리는 약속입니다. 저희는 또한 기간 한정 판매도 하고 있습니다. ⁷³**이번 주에 카메라를 구입하시는 고객들은 여분의 배터리를 무료로 받으실 수 있습니다!**

어휘

affordable [가격 등이] 알맞은, 저렴한
amateur 아마추어의, 취미로 하는   professional 전문적인
consistently 일관되게   full refund 전액 환불
limited-time offer 기간 한정 판매   spare 여분의, 예비용의

71.

광고되는 것은 무엇인가?

(A) 디지털 카메라
(B) 노트북 컴퓨터

(C) 보안 장치
(D) 전동 공구

72.

화자가 언급하는 제품의 이점은 무엇인가?

(A) 자주 충전할 필요가 없다.
(B) 스마트폰 애플리케이션으로 사용할 수 있다.
(C) 경량 설계가 되어 있다.
(D) 환불 보증이 딸려 있다.

어휘

recharge 재충전하다   application 애플리케이션
lightweight 경량의   come with ~이 딸려 있다
money-back guarantee 환불 보증

패러프레이징

a full refund → a money-back guarantee

73.

고객들이 이번 주에 받을 수 있는 것은 무엇인가?

(A) 쿠폰
(B) 무료 배송
(C) 회원 할인
(D) 여분의 배터리

패러프레이징

a free spare battery → An extra battery

[74-76] 미녀 🎧

Questions 74-76 refer to the following tour information.

> W I'd like to welcome you all to the Kendall factory tour. I'm your guide, Kathy. Today, I'll be showing you ⁷⁴how we produce our range of shoes. You'll see that we give special attention to the shoes at every stage of the manufacturing process. ⁷⁵This helps to ensure that our products last for a long time. In fact, that's what we're famous for. Now, we're about to enter the production floor, so ⁷⁶I'm passing out the safety goggles that you'll need to wear. I'll collect them again once we're out.

해석

74-76번은 다음 견학 정보에 관한 문제입니다.

여 켄델 공장 견학에 오신 여러분 모두를 환영합니다. 저는 여러분의 가이드인 케시입니다. 저는 오늘 ⁷⁴**우리가 다양한 신발을 어떻게 생산하는지** 보여 드리겠습니다. 여러분은 우리가 제조 공정의 모든 단계에서 신발에 특별한 주의를 기울이는 것을 알게 되실 겁니다. ⁷⁵**이는 우리 제품이 오랫동안 지속되도록 하는 데 도움이 됩니다.** 사실, 그것이 우리가 유명한 이유입니다. 이제, 우리는 곧 생산 현장에 들어갈 거라서, ⁷⁶**여러분이 착용하셔야 할 안전 고글을 나눠 드리겠습니다.** 우리가 나오면 그걸 다시 수거할 것입니다.

어휘

a range of 다양한 give attention to ~에 주의를 기울이다
stage 단계 manufacturing process 제조 공정
ensure ~을 확실하게 하다, 보증하다 last 지속되다
production 생산 floor 바닥, 작업장 pass out 나누어 주다
collect 모으다, 수집하다

74.
회사가 만드는 것은 무엇인가?
(A) 사무용품
(B) 가구
(C) 캠핑 장비
(D) 신발

패러프레이징
shoes → Footwear

75.
화자에 따르면, 회사는 무엇으로 유명한가?
(A) 훌륭한 고객 서비스
(B) 오래가는 제품
(C) 친환경 소재
(D) 폭넓은 선택권

어휘
long-lasting 오래가는
environmentally friendly 환경친화적인 selection 선택

패러프레이징
our products last for a long time
→ Its long-lasting products

76.
청자들이 다음에 할 것 같은 일은 무엇인가?
(A) 정보 수집하기
(B) 단체 사진 찍기
(C) 보호 장비 착용하기
(D) 질문 제출하기

패러프레이징
safety goggles that you'll need to wear
→ Put on protective gear

[77-79] 호남 🎧
Questions 77-79 refer to the following excerpt from a meeting.

> M To begin today's staff meeting, ⁷⁷ I'd like to tell you about the new tablets we purchased for taking inventory. They will help us to keep our records updated more easily. If you are assigned an inventory task, ⁷⁸ check one of these tablets out from the IT department. You'll need your employee number to do that. After Thursday's training session on how to use the software, we're buying pizza for the staff to

> thank you for your hard work. So, ⁷⁹ if there's a certain type of pizza that you would like, don't forget to let Monica know before she places the order. Thanks.

해석
77–79번은 다음 회의 발췌에 관한 문제입니다.

남 오늘 직원 회의를 시작하면서, ⁷⁷ 우리가 구입한 새 태블릿에 대해 말씀드리겠습니다. 그것들은 우리의 기록을 더 쉽게 업데이트하는 데 도움이 될 것입니다. 재고 조사 업무를 할당받는다면, ⁷⁸ IT 부서에서 이 태블릿 중 하나를 빌리세요. 그렇게 하려면 사원 번호가 필요할 겁니다. 목요일 소프트웨어 사용법에 대한 교육이 끝난 후, 우리는 여러분의 노고에 감사하기 위해 직원들에게 피자를 사 드릴 겁니다. 그러니, ⁷⁹ 만약 여러분이 원하는 특정 종류의 피자가 있다면, 모니카가 주문하기 전에 알려 주는 걸 잊지 마세요. 감사합니다.

어휘
take inventory 재고 조사를 하다 record 기록
assign 할당하다, 배정하다 inventory 재고품, 재고 조사
check ~ out (책·차 등을 수속에 의해) 빌리다
training session 교육 (과정) place an order 주문하다

77.
회의의 주된 내용은 무엇인가?
(A) 자원봉사 기회
(B) 업계 행사
(C) 새로운 장비
(D) 정책 변경

어휘
volunteer 자원봉사 opportunity 기회 industry 산업, 업계
policy 정책, 방침

패러프레이징
the new tablets → some new equipment

78.
화자에 따르면, 청자들이 ID 번호가 필요한 이유는 무엇인가?
(A) 강좌를 신청하기 위해
(B) 급여를 받기 위해
(C) 데이터베이스에 접근하기 위해
(D) 물품을 빌리기 위해

어휘
sign up for ~을 신청하다 course 강좌, 강의
payment 지불, 보수 access 접근하다

패러프레이징
check one of these tablets out → borrow an item

79.
화자가 청자들에게 하도록 상기시키는 것은 무엇인가?
(A) 소프트웨어 프로그램 다운로드하기
(B) 일정 확인하기
(C) 선호 표현하기

(D) 일찍 출근하기

[80-82] 영녀 🎧

Questions 80-82 refer to the following broadcast.

> W Thanks for listening to *Entertainment Talk* on Radio 22. My guest in the studio today is 80 Matthew Foster, owner of Europa Max, which leads group tours throughout Europe. Mr. Foster has been in the business for over three decades. 81 He can speak Spanish, French, and German at an advanced level as well as several other languages at a basic level. I'm sure this has been useful throughout his career. Mr. Foster plans to sell his business after the summer season, but that won't be the end of his travels. 82 He plans to build an online travel guide for others to use. We'll hear more about this in just a moment.

해석

80-82번은 다음 방송에 관한 문제입니다.

여 Radio 22의 〈연예 토크〉를 들어 주셔서 감사합니다. 오늘 스튜디오에 오신 손님은 80 유럽 전역의 단체 여행을 이끌고 있는 유로파 맥스의 소유주인 매튜 포스터 씨입니다. 포스터 씨는 30년 넘게 그 사업에 종사해 오셨습니다. 81 그는 고급 수준의 스페인어, 프랑스어, 독일어뿐만 아니라 기초 수준의 여러 다른 언어를 구사할 수 있습니다. 저는 이것이 그의 경력 내내 유용했다고 확신합니다. 포스터 씨는 여름 시즌이 끝난 후 그의 사업을 매각할 계획이지만, 그것이 그의 여행의 끝은 아닐 겁니다. 82 그는 다른 사람들이 이용할 수 있도록 온라인 여행 가이드를 만들 계획입니다. 잠시 후에 이에 대해 좀 더 들어 보겠습니다.

80.

포스터 씨가 일하는 곳은 어디인가?

(A) 항공사
(B) 헬스 클럽
(C) 여행사
(D) 기업 연구소

패러프레이징

Europa Max, which leads group tours throughout Europe → a tour company

81.

화자에 따르면, 포스터 씨가 갖고 있는 기술은 무엇인가?

(A) 여러 언어 구사하기
(B) 전문적인 사진 찍기

(C) 그룹 팀워크 향상시키기
(D) 여러 지점 관리하기

82.

포스터 씨가 사업을 매각한 뒤에 하려고 계획하는 것은 무엇인가?

(A) 은퇴 시작하기
(B) 웹사이트 만들기
(C) 해외로 이주하기
(D) 수업 듣기

패러프레이징

build an online travel guide → Create a Web site

[83-85] 호남 🎧

Questions 83-85 refer to the following excerpt from a meeting.

> M Alright, everyone. The summer season is starting soon, so once again 83 we'll have a special section in the newspaper about the country's beaches. I'll assign an article about a specific beach to each one of you. Some of the beaches are remote, so 84 I'll send you driving directions later today. 85 Now, this may feel like a casual task, but just remember to think about our readers. They look forward to this every year.

해석

83-85번은 다음 회의 발췌에 관한 문제입니다.

남 좋습니다, 여러분. 여름 시즌이 곧 시작되므로, 다시 한번 83 우리는 신문에 우리나라의 해변에 관한 특별 코너를 게재할 것입니다. 여러분 각자에게 특정 해변에 관한 기사를 배정하겠습니다. 일부 해변은 외진 곳에 있어서, 84 여러분에게 오늘 오후에 운전 경로를 보내드리겠습니다. 85 자, 이것이 가벼운 업무로 느껴질 수도 있지만, 우리 독자들에 대해 생각해 볼 것을 기억하세요. 그들은 매년 이걸 기대하고 있습니다.

83.

청자들은 누구일 것 같은가?

(A) 회계사
(B) 기자
(C) 판매원
(D) 투자자

84.

오늘 화자가 청자에게 보낼 것은 무엇인가?
(A) 업데이트된 일정
(B) 계정 비밀번호
(C) 운전 경로
(D) 사진 찍는 것에 대한 조언

어휘

account 계정, 계좌 password 비밀번호

85.

화자가 "그들은 매년 이걸 기대하고 있습니다"라고 말한 이유는 무엇인가?
(A) 청자들에게 도움을 요청하도록 상기시키기 위해
(B) 청자들의 빠른 작업에 감사하기 위해
(C) 업무의 중요성을 강조하기 위해
(D) 예산이 증가된 이유를 설명하기 위해

어휘

remind 상기시키다 highlight 강조하다 significance 중요성
budget 예산

[86-88] 미남 🎧

Questions 86-88 refer to the following announcement.

> M Good morning, and ⁸⁶ welcome to the Wallingford Library's third annual Job Skills Event. It's great to see so many people here to learn more about improving their skills. We wish you all the best of luck in your job search. ⁸⁷ We'll be proofreading and reviewing résumés for free all day. Mistakes on your résumé can make a bad impression with potential employers, and some of these are hard to see. Also, ⁸⁸ there is a lecture on interview strategies starting shortly in the Sunrise Room. You won't want to miss that.

해석

86-88번은 다음 공지에 관한 문제입니다.
남 안녕하세요, ⁸⁶ 월링포드 도서관의 제3회 연례 직무 기술 행사에 오신 걸 환영합니다. 이렇게 많은 분들이 기술 향상에 대해 더 많이 배우기 위해 여기 계신 걸 보니 좋습니다. 여러분의 구직 활동에 행운이 가득하길 빕니다. ⁸⁷ 우리는 하루 종일 무료로 이력서를 교정하고 검토해 드릴 것입니다. 이력서의 오류는 잠재적인 고용주들에게 안 좋은 인상을 줄 수 있는데, 이것들 중 일부는 알아보기 어렵습니다. 또한, ⁸⁸ 잠시 후 선라이즈 룸에서 면접 전략에 관한 강의가 있을 것입니다. 그걸 놓치고 싶지 않을 거예요.

어휘

job search 구직 활동 proofread 교정하다 review 검토하다
résumé 이력서 for free 무료로 mistake 실수, 오류
make an impression 인상을 주다
potential 잠재적인, 가능성 있는 lecture 강의 strategy 전략

miss 놓치다, 그리워하다

86.

청자들이 있을 것 같은 곳은 어디인가?
(A) 기업 연구소
(B) 채용 대행업체
(C) 서점
(D) 도서관

패러프레이징

Wallingford Library → a library

87.

화자가 "이것들 중 일부는 알아보기 어렵습니다"라고 말한 이유는 무엇인가?
(A) 불편에 사과하기 위해
(B) 시력 검사의 중요성을 설명하기 위해
(C) 사람들이 서류를 확인받도록 권장하기 위해
(D) 일부 글자의 크기를 변경할 것을 권하기 위해

어휘

apologize for ~에 대해 사과하다 inconvenience 불편
importance 중요성 encourage 권장[장려]하다

88.

청자들에게 지금 하도록 권하는 것은 무엇인가?
(A) 질문 공유하기
(B) 동영상 시청하기
(C) 강연에 참석하기
(D) 고용주 만나기

패러프레이징

a lecture on interview strategies → a talk

[89-91] 미녀 🎧

Questions 89-91 refer to the following speech.

> W Hello, I'm Wanda from Mesa Furnishings. In this video, I'm going to be talking about curtains. ⁸⁹ When you need new curtains, there are a lot of factors to consider. Today I'll be giving you some advice to help you find the right ones. First, think about which color or pattern would go well with the rest of the room. Second, think about the fabric. For example, ⁹⁰ silk is very delicate and can be damaged by the sun, so it is best for north-facing rooms. Last, think about how much light you want to block out. For further help, ⁹¹ one of our consultants will visit your home and advise you at no charge.

해석

89-91번은 다음 연설에 관한 문제입니다.
여 안녕하세요, 저는 메사 퍼니싱즈의 완다입니다. 이 동영상에서,

저는 커튼에 대해 이야기할 것입니다. **89 새 커튼이 필요할 때 고려해야 할 요소가 많습니다.** 오늘 제가 여러분에게 맞는 것을 찾는 데 도움이 되는 조언을 해 드리겠습니다. 먼저, 어떤 색깔이나 무늬가 방의 나머지 부분과 잘 어울릴지 생각해 보세요. 두 번째로, 천에 대해 생각해 보세요. 예를 들어, **90 비단은 매우 섬세하고 태양에 의해 손상될 수 있기 때문에 북향의 방에 가장 좋습니다.** 마지막으로, 여러분이 얼마나 많은 양의 빛을 차단하고 싶은지 생각해 보세요. 더 많은 도움을 드리기 위해 **91 저희 상담사 중한 명이 여러분 댁에 방문하여 무료로 조언을 해 드릴 것입니다.**

어휘

factor 요소 consider 고려하다 go well with ~와 잘 어울리다
fabric 직물, 천 delicate 섬세한, 연약한 damage 손상을 주다
block out (빛·소리를) 가리다[차단하다]
consultant 상담가, 컨설턴트 at no charge 무료로

89.

화자가 주로 논의하고 있는 것은 무엇인가?
(A) 커튼을 청소하는 것
(B) 커튼의 치수를 재는 것
(C) 커튼을 선택하는 것
(D) 커튼을 바느질하는 것

어휘

measure 측정하다, ~의 치수를 재다 select 선택하다
sew 바느질하다

90.

화자가 비단에 대해 말한 것은 무엇인가?
(A) 햇빛에 민감하다.
(B) 쉽게 얼룩질 수 있다.
(C) 가볍다.
(D) 매우 비쌀 수 있다.

어휘

sensitive to ~에 민감한 stain 얼룩지다; 얼룩

패러프레이징

can be damaged by the sun → is sensitive to sunlight

91.

청자들이 메사 퍼니싱즈에서 받을 수 있는 것은 무엇인가?
(A) 직물 견본
(B) 할인 코드
(C) 제품 카탈로그
(D) 무료 상담

어휘

consultation 상담

패러프레이징

advise you at no charge → A free consultation

[92-94] 미남 🎧

Questions 92-94 refer to the following telephone message.

M Hi, Ms. Martinez. This is Brandon Becker, the owner of Odin's. **92 I just wanted to call to thank you for the article you wrote about my restaurant.** It's important for us to get publicity like that. I'm glad that you liked the dishes that you tried, but I noticed that **93 you expressed dissatisfaction with the prices.** The thing is, we source our ingredients from farms in the area to help the local community. This is a complex issue. **94 I'd love the opportunity to explain our supply chains in greater detail.** If you have time, please call me back so I can do so.

해석

92-94번은 다음 전화 메시지에 관한 문제입니다.

남 안녕하세요, 마르티네즈 씨. 저는 오딘즈의 소유주인 브랜던 베커입니다. **92 제 식당에 대해 써 주신 기사에 감사 전화를 드리고 싶었어요.** 우리에게는 그런 명성을 얻는 게 중요하거든요. 귀하가 드셔 보신 요리가 마음에 드셨다니 기쁩니다만, **93 가격에 불만을 표하셨군요.** 중요한 건, 우리는 지역 사회를 돕기 위해 우리 재료를 이 지역 농장에서 구한다는 겁니다. 이것은 복잡한 문제입니다. **94 우리의 공급망을 더 상세히 설명할 기회를 갖고 싶습니다.** 시간이 되시면 제가 그렇게 할 수 있도록 전화해 주세요.

어휘

article 기사, 조항 get publicity 명성을 얻다, 평판이 나다
dissatisfaction 불만 source 얻다, 공급자를 찾다; 원천, 출처
ingredient 재료 community 지역 사회 complex 복잡한
opportunity 기회 supply chain 공급망 in detail 상세히
call back 다시 전화하다

92.

화자가 청자에게 고마워하는 것은 무엇인가?
(A) 그의 사업체를 널리 알린 것
(B) 메뉴의 오류를 지적한 것
(C) 식당에 투자한 것
(D) 새로운 요리사를 소개한 것

어휘

give publicity ~을 널리 알리다 point out ~을 지적하다
invest in ~에 투자하다 introduce 소개하다

93.

화자가 "이것은 복잡한 문제입니다"라고 말한 의도는 무엇인가?
(A) 어떤 요리는 만드는 데 오랜 시간이 걸린다.
(B) 제안된 기한이 너무 촉박하다.
(C) 더 많은 직원들이 필요할 수 있다.
(D) 가격에는 몇 가지 요인이 작용한다.

어휘

propose 제안하다 tight 단단한, (여유가 없이) 빠듯한
factor 요인 contribute to 기여[공헌]하다, (~의) 한 원인이 되다

94.

화자가 회신 전화를 원하는 이유는 무엇인가?

(A) 동료를 추천하기 위해

(B) 자세한 정보를 제공하기 위해

(C) 주소를 확인하기 위해

(D) 순서를 조정하기 위해

adjust 조정하다

to explain our supply chains in greater detail

→ To provide further information

[95-97] 호남 🎧

Questions 95-97 refer to the following talk and map.

> M I'd like to welcome you all to the grand opening of Newbury Park. ⁹⁵ I'm Dean Murray, the director of the Parks and Recreation Department. This project would not have been possible without support from Mayor Collins and residents like you. ⁹⁶ We'll be serving a picnic lunch at noon at the sports field between Willis Pond and the playground. This is available for free to all attendees. Also, ⁹⁷ I'm looking for a few volunteers to help pick up trash from the area after this event. Please speak to me if you have time to help. We don't want to leave behind a mess for future park users.

95-97번은 다음 담화와 지도에 관한 문제입니다.

남 뉴베리 공원 개장식에 오신 여러분 모두를 환영합니다. ⁹⁵ 저는 **공원 및 위락 시설 관리국의 책임자인 딘 머레이입니다.** 이 프로젝트는 콜린스 시장과 여러분과 같은 주민들의 지원이 없었다면 가능하지 않았을 겁니다. ⁹⁶ **우리는 정오에 윌리스 연못과 놀이터 사이에 있는 운동 경기장에서 소풍 도시락을 제공할 것입니다.** 이는 모든 참석자에게 무료로 제공됩니다. 또한, ⁹⁷ **저는 이 행사 후에 이 지역에서 쓰레기 수거를 도울 몇 명의 자원봉사자를 찾고 있습니다.** 도울 시간이 있으면 제게 말씀하세요. 우리는 향후 공원 사용자들을 위해 엉망인 상태로 남겨 두고 싶지 않습니다.

support 지지, 도움 resident 주민, 거주자 serve 제공하다
playground 놀이터, 운동장 attendee 참석자
volunteer 자원봉사자 pick up 정리 정돈하다[치우다]
trash 쓰레기 mess 엉망인 상태

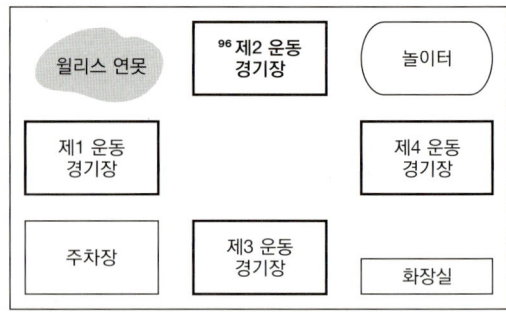

95.

화자는 누구인가?

(A) 도시의 시장

(B) 기자

(C) 관광 가이드

(D) 부서장

the director of the Parks and Recreation Department

→ A department head

96.

시각 자료를 보시오. 어느 운동 경기장이 사용될 것인가?

(A) 제1 운동 경기장

(B) 제2 운동 경기장

(C) 제3 운동 경기장

(D) 제4 운동 경기장

97.

현장에 자원봉사자들이 필요한 이유는 무엇인가?

(A) 진행 중인 활동을 계획하기 위해

(B) 지역을 청소하기 위해

(C) 표지판을 걸기 위해

(D) 식물을 돌보기 위해

ongoing 진행 중인 activity 활동
clean up (~을) 치우다[청소하다] hang up ~을 걸다
sign 표지판 take care of ~을 돌보다

to help pick up trash from the area

→ To clean up an area

[98-100] 영녀 🎧

Questions 98-100 refer to the following announcement and survey form.

> W Since ⁹⁸ our hardware store is looking for new ways to get customers interested in our products, we are offering several free demonstrations. These will cover various projects that beginners can make. I think our customers will enjoy them, but ⁹⁹ I also want

the staff to learn some basic skills related to plumbing. Since many of our customers visit us because of those problems, those skills will help you recommend the best tools for different jobs. To help with that goal, I'll be conducting a series of workshops just for the staff. I'm trying to find the best day and time to do it. So, I ask that you complete this brief survey. And, if needed, ¹⁰⁰ I can change the morning session because my schedule is flexible that day, but I can't add any other weekend times.

(C) 통솔력 장려하기
(D) 새로운 기술 가르치기

패러프레이징

some basic skills related to plumbing → new skills

100.

시각 자료를 보시오. 어떤 요일에 화자의 일정이 유동적인가?

(A) 화요일

(B) 목요일

(C) 금요일

(D) 일요일

해석

98-100번은 다음 공지와 설문지에 관한 문제입니다.

여 **⁹⁸ 우리 철물점**은 고객들이 우리 제품에 관심을 가질 수 있는 새로운 방법을 찾고 있기 때문에, 몇 가지 무료 시연을 제공하고 있습니다. 이것들은 초보자들이 만들 수 있는 다양한 프로젝트를 다룰 것입니다. 고객들이 그것들을 즐길 거라고 생각하지만, **⁹⁹ 직원들 또한 배관 관련 기본 기술을 배우면 좋겠습니다.** 많은 고객들이 그 문제로 우리를 방문하기 때문에, 그러한 기술은 여러분이 다양한 작업에 가장 적합한 도구를 추천하는 데 도움이 될 것입니다. 그 목표에 도움이 되도록, 저는 직원만을 위한 일련의 워크숍을 진행할 것입니다. 저는 그것을 할 가장 좋은 날짜와 시간을 찾으려고 노력하고 있습니다. 그러니 이 간단한 설문 조사를 작성해 주시기 바랍니다. 그리고 필요하다면, **¹⁰⁰ 그날 제 일정이 유동적이기 때문에 오전 과정을 변경할 수는 있지만** 다른 주말 시간은 추가할 수 없습니다.

어휘

hardware store 철물점 demonstration 시연
cover 다루다 plumbing 배관, 배관 작업 goal 목표
conduct 지휘하다, 수행하다 a series of 일련의 brief 간단한
survey 설문 조사, 조사서[표] session 회기, 수업 (시간)

가능한 날짜에 체크하세요.
[ ] 화요일 오후 3시
[ ] ¹⁰⁰ 목요일 오전 10시 30분
[ ] 금요일 오후 2시 30분
[ ] 일요일 오후 1시

98.

화자가 일할 것 같은 곳은 어디인가?

(A) 공동체 텃밭

(B) 슈퍼마켓

(C) 철물점

(D) 제과점

99.

화자의 목표는 무엇인가?

(A) 비용 절감하기

(B) 팀워크 향상시키기